International Business

Environments & Operations

Seventeenth Edition

John D. Daniels

University of Miami

Lee H. Radebaugh

Brigham Young University

Daniel P. Sullivan

University of Delaware

Reid W. Click

George Washington University

Pearson

Please contact https://support.pearson.com/getsupport/s/ with any queries on this content

Cover Image by Liu Zishan/123RF

Library of Congress Cataloging-in-Publication Data

Names: Daniels, John D., author. | Radebaugh, Lee H., author. | Sullivan, Daniel P., author. | Click, Reid W., author.
Title: International business: environments & operations / John D. Daniels, University of Miami, Lee H. Radebaugh, Brigham Young University, Daniel P. Sullivan, University of Delaware, Reid W. Click, George Washington University.
Description: Seventeenth Edition. | Hoboken: Pearson, 2021. | Revised edition of International business, [2017] | Includes bibliographical references and index. | Summary: "For nearly half a century, students, teachers, scholars, managers, and officials have praised our text for insightfully integrating authoritative theory with meaningful practice within the context of rigorous analysis of trends and circumstances in international business (IB). Commanding a sharper sense of the political, legal, technological, competitive, and cultural factors sharpens decision-making and improves performance. The standards of success that inspire our efforts, we believe, make this edition the best yet. Our collective efforts result in a text that provides instructors and students a powerful, productive, and meaningful understanding of the dimensions and dynamics that define the world of business."— Provided by publisher.
Identifiers: LCCN 2020038596 | ISBN 9780135899915 (hardcover)
Subjects: LCSH: International business enterprises. | International economic relations. | Investments, Foreign.
Classification: LCC HD2755.5 .D35 2021 | DDC 658.1/8—dc23
LC record available at https://lccn.loc.gov/2020038596

4 2021

Pearson

ISBN-10: 0-13-589991-5
ISBN-13: 978-0-13-589991-5

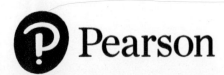

Brief Contents

Contents

Preface

The 17th edition of *International Business: Environment and Operations*, besides the latest, we believe is the greatest version of our work. It is a best-selling international business (IB) textbook—both in the United States and worldwide. The long-running choice in many international business studies and MBA programs, it is used around the globe in undergraduate and graduate education. To date, it has been translated into Albanian, Chinese, Korean, Macedonian, Russian, Spanish, and Thai. Its first edition in 1976, according to many professors, defined the intellectual structure of the IB domain. The subsequent 16 editions have fortified its status as the global standard for studying the environments and operations of IB.

For nearly half a century, students, teachers, scholars, managers, and officials have praised our text for insightfully integrating authoritative theory with meaningful practice within the context of rigorous analysis of trends and circumstances in IB. Commanding a sharper sense of the political, legal, technological, competitive, and cultural factors sharpens decision-making and improves performance. The standards of success that inspire our efforts, we believe, make this edition the best yet. Our collective efforts result in a textbook that provides instructors and students a powerful, productive, and meaningful understanding of the dimensions and dynamics that define the world of business.

NEW TO THE SEVENTEENTH EDITION

The changing business world calls on us to change our understanding and interpretation, aspiring to make sense of the environments and operations of IB. This edition shares our latest views on a wide variety of topics, issues, challenges, and opportunities in IB. Throughout, we strive to help readers interpret what it all means for professional and personal choices. To that end, we have aggressively revised the text to reflect current research and best practices, both academic and practitioner. We have updated and added countless examples of managers and companies around the world, relying on reports from many sources. Specific features and changes include:

- Reid Click of George Washington University joined the author team. Reid brings a wealth of experience and expertise in the areas of international economics, global financial markets, international business finance, and business in emerging markets. His analyses and insights greatly improve the rigor and relevance of the text.
- The chapter structure of the text replicates that used in the 16th edition. However, we've revised and, in some cases, revamped materials, given dramatic political, economic, social, and institutional changes, let alone the unfolding consequences of the COVID-19 pandemic.
- Coverage of recent developments has been added throughout the text to put a spotlight on the dynamic nature of IB. For example, new content on the COVID-19 pandemic focuses attention on changes in the environments and operations of IB, with special emphasis on institutions, supply chains, and trade.
- The expanding migration of the text into digital delivery formats, in conjunction with the MyLab platform, spurred us to address the concerns of all users, no matter their preferred format.
- Discussion of new legislation and regulation underscores the need for reevaluation of corporate policies and strategies, such as those brought on by the overhaul of multinational corporate taxation in the United States enacted by the Tax Cuts and Jobs Act and recent rounds of trade negotiations by nations worldwide.

- Nearly all figures, tables, and maps are updated to track the changing context of globalization and the conduct of IB. Several new figures, tables, and maps are added to enrich analysis.
- All new photographs provide contemporary illustrations of traditional and expanded topics.
- Four new cases address contemporary issues in IB.
    - International Students and International Business in Chapter 2
    - Open Sesame: Alibaba Isn't Poor Anymore in Chapter 11
    - Amazon.com in Chapter 13
    - Alibaba: Redefining Export Pathways, Platforms, and Performance in Chapter 14
- All other chapter opening and closing cases, 36 in total, have been revised to provide fully up-to-date analysis of issues, institutions, countries, and companies.

CHAPTER-BY-CHAPTER UPDATES

Part One: Background for International Business	
Chapter 1 | Globalization and International Business	• Updated material on the downside of globalization, including new examples of corruption and cheating in sports. • Enhanced presentation of the role of technology in global production with discussion of China becoming the world's workshop. • Added material on the escalation of US-China trade restrictions. • Expanded coverage of reasons for anti-globalization, including the concern for becoming a minority in one's own country. • Added discussion on the effect of stress from globalization, using French protests as an example. • Added material on the COVID-19 pandemic, covering how it negatively affects supply chains and the cruise business, but also provides a reason for global cooperation to fight pandemics. • Updated the "Why Study IB?" section. • Added coverage of de-globalization.
Part Two: Comparative Environmental Frameworks	
Chapter 2 | The Cultural Environments Facing Business	• Extended discussion of cultural dynamics, including recent gains of women's rights in Saudi Arabia. • Added content on the concept of the Anglosphere. • Extended discussion on how the meaning of gestures can change, using the example of the U.S. OK sign being used for white supremacy. • Added information on how people adjust abroad by degree, such as accepting some foods but not others. • New closing case on international students' effects on themselves, organizations, and nations.
Chapter 3 | The Political and Legal Environments Facing Business	• Updated opening case profile of China capturing ongoing political and legal developments, highlighting the implications of pro-democracy protests in Hong Kong as well as the COVID-19 pandemic. • Streamlined interpretation of political freedom and continuing tension between democracy and totalitarianism. • Added profile and assessment of populism and the challenges it poses to political freedom. • Updated profile of intellectual property regulation, piracy, and counterfeiting within the political context of IB.

Chapter 4 | The Economic Environments Facing Businesses

- Updated profile of emerging economies, highlighting long-running trends as well as recent developments, both pro and con, notably on the One Belt, One Road initiative.
- Revised profiles of developed, developing, and emerging economic systems.
- Updated and streamlined discussion of economic freedom in light of the ongoing changes in different types of economic systems, and revised discussion of the relationship between economic freedom and standard of living, strengthening the connection between the concepts.
- Modified discussion of the mixed economic system given political trends in developed countries, most notably expanding socialism and populism.
- Expanded discussion of the shadow economy as a key component of national and global economies.
- Refined coverage of key economic indicators and expanded discussion of indicators used to integrate economic analysis.
- Revised, updated, and expanded closing case on economic environments of the West covering ongoing problems, puzzles, and the implications of the fourth industrial revolution.

Chapter 5 | Globalization and Society

- Added discussion on the interaction between the Corporate Ethical Values (CEV) set by a company and the degree of corruption (using the Corruption Perceptions Index) in a country where the company is operating.
- Added material on how companies and governments have to deal with greenhouse gas emissions and air and water pollution in their overall environmental strategy.
- Updated presentation of the Paris Agreement on Climate Change and what countries are doing to deal with greenhouse gas emissions.

Part Three: Theories and Institutions: Trade and Investment

Chapter 6 | International Trade and Factor Mobility Theory

- Updated opening case on Taiwan's trade using new data and recent political developments.
- Improved coverage of international migration with new data and discussion of contemporary issues.
- Expanded discussion of international capital movement, and its effects, within the context of foreign direct investment.
- Enhanced material on domestic labor mobility in the context of trade effects, including discussion of the immobility of labor in sectors shrinking due to competition from imports to move into sectors that are expanding.

Chapter 7 | Governmental Influence on Trade

- Updated opening case on the U.S.-Vietnamese catfish dispute providing new industry data, insights on unintended consequences in the U.S., and perspective setting the stage for Vietnam's response in a new section, entitled "Vietnam Fights Back," covering new developments at the World Trade Organization (WTO).
- Added analysis of the 2018 tariffs on U.S. imports, including expanded attention to the effects on prices and the question of who pays.
- Expanded discussion of "comparable access" and "fairness" in trade given the discourse in the United States during 2018–2019.
- Added coverage of the effects of the coronavirus pandemic on trade by highlighting examples of export restrictions designed to keep medical supplies at home.
- Revised closing case incorporating recent proposals to allow more imports of pharmaceuticals from Canada.

Chapter 8 | Cross-National Cooperation and Agreements

- Updated discussion on the European Union reflecting the exit of the United Kingdom (Brexit) and its impact on global trade.
- Added coverage of changes in the North American Free Trade Agreement resulting in the new United States–Mexico–Canada Agreement (USMCA) and policies designed to increase manufacturing production in North America.
- Added discussion of how political changes and a move to stronger nationalism can result in national self-interest and greater reliance on bilateral rather than multilateral trade agreements.
- Added analysis on how, even though the U.S. is no longer actively involved in the Trans-Pacific Partnership, some of the trade rules developed in the agreement are incorporated in the USMCA.

Part Four: World Financial Environment

Chapter 9 | Global Foreign-Exchange Markets

- Revised discussion of foreign exchange trading capturing institutional and technological changes.
- Expanded "Looking to the Future" including recent developments regarding the rise of the Chinese yuan as a global currency and the new landscape of cryptocurrencies, including Facebook's Libra.
- Extended closing case on the Chinese yuan renminbi highlighting the importance of the 2015 reforms, the U.S. declaration of China as a currency manipulator, and the slow movement away from a fixed exchange rate regime toward a floating exchange rate regime.

Chapter 10 | The Determination of Exchange Rates

- Revised discussion of the International Monetary Fund, including its response to the COVID-19 pandemic.
- Updated Point/Counterpoint on a common currency for Africa incorporating recent developments.
- Improved content on the breakdown of Zimbabwe's financial system and the rise of a black market for foreign exchange, covering recent developments including introduction of an electronic currency and subsequent introduction of a new paper currency.
- Expanded presentation of the Big Mac Index conveying the concept of Purchasing Power Parity and extending analysis to include price changes.
- Modified discussion of the "flight to safety" in currency markets using the COVID-19 pandemic as a new example.
- Revised "Looking to the Future" on changes in the relative strength of global currencies capturing recent developments with China and the yuan, as well as Brexit.
- Updated closing case on Sony and the Japanese yen introducing recent events in Japan, developments with the yen, and current company data.

Chapter 11 | Global Capital Markets

- Revised opening case on Pfizer and international taxation introducing new U.S. policies on corporate inversions and the overhaul of multinational corporate taxation brought by the Tax Cuts and Jobs Act of 2017.
- Added examples of recent international cross-listings and de-listings.
- Revised discussion of corporate tax rates updating data and highlighting the effects of the Tax Cuts and Jobs Act of 2017.
- Modified discussion of worldwide and territorial taxation accounting for changes in the U.S. engendered by the Tax Cuts and Jobs Act of 2017.
- Added coverage of the new global intangible low tax income (GILTI) in the U.S. and the complexity of its implementation.

	• Revised "Looking to the Future" on capital markets and taxes covering recent developments. • New closing case on Alibaba's record-breaking initial public offering on the NYSE in 2014 and its cross-listing on the Hong Kong exchange in 2019, featuring discussion of corporate governance, the investment banking process, and a contrast to the Saudi Aramco record-breaking listing on the Tadawul stock exchange.
Part Five: Global Strategy, Structure, and Implementation	
Chapter 12 | The Strategy of International Business	• Revised material on strategic planning better connecting concepts from strategic management and international business. • Refined presentation on the contrast between industrial organization and resource-based perspectives of strategy. • Improved discussion of location economics as a moderator of strategy given technological trends in artificial intelligence and automation. • Modified specifications of international, localization, global, and transnational strategies. • New Figure 12.5 communicating the implication of the integration-responsiveness grid to strategy type in IB. • Updated and revised closing case improving specifications of alternative scenarios for the multinational enterprise of the future.
Chapter 13 | Country Evaluation and Selection	• Updated opening case on Burger King reflecting recent financial information and operating strategies. • Added example in the discussion of social and economic conditions explaining the effects of the 2019 anti-government protests in Algeria on Exxon-Mobil. • Modified information in the section on debilitating diseases introducing the novel coronavirus COVID-19. • New ending case on the evolution of country selection strategy at Amazon.com, featuring discussion of initial expansion in Europe and recent expansion attempts in China and India, and introducing a new map with Amazon's localized online storefronts.
Chapter 14 | Export and Import	• Updated opening case improving coverage of managerial and market dynamics in the export process. • Added detail on export/import profiles at the national level, highlighting the top three merchandise importers and exporters. • Streamlined coverage of the alternative approaches to exporting. • Updated profile of exporting e-waste developing the elements supporting it and better balancing the arguments against it. • Revised and streamlined profile of "Exporting and Importing: Problems and Pitfalls." • New Figure 14.1 illustrating key categories of barriers to trade and improving intellectual accessibility. • New closing case: "Alibaba: Redefining Export Pathways, Platforms, and Performance."
Chapter 15 | Direct Investment and Collaborative Strategies	• Updated opening case on Meliá Hotels highlighting changes in type and location of foreign operations. • Extended discussion of appropriability theory showing that operating forms other than direct investment can be employed. • Added material presenting the effect of firms' operating experience on their choices of new entry modes, with emphasis on recent trends. • Added coverage of the effects of airline deregulation on the number of airlines. • Revised closing case on the oneworld Alliance updating participants.

Chapter 16 | The Organization of International Business	• Improved opening case on W. L. Gore utilizing imagery, interviews, and updated information. • Reinterpreted ideas of centralization in terms of traditional organizational theory perspectives. • Added material on the ongoing expansion and influence of automation and artificial intelligence to radically reconfigure organizations. • Revised organizational charts highlighting vertical and horizontal differentiation more effectively. • Added Figure 16.7 on the mixed structure. • Amplified discussion of neoclassical structures, particularly highlighting their point of differentiation with classical counterparts. • Updated graphical representation of the network structure, better communicating the interrelationships among its key elements. • Improved discussion of the virtual structure by highlighting forms found in emerging firms such as Airbnb, Uber, and Upwork. • Revised profiles of coordination by plan and mutual adjustment, taking into account the potential of automation and artificial intelligence. • Reorganized closing case on Johnson & Johnson highlighting the interactions between structure, systems, and corporate culture.
Part Six: Managing International Operations	
Chapter 17 | Marketing Globally	• Added content on how marketing practices evolve, such as Hilfiger's use of different models and introduction of retro designs. • Expanded coverage of different country legal and environmental standards on products and promotion. • Revised examples of companies' product offerings in developing countries that differ from those in their home markets. • Enhanced discussion of distributional cost differences in developing economies. • Added ending case question asking whether Grameen-Danone should continue Bangladeshi operations if it is not profitable.
Chapter 18 | Global Operations and Supply-Chain Management	• Added discussion of the impact of COVID-19 on supply chains using Apple as an example of a company relying significantly on China for suppliers and contract manufacturing. • Added material on the importance of quality in the manufacturing sector using the example of Boeing and their popular 737 MAX airplane and how a quality disaster can affect a company's competitive position and profitability. • Added coverage of how the pressure to meet the profitability and speed to market of competitors forced many Japanese companies to sacrifice quality and falsify quality records, resulting in a drop in reputation. • New section on blockchain technology and how it can be used in supply chain management. • Revised "Looking to the Future" discussing how the COVID-19 pandemic has affected current global supply chains and how scenario planning for future pandemics could affect supply chains permanently.
Chapter 19 | International Accounting and Finance Issues	• Revised opening case showing how GPS Capital Markets has expanded the scope of its services to meet competitive challenges. • Updated discussion of International Financial Reporting Standards (IFRS) covering recent changes and possible impacts on U.S. GAAP.

- Refined coverage on the international dimensions of the financial role of the Controller.
- Added explanations of why it is so complicated for a company engaged in global operations to deal with accounting issues.
- Updated foreign currency translation examples reflecting changes in revenue recognition in the United States and how the changes alter the way exchange rates impact the financial statements.
- Updated closing case on H&M including changes in IFRS and impacts on H&M's financial reporting.

Chapter 20 | International Human Resource Management

- Updated opening case on "Globalizing Your Career" expanding the points of perspective reported.
- Expanded discussion of mainstream HRM in order to better contrast and develop the ideas of IHRM.
- Added profile of the evolution of IHRM and expatriate management from pre-1970 though the 2020s.
- New Figure 20.3 presenting the chronology of outlooks and outcomes in expatriate selection.
- Expanded discussion of commuter/flexpatriate assignment incorporating the emerging class of gig-pats.
- Revised profile of IHRM staffing frameworks introducing the regiocentric perspective, thereby complementing the ethnocentric, polycentric, and geocentric profiles.
- Updated Table 20.1 providing a summary profile of the regiocentric staffing framework.
- Revised Figure 20.5 and discussion on the leading concerns of expatriates ahead of moving to their foreign assignment.
- Revised Figure 20.6 and discussion on factors most commonly responsible for expatriate assignments not going as planned.
- Revised closing case incorporating discussion of company strategy as a moderator of its staffing network and directly framing the expatriate selection decision within the context of the company's selection framework.

SOLVING TEACHING AND LEARNING CHALLENGES

Helping you, as a teacher, deliver the best possible learning experience to your students motivates us to incorporate productive resources and powerful pedagogies throughout the text. We, as teachers of IB, have been in your position for many years. Hence, we believe we understand the challenge you face and the opportunity you have to teach the principles and practices of IB. To that end, we have developed a range of resources to help you inspire your students to engage the text and, for your students, to master the material.

CASES

We develop all cases with the explicit objective to fit with the topics, themes, ideas, and examples covered in the chapter. Our cases span the wide world of business, engaging an extensive range of topics from environmental, institutional, country, industry, business, executive, and individual perspectives. They include a range of company perspectives, from large MNEs to small exporters, from old-line manufacturers to emergent digital

CASE

The Globalized Business of Sports[1]

Sports may be the world's most globalized business. Fans demand to see the best, and "best" has become a global competitive standard. (The opening photo shows tourists from several countries in Moscow for the 2018 World Cup.) Satellite TV brings live events from just about anywhere in the world to fans just about anywhere else. This gives the key sports-business participants—athletes, team owners, league representatives, and sports associations—broadened audience exposure, expanded fan bases, and augmented revenues.

National sports federations' sponsorship of international competitions is common, most notably the long-standing World Cup in football (soccer) and the Olympics. More national organizations participate in these events than there are United Nations (UN) members, and probably more people follow them than follow most of the UN's businesses, and from product manufacturers to service providers. All cases are written from the perspective of assessing an opportunity, analyzing a challenge, and making a decision.

CASE

Saudi Arabia's Dynamic Culture[1]

Saudi Arabia (see Map 2.1) can be perplexing to foreign firms as they try to exercise acceptable personal and business behavior. Its mixture of strict religious convictions, ancient social customs, and governmental economic policies results in laws and customs that often contrast with those elsewhere, shift with little advance notice, and vary by industry and region. (The opening photo illustrates the contrast between tradition and modern, i.e., people in religiously fostered traditional dress at an ultramodern structure.) Thus, foreign companies and employees must determine what these differences are and how to adjust to them. A brief sample of Saudi traditions, cultural norms, and foreign operating adjustments should help you understand the importance of culture in IB.

A LITTLE HISTORY AND BACKGROUND

Although the land encompassing the Kingdom of Saudi Arabia has a long history, during most of that history invaders controlled a divided land and most inhabitants had a tribal rather than national loyalty. Nevertheless, the inhabitants have shared a common language (Arabic) and religion (Islam). In fact, Saudi Arabia is the birthplace of Islam and the location of its two holiest cities, Mecca and Medina. King Ibn Saud, a descendant of Mohamad, took power in 1901, merged independent areas, created a political and religious entity, and legitimized his monarchy and succession by defending Islamic holy areas, beliefs, and values.

The growing importance of oil for Saudi Arabia, particularly since the 1970s, led to rapid urbanization and gave the government the means to offer social services such as free education. These

The Opening Case Each chapter opens with a case profile of a big topic issue in IB. It familiarizes the students with the upcoming topics in the chapter by introducing themes within a practical context that speak to the key topics explained in the chapter. Much like the overture of a symphony, the opening case highlights critical ideas and issues for the students that are developed through academic perspectives and applied interpretation throughout the chapter, thereby stimulating their thinking engines.

CASE

It's a Knockoff World

Worldwide, companies are plagued by piracy—the illegal imitation, copying, or counterfeiting of their intellectual property. It's a tense issue given that it cuts to issues of history, culture, politics, income, development, innovation, competitiveness, and prosperity. Making matters worse is that pirates, besides being everywhere, come in every form: individuals making copies at work, imitators laboring in dingy sweatshops, modern enterprises build to steal, deni- the latter provides cheap, easily accessible marketing platforms and distribution channels. The costs of counterfeit IP, from lost sales, eroded consumer confidence, diminished brand reputation, lower tax revenue, and higher enforcement expenses, is staggering. The International Anti-Counterfeiting Coalition (IACC) estimates that international trade in illegitimate goods runs $1.77 trillion—approximately 10 percent of world merchandise trade. To top it off, piracy has grown more than 10,000 percent in the past three decades—it was a paltry $5.5 billion in 1982.[107]

The Closing Case Each chapter closes with a case profile of a big topic in IB that extends and elaborates key ideas reported in the chapter. It provides a student a real-world situation to apply the principles covered throughout the chapter. It gives the student a great opportunity to ask what would they do, as an observer, executive, or official, to make sense of the situation and, importantly, to make a decision in the real-world context of IB.

POINT

Should Africa Develop a Common Currency?

YES So far, we've looked at the success of the EU in initiating a common currency. But what about Africa, the continent of some of the world's fastest-growing frontier economies? The success of the euro and the deep economic and political problems in Africa have caused many experts to wonder whether the continent should attempt to develop one common currency with a central bank to set monetary policy.[15] In 2003, the Association of African Central Bank Governors of the African Union (AU)

COUNTERPOINT

Should Africa Develop a Common Currency?

NO There is no way the countries of Africa will ever establish a common currency, even though the African Union hopes to do so. The institutional framework in the individual African nations is simply not ready. Few of the individual central banks are independent of the political process, so they often have to stimulate the economy to respond to political pressures. If the process is not managed properly and the currency is subject to frequent devaluation, there will be no pride in

Point-Counterpoint This feature reflects the fact that many issues in IB, depending upon one's perspective, have different characteristics that support different decisions. It gives students a great opportunity to study an issue, examining two contrasting perspectives, and make sense of overlaps and contradictions. This allows students to apply the principles learned in the chapter to resolve the contrasting points of view. Importantly, this feature helps students understand that, depending on the perspective one applies, one can come up with different, but still credible interpretations and conclusions.

CONCEPT CHECK

Chapter 2 notes that globalization spurs a variety of managerial approaches. Similarly, Chapters 3 and 4 emphasize that MNEs invariably encounter different political, legal, and economic practices. Likewise, here we highlight that global imperatives and local constraints shape planning in the MNE.

Concept Checks Concept checks support the student's understanding of relationships between fundamental principles introduced in one chapter with overlapping principles reported in other chapters. Concept checks are used thoughtfully, highlighting key foundational aspects of IB. Each shows how linkages and connections are an important aspect of studying IB. Each is positioned in the margin, adjacent to the corresponding topic.

LOOKING TO THE FUTURE Digits, Widgets, and Changing Location Advantages

Since business began, location advantages have influenced how companies configure value activities. Searching for raw materials, seeking productive, low-cost labor, arbitraging taxes and tariffs, and the like push MNEs to travel the world, continually seeking optimal locations. Making products there yet moving products here required an expansive, often expensive logistics matrix. Today, in a bit of understatement, "the times they are a changin." Revolutionary developments in digitalization, robots, and 3-D printers spur radically rethinking the implication of location advantages to configuring value activities.

Similar trends, for instance, disrupt location effects in value activities such as regulatory registration or evaluation. Digitization disperses these activities. Indeed, it has created a new global model for financial services, unleashing disruptive innovations that change the gameboard. Arguably, we have never seen disruption of this magnitude in history. Companies respond in kind, rethinking the location of value activities. Some see digitization "creating a second economy that's vast, automatic, and invisible—thereby bringing the biggest change since the Industrial Revolution."[54]

Looking to the Future Each chapter covers issues that have implications to apparent trends and the possible future for IB. The feature helps students realize the importance of understanding the past and the present in order to anticipate the future. The ideas and perspectives covered in the corresponding chapter position them to forecast possible future IB scenarios by understanding how current trends and contemporary events create opportunities and threats. Notably, given the unfolding consequences of the COVID-19 pandemic, looking to the future is fundamentally important to making sense of IB—and throughout the text, this feature does precisely that.

Maps Besides orienting students to the scale and scope of IB, maps are helpful for learners to understand the practical geography of IB – whether it involves understanding a company situation reported in the course of the chapter, a feature of an opening or closing case, or just simply an aspect of class discussion. Time and time again, maps have helped us help our students visualize patterns and processes in the global business environment. Indeed, maps consistently help us convey information and findings that are often tough to express verbally, but, once a student "sees" it in the context of a map, the student "gets it."

> Global integration standardizes worldwide activities to maximize efficiency, whereas local responsiveness adapts local activities to optimize effectiveness.

Margin Notes These are selectively included throughout each chapter to highlight important ideas and concepts. Students moving through the text can more effectively orient their learning experience by quickly reviewing a section or chapter, getting a general sense of the structure and flow of the materials. Too, they make for efficient note-taking and study aids. Our students report the value of adding their own margin notes to improve their learning as well as prepping for assessments.

A Diversity of Perspectives Our teaching experiences and research activities confirm the value a student gains by understanding the wide-ranging facets of IB. Hence, we present materials from a diversity of perspectives. Consistently, the material puts students in a position to apply a managerial perspective. However, it also puts them in a position to apply it from institutional to strategic to tactical viewpoints. Inevitably, students see the value of applying different levels of analysis to interpret how policies, whether set by a transnational institution, national government, multinational enterprise, or local entrepreneur, influence their personal lives and professional ambitions.

DEVELOPING SKILLS TO HELP YOU GET A JOB AND ENHANCE YOUR CAREER

As students consider whether or not to take an IB class and use this text, they ask themselves two fundamental questions: First, how will studying this text help me get a job and, second, from then on, how will it enhance my career? Fundamentally, we see the test of the usefulness of our text in terms of preparing students with the knowledge, skills, and abilities that employers require in a competitive labor market. Consistently, reports by various institutions, such as the Graduate Management Admission Council, World Economic Forum, Workplace, and the U.S. Department of Labor, highlight the importance of the following:

Complex Problem-Solving	Find solutions to difficult scenarios and complicated issues.
Comprehension and Logic	Apply critical and logical reasoning skills to evaluate facts and arguments in developing valid conclusions.
Critical Thinking	Objective analysis and evaluation of an issue in order to form a judgment.
Cultural Awareness	Understanding the differences between oneself and people from other countries or other backgrounds, especially differences in attitudes, outlooks, and values.
Ethics	Assess and interpret the relationship between right and wrong in the world of business.
Global Mindset	Outlook and orientation that helps one work more effectively with individuals, groups, and organizations unlike themselves.
Integrated Reasoning	Organize, manipulate, and evaluate information from different sources to identify relationships, synthesize connections, and solve multiple, interrelated problems.

The breadth and depth of our text offers many opportunities to develop this skillset. We cover a panorama of topics from all business domains along with materials from allied disciplines, including anthropology, political science, sociology, law, economics, geography, demography, psychology, international relations, public policy, comparative politics, and institutional theory. In addition, we apply a diversity of intellectual, philosophical, and cultural perspectives. Throughout, the text integrates key concepts that span these domains. Collectively, these ambitions and outcomes develop several of the skills that employers seek.

Each chapter's primary content along with showcase features develop employability skills in broad as well as precise terms. The scale and scope of the primary chapter material encourage the student to develop the full set of skills listed above. Furthermore, features, such as Business Cases, Looking to the Future Profiles, and Point-Counterpoint Debates, showcase a variety of issues and questions, highlight different perspectives, introduce different information sources, and emphasize synthesizing connections among concepts. Each and all encourage students to develop a robust skillset that the workplace confirms and supports professional success. Given the different objectives of the different features, some emphasize certain skills while others develop different ones—as we see here.

EMPLOYABILITY SKILLS MATRIX					
Skill	Opening Chapter Case	Chapter Content	Point-Counterpoint	Looking to the Future	Closing Chapter Case
Complex Problem-Solving	X	X		X	X
Comprehension and Logic	X	X			X
Critical Thinking	X	X	X	X	X
Cultural Awareness		X	X		
Ethics		X	X		
Global Mindset	X	X		X	X
Integrated Reasoning		X	X	X	X

INSTRUCTOR RESOURCES

Your Pearson team recognizes the importance of diverse, effective teaching resources to support the design and delivery of your class. Presently, we offer a full slate of resource options for you and we continually look for ways to expand and enhance your resources. Please visit www.pearson.com to see your latest options.

ACKNOWLEDGMENTS

We have received many suggestions, recommendations, and constructive criticisms from adopters and reviewers. In addition, our editorial staff has shared invaluable insights on significant design and delivery issues. Notwithstanding the importance of each, it is impossible to implement every recommendation. Ever-present constraints on the scale of the textbook impose tough page boundaries. Developing the text with an eye toward supporting its digital formats adds other constraints. Nevertheless, we, along with our editorial team, are always mindful of ensuring the text offers compelling value to the student. Generally, external reviewers are anonymous to us. Nevertheless, we humbly thank them for the insights and effort. Inevitably, we learn a great deal from listening to you, and your comments significantly improve the value of the text to adopters and students worldwide.

Beginning with researching and writing nearly half a century ago, this text, first published in 1976, now heads into its 17th edition. Over that span, many contributors, colleagues, and critics have shared their views; the collective set is far too lengthy to list here. Nevertheless, the text could have attained its present position only with their ideas and insights. Once again, our sincere gratitude.

We also acknowledge people whom we interviewed in writing cases. These are Brenda Yester (Carnival Cruise Lines); Omar Aljindi, Nora al Jundi, and Talah Tamimi (Saudi Arabia's Dynamic Culture); Mauricio Calero (Ecuador: A Rosy Export Future?); Raul Arguelles, Diaz Gonzales, and Francisco Suarez Mogollon (Walmart Goes South); Jonathan Fitzpatrick, Julio A. Ramirez, Arianne Cento, and Ana Miranda (Burger King); several executives at American Airlines and oneworld who wish to remain anonymous (The oneworld Airline Alliance); and Ali R. Manbien (GPS Capital Markets Inc).

In addition, we would like to thank several people who authored or coauthored cases for us: Terence Mughan at Royal Roads University for International Students and International Business: Leveraging Global Knowledge (Chapter 2), Lichung Jen at National Taiwan University for The Evolution of Taiwan's International Trade (Chapter 6), various executives at Walmart for their assistance with Walmart Goes South (Chapter 8), Fidel León-Darder and Cristina Villar at Universitat de València for Meliá Hotels International (Chapter 15), Jon Jungbien Moon at Korea University for Grameen Danone Foods in Bangladesh (Chapter 17), and Manuel Serapio at the University of Colorado Denver and Steve Katsaros, founder and CEO of Nokero, for Nokero: Lighting the World (Chapter 18). Others who helped with administrative and research matters include Ian G. Daniels, Maddison Daines, Lisa Curlee, Allison Johnson, and Katie Cooper Redding.

It takes a dedicated group of individuals to take a textbook from first draft to final manuscript. We would like to thank our partners at Pearson Education for their tireless efforts in bringing the 17th edition of this book from aspiration to reality. Our thanks go to Director of HE Global Content Strategy, Lacey Vitetta; Manager—HE Global Content Strategy, Lynn Huddon; Managing Editor—US and UK, Sutapa Mukherjee; Sr. Sponsoring Editor, Neeraj Bhalla; Product Managers, Olutosin Aje-Adegbite and Ellen Geary; Content Producers, Sugandh Juneja and Shweta Jain; and Project Manager at Integra, Allison Campbell.

About the Authors

From left to right: John Daniels, Reid Click, Lee Radebaugh, and Daniel Sullivan

Four respected and renowned scholars show your students how dynamic, how real, how interesting, and how important the study of international business can be.

John D. Daniels, the Samuel N. Friedland Chair of Executive Management emeritus at the University of Miami, received his BBA, MBA, and PhD respectively at the University of Miami, University of the Americas, and the University of Michigan. He holds an honorary doctorate from UPAO in Peru and served as Chancellor (Honorary) of the University College of the Caribbean in Jamaica. His dissertation won first place in the award competition of the Academy of International Business, and he won a decade award from the *Journal of International Business Studies* along with a silver medal award for contributions. His articles have appeared in such journals as *Academy of Management Journal, Advances in International Marketing, California Management Review, Columbia Journal of World Business, International Marketing Review, International Trade Journal, Journal of Business Research, Journal of High Technology Management Research, Journal of International Business Studies (JIBS), Management International Review, Multinational Business Review, Strategic Management Journal, Transnational Corporations,* and *Weltwirtschaftliches Archiv.* He has published 15 books, most recently *Multinational Enterprises and the Changing World Economy* (coedited with Ray Loveridge, Tsai-Mei Lin, and Alan M. Rugman), three volumes on Multinational Enterprise Theory, and three volumes on International Business and Globalization (all coedited with Jeffrey Krug). On its 30th anniversary, *Management International Review* referred to him as "one of the most prolific American IB scholars." He served as president of the Academy of International Business and dean of its Fellows, as well as chairperson of the international division of the Academy of Management, which named him Outstanding Educator of the Year in 2010.

Professor Daniels has worked and lived a year or longer in seven different countries, worked shorter stints in approximately 30 other countries on six continents, and traveled in many more. His foreign work has been a combination of private sector, governmental, teaching, and research assignments. He was formerly a faculty member at Georgia State University and The Pennsylvania State University, director of the Center for International Business Education and Research (CIBER) at Indiana University, and holder of the E. Claiborne Robins Distinguished Chair at the University of Richmond. He and his wife, Letty, have been married since 1963, and they have two sons.

Lee H. Radebaugh is the Emeritus Whitmore Professor of International Business and former Director of the Kay and Yvonne Whitmore Global Management Center/CIBER at Brigham Young University (BYU). Previously, he was the Associate Dean of the Marriott School of Management, Associate Director of the MBA program, and Director of the School of Accountancy. In his prior position as CIBER Director at BYU, he was responsible for international business programs in the Marriott School of Management at BYU, outreach to the business and academic communities and establishing exchange agreements with universities abroad. He led student and faculty groups to Asia, the Middle East, and South America. From 2000–2003, he was the President of the Brazil Porto Alegre South Mission of the Church of Jesus Christ of Latter-day Saints. He received his DBA and MBA from Indiana University and his BS in accounting from BYU. He taught at The Pennsylvania State University from 1972 to 1980 and was a visiting professor at ESAN in Lima, Peru and at Glasgow University in Glasgow, Scotland. He is the coauthor of several books, including *International Business Environments and Operations* and *International Accounting and Multinational Enterprises*, both of which have been translated into several languages, including Mandarin Chinese. He has also published several monographs and articles on international business and international accounting. In 2019, he was awarded the Silver Medal for Scholarship by the Academy of International Business for substantive contributions to JIBS. His international research interests include the impact of exchange rates on operations, accounting, and financial reporting; the global implementation of IFRS; and the role of culture and institutional factors on international accounting and international business. He was recognized as the International Person of the Year for the State of Utah in 1998 for his service to the Utah business community. A past president of the International Accounting Section of the American Accounting Association, he was given the Outstanding Service Award for the section in 2007, and in 1998, he was named the "Outstanding International Educator" of the International Section of the AAA. He was elected to the Fellows of the Academy of International Business in 1990. Lee and his wife, Tanya, are the parents of six children and 14 grandchildren.

Daniel P. Sullivan, Professor of Global Studies at the Alfred Lerner College of Business of the University of Delaware, received his doctorate from the University of South Carolina. He researches a range of topics, including globalization and business, international management, global strategy, competitive analysis, and corporate governance. His work on these topics has been published in leading scholarly journals, including the *Journal of International Business Studies, Management International Review, Law and Society Review, Academy of Management Journal, Academy of Management Perspectives*, and the *Online Learning Journal*. He has served on the editorial boards of the *Journal of International Business Studies* and *Management International Review*. Professor Sullivan has been honored for both his research and teaching, receiving grants and winning awards for both activities while at the University of Delaware and, his former affiliation, the Freeman School of Tulane University. He is a recipient of the Academy of International Business, JIBS Silver Medal in recognition for intellectual contributions published in the *Journal of International Business Studies* (JIBS), the premier journal in the international business domain. The Silver Medal was awarded to 48 IB scholars who have published at least five significant papers in JIBS since its inception. He has been awarded numerous teaching honors—most notably, he has been voted Outstanding Teacher by the students of 19 different executive, MBA, and undergraduate classes at the University of Delaware and Tulane University. Professor Sullivan has taught, designed, and administered a range of in-class and online graduate, undergraduate, and nondegree courses on topics spanning globalization and business, international business operations, international management, strategic perspectives, executive leadership, and corporate strategy. In the United States, he has delivered lectures and courses at several university and companies. In addition, he has led courses in several foreign countries, including China, Hong Kong, Bulgaria, the Czech Republic, France, South Korea, Switzerland, Taiwan, and the United Kingdom. Finally, he has worked with many managers and consulted with several multinational enterprises on issues of international business.

Reid W. Click is Associate Professor of International Business and International Affairs at George Washington University in Washington, DC. He received his MBA and PhD degrees from the University of Chicago Booth School of Business, where he studied economics and international business, and his undergraduate B.A. in economics from Kenyon College in Ohio. His research and teaching interests are in the fields of global financial markets, international financial management, macroeconomics in the global economy, and finance for development. An expert on international financial risk and risk management, his academic work has been published in leading journals, including the *Journal of International Business Studies* and the *Journal of Money, Credit and Banking*. After research appointments in Asia, including one as a Fulbright Scholar at the Asian Institute of Management in the Philippines, he became Associate Editor of the *Journal of Asian Economics* in the field of international finance. At George Washington University, he has served in leadership positions to develop the international business programs, most recently as the founding Director of the joint International Finance Corporation—Milken Institute Capital Markets Program. Previously, he served as the Faculty Director of the Center for International Business Education and Research (GW-CIBER), part of the national CIBER network funded by a grant from the U.S. Department of Education. He has also served as chairperson of George Washington's renowned Department of International Business, and has run eight student and faculty programs investigating business institutions, finance, and economic development in Rwanda. In addition to his academic work, he has been a consultant to several international organizations, notably the U.S. Agency for International Development (USAID) Office of Development Credit and the U.S. International Development Finance Corporation, on matters pertaining to international banking, financial risk, and risk management.

Atlas

Satellite television transmission now makes it commonplace for us to watch events as they unfold in other countries. Transportation and communication advances and government-to-government accords have contributed to our increasing dependence on foreign goods and markets. As this dependence grows, updated maps are a valuable tool. They can show the locations of population, economic wealth, production, and markets; portray certain commonalities and differences among areas; and illustrate barriers that might inhibit trade. In spite of the usefulness of maps, a substantial number of people worldwide have a poor knowledge of how to interpret information on maps and even of how to find the location of events that affect their lives.

We urge you to use the following maps to build your awareness of geography.

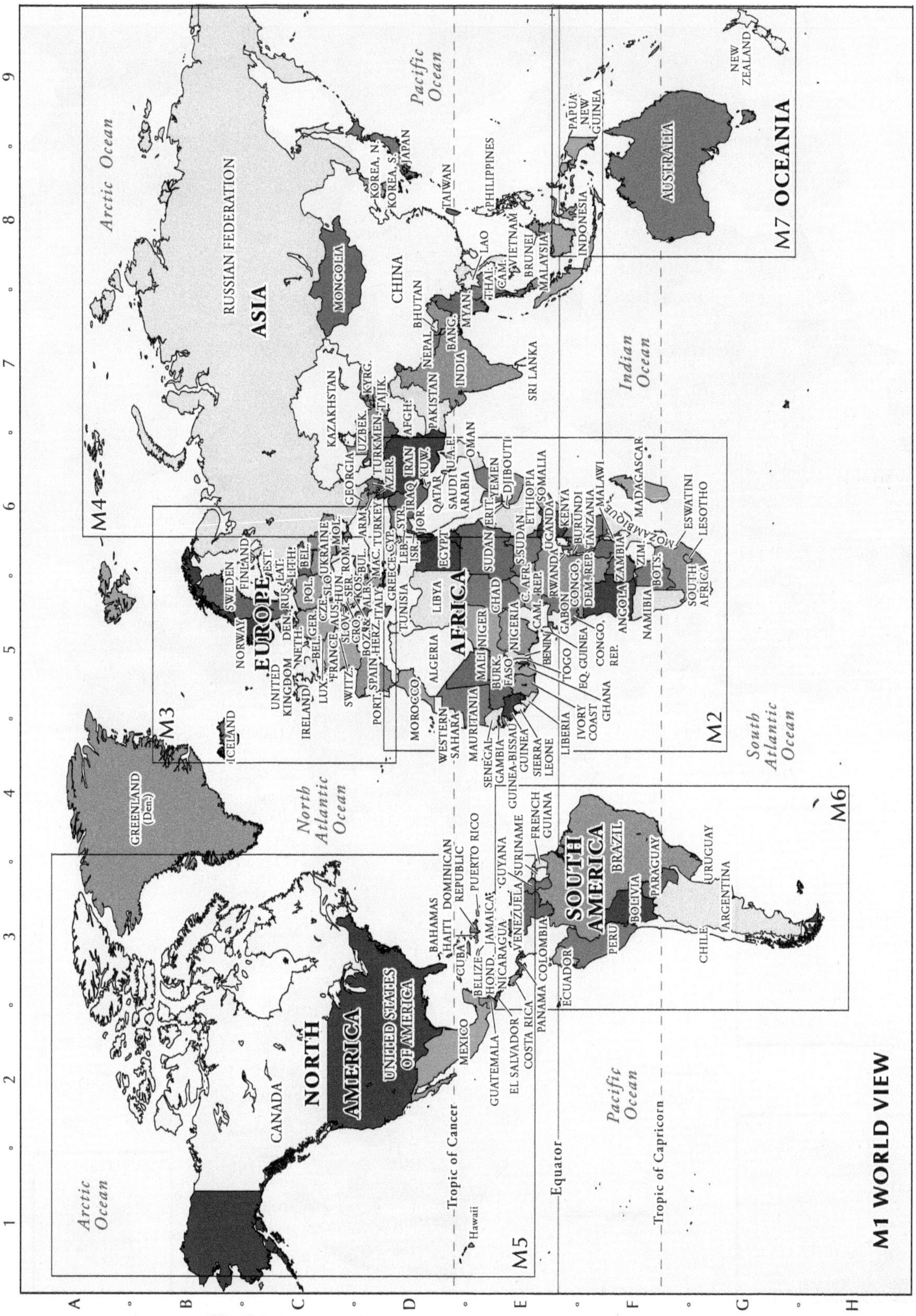

M1 WORLD VIEW

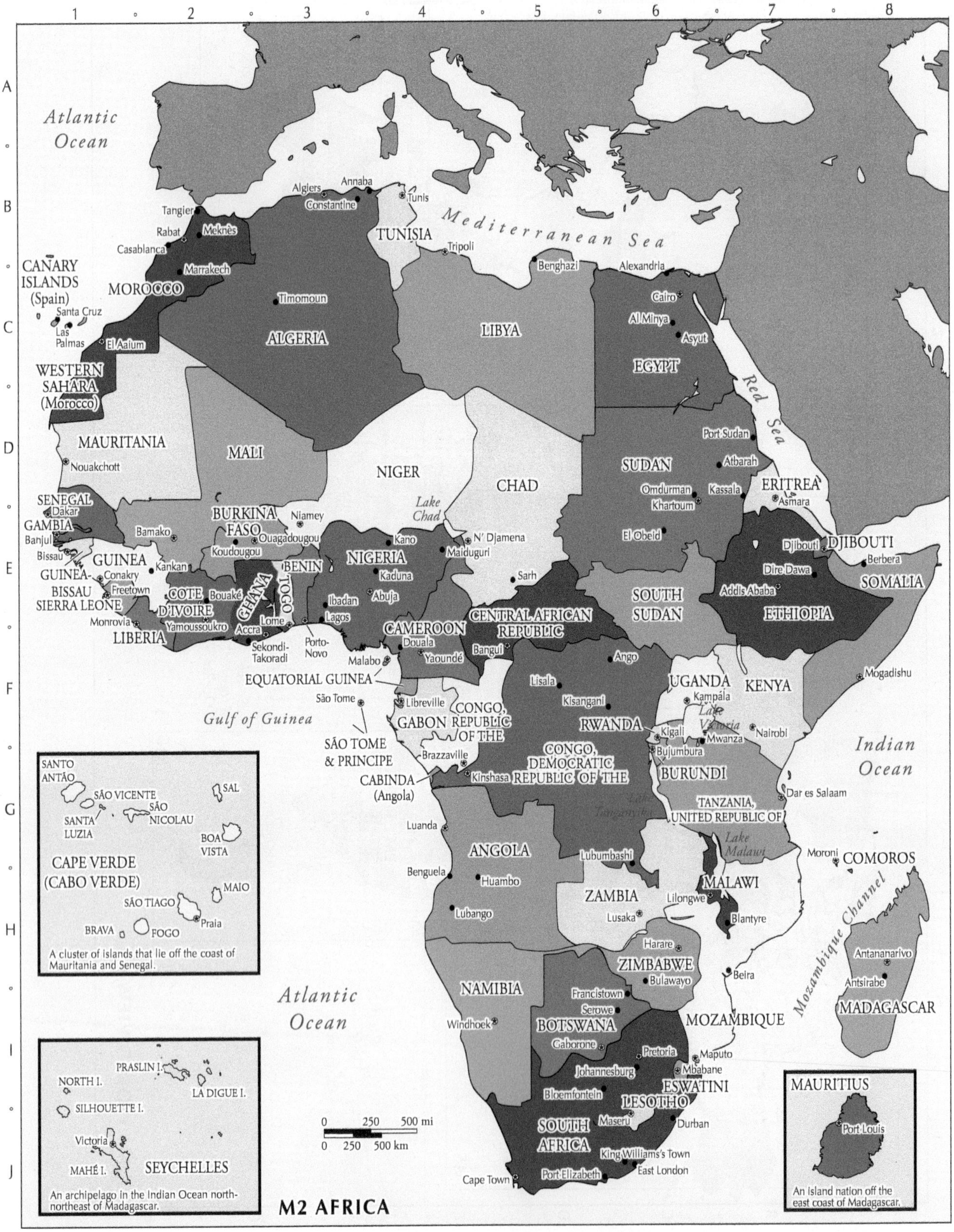

1
2
3
4
5
6
7
8
A
B
C
D
E
F
G
H
I
J
Atlantic Ocean
Mediterranean Sea
Red Sea
Gulf of Guinea
Indian Ocean
Mozambique Channel
Lake Chad
Lake Victoria
Lake Tanganyika
Lake Malawi
CANARY ISLANDS (Spain)
Santa Cruz
Las Palmas
MOROCCO
Tangier
Rabat
Meknès
Casablanca
Marrakech
El Aaiun
WESTERN SAHARA (Morocco)
Algiers
Annaba
Constantine
Tunis
TUNISIA
Tripoli
Benghazi
Alexandria
Cairo
Al Minya
Asyut
EGYPT
ALGERIA
Timomoun
LIBYA
MAURITANIA
Nouakchott
MALI
NIGER
CHAD
SUDAN
Port Sudan
Atbarah
Omdurman
Khartoum
Kassala
El Obeid
ERITREA
Asmara
DJIBOUTI
Djibouti
Berbera
Dire Dawa
Addis Ababa
ETHIOPIA
SOMALIA
Mogadishu
SENEGAL
Dakar
GAMBIA
Banjul
Bissau
GUINEA-BISSAU
GUINEA
Conakry
Kankan
Freetown
SIERRA LEONE
Monrovia
LIBERIA
Bamako
BURKINA FASO
Ouagadougou
Koudougou
Niamey
COTE D'IVOIRE
Bouaké
Yamoussoukro
GHANA
Accra
Sekondi-Takoradi
TOGO
Lome
BENIN
Porto-Novo
NIGERIA
Kano
Kaduna
Abuja
Ibadan
Lagos
Maiduguri
N' Djamena
Sarh
CAMEROON
Douala
Yaoundé
Malabo
EQUATORIAL GUINEA
São Tome
SÃO TOME & PRINCIPE
CENTRAL AFRICAN REPUBLIC
Bangui
SOUTH SUDAN
Libreville
GABON
CONGO, REPUBLIC OF THE
Brazzaville
Kinshasa
CABINDA (Angola)
Ango
Lisala
Kisangani
CONGO, DEMOCRATIC REPUBLIC OF THE
UGANDA
Kampala
KENYA
Nairobi
RWANDA
Kigali
Mwanza
Bujumbura
BURUNDI
TANZANIA, UNITED REPUBLIC OF
Dar es Salaam
Luanda
ANGOLA
Benguela
Huambo
Lubango
Lubumbashi
ZAMBIA
Lusaka
Lilongwe
MALAWI
Blantyre
Moroni
COMOROS
Harare
ZIMBABWE
Bulawayo
Beira
MOZAMBIQUE
Antananarivo
Antsirabe
MADAGASCAR
NAMIBIA
Windhoek
Francistown
Serowe
BOTSWANA
Gaborone
Pretoria
Maputo
Mbabane
ESWATINI
Johannesburg
Bloemfontein
LESOTHO
Maseru
Durban
SOUTH AFRICA
King Williams's Town
East London
Port Elizabeth
Cape Town
0 250 500 mi
0 250 500 km
SANTO ANTÃO
SÃO VICENTE
SANTA LUZIA
SÃO NICOLAU
SAL
BOA VISTA
CAPE VERDE (CABO VERDE)
MAIO
SÃO TIAGO
Praia
BRAVA
FOGO
A cluster of islands that lie off the coast of Mauritania and Senegal.
PRASLIN I.
NORTH I.
LA DIGUE I.
SILHOUETTE I.
Victoria
MAHÉ I.
SEYCHELLES
An archipelago in the Indian Ocean north-northeast of Madagascar.
MAURITIUS
Port Louis
An island nation off the east coast of Madagascar.

M2 AFRICA

1
2
3
4
5
6
7
8
A
B
C
D
E
F
G
H
I
J
JAN MAYEN IS.
(Denmark)
Arctic
Ocean
Barents Sea
Denmark Strait
Murmansk
ICELAND
Reykjavík
Norwegian
Sea
RUSSIAN
FEDERATION
SWEDEN
FINLAND
FAEROE IS.
(Den.)
Lake
Ladoga
NORWAY
SHETLAND IS.
(U.K.)
Helsinki
St. Petersburg
Kostroma
Bergen
Tallinn
Oslo
Stockholm
ORKNEY IS.
ESTONIA
Moscow
Riga
Göteborg
LATVIA
Tula
North
Sea
Baltic
Sea
Smolensk
Glasgow
Edinburgh
DENMARK
LITHUANIA
UNITED
KINGDOM
Belfast
Copenhagen
Malmo
Vilnius
Orel
Minsk
RUS.
Kaliningrad
Kursk
Dublin
Irish
Sea
Manchester
Gdansk
BELARUS
Liverpool
IRELAND
Hamburg
Homyel'
Bydgoszcz
NETHERLANDS
Birmingham
Amsterdam
Berlin
POLAND
Kiev
The Hague
GERMANY
Warsaw
London
Essen
Leipzig
Lódz
BELGIUM
Düsseldorf
Dresden
UKRAINE
Dnipropetrovsk
Atlantic
Ocean
English Channel
Brussels
Liège
Bonn
Wroclaw
Lvov
Prague
Krakow
Le Havre
LUXEMBOURG
Frankfurt
Chernivtsi
CZECHIA
Brno
Luxembourg
SLOVAKIA
MOLDOVA
Mykolayiv
Paris
Stuttgart
Vienna
Bratislava
Debrecen
Le Mans
Munich
Linz
Chisinau
Odesa
FRANCE
Zurich
LIECHTENSTEIN
Budapest
ROMANIA
AUSTRIA
HUNGARY
SWITZERLAND
Arad
Bay of
Biscay
Limoges
Geneva
Bern
Ljubljana
SLOVENIA
Timisoara
Black Sea
Lyon
Zagreb
Bordeaux
Milan
Padova
Venice
Belgrade
Bucharest
St. Etienne
BOSNIA &
HERZE-
GOVINA
SAN
MARINO
Turin
CROATIA
EUROPE PORTION
OF TURKEY
A Coruña
SERBIA
Nîmes
Genoa
BULGARIA
Toulouse
Sarajevo
MONACO
Florence
Marseille
Livorno
MONTE-
NEGRO
KOSOVO
Sofia
Istanbul
ASIA PORTION
OF TURKEY
Porto
ITALY
Pristina
Adriatic Sea
ANDORRA
Skopje
CORSICA
Rome
Tirana
NORTH
MACEDONIA
PORTUGAL
Barcelona
VATICAN
CITY
TURKEY
Madrid
Bari
ALBANIA
Thessaloniki
Lisbon
SARDINIA
Naples
Taranto
SPAIN
Aegean
Sea
GREECE
Valencia
Tyrrhenian
Sea
Ionian
Sea
BALEARIC IS.
Sevilla
Granada
Piraiévs
Athens
Palermo
Messina
Cartagena
Málaga
Mediterranean Sea
SICILY
Strait of
Gibraltar
CYPRUS
CRETE
Valetta
MALTA
0
300 mi
0
300 km
M3 EUROPE

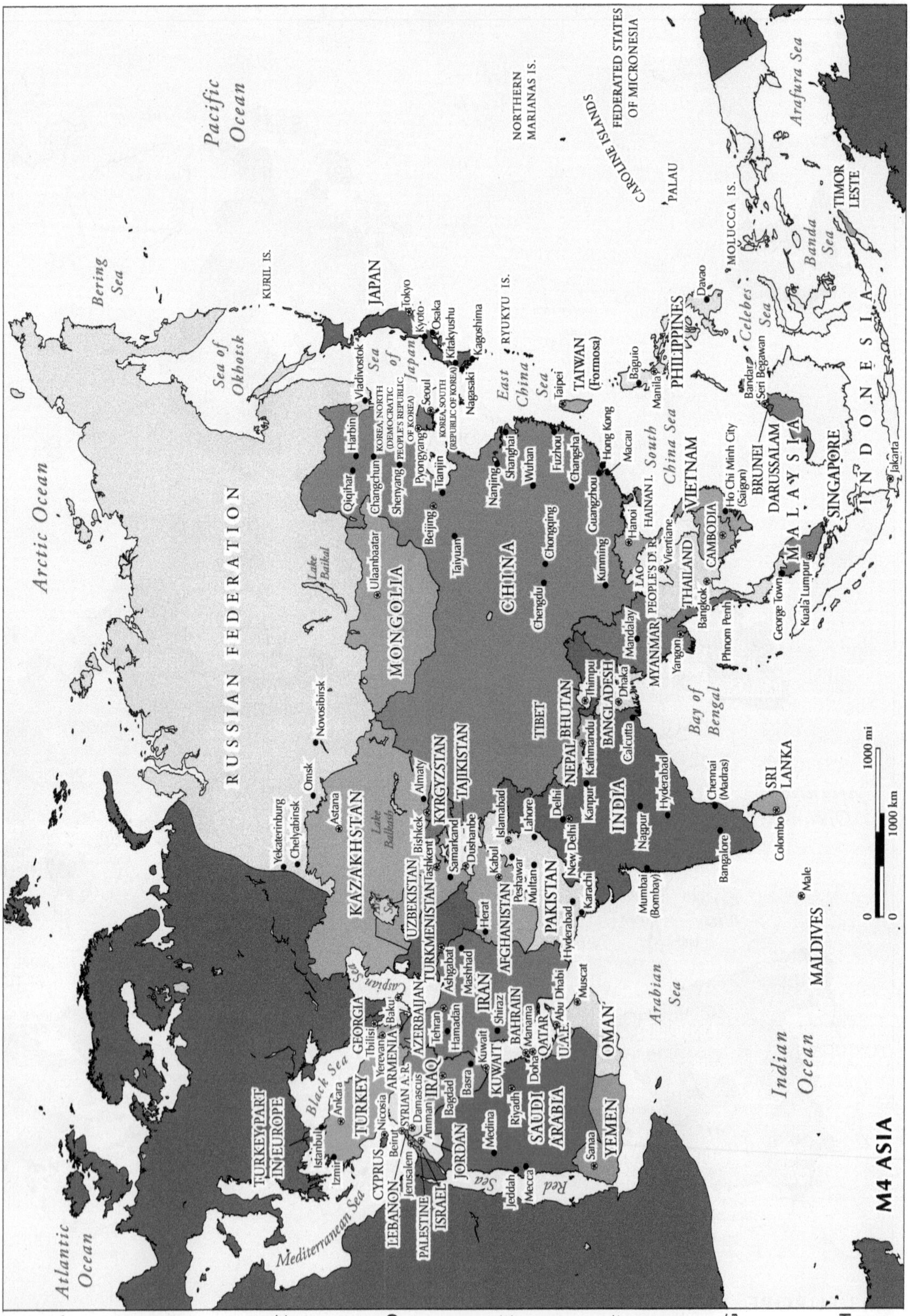
Arctic Ocean
Pacific Ocean
Atlantic Ocean
Indian Ocean
Bering Sea
Sea of Okhotsk
Sea of Japan
East China Sea
South China Sea
Bay of Bengal
Arabian Sea
Red Sea
Black Sea
Caspian Sea
Mediterranean Sea
Celebes Sea
Banda Sea
Arafura Sea
Lake Baikal
Lake Balkash
RUSSIAN FEDERATION
KAZAKHSTAN
MONGOLIA
CHINA
TIBET
INDIA
PAKISTAN
AFGHANISTAN
IRAN
IRAQ
TURKEY
TURKEY PART IN EUROPE
SAUDI ARABIA
YEMEN
OMAN
U.A.E.
QATAR
BAHRAIN
KUWAIT
JORDAN
ISRAEL
PALESTINE
LEBANON
CYPRUS
SYRIAN A.R.
ARMENIA
GEORGIA
AZERBAIJAN
TURKMENISTAN
UZBEKISTAN
KYRGYZSTAN
TAJIKISTAN
NEPAL
BHUTAN
BANGLADESH
MYANMAR
THAILAND
LAO PEOPLE'S D.R.
VIETNAM
CAMBODIA
MALAYSIA
SINGAPORE
BRUNEI DARUSSALAM
INDONESIA
PHILIPPINES
TAIWAN (Formosa)
JAPAN
KOREA, NORTH (DEMOCRATIC PEOPLE'S REPUBLIC OF KOREA)
KOREA, SOUTH (REPUBLIC OF KOREA)
SRI LANKA
MALDIVES
TIMOR LESTE
PALAU
NORTHERN MARIANAS IS.
CAROLINE ISLANDS
FEDERATED STATES OF MICRONESIA
KURIL IS.
RYUKYU IS.
MOLUCCA IS.
HAINAN I.
Yekaterinburg
Chelyabinsk
Omsk
Novosibirsk
Astana
Almaty
Bishkek
Tashkent
Samarkand
Dushanbe
Ashgabat
Mashhad
Herat
Kabul
Islamabad
Peshawar
Lahore
Multan
Karachi
Hyderabad
New Delhi
Delhi
Kanpur
Kathmandu
Thimpu
Dhaka
Calcutta
Nagpur
Mumbai (Bombay)
Bangalore
Chennai (Madras)
Colombo
Male
Istanbul
Izmir
Ankara
Nicosia
Beirut
Jerusalem
Amman
Damascus
Baghdad
Basra
Kuwait
Riyadh
Medina
Jeddah
Mecca
Sanaa
Doha
Manama
Abu Dhabi
Muscat
Shiraz
Tehran
Hamadan
Tbilisi
Yerevan
Baku
Ulaanbaatar
Qiqihar
Harbin
Changchun
Shenyang
Vladivostok
Beijing
Tianjin
Pyongyang
Seoul
Taiyuan
Nanjing
Shanghai
Wuhan
Chengdu
Chongqing
Kunming
Guangzhou
Changsha
Fuzhou
Hong Kong
Macau
Taipei
Tokyo
Kyoto
Osaka
Kitakyushu
Nagasaki
Kagoshima
Mandalay
Yangon
Bangkok
Vientiane
Hanoi
Phnom Penh
Ho Chi Minh City (Saigon)
Kuala Lumpur
George Town
Bandar Seri Begawan
Manila
Baguio
Davao
Jakarta
0 1000 mi
0 1000 km
A B C D E F G H
1 2 3 4 5 6 7 8 9
M4 ASIA

M5 NORTH AMERICA

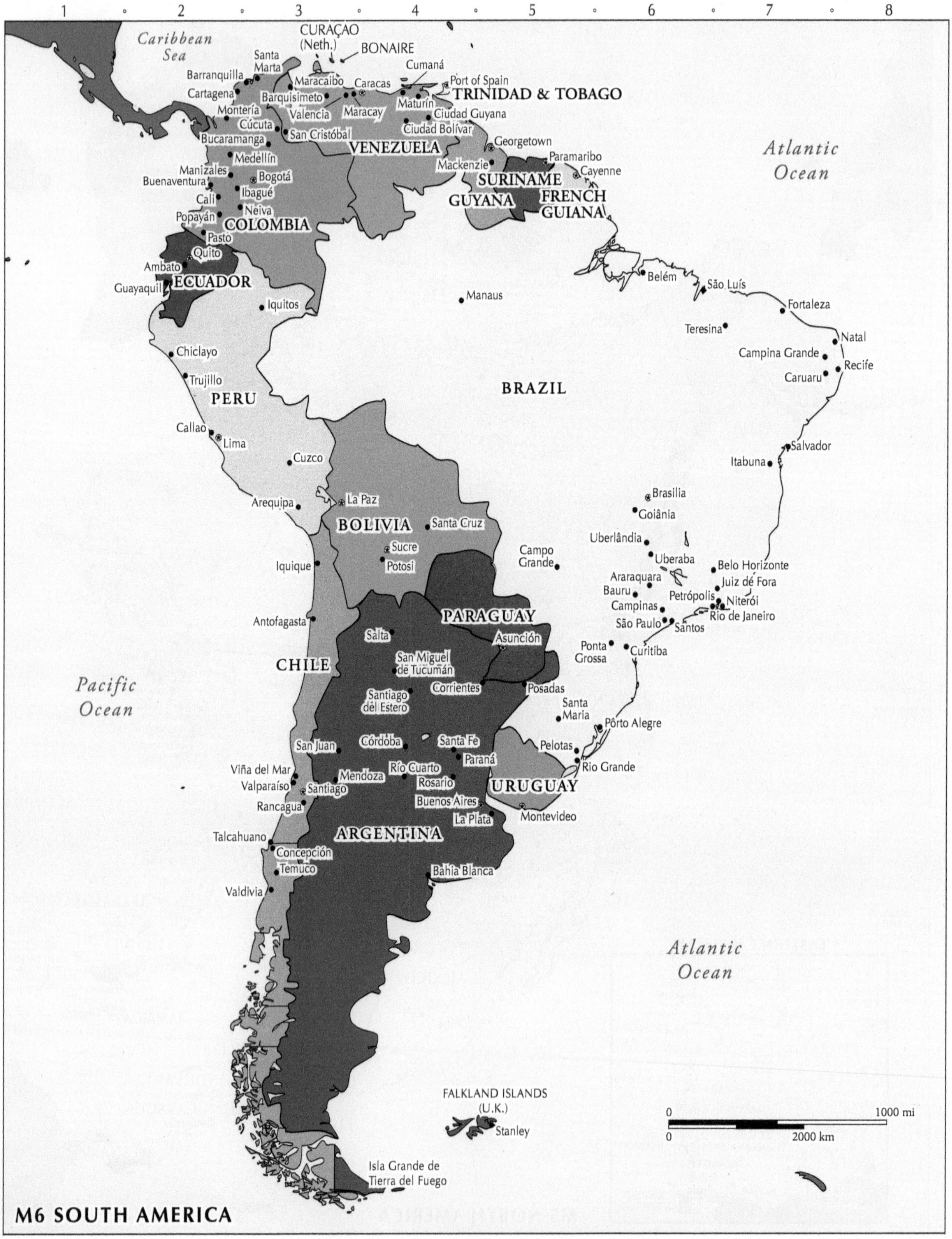
1
2
3
4
5
6
7
8
A
B
C
D
E
F
G
H
I
J
Caribbean Sea
CURAÇAO (Neth.)
BONAIRE
Santa Marta
Barranquilla
Cartagena
Maracaibo
Caracas
Cumaná
Port of Spain
TRINIDAD & TOBAGO
Barquisimeto
Valencia
Maracay
Maturín
Montería
Cúcuta
Ciudad Guyana
Ciudad Bolívar
San Cristóbal
Bucaramanga
VENEZUELA
Georgetown
Medellín
Manizales
Buenaventura
Bogotá
Ibagué
Cali
Popayán
Neiva
COLOMBIA
Pasto
Quito
Ambato
Guayaquil
ECUADOR
Mackenzie
Paramaribo
Cayenne
SURINAME
GUYANA
FRENCH GUIANA
Atlantic Ocean
Belém
São Luís
Manaus
Iquitos
Fortaleza
Teresina
Natal
Campina Grande
Recife
Caruaru
Chiclayo
Trujillo
PERU
BRAZIL
Callao
Lima
Cuzco
Salvador
Itabuna
Brasília
Goiânia
Arequipa
La Paz
BOLIVIA
Santa Cruz
Uberlândia
Uberaba
Campo Grande
Sucre
Potosí
Iquique
Belo Horizonte
Juiz de Fora
Araraquara
Bauru
Petrópolis
Niterói
Campinas
Rio de Janeiro
São Paulo
Santos
Antofagasta
PARAGUAY
Salta
Asunción
Ponta Grossa
Curitiba
CHILE
San Miguel de Tucumán
Corrientes
Posadas
Pacific Ocean
Santiago del Estero
Santa Maria
Pôrto Alegre
San Juan
Córdoba
Santa Fe
Paraná
Pelotas
Rio Grande
Viña del Mar
Valparaíso
Mendoza
Río Cuarto
Rosario
Santiago
Rancagua
URUGUAY
Buenos Aires
La Plata
Montevideo
ARGENTINA
Talcahuano
Concepción
Temuco
Bahía Blanca
Valdivia
Atlantic Ocean
FALKLAND ISLANDS (U.K.)
Stanley
0
1000 mi
0
2000 km
Isla Grande de Tierra del Fuego

M6 SOUTH AMERICA

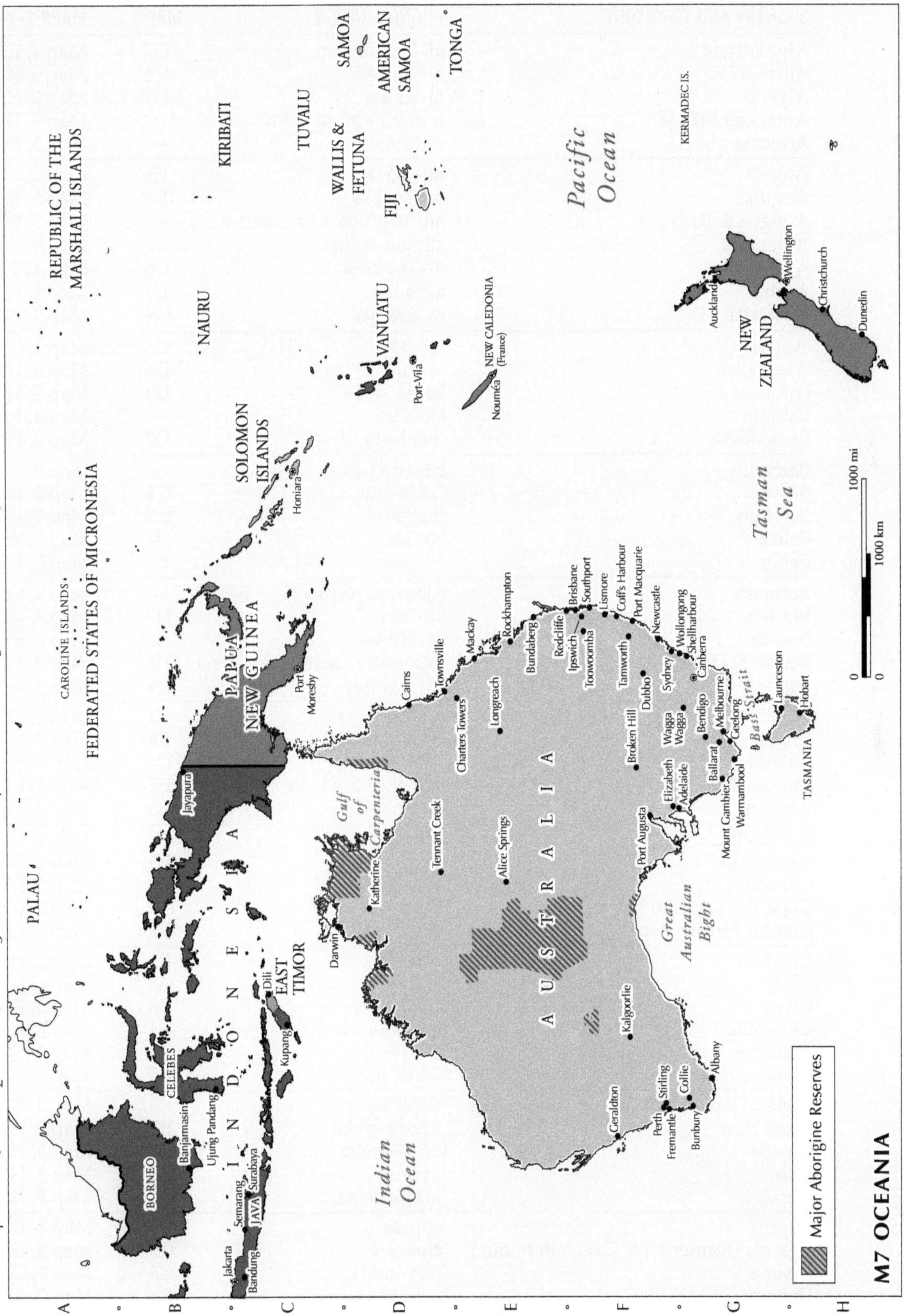
Major Aborigine Reserves
REPUBLIC OF THE MARSHALL ISLANDS
KIRIBATI
TUVALU
SAMOA
AMERICAN SAMOA
TONGA
WALLIS & FETUNA
FIJI
KERMADEC IS.
Pacific Ocean
NAURU
VANUATU
Port-Vila
NEW CALEDONIA (France)
Nouméa
SOLOMON ISLANDS
Honiara
CAROLINE ISLANDS
FEDERATED STATES OF MICRONESIA
PALAU
PAPUA NEW GUINEA
Port Moresby
Jayapura
INDONESIA
BORNEO
CELEBES
Banjarmasin
Ujung Pandang
JAVA
Jakarta
Bandung
Semarang
Surabaya
Kupang
Dili
EAST TIMOR
Indian Ocean
Gulf of Carpentaria
AUSTRALIA
Darwin
Katherine
Tennant Creek
Alice Springs
Cairns
Townsville
Charters Towers
Mackay
Longreach
Rockhampton
Bundaberg
Redcliffe
Brisbane
Ipswich
Southport
Toowoomba
Lismore
Coffs Harbour
Tamworth
Port Macquarie
Newcastle
Dubbo
Sydney
Wollongong
Shellharbour
Canberra
Broken Hill
Wagga Wagga
Bendigo
Melbourne
Geelong
Ballarat
Port Augusta
Elizabeth
Adelaide
Mount Gambier
Warrnambool
Kalgoorlie
Geraldton
Perth
Stirling
Fremantle
Collie
Bunbury
Albany
Great Australian Bight
Bass Strait
Launceston
Hobart
TASMANIA
Tasman Sea
NEW ZEALAND
Auckland
Wellington
Christchurch
Dunedin
0 1000 mi
0 1000 km
1 2 3 4 5 6 7 8 9
A B C D E F G H

M7 OCEANIA

COUNTRY AND TERRITORY	PRONUNCIATION	MAP 1	MAPS 2–7
Afghanistan	af-ˊgan-ə-ˌstan	D7	Map 4, E3
Albania	al-ˈbā-nē-ə	C5	Map 3, I6
Algeria	al-ˊjir-ē-ə	D5	Map 2, C3
American Samoa	ə-merˊi-kən sə-mōˊə	F9	Map 7, D9
Andorra	an-ˊdȯr-ə	—	Map 3, H2
Angola	an-ˊgō-lə	E5	Map 2, G4
Anguila	an-ˊgwi-lə	E3	Map 5, I2
Antigua & Barbuda	an-ˊtē-g(w)ə / bär-ˈbüd-ə	—	Map 5, I3
Argentina	ˌˌär-jen-ˊtē-nə	G3	Map 6, G3
Armenia	är-ˊmē-ne-ə	C6	Map 4, D2
Aruba	ə-ˈrü-bə	E3	Map 5, I7
Australia	ȯ-ˊstrāl-yə	G8	Map 7, E4
Austria	ˊȯs-trē-ə	C5	Map 3, G5
Azerbaijan	ˊaz-ər-ˈbī-ˊjän	D6	Map 4, D2
Bahamas	bə-häˊ-məz	D3	Map 5, H7
Bahrain	bä-ˊrān	—	Map 4, E2
Bangladesh	ˈbänJ-glə-ˊdesh	D7	Map 4, F5
Barbados	bär-ˈbād-əs	—	Map 5, J3
Belarus	ˈbē-lə-ˊrüs	C5	Map 3, F6
Belgium	ˈbel-jəm	C5	Map 3, F3
Belize	bə-ˈlēz	D2	Map 5, I6
Benin	bə-ˊnin	E5	Map 2, E3
Bermuda	(ˊ)bər-ˊmyüd-ə	—	Map 5, G8
Bhutan	bü-ˊtan	D7	Map 4, F5
Bolivia	bə-ˈliv-ē-ə	F3	Map 6, E4
Bosnia & Herzegovina	ˈbäz-nē-ə / ˈhert-sə-gō-ˊvē-nə	D5	Map 3, H5
Botswana	bät-ˊswän-ə	F5	Map 2, I5
Brazil	brə-ˊzil	F3	Map 6, D6
Brunei	brōō-nīˊ	E8	Map 4, G7
Bulgaria	ˈbəl-ˊgar-ē-ə	D5	Map 3, H6
Burkina Faso	buˊr-ˈkē-nə-ˊfaˊ-sō	E5	Map 2, E2
Burundi	buˊ-ˊrün-dē	E6	Map 2, G6
Cambodia	kam-ˈbd-ē-ə	E7	Map 4, G6
Cameroon	ˊkam-ə-ˊrün	E5	Map 2, F4
Canada	ˊkan-əd-ə	C2	Map 5, E5
Cape Verde (Cabo Verde)	ˊvard	—	Map 2, G1
Central African Rep.		E5	Map 2, E5
Chad	ˊchad	E5	Map 2, D5
Chile	ˊchil-ē	G3	Map 6, F3
China	ˊchī-nə	D8	Map 4, E5
Colombia	kə-ˈləm-bē-ə	E3	Map 6, B3
Comoros	kä-mə-ˌrōz	—	Map 2, G7
Congo, Democratic Republic of the	ˊkänJ(ˊ)gō	E5	Map 2, G5
Congo, Republic of the	ˊkänJ(ˊ)gō	E5	Map 2, F4
Costa Rica	ˊkäs-tə-ˊrē-kə	E2	Map 5, J7
Croatia	krō-ˊā-sh(ē)ə	D5	Map 3, H5
Cuba	ˊkyü-bə	E3	Map 5, H7
Curaçao	ˊk(y)ür-ə-ˊsō	—	Map 5, J1
Cyprus	ˊsī-prəs	D6	Map 4, D2
Czechia (formerly the Czech Republic)	ˊchek-ē-ə	C5	Map 3, G5
Denmark	ˊden-ˊmärk	C5	Map 3, E4
Djibouti	jə-ˈbüt-ē	E6	Map 2, E7
Dominica	ˊdäm-ə-ˊnē-kə	—	Map 5, I3
Dominican Republic	də-ˊmin-i-kən	E3	Map 5, H8
Ecuador	ˊek-wə-ˊdȯ(ə)r	E3	Map 6, C2
Egypt	ˊē-jəpt	D5	Map 2, C6
El Salvador	el-ˊsal-və-ˊdȯ(ə)r	E2	Map 5, I6
Equatorial Guinea	ē-kwaˊ-tōr-ēal ˋgi-nē	E5	Map 2, F4

COUNTRY AND TERRITORY	PRONUNCIATION	MAP 1	MAPS 2–7
Eritrea	ˊer-ə-ˊtrē-ə	E6	Map 2, D7
Estonia	e-ˊstō-nē-ə	C5	Map 3, D6
Eswatini (formerly Swaziland)	es-wa-ˊtē-nē	F6	Map 2, I6
Ethiopia	ˊē-thē-ˊō-pē-ə	E6	Map 2, E7
Falkland Islands	ˊfò(l)-klənd	—	Map 6, J4
Faroe Islands	fer - (ˌ)ō	—	Map 3, C2
Fiji	ˊfē-jē	—	Map 7, D8
Finland	ˊfin-lənd	B5	Map 3, C6
France	ˊfran(t)s	C5	Map 3, G3
French Guiana	gē-ˊan-ə	E3	Map 6, B5
Gabon	ga-ˊbōn	E5	Map 2, F4
Gambia	ˊgam-bē-ə	E4	Map 2, E1
Georgia	ˊjòr-jə	C6	Map 4, D2
Germany	ˊjerm-(ə-)nē	C5	Map 3, F4
Ghana	ˊgän-ə	E5	Map 2, E2
Greece	ˊgrēs	D5	Map 3, I6
Greenland	ˊgrēn-lənd	A4	Map 5, B7
Grenada	grə-nāˊdə	—	Map 5, J3
Guam		—	
Guatemala	ˊgwät-ə-ˊmäl-ə	E2	Map 5, I6
Guinea	ˊgin-ē	E4	Map 2, E1
Guinea-Bissau	ˊgin-ē-bis-ˊauˊ	E4	Map 2, E1
Guyana	gī-ˊan-ə	E3	Map 6, B4
Haiti	ˊhāt-ē	E3	Map 5, H8
Honduras	hän-ˊd(y)uˊr-əs	E2	Map 5, I7
Hong Kong	ˊhänJ-ˊkänJ	—	Map 4, F6
Hungary	ˊhənJ-g(ə)rē	C5	Map 3, G5
Iceland	ˊī-slənd	B4	Map 3, B1
India	ˊin-dê-ə	D7	Map 4, F4
Indonesia	ˊin-də-ˊnē-zhə	E8	Map 4, H7; Map 7, B3
Iran	i-ˊrän	D6	Map 4, E3
Iraq	i-ˊräk	D6	Map 4, D2
Ireland	ˊī(ə)r-lənd	C5	Map 3, F1
Israel	ˊiz-rē-əl	D6	Map 4, D2
Italy	ˊit-əl-ē	D6	Map 3, H4
Ivory Coast (Cote D'Ivoire)	īˊvə-rē	E5	Map 2, E2
Jamaica	jə-ˊmā-kə	E3	Map 5, I7
Japan	jə-ˊpan	D8	Map 4, D7
Jordan	ˊjòrd-ən	D6	Map 4, D2
Kazakhstan	kə-ˊzak-ˊstan	D7	Map 4, D4
Kenya	ˊken-yə	E6	Map 2, F7
Kiribati	kîr-ì-bàsˊ	—	Map 7, B8
Korea, North (Democratic People's Republic of Korea)	kə-ˊrē-ə	D8	Map 4, D7
Korea, South (Republic of Korea)	kə-ˊrē-ə	D8	Map 4, D7
Kosovo	ˊKo-sō-vō	C5	Map 3, H6
Kuwait	kə-ˊwāt	D6	Map 4, E2
Kyrgyzstan	kîr-gē-stänˊ	D7	Map 4, D4
Laos (Lao People's Democratic Republic)	ˊlauˊs	D7	Map 4, F5
Latvia	ˊlat-vē-ə	C5	Map 3, E6
Lebanon	ˊleb-ə-nən	D6	Map 4, D2
Lesotho	lə-ˊsō-(ˊ)tō	F6	Map 2, J6
Liberia	lī-ˊbir-ē-ə	E5	Map 2, F2
Libya	ˊlib-ē-ə	D5	Map 2, C4
Liechtenstein	likˊtən-stīnˊ	—	Map 3, G4
Lithuania	ˊlith-(y)ə-ˊwā-nē-ə	C5	Map 3, E6
Luxembourg	ˊlək-səm-ˊbərg	C5	Map 3, G3
Macao SAR	mə-ˊkaů	—	Map 4, F6

COUNTRY AND TERRITORY	PRONUNCIATION	MAP 1	MAPS 2–7
Madagascar	´mad-ə-´gas-kər	F6	Map 2, I8
Malawi	mə-´lä-wē	F6	Map 2, H6
Malaysia	mə-´lā-zh(ē-)ə	E8	Map 4, G6
Maldives	môl´dīvz	—	Map 4, H3
Mali	´mäl-ē	D5	Map 2, D2
Malta	´mȯl-tə	—	Map 3, J5
Marshall Islands	mär´shəl	—	Map 7, A8
Mauritania	´mȯr-ə-´tā-nē-ə	D5	Map 2, D1
Mauritius	mȯ-´rísh´əs	—	Map 2, J8
Mexico	´mek-si-´kō	D2	Map 5, I5
Micronesia	mī´krō-nē´zhə	—	Map 7, A5
Moldova	mäl-´dō-və	D6	Map 3, G7
Monaco	män-a-kō	—	Map 3, H4
Mongolia	män-´gōl-yə	D8	Map 4, D5
Montenegro	´män-tə-´nē-grō	—	Map 3, H6
Morocco	mə-´räk-(´)ō	D5	Map 2, B2
Mozambique	´mō-zəm-´bēk	F6	Map 2, H6
Myanmar	´myän-´mär	E7	Map 4, F5
Namibia	nə-´mib-ē-ə	F5	Map 2, I4
Naura	nä´-ü-rü	—	Map 7, B7
Nepal	nə-´pȯl	D7	Map 4, F4
Netherlands	´neth-ər-lən(d)z	C5	Map 3, F3
New Caledonia	´kal-ə-´dō-nyə	—	Map 7, E7
New Zealand	´zē-lənd	G9	Map 7, H7
Nicaragua	´nik-ə-´räg-wə	E3	Map 5, I7
Niger	´nī-jər	E5	Map 2, D4
Nigeria	nī-´jir-ē-ə	E5	Map 2, E4
North Macedonia	´mas-ə-´dō-nyə	D6	Map 3, H6
Norway	´nȯ(ə)r-´wā	C5	Map 3, D4
Oman	ō-´män	E6	Map 4, F2
Pakistan	´pak-i-´stan	D7	Map 4, E3
Palau	pä-lou´	—	Map 7, A3
Palestine	pa-lə-´stīn	—	Map 4, D1
Panama	´pan-ə-´mä	E3	Map 5, J8
Papua New Guinea	´pap-yə-wə	F9	Map 7, C5
Paraguay	´par-ə-´gwī	F3	Map 6, E4
Peru	pə-´rü	F3	Map 6, D2
Philippines	´fil-ə-´pēnz	E8	Map 4, F7
Poland	´pō-lənd	D5	Map 3, F5
Portugal	´pōr-chi-gəl	D5	Map 3, I1
Puerto Rico	´pōrt-ə-´rē(´)kō	E3	Map 5, I2
Qatar	´kät-ər	D6	Map 4, E2
Romania	rō-´ā-nē-ə	D5	Map 3, H6
Russia (Russian Federation)	´rəsh-ə	C7	Map 3, D7; Map 4, C5
Rwanda	ru˙-´än-də	E6	Map 2, F6
St. Kitts & Nevis	´kits / ´nē-vəs	—	Map 5, I3
St. Lucia	sānt-´lü-shə	—	Map 5, I3
St. Martin	sānt-´mär-tᵊn	—	Map 5, I2
St. Vincent and the Grenadines	grèn´ə-dēnz´	—	Map 5, J3
Samoa	sa-mō´a	F9	Map 7, D9
San Marino	sàn mə-rē´nō	—	Map 3, H4
São Tomé and Príncipe	soun tōə-mè´prēn´-sēpə	—	Map 2, F3
Saudi Arabia	´sau˙d-ē	E6	Map 4, E2
Senegal	´sen-i-´g˙l	E4	Map 2, D1
Serbia	´sər-bē-ə	D5	Map 3, H6
Seychelles	sā-shèlz´	—	Map 2, J1
Sierra Leone	sē-´er-ə-lē-´ōn	E4	Map 2, E1

COUNTRY AND TERRITORY	PRONUNCIATION	MAP 1	MAPS 2–7
Singapore	´sinJ-(g)ə-´pō(ə)r	—	Map 4, H6
Slovakia	slō-´väk-ē-ə	C5	Map 3, G5
Slovenia	slō-´vēn-ē-ə	C5	Map 3, H5
Solomon Islands	´säl-ə-mən	—	Map 7, C6
Somalia	sō-´mäl-ē-ə	E6	Map 2, F8
South Africa	´a-fri-kə	F6	Map 2, J5
South Sudan	sü-´dan	E6	Map 2, E6
Spain	´spān	C5	Map 3, I1
Sri Lanka	(´)srē-´länJ-kə	E7	Map 4, G4
Sudan	sü-´dan	E6	Map 2, E6
Suriname	su˙r-ə-´näm-ə	E3	Map 6, B5
Sweden	´swēd-ən	B5	Map 3, C5
Switzerland	´swit-sər-lənd	C5	Map 3, G4
Syria (Syrian Arab Republic)	´sir-ē-ə	D6	Map 4, D2
Taiwan	´tī-´wän	D8	Map 4, E7
Tajikistan	tä-´ji-ki-´stan	D7	Map 4, E4
Tanzania, United Republic of	´tan-zə-´nē-ə	F6	Map 2, G6
Thailand	´tī-land	E8	Map 4, F5
Timor Leste	tē-mōr-´lesh-ˌtā	—	Map 4, H8
Togo	´tō(´)gō	E5	Map 2, E3
Tonga	´tän-gə	—	Map 7, D9
Trinidad & Tobago	´trin-ə-´dad / tə-´bā-(´)gō	—	Map 5, J3
Tunisia	t(y)ü-´nē-zh(ē-)ə	D5	Map 2, B4
Turkey	´tər-kē	D6	Map 4, D2
Turkmenistan	tûrk´-men-i-stàn´	D6	Map 4, D3
Turks and Caicos Islands	tərks-ənd-´kā-kəs	—	Map 5, H8
Tuvalu	tü´-vä-lü	—	Map 7, C9
Uganda	(y)ü-´gan-də	E6	Map 2, F6
Ukraine	yü-´krān	C6	Map 3, F7
United Arab Emirates	yoo-nī´tid à r´əb i-mîr´its	D6	Map 4, E2
United Kingdom	king´dəm	C5	Map 3, F2
United States	yu˙-´nīt-əd-´stāts	D2	Map 5, F5
Uruguay	´(y)u˙r-ə-gwī	G3	Map 6, G5
Uzbekistan	(´)u˙z-´bek-i-´stan	C6	Map 4, D3
Vanuatu	van-ə-´wät-(´)ü	—	Map 7, D7
Vatican City	vàt´ ì-kən	—	Map 3, H4
Venezuela	´ven-əz(-ə)-´wā-lə	E3	Map 6, A4
Vietnam	vē-´et-´näm	E8	Map 4, G6
Virgin Islands (U.S. - Br.)		—	Map 5, I2
Western Sahara	sə-hâr´ə	D4	Map 2, C1
Yemen	´yem-ən	E6	Map 4, F2
Zambia	´zam-bē-ə	F5	Map 2, H5
Zimbabwe	zim-´bäb-wē	F6	Map 2, H6

CHAPTER 1

Globalization and International Business

OBJECTIVES

After studying this chapter, you should be able to

1-1 Explain why and how the study of international business (IB) is important

1-2 Understand the relationship between globalization and IB

1-3 Grasp the forces driving globalization and IB

1-4 Discuss the major criticisms of globalization

1-5 Assess the major reasons companies seek to create value by engaging in IB

1-6 Define and illustrate the different operating modes for companies to accomplish their international objectives

1-7 Recognize why national differences in companies' external environments affect how they may best improve their IB performance

The world's a stage; all play their parts and take their share.

—Dutch proverb

Source: aarows/Shutterstock

▲ International tourists visiting for the 2018 World Cup in Russia.

CASE

The Globalized Business of Sports[1]

Sports may be the world's most globalized business. Fans demand to see the best, and "best" has become a global competitive standard. (The opening photo shows tourists from several countries in Moscow for the 2018 World Cup.) Satellite TV brings live events from just about anywhere in the world to fans just about anywhere else. This gives the key sports-business participants—athletes, team owners, league representatives, and sports associations—broadened audience exposure, expanded fan bases, and augmented revenues.

National sports federations' sponsorship of international competitions is common, most notably the long-standing World Cup in football (soccer) and the Olympics. More national organizations participate in these events than there are United Nations (UN) members, and probably more people follow them than follow most of the UN's activities. How do these international competitions relate to business? Cities and countries compete to host events to attract tourists and publicize their business opportunities. In turn, companies pay for marketing rights as sponsors. Finally, individual athletes compete not only for medals, but also for lucrative contracts to endorse products.

While the Olympics and the World Cup participations have long been global, the competitive location is increasingly so. The World Cup has recently moved about to such locales as South Africa, Brazil, Russia, and on to Qatar in 2022. Likewise, the Olympics have bounced among Canada, China, Russia, and Brazil over the past few years and are likely headed to Japan, China, France, and the United States.

THE INTERNATIONAL JOB MARKET

The search for talent has become worldwide. Professional basketball scouts search remote Nigerian areas for tall high-potential youngsters. Baseball agents provide live-in training camps for Dominican Republic teenagers in exchange for a percentage of their future professional signing bonuses. (However, overzealous agents are criticized for promising teenagers more than they can deliver in terms of education, training, and living standards.) But just assembling talent, although necessary, is insufficient for making a sports business successful. Shrewd marketing and financial management are crucial too. For instance, Fútbol Barcelona, one of recent years' best professional soccer teams, turned to young business graduates to help improve its finances.

Most of today's top-notch athletes are willing to follow the money anywhere. Most of the top professional sports leagues in North America and Europe share an important trait: Their composition is more international than ever before. England's professional soccer league (Premier) and Spain's La Liga have players from 66 and 50 countries respectively. Besides improving the caliber of play, foreign players expand the international fan base.

How the ATP Courts Worldwide Support

You've probably noticed that individual sports professionals are globe hoppers. Take tennis. No country boasts enough fans to keep players at home for year-round competition, yet today's top-flight tennis pros come from every inhabited continent. For 2019 the Association of Tennis Professionals (ATP) sanctioned 64 tournaments in 31 countries—and thus players travel to many countries. Logistics, compounded by fatigue, means that no tennis pro can compete in every ATP event.

Tournaments earn money through ticket sales, corporate sponsorship agreements, television contracts, and leasing of advertising space. The larger the stadium and TV audiences, the more backers and advertisers will pay to get their attention. Moreover, international broadcasts attract sponsorship from companies in various industries and countries. Consequently, organizers compete for top draws to fill stadium seats and land lucrative media contracts. Prizes are extremely generous—about US 50 million for competitors at the 2020 Australian Open.

From National to International Sports Pastimes

Some countries have legally designated a national sport to help preserve traditions; others effectively have one. Map 1.1 shows a sample of these. However, other sports have sometimes replaced national sports in popularity, such as cricket replacing field hockey as India's most popular sport.

Historically, baseball was popular only in its North American birthplace. Today the International Baseball Federation lists more than 100-member countries. As media revenues flattened in North America, Major League Baseball (MLB) broadened its fan base by broadcasting games to international audiences, which also showed youngsters all over the world how the game was played. The average MLB clubhouse is now a bastion of multilingual camaraderie, with players and coaches talking baseball in Spanish, Japanese, Mandarin, and Korean as well as English.

THE WIDE WORLD OF TELEVISED SPORTS

Not surprisingly, other professional sports have expanded their global TV coverage (and marketing programs). Most viewers of Stanley Cup hockey watch from outside North America. Fans can watch NASCAR races (National Association for Stock Car Auto Racing) and National Basketball Association (NBA) games in most countries.

TV isn't the only means by which sports organizations are seeking foreign fan bases and players. The U.S.'s National Football League (NFL) underwrites football programs in Chinese schools and plays some regular games in Europe. The NBA is helping to build youth leagues in India.

The Top-Notch Pro as Upscale Brand

Many top players are effectively global brands, such as U.S. tennis pro Serena Williams and Portuguese soccer forward Cristiano Ronaldo. Because of their sports success and charisma, companies within and outside the sports industry pay them handsomely for endorsing clothing, equipment, and other products. Swiss tennis star Roger Federer, long affiliated with Nike, parted ways with the swoosh to join Japanese casual clothing brand Uniqlo—for a guaranteed US $300 million over 10 years.

Promotion as Teamwork

A few teams, such as the New York Yankees in baseball, the New Zealand All Blacks in rugby, and Manchester United (Man U) in soccer, also have enough brand-name cachet to be global brands for selling clothing and other items. Just about every team can get something for the rights to use its logo, while some have enough name recognition to support global chains of retail outlets. Similarly, companies both sponsor and seek endorsements from well-known teams, such as the placement of "Fly Emirates" on Real Madrid's soccer jerseys.

Still others pay for naming rights to arenas and other venues. Of course, teams themselves can be attractive international investments. For instance, U.S. investors bought the Liverpool Football Club of the United Kingdom.

The Upsides and Downsides of Globalized Sports

What does all this mean to a sports fan? Now that pro sports have become a global phenomenon, fans can enjoy a greater variety of sports—and a higher level of competition—than any former

MAP 1.1 Examples of National Sports

Some 62 countries have a national sport; 16 have declared it by law, the rest by de facto. Some national sports are shared by more than one country, such as cricket by England and seven of its former colonies. Others protect the historical heritage, such as tejo in Colombia, kabaddi in Bangladesh, or pato in Argentina. Several countries have more than one national sport, such as Canada with hockey in the winter and lacrosse in the summer.

Source: The information on sports was taken from Wikipedia, http://en.wikipedia.org/wiki/National_sport (accessed March 18, 2016).

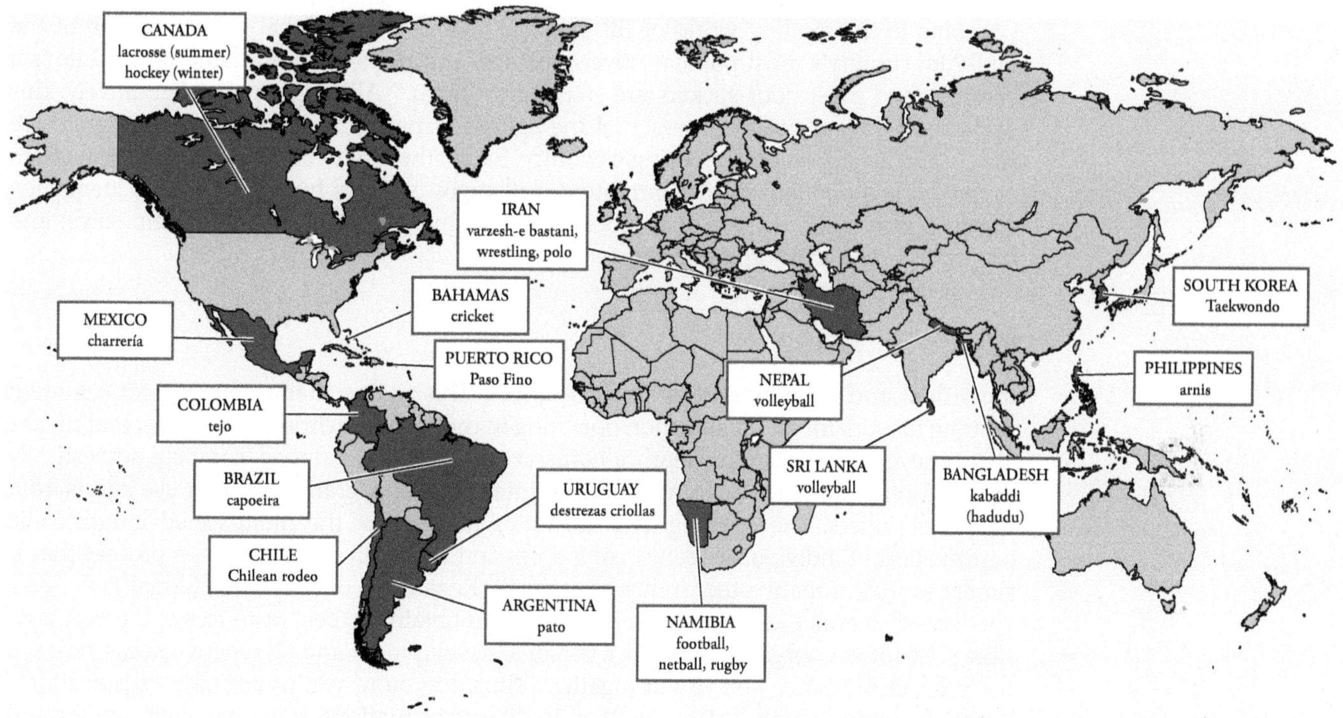

generation. That's the upside, but people don't always take easily to another country's sport. Despite many efforts, cricket, although popular in countries that once were British colonies, is popular elsewhere only where there are many immigrants from cricket-popular countries, such as in Germany where the Pakistani population is large. Nor has American football gained much popularity outside the United States. One possible reason is that rules for cricket and American football are so complicated. However, basketball and soccer have traveled to new markets more readily because they are easier to understand and require little specialized equipment.

Further, there is disagreement about the economic effect of successfully winning a bid to host big international competitions such as the World Cup and Olympics. On the one hand, they help spur tourism, foreign investment, infrastructure construction, and improvement of blighted areas. On the other hand, threats from terrorism boost the cost of security, while hosts may have to spend on stadiums and facilities that have no use afterward. Further, political disturbances, natural disasters, and contagious health conditions may play havoc with competitions. At this writing, the 2020 Summer Olympics in Japan has already been delayed until 2021 because of the global COVID-19 pandemic. Further, other sports have had to adjust to attendance limits at games and restrictions on the international movements of players and fans. Finally, many competitions have ended with substantially increased debt. Critics, therefore, often believe the funds would have been better spent on social services.

Nor is everyone happy with the unbridled globalization of sports—or at least with some of the effects. Brazilian soccer fans lament the loss of their best players, Cuban baseball fans fret about the movements of its players to U.S. and Japanese teams, and French fans protested the Qatar Investment Authorities' purchase of the Paris Saint-Germain (PSG) football club. Some factions within England have contended that the large influx of foreign players has disadvantaged the development of native players. Further, the income and publicity from winning and hosting in international competition have influenced cheating, such as by using illegal performance-enhancing drugs and bribing officials who decide the location of competitions. Finally, the high stakes of professional sports have led to vast gambling, which tempts corruption. It has shown up in sports both obscure, such as handball and sumo wrestling, and prominent, like soccer, baseball, and tennis.

QUESTIONS

1-1 Professional athlete A is a star, and athlete B is an average professional player. How has the globalization of professional sports affected each of these both positively and negatively?

1-2 As you read the chapter, identify and show an example of each international mode of operations that is illustrated in the globalization of professional sports.

THE WHY, WHAT, AND HOW OF STUDYING INTERNATIONAL BUSINESS (IB)

1-1 Explain why and how the study of international business (IB) is important

Welcome to the exciting world of IB! The title character and global traveler in one of the mid-20th century's most popular novels, movies, and plays (Auntie Mame) said, "Life is a banquet, and most poor suckers are starving to death." Although meant figuratively, this declaration rings of reality. In essence, the figurative message is that the world offers more variety and attraction than any single country. Sadly, the reality of the message is that much of the world's population faces profound challenges, such as hunger, sickness, inequality, and insecurity. Still, every global problem is also an opportunity for IB to help solve, and you'll play a part in finding solutions.

WHY STUDY IB?

Individual and Organizational Performance This text's material is critical for a student aspiring to work for an organization operating in the global environment. Today, that means virtually every organization. Nearly all organizations compete abroad, compete domestically against foreign or domestic companies with international operations, and/or use inputs from foreign suppliers. The opening case illustrates reasons for the multifaceted international participation of individuals, teams, companies and associations in sports—a process that is similar to that in many other industries as well. Regardless of your professional ambitions, you'll need to evaluate (1) where in the world you obtain the best resources at the best possible price for your organizational and personal development and (2) where you can best sell the product or service you've put together. Thus, the more you understand organizations' operating environments and experiences in different situations, the more likely you'll stand out and either attract the attention of recruiters as you prepare to enter the job market or, if already working, position yourself for promotion.

Making Nonbusiness Decisions Even if you don't anticipate direct IB activities, understanding the subject matter will likely prove useful. The international operations of companies, both big and small, along with the policies of their governments affect overall national conditions—economic growth, employment, consumer prices, national security—as well as the success of individual industries and firms. Currently, for example, nations grapple with questions on the degree to depend on foreign production and markets, ally with other countries for defense, and cooperate to solve problems that transcend national borders. A better understanding of IB will help you make more informed decisions, such as where to work and what governmental policies to support.

Let's also not overlook what Auntie Mame called a banquet. Growing knowledge about the variety of world attractions has powered a tremendous expansion in international travel. As you study the content in this text, you'll improve your understanding not only of the business opportunities that exist worldwide, but also the tools to better interpret national behavioral and opinion differences in your future travel. So, enjoy your global banquet!

Studying IB is important because

- most organizations are either international or compete with international companies,
- modes of operations may differ from those used domestically,
- it helps managers to decide where to find resources and to sell,
- the best way of conducting business may differ by country,
- an understanding helps you make better career decisions,
- an understanding helps you decide what governmental policies to support.

WHAT TO STUDY IN IB

Some of you may aspire to work directly in IB in your home or a foreign country. Some of you may work within your home country for companies dealing with foreign clients, suppliers, and competitors. In either case, your organization's performance depends on making sense of operating environments, identifying your objectives, and developing the means to achieve them. Thus, we have divided this text into two main sections—the environments and operations of IB—as you see illustrated in the text's title as well as Figure 1.1.

In your professional future, you'll discover that the way you do business in your home market is often not the best way to do business internationally. Why? First, companies operating internationally engage different modes of business, such as exporting

FIGURE 1.1 Factors in IB Operations

The conduct of an organization's international operations depends on two factors: its objectives and its means to achieve them. Likewise, its operations affect, and are affected by two sets of factors: physical/social and competitive.

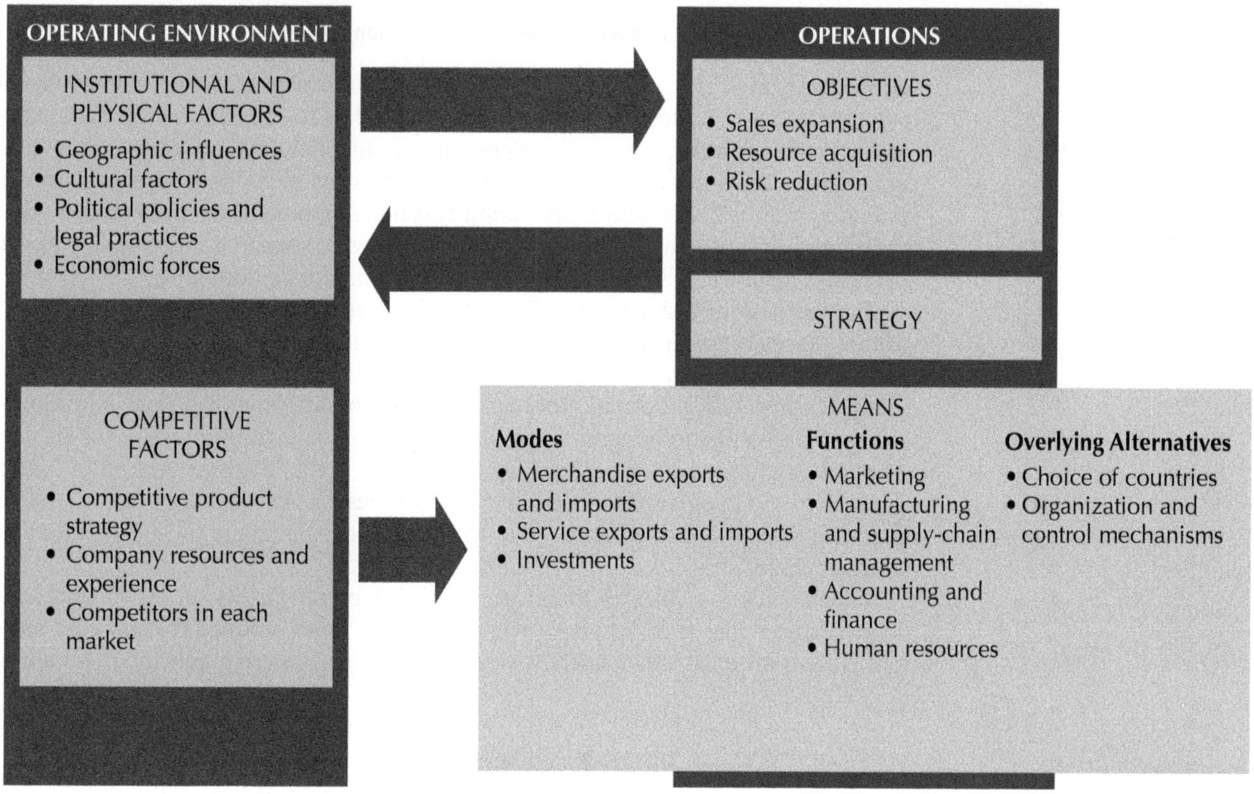

and importing. Second, physical, institutional, and competitive conditions differ among countries; these differences inevitably affect the optimum ways to do business. Thus, international companies have more diverse and complex operating environments than purely domestic ones.

HOW TO STUDY IB TO DEVELOP A CRITICAL SET OF SKILLS

The text broadly profiles the environments and operations of IB. We cover a lot of ideas and issues in order to help you develop skills that support your employability and professional success. Although we cover a lot about a lot, you'll find many features that help you study, understand, and use the materials. We summarize key points in the margin and highlight fundamental connections to ideas in other chapters. Similarly, we highlight, in bold type, the introduction of foundation terms that anchor an understanding of IB; too, we compile these in the Glossary. We link your learning experience to your development of important employability skills. Specifically, in the Preface, on pp. xxviii–xxix, you'll find seven skills that institutions, such as the Graduate Management Admissions Council (GMAC) and World Economic Forum, identify as critical to getting and being successful in a job. A quick look at this section shows you how we incorporate each into the main features of your text. For example, the Opening and Closing Chapter Cases, "Point-Counterpoint," and "Looking to the Future" features, included in all chapters, help you develop your skills on complex problem-solving, comprehension and logic, critical thinking, cultural awareness, ethics, global mindset, and integrated reasoning. Each and all help you improve your talents for evaluating ideas, interpreting complex information, reconciling contradictions, synthesizing diverse recommendations, and making insightful decisions. Undoubtedly, you have already begun developing these skills in previous coursework. Our text helps you improve them within the fascinating context of the environments and operations of IB. Eventually, you'll showcase these skills in job interviews, and then use them to build a rewarding and successful career. Along the way, you'll probably even enjoy your global banquet!

THE RELATIONSHIP BETWEEN GLOBALIZATION AND IB

1-2 Understand the relationship between globalization and IB

Globalization is the widening and deepening of interdependent relationships among people from different nations. The term sometimes refers to the elimination of barriers to international movements of goods, services, capital, technology, and people that influence the integration of world economies.[2] Throughout history, expanded human connections have extended people's access to more varied resources, products, services, and markets. We've altered the way we want and expect to live, and we've become more deeply affected (positively and negatively) by conditions outside our immediate domains.

Industries and organizations, like those described in the opening case, have expanded to distant places to gain supplies and markets. As consumers we know from "Made in" labels that we commonly buy products from all over the world, but these labels do not tell us everything. For instance, a Belgian Neuhaus bonbon and an American Ford automobile contain so many different components, ingredients, and specialized business activities from diverse countries that pinpointing where they were made is challenging.[3] Although Apple ships its iPhones from China and they appear to be Chinese products, very little value is created in China. For example, the iPhone 7 had a factory-cost estimate of $237.45; all that's earned in China is $8.46.[4]

Globalization enables us to get more variety, better quality, or lower prices. Our meals contain spices that aren't grown domestically and fresh produce that may be out of season locally. Our cars cost less than they would if all the parts were made and the labor performed in one place.

HOW DOES *IB* FIT IN?

IB consists of all commercial transactions between two or more countries.

- The IB goal of private business is to make profits.
- Government IB may or may not be motivated by profit.

The Relation to Globalization The global connections between supplies and markets result from the activities of **international business** (IB), which are all commercial transactions (including sales, investments, and transportation) that take place among countries. Private companies undertake such transactions for profit; governments may undertake them either for profit or for other reasons.

THE FORCES DRIVING GLOBALIZATION AND IB

1-3 Grasp the forces driving globalization and IB

Although hard to measure, globalization

- has been growing, although sporadically,
- is less pervasive than generally thought,
- has economic and noneconomic dimensions,
- is stimulated by several factors.

Measuring globalization is a problem, especially for historical comparisons. First, a country's interdependence must be measured indirectly.[5] Second, when national boundaries shift, such as Ukraine's territorial loss to Russia, domestic business transactions can become international ones and vice versa. Nevertheless, various reliable indicators assure us that economic interdependence has been increasing, although sporadically, at least since the mid-twentieth century. Currently, about a quarter of world production is sold outside its country of origin, compared to about 7 percent in 1950. Restrictions on imports have generally been decreasing (once again sporadically), and output from foreign-owned investments as a percentage of world production has increased. In periods of rapid economic growth, such as most years since World War II, world trade grows more rapidly than world production. However, in economic downturns, such as the one caused by the COVID-19 pandemic, global trade and investment shrink even more than the global economy.

At the same time, however, globalization is less pervasive than you might suppose. In fact, many people in the United States are surprised to learn that only about 15 percent of the value of U.S. consumption comes from other countries. In much of the world (especially in poor rural areas), people lack the resources to connect much beyond their isolated domains. Such isolation is changing quickly, though, especially since the advent of mobile phones.[6] (The adjacent photo shows two young Rwandan boys caring for a power stall for people who wish to charge their communications devices.) Only a few countries—mainly very small ones—either sell over half their production abroad or depend on foreign output for more

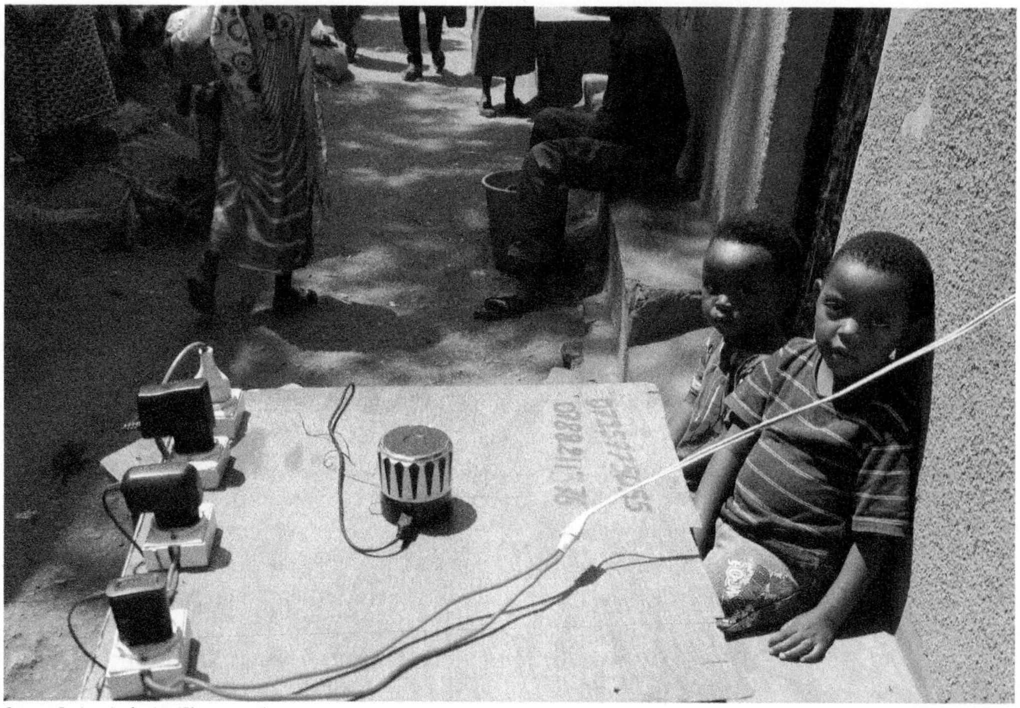

Two young Rwandan boys take ▶ care of a "power" stall at the local market, where they provide customers with charging outlets and phone chargers.

Source: Sarine Arslanian/Shutterstock

than half their consumption. This means that most of the world's goods and services are still sold in the countries where they're produced. Moreover, the principal source of capital in most countries is domestic rather than international.

Granted, these measurements address only *economic* aspects of globalization. More comprehensive comparisons include people-to-people contacts through travel and communications, technological interchanges, government-to-government relationships, and acceptance and adaptation of attributes from foreign cultures such as words from other languages.[7] These comparisons have several commonalities:

- Size of countries—Smaller countries tend to be more globalized than larger ones, mainly because their smaller land masses and populations permit a lower variety of production.
- Per capita incomes—Countries with higher per capita incomes tend to be more globalized than those with lower ones because their citizens can better afford foreign products, travel, and communications.
- Variance among globalization aspects—Although a country may rank as highly globalized on one dimension, it may be low on another, such as the United States being high on technological scales but low on economic ones.

FACTORS IN INCREASED GLOBALIZATION

What factors have contributed to the growth of globalization in recent decades? Most analysts cite the following interrelated factors:

1. Rise in and application of technology
2. Liberalization of cross-border trade and resource movements
3. Development of services that support IB
4. Growth of consumer pressures
5. Increase in global competition
6. Changes in political situations and government policies
7. Expansion of cross-national cooperation

Rise in and Application of Technology Many of the proverbial "modern marvels" and efficient means of production have come about recently. These include new products, such as handheld mobile communications devices, as well as new applications of old products, such as biodegradable plastic made from mushrooms, tin in circuit boards, or Indian guar beans in oil and natural gas mining.[8] The shift in demand for older products has also altered production locations, such as the demand for air conditioners that has turned southern China into the workshop of the world.[9] Thus, much of what we trade today either did not exist or was unimportant in trade a decade or two ago. Why have technical developments increased so much? More than half the scientists who have ever lived are alive today. One reason, of course, is population growth. But another is rising productivity—taking less time to produce the same thing—which frees up more people to *develop* new products because fewer people are necessary to *produce* them. This rising productivity also means that on average people can buy more, including the new products, by working the same number of hours. The entry of new products into the market creates a need for other complementary products (such as apps for smartphones), thus accelerating the need for scientists and engineers.

Production of many new products cannot successfully take place in a single country. Much new technical innovation takes so many financial and intellectual resources that companies from different countries must cooperate to take on portions of development. Further, when new products are developed, the optimum scale size of production seldom corresponds with the market demand in a single country. Consequently, companies may need to sell both domestically and internationally to spread the fixed developmental and production costs over more units of production.

Advances in Communications and Transportation Strides in communications and transportation now allow us to discover, desire, and demand goods and services from abroad. Meanwhile, the costs of these strides have risen more slowly in most years than costs in general, thus increasing affordability. A three-minute phone call from New York to London that cost $10.80 in 1970 costs less than $0.20 today, while a call using Voice over Internet Protocol (VoIP) is virtually free. Similarly, passenger airfares have been falling for years. Between 1995 and 2014, they fell by half in real terms.[10]

Innovations in transportation mean that more countries can compete for sales to a given market. U.S. purchases of foreign-grown flowers used to be largely impractical and aimed only at high-income consumers; today, however, flower producers from as far away and dispersed as Ecuador, Israel, the Netherlands, and New Zealand compete for the U.S. market because growers can ship flowers quickly and economically.

Improved communications and transportation also enhance a manager's ability to oversee foreign operations, such as more easily visiting foreign facilities and communicating with managers therein. Thanks to the Internet, companies can instantly exchange pictures of samples. Even small companies can reach global customers and suppliers. However, you may ponder the following question: Has the Internet been a bigger force in globalization than the laying of the first transoceanic cable across the Atlantic in 1858 that reduced communication time from 10 days to a matter of a few minutes?

Liberalization of Cross-Border Trade and Resource Movements To protect its own industries, every country restricts the entry and exit of not only goods and services but also the resources—workers, capital, tools, and so on—needed to produce them. Such restrictions, of course, set limits on IB activities and, because regulations can change at any time, contribute to uncertainty. For example, the United States and China escalated restrictions on each other's products in the late twenty-teens. Over time, however, most governments have reduced such restrictions, primarily for three reasons:

1. Their citizens want a greater variety of goods and services at lower prices.
2. Competition spurs domestic producers to become more efficient.
3. They hope to induce other countries to lower their barriers in turn.

Services That Support IB Companies and governments have developed services that facilitate global commerce. For example, because of bank credit agreements—clearing arrangements that convert one currency into another and insurance that covers such risks as nonpayment and damage en route—most producers can be paid relatively easily for their sales abroad. When Nike sells sportswear to a French soccer team, a bank in France collects payment in euros from the soccer team when the shipment arrives at French customs and pays Nike in U.S. dollars through a U.S. bank.

Growth in Consumer Pressures More consumers know more today about products and services available in other countries, can afford to buy them, and want the greater variety, better quality, and lower prices offered by access to them. However, this demand is spread unevenly because of uneven affluence, both among and within countries as well as from year to year.

Consumer pressure has also spurred companies to spend on research and development (R&D) and to search worldwide for innovations and products they can sell to ever-more-demanding consumers. By the same token, consumers are more proficient today at scouring the globe for better deals, such as searching the Internet for lower-priced prescription drugs abroad.

Increase in Global Competition Increased competitive pressures can persuade companies to buy or sell abroad. For example, a firm might introduce products into markets where competitors are already gaining sales, or seek supplies where competitors are getting cheaper or more attractive products. Once a few companies respond to foreign opportunities, others inevitably follow suit. And they learn from each other's foreign experiences. As the opening case suggests, the early success of foreign-born baseball players in U.S. leagues spurred U.S. basketball and football organizations to look for and develop talent abroad.[11]

So-called **born-global companies** start out with a global focus because of their founders' international experience[12] and because advances in communications give them a good idea of the location for global markets and supplies. Take SoundCloud, a Swedish audio-sharing web service. Its cofounders—one born in England and one in Sweden—were previously knowledgeable enough about the German and U.S. markets to move into both within months of starting up.[13] Meanwhile, some startups, like Airobotics of Israel, maker of drones, develop compelling technical solutions.[14] Akin to the idea "build a better mousetrap, and the world will beat a path to your door," they developed customers worldwide from their beginning. Regardless of industry, most firms and individuals must become more global; in today's competitive business environment, failure to do so is costly.

Changes in Political Situations and Government Policies For nearly half a century after World War II, business between Communist countries and the rest of the world was minimal. Today, only a few countries are heavily isolated economically or do business almost entirely within a political bloc. Nevertheless, governments still deny business with others for political reasons, such as many countries' sanctions against doing business with North Korea and Iran. However, government policies may open markets as well as close them.

Governments support programs, such as improving airport and seaport facilities, to foster efficiencies for delivering goods internationally. They also now provide an array of services to help domestic companies sell more abroad, such as collecting information about foreign markets, furnishing contacts with potential buyers, and offering insurance against nonpayment in the home-country currency.

Expansion of Cross-National Cooperation Governments have come to realize that their own interests can be addressed through international cooperation by means of treaties, agreements, and consultation. The willingness to pursue such policies is due largely to these three needs:

1. To gain reciprocal advantages
2. To attack problems jointly that one country acting alone cannot solve
3. To deal with areas of concern that lie outside the territory of any nation

Gain Reciprocal Advantages Essentially, companies don't want to be disadvantaged when operating internationally, so they lobby their governments to act on their behalf. Thus, governments join international organizations and sign treaties and agreements for a variety of commercial activities. For instance, some treaties and agreements allow countries' commercial ships and planes to use each other's seaports and airports; some cover commercial-aircraft safety standards and flyover rights; and some protect property, such as foreign-owned investments, patents, trademarks, and copyrights. Countries also enact treaties for reciprocal reductions of import restrictions.

Multinational Problem Solving Governments often act to coordinate activities along their mutual borders by building highways, railroads, and hydroelectric dams that serve the interests of all parties. However, there are still legacy border problems. For instance, fears of invasions from a rail-borne foreign army spurred nations to install wider or narrower rail tracks. Russia uses wider tracks than the standard Chinese gauge while in Europe trains between Italy and Sweden must change locomotives three or four times because of different national systems.[15]

Governments cooperate to resolve problems that they either can't or won't solve alone. First, the needed resources may be too great for one country to manage. Further, sometimes no single country is willing to pay all the cost for a project that will also benefit another country. In any case, many problems are inherently global—think of countering global climate change, terrorism, and diseases.

Second, one country's policies may affect those of others. Higher real-interest rates in one country, for example, can attract funds very quickly from individuals and firms in countries with lower rates, thus creating a shortage of investment funds in the latter. This movement is particularly disruptive to small developing economies.[16] Similarly, a country may weaken the value of its currency so that its products are cheaper in foreign markets. Thus, buyers may divert purchases to the newly cheaper country, hence contributing to unemployment in the country they forsook. To coordinate economic policies in these and other areas, the most economically important countries meet regularly to share information and pool ideas. The most notable coordination, known as the G20 countries, consists of 19 of the world's most economically important countries plus representation from the European Union of its members not included in the 19. These countries account for about 90% of world production, 80% of world trade, two-thirds of the world population, and approximately half of the world land area.[17]

Areas Outside National Territories Three global areas belong to no single country: the noncoastal areas of the oceans, outer space, and Antarctica. Until their commercial viability was demonstrated, they excited little interest for either exploitation or multinational cooperation. The oceans, however, contain food and mineral resources and constitute the surface over which much international commerce passes. Today, we have agreements to specify the amounts and methods of fishing, to address questions of oceanic mineral rights (such as on oil resources below the Arctic Ocean), and to deal with the piracy of ships.[18]

Likewise, there is disagreement on the commercial benefits to be reaped from outer space. Commercial satellites, for example, pass over countries that receive no direct benefit from them but argue that they should. If that sounds a little far-fetched, remember that countries do charge foreign airlines for flying over their territories.[19]

Antarctica, with minerals and abundant sea life along its coast, attracts thousands of tourists each year and has a highway leading to the South Pole and a Russian Orthodox church. Thus, it has been the subject of agreements to limit commercial exploitation, such as the Antarctic Treaty of 1959 that dedicated the continent to research. Since then, several countries have constructed research facilities there that use state-of-the-art architecture.[20] However, there is still disagreement about the continent's development—how much there should be and who does it.

THE CRITICISMS OF GLOBALIZATION

1-4 Discuss the major criticisms of globalization

Critics of globalization claim
- countries' sovereignty is diminished,
- the resultant growth hurts the environment,
- some people lose both relatively and absolutely,
- greater insecurity increases personal stress.

Although we've discussed interrelated reasons for and the benefits from the rise in IB and globalization, the consequences of the rise are controversial. *Antiglobalization* forces regularly protest at home and at international conferences about governmental policies—sometimes violently. We focus here on three issues: *threats to national sovereignty, environmental stress,* and *growing income inequality and personal stress.*

THREATS TO NATIONAL SOVEREIGNTY

You've probably heard the slogan "Think globally, act locally," which means giving precedence to local interests over global ones. Some observers worry that the proliferation of international agreements, particularly those that undermine local regulations on how goods are produced and sold, will diminish a nation's **sovereignty**—its freedom to "act locally" and without externally imposed restrictions.

The Question of Local Objectives and Policies Countries seek to fulfill their citizens' objectives by setting policies reflecting national priorities, such as those governing worker protection and environmental practices. However, critics argue that these priorities are undermined by opening borders to trade. For example, if a country has stringent regulations to improve labor conditions and promotes clean production methods such as by taxing companies' carbon emissions, it may not be able to compete with countries that have less rigorous rules. [21] By opening its borders to trade, it must either forgo its labor and environmental priorities to be competitive or face the downside of fewer jobs and less economic output.

The Question of Small Economies' Overdependence Critics complain that economically small countries depend too much on larger ones for supplies and sales. Thus, they are vulnerable to foreign mandates, including everything from defending certain UN positions to supporting a large economy's foreign military or economic actions. Nobel economist George Akerlof has noted that this dependence is intensified by poor countries' inadequate administrative capacity to deal with globalization.[22] Similarly, critics complain that large international corporations are powerful enough to dictate their operating terms (say, by threatening to relocate), exploit legal loopholes to avoid political oversight and taxes, and counter the small economies' best interests by favoring their home countries' political and economic interests.

The Question of Cultural Homogeneity Finally, critics charge that globalization homogenizes products and how they are made, social structures, and even language, thus undermining the cultural foundation of sovereignty. In essence, they argue that countries have difficulty maintaining the traditional ways of life that unify and differentiate them. Fundamentally, they claim helplessness in stopping the incursion of foreign influences by such means as satellite television, print media, and Internet sites.[23]

ENVIRONMENTAL STRESS

Much critique of globalization revolves around the economic growth it brings. One argument is that growth in both production and international travel consumes more nonrenewable natural resources and increases environmental damage—despoliation through toxic runoff into rivers and oceans, air pollution from factory and vehicle emissions, and deforestation that can affect weather and climate. In addition, critics contend that buying from more distant locations increases transportation, hence increasing the *carbon footprint,* which refers to the total set of greenhouse gases emitted.[24] They point further to the more than 1,000 container ships plying the seas and relying on heavy oil as a fuel; each pollutes as much as 50 million cars do. Indeed, the emissions from 15 mega-ships match those from all the cars in the world.[25]

The Argument for Global Growth and Global Cooperation However, other factions assert that globalization is positive for conserving natural resources and maintaining an environmentally sound planet—the former by fostering superior and uniform environmental standards and the latter by promoting global competition that encourages companies to seek resource-saving and eco-friendly technologies. A case in point is the automobile industry that has progressively produced cars that use less gas and emit fewer pollutants.

The positive effects of pursuing *global* interests may, nevertheless, conflict with *national* interests. Consider the effect of global pressure on Brazil to help protect the world's climate by curtailing logging and agricultural activity in the Amazon region. Unemployed Brazilian workers have felt that national job creation is more important than climate protection outside Brazil.

GROWING INCOME INEQUALITY AND PERSONAL STRESS

In terms of economic well-being, we look not only at our absolute situations but also compare ourselves to others (our relative situations). We generally don't find our economic status satisfactory unless we're doing better *and* keeping up with others.[26]

Income Inequality By various measurements, income inequality, with some notable exceptions, has been growing both among and within many countries.[27] Critics claim that globalization has affected this disparity by helping to develop a global superstar system, creating access to a greater supply of low-cost labor, and developing competition that leads to winners and losers.

The superstar system is especially apparent in sports, where today's global stars (as compared to past years) earn far more than the average professional player or professionals in less popular sports. The system carries over to other professions, such as in business, where charismatic leaders can command many times what others can.

Although globalization has brought unprecedented opportunities for firms to profit by gaining more sales and cheaper or better supplies, critics argue that profits have gone disproportionately to the top executives and shareholders rather than to the rank and file. Nobel economist Robert Solow has supported this criticism by arguing that greater access to low-cost labor in poor countries has reduced the real wage growth of labor in rich countries.[28] And even if overall worldwide gains from globalization are positive, there are bound to be some absolute or relative losers (who will probably oppose globalization). The speed of global technological and competitive expansion creates more winners and losers along with changing the relative positions of individuals, companies, and countries. As an example, recent manufacturing and foreign sales growth in China and India have helped them to grow more rapidly than the United States, thus lessening the *relative* economic leadership of the United States over those countries.[29] Likewise, some workers have lost economic and social standing as manufacturing jobs have shifted to other countries. The challenge, therefore, is to maximize the gains from globalization while simultaneously to minimize the costs borne by the losers.

Personal Stress Some repercussions of globalization can't be measured in strictly economic terms, such as people's stress from real and potential loss of relative economic and social positions.[30] Many worry also that immigration will lead them to become minorities rather than members of their countries' dominant group.[31] Further, stress, if widespread, goes hand in hand with costly social unrest.[32] The adjacent photo shows part of a violent protest influenced by such stress that rocked French politics in 2018–19. Although few of the world's problems are brand new, we may worry about them more now because globalized communications bring exotic sagas of misery into living rooms everywhere.[33]

The Paris protests in the photo ▶ were largely in response to an increase in gasoline taxes to help reduce global carbon emissions at the sacrifice assumed by French consumers.

Source: Alexandros Michailidis/Shutterstock

POINT

Is Offshoring of Production a Good Strategy?

YES Offshoring is the dependence on production in a foreign country, usually by shifting from a domestic source. If offshoring succeeds in reducing costs, it's good. This is happening with many companies. Most branded clothing companies depend on production offshore to have work done by cheaper sewing machine operators. Many investment companies, such as Fidelity in India, are hiring back-office workers in lower-wage countries to cut the cost of industry research. What good are cost savings? It's basic. If you can cut your costs, you can cut your prices or improve your product. Thus, by offshoring work to India, Claimpower, a small U.S. medical-insurance billing company, cut costs, lowered its prices to doctors, quadrupled its business in two years, and hired more U.S. employees because of the growth.[34]

What's the main complaint about offshoring? Too many domestic jobs end up abroad. As we discuss this, keep in mind that employment results from offshoring are difficult to isolate from other reasons for employment changes. Sure, many workers in high-income countries have lost jobs, but this has probably been due mainly to improvements in production technology. Let's try to pinpoint direct results of offshoring.

Samsung is a good example. By offshoring mobile phone assembly from Korea to Brazil, China, India, and Vietnam, the company was able to lower costs and sell more units, thereby maintaining the same number of low-paying domestic jobs while increasing high-paying jobs at home in R&D, engineering, design, and marketing.[35] If Samsung failed to enact such cost savings, its competitors in low-wage countries could underprice it with competitive products and services. In summary, cost savings generate growth, and growth creates more jobs.

Not just any jobs, either: This process lets companies create more high-value jobs at home—the ones performed by people like managers and researchers, who draw high salaries. When that happens, demand for qualified people goes up. In the United States, that process has already resulted in a higher percentage of white-collar and professional employees in the workforce. These are high-income people, and more of them are employed as a result of sending low-income jobs to countries with lower labor costs.[36]

Further, offshoring is a natural extension of outsourcing, the process of companies' contracting work to other companies so that they can concentrate on what they do best.[37] This contributes to making a company more efficient. What is the difference, then, of outsourcing to a domestic versus a foreign location?

Admittedly, workers do get displaced from offshoring, but aggregate employment figures show that these

COUNTERPOINT

Is Offshoring of Production a Good Strategy?

NO Some things are good for some of the people some of the time, and that's almost the case with offshoring. Unfortunately, it is good for only a few people but not for most. I keep hearing about the cost savings, but when I buy goods or services I rarely find anything that's cheaper than it used to be. Whether buying a Ralph Lauren shirt, getting medical services from a doctor who is saving money through Claimpower, or having Fidelity manage my assets, I have seen no lower prices for me. Instead, the lower production costs have resulted in higher compensation for already high-paid managers and for shareholders. Further, Claimpower's growth had to be at the expense of other companies in the business, not because of growth in the number of people getting medical services. In fact, studies show that the share of the economy going to employee wages steadily decreases while the share of national income going to profits steadily increases.[43] Meanwhile, the extreme pay gap between CEOs and workers expands.[44]

Here's a key problem: When you replace jobs by offshoring, you're exchanging good jobs for bad ones. Most of the workers who wind up with the short end of the offshoring stick struggled for decades to get reasonable work hours and a few basic benefits, such as health-care and retirement plans. More important, their incomes allowed them to send their kids to college, and the result was an upwardly mobile—and productive—generation.

Now many of these employees have worked long and loyally for their employers and have little to show for it in the offshoring era. Yes, governments give them unemployment benefits, but these never equal what the employees had before, and they run out.[45] On top of everything else, they may have no other usable skills, and at their age, who's going to foot the bill for retraining them? The increase in what is called "high-value jobs" doesn't do them any good. Further, when reshoring occurs (usually because managers didn't think through the offshoring decision adequately in the first place), you can bet they rehire domestic workers at less cost than before they offshored those jobs. Offshoring may lead to short-term cost savings, but it merely diverts companies' attention from taking steps to find innovative means of more efficient production, such as productivity-enhancing technologies.[46] Concentrating on these innovative means may cut costs, increase production, maintain the jobs that are going abroad, and permit incomes of workers to rise. In addition, offshoring brings additional risks to companies, primarily because their governments may impose import workers find other jobs, just like workers who get displaced for other reasons. In a dynamic economy, people are constantly shifting jobs, partly due to technology. The prevailing employment for U.S. women was once as telephone operators; direct dialing technology changed that. Attendants used to pump all the gas, but most is now self-service. Passenger aircraft used to carry five cockpit crew members; technology eliminated the need for the navigator, flight engineer, and radio operator. On the near-future horizon, pilotless passenger aircraft and package-carrying drone helicopters will reduce the cockpit crew to one or even zero,[38] while driverless cars will reduce demand for traffic policemen, auto insurers, emergency room personnel, auto-accident lawyers, and makers of such products as road signals and guard rails.[39] In fact, reports predict that in the United States, computerization threatens 47 percent of jobs, while in the European Union, estimates range up to 55 percent.[40] Furthermore, some predictions are that by 2030, as many as 800 million jobs could be lost worldwide to automation and artificial intelligence.[41]

What all this means is that the shifting of jobs because of offshoring is no different from shifting for any other reason. In any case, because there are bound to be upper limits on the amount of outsourcing work a country can do, the direst predictions about job loss are exaggerated: There simply aren't enough unemployed people abroad who have the needed skills and who will work at a sufficiently low cost. Further, as production increases in outsourced facilities abroad, wage rates go up there.

Offshoring isn't for all companies or all types of operations. Some firms are bringing many operations back from abroad, a situation known as **reshoring** or **rightshoring**, because of miscalculating offshoring advantages to begin with as well as poor quality, consumer pressure, concerns about competitive security, fear of transportation risks, and advantages of locating production near technical development.[42] That brings us back to what we said explicitly at the outset: Offshoring works when you cut operating costs *effectively*.

restrictions on what they are buying abroad, such as occurred for the U.S. auto producers in the late 2010s. Finally, the dependence on foreign production makes them vulnerable to shortages created by natural disasters or export restrictions elsewhere. For example, U.S. companies offshored almost all the production of face masks to China, but with the global spread of the COVID-19 pandemic in 2020, China limited the export of those masks.

While we're on the subject of job "value," what kinds of jobs are we creating in poor countries? Because countries are competing with lower wages, they are encouraged to keep wages from rising, a sort of race to the bottom. However, multinational enterprises (MNEs) no doubt pay workers in low-wage countries more than they could get otherwise, and admittedly some of these jobs—the white-collar and technical jobs—are pretty good. But for most people, the hours are long, the working conditions are brutal, and the pay is barely enough to survive. Take Bangladesh. Workers were killed when locked doors prevented their escape from a fire, and others were killed when their ramshackle workplace building collapsed, which caused a backlash against and loss of reputation for companies that had used those suppliers. There is also little job security. If salaries creep up where companies are offshoring, the companies merely move to even cheaper places to get the job done.

Admittedly, in a dynamic economy, people must change jobs more often than they would in a stagnant economy—but not to the extent caused by offshoring. There's still some disagreement about the effects of offshoring on a country's employment rate. Researchers are looking into the issue, but what they're finding is that more of the so-called better jobs are also being outsourced, such as in finance and IT. So, are we really creating higher-level jobs at home? Here's the bottom line: In countries like the United States, workers simply aren't equipped to handle the pace of change when jobs can be exported faster than the average worker can retrain for different skills.

WHY COMPANIES ENGAGE IN IB

1-5 Assess the major reasons companies seek to create value by engaging in IB

Let's now focus on some of the specific ways firms can create value through IB. Take another look at Figure 1.1, where you'll see three major IB operating objectives:

- Sales expansion
- Resource acquisition
- Risk reduction

Normally, these three objectives guide all decisions about whether, where, and how to engage in IB. Let's examine each in more detail.

SALES EXPANSION

Pursuing international sales usually increases the potential sales and potential profits.

A company's sales depend on consumers' demand. Obviously, there are more potential consumers in the world than in any single country. Now, higher sales ordinarily create value, but only if the costs of making the additional sales don't increase disproportionately. Recall, for instance, the opening case. Televising sports competitions to multiple countries generates advertising revenue greater than increased transmission costs. In fact, additional sales from abroad may enable a company to reduce its per-unit costs by covering its fixed costs—say, up-front research costs—over a larger number of consumers. Because of lower unit costs, it can boost sales even more.

So increased sales are a major motive for expanding into international markets, and many of the world's largest companies derive more than half their sales outside their home countries. It is also true that IB is not the purview only of large companies. Some 280,000 small and medium-size enterprises (SMEs)—specifically, companies with fewer than 500 workers—account for 98 percent of U.S. exporters.[47] Nevertheless, some 7,000 large companies in the United States—such as Caterpillar, Boeing, General Electric, and Intel—generate just over two-thirds of export value.

RESOURCE ACQUISITION

Foreign locations may give companies

- lower costs,
- new or better products and components,
- additional operating knowledge.

Producers and distributors seek out products, services, resources, and components from foreign countries—sometimes because domestic supplies are inadequate (such as industrial diamonds in the United States). They're also looking for anything that will create a competitive advantage. This may mean acquiring any resource that cuts costs. For instance, think again of Apple's call to make the iPhone in China and its aims to access inexpensive, productive local expertise in tooling engineering, materials management, and assembly. Those resources are available elsewhere but, as Apple's CEO explained, the "Chinese have developed and scaled these skills over the last three decades while the U.S. and other countries have gone the other direction."[48]

Sometimes firms gain competitive advantage by improving product quality or differentiating their products from those of competitors; in both cases, they're potentially increasing market share and profits. This process often takes them abroad. Most automobile manufacturers, for example, hire design companies in northern Italy to help with styling. Many companies establish foreign R&D facilities to tap additional scientific resources.[49] Indian firms have followed foreign acquisition strategies to gain knowledge needed to compete globally.[50] Further, by operating abroad, companies gain diversity among their employees that can bring them new perspectives.

RISK REDUCTION

International operations may reduce operating risk by

- smoothing sales, profits, and supplies,
- preventing competitors from gaining advantages.

Selling in countries with different timing of business cycles can decrease swings in sales and profits (e.g., increasing sales stability through operations in countries that enter and recover from recessions at even slightly different times). Moreover, by obtaining supplies of products or components both domestically and internationally, companies may be able to soften the impact of price swings or shortages in any one country.

Finally, companies often go international for defensive reasons. Perhaps they want to counter competitors' advantages in foreign markets that might hurt them elsewhere. By operating in Japan, for instance, Procter & Gamble (P&G) delayed potential Japanese rivals' foreign expansion by slowing their amassment of the resources needed to enter into other international markets where P&G was active. Similarly, Tredegar Industries followed its main U.S. customer into the Chinese market to prevent that customer from finding an alternative supplier who might then threaten Tredegar's U.S. position.

IB OPERATING MODES

1-6 Define and illustrate the different operating modes for companies to accomplish their international objectives

When pursuing IB, an organization must decide on suitable *modes of operations* included in Figure 1.1. In the following sections, we define and introduce each of these modes.

MERCHANDISE EXPORTS AND IMPORTS

Merchandise exports and imports are the most popular IB modes.

Exporting and importing are the most popular IB modes, especially among smaller companies. **Merchandise exports and imports** are tangible products—goods—that are respectively sent *out* of and brought *into* a country. Because we can actually *see* these goods, they are sometimes called *visible exports* and *imports*. For most countries, the export and import of goods are the major sources of international revenues and expenditures.

SERVICE EXPORTS AND IMPORTS

Service exports and imports are international nonproduct sales and purchases.

- They include travel, transportation, banking, insurance, and the use of assets such as trademarks, patents, and copyrights.
- They are very important for some countries.
- They include many specialized IB operating modes.

The terms *export* and *import* often apply only to *merchandise*. For non-merchandise international earnings, the terms are **service exports and imports** and are referred to as invisibles. The provider and receiver of payment makes a *service export*; the recipient and payer makes a *service import*. Services constitute the fastest growth sector in international trade and take many forms. In this section we discuss the following:

- Tourism and transportation
- Service performance
- Asset use

Tourism and Transportation Let's say that some Australian fans take Air France to watch the Tour de France bicycle competition. Their tickets on Air France and travel expenses in France are service exports for France and service imports for Australia. Obviously, then, tourism and transportation are important sources of revenue for airlines, shipping companies, travel agencies, and hotels. The economies of some countries depend heavily on revenue from these sectors, such as Greece from foreign cargo carried on their shipping lines and the Bahamas from foreign tourists.

Service Performance Some services, including banking, insurance, rental, engineering, and management services, net companies' earnings in the form of *fees*: payments for the performance of those services. On an international level, for example, companies receive fees for engineering services rendered in **turnkey operations**, which are contracted construction projects transferred to owners when they're operational. For instance, the Spanish turnkey operator Sacyr Vallehermoso constructed the Panama Canal expansion. Companies also receive fees from **management contracts**—arrangements in which they provide personnel to perform management functions for another, such as Disney's management of theme parks in France and Japan.

Asset Use Companies receive **royalties** from **licensing agreements**, whereby they allow others to use some assets—such as trademarks, patents, copyrights, or expertise. For example, the Real Madrid football team receives a royalty from Adidas' use of its logo on merchandise. Companies also receive royalties from **franchising**, a contract in which a company assists another on a continuous basis and allows use of its trademark. For instance, McDonald's assists individually owned McDonald's' trademarked restaurants by providing supplies, management services, technology, and joint advertising programs.

INVESTMENTS

Dividends and interest from foreign investments are also service exports and imports because they represent the use of assets (capital). The investments themselves, however, are treated separately in national statistics. Note that *foreign investment* means ownership of foreign property in exchange for a financial return, such as interest and dividends, and it may take two forms: *direct* and *portfolio*.

Direct Investment In **foreign direct investment (FDI)**, sometimes referred to simply as *direct investment*, the investor takes a controlling interest in a foreign company. When, for example, the owner of the Boston Globe and Boston Red Sox bought the Liverpool Football Club, it became a U.S. FDI in the United Kingdom. Control need not be a 100 percent or even a 51 percent interest; if a foreign investor holds a minority stake and the remaining ownership is widely dispersed, no other owner may effectively counter the investor's decisions.

When two or more companies share ownership of an FDI, the operation is a **joint venture.** (There are also non-equity joint ventures.)

Key components of portfolio investment are

- noncontrolling interest of a foreign operation,
- extension of loans.

Portfolio Investment A **portfolio investment** is a *noncontrolling* financial interest in another entity. It consists of shares in or loans to a company (or country) in the form of bonds, bills, or notes purchased by the investor. They're important for most international companies, which routinely move funds from country to country for short-term financial gain.

TYPES OF INTERNATIONAL BUSINESS ORGANIZATIONS

Basically, an "international company" is any company operating in more than one country, but a variety of terms designate different ways of operating. The term **collaborative arrangements** denotes companies' working together—in *joint ventures, licensing agreements, management contracts, minority ownership,* and *long-term contractual arrangements.* The term **strategic alliance** is sometimes used to mean the same, but it usually refers to either an agreement that is of critical importance to a partner or one that does not involve joint ownership.

A multinational enterprise or MNE (sometimes called MNC or TNC) is a company with foreign direct investments.

Multinational Enterprise A **multinational enterprise (MNE)** usually signifies any company with foreign direct investments. This is the definition we use in this text. However, some writers use the term only for a company that has direct investments in some minimum number of countries. The term **multinational corporation or company (MNC)** is often used as a synonym for MNE, while the United Nations uses the term **transnational company (TNC).**

Does Size Matter? Some definitions require a certain size—usually giant. However, a small company can have foreign direct investments and adopt any of the operating modes we've discussed. Note, though, that if successful, small companies become medium or large ones.[51] Vistaprint (now Cimpress) is a good example. Founded in 1995, its sales grew to $6.1 million in 2000 and to over $1 billion by 2012 with operations mainly in North America and Europe.

WHY DO COMPANIES' EXTERNAL ENVIRONMENTS AFFECT HOW THEY MAY BEST OPERATE ABROAD?

1-7 Recognize why national differences in companies' external environments affect how they may best improve their IB performance

Although foreign external environmental differences are problematic

- some anecdotes of IB failures are merely myths,
- they must be weighed against domestic opportunities and risks,
- understanding institutional factors and how they affect all business functions helps assure success abroad.

Let's now turn to the conditions in a company's *external environment* that may affect its international operations. Although there are many anecdotes illustrating operational problems when companies have failed to consider foreign environmental differences, these differences are not so daunting that they prevent success. First, some of the anecdotes are merely myths that have been repeated so often their validity is seldom challenged. Second, gaining start-up success domestically is also problematic; thus, when companies look objectively at their domestic versus foreign opportunities and risks, foreign entries may seem comparatively less formidable. Third, a good understanding of what one will encounter helps reduce operating risks, and smart companies develop the means to implement international strategies by examining the following conditions that can affect their success:

- *Physical factors* (such as geography or demography)
- *Institutional factors* (such as culture, politics, law, and economy)
- *Competitive factors* (such as the number and strength of suppliers, customers, and rival firms)

In examining these categories, we delve into external conditions that affect patterns of companies' behavior in different parts of the world and that influence companies to alter what they do domestically to fit foreign needs.

PHYSICAL FACTORS

Physical factors affect

- where different goods and services can be best produced,
- operating risks.

Physical factors, such as geography and demography, can affect how companies produce and market products, employ personnel, and even maintain accounts. Remember that any of these factors may require a company to alter its operation abroad (compared to domestically) for the sake of performance.

Geographic Influences Managers who are knowledgeable about geography can better determine the location, quantity, quality, and availability of the world's natural resources and conditions. Their uneven global distribution helps explain why different products and services are produced in different places.

Again, take sports. Norway fares better in the Winter Olympics than in the Summer Olympics because of its climate, and except for the well-publicized Jamaican bobsled team (whose members actually lived in Canada), you seldom hear of tropical countries competing in the Winter Olympics. East Africans' domination in distance races is due in part to their ability to train at higher altitudes than most other runners.

Geographic barriers—mountains, deserts, jungles, and land-locked areas—often affect communications and distribution channels. And the chance of natural disasters and adverse climatic conditions can make business riskier in some areas than in others by affecting supplies, prices, and operating conditions. Keep in mind also that climatic conditions may have short- or long-term cycles and changes. For instance, recent melting of Arctic ice floes along with new ship technologies have allowed more ships to use a Northwest Passage between the Atlantic and Pacific Oceans to cut transport costs by saving as many as 15 days at sea.[52]

Demographic Influences Finally, countries' populations differ in many ways, such as density, education, age distribution, and life expectancy. These differences impact IB operations, such as market demand and workforce availability.

INSTITUTIONAL FACTORS

Institutions refer to "systems of established and prevalent social rules that structure social interactions. Language, money, law, systems of weights and measures, table manners and firms (and other organizations) are thus all institutions."[53] We will now examine a sample of these.

Politics often determines where and how IB can take place.

Political Policies Not surprisingly, a nation's political policies influence how and if IB takes place. For instance, before Cuba and the United States severed diplomatic relations in the 1960s, Havana had a minor league baseball franchise. Not only did that disappear, but also the facility by which Cuban baseball players could join U.S. professional teams. Many of them did so, although most had to defect from Cuba to play abroad. That changed sporadically with some political normalizations since 2013.[54]

Obviously, political disputes—particularly military confrontations—can disrupt trade and investment. Even conflicts that directly affect only small areas can have far-reaching effects since these areas may produce important components needed for production elsewhere and because tourists' and companies' fear prevents their interactions abroad.

Each country has its own laws regulating business. Agreements among countries set international law.

Legal Policies Domestic and international laws play a big role in determining how a company can operate abroad. *Domestic law* includes both home- and host-country regulations on such matters as taxation, employment, and foreign-exchange transactions. British law, for example, determines how the U.S.-investor-owned Liverpool Football Club is taxed and which nationalities of people it employs in the U.K. Meanwhile, U.S. law determines how and when the earnings from the operation are taxed in the United States.

International law—in the form of legal agreements between countries—determines how earnings are taxed by *all* jurisdictions. As we point out in our closing case, international agreements permit ships' crews to move about almost anywhere. Sometimes, transactions between countries devolve into disputes, such as whether a French football team, questioning the quality of uniforms provided by U.S. incorporated Nike, withholds payment. Sales contracts usually include a choice-of-law clause that stipulates which nation's laws, when necessary, govern dispute resolution. Similarly, companies can include an arbitration provision in the contract, agreeing in advance to resolve potential disputes outside of court. Finally, the ways in which laws are *enforced* also affect a firm's foreign operations. In the realm of trademarks, patented knowledge, and copyrights, most countries have joined in international treaties and enacted domestic laws dealing with violations. Many, however, do very little to enforce either the agreements or their own laws. Therefore, companies must determine how fastidiously different countries implement their laws.

Behavioral Factors The related disciplines of anthropology, psychology, and sociology can help managers better understand different values, attitudes, and beliefs to enable

Countries' behavioral norms influence how companies should operate there.

them to make operational decisions abroad. Let's return once again to the opening case. Although professional sports are spreading internationally, the popularity of specific sports differs among countries, while rules and the customary way of play for the same sport sometimes differ as well. Because of tradition, tennis's grand slam tournaments are played on hard courts in Australia and the United States, on clay in France, and on grass in England. A baseball game in the United States continues until there is a winner, while Japanese games end with a tie if neither team is ahead after 12 innings. Presumably the reason for the baseball difference is that the Japanese value harmony more than Americans do, whereas Americans value competitiveness more than the Japanese do.

Economics helps explain country differences in costs, currency values, and market size.

Economic Forces Economics helps explain why countries exchange goods and services, why capital and people travel among countries in the course of business, and why one country's currency has a certain value compared to another's. Recall the internationalization of sports. Non-U.S.-born players make up an increasing portion of major league baseball rosters, and players from the Dominican Republic form the largest share. Obviously, higher incomes in the United States and Canada enable major league teams to offer salaries that attract Dominican players. Further, putting a major league baseball team in the Dominican Republic isn't practical because too few Dominicans can afford the ticket prices necessary to support a team.

Economics also helps explain why some countries can produce goods or services for less. And it provides the analytical tools to determine the impact of an international company's operations on the economies of both host and home countries, as well as the impact of the host country's economic environment on a foreign firm.

THE COMPETITIVE ENVIRONMENT

Companies' competitive situations may differ by

- their relative size in different countries,
- the competitors they face by country,
- the resources they can commit internationally.

In addition to its physical and social environments, every globally active company operates within a competitive environment. Figure 1.1 highlights some key competitive factors in the external environment of IB: product strategy, resource base and experience, and competitor capability.

Competitive Product Strategy Products compete by means of *cost* or *differentiation strategies*, the latter usually by

- developing a favorable *brand image*, usually through advertising or from long-term consumer experience with the brand; or
- developing *unique characteristics*, such as through R&D efforts or different means of distribution.

Using either approach, a firm may mass-market a product or sell to a niche market (the latter approach is called a *focus strategy*). Different strategies can be used for different products or for different countries, but a firm's choice of strategy plays a big part in determining how and where it will operate. Take Fiat Chrysler Automobiles (FCA), an Italian and U.S. MNE that is one of the world's largest auto makers. FCA competes with its best-selling models, like the Fiat UNO, primarily through a cost strategy targeting mass-market sales. This strategy led FCA to shift some engine plants to China, where production costs are low, and to target price-sensitive markets like Brazil, India, and Mexico. At the same time, FCA concentrates production of its premium Alfa Romeo and Maserati brands in Italy, using a high-priced focus strategy that requires access to the innovative design expertise as well as playing to customers' sense of sophistication. FCA then targets affluent, status-sensitive customers in higher-income countries such as Germany and the United States.

Company Resources and Experience Other competitive factors are a company's size and resources compared to those of its competitors. A market leader, for example—say, Coca-Cola—has resources for much more ambitious international operations than a smaller competitor like Royal Crown. Royal Crown sells in about 60 countries, Coca-Cola in more than 200.

In large markets (such as the United States), companies must invest much more to secure national distribution than in small markets (such as Singapore). Further, they'll probably face more competitors in large markets than in small ones. Conversely, national market share and brand recognition have a bearing on operating in a given country. A company with a long-standing dominant national market position uses operating tactics that are quite different from those employed by a newcomer. Such a company, for example, has much more clout with suppliers and distributors. Remember, too, that being a leader in one country doesn't guarantee being a leader anywhere else. For example, in terms of global market share, Volkswagen, Toyota and General Motors vie to be the biggest carmaker. In many countries, however, none of them hold any of the top three positions. Maruti Suzuki, Hyundai, and Mahindra & Mahindra, for instance, claim the top three rankings in India.[55]

Competitors Faced in Each Market Finally, market success, whether domestic or foreign, often depends on the strength of competition and whether it is international or local. Large commercial aircraft makers Boeing and Airbus, for example, compete almost only with each other in every market they serve. What they learn about each other in one country is useful in predicting the other's strategies elsewhere. In contrast, Walmart faces different local competition with customized local strategies in almost every foreign market it enters.

LOOKING TO THE FUTURE Three Major Scenarios on Globalization's Future

At this juncture, opinions differ on the future of IB and globalization. Basically, there are three major scenarios:

- Further globalization is inevitable.
- IB will grow, but more regionally than globally.
- Forces working against further globalization and IB will slow down the growth of both.

Globalization of Business Is Inevitable

The view that globalization is inevitable reflects the premise that advances in human connectivity are so pervasive that consumers everywhere will know about and demand the best products for the best prices regardless of their origins. This view, known as *connectography*, premises that internationally connecting infrastructure will accelerate.[56] Those who hold this view also argue that because MNEs have built so many interconnecting international production and distribution networks, they'll pressure their governments to place fewer restrictions on international movements of goods and means to produce them.

Even if we accept this view, we must still meet at least one challenge to riding the wave of the future: Because the future is what we make of it, we must figure out how to spread the benefits of globalization equitably while minimizing the hardships placed on those parties—both people and companies—who suffer from increased international competition.

The *Wall Street Journal* posed a question to Nobel Prize winners in economics: "What is the greatest economic challenge for the future?" Several responses addressed globalization and IB. Robert Fogel said it's the problem of getting available technology and food to people who are needlessly dying. Both Vernon Smith and Harry Markowitz specified the need to bring down global trade barriers. Lawrence Klein called for "the reduction of poverty and disease in a peaceful political environment." John Nash felt we must address the problem of increasing the worldwide standard of living while the amount of the earth's surface per person is shrinking.[57] Clearly, each of these responses projects both managerial challenges and opportunities.

IB Growth That Is Less Global

The second view—that IB growth will be less global—is based on studies showing that almost all the companies we think of as "global" conduct most of their business in home and neighboring countries.[58] Most world trade is regional, and many treaties to remove trade barriers are regional. Additionally, recent years have witnessed a greater growth in bilateral agreements between two countries rather than multilateral ones that encompass huge swaths of nations. Transport costs favor regional over global business. And regional sales may be sufficient for companies to gain scale economies to cover their fixed costs adequately. Nevertheless, regionalization of business may be merely a transition stage. In other words, companies may first promote international business in nearby countries and then expand their activities once they've reached certain regional goals.

Globalization and IB Will Slow

The third view argues that the pace of globalization will slow or may already have begun collapsing.[59] This is often referred to as *deglobalization*. In light of the antiglobalization sentiments mentioned earlier, it's easy to see that some people are adamant and earnest in voicing their reservations. The crux of the antiglobalization movement is the perceived schism between parties (including MNEs) who are thriving in a globalized environment and those that aren't. For example, in 2019, about 10 percent of the world's population—over 700 million people—lived in extreme poverty, surviving on no more than $1.90 per day. However, it was 47 percent in 1990. Most of the improvement results from the economic transformation in China. In 1981, 500 million people, about 90 percent of China, lived in extreme poverty; today, 6.5 percent do.[60]

Antiglobalists pressure governments to promote nationalism by raising trade barriers and rejecting international organizations and treaties. Historically, they have often succeeded (at least temporarily) in obstructing either technological or commercial advances that threatened their well-being. Recently, antiglobalization sentiments have grown in many countries, such as law changes in some U.S. states that hinder activities of undocumented aliens, the deportation by France of ethnic Roma (gypsies), the backlash against accepting refugees in several countries, and new import restrictions in China and the United States on each other's products. In Brazil and South Africa, the governments have authorized domestic companies to copy pharmaceuticals under global patent protection. Bolivia and Venezuela have nationalized some foreign investments, and Canada prevented the Malaysian state energy firm, Petronas, from buying Progress Energy, a natural gas producer. The sparring between pro- and anti-globalists is one reason why the globalization process has progressed in fits and starts.

Other uncertainties may hamper globalization. First is the question of oil prices, which affect international transportation because they can constitute more than 75 percent of operating costs on large ships.[61] Not only have global oil prices fluctuated widely, but technology for fracking and shale oil conversion has altered production locations when prices are high. Further, continuing political disturbances in the Middle East disrupt the global energy market. Many U.S. companies, such as furniture manufacturers, have responded by reshoring rather than facing transport cost and trade restriction uncertainty. Second, safety concerns—property confiscation, terrorism, piracy of ships, and outright lawlessness—may inhibit companies from venturing abroad as much.

Finally, one view holds that for globalization to succeed, efficient organizations with clear-cut mandates are necessary; however, there is concern that neither the organizations nor the people working in them can adequately handle the complexities of an interconnected world.[62]

Going Forward

Only time will tell, but one thing seems certain: If a company wants to capitalize on international opportunities, it can't wait too long to see what happens on political and economic fronts. Investments in research, equipment, plants, and personnel training can take years to pan out. Forecasting foreign opportunities and risks is always challenging. Yet, by examining different ways in which the future may evolve, a company's management has a better chance of avoiding unpleasant surprises. That's why each chapter of this book includes a feature that shows how certain chapter topics can become subjects for looking into the future of IB.

CASE

Carnival Cruise Lines[63]

I must go down to the seas again,
for the call of the running tide
Is a wild call and a clear call that may not be denied.
—John Masefield, *Sea Fever*

The call of the sea spurs the cruise business. Sea voyages have had an aura of mystique for centuries, but only in recent decades have they been available to a mass market. Historically, recreational sea voyages were an essentially elitist endeavor. Certainly, individuals with lower incomes occasionally found themselves on the open sea, but usually as displaced job seekers or ships' crew members. In recent years, however, the cruise industry has targeted the working middle class as well as the idle rich.

What's a Cruise, and What Happened to the Cruise Industry?

A "cruise" is a sea voyage taken for pleasure (as opposed to, say, working aboard a ship or conveying oneself from point A to point B). Typically, passengers enjoy cabin accommodations for the duration of a fixed itinerary that brings them back to their original point of embarkation.

There was a time when ships (called *liners*) transported people across waters for business or pleasure, but the advent of transoceanic air service after World War II offered a speedier and less expensive alternative, and airlines captured liners' passengers. The competitive balance tipped decisively in the 1960s, when advances in jet technology made air travel a viable option for a growing mass market of budget-minded travelers. One by one, shipping companies retired the great luxury liners that had plied the seas for decades.

The Contemporary Cruise Industry

Today, the cruise industry is dominated by two companies: Carnival and Royal Caribbean, which command a combined 71 percent of the market. By far, the largest is Carnival, whose ships cruise every continent. It operates 9 branded lines, such as Costa, Cunard, Holland, and Seabourn. Map 1.2 shows the headquarters of each.

Carnival was born when its founder saw an opportunity to expand mass-market sea travel by promoting the idea of the "Fun Ship" vacation—an excursion designed to be a little less formal and luxurious than the traditional ocean liner. The timing was right. Sea travel still projected a certain aura, and more people could afford an ocean-borne vacation. Further, a lot of vacationers preferred to spend their holidays in ways that were compatible with the Fun Ship concept, such as on group tours, theme-park visits, and sojourns to Las Vegas. Carnival bought a retired liner at a good price, refurbished it in bright colors and lights, and installed discos and casinos. On its maiden voyage in 1972, the ship ran aground with 300 journalists on board; fortunately, neither the ship nor the business concept were

MAP 1.2 Where Carnival's Cruise Lines (Brands) Are Headquartered

Countries designated on the map denote headquarters locations of each company/brand (e.g., four lines operate out of North America and two out of the United Kingdom). Carnival has the most recognized brands in North America, the United Kingdom, Germany, Italy, Australia, and Hong Kong/China—areas that account for more than 90 percent of the world's cruise-line passengers.

Source: Data from "Corporate Information," https://www.carnivalcorp.com/corporate-information, accessed January 20, 2020.

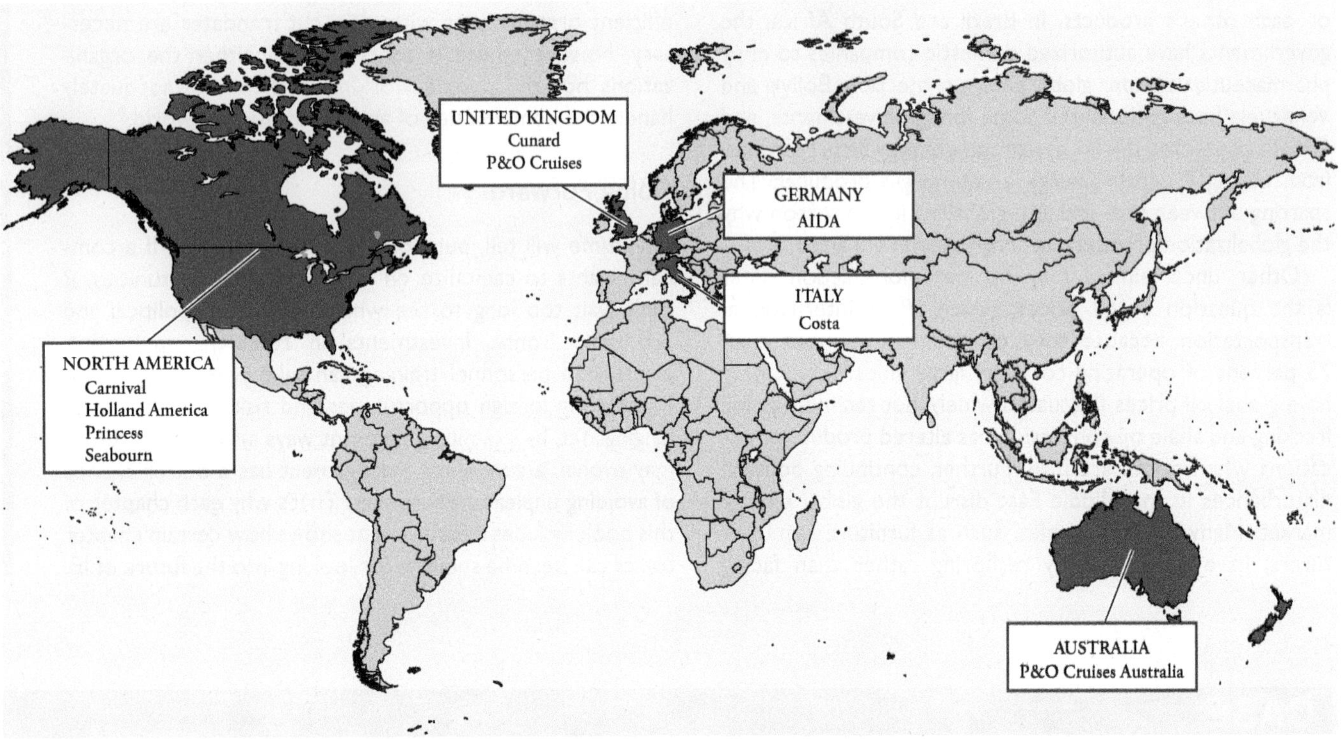

sunk. Over time, Carnival added not only ships but also whole cruise lines to its fleet. Today, each brand operates primarily in a designated region and is differentiated from other Carnival brands in terms of geographically pertinent themes (in Italy, for instance, Costa boasts a Mediterranean flavor) and in terms of cost (cruises on Cunard and Seabourn cost much more per night than on Carnival).

Doing Business in International Waters

Almost the whole cruise-line industry is international in scope. Take the nationality of competitors. Companies can obtain *flags of convenience* from about 30 different countries. By registering as, say, a Liberian legal entity, a company can take advantage of lower taxes and less stringent employment rules. Legally, Carnival is a Panamanian company, even though it's listed on the New York Stock Exchange, has operating headquarters in Miami and London, and caters mainly to passengers who set sail from the United States. Although cruise-line revenue is subject to neither Panamanian nor U.S. income taxes, Carnival does have to pay substantial "port fees." In fact, ports compete for cruise stopovers because of fees and tourist expenditures. However, the 2020 COVID-19 pandemic showed the downside of flags of convenience. Many ports delayed permission for the cruise ships to dock and unload because many passengers had contracted the virus and the ships were seen as being foreign. Several months after the outbreaks, over 100 thousand crew members were still trapped aboard the ships.

Only a few cruise-line offerings—such as excursions along the Mississippi River—can be characterized as purely domestic. Even trips from the U.S. West Coast to Alaska are "international" because they stop in Canada. By far the most popular destination for cruise passengers is the Caribbean/Bahamas, largely because the area boasts balmy weather year-round. During summer months, Carnival shifts some of its ships from Caribbean/Bahamas to Alaskan and Mediterranean routes.

Obviously, cruise ships go only where there are seaports, but Carnival, along with independent agents, for a fee, offers more than 2,000 onshore excursions. Carnival estimates that half its passengers to the Caribbean take shore excursions to such sightseeing attractions as the Mayan ruins in Belize. Nevertheless, critics contend that passengers see and spend too little in the countries they visit, going only to cruise-line-sanctioned locations and stores.

What It Takes to Operate a Cruise Line

Ship Shopping

Ships constitute the biggest investment for cruise lines. Carnival introduces two to three new ships per year. Governments in several countries subsidize shipbuilding because it employs many people and uses locally produced steel—a practice that gives the cruise-line industry less expensive ships.

Where to Find Crew Members

Shipping companies scour the world for crew members who can perform specialized tasks, are properly certified (by international agreement, a registered crew member can enter almost any port in the world), and who can interact with passengers, especially in English. On a typical Carnival ship, crew members hail from over 100 countries, but about a third of the world's ship crews are Filipino because of their English fluency and willingness to work for low wages. The mix of nationalities created obstacles for Carnival during the COVID-19 pandemic to find means of returning crew members to their home countries.

Casinos and Other Amenities

Each of its Carnival's cruises offers one or two formal nights per week; theme-based dinners centering on national cuisines; a variety of musical entertainment, games, and contests; spas and athletic facilities; and onboard shopping. Casinos are onboard fixtures because cruises, by operating outside the jurisdiction of any national authority, are not subject to any national laws restricting gambling.

The Overseas Environment

Because Carnival operates around the world, it has the advantage of treating the whole world as a source of both customers and supplies. In addition, because its chief assets are ocean-borne, Carnival can move them where they can best serve the company's needs. However, it's also vulnerable to a wide range of environmental disturbances. Let's look at a few of these.

Safety Issues

After terrorists seized a cruise ship in the Mediterranean in 1985, the major cruise lines instituted strict security checks for boarding passengers; thus, they had in place a security protocol before 9/11 and before the airline industry had one.

In the wake of 9/11, when cancellations started to exceed bookings, Carnival increased the number of U.S. ports from which its ships embarked so that passengers with a heightened fear of flying could reach points of departure by land. Carnival also redeploys cruises to avoid areas of political upheaval or crime. During the mosquito-borne Zika virus outbreak, Carnival offered cancellations with credit for future cruises to pregnant women and their families.

Fortunately, shipboard emergencies are infrequent, but when they do occur they are problematic. For instance, the Costa Concordia hit a rock and sank off Italy, causing 32 people to die. A generator fire on the Carnival Triumph stranded 4000 passengers for four days. Sporadically, viruses causing diarrhea and vomiting strike cruise ships, causing Carnival to take an infected ship out of service to eradicate all traces of the virus by sanitizing nearly every object on board. The 2020 COVID-19 pandemic led to passenger quarantines and the eventual global shutdown of almost all cruise activity. Although these incidents are costly, the cruise industry has a fatality rate three times better than airlines.

Economic Issues

Spending for a cruise is generally considered discretionary. During recessions, people are more apt to take shorter cruises and to embark from nearby ports rather than flying to faraway points of departure. Interestingly, however, in comparison with other segments of the tourist industry, cruise lines have fared well during economic downturns, partly because of offering discounts and partly because fixed cruise-line prices spare passengers the added risk of encountering unforeseen unfavorable exchange rates.

The Weather

Whenever there is extreme weather, Carnival may have to cancel trips, switch embarkation points, or change destinations. Typically, passengers on canceled trips receive full refunds and those on shortened cruises partial refunds.

The Future

Overall, the outlook for Carnival and the cruise-line industry is mixed. The number of passengers grew by seven percent in 2018. On the one hand, with prospects for growing incomes in many countries, such as China, more people will have discretionary income to spend on tourism. There are still relatively untapped cruise destinations that Carnival has either not exploited or has only recently begun to serve, such as the addition of ports in Vietnam, Indonesia, and Papua New Guinea. Changes in U.S.–Cuban relations led to cruises from the U.S. to Cuba in 2016. However, the U.S. disallowed these in 2019.

Since only 20 percent of the U.S. population has taken a cruise, there is growth potential. On the other hand, people who have taken a cruise continue to be repeat customers, but the percentage of first-time customers is declining. On the downside, then, industry observers worry that experienced cruisers will tire of visiting one port that's pretty much like another and that noncruisers will still prefer to fly to resorts where they can spend more time in a single place than they can on cruises.

A big unknown is the effect of COVID-19 on future cruise business, not only because of lower incomes caused by higher unemployment, but also how it will affect the perception of safety aboard ships.

There is also concern about the uncertainty of operating costs created by oil prices and pressures to be more environmentally friendly by becoming more fuel-efficient and by not dumping wastes into the oceans.

QUESTIONS

1-3 What specific steps has Carnival Cruise Lines taken to benefit from global social changes?

1-4 What economic factors influence success of the international cruise industry? Explain how each affects such success.

1-5 Although most cruise-line passengers are from the United States, the average number of annual vacation days taken by U.S. residents is lower than that of workers in most other high-income countries (13 days, compared to 5 weeks in France and Germany). How might cruise lines increase sales to people outside the United States?

1-6 What threats exist to the future performance of the cruise-line industry and specifically of Carnival Cruise Lines? If you were in charge of Carnival, how would you (a) try to prevent these threats from becoming reality and (b) deal with them if they were realized?

CHAPTER 2

The Cultural Environments Facing Business

OBJECTIVES

After studying this chapter, you should be able to

2-1 Explain why culture, especially national culture, is important in IB but tricky to assess

2-2 Grasp the major causes of national cultural formation and change

2-3 Discuss major behavioral factors influencing countries' business practices

2-4 Recognize the complexities of cross-cultural communications

2-5 Analyze guidelines for cultural adjustment

What is learned in youth is carved in stone.

—Arab proverb

Source: View Pictures/Hufton + Crow/VIEW/Newscom

▲ Part of complex by Zaha Hadid Architects at King Abdullah Petroleum Studies in Riyadh, Saudi Arabia.

CASE

Saudi Arabia's Dynamic Culture[1]

Saudi Arabia (see Map 2.1) can be perplexing to foreign firms as they try to exercise acceptable personal and business behavior. Its mixture of strict religious convictions, ancient social customs, and governmental economic policies results in laws and customs that often contrast with those elsewhere, shift with little advance notice, and vary by industry and region. (The opening photo illustrates the contrast between tradition and modern, i.e., people in religiously fostered traditional dress at an ultramodern structure.) Thus, foreign companies and employees must determine what these differences are and how to adjust to them. A brief sample of Saudi traditions, cultural norms, and foreign operating adjustments should help you understand the importance of culture in IB.

A LITTLE HISTORY AND BACKGROUND

Although the land encompassing the Kingdom of Saudi Arabia has a long history, during most of that history invaders controlled a divided land and most inhabitants had a tribal rather than national loyalty. Nevertheless, the inhabitants have shared a common language (Arabic) and religion (Islam). In fact, Saudi Arabia is the birthplace of Islam and the location of its two holiest cities, Mecca and Medina. King Ibn Saud, a descendant of Mohamad, took power in 1901, merged independent areas, created a political and religious entity, and legitimized his monarchy and succession by defending Islamic holy areas, beliefs, and values.

The growing importance of oil for Saudi Arabia, particularly since the 1970s, led to rapid urbanization and gave the government the means to offer social services such as free education. These changes have furthered its citizens' sense of national identity, while diminishing their traditional (particularly nomadic) lifestyle. Cities have modernized physically. However, below the physical surface, Saudis hold some attitudes and values that are neither like the norm elsewhere nor easily discerned.

Modernization has been controversial within Saudi Arabia. A liberal group, supported by an elite foreign-traveled segment, wants economic growth to provide more choices in products and lifestyles. A conservative group, supported by religious leaders, is fearful that modernization will upset traditional values and strict Koranic teachings. The government (the Royal Family) must satisfy conservative viewpoints, lest its leadership becomes vulnerable. For instance, Iran's Islamic Revolution was spearheaded in part by dissenters who viewed the Shah's modernization movements as too secular. Meanwhile, liberals have been largely pacified by taking well-paid government jobs and slowly gaining their desired transformation. The government has sometimes made trade-offs to appease conflicting groups, such as requiring women to wear longer robes (women must wear *abayas* and men customarily wear *thobes*) in exchange for advancing women's education. However, the abayas, traditionally black, are increasingly in more modern designs and bright colors.

THE RELIGIOUS FACTOR

If you are accustomed to fairly strict separation between religion and the state, you will probably find the pervasiveness of religious culture in Saudi Arabia daunting. Religious proscriptions prohibit pork products and alcohol. During the holy period of Ramadan, when people fast during the day, restaurants serve customers only in the evening. Restaurants such as McDonald's dim their lights and close their doors during the five times a day that Muslim men are called to prayer. Many companies convert revenue-generating space to prayer areas; Saudi Arabian Airlines does this in its planes, the British retailer Harvey Nichols in its department store.

However, there are regional differences. In Riyadh, women customarily wear *niqabs* that cover their faces. But fewer women wear them in Jeddah, which has more contact with foreigners, is less conservative, and has more relaxed dress codes. Nevertheless, merchants routinely remove mannequins' heads and hands and keep them properly clad to prevent public objections. IKEA even erased pictures of women from its Saudi catalogue.

Rules of behavior may also be hard to comprehend because religious and legal rules have sometimes been adapted to contemporary situations. Islamic law, for instance, forbids charging interest and selling accident insurance (strict doctrine holds there are no accidents, only preordained acts of God). In the case of mortgages, the Saudi government offers interest-free mortgage loans instead. It allows accident insurance because Saudi businesses, like businesses elsewhere, need the coverage.

Nor are expected behaviors necessarily the same for locals and foreigners. Non-Muslim foreign women are not required to wear

MAP 2.1 Saudi Arabia and the Arabian Peninsula

The kingdom of Saudi Arabia comprises most of the Arabian Peninsula in Southwest Asia. The capital is Riyadh. Mecca and Medina are Islam's holiest cities. Jeddah is the most important port. All of the country's adjacent neighbors are also Arabic—that is, the people speak Arabic as a first language. All the nations on the peninsula are predominantly Islamic.

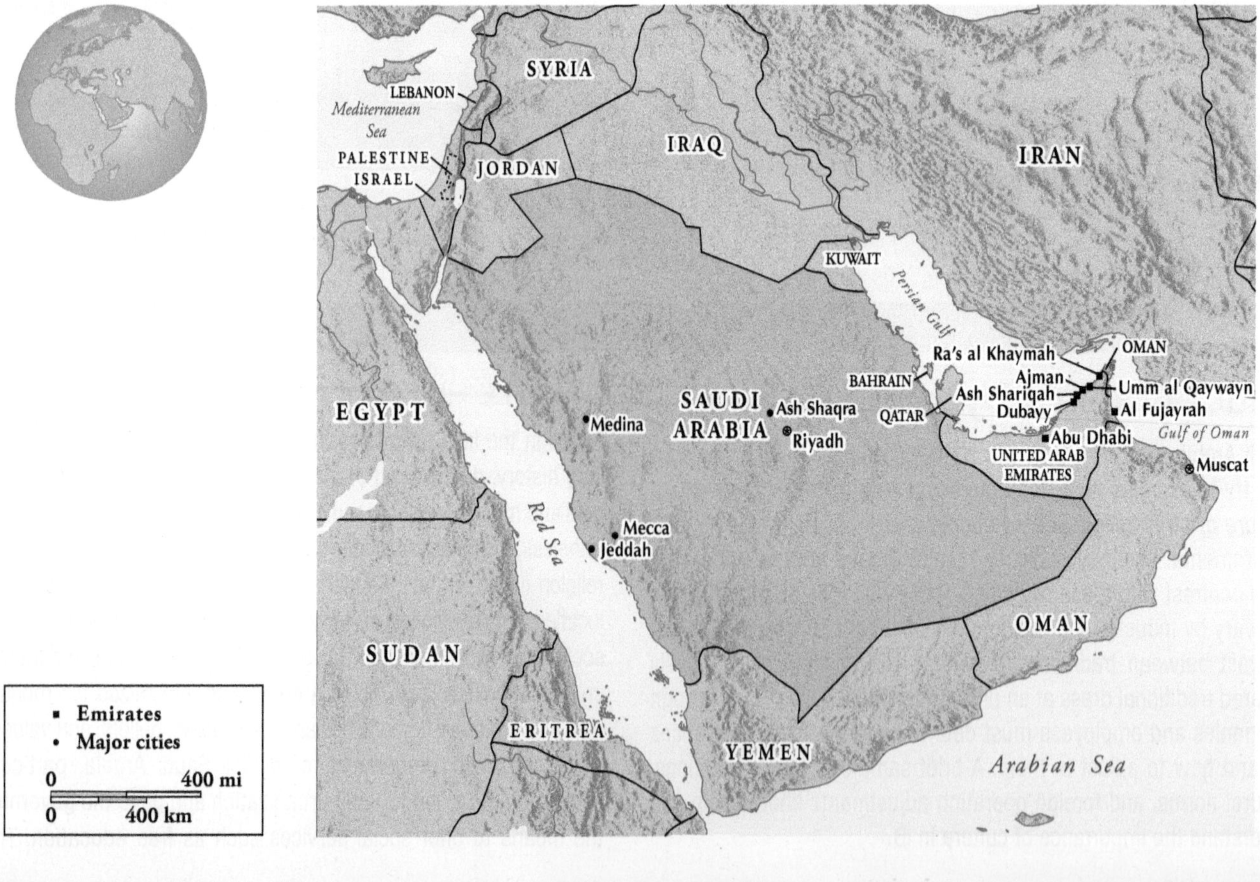

head scarves, although they may be admonished by religious patrols. Saudi Arabian Airlines does not hire Saudi women as flight attendants (being in direct contact with men might tempt promiscuous behavior), but it hires women from abroad. In addition, the government permits residents of compounds, inhabited largely by Americans and Europeans, to dress therein much the way they do back home. However, in an example of a reverse dress code, some compounds prohibit residents and their visitors from wearing *abayas* and *thobes* in their public areas.

TRADITIONAL FACTORS

Some Saudi traditions grew from its tribal and nomadic past. For instance, the oft-quoted saying "Me against my brother, my brothers and me against my cousins, then my cousins and me against strangers" illustrates a family-centered society where trust of others is highly correlated with the degree of familiarity with them.

Given the trust factor, most Saudi businesses have historically been family owned and operated, preferring to hire family members or people they know well even though others might be better qualified technically. However, as companies have needed to partner with foreign firms to gain expertise, the partnering process has usually been lengthy. Saudis take time to know the foreigners well and are reluctant to make full financial disclosures outside the family. They generally prefer to get to know you well, perhaps invite you into their homes, and develop a certain level of friendship before ever turning to business.

Not understanding this norm, a British publisher dispatched two sales representatives to Saudi Arabia and paid them on commission. The sales reps moved aggressively to make the same number of calls—and sales—per day as they made in Britain, where they were used to punctual schedules, undivided attention of potential clients, and conversations devoted only to business. To them, time was money. In Saudi Arabia, however, they found that appointments seldom began at the appointed time, usually taking place at cafés over cups of coffee. They felt that Saudis spent too much time in idle chitchat while ignoring business to talk with friends. Eventually, both sales reps showed their irritation, and their Saudi counterparts regarded them as rude and impatient. The publisher had to recall them.

Saudis' preference for dealing with people they know has led to a system known as *wasta*, which roughly translates into English as "connections." Thus, who you know helps a great deal in almost everything, such as moving a résumé to the top of a pile, gaining approval of a zoning request, getting a passport, and obtaining a visa to bring in a visitor from headquarters.

Gender Roles

Perhaps the most baffling aspect of Saudi culture to outsiders is the role of gender. Based largely on a Koranic prescription whereby daughters receive half the inheritance that sons receive, females are placed in a separate and often seemingly subservient position. Their role has been to be virtuous, marry young, and have offspring, while males take responsibility as their protectors and the family breadwinners. The *appearance* of female virtue is also required because a negative perception of one family member reflects on all. These beliefs have led to prohibitions for women, such as for traveling abroad without a male relative's permission and studying abroad without a male relative escort. Basically, nonkin males and females may interact personally only in "open areas," or in "closed areas" when the females are accompanied by a male relative. However, applying this restriction may seem a bit confusing to outsiders. For instance, restaurants are considered closed areas, and proprietors must maintain separate dining rooms and entrances for men without female companions. However, the food malls at most shopping centers are considered open areas where members of both sexes intermingle.

Nevertheless, several recent events foretell possibly fewer future differences in gender requirements: women can now vote, hold political offices, drive automobiles, and take physical education classes for females. A limited number of women athletes now participate in the Olympics, and as of 2019 women can attend sports competitions within Saudi Arabia, but must sit in the family section. In 2019, the World Wrestling Entertainment (WWE) held a women's wrestling match in Riyadh. Divorced women and widows can now manage their family affairs.

Men and women may mix in the workplace, but the situation is complex. Male and female employees within the public sector work in separate buildings. To meet together, they do so within special meeting rooms, where they must use separate entrances. Men and women may work together within the private sector, but there are other limitations.

Although females now outnumber males as university graduates, only about 15 percent of the Saudi workforce is female. This drives up the need for and added expense of foreign workers. Why are women so underrepresented? Some women prefer traditional family roles. Some families prohibit female members from working because of family honor ("What will people think?"). Economic factors blend with cultural ones as well, such as companies' reluctance to hire women so as to avoid incurring the cost of providing separate entrances and toilet facilities. Nevertheless, the genders do interact in multinational companies as long they adhere to dress codes. However, females are limited in foreign business travel because they need permission from their male relatives. Some multinationals ease this problem by paying the travel costs for a male relative to accompany a woman abroad.

At one time, visas for single women to enter Saudi Arabia were nearly unobtainable. However, Saudi Arabia promotes investments by MNEs, and they need visas to send female executives there. While these visas are not given automatically, they can be obtained—more easily for women over 40, but also possible for younger women, especially with the use of *wasta.* Restrictions on gender interactions also lead to other adjustments. For instance, four young Saudis, who had lived abroad, needed market research before opening an upscale restaurant in Jeddah. Such research is difficult because limitations on male–female interactions restrain family-focused interviews. In this case, however, consultants interviewed apparently affluent families by approaching them in restaurants. How did they know they were affluent? Aside from the caliber of restaurants, they noted clients' comportment, whether they wore custom-made versus off-the-rack robes, the quality of wristwatches showing beneath long sleeves, and how well the men kept their beards. These were indicators that researchers unfamiliar with the society would probably overlook.

At upscale foreign-based department stores like Saks Fifth Avenue, only the lower floors have mixed shopping. There, all salespeople are men (even those specializing in such products as cosmetics and lingerie), and there are no changing rooms or places to try cosmetics. Meanwhile, the upper floors are for women only, and female shoppers can check their *abayas* and shop in whatever they choose. (Meanwhile, the men who drove the women there can relax in a store-provided lounge.) One problem: Because male managers can visit these upper floors only when a store is closed, they are limited in their ability to observe operations.

CULTURAL DYNAMICS

Almost all aspects of culture evolve, and we have shown that Saudi Arabia is no exception. Since the first public school for girls opened in 1960, there has been a gradual increase in years of study and curriculum for females. On the one hand, economic need has spurred changes in education and its use within the workforce. On the other hand, critics have had to be persuaded that changes for women are compatible with their roles. One of the first acceptances of working women (alongside men) was in the medical field because of the shortage of doctors, the high cost to separate male and female specialists, and the compatibility of healing with women's role as nurturers.

The Saudi business world has seen much change. Consider that women own about 20 percent of all Saudi businesses, or that a woman is CEO of one of the country's largest concerns, the Olayan Financing Company. Five things will likely boost Saudi female workforce participation: (1) an increase in inward FDI, (2) more women studying abroad, (3) women's psychological drive to prove themselves, (4) social media access that connects genders and provides Saudis with more outside information, and (5) the uncertainty of income from oil as prices fluctuate. In addition, Saudi Arabia is promoting international tourism as a means to help diversify its economy. Bear in mind, however, that changes tend to be uneven, particularly among the country's geographic areas and among people with different income and educational levels.

QUESTIONS

2-1 Assume you are an MNE manager who needs to send a team to Saudi Arabia to investigate the feasibility of selling your products there. What advice should you give them to help assure that cultural problems do not impede their success?

2-2 Assume your company is from North America or Europe and considering the establishment of an office in Saudi Arabia. What additional operating costs might it have to assume because of the Saudi culture?

CULTURE'S IMPORTANCE IN IB AND TRICKINESS TO ASSESS

2-1 Explain why culture, especially national culture, is important in IB but tricky to assess

CONCEPT CHECK

In Chapter 1, we explained that behavioral factors, values, attitudes, and beliefs can be studied as keys to developing suitable business practices abroad.

Our opening case illustrates companies' need to understand and be sensitive to the culture where they operate. The adjacent Figure 2.1 shows the relation of culture to IB.

NATIONAL CULTURES AS A POINT OF REFERENCE

All individuals have values, and these are all learned. They are reflected in their attitudes, beliefs, and actions. Their **core values** are so strong that they are not negotiable, whereas their **peripheral values** are less dominant and more pliable.[2] The shared values, attitudes, and beliefs of a group of individuals constitute a **culture**.

FIGURE 2.1 Cultural Factors Affecting IB Operations

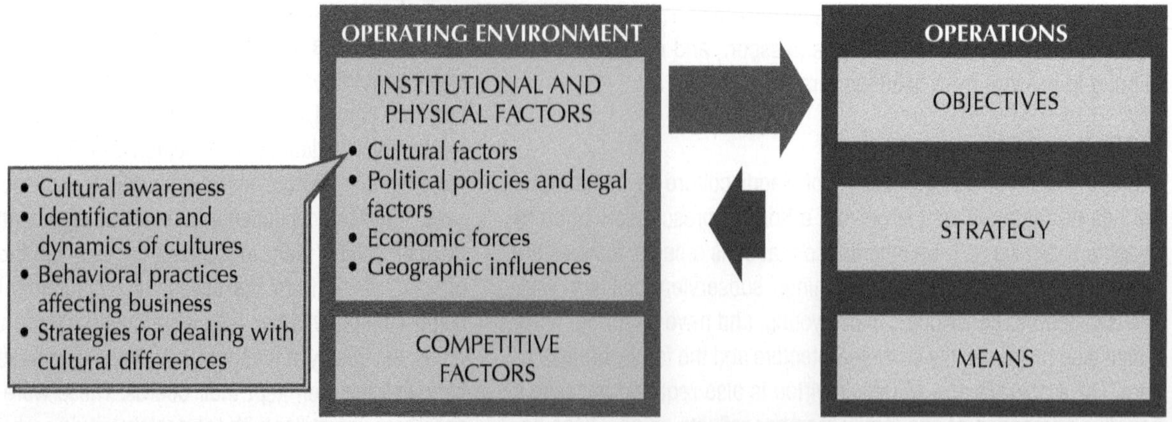

The nation is a useful definition of society because
- similarity among people is a cause and an effect of national boundaries,
- it is a reference people make to "we" versus "they."

Culture is elusive to study, partly because people belong to multiple cultures based on their nationality, ethnicity, religion, gender, work organization, profession, age, and income level. We emphasize *national cultures,* but also discuss how major cultural memberships differ among countries.

The nation provides a workable definition of culture because similarity among people is both a cause and an effect of national boundaries. Within a nation, people chiefly share such essential attributes as values and language. The feeling of "we" casts foreigners as "they." National identity is perpetuated through rites, symbols, and respect for national heroes, while the preservation of national sites, documents, monuments, and museums promotes a common perception of "we."

Despite using the nation as a cultural reference point
- not everyone therein shares the same values and attitudes,
- subcultures exist within nations,
- some people have internalized more than one culture,
- cultural similarities link groups from different countries.

The Nation as Cultural Mediator Obviously, not everyone in a country shares all the same values, nor is each country unique in all respects. Nations include various subcultures, and a nation must be flexible enough to accommodate and mediate its diversity;[3] those that fail sometimes dissolve. Yet a nation's shared and mediated characteristics constitute its national identity and affect the practices of any company that does business there. At the same time, some people (probably a growing number) are **bicultural** or **multicultural**, meaning that they have internalized more than one national culture because of having dual or multiple citizenships, parents or spouses from another country, or lived abroad at an impressionable age.

Groups can hold more similar attitudes with like groups abroad than with dissimilar groups in their own countries. For instance, urban people in Country A may have more in common with urban people in Country B than with rural people in their own country. As a consequence, when comparing nations culturally, one must be careful to examine *relevant groups*—differentiating between, say, the typical attitudes of rural and urban dwellers, or between managers and production workers.

THE PEOPLE FACTOR

IB involves people from different national cultures, which affects every business function—managing a workforce, marketing and transporting output, purchasing supplies, dealing with regulators, securing funds.

Cultural diversity can be a competitive advantage, but managing it can be difficult.

Cultural Diversity As nationalities come together through projects and teams, their diverse perspectives and experiences often enable businesses to gain a deeper knowledge of how to create and deliver products and services. However, successful cultivation of diversity is difficult because of conflicts when individuals interact as they do within their own cultures. Fortunately, there is an emerging body of research on nationally diverse teams that helps make them more effective. For instance, problems occur when some nationalities are accustomed to compete with team members while others are accustomed to cooperate, when some await precise directions while others take self-initiative, and when some expect to divide tasks while others seek a cooperative solution to each. Similarly, language differences inhibit a common understanding of team roles, priorities, and sentiments.[4] The more successful teams work to understand each other's cultures before dealing with the tasks at hand.[5] When team members expect diversity, they are more prone to realize the need to prepare to deal with differences, keep open minds, and develop a nonthreatening atmosphere, especially for dealing with others who may feel insecure in the language or threatened when expressing minority and divergent viewpoints.[6]

Cultural collision may cause
- ineffective business practices,
- personal distress.

Cultural Collision When contact among divergent cultures creates problems, the situation is known as **cultural collision**. Such collision may result in a company's implementation of practices that are less effective than intended. It may also cause distress to its employees sent abroad because of difficulty in adjusting to different behaviors.

Our opening case illustrates both problems: the publisher failed to meet its sales objectives, and its sales reps became distressed because they wrongly assumed their potential Saudi customers would be punctual and give them their undivided attention. Specifically, the British sales reps came from a **deal-focus (DF) culture**, where people are primarily task-oriented; whereas the Saudis came from a **relationship-focus (RF) culture**.[7] The latter had less compulsion to wrap things up, regarded small talk at a café as a means to identify acceptable business partners, and put dealings with friends ahead of business dealings. **DF** people typically view **RF** people as time-wasters, whereas **RF** people view **DF** people as offensively blunt.

BUILDING CULTURAL AWARENESS

A firm doing business abroad must determine which foreign business practices differ from its own and then decide what adjustments, if any, it should make. Some cultural differences, such as acceptable attire, are fairly obvious; others aren't. And people often react to given situations by expecting the same responses they would likely get in their own countries.

Most cultural variables—daily routines and rules, codes of social relations, language, emotive expression, concepts of luck—exist everywhere; however, the forms they take differ among cultures. Every national culture, for instance, features dancing, but types of and participation in dancing vary among and even within cultures.[8]

Almost everyone agrees that national cultures differ, but they disagree on what the differences are and the importance of them.

No foolproof method exists for building cultural awareness.[9] Travelers remark on cultural differences, experts write about them, and international managers note how they affect operations. Even so, people disagree on what they are, whether they're widespread or limited, and whether they are caused by core versus peripheral values.

Cultural research can improve a person's awareness and sensitivity.

Some people have an innate ability to say and do the right thing at the right time, while others offend unintentionally or seem ignorant. Experts note, however, that businesspeople can improve their awareness and sensitivity and, by educating themselves, enhance their likelihood of succeeding abroad. Although research on another culture can be instructive, one must assess information carefully to determine if it perpetuates unwarranted stereotypes, covers only limited segments of a country's culture, or is obsolete. One should also observe the behavior of those people who have garnered the kind of respect and confidence they themselves will need.

Of course, cultural variations are too numerous to list, much less to memorize completely. Just consider one—the many different ways to address people. Should you use a given name or a surname? Does a surname come before or after a given name? Do people take a parent's name as a surname? If so, is it taken from a parent's first or last name? If so, is it from one or both parents? Does a wife take her husband's name? What titles are appropriate for different professions? Note also that many countries use pronouns and verb forms (familiar and polite) that reflect status and familiarity. Mistakes that may seem minor can be perceived as ignorance or rudeness. Fortunately, you can consult guidebooks and speak with knowledgeable people. Fortunately, many studies on cross-cultural attitudes and practices concern businesspeople.[10] Nevertheless, many attitudes, practices, and cultures remain insufficiently studied.

SHORTCOMINGS IN CULTURAL ASSESSMENTS

Sometimes differences are attributed only to culture, although other factors may be influential.

Too often when we can't explain some difference—say, why the Irish consume more cold cereal than the Spanish do—we attribute it to culture without probing why. (Perhaps the difference is simply that cereal companies have marketed more in Ireland.) Nor is it easy to isolate culture from economic and political conditions. Entrepreneurial practices, for example, could be influenced not only by risk-taking values but also by current economic conditions.[11] China's changing preference for male versus female offspring offers an example of cultural and economic interaction. When China had its one-child policy, millions of families aborted female fetuses. Why? Because males could carry on a family name (cultural), help work fields in rural areas (economic), and care for parents in old age (cultural and economic). Recently, however, China has seen a shift toward more fondness for female offspring. Why? Urbanization requires fewer male workers on farms (economic), while rising property values (economic) have taken a toll on families' tradition (cultural) of buying living quarters for sons before they can marry.[12]

Shortcomings in cultural research include

- erroneous responses to questions,
- relying on averages when there are variations,
- overlooking changes.

We should also emphasize a few common shortcomings in interpreting cultural research:

1. Comparing countries by people's responses can be risky because they may be colored by the very culture one tries to understand. Some groups may be happiest when they're complaining; some respond with what they think questioners want to hear. In responding to degrees of agreement, say on a scale of one to five, some cultures are more apt to select the middle point, others the extremes.[13]
2. Researchers focusing on national differences in terms of *averages* may overlook variations within countries. For instance, the *average* Scandinavian may be uncomfortable with bargaining, but assuming that a Swedish buyer for IKEA doesn't expect to bargain on prices could be a grave mistake.[14] And of course, personality differences make some people outliers in their own cultures.[15] Nevertheless, there is a marked difference among countries in the extent that people conform close to the countries' average. When most people are close to the average, it is known as *cultural tightness*. When people are not, it is known as *cultural looseness*.[16]
3. Because cultures evolve, research may be outdated. Our opening case, for instance, details some changing Saudi practices toward gender differences.

INFLUENCES ON CULTURAL FORMATION AND CHANGE

2-2 Grasp the major causes of national cultural formation and change

Culture is transmitted in various ways—from parent to child, teacher to pupil, social leader to follower, peer to peer. Developmental psychologists believe that most people acquire their basic value systems, especially core values, as children, including such concepts as evil versus good, dirty versus clean, ugly versus beautiful, unnatural versus natural, abnormal versus normal, paradoxical versus logical, and irrational versus rational.[17]

SOURCES OF CHANGE

Cultural value systems, especially core values, are set early in life but may change through

- choice or imposition,
- contact with other cultures.

Examining individual and collective evolution of values helps explain how cultures come to accept (or reject) certain business practices—a useful examination for companies attempting to introduce their business practices abroad. The important thing here is willingness to accept a *change*, which may result from either *choice* or *imposition*.

Change by Choice Change by choice may occur because social and economic situations present people with new alternatives. When rural people choose to accept factory jobs, for example, they change some basic customs—notably, by working regular hours they give up work-time social interactions that farm work allowed.

Change by Imposition Change by imposition—sometimes called **cultural imperialism**—involves imposing certain elements from an alien culture, such as a forced change in laws by a dominant country that, over time, becomes part of the subject culture.

Generally, contact among countries brings change, known as *cultural diffusion*. When the change results in mixing cultures, we have *creolization*. For example, the U.S. popularity of Mexican tortillas is a result of *cultural diffusion*. Subsequent adaptions of them to U.S. tastes, such as tortilla chips and burritos, are *creolization*. Some groups and governments have tried without full success to protect national cultures. Their efforts have been hampered by their citizens' foreign travel, access to information abroad, and desire to adopt economic enhancing foreign technology. Thus, most countries seek to preserve traditions that help maintain national cohesiveness while being open to changes that grow their economies. South Korea, for example, has become more multiethnic because of the influx of foreigners needed to work in its factories. To help maintain traditions, the government now sponsors programs and language centers to "Koreanize" the foreigners.[18]

LANGUAGE AS BOTH A DIFFUSER AND STABILIZER OF CULTURE

A common language is a unifying force, but many countries

- have multiple language groups,
- depend on a second language that is common regionally.

Language is a noticeable aspect of culture because it limits contact among people who can't communicate with each other. Although a nation may have a single official language, the reality is much more complex.[19] For instance, there is disagreement as to what constitutes a separate language versus being merely a dialect of another.[20]Many nations contain multiple languages, of which more than one may be official. Further, many people are bilingual or multilingual. Nevertheless, language is at the heart of social identity. When people from different countries speak the same language, culture spreads more easily among them. Commerce also expands because a common language fosters a sense of shared identity, and, on a practical level, there is less need to translate everything. When a group, especially one with few people, has a language not spoken elsewhere, people therein either learn other languages or they become isolated.

Certain languages have long been common regionally as a second language, such as French in parts of Africa and Russian in Eastern Europe and Central Asia. This leads native speakers of regional or very widely spoken languages to be complacent about learning foreign languages because they can so often get by without doing so. Further, these languages are often seen as the languages of power, influence, and opportunity. For instance, as English has emerged as the most common second language, people in native English-speaking countries tend to be more monolingual than people in most other countries. This has made native English speakers more dependent on others (whom they often hardly know) to mediate in multicultural and multilingual business settings. There is a simple consequence to this: If you speak the languages of both parties, you need not depend on an intermediary who may confuse the communication. (Map 2.2 shows the distribution of the world's major language groups.)

MAP 2.2 Distribution of the World's Major Languages

Globally, people speak over 7,000 different languages, but 23 of these are the mother tongue for about 57 percent of the world's population. Some estimates are that 50 to 90 percent of languages may be extinct by the end of the twenty-first century; however, recent efforts to bolster indigenous peoples may save many languages. Only a few languages remain important in the dissemination of culture. A significant portion of countries, for example, speak Arabic, English, French, or Spanish. But take a look at Mandarin Chinese. It's important in IB because China comprises a lot of people and has become the world's second-largest economy. The classification "Regional" actually takes in two categories: (1) countries in which the dominant language is not dominant anywhere else (e.g., Japan) and (2) countries in which several different languages are spoken (e.g., India).

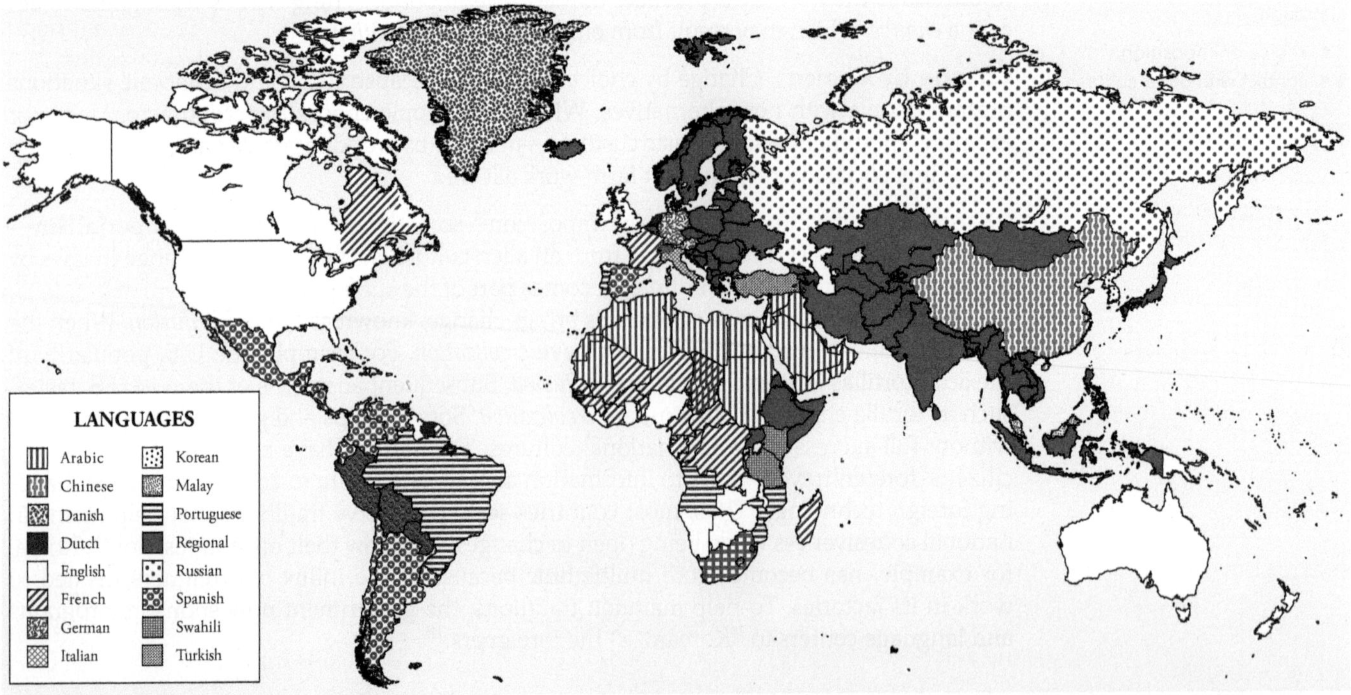

English has become the "international language of business"

- because native English language countries account for so much of world production,
- because it is the world's most important second language,
- but it may lose some relative importance in the future,
- but it may lead to overvaluing employees with English competence.

Why English Travels So Well Although the countries where English is spoken as a first language have only 6 percent of the global population, they account for 25 percent of the world's output.[21] As such, the five economically most important English language countries (Australia, Canada, New Zealand, the United Kingdom, and the United States) are collectively called the *Anglosphere* and are the preferred destination for people who wish to immigrate and for highly skilled immigrants.[22] This difference helps to explain why English is the world's most important *second* language. (About 1.5 billion people are studying English as a second language. French is the second most important and it has 82 million.)[23] Remember, too, that MNEs—which are largely headquartered in English-speaking countries—decide on the common language for communication among their employees in different countries. Not surprisingly, they usually select English because many of their managers either speak only English or have English as a second language. In addition, some MNEs from non–English-speaking countries have adopted English—the "international language of business"—as their operating language. Nevertheless, this policy can have some negative effects, such as overvaluing people with English language competence in hiring and evaluation decisions.[24] More competent individuals may be overlooked and eventually leave the company. However, at the same time, a common corporate language is often an illusion as individuals continue to use other languages informally.

Monolingual English speakers may eventually experience more difficulty in communicating worldwide. Why? Because the percentage of them will decrease, while the languages of such countries as China and India will grow rapidly along with their economies.[25] As is often the case, history may teach us about this matter: Latin and French were once the languages of scholarship and diplomacy, respectively. Aramaic was once dominant in the Middle East.[26] But the use of these languages has long since been diminished or supplanted.

The Evolvement of Languages Languages add and delete words. Over time, if groups of people become sufficiently isolated from each other, a common language may evolve into more than one, such as occurred with the various Romance languages that developed from Latin. At the same time, languages coexist and influence each other. When, say, a U.S. product enters a foreign market, its vocabulary often enters the language as well—sometimes in a strange form. In a Spanish-speaking country, for instance, you might see a sign announcing *Vendemos blue jeans de varios colores* ("We sell various colors of blue jeans"). It might appear that the use of the word "jeans" in this context is an example only of English predominance. However, the English language adapted the word "Gênes," the French word for the Italian city of Genoa and the fabric (now referred to as denim) that originated there. This cross-pollination of languages is an ongoing phenomenon that coincides with the diffusion of cultures.

RELIGION AS A CULTURAL STABILIZER

Many strong values are the result of a dominant religion.

Map 2.3 shows the approximate distribution of the world's major religions. Religion has been a cultural stabilizer because centuries of religious influence continue to shape cultural values even in those societies where the practice of religion has been declining.[27] The role of religion in shaping behavior is even stronger among people and countries with strong religious convictions.

Religions—such as Buddhism, Christianity, Hinduism, Islam, and Judaism—influence beliefs that affect business. Each religion is too complex to make meaningful brief realistic generalizations about it, so be cautious in accepting cultural explanations that rely very heavily on simplifications. For one, there are divisions within religions, such as between Theravada and Vajrayana Buddhists, Evangelical and Catholic Christians, Sunni and Shite Muslims (in Islam), and Orthodox and Reform Jews. Nevertheless, religious pervasiveness causes companies to make operating adjustments. For instance, McDonald's limits sales of beef and pork in India to keep from offending, respectively, its Hindu and Muslim populations. El Al, the Israeli national airline, does not fly on Saturday, the Jewish Sabbath. In fact, religion has an impact on almost every business function. To be viewed legitimately, companies must take religious beliefs into account.[28]

MAP 2.3 Distribution of the World's Major Religions

About 84 percent of the world's population identifies with a religious group. Most countries are home to people of various religious beliefs, but a nation's culture is typically influenced most heavily by a dominant religion. The practices of the dominant religion, for instance, often shape customary practices in legal and business affairs.

Source: The numbers for adherents are taken from Pew Research Center, "The Global Religious Landscape," (December 18, 2012) http://www.pewforum.org/2012/12/18/global-religious-landscape-exec/?utm_content=bufferf682f&utm_source=buffer&utm_medium=twitter&utm_campaign=Buffer (accessed February 6, 2016) and from "Major Religious Groups," *Wikipedia* (accessed April 15, 2019).

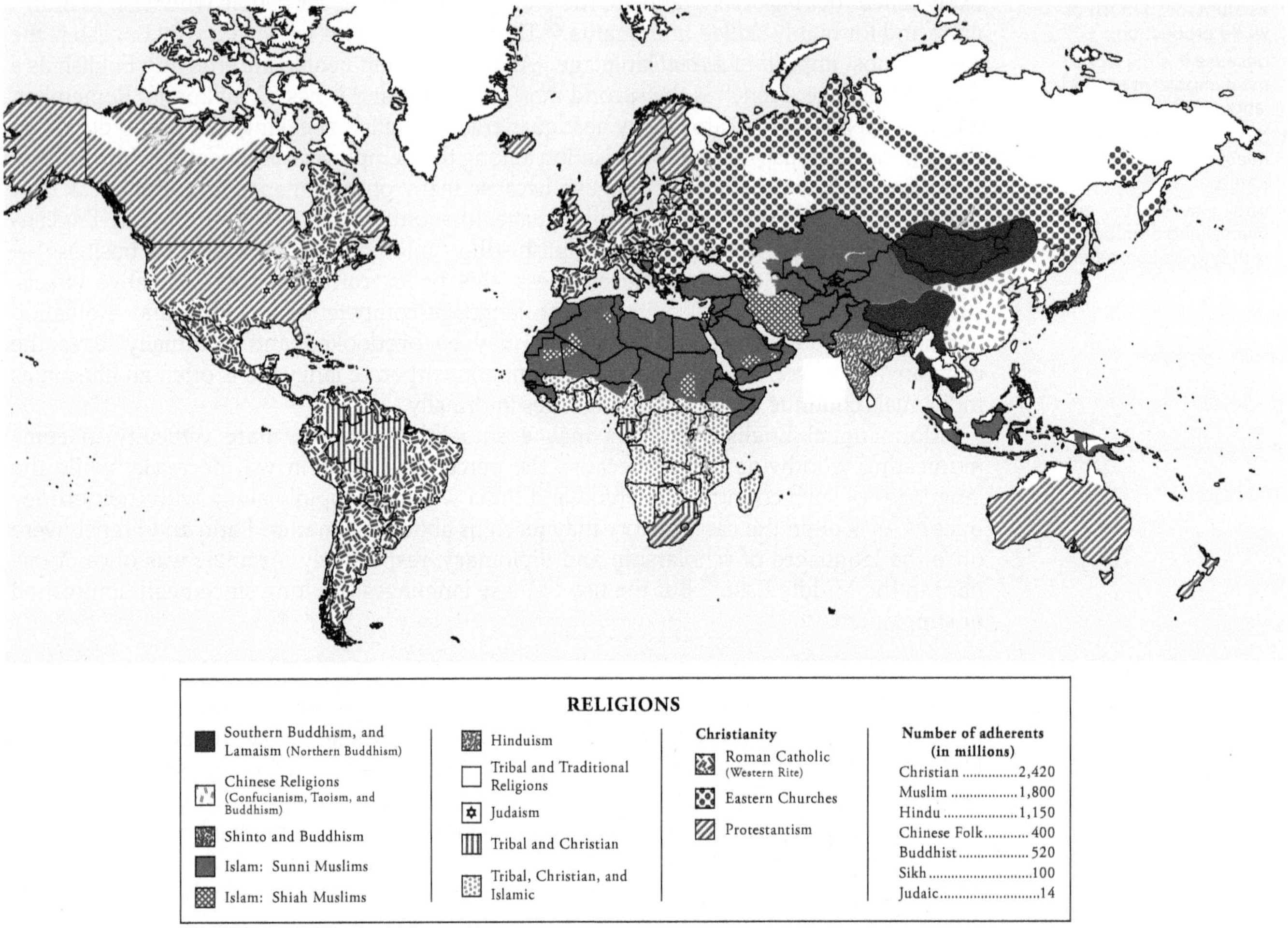

But not all nations with the same dominant religion impose the same business constraints. For example, Friday is a day of worship in Islam, but Turkey (a secular Islamic country) has Friday as a workday to adhere to the Christian work calendar in European countries. Where rival religions vie for political control, strife can cause business upheaval. Unfortunately, the problem is substantial. In recent years, religious violence has erupted in such countries as India, Iraq, Sri Lanka, Sudan, and Syria.

MAJOR BEHAVIORAL PRACTICES AFFECTING BUSINESS

2-3 Discuss major behavioral factors influencing countries' business practices

Cultural variables are sometimes defined differently and given various names for slightly different and sometimes overlapping concepts. Because of these nuances, there are thousands of possible ways to relate culture to business—far too many to cover in one chapter. We'll settle for hitting the highlights.

ISSUES IN SOCIAL STRATIFICATION

Every culture ranks people. Such *social stratification* creates hierarchies and influences a person's class, status, and financial rewards within that culture. In business, this practice may entail ranking and rewarding members of managerial groups more highly than production group members. Social stratification is determined by (1) individuals' achievements and talents (*meritocracy*) and (2) their group identifications. These two factors interact, but the importance of one versus the other varies among cultures. Further, more formal cultures expect more status-oriented communications between hierarchical levels. Higher-status individuals, for example, may be offended if people from a lower status address them by a first name or without using a title.

Businesses reward meritocracy more highly in some societies.

Individual Qualifications and Their Limitations In most societies, meritocracy is important in business, such as in choosing a star athlete to promote sportswear or a highly educated and motivated person to handle competitive responsibilities. However, we shall see that this is not always the case.

Because societies value group affiliations differently, business practices differ among countries. For example, Japanese companies generally place more weight on seniority than companies in other countries, and seniority favors older employees.[29] In another example, a study comparing British and German banks' staff-reduction practices, the former were more prone to save costs by discharging on a performance-to-salary basis (targeting, say, a middle-aged manager with a high salary and average performance), whereas the latter were more inclined to minimize personal hardship (targeting younger managers, regardless of performance, because they could find new jobs more easily).[30]

Group affiliations can be
- ascribed or acquired,
- a reflection of class and status.

The above examples deal largely with age groups, but there are many other ways to classify people's group memberships. Those usually determined by birth are **ascribed group memberships**, including gender, family, age, caste, and ethnic, racial, or national origin. **Acquired group memberships** include those based on religion, political affiliation, educational place and achievement, and profession.

Laws and policies often try to influence the importance of group difference. For example, policies that exclude female access to education in much of sub-Saharan Africa reinforce females' lower earning potential. The Nobel economist Amartya Sen referred to this exclusion from the workforce as *unfreedom* and pointed out its negative effect on economic advancement.[31] In contrast, European policies that require large companies to include a minimum percentage of women on their boards are aimed at overcoming male dominance therein.

Even when individuals qualify for given positions and no legal barriers exist to hold them back, opposition to certain groups—by other workers, customers, shareholders, or government officials—may limit their equal access to employment.

Country-by-country attitudes vary toward
- social connections,
- race and ethnicity,
- male and female roles,
- rules and expectations based on age,
- family ties.

The following sections focus on some of the group memberships that influence how a person is viewed from country to country. An additional factor that is often important is a person's *social connections*,[32] which corresponds to the old adage, "It's *who* you know, not *what* you know."

Ethnic and Racial Groups Malaysia, for example, defines political parties and employment quotas explicitly by three ethnic groups—Malays, Chinese, and Indians. The employment quotas are primarily to upgrade the economic position of Malays because the Chinese and Indian minorities long dominated business ownership and the professions, respectively.[33] The system requires companies to maintain expensive record-keeping systems of their hiring.[34] India has employment and university entrance quotas aimed at bettering the lot of lower income and caste levels.[35] Brazilian common language usage has many terms to designate skin color, of which five are official classifications within its census. The country has racial quotas in universities and pressures to enact employment quotas.[36] (But only competence counts in selecting the national football team.)

Gender-Based Groups Country-specific differences in equality and attitudes toward gender are sometimes quite pronounced.[37] In our opening case, we discussed Saudi Arabian cultural attitudes toward gender, resulting in almost seven employed men for every employed woman. Compare that with Norway, where only 1.1 men are employed for every woman. In Lithuania, more than 50 percent of both males and females agreed with the following statement: "When jobs are scarce, men have a better right to a job than women"; in Sweden and Iceland, the number was under 10 percent.[38]

Most countries have some laws hindering women's ability to work. Although many of these laws are intended to protect women, the results are sometimes discriminatory. For example, France prohibits women from working in jobs requiring them to lift more than 25 kilos (55 pounds), even though that's about the weight of a 5-year-old that they regularly lift. It also cuts them off from working, for example, to deliver FedEx packages.[39] In many places, however, gender barriers in employment practices are coming down because of changes in attitudes and work requirements. A noticeable U.S. change is reflected in the number of people of one gender employed in occupations previously dominated by the other, such as more male nurses and more female physicians. But some of this change may be economic rather than attitudinal.[40] The change in work requirements is reflected in the decrease in jobs requiring brawn and increase in jobs needing specialized education, such as X-ray technology and psychiatric casework.

Age-Based Groups All countries enforce age-related laws such as on employment, driving privileges, rights to obtain products and services (alcohol, cigarettes, certain pharmaceuticals, bank accounts), and civic duty (voting, serving in the military or on juries). Sometimes the logic of these laws seems paradoxical. For example, Americans can vote, marry, drive, and die for their country before they can legally buy alcohol at age 21. In contrast, Luxembourgers can legally buy distilled alcohol at age 16.[41] U.S. firms bombard children with TV advertising, but Sweden prohibits ads targeted to children.

National differences toward employment age are substantial. Both Finland and the Netherlands enforce mandatory retirement ages, but with few exceptions (e.g., airline pilots) U.S. law specifically prohibits the practice. In Britain, age discrimination laws apply to all ages, whereas U.S. law (except for child labor) protects only people over age 40.[42] When the proposition "When jobs are scarce, people should be forced to retire early" was put to people in different countries, almost three-quarters of Bulgarians agreed, but only 10 percent of Japanese.[43] Why this latter difference? For one thing, Japanese hold strongly to the assumption that there's a correlation between age and wisdom.

Family-Based Groups In some cultures, such as in much of Latin America, family is the most important group. A person's position in society depends heavily on the family's social status or "respectability" rather than on individual achievement. When family ties are strong, small family-run companies are quite successful; however, they often encounter growth difficulties because owners are reluctant to share responsibility with technically competent professional managers hired from outside the family. When its business culture is thus hampered, a country may lack sufficient numbers of indigenously owned *large-scale* companies that are usually necessary for long-term economic development.[44]

WORK MOTIVATION

Highly motivated employees (toward work) are normally more productive than workers who aren't. Further, higher worker productivity impacts companies' efficiency and countries' economic development. We now summarize major studies showing some differences in how and why nations differ in this motivation.

The desire for material wealth is
- a prime motivation to work,
- positive for economic development.

Materialism and Motivation When developing his *Protestant work ethic* theory, Max Weber observed that predominantly Protestant countries were the most economically developed. He attributed this to an outgrowth of the Protestant Reformation in sixteenth-century Europe, which reflects the "ethic" that work is a pathway to salvation and that material success does not impede redemption. Although we no longer strictly accept this distinction for Protestants, we do tend to adhere to some of Weber's underlying notions: namely, that self-discipline, hard work, honesty, and a belief in a just world foster work motivation and, thus, economic growth.[45]

On one hand, evidence indicates a positive correlation between the intensity of religious beliefs per se (regardless of specific belief systems) and adherence to some attributes that lead to economic growth (say, confidence in the rule of law and belief in the virtue of thrift).[46] Moreover, individuals' desire for material wealth motivates them to work hard, which in turn leads to community-wide economic development.[47] On the other hand, some religious values, such as predetermination, may lessen work motivation because "what will be, will be."[48] Further, in societies such as Myanmar and Laos, a large portion of the population vanishes

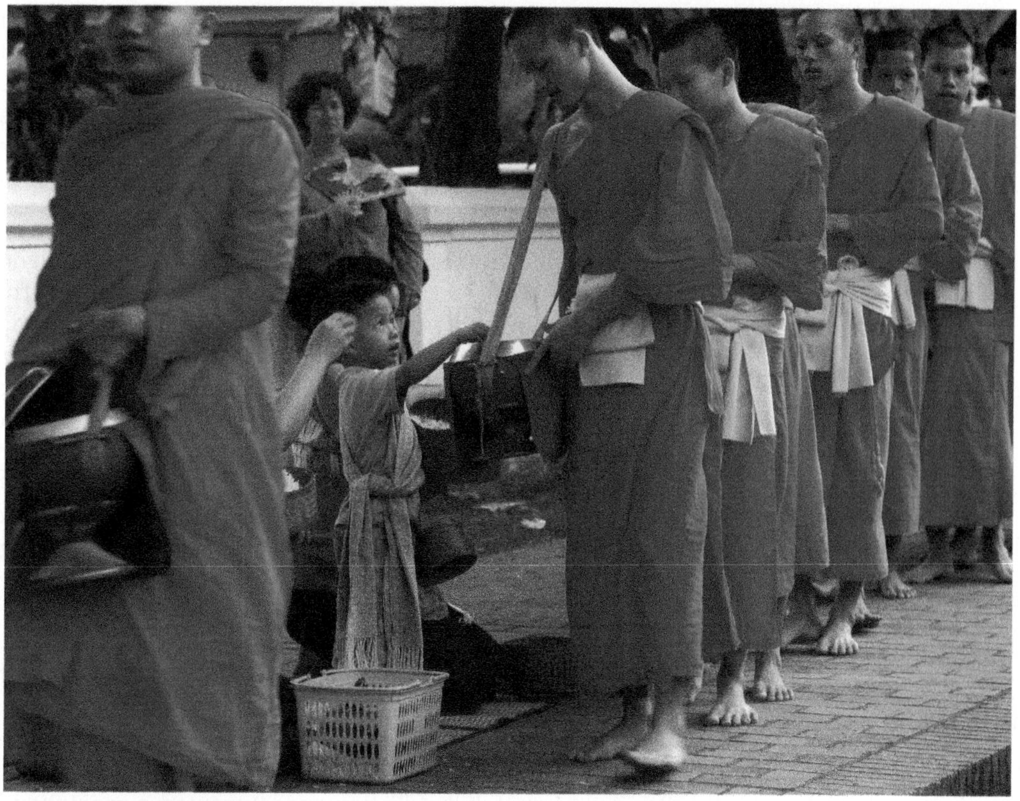

Monks going on alms round in ▶ Luang Prabang, Laos.

Source: Barbara Walton/EPA/Shutterstock

from the economic workforce temporarily or permanently while pursuing religious activities and being supported by others. (See the adjacent photo in Laos.)

People are more eager to work if
- rewards for success are high relative to failure,
- there is some uncertainty of success.

Expectation of Success and Reward The perceived likelihood of success and its rewards versus failure influence work motivation. Generally, people have little enthusiasm for effort when the likelihood of success seems overly easy or difficult. Few would care to run a race against either a snail or a racehorse; in either case, the outcome is too predictable. Enthusiasm peaks when uncertainty of success is high, such as the challenge of racing another human of roughly equal ability. Likewise, the reward for a successfully completed task—say, winning a fair footrace—may be high or low, and most of us usually exert more effort when the expectation of reward from success is much higher than for failure.

Success and Reward Across Borders Performed in different countries, the same tasks come with different probabilities of success and different rewards for success versus failure. In cultures where the probability of failure from work is almost certain and the perceived rewards of success versus failure are not much different, people tend—not surprisingly—to view work as unsatisfying, mainly because they foresee little benefit to themselves. This attitude may prevail in harsh climates, in very poor areas, or in subcultures subject to discrimination. Likewise, there is less motivation to work hard where public policy allocates output from productive workers to unproductive workers. When high outcome uncertainty is combined with a positive reward for success and little or no reward for failure, we find the greatest work enthusiasm.[49]

Performance and Achievement

A high-masculinity culture prefers to "live to work," and a high-femininity culture prefers to "work to live."

The Masculinity–Femininity Index The **masculinity–femininity index** measures attitudes toward achievement rather than physical attributes of males and females. A high-masculinity score indicates a preference for "live to work," whereas a high-femininity score indicates a preference for "work to live." In essence, high-masculinity individuals show admiration for successful work achievers, lower sympathy for the unfortunate, preference to be better than others rather than on a par with them, and a money-and-things orientation. (They also strongly prefer role differences between the genders.) A high-femininity score denotes the opposite. It indicates a people orientation rather than work orientation and a preference for quality of life and the environment over economic performance and growth.[50]

This index helps explain national differences in behaviors. Let's say a firm in a high-masculinity country such as Austria sets up operations in a high-femininity country such as Sweden. Purchasing managers in Sweden, if they are high-femininity individuals, probably prefer smooth social relationships, amiable and ongoing dealings with suppliers, and employee and social welfare, whereas employees of the Austrian firm prefer lower costs, faster delivery, and minimized compensation for workers.

The hierarchy of needs
- may differ among countries,
- is useful in deciding how to motivate differently among countries.

Hierarchies of Needs According to the **hierarchy-of-needs theory** of motivation, people try to fulfill lower-level needs before moving on to higher-level ones.[51] The most basic needs are *physiological*: food, water, sex, warmth, and rest. These must be satisfied (or nearly satisfied) before activating *security* needs—safe physical and emotional environments—to become motivators. These must be satisfied before triggering *affiliation* needs—peer acceptance. Then motivation is to satisfy *esteem* needs—bolstering self-image through recognition, attention, and appreciation. The highest-order need calls for *self-actualization*—self-fulfillment of one's potential. Finally, the theory infers that once a need is satisfied, its motivation value diminishes.

This theory helps in distinguishing among employees' reward preferences in different parts of the world. In very poor countries, for example, a large portion of workers are likely engaged in very menial and unskilled jobs;[52] thus, a company may motivate them simply by providing enough compensation to satisfy needs for food and shelter. Elsewhere, a larger portion of workers are motivated by other needs.

Compensation (even at low levels of income) cannot fully explain differences in work motivation. A long-term study among a U.S. airline's back-office employees (almost all female) found that those in the United States and the Dominican Republic saw the job as a stepping-stone to higher-level positions. However, few in Barbados (because of using work largely to help fulfill affiliation needs) wanted a promotion because it would change relationships with friends. U.S. workers dressed very casually because they perceived choice of attire in a back-office job to be insignificant in fulfilling their esteem needs. But Barbadians dressed up to be seen en route to what they considered a prestige job. In fact, the company offered the Barbadians free company-owned bus transport, but they preferred to use slower public transportation where others could see them. The Barbados staff had low absenteeism and turnover rates because Barbados has a history of women working long-term. In the Dominican Republic, however, most female employees stayed on only until they married.

RELATIONSHIP PREFERENCES

So far, we've discussed two categories of behavioral practices affecting business: social stratification systems and work motivation. Next, we examine some of the values underlying interpersonal differences in behavior.

There are national variations in the preference for autocratic versus consultative management.

Power Distance **Power distance** is a measurement of employee preferences of interaction between superiors and subordinates. Evidence suggests that people perform better when these interactions fit their preferences, thus companies should consider aligning relationship styles effectively.

With *high* power distance, people prefer little consultation between bosses and subordinates. They also prefer management styles that are *autocratic* (ruling with unlimited authority). With *low* power distance, they prefer "consultative" styles.[53] What might happen, therefore, if a Dutch manager, who typically prefers low power distance, were sent to work in Morocco, where workers typically prefer high power distance? The Dutch manager might consult with Moroccan subordinates, who lose confidence in the manager, believing "Why doesn't the boss know what to do?" Thus, performance deteriorates rather than improves.

Interestingly, managers who prefer an autocratic relationship style are generally willing to delegate and accept decision-making by subordinates. What they don't accept well is consultative interaction between the two tiers, which implies a more equal relationship between them. Clearly, worker-participation methods may need to be adjusted to fit different countries.

Provision of better workplace conditions motivates collectivists. Challenges motivate individualists.

Individualism Versus Collectivism *High* **individualism** describes a preference to fulfill leisure time, build friendships, and improve skills independently of the organization. People with high individualism also prefer to receive direct monetary compensation as opposed to fringe benefits, and they prefer to engage in personal decision-making and on-the-job challenges. *High* **collectivism**, in contrast, typifies a penchant for dependence on the organization through training, satisfactory workplace conditions, and good benefits. For example, the United States is a highly individualist country, and employees socialize less with close work colleagues outside of work than employees do in more collectivist societies.[54] In countries with high individualism, a self-actualization opportunity is a prime motivator because employees want challenges. In those with high collectivism, fulfilling security needs is a prime motivator.[55]

Degrees of individualism and collectivism also influence on-the-job interactions. Levi Strauss attempted to introduce team-based production into U.S. plants after its management observed its high productivity within Japan's highly collectivist culture. However, Levi Strauss's U.S. employees, especially the most skilled workers, balked at group methods to improve work methods and solve problems; productivity went down, and Levi Strauss returned to a more individualistic system that better suited its U.S. workforce culture.

RISK-TAKING BEHAVIOR

Risk-taking behavior differs among nationalities because of their

- comfort in handling uncertainties,
- degree of trust among people,
- future orientation.
- attitudes of self-determination versus fatalism.

Cultures differ in people's satisfaction with the status quo versus taking risks to change situations. The following discussion examines four types of *risk-taking behavior* that reflect these attitudes: *uncertainty avoidance, trust, future orientation,* and *fatalism.*

Uncertainty Avoidance **Uncertainty avoidance** describes a trait of being uncomfortable with ambiguity. Where this trait is strong, most employees prefer to follow set rules even if they believe that breaking them may be in the company's best interests. They also tend to stay with current employers for a long time, preferring the certainty of present positions over the uncertainty of their future elsewhere.[56] In such situations, superiors may need to be more precise in their directions to subordinates, who typically don't want to be responsible for actions that counter what their superiors want.

Trust Surveys on *trust* indicate national response differences to such statements as "Most people can be trusted" and "You can't be too careful in dealing with people." Many more Norwegians than Brazilians, for example, regard most people as trustworthy.[57] Where trust is high, business costs tend to be lower because managers spend less time fussing over every possible contingency and noncompliance, thus giving them more time to produce, sell, and innovate.[58] At the same time, people's trust may differ toward their in-group and others.[59] For instance, we discussed that in some family-oriented societies, people have high trust of other family members, but low trust of people they know less well.

Future Orientation A **future orientation** denotes a willingness to delay gratification in order to reap more in the future. People develop this characteristic as preschoolers and it relates positively to their economic success as adults. It also relates positively to trust (e.g., belief in whether they'll receive the postponed rewards).[60] Future orientation is more pronounced in, for example, Switzerland, than in Italy.[61] In the former, it may be easier for companies to motivate workers through such delayed-compensation programs as retirement plans.

Fatalism If people are *fatalistic* (believing that events are predetermined and inevitable), they're less likely to accept the basic cause-and-effect relationship between work and reward. Thus, managers are less apt to sway them with cause-and-effect logic than by making personal appeals or by offering them rewards for complying with requests.[62]

INFORMATION AND TASK PROCESSING

"Beauty," we're often told, "is in the eye of the beholder." So, apparently, are perceptions and judgments, both of which are based on what people consider accurate *information.* The following discussion examines some of the ways in which people perceive, obtain, and process information.

Perception of Cues As a rule, we selectively perceive *cues*—features that inform us about the nature of something. We may identify things through any of our senses, and each sense

Differences in perception of cues may result from genetics and language.

can provide information in various ways, such as seeing color, depth, and shape through vision. People rely on cues that are partly physiological because evolution and genetics play a role in how different groups perceive.[63] Genetic differences in eye pigmentation, for instance, allow some people to differentiate colors more precisely than others.

Cultural differences, especially language, also reflect perceptual differences. The richness of a language's descriptive vocabulary allows its speakers to note and express very subtle nuances that nonspeakers do not discern. For instance, the Arabic language has many more words for camels, their body parts, and the equipment associated with them than other languages,[64] and Arabic speakers who work around camels can express nuances about them that most other people overlook.

Managers are helped by knowing whether cultures favor

- focused or broad information,
- a particular way of classifying information,
- sequential or simultaneous handling of situations,
- handling principles versus small issues first.

Obtaining Information: Low-Context Versus High-Context Cultures Some countries (including the United States and most of northern Europe) are **low-context cultures**, ones where people generally regard as relevant only firsthand information that bears directly on the subject at hand. Businesspeople spend little time on small talk before getting to the point. In **high-context cultures**, people tend to understand and regard indirect information as pertinent. Differences can result in miscommunication. For example, in Japan, a high-context culture, subordinates typically understand superiors' indirect instructions. But Japanese managers in the United Kingdom, a low-context culture, have been challenged in conveying instructions there because the subordinates expect more explicit explanations.[65]

Information Processing All cultures process information inasmuch as they categorize, plan, and quantify. However, every culture has its own systems for ordering and classifying information. In U.S. directories, people's names appear in alphabetical order by last (family) name; in Iceland, they're organized by first (given) name. U.S. street numbers are generally odd on one side of the street and even on the other; in much of the Americas, the numbers indicate the distance from where the street begins; in much of Japan, the numbers refer to the construction date; and in Berlin, numbers often go up sequentially on one side of the street and then down the other.[66] To perform efficiently in a foreign environment, you need to understand such differences in processing systems. Further, different processing systems create challenges in sharing global data. Even global personnel directories are problematic because of different alphabets, alphabetizing methods, and number systems.

Monochronic Versus Polychronic Cultures In **monochronic** cultures people normally prefer to work sequentially, such as finishing transactions with one customer before dealing with another. Conversely, **polychronic** people (and cultures) are more comfortable working simultaneously on a variety of tasks (multitasking), such as dealing simultaneously with multiple customers who need service. Imagine the potential misconceptions when monochronic businesspeople think their polychronic counterparts are uninterested in doing business with them because they don't bother to give them their undivided attention. Further, firms combine people in teams from both types of cultures, the monochronic members sometimes feel that the polychronic ones delay results by wasting time before finishing with any items in the program.[67]

Idealism Versus Pragmatism Some cultures tend to focus first on the whole and then on the parts; others do the opposite. When asked to describe an underwater scene in which one large fish was swimming among some smaller fish, most Japanese first described the overall picture, whereas most Americans first described the large fish.[68] Similarly, some cultures prefer to establish overall principles before they try to resolve small issues—an approach sometimes labeled **idealism**. Cultures in which people focus more on details than on abstract principles are said to be **pragmatic**.

These different approaches can affect business in a number of ways. In a pragmatic culture (as in the United States), labor negotiations tend to focus on specifically defined issues—say, hourly pay increases for a specific bargaining unit. In an idealist culture (as in Argentina), labor disputes tend to blur the focus on specific demands as workers are inclined to rely first on mass action, such as general strikes or political activities, to gain support for basic principles.

PROBLEMS IN COMMUNICATING ACROSS CULTURES

2-4 Recognize the complexities of cross-cultural communications

We now look at problems in *communicating across cultures*—especially translating and differences that occur by means other than spoken and written language (a so-called "silent language").

TRANSLATION OF SPOKEN AND WRITTEN LANGUAGE

Cross-border communications do not always translate as intended.

Translating one language into another is not as straightforward as it may seem. Some words simply don't have common direct translations. In English, for example, *children* may mean either "young people" or "offspring." In Spanish, *niños* and *hijos* distinguish between the two, and there is no word that encompasses both meanings that exist in English. Thus, despite recent strides in machine translations, many errors still occur. Moreover, many translations—say, Galician into Welsh—go through an intermediate language, usually English.[69]

Language is constantly evolving. When Microsoft purchased a thesaurus code for its Spanish version of Word, the connotations of many synonyms had shifted by the time it implemented the software; some, in fact, were transformed into outright insults that alienated potential customers.[70] Of course, in any language, words mean different things in different contexts. For example, the English word "old" can mean "former" or "long-standing." Imagine the confusion of "We are the old leader in banking."

Finally, grammar is complex and the seemingly slight misuse (or even placement) of a word can substantially change the meaning. The following, each originally composed to assist English-speaking guests, have appeared on signs in hotels around the world:

JAPAN: "You are invited to take advantage of the chambermaid."

NORWAY: "Ladies are requested not to have children in the bar."

SWITZERLAND: "Because of the impropriety of entertaining guests of the opposite sex in the bedroom, it is suggested that the lobby be used for this purpose."

These examples offer a comical look at language barriers that usually result in only a chuckle or a little embarrassment. Poor translations, however, can cause commercial disputes; the Shanghai Maritime Court has dealt with thousands of such disputes between Chinese and foreign companies.[71] So choose your words carefully. Although there's no foolproof way of ensuring translations, experienced IB personnel rely on suggestions such as the following:

- Get references for the people who will be translators.
- Make sure your translator knows the technical vocabulary of your business.
- For written work, do *back translations*: Have one person go from, say, English to French and a second from French back to English. If your final message says what you meant originally, it's probably satisfactory.
- Make sure that the tone, not just the words, fit both your own intentions and the expectations of recipients.
- Use simple words whenever possible (such as *ban* instead of *interdiction*).
- Avoid slang. U.S. slang, especially words or phrases originating from sports such as baseball—*off base, out in left field, threw me a curve, ballpark figure*—are probably meaningless to most businesspeople outside the United States.[72]
- When either you or your counterpart is dealing in a language other than your first language, clarify communications in several ways (repeat things in different words and ask questions) to ensure that all parties have the same interpretation.
- Budget from the start for the extra time needed for translation and clarification.

Be careful with humor because it sometimes lacks universal appeal. A Microsoft executive quipped to Indian executives that he lacked qualifications to speak because he did not complete his MBA. The comment was badly received because most Indians place high importance on education and on persevering rather than dropping out.[73]

TABLE 2.1 Dangers of Misspeaking the Language(s) of Business

Below is a short list of business words whose meanings are different in the United States and the United Kingdom—"two countries separated by a common language," as the Irish playwright George Bernard Shaw once quipped. There are approximately 4,000 English words with the potential to cause problems for people who—in theory—speak the same language.

United States	United Kingdom
turnover	redundancy
sales	turnover
inventory	stock
stock	shares
president	managing director
chapter 11	receivership

Finally, even when all parties to a communication come from countries that share an official language, don't assume that understanding will go smoothly. Table 2.1, for instance, lists a few business terms that have different meanings in British and American English. What could go wrong? When Hershey's launched its Elegancita candy bar in Latin America, it advertised the *cajeta* in the product. Unfortunately, although *cajeta* means "goat's-milk caramel" in Mexico, in much of South America it's vulgar slang for a part of the female anatomy.[74]

SILENT LANGUAGE

Silent language includes color associations, sense of appropriate distance, concept of time, body language, and prestige cues.

We constantly exchange messages through a host of nonspoken and nonwritten cues that form a **silent language**.[75] Recall from our opening case that in the process of conducting market research for a new restaurant, researchers depended on several such cues to deduce who was affluent.

Colors For a product to succeed, its colors must coincide with consumers' frame of reference. Colors invoke distinct connotations in different countries, such as being lucky or unlucky or being associated with a specific business (e.g., yellow cabs in the United States and black ones in the United Kingdom). In most Western countries, black is a color for mourning death; in parts of Africa, it's white. United Airlines' promotion of a new passenger service in Hong Kong backfired because of color. Why? It handed out white carnations to boarding customers, but Hong Kong residents give white carnations in sympathy for a death in the family.

Distance Comfortable distances among people vary. For example, in the United States people tend to maintain larger distances during conversations or when conducting business than people in Mexico do. And except for handshakes, there is little or no touching in the United States, whereas touching one another in Mexico is quite common.[76] Thus, U.S. and Mexican managers when conducting business with each other may find themselves constantly moving to maintain their accustomed distances and body contact. At the end of the discussion, both parties may well feel uneasy about each other without realizing why.

However, at this writing the COVID-19 pandemic is altering norms for physical contact and distance among people globally. We must wait and see whether and how people revert to old habits at the end of the pandemic.

Time and Punctuality Different perceptions of time and punctuality also may create confusion. U.S. businesspeople usually arrive ahead of a business appointment time, a few minutes late for dinner at someone's home, and a bit later still for large social gatherings. In another country, the concept of punctuality in any or all of these situations may be different. A Latin American host may be astonished and find U.S. guests perhaps discourteous if they arrive only a few minutes later than the stated time for dinner.

Is time a scarce commodity or an event? People who value time as a scarce commodity believe that if it's lost, it can't be recouped.[77] They tend to stick to schedules, even if taking longer would yield better results. In contrast, people who view time as an event prefer to take as long as necessary to complete a task to their satisfaction. In one case, a U.S. management team was so confident of winning a contract on the basis of better technology that it

FIGURE 2.2 Body Language Is Not a Universal Language

The fine line between approval and put-down: Very few gestures have universal meanings. In the United States, you'd probably be safe in approving of another person's statement by forming an O with your thumb and index finger (the so-called high sign). In Germany, Greece, and France, however, you'd be expressing a very different meaning.

Source: The meanings are based on descriptions in Roger E. Axtell, *Gestures* (New York: John Wiley, 1998). Reprinted by permission of John Wiley & Sons, Inc.

scheduled a tight, one-day meeting in Mexico City, thinking this was sufficient for its presentation and questions. Unfortunately, the Mexican team arrived one hour after the scheduled start. Then, when an urgent phone call caused a Mexican team member to leave the room, the whole Mexican group got upset when the U.S. team tried to proceed without him. The competing French team, in contrast, allocated two weeks for discussions and won the contract with less sophisticated technology.[78]

Body Language Body language, or *kinesics*, is the way people walk, touch, and move their bodies. Very few have universal meanings. A Greek, Turk, or Bulgarian may indicate "yes" with a sideways movement of the head that could be construed as "no" in the United States and much of Europe. As Figure 2.2 shows, certain gestures may have several, even contradictory meanings. Further, meanings can change. The gesture in Figure 2.2 that ordinarily means it's fine or O.K. in the United States has come to indicate "white supremacism" as well.[79]

Prestige Another factor in silent language relates to a person's status, particularly in an organizational setting. U.S. managers typically place great faith in physical things as cues to prestige and may underestimate the status of foreign counterparts who lack large, plush corner offices on high floors. Foreigners may underestimate U.S. counterparts who perform their own services, such as opening doors, fetching coffee, and answering unscreened phone calls.

GUIDELINES FOR CULTURAL ADJUSTMENT

2-5 Analyze guidelines for cultural adjustment

After managers identify key cultural differences abroad, must they alter their customary practices to succeed there? Can people overcome culturally related adjustment problems when working abroad? There are no easy answers to these questions, but the following discussion highlights four issues that affect *degrees* of successful adjustment:

1. The extent to which a culture is willing to accept the introduction of anything foreign
2. Whether key cultural differences are small or great
3. The ability of individuals to adjust to what they find in foreign cultures
4. The general management orientation of the company involved

The following sections address each of these issues.

HOST SOCIETY ACCEPTANCE

Host cultures do not always expect foreigners to adjust to them.

Although our opening case illustrates the advantages of *adjusting* to a host country's culture, international companies sometimes succeed in introducing new products, technologies, and operating procedures with relatively little alteration. They pull it off because what they're introducing does not run counter to core values or because the host culture is willing to accept foreign products or practices as an agreeable trade-off to its peripheral values. Bahrain needs non-Muslim workers, so it permits the sale of pork products (ordinarily prohibited by religious law) as long as transactions are limited to special places in which Muslims can neither work nor shop.

DEGREE OF CULTURAL DIFFERENCES

When doing business in a similar culture, companies

- usually have to make fewer adjustments,
- may overlook subtle differences.

Obviously, a country can be much like some others, usually because it shares many characteristics with them, such as language, religion, geographic location, ethnicity, and level of economic development.

Cultural Distance A human values study comparing 43 societies on 405 cultural dimensions[80] calculated their **cultural distance**, which is the average number of countries they are apart on the dimensions. When a company moves into a culturally close foreign country, such as an Ecuadoran company into Colombia, it should encounter fewer cultural adjustments than when entering a culturally distant country, such as Thailand.

Even among culturally close countries, however, differences could still undermine business dealings. Managers may assume that countries are more alike than they really are, thus overlooking important subtleties or some differences that are not noted in overall cultural distance analysis. For instance, Arab countries are culturally close to each other overall, but women's roles and behavior differ substantially from one Arab country to another.

Hidden Cultural Attitudes Even if the home and host countries have seemingly similar cultures, people in the host country may reject the influx of foreign practices because they see them as additional steps that threaten their self-identities.[81] And with thousands of *minute* cultural dimensions, it may not be easy to discern operating impediments by comparing countries on the *broad* ones that are both obvious and studied. For instance, Disney had much more success in opening a theme park in Japan than in France, even though France is culturally closer to the United States. Why? First, many French were concerned about loss of the country's individuality, especially vis-à-vis the United States because of encroachment of American English words into French, fast-food restaurants' threat to customary long lunches with traditional cuisine, and U.S. companies' acquisition of French firms considered focal to French distinctiveness. Next, subtle differences separated the Japanese from the French. The Japanese were more receptive to Disney because (1) both Japanese children and adults perceived Mickey Mouse as a wholesome, nonthreatening figure, (2) the Japanese had a tradition of buying souvenirs on family excursions, and (3) Disney's reputation for super-cleanliness and smiling faces fit well with Japanese preferences for harmony and order. The French, in contrast, knew Mickey Mouse only as a comic schemer. They regarded Disney souvenirs as tacky and policies requiring personnel to dress uniformly and smile mindlessly as violations of personal dignity.[82]

ABILITY TO ADJUST: CULTURE SHOCK

Some people get frustrated when entering a different cultural environment.

When individuals go abroad, they encounter different customs and practices. Some of these may be potentially traumatic to them. At an extreme, some cultural practices are considered by many outsiders as downright wrong, such as polygamy, child marriage, the punishment of people (sometimes severe) for activities not considered crimes at home, and the public display of executions and executed bodies. Both companies and individuals must decide if they're ready to work in places that countenance such practices.

Even in countries whose practices aren't necessarily traumatic to them, workers who go abroad often encounter **culture shock**—the frustration that results from having to absorb a vast array of new cultural cues and expectations. Even such seemingly simple tasks as using a different type of toilet or finding how to obtain specific merchandise or services can be taxing experiences at first. As such, some people may pass through certain adjustment stages. At first, much like tourists, they're delighted with quaint differences. Later, however, they grow depressed and confused (the *culture shock* phase), so their effectiveness in the foreign environment suffers. Fortunately for most people, culture shock begins to ebb after a month or two as they grow more comfortable. In fact, some people experience **reverse culture shock** when they return, having become partial to aspects of life abroad that are not options back home.

COMPANY AND MANAGEMENT ORIENTATIONS

Whether and how a company and its managers adapt abroad depends not only on the host-country culture but also on their own attitudes and behaviors. The following sections discuss three such attitudes or orientations: polycentrism, ethnocentrism, and geocentrism.

Polycentric management may be so overwhelmed by national differences that it won't introduce workable changes.

Polycentrism A *polycentric* organization believes it should act abroad like companies there. Given the uniquely publicized problems of not adapting to foreign cultures, companies' development of polycentric perspectives is not surprising. However, polycentrism may be an overly cautious response to cultural variety, causing a firm to shy away from certain countries or avoid transferring home-country practices or resources that will actually work well abroad.

Look at it this way. To compete effectively, an international company must usually perform some functions differently from its competitors abroad in order to have an advantage over them. They may, for instance, need to sell and market new products or produce old ones differently. Thus, the overly polycentric firm may rely too heavily on imitating proven host-country practices and, in the process, lose the innovative edge it has honed at home.

Ethnocentric management overlooks national differences and

- ignores important factors,
- believes home-country objectives should prevail,
- thinks acceptance by other cultures is easy.

Ethnocentrism **Ethnocentrism** reflects the conviction that one's own practices are superior to those of other countries. In IB, the term is usually applied to a company (or individual) so strongly committed to the principle of "What works at home will work abroad" that its foreign practices ignore differences in cultures, markets, and institutions. In turn, it underestimates the complexity of introducing new management methods, products, or marketing means, which likely leads to poor performance.

However, ethnocentrism isn't entirely an inappropriate way of looking at things. From a company standpoint, much of what works at home will in fact work abroad. Further, concentrating on national differences in terms of *averages* overlooks specific variations within countries. A company may be able to deal with outliers even though the *average* person in the country has a strong cultural bias against what the company does. For example, although the average person in India has a strong cultural bias against eating meat, a company could sell meat products to the many Indians who do eat meat. Likewise, a company may identify partners, suppliers, and employees among a population's minority whose attitudes don't fit the cultural average (for instance, there are always individualists in even the most collectivist societies).

Likewise, people may adjust abroad by degree. Take food, for example. Most of us are delighted with new dishes when we go abroad, but not all dishes. The Museum of Disgusting Food in Malmö, Sweden offers food samples acceptable in some places, but disgusting in others. Many people who have not grown up with them become physically sick even by their description. Although people can learn to tolerate food and other things they first found revolting, they are likely able to adjust abroad sufficiently without having to accept everything.[83]

Geocentric management often uses business practices that are hybrids of home and foreign norms.

Geocentrism Between the extremes of polycentrism and ethnocentrism, **geocentrism** integrates home- and host-country practices as well as introducing some entirely new ones.[84] In our opening case, Saks Fifth Avenue adjusted to Saudi customs by setting aside women-only floors, introduced many home-country merchandising practices, and introduced the new practice of providing lounges for the drivers of female customers.

Geocentrism requires companies to balance informed knowledge of their own organizational cultures with home- and host-country needs, capabilities, and constraints. Because it encourages innovation and improves the likelihood of success, geocentrism is the preferred approach for most companies to succeed in foreign cultures and markets.

STRATEGIES FOR INSTITUTING CHANGE

Because people do not necessarily accept change readily, the management of change is important.

As we've seen, companies may need to compete by operating differently in some ways from other companies abroad (i.e., they introduce some degree of change into foreign markets). Thus, they need to bear in mind that people don't always accept change very readily. The methods they choose for managing such changes are important for ensuring success.

Fortunately, we can gain a lot of insight by examining organizations' international experiences. Moreover, a great deal of material is available on potential methods and so-called *change agents* (people or processes that intentionally cause or accelerate social, cultural, or behavioral change). The following sections discuss both experiences with and approaches to successful change, focusing on the following areas:

- Value systems
- Resistance to too much change
- Participation
- Reward sharing
- Opinion leadership
- Biculturals as mediators
- Timing
- Learning abroad

Value Systems If something contradicts core values, it will likely not be accepted. But even contradictions to peripheral values face obstacles. In Eritrea, for example, seafood consumption is very low despite its periods of agricultural famine and long coastline rich in seafood. One reason is that Eritrea's Cushitic speakers have religious taboos against eating much of the seafood that is available. Since seafood consumption goes against their core dietary value, the Eritrean government and the United Nations World Food Program have not been fully successful in persuading them to change their eating habits. But non-Cushitic speakers also eat little seafood. Part of the reason is economic. Poverty has prevented most of them from accessing ice and refrigeration to prevent seafood spoilage. Thus many adults have never developed a taste for seafood, worry about its safety, and believe it has a foul taste. Among schoolchildren, however, whose value systems and habits are still flexible, officials have faced little opposition.[85]

Resistance to Too Much Change The German magazine publisher G + J bought U.S.-based *McCall's* and immediately overhauled the magazine's format: changed editors, eliminated long stories and certain features, increased celebrity coverage, made layouts more robust, supplemented articles with sidebars, and refused discounts for big advertisers. Before long, morale declines led to greater employee turnover. More important, revenues fell because advertisers saw the change in format as too radical.[86] According to most observers, G + J might have received more employee and advertiser acceptance had it phased in its plans for change a little more gradually.

POINT

Does IB Lead to Cultural Imperialism?

YES The idea is pretty well accepted: IB influences globalization and globalization influences culture. Now, I have nothing against IB or globalization—at least part of it. What I don't like is modern cultural imperialism, which is what happens when the West, especially the United States, imposes its technical, political, military, and economic supremacy on developing countries.[87]

U.S. firms are in the business of exporting U.S. culture—mostly through tactics that are rarely in the best cultural interests of the nations it targets for economic domination. Because these firms nearly monopolize the international entertainment media, people all over the world are bombarded with U.S. movies and television, not to mention the barrage of accompanying ads from U.S. companies.

And what about the hordes of U.S. tourists who pay more for a night's lodging in a developing country than the hotel maid makes in months? The fact is they're selling the U.S. lifestyle to a market that can't afford it and that's probably better off without it. The

COUNTERPOINT

Does IB Lead to Cultural Imperialism?

NO You imply that people in poor countries passively accept everything they see in movie theaters and on TV. But they've turned their backs on a lot of products that international companies have promoted. Like most of us, they pick and choose.[89] You also imply that cultures in developing countries are the same. They aren't. They interpret what they see and hear—and what they buy—quite differently.

Like cultural purists everywhere, you've overlooked how cultural diffusion works. Through contact, culture heads in both directions and evolves. Of course, American English is seeping into other languages, but Americans have added a lot of foreign words as well. If you're a macho (Spanish) guy in charge of the whole enchilada (Spanish), for example, you're probably called the "head honcho" (Japanese).

Similarly, although U.S.-style fast food is almost everywhere, it has not entirely displaced local foods anywhere. When it comes to food, the result of IB is greater combination of media, advertisements, and tourists means that people in developing countries are exposed to U.S. possessions, practices, and lifestyles to their hearts' content. Never mind that they get an erroneous impression. According to TV and the movies, the United States is mainly populated by the super-wealthy and by cops and psychotic malcontents whose daily lives are taken up with bullet-spattered body parts, round-the-clock sex, and inane family relationships. The lifestyle is, nevertheless, seductive. That's why people everywhere are eating and consuming soft drinks at U.S. franchised fast-food restaurants and starting to behave and even talk like fictional Americans. Every speech from Manila to Managua is now peppered with U.S. slang. Along the way, people are letting their own cultural identities slip away.

I admit, if a country is rich enough, it can afford to resist most cultural exploitation. Canada says no to foreign investment in culturally sensitive industries and makes sure there's Canadian content in local entertainment media. France shuns outside languages and subsidizes a national motion picture industry. But even rich countries are affected. Some French TV programs and films are now being produced in English to cater to international audiences, and more of their university courses are being taught in English.[88] In the developing world, where there's precious little cash for fighting off cultural extinction, people are at the mercy of foreign culture brokers.

diversity for everybody. What we're witnessing is not "cultural imperialism" but cultural hybridization. In most countries, U.S. hamburgers, Japanese sushi, Italian pizza, Mexican tacos, and Middle Eastern pita bread coexist with the local cuisine. Mexico's Grupo Bimbo (owner of Sara Lee from the United States) sells tortillas in the United States and U.S.-style bagels in Mexico.[90]

Also, just because people in developing countries have taken a liking to soft drinks and fast food doesn't mean their tastes are permanent. Some evidence suggests that, although young people are most likely to adopt elements from a foreign culture, they tend to revert to traditional values and habits as they get older.[91]

As people seek to fulfill different wants, they must make trade-offs. But are people (and societies) worse off because they give up, say, lunch with the family by accepting a factory job to be able to afford certain consumer goods that will satisfy the whole family's needs? Globalization simply gives people more options. And tourism is also a two-edged sword. Rather than having a primarily negative effect, quite often it has helped maintain certain features of a traditional culture, such as the revival of traditional Balinese dancing because tourists want to see it.

Rather than simply imposing a foreign culture, a successful business, whether local or foreign-owned, must accommodate itself sufficiently to the culture in which it operates. This may mean revising plans to respond to local demands, which many foreign companies have done.

Participation One way to avoid problems is to discuss proposed changes with stakeholders (employees, suppliers, customers, and the like) in advance. The discussion might help management assess the strength of the resistance, stimulate stakeholders to recognize the need for change, and ease fears about the consequences. Stakeholders might be satisfied that management has at least listened to them, regardless of the decisions it ultimately makes.[92]

Companies sometimes mistakenly think that stakeholder participation in decision-making is effective only with educated people who are willing to speak up. Anyone who has had to deal with foreign aid programs can tell you that participation can be extremely important even in countries where education levels are low and power distance and uncertainty avoidance high.

Reward Sharing Sometimes a proposed change may have no foreseeable benefit for those whose support is needed. Production workers, for example, may have little incentive to try new work practices unless they see some imminent benefit for themselves. What can an employer do? It might develop means of sharing gains with stakeholders. For example, China National Petroleum has faced property damage from angry Iraqi farmers who have perceived problems without gains from living near drilling operations.[93] In contrast, a U.S.–Peruvian gold-mining venture won the support of skeptical Andean villagers simply through sharing the benefit by donating sheep to them.[94]

Opinion Leadership By making use of channels of influence, or *opinion leaders,* a firm may be able to facilitate the acceptance of change. Opinion leaders may emerge in unexpected places. When Ford wanted to install U.S. manufacturing methods in a Mexican plant, management relied on Mexican production workers—rather than either Mexican or U.S. supervisors—to observe operations at U.S. plants. The advantage was that the production workers had more credibility with the Mexican workforce who would have to implement the new methods.[95]

Biculturals and Multiculturals as Mediators Stakeholders are persuaded not only by the details presenters point out in proposed changes, but also by their confidence in the presenters' technical qualifications, understanding of host-country constraints, and flexible attitudes toward reaching solutions. In this respect, companies may rely on bicultural or multicultural individuals, to present and explain changes to stakeholders.[96] These bicultural and multicultural individuals may be especially adept at serving in mediator roles, especially if their cultures are from both the company's home and host countries. Even if the cultures are from other countries, these individuals may understand cultural nuances more easily than unicultural individuals. Further, their demonstrated empathy for divergent viewpoints may be more positively perceived by host country stakeholders simply because they seem less likely to be pushing an ethnocentric agenda.[97]

Timing Many well-conceived changes fail simply because they're ill-timed. A proposed labor-saving production method, say, might make employees nervous about losing their jobs no matter how much management tries to reassure them. If, however, the proposal is made during a period of labor shortage, the firm will likely encounter less fear and resistance.

In certain cases, of course, crisis precipitates the acceptance of change. In Turkey, for example, where family members have traditionally dominated business organizations, poor performance stimulated a rapid change in this practice: rather than "running" the business, many families now serve in "advisory capacities" (often on the board of directors).

Learning Abroad Companies' experience in foreign operations enables them to learn as well as impart valuable knowledge—knowledge that proves just as useful at home as in the host country. Such learning may concern any business function; however, access to R&D personnel is a particularly potent advantage in operating abroad. Nevertheless, going abroad with the belief that one already knows everything provides little chance to learn. But there are many examples of good results from being open-minded.

Finally, companies should examine the economies and businesses abroad that are performing well in order to determine practices they can emulate. For example, some large Indian companies have recently performed extremely well because of stressing social missions and investing heavily in their employees.[98] Can non-Indian companies learn from and emulate this experience successfully?

LOOKING TO THE FUTURE Scenarios on the Evolvement of National Cultures

Scenario 1: New Hybrid Cultures Will Develop and Personal Horizons Will Broaden

International contact is growing at a rate perhaps unimaginable a few decades ago—a process that should lead to a certain mixing and greater similarity among national cultures. At first glance, that's exactly what's happening. The mixing seems evident when one sees, say, Japanese tourists listening to a Philippine band perform an American pop song at a British hotel in Indonesia. Likewise, combinations of languages such as "Spanglish" have emerged. The growing mix seems apparent when people in every corner of the world wear similar clothing and listen to international recording stars alongside other people wearing local styles and listening to local recording artists. Competitors headquartered in far-flung global areas are increasingly copying each other's operating practices, thus creating a competitive work environment that's more global than national. As companies and people get used to operating internationally, they're apt to continue gaining confidence in applying the benefits of cultural diversity and globally inspired operating procedures to explore new areas in both workplace productivity and consumer behavior.

Historically, most people who immigrated to foreign countries were able to return to their birthlands perhaps once in their lives. They were thus usually compelled to accept the cultures of their adopted countries, sacrificing much of their native cultural identity in the process. Today, however, many obtain dual citizenship and maintain contact with their native cultures through travel, direct-dial phone calls, and Internet communications. On the one hand, these immigrants tend to transfer culture in both directions, bringing greater diversity to both host and home countries. Further, as people travel more abroad, marriage among different nationalities increases; the number of Americans with foreign-born spouses doubled between 1960 and 2010.[99] Evidence suggests that children in these circumstances are becoming bi- or multicultural, resulting in a class of international managers whose traditional ties to specific cultures are much looser than those of most people. On the other hand, multiculturalism appears to be failing in many places because the number of immigrants is so large that they no longer have to assimilate into the culture of their new residency. This may lead to more restrictions on immigration and cultural strife within nations.[100]

Scenario 2: Although the Outward Expressions of National Culture Will Continue to Become More Homogeneous, Distinct Values Will Tend to Remain Stable

Beneath the surface of the visual aspects of culture (including the elements touched on in Scenario 1), people continue to hold fast to some of the basics that distinguish national cultures. In other words, although certain material and even behavioral facets of cultures will become more universal, certain fundamental values and attitudes will continue to differentiate them. Religious differences are as strong as ever; language differences still bolster ethnic identities. What's important is that such differences are still powerful enough to fragment the world culturally and stymie the global standardization of products and operating methods.

Scenario 3: Nationalism Will Continue to Reinforce Cultural Identity

If people didn't perceive the *cultural* differences among themselves and others, they'd be less likely to regard themselves as distinct *national* entities. That's why appeals to cultural identity are so effective in mobilizing people to defend national identity. Typically, such efforts promote the "national culture" by reinforcing language and religion, subsidizing nationalistic programs and activities, and propagandizing against foreign influences on the national culture. Further, even if people will be more internationally mobile, peer pressure will force them to adhere to their national cultures.

Scenario 4: Existing National Borders Will Shift to Accommodate Ethnic Differences

Several countries are showing more evidence of subcultural power and influence. Why? Among basic factors are immigration and the rise of religious fundamentalism. Equally important seems to be the growing desire among ethnic groups for independence from dominant groups where they reside. Both Yugoslavia and Czechoslovakia broke up for this reason, while people within ethnic groups in Britain and Spain (Scots, Catalons, and Basques) are currently pushing for independence. Meanwhile, some subcultures—such as the Inuits in the Arctic and the Kurds in the Middle East—transcend national boundaries and simply resist being "nationalized." Because they have less in common with their "fellow citizens" than with ethnic brethren in other countries, it's hard to assign them an identity on the basis of present political geography.

Regardless of the scenario that unfolds in any given arena, IB personnel must learn to examine specific cultural differences if they hope to operate effectively in a foreign environment. In the future, analysis based only on national characteristics won't be sufficient; business will have to pay attention to all the other myriad factors that contribute to distinctions in values, attitudes, and behavior.

CASE

International Students and International Business[101]

— Terry Mughan, Portland State University

Erasmus, the Dutch Christian humanist (1466–1536), studied at universities in Holland, France, England, and Switzerland. He is recognized as the greatest scholar of the northern Renaissance. His cultural integration to England was not fully successful, however, as he never came to enjoy the weather or the beer. Like Erasmus, not all international students fully integrate culturally to every country where they study.

In 2017, about 5.3 million students enrolled in university education outside their country of citizenship. Students enroll in degree programs or to study temporarily, such as on study abroad programs through their home country universities. The scale of this mobility affects all stakeholders (financially and culturally)—students themselves, home and host universities and the home and host countries. The subject may be examined at a national (macro), university (meso) and individual (micro) level. Further, it may be examined from the standpoint of home countries (those from which they come) and host countries (those to which they go).

The National Level

At a national level, the United States (US) is the largest recipient country. However, its international students represent only a little over four percent of the total US student population. International students account for a substantially larger percentage in some other countries, i.e. just under 11 percent in Canada, about 19 percent in the United Kingdom (UK), and 25 percent in Australia.

Diverse countries see international student recruitment as an essential part of their economic and trade achievements, educational mission, and global diplomatic influence. For example, although the US ran a deficit in merchandise trade in 2017, the international students' $39 billion expenditure in the US economy contributed to the US surplus in service trade and supported about

400,000 jobs. In the UK in 2014/15, the economic activity and employment sustained by international students' off-campus spending generated GBP 1 billion in tax revenues. Thus, international students' economic contribution to host countries is much higher than the fees they pay to universities.

There is a near consensus that a prime future determinant of international competitiveness is the availability of highly skilled employees, who are needed in every type of university-gained specialty. For example, one sub-group is referred to as STEM (science, technology, engineering, and math). The employment of STEM professionals is expected to grow substantially more than employment in general. Because of a shortfall, developed countries depend on immigrants to fill the gaps. For example, in 2015 almost 40 percent of software engineers and a quarter of nuclear engineers and physicians in the United States were foreign born. Other growth areas are in the cultural industries and media because global trade in tourism, film and music generate demand for graduates with a global mind-set.

But, what does this mean to international students and universities? Canada offers a good example. It, like the United States, has had a very low birth rate and skills shortage in the 21st century and would face a declining population if it were not for immigration. The Canadian government encourages international students to remain in Canada after their studies, obtain employment, and then permanent residency. Thus, aligning educational policy with immigration policy is a key government challenge. The influx of international students can also contribute to diplomatic influence if they view their experiences abroad favorably. For example, in 2018 among monarchs, presidents, and prime ministers, 58 had studied in the US, 57 in the UK, and 40 in France. These individuals usually become levers of international diplomacy, promoting trade and international understanding. However, once in a while a leader turns unfriendly despite studying abroad, such as North Korea's leader Kim Jong Un who studied in Switzerland.

Apart from diplomatic connections, domestic and international students get to know one another. Their formation of friendships can lead to international business connections once the international students return home. In essence, students see different products and technologies while abroad that they think are adoptable in their home countries. In the process, the friendship and mutual trust developed through studying abroad may then serve as connections to transfer adoptable assets internationally, thus promoting international business.

Despite the positive consequences of international student movements just discussed, there are criticisms from some quarters. Many of these are related to backlashes against immigration per se. Additionally, keep in mind the following (sometimes contradictory) contentions:

- Although host (usually high income) countries gain valuable human resources when international students immigrate, this is a brain drain for developing countries.
- The full cost for educating a university student is seldom covered completely through tuition, thus international students are subsidized by host country taxes and expenditures.
- When admission demand and/or enrolment exceeds university space, international students may displace domestic students, and this may generate resentment.
- Some perceive that international students learn abroad, return home, and then compete against the country that educated them. This can cause tensions in internal politics of host countries.

The University Level

The host universities are the main agents of welcome and orientation for international students. They are responsible for ensuring the students meet their visa requirements and help them acclimatize to a new way of life and learning. Their help may range from accommodation assistance to guidance on what is good academic and adjustment practice. These responsibilities are exercised across the institution by executives, professors and administrators. As more students have signed up for entire programs of study, as opposed to short courses and exchange programs, responsibilities have evolved into a mainstream part of the university structure and services. Increasingly, international students are integrated into regular courses with domestic students. Universities' handling of larger international student populations that are matriculating for longer periods has placed additional demands on all their levels (central services, faculties, employees) because they have had to meet a diverse range of student needs, which are often different from those of domestic students. At the same time, the need for international students to accomplish demanding bureaucratic and academic tasks, often with language difficulties, is often overlooked by host universities. If international students adjust to academic requirements abroad, they can contribute to host country students' international perspectives. For example, they may provide diverse viewpoints in the classroom. In addition, they may serve as resources for information about other parts of the world. The adjacent photo shows an example of such a planned activity.

Universities all over the world are responding to pressures by employers, parents and accrediting organizations to prepare students to have a global perspective that includes intercultural competence. For example, AACSB is the world's foremost accreditor of university business programs (more than 850 programs in 56 countries), and it requires preparation of students to work effectively in diverse and multicultural environments. Understandably, many business schools have similarly stated missions, such as that of IÉSEG, a leading French business school in Lille and Paris, whose mission statement is "to educate managers to be inspiring, intercultural and ethical pioneers of change." Nevertheless, there is considerable variance and discussion on how best to achieve this. Each university has to develop its own policy for relations with the diverse members

International students from over 80 countries at Viadrina University in Frankfurt (Oder), Germany have set up exhibition booths to describe their countries to both domestic and international students.

Source: dpa picture alliance/Alamy Stock Photo

of its community and this is not always agreed upon, as the following situation illustrates:

A director of graduate studies at a prestigious American university stepped down after she wrote to Chinese students asking them to speak only in English while on campus.

The students were very unhappy with the intrusion into their privacy and they received a second email shortly after from the dean telling them that there are no restrictions on the languages they may speak when on campus.

—Adapted from *The Independent Newspaper,* London, UK, 29 January 2019.

Another challenge is to infuse international content into program curricula because many faculty members have little or no experience abroad, have not been trained in the international nuances of their specialties, and have time constraints in adding anything to already jam-packed courses. To help mitigate this challenge, many programs have added specialized international courses (sometimes required) and some have developed faculty exchange programs with universities in other countries so that they experience life and work in another cultural setting that will broaden their class presentations when returning. In addition, some business schools, such as at the University of South Carolina, have developed short-term training programs for faculty from diverse universities to learn about the international content of their fields. Some others are offering study trips for groups of professors to visit a specific foreign geographic area, typically including not only tourist sites, but also visits to companies and government offices that inform them about the local business environment. In addition, a few universities, such as Nottingham University, have established campuses abroad that facilitate the foreign experience of both faculty and students as well as the intermingling among nationalities.

Many surveys are carried out by universities, governments, and education agencies to ascertain international students' satisfaction with their university's provision of and the degree of institutional "internationalization." Unsurprisingly, these surveys boast high levels of student satisfaction. However, there is concern that too little information is gathered on student impact.[102] Instead, most surveys are based on 'structural' measures, such as the number and proportions of types of students and faculty, home versus international students, and participation in international exchanges.

Many agree that other, more routine kinds of actions can be promoted to increase interaction between international and domestic students[103]. Faculty might organize events to enable students to share their international study experiences and help student associations become more open and inclusive of international students. Allowing coursework outside the major helps mix up classes and groups, thus providing more opportunities to make friends. New programs in particular could create space for projects and teamwork with designated, cross-national membership and outputs requiring interdependence of the team members.

The Student Level

Students' motives for studying abroad differ between those pursuing a degree in a foreign country and those studying short-term abroad or on student exchanges. The former become international students primarily for any of a number of reasons: (1) the cachet of a degree from a foreign university, often one in a developed economy, (2) acquisition of a foreign language and cultural knowledge to add to their resumes, (3) unavailability of specialized courses within their home countries, and (4) the possibility of employment and post-graduation residency in the host-country. Short-term study abroad programs are less extensive and aim primarily to add value to the home study program at less cost and with less risk of academic failure while imparting the benefits of living and learning in another culture.

International students face some similar adjustment challenges as those of expatriate managers, i.e. cultural adaptation, performance challenges, and new social experiences. For expatriate managers, there is generally cross-cultural training and many tools and methods to facilitate this learning. Most existing practices for the executive have been built around a corporate portfolio of pre-departure training, support, and in-country development that sometimes includes the family. These have been designed to address specifically the nature and needs of corporate operations. Given the massive growth in student mobility and the importance of international students to the global economy, much thought has been given to what business experiences can be applied from corporate experiences and vice versa.

Intercultural Competence Model

Although universities take diverse approaches to make students more culturally competent based on their internal and external situations, Figure 2.3 shows a model to approach training. One suggestion in addition to students' immersion in another culture is to plan an intercultural curriculum over the duration of students' study programs. Such an approach could develop their competences over time to suit situations like the workplace and roles in the broader community where their knowledge and abilities can help improve inter-community and international relations.

Intercultural competence[104] embraces a range of competences such as empathy, flexibility, learning, resilience and anxiety management and skills such as active listening and foreign language proficiency. The model shows how the students' attitudes are the starting point for their personal journey in learning to work with other cultures. By improving their knowledge and skills about culture, they then progress from the personal level to the interpersonal level (intercultural interaction with others).

Conclusion

Recent research[105] corroborates the usefulness of this approach. Based on extensive studies, the path to intercultural competence for international students is best supported by overseas immersion accompanied by an "integrated intercultural program, followed by culture-based teaching materials, teaching strategies and classroom activities."[106]

FIGURE 2.3 Process Model of Intercultural Competence

The model is based on wide-scale research in U.S. universities and includes components of attitudes, knowledge and comprehension, desired internal outcome, and desired external outcome.

Source: From "The Identification and Assessment of Intercultural Competence as a Student Outcome of Internalization at Institutions of Higher Education in the United States" in *Journal of Studies in International Education*, Fall 2006, 10, pp. 241–266 and in *The SAGE Handbook of Intercultural Competence*, 2009 (Thousand Oaks, CA: Sage). Copyright 2006 by D. K. Deardorff.

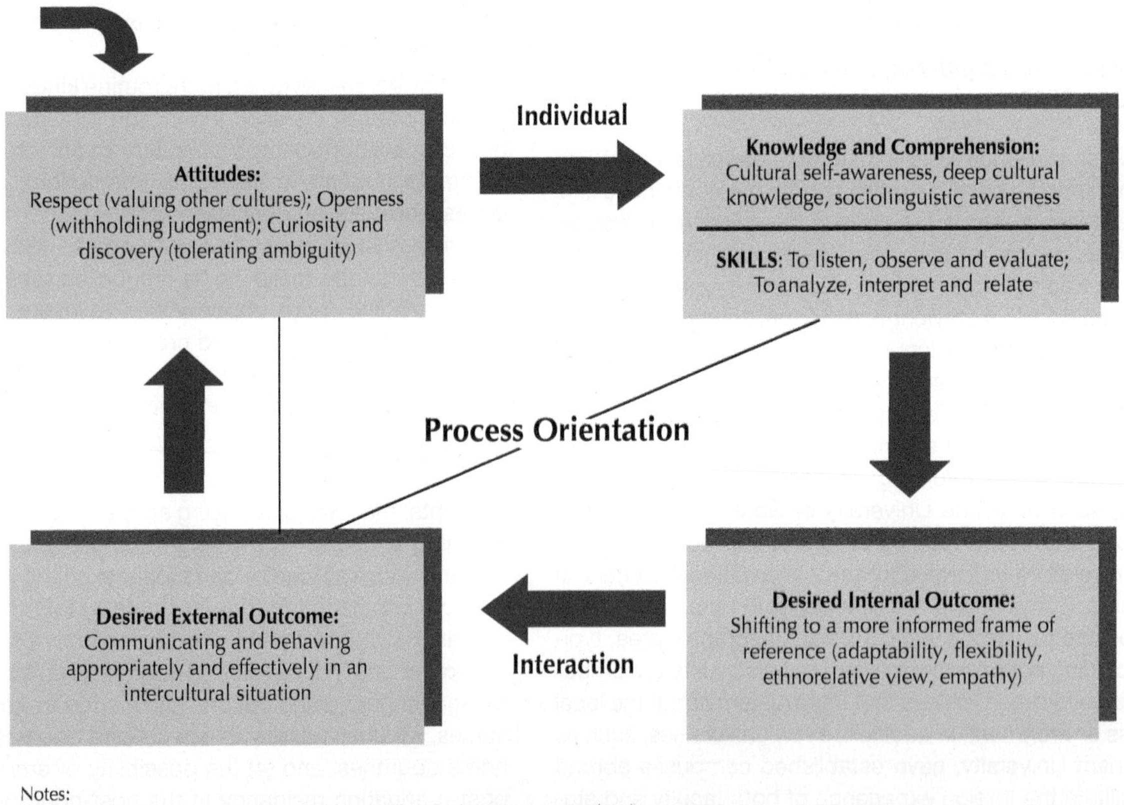

Notes:
- Begin with attitudes; move from individual level (attitudes) to interaction level (outcomes)
- Degree of intercultural competence depends on acquired degree of attitudes, knowledge/comprehension, and skills

International students are an established feature of university life almost everywhere. They make a solid financial contribution to the communities where they study. They probably have the potential to contribute as well by linking those communities. Governments and universities are beginning to adjust to the nature of this contribution by supporting students' university integration as well as their activities beyond the duration of the program. Like Erasmus in England, some students can be successful academically without necessarily adjusting completely to their host environments, though most will be happier if they integrate well and get to share social activities with domestic students. Universities should constantly be seeking to do more to bring international and domestic students together in the classroom, on campus and elsewhere to facilitate friend-making, cultural immersion and new knowledge generation.

If students are to develop and retain friendly links with the host community and advance professional and cultural links that sustain their contribution to it, integrated programs of intercultural cultural learning will help students bond with that community and establish lasting ties with it. These may create a foundation for ongoing communication and relations between the home and host communities whereby international graduates may be cultural and economic "bridges" or "boundary-spanners" more effectively in the years after graduating. This may be in the areas of trade, reciprocal business and economic development, and the advancement of global leadership skills and projects leveraging business and cultural links across borders.

QUESTIONS

2-3 Assume someone from another country asks to understand the most important cultural things about your country, how would you respond?

2-4 If you are planning to visit another country as a student or tourist, what preparations can you make that will help you to understand that culture better?

2-5 If you have visited other countries, did the experience make you think more about yourself or your home country?

2-6 Can you think of an occasion when a student from another culture has made a contribution to student life that you valued?

2-7 Have you made any friends with students from other countries? Is so, describe how it happened. If not, why do you think you haven't?

2-8 Assume on post-graduation that you are launching a new global start-up and are seeking new partners. How might you start building your global business networks now?

CHAPTER 3

The Political and Legal Environments Facing Business

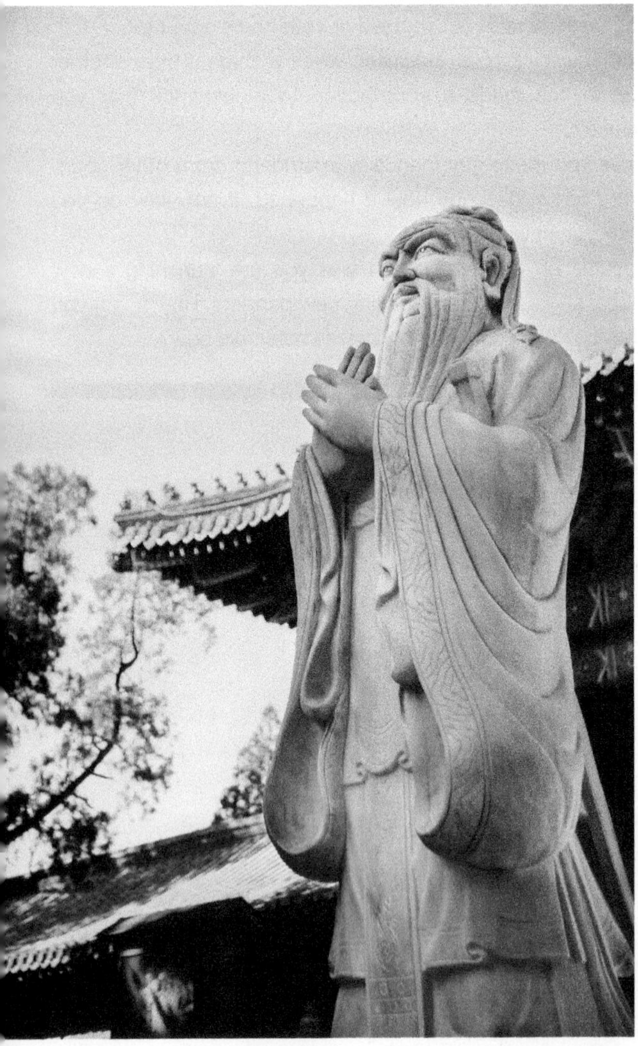

Statue of the Chinese philosopher Confucius. ▲

OBJECTIVES

After studying this chapter, you should be able to

3-1 Explain how politics and laws influence business activities

3-2 Interpret the principles and practices of a political environment

3-3 Discuss the principles and practices of political freedom

3-4 Describe the idea of political risk

3-5 Interpret the principles and practices of a legal environment

3-6 Describe legal issues facing international companies

3-7 Relate the ideas of politics, law, and business

Every road has two directions.

—Russian proverb

CASE

China: Big Opportunities, Complicated Risks[1]

From 1949 to the late 1970s, China was autarkic, championing a self-sufficient economy that relied on its own resources. Leaders of the governing Chinese Communist Party (CCP) feared interaction with foreigners would corrupt its politics and pollute its culture; hence, they prohibited foreign investment and restricted foreign trade. Near the end of the 1970s, China's increasing economic struggles pushed its leaders to rethink this outlook. In 1978, China instituted the *Law on Joint Ventures Using Chinese and Foreign Investment* and began opening its market to the world. Since then, China's economic liberalization has powered extensive industrialization, fueled booming exports, and attracted waves of foreign investment. Throughout all, the CCP maintains its monopoly on political power. As one Beijing scholar observed, "The Party (CCP) is like God. He is everywhere. You just can't see him."[2]

Transformation has yielded astonishing results. Over the past few decades, China has prospered more from globalization than any other country, outsmarting and outperforming many on the world stage. Tens of millions have moved from simple structures to stunning high-rises. China's per capita income increased fivefold between 1990 and 2000, from $200 to $1,000. Between 2000 and 2010, its per capita income rose by the same rate, from $1,000 to $5,000. In 2018, it hit $10,200, moving China into the ranks of middle-income countries. Along the way, some 800 million moved out of poverty while 420 million joined the middle class. Chinese companies have spun from woeful state-owned enterprises into world-class multinationals. Steadily, China, in building the largest economy, has accumulated the greatest financial reserves in the world. Consequently, many see its ascendency as a global event without parallel.

Since the 1980s, MNEs of virtually every sort, size, and nationality have opened Chinese operations. Total FDI in China, literally nonexistent in 1978, passed $1.5 trillion in 2018. Why have thousands of foreign firms made huge bets on China? Quite simply, they see amazing opportunities in terms of consumer demand, worker productivity, ingenuity and innovativeness, infrastructure buildouts, and market potential.

THE CALL AND COMPLICATION OF CHINA

Foreign investors have entered China successfully, opened operations, managed activities, and earned profits. For many, success has not come easily. China's political system imposes hardships while its legal system complicates activities. Generally, MNEs report that China's political and legal systems make operating in China a hazy, frustrating process. Those accustomed to democratic governance in Western markets, in which they have political freedom and legal safeguards, run into different circumstances in the Middle Kingdom. There, the government, under the control of the CCP, practices "State Capitalism," manipulating market activities to achieve political objectives that support its quest of "*Qiang Zhong Gwo Meng*"; the latter, explains Xi Jinping, CCP Chief and China's President, refers to "the Chinese dream" to regain its status as the guiding global power.[3] Consequently, MNEs doing business in China find themselves struggling to make sense of political policies and legal regulations. Ambitious Western firms such as ExxonMobil, ABB, Google, eBay, Best Buy, Home Depot, Uber, Caterpillar, and Vodafone started operations or purchased stakes in Chinese companies. Political problems and legal difficulties short-circuited their plans. Eventually, like many others, they sold their stakes and reset their strategies.[4]

China's rapid economic emergence accentuates long-running idiosyncrasies. Its mix of ancient and contemporary outlooks creates many gray zones. Some argue that, when it comes to doing business in China, the first rule is to throw away the rulebook. Foreign investors forsake the notion that Western ideas automatically work in China. Opening operations in China, for instance, requires informing the government—in excruciating detail—who you are, what you want to do, how you plan to do it, how much you intend to invest, how many jobs you will create, and on and on. Each stop along the long negotiations march finds national, provincial, and local officials asking how the proposed investment encourages capital formation, promotes exports, creates jobs, and transfers technology. Proposals that hit the right targets, as set by the government, not by the market, get the green light.

CALMING DRAGONS AND CHARMING SNAKES

Governments in many countries, as does China's, use their political and legal environments to set the path and pace of their economic development. China, however, is a notoriously tough case. The complexity of its political and legal systems imposes daunting barriers. China's intricate bureaucracy and fledgling legal system can stack the odds against foreigners that are bold enough to forge ahead.[5] "If the great invention of European civilization was a legal system," quipped an observer, "then China's was bureaucracy."[6]

Exasperated investors often point to a byzantine system based on reasonable regulations but arbitrary agendas. Personal connections, not professional competencies, often matter more in doing deals and righting wrongs. Managers who reason that objective economics should determine the means of running business operations see this as illogical. Still, it is utterly logical to Chinese leaders who regard state direction of the economy as the most reliable path toward harmonious prosperity—and, one mustn't forget, staying in charge of the show. Consequently, foreign investors navigate often-mysterious political channels.

The long-running conflict between central and local Chinese authorities compounds complications. The vastness of China means that local officials, whether headquartered in the smallest village or the largest city, are often left alone by their comrades in Beijing, the capital of China. Certainly, there are national laws. How they move from Beijing to the other 33 provinces is an entirely different story. "The center," notes one observer, often "has no control over the provinces. When it sends people to investigate illegal pirating of CDs, local governors block access to the factories."[7] As Chinese folklore warns, "The mightiest dragon cannot crush the local snake," cautioning that even though officials in Beijing may appear to be all-powerful, the politics of local fiefdoms often subvert their authority. Consequently, foreign investors must develop the fine art of calming dragons and charming snakes.

PREDICTABLE LAWS OR AMBIGUOUS GUIDELINES?

China had a basic legal system in 1978 when it launched one of the greatest campaigns of legal reform in history. Ongoing developments have stabilized what had been an unpredictable, periodically chaotic legal environment. Despite great progress, China's legal environment is still marked by policy gaps, hazy interpretation, and arbitrary enforcement. Laws are chock-full of ambiguities, and some say it will take a generation to make things predictable. Others are less optimistic, comparing the state of China's legal system with that of the United States in the early 1900s—then an antiquated composite of statutes and codes that took decades to modernize. Certainly, calls for China to institute transparency, accountability, and objectivity may one day prove successful. Still, the powerful influence of China's 4000-year legal legacies, as one analyst concluded, makes doing so "one of the largest social infrastructure projects in the history of mankind."[8]

Challenges in China's legal system reflect a profound difference in its interpretation of legality. Western legal systems rest on the rule of law and its doctrine of legitimate regulations impartially administered by public officials who are held accountable for their just enforcement. In contrast, China practices the philosophy of the rule of man, seeing the right of the "man" (once in the person of the Emperor, today in the form of the CCP) to act free of checks and balances for as long as "he" honors his "mandate of heaven." The latter holds that *tiān* (heaven) grants an emperor the right to rule unilaterally, as long as he rules virtuously. Hence, besides being the law, the CCP has the legitimacy, based on its mandate of heaven, to operate above the law. So, in practice, rarely does a criminal court, under the direction of the CCP, end with anything other than a guilty verdict. Explained an FBI Special Agent and legal attaché at the U.S. Embassy in Beijing, "there is really no rule of law here. . . they (CCP) make a decision ahead of time to make a point."[9]

THE LEGALITY OF ILLEGALITY

China's legal practices, combined with the growing pains of its novel commercial codes and evolving political norms, tests foreign companies. A flashpoint is the protection of intellectual property—the latter refers to a work or invention that its creator has the right to determine its use as conferred by a patent, copyright, trademark, etc. MNEs complain that the theft of their intellectual property fuels China's economic surge. Early on, aggressive estimates linked nearly a third of the Chinese economy to piracy.[10] Its share has declined in tandem with China's expansion. Still, the U.S. estimates that American companies lose hundreds of billions annually to Chinese piracy. To wit, China consistently ranks as the leading source of seized counterfeits. In the United States, customs officials report that the bulk of counterfeits seized originated in China.[11] U.S. authorities, noting the rarity of legal punishment, charge Chinese officials with tolerating local counterfeiters. The United States, to slight success, has appealed to transnational institutions to redress China's "inadequate enforcement" of intellectual property regulations.[12]

What accounts for China's status as the world's premier counterfeiter? Analysts point to a mix of factors, including its quest to catch the West, collectivist orientation, rule-of-man legacy, and dubious enforcement of ambiguous laws. Combined, these create an epic muddle. Noted an observer, "We have never seen a problem of this size and magnitude in world history. . . . There's more counterfeiting going on in China now than we've ever seen anywhere."[13] Problems threaten to escalate. Government policies have "left a deep impression on companies that intellectual property is there for anyone to use it." Local and provincial authorities look to pirates to power economic growth. Moreover, China excels in making high-quality knockoffs. As some say in Shanghai, "We can copy everything except your mother."[14]

WHAT'S NEXT?

Inevitably, foreign investors question how an opaque, single-party political system, nested in a shadowy legal environment, can fairly regulate their activities and justly protect their property rights. Some had thought that external institutions would exert decisive influence. China's 2001 ascension to the World Trade Organization (WTO), for example, required it to accept rules on all sorts of business matters, including tariffs, subsidies, and intellectual property. China has steadily amended its legal codes to comply with WTO standards. Still, problems persist, due not to a shortage of regulations, critics charge, but their inconsistent enforcement.

Bigger changes may be afoot that challenge Xi Jingping's "Chinese Dream" of national ascendancy. Credit concerns in the banking and real estate sectors, questionable infrastructure investments, slowing market growth, reliance on assembly line jobs, and the "middle income trap" pose economic problems.[15] Persistent pro-democracy protests in Hong Kong and ongoing tariff battles with the United States pose potentially big problems for China. Then again, these might seem trivial as the fallout of the COVID-19 pandemic diminishes China's role in the globalization game. The pandemic showed that anchoring supply chains in China, great when things go well, can collapse quickly into bottlenecks, shortages, and stoppages. Hence, MNE worldwide began evaluating the "ABC" strategy, namely, "anywhere but China," looking to disperse supply centers in multiple parts of the world.[16] Apple, for example, planned to move a fifth of its Chinese production to India while Taiwanese computer chipmaker TSMC move ahead building a $12 billion factory in Arizona.

CHINA'S CHOICE

As will see in this chapter, the path of productive change is, ultimately, and legitimately, China's sovereign right. Some point to the CCP's growing support of Confucian ideals foreshadowing its future standards. Xi Jinping champions Confucian virtues, seeing the homegrown thoughts of the ancient sage, codified in his collected teachings, "The Analects," as useful guides for China's political and legal evolution. Confucianism holds that people are fundamentally good and, rather than being coerced via government regulations and penal law, are better governed through the virtuous abstraction of *Li*—namely, traditional values, ritual, decorum, rules of propriety, customs, and norms. Internalizing the ideals of *Li*, goes Confucian reasoning, culminates in a harmonious social order where all willingly behave properly. Certainly, formal laws are needed, but only for "bad actors" that selfishly pursue their self-interests at the expense of collective harmony. Foreign investors, naturally, wondered what blending Confucian virtues, ideals of *Li*, and social harmony meant to their activities.

Despite intimidating political situations and confusing legal circumstances, legions of foreign investors profitably answer the siren call of China. Whether driven by bright forecasts, confidence in continued progress, or desperation not to miss this megatrend, many foreign companies have successfully left the sanctuary of familiar markets for the unique ways of the Middle Kingdom. Then, once they convince skeptical bureaucrats, clear immigration, and cross the modern-day Rubicon, they determine how to navigate China's political and legal systems.

QUESTIONS

3-1 What general perspective do you advocate to make sense of China's political environment?

3-2 How would you advise an MNE to manage the intricacies of China's legal environment?

POLITICS, LAWS, AND OPERATING INTERNATIONALLY

3-1 Explain how politics and laws influence business activities

Politics and laws, everywhere and always, are dynamic. At different times, different groups champion different principles that endorse different practices. Consequently, investing and operating internationally exposes MNEs to risks that arise from changes in a country's political and legal systems.[17] Map 3.1, for example, identifies the degree of political risk in

MAP 3.1 Map of Political Risk, 2019

The distribution of political risk worldwide shows that it is a fundamental feature of the global business environment. Some countries have a little, some countries have a lot, but all have some that influence an MNE's strategic choices and operating decisions.

Source: Marsh, Political Risk Index Map 2019; https://www.marsh.com/us/campaigns/political-risk-map-2019.html.

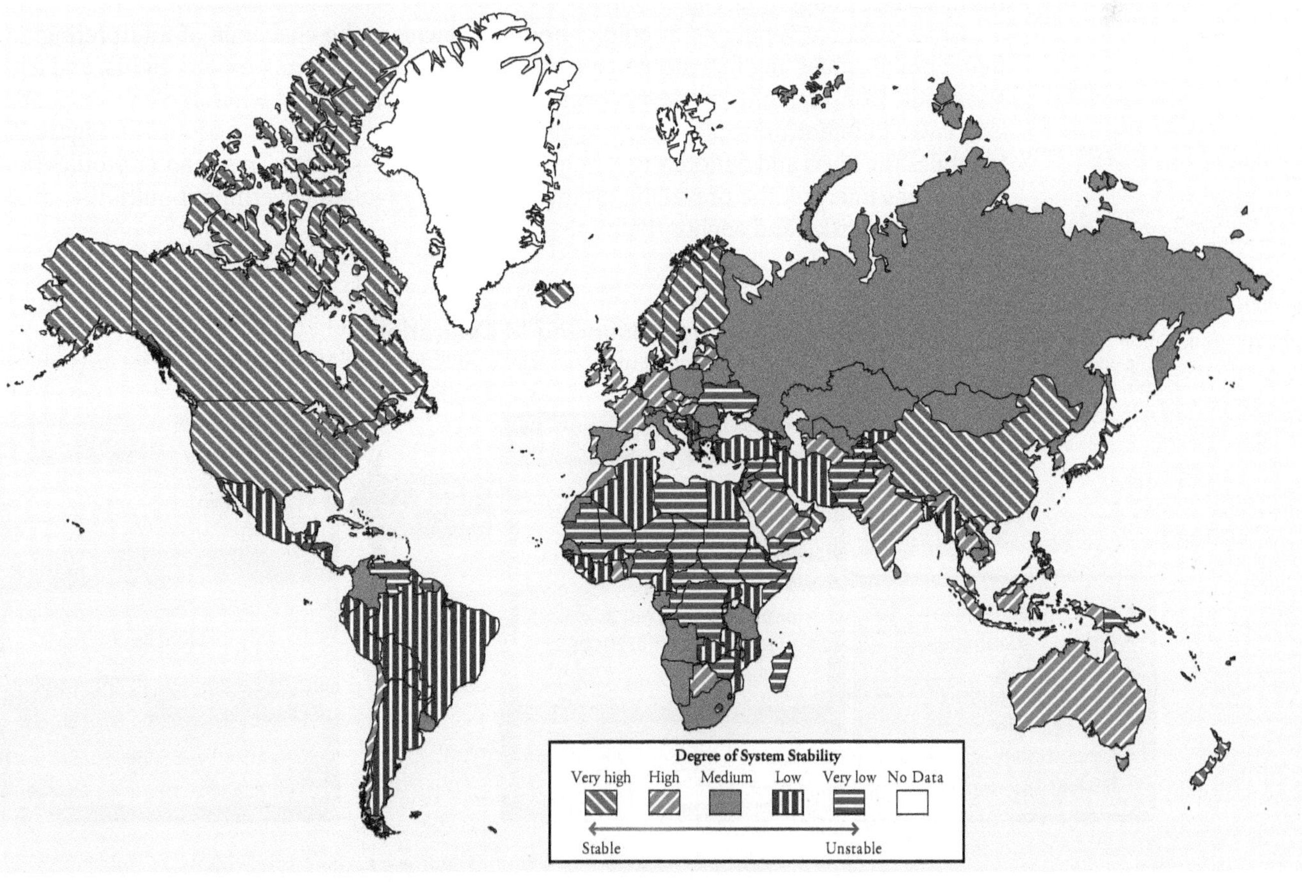

countries worldwide. We profile this idea later in the chapter, but, at this point, this map highlights an enduring reality of IB: every market in the world has some, with most having high, degree of political risk that threatens the short-term profit and long-term sustainability of business activity. Therefore, managers evaluate politics and laws, making sense of their essential principles and applied practices, and estimating the resulting risks to the operation, profitability, and sustainability of their activities.

The interplay of political ideologies, conceptions of political freedom, legacies of legality, presumptions of fairness, and standards of accountability in different market makes for challenging situations. Navigating situations requires studying how political and legal circumstances overlap and differ. Generally, managers evaluate whether political freedom is a practical ideal or a wishful abstraction. They study how officials exercise authority, legislate policies, regulate enterprise, and punish wrongdoers. They assess the interplay between the rule of law versus the rule of man. They monitor how politicians are elected and whether, and how, they depart. Then, based on their analyses, they forecast political and legal challenges, synthesize scenarios, and determine the optimal plan to acquire resources, make investments, adapt operating modes, and manage risks.

Making sense of some situations is straightforward; Australian companies find few surprises in New Zealand, for instance. In other cases, managers face profound differences; an ill-prepared Canadian company will hit big bumps and hard times in, for instance, Russia. Home to 144 million people, Russia is the world's largest country in terms of territory. It possesses vast natural resources and its government looks to foreign MNEs to help modernize its energy-dependent economy. Still, its political risks pose problems for foreign investors. An executive at IKEA explained that the Russian political environment is "a bit of a roller coaster. . . . [Y]ou don't know exactly what will happen tomorrow."[18] Doing business in Russia means you had better be "big enough to defend yourself against bureaucratic attacks [and] . . . ready to hold your nose when elections are rigged and political opposition is crushed."[19] Then again, that might be insufficient—its President authorized Russian prosecutors, if inclined, to declare foreign organizations "undesirable" and unilaterally close them. Besides political risk, Russia ranks high in terms of corruption and crony capitalism.[20] Still, despite these problems, Russia attracts significant investment from clever, confident foreign companies.

Cross-national variations in politics and laws increase the challenge of interpreting different philosophies, regulations, and attitudes on political freedom, property rights, and legal standards. Consequently, managers begin with the realization that when it comes to politics and laws, different principles result in different practices in different countries. Figure 3.1 identifies the ideas and outlooks that help frame their assessments. This chapter profiles how these ideas interpret the prevailing political ideology, regulate government authority, influence political risks, and anchor the legal system.

FIGURE 3.1 Political and Legal Factors Influencing IB Operations

The political and legal environments are broad-stroke concepts that defy straightforward classification. Nevertheless, here we see key points that help managers develop useful perspectives.

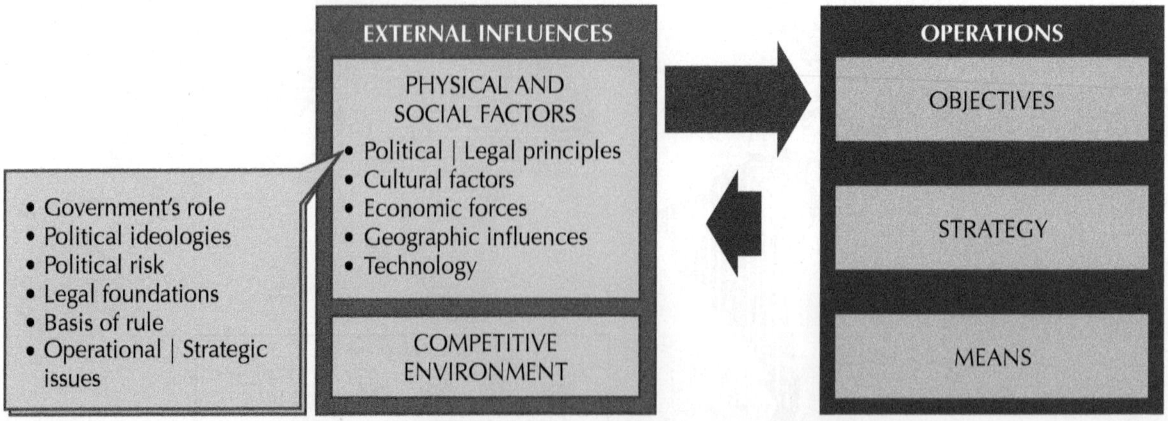

THE POLITICAL ENVIRONMENT

3-2 Interpret the principles and practices of a political environment

An effective political system integrates the diverse elements of a society. Its test is uniting society in the face of divisive viewpoints.

Whether targeting Afghanistan, Zimbabwe, or any of the 200-plus markets in between, managers study a nation's **political system**—namely, the structural dimensions and power dynamics of the government that (1) specify institutions, organizations, and interest groups and (2) define the norms and rules that govern political activities. The mission of a political system is straightforward: integrate diverse groups into a functioning, self-governing society. Likewise, its acid test is its capacity to sustain society in the face of divisive viewpoints. Success supports peace and prosperity, as we see in Austria, Botswana, Canada, New Zealand, Rwanda, and Singapore. Failure leads to the systemic instability and institutional fragility of the sort seen in Afghanistan, Bangladesh, Libya, Sudan, Venezuela, and Yemen.[21]

CONCEPT CHECK

Chapter 2 explained that culture moderates the practices of international business. Many points of interpretation, both from an academic and managerial perspective, are shaped by the ideas of individualism and collectivism.

Explaining the similarities and differences of political systems has intrigued a long line of thinkers, beginning with Plato and Confucius and moving on to Herodotus, Machiavelli, Smith, Rousseau, Marx, Gandhi, and Friedman.[22] Each wrestled with enduring philosophical issues: How should society balance individual rights versus the needs of the community to sustain a rational, righteous, and peaceful system? What is the basis of the state's authority over its citizens? Should society grant an individual the freedom to pursue personal interests? Does society fare better when individual rights are subordinated to collective goals? Should society champion equality or institute hierarchy? Are human rights inalienable to all individuals or conferred by the collective? Engaging these and like-minded questions, vital to interpreting any and all political environments, directs our attention to the ideas of individualism and collectivism.

INDIVIDUALISM

Individualism champions the primacy of the individual over the group.

The doctrine of individualism emphasizes the primacy of individual freedom, self-expression, and personal independence—think of the stipulation in the U.S. Declaration of Independence that people have "certain inalienable Rights, that among these are Life, Liberty and the pursuit of Happiness."[23] Individualism champions the exercise of one's ambitions while opposing regulations that constrain them. In an individualistic system, social ideals encourage people to be strong, self-reliant, and assertive; people aspire to independence and autonomy—"I," rather than "We," is the predominant perspective. The government protects the liberty of individuals to act as they wish, as long as their actions do not infringe upon the liberties of others. Individualism strongly influences politics in a range of countries, notably Australia, Canada, Hungary, Italy, Israel, Netherlands, New Zealand, South Africa, Switzerland, and the United States.

The business implications of individualism are direct: every person has the right to make decisions free of onerous rules and regulations. Individuals have the freedom to decide how to work, produce, consume, save, invest, and innovate. Countries with an individualistic orientation shape their marketplace with the idea of **laissez-faire**; literally translated as "Let do," it advises "Let it be" or "Leave it alone." Hence, laissez-faire recommends letting business affairs take their own course, free from government interference. Similarly, neoliberal principles reason that individuals, behaving fairly and justly in pursuing personal ambition, do not threaten collective welfare. In reality, gaps between idealistic principles and opportunistic practices can fan adversarial relationships between governments and businesses in individualistic societies. Apprehension that some individuals maximize self-interest at the expense of collective welfare leads governments to institute laws and regulations that protect individuals from market inefficiencies (e.g., deficient consumer knowledge, unclear property rights, and excessive producer power).

COLLECTIVISM

Collectivism advocates the primacy of the group over the individual.

The doctrine of collectivism emphasizes the primacy of the collective (e.g., in the form of a group, party, community, class, society, or nation) over the interests of the individual. No matter the importance of those who compose it, the whole of the collective trumps the sum of its individual parts. Relationships with other members of the group and the corresponding interconnections are a central aspect of personal identity. In a collectivist system, social ideals encourage people to be self-sacrificing, dependable, generous, and helpful to others; people aspire toward interdependency and interactions—"We," rather than "I," is the predominant perspective. More pointedly, popular proverbs in the United States, an individualistic society, include "The squeaky wheel gets the grease" or "There is no I in team." In contrast, one finds different outlooks in a collectivist society; one is likely to hear in China, "The loudest duck gets shot," or, in Japan, "The nail that sticks out gets hammered down." Collectivism strongly influences politics in a range of countries, such as Guatemala, Indonesia, Kuwait, Pakistan, Peru, South Korea, Taiwan, and Vietnam.

A collectivist outlook encourages the political system to develop regulations that promote social justice, labor rights, income equality, and workplace harmony. Then, the "welfare of the nation takes precedence over the selfishness of the individuals."[24] The strong, swift response to COVID-19 in collectivist cultures, notably China, Japan, South Korea, and Singapore, relative to the situations in individualistic cultures, notably Italy, Spain, and the United States, highlighted this orientation.[25] More practically, collectivism in the business world holds that the ownership of assets, the allocation of resources, the structure of industries, the conduct of companies, and the actions of managers share a common goal: make decisions and conduct activities that benefit the collective. In extreme cases, such as Iran, North Korea, or Saudi Arabia, political leaders limit individual property rights and police mass media to enforce collective standards.

POLITICAL IDEOLOGY

A political ideology encapsulates the doctrine of political behavior and change. It describes the path to convert ideals into outcomes.

A nation's orientation toward individualism or collectivism is a key anchor of its political system. It profoundly influences its predominant **political ideology**. In theory, an ideology is an integrated vision that defines a holistic conception of an abstract ideal and its normative thought processes. For example, the ideal of freedom, a vision of democratic ideologies, advocates corresponding principles, doctrines, goals, practices, and symbols. Likewise, the ideal of harmony, a vision of totalitarian ideologies, does the same. Practically, a political ideology stipulates how society ought to govern itself and explains the methods by which it will do so. An effective political ideology moves beyond merely describing a vision of a better, brighter future—it specifies the means to achieve it.

Figure 3.2 interprets prominent political ideologies in terms of a **political spectrum**. Spectrum analysis, in specifying a basic conceptual structure, guides the assessment of a complex issue—in this case, political ideology. Configuring ideologies in relation to the central axis lets us model different ones relative to the others. The starting point is specifying reasonable endpoints. Once set, one can then position other ideologies. Determining the standard of "reasonable endpoints" is open for interpretation, given the range of the candidates. Possibilities include anarchism, conservatism, secularism, environmentalism, liberalism, feminism, nationalism, socialism, theocracy, to name just a few.

From a Western perspective, for example, one is likely to set the endpoints as conservative versus liberal interpretations of democratic governance (i.e., Republican versus Democrat in the United States, Conservative vs. Labour in the United Kingdom, or Bharatiya Janata

FIGURE 3.2 The Political Ideology Spectrum

Purely democratic and totalitarian systems are exceptions. Looking around the world, one sees wide variation in the interpretation, expression, and application of each type.

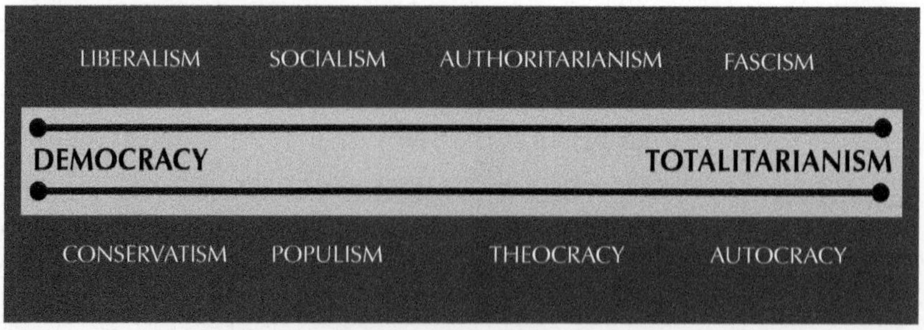

Party versus National Congress in India). Other endpoints command greater relevance in other contexts. A political spectrum in an Islamic country, such as Iran or Saudi Arabia, is bounded by theocracy versus secularism to reflect the role of the clergy in the government. In the case of Taiwan, those endorsing Taiwanese independence oppose those advocating reunification with China. In Belgium, the ends would reflect the ethnic and socioeconomic differences between the Dutch-speaking Flanders region and the French-speaking Walloon region. In Canada, the ends might reflect those advocating inclusive nationalism versus Bloc Québécois's call for the sovereignty of predominantly French-speaking Québec.

To sort through these options, we interpret the idea of political ideology in terms of its vision of freedom. This choice originates in the principles of politics in ancient Greece and has since been inseparable from interpreting the practices of politics. Technically, a political system institutes **political freedom** by its choices on matters like fair and competitive elections, individual and group freedoms, the rule of law, and civil and human rights. While some insist otherwise, political freedom, rather than being inalienable, is open to debate. Some, like the United States, champion a lot. Others, like Saudi Arabia, advocate a little. A few, like North Korea, justify nearly none. Consequently, managers' freedom to run local operations is conditional upon prevailing outlooks and attitudes.

Freedom sets the political ideology spectrum that we use in this text (see Figure 3.2). Freedom as the criterion encourages setting democracy as one endpoint, and totalitarianism, the other. One sees different interpretations of democracy, including forms classified as liberal, conservative, or social. Fundamentally, all advocate the legitimacy of individualism and, in turn, personal freedoms to pursue happiness. Likewise, one sees different interpretations of totalitarianism, including forms classified as authoritarianism, theocracy, and autocracy. Fundamentally, all advocate the legitimacy of control to subordinate personal freedoms to the pursuit of collective harmony. Consequently, in democracies, managers have many freedoms, whereas in totalitarian systems, they have few to none. Hence, managers study how a political system interprets freedom, and gauge its implications for how the state regulates the market and, thus, their operations. Each ideology in Figure 3.2 is noteworthy; we lack the space to profile each. Understanding the ideals and the means of the two endpoints, democracy and totalitarianism, helps interpret the others.

DEMOCRACY

Democracy and individualism are intrinsically related and mutually reinforcing; individualism legitimates principles of democracy and democracy fortifies standards of individualism.

Abraham Lincoln held that **democracy** is a government "of the people, by the people, for the people." Modern-day democracies translate this ideology into the principles that all citizens are politically equal, entitled to freedom of thought, opinion, belief, speech, and association, and command ultimate authority over public officials.[26] Effectively, democracy calls for equal and open participation by citizens in a fair and just decision-making process. A democratic government institutes personal and political rights, civil liberties, fair and free elections, and independent courts of law.[27] These principles and practices institutionalize political freedoms and civil liberties that, by endorsing equality, liberty, and justice, endorse individualism.

Different legacies shape the performance of democracy in a nation. Practically, the scale and scope of modern society impose logistical constraints, particularly when the size of the population precludes all voters from participating directly. Table 3.1 shows that countries respond with different types of democracies. Notwithstanding variance, all advocate the authority of the many over the few. Looking forward, we may see more direct democracy. Evolving technologies increasingly support a virtual assembly of citizens who express their votes directly, rather than through representatives, via electronic signature or blockchains.

Business Implications In modern democracies, political and economic freedoms are increasingly interconnected. In political terms, freedom legitimizes rights and liberties. In economic terms, freedom legitimizes profits and prosperity. In a democracy, managers have the freedom to invest and operate based on economic, not political, standards. The belief in individualism promotes the idea that private companies, not public officials, lead economic development. Officials see a business environment that maximizes the freedom of activity, investment, and trade as the path toward economic, social, and political progress. The signaling devices of free market activities, not bureaucratic regulation, let managers optimally organize resources.

TABLE 3.1 Prominent Types of Democracies

The elemental definition of democracy stems from the Greek *dēmokratía*: "rule by the people." Translating the ideal of the "rule by the people" into a functioning political system takes various forms.

Form	Profile	Examples
Multiparty	System whereby three or more parties govern, either separately or as part of a coalition. One party negotiates with opposition parties to legislate policy.	Canada, Germany, Italy, Israel, Mexico
Parliamentary	Citizens exercise political power by electing representatives to a legislative branch, the Parliament. It is the basis of legitimacy for the various ministers who then direct the executive branch.	Australia, India, New Zealand, United Kingdom
Representative	Originates in a constitution that protects individual freedoms and liberties. The law treats all citizens equally. Elected representatives, while ultimately autonomous, act in the people's interest. Officials represent voters and, while mindful of voters' preferences, have the authority to act as they see fit.	Japan, United States
Social	Applies democratic means to transition from capitalism to socialism. The government promotes egalitarianism while also regulating capitalism's tendency toward opportunism.	Denmark, Finland, Norway, Sweden

The stability and transparency of democracies support private enterprises, creating business opportunities, encouraging investments, and sustaining productive enterprises. Democracy institutes checks and balances that reduce red tape, trade barriers, rent seeking, regulatory capture, corruption, and cronyism. Regular election and rotation of officials reduces market manipulations. The sanctity of political rights and civil liberties promotes openness to different people in different places. Interest in expanding cross-national contacts, communication, and collaboration expands the scale and scope of IB.[28]

TOTALITARIANISM

A totalitarian system consolidates power in a single agent who then controls political, economic, and social activities.

Totalitarianism subordinates the interests of the individual to that of the collective. An agent, in some form, such as an individual, a committee, an assembly, a junta, or a party, monopolizes political power and uses it to regulate many, if not all, aspects of public and private life. The agent believes it has noble intentions, protecting people from the hazards of individual choice on the path to a utopian society.[29] Fair game includes regulating residents' occupation, income, interests, religion, and even family structure. Table 3.2 profiles types of totalitarian systems.

A totalitarian government eliminates dissent through indoctrination, surveillance, propaganda, censorship, and violence. It tolerates few, if any, ideas, interests, or activities that oppose

TABLE 3.2 Prominent Types of Totalitarianism

First noted in reference to Italian fascism, "totalitario" meant "complete, absolute" control of an individual's life by an autocratic state. Here, we see approaches that an autocrat can take to control society.

Form	Profile	Examples
Authoritarian	Tolerates no deviation from state ideology. Day-to-day life reflects submission to state authority; resistance incurs punishment. Officials control politics, but pay less attention to the economic and social structure of society.	Kazakhstan, North Korea, Chad, and Turkmenistan
Fascist	Advocates a single-party state that controls, through force and indoctrination, people's minds, souls, and daily existence. Calls for the merger of state and corporate power to standardize values and systems. There have been few fascist political systems; nearly all prevailed during World War II.	Italy, Germany, Japan, circa 1920s–1945
Secular	A single party controls elections, tolerates dissent if it does not challenge the state, and suppresses other ideologies. The state does not prescribe a grand, all-encompassing vision. It grants an individual some economic and civil freedoms provided one does not contest state authority or disrupt social harmony.	China, Vietnam, Rwanda, Russia, and Venezuela
Theocratic	Government is an expression of the favored deity. Leaders profess to represent its interests on earth. The State applies ancient dogma in place of modern principles. Strict social regulation and gender regimentation typically prevails.	Iran, Afghanistan, and Saudi Arabia

state ideology.[30] Private ownership of satellite dishes, for instance, is illegal in Iran and Saudi Arabia given the view that it lets people access media that glorifies individualism.[31] In extreme situations, personal survival is linked to that of the regime. These conditions merge the interests of individuals with those of the state.

CONCEPT CHECK

Recall our discussion in Chapter 2 of "Major Behavioral Factors Affecting Business." These variables change as people change—or as state authority influences them. Shaping people's behavior to support the state's interests leads a totalitarian government to manipulate, if not dictate, norms, including work motivation, risk taking, communication practices, and consumption preferences.

Totalitarianism and collectivism are intrinsically related and mutually reinforcing; collectivism legitimates principles of totalitarianism, and totalitarianism supports standards of collectivism.

The dynamics of change in a totalitarian state highlight the means used to enforce its ideology. Rejecting preceding forms of society as corrupt, immoral, and beyond reform, a single leader advocates a new society that corrects wrongs, redresses injustice, and institutes harmony. In place of private property, the state allocates power and status to reward supporters (who often monetize privileges through cronyism and corruption). It uses propaganda, indoctrination, and incarceration to coerce citizens; an individual conforms or is cast out. State-controlled media filters information, state-controlled education filters ideas, and state-controlled courts, police, and security squads suppress dissent. Totalitarianism is a condition in which politics invades all aspects of life and, in extreme cases, the cumulative result is a "virtual mind prison" that fuses leader and the state.[32]

Business Implications Managers in totalitarian systems face radically different markets than those found in democracies. Private enterprise, when allowed, supports the state. For instance, the Chinese government, under the direction of the CCP, owns and manages large swathes of its economy. The state is the majority owner of many of the largest publicly listed Chinese companies, some of which are among the biggest firms in the world.[33] Similarly, conglomerates in finance, media, mining, metals, transportation, communication, and so on answer to the CCP. Likewise, China's provincial and municipal officials control tens of thousands of medium-sized and smaller ones.[34] Add it all up and you have an authoritarian system that rejects the laissez-faire outlook typically found in democracies.

Managers operating in these sorts of markets adjust decision making for the fact that the government's imperative is sustaining state power, and it sees the market as a powerful tool to do so. Political risks affect all companies, but typically target foreign investors. The state favors local companies at the expense of foreign competitors, providing them with advantageous financing, preferential tax programs, relaxed work regulations, and other benefits.[35] The state manipulates markets for political purposes, thereby distorting resource valuations and blurring risk–return relationships. For example, China requires that foreign enterprises provide the "necessary conditions" for Communist Party cells in their local operations. Local governments can require that private companies contribute a share of their payrolls to finance Party activities.[36] The cells then advise companies to behave lawfully, fulfill their social responsibilities, promote stable labor relations, and maintain social harmony.

THE STATE OF FREEDOM

3-3 Discuss the principles and practices of political freedom

Since 1972, Freedom House annually assesses the state of freedom around the world. It declares that "Freedom is possible only in democratic political systems in which the governments are accountable to their own people; the rule of law prevails; and freedoms of expression, association, and belief, as well as respect for the rights of minorities and women, are guaranteed."[37] Freedom House estimates freedom worldwide based on measures derived from the Universal Declaration of Human Rights; the latter proclaims the 30 rights to which all people are inherently entitled, including the right to life, equality, thought, expression, public assembly, nationality, mobility, religion, fair and free world, education, marriage and family. Rather than the freedoms declared by governments, Freedom House looks at those practiced by individuals. A country's performance rates as:

- A *"free" country* exhibits open political competition, respect for civil liberties, robust rule of law, independent civic life, and independent media. There are inalienable freedoms of expression, assembly, association, education, and religion. Examples include Australia, Brazil, India, and the United States.

- A *"partly free" country* exhibits limited political rights and civil liberties, corruption, weak rule of law, ethnic and religious strife, unfair elections, and censorship. Examples include Guatemala, Hungary, Pakistan, and Tanzania.
- A *"not free" country* has few to no political rights and civil liberties. The government allows minimal to no exercise of personal choice, relies on the rule of man as the basis of law, constrains religious and social freedoms, and controls a large share, if not all, of business activity. Examples include China, Russia, Saudi Arabia, and Iran.

Currently some 2.9 billion people live in a free country. Although remote to many in Western democracies, most people in the world live in various forms of authoritarian political systems. As seen in Map 3.2, roughly 24 percent of the world population resides in partly free countries whereas 36 percent live in not free countries.

THE PREVALENCE OF POLITICAL FREEDOM

The Third Wave of Democratization refers to the third surge of democratically governed nations in the latter twentieth century.

Various forces powered past the Third Wave of Democratization:

- Failure of totalitarian regimes to deliver prosperity
- Improving communication technology
- Economic dividends of political freedom

The second half of the twentieth century saw the steady diffusion of democracy worldwide. Between 1950 and 2016, the number of electoral democracies grew from 22 to 129.[38] Many had been totalitarian, but steadily instituted democratic ideologies. The scale and scope of this ideological shift represented the so-called **Third Wave of Democratization**. This movement expanded individual freedoms and civil liberties worldwide.[39] Countries began building just institutions, civil societies, fair property rights, independent media, and impartial judiciaries. As a result, by 2000, nearly half the world's population, more than at any time in history, lived in a democracy of some sort.

Beginning in the mid-1970s, a confluence of trends had begun accelerating the Third Wave of Democratization. By the late 1980s, they culminated in toppling the Berlin Wall, undoing the Communist Bloc, and ending the Cold War. First, the growing failure of totalitarian regimes to deliver prosperity eroded their legitimacy. Aggrieved citizens, weary of declining living standards, rebelled. Formerly communist countries, shifting to freer markets, endorsed entrepreneurialism. The movement toward more individualism promoted civil

MAP 3.2 The Distribution of Political Freedom

Freedom House, classifying countries in terms of their degree of freedom, identifies three types—Free, Partly Free, and Not Free.

Source: Freedom House, "Freedom in the World, 2019 Map." Used by permission of Freedom House.

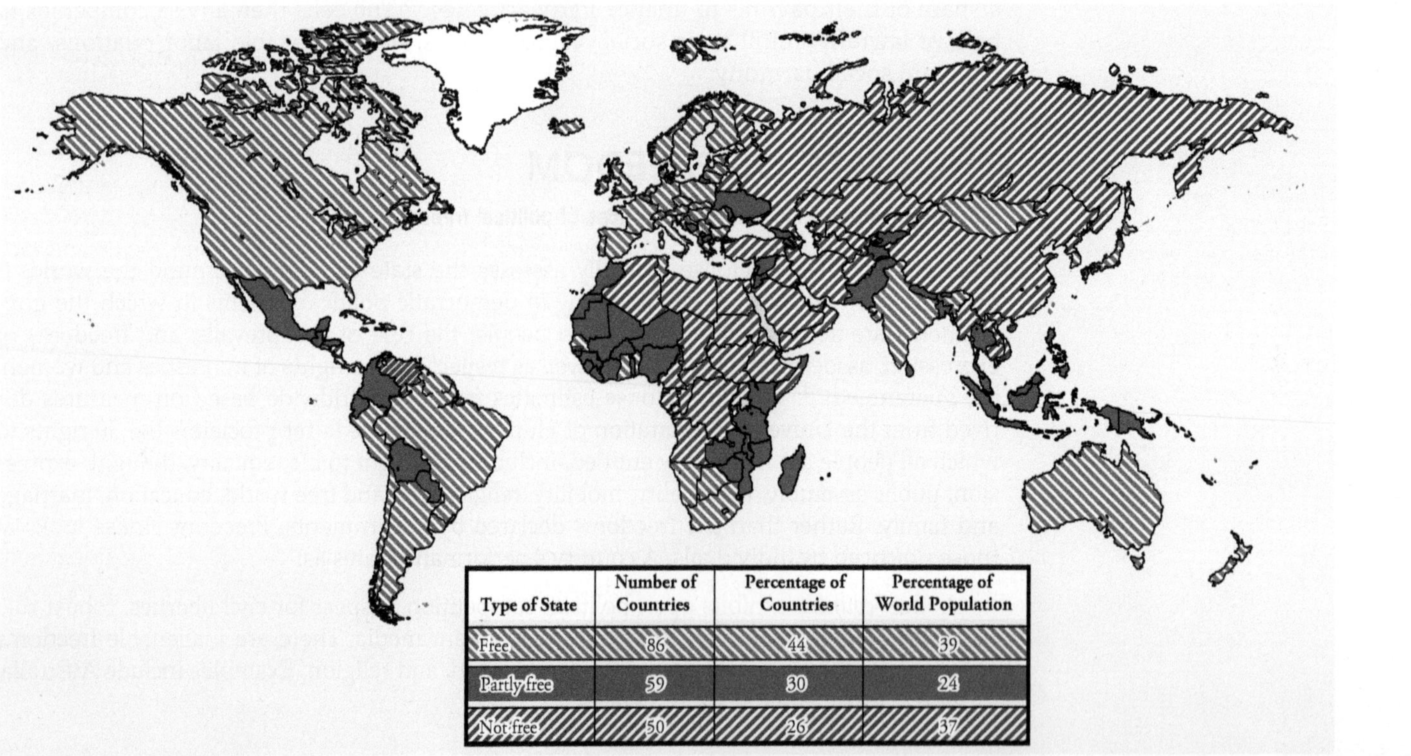

Type of State	Number of Countries	Percentage of Countries	Percentage of World Population
Free	86	44	39
Partly free	59	30	24
Not free	50	26	37

Source: Stephane Bidouze/Shutterstock

Once unusual, satellite dishes ▶ are ubiquitous throughout the world. This rooftop view in Bordeaux, France, shows many homes tagged, each able to tap the expanding information flowing throughout the world.

liberties and encouraged political freedom. Second, improving communications technologies eroded totalitarian regimes' control of information. Whereas once it took weeks, if ever, for news to spread, improving connections quickly circulated information. Expanding access to uncensored news, in light of Thomas Jefferson's thesis that "Information is the currency of democracy," inspired pro-democracy movements worldwide.

CONCEPT CHECK

Chapter 1 identifies the "Expansion of Technology" as a driving force of globalization. Advances in telecommunications liberated the flow of information, thereby challenging and changing social and political attitudes in many countries.

CONCEPT CHECK

In profiling "The Forces Driving Globalization" in Chapter 1, we noted the power of changing political situations. Until recently, we have witnessed the diffusion of democracy and the corresponding decline in totalitarianism. Growing acceptance of the legitimacy of democracy accelerated the expansion of international business.

Finally, freedom yielded economic dividends, most notably moving people from poverty to prosperity. The median per capita gross domestic product, a measure of the standard of living, is nearly seven times greater in free versus not free countries. Growing prosperity moved people to demand property rights, the rule of law, education opportunities, gender equality, media vigilance, and social tolerance.[40] An expanding middle class, freed from the tyranny of ceaselessly seeking sustenance, shelter, and security, had growing resources to support the ideals of individuality, justice, and liberty. Rising prosperity supported political stability and a belief in a brighter future.

As the twentieth century ended, the multi-decade march toward greater political freedoms and expansive civil liberties fueled a belief in the inevitability of democracy. Some saw this surge symbolizing the "end of history," whereby the universalization of Western liberal democracy represented the endpoint of humanity's ideological evolution and the final stage of human governance.[41] This megatrend had huge consequences for the growth and expansion of IB. Democratic governance steadied many unstable business environments. This, in turn, encouraged MNEs to expand their investment horizon to include markets, such as China, Russia, and Eastern Europe, that had previously been off-limits given extreme political risks. Steadily, industries developed, middle classes emerged, globalization accelerated, and freedom flourished worldwide.

FREEDOM STRUGGLES

Several indicators show slowing adoption of democracy throughout the world.

Democracy's advocacy of individualism, freedom, prosperity, and peace made it the most successful political idea of the 20th century. Troubling data, Freedom House reports, question its momentum in the 21st century. In 2008, its slowing momentum suggested a "democracy recession." In 2012, data signaled democracy's retreat worldwide. In 2015, retreat gave way to reversal and the "return of the iron fist." In 2018, events and trends indicated a state of "democracy in crisis." 2019 found democracy's retreat accelerating worldwide.[42] Consequently, managers qualify their political interpretations with the possibility that "history," rather than ending, continues onward.

FIGURE 3.3 Freedom in the World: Gains and Declines by Country

The momentum of political freedom has changed over the past decades, as early gains have given way to increasing decline.

Source: "Freedom in the World 2019: Democracy in Retreat," www.freedomhouse.org. Used by permission of Freedom House.

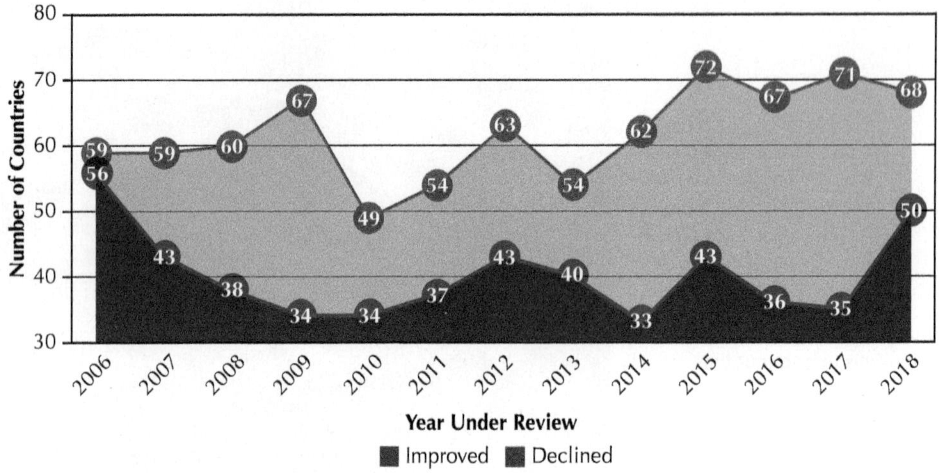

Certainly, many gains in many democracies seen during the Third Wave of Democratization endure. Individuals and institutions, however, struggle to promote free elections, defend human rights, constrain state power, and safeguard regulatory integrity. Sham elections, police crackdowns, kangaroo courts, and persecution of dissidents gain traction. Worldwide, influential totalitarian regimes suppress advocates, and, ultimately, the very idea of democracy itself. Many echo the outlook of the President of Belarus, who declared on the heels of a rigged election victory, "There will be no more mindless democracy in this country."[43]

As a result, the political environment in many countries is in play. Collectively, Freedom House reports that 2018 marked the 13th consecutive year that political freedom declined worldwide—the longest consecutive period of setbacks in modern times.[44] Democracy faces its most profound crisis in decades as its fundamental precepts are challenged, and increasingly rejected, worldwide. In 2018, 68 nations saw net declines in political rights and civil liberties; 50 reported gains. Since democracy's slide began in 2006, 113 countries have seen a net decline in freedom while 62 report a net improvement (see Figure 3.3).[45] Correspondingly, in 2019, the EIU's Democracy Index set an an all-time global low, averaging 5.44 (on a scale of 1 to 10) for 165 countries and two territories.

The *Economist Intelligence Unit* identifies four types of political systems:

- Full democracy
- Flawed democracy
- Hybrid regime
- Authoritarian regime

Gauging the Scale of Struggle: The Texture of Democracy Democracy, narrowly defined, is easily achieved—if merely holding elections were sufficient, most countries, including many that are partly and not free, would qualify. The Economist Intelligence Unit (EIU) resolves this distortion by assessing the degree that day-to-day life demonstrates the legitimate practice of political freedom. Specifically, the EIU evaluates the "texture of democracy" in a country in terms of the degree that its electoral process, pluralism, civil liberties, government performance, political participation, and political culture support democratic governance. The EIU translates these dimensions into 60 indicators to measure the texture of democracy in 165 independent states and two territories; this set is home to nearly the entire global population. A political system is classified as either a *full democracy, flawed democracy, hybrid regime,* or *authoritarian regime.* Table 3.3 profiles the characteristics found in the different types. Map 3.3 reports their distribution worldwide.

The Distribution of Democracy The EIU classifies 76 countries as democracies—that is, each meets the minimum expectation of regularly running nominally fair elections. Evaluated in terms of the texture of democracy, however, many are found to be "democracies" in name only. Just 22 are full democracies. The remaining 54 are flawed democracies. One sees most full democracies in the West, few in Latin America, Eastern Europe, and Africa. More precisely, the developed OECD countries of Europe and North America dominate the "full democracies" set; there are also the two Australasian countries (but no Asian ones), two Latin American countries (Uruguay and Costa Rica), and one African country (Mauritius).

TABLE 3.3 The Texture of Democracy: Types, Characteristics, and Examples

Type	Characteristics[46]	Examples
Full Democracy	• Mature political culture promotes and protects political freedoms and civil liberties. • Government discharges responsibilities transparently. • An effective system of checks and balances regulates politics. • The judiciary is independent, its decisions are impartially enforced, and the rule of law predominates. • Media are independent, vigilant, and diverse.	Australia, Austria, Costa Rica, Denmark, New Zealand, Norway, Switzerland, Uruguay
Flawed Democracy	• The State respects basic civil liberties. • Free and fair elections regularly occur but experience fraud or media restrictions. • Governance problems and low political participation make for a weak political culture. • Leadership and policy change occur frequently.	Brazil, Estonia, Hungary, India, Indonesia, Mexico, Senegal, Singapore, South Africa, South Korea, United States, Taiwan
Hybrid Regime	• Electoral irregularities undermine freedom and justice. • The state limits opposition parties and candidates. • Judicial bias favouring the "man" undermines the rule of law. • Political culture, public administration, and political participation struggles. • Corruption is extensive, civil society fades, and media are regulated.	Bangladesh, Cambodia, Honduras, Kyrgyzstan, Nigeria, Pakistan, Tanzania, Thailand, Ukraine
Authoritarian Regime	• Political pluralism is absent or repressed by the state. • Democratic institutions may exist but the state uses them to legitimate single-party rule. • Elections, if they do occur, are neither free nor fair. • The state systematically disregards civil liberties. • There is no independent judiciary and the rule of man predominates. • Media are typically state-owned or controlled by groups connected to the state. • Censorship suppresses criticism of the state. • Propaganda promotes the state ideology.	Afghanistan, Belarus, China, Gabon, Kuwait, Nicaragua, Mozambique, Russia, Saudi Arabia, Zimbabwe

MAP 3.3 The Texture of Democracy: Worldwide Distribution of System Type

The scale and scope of democracy varies worldwide.

Source: Adapted from "Democracy Index 2019: A Year of Democratic Setbacks and Popular Protest," The Economist Intelligence Unit (2019).

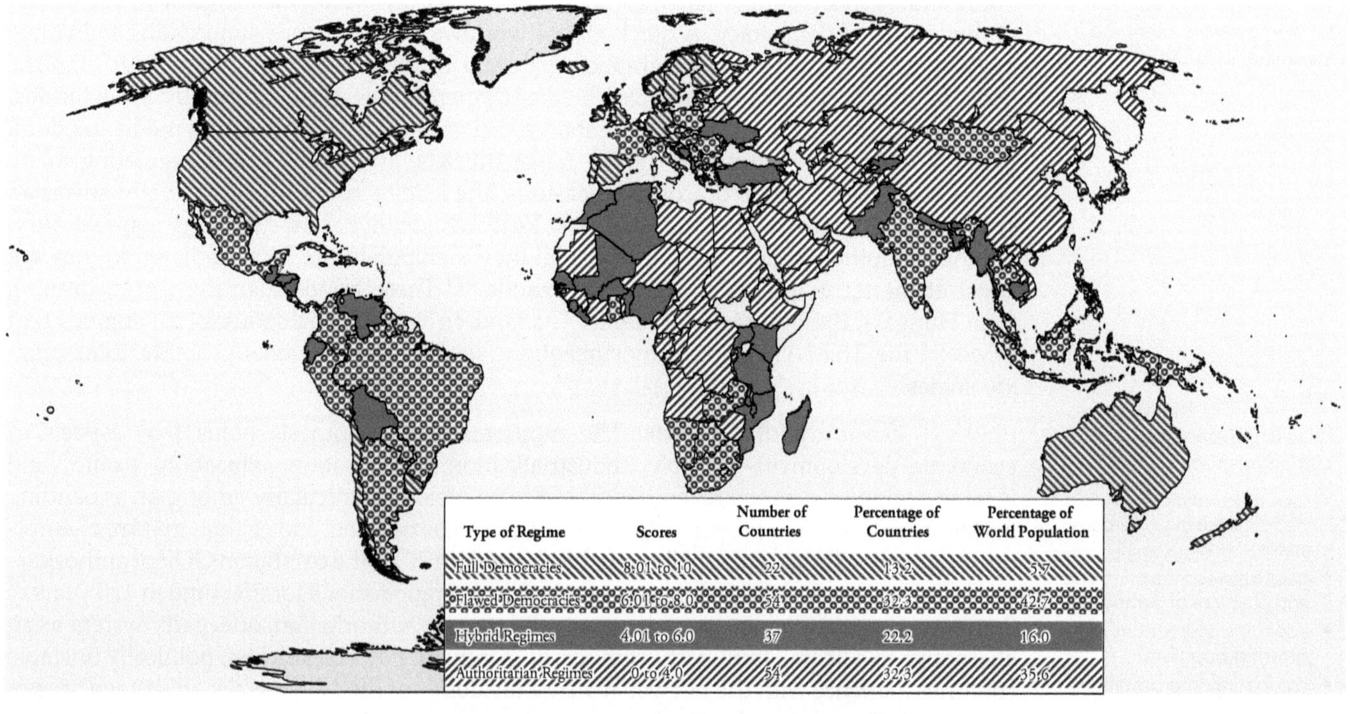

Type of Regime	Scores	Number of Countries	Percentage of Countries	Percentage of World Population
Full Democracies	8.01 to 10	22	13.2	5.7
Flawed Democracies	6.01 to 8.0	54	32.3	42.7
Hybrid Regimes	4.01 to 6.0	37	22.2	16.0
Authoritarian Regimes	0 to 4.0	54	32.3	35.6

The predominance of OECD countries among "full democracies" suggests a relationship between democratic governance and economic development.[47]

Map 3.3 shows that flawed democracies are found worldwide but prevail in Eastern Europe along with Latin and South America. Here, one finds fragile institutional structures and low political participation constrain freedom. Likewise, their governments' response to corruption, terrorism, and drug trafficking complicate governance. Often, democracy serves as a convenient slogan for the single party that dominates within a façade of regulated pluralism. Hong Kong, for example, exemplifies a flawed democracy. It has telltale aspects of a democracy, such as an impartial judiciary, civil liberties, independent media, and political parties. Still, procedural irregularities thwart democratic governance. Consider, for instance, its electoral process. Its Chief Executive (effectively its president) is chosen not by Hong Kong's 7.4 million residents, but by a 1,200-person "Election Committee" composed of handpicked elites. Fervent opposition to this procedure, along with other state policies, has fueled widespread protests. Hong Kong, by the way, tops the crony-capitalism world league table and, as you'll see in Chapter 4, leads the world in economic freedom.

The EIU reports that 37 countries are hybrid regimes that mix democratic and authoritarian practices. Many hybrid regimes manifest the markings of democracies. However, systematic abuses corrupt free and fair processes that, in turn, erode freedom. Authoritarian regimes predominate in 54 countries. As do hybrid regimes, many of these states proclaim democratic practices, such as popular elections, open debates, and civil rights. In practice, they are largely Potemkin designs—citizens have the freedom, for instance, to vote only for candidates that have been preapproved by the ruling elite. China, classified as an authoritarian state by the EIU, for example, declares its "intraparty democracy" permits eight other legal democratic parties to participate in the political system; they are, though, forbidden from challenging the Communist Party.[48] Day-to-day life often evidences aspects of authoritarianism, including personal restrictions, public corruption, state-owned media, omnipresent state security, pervasive censorship, and a biased judiciary.

Qualifying Democracy by Demography The distribution of political systems in terms of demography extends the interpretation of the texture of democracy. Roughly 3.7 billion (48 percent) of the world's population lives in some form of democracy. However, just 4.5 percent, or, about 340 million, live in a full democracy. Some 1.2 billion (17 percent) live in hybrid regimes and 2.7 billion (36 percent) reside in authoritarian regimes.

THE ALLURE OF AUTHORITARIANISM

Worldwide, few people live in full democracies; many more live in authoritarian regimes.

The re-emergence of, single-party, authoritarian states worldwide indicates growing scepticism of the virtues of democracy. A quick glance worldwide finds Russia suppressing individual freedoms through arbitrary governance, Bahraini officials responding harshly to opposition, Venezuela restricting dissenting media, Cameroon elections marred by irregularities, Mali relying upon state security to maintain social order, Egypt constraining media freedom, Nicaragua consolidating power among fewer officials, and Saudi Arabia regulating many personal choices. Despite draconian measures, the leaders of these and similarly governed states display improving political deftness. Research spotlights the "growing sophistication of modern authoritarians. They are flexible; they manipulate the legal framework; they are adept at the techniques of modern propaganda."[49] These trends span the world, running from Hungary, Burkina Faso, Lithuania, Thailand, to Turkey. Analogous to the engines that powered the Third Wave of Democratization, several developments promote totalitarian ideologies.

Powering expanding authoritarianism is

- robust economic performance in single-party states,
- gaps between the principles and practices of democracy,
- economic insecurities and growing populism,
- competing interpretations of the idea of democracy.

Political Economy of Growth The modernization hypothesis holds that aspects of economic development—notably, industrialization, urbanization, education, health, and income—support democratic governance. Rising wealth, particularly among an expanding middle class, promotes property rights and encourages personal choice that, in turn, champions democracy. Today, data challenges this thesis.[50] In 2019, the combined GDP of authoritarian nations surpassed the economic output of democratic nations for first time in 120 years.[51] Some see China's economic performance validating its authoritarian, one-party system as an alternative to a liberal, multiparty democracy. For many poverty-stricken, politically unstable countries, patience with the not-yet-realized dividends of the "democracy advantage" thesis wears thin. Despite nearly 75 years of uninterrupted democratic governance, for instance, many of India's citizens struggle to improve health, education, and security. Consequently, China's model of a so-called "People's Democratic Dictatorship" gains credibility.[52]

Rhetoric Versus Reality Democracy setbacks in several Western nations, notably Italy, France, Spain, and the United States, give pause to some 70 strategically significant countries at the political crossroads. If democracy can't work there, how could it work here, wonder some in places like Afghanistan, Argentina, Bangladesh, and Mozambique.[53] Symbolically, the United States' fall from a full to a flawed democracy in 2017 tested the legitimacy of long-running principles. Likewise, charges of hypocrisy against Western countries (owing to incursions in Iraq, Libya, Syria, and Afghanistan, along with the implications of antiterrorist activities to political freedoms and civil liberties) jumble democratic ideals. Double standards in foreign policy (i.e., some autocratic countries are allies, such as Saudi Arabia or Thailand, whereas others are foes, like Iran or Venezuela) discredit democracy's promoters.[54]

Likewise, confidence in institutions has declined throughout the West. Fewer than one in five Europeans trust political parties, while only one in three regards governments and parliaments as trustworthy.[55] Likewise, more than a quarter of Europeans indicated they would prefer political decisions made by artificial intelligence instead of elected officials; it climbed to one in three in Germany, Netherlands, and the United Kingdom.[56] In the United States, 11 percent in 2019, versus 42 percent in 1973, report "a great deal/quite a lot" of confidence in Congress; this is the lowest score among 15 major institutions, including the military, big business, public schools, banks, newspapers, and the presidency.[57]

Economic Problems Persistent unemployment, slow growth, higher taxes, and rising debt in many Western countries call into question the capacity of democracy to create a fairer, brighter, prosperous future.[58] Authoritarian movements often draw support from folks fearful of fading prospects. Conflict between the *gilets jaunes* (yellow vests) and the state in France, for example, highlights anxieties over democracy's effectiveness. Similar situations in the United States, notably controversial presidential politics, and in the United Kingdom, the polarizing BREXIT saga, spotlight similar scenarios.

Folks fearing declining prospects, especially for their children, are often open to an alternative ideology, even given objectionable elements, if it restores their confidence in the future. For example, **populism** grows worldwide, as ordinary people who believe that corrupt elites disregard their concerns consider ideological alternatives to democracy. The Global Populism Index, for instance, finds support for populist parties escalating significantly worldwide; currently, it reports degrees of support last seen in the early 1940s. Evidence indicates, in line with expectations of folks questioning democracy's effectiveness, that populist policies reduce economic inequality.[59]

Source: Alexandros Michailidis/Shutterstock

Sparked in France, the yellow vest movement has spread outward from France. Here, we see marchers in Brussels, Belgium, protesting growing oppression of the working and middle class.

Who Defines Democracy? The legitimacy of Western notions of democracy travels poorly to countries that endorse different ideals. China's former president spoke of "democracy" with a different meaning from that commonly used in the West. In his view, calls for multiparty democracy are taboo, opposition cannot officially organize, reform must obey the "correct political orientation," and "orderly" change must respect and preserve the authority of the CCP.[60] China's president, Xi Jinping, advises the West that "your democracy is the democracy of Greece and ancient Rome, and that's your tradition. We have our own traditions."[61]

Similarly, Russia's president, Vladimir Putin, declares himself "a true democrat" and argues that the West misinterprets the virtues of authoritarianism. He charges "some of the participants in the international dialogue believe that their ideas [of democracy] are the ultimate truth."[62] Instead, he oversees a "sovereign democracy," an approach that appeals to many Russians who prefer stable, autocratic leadership to a chaotic, liberal democracy. Others add that Western-style democracy, rather than promoting individual rights and civil liberties, is an ideological ruse that disguises inequities in class, wealth, and power. Various leaders contend that the advocates of Western-style democracy no longer speak for the world, having lost the moral authority to dictate solutions to developing countries.[63]

LOOKING TO THE FUTURE Political Ideology and MNEs' Actions

Like you, managers wonder what a political map of the world might look like in the next decade. Will democracy regain its intellectual and practical appeal? Will totalitarianism gain more ground? Will new ideologies arise? It is tempting to regard these questions as academic straw men, best left to the folks in ivory towers to wonder about. The latest data indicate they are anything but. As faltering political freedom and resurgent authoritarianism accelerate democracy's retreat, countries reset marketplaces and MNEs adjust strategies. Trends highlight the contemporary political ideologies competing for supremacy—namely, the Washington Consensus versus the Beijing Consensus, What, pray tell, might these mean to managers?

The Washington Consensus

Increasingly prominent after the close of the Cold War, the Washington Consensus centers on free-market, pro-trade, and pro-globalization policies. Promoted by the United States, it advocates democracy, political freedom, rule of law, and human rights in the pursuit of life, liberty, and happiness. In terms of timing, the collapse of the Moscow Consensus, symbolized by the fall of the Berlin Wall in 1989, set Washington as the global philosophical center in an America-dominated unipolar world. Its idealized Consensus—promoted by executives, politicians, generals, media, and institutions—called upon countries to reform in ways that reflected the neoliberal political economy of the United States. Powering this call was a set of interrelated beliefs: right-minded market reform led to economic growth, which created a middle class that supported property rights, which, in turn, instituted the rule of law.

Successfully navigating this sequence, reasoned the United States, would build nations that steadfastly championed prosperity and peace. The Washington Consensus holds that the universality of these beliefs, much like the universality of the ideals of life, liberty, and happiness, offset the limitations imposed by a country's legacy of authoritarianism, rule of man, and systemic suppression. Adopting the steps and sequences of the Washington Consensus implemented the policies that set, support, and sustain a legitimate neoliberal democracy. Institutionalizing its ideals into day-to-day life meant that individuals had the intrinsic freedom to live life as they choose. Ultimately, the diffusion of the Washington Consensus creates a world of nations practicing U.S.-style pro-peace democracy. Attainment, argued political theorists, signified the endpoint of humanity's sociocultural evolution.

The Beijing Consensus

Alternatively, some say the growing appeal of the Beijing Consensus signals the next political era rather than the end of history. Indeed, just as the twentieth century was marked by an ideological contest between Moscow and Washington, with each advocating its preferred consensus, so the twenty-first century sees history ready to rhyme—this time though, with the ideological contest being that between Washington and Beijing. A euphemism for China's self-proclaimed "People's Democratic Dictatorship," the Beijing Consensus advocates a single-party system in which elected representatives, preapproved by the ruling party, oversee a nominal democratic system whose citizens, though granted the right to vote, do not participate in decision making. Elections, while free, are not fair. The state, in the form of the Communist Party of China (CCP), aspires to rule by consent, preferring benevolent persuasion to the iron fist. Still, the state swiftly suppresses those who challenge its authority. Spontaneity in a single-party system, no matter how apolitical, symbolizes protest. As CCP officials routinely explained, "Stability trumps everything."

Unlike the ideologically interventionist Washington Consensus, the Beijing Consensus is ideologically agnostic. It prizes economic development and international trade as the means to generate growth, accumulate wealth, and create harmony within its borders. It uses fast-growing prosperity to subvert political choice, reasoning that its citizens value higher wages, social stability, and economic security more than political freedoms. The Beijing Consensus does not pass judgment on another country's politics; in turn, it expects not to be judged. It advocates trade "with no strings attached" (which, in the case of the Washington Consensus, are democracy, freedom, human rights, and the rule of law). To this end, China invests throughout Asia, Africa, the Middle East, and South America without call for political reform.

China's policy of harmonious stability within a single-party state has gained credibility worldwide, especially given its economic performance over the past 40 years. Said one analyst, "[T]he 'China model' of authoritarian capitalism is gaining currency. Governments from Syria to Vietnam have sung its praises." Some argue that state control that weds liberal economics with authoritarian politics, rather than the union of liberal economics and multiparty democracy, now represents the superior political path to prosperity and harmony.

What's Next, Managers Ask?

Democracy's ongoing retreat questions long-cherished ideals. Managers study the direction that political ideologies might track. Will liberal democracy à la the Washington Consensus regain the commanding heights? Ongoing developments worldwide, led by an expanding middle class that is progressively connected through expanding cross-national networks, support that forecast. Alternatively, will the authoritarian ethos of the Beijing Consensus set political standards? Supporters point to China's growing involvement in receptive countries worldwide as persuasive validation.

No matter the scenario, history reminds us that it matters. The first and second waves of democratization (1828–1926 and 1943–1962, respectively) were followed by periods of freedom backlash, democracy's retreat, and surging authoritarianism. The end of the second wave saw more than 20 countries revert from totalitarianism, symbolized by the ensuing ideological war between Washington and Moscow. Hence, the question arises: Are we once again facing a cycle of transition and consolidation? Whatever the answer, only the ill-advised underestimate the consequence of political change. If the Washington Consensus proves resilient, managers must adjust operations to the growing pains of countries that endorse individualism, champion freedom, advocate human rights, and adopt the rule of law. Prosperity may come with difficulty, but there will be prosperity for many. If the Beijing Consensus predominates, managers must rethink business in a world that advocates collectivism, seeks harmony, and relies on the state to deliver economic prosperity in exchange for political freedoms. Prosperity may come a bit easier, but its price will constrain choice.

POLITICAL RISK

3-4 Describe the idea of political risk

Political risk refers to the threat that decisions or events in a country will negatively affect the profitability and sustainability of an investment.

Map 3.1 profiles the scale and scope of political risk that MNEs face worldwide. No matter whether it operates in Canada, Cambodia, Cameroon, Chad, China, or Chile, for instance, an MNE faces risks that the political events in the host country will adversely affect its operational objectives, strategic goals, and profitability. Technically, **political risk** is the chance that political decisions, events, or conditions change a country's business environment in ways that force a company to accept lower rates of return, cost it some or all of its investment, or threaten the sustainability of its operation.

Various trends increase political risk. Declining political freedom destabilizes the play of politics across markets. Many countries lack the texture of democracy to sustain consistent governance. Earlier, given the expanding Third Wave of Democratization, managers saw the principles of political freedom, not authoritarian control, shaping national affairs. The fair, just principles of democracy, not the arbitrary, opportunistic hallmarks of authoritarianism, systemically reduced political risks in more countries. IB flourished, expanding into markets that steadily instituted democratic governance. Now, policies decreasing political freedom in countries worldwide, by increasing the uncertainty of politics, increase political risks.

CONCEPT CHECK

Chapter 1 notes that some interest groups fear that globalization severely weakens national sovereignty—that is, growing cross-national connections constrains a nation's right to act in its own interests. This outlook often intensifies political risk, pushing a government to protect its national sovereignty by aggressively regulating foreign investors.

Compounding problems is the fact that many emerging markets are rife with flashpoints. Operationally, foreign investors often compete with state-run rivals whose political allegiance complicate economic situations; government favoritism for homegrown champions makes for risky situations. More fundamentally, arbitrary laws, fragile institutions, volatile societies, and corrupt regimes fuel uncertainty. Matters that had been peripheral in 2000, such as populism, unemployment, income inequality, large-scale migration, escalating nationalism, and civil polarization, have moved to the center stage in many places. Complicating matters is the fact that political risks triggers differ from market to market. In Venezuela, managers face economic nationalism amid expanding socialism; in Brazil, managers must decrypt Congress's shifting, multiparty alliances; in China, one must decipher the power and play of the CCP; in Saudi Arabia, a manager must decode the internal dealings of the ruling family. In the United States and Great Britain, managers must make sense of the implication of rising nationalism to cross-national integration. Consequently, political analytics that work in one country often travel poorly to others.

CLASSIFYING POLITICAL RISK

Our evaluation of political risk applies a macro-micro scale (see Figure 3.4). Macro risks affect all companies, both domestic and foreign alike, in a given country. Micro risks are agent-specific actions that affect specific, usually foreign-owned, companies. Let's take a closer look at each type.

Systemic Political Risk Generally, a country's political processes do not punish companies arbitrarily. Otherwise, few would hazard investing there. Rather, firms commonly face ordinary sorts of political risk, typically resulting from shifting public policies, that influence local business activities. Newly elected officials, for instance, typically launch programs that differ from those of their predecessors—say, instituting new fiscal policies, authorizing new regulations, or changing monetary policy. Sometimes the importance of a national market leaves MNEs few practical options to evade systemic risks. Most don't consider the United States, for instance, a hotbed of political risk. If you're in the cigarette business, however, the United States is a hazardous market. The U.S. government aggressively regulates cigarette makers (both domestic, like Philip Morris, and foreign, like British American Tobacco) on matters of taxation, business practice, and liability. Preserving access to politically risky yet strategically important markets requires adeptly navigating dynamic situations.

FIGURE 3.4 Classes and Characteristics of Political Risk

Political risks have telltale characteristics in terms of types, techniques, and outcomes.

Scale	Class	Type	Outcome
Micro ↑		Financial Anomalies	Regulatory policies that make it difficult for the company to get credit or arrange overseas loans.
	Systemic ↕	Competing Perspectives	The host government's policies on, for instance, human rights, labor conditions, or environmental sustainability, create public relations problems for a foreign company at home.
		Unilateral Breach of Contract	The host government repudiates a contract negotiated with a foreign company or approves a local firm's doing the same.
	Procedural ↕	Tax Discrimination	A foreign company is saddled with a higher tax burden than a local competitor.
		Restrictions on Profit Repatriation	The host government arbitrarily limits the amount of profit that a foreign company can remit from its local operations to the home office.
	Distributive ↕	Destructive Government Actions	Unilateral trade barriers, often via local-content requirements, interfere with the distribution of products to local consumers.
		Harmful Action Against People	Local employees of a foreign company are threatened by kidnapping, extortion, or terrorist actions.
	Catastrophic	Expropriation/Nationalization	The host government or a political faction seizes a company's local assets. Compensation, if any, is usually trivial. Resurgent totalitarianism and resource nationalism increase this risk.
↓ Macro		Civil Strife, Insurrection, War	Military action damages or destroys a company's local operations.

Systemic political risks, by influencing investment and operating conditions in a nation, affect the activities of all firms.

Occasionally, a government may target a strategic sector that it sees dominated by companies, both local and foreign, such as Venezuela nationalizing its energy industry, Argentina nationalizing its railways, or Russia re-nationalizing its space industry. Likewise, Saudi Arabia's plan to create jobs for Saudi citizens in the private sector, in place of the many foreigners who filled those slots, led to widespread prohibitions; the resulting exodus of foreign workers increased wage rates throughout the country. In these sorts of situations, politically motivated policies alter the macro environment, thereby creating systemic political risks that affect all firms.

Procedural political risk institutes impediments that constrain efficiently running activities.

Procedural Political Risk Products and resources ceaselessly move through the global market. Each move creates a procedural transaction between individuals, subsidiaries, companies, institutions, or countries. Political policies sometimes impose frictions that slow or stop these transactions. Opportunistic officials, for instance, might pressure a firm to pay additional monies to clear goods through customs, obtain a permit to transfer technology, or authorize capital repatriation. For example, Nigeria's business environment is rife with procedural risks. "The entire state machinery exists to siphon off cash," complained one observer. "Many functions of government have been adapted for personal gain . . . A universe of red tape engulfs the economy . . . In some Nigerian states, governors must personally sign off on every property sale; many demand a fee."[64] Political interference escalates expenses, thereby lowering returns. Procedural political risk generally affects some, but not all, companies. MNEs manage it by monitoring industry developments, minding their relationship with officials, and practicing good citizenship.

Distributive political risks progressively eliminate the local property rights of foreign companies.

Distributive Political Risk Countries see successful foreign investors as agents of innovation and sources of prosperity. Often, as MNEs grow profits in the local economy, the host government questions its share of the rewards. Many conclude they should receive a larger cut and impose policies to reset the distribution. Often, governments apply processes of **creeping expropriation**, whereby the gradual reduction of a MNE's local property rights, via legislation, regulation, and taxation, progressively captures a bigger share of its profits.

Vigilance helps MNEs reduce exposure to distributive political risk. Preemptive moves include configuring activities to disaggregate and disperse operations. Chrysler deterred creeping expropriation in Peru by having its local factory make many, but not all, of the parts needed to assemble a car; importing the rest meant the local facility was useless if the government expropriated it. Likewise, Japan's periodic tension with China pushes Japanese MNEs, who have extensive operations in China, to hedge their political risk. Some apply a "China-plus" approach whereby they backstop their supply chains, largely anchored in China, with a shadow hub in another Asian market such as Thailand, Vietnam, or the Philippines. Although inefficient, secondary locations safeguard their operations if tensions escalate.[65]

Catastrophic political risk devastates the business environment for all companies.

Catastrophic Political Risk Extraordinary political events, such as ethnic conflict, illegitimate regime change, civil disorder, or insurrection, directly and dramatically affect the investments and operations of every firm in a country. No matter the cause, these sorts of calamities fundamentally disrupt markets. Anti-state activities in Egypt during the Arab Spring movement, for example, paralyzed its economy. Foreign commerce and domestic business halted, channels seized, and supplies of all sorts vanished. Auspiciously, Egypt pulled back from the brink. In other situations, especially in so-called failed states, like Chad, Libya, or Somalia, spiralling disruptions devastate the business environment for all firms.[66] Likewise, the COVID-19 pandemic initially triggered large-scale quarantines, travel restrictions, and social-distancing measures that drove a sharp fall in consumer and business spending. Soon, layoffs, business closures, and bankruptcies fed into a self-reinforcing downward spiral, and some countries felt recession, if not depression.[67]

POINT

Proactive Political Risk Management: The Superior Approach

YES Companies take politics seriously, keenly aware that governments regulate the business environment and, hence, influence their performance. Consequently, MNEs need sharp-minded political risk management strategies. All have a choice: apply a proactive or a passive approach. Those who advocate proactive political risk management reason that the best defense is a good offense. In my opinion, they're right. Taking charge, applying analytics, and predicting problems, in order to take preemptive actions, is the optimal approach to manage risk.

What to Do Executives use battle-tested tactics. First, they apply state-of-the-art statistical modeling and big data analytics to quantify political risks. They begin with the thesis that political events are neither independent nor chance events. Civil strife, creeping expropriation, regime change, ethnic tension, terrorism, and the like do not happen randomly. They unfold in observable patterns that bright folks applying incisive analytics can measure to estimate the odds of future outcomes. Then, they can consult experts on the political drama in a country to test the validity of their models. Applying rigorous analytics that detect, measure, and frame scenarios moves an MNE ahead of the curve, proactively managing its political risk exposure.

What to Track Measuring the right set of discrete events is the key to modeling political risk—success depends on identifying valid indicators that one can reliably track. Research identifies useful candidates such as the frequency of government crises, pervasiveness of corruption, extent of crony capitalism, scope of counterfeiting, number of military officers holding political office, pace of urbanization, freedom of the press, ethno-lingual fractionalization, and so on. Evolving methods fortify analyses. For example, sentiment analysis, opinion mining, and computational linguistics track emotionally charged words and phrases used in online communications. Comparing the relative frequency of positive and negative words used in millions of exchanges, feeds, streams, and posts produces national and global heat maps of how people "feel." Sentiment analysis, for example, indicated that people's resentment of autocratic rule crossed critical thresholds in Egypt and Libya weeks before violence erupted.[68] Sentiment analysis confirms that the challenge is not identifying individual measures, but rather identifying the right mix. Once done, skillful statistical modeling objectively estimates risk exposure.

COUNTERPOINT

Proactive Political Risk Management: The Superior Approach

NO Unquestionably, a proactive approach exhibits the hallmark of good management—enterprising, confident, objective, and decisive. However, it fails to explain why some MNEs do the exact opposite, opting to manage political risk passively by treating it as an unpredictable hazard. Essentially, these companies reason that no model, regardless of how brilliantly it has been conceptualized, how systematically it has been specified, and how precisely it has been analyzed, can consistently predict political risk. Granted, shrewd models extrapolate meaningful insights from economic, political, and social reports about who may take office, what policies may pass, and how these sorts of events may affect markets. Unquestionably, these insights make a political system and its risks understandable. They do not, however, make it predictable.

What to Hedge Insights do not qualify as predictions precisely because of the impracticality of reliably measuring messy, ill-structured situations. The political world is complex, its inalienable feature is ambiguity, and its tendency to change is absurdly high. Compounding the difficulty are the innumerable variables and their interaction that constitute a political system—think, for example, of the 60 indicators that estimate the texture of democracy in a nation.

This situation becomes more challenging as MNEs venture into developing markets, each with its own political peculiarities. Going from the United States to Mexico may be a stretch, but that pales in comparison to expanding from the United States to, say, Saudi Arabia, Kazakhstan, or Zimbabwe. No matter how comprehensive the spreadsheet or insightful the expert, the dimensions and dynamics of a political environment ultimately defy precise specification. Yes, developing broad frameworks that anticipate potential hazards makes good business sense. However, prudently managing political risk starts by rejecting the delusion that one can. The objective is protection, not prediction—or, put differently, the best offense is a good defense.

How to Hedge How does one hedge exposure to political risk? Typically, an MNE purchases political risk insurance. Policies provide single-country coverage or broad, multi-country, regional, or global coverage for several risks, including creeping expropriation, political violence, currency inconvertibility, nonpayment, and contract frustration. A range of public agencies, international organizations, and private companies offer coverage options.

- Multilateral Development Banks are international financial institutions funded and owned by member governments that promote growth in member countries by providing financial incentives to potential investors. Reducing the capital at risk encourages firms to expand

What to Add Yes, the proactive approach faces limits. Spreadsheet estimation, no matter how rigorous, carries analysis only so far. Reaching this bound need not halt risk management. One can complement quantitative measures with in-depth, country-specific qualitative indicators. Surveying country experts taps interpretations of a country's political drama in ways that numbers may struggle to represent. Specialists make sense of subtle intricacies, enhancing quantitative analyses with their expertise on subjective conditions. Then, what may seem idiosyncratic circumstances, given their insights, become systematic patterns. Integrating expert assessments into a political risk strategy is straightforward. Begin by running standardized interviews with experts to assess a country's political environment. If stuck, a useful starting point is the Internet; searching "political risk management" generates resources. Collectively, they support projecting realistic scenarios and objectively assigning probabilities to reasonable outcomes—the hallmarks of proactive political risk management.

What to Realize Modeling the ambiguous, subjective, unpredictable dynamics of political change strikes many as more delusional than definitive. Nonetheless, operating internationally means managers deal with endless questions and complexities; part of the daily drama is political. As tough as that sounds, the track record of MNEs confirms that managers consistently make it happen, devising political risk strategies that find ingenious ways to run profitable enterprises.

into otherwise unacceptably risky environments. Examples include the African Development Bank, the Asian Development Bank, and the World Bank Group.

- The Overseas Private Investment Corporation (OPIC) encourages U.S. investment projects overseas by protecting ventures against various forms of risk, including civil strife, expropriation, and currency inconvertibility. OPIC prefers promoting investments in developing markets that support the foreign policies of the United States.
- Private insurance companies underwrite political risk protection. Many cover "routine" procedural and distributive risks that involve property and income, such as contract repudiation and currency inconvertibility. Private insurers are reluctant, given the potential scale of loss, to cover catastrophic risks that result from civil strife, insurrection, or war.

What to Realize Ultimately, we have no quarrel with the notion that prediction and control are touchstones of professional management. Still, politics are anything but predictable and controllable. Few, if any, predicted the political turmoil of the Arab Spring. Likewise, Britain's vote to depart the European Union surprised many as did the election of Donald Trump in the United States. Moreover, few forecast democracy's retreat a decade ago; instead, analysts proclaimed the "end of history." Not to put too sharp a point on it, but if one cannot predict these sorts of mega-events, then exactly what can one predict? Therefore, it just makes more sense—and, we might add, more cents—to resist the proactivity delusion and opt for the practicality of passively managing political risk.

THE LEGAL ENVIRONMENT

3-5 Interpret the principles and practices of a legal environment

Just as politics differ among countries, so do legal systems. Thus, a key aspect of the environments of IB is how a country develops, interprets, and enforces its laws. Understandably, managers champion consistency in laws from country to country. Uniform, transparent laws make it easier to decide where to invest and, once there, how to compete on professional competencies, not personal connections. In theory, legitimate rules that apply without prejudice to an individual or a company, regardless of political, cultural, or economic status, anchor a just and fair legal environment. Done judiciously, individuals and companies can make lawful decisions that support peace and prosperity. Done arbitrarily, individuals and companies suffer because, as Honoré de Balzac warned, "To distrust the judiciary marks the beginning of the end of society."

The legal system is the mechanism for developing, stipulating, interpreting, and enforcing the laws in a formal jurisdiction.

The **legal system** of a nation specifies the rules that regulate behavior, the processes that enforce laws, and the procedures that resolve grievances. All things being equal, every legal system institutes rules that support business formation, regulate transactions, and formalize relationships. Doing so ensures that a society can pursue economic development and, when disagreements arise, resolve them without resorting to lawlessness. However, legal systems differ across countries due to variations in tradition, precedent, usage, custom, or religious precepts. Moreover, with the exception of the members of the European Union, countries rarely recognize the legitimacy of legal practices or court judgments from other nations; explained one observer, "Products move very easily across borders. Legal judgments, not so much."[69]

Modern legal systems evidence three components:
- constitutional law
- criminal law
- civil and commercial law

Modern legal systems have three essential components: (1) **constitutional law**, which translates a country's constitution into an open and just legal system, setting the framework for government and defining the authority and procedure of political bodies to establish laws; (2) **criminal law**, which safeguards society by specifying what conduct is criminal, and prescribing punishment to those who breach those standards; and (3) **civil and commercial laws**, which ensure fairness and efficiency in business transactions by stipulating private rights and specific remedies in order to regulate conduct between individuals and/or organizations. No single legal component in and of itself guarantees a functioning legal system. Success depends on the collective effectiveness of all components to institute philosophical integrity, procedural justice, and personal security.

Aspects of each component influence MNEs' actions in a host country. Our opening case, for example, profiled how China's legal traditions and practices attract, retain, as well as deter investment. Whereas Western investors are accustomed to transparent bankruptcy laws that protect creditors, for instance, Chinese law protects debtors. Likewise, one in six business practitioners in Russia has been prosecuted for alleged economic crime over the past decade; most cases have no plaintiff, acquittals are rare, and a company's assets are often expropriated by the state. Russian law, contends critics, "is the property of those who enforce it, and written exclusively for them."[70] Managers must find the path to navigate these situations. Sometimes the path is straight and narrow, while sometimes it is marked by twists and turns.

TYPES OF LEGAL SYSTEMS

A country's legal system regulates the conduct of business transactions, the rights and obligations of those doing business, and the legal redress open to those who have been wronged. Understanding its nuances encourages executives to assess a variety of issues: Are laws based on abstractions or practicality? Do judges or juries pass judgment? Is justice based on objective principles or is it seen as the province of divinity? Do personal connections trump case facts? Peculiar as these and similar sorts of questions sound, IB puts managers into situations wherein different interpretations set different standards that regulate the legality of their actions.

MAP 3.4 The Wide World of Legal Systems

Managers operating internationally face legal environments anchored in various philosophies and principles. Here we see the world organized by predominant types.

Source: University of Ottawa, "World Legal Systems," retrieved January 15, 2020, from www.juriglobe.ca/eng/index.php. Used by permission.

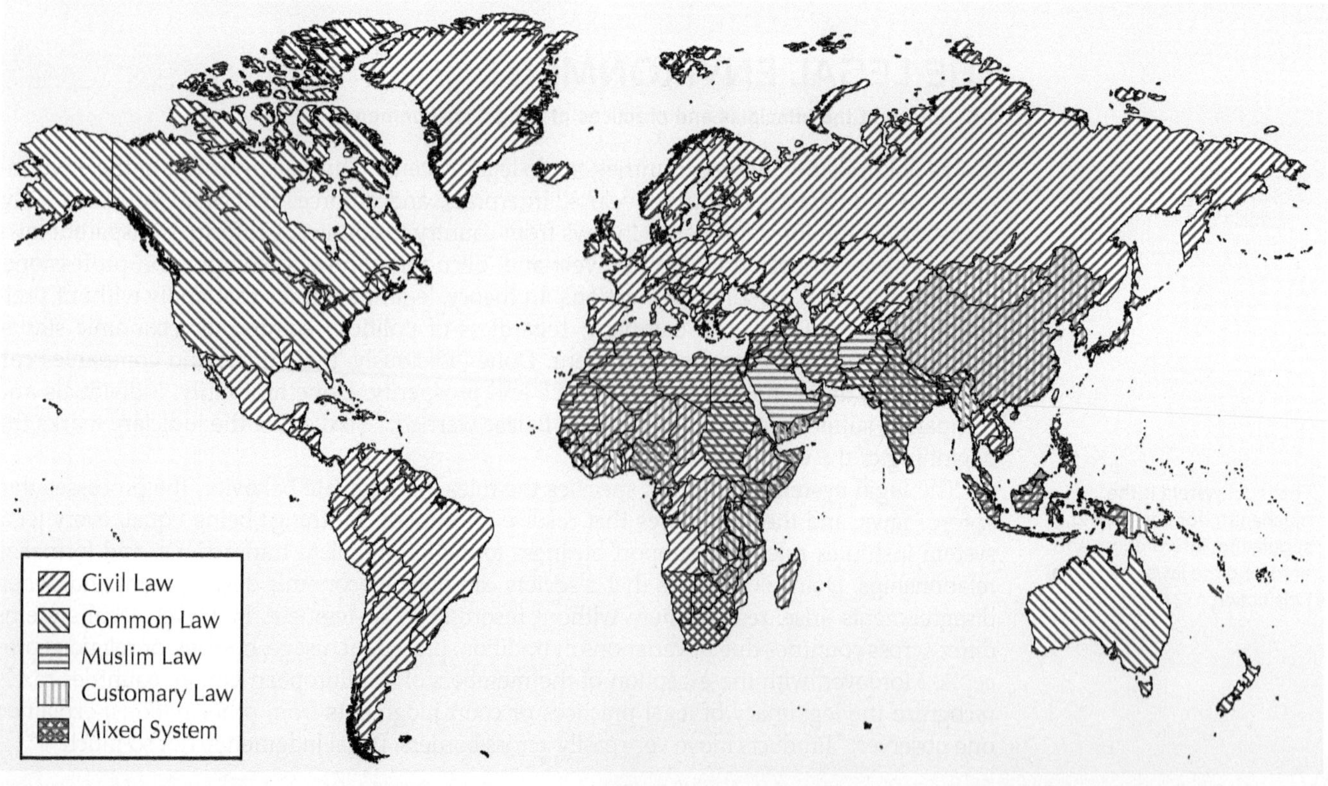

The globalization of business, especially expanding cross-national contact, communication, and collaboration, promotes the standardization of legal principles and practices. Transnational institutions, notably the UN, OECD, IMF, and WIPO, in advocating universal outlooks, ease convergence across countries. Still, enduring philosophical outlooks and political policies sustain distinct types of legal systems. Map 3.4 identifies the primary types that prevail today, namely common law, civil law, theocratic law, customary law, and mixed systems.[71]

Common law is derived from judicial decisions of courts; its defining characteristic is that it emerged as precedent.

Common Law The **common law** system relies on tradition, judge-made precedent, and usage. Philosophically, it is based on English common law concepts and gives precedence to case law. Judicial officers consult statutory codes and legislation, but only after considering the rules of the court, custom, judicial reasoning, prior court decisions, and principles of equity. The doctrine of *stare decisis* is a distinguishing feature—it obliges judges to respect the precedent of prior court rulings.[72] Common law has Anglo-American legacies; it prevails in, among others, Australia, Canada, England, Hong Kong, New Zealand, and the United States.

Civil law codifies core principles that serve as the primary source of law.

Civil Law The **civil law** system relies on the systematic codification of detailed laws. Philosophically, civil (derivative of *civilian*) law draws its inspiration from Roman law and gives precedence to the written law. Political officials, rather than judges, translate legal principles into a compendium of regulatory statutes. Rather than create law, as they do in the common law system, judges apply the relevant statutes to resolve disputes. Likewise, in contrast to *stare decisis*, judicial officers in the civil law system are not bound by precedent. Statutory codes, however, regulate their authority. Similarly, notaries public play minor roles in the common law system, but are important gatekeepers as well as regulators of contracts and certificates in the civil law system. Civil law is the most widespread type of legal system in the world; we find it in approximately 150 countries, including Azerbaijan, Chile, France, Germany, Japan, Kuwait, Mexico, Russia, Switzerland, and Thailand.

Theocratic law applies the inspirations and instructions of religious teachings.

Theocratic Law The **theocratic law** system relies on religious doctrine, precepts, and beliefs. Ultimate authority is vested in religious leaders, who regulate business transactions and social relations based on their interpretation of a sacred text. For instance, Iran's President Hassan Rouhani defers to the final say of Iran's Supreme Leader, cleric Ayatollah Ali Khamenei. Theocratic laws see no separation of church and state; government, law, and religion are one. The most prevalent theocratic system, Muslim or Islamic law, *Shari'a*, is based on the Qur'an (Koran), the *Sunnah* (decisions and sayings of the Prophet Muhammad), the writings of Islamic scholars, and the consensus of legal communities in Muslim countries.[73] Muslim law prevails in the Middle East and North Africa. However, modernists (e.g., Turkey, Indonesia), traditionalists (e.g., Kuwait, Malaysia), and fundamentalists (e.g., Iran, Saudi Arabia) advocate different interpretations of *Shari'a*.

Customary law is based on norms of behavior that gain legitimacy through ongoing practice.

Customary Law The **customary law** system reflects the wisdom of the routines and rituals of everyday life or, more formally, enduring spiritual legacies and time-honored philosophical outlooks. It anchors legal systems in many indigenous communities, defining the rights and responsibilities of members. The legitimacy of customary law follows not from the stamp of a powerful person or institution, but from individuals willingly accepting the benefits of complying with community standards. Offenses are treated as torts (i.e., private wrongs or injuries rather than crimes against the state or society). Customary law prevails in many developing countries, particularly in Africa. Few nations, notably Andorra, Guernsey, and Jersey, operate under a wholly customary legal system. Rather, this type often plays a role in countries that use a mixed legal system.

Mixed System The **mixed legal system** results when a nation uses two or more of the preceding types; each type applies cumulatively or interactively, as well as locations where no type clearly predominates. Map 3.4 shows that one finds most mixed systems in Africa and Asia. Potential mixes run the gamut—one finds countries blending two to four types. The Philippines, South Africa, and Guyana, for instance, blend civil and common law. Bangladesh, Singapore, and Pakistan blend common and theocratic law. Indonesia, Djibouti, and Oman blend theocratic law with civil codes. India, Nigeria, Malaysia, and Kenya mix common, theocratic, and customary law. Lastly, Bahrain, Qatar, Somalia, and Yemen combine common, civil, theocratic, and customary law.

THE CONTEXT OF LEGALITY

CONCEPT CHECK

As we saw in Chapter 1, national business environments vary. Unquestionably, there are points of convergence. Still, IB activity requires recognizing enduring differences across countries. Here, we stress that the foundations of legal systems differ in terms of principles and practices.

In general, legality is that which makes something legal or, for that matter, illegal; to wit, "no crime exists if an action is not a crime in that specific jurisdiction."[74] The context of legality creates confidence or, if absent, fans anxieties, in the legal system. If legitimately established, the legal system gives managers confidence in the sanctity of property rights, quality of contract enforcement, integrity of the police, fairness of the courts, and protection from crime and violence. Hence, legal environments marked by accountability, transparency, legitimacy, and justice, all of which constitute the context of legality, inspire different choices, and elicit different consequences than those environments marred by uncertainty, arbitrariness, and illegitimacy. The preceding profile of the types of legal systems in the world gives a sense of how countries institute a system of legality. In principle, all systems function effectively. In practice, questions often arise. Assessing the gap between principle and practice calls for assessing the context of legality in terms of the basis of rule in a nation.

The World Bank helps managers appraise the basis of rule in a nation. Specifically, as seen in Map 3.5, the World Bank assesses a nation's legal system to determine whether its basis of rule favors the law or favors the "man." Before explaining those ideas, a quick look at Map 3.5 shows that the rule of law prevails in westernized countries, notably, the United States, Canada, Japan, New Zealand, Australia, and most of Europe. Alternatively, the countries that fall in the long arc that starts in northern Russia, cuts southward through China, veers to South East Asia, travels toward the Middle East, and moves through Africa over to South America spotlight the pervasiveness of the rule of man. Conclusion? Diametrically different interpretations of legality in different nations require that managers ask, "What is the basis of rule in a country—is it the law or is it the man?"

MAP 3.5 The Basis of Rule

The coding of this map profiles the basis of rule worldwide. Canada's classification at the 90th percentile indicates the pervasiveness of the rule of law in its legal environment. Conversely, Afghanistan's classification below the 10th percentile indicates its absence or, alternatively, the pervasiveness of the rule of man in its legal environment.[75]

Source: Kaufmann, D., A. Kraay, and M. Mastruzzi (2010). The Worldwide Governance Indicators: Methodology and Analytical Issues. The Worldwide Governance Indicators are available at: www.govindicators.org. © 2018 The World Bank Group. All Rights Reserved.

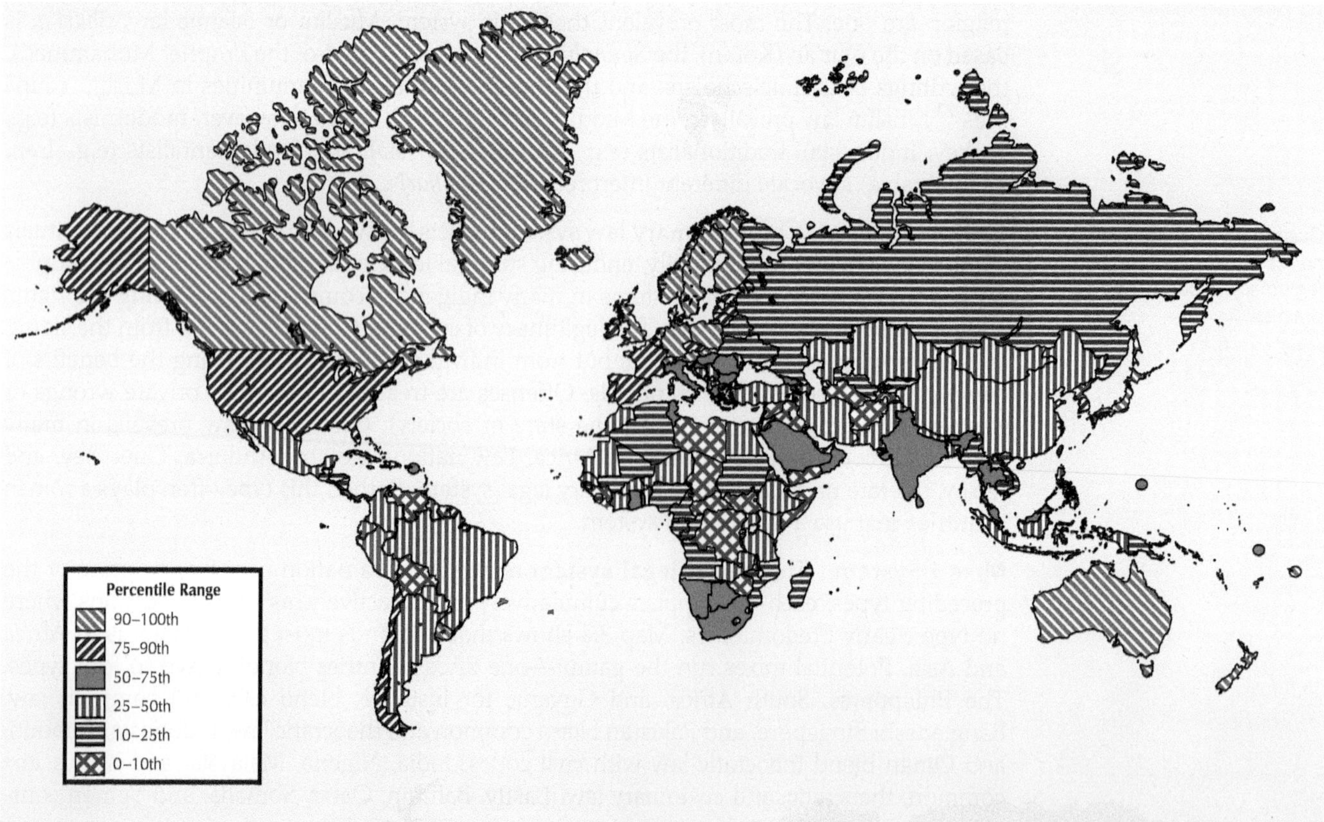

The rule of law holds that no individual, from president to peon, is above laws that are clearly specified, commonly understood, and fairly enforced.

The Rule of Law The Magna Carta, signed in 1215, is seen as the genesis of the **rule of law**; it established the principle that everyone, from king to peasant, is subject to the same laws, which are enforced in the same way. Likewise, in 1776, the U.S. Declaration of Independence's decree that "all men are created equal" reiterated that everyone, no matter how powerful or powerless, is subject to the same laws.[76] Today, one sees various expressions of this outlook. For instance, in front of courthouses worldwide stands a statue of Lady Justice, carrying a sword and measuring balance, sometimes wearing a blindfold, sometimes with eyes closed. Her sword symbolizes the power of the court; her scales the competing claims of the petitioners; and her "blindness" that justice is meted objectively, without fear or favor, to each and all. Justice is impartial and transparent, not arbitrary and self-serving. In the abstract, the rule of law is a transcendent principle. Operationally, it safeguards equality and fairness in society.

The rule of law advocates a legal system that is clear, publicized, and protective of fundamental rights. Laws are developed, administered, and enforced transparently; all citizens have access to a competent, independent, and ethical judiciary; all officials are accountable to the law of the land; and governmental authority is legitimately exercised in accordance with written, publicly disclosed laws.[77] Successfully instituted, citizens then regard constitutional principles as legitimate, criminal codes as just, and commercial/civil matters as fair.

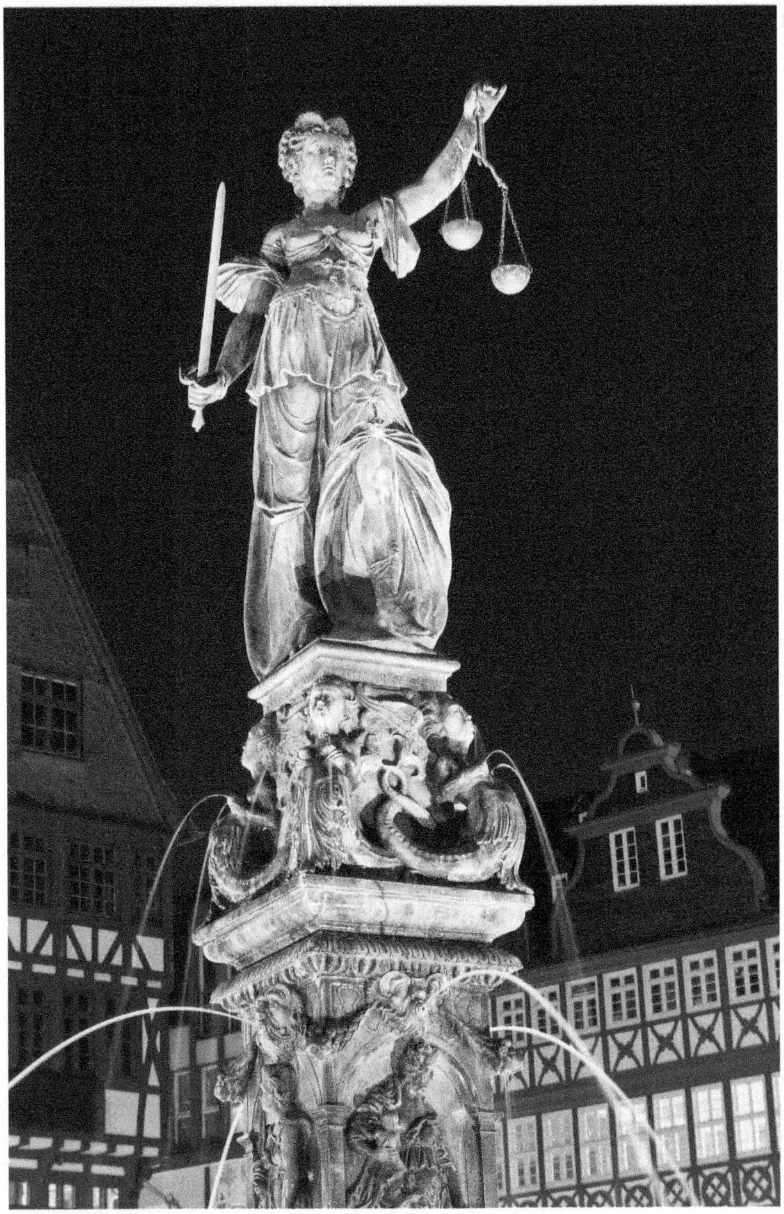

Source: Patrick/123RF

Lady Justice, here seen in Römer Square in Frankfurt, Germany, is an allegorical personification of the moral force of the rule of law.[79]

Democracy, fortified by the rule of law, works precisely because it has the legal tools to regulate power, in any and all forms.[78] Besides instituting a just political environment, the rule of law guarantees the enforceability of commercial contracts, business transactions, and the sanctity of property rights. Companies rely on its legitimacy to validate the laws, codes, and statutes that regulate their activities.

The rule of man holds that the ruler, in whatever form, commands authority that is above the law.

The Rule of Man The thesis that ultimate authority resides in a person whose word and whim, no matter how unfair or unjust, is the law anchors the doctrine of the **rule of man**. For much of history, rulers and law were one and the same—the law was the will of the ruler, whether in the form of king, empress, shogun, tsar, maharajah, chief, caliph, etc. Today, these titles have given way to others, such as chairman, commandant, comrade, generalissimo, or supreme leader. No matter the title, the rule of man defines a legal system in which the actions of the leader are unrestricted by a constitution, unregulated by criminal codes, and beyond civil challenge. For example, Saddam Hussein, former president of Iraq, imperiously declared the "law is anything I write on a scrap of paper."[80] In China, party members accused of wrongdoing answer to the CCP first, not to the law of the land, precisely because "the Party sits outside, and above the law."[81]

Nations that set the basis of rule in terms of the rule of man institute a legal system where the sovereign leader creates the law, officials are obedient agents, and citizens are powerless subjects. The law is an apparatus of the state, used to suppress threats to, and reward support for, its authority. Constitutional issues are discretionary, criminal law is arbitrary, and opportunism taints commercial and civil matters. The rule of man is an instrumental device of totalitarianism.

In countries where the rule of man is the basis of law, acceptable marketplace behavior is unpredictable. Managers stay alert to trumped-up charges, solicitation of bribes, favoritism of local rivals, and the primacy of cronyism over competencies. For example, in the West, property rights—namely, the legal authority to determine how one controls, benefits from, and transfers property—are so taken for granted that they rarely cross our minds. One cannot say the same for many countries in Asia, Africa, the Middle East, and South America. There, the historic centrality of the rule of man makes the principles and practices of the rule of law remote abstractions and, hence, ambiguous property rights. Put differently, the rule of law has a negligible legacy in the legal traditions of many now emerging economies, most with legacies of authoritarian governance by the "man." As a result, vague property rights in countries like Russia, China, Venezuela, Malaysia, Ukraine, Saudi Arabia, and Vietnam pose ongoing concerns.[82]

THE BASIS OF RULE: LEGACIES AND TRENDS

CONCEPT CHECK

As developed in Chapter 2, a country's cultural orientation toward notions of power, status, accountability, equity, and fairness shape the principles that anchor its legal environment.

From 1215 to 1776 and onward, the rule of law anchored the legal evolution of several nations, most notably Great Britain, the United States, France, and Germany. By the late twentieth century, it was the undisputed foundation of legality in westernized countries. The Third Wave of Democratization, in diffusing neoliberal ideals of democracy, championed an individual's inalienable legal rights and instituted systems of due process to protect them. These changes spread the rule of law worldwide. In many countries, both developed and developing, the law grew more transparent, the courts more impartial, and officials more accountable. Executives increasingly looked to the law, not the "man," to interpret matters in a fair, just manner in more nations. Markets once considered unduly risky grew politically stable and legally predictable as the rule of law gained legitimacy.

CONCEPT CHECK

Chapter 1 suggests that democratic political systems offer MNEs the freedom to engage in their preferred modes of international business. Democracy's retreat creates big questions about how countries might use their legal system to regulate business activity.

History shows that as countries moved from agrarian to industrial economies, increasingly prosperous citizens called for laws to protect their increasingly vital property rights. Sustaining economic development, as well as protecting growing wealth, required a legal system not under the direction of the "man," but based on just, fair, and transparent laws. Therefore, extrapolating from history, the shift from agrarianism to industrialism in emerging economies, goes the reasoning, should see countries, such as China, Nigeria, Peru, Thailand, and Malaysia, following precedent and moving from the rule of man to the rule of law.

Ominous Trends Contemporary developments complicate predictions. Democracy's ongoing decline has slowed the diffusion of the rule of law. Whereas the rule of law is the cornerstone of democracy, the rule of man is the cornerstone of authoritarianism—simply put, one cannot be the "man" if one must answer to the law. Fading freedom and struggling democracy, hence, relieve pressure on the "man" to institute the rule of law. Similarly, China's market performance challenges, if not rejects, the thesis that a direct relationship exists between the rule of law and economic growth.[83] China's status as the world's largest recipient of foreign investment over the past few decades, notwithstanding its record of opaque governance, crony capitalism, and persistent corruption, questions the absolute necessity of the rule of law. One sees similar situations in Russia, Saudi Arabia, Belarus, Rwanda, Turkey, and Turkmenistan. Increasing foreign investments in those sorts of markets, by the way, highlights foreign investors' ingenuity to prosper in places where the basis of rule is not the law but the "man."

The growing confidence of emerging economies increasingly questions the presumption that "the West knows best."

Philosophical Perspectives Different philosophical legacies in different nations moderate the preferred basis of rule. The forecast of the rule of law as the inevitable end-state for all nations presumes that the legal philosophies of the West apply to all. Instead, some counter that the "West does not know best," reasoning that the efficiency, stability, and harmony of authoritarianism matter more than the liberty, freedom, and happiness of a democracy. Explained a prominent Western commentator, "One-party autocracy certainly has its drawbacks. But when it is led by a reasonably enlightened group of people, as China is today, it can also have great advantages."[84] Interestingly, the current leader of China, Xi Jinping, advises the West that "your democracy is the democracy of Greece and ancient Rome, and that's your tradition. We have our own traditions."[85] Indeed, throughout its storied 4000-year history, Chinese civilization has never practiced Western conceptions of legality. Rather, as dynasties came and went, each followed its "mandate of heaven," adopted authoritarianism, and instituted the rule of man. Today, in the realm of IB, China is the exemplar; other countries apply similar principles and practices.

IMPLICATIONS TO MANAGERS

Uncertainty about the basis of rule and the goals of government throughout much of the world creates risky legal environments. Yes, operating in markets regulated by the rule of law sees the consistent application of legitimate laws. However, operating in markets regulated by the rule of man sees arbitrary regulation. A glance at Maps 3.2 and 3.3 helps explains the situation. Countries that Freedom House rates as "Partly Free" or "Not Free" or that the EIU classifies as "hybrid regime" or "authoritarian regime" lie in the "rule of man arc" identified in Map 3.5. Collectively, these maps highlight that rising authoritarianism in many countries calls into question the thesis of their progressive adoption of the rule of law. Generally, authoritarian governments use the legal system, in the context of the rule of man, to regulate business activity to support and sustain the state. As authoritarianism surges and democracy retreats, the basis of rule moves from the law to the man.

Recall earlier observations on legal affairs in China. Doing business there, said an observer, means dealing with "a society that had . . . plenty of rules, but they were seldom enforced. China appeared to be run by masterful showmen: appearances mattered more than substance, the rules were there to be distorted."[86] Moreover, the CCP's official status above the law further complicates determining what is right and what is wrong. China is not the exception. The ambiguities that permeate Russia's legal code means businesses "cannot even keep track of the law, let alone decide whether to follow it."[87] Likewise, in Belarus, Kazakhstan, or Venezuela, all rule-of-man systems, writs, injunctions, and lawsuits are trapped in a slow-grinding legal machine that answers to the leader, not to impartial legal standards.[88] Folks who are in the good graces of the "man," whether Alexander Lukashenko of Belarus, Kassym-Jomart Tokayev of Kazakhstan, or Nicolás Maduro of Venezuela, flourish.[89]

Market Realities Certainly, as had long been the case, Western companies could opt to bypass these sorts of legally risky markets. Throughout the 20th century, this was a reasonable option. Western markets provided ample opportunities for productive, profitable activity. Generally, markets that practiced the rule of man were on the periphery of the global economy, typically providing raw materials or low-cost labor. The occasional dispute between an adventurous Western company and the locals was usually resolved in the favor of the former. Hence, for Western MNEs, the basis of rule was important, but not decisive, and managers had various means to deflect the arbitrariness of the "man."

Today, slow growth in the West moves the fast-growing emerging economies to the center of the global market. Abundant supply of inexpensive, productive resources along with accelerating local demand is a siren call few MNEs can resist. As GE's former CEO explained, "We've globalized around markets . . . Today we go to Brazil, we go to China, we go to India because that's where the customers are."[90] Looking forward, 400 midsize emerging-market cities (many unfamiliar to the West, such as Bamako, Chittagong, Ibadan, Kinshasa, Ouagadougou, and Sanaa) will generate nearly 40 percent of global growth over the next 15 years.[91] Almost all fall within the rule of man arc identified in Map 3.5.

Operating in different markets with different conceptions of legality requires assessing the foundation of legality to understand how local officials will regulate activities.

MNEs, long accustomed to operating by the rule of law in markets like Germany and Japan, increasingly operate in markets anchored in the rule of man, like China and Russia. Hence, managers navigate legal systems based on the rule of man found in vital markets of the global economy. Lastly, growing demands from increasingly wealthy citizens for stronger property rights, by forcing the accountability of public officials, may gradually push for the protection instituted by the rule of law.[92] Currently, though, as seen in fading freedom and democracy's retreat, authoritarianism and its instrumentality, the rule of man, influence IB.

LEGAL ISSUES FACING INTERNATIONAL COMPANIES

3-6 Describe legal issues facing international companies

CONCEPT CHECK

A theme of the text is the expanding linkages among individuals, companies, countries, and institutions. Here, we emphasize the importance of relationships between ideas and ideals, namely the interplay among a country's political system and legal doctrine. Making these connections helps managers assess the systemic nature of a country's business environment.

The globalization of markets progressively standardizes many aspects of the legal environment. Countries intent on attracting foreign investment develop consistent politics to build attractive markets. Likewise, officials fortify positive reputations with transparent regulations that are easily accessible and objectively administered. Well-designed rules discourage corruption, improve accountability, and boost economic growth. Expanding membership in transnational organizations accelerates these trends. For instance, the European Union requires that member countries meet standards of the rule of law; the World Bank requires borrowers agree to legal reforms; and the WTO institutes trade regulations that supersede national statutes.

Despite convergence, different countries regulate business activity differently. Variability follows from differences in orientation toward individualism versus collectivism, ideals of freedom, political ideologies, and outlook on the basis of rule. Moreover, new forms of business activity along with changing patterns of trade and investment create legal uncertainties. Consequently, managers adjust operations and strategies to obey local laws.

THE LEGALITY OF BUSINESS PRACTICES

The legal system moderates practical aspects of business operations, including how managers

- start a business,
- enter and enforce contracts,
- hire and fire workers,
- close a business.

The World Bank maintains that productive business activity requires fair, just, and transparent rules that (1) set and sustain property rights, (2) minimize the costs and complications of resolving disputes, (3) specify rules that reduce the riskiness of transactions, and (4) organize rules to protect contractual partners against abuse. Annually, the World Bank assesses how well countries meet these standards in terms of the influence of local laws on the day-to-day operations of private companies. It tracks microlevel characteristics of the regulatory frameworks in 190 countries, looking at the costs, requirements, and procedures in terms of starting a business, dealing with construction permits, employing workers, registering property, getting credit, protecting investors, taxes, trading across borders, enforcing contracts, getting an electricity connection, and closing a business. To get a sense of the situation, let's take a look at the ins-and-outs of starting, running, and closing a business around the world.

Starting a Business Starting a business involves activities such as registering its name, identifying the appropriate tax classification, obtaining licenses and permits, arranging credit, and securing insurance. Some countries expedite this process, others complicate it. For instance, India imposes a battery of regulations on multi-brand foreign chains, such as Walmart, Carrefour, and IKEA. They must operate as joint ventures, have no higher than a 51 percent ownership share, direct at least half of their capital investments into processing infrastructure, and open outlets only in cities that have at least one million residents.[93]

At the micro level, a Brazilian entrepreneur recalled his experience starting his company in his home country; obtaining authorizations, licenses, and permits from seven different ministries took about 150 days. Subsequently, he launched a U.S.-based business and noted that "within a week I had formed an LLC (limited liability corporation), incorporated in Delaware, and set up bank accounts."[94] Similarly, start-up is a straightforward process in Canada, requiring two registration procedures that cover tax, labor, and administrative declarations. Conversely, Vietnam imposes eight procedural requirements, including regulations for bank deposits, court registration, health benefits, and so on. The upshot: it takes about a day and a half to start a business in Canada versus 17 days in Vietnam.

Entering and Enforcing Contracts Once up and running, companies enter contracts with buyers and sellers.[95] The sanctity of a contract is vital to business transactions. The United Nations Convention on Contracts for the International Sale of Goods sets guidelines for negotiating and enforcing contracts. Still, practices vary across legal systems. Countries using a common law system, for instance, encourage precise, detailed contracts, whereas a civil law system allows broader agreements. Similar tendencies show up in contract-enforcement policies. Australia, Norway, and the United Kingdom impose the fewest number of enforcement procedures. Burundi, Angola, Bolivia, Cameroon, El Salvador, Mexico, and Panama require many. Hence, Australia needs 402 days to enforce a contract, Bolivia, 591 days, and Cameroon, 800 days.

Hiring and Firing No matter where a firm operates, it must hire and, when necessary, fire workers. Worldwide, workplace regulation and employment law speak to how workers are hired, what they are paid, how many hours they can work, and how they are fired. Singapore, New Zealand, and the United States have flexible labor-regulation statutes. China allows greater flexibility in hiring, firing, and setting employment conditions (e.g., work hours, minimum wages, and benefits). In contrast, Angola, Belarus, India, and Paraguay strictly regulate how companies terminate employees as well as require generous severance payments. For instance, India's national government specifies nearly 60 labor laws, including its Industrial Disputes Act, which requires a company employing 100 or more workers to obtain state permission before firing anyone, even if it has hit hard times.[96] Meanwhile, India's 28 states and 9 union territories enforce many more laws. Add it all up and companies are reluctant to hire, given how difficult it is to fire workers.

Getting Out or Going Under Closing a business involves more than turning out the lights, padlocking the doors, and slinking away. In Western markets, the bankruptcy process is anchored in the English bankruptcy law of 1732, the first modern law to address this issue, and its progressive revision, beginning in 1800, by the United States. Ireland, Japan, Canada, and Hong Kong, for instance, make shutting down "fast" (between four to eight months) and cheap (between 1 and 10 percent of the estate).[97] The situation differs in developing countries. India's lack of a comprehensive bankruptcy code complicates dealing with creditors, officials, and courts, which in turn discourages bankruptcy; about 25 percent of Indian creditors get their money back when the typical company goes bust versus 77 percent in Europe and the United States.[98] Hence, fewer firms file for bankruptcy in India than in the West. Bankruptcy in Indonesia, Vietnam, and Ecuador is slow (between five to eight years) and expensive (between 10 and 30 percent of the estate). Alternatively, Burundi, Cambodia, Dominica, and Guinea-Bissau, among others, stipulate no standards to govern dissolution.

THE LEGALITY OF BUSINESS STRATEGIES

The legal system moderates strategic aspects of business operations, including

- product origin and local content,
- marketplace behavior,
- legal jurisdiction,
- product safety and liability,
- intellectual property protection.

Day-to-day business activities focus managers' attention on the practicalities of opening, running, and closing a business. Strategic concerns direct their attention to long-term issues that shape the competitiveness, profitability, and sustainability of the firm. This section takes a look at how a country's legal environment influences an MNE's s business strategies in terms of making a product, marketing it, and safeguarding its proprietary features.

Product Regulation National laws affect the flow of products across borders. Host governments set laws that regulate access based on the product's **country of origin**—the country where it was extracted, grown, produced, or manufactured. Some countries apply this policy to product labels, under the title COOL (country-of-origin labeling), to inform consumers and support local producers. National security concerns also shape country-of-origin regulations. Suspicions concerning the espionage capabilities of their communication products, for example, plague Chinese MNEs Huawei and ZTE. Officials in the West object to their opaque governance and linkages to the Communist Party of China. National security concerns have led Australia, Canada, and the United States, among others, to exclude their network equipment from public contracts.[99]

Politicians also enact regulations to protect jobs, appease voters, placate special interests, and preserve tax revenue. Understandably, host governments prefer that MNEs make the greatest possible portion of their product(s) locally. Besides boosting local enterprise, technology transfers and knowledge spillovers support domestic innovation. To spur reluctant companies, governments enforce **local content** regulations, thereby requiring that a certain percentage of intermediate goods used in the production processes come from domestic suppliers.

Russia, for example, imposes aggressive data localization laws that require data collected electronically be processed and stored locally before being allowed to move beyond its borders. India requires single-brand retail stores, like Apple or Nike, to source at least 30 percent of the local value of their goods from Indian firms. The United States' Buy American Act requires its public agencies look first to homemade products, then, if necessary, foreign alternatives. Similarly, its Jones Act requires that ships moving goods or people between U.S. ports be owned and operated by citizens of the United States. Likewise, China requires foreign film makers to meet quotas on the number of foreign films released, profit-sharing agreements, and requirements to sell rights to domestic companies. So, for example, U.S. companies can export 34 films per year into China on a revenue-sharing basis and a further 30 to 40 films on a flat-fee basis; in the latter, Chinese companies license them for foreign distribution but do not share box office revenue with the licensor.

Product Safety and Liability Regulation Countries impose product-safety and liability laws that require an MNE adapt a product or else forsake market access. As a rule, wealthier countries impose stringent standards, whereas poorer countries, reflecting developing legal codes and rule of man legacies, inconsistently apply broader regulations. Currently, the European Union's product-liability directive shapes global standards.[100] It outlines the legal responsibility of manufacturers and stipulates the process of liability compensation claims. Then again, some MNEs preempt risks. The Danish toy maker Lego, for instance, noted consumers' fear of the possible toxicity of plastic toys made in China and did not open a factory there. Instead, Lego opened factories in comparatively more expensive, but less worrisome, Mexico and Eastern Europe.[101]

Legal Jurisdiction IB transactions, by definition, cross national borders. In the event of a dispute, determining which country's legal system takes precedence is the matter of legal jurisdiction. Expectedly, each company in a contract dispute claims its laws apply in the belief that it will receive favorable treatment from its home courts. This situation is especially pressing when an MNE from a rule of law system, say Canada, has legal difficulties in a rule of man environment, say Bolivia. Moreover, intricate ownership patterns coupled with interdependent operations spanning multiple countries often make it difficult to determine legal jurisdiction. Hence, MNEs specify a **choice-of-law clause** in contracts that stipulates whose laws, when necessary, govern dispute resolution. Similarly, contracts usually include arbitration provisions, whereby companies agree to resolve potential disputes outside of court through agencies such as the International Court of Arbitration.

Intellectual Property In Adam Smith's time, countries drew strength from their agricultural prowess. Later, smokestack industries defined a nation's prosperity and power. Now, countries look to their brainpower to create might, prestige, and wealth. We call this output **intellectual property (IP)**—the creative ideas, proprietary works, innovative expertise, or intangible insights, often in the form of inventions, literary and artistic works, symbols, names, images, designs, or processes, that create a competitive advantage for an individual, company, or country. The rising power of ideas in the global economy has made protecting IP a growing concern.

CONCEPT CHECK

Chapters 1 and 2 note that income levels influence how countries, both rich and poor, develop their business environments. It also influences countries' approach to regulating MNEs' operations and strategies.

Mainstream thought holds that an individual's right to own IP stimulates innovation. Effectively, it you make it and register ownership, then it's your legal right to decide who may use it; fundamentally, this perspective taps the ideals of individualism. Alternatively, others advocate less-stringent protection, arguing that IP rights are state-created monopoly privileges that inhibit local development and lower global welfare by constraining the use of knowledge. Effectively, if you create something, it should benefit the collective. For example, when asked about software piracy in his country, a South Korean diplomat explained, "[H]istorically, Koreans have not viewed intellectual discoveries or scientific inventions as the private property of the discoverers or inventors. New ideas or technologies [are] 'public goods' for everybody to share freely. Cultural esteem rather than material gain [is] the incentive for creativity."[102]

Currently, the individualistic perspective predominates. Transnational institutions—notably, the World Intellectual Property Organization (WIPO), along with governments and industry associations—push for stronger protection. The primary safeguard is an **intellectual property right (IPR)**; it grants the registered owners of IP the legal authority to decide who may use its property and under what circumstances. Essentially, an IPR constitutes a legally enforceable, but limited monopoly granted by a country to the innovator.

Matters of jurisdiction complicate protecting IPRs. A U.S. patent, for example, establishes an IPR only in the United States and its territories and possessions; it does not extend to other nations. There's no shortcut to worldwide protection—a company cannot register a "global" patent, trademark, or copyright. Although an IPR sounds secure, enforcing it is difficult. For example, in the United States, companies can go after the makers and sellers, not users, of counterfeit goods.[103] Worldwide, governments claim to abide by these agreements and enforce IPRs. However, pirates continue counterfeiting popular, pricey, and vital products.

MNEs invest great effort to safeguard their intellectual property. The pervasiveness of piracy worldwide makes for a mind-boggling challenge. Our closing case, "It's a Knockoff World," profiles this situation. Weak enforcement in some countries, particularly those marked by a rule of man bias and authoritarian politics, imposes tough obstacles. Other problems arise because some advocate a collectivist interpretation that rejects individual property rights. Expectedly, countries that observe the rule of law, as opposed to the rule of man, more aggressively protect intellectual property rights. Hence, the predominant share of counterfeit products is made in countries in which the rule of man prevails.

Lastly, complications follow from the fact that not all countries endorse agreements that protect IPRs—primarily, the Paris Convention for the Protection of Industrial Property and the Berne Convention for the Protection of Literary and Artistic Works. Both emerged in the 1880s and are periodically updated. The WTO's Trade-Related Aspects of Intellectual Property Rights (TRIPS) broadens IP protection. Meanwhile, the EU continues moving toward instituting a "unitary patent" that is legally binding in all member countries.

POLITICS, LAW, AND BUSINESS

3-7 Relate the ideas of politics, law, and business

Table 3.4 identifies the top- and bottom-ranked countries whose political and legal policies institute, respectively, the most or least supportive business environments. In terms of the former, politically stable and legally predictable Singapore fosters the most favorable business environment in the world. Conversely, the Central African Republic's political instability and legal shortcomings create the world's least favorable business environment. Digging deeper into the data highlights a key relationship: most of the top-ranked countries have a democratic political system and a common or civil law legal system anchored in the rule of law. In contrast, most bottom-ranked countries exhibit authoritarian politics and a mixed legal system anchored in the rule of man.

TABLE 3.4 Easy Here, Hard There: Doing Business in Various Countries

The World Bank ranks 190 countries on their respective ease of doing business—the higher the score, the more favorable the business environment. Technically, the index averages the country's percentile rankings on ten dimensions: starting a business, dealing with construction permits, employing workers, registering property, getting credit, protecting investors, paying taxes, trading across borders, and enforcing contracts. Here we see the best and worst performers.

Country	Ranking	Country	Ranking
New Zealand	1	Timor-Leste	181
Singapore	2	Chad	182
Hong Kong SAR, China	3	Congo, Dem. Rep	183
Denmark	4	Central African Republic	184
South Korea	5	South Sudan	185
United States	6	Libya	186
Georgia	7	Yemen	187
United Kingdom	8	Venezuela	188
Norway	9	Eritrea	189
Sweden	10	Somalia	190

Source: Doing Business 2020. The World Bank. Retrieved January 29, 2020 from https://www.doingbusiness.org/en/doingbusiness

CASE

It's a Knockoff World

Worldwide, companies are plagued by piracy—the illegal imitation, copying, or counterfeiting of their intellectual property. It's a tense issue given that it cuts to issues of history, culture, politics, income, development, innovation, competitiveness, and prosperity. Making matters worse is that pirates, besides being everywhere, come in every form: individuals making copies at work, imitators laboring in dingy sweatshops, modern enterprises build to steal, denizens of the dark web dealing in the shadows, and hardened criminals running global syndicates.

The problem is straightforward: intellectual property (IP), in the form of books, music, product designs, brand names, process innovations, software, film, and the like, is tough to create but easy to copy. Moreover, notwithstanding moral shortcomings, pirates do not lack initiative or imagination. In our knockoff world, if it's being made, it's likely being faked. Fair game includes virtually everything—from the humble aspirin to the flashy Ferrari.[104] And, for the kicker, although knockoffs sell for a fraction of the price of the real thing, piracy is astoundingly profitable; gross margins of 500 to 50,000 percent are common.[105] Counterfeit medicines are more profitable than heroin, copywatches may run a couple of bucks to make but sell for $40 in Beijing's Silk Market and $250 on Internet sites, and sales of high-end counterfeit software rival the return from cocaine trafficking.[106]

Big Opportunity, Big Money

IP theft is big business. Globalization and the Internet feed the perfect storm. The former moves much of the world's manufacturing to countries with poor IP protection, while the latter provides cheap, easily accessible marketing platforms and distribution channels. The costs of counterfeit IP, from lost sales, eroded consumer confidence, diminished brand reputation, lower tax revenue, and higher enforcement expenses, is staggering. The International Anti-Counterfeiting Coalition (IACC) estimates that international trade in illegitimate goods runs $1.77 trillion—approximately 10 percent of world merchandise trade. To top it off, piracy has grown more than 10,000 percent in the past three decades—it was a paltry $5.5 billion in 1982.[107]

Microsoft's predicament in China highlights common problems. Copies of its Office and Windows programs are peddled in market stalls for a few dollars, a fraction of their retail price. Rampant software piracy means Microsoft's revenue in China is a small fraction of its U.S. sales—even though personal-computer sales are higher in China. Early on, Microsoft's total revenue in China, with its population of 1.34 billion, was less than what it collected in the Netherlands, a country of 17 million.[108] This situation is not unique to Microsoft; companies worldwide struggle with similar challenges.

Nothing Is Off-Limits

Many think piracy is a problem for snobby brands. Certainly, pirates target high-end brands like Nike, North Face, Hermès, Lipitor, Adidas, and Louis Vuitton. Then, they easily knock off Chloé ankle boots, Chanel Le Boy bags, Saint Laurent wallets, or c Ray-Ban shades. Luxury fakes, however, account for about 5 percent of the problem. The remaining 95 percent include copies of everyday products. Nothing is off-limits; "If it's making money over here in the U.S., it's going to be reverse-engineered or made overseas."[109]

The pharmaceutical supply chain, for instance, is a pirate's paradise. Rampant counterfeiting threatens global health and safety; imitation medicines annually kill tens of thousands. It's anyone's guess how much fake medicine is floating around the world. The Food and Drug Administration estimates that counterfeits account for 10 percent of all drugs sold in the United States even though that country's drug supply chain is among the safest in the world. Studies of anti-infective treatments in Africa and Southeast Asia peg up to 70 percent as fake.[110] The United Nations estimates that half of the anti-malarial drugs sold in Africa are counterfeits. Pfizer reports finding copies of best-selling drugs, such as Prevnar 13, Lipitor, and Lyrica, in the legitimate supply chains in more than 40 countries.

Waging a Multifront War

Companies, industry associations, and governments use a battery of legal weapons to wage war on the pirates. An enduring approach relies on dispatching squads of lawyers on search-and-destroy missions. Companies lawyer-up to lobby officials, monitor the web, prod Internet providers to take down copycat sites, and file injunctions against illegal sellers. UGG Australia began enforcing its IP upon realizing the prevalence of counterfeit boots. It has shut down thousands of websites selling fake UGGs and blocked many thousands more of illegal online listings. Liz Claiborne, owner of the Juicy Couture and Kate Spade brands, fights legions of websites selling counterfeits; it removed nearly 30,000 auction listings of counterfeits in just a few months.

Some companies prefer high-tech assault. One approach embeds radio frequency identification (RFID) chips in the product packaging to allow precise tracking; IBM, 3M, and Abbot Laboratories are pacesetters. Others provide software programs that track products from factories to consumers. In Ghana, mPedigree's product serialization strategy lets consumers use their mobile phones to authenticate the product; buyers call in a code embossed inside the package to verify its genuineness.[111] Eventually, some anticipate weaving microscopic markers and tags into a product's packaging and, eventually, its formulation.

Governments, pressed by legitimate businesses and watching tax revenues decline, devise aggressive protection programs. The European Union ranks IP theft as a high priority. The United States elevated software piracy from a misdemeanor to a felony and boosted enforcement efforts by threatening to sanction notorious pirates with records of "onerous and egregious" IPR violations (including countries such as China, Russia, Argentina, India, Thailand, Turkey, and Ukraine). Likewise, its Federal Drug Administration has opened offices in China, India, South Africa, and Mexico, among others, taking the fight to the front lines. Elsewhere, rhetoric escalates. The U.S. Trade Representative, for instance, declared, "We must defend ideas, inventions, and creativity from rip-off artists and thieves."[112]

MNEs, officials, and trade associations lobby transnational institutions to build stronger defenses. Industry associations, like the IACC, spearhead efforts to toughen laws. Governments worldwide provide global services in public policy, business development, and consumer education. The World Intellectual Property Organization (WIPO) fortifies IP treaties and spurs members to bolster antipiracy programs. Likewise, the WTO applies the Trade-Related Aspects of Intellectual Property Rights (TRIPS) program to regulate enforcement. It requires member nations to enforce IPRs according to global, not local, standards.

A barrage of legal assaults, novel technologies, smarter investigations, diplomatic efforts, industry initiatives, consumer education, stronger IP policies, aggressive law enforcement, and concerted political, commercial, and institutional action, one would think, should prove more than enough. Then, to make things a bit more interesting, throw in the firepower of the global reach of vigilant MNEs, high-profile legal proceedings, expanding government coordination, and tougher trade agreements. Such a shock-and-awe campaign should devastate the pirates, right? Surprise, surprise: Piracy steadily expands.

"The Bandits Are Everywhere"

The global cat-and-mouse game between MNEs and pirates, far from winding down, escalates. Booming piracy in big, fast-growing emerging markets like China, India, and Nigeria spells big, fast-growing troubles. Inexorably, more and more people enter the global market, many of whom, although poor, are eager to consume the latest, greatest IP for the lowest possible price. Experts warn that this endless quest, shared among billions worldwide, turbocharges piracy.

Crafty pirates quickly overcome IP defenses. They crack licensing codes, duplicate holograms, falsify e-mail headers, manipulate instant messenger apps, spam bots, deploy botnets, and utilize crypto-currencies. Staying one step ahead of the IP police is a widespread competency. "Like drug trafficking, the counterfeiting problem is so massive [that] you don't know how to get a handle on it. The bandits are everywhere."[113] Worrisomely, successful pirates evolve from clever entrepreneurs to sophisticated global networks. "When you are dealing with high-end counterfeits, you are talking about organizations that have a full supply chain, a full distribution chain, a full set of manufacturing tools all in place and it is all based on profits."[114] Lamented one analyst, "Counterfeiting is like a balloon filled with water. You push it on one side, but when you remove your hand, it bounces back even stronger."[115]

Piracy gets a huge boost from the increasing availability of counterfeit goods through Internet channels, such as P2P file-sharing sites, mail-order sites, auction sites, or the dark web. Outgunned and outfoxed, some companies surrender. Foley & Corinna, a high-end handbag maker, explained that as it saw more Internet fakes, it stopped looking altogether. "It's just too frustrating. You can try to do something, but it's so big and so fast."[116] Then again, there are those who see IP theft as the price of doing business. Despite everyday piracy of his products in the Chinese market, an executive reasoned that the profitability of his legal sales more than offset the losses due to counterfeits.[117]

Is Piracy Inevitable?

The pervasiveness of piracy, in the face of aggressive lawyering, sophisticated tracking and tagging technologies, and tighter controls, poses profound questions for protecting IP. Some worry that different legal legacies and political ideologies among countries irresolvably complicate basic issues. The WTO's program, TRIPS, by standardizing codes and norms, should have settled troublesome issues. Still, cross-country variation in the basis of rule, as well as cultural orientation in terms of individualism versus collectivism, constrains its impact.

Despite winning an occasional battle, some fear that companies and countries have lost the war on piracy. Its mind-boggling scale and scope indicate that consumers and businesses worldwide have few ethical qualms about making, buying, and using counterfeits. Take software, for instance. Global software piracy, besides being prevalent, persists. Currently, the worldwide PC software piracy rate runs 37 percent. Put differently, of all the packaged software installed on PCs worldwide, 37 percent was obtained illegally; the cost to companies was nearly $47 billion, up from losses of $29 billion in 2003. For many nations, such as Armenia, Indonesia, Nigeria, Thailand, Ukraine, Venezuela, and Vietnam, software piracy rates run anywhere from 60 to 90 percent. Even the best-behaved nations, like France, Japan, and the United States, report software piracy rates north of 15 percent.[118] Consequently, Microsoft's biggest rival is not another software company—it is counterfeiters.

Right or wrong, the quest to live better lives on tight budgets pushes people to seek counterfeits. Many in collectivist cultures rationalize that IP holders should honor society by abandoning their intrinsically selfish, profit-maximizing business models. Sharing knowledge to benefit all, not protecting it for personal gain, is the moral imperative. Others, championing enterprising individuals pursuing fame and fortune, counter that without protection, ultimately there will be no IP to share or, for that matter, steal. In the meantime, an immense volume of IP is stolen everywhere and anywhere. Companies and countries, looking to sustain innovation and prosperity, scramble for solutions.

QUESTIONS

3-3 Would you expect piracy to thrive in a democracy or, alternatively, a totalitarian state? Why?

3-4 Can you envision a scenario where developers and consumers of IP develop a relationship that eliminates the profitability of piracy?

3-5 Put yourself in the place of a poor individual in a poor country struggling to improve the quality of your life. What thoughts might shape how you interpret the legality of IPRs? Would it matter if those IPRs were held by Western MNEs?

CHAPTER 4

The Economic Environments Facing Businesses

OBJECTIVES

After studying this chapter, you should be able to

4-1 Explain the value of economic analysis

4-2 Distinguish the types of economic environments

4-3 Discuss the idea of economic freedom

4-4 Distinguish the types of economic systems

4-5 Interpret indicators of economic development, performance, and potential

4-6 Discuss elements of economic analysis

4-7 Profile approaches to integrate economic analysis

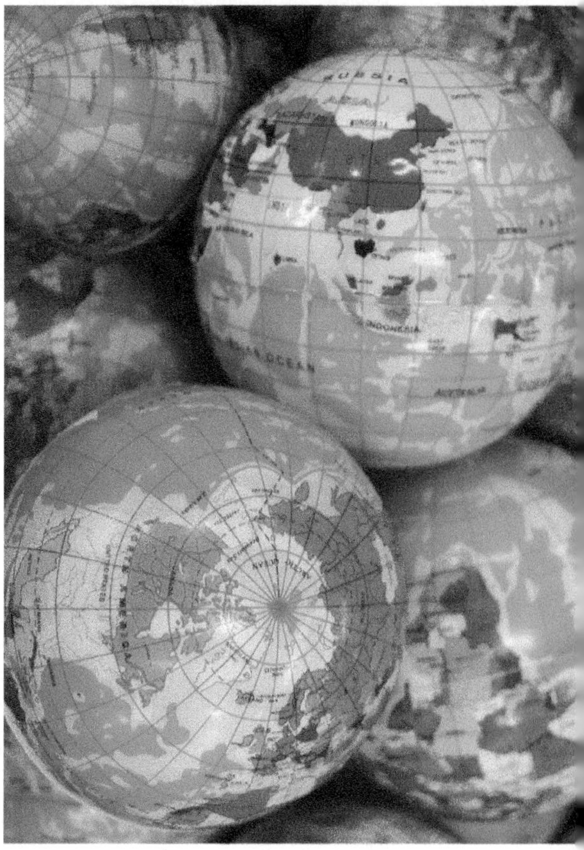

Source: Gumpanat/Shutterstock

▲ Worlds of opportunities and challenges.

One who owes nothing is rich.

—French proverb

CASE

Emerging Economies: Comeback or Collapse?[1]

Worldwide, we watch an epochal shift in the structure of the global economy. By 2050, most of the biggest economies in the world, notably China, India, Japan, Indonesia, and Russia, will be in greater Asia. Their growth will create a second tier of robust economies among their Asian neighbors, such as Australia, Singapore, Philippines, Cambodia, South Korea, Taiwan, Malaysia, Kyrgyzstan, Vietnam, and Thailand. Economies in other, long-sluggish parts of the world, notably Africa and South Africa, will progress along with their Asian counterparts. Although the pace varies, all are moving from the periphery to the center of the global economy.

Figure 4.1 highlights the unfolding consequence. It profiles the shifting **economic center of gravity** in our world—technically, it's estimated by weighting the approximate center of landmass of a country by its total economic output production. Currently, the economic center of gravity is moving from the West, primarily Europe and the United States, toward the East, notably China and India. Earlier, in the 1800s, the productivity and prosperity of the Industrial Revolution had pulled it from the East to the West. Then, soon after World War II, it began cycling back, steadily gaining speed. Presently, it's shifting approximately 140 kilometers/85 miles eastward per year, faster than ever before in history.[2]

Extrapolating from 2020 to 2050, unquestionably, is more speculation than specification. Still, many emerging economies are applying potent pro-growth policies to markets sitting atop of billions of workers and consumers. Hard data confirm their success so far. In 1980, the combined output of emerging economies accounted for 36 percent of total world production. They crossed a milestone in 2009, accounting for more than half. In 2019, their share had climbed to 59 percent. Besides big changes in big places like Shanghai and Mumbai, we see big changes elsewhere. The IMF reports that the 10 fastest-growing markets in the years ahead are in emerging economies. Likewise, 400 midsize emerging-market cities, many unfamiliar in the West, such as Abidjan, Chittagong, Khartoum, Kinshasa, Luanda, and Ouagadougou, will produce about 40 percent of global growth over the next 15 years.[3]

Institutionally, the G-7, originally a Western stronghold, has expanded into the G-20. New members, notably China, India, Brazil, Mexico, and South Korea, now have a greater say in global governance. These new stakeholders advocate different views of economic development than those historically championed in the West. Issues like economic freedom and free markets, long-running anchors in the developed economies, now make room for the ideas of state capitalism and authoritarianism that anchor many emerging economies. Moreover, emerging economies are building transnational institutions, such as the Asia-Pacific Economic Cooperation (APEC) and Asian Infrastructure Investment Bank (AIIB), to advocate their agenda as well as new instrumentalities, such as the China International Payments System (CIPS) and Russia's System for Transfer of Financial Messages (SPFS), to implement it. Collectively, the

FIGURE 4.1 Mapping the Earth's Economic Center of Gravity: 1 CE to 2025

In a shift of millennial significance, the economic center of gravity is returning to Asia.

Sources: Dobbs, R., Jaana Remes, James Manyika, Charles Roxburgh, Sven Smit, and Fabian Schaer. *Urban World: Cities and the Rise of the Consuming Class*. McKinsey Global Institute, 2012. "Asia's Future Is Now | McKinsey." Accessed February 10, 2020. https://www.mckinsey.com/featured-insights/asia-pacific/asias-future-is-now.

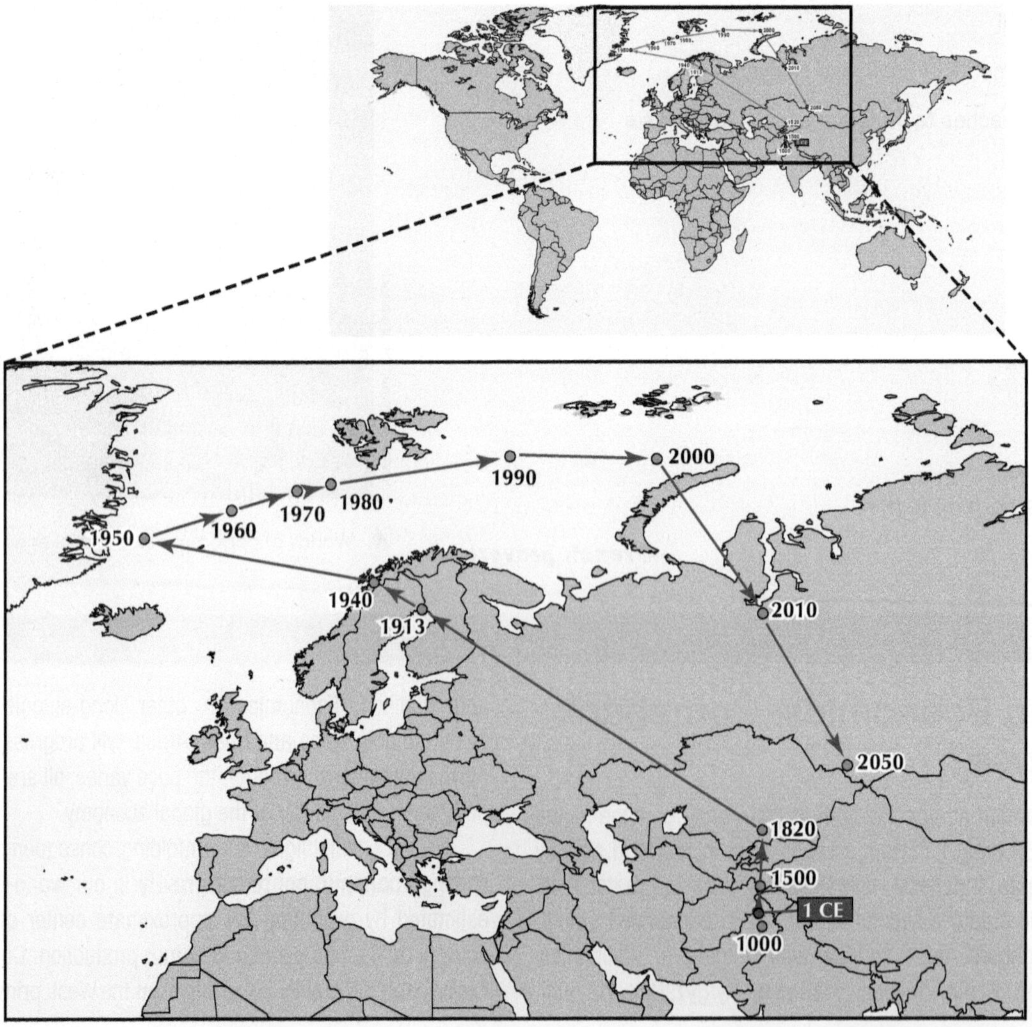

accelerating rise of emerging economies signalled that the wealthier countries of the twentieth century would not dictate the principles and practices of the global economy in the twenty-first century.

The momentum of progress and prosperity in emerging economies suggests the revolution has only begun. Their ambitions to improve infrastructure, increase productivity, create jobs, alleviate poverty, and expand consumption has put into motion what will likely be the biggest economic stimulus in history. The last transformation of similar magnitude—the Industrial Revolution—involved far fewer people in far fewer nations, but still powered a century-and-a-half expansion that changed lives everywhere. Today's revolution spans the globe, includes far more people in far more countries, and represents the biggest opportunity in the history of capitalism.[4]

The transfer of the leadership baton from developed countries to emerging economies, for better and for worse, reorganizes our interpretation of the development, performance, and potential of economic environments. Consequently, managers fine-tune analytics anchored in the developed economies for the radically different circumstances routinely found in emerging economies. Issues like property rights, government regulation, and economic freedom, long taken for granted, are back in play.

TRENDS AND TRANSITIONS

Tracking the past millennium puts the current drama into perspective. Before the steam engine and the power loom pulled economic might from Asia to the West, today's emerging economies dominated world output. From 1000 to the mid-1880s, they produced, on average, 70 to 80 percent of it (see Figure 4.2). Over this span, China and India were the world's two biggest economies; China alone generated one-third of global output in 1850. Beginning in the 1880s, Great Britain converted its booming industrial might into global leadership, and soon supplanted China as the driver of the global economy. Then, as history unfolded, the twentieth century saw the United States roar to global dominance, knocking Great Britain from the top spot.

The United States, along with other developed economies, notably Great Britain, Germany, and France, flipped the global economy via the tools of the Industrial Revolution. Developed economies' advocacy of free market ideologies, institution of economic freedoms, and application of productivity innovations dramatically shifted the economic center of gravity. By 1950, emerging economies' share of global output had fallen by half; China's share had collapsed to five percent. Many others, from India to Indonesia, floundered as internal struggles, aggravated by political strife, colonialism, and dubious trade agreements, spurred isolationism and xenophobia.

FIGURE 4.2 Emerging Markets Make a Comeback

Throughout much of the past millennium, today's emerging economies, notably China and India, accounted for the bulk of global output. Trends suggest that by 2025, emerging economies will again dominate the global economy.

Sources: Based on Development Centre Studies, *The World Economy: A Millennial Perspective*, OECD Publishing, 2006; *Looking to 2060: A Global Vision of Long-Term Growth*, OECD Economic Policy Papers, November 2012; Loayza, N., & S Pennings, *The Long-Term Growth Model*, World Bank: Washington DC, 2018.[5]

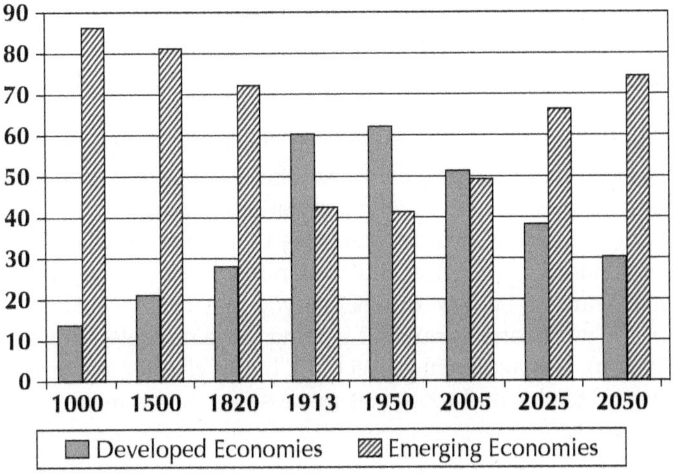

NEW GAMES, NEW WORLD

The ambition of emerging economies is logical: Restore their historic stature as the driver of the global economy. This goal will culminate in their comeback, where, once again, they account for the lion's share of global activity. Symbolizing this change, in 2009 China reclaimed the status it had last held in 1850—then, as now, it produced the greatest share of goods in the world. The United States, leader for the previous 110 years, slipped to second. Likewise, the IMF reported that China has become the central trading power in the world—it is the biggest trading partner with 124 countries. Some 76 countries have that relationship with the United States.[6]

The matters of development, performance and potential in the realm of emerging economies are powerfully represented in the vision of China's One Belt One Road (OBOR) program. Begun in 2013, OBOR involves a large swath of the global marketplace; it spans more than 70 percent of the global population, 35 percent of global GDP, and some 90 countries, most of which are fast-growing emerging economies. Some see OBOR positioning China as the center of the world's most expansive commercial empire. The planned network of roads, pipelines, railways, ports, and power plants is building a mind-boggling platform for market connectivity and transnational collaboration. Besides terrestrial and sea-based paths, OBOR is laying the Digital Silk Road, using fiber-optic cables and 5G connections to modernize ancient trade routes.

MAKING SENSE TO MAKE CENTS

Megatrends such as the comeback of the emerging economies are millennial events. This profile spotlights its unfolding benefits and pending dividends. Unquestionably, megatrends can go dramatically awry. Emerging economies face demographic, environmental, equity, ideological, and institutional challenges, among many others. Moreover, as exemplified in the COVID-19 pandemic, so-called "black swan" events that test, if not reset, systems is an ongoing threat. Nevertheless, consumers, workers, investors, executives, and policymakers wrestle with the unfolding revolution powered by the comeback, or, as the case may be, the fallout of the possible collapse.

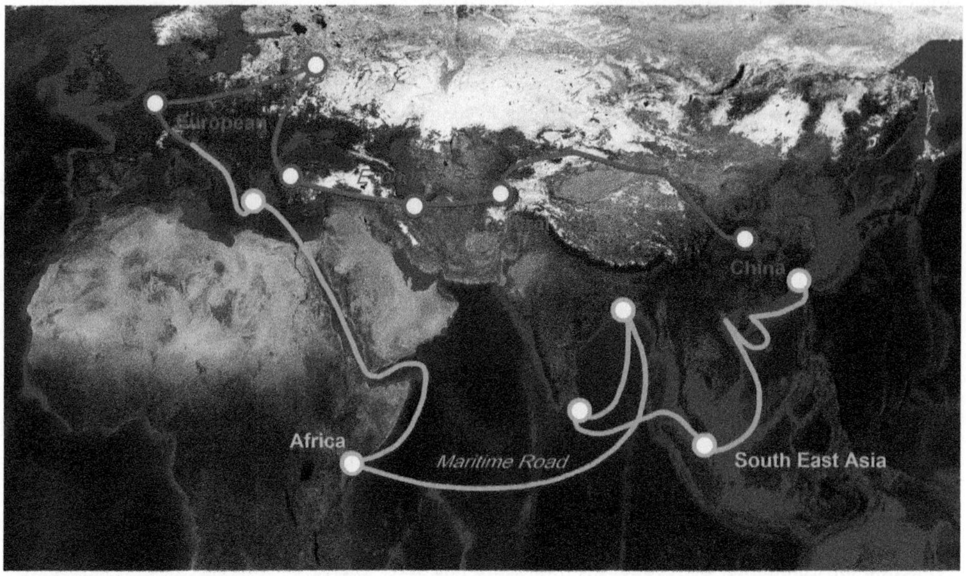

China's One Belt One Road program aims to improve connectivity, promote cooperation, and expand commerce among countries spanning Asia, Africa, and Europe. Here we see its broad geographic scope. The fact that within this zone lives most of the global population highlights its potential scale.

Source: YIUCHEUNG/Shutterstock

Watchfully, managers study economic environments to assess the development, explain the performance, and estimate the potential of the emerging economies. Making investments, positioning assets, and running operations, in terms of the comeback or, as may unfold, the collapse, depends on making sense of the possibly good, possibly bad, brave new global business environment. All the while, managers realize that the analytics anchored in the developed markets of the West do not automatically translate to the economies in the East. Instead, as we will see in this chapter, new perspectives, principles, and practices emerge.

QUESTIONS

4-1 Transformations such as the comeback of the emerging economies happen rarely. This amplifies their impact on our lives. Estimate how your life has changed, or will likely change, given the comeback to date and, significantly, its ongoing successes.

4-2 Now, flip the analysis and consider what might happen if the ambitions of the emerging economies prove far too ambitious and rather than come back, they collapse. If so, what might that mean to your life?

INTERNATIONAL ECONOMIC ANALYSIS

4-1 Explain the value of economic analysis

This chapter extends our profile of the environmental domains of IB. It explains, as we did with cultural, political, and legal systems, how economic environments influence a company's decision on where, when, and how to do business. We profile the general ideas and specific tools that analyze an economy as well as the perspectives and frameworks that integrate interpretation.[7] Throughout the chapter, we profile the relevance of economics to citizens, executives, companies, and officials given the thesis that understanding its dimensions and dynamics helps all make better consumption, investment, operating, and policy decisions.

Assessing the economic environments of IB is a fascinating challenge. To begin, just think about the scale and scope of the task. The World Bank identifies 217 discrete economic environments—189 countries along with 28 economies with populations of more than 30,000 that report economic statistics.[8] The set of 189 includes countries that we're familiar with, such as Australia, China, Germany, Indonesia, Nigeria, and the United States. The set of 28 includes some that you might have heard of, but also others that you may not have, such as the Isle of Man, Macao, San Marino, Tuvalu, and Vanuatu. Mapping these markets, from the biggest (China) to the smallest (Tuvalu), is an essential aspect of IB. In this chapter, we profile how managers do so, highlighting principles and tools that make sense of the remarkable diversity of economies.

Managers study an economic environment to interpret its development, assess its performance, and estimate its potential.

Few, if any, MNEs can fund and run operations in all 217 economic environments. Resource constraints require managers prioritize options, targeting markets that offer the greatest return with the least risk. Improving the odds of success depends on assessing the development, performance, and potential of an economy. Economics identifies a range of ingenious ideas and rigorous tools that systematize evaluation. Familiar metrics, such as production, interest rates, inflation, and unemployment, estimate important features. Integrating analysis taps scientific principles, like production functions, marginal analysis, and the general equilibrium model, as well as behavioral assumptions, like rationality and incentives. Together, these principles and analytics help managers understand consumer choice, firm conduct, industry structure, and market patterns.[9]

Mapping an economic system is difficult—like any system, an economy is a cohesive conglomeration of interrelated, interconnected, interdependent, and interacting parts. Expanding analysis to include any number of the 217 economies in the global market quickly proves daunting—especially given the tremendous differences one finds from Afghanistan to Zimbabwe and all points in-between. Moreover, each and every economy is fundamentally interconnected—as the COVID-19 pandemic vividly showed. The intricacy of even the simplest economic system defies straightforward specification. Stipulating models that definitively represent an economy's performance and potential and then work reliably in other places is challenging. Hence, managers wrestle with identifying valid perspectives and reliable measures, modeling their relationships, mapping them onto an economy, tracking key trends, and inferring their implications. Repeatedly, as this chapter highlights, managers find ingenious ways to do so and, in the process, run multinational activities successfully.

CONCEPT CHECK

A principle of globalization is the broadening network of relationships among people, companies, countries, and institutions. Philosophically, the same principle applies to the emergence and evolution of economies.

CONCEPT CHECK

Chapter 1 notes that changing environmental conditions promote and constrain globalization, Chapter 2 notes the same for changing cultural identities, and Chapter 3 follows with changing political philosophies and legal outlooks. The same perspective applies here as well—the changing economic environments of IB create opportunities and difficulties. Collectively, engaging these issues pinpoints where investments should go and, perhaps more importantly, where they should not.

MAKING CHOICES, NAVIGATING CHALLENGES

Figure 4.3 shows how managers make choices and navigate challenges—whether in their home market or in faraway places. It holds that economic conditions shape a country's development, performance, and potential. It highlights the elements that frame assessment and emphasizes the significance of theoretical and applied analysis. Clarifying the interactions among these features helps managers map development paths and estimate potentials. Hence, Figure 4.3 endorses a systems perspective that qualifies interpretation in terms of the (1) type of economic environment in terms of its state of development; (2) economic freedom managers have to make investments and run operations; (3) orientation of the economic system that shapes market standards and situations; (4) drivers of economic change; and (5) foundations of economic performance, especially in terms of innovation and competitiveness. In turn, this chapter evaluates each.

FIGURE 4.3 Economic Factors Affecting International Business Operations

Economic environments vary from country to country. Still, they share telltale principles and practices. Managers focus on these, as well as their interactions, to organize economic analysis.

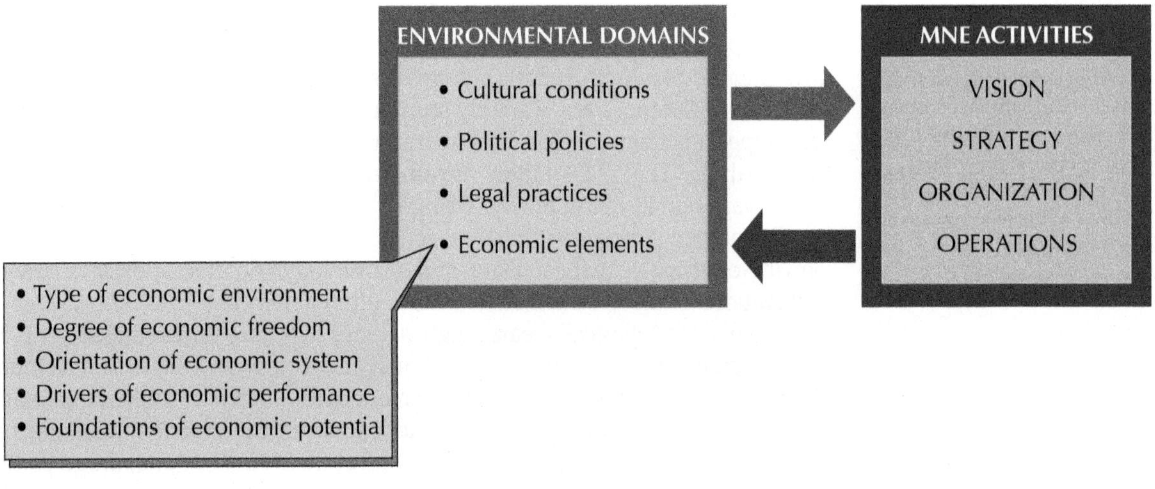

WHO'S WHO IN THE GLOBAL BUSINESS ENVIRONMENT

4-2 Distinguish the types of economic environments

In absolute terms, business activity, largely powered by growing globalization, has increased significantly. Gross world output increased nearly sevenfold between 1970 and 2020, growing from $12 trillion to $88 trillion. In relative terms, this expansion saw many countries prosper, some more than others, and a few not much. Uneven national performance requires that managers track economies, evaluating events and trends to spot opportunities and preempt risks. Interpreting the complexity, dynamism, and interdependencies spanning 217 countries, to say the least, is challenging.

Complicating analyses is that despite extensive overlaps, fundamentally no two economies are identical. Sources of differences run the gamut, including but by no means limited to demography, geography, resource endowment, national output, wages, productivity, and trade activity. These sorts of characteristics, in turn, shape the ease of doing business by influencing elemental features such as the organization of productive activity, attitudes toward foreign investors, transparency of regulations, sophistication of market systems, and scale of aggregate demand.

Getting one's bearings on these aspects of economic environments begins by identifying who's who. In IB, the single most comprehensive indicator is the development level of a country. It centers analysis on a country's ability to improve living standard, increase per capita income, institute civil stability, and provide social amenities like education, medical care, and social services to its citizens. We follow the lead of the IMF, United Nations, and World Bank, within the context of world-systems theory, to identify who's who. These reports endorse a trichotomous framework that classifies a nation as a developed economy, developing economy, or emerging economy.[10]

DEVELOPED ECONOMIES

Developed economies generally have high income levels, advanced technologies, sophisticated infrastructure, high living standards, but slowing growth.

Most members of the Organization for Economic Cooperation and Development (OECD) and European Union (EU), namely, Australia, Canada, Japan, New Zealand, Norway, Switzerland, and the United States, are developed economies. Generally, **developed economies** champion political freedom, institute democratic governance, enforce the rule of law, and endorse free markets. Residents enjoy a high standard of living, social stability, long lives, educational opportunities, reasonable nutrition, advanced health care, public hygiene, and a variety of goods and services. Developed economies exhibit efficient capital movement, stable institutions, extensive infrastructure, and cutting-edge technologies. Today, approximately 1.1 billion people (14 percent of the world's population) live in developed economies. Collectively, they generate 41 percent of the current gross world product; in 2000, their share was 57 percent.[11]

A distinctive feature of the developed economies is the income earned, on average, by its typical resident. Specifically, the average per capita income in high-income developed economies, such as United States, France, Japan, or Switzerland, is $40,142. In contrast, it can drop up to 99 percent in developing economies. For example, the average income in a low-income developing economy, such as Chad, Uganda, Tajikistan, or Afghanistan, is $744. Absolute differences are similarly stunning. The annual income per person in Singapore, a developed economy, is $54,530; in Burundi, a developing economy, it is $280.[12] Observed one analyst, "That's absolutely astounding, to be on the same planet and to have that extreme variation in material well-being."[13]

CONCEPT CHECK

"The Forces Driving Globalization" profile in Chapter 1 explained how economic environments respond to technology, trade, competition, consumer attitudes, and cross-border relationships. These conditions differ given the level of development in an economic system.

Developed economies' historic reliance on manufacturing steadily shifts to diversified, service-oriented activities. Data and technology, not factories and assembly lines, drive innovation. Skilled, educated workers, often referred to as "knowledge workers" or the "creative class," typically earn high salaries working in urban centers. Manufacturers in developed economies have offshored many activities to factories in developing and emerging economies. Manufacturing jobs as a percent of total workers in the United States, for instance, have fallen from 26.4 percent in 1970 to just under 10 percent in 2020. Recently, automation, robotics, and the like support manufacturing methods that encourage companies to reshore activities (i.e., returning jobs to developed economies).

Still, a dominant trend in developed economies for the past generation has been offshoring manufacturing to higher productivity factories in lower-cost emerging and developing economies. Offshoring, as you saw in Chapter 1, significantly influences manual as well as professional career options in developed economies. A growing share of folks struggle with unemployment as well as underemployment in developed countries. For instance, wages grew at 98 percent for households in nearly every developed economy from 1995 to 2004. From 2005 to 2014, however, wage stagnation prevailed. Since then, wage income has decreased for many households in developed economies. In the United States, for example, income inequality, namely the disparity in the distribution of income between individuals, had, in 2020, reached its highest degree in 50 years; forecasts see the gap expanding. Consequently, income inequality is a growing problem in most developed economies, whereby the rich get richer while the poor get poorer.[14]

The movement from manufacturing to service as the driver of prosperity prompts referring to developed countries as high-income economies, advanced markets, advanced industrial economies, or post-industrial economies. In the future, we may see the term "established market economies," given their higher per capita income, higher standard of living, and sophisticated institutional framework but slower growth relative to developing and emerging economies.

DEVELOPING ECONOMIES

Developing economies generally have low incomes, limited industrialization, basic infrastructure, challenging living standards, and chronic civil difficulties.

Currently, there are approximately 120 developing economies; they span Africa, Asia, Eastern Europe, Latin America, South America, and the Middle East. Today, about 2 billion (26 percent of the world's population) reside in these nations. Collectively, they generate about 10 percent of total world output. Generally, a **developing economy** has fragile institutions, heavy indebtedness, inconsistent regulation, and civil instability. Governments struggle managing sovereign responsibilities. Developing economies cope with inefficient capital movement, suspicion of foreign ownership, trade barriers, imperfect competition, and patchy infrastructure. Corruption, cronyism, and crime complicate efforts to regulate society consistently or implement prudent policies.

Developing economies, as a rule, have a low gross national income per capita. At the low end, average annual incomes are in the mid- to high-hundreds (US$). In higher performing developed economies, like Cameroon, Nicaragua, Nigeria, Uzbekistan, and Yemen, average annual incomes run in the low thousands (US$).[15] Developing economies often have pockets of great wealth; still, many endure extreme poverty, low living standards, scarce opportunities, and limited access to few goods and services. Workers, often lacking formal education or practical training, have few career options. Pervasive underemployment compounds high unemployment. Many people live in rural areas and work in agriculture. For instance, 1 to 3 percent of workers in developed economies work on a farm whereas, in developing economies, many to most do; for example, in Ethiopia, Nepal, and Burundi, respectively, some 62, 68, and 91 percent do.

Developing countries have strong communities and social ties, extraordinary self-sufficiency, and inspiring work ethics. Nonetheless, life differs on innumerable aspects between developed and developing economies. In the latter, one finds higher infant mortality, shorter life expectancy, lower literacy levels, poorer public hygiene, insufficient health care, and inadequate nutrition. Harsh conditions largely follow from widespread poverty. Certainly, poverty influences markets everywhere, from the wealthiest developed to the poorest developing economies. However, poverty profoundly influences life in developing economies. Technically, earning less than $1.90 a day qualifies as extreme poverty; currently, nearly 700 million people, roughly 1 in 10 people worldwide, fall in this cluster. Most reside in developing economies.

Poverty in terms of day-to-day life expands interpretation. Prevalent poverty in developing economies forces ongoing personal struggles for food, shelter, clothing, clean water, and health services, to say nothing of safety, education, and opportunity. Deprivation contributes to malnutrition, illness, famine, criminality, conflict, and crises. Governments struggle to provide social services, health care, education, and civil stability. Markets are prone to corruption, cronyism, and political risk. The grinding struggle for survival deters enterprise, stymies

Source: Sarine Arslanian/Shutterstock

The idea of economies in transition can be a bit abstract. Here, though, on a dusty street in Kampala, Uganda, we see the transition on the front lines of the market, with one stall selling firewood, the other cell phone and fintech services.

entrepreneurs, and slows productivity, thereby recharging a brutal cycle of persistent poverty. Sustaining IB's expansion ultimately depends on alleviating poverty.

The Base of the Pyramid is the largest, but poorest, socioeconomic group in the world.

MNEs adjust analytics anchored in the context of wealthy developed economies for the radically different markets of developing economies. For instance, product development strategies in affluent developed economies must reset to fit the economics of poor markets. In the former, customers prefer, and can afford, robust product functionality, whereas inexpensive simplicity matters more in the latter. Recent trends, however, refine interpretations. Notably, the **Base of the Pyramid** spotlights the poorest two-thirds of the economic human pyramid, a group of more than four billion people who earn a few dollars per day; most residents of developing economies qualify. Though long seen as inaccessible and unprofitable, collectively, these billions of consumers represent immense demand; some see it as the next frontier of the global economy.[16] Throughout it all, managers' economic instincts, tried and tested for developed economies, adapt to the changing, often contradictory circumstances in developing economies.

EMERGING ECONOMIES

Emerging economies exhibit improving productivity, rising income, and growing prosperity, particularly relative to slower growing developing economies.

Great range marks the performance among countries precisely because different economies experience different levels of development at different rates. Some developing economies are fast-growing, quickly industrializing countries. They are referred to as economies in transition, emerging markets, frontier markets, or newly industrializing countries; generally, terminology defaults to **emerging economies**. They are applying structural transformations that institute market-based principles and practices. An emerging economy has some, but not all, of the features of a developed economy. Unlike developing economies, it is well on its way to instituting them.

Currently, some 35 or so economies qualify as emerging (see Map 4.1).[17] These nations report accelerating growth in productivity, industrialization, and per capita income. Their financial systems, political institutions, and market infrastructure steadily modernize. Market liberalization promotes foreign investments and growing exports, deregulation and privatization improve business efficiency, and expanding opportunities encourage entrepreneurialism. Prosperity and progress support a growing middle class whose aspirations and rising expectations drive improving living standards.

MAP 4.1 Emerging Economies of the World

Various designations organize economic environments. Here we highlight markets commonly referred to as emerging economies, specifically those experiencing accelerating development.

Source: MSCI Emerging Markets Index. Retrieved January 22, 2020, from https://www.msci.com/market-classification

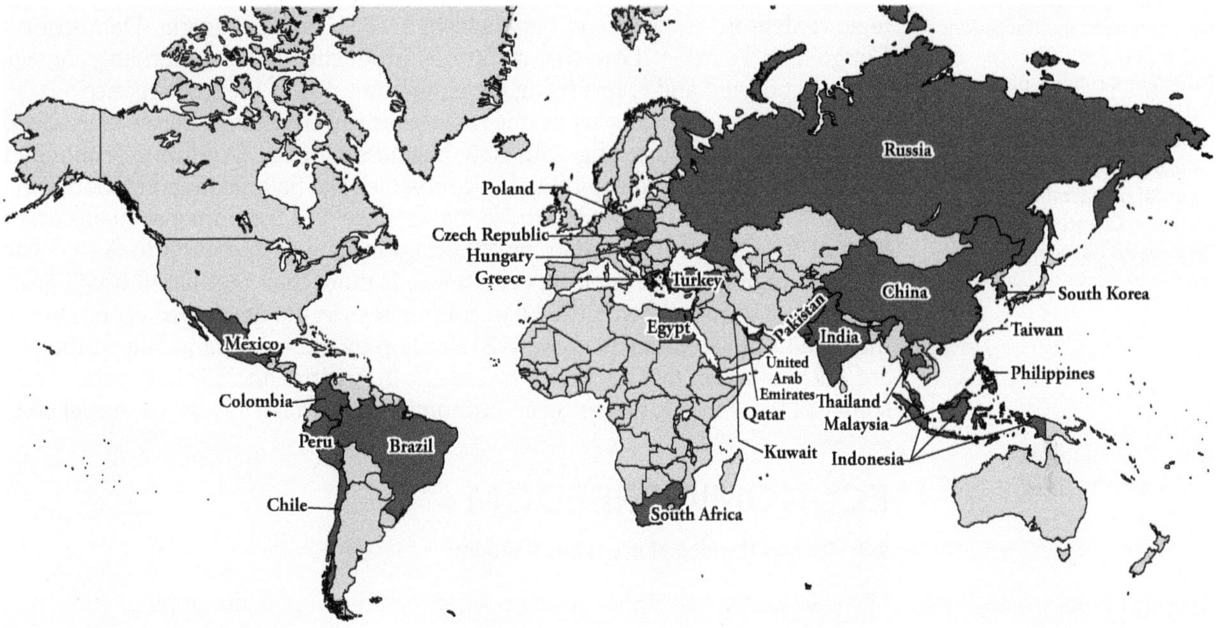

Today, roughly 60 percent of the world's population (about 4.2 billion people) lives in emerging economies—the big two, China and India, are home to 2.7 billion. Collectively, emerging economies generate roughly 50 percent of the current gross world product; in 2000, their share was 32 percent.[18] Correspondingly, residents in emerging economies average around $9,000 in annual income versus $40,142 in developed countries.[19] Other countries, although not yet qualifying as emerging, show improving productivity and prosperity. Table 4.1 identifies popular groupings.

TABLE 4.1 The Alphabet of Emerging Economies

A range of acronyms classify various sets of emerging economies. As different countries emerge, observers have coined a variety of shorthand codes.

Acronym	Specification
BRIC	B for Brazil, R for Russia, I for India, C for China
BASIC	Add AS for South Africa, Remove R for Russia
BIC	Remove R for Russia
BRICA	Add A for Arab countries—Saudi Arabia, Qatar, Kuwait, Bahrain, Oman, and the United Arab Emirates
BRICET	Add E for Eastern Europe, T for Turkey
BRICIT	Add I for Indonesia, T for Turkey
BRICK	Add K for South Korea
BRICS	Add S for South Africa
BRIIC	Add I for Indonesia
BRIMC	Add M for Mexico
CARBS	Canada, Australia, Russia, Brazil, South Africa
CIVETS	Colombia, Indonesia, Vietnam, Egypt, Turkey, South Africa
MIST	Mexico, Indonesia, South Korea, Turkey
N-11 (*The Next 11*)	Bangladesh, Egypt, Indonesia, Iran, Mexico, Nigeria, Pakistan, Philippines, South Korea, Turkey, Vietnam
PPICS	Peru, Philippines, Indonesia, Colombia, Sri Lanka

CONCEPT CHECK

The market potential of emerging and developing economies is undeniably attractive. Still, managers heed the discussions of Chapters 2 and 3 concerning the different cultural, political, and legal environments found in these countries. Keep in mind, though, that powerful drivers of globalization, profiled in Chapter 1, steadily narrow gaps between them and the developed countries.

Estimates see more than 70 percent of the world's growth over the next few years in emerging economies and, to a lesser degree, secondary developing economies. Some 400 midsize emerging-market cities will generate about 40 percent of global growth over the next 15 years. Many of these, such as Chittagong, Bamako, Kampala, Kano, Kinshasa, and Sanaa, are strategic centers in, respectively, Bangladesh, Mali, Uganda, Nigeria, Democratic Republic of Congo, and Yemen.[20] Low-cost resources, productive labor, expanding consumption, pro-business policies, and enterprising conglomerates power their emergence.

Managers in emerging economies are cleverly reinventing systems of production and distribution and experimenting with new business models. From mobile money in Kenya to frugal innovation in India, pioneering companies like Safari.com and Goonj fuel accelerating performance. At the low end of these markets, we find the immense needs and wants of the Base of the Pyramid. Likewise, middle-class consumer spending in Asia–Pacific, home to many emerging and developing economies, is more than $6 trillion. It will grow more than 500 percent to $33 trillion by 2030. In comparison, in the developed economies, it is approximately $15 trillion and will grow to $17 trillion by then.[21] Meanwhile, at the pinnacle, there are 719 billionaires in Asia, versus 631 in North America and 559 in Europe. Add it all up, and some see these trends powering an economic surge unlike any we have ever seen.[22]

ECONOMIC FREEDOM

4-3 Discuss the idea of economic freedom

Economic freedom holds that one has the right to work, produce, consume, save, and invest in the way that one prefers.

The scale and scope of the differences between developed, developing, and emerging economies challenge analysis. A key idea, namely economic freedom, provides a useful perspective. Think back, for a moment, to Chapter 3's use of political freedom to anchor the evaluation of political environments. Analysis of politics, no matter the terminology, dimensions, or dynamics, ultimately engages the issue of what one is free to do. We apply the same logic here, holding that the idea of economic freedom is a robust perspective to assess the principles and practices of an economy.

Formally, **economic freedom** is the "absolute right of property ownership, fully realized freedoms of movement for labor, capital, and goods, and an absolute absence of coercion or constraint of economic liberty beyond the extent necessary for citizens to protect and maintain liberty itself."[23] More simply, economic freedom is about diffusing economic decision making from the state throughout the economy and, in doing so, empowering ordinary people with more opportunities and more choices. In practical terms, the greater the degree of economic freedom in an economy, the greater the freedom an individual has to decide how to work, produce, consume, save, invest, and innovate. In many countries, primarily developed economies, aspects of economic freedom are so taken for granted that they rarely cross our minds. In many others, namely developing and emerging economies, they are so restricted that they serve as topics of ongoing fascination and, often, flashpoints.

For businesses, economic freedom supports confidence in the legitimacy of property rights, liberty to use the factors of production, flexibility to organize goods and services, and protection from undue political interference. Managers, not the state, decide investments, allocate resources, hire and fire, and compete with rivals. Economic freedom creates opportunities and boosts productivity, functioning as the critical link between ambition and action. Economically free countries support activities that generate income and wealth. Successful entrepreneurs map paths that others follow to build better lives.

Economic freedom does not unconditionally advocate the absence of government from the marketplace. Rather, safeguarding economic freedom requires protection via enlightened governance. Think of, for example, the police force that protects property rights, market regulators that ensure fair competition, monetary authorities promote stability, or an impartial judiciary that enforces contracts. Certainly, these sorts of safeguards reduce economic freedom. Ideally, each does so only to the degree needed to protect and sustain individual choice. State intervention, when excessive, overly substitutes political judgment in place of individual choice. Data indicates this then constrains enterprise, deters entrepreneurialism, and reduces market efficiency.

Economic freedom measures the absence of government constraint on the production, distribution, or consumption of goods and services beyond the extent necessary for citizens to protect and maintain liberty.

Measuring Economic Freedom The **Economic Freedom Index** estimates economic freedom in 180 countries worldwide. In principle, it measures the degree that a nation

TABLE 4.2 Dimensions of the Economic Freedom Index

Category	Component	Measure
Rule of Law	Property Rights	Ability of individuals to accumulate, use, trade, and sell private property, protected and safeguarded by clear, specific, and explicit laws that are fully and fairly enforced by the state.
	Government Integrity	How does corruption, in forms such as cronyism, extortion, graft, bribery, patronage, nepotism, and self-dealing, by creating insecurity, coercion, uncertainty, and opportunism, subvert economic transactions, activities, and relationships.
	Judicial Effectiveness	Degree that the judicial system impartially interprets the legal framework and justly applies the law in order to sustain the public's confidence that the legal system operates with an absence of bias against parties.
Limited Government	Fiscal Health	Extent that a government institute systematic policies that manage taxation, public revenues, and public debt to support and sustain stable economic conditions.
	Government Spending	The burden imposed on the economic system by the monies spent by government agents in acquiring goods, providing services, and transferring income payments to its citizens.
	Tax Burden	The proportion of total income and profits that residents and companies pay, in the form of taxes such as income, payroll, consumption, tariff, sales, and property, to the local, state, regional, and federal government.
Regulatory Efficiency	Labor Freedom	The legal codes and regulatory policies that influence workers' rights in the workplace on matters such as occupational safety and health, wages and hours of work, collective bargaining, and employment discrimination.
	Business Freedom	The legal, regulatory, infrastructure contexts that influence an enterprise's efficient management of matters such as the ease of starting, operating, and closing a business.
	Monetary Freedom	Measure of price stability and scale and scope of price controls in terms of their support and distortion of market activity.
Open Markets	Trade Freedom	The openness of an economy to the export and imports of goods and service as moderated by the scale and scope of tariff and nontariff barriers applied by the government to regulate trade.
	Investment Freedom	The absence of investment restrictions, such as burdensome bureaucracy, private property regulation, and foreign exchange controls, that complicate or control an individual's choice to allocate resources to activities and opportunities.
	Financial Freedom	The independence an individual or company attains that buffers, defends, and protects them from interference by government agents, officials, and policies.

Adapted from "Methodology," *2019 Index of Economic Freedom*, The Heritage Foundation, in partnership with *the Wall Street Journal*, from www.heritage.org/index/pdf/2019/book/methodology.pdf and TCdata360, The World Bank, from https://tcdata360.worldbank.org/, retrieved September 13, 2020

accepts Adam Smith's thesis that "basic institutions that protect the liberty of individuals to pursue their own economic interests result in greater prosperity for the larger society."[24] In practice, it specifies four key categories and disaggregates those into 12 quantitative and qualitative measures of freedomsee Table 4.2). A country's performance in terms of some 50 estimators earns it a score from zero (no freedom) to 100 (full freedom). As we see in Table 4.3, a country then qualifies as *free, mostly free, moderately free, mostly unfree,* or *repressed.*

Table 4.3 highlights characteristics of each category as well as identifies representative nations. Table 4.3 highlights the operational implications of the dimensions of economic freedom. For instance, in a free economy, individuals and companies face little corruption and slight risk of unilateral expropriation; hence they have a great deal of confidence in acquiring and using property. In contrast, in a repressed economy, corruption is pervasive and private property is, at best, weakly protected and, at worst, outlawed. Likewise, individuals in a free economy confidently expect slight government interference in the marketplace, those in a moderately free economy see more extensive involvement, and those in a repressed economy endure oppresive regulation of virtually any and all market activity.

CONCEPT CHECK

Chapter 1 suggests that income inequality and poverty should diminish as IB improves the efficiency of resource allocation. Chapter 3 highlighted the importance of people's political freedom to champion helpful policies. Here we add to the mix the idea of economic freedom and its thesis that productive use of ambition and investment increases prosperity.

THE VALUE OF ECONOMIC FREEDOM

Economies that implement policies that institute economic freedom enjoy a range of benefits. Economic freedom supports higher growth in the short- (5 years), medium- (10 years), and long-term (20 years). Higher growth, in turn, supports higher personal income; in economically free countries, it is more than double the worldwide average and four times higher than that in mostly unfree and repressed economies. Higher growth and higher income combine to support higher living standards (see Figure 4.4).

TABLE 4.3 Economic Freedom: Classification and Characteristics[25]

Economic Freedom Score	Class	General Characteristics	Representative Nations
80–100	Free	• Companies, both domestic and foreign, face none to few restrictions making or selling products. • Government institutes enforces extensive property rights. • Negligible government interference in the marketplace. • Slight corruption or risk of expropriation. • Government endorse openness to international trade and investment. • Regulation is minimal and centers on improving transparency, fairness, and firm conduct.	Australia, Hong Kong, New Zealand, Singapore, Switzerland, Ireland
70–79.9	Mostly Free	• Limited state interference in the movement of labor, capital, and goods. • Property rights are acknowledged and protected. • Foreign companies are subject to few discriminatory restrictions. • Judicial system is subject to delays and may inconsistently enforce contracts. • Corruption is unusual; the risk of expropriation is low. • Sizable government ownership of companies in key sectors.	Canada, Chile, Colombia, Estonia, Israel, Lithuania, South Korea, St. Lucia, Sweden, Taiwan, United States
60–69.9	Moderately Free	• Inflexible, often rigid, labor regulations. • Inward and outward capital movements face restrictions. • Moderate government interference in economic affairs. • Regulations are somewhat burdensome and costly. • The government exercises ownership and control of significant economic sectors. • The judiciary may be unduly influenced by public officials and private agents.	Azerbaijan, Belgium, Botswana, Ghana, Italy, Jamaica, Kazakhstan, Kuwait, Mexico, Morocco, Oman, Peru, Philippines, Rwanda, Saudi Arabia
50–59.9	Mostly Unfree	• Considerable state action interferes with individual choice. • Government owns or controls some to many companies. • Foreign companies are subject to cursive policies. • Regulations restrict repatriation of funds foreign headquarters. • Private use of capital faces significant barriers. • Laws are often opaque and arbitrarily enforced. • The court system is inefficient and subject to delays. • The State hinders the free flow of foreign commerce.	Bangladesh, Brazil, Cambodia, Cameroon, China, Ethiopia, Fiji, Greece, India, Lebanon, Nepal, Nicaragua, Pakistan, Russia, Sri Lanka, Swaziland, Tunisia, Vietnam
0–49.9	Repressed	• An oppressive bureaucracy administers burdensome regulations. • Corruption is pervasive and endemic. • Foreign companies, if permitted, navigate extensive barriers to entry and mobility. • Private property ownership is, at best, weakly protected, at worst, outlawed. • Supervision and regulation restrict, if not eliminate, personal choice in the marketplace. • The State owns some to all property and directly produces goods and services. • Coercion and constraint pervade an unfair market system.	Angola, Argentina, Belarus, Burma, Bolivia, Chad, Ecuador, Iran, North Korea, Turkmenistan, Venezuela, Zimbabwe

Source: Adatpted from Terry Miller, Anthony B. Kim, James M. Roberts, and Patrick Tyrrel, *2020 Index of Economic Freedom*, The Heritage Foundation.

The track record of economic freedom in countries worldwide indicates a direct relationship with higher productivity, greater prosperity, and less poverty.

Higher economic freedom promotes macroeconomic stability that, in turn, lowers inflation and increases employment. Operationally, economic freedom helps managers balance risk and return given their confidence in legitimate property rights, efficient capital markets, and prudent monetary policy. Streamlining regulation institutes incentives that inspire entrepreneurial activity, opening opportunities for innovation and paths to optimize resource usage. Improving opportunities reduces the gap between the rich and poor; poverty rates in mostly free and repressed economies are about four times those in freer markets. Growing prosperity

FIGURE 4.4 Economic Freedom and the Standard of Living

Economic freedom has significant relationships with a variety of income, market, social, and political measures. Here we see the link between economic freedom and a broad indicator of the standard of living, specifically gross domestic product per capita.

Sources: Terry Miller, Anthony B. Kim, James M. Roberts, and Patrick Tyrrel, *2020 Index of Economic Freedom* (Washington: The Heritage Foundation, 2020), http://www.heritage.org/index and International Monetary Fund, World Economic Outlook Databasehttps://bit.ly/3eWOIHl (accessed July, 20, 2020).

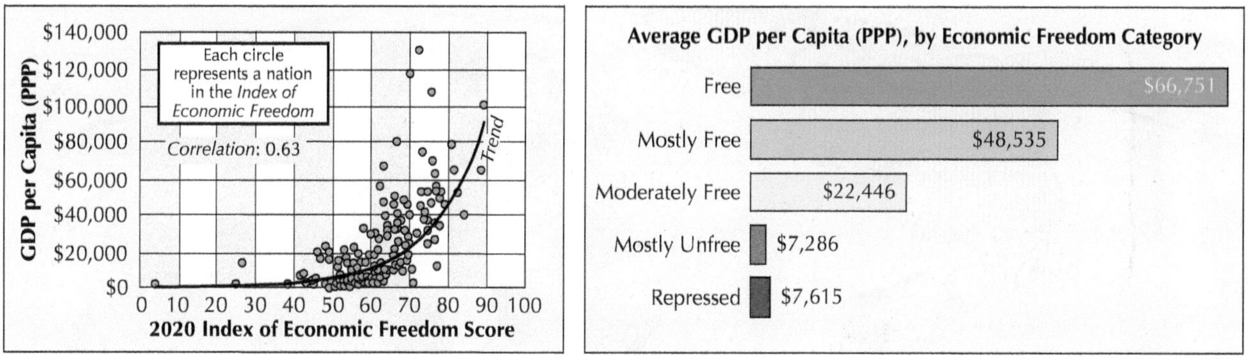

opens access to education, promotes literacy, improves health care, and expands the middle class—the latter, as Chapter 3 reported, is a precondition of democratic governance.

Market liberalization encourages connections with other countries in trade networks (e.g., the EU or USCMA), multilateral financial institutions (e.g., the AIIB, IMF, or World Bank), and transnational institutions (e.g., the UN, WTO, or WHO). Expanding connectivity institutionalizes elements of economic freedom into organizations worldwide, thereby encouraging entrepreneurs and companies to pursue international opportunities. In summary, individuals and firms' economic freedom to choose how to operate innovatively, productively, and responsibly is a commonality of the world's most competitive nations.[26]

THE PREVALENCE OF ECONOMIC FREEDOM

Map 4.2 displays the Economic Freedom Index for 180 economies. North America (Canada, Mexico, and the United States) enjoys the highest levels of economic freedom, with an average score, 73.7 versus the global average, 61.6. Europe, the Middle East and North Africa, Asia and the Pacific, and Central and South America cluster around the world average at, respectively, 69.8, 61.8, 61.1, and 58.2. Sub-Saharan Africa clocks in at 55.2. Some 37 countries score above 70, effectively providing individuals and private enterprises high degrees of economic freedom. Some 62 markets, with scores between 60 and 70, are "moderately free." Finally, 81 economies score below 60; of those, 63 are considered "mostly unfree" (scores of 50–60) while the remaining 18 rate as "repressed" (score below 50).[27] Other than sub-Saharan Africa, every region has at least one representative among the top 20 freest economies. Ten of these are in Europe, five are in Asia–Pacific, three represent the Americas, and one hails from the Middle East and North Africa.

National outcomes amplify these standings. The freest economies are Singapore (89.4) Hong Kong (89.1), New Zealand (84.1), Australia (82.6.), Switzerland (81.9), and Ireland (80.9). Alternatively, the least free are the Eritrea (38.5), Cuba (26.9), Venezuela (25.2), and North Korea (4.2). Some 99 countries, with economic freedom scores above 60, grant individuals and private enterprises a moderate degree of economic freedom. Prominent emerging economies, notably Brazil (53.7), China (59.5), and India (56.5), continue their long-running trend as mostly unfree. The United States is a "mostly free" economy, with a score of 76.6. In 2007, before the great financial crisis, it ranked as a "free" economy with a score of 81.2, its all-time high.

Worldwide, the recent growth in economic freedom has been evolutionary rather than revolutionary: in 1999, the world average was 57.6; in 2009, it was 59.5; and in 2020, it is 61.6. Certainly, the pace of change varies from country to country, as governments loosen

MAP 4.2 The Distribution of Economic Freedom

The worldwide distribution of economic freedom varies, from a little to a lot, from country to country.

Source: Terry Miller, Anthony B. Kim, James M. Roberts, and Patrick Tyrrel, *2020 Index of Economic Freedom* (Washington, DC: The Heritage Foundation and Dow Jones & Co., Inc., 2020).

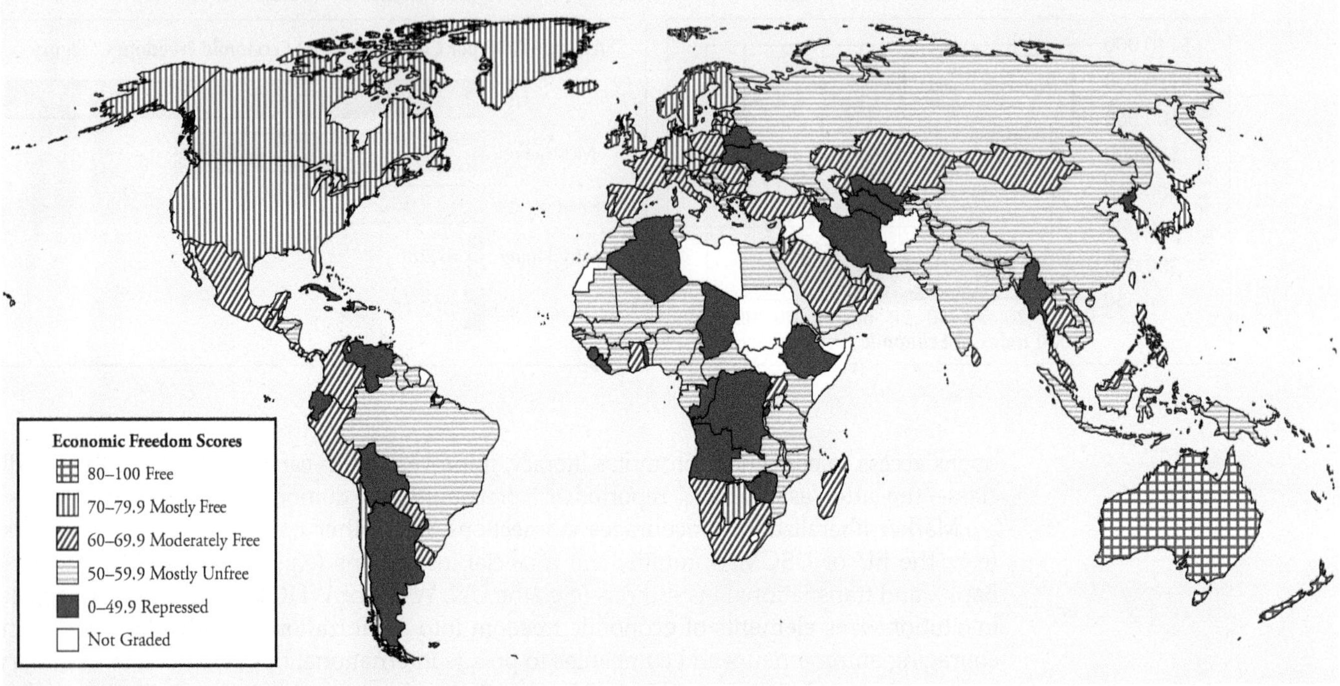

or tighten controls; in 2020, for instance, we see a range from 89.4 for Singapore to 4.2 for North Korea. Variability, despite steady growth, calls on managers to monitor economic environments, assessing policies and practices in determining government intentions and their implications for economic freedom.

ECONOMIC FREEDOM BY TYPE OF ECONOMIC ENVIRONMENT

Table 4.4 reports the average economic freedom score, as well as for its 12 components, by type of economic environment. The characteristics of economic freedom, controlling for the level of development, highlight the scale and scope of difference facing managers. Consistently, the developed economies devise policies that promote and protect individual choice as seen in their higher score. Notably, property rights, freedom from corruption, and confidence in government integrity differ significantly from levels seen in emerging and developing economies. As discussed in Chapter 3, these gaps largely follow from the prevalence of democracy and the rule of law in developed economies versus authoritarianism and the rule of man in many developing and emerging economies. Beside regulating business more aggressively, developing economies constrain investment and trade freedoms more strictly then do developed and emerging economies.

Richer countries typically regulate business activities less. Poorer countries typically regulate them more.

Operationally, these tendencies contribute to an inverse relationship between a nation's income levels and its scope of regulation—generally, the richer, developed countries regulate less, and the poorer, developing countries regulate more. In high-income developed countries (e.g., the United States, France, Japan), starting a business requires an average of 6.28 procedures, spans 18 days, and costs 7 percent of per capita income. Doing the same in the middle-income emerging economies (e.g., Mexico, Poland, Malaysia, China, India, South Africa), requires an average of 7.8 procedures, spans 36 days, and costs 28 percent of per capita income. Lastly, in the low-income developing countries (e.g., Bangladesh, Ethiopia, Nepal), one is facing 7.5 procedures, a 90-day span, and 37 percent of per capita income. [28] Furthermore, legal systems in wealthier nations tend to regulate operational activities more consistently than do those in poorer countries—as one would expect, given the prevalence of the rule of law in the former and the rule of man in the latter.

TABLE 4.4 Average Freedom Scores by Type of Economic Environment (in %)

The development status of an economic environment significantly influences managers' freedom to make investments, build operations, and run businesses. The higher the score, as we see below, the greater the freedom an individual has in that domain.

Dimension		Developed Economies	Emerging Economies	Developing Economies[29]
Overall Economic Freedom Score		73.3	66.9	57.1
Rule of Law	Property Rights	82.9	61.1	45.3
	Judicial effectiveness	72.1	52.6	34.3
	Government Integrity	76.7	45.8	34.3
Government Size	Tax Burden	62.7	79.9	79.5
	Fiscal Health	82.2	75.1	61.4
	Government Spending	43.3	71.1	66.9
Regulatory Efficiency	Labor Freedom	65.7	61.5	57.9
	Business Freedom	81.6	70.9	59.0
	Monetary Freedom	82.6	76.4	73.5
Open Markets	Trade Freedom	85.9	80.1	71.1
	Investment Freedom	82.5	59.8	52.0
	Financial Freedom	73.8	56.5	42.5

Note: Scores range from zero (no freedom) to 100 (full freedom).

THE PARADOX OF PROMISE VERSUS PREVALENCE

The fall of the Berlin Wall in 1989 symbolized the triumph of capitalism over communism. More pointedly, it signified the supremacy of economic freedom over state control to promote development, improve performance, and boost potential. Countries progressively abandoned the policies of state control and instituted the hallmarks of economic freedom: property rights, governmental transparency, regulatory efficiency, and fair competition. Worldwide, governments increasingly deferred to the laws of supply and demand—the invisible hand of the marketplace rather than the visible hand of politicians—to direct their economy. Since then, more folks in more countries have more choices to improve their standard of living.

Notwithstanding progress, there is a paradox in the promise and the prevalence of economic freedom. Specifically, given the benefits of economic freedom, one likely wonders why so few countries maximize it. Regarding benefits, countries that improve economic freedom achieve higher growth, gain greater prosperity, and enjoy more socioeconomic development; those that restrict economic freedom do not. More directly, Figure 4.4 reports that the average GNP per capita in a free economy is $66,751; it falls to $48,535 in a mostly free economy, $22,446 in a moderately free economy, $7,286 in a mostly unfree economy, and $7,615 in a repressed economy. The message is clear: improving economic freedom improves prosperity.

Paradoxically, despite the benefits of economic freedom, just six countries out of 180 rank as a "free" economy.

Map 4.2 shows that Hong Kong, Singapore, New Zealand, Switzerland, Australia, and Ireland are the only "free" economies in the world; they are home to just over 50 million people. Some 31 other countries are mostly free, including Canada, the United States, Germany, Sweden, South Korea, and Malaysia; they are home to another billion or so. In contrast, 62 countries are moderately free, 62 are mostly unfree, and 19 are repressed; they are home to approximately 6.3 billion people. Put differently, 37 of 180 countries—home to around 15 percent of the world population—grant their residents significant economic freedom.

Increasing Effectiveness of the State Managers study this situation, gauging its implications to where to open and then how to run a business. As economies in the mostly free markets in the West struggle to grow, the focus of our closing case, managers wonder if economic freedom will prevail. Elsewhere, in less free markets, authoritarian governments increasingly control the economy, directing its development, regulating its performance, and determining its potential. Results complicate interpretation, raising the question of whether optimizing economic freedom is still necessary to anchor a productive economic system.[30] Specifically, the record of various countries, such as China, Russia, Ethiopia, Mexico, and Rwanda, indicates that improving economic freedom is not necessarily required to improve productivity and prosperity.

Managers watch key events to gauge the contest between economic freedom and state control. These include how the government

- regulates the economy,
- protects property rights,
- sets fiscal and monetary policies,
- promotes transparent decision making.

Since 2008, real cumulative growth in prominent developed economies, historically strong advocates of economic freedom, has struggled and in some cases, fallen. In comparison, China, technically a mostly unfree economy, has seen its real growth more than double its total production. Likewise, annual per capita income in China has increased from $940 in 2000 to $10,262 in 2098, lifting more than 800 million Chinese out of extreme poverty and expanding its middle class from four percent, in 2002, to now 31 percent.[31] The success of China follows not from maximizing economic freedom, but from the state's direction of development. China is not an isolated case. Many fast-growing emerging and developing economies similarly deemphasize economic freedom in favor of pervasive state involvement. As China has done, they institute an alternative relationship between individuals, markets, and governments. This relationship, as we profile in our *Looking to the Future* insert, spotlights the idea of **state capitalism**.

LOOKING TO THE FUTURE State Capitalism: Detour or Destination?

An epic philosophical contest is underway. In one corner, we have the ideals of economic freedom, anchored in notions popularized by Adam Smith and instituted via free markets. In the other, we have models of state power, loosely linked to notions popularized by Karl Marx and Vladimir Lenin and instituted via state capitalism. A generation ago, the state-controlled economy was seen as a way station on the path to a free market. Now, improving performances in many emerging and developing economies suggests that free market economics is no longer the only practical route to modernization. Worldwide, managers watch and wait as the contest between "Smith's" free markets and "Marx's" state power determines the sort of economy that works best in the twenty-first century.

What Is It?

State capitalism is an economic system whereby political officials firmly influence, but do not directly control, the valuation and use of the factors of production.[32] The state nurtures national champions, manages trade relations and exchange rates to promote exports and discourage imports, mediates the financial system to provide low-cost capital to domestic industries, and runs nationalist legal systems. State capitalism, unlike market capitalism or state communism, does not overly advocate an ideology. Rather, it encourages the state to manage the economy to set and sustain its political legitimacy, not to enforce an abstract ideal or promote a personality cult. Instead of politicized revolutionaries promising utopia, state capitalism relies on pragmatic technocrats who, applying sophisticated management principles, build a prosperous, productive economy. Unburdened of an ideological agenda, the state assumes anonymity. As long as a growing economy supports stability, officials stay in the shadows, influencing activities and shaping outcomes. In the event that plans go awry, the veiled hand quickly turns visible. The state steps in, revises policies, resets funding, and redirects activities.

Manipulating market outcomes for political purposes inevitably reduces economic freedom. This trade-off, officials explain, helps stabilize market cycles, equalizes income distribution, and preempts the self-interests that threaten social harmony. History shows that when allowed to run free, market economies can encourage the psychology that greed is good. Only a proactive state, goes the reasoning, stops this outlook from descending into psychosis. Hence, the state manages the economy to promote stability and growth, thereby creating the prosperity that legitimates its ongoing rule. The payoff is plain: subverting political freedom with economic prosperity fortifies the authority of the state.[33]

Who Owns Whom?

State capitalism calls for the government to own, either directly or indirectly, its national champions, using them to influence market activity as well as consolidate its authority. For instance, the Chinese Communist Party (CCP) is the majority owner of many of the largest publicly listed Chinese companies, including major banks, energy producers, telecom carriers, media conglomerates, and construction firms. Its managers ultimately answer to the CCP.[34] Furthermore, party officials in China's provinces and cities own and run thousands of medium-sized and smaller ones. State officials, while discreet, are not shy. At all levels, "the tentacles of state-owned enterprises extend into every nook where profits can be made."[35] Similar situations in Brazil, Rwanda, Russia, Saudi Arabia, and South Africa, for instance, highlight the state's economic clout.

Telltale Marks

State capitalism institutes economies with telltale marks. Public investment, public wealth, and public enterprise prevail. Officials fan economic nationalism, encouraging consumers to "buy local." The state promotes domestic markets as sanctuaries for national champions, thereby giving them the platform to develop global competitiveness. State capitalism promotes the growth of specific industrial sectors and companies in order to speed economic development. For example, besides supervising the ambitious OBOR project, the Chinese state also directs "Made in China 2025. The latter guides transforming China from the world's factory floor to the inventor of innovative products in aerospace, pharmaceuticals, automotive, industry, semiconductors, communications, and robotics.[36]

State capitalism advocates installing trade and investment barriers to spur local development. The state attracts innovative foreign companies, using state-owned banks to provide cheap loans, favorable regulations, and stable markets. Regulators often require that foreign investors accept joint ventures with local companies as the price of entry. However, if difficulties emerge, and push comes to shove, foreign companies often receive scant protection and even weaker legal defense. State capitalism has little need for an independent judiciary; the legal system legitimates state policies as needed. Similarly, the state uses the tax code as a tool for economic, not social, engineering.

Gaining Momentum

Some 70 or so strategically important countries worldwide are at a crossroads in determining their political and economic futures.[37] For many, the economic choice is stark: institute a free market or state capitalism. Many see China as the bellwether. It has used state capitalism to develop and direct the world's fastest-growing economy, which, in turn, has powered the swiftest, most extensive rise out of poverty any nation has ever seen. Its success, not just surviving, but prospering during the great financial crisis, convinced "Chinese leadership that state control of much of the country's economic development is the steadiest path toward prosperity, and, therefore, domestic tranquility."[38] The aftermath of the COVID-19 pandemic fortified this outlook.

What then of those that dismiss state capitalism as inevitably unacceptable, forecasting growing pressure from folks clamoring for greater economic freedom. Survey data paint an interesting picture. In 2002, asked whether the country's economic situation is "good" or "bad," some 52 percent of Chinese versus 46 percent of United States respondents affirmed it as good. In 2009, asked the same, some 88 percent of Chinese versus 17 percent of United States respondents affirmed it as good. In 2016, when asked the same question, 87 percent of Chinese while 44 percent of United States saw good times.[39] Meanwhile, over this period, economic freedom scores consistently placed China in the mostly unfree category, whereas the United States had slipped from a free to mostly free economy.

Given growing challenges and competition, it's not surprising to see other economies, particularly those using authoritarianism, institute elements of state capitalism. Throughout Africa, Asia, Middle East, Latin, and South America, countries broadly emulate China's model.[40] Their state-backed companies grow and expand, generating progress and prosperity. The success of state capitalism, besides clarifying the prevalence of authoritarianism, helps explain why many countries, collectively home to several billion people, restrict economic freedom.

TYPES OF ECONOMIC SYSTEMS

4-4 Distinguish the types of economic systems

An economic system organizes the production, distribution, and consumption of goods and services.

Wherever they go, managers question how the host government might regulate the market, implement fiscal and monetary policies, and interpret the idea of economic freedom. Evaluating these sorts of issues in the context of a county's **economic system** helps organize analysis. That is, evaluating how a country has configured its market to allocate resources and trade goods and services explains the means and methods managers use to run operations. Specifically, classifying an economic system in terms of whether it is a market, mixed, or command economy clarifies the drivers of supply and demand, the role of price as a signaling device, the efficiency of resource allocation, and the degree of economic freedom. Figure 4.5 shows that fundamental features distinguish the market, mixed, and command economies. Let's take a closer look at each.

THE MARKET ECONOMY

Capitalism and its advocacy of the private ownership of the factors of production anchors a market economy.

The economic system whereby individuals, rather than the government, make most decisions is a **market economy**. It is anchored in the doctrine of **capitalism** and its thesis that private ownership confers inalienable property rights that legitimize the profits earned by one's initiative, investment, and risk. Optimal resource allocation follows from consumers exercising their freedom of choice in the goods and services they buy, and producers responding accordingly. Market economies are commonly found in developed economies, such as Australia, Canada, Hong Kong, Switzerland, and the United States. The market economy champions economic freedom in order to institute a system that gives individuals a lot of choice to decide where to work, what to do and for how long, how to spend or save money, and whether to consume now or later.

FIGURE 4.5 Types of Economic Systems

The principal types of economic systems endorse different philosophies, advocate different principles, and apply different methods.

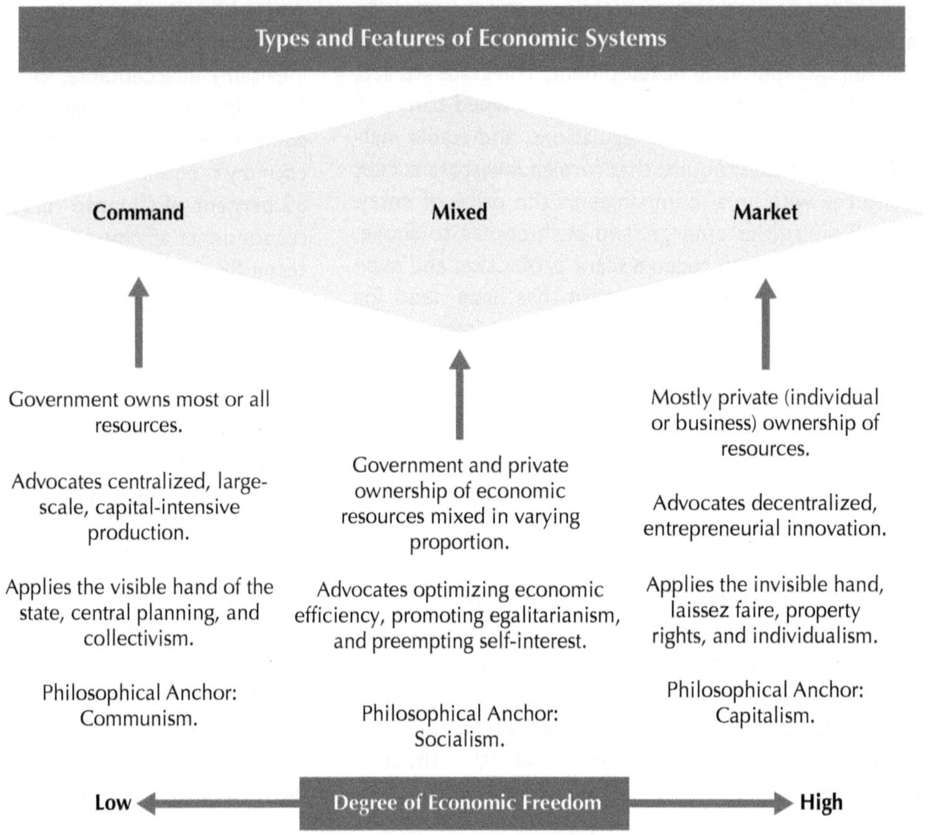
Types and Features of Economic Systems
Command
Mixed
Market
Government owns most or all resources.
Advocates centralized, large-scale, capital-intensive production.
Applies the visible hand of the state, central planning, and collectivism.
Philosophical Anchor: Communism.
Government and private ownership of economic resources mixed in varying proportion.
Advocates optimizing economic efficiency, promoting egalitarianism, and preempting self-interest.
Philosophical Anchor: Socialism.
Mostly private (individual or business) ownership of resources.
Advocates decentralized, entrepreneurial innovation.
Applies the invisible hand, laissez faire, property rights, and individualism.
Philosophical Anchor: Capitalism.
Low
Degree of Economic Freedom
High

CONCEPT CHECK

Chapter 3 notes that the individual voter is the cornerstone of a democracy. Similarly, the individual, as a consumer, is the cornerstone of a market economy. Whereas democracy recognizes the supremacy of voter sovereignty, the market economy recognizes the supremacy of consumer sovereignty.

The market economy champions the "invisible hand" of economically free, self-interested, utility-maximizing consumers as the driver of productive efficiency. Consumers, through their interactions with producers, optimize the relationships among price, quantity, supply, and demand. The market economy pushes producers, spurred by the quest to maximize profits, to make products that consumers, spurred by the quest to maximize utility, buy. Consequently, by virtue of what they buy, and, for that matter, do not, consumers direct the efficient allocation of resources and the optimal valuation of assets.

An enduring bias toward minimal government intervention anchors the market economy. The less visible the "hand" is due to government intervention, the more efficiently the market economy performs. Fundamentally, the market economy endorses the notion of *laissez-faire*, which can be literally translated as "Let do," and more broadly advises "Let it be" or "Leave it alone." A *laissez-faire* outlook opposes governmental interference in economic affairs beyond the minimum necessary to support safety and sustain stability. The outcome, as Adam Smith reasoned, is a market whereby "Every man, as long as he does not violate the laws of justice, is left perfectly free to pursue his own interest his own way, and to bring both his industry and capital into competition with those of any other man or order of men."[41]

A market economy endorses the ideals of economic freedom, the doctrine of capitalism, and the principle of the invisible hand.

The need for the government to provide public goods (e.g., traffic lights, highways, schools) and protect society (e.g., minimum wage, product safeguards, environmental standards) makes a bit visible the otherwise invisible hand. Therefore, notwithstanding advocacy of economic freedom and *laissez-faire*, the market economy relies on the state to enforce contracts, protect property rights, ensure fair and free competition, and provide general safety and stability.

THE COMMAND ECONOMY

In the command economy, the visible hand of the state supersedes the invisible hand of the market.

Communism champions the state's ownership of resources and control of economic activity. Nominally a political ideology, communism calls for an egalitarian, classless, and ultimately stateless society based on the government's command of the economy (the instrumentality of attaining the Marxian mandate, "From each according to his ability, to each according to his need").[42] Instituting a communist system requires that the state impose a **command economy** whereby it owns and controls the factors of production. Public officials, not private agents, then decide what products to make, in what quantity, at what price, and in what way.

Making the invisible hand explicitly visible means that government officials, not private consumers, determine the prices of goods and services and, hence, the allocation of resources. For example, in the market economy, if the government needs automobiles, it collects taxes and buys cars at market prices from privately-owned carmakers. In the command economy, the visible hand of the government, with slight regard for price, orders state-owned carmakers to produce them. Consequently, in the command economy, product quality is often erratic and, absent profit-maximizing incentives, typically deteriorates. Products are usually in short supply and there are few substitutes. State-owned enterprises, often large-scale, inefficient, and unprofitable, have fewer resources to upgrade or incentives to innovate.

CONCEPT CHECK

Totalitarianism subordinates people's day-to-day lives—including their market behavior and economic outlook—to the state. Commanding the economy, by determining asset valuation and directing resource allocation, lets the government control economic freedom.

Certainly, the command economy can outperform the market economy for short periods. Controlling everyone and everything lets the state mobilize idle resources, usually labor, to generate growth spurts. High productivity continues as long as the state competently manages the supply of slack, low-cost resources. Improving performance often inspires officials to proclaim the command economy's superiority to a free market. History, however, shows otherwise. Central planning commonly proves counterproductive, given that officials, no matter how astute, cannot consistently predict consumers' preferences, craft incentives for entrepreneurs, and efficiently allocate resources. Eventually, the command economy struggles with diminishing productivity, compounded by growing inequality, cronyism, corruption, and, ultimately, the failure to improve living standards. Command economies have included the Soviet Union (which, at its peak in 1966, was the world's second-largest economy), China during its Great Leap Forward era circa 1960, India prior to its economic reforms in 1991, and Afghanistan during the rule by Soviet occupation and the Taliban. Today, we see few pure examples, other than North Korea—as exemplified by its economic freedom score of 7.6.

Qualification The command economy and state capitalism overlap on some elements. Surveying the economic environments of various countries practicing state capitalism, such as China, Iran, Rwanda, Russia, Saudi Arabia, and Vietnam, finds the visible hand of an authoritarian state influencing resource allocation, controlling some to many companies, and regulating individual choice. Correspondingly, many of these economies routinely fall in the "mostly unfree" and "repressed" categories of the Economic Freedom Index. Hence, state capitalism exhibits the hallmarks of state control that are suggestive of the command economy. Fundamentally, however, they differ. As noted in the *Looking to the Future* profile, instead of organizing the command economy in terms of a grand ideological agenda, a government instituting state capitalism manipulates the economy with the goal of improving prosperity in order to legitimate and sustain its authority. So, despite points of overlap, state capitalism differs from communism; most notably, the former promotes the authority of the state whereas the latter promotes the ideology of the state.

THE MIXED ECONOMY

The mixed economic system combines elements of the market and command economic systems; both government and private enterprise influence production, consumption, investment, and savings.

Many economies, in some form of the **mixed economy**, fall between the market and command formats. Generally, the mixed economy is a system in which economic decisions are principally market driven and ownership is largely private, but the government intervenes, from a little to a lot, in valuing assets, allocating resources, regulating activities, and organizing commerce. The notion of "mix" follows from the state letting the market allocate resources, as does capitalism, while simultaneously regulating their use given political goals, as does communism. Essentially, the state reasons that it must make strategic decisions about strategic industries in order to optimize market performance. Doing so leads it to institute a mixed economy that blends elements of the market and command systems. Operationally, in shades of the command economy, the state owns some resources, centralizes some planning functions, and regulates some systems. Still, in echoes of the market economy, the state institutes some economic freedoms.

The mixed economy largely relies on the interaction of supply and demand, signaled to producers through the choices that consumers make, rather than state direction, to organize production.[43] For example, in the mixed economy, the government may partially own a carmaker. Rather than dictating the type, quantity, and style of cars it must make, the state grants the carmaker freedom to decide—subject to optimizing public programs and social objectives. Generally, the mixed economy falls short of the productivity of the market economy but outperforms that seen in the command economy. Presently, countries classified as mixed economies include Japan, South Korea, Sweden, France, Brazil, Germany, and India. They typically fall in the "mostly" and "moderately" free categories of the Economic Freedom Index.

The market economy is anchored in capitalism, the command economy is anchored in communism, and the mixed economy is anchored in socialism.

Democracy and the market economy are philosophically congruent. The same goes for communism and the command economy. Likewise, **socialism** is philosophically congruent with the mixed economy. Socialism holds that a fair and just economy, besides optimizing productivity, promotes common cause by maximizing employment, prevents the consolidation of wealth and privilege, helps the poor by redistributing income, stabilizes society by mediating market failures, and protects the public by limiting abuses of market power. Advocates of socialism, and by extension the mixed economy, reason that governments more conscientiously institute an egalitarian ethos that deters the opportunistic individualism found in the market economy while lessening the oppressive collectivism found in the command economy.

Like many aspects of IB, the extent of state intervention in the mixed economy varies. Political leadership, social agendas, and market circumstances differently shape how the state interprets mixing economic freedom and central planning. In Sweden, like fellow Nordic countries, the state applies the idea of *lagom* ("just the right amount") to promote work–life balance, income equality, and inclusive social relations. The state does so by setting employment, social, welfare, environmental, and market standards. Alternatively, France champions the notion of *dirigisme* ("to direct"), whereby the state shapes market conduct, often taking control of key sectors, but refrains from stipulating social standards. Hence, although both are mixed economies, the extent of the French government's direction is less than that seen in Sweden.

ASSESSING ECONOMIC DEVELOPMENT, PERFORMANCE, AND POTENTIAL

4-5 Interpret indicators of economic development, performance, and potential

Managers tap a broad portfolio of macro and micro measures to assess an economy. If anything, executives increasingly face too much, not too little, data. Some, looking for a competitive edge or unique insight, consider informal or idiosyncratic indicators; topics like the number of wireless subscriptions, Internet searches for telltale terms, scale of family-owned conglomerates, or prevalence of military officers controlling companies come into play.[44] Typically, though, convention dominates practice and managers rely on monetary measures to estimate productivity, income, and wealth. Growing concern for climate change and environmental disruption encourages managers to improve analysis with estimators of sustainability and stability. Let's take a look at each perspective.

MONETARY MEASURES

Comprehensive, single-item monetary measures are incisive indicators of whether an economy (1) is expanding or contracting, (2) needs a boost or the brakes, and (3) is threatened by inflation or recession. Consider that taking the temperature of a patient is a simple procedure but quickly highlights the performance of vital activities that are essential to life. The same holds true for single-item monetary measures. Standards, notably gross national income (GNI), gross domestic product (GDP), or gross national product (GNP), take the "temperature" of the economy, efficiently summarizing the activity of households, businesses, and government in terms of their consumption, investment, spending, and trading. Furthermore, tracking real change in an aggregate measure, like GDP, estimates overall production, maps the direction of the market, and indicates the general health of an economy. The GDP statistic, for instance, is regarded as "truly among the great inventions of the twentieth century, a beacon that helps policymakers steer the economy toward key economic objectives."[45]

Among monetary aggregates, GNI provides the broadest measure of economic performance.

Gross national income (GNI) is the broadest measure of a country's economic performance. It has four principal components: personal consumption, business investments, government spending, and net exports of goods and services. It measures the value of all production in the domestic economy together with the income that a country receives from other countries in the forms of profits, interest, and dividends, less the same sorts of payments that it has made to others. For example, the value of a smartphone made by Samsung, a South Korean MNE, as well as the value of a Samsung smartphone made in Japan using Samsung's resources is counted in South Korea's GNI. Similarly, the value of a smartphone made by Sony, a Japanese MNE, in South Korea using Sony's resources counts in the GNI of Japan.

For most countries, the income received versus the payments made generally offset each other. In this situation, there is little difference between GNI and other estimators, like GDP, and managers can confidently use either estimator. For instance, GNI for the United States was less than 1 percent higher than its GDP in 2019. For some countries, MNEs play an outsized role and, consequently, flows are uneven. Large-scale repatriation of profits from the foreign subsidiaries of a country's MNEs, for instance, can drop its GDP below its GNI, thereby understating its performance. In 2019, for instance, Japan's GNI hit $5.263 trillion, given the extensive international operations of its domestic companies; its GDP, however, was $4.97 trillion.

GDP is the total market value of goods and services produced by workers and capital within a nation's borders; it provides the truest measure of a nation's economic activity.

Gross domestic product (GDP) is the total market value of all output produced within a nation's borders, no matter whether it is generated by a domestic or a foreign-owned enterprise; basically, if it's made within a country's borders, GDP counts it.[46] GDP estimates the output from a sample of businesses in every part of a nation's economy, from agriculture to social media. The weight of each sector reflects its relative importance in the national economy. As such, GDP measures the total value of finished goods and services that have been produced for consumers, business, and government within a nation. Measuring the flow of economic activity in terms of the production of, not simply its stock of productive assets, indicates whether an economy is expanding or contracting. Currently, GDP is the most commonly used estimator of economic performance. It functions as a universal benchmark of productivity and prosperity. Table 4.5 lists the largest economies by GDP.

Unlike GNI's sensitivity to ownership, GDP emphasizes the geography of production. That is, it measures the economic activity done by any and all workers within a country's borders. For instance, smartphones made by Samsung and Sony in South Korea contribute to South Korea's GDP. A smartphone made by Samsung in Japan does not. Instead, it counts toward Japan's GDP. Therefore, GDP better estimates performance in those markets, such as South Korea, Ireland, or China, where foreign MNEs' local output is a significant share of business activity. Furthermore, GDP, by tracking only national production, supports short-term analysis and facilitates cross-national comparisons. Countries began emphasizing GDP in the 1960s. By the 1990s, it had eclipsed GNP, the previous standard.[48]

TABLE 4.5 The 10 Largest Economies by GDP[a]

Rank	Country	Type of Economy	GDP ($, trillions)	Percent of World Economy	Economic Freedom Score
1	United States	Developed	22.32	26.31	76.8
2	China	Emerging	15.27	18	58.4
3	Japan	Developed	5.41	6.38	72.1
4	Germany	Developed	3.98	4.69	73.5
5	India	Emerging	3.2	3.77	55.2
6	France	Developed	2.77	3.27	63.8
7	United Kingdom	Developed	2.72	3.21	78.9
8	Italy	Developed	2.01	2.37	62.2
9	Brazil	Emerging	1.89	2.23	51.9
10	Canada	Emerging	1.81	2.13	77.7
	World		84.83	72.36	60.8

Sources: International Monetary Fund 2019 and 2019 Index of Economic Freedom.[47]

GNP is the total value of all final goods and services produced within a nation in a particular year.

Gross national product (GNP) begins by estimating the market value of goods and services produced in a given year by the labor, assets, and capital supplied by the resident of a country. It then adds the income that its citizens earned working abroad, but removes the income earned by foreigners working within its national borders—the latter counts toward their home nation's GNP. Effectively, GNP estimates economic performance in terms of the location of ownership, including production done locally as well as when the country's capital or labor produces value outside its borders. As such, unlike GDP, GNP tallies all of the activity by citizens and companies of a nation—even if this activity takes place in another country.

IMPROVING ECONOMIC ANALYTICS

Managers improve the usefulness of economic indicators by adjusting for the

- growth rate of the economy,
- the nation's population,
- local cost of living.

GNI, GDP, and GNP estimate an economy's absolute performance. Despite strengths, they can distort estimations and comparisons. For example, economic powers like the United States, Japan, and Germany consistently claim the top rankings in the league tables for GNI, GDP, and GNP. Some may infer that their economies are also more productive than lower-ranked countries. Often, the opposite is true. Therefore, managers improve the usefulness of economic indicators by adjusting for the (1) rate of economic growth, (2) number of people in a country, and (3) purchasing power of the local currency.

Rate of Economic Growth Monetary aggregates take a snapshot of an economy at a point in time. Hence, they do not measure its rate of change. A key aspect of an economy's performance is its growth rate. In the short term, an expanding economy, indicated by positive growth in, say, GDP, means that business, jobs, and personal income are expanding. Longer term, GDP's growth rate estimates a country's economic potential: if it is growing faster (or *slower*) than the growth rate of its population, then the country's standards of living are rising (or *falling*).

Qualifying measures by their growth rate helps identify promising business opportunities. Looking at the 217 countries that compose the global business environment, one finds, as expected, variability in the growth rates from country to country. Notably, GDP in many emerging and developing economies, such as Ghana, Ethiopia, India, or Côte d'Ivoire, is rising at up to 10 times faster than that seen in the developed economies. China, for instance, has been one of the fastest-growing economies over the past three decades; on average, it has grown more than 8 percent annually since 1995. Commensurately, its GDP has gone from about $600 billion at that time to $15 trillion in 2018. Its expanding market has created many jobs, boosted workers' income, increased aggregate demand, attracted foreign investors, and raised living standards.

Population Size Managers routinely adjust indicators by the number of people who live in a country. This conversion is sensible given how unevenly the world's population of 7.63 billion is distributed (e.g., from a high of 1.389 billion in China to a low of 50 in the Pitcairn Islands).[49] China is the world's second-largest economy when ranked by GDP. Adjusting its performance for its population, however, moves it to the lower-middle tier. Similarly, in 2018, Switzerland's GDP of $705 billion is 3.7 percent of the $20.5 trillion reported by the United States. However, given its population of 8.57 million residents, Switzerland's GDP per capita is $80,450. In comparison, GDP per capita in the United States is $62,794 given its 327 million citizens.[50]

Purchasing power parity controls for differences in the relative cost of living between countries.

Purchasing Power Parity The prices of goods and services vary from country to country due to, among other things, differences in factor endowments, productivity rates, and regulations. Some prices vary little, say from one developed economy to another developed economy. Some vary a lot, say from a developed country to a developing country. A liter of gasoline, for instance, sells for $1.90, $1.93, or $2.30 in Netherlands, Iceland, or Hong Kong, respectively. Meanwhile, the same liter costs $0.01, $0.11, or $0.35 in Venezuela, Iran, or Kuwait, respectively.[51] Consequently, simple comparisons of GDP per capita, while giving a quick sense of conditions among countries, can misrepresent key differences. Overlooked, price differentials confound analysis. Understandably, managers adjust monetary measures to account for the fact that a dollar of income in Miami does not have has the same purchasing power as a dollar of income in Mumbai given the dramatic difference in the cost of living between India and the United States.

Adjusting for **purchasing power parity (PPP)** between countries resolves this problem. It controls for how many goods and services one can buy with a unit of income in one country versus how much one can buy with an equivalent unit of income in another country. Technically, one applies the rate at which the currency of one country converts into that of another country in order to buy an equivalent "basket" of goods and services. The basket commonly includes items such as a liter of cooking oil, cell-phone plan, liter of gasoline, and even a McDonald's Big Mac. Setting equivalent baskets and then calculating their local price given the relative cost of living and currency effects between countries—say, India and the United States—makes the purchasing power of a dollar in Mumbai equivalent to that in Miami. Historically, the PPP conversion rate is set in terms of the number of units of a country's currency needed to buy a basket of goods and services with an equivalent basket in the United States.

Table 4.6 shows the effect of adjusting national economic performance by PPP. The rankings by GDP reported in Table 4.5 change significantly. For instance, China displaces the United States as the largest economy in the world—its GDP of $15.27 trillion, adjusted for PPP, nearly doubles to $29.47 trillion. Similarly, PPP adjustments boost India and Russia, drop Japan, Germany, the United Kingdom, and France, and replace Italy with Indonesia. Likewise, PPP adjustments reduce some of the otherwise extreme variability in country-to-country per capita comparisons. For instance, Switzerland's GDP per capita of $80,450 falls to $68,060 when adjusted for the reduced purchasing power that a unit of its currency has in its high-priced market. We see the opposite in countries with less expensive standards of living, such as India; its GDP per capita of $2,041 more than triples to $7,762 when adjusted for PPP.[52] These sorts of adjustments help explain the appeal of the Base of the Pyramid, highlighting the real economic potential of the billions of poorer people spanning the globe. Map 4.3 profiles countries in terms of GDP per capita adjusted for PPP.

THE WILDCARD: THE SHADOW ECONOMY

Estimating and adjusting GNI, GDP, and GNP, as well as a host of similar indicators, requires data that fully represents activity in a national economy. Throughout the world, governments ably collect data and generate statistics. Their efforts are complicated by the **shadow economy**—sometimes called the black, gray, or parallel market, informal economy, or System D. Found anywhere and everywhere, the shadow economy includes extralegal activities (e.g., driving an unlicensed shuttle, covert payoffs, travel-visa violations, under-the-table activity, unregistered day-care centers, and similar sorts of shady transactions) as well as illegal doings (e.g., drug slinging, prostitution, illicit gambling, cigarette and alcohol smuggling, product piracy) that fall beyond the official statistics. Besides conducting business in hard-to-track cash, shadow players typically go to great lengths to hide illicit transactions or dodge taxes. The off-the-books activities of the shadow economy evade and, therefore, confound estimates of the scale and scope of economic activity in a country.[53]

TABLE 4.6 The 10 Largest Economies, GDP Adjusted for Purchasing Power Parity

Rank	Country	Population (millions)	GDP by PPP (US$ trillions)	Percent of World Economy	Economic Freedom Score
1	China	1,341	29.47	21.62	58.4
2	United States	322	22.32	16.38	76.8
3	India	1,267	12.36	9.07	62.2
4	Japan	127	5.89	4.32	72.1
5	Germany	83	4.59	3.37	73.5
6	Russia	142	4.52	3.32	58.9
7	Indonesia	252	4	2.93	65.8
8	Brazil	203	3.6	2.64	51.9
9	United Kingdom	63	3.24	2.38	78.9
10	France	64	3.16	2.32	63.8
	World	7,556,278	$135.24	68.34	

Sources: International Monetary Fund 2019 and the 2019 Index of Economic Freedom.

MAP 4.3 GDP per Capita, Adjusted for Purchasing Power Parity

Source: Based on World Bank Indicators. Retrieved January 21, 2020 from http://data.worldbank.org/indicator/NY.GDP.PCAP.PP.CD/countries?display=map.

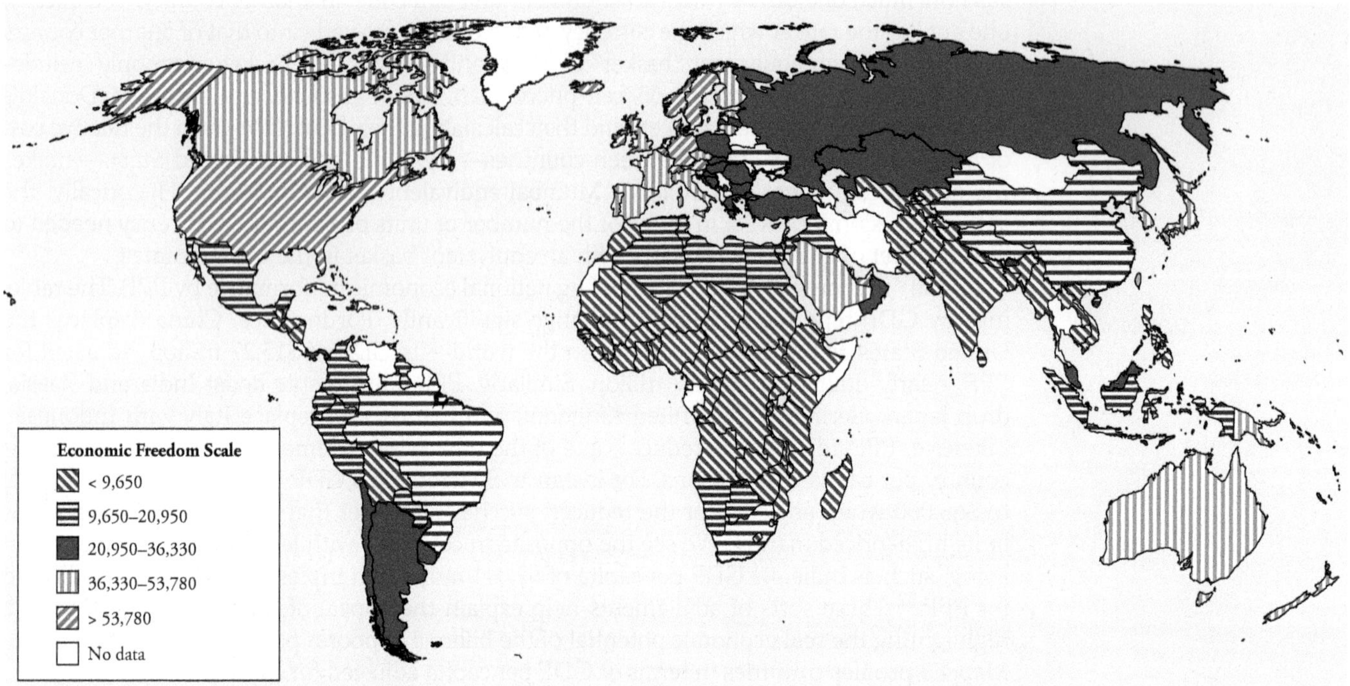

Developed economies, such as Canada, Germany, and the United States, tend to have a smaller shadow economy than emerging and developing economies, such as Greece, India, and Mexico. In the developed economies, the shadow economy generally runs 5 to 15 percent of GDP. In developing economies, it runs much higher—reports estimate up to 60 percent of GDP in, for example, Georgia, Bolivia, Azerbaijan, Tanzania, Thailand, Uruguay, and Guatemala. The IMF reports that the average size of the shadow economy in 158 countries from 1991 to 2015 was 31.9 percent. Similarly, the OECD reports that the informal economy in developing and emerging countries employs 70 percent of all workers; it's about 18 percent in developed countries.[54] Some estimate that worldwide, the shadow economy is approximately a quarter of global GDP.[55]

The scale and scope of shadow economies spur some governments to rethink how they tally GDP. For example, growing pressure to keep a nation's debt and deficits, relative to the size of its reported GDP, within the EU's prescribed targets spurs some European countries to find ways to increase the size of their economy. Ireland, Italy, and the United Kingdom, among others, move to include shadow activities when measuring national production. The United Kingdom, for example, estimated that including the value of illicit drug trade (about $7.5 billion) and prostitution activity (about $9 billion) would boost its GDP by 0.7 percent.[56] Including all extralegal and illegal activities that go uncounted would lift British GDP by more than 10 percent.[57]

SUSTAINABILITY AND STABILITY

CONCEPT CHECK

Chapter 1 notes that some groups oppose globalization, Chapter 2 discussed cultural objections, and Chapter 3 identified political reasons that inspire opposition. Here, we add that critics charge that overly emphasizing monetary measures misrepresents the economic benefits of globalization.

Representing the performance of an economy beyond the information provided by monetary aggregates directs our attention to estimating its sustainability and stability. Specifically, GNI, GDP, and GNP, even after adjusting for growth rates, population size, and purchasing power, partially profile a country's performance and potential. Besides the complications posed by the shadow economy, underestimating the costs and consequences of growth erodes the validity of analysis. Furthermore, anchoring GNI, GNP, and GDP in terms of "gross" rather than "net" signifies that the cost of the resources used in production is not deducted from the value of total output. Moreover, monetary aggregates miss other costs, so-called externalities like air, water, or noise pollution, which result from economic activity. Measuring the monetary quantity of market activity without accounting for the associated costs that result from those

These street vendors in Nha Trang, Vietnam are far off the official market grid. Their sales, each small, but when combined, immense, fall in the realm of the shadow economy.

Source: Busurmanov/Shutterstock

activities misestimates performance and misrepresents potential. Improving estimation and interpretation calls for expanding analytics in terms of standards of sustainability and stability.

SUSTAINABILITY

Green economics advocates assessing economic performance in terms of the effect of current choices on long-term sustainability.

Green economics holds that an economy is a component of, and ultimately dependent on, the natural world. Sustaining productive business activity hinges on minimizing its environmental impact. In this context, **sustainability** advocates accounting for the gains and the costs of growth by complementing monetary metrics with measures of economic performance that estimate "meeting the needs of the present without compromising the ability of future generations to meet their own needs."[58] Presently Sweden, Norway, Iceland, Finland, and Denmark top the world rankings for sustainability. At the other extreme, Iraq, Yemen, the Seychelles, South Sudan, and Haiti face the greatest challenge. Several proposals outline paths to "greenify" GNI, GNP, or GDP. Current candidates include the following:

- **Net national product (NNP)** In theory, a country can measure the depletion of natural resources and degradation of the environment that result from making and consuming products. Just as a company depreciates its assets when making a product, green economics argues so too should countries. NNP does so by depreciating the country's assets commensurate with their use in generating output.[59]
- **Genuine Progress Indicator (GPI)** This measure begins by applying the same accounting framework used to estimate GDP. It then adjusts for the corresponding costs of reduced environmental quality, health and hygiene, security, equity, free time, and education. For example, unlike GDP, GPI counts voluntary and unpaid household work as paid labor and subtracts the costs linked to crime, pollution, and family stress. Effectively, GDP versus GPI is analogous to gross profits versus net profits—accounting for the costs incurred to create economic value converts gross GDP to net GPI. Accordingly, GPI equals zero if the costs of pollution, crime, and family stress, holding all other factors constant, equal the monetary gains from the production of goods and services.
- **Human Development Index (HDI)** The matters of human development do not show up immediately in performance measures. Ultimately, the reasoning goes, they will, given that improving the human condition through nutrition, education, health care, and hygiene improves performance. So, estimating a country's degree of human development in terms of the physical, intellectual, and social standards that shape its overall quality of life helps managers more comprehensively assess its economy. The United Nations translates this view into the HDI and its primary components: *Longevity*, measured by life expectancy at birth; *Knowledge*, measured by the adult literacy rate and the combined primary, secondary, and tertiary gross enrollment ratio; and *Standard of Living*, measured by GNI per capita (PPP). Nations scoring high on the HDI include Norway, Australia, Switzerland, Denmark, and the Netherlands. Laggards include Benin, Uganda, Rwanda, Haiti, and Togo.[60]

STABILITY

Sustainability and stability perspectives hold that the objective of economic activity is to create an environment for people to enjoy long, healthy, and happy lives.

Universal affluence, despite its appeal, is practically impossible: the earth lacks sufficient resources to support and sustain high consumption for its 7.6 billion inhabitants, to say nothing of the projected population of 9.7 billion by 2050. Indeed, warns the WorldWatch Institute, if all countries were to consume resources and produce pollution at the current per capita level in the United States, an affluent country, we would require five planet Earths to provide the resources needed to meet demand, process waste, and sustain the system. Rather than assessing an economy's potential for increasing affluence, perspectives like **happynomics** and welfare economics encourage including elements of psychology, health, security, and sociology. More fundamentally, they advocate redefining the traditional performance standards of wealth, income, or profit to reflect principles of well-being, quality of life, and life satisfaction. As the United Nations declares, "Happiness is increasingly considered a proper measure of social progress and a goal of public policy."[61]

Green economics argues that fully measuring growth, progress, and prosperity calls for assessing the consequences of economic choice on sustainability and stability.

Happynomics encourages moving "from the concept of financial prosperity to the idea of emotional prosperity."[62] The constitution of Bhutan, for instance, advocates making its citizens happier, not richer, every year; goals include boosting the happiness of society, people's satisfaction with their lives, and national well-being independent of monetary achievement. Rethinking economic activity in terms of happiness, the argument goes, promotes the sustainability and stability that better represents performance and estimate potential. For instance, happynomics reports that nearly 70 percent of personal satisfaction is determined by the quantity and quality of interpersonal relationships, not by production, income flow, or wealth accumulation.[63] The United States, when rated on monetary metrics, leads Australia, the Netherlands, and Sweden. Re-sorting performance in terms of life expectancy, leisure time, income equality, freedom to make life choices, generosity, and trust, however, moves Australia, the Netherlands, and Sweden ahead of the United States. Currently, according to the United Nations, the league table of the happiest countries in the world is topped by Finland, followed by Denmark, Luxembourg, Norway, Iceland, and the Netherlands.[64]

Estimating stability, happiness, and the like is difficult. For instance, happiness, like beauty, is often in the eye of the beholder. Potential indicators such as enjoyment, altruism, engagement, or, conversely, depression, sadness, and stress, are notoriously difficult to pin down. In addition, how does one assign a monetary value to reasonable goals, like safe streets and clean air, which one can measure objectively? Some contend that mapping happiness unnecessarily confuses economic analysis. Others counter that an unhappy citizenry may be a leading indicator of a secular shift in consumption or social instability that threatens economic performance. Too, measuring subjective well-being encourages officials, for instance, to improve the design of public spaces and the delivery of public services, thereby increasing economic potential.

The intricacies of happiness capture increasing attention. Insights progressively improve measurement. The United Nations, for instance, is progressively operationalizing its resolution, *Happiness and Well-Being: Defining a New Economic Paradigm,* into practical measurements.[65] In the meantime, managers consult the following indicators:

- **Your Better Life Index (YBLI)** Developed by the OECD, the YBLI advocates evaluating economic performance in terms of 11 aspects of life that people worldwide believe are important (e.g., housing, jobs, relationships, health, security, family–life–work balance, education), but that fall beyond the scope of monetary measures. The YBLI redirect attention to assessing people's well-being and perceptions of living standards. Explained the OECD, YBLI pushes the "boundaries of knowledge and understanding in a pioneering and innovative manner. . . It has extraordinary potential to help us deliver better policies for better lives."[66]
- **Gross National Wellness (GNW)** This outlook holds that that material and spiritual development occur side by side; one reinforces the other or both suffer. It stipulates that the purpose of government is promoting happiness. GNW measures a country's capacity to use its resources to promote individual well-being in terms of economic, environmental, physical, mental, work, social, and political dimensions of life.
- **Gross National Happiness (GNH)** This index emphasizes collective happiness and well-being of the population. GNH emphasizes equitable and sustainable socioeconomic

development, elevating spirituality, preserving cultural values, conserving the natural environment, and championing fair, just governance. Philosophically, it's anchored in the precepts of Buddhism. Practically, the Constitution of Bhutan, notably, endorses this view and stipulates happiness as the goal of the government.

- **Happy Planet Index (HPI)** The utilitarian view holds that people aspire to live long, healthy, ecologically sensitive lives. How well an economy helps its citizens to do so, while not infringing on the opportunity of people in other countries as well as future generations to do the same, fully represents its performance and potential. HPI defines progress not in terms of economic development, but success in achieving sustainable well-being for all.[67] Currently, the HPI ranks 140 countries. Costa Rica leads the world table; Mexico, Colombia, Vanuatu, and Vietnam follow it. At the other end, Chad, Luxembourg, and Togo face the biggest tests.

CONCEPT CHECK

As we saw in Chapter 1, critics of globalization point to the inefficient use of resources to promote economic activity. Hence, some advocate including measures of sustainability and stability to better estimate the benefits and costs of globalization.

POINT

Growth: Positive and Productive?

YES Growth is not only good, it is an absolute necessity. Growth is life, the instrumentality to actualize the productive potential of individuals, communities, and countries. Growth creates benefits for everyone, everywhere. It morally stabilizes society. It liberates those trapped in poverty. It reduces violent conflict. It raises living standards. It funds safety nets and government backstops. It inspires material improvements that make life comfortable. It creates jobs, income, wealth, and prosperity for individuals and society. Let's take a closer look at the positive and productive benefits of growth.

Poverty Reduction Notwithstanding the kindness of strangers, growth is the only means to alleviate poverty for the billions struggling to sustain life. Growth has greatly reduced the number of people living in abject poverty. Some 1.94 billion people, or 43 percent of the world population, lived in extreme poverty in 1981. Today, as freer markets fuel growth, it has dropped to 10 percent—about 800 million people.[68] Without growth, humanity loses the war against poverty and countless millions suffer.

Civil Stability Growth rallies social attitudes and fortifies political institutions; both anchor civil stability. People experiencing rising incomes are more tolerant of and benevolent toward each other. In a word, wealth engenders humanity. Growth creates the resources that promote transparency of authority, openness of opportunity, tolerance of diversity, pathways of social mobility, and fair and just laws.

Business Dividend Growth stimulates employment, inspires investment, and improves productivity. Rising asset valuations, stabilizing wealth effects, and confidence in overcoming tough times fortifies individuals and companies. Amidst the panic of the global financial crisis, for instance, people drew support from the virtue of growth. Some 76 percent of Americans agreed

COUNTERPOINT

Growth: Positive and Productive?

NO We accept the premise that growth supports life, powerfully fostering morality, transparency, tolerance, mobility, equality, justice, and liberty. However, ignoring or, worse, denying the costs of these benefits, costs that seem to grow faster than growth itself, imperils civil society and, ultimately, the stability of humanity and the sustainability of the planet. Once you untangle the strands of half-truths, falsehoods, and self-interests that lace deceptive pro-growth arguments, the promise of endless milk and honey for all devolves into a bitter delusion. The problems of growth span the present and the future; where one stops and the other starts is tough to pinpoint. Still, as we contend, each hits humanity hard.

Growth Privileges Few The quintessential promise of growth is "a rising tide lifts all boats." In theory, as an economy grows, it generates higher wages and income for all. In reality, the benefits of growth are unevenly distributed, thereby creating and perpetuating extreme inequalities of wealth and power. Unquestionably, increasing growth has raised the tide worldwide. However, a share of the global population has seen their patchwork-rafts capsize, many struggle to keep their leaky boats afloat, and a tiny set have upgraded to even more stunningly ostentatious yachts.

Growth Is Misleading Despite the hype and hoopla, ultimately growth does not deliver the benefits it promises. It rewards the financially strong but punishes the economically weak. It liberates people from old routines, but enslaves them to new habits. It creates free time to spend with family and community but then demands mobility and migration that cut connections. It promises newer, cooler products to enable self-fulfillment but insidiously traps consumers in a never-ending cycle of hope, deception, and disappointment. Put simply, growth oversells and underdelivers, condemning people that U.S. strength is "mostly based on the success of American business" and 90 percent stated that they respect people who "get rich by working hard."[69]

Fiscal Dividend Government finances are ultimately at the mercy of growth. A thriving economy boosts tax revenues, thereby providing local, state, regional, and national governments the funds to finance spending projects that support, enrich, and sustain society. Besides investing in a brigher future, fiscal dividends support transition times for people experiencing difficulties whether from unemployment, family struggles, and even the consequences of natural disasters. Although appealing, history shows cheap government does not translate into good government. Growing fiscal and monetary stability grows good governance.

Peace Dividend Growth creates more opportunities for more people in more places. People who see the potential for prosperity behave peacefully. Poor people who move into the middle class, for example, think and behave differently. Freed from the tyranny of ceaselessly seeking sustenance, shelter, and security, they become more open-minded, more concerned about their children's future, more influenced by abstract values than traditional norms, more inclined to settle conflicts peacefully, more supportive of free markets and democracy, and more confident in a brighter future. People safeguarding their assets see immense value in maintaining stable communities. Ultimately, progressive outlooks on people, processes, principles, and prospects promote peacefulness.

Environmental Benefits Growth encourages innovation, spurring people to specialize in what they do best and outsource the rest. Ingenious plans to do more with less optimize resource allocation and maximize productivity. The falling ratio of energy consumption per unit of GDP, in the face of the growing abundance of goods and services, testifies to the efficiencies of growth. By making resources valuable, growth makes us consume them wisely.

Quest to Excel Growth incentivizes people to bring to bear their initiative, imagination, and industriousness to find a better way, every day, to make a difference. Pushing back the frontier of human experience—whether it involves the trivial (e.g., the latest social fad) or the substantive (e.g., alternative energy)—is powered by the quest to grow. Eliminating the pursuit of profit, by diminishing the quest to excel, saps society's vibrancy.

Life Growth supports longer lives. In 1900, life expectancy at birth was 47 years in the United States. In 2020, after a century marked by an epic burst in growth, it was 78 years. Earlier, in the 1990s, work, and life as well, was likely to be "solitary, poor, nasty, brutish, and short."[70] Following a century of progress, people now must work just half the time they once had to, leveraging improving tools to boost productivity, benefiting from rising quality of life, taking solace in better health care, and finding inspiration in brighter prospects.

to "spiritual despair scarcely concealed by the frantic pace of life."[71] People, trapped on hedonic treadmills, endlessly searching for newer, shinier, better, bigger, smaller, faster, or fancier, confuse consumption of the latest and greatest as the path toward actualization—i.e., "I shop, therefore I am."

Growth Threatens Life Polluted air, poisoned water, and toxic land, let alone climate change, biodiversity collapse, and resource depletion, are the inevitable by-products of growth. Indisputably, some production provides crucial goods and services. Overproduction, however, destabilizes the basis of life. Ironically, when we measure the value created by an economy, say, with GDP or GNI, no costs are tallied. Rather, they are labeled "externalities," mysteriously understood to affect society but conveniently excluded while we sing the praises of the wondrous benefits of growth in the church of conspicuous consumption. Effectively, since "nobody" is responsible for the costs of externalities, "nobody" pays for them, and the growth engine chugs merrily along. Ultimately, "everybody" pays with a despoiled environment, financial servitude, warped values, and growing alienation and anomie.

Growth Diminishes Individuality Growth's mandate to maximize efficiency demands massification—mass production, mass consumption, mass distribution, mass markets, mass media, and so on. Maximizing massification delivers tremendous economic benefits but at extreme social costs. One analyst notes that "a part of the price that people in the West pay for this unending procession of shiny assembly-line products is the concomitant loss of those now rarer things that once imparted zest and gratification—the loss of individuality, uniqueness and flavor; the loss of craftsmanship, local variety and richness; the loss of intimacy and atmosphere, of eccentricity and character."[72] Sadly, growth for the sake of growth replaces material poverty with moral poverty.

Current Growth Is Unsustainable Humanity plunders the earth at an unprecedented rate. Presently, human consumption is 30 percent greater than nature's capacity to regenerate. By 2050, at current trends, humanity will require three to five planets of natural resources just to keep the game going. "For more than 20 years we have exceeded the Earth's ability to support a consumptive lifestyle that is unsustainable, and we cannot afford to continue down this path," warns the WorldWatch Institute.[73] Barring black-swan innovations in mining, agriculture, manufacturing, and recycling, no matter how hard we wish otherwise, Mother Earth will stop current growth patterns sooner rather than later.

Change the Game Our position is straightforward. Epic poverty for billions, slow-motion death spiral of ecosystems, false hope of actualization through consumption, binge-buying alienation, and the deterioration

Progress or Decline Unquestionably, as the Counterpoint argues, growth imposes costs on individuals, humanity, and the planet. We agree that these costs are striking, but in the grand scheme, understandable and ultimately manageable. The benefits of growth continually inspire bright people to imagine bright solutions that build a brighter future. In sum, our position is unequivocal: No matter the costs of growth, they pale in comparison to the unacceptable price and indefensible policy of no growth. Bluntly put, when growth stops, decay starts.

of nominal democracies into shadow plutocracies puts us at the proverbial fork in the road. We can remain blissfully ignorant of the price of growth, seduced by the endless rush of apparent gains, but continually surprised by inevitable and underestimated externalities. Alternatively, we can face the issue full on, applying the standards of sustainability and radically resetting the economy so that growth "meets the needs of the present without compromising the ability of future generations to meet their own needs."

ELEMENTS OF ECONOMIC ANALYSIS

4-6 Discuss elements of economic analysis

Estimating a market's attractiveness as a place to do business and, once there, making smart investment and sound operating decisions centers on understanding the fundamental features of its economy. Narrow (e.g., GNI, GDP, and GNP) and broad (e.g., HDI, HPI, and NNP) measures estimate absolute and relative economic conditions. In theory, partial equilibrium analysis encourages assessing a restricted range of discrete indicators to refine analyses and elaborate interpretation. For instance, central bankers' monetary policies directly influence interest and inflation rates. Hence, managers keen to the performance of capital markets concentrate on those sorts of indicators. Managers in other industries similarly focus on measures critical to their activities. Table 4.7 profiles several indicators that managers track to make sense of an economy.

TABLE 4.7 Key Components of Economic Analysis

Dimension	Specification	Implication
Balance of Payments (BOP)	Summary of an economy's trade and financial transactions, as conducted by individuals, businesses, and government agencies, with the rest of the world.	Indicates if a country has sufficient savings to pay for its imports as well as if it produces enough income to finance growth.
Deflation	General decline in prices, often caused by a reduction in the supply of money or credit or declining aggregate demand.	Slows economic growth; anticipating lower prices, consumers defer purchases, thereby risking a deflationary spiral. Increases the real value of debt.
Foreign Direct Investment	Controlling ownership in a business enterprise in one country by an entity based in another country.	Promotes development, job expansion, industrialization, and exports. Transfers skills and technologies.
Income Distribution	The distribution of income among a nation's population; estimated by the GINI coefficient.[74]	Equality stabilizes society and opens opportunities; inequality promotes debt, stress, and risks.
Inflation	The sustained rise in consumer prices measured against a standard level of purchasing power.	Influences interest rates, living costs, consumer confidence, and, ultimately, political stability.
Misery Index	The sum of a country's inflation and unemployment rates. The higher the sum, the greater the economic misery.	Higher misery discourages spending and investment in the face of growing austerity.
Poverty	Multidimensional condition whereby a person or community lacks the essentials for a minimum standard of well-being and life.	Persistent poverty destabilizes performance and constrains potential. Creates stress points that challenge civil society.
Public Debt	The total of a state's financial obligations; measures what the government borrows from its citizens, foreign organizations, foreign governments, and international institutions.	Decreasing debt opens growth opportunities. Growing debt signals increasing austerity, rising taxes, and, if uncontrolled, debt crises that impose political, economic, and social costs.
Unemployment	The share of out-of-work citizens actively seeking employment for pay relative to the total civilian labor force.	People gainfully employed testify to the competency of policymakers to sustain a productive economy. Persistent unemployment indicates government ineptitude.

INTEGRATING ECONOMIC ANALYSIS

4-7 Profile approaches to integrate economic analysis

The scale and scope of an economic environment make it impossible to fully represent its performance and potential in terms of a set of individual estimators. Just as no one is an island, no country is isolated. Likewise, economic environments are dynamic systems that, given the catalysts of globalization, encourage expanding networks of people, processes, and products. Studying the connections among the elements of a system refines analysis. Popular indices include the following:

The Global Competitiveness Index (GCI) The World Economic Forum holds that increasing prosperity hinges on how effectively a country develops institutions, regulates activity, and uses resources to improve productivity. A country's proficiency in developing these domains, in turn, determines its international competitiveness.[75] The GCI integrates relationships among 110 variables spanning 12 "pillars of competitiveness." Pillars tap dimensions like financial market development, macroeconomic environment, technological readiness, market efficiency, and innovation.

CONCEPT CHECK

Making sense of the different domains in a big world, as we saw in Chapters 1, 2, and 3, encourages integrating indicators into a comprehensive index. Indices of the sort we see here help managers develop a holistic profile of an economy in terms of productivity, competitiveness, and innovation.

An economy's productivity, namely its efficiency in converting inputs into useful outputs, is a key determinant of its competitiveness.

The impact of each pillar on competitiveness varies across countries, given the stage of economic development, as indicated by GDP per capita. Competitiveness in developed economies, like Sweden or Taiwan, is driven by ideas and innovations. Alternatively, it's determined by endowments of labor and natural resources in developing economies like Ghana or Cambodia. Currently, developed countries claim the top spots in the GCI standings: the United States is the global leader, followed by Singapore, Germany, Switzerland, and Japan. Of the big emerging economies, China and India steadily rise in the rankings. Some smaller markets, notably Taiwan, Qatar, Malaysia, the Czech Republic, and the United Arab Emirates, are rising quickly.[76]

The World Competitiveness Index (WCI) The World Competitiveness Project assesses a nation's ability to set and sustain a business environment that enables enterprises to compete, prosper, and create wealth. Four factors determine a nation's competitiveness: economic performance, government efficiency, business efficiency, and infrastructure. Each category has sub-measures that tap dimensions such as international trade, employment, prices, business legislation, productivity, and management practices. Ultimately, the WCI evaluates more than 300 criteria to summarize a nation's performance. Singapore, on the strength of its business efficiency, financial sector, innovation, and infrastructure, tops the WCI scoreboard. The performance of other high-ranking counties, such as Hong Kong, Switzerland, Sweden, and Germany, highlights the importance of improving business efficiency, supporting new business development, and promoting international connectivity. Notably, trade tensions between China and the United States weakened their competitiveness; the latest rankings dropped China to 20th (it had been 14th) while the United States dropped to 10th (it had been 3rd).[77]

The Global Innovation Index (GII) Countries increasingly look to brainpower for innovations that boost productivity, fortify competitiveness, and increase prosperity. The growing power of ideas makes a country's capacity for innovation a key determinant of its performance and potential in the global market. Rather than focus on the scale of research and development, the GII estimates a nation's capacity to imagine ideas, leverage them into pioneering products, and, in the process, generate knowledge, fortify competitiveness, and sustain prosperity.

The GII anchors analysis in terms of inputs and outputs. Inputs, which promote and enable innovation, include institutions and policies, human capacity, infrastructure, technological sophistication, business markets, and capital. Alternatively, outputs include knowledge, competitiveness, and wealth. Collectively, these indicators measure a country's competency in promoting technologies, expanding human capacities, streamlining organizational capabilities, and improving institutional responsiveness. The GII indicates that economies that consistently transform neat ideas into real innovations excel.[78]

Currently, developed countries claim the top spots in the GII standings: Switzerland ranks first, followed by the Netherlands, Sweden, and the United Kingdom. Accelerating innovation in Eastern Europe, notably Estonia, Slovenia, and the Czech Republic, and Asia, notably South Korea, Hong Kong, and China, improve their positioning. Collectively, the data show emerging economies shifting from practices that had optimized industrial efficiency to policies that improve the environment for innovation—such as seen in China's OBOR and "Made in China 2025" initiatives.

The Best Countries Index (BCI) The BCI sees a country's wealth and success resulting from policies that create possibilities, the people that achieve them, and the history that anchors its outlook and orientation. The BCI evaluates 65 characteristics in terms of global perceptions that influence trade, travel, and investment that, in turn, productively shape a nation's economy. Dimensions include citizenship, cultural influence, entrepreneurship, heritage, and quality of life. A survey of more than 20,000 people worldwide considered 80 countries. Switzerland ranks first, followed by Japan, Canada, Germany, and the United Kingdom. Of the top 25 countries, 22 are developed economies while three are emerging economies, specifically, China, United Arab Emirates, and Russia.

The Where-To-Be-Born Index (WTBBI) Looking a bit further into the future, the WTBBI holds that how well a country provides opportunities for a healthy, safe, and prosperous life helps explain its current and future performance.[79] The WTBBI evaluates 11 indicators, such as geography, demography, quality of life, per capita income, and life expectancy. The "lucky baby" league table, comprising 80 countries, is topped by Switzerland, followed by Australia, Norway, Sweden, and Denmark. Smaller nations lead the rankings, accounting for the top 15 countries in the lottery of life. Large, wealthy countries—notably the United States, Japan, France, and Great Britain—populate the next tier. Emerging and developing economies run from the middle to the bottom of the ranking.

ECONOMIC FREEDOM, INNOVATION, AND COMPETITIVENESS

Economic freedom has a direct relationship with a country's relative competitiveness and innovation performance.

We close by profiling the connection of the conceptual anchor of this chapter, economic freedom, to meta-measures of economic vitality. Specifically, Table 4.8 reports the economic freedom score for various countries as well as their ranking on the preceding indices. Countries with higher degrees of economic freedom consistently exhibit higher degrees of competitiveness and innovation. Smaller markets, notably Singapore, Switzerland, and Sweden stand out; each has high economic freedom and ranks highly in terms of competitiveness, innovation, and, incidentally,

TABLE 4.8 Integrating Economic Freedom, Innovation, and Competitiveness[80]

Nation	Economic Freedom Score	Type of Economy	Global Competitiveness Index, Rank	World Competitiveness Index, Rank	Global Innovation Index, Rank	Best Countries Index, Rank	Where-To-Be-Born Index Rank
Singapore	89.4	Developed	1	1	8	15	6
Switzerland	81	Developed	5	3	1	1	1
Australia	80.9	Developed	16	18	22	7	2
Canada	77.1	Developed	14	8	17	3	9
United States	76.2	Developed	2	10	3	8	17
Sweden	75.2	Developed	8	6	2	6	4
Malaysia	74	Emerging	27	27	35	38	36
Germany	73.5	Developed	7	17	9	4	16
South Korea	72.3	Developed	13	23	11	22	19
Japan	72.1	Developed	6	34	15	2	25
Poland	67.8	Emerging	37	39	39	33	33
Colombia	67.3	Emerging	57	54	63	66	42
Indonesia	65.8	Emerging	50	40	85	43	71
Mexico	64.7	Emerging	48	53	56	35	39
Philippines	63.8	Emerging	64	45	54	50	63
Saudi Arabia	60.7	Developing	36	24	68	32	38
Russia	58.9	Emerging	43	50	46	24	72
China	58.4	Emerging	28	20	14	16	49
South Africa	58.3	Emerging	60	59	63	*	53
India	55.2	Emerging	68	43	52	27	66
Brazil	51.9	Emerging	71	56	66	28	37

as a promising place to be born. Among larger systems, the United States is the standard setter. Overall, the data indicate that countries that champion economic freedom, purposefully improving the efficiency of business activity and flexibility of individual choice, are more likely to sustain productive economies. In turn, they reap the rewards of world-class innovation and competitiveness. Ultimately, these accomplishments support improving living standards.

CASE

Economic Environments of the West: Problems, Puzzles, and the Fourth Industrial Revolution

Scanning the emerging economies, such as China, India, Brazil, and Indonesia, we find entrepreneurial folks and enterprising companies seeking brighter futures. Scanning the developed economies of the West, such as Canada, Germany, Italy, and the United States, we find folks chasing similar dreams. Different economic circumstances, however, means those in the developed economies face different opportunities and challenges than their counterparts in the emerging economies.

The sheer stature of Western markets—although 14 percent of the global population, they account for 40 percent of global GDP—makes them big, powerful players in the global economy. Still, ongoing trends and tough situations give pause. Yes, the developed economies currently account for 40 percent of global GDP, but their share was 57 percent in 2000 and is heading to 37 percent by 2025.[81] Yes, companies in the developed economies are the makers of innovative, world-class processes and products. Their competitors in emerging economies, meanwhile, are cleverly reinventing systems of production and distribution and experimenting with new business models. So, from a big picture point of view, managers ask a basic question: as production frontiers shift, market systems transform, economic environments evolve, and emerging economies steadily predominate, what will the developed economies of the West do?

Persistent Problems and Troublesome Anomalies

Since the 2008 financial crisis, a phenomenon largely made in the West, real cumulative growth in the developed economies has struggled—the EU recorded negative 2 percent while the United States hit 34 percent versus 139 percent in China and 96 percent in India.[82] Slow growth fuels a cascade of problems. The West wrestles with persistent unemployment, slowing wage growth, fraying social security nets, and worsening income inequality. For instance, wages grew at 98 percent for households in nearly every developed economy from 1995 to 2004. From 2005 to 2014, however, wage stagnation prevailed. Since then, wage income had decreased for many households in France, Netherlands, United Kingdom, and Italy. The United States had it even worse. Four out of five households saw flat or falling income before factoring in taxes and transfers.

Likewise, real median net wealth has not recovered in 13 countries since the financial crisis; it declined from $104,371 to $80,659 on average in 22 developed economies between 2007 and 2018. This has hit workers the hardest. In the United States, again, the average net worth per household $692,100. However, the median net worth is $97,300–median is the middle point where half the households have more, and half have less. Why the big difference? The average, or the "mean, is skewed by the super-rich. Consequently, income inequality, compounded by wealth disparities, are growing problems throughout developed economies, as the rich reap disproportional rewards and leave workers farther behind.[83]

On the policy front, low and zero interest rate policies implemented by anxious central bankers meant that real interest rates were not just low within the context of modern times—they were at the lowest levels in 5,000 years.[84] Movement in some markets, notably Japan, Sweden, and Switzerland, toward negative interest rate policies created the unprecedented situation whereby investors paid governments to hold their money. In 2019, in the latest sign of ebbing confidence, Japanese and European investors paid their governments to hold more than $11 trillion of their bonds.[85] These trends only worsened in the financial fallout of the COVID-19 pandemic,

Notwithstanding extraordinary monetary expansion and increasing fiscal stimulus in nearly every Western market, falling aggregate demand meant that, for the first time since the Great Depression, deflation, not inflation, posed the greatest systemic risk. Countries, with fewer and fewer policy options, resorted to competitive currency devaluations while central bankers speculated about "helicopter money" and politicians debated universal basic income schemes.[86] Public debt and unfunded nondebt liabilities grew ominously high, weighing down public-sector balance sheets. Fading public-sector investment, given growing debt burdens and falling aggregate demand, aggravated market shortfalls.

Problems and puzzles in the West have significant policy consequences. Notably, growing state intervention in the marketplace tests the legitimacy of economic freedom in the developed economies. In the United States, long the chief advocate of the free market ideology and *laissez-faire* outlook, growing government involvement in its economy had dropped it from a free to mostly free ranking in 2016.

Similarly, its economic problems have triggered political difficulties; as reported in Chapter 3, the United States fell from a full to a flawed democracy in 2017. Elsewhere, economic nationalism, notably BREXIT, and escalating populism, such as seen in the "*mouvement des gilets jaunes*" (yellow vest movement) in France or the "Anti-Extradition Law Amendment Bill (Anti-ELAB)" movement in Hong Kong, and social unrest and civil strife, dramatically highlighted by the Black Lives Matter movement, complicated economic policies. The COVID-19 pandemic tumbled national economies, particularly in developed countries, into recession. The global economy shrank almost 4.9 percent, the United States's GNP fell eight percent, and market problems worldwide echoed the Great Depression of the 1930s.

What's Next for the West?

Increasingly, mindful of the comeback of emerging economies, managers ask what's next for the West. Would aggressive growth stimuli and fiscal engineering finally revitalize aggregate demand? Could even looser monetary policy generate organic growth? Would the unemployed in Portugal, Italy, France, and Spain, among others, rejoin the workforce? How might consumers, from Australia to the United States, regain their mojo and resume spending? Others raised far more worrisome questions. Might long-term stagnation be the price the West must pay for using extreme monetary and fiscal policies to pull consumer demand forward? Was it finally time to complement, if not replace, conventional monetary measures with estimators of happiness, stability, and sustainability to better estimate productivity and prosperity? Ideologically, would economic freedom survive growing state intervention? Ultimately, how might the developed economies compete, presuming they can, against enterprising emerging economies?

Searching here, there, and everywhere for answers, analysts projected wide-ranging scenarios. But, as growth stayed stuck in a rut and policymakers applied drastic tactics, attention turned to a provocative possibility. Looking to the past for insight centered on preceding growth spurts in the West, especially those associated with the Industrial Revolution and its subsequent iterations. Then, radical productivity innovations led to booming growth, growing income, and expanding employment. Now, scanning the emerging techno-landscape, analysts wondered what the heck was truly happening. Might the economies of the West, given the emergent Fourth Industrial Revolution, be in the early stage of a fundamental shift in how people work, consumers spend, companies compete, officials regulate, and markets perform?[87]

The Promise and Peril of the Fourth Industrial Revolution

Table 4.9 profiles the pivotal stages in how we have produced, consumed, and worked over the past 250 years or so. Every few generations a wave of technology rolls in that transforms economies and opens new frontiers. Today, the systemic convergence of the physical and digital world ushers in the Fourth Industrial Revolution. This era, even if it only faintly echoes preceding stages, will unleash tools and techniques that radically disrupt the idea of work, productivity, and prosperity.

The "Internet of things" steadily digitizes the physical world, tracking data feeds among sensors loaded in billions of objects. Clever folks synthesize ingenious materials and redesign production and consumption systems to maximize resource efficiencies. 3-D printing, as "one of the pillars of the future of manufacturing," signals that big factories in faraway places may be unnecessary to achieve efficient production. The falling cost of making smaller batches of a wider variety of products opens scenarios where companies make items tailored to a customer's request. Robotic platforms steadily support small-scale factories, located anywhere and everywhere, that support mass customization. Already, robot makers contend that machines are more cost-effective than humans in an expanding range of applications, suggesting that "We're on the cusp of completely changing manufacturing and distribution. I think it's not as a singular event, but it will ultimately have as big an impact as the Internet."[88] Likewise, cheap smartphones, each equivalent to the supercomputers of a generation or two ago and increasingly in everyone's pocket, turbocharge the techno sphere.

TABLE 4.9 Stages of the Industrial Revolution

Stage	Start	Catalyst	Key Outcomes
I	1784	Water- and steam-powered mechanical production equipment.	Transition from an agrarian to industrial economy.
II	1870	Electrical energy and division of labor supported widespread, large-scale industrialization. Mass production, mass consumption, mass media, and mass distribution ensued.	Moved many workers from agrarian to industrial lifestyles. Resulting jobs and careers fueled the rise of the middle class and, by extension, property rights, the rule of law, and democracy.
III	1970	Electronics and information technology opened a digital world. Exploration opened business frontiers and career paths.	Connectivity resets automation, production, communication, and collaboration standards. Emergence of knowledge workers and the creative class.
IV	2020	Ubiquitous connectivity, artificial intelligence–based software, big data platforms, and robotic technologies expand the scale and scope of the techno sphere.	Emerging cyber-physical systems transform production and consumption processes. Revolutionary efficiencies drive a new cycle of global economic activity.

Timing Revolutions

Preceding iterations of the Industrial Revolution transformed economic logics, marketplace activities, and workplace standards. Earlier, for instance, machine power replaced farm labor—in 1800, 83 percent of the U.S. labor force was employed in agriculture; in 1900, it was 41 percent; today, it's less than 2 percent. Likewise, automation replaced factory labor—in 1965, 28 percent of the U.S. labor force was employed in manufacturing; today, it's about 10 percent.[89] Now, as had happened in farming and manufacturing, business processes, historically the realm of white-collar jobs, are becoming automated via machine learning that progressively taps artificial intelligence to turbocharge the system. Workers in a wide range of professions (i.e., accounting, education, and medicine) and industries (i.e., transportation, manufacturing, energy) face growing job insecurity. Some expect emerging techno-systems, in the form of frightfully powerful thinking machines applying increasingly sophisticated learning-based algorithms, joining, and perhaps replacing, executives.[90]

Unlike before, where these shifts unfolded over three or four generations, the West faces the unprecedented challenge of experiencing the latest shift in a single generation. Forecasts are dire: estimates see nearly half of the jobs in developed economies at high risk from the changes underway in digitization and automation.[91] Artificial intelligence and robots will eliminate 75 million jobs worldwide by 2022. Worse still, more than half of all tasks in the workplace will be done by machines by 2025.

Still, there are bright linings in the apocalypse. The World Economic Forum estimates that more than 130 million new jobs will be created by machines in that time frame. Indeed, it advised that "Despite bringing widespread disruption, the advent of machines, robots and algorithm could actually have a positive impact on human employment."[92] People, however, must learn new ideas, master new skills, and acquire new abilities to stay ahead of the "seismic shift" in how we use machines. Longer term, people anticipate lifelong learning and continual adaptation as the Fourth Industrial Revolution transforms the economic environment.

Change and Consequences

By definition, a revolution radically disrupts, if not resets, existence. In the economic realm, the West faces daunting prospects. In the least, expanding challenges from fast-growing, competitive, and innovative competitors from the East are unavoidable. The improving performance and potential of emerging economies, as spotlighted throughout the chapter, increasingly determines the economic center of gravity for the world. Initiatives, notably China's One Belt, One Road, open immense possibilities to blaze brighter futures. Built on a demographic base of billions of people, many of whom are willing to work far harder for far less than others, the East threatens intense, immense competition to the West.

The prospect of tech-utopia in the form of the Fourth Industrial Revolution signaled an alternative path. Robots, 3-D printing, artificial intelligence, infinite connectivity, to say nothing of nanotechnology, implantable devices, wearable tech, and sentient machines, arguably reset the dimensions and dynamics of economic environments in the favor of the West. Various meta-measures, notably the GCI, GII, and WCI indices, indicate that the West is superbly positioned to imagine and invent the tools of the future—as we see in Table 4.8, countries like Switzerland, Sweden, United States, and Germany consistently rank in the top. As had happened in the early days of the first Industrial Revolution, the West's development of the then tools of the future shifted the economic center of gravity. Once again, some believed, and many in the West hoped, history would repeat. Those in the East, understandably, forecast a different future, essentially calling for going back to the future, circa 1799; then, the East dominated the global economy.

The drama and trauma of economics are endlessly fascinating. Currently, few other issues captivate folks more than mapping the performance and forecasting the potential of economic environments worldwide. From Beijing to Washington, from Tokyo to New Delhi, from Jakarta to Berlin, workers, consumers, companies, citizens, regulators, and governments, as you yourself are doing right now, wonder what it all means to their lives and their livelihoods.

QUESTIONS

4-3 Forecast your *personal* future given (1) the ongoing comeback of emerging economies and then (2) the techno-transformations powered by the Fourth Industrial Revolution. Which scenario do you prefer? Why?

4-4 Forecast your *professional* future given (1) the ongoing comeback of emerging economies and then (2) the techno-transformations powered by the Fourth Industrial Revolution. Which scenario do you prefer? Why?

4-5 Historically, those in the West hold that economic freedom is the catalyst of prosperity. Given the recent performance of emerging economies, do you think state capitalism might do a better job?

4-6 In the realm of the Fourth Industrial Revolution, should governments estimate performance with monetary aggregates, like GDP, or sustainability and stability, like human development or happiness?

4-7 Working in the Fourth Industrial Revolution signals the increasing likelihood of working alongside ever-smarter machines. Some advice workers to complement, not compete with, AI-powered tools. How would you do so?

4-8 Who will likely benefit more from the Fourth Industrial Revolution: workers in developed, emerging, or developing economies? Why?

CHAPTER 5
Globalization and Society

OBJECTIVES

After studying this chapter, you should be able to

5-1 Describe the trade-offs among different stakeholders in MNE activities

5-2 Evaluate the major economic effects of MNEs on home and host countries

5-3 Explain the broad foundations of ethical behavior

5-4 Identify the cultural foundations of ethical behavior

5-5 Illustrate how ethical behavior is affected by different legal attitudes

5-6 Show how corruption and bribery affect and are affected by cultural, legal, and political forces

5-7 Summarize what the roles are of governments and companies in resolving environmental issues

5-8 Demonstrate how global labor issues need to be addressed by MNEs to their stakeholders

5-9 Restate how codes of conduct can help MNEs respond to concerns by stakeholders over responsible corporate behavior

Source: Katarzyna Mazurowska/Shutterstock

▲ This wind farm on an island in the North Sea just off the coast of Germany is part of the future of sustainable energy in Germany, and GE's new turbines will be a key part of that strategy.

When the last tree has been cut down, the last river has been polluted and the last fish has been caught—only then do you realize that money can't buy everything.

—Native American proverb

CASE

The Global Greening of GE[1]

As noted on Map 5.1, a recent TV ad invites viewers to "accompany" a small green frog as it does a little globe hopping from one exotic location to another. The frog, however, doesn't seem intent on hitting the usual tourist spots, instead preferring stopovers at such places as a solar farm in South Korea, a water-purification plant in Kuwait, and a wind farm in Germany. To begin the second leg of his tour, he hops on a GE90 aircraft engine flying over China and takes viewers to a "clean" coal-powered facility somewhere in Florida. Then he boards a GE Evolution locomotive in the Canadian Rockies as a voiceover explains the point of all this seemingly ordinary sightseeing: "At GE, we're combining imagination with advanced technology around the world to make it a better place to live for everyone." The journey's end finds our frog in the midst of a lush, green tropical rain forest.

MAP 5.1 Global Travels of GE's "Green Frog," Its Symbol of Commitment to the Environment

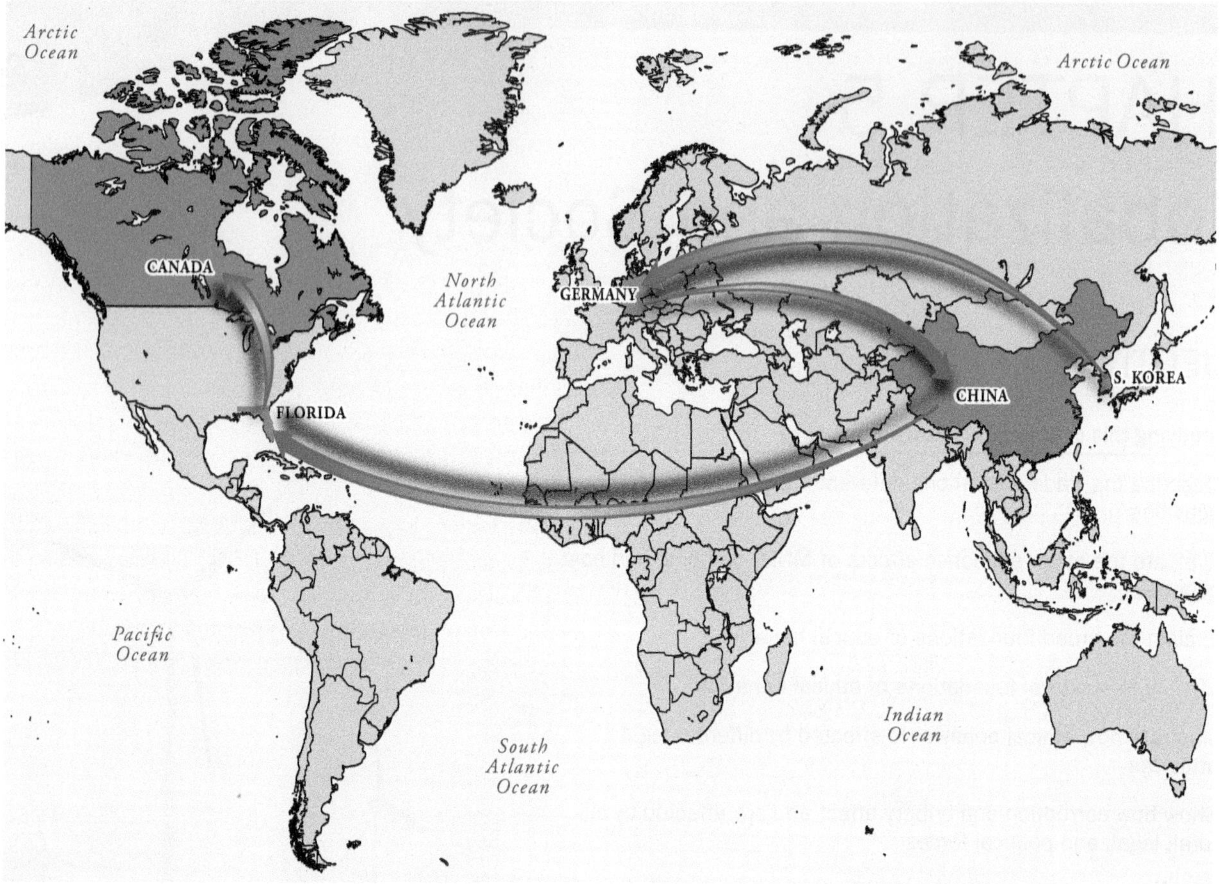

"GREEN IS GREEN"

The ad was part of a major promotional campaign by General Electric Company (GE) for its Ecomagination Initiative. Announced in 2005 by then-CEO Jeffrey Immelt, Ecomagination was an ambitious strategy designed to demonstrate that an ecologically conscious conglomerate can cultivate the bottom line while doing its duty toward the global environment—hence, the campaign motto "Green Is Green." Although GE has gone through leadership changes and serious problems since 2005, the greening of GE is still an important strategy.

GE, one of the leaders in power generation worldwide, has run into hard times in recent years, having lost $200 billion in market value in 2017 and 2018, forcing GE to make significant business and leadership changes. For example, GE announced in 2018 that it would spin off its $19 billion GE Healthcare business into a separate business sometime in 2019 to reduce debt and increase cash flow. That would allow GE to concentrate on its aviation, power, and renewable energy businesses.

When the company announced its plan to launch an internal green revolution, GE surprised both investors and industrial customers who had long seen the firm as an ally in the struggle against environmental activists and lobbyists. But as more and more evidence supports the claim that carbon dioxide emitted from human-made sources is heating up average global temperatures, GE decided to ally itself with a growing number of companies that regard investor and environmental interests as intrinsically interlocked rather than diametrically opposed.

COMMITMENTS AND GOALS

GE's Ecomagination initiative focused on several areas, including a commitment to plans to reduce greenhouse emissions, improve the energy efficiency of operations, and reduce its global use of water. The company's overall target was a 1 percent reduction in carbon dioxide emissions from 2004 levels by 2012. At first glance, the goal didn't seem to have been overly ambitious, but that number represents a significant improvement if you account for the fact that, given GE's projected growth, levels would otherwise soar to 40 percent above 2004 levels. Immelt also committed the company to reducing the intensity of GHG emissions—its level of emissions in relation to the company's economic activity—30 percent by 2008 and to improving energy efficiency 30 percent by 2012. To ensure that these goals were met, Immelt assembled a cross-business, cross-functional team to oversee planning and monitor progress. In spite of Immelt's retirement and a rapid succession of two CEOs, the goals to meet the environmental standards continued as part of GE's culture. For example, from 2011 to 2017, GE had reduced GHG emissions by 27 percent, compared with its target of 20 percent for 2020, and reduced its freshwater reduction by 25 percent compared with a target of 20 percent by 2020.

A LITTLE CONSENSUS SEEKING

In addition to instituting the internal changes necessary to curb GHG emissions, Immelt considered GE's global political environment. He enlisted the Belgian and Japanese governments in the global ecological discussion and allied GE with other green-minded corporations to lobby American lawmakers on such matters as mandatory GHG reductions. Working with the Environmental and Natural Resources Defense Council and the Pew Center on Global Climate Change, GE also joined other companies to form the U.S. Climate Action Partnership to help shape the international political debate over global warming.

GE and its allies want to be known for developing forward-looking strategies and making long-term investments in an increasingly fragmented regulatory environment. With half of its markets located outside the United States, GE is already under the jurisdiction of foreign governments that are more active than the United States in addressing environmental issues.

TECHNOLOGICAL TACTICS AND ECO-FRIENDLY PRODUCTS

Under Immelt's direction, GE geared up to double R&D investment in clean technologies, including renewable-energy, water-purification processes, and fuel-efficient products from which it expects significant revenue growth. GE had already spent $10 billion on R&D investment between 2010 and 2014. In 2006, GE announced that it would reduce water usage by 25 percent from its 2006 baseline, and it achieved a 42 percent reduction by 2014.

When the Ecomagination initiative was first launched, GE marketed only 17 products that met its own Ecomagination criteria; by 2009, there were 90 such products, and by 2011, there were 140 products and solutions generating $105 billion in revenues. By 2014, revenues over the 2010–2014 period had increased to $200 billion. GE wind was generating $30 billion in revenues, and there were over 30,000 wind turbines in operation. In 2016, GE purchased the energy business of French-based Alstom, giving GE access to Alstom's giant offshore wind turbine technology.

In addition to making other products, such as appliances and light bulbs, energy efficient, GE intends to establish itself as an "energy-services" consultant and to bid on contracts for maintaining water-purification plants and wind farms, a venture that could be five times as lucrative as simply manufacturing the products needed for such projects. The use of its website to communicate information about its green products and the efforts to improve its own GHG emissions reduction is an example of commitment to keep the public informed.

"SOLVING ENVIRONMENTAL PROBLEMS IS GOOD BUSINESS"

GE insists that the markets for such products and services are both growing and profitable, and Immelt was convinced that taking advantage of them not only helps the environment but also strengthens the company's strategic position with major profit opportunities.

GE also regards its Ecomagination strategy as a necessary response to customer demand. In spite of carefully trying to read customer demand, GE miscalculated the shift from fossil fuels to renewable energy, which hit their power division hard.

The power division focuses on energy production, including gas and steam turbines, engines, generators, and high-voltage equipment that supply about 30 percent of the world's energy. The renewable energy division concentrates on onshore and offshore wind turbines and blades as well as hydropower solutions. Germany's goal is to generate 65 percent of all electricity from renewables by 2030, and GE has developed a massive wind farm for Germany offshore in the North Sea, utilizing 66 massive wind turbines.

The aviation business specializes in commercial and military engines and services. The GE 9X jet engine developed by the aviation division is the largest jet engine ever made, and it will power Boeing's long-range 777x. It will produce 10 percent less CO_2 greenhouse gas emissions and 45 percent less smog-causing emissions than the engine it will replace.

MIXED REACTIONS

Not surprisingly, GE has been praised for its efforts to go green. At the same time, however, the company has generated a certain amount of skepticism. What happens, for example, if the markets it's betting on don't materialize fast enough (or at all)?

Another potential risk revolves around the participation of developing nations in the clean-technology push. In particular, will they be willing to pay prices that developed countries pay for the technology that reaches the market? GE also faces the challenge of implementing the internal changes entailed by its green strategy. Traditionally, the firm's culture has been accustomed to strategies of incremental change in time-tested products and services. Management may have its work cut out when it comes to persuading marketing, sales, and production teams that untested, early-stage Ecomagination products are worth the risk. Not only that, but GE must continue its push to remain green during a time of turmoil, leadership change, poor economic performance, and skeptical stakeholders.

QUESTIONS

5-1 What are the major challenges GE faces in adopting a green strategy while keeping all of its stakeholders happy?

5-2 From the standpoint of environmental impact, do you think it's more important for GE to reduce its carbon footprint or to develop products that fit their Ecomagination strategy of being energy efficient?

In this chapter, we'll examine how globalization affects society and managers' judgments as they interact with different laws and cultures and try to be socially responsible. This will help you as new graduates to be better positioned to be successful in today's socially responsible environment. Doing business abroad is not easy. The greater the "distance" from one's home country, the more complicated it is to do business. Distance can be described in many different ways, but one way to identify it is the acronym CAGE: cultural (also known as psychic distance), administrative (such as political and institutional policies), geographic, and economic.[2] Given the criticisms of globalization and the challenge of companies and individuals doing business in areas of the world that are quite distant, as defined above, how can companies and individuals be successful, or at least not create serious mistakes?

STAKEHOLDER TRADE-OFFS

5-1 Describe the trade-offs among different stakeholders in MNE activities

Companies must satisfy the demands of

- shareholders,
- employees,
- customers,
- suppliers,
- society.

To prosper—indeed, to survive—a company must satisfy different groups of **stakeholders**, including shareholders, employees, customers, suppliers, and society at large. Obviously, this juggling act can be quite tricky. The shareholder (or stockholder)-versus-stakeholder dilemma pits the demands of one stakeholder against all the others. There is a debate on the idea of shared value, which implies that companies can increase profits while at the same time addressing critical social problems. It is tricky to do both successfully, but many MNEs feel it is worth the effort.[3] In essence, that is what GE is doing by trying to increase profits and positive cash flow while at the same time being environmentally responsible. The basic idea of focusing on stakeholders more broadly is that companies can consider various socially important groups when making decisions.[4] In the short term, for example, group aims often conflict. *Shareholders* want additional sales and increased productivity (which result in higher profits and returns). *Employees* want safer workplaces and higher compensation. *Customers* want higher-quality products at lower prices. *Society* would like to see more jobs, increased corporate taxes, more corporate support for social services, and more trustworthy behavior on the part of corporate executives.

In the *long* term, all of these aims must be adequately met. If they aren't, there's a good chance that none of them will be, especially if each stakeholder group is powerful enough to bring operations to a standstill. In addition, pressure groups—which may reflect the interests of any stakeholder group—lobby governments to regulate MNE activities both at home and abroad.

As we noted in our opening case, for example, GE's Ecomagination initiative has generated pressure from various constituencies, including clients and shareholders concerned about profitability, various governments concerned with drafting regulations, employees wondering about changes in the company's strategies and goals, and environmental lobbyists, NGOs, and fellow businesses trying to preserve the environment. Each group has a powerful influence on how GE does business and on how successful it is in the marketplace. However, GE has to satisfy a variety of stakeholders with different concerns. For that reason, it has many different initiatives working with different stakeholders, not just those interested in climate change.

THE ECONOMIC IMPACT OF THE MNE

5-2 Evaluate the major economic effects of MNEs on home and host countries

As we examine globalization and society, let's begin with a discussion of the impact of MNEs on the countries where they operate. As discussed in Chapter 1, there are many ways a company can do business abroad, and its success or failure can be strongly affected by the operating environment as illustrated in Figure 1.1. In addition, the MNE's activities can also affect the operating environment, such as through corruption and bribery, environmental impact (i.e., air and water pollution), and labor policies.

FIGURE 5.1 What MNEs Have to Offer

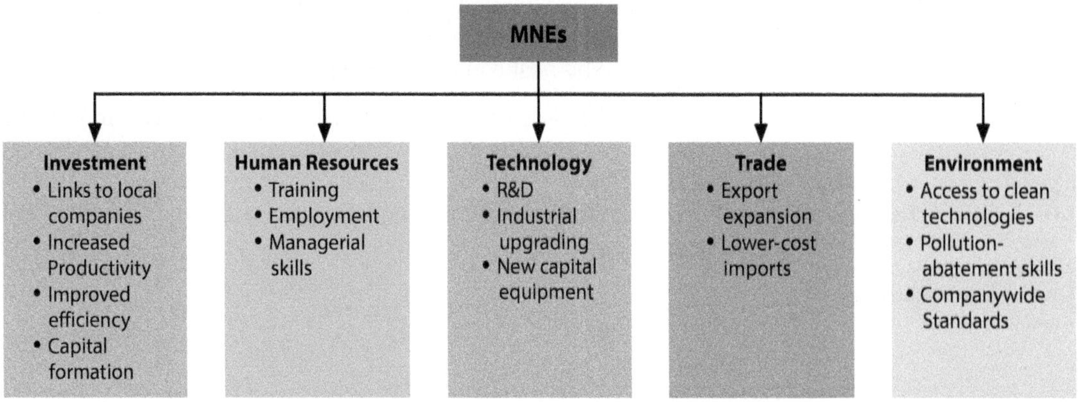

Although not all companies engage in foreign production, the dynamics involved in this decision raise lots of interesting issues. According to the eclectic paradigm of international production, there are three conditions that help explain the foreign production decision: ownership-advantages of MNEs that give them an advantage over companies in the host countries, location-specific advantages of the host country that make them attractive locations for FDI, and internalization advantages for the MNEs to utilize their specific ownership advantages rather than sell or license them to outsiders to exploit.[5] Figure 5.1 identifies some of the ownership-specific advantages of the MNE, focusing on what the MNE has to offer.

Measuring the impact of the MNE on home and host societies depends on its stakeholders, the ability to understand cause-and-effect relationships, and individual versus aggregate effects.

It is hard to determine whether or not the actions of MNEs affect societal conditions.

Cause-and-effect relationships refer to the true impact of an MNE on a host country. Opponents of FDI persist in trying to link MNE activities to such problems in host countries as inequitable income distribution, political corruption, environmental debasement, and social deprivation.[6] In contrast, proponents of MNE activities tend to assume a positive link between their activities and such effects in recipient countries as higher tax revenues, increased levels of employment and exports, and greater innovation. There may or may not be a link, but each side needs to provide evidence to back up their position.

The philosophy, goals, and actions of each MNE are unique, making it difficult to know how to deal with them.

Some countries evaluate MNEs and their activities on an individual or case-by-case basis. Other countries assume that all foreign companies affect the local economy the same way. It's probably more accurate to treat foreign investors on a case-by-case basis, but it's easier to treat all foreign companies the same. Only experience will help policy makers know which is best.

BALANCE-OF-PAYMENTS EFFECTS

The effect of an individual MNE may be positive or negative.

BOP effects refer to trade and capital flows resulting from FDI. Under different conditions, these effects may be positive or negative, either for the host country or the home country.

Host countries want capital inflows because they provide the foreign exchange needed to import goods and services and to pay off foreign debt. However, FDI results in both capital inflows and capital outflows. Money flows in with the initial investment but flows out when earnings are repatriated to the parent company.

CONCEPT CHECK

On page 117 of Chapter 4, we mention how balance of payments is a key feature of a country's economy.

Effect of Individual FDI To appreciate better why countries must evaluate the effect of each investment on their balance of payments, we can examine two extreme hypothetical scenarios reflecting the effects of FDI on a nation's balance of payments:

- *Scenario 1:* Assume that a Mexican MNE makes an FDI when purchasing a Jamaican-owned company as a portfolio investment. If the MNE makes no changes in management, capitalization, or operations, profitability remains the same for the Jamaican company. Dividends, however, now go to the Mexican owners rather than remaining in Jamaica. This results in a drain on Jamaica foreign exchange and a corresponding inflow to Mexico.

- *Scenario 2:* A Mexican MNE purchases idle resources (land, labor, materials, equipment) in Jamaica and converts them to the production of formerly imported goods. Rising consumer demand leads the MNE to reinvest its profits in Jamaica, where import substitution increases the host country's foreign-exchange reserves.

Most FDI falls somewhere between these two extreme examples. That's why they're hard to evaluate, particularly when policymakers try to apply regulations to all in-bound investments.

The formula to determine the balance-of-payments effect is simple, but the data used must be estimated and are subject to assumptions.

There is, however, a basic equation for analyzing the effect of FDI on a host country's balance of payments:

$$B = (m - m_1) + (x - x_1) + (c - c_1)$$

Where

B = balance-of-payments effect
m = import displacement
m_1 = import stimulus
x = export stimulus
x_1 = export reduction
c = capital inflow for other than import and export payment
c_1 = capital outflow for other than import and export payment

On the import side, the balance of payments is positive if the FDI results in a substitution for imports and negative if it results in an increase in imports.

Calculating Net Import Effect Even though the equation itself is pretty straightforward, determining the value for each variable can be a challenge. Let's examine the effect of the decision to locate a Toyota automobile plant in Brazil—an instance of FDI by a Japanese MNE. The easy answer is that import displacement assumes that Brazilian-made Toyotas will take the place of Toyotas previously imported into Brazil. Those locally-made Toyotas could also take the place of other brands of autos being imported into Brazil to service the Brazilian market, such as Fiats or VWs. The import stimulus of the FDI implies that Toyota has to import parts, components, and machinery into Brazil to set up the plant, assuming that it doesn't source those items inside Brazil. Once the plant is up and running, Toyota might be able to use local suppliers of parts and components, thus reducing the amount of import stimulus. In addition, Toyota's Japanese suppliers might invest in Brazil, further reducing Toyota's import of parts.

The net export effect is the *export stimulus* minus the *export reduction* $(x - x_1)$, but bear in mind that this figure is complicated. Let's go back to our Toyota example. In this case, we can make the assumption that the Brazilian plant merely substitutes for imports from and production in Japan. If, in fact, we proceed on this assumption, we get no net export effect for Brazil. For Japan, we arrive at a negative net export effect because of Toyota's export reduction (it's now selling cars made in Brazil to Brazilian consumers instead of exporting Japanese-made cars to Brazil). Toyota, however, might well defend itself on the grounds that its moves abroad are (largely) defensive. How so? Under this assumption, Toyota can argue that it is capturing sales that would otherwise go to non-Japanese carmakers in Brazil, such as Fiat or VW. In that case, Toyota's export reduction from Japan amounts only to the export replacement (loss) resulting from the decision to build a production plant in Brazil, although it is still capturing sales in Brazil, although from production in Japan. Also, Toyota might sell Brazilian-made cars to surrounding countries, thus increasing exports from Brazil.

The balance-of-payments effects in terms of capital flows for FDI are usually

- positive for the host country initially and negative for the home country,
- negative for host country and positive for the home country later.

In some cases, MNEs have argued that their overseas investments stimulate home-country exports of complementary products (say, in Toyota's case, auto parts) that they can sell in host countries through foreign-owned facilities.

Calculating Net Capital Flow *Net capital flow* $(c - c_1)$ is the easiest figure to calculate because of controls maintained by most central banks. There are, however, a few sticking points. Basing your evaluation on a given year is problematic because there's a time lag between a company's outward flow of investment funds and the inward flow of remitted earnings. Because companies eventually plan to take out more capital than they originally put in, what appears at a given time to be a favorable (or unfavorable) capital flow may prove, over a longer period, to be the opposite. The time it takes Toyota to recoup its capital outflow to Brazil depends on such factors as the need to reinvest funds in the host country, the ability to borrow locally, estimates of future exchange rates, and rules on the repatriation of capital.

As a rule, MNE investments are initially favorable to the host country and unfavorable to the home country in the short run. After some time, however, the situation usually reverses.[7] Why? Because nearly all foreign investors eventually plan to have their subsidiaries remit dividends back to the parent company in excess of the amount they sent abroad. If the net value of the FDI continues to grow through retained earnings, dividend payments for a given year may ultimately exceed the total amount of capital transfers composing the initial investment.

GROWTH AND EMPLOYMENT EFFECTS

Growth and employment effects are not a zero-sum game because MNEs may use resources that were unemployed or underemployed.

In contrast to balance-of-payments effects, MNE effects on growth and employment don't necessarily amount to *zero-sum games* (where gains must equal losses) between home and host countries. Classical economists assumed that production factors were always at full employment; consequently, any movement of any of these factors from home to abroad would result in an increase in foreign output abroad and a decrease in domestic output. Even if this assumption were realistic, it's still possible that gains in the host country will be greater or less than the losses in the home country.

The argument that both home and host countries may gain from FDI rests on two assumptions: (1) resources aren't necessarily being fully employed and (2) capital and technology can't be easily transferred from one industry to another. Let's say, for example, that a soft-drink maker is producing at maximum capacity for the domestic market but is limited (say, by high transportation costs) in generating export sales. In addition, moving into other product lines or using its financial resources to increase domestic productivity aren't viable options.

Setting up a foreign production facility is appealing because it would allow the company to develop foreign sales without reducing resource employment in its home market. In fact, it may wind up hiring additional domestic managers to oversee international operations; perhaps it will also end up earning dividends and royalties from the foreign use of its capital, brand, and technology.

For example, many U.S. and European garment manufacturers moved production operations to low-wage countries to realize cost advantages as their consumers demand lower-cost garments.[8] In the process, they shut down—or at least declined to expand—home-country operations. Thus, overseas FDI in the garment-making industry has resulted in a loss of jobs in home countries while creating jobs abroad. However, FDI into the U.S. and European countries has also taken place, creating domestic jobs in companies totally or partially owned by foreign investors. Host countries in apparel have gained through the transfer of capital and technology. If that capital is used to acquire host-country operations that are going out of business, then the foreign investor may very well save host-country jobs and, through the import of technology and managerial ability, even create new jobs.

Critics, however, contend that MNEs often make investments that domestic companies could otherwise make, thereby locking out local entrepreneurs. Likewise, they say, foreign investors often bid up prices when competing with local companies for labor and other resources. Critics also claim that FDI destroys local entrepreneurship in ways that affect national development. Because entrepreneurs are inspired by the reasonable expectation of success, the collapse in several countries of small cottage industries, especially in the face of MNE efforts to consolidate local operations, may have played a role in undermining the competitive confidence of local businesspeople.

A complicating factor is that foreign investors are constantly shifting resources to adjust to changes in market conditions. For example, Ford announced in 2019 that it was going to close down some operations in Brazil due to changes in market conditions and focus more on products that were more popular in Brazil rather than in products that could be exported back to the United States. Their decision would have a major impact on growth and employment in Brazil.[9]

THE FOUNDATIONS OF ETHICAL BEHAVIOR

5-3 Explain the broad foundations of ethical behavior

Many actions elicit universal agreement on what is right or wrong, but other situations are less clear.

Companies and those who work for them must act *responsibly* wherever they go. However, a look at ethical behavior tends to focus on individuals—those who finally make the decision of how to behave. But top management can determine the values a company espouses and to which employees must adhere. Such values are generally included in a Code of Conduct (discussed at the end of the chapter) and in the behavior of other individuals in the organization, especially peers and superiors. In order to ensure adherence to those values, management will try to hire individuals who are willing to work in the type of ethical environment it is trying to create. However, people still must make the decision about how they are going to act in any given situation, and not every situation is clear-cut.

There are three levels of moral development:

- Preconventional
- Conventional
- Postconventional, autonomous, or principled

The sections below will examine the cultural and legal dimensions of ethical behavior in a global context. First, though, let's briefly examine the broad foundations of ethical behavior. There are three levels of moral development:[10]

- Level 1, the *preconventional* level, where children learn what is right and wrong but don't necessarily understand *why* their behavior is right or wrong.
- Level 2, the *conventional* level, where we learn role conformity, first from our peers (including parents), then from societal laws. One could argue that company codes of conduct are also part of the *conventional* level of behavior in the narrow context of a company rather than a society. However, behavior espoused by companies likely reflects the values of the company's home country.
- Level 3, the *postconventional, autonomous, or principled* level, where individuals internalize moral behavior, not because they are afraid of sanctions, but because they truly believe such behavior is right.

It is possible that behaviors under Level 2 and Level 3 are the same as long as individuals accept the laws where they live, or the codes of conduct of the companies they work for.[11]

Teleological Approach: Decisions are based on the consequences of the action.

Utilitarianism: An action is right if it produces the greatest amount of good.

Deontological Approach: Moral judgments are made and moral reasoning occurs independent of consequences.

When individuals confronted with ethical decisions enter the realm of moral reasoning, they examine their moral values, especially as related to Levels 2 and 3 above, and decide what to do. One method of doing so, the **teleological approach**, holds to the idea that decisions are based on the consequences of the action. **Utilitarianism**, a consequences-based theory of moral reasoning, means that "an action is right if it produces, or if it tends to produce, the greatest amount of good for the greatest number of people affected by the action. Otherwise, the action is wrong."[12] A second method, the **deontological approach**, asserts that we make moral judgments or engage in moral reasoning independent of consequences. It implies that actions are right or wrong *per se.*[13] In other words, ethics teaches that "people have a responsibility to do what is right and to avoid doing what is wrong."[14] When individuals engage in moral reasoning, they use one or the other of these methods, or possibly some mixture of the two.

As noted in current research, there is a possibility that in addition to individuals with a strong moral compass, there are also bad apples—individuals for whom the love of money is a strong motivator and likely to result in dishonest behavior. There are two external moderating forces to counterbalance the bad apple behavior, however. One is corporate ethical values (CEV) and the other is the degree of corruption in the country where the individual is operating (CPI or the Corruption Perceptions Index as described below). When a company establishes strong CEV and the country in which the company is operating has a strong CPI, the less likely the individual is to engage in dishonest behavior.[15] Although the company cannot influence the CPI, it can establish strong CEV as we'll show below. As you begin to work in international assignments, moral reasoning becomes very complicated. Consequences may vary due to legal differences, and what is right or wrong may depend to an extent on local values. People need to figure out how make moral decisions—and so do the companies they work for. Two questions arise here: Why should companies and individuals care about ethical behavior? And what are the cultural and legal foundations of ethical behavior when it comes to adapting to a foreign environment?

WHY DO COMPANIES CARE ABOUT ETHICAL BEHAVIOR?

Why should companies worry about ethical behavior at all? From a business standpoint, ethical behavior can be instrumental in achieving one or both of two possible objectives:

1. To develop competitive advantage
2. To avoid being perceived as irresponsible

First, some argue that responsible behavior contributes to strategic and financial success because it fosters trust, which in turn encourages commitment.[16] For instance, GE's Ecomagination program reflects top managers' belief that by actively responding to social concerns about global warming, GE can gain a strategic advantage over competitors, perhaps developing an edge in emerging markets that are facing severe environmental problems.

NGOs are active in prodding companies to comply with certain standards of ethical behavior.

Second, companies are aware that more and more Non-Governmental Organizations (NGOs) and other groups and individuals are becoming active in monitoring—and publicizing—international corporate practices. Governments also want to ensure that individual and corporate behavior is consistent with the best interests of the broader community and that laws are being duly followed. Even worse than perception is reality. Unethical behavior can result in serious sanctions against companies and legal action against individuals.

THE CULTURAL FOUNDATIONS OF ETHICAL BEHAVIOR

5-4 Identify the cultural foundations of ethical behavior

RELATIVISM VERSUS NORMATIVISM

Values differ from country to country and between employees and companies.

CONCEPT CHECK

Recall from Chapter 2, page 30, our discussion of "cultural awareness" and the various ways in which social and cultural distinctions can characterize a country's population. We also observed that companies doing business overseas need to be sensitive to internal diversity: They should remember that people in most nations are often members of multiple cultures and in some cases have more in common with certain foreign groups than with domestic groups.

As discussed in Chapter 2, despite the cultural differences found among countries, it is tempting to assume that there is almost universal agreement on what's right and what's wrong. In the real world, however, managers face situations in which the whys and hows of applying cultural values are less than crystal clear. Everything that complicates dilemmas in the domestic business environment tends to complicate them even further in the international arena. So, does ethical behavior vary by country, or are there uniform values that everyone should share?

Relativism One point of view is to accept that there are significant differences from country to country that might affect our behavior. "When in Rome, do as the Romans do" is an oft-quoted expression that dates to the fourth century AD, which implies that in different environments, one must adapt to local customs out of respect for them.[17]

Applying this expression in an international environment may depend on whether we assume that decisions are based on the consequences of our actions or on a strongly held view of right and wrong. **Relativism** holds that ethical truths depend on the values of a particular society and may vary from one society or country to another.[18] The implication is that it would not be appropriate to inject or enforce one's ethical values on another, or that a foreigner must adopt local values or morals whether or not they are consistent with the foreigner's own home values and beliefs.

Relativism: Ethical truths depend on the groups holding them.

Normativism In contrast, **normativism** holds that there are indeed universal standards of behavior that, although influenced by different cultural values, should be accepted by people everywhere. Even a pluralistic society such as the United States has a large core of

CONCEPT CHECK

In discussing "guidelines for cultural adjustment" on page 43 in Chapter 2, we demonstrate that successful accommodation to a host country's culture depends not only on that culture's willingness to accept anything foreign but also on the extent to which foreign firms and their employees are able to adjust to the culture in which they find themselves.

Normativism: There are universal standards of behavior that all cultures should follow.

Managers need to exhibit ordinary decency—principles of honesty and fairness.

Social responsibility requires human judgment, which is subjective and ambiguous.

CONCEPT CHECK

Note that on page 75 in Chapter 3 we define a country's legal system as the fundamental institution that creates a comprehensive legal network to regulate social interaction; its purpose is to stabilize political and social environments as well as to ensure a fair, safe, and efficient business environment.

Legal justification for ethical behavior may not be sufficient because not everything that is unethical is illegal.

The law is a good basis for ethical behavior because it embodies local cultural values.

commonly held values and norms.[19] However, people may adopt other values and norms as their own. The key is to distinguish between what is common to all and what is unique to the individual.

Walking the Fine Line Between Relative and Normative Companies and their employees struggle with the problem of how to implement their own ethical principles in foreign business environments: Do those principles reflect universally valid "truths" (the normative approach)? Or must they adapt to local conditions on the assumption that every place has its own "truths" and needs to be treated differently (the relative approach)?

Many individuals and organizations have laid out minimum levels of business practices that they say a company (domestic or foreign) must follow regardless of the legal requirements or ethical norms prevalent where it operates.[20] One could consider this as behavior based on principles of honesty and fairness, or "ordinary decency."[21]

THE LEGAL FOUNDATIONS OF ETHICAL BEHAVIOR

5-5 Illustrate how ethical behavior is affected by different legal attitudes

Dealing with *ethical dilemmas* is often a balancing act between *means* (the actions we take, which may be right or wrong) and *ends* (the consequences of our actions, which may also be right or wrong). Legal foundations for ethical behavior can provide guidance here, but legal justification is more rooted in the teleological approach to moral reasoning and moral behavior (consequences) than in the deontological approach (right vs. wrong behavior). However, there are good reasons to consider the law as a foundation of ethical behavior, just as there are limitations to using the law. Another concern is whose laws take precedence? Should the MNE only worry about local laws, or do they have to worry about the laws of the country where their headquarters are located? If there is a conflict between home country and host country laws, which laws take precedence?

LEGAL JUSTIFICATION: PRO AND CON

According to the legal argument, an individual or company can do anything that isn't illegal. However, there are five good reasons why this is inadequate:

1. Some things that are *unethical* are not *illegal*. Some forms of interpersonal behavior, for example, can clearly be wrong even if they're not against the law.
2. The law is slow to develop in emerging areas, and it takes time to pass and test laws in the courts. Moreover, because laws essentially respond to issues that have already surfaced, they can't always anticipate dilemmas that will arise in the future.
3. The law is often based on imprecisely defined moral concepts that can't be separated from the legal concepts they underpin.
4. The law often needs to undergo scrutiny by the courts. This is especially true of case law, in which the courts create law by establishing precedent.
5. The law simply isn't very efficient. "Efficiency" in this case implies achieving ethical behavior at a very low cost, and it would be impossible to solve every ethical behavioral problem with an applicable law.[22]

In contrast, there are also several good reasons for using the law to justify ethical behavior:

1. The law embodies many of a country's moral principles, making it an adequate guide for proper conduct.
2. The law provides a clearly defined set of rules, and following it at least establishes a good precedent for acceptable behavior.
3. The law contains enforceable rules that apply to everyone.
4. Because the law represents a consensus derived from widely shared experience and deliberation, it reflects careful and wide-ranging discussions.[23]

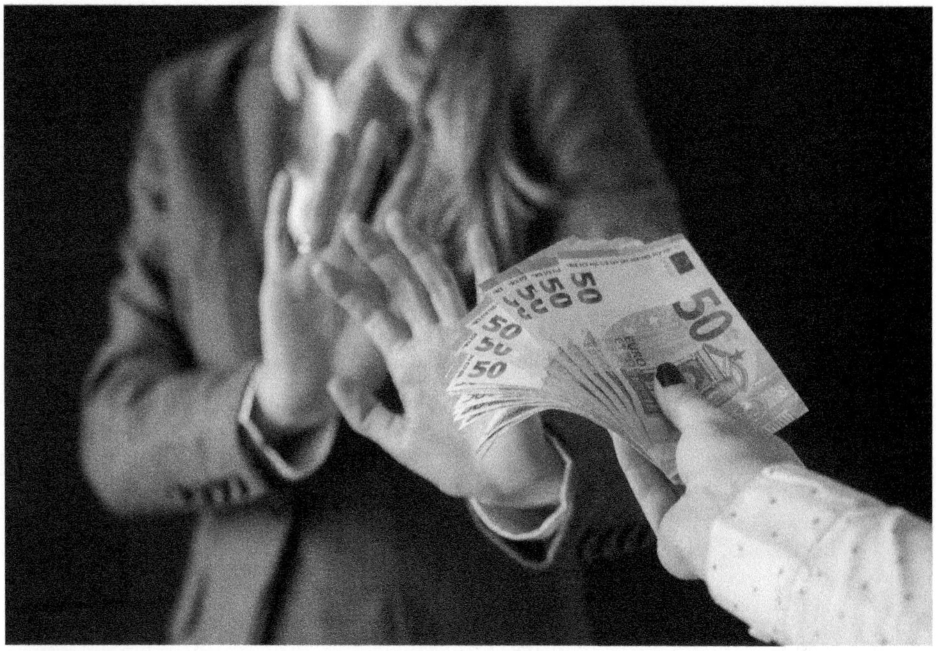

Company codes of conduct and a manager's moral compass to do what is right are often needed to reject bribes.

Source: Kaspars Grinvald/Shutterstock

CORRUPTION AND BRIBERY

5-6 Show how corruption and bribery affect and are affected by cultural, legal, and political forces

Bribery of public officials takes place to obtain government contracts or to get officials to do what they should be doing anyway.

Bribes are payments or promises to pay cash or anything of value.

Bribery is one facet of *corruption.* The determinants of corruption include cultural, legal, and political forces.[24] As defined by Transparency International, corruption is "the abuse of entrusted power for private gain. When government officials are involved, bribes can be paid to obtain government contracts, or they can be as minor as trying to get government officials to do what they should be doing anyway. It can be grand, petty, and political depending on the amounts of money and the sector where it operates."[25] Bribes are payments or promises to pay cash or anything of value.

Figure 5.2 provides information on the Corruption Perceptions Index for 2018 by identifying the perceived levels of public-sector corruption for a small sample of the 180 countries included in the data set. Although no country is free of corruption, it is depressing to note that the most corrupt countries tend to be in high-conflict regions, especially in Africa. Clearly poverty is an issue, although corruption and bribery occur at all income levels. Higher levels of corruption and bribery can also lead to or result from destabilized political environments, which can create problems for foreign investors as well as local companies. Transparency International publishes not only a Corruption Perceptions Index but also a Bribe Payers Index, which identifies which of the top 28 countries in the world are likely to have companies that pay bribes to do business abroad. In a recent survey, they reported that companies from Russia, China, Mexico, Indonesia, and the United Arab Emirates were most likely to pay bribes, either to foreign government officials or to other private sector companies.[26] However, it is hard to follow trends in this index since it is not published on an annual basis like the CPI.

CORRUPTION WITH A GLOBAL TWIST

Corruption is a widespread phenomenon. Sometimes it occurs within a country involving local politicians and companies or between companies and individuals outside the political system. It can also involve countries with a low CPI as well as those with a high CPI. In addition, corruption can also involve foreign actors. One example is the Car Wash scandal involving Petrobras, the Brazilian national oil company, which resulted in the disclosure

FIGURE 5-2 Where Bribes Are (and Are Not) Business as Usual

Transparency International asked country experts, nonresidents, and residents about the overall extent of corruption (frequency and/or size of bribes) in the public and private sectors. The scale runs from 0 to 100, where 0 means that a country is perceived as highly corrupt and 100 means it is perceived as very clean. The figures include a sample of countries.

Source: Based on Transparency International, "TI Corruption Perceptions Index" (2018), transparency.org/cpi201 (accessed February 22, 2019).

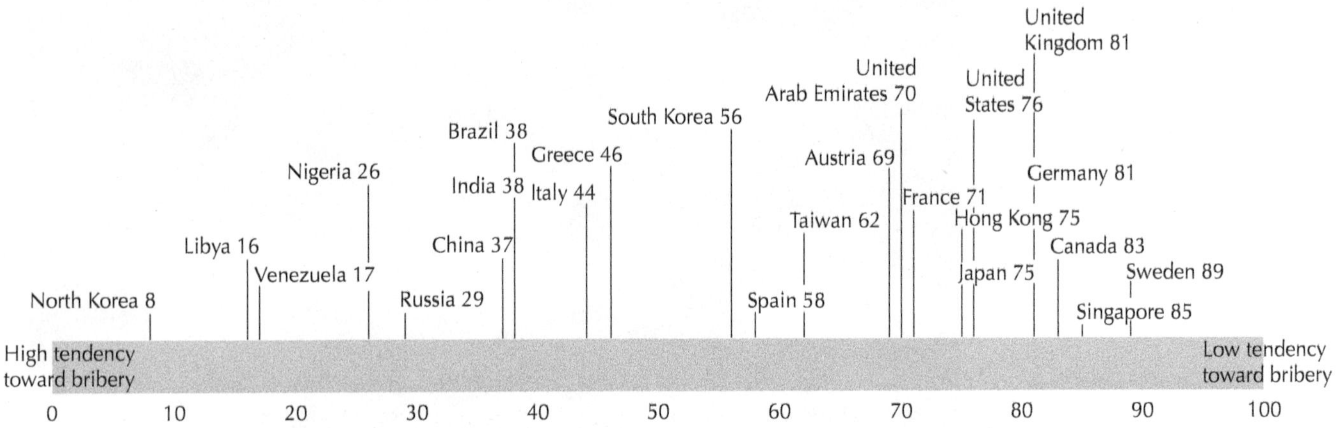

of at least $3 billion in bribes, kickbacks, and money laundering, involving payments to company executives, the ruling Brazilian Worker's Party, and more than 50 sitting politicians and numerous companies trying to secure lucrative contracts with Petrobras. The speaker of Brazil's lower house of Congress and a powerful senator close to Brazil's president were also implicated.[27] On the international side, British Engineering group Rolls-Royce was also accused of paying bribes to Petrobras to secure contracts.[28] Other foreign engineering companies are also being investigated for overinflating services and funneling bribes to Petrobras officials and political parties. The Petrobras corruption scandal is one of nine such scandals targeted by Transparency International for a campaign called "Unmask the Corrupt." Petrobras was forced to pay $2.95 billion in restitution.

THE CONSEQUENCES OF CORRUPTION

Corruption affects company performance and local economies. Higher levels of corruption, for instance, correlate strongly with lower national growth rates and lower levels of per capita income.[29] Corruption can also erode the authority of governments that condone it. Over the years, bribery-based scandals have led to the downfall of numerous heads of state, with many government officials and business executives being imprisoned, fined, or forced to resign. President Dilma Rousseff of Brazil was impeached in 2016, and her predecessor, Luiz Inacio Lula da Silva, was sentenced to 13 years in prison over the Car Wash and other bribery scandals. Moreover, disclosures of corruption not only damage the reputations of companies and whole countries, they also compromise the legitimacy of MNEs in the eyes of local and global communities when they become involved in the scandals.[30] Finally, corruption is expensive, inflating a company's costs and bloating its prices. Nevertheless, it persists as one of the most challenging concerns in international business and politics in the world today.

WHAT'S BEING DONE ABOUT CORRUPTION?

Many efforts are underway to slow the pace of bribery as an international business practice at international and national levels. International efforts to combat bribery include those established by the OECD (Organization for Economic Cooperation and Development), the ICC (International Chamber of Commerce), and the United Nations through UNCAC (United Nations Convention against Corruption). The problem is that none of the conventions have the force of law behind them. They can identify key issues in corruption and shine the spotlight on offenders, but legal action under the control of national governments must be taken for the fight against corruption to be effective.

The OECD comprises 36 mostly high-income countries from around the world. Its Anti-Bribery Convention, signed in 1997, establishes legally binding standards to criminalize bribery of foreign public officials in international business transactions and provides recommendations to the countries that adopted the 2009 Anti-Bribery Recommendation. Prior to the signing of the convention, only one country had made foreign bribery a crime, and most others treated foreign bribe payments as legitimate tax-deductible expenses. Of course, the member countries have to implement the recommendations into national law in order for them to have any weight. In addition, the countries have to do a better job of enforcement.[31] For example, a 2015 study by Transparency International found active enforcement in only 4 of the signatory countries, moderate enforcement in 6, and limited, little, or no enforcement in 29 countries.[32] However, the OECD is continuing to strengthen its recommendations, launching in December 2018 a review of the 2009 Recommendation for Further Combating Bribery of Foreign Public Officials in International Business. The review is projected to be completed in 2020.[33]

The European Union The European Commission confirmed its support for strong anticorruption measures within the EU in a 2007 communication to the European Council, Parliament, and Economic and Social Committee. This included the adoption of the UN's official definition of corruption and support for many of the policies contained within international agreements. The communication also sanctions the work of the Commission's office of antifraud (OLAF), which conducts the affairs of the EU relevant to corporate and individual corruption, as well as an internal auditing service that monitors the activities of all of the Commission's departments. The EU does not have specific anticorruption legislation, but it encourages member nations to adopt high standards and follow them. In its most recent Anti-Corruption Report, the EU noted that corruption costs the EU 120 billion euro per year, and that efforts to combat corruption are very uneven across the EU[34]—thus the importance of national legislation.

The Foreign Corrupt Practices Act is U.S. legislation that makes bribery illegal. It applies to domestic or foreign operations and to company employees as well as their agents overseas.

National Initiative: The United States Many countries have established their own anti-corruption initiatives, utilizing international best practices. One example is the United States. There are several ways the United States has gotten involved in foreign corruption. For example, the **Foreign Corrupt Practices Act (FCPA)** outlaws bribery payments by U.S. firms to foreign officials, political parties, party officials, and political candidates. The coverage of the FCPA was extended in 1998 to include bribery by foreign firms operating in any U.S. territory. The FCPA applies not only to companies registered in the United States but also to any foreign company quoted on any U.S. stock exchange.

Although it is legal to make payments to officials to expedite otherwise legitimate transactions (officially called *facilitating payments* but sometimes referred to as *speed money* or *grease money*), payments can't be made to officials who aren't directly responsible for the transactions in question. In 1988, an amendment to the FCPA actually excluded facilitating payments from the definition of *bribery*. Now, for example, payment to a customs official to clear legitimate merchandise is legal, whereas paying a government minister to influence a customs official is not.

Both the U.S. Securities and Exchange Commission and the U.S. Justice Department also play roles in the fight against global corruption even when it doesn't affect government officials. For example, an estimated $150 million bribery scandal involving FIFA, the Swiss-based governing body of football (or soccer in the United States), was brought to light by the U.S. Justice Department because of income tax evasion in the United States by some of the parties, and because of the use of the U.S. financial system to facilitate the flow of funds. Even U.S.-based Nike was brought into the picture because of possible bribes paid to the Brazilian soccer federation. However, the allegations against Nike would not be prosecuted under the FCPA since it didn't involve a foreign government. The scandal became truly global, and the powerful head of FIFA was forced to resign.[35]

Sarbanes–Oxley legislation in the United States is helpful in combating corruption through more effective corporate governance, financial disclosure, and public accounting oversight.

Another major legislative effort in the United States is the Sarbanes–Oxley Act (SOX), which was passed in 2002 as a response to an epidemic of well-known corporate scandals. SOX toughened standards with regard to corporate governance, financial disclosure, strong internal controls, and oversight of accounting and auditing practices. With its passage, the Justice Department began to use the FCPA more aggressively to combat bribery.

ETHICS AND THE ENVIRONMENT

5-7 Summarize what the roles are of governments and companies in resolving environmental issues

Companies that extract natural resources, generate air or water waste, or manufacture products such as autos that generate pollution need to be concerned with their environmental impact.

In this section, we refer to the environment more narrowly in the context of pollution, both air and water, and global warming. All three are important for company policy and strategy. Companies can create water pollution through disposal of industrial waste into water systems as well as the inefficient use of water, which results more in water shortage than in water pollution. There is a link between air pollution and global warming, but the dominant greenhouse gas (GHG) that causes global warming is carbon dioxide, whereas air pollution is more affected by ozone (also a GHG), sulfur dioxide, nitrogen oxide, and particulates. In terms of air quality, India, Pakistan, Bangladesh, and China are the worst, and 7 of the world's 10 worst polluted cities are in India.[36] Even though the advanced industrial countries have seen a reduction in air pollution due to industrial decline and clean air policies, there are still major issues. The European Union estimates that more than 400,000 Europeans die prematurely each year due to air pollution and that health-related issues from air pollution cost 3–7 percent of GDP.[37] Even as the world struggles with global warming, it still has to fight against air pollution.

As we saw in our opening case, GE has come to see eco-responsibility as a matter of protecting not only the future of the environment but also its own future. Like GE, companies contribute to environmental damage in a variety of ways. Some, for example, contaminate the air, soil, or water during manufacturing, or make products such as automobiles or electricity that release fossil-fuel contaminants into the atmosphere.

In extracting natural resources, other companies also have a direct and unmistakable effect on the environment. But even in these cases the issue isn't necessarily clear-cut. Granted, although some resources (such as minerals, gas, and oil) may not be renewable, others (such as timber) are, and some observers even suggest that resources can never really become scarce. Why? Because as they become less available, prices go up and technology or substitutes compensate.

WHAT IS "SUSTAINABILITY"?

Sustainability involves meeting the needs of the present without compromising the ability of future generations to meet their own needs while taking into account what is best for the people and the environment.

Sustainability is no longer just good business practice. New businesses are emerging that are combining the idea of environmental responsibility and profitability.

Sustainability means meeting the needs of the present without compromising the ability of future generations to meet their own needs. In this section, we use sustainability from the perspective of environmental sustainability. Proponents of the concept argue that sustainability considers what's best for both people and the environment. It is important that companies that affect the environment establish policies for responsible behavior toward the earth—a responsibility that has both cultural and legal ramifications.

But is it possible that sustainability is not only a good business practice, but also good business? GE has demonstrated that it makes good business sense to adopt a strong policy of sustainability, but it also has vast resources at its disposal. However, even born-global companies can adopt a sustainable strategy and generate export revenues at the same time.

GLOBAL WARMING AND THE PARIS AGREEMENT ON CLIMATE CHANGE

Global warming results from the release of greenhouse gases that trap heat in the atmosphere rather than allowing it to escape.

At the core of the United Nations Framework Convention on Climate Change talks, held in Paris in December 2015, is the concept that global climate change results from an increase in carbon dioxide and other gases that act like the roof of a greenhouse, trapping heat that would normally radiate into space, and thereby warming the planet. If carbon dioxide emissions aren't reduced and controlled, rising temperatures could have catastrophic consequences, including melting the polar ice cap, flooding coastal regions, shifting storm patterns, reducing farm output, causing drought, and even killing off plant and animal species.[38]

However, the Paris Agreement, which entered into force in November 2016, changed everything. One hundred eighty-seven countries agreed to keep the increase in the global average temperature to 2°C above pre-industrial levels and try to achieve 1.5°C. The countries also agreed to try to shoot for a target of zero net GHG emissions by the second half of the century.[39] That would involve moving away from fossil fuels for electricity and

The Paris Climate Agreement involving 187 countries targeted policies to reduce GHG emissions in order to keep the global average temperature to 2°C above pre-industrial levels.

transportation, the two primary creators of GHG emissions, and moving more toward sustainable energy, such as solar and wind. To achieve this ambitious and improbable goal, all countries, including the emerging markets, intended to set national goals called "intended nationally determined contributions or INDCs." In addition, the developed countries agreed to provide $100 billion per year by 2020 to developing countries to help them adapt to climate change. The Paris Agreement discussed how to not only stabilize atmospheric concentration of GHG emissions, but also to avoid dangerous anthropogenic (human) interference with the climate. A big target of the latter concern is reducing deforestation and forest degradation in countries like Indonesia and Brazil. The problem is that shrinking forests contribute to GHG emissions, and their disappearance also eliminates a major natural way to sop up and store carbon dioxide.[40] The United States, one of the major sources of GHG emissions, signed the agreement in 2015 by executive order of the President of the United States. However, after a new election in 2017, the United States announced it would cease all participation in the Paris Agreement. According to the Agreement, the United States cannot withdraw until four years have passed since it originally signed the agreement; therefore, the earliest effective withdrawal date would be November 4, 2020.

The success of the Paris Agreement to slow global warming has to come from two sources—the public sector and the private sector. The problem with the public sector is that countries still rely heavily on fossil fuels for energy. Even Germany, which is trying desperately to eliminate the use of coal, still relies on it for 37 percent of its energy needs, even as renewable energy has risen from 6 percent of Germany's energy supply to 33 percent in 2018.[41] Reliance on renewable energy is a positive move, but experts point out that we are far from being able to eliminate the use of fossil fuels. Thus, GHG emissions will still be a problem in the foreseeable future. The fall in oil prices since mid-2015 will require significant government subsidies to shift the supply of energy to solar and wind energy. The second source is the private sector. Part of the private sector solution is to reduce the level of GHG emissions through improvements in technology as well as developing products, such as automobiles, that use electricity. Unfortunately, power plants generate electricity, and the world still relies on power plants that use fossil fuels. Stakeholders are pushing companies to reduce their carbon footprint, but a major challenge will be enticing companies to invest heavily in the development of alternative sources of energy without government subsidies to fund growth and money from outside investors. If investors don't see a viable return from investing in alternative energy, they decide not to invest in the renewable energy sector. A good example of this is when PG&E, the California utility, went bankrupt as the stock price plunged in response to concerns over potential liabilities resulting from PG&E's equipment problems contributing to the California wildfires in 2018. Even though PG&E received high marks from the investing community because of their increased usage of renewable energy and a strong reputation in Environmental, Social and Governance (ESG) metrics, investors didn't pay enough attention to risks.[42]

Finally, MNEs have the task of adapting to different standards in different countries. A European-based MNE with operations in, say, the United States, Germany, and China, and a U.S.-based MNE with plants in the same countries are faced with a smorgasbord of regulatory environments. On the one hand, the *legal* approach to responsible corporate behavior says an MNE should settle for adopting local environmental standards in accord with local laws. The *ethical* approach, on the other hand, urges companies to go beyond the law to do whatever is necessary and economically feasible to reduce GHG emissions, given that they still have multiple stakeholders to satisfy.

ETHICAL DILEMMAS OF LABOR CONDITIONS

5-8 Demonstrate how global labor issues need to be addressed by MNEs to their stakeholders

A major challenge facing MNEs today is the labor conditions of foreign workers, whether in their own offshore operations or their outsourced supply chains. They're especially critical in retail, clothing, footwear, electronics, and agriculture—industries in which MNEs typically outsource huge portions of production to independent companies abroad.

POINT

Should MNEs Accept Full Responsibility for the Unethical Behavior of Their Employees?

YES However, it is hard to know where the corruption begins and who knows what. On September 18, 2015, the U.S. Environmental Protection Agency announced that it was going to order German auto company, Volkswagen AG, one of the world's leading auto manufacturers and the largest in Europe, to recall over 500,000 vehicles in the United States because they were equipped with software that allowed them to evade emissions standards for reducing smog during testing. The software would recognize when a car was being tested and turn up emissions controls. Then when the car wasn't being tested, the software turned down the emissions controls, which resulted in better driving performance and fuel economy. It was estimated that in normal driving conditions, cars would emit up to 40 times the amount of pollutants allowed by U.S. government regulations. VW announced that the software designed to trick or "defeat" the emissions tests had been installed in millions of vehicles.[43] Eventually, this spread to certain models in Audi and Porsche, two other VW brands. How could this have happened? There were several very interesting dimensions to the case—different regulatory environments in Europe and the United States; VW's desire to increase its market share in the United States, especially in diesel cars; and the efforts of the regulators and VW itself to find out who knew what was going on.

One of the real ironies is that in its 2014 Sustainability Report, VW claimed that it was selling environmentally friendly products and meeting the guidelines for emissions of carbon dioxide, nitrogen oxide, and other pollutants. It also said it was in compliance with the Global Reporting Initiative (G4), the UN Global Compact, and the German Sustainability Code. PricewaterhouseCoopers, one of the leading global public accounting firms, certified that the Sustainability Report was accurate. Not only did VW claim that it was operating according to high standards, but it also had a program to make sure its employees understood what the company stood for.

Different legal and regulatory systems also contributed to differences between U.S. and German stakeholders. Given that VW is a German Company and therefore under the regulatory environment of the European Union, it claimed that even though it was violating U.S. regulatory guidelines, it was not violating European regulatory guidelines. Is it possible that the software was not illegal in Europe, even though it was in the United States? There are not only different standards in the United States and EU, but there are also different testing procedures. In the United States, California has

COUNTERPOINT

Should MNEs Accept Full Responsibility for the Unethical Behavior of Their Employees?

NO VW obviously must take responsibility for installing the "defeat" software into some of the diesel models it was selling worldwide, but who was responsible for this happening? Wolfgang Hatz, the head of engines and transmissions for VW, was one of the key people in this scandal. He was also one of the first employees suspended by VW when the crisis broke in September 2015. One of his first concerns at VW was to figure out how to develop a diesel engine that would meet the stringent antipollution requirements set by the State of California. He was hired from the same position at Audi, one of VW's brands, which also includes Porsche. Hatz loved fast cars, and he realized that to meet emission requirements VW would have to introduce more diesels into the United States. But how could they develop a car that would still be alluring and peppy, something that American drivers wanted? Diesels have better fuel economy and lower GHG emissions, but they also have higher smog-forming pollutants. One strategy being considered at VW was to build an alliance with Mercedes-Benz and BMW to develop new technologies, but Mr. Hatz and others at VW decided they wanted to develop a less expensive alternative. However, it was clear that this would not meet the emissions requirements. Rather than scale back their strategy to increase the sales of diesels in the U.S. market, someone decided to cheat.

But who was behind the scheme to introduce the "defeat" software? An internal whistle-blower at VW was responsible for uncovering exaggerated carbon dioxide and fuel economy claims, but the U.S. EPA uncovered the "defeat" software strategy for pollutants in the United States. VW decided to offer amnesty to anyone at VW who could shed any light on this subject. The first person sent to prison for the scandal was a VW engineer who also implicated other VW executives. By 2016, five former executives were indicted, and in May 2018, VW's former CEO was indicted for giving approval for the use of the "defeat" software strategy.[45]

Offering amnesty for information is relatively rare in these cases, but a similar thing happened in 2008 when the Siemens bribery scandal broke. In this case, it was determined that Siemens diverted funds filed under bogus consulting contracts into a network of "black accounts" for bribing officials in countries like Italy, Greece, Argentina, and Saudi Arabia. One thing that came out of the investigation is that Siemens had created a culture of corruption. Although the VW example doesn't involve bribery, it obviously involved corrupt behavior in the sense that somebody felt comfortable breaking regulatory guidelines in the United States and Europe in order to enhance sales. As noted by Hans-Dieter Potsch, VW's a stringent antipollution regulatory environment, and VW realized it had to find a way to be successful there if it wanted to increase the sale of its diesel engines. Also, U.S. regulators conduct their own tests to see if auto manufacturers' claims are accurate, whereas European regulators leave the testing and verification to the manufacturers themselves.[44] In order to keep from losing its U.S. customers, VW offered payments to customers who had bought cars with the diesel engines that had the "defeat" software installed. Of course, the legal environment in the United States that allows for class-action suits probably had something to do with that. Class-action lawsuits are relatively unknown in Europe, and payments were not offered to European customers, especially since VW didn't feel it was violating any law in Europe.

chairman, "There was a tolerance for breaking the rules. It proves not to have been a onetime error, but rather a chain of errors that were allowed to happen."[46] As a result of the scandal, VW paid over $20 billion in fines and penalties. Given what we know about VW's supposed commitment to a high level of corporate behavior, why didn't someone step forward and say "no!"

QUESTION

If you were an engineer working on the project to develop the software that would allow VW to avoid providing regulators and consumers accurate data about GHG and pollution emissions, would you have said "no"? Explain why or why not.

Major labor issues that MNEs get involved in through FDI or purchasing from independent manufacturers in developing countries are fair wages, child labor, slave labor, working conditions, working hours, and freedom of association.

The concerns over the ethical treatment of labor deal directly with a company but also indirectly through its suppliers. Increased pressure is being placed on companies to adopt policies to protect workers as well as to disclose to shareholders the policies and their effectiveness. Figure 5.3 highlights the multiple pressures external stakeholders place on companies to encourage them to adopt responsible worker-related practices in their overseas operations. The issues that raise concerns are identified by a variety of organizations, principally the U.N.-based International Labor Organization, the U.N. Global Compact, and others that use many of their benchmarks, such as the Ethical Trading Initiative and the California Transparency in Supply Chains Act of 2010. A more specific listing of worker issues was developed by the Ethical Trading Initiative (ETI), a British-based organization that focuses on MNEs' employment practices and whose standards are consistent with those adopted by the UN-based International Labor Organization. Its members include representatives from GAP Inc., Inditex, H&M, Marks & Spencer, The Body Shop International, and other companies, as well as from trade union organizations, NGOs, and governments. The objective of ETI is to

FIGURE 5.3 Sources of Worker-Related Pressures in the Global Supply Chain

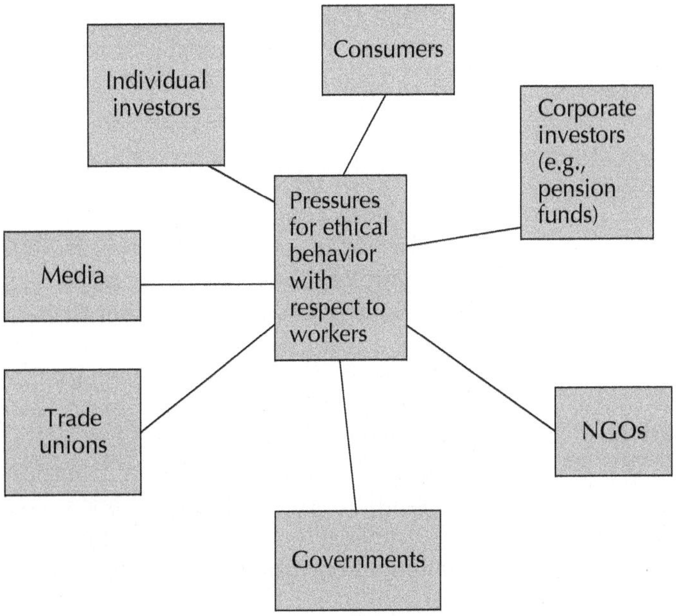

get companies to adopt ethical employment policies and then monitor compliance with their overseas suppliers. ETI's trading initiative base code identifies the following issues:

1. Employment is freely chosen.
2. Freedom of association.
3. Working conditions are safe and hygienic.
4. Child labor shall not be used.
5. Living wages are paid.
6. Working hours are not excessive.
7. No discrimination is practiced.
8. Regular employment is provided.
9. No harsh or inhumane treatment is allowed.[47]

Although all issues identified by each of these organizations are important, there are several sources of concern, including forced labor, modern slavery, human trafficking, and child labor.

Let's start by considering a couple of very brief cases that deal with child labor:

- There are two arguments for the use of children in the Indian carpet industry: (1) they're better suited than adults to perform certain tasks, and (2) if they weren't employed, they'd be even worse off. In fact, children in India are often put to work because parents don't earn enough to support families; if parents can't pay off debts, their children are often *indentured* to creditors.
- In the 1990s, the impoverished Asian nation of Bangladesh was pressured to stop employing thousands of child workers or face U.S. trade sanctions. In this case, the plight of the children did in fact go from bad to worse. Between 5,000 and 7,000 young girls, for example, went from factory work to prostitution.[48]

According to the International Labor Organization (ILO), 218 million children between the ages of 5 and 17 are in employment.[49] The ILO has very specific guidelines describing what it considers child labor to be and what the worst forms of child labor are. In particular, the worst forms involve slavery and prostitution—illicit activities that are a danger to the health, safety, and morals of a child. ILO guidelines state that children who are at least 12–14 years old may be employed in "light" work that's not harmful to their health, is less than 14 hours a week, and doesn't interfere with school. All children under the age of 18 should be protected against the most abusive labor conditions.[50]

The concerns over slavery and human trafficking involve more than just child labor. They are defined by the ILO as "all work or service which is exacted from one person under threat of a penalty and for which the person has not offered himself voluntarily."[51] This tends to occur more in the supply chain for an MNE than it would directly for their own facilities abroad. It could also occur with contract manufacturers.

WHAT MNES CAN AND CAN'T DO

In spite of these difficulties, MNEs are not powerless when it comes to labor-related matters in overseas facilities. When the Swedish retailer IKEA ran into trouble in India for buying carpets from local companies that relied heavily on extensive child labor, it identified and tackled two different problems rather than try to force suppliers to stop exploiting the children. First, it helped working mothers increase family earning power so they could escape the clutches of the loan sharks to whom they were putting up their children as collateral. Second, it set up "bridge schools" to enable working children to enter mainstream education channels within a year.[52]

Some companies avoid operating in countries where child labor is employed, whereas others try to establish responsible policies in those same countries.

Frequently, MNEs operating in countries with very different labor policies succumb to the pressure to simply leave the market. Usually, this turns out to be a shortsighted decision. Research shows, for instance, that companies like IKEA have substantially improved the conditions of workers in overseas facilities.[53]

CORPORATE CODES OF ETHICS: HOW SHOULD A COMPANY BEHAVE?

5-9 Restate how codes of conduct can help MNEs respond to concerns by stakeholders over responsible corporate behavior

MOTIVATIONS FOR CORPORATE RESPONSIBILITY

Companies need to act responsibly because unethical and irresponsible behavior

- could result in legal sanctions,
- could result in consumer boycotts,
- could lower employee morale,
- could cost sales because of bad publicity.

Companies generally experience four strong motivations for acting responsibly:

1. Unethical and irresponsible behavior can result in *legal headaches,* especially in such areas as financial mismanagement, bribery, and product safety.
2. Such behavior could also result in *consumer action* such as a boycott.
3. Unethical behavior can affect *employee morale.* Conversely, responsible behavior can have a positive influence on a workforce, both at corporate headquarters and in overseas facilities.
4. You never know when *bad publicity* is going to cost you sales. Perhaps this concern is one reason why many global apparel and clothing companies responded so quickly to criticism about unfair employment practices in developing countries.

DEVELOPING A CODE OF CONDUCT

A major component in a company's strategy for ethical and socially responsible behavior is a code of conduct.

A **code of conduct** is a major component of most companies' strategies for ethical and socially responsible behavior. In the context of international operations, it can take the form of two perspectives: external and internal. Codes of conduct are useful insofar as they give companies some general guidance on how to operate. The practical challenge for the company is familiarizing itself with the codes of many different organizations and using them to fashion its own *internal code of conduct.*

Codes of conduct involve four dimensions:

- Setting a global policy that must be complied with wherever the company operates,
- Communicating the code to employees, suppliers, and subcontractors,
- Ensuring that policies are carried out,
- Reporting results to external stakeholders.

What makes a good internal code of conduct? Here are four criteria:

1. *It sets global policies with which everyone working anywhere for the company must comply.* A good example is the code promulgated by the Finnish cell-phone company Nokia, which discusses how its code was set, who approved it, how it is communicated to its employees, and what its foundation values are.
2. *It communicates company policies not only to all employees but to all suppliers and subcontractors as well.*
3. *It ensures that the policies laid out in the code are carried out.* This usually occurs through training programs where employees sign off on their compliance and sometimes through internal audits.
4. *It reports the results to external stakeholders.* This usually occurs in a company's annual report to shareholders, but GE uses social media to communicate with external stakeholders, a common practice of most MNEs. In addition, a major contributor to enhanced transparency is the Global Reporting Initiative (or GRI), which has issued G4 sustainability reporting guidelines that identify several different areas related to the environment, society, and the economy.[54]

LOOKING TO THE FUTURE Dealing with Ethical Dilemmas in the Global Economy

As you prepare to work globally, it is essential that you understand the environmental, social, and governance structure (often known as ESG) of the company you work for. This chapter has continued the discussion from Chapter 1 on the effects of globalization, but with more focus on the ethical issues and how companies can be more responsible as they operate abroad. Chapter 1 identified three scenarios on the future of globalization:

- Further globalization is inevitable.
- International business will grow primarily along regional rather than global lines.
- Forces working against further globalization and international business will slow down the growth of both.

Regardless of what happens, the more companies expand abroad, the greater the likelihood they will have

(continued)

hard decisions to make on how they should operate in a socially responsible manner. As discussed by Bartlett and Beamish,[55] MNEs can operate in four major ways. They can be exploitative, which is the model of the past. However, some MNEs still operate exploitatively in poorer countries that do not have the strength to stand up for what they think is best. Second, they can operate on a transactional basis where they engage in doing deals and respecting the law. The challenge is that they may have to choose between local law and the law of the country where their corporate headquarters is domiciled. Third, they can be responsive in the sense of trying to make a difference in the countries where they operate. This is clearly the direction that most large MNEs find themselves going. Many of them have signed on to the UN Global compact and try to make a difference in human rights, labor standards, the environment, and anticorruption. Finally, they can be transformative in terms of taking the lead in generating broad change. This is far more difficult and requires a joint partnership with NGOs and local governments, often responding to the wishes of their stakeholders.

It is clear that social media will have a greater impact on socially responsible behavior in the future. Historically, we have always thought that one of the keys to transparency is an independent press willing to investigate and report on wrongdoings. But now social media, such as Facebook, Twitter, YouTube, and so on, have added an important new dimension to transparency. Neither companies nor governments can hide in the shadows, so it is critical for socially responsible companies to be transparent, and a solid social media strategy is an important dimension of their transparency.

CASE

Anglo American PLC in South Africa: How Can You Make a Difference in the Fight Against HIV/AIDS?[56]

By now it should be obvious that, regardless of where it chooses to do business, an MNE is going to face quite a variety of threats and disruptions to its plans and operations, ranging from bureaucratic corruption and political instability to terrorism and war. In 2019, Anglo American PLC, one of the world's largest mining companies, found itself involved in a global campaign to eradicate the HIV/AIDS epidemic in South Africa.

In 2002, Anglo American made a landmark decision to provide free antiretroviral therapy (ART) to HIV-infected employees there, and expanded these efforts in 2008 to include treatment for the dependents of their employees. Now the U.K.-based company is asking itself, "Where do we go from here?"

AIDS in South Africa

How bad must a disease be to be accorded the status of an "epidemic"? When Anglo American was first confronted with the issues of HIV/AIDS, sub-Saharan Africa was home to just over 10 percent of the world's population and 60 percent of all people infected with HIV, the virus that causes AIDS. South Africa had the highest number of people living with HIV/AIDS and one of the world's highest rates of HIV infection and mortality from AIDS-related diseases. Even in 2017, approximately 75 percent of all people living with HIV live in sub-Saharan Africa.

Thus, over the past decade the spread of HIV/AIDS has had a profound impact on the people of South Africa and their economy. Life expectancy is 56.1 years compared to, say, 76.8 years in Poland, a country with a similar population size and per capita GDP. AIDS has also devastated the country's economy. Between 1992 and 2002, South Africa lost $7 billion annually—around 2 percent of GDP—as a result of AIDS-related worker deaths.

Anglo American Operations in South Africa

Anglo American PLC is a diversified mining conglomerate operating worldwide with 69,000 employees who produce diamonds, precious metals (platinum), base metals (copper, nickel, zinc, and phosphates), and bulk metals (such as iron and coal). Founded in 1917 as the Anglo American Corporation of South Africa, it is a multinational firm headquartered in London with mining operations worldwide.

Anglo American and ART

With such a huge investment in South Africa, Anglo American has been hit hard by the HIV/AIDS epidemic. Having recognized the threat as far back as the early 1990s, Anglo was one of the first corporations to develop a comprehensive, proactive strategy to combat the ravages of the disease on its workforce.

Originally, the program consisted of prevention initiatives aimed at education and awareness, the distribution of condoms, financial and skill-related training to alleviate poverty, and a survey system to monitor the prevalence of the infection. Eventually, these policies were expanded to include voluntary counseling, testing, and care-and-wellness programs, and the services of all programs were extended to cover not only the families of employees but also the populations of surrounding communities.

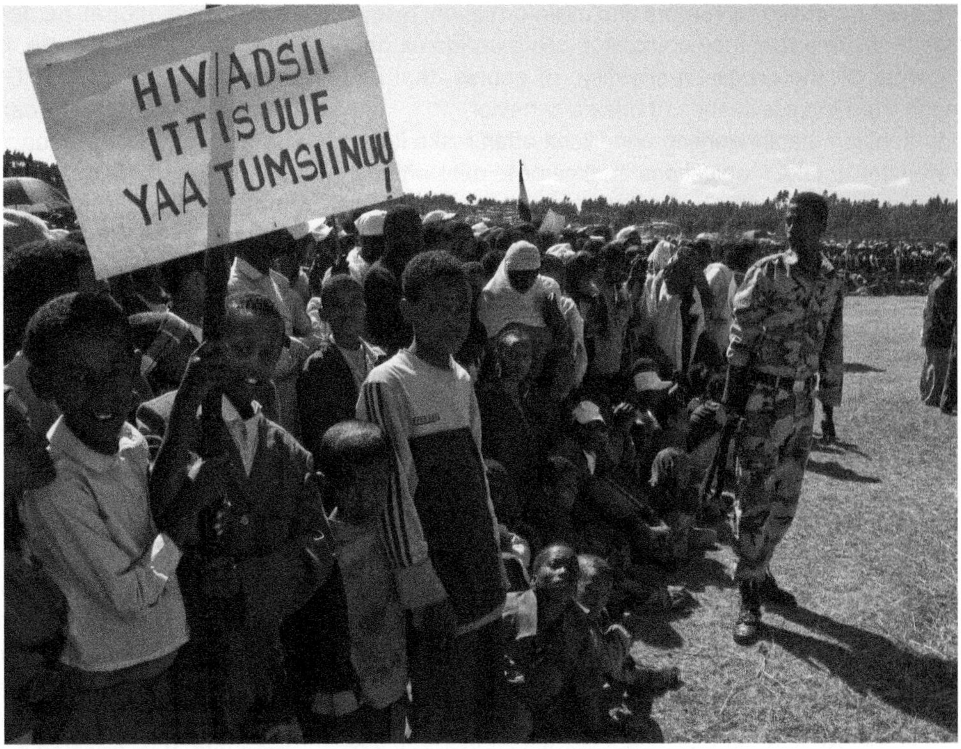

Children all over Africa demonstrate against AIDS, including these children in Fitche, Ethiopia, on the 20th World AIDS Day event on January 13, 2008.

Source: Clive Chilvers/Shutterstock

By adopting these strategies so early, Anglo American became a de facto leader in the private-sector fight against HIV/AIDS in Africa. Many other MNEs soon followed Anglo's example. However, the majority of companies operating in South Africa still hesitated, which is why Anglo's 2002 announcement that it would provide ART to its South African workforce (at company expense) was met with wide approval by organizations such as the World Health Organization and the Global Business Council on HIV/AIDS.

The Costs of Operating in an Epidemic

The incentive for Anglo American's ART program largely came from the failure of its AIDS-prevention efforts to make much headway in stemming the spread of the disease. By 2001, the prevalence of HIV-positive workers had risen to an average of 21 percent across all operations—a figure that was climbing steadily at a rate of 2 percent annually. It was estimated that HIV/AIDS was adding as much as $5 to the cost of producing one ounce of gold, thereby tacking on $11 million a year to the company's production costs. Then there was the $7 million it was spending annually to combat such AIDS-related illnesses as tuberculosis (which was five times as prevalent as it had been just a decade earlier).

Finally, in addition to losses in productivity, the company had to bear the costs entailed by high levels of absenteeism, the constant retraining of replacement workers, and burgeoning payouts in health, hospitalization, and death benefits. Studies conducted at the time indicated not only that the costs of AIDS could reach as much as 7.2 percent of the company's total wage bill but also that the costs of leaving employees untreated would be even higher than the cost of providing ART.

Nine years after it rolled out its ART program, Anglo found itself struggling to please various stakeholders and determine whether all of its efforts are making a difference in the underlying problem or merely masking its effects. By the end of 2009, for instance, although 27 percent of the HIV-infected workforce was receiving ART, the company still struggled with high rates of non-adherence and dropout from treatment regimens.

Anglo also faces the problem of spiraling costs for the program itself. Even though the prices of most of the necessary drugs have been decreasing, the cost of distributing them remains high, and the treatment regimen costs the company an estimated $4,000 per year per employee—quite expensive, especially compared to the wages and benefits that Anglo typically offers mineworkers. (Average monthly wages in the South African mining industry are about 5,100 rand, or US$830.) Meanwhile, as Anglo officials continued to remind investors that treating workers ultimately serves the bottom line, estimates projected a total cost to the company of $1 billion or more over 10 years.

On the upside, cost per patient should decrease as the number of workers participating in the program increases. Unfortunately, one of the biggest challenges facing Anglo is encouraging participation among a migrant and largely uneducated workforce laboring under harsh conditions in an unstable environment. In South Africa, HIV/AIDS still carries a severe stigma, and many South Africans refuse to be tested or to admit they've been infected for fear of discrimination by managers, fellow employees, and even society at large. Moreover, many of those who agreed to participate have been confused by rumors and misinformation, leading them to assume that they could stop using condoms once they were on the drugs—a situation, of course, that only exacerbated the prevalence of unsafe behavior.

In addition, harsh working conditions often make it hard for workers to take medications on time or to deal with certain side-effects. Finally, migrant workers—about four-fifths of the total workforce—who come from isolated villages hundreds of miles away are 2.5 times more likely to contract the disease, which they take with them back to their villages.

Constituencies, Critics, and Progress

Anglo American also faces the problem of pressure from various stakeholders. Anglo has countered many of these criticisms, insisting that it's beyond the resources and capacity of a single company to combat the overall problem, and it has called for more involvement on the part of the South African government. Instead of cooperation, however, the company initially encountered outright opposition from political leaders.

In addition, dealing with pharmaceutical companies has proved a tricky proposition. On the one hand, Anglo has a deal with GlaxoSmithKline allowing it to purchase ART drugs at a tenth of the market price in the industrialized world (the same that GSK charges not-for-profit organizations). At the same time, however, other pharmaceutical companies have been hesitant and unreliable at best, promising price cuts and then reneging over fears of violating intellectual property rights. In spite of that, new and more effective drugs are now available to treat HIV/AIDS.

Given the many challenges Anglo has faced, not to mention the opposition from some stakeholders, some have suggested that the company would be better off simply pulling back on its HIV/AIDS treatment program. In the long run, however, Anglo must consider the continued pressure it will get from ethically minded shareholders as well as its own sense of moral responsibility.

There are also indications that the future may not be as bleak as it initially appeared. In 2017, due to an aggressive global campaign to deal with HIV/AIDs, 59 percent of the people living with HIV worldwide were receiving ART, and AIDS-related deaths had dropped by more than 51 percent since the peak in 2004. For its part, Anglo American's efforts resulted in 86 percent of its employees and dependents receiving free ART therapy, testing, and treatment. UNAIDS is leading the charge to eliminate AIDS as a public health threat by 2030, a strategy endorsed by Anglo American. UNAIDS has announced a 90-90-90 strategy: By 2020, 90 percent of all people living with HIV will know their status; 90 percent of all people diagnosed with HIV infection will receive sustained ART; and 90 percent of all people receiving ART will have viral suppression.

However, the introduction and spread of COVID-19 in 2020 has added a new complexity to the challenges faced by Anglo American, as over 7.000 people have died in South Africa from the pandemic, and nearly 500,000 people have been diagnosed with the virus. Although the AIDS virus has created problems with employees and their families, the COVID-19 pandemic has had a far greater impact on Anglo American's operations because of the devastating effects on the global economic and the demand for their products. It is amazing how two different viruses can have such an huge impact on the global operations of an MNE and their employees worldwide.

QUESTIONS

5-3 Because such a large percentage of its workforce consists of migrant workers who are more likely to acquire and spread HIV/AIDS, should Anglo adopt the policy of not hiring migrant workers? Should the South African government close the doors to migrant workers?

5-4 What role do pharmaceutical companies play in responding to the HIV/AIDS epidemic in South Africa? Given that HIV/AIDS drugs can be exported from India at a lower cost than from the pharmaceutical companies themselves, should Anglo just import the drugs to be used for their employees?

CHAPTER 6

International Trade and Factor Mobility Theory

OBJECTIVES

After studying this chapter, you should be able to

6-1 Understand why policymakers and managers rely on international trade and factor mobility theories to help achieve economic objectives

6-2 Illustrate the historical and current rationale for interventionist and free trade theories

6-3 Describe theories that explain national trade patterns

6-4 Explain why a country's export capabilities are dynamic

6-5 Summarize the reasons for and major effects of international factor movements

6-6 Assess the relationship between foreign trade and international factor mobility

A market is not held for the sake of one person.

—African (Fulani) proverb

Source: Panther Media GmbH/Alamy Stock Photo

▲ Modern highway infrastructure in Taiwan.

CASE

The Evolution of Taiwan's International Trade

—Used with permission of the author, Lichung Jen.[1]

Taiwan, officially the Republic of China, is a small Southeast Asian island country (slightly larger than the U.S. state of Maryland), with a 2019 population of about 23.6 million. Given a lack of natural resources, Taiwan's main natural advantage is its location on the important seaway connecting the east-Asian mainland with the rest of the world. (Map 6.1 shows Taiwan's location and major export markets.)

Taiwan has been called one of the "Asian Tigers" because of its rapid economic growth. (The opening photo shows modern highway infrastructure in Taiwan.) International trade has been an important locomotive of economic growth, and in 2017 Taiwan was the world's 18th-largest exporter. During the last half century, Taiwan's

MAP 6.1 Taiwan and Its Major Export Markets

Estimates for 2018 indicate that 64.9 percent of Taiwan's exports went to only five countries/territories.

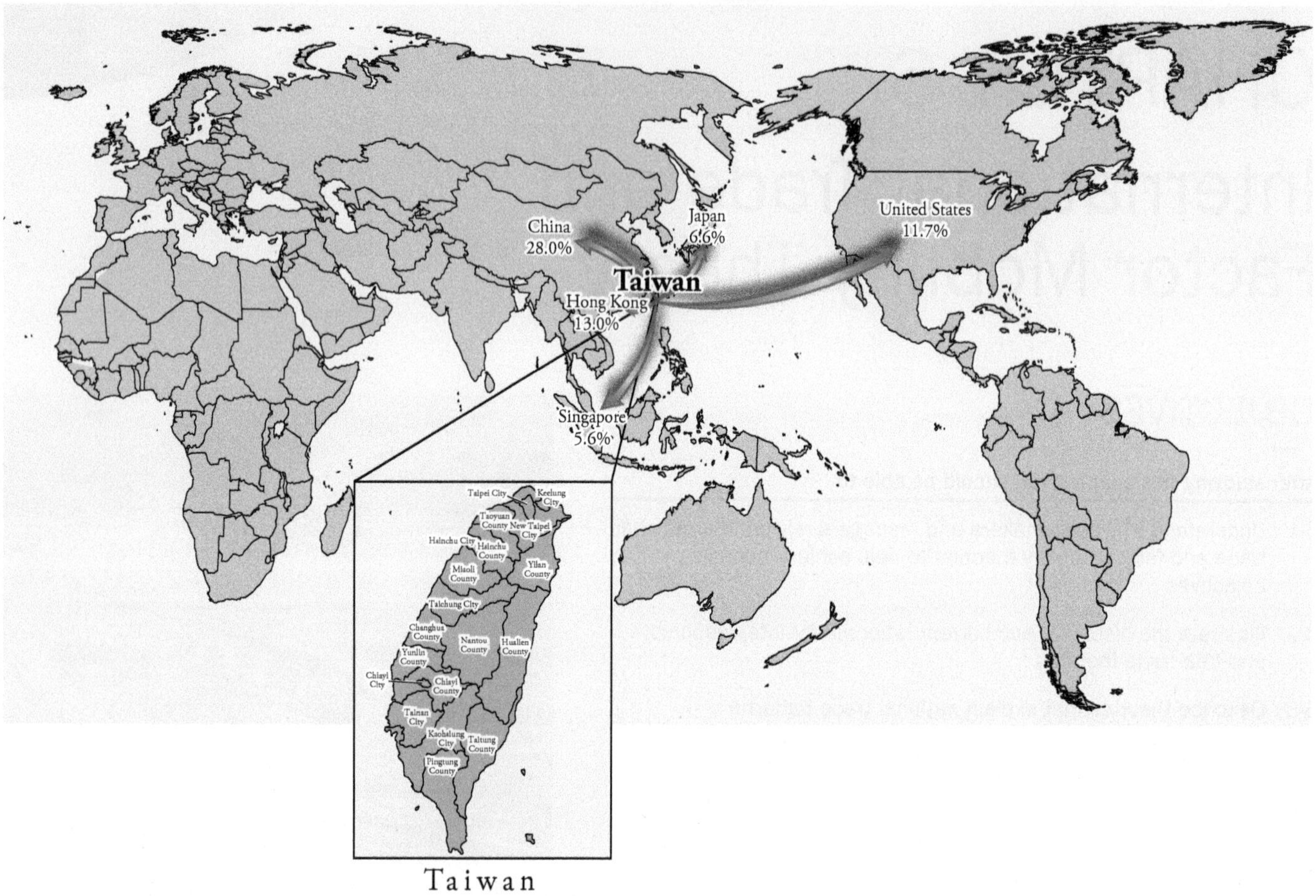

economic and export dependence have shifted from agricultural to industrial products. Evidence of Taiwan's habitation goes back about 10,000 years, but we will overview its trade policies only since the beginning of the Japanese occupation in 1895.

THE JAPANESE OCCUPATION (1895–1945)

Japan took over Taiwan (a Chinese province since 1885) in 1895 after defeating China at war. At that time, Taiwan depended almost entirely on agricultural exports—mainly tea, sugarcane, and rice. In fact, its only significant manufactured export was fake Panama hats. This dependence changed little under Japanese occupation; however, the Japanese did much to improve Taiwan's business environment to be competitive. With funds and Japanese technical experts, it modernized the infrastructure and social structure through the building of roads, railroads, dams for electricity, hospitals, schools, and irrigation systems. It also brought law and order, often brutally, through strict police control. At the same time, Japan absorbed almost all Taiwanese exports at higher-than-world-market prices in order to feed its agricultural needs because a considerable portion of the Japanese population was moving from agriculture into the manufacturing sector.

THE PERIOD OF IMPORT SUBSTITUTION (1945–1958)

At the end of World War II in 1945, Taiwan once again became a part of China, but this was short-lived. The communists took power in the mainland the same year, the nationalist government moved to Taiwan, and business between the mainland and Taiwan came to a virtual halt. Taiwan expelled nearly all Japanese (over 400,000) and lost its protected Japanese export market. It faced a food shortage, high inflation, unemployment, and insufficient foreign earnings to buy the imports needed. The government focused on increasing production and exports while decreasing imports. To do this, the government strictly controlled imports and gave production subsidies to many sectors so that domestic consumers would buy domestically produced goods rather than imported ones (known as an *import substitution*) and so that its traditional primary products would be competitive in external markets.

These policies allowed domestic industries to develop and increased Taiwan's foreign earnings and reserves. For example, in 1950 Taiwan forbade the import of radios, but not radio parts, thus encouraging local assembly of radios to sell domestically. In addition, the policies helped the survival of some light, simple-technical and labor-intensive industries, such as textiles, plywood, and home appliances. During this period, Taiwan's economy boomed, with the real GDP increasing steadily at 7.1 percent a year.

However, the negative effects of the import substitution policy included (1) overproduction of some goods because of insufficient domestic demand coupled with a lack of scale economies to compete internationally; (2) industry inefficiency because noncompetitive manufacturers were not eliminated through market competition; and (3) the emergence of several monopolies that damaged consumer and societal welfare.

THE PERIOD OF EXPORT EXPANSION (1958–1969)

Given the negative effects of import substitution, especially the reliance of production for the domestic market, the government changed its trade policy to promote export expansion. It promoted a series of policies to encourage exports. First, Taiwan depreciated its currency (the NT dollar) by 50 percent to make its products cheaper when bought in foreign currencies. Second, the government set up a system whereby companies could be rebated for the taxes (duties) they paid on imported raw materials when they used them in exported finished goods. Third, companies could avoid duties altogether if imports were processed in bonded factories or warehouses and then exported. Fourth, the government set up export processing zones (the first in the world) in three cities. There were no import duties in these zones as long as companies exported all the finished goods produced therein.

In the meantime, companies in industrially advanced countries, such as Japan and the United States, invested in Taiwan to take advantage of its abundant low-cost labor. This furthered Taiwan's economic growth. The result was that by 1966, the export value of Taiwan's industrial goods exceeded those of agricultural goods for the first time, despite continued agricultural growth resulting from productivity gains that took place in the so-called "green revolution." In turn, this growth freed agricultural workers to move into the manufacturing sector. The economic structure of the economy had also changed from dependence on domestic to export demand. Meanwhile, Taiwan became a bigger part of the global economy, and its exports became the principal thrust of its economic growth.

THE SECOND PERIOD OF IMPORT SUBSTITUTION (1969–1980)

Whereas the first period of import substitution sought to reduce dependence on finished foreign consumer goods, the aim during a second import substitution period was to reduce foreign dependence on the equipment and components needed to produce finished goods.

During this period, the government sought to improve competitiveness by investing in what was referred to as the "The Big Ten Constructions." These focused on six transportation projects (a new freeway, extended railroad, railroad electrification, two harbor developments, and an international airport) and four projects in heavy industries (steel, shipbuilding, petrochemicals, and nuclear power). In addition to decreasing foreign dependence, "The Big Ten Constructions" sped up economic growth and created 146,000 new jobs. However, not all of the heavy industries were equally successful; petrochemicals were more successful than shipbuilding and steel.

The 1970s also saw the growth of small- and medium-sized companies, most of which were family owned, dependent on private loan clubs, labor intensive, export oriented, and involved in processing inputs from other companies. The portion of these companies' sales in export markets grew from 56 percent in 1972 to 75 percent in 1983. This period also saw the growth of foreign investment in export industries. The number of foreign companies exporting from Taiwan increased from 52 in 1966 to 300 in 1980. FDI in exporting businesses increased from US$10 million to US$380 million in the same time frame.

THE PERIOD OF ECONOMIC REFORM AND CONTINUOUS EXPORT EXPANSION (1981–1989)

Although exports continued to expand during this period, the basic government policy was "Liberalization and Globalization." The aim was to increase competition and to open the economy more to imports. The first step was to reduce import duties. This was done gradually to lower the impact on domestic industries. The average nominal import duty fell from 31.71 percent in 1980 to 9.65 percent in 1989. The second step was to liberalize finance and banking, such as by the deregulation and establishment of private banking institutions, the use of market forces to determine interest rates, and the relaxation of foreign currency controls.

THE ECONOMIC POLICIES IN THE 1990S

A major change for Taiwan during the 1990s was its renewal and growth of trade and investment with China. While part of this change was caused by political leadership change, economic factors influenced the growth. By this time, Taiwan was no longer engaged primarily in the labor-intensive processing of components from abroad. Instead, its economic growth, rise in technology, and accompanying higher-wage rates required it to offshore and outsource assembly (e.g., laptop computers) to a lower wage-rate country in order to be competitive. Chinese coastal cities across the strait from Taiwan were ideal for this, and China needed the jobs it would create. At the same time, many Taiwanese firms made investments in the Chinese assembly operations and moved machinery and equipment into China as part of their investment. The result was that China became Taiwan's largest export market and recipient of its direct investment. Concomitantly, Chinese exports to and direct investment in Taiwan have consistently been lower than Taiwan's exports and investments in China. However, official statistics obscure both the value and direction of trade. For instance, when Taiwan ships components to China, those components may be reshipped in finished products that go, say, to the United States. But U.S. and Taiwanese trade figures show the reshipment merely as Chinese exports.

MASSIVE FDI AND FACTOR MOBILITY (2000–PRESENT)

Since the millennium, Taiwan has continued to reduce its trade restrictions, such as by joining the World Trade Organization (WTO) in 2002. (We will discuss the WTO's functions in Chapter 8.) Between 2000 and 2018, both its exports and its imports have more than doubled. Because unemployment rates have been very low, Taiwan has had to utilize foreign contract workers to help keep its production increasing—more than 700 thousand of them in 2018. These are almost all from other Southeast Asian countries—about 70 percent from Vietnam and Indonesia—and are employed at the bottom rung of the socioeconomic ladder. Meanwhile, Taiwan's outward FDI has increased by 150 percent between 2000 and 2018. By 2018, its stock of direct investment abroad was almost four times greater than the FDI within Taiwan.

At the same time, the Taiwanese government has indicated that it needs to make two changes: it needs to change its production base from an efficiency-seeking model to one of innovation, and change its primary export market dependence on China. The government recognizes that it needs to shift more exports to Japan and the United States, but in September 2016 it also introduced an initiative, the "New Southbound Policy," to promote Taiwanese brands and enhance exchanges with 18 countries in Southeast Asia, South Asia, and Australasia.

QUESTIONS

6-1 Using the framework in Table 6.1, explain which of the theories relate to Taiwan's trade policy during each of the eras described in the case.

6-2 Map 6.1 shows that 64.9 percent of Taiwan's exports go to only five countries/territories. Which trade theories may help to explain this concentration and why?

WHY DO POLICYMAKERS AND MANAGERS RELY ON INTERNATIONAL TRADE AND FACTOR MOBILITY THEORIES?

6-1 Understand why policymakers and managers rely on international trade and factor mobility theories to help achieve economic objectives

Trade theory helps government policymakers and firm managers focus on these questions:

- What products should we import and export?
- How much should we trade?
- With whom should we trade?

Some trade theories prescribe that governments should influence trade patterns; others propose a laissez-faire treatment for free trade.

Countries are linked through trade and factor mobility (movement of people, capital, and technology). The preceding case illustrates Taiwan's use of these links to help achieve its economic objectives. Not only are trade and factor mobility important in growing portions of the global economy, the theories to explain them help all governments and firms wrestle with the decisions of what, how much, and with whom to trade. These questions are intertwined with considerations of what they can produce competitively by boosting the quality and quantity of worker skills, capital, and technical competence.

This chapter will first examine theories that endorse government intervention in trade (*mercantilism* and *neomercantilism*) versus a laissez-faire approach without governmental intervention (*free-trade theories of absolute advantage and comparative advantage*). It will then look at theories to explain trade patterns (how much countries depend on trade, in what products, and with whom), including theories of *country size, factor proportions,* and *country similarity.* It will subsequently consider theories dealing with the dynamics of countries' trade competitiveness for particular products, which include the *product life cycle theory* and the *diamond of national competitive advantage theory.* Because the stability and dynamics of countries' competitive positions depend largely on the quantity and quality of their production factors (land, labor, capital, technology), we'll conclude this chapter with an overview of factor mobility. Whether taking a laissez-faire or interventionist approach, countries rely on trade and factor mobility theories to guide policy development. In turn, companies respond by basing their location decisions on these policy developments, as shown in Figure 6.1.

Table 6.1 summarizes the major trade theories and their emphases. These different theories expand our understanding of how government trade policies might affect business competitiveness. For instance, they provide insights on favorable locales and products for exports, thereby helping companies determine where to locate their production facilities when governments do or do not impose trade restrictions.

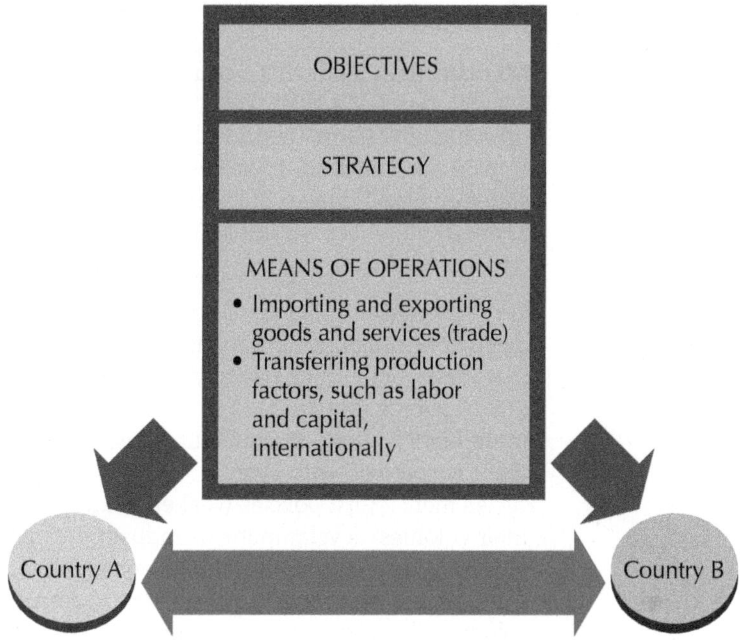

FIGURE 6.1 International Operations and Economic Connections

To meet its international objectives, a company must gear its strategy to trading and transferring its means of operation across borders—say, from (Home) Country A to (Host) Country B. Once either of these processes has taken place, the two countries are connected economically.

TABLE 6.1 What Major Trade Theories Do and Don't Discuss: A Checklist

A check mark indicates that a theory of trade addresses the question asked at the head of the column; if there's a dash, it doesn't.

	Description of Natural Trade			Prescription of Trade Relationships			
Theories	**How Much Is Traded?**	**What Products Are Traded?**	**With Whom Does Trade Take Place?**	**Should Government Control Trade?**	**How Much Should Be Traded?**	**What Products Should Be Traded?**	**With Whom Should Trade Take Place?**
Interventionist & free trade							
Mercantilism	—	—	—	yes	✓	✓	✓
Neomercantilism	—	—	—	yes	✓	—	—
Absolute advantage	—	✓	—	no	—	✓	—
Comparative advantage	—	✓	—	no	—	✓	—
National trade patterns							
Country size	✓	✓	—	—	—	—	—
Factor proportions	—	✓	✓	—	—	—	—
Country similarity	—	✓	✓	—	—	—	—
Export dynamics							
Product life cycle (PLC)	—	✓	✓	—	—	—	—
Diamond of national competitive advantage	—	✓	—	—	—	—	—

INTERVENTIONIST AND FREE TRADE THEORIES

6-2 Illustrate the historical and current rationale for interventionist and free trade theories

At one extreme of trade policies, governments intervene a great deal in trade. Let's begin with mercantilism because it is the oldest trade theory, out of which neomercantilism has more recently emerged.

MERCANTILISM

According to mercantilism, countries should export more than they import.

Mercantilism holds that a country's wealth is measured by its holdings of "treasure," which usually means its gold. This theory, which formed the foundation of economic thought from about 1500 to 1800,[2] holds that countries should export more than they import (run a trade surplus) and, if successful, receive gold from countries that run deficits. Nation-states emerged during this period, and gold empowered governments to raise armies and invest in national institutions that helped to solidify people's primary allegiance to the new nations.

Governmental Policies To run a trade surplus, governments restricted imports and subsidized noncompetitive production. Countries with colonies imported commodities from them that they would otherwise have to purchase elsewhere. They monopolized colonial trade in order to force the colonies to export less highly valued raw materials to them and import more highly valued manufactured products from them. This way, the colonies ran deficits that they paid off with gold.

As mercantilist policies weakened after about 1800, governments seldom directly limited their colonies' development of industrial capabilities. However, their home-based companies had technological leadership, ownership of raw material production abroad, and usually some degree of protection from foreign competition—a combination that continued to make colonies dependent on raw material production and tie their trade to their industrialized mother countries. We still see vestiges of these relationships, which we discuss in the next chapter.

Running a favorable balance of trade is not necessarily beneficial.

The Concept of Balance of Trade Some mercantilist terminology has endured. For example, a **favorable balance of trade** (also called a **trade surplus**) still indicates that a country is exporting more than it imports. An **unfavorable balance of trade** (also known as a **trade deficit**) indicates the opposite. These terms are misnomers because the word *favorable* implies "benefit," and the word *unfavorable* suggests "impairment." In fact, running a trade surplus is not necessarily beneficial, nor is running a trade deficit necessarily detrimental. A country with a favorable balance of trade is supplying people in foreign countries with more than it receives from them.[3] In the mercantilist period, the deficit was paid by a gold transfer. Today, the surplus country, say China, grants credit to the deficit country, say the United States, by holding its currency (U.S. dollars) or investments denominated in U.S. dollars. If that credit cannot eventually buy sufficient goods and services, the so-called favorable trade balance actually may turn out to be disadvantageous for the country with the surplus.

NEOMERCANTILISM

A country that practices neomercantilism attempts to run an export surplus to achieve a social or political objective.

Neomercantilism is the running of a favorable balance of trade to achieve some social or political objective. For example, a country may reduce unemployment by encouraging its companies to produce in excess of the home demand and send the surplus abroad. Or it may attempt to maintain political influence in an area by sending more merchandise there than it receives, such as a government granting merchandise aid or loans to a foreign government.

FREE TRADE THEORIES

CONCEPT CHECK

Chapter 1 observes that nations have been reducing barriers to the movement of trade and production factors because competition spurs efficiency and consumers want a greater variety of goods and services at lower prices.

Why do countries need to trade at all? Why can't Taiwan (or any other country) be content with the goods and services it produces? To begin with, no nation has all the natural resources, geographic conditions, and technology necessary to produce everything we consume today. In addition, two free trade theories further help answer this question: *absolute advantage* and *comparative advantage.*

Both theories hold that nations should let the market determine producers' survival based on what consumers choose to buy.[4] Both theories also imply *specialization.* Just as individuals and families produce an excess of specialized goods and services and exchange them for others' excess specialized goods and services, nations export their specialized surpluses and pay for imports with their export earnings.

THEORY OF ABSOLUTE ADVANTAGE

According to Adam Smith, a country's wealth is based on available goods and services for its residents rather than on gold.

In 1776, Adam Smith declared that a country's well-being is its citizens' access to goods and services rather than the mercantilists' concept of its ownership of gold. His theory of **absolute advantage** holds that different countries produce different things more efficiently than others and that consumers should not have to buy domestically produced goods when they can buy them more cheaply from abroad. Smith reasoned that unrestricted trade would lead a country to specialize in those products that gave it a competitive advantage. Its resources would shift to the efficient industries because it could not compete in the inefficient ones. Through specialization, it could increase its efficiency for three reasons:

Specialization increases efficiency because
- labor skills improve,
- less time is lost by not switching production,
- it incentivizes better working methods.

1. Labor could become more skilled by repeating the same tasks.
2. Labor would not lose time in switching production from one kind of product to another.
3. Larger amounts of production would provide incentives for developing more effective working methods.

In what products should a country specialize? Although Smith believed the marketplace would make the determination, he thought that a country's advantage would be either *natural* or *acquired.*

Natural advantage considers climate, natural resources, and labor force availability.

Natural Advantage A country's **natural advantage** in production comes from climatic conditions, access to certain natural resources, or availability of certain labor forces. As we saw in our opening case, Taiwan's major export used to be tea, a product it still exports and has advantages in producing because its high elevations give its oolong tea a unique taste. Taiwan imports wheat. If it were to increase its wheat production, for which its climate and terrain are less suited, it would have to use land now devoted to tea as well as workers in some of its high-tech industries, thus reducing those earnings.

Conversely, the United States produces a small quantity of tea. To become self-sufficient in tea production would require diverting resources away from products such as wheat, for which its climate and terrain are naturally suited. Trading tea for wheat achieves more efficiency than if these two countries were to try to become self-sufficient in the production of both. The more the two countries' natural advantages differ, the more likely they will favor trade with one another.

Variations among countries in natural advantages also help explain where certain manufactured or processed items might best be produced, particularly if a company can reduce transportation costs by processing an agricultural commodity or natural resource prior to exporting. Processing tea leaves reduces bulk and is likely to reduce transport costs on tea exports; producing bottles of a prepared tea drink would add weight, lessening the industry's internationally competitive edge.

Acquired advantage occurs through either product or process technology.

Acquired Advantage Most of today's world trade is in manufactured goods that compete through an **acquired advantage**, usually in either product or process technology. A *product technology* enables a country to produce a unique product or one that is easily distinguished from those of competitors. For example, Denmark exports silver tableware, not because there are rich Danish silver mines but because Danish companies have developed distinctive products. A *process technology* enables a country to efficiently produce a homogeneous product (one not easily distinguished from that of competitors). Iceland now exports tomatoes grown near the Arctic Circle, while Brazil exports quality wine produced near the equator—both of which were impossible until the countries developed fairly recent process technology.[5] Countries that develop product or process technologies have acquired advantages, but only until producers in another country emulate or surpass them successfully. Such dynamics are commonplace as new products replace old ones, as new uses develop for old products, and as different ways of production come into play.

Free trade will bring
- specialization,
- higher global output.

How Does Specialization Increase Output? We can demonstrate absolute trade advantage by examining two countries and two commodities. Because we are not yet considering the concepts of money and exchange rates, we define the cost of production in terms of the resources needed to produce either commodity. This example is realistic because real income depends on the output of goods compared to the resources used to produce them.

FIGURE 6.2 Production Possibilities Under Conditions of Absolute Advantage

In short, specialization increases potential output.

ASSUMPTIONS
for Taiwan

1. 100 units of resources available
2. 10 units to produce a ton of wheat
3. 4 units to produce a ton of tea
4. Uses half of total resources per product when there is no foreign trade

ASSUMPTIONS
for United States

1. 100 units of resources available
2. 5 units to produce a ton of wheat
3. 20 units to produce a ton of tea
4. Uses half of total resources per product when there is no foreign trade

PRODUCTION	Tea (tons)	Wheat (tons)
Without Trade:		
Taiwan (point *A*)	$12\frac{1}{2}$	5
United States (point *B*)	$2\frac{1}{2}$	10
Total	15	15
With Trade:		
Taiwan (point *C*)	25	0
United States (point *D*)	0	20
Total	25	20

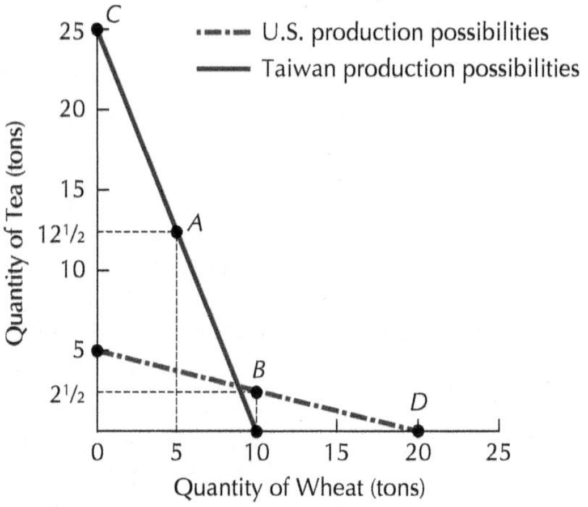

Say that Taiwan and the United States are the only two countries and each has the same amount of resources (land, labor, and capital) to produce either tea or wheat. Using Figure 6.2, let's say that 100 units of resources are available in each country. In Taiwan, assume that it takes 4 units to produce a ton of tea and 10 units per ton of wheat. The purple Taiwanese production possibility line shows that Taiwan can produce 25 tons of tea and no wheat, 10 tons of wheat and no tea, or some combination in between the two.

In the United States, it takes 20 units per ton of tea and 5 units per ton of wheat. The green U.S. production possibility line indicates that the country can produce 5 tons of tea and no wheat, 20 tons of wheat and no tea, or some combination of the two. Taiwan is more efficient in tea production (that is, requires fewer resources to produce tea), while the United States is more efficient in wheat production.

How can production be increased through specialization and trade? Let's say the two countries have no foreign trade. We could start from any place on each production possibility line; for convenience, let's assume that if each country devotes half of its 100 resources to production of each product, Taiwan can produce 12.5 tons of tea (divide 50 by 4) and 5 tons of wheat (divide 50 by 10), shown as point A in Figure 6.2, while the United States can produce 2.5 tons of tea (divide 50 by 20) and 10 tons of wheat (divide 50 by 5), shown as point B in Figure 6.2.

Because each country has only 100 units of resources, neither can increase wheat production without decreasing tea production, or vice versa. Without trade, the combined production is 15 tons of tea (12.5 + 2.5) and 15 tons of wheat (5 + 10). If each country specialized in the commodity for which it had an absolute advantage, Taiwan could then produce 25 tons of tea and the United States 20 tons of wheat (points C and D in the figure).

You can see that specialization increases the production of both products. By trading, global efficiency is optimized, and the two countries can have more tea and more wheat than they would without trade.

THEORY OF COMPARATIVE ADVANTAGE

Gains from trade will occur even in a country that has absolute advantage in all products, because the country must give up less efficient output to produce more efficient output.

We have just described absolute advantage, which requires each country to be more efficient than the other in producing one of the two goods. In 1817, David Ricardo examined the question, "What happens when one country can produce all products at an absolute advantage?" His resulting theory of **comparative advantage** says that global efficiency gains may still result from trade if a country specializes in what it can produce most efficiently—regardless of other countries' absolute advantage.

Comparative Advantage by Analogy Although this theory may seem initially incongruous, an analogy should clarify its logic. Imagine that the best physician in town also happens to be the best medical administrator. It would not make economic sense for the physician to handle all the office's administrative duties because the physician can earn more money by concentrating on medical duties, even though that means having to hire a less-skilled office administrator. In the same manner, a country gains if it concentrates its resources on the commodities it can produce most efficiently. It then trades some of those for commodities produced abroad. The following discussion clarifies this theory.

Production Possibilities Assume the United States is more efficient in producing tea and wheat than Taiwan is, thus having an absolute advantage in the production of both.[6] Take a look at Figure 6.3. As in our earlier example, there are only two countries, each with a total of 100 units of resources available, and half of each used in each product. It takes Taiwan 10 units of resources to produce either a ton of tea or a ton of wheat, whereas it takes the United States only 5 units to produce a ton of tea and 4 for a ton of wheat. Taiwan can produce 5 tons of tea and 5 tons of wheat (point A on the purple line), and the United States can produce 10 tons of tea and 12.5 tons of wheat (point B on the green line). Without trade, neither country can increase its tea production without sacrificing some wheat production, or vice versa.

Although the United States has an absolute advantage in producing both commodities, its comparative advantage is only in wheat. This is because its wheat production is 2.5 times that of Taiwan, whereas its tea production is only twice as much. Although Taiwan has an absolute disadvantage in the production of both products, it has a comparative advantage (or less of a comparative disadvantage) in tea. Why? Because its production is half as efficient in tea and only 40 percent as efficient in wheat.

Without trade, the combined production is 15 tons of tea (5 in Taiwan plus 10 in the United States) and 17.5 tons of wheat (5 plus 12.5). Through trading, the combined production of the commodities within the two countries can be increased. For example, if the combined wheat production is unchanged from when there was no trade, the United States could produce all 17.5 tons by using 70 units of resources (17.5 tons times 4 units per ton). The remaining 30 resource units could be used for producing 6 tons of tea (30 units divided by 5 units per ton), shown by point D in Figure 6.3. Taiwan would use all its resources to produce 10 tons of tea (point C). The combined wheat production has stayed at 17.5 tons, but the tea production has increased from 15 to 16 tons.

FIGURE 6.3 Production Possibilities Under Conditions of Comparative Advantage

There are advantages to trade even if one country enjoys an absolute advantage in the production of all products.

ASSUMPTIONS
for Taiwan

1. 100 units of resources available
2. 10 units to produce a ton of wheat
3. 10 units to produce a ton of tea
4. Uses half of total resources per product when there is no foreign trade

ASSUMPTIONS
for United States

1. 100 units of resources available
2. 4 units to produce a ton of wheat
3. 5 units to produce a ton of tea
4. Uses half of total resources per product when there is no foreign trade

PRODUCTION	Tea (tons)	Wheat (tons)
Without Trade:		
Taiwan (point *A*)	5	5
United States (point *B*)	10	12½
Total	15	17½
With Trade (increasing tea production):		
Taiwan (point *C*)	10	0
United States (point *D*)	6	17½
Total	16	17½
With Trade (increasing wheat production):		
Taiwan (point *C*)	10	0
United States (point *E*)	5	18¾
Total	15	18¾

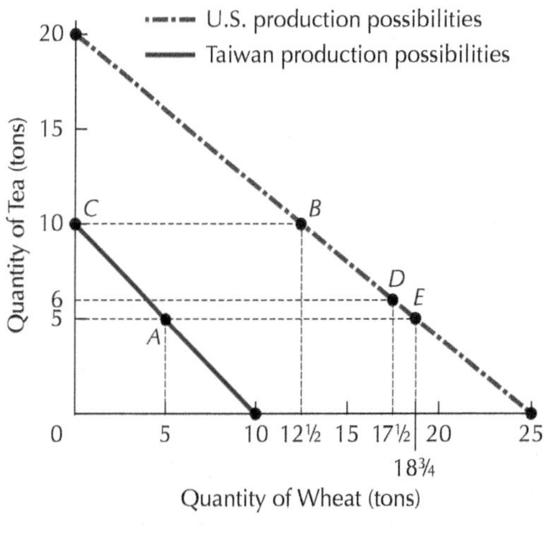

If the combined tea production is unchanged from the time before trade, Taiwan could use all its resources to produce tea, yielding 10 tons (point C in Figure 6.3). The United States could produce the remaining 5 tons of tea by using 25 units, with its remaining 75 units being used to produce 18.75 tons of wheat (75 divided by 4). This production possibility is point E. Without sacrificing any of the tea available before trade, wheat production has increased from 17.5 to 18.75 tons.

If the United States were to produce somewhere between points D and E, both tea and wheat production would increase over what is possible without trade. Whether the production target is a rise in tea or wheat or a combination of the two, both countries can gain by having Taiwan trade some of its tea production to the United States for some U.S. wheat output.

Don't Confuse Comparative and Absolute Advantage Most economists accept the comparative advantage theory, which influences them to promote policies for freer trade. Nevertheless, many people confuse comparative advantage with absolute advantage and do not understand how a country can simultaneously have a comparative *advantage* and absolute *disadvantage* in the production of a given product.

FREE TRADE THEORIES: SOME ASSUMPTIONS AND LIMITATIONS

Both absolute and comparative advantage claim increased production through specialization and trade. However, these theories make assumptions, some of which are not always completely valid.

Full employment is not necessarily a valid assumption of absolute and comparative advantage.

Full Employment Our earlier physician/administrator analogy assumed that the physician could be fully employed practicing medicine. If not, the physician might perform the administrative work without sacrificing earnings from medical duties. The free trade theories assume fully employed resources. When countries have many unemployed or unused resources, they may restrict imports to employ or use idle resources.

Countries' goals may not be limited to economic efficiency.

Economic Efficiency Our analogy also assumes that the physician is interested primarily in maximizing income. Yet there are a number of reasons for choosing not to work full time at medical tasks, such as finding administrative work relaxing and self-fulfilling, fearing that a hired administrator would be unreliable, or wishing to maintain administrative skills in the unlikely event that administrators will command higher wages than physicians in the future. Often, countries also pursue objectives other than output efficiency. They may avoid overspecialization because of the vulnerability created by changes in technology and by price fluctuations or because they do not trust foreign countries to always supply them with essential goods.

CONCEPT CHECK

Recall from Chapter 1 that individuals evaluate their well-being on both an absolute and a comparative basis. Chapter 2 notes national differences in preference for "live to work" versus "work to live."

Division of Gains Although specialization brings potential economic benefits to all trading countries, the earlier discussion did not indicate how countries will divide increased output. In the case of our wheat and tea example, if both the United States and Taiwan receive some share, they will both be better off in an absolute sense. However, people and nations are concerned with relative as well as absolute economic gains. If they perceive that a trading partner is gaining too large a share of benefits, they may prefer to forgo absolute gains for themselves so as to prevent others from gaining a relative economic advantage.[7]

Transport Costs If it costs more to transport the goods than is saved through specialization, the advantages of trade are negated. In other words, in our two-country scenario, some workers would need to forgo producing tea or wheat in order to work in transporting the tea and wheat abroad. However, as long as the diversion reduces output by less than what the two countries gain from specialization, there are still gains from trade.

Insufficient Demand If trade increases production by more than normally acceptable tea and wheat consumption, is there still an advantage? Yes. The consumers in the two countries can gain access to sufficient output by working fewer hours, thus giving them more leisure time.

Countries' absolute and comparative advantages can change.

Statics and Dynamics The theories of absolute and comparative advantage address countries statically—by looking at them at one point in time. However, countries' abilities change. Recall in our opening case how Taiwan's production and exports have evolved. In our two-product example, the resources needed to produce tea or wheat in either Taiwan or the United States could change, such as because of advancements in mechanized tea harvesting and acceptance of genetically modified crops.[8] Thus, we should not assume that future absolute or comparative advantages will remain as they are today. We return to this theme later in the chapter as we examine theories to explain the dynamics of competitive production locations.

Free trade advantages apply to services as well as physical products.

Services The theories deal with products rather than services. However, with a growing portion of world trade made up of services, the theories apply because resources must also go into service production. For instance, the United States sells an excess of such services as education to foreign countries (many foreign students attend U.S. universities). At the same time, it buys an excess of foreign shipping services. To become more self-sufficient in international shipping, the United States might have to divert resources from its more efficient use of them in higher education or in the production of other competitive products.

CONCEPT CHECK

Chapter 1 explains that many products are partially made in different countries. Nevertheless, the concepts of absolute and comparative advantage hold in these instances.

Production Networks Although portions of products increasingly may come from different countries, this development fits well with the concept of advantages through specialization. In other words having portions of products produced in those countries where there is an absolute or comparative advantage saves costs.

Neither domestic labor mobility nor international labor immobility is as great as implied by the free trade theories.

Mobility Perhaps the greatest criticism of the theories is that they assume resources can move domestically from the production of one good to another—and at no cost. But this assumption is not completely valid. For example, factory workers who lose their jobs to imports do not easily find work in an expanding high-tech sector. In the model of wheat and tea, wheat farmers might not easily become tea harvesters. In both situations, required skills are different and retraining might be costly and time-consuming. Furthermore, workers may not readily move to new locations because of family ties, property ownership, local networks of friends, inadequate information about distant opportunities, lack of connections elsewhere, and general aversion to uncertainty.[9] Even if they do, they may be less productive than before.[10]

The theories also assume that resources are immobile internationally. Increasingly, they are mobile, thus affecting countries' production capabilities. For instance, nearly half a million contract workers are in Taiwan, mainly because of better job opportunities there.[11] Further, foreign companies have moved both managers and capital to support their investments there, which has contributed to changing Taiwanese capabilities. Such movement is clearly an alternative to trade, a topic discussed later in the chapter. However, it is safe to say that resources are more mobile domestically than they are internationally.

THEORIES TO EXPLAIN NATIONAL TRADE PATTERNS

6-3 Describe theories that explain national trade patterns

The free trade theories demonstrate how output growth occurs through specialization and free trade; however, they do not deal with trade patterns such as how much a country trades, what products it trades, or who will be its trading partners. In this section, we discuss the theories that help explain these patterns.

HOW MUCH DOES A COUNTRY TRADE?

Free-trade theories of specialization neither propose nor imply that only one country should or will produce a given product or service. **Non-tradable goods**—products and services (haircuts, retail grocery distribution, etc.) that are seldom practical to export because of high transportation costs—are produced in every country. However, among tradable goods, we'll now discuss theories to explain why some countries depend on imports and exports more than others.

Bigger countries (in terms of land mass) differ in several ways from smaller countries. They

- tend to export a smaller portion of output and import a smaller part of consumption,
- have higher average transport costs for foreign trade.

Theory of Country Size The **theory of country size** holds that countries with larger land masses usually depend less on trade than smaller ones. They are apt to have more varied climates and an assortment of natural resources that make them more self-sufficient. Most large countries (such as Brazil, China, India, the United States, and Russia) import less of their consumption and export less of their production output than do small nations (such as Uruguay, Belgium, and Sri Lanka).

Furthermore, distance to foreign markets affects large and small countries differently. Normally, the farther the distance, the higher the transport costs, the longer the inventory carrying time, and the greater the uncertainty and unreliability of timely product delivery. The following example illustrates why distance is more pronounced for a large country than for a small one.

Assume that the normal maximum distance for transporting a product is 100 miles because costs rise too much at greater distances. Although almost any location in Belgium is within 100 miles of a foreign country, the same isn't true for its two largest neighbors, France and Germany. This shorter distance to foreign markets for Belgium additionally helps to explain its higher dependence on trade as a percentage of its production and consumption.

Larger economies are the biggest traders because they produce and consume more.

Size of the Economy While land area helps explain the *relative* dependence on trade, countries' economic size helps explain *absolute* differences in the amount of trade. The world's largest four economies in 2017 were also the top four exporting countries. Simply put, the largest economies produce so much that they have more to sell, both domestically and internationally. At the same time, most of developing countries' trade is with developed countries. There has, however, been a recent upsurge of trade among developing countries, mainly because the economic growth in China and India has increased their demand for raw materials found mainly in developing countries.[12]

Related to levels of economic development is landlocked countries' disadvantage in trade. With few exceptions, these countries lag maritime countries in both trade and GDP per capita. They must depend on other countries to build infrastructure to gain their access to the sea, and there is little incentive for them to do this. At the same time, landlocked countries generally have higher transport costs for exporting. Further, potential trading partners view suppliers from landlocked countries as less reliable because conditions in transit countries can impede trade. Those exceptional landlocked countries' success hinges on forgoing transit problems by depending on service exports (e.g., Switzerland with financial services) or on goods exported by air (e.g., Botswana with diamonds).[13]

The United States offers a good example of the difference between relative and absolute dependence on trade because it is the third-largest country in area and the largest economically. Although its dependence on either imports or exports is comparatively low as a percentage of either production or consumption, it is the world's largest trader (imports + exports). In fact, the output of each U.S. state is so high that states have plenty of opportunity to buy and sell with each other. Map 6.2 illustrates the large U.S. economic size by showing how each of its states compares economically with foreign countries.

WHAT TYPES OF PRODUCTS DOES A COUNTRY TRADE?

According to the factor proportions theory, countries have their best trade advantage when depending on their relatively abundant production factors.

We won't delve again into those factors we've already discussed (climate and natural resources) that give a country a natural advantage; instead, we will examine the factor endowment theory of trade and the importance of process and product technology.

Factor Proportions Theory Eli Heckscher and Bertil Ohlin developed the **factor proportions theory**, maintaining that differences in countries' proportional endowments of labor, land, and capital explain differences in these endowments' costs. For instance, if labor were abundant in comparison to land and capital, labor costs would be low relative to land and capital costs; if scarce, the costs would be high. These relative factor costs would lead countries to excel in the production and export of products that used their abundant—and therefore cheaper—production factors.[14]

MAP 6.2 U.S. States' Economies Compared to National Economies

The U.S. size, both geographically and economically, results in its being one of the world's largest traders while also depending relatively less than most countries on imports and exports.

GDP figures for the U.S. states are based on 2018 data from https://en.wikipedia.org/wiki/List_of_U.S._states_and_territories_by_GDP, retrieved January 15, 2020. Country GDP figures for 2018 are from IMF World Economic Outlook (WEO), October 2019.

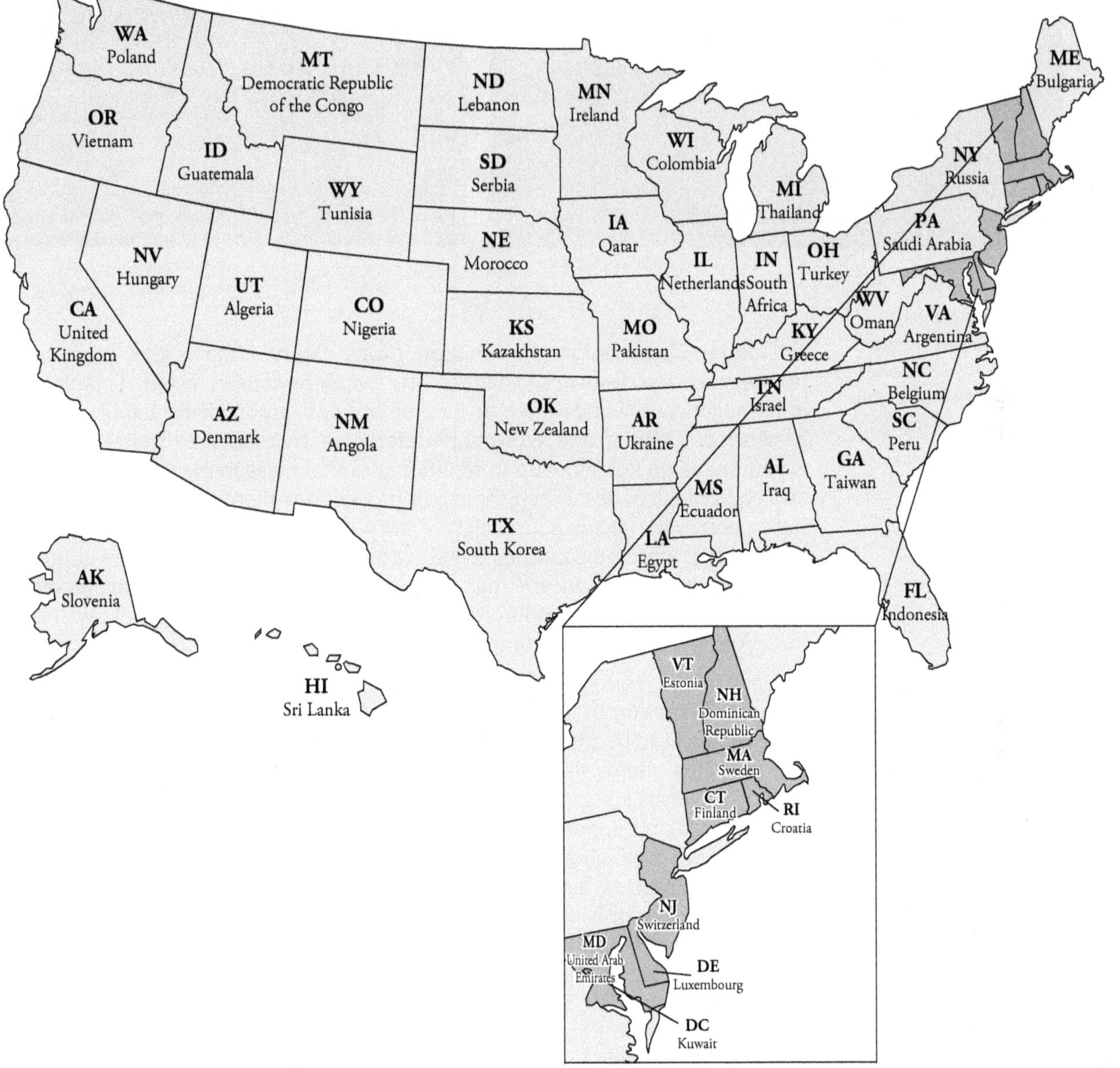

General Observation Factor proportions theory appears logical, and a general observation gives many examples that conform to the theory. For instance, densely populated Hong Kong uses little land for agriculture and produces manufactured products not requiring large amounts of land. Canada is the opposite. Hong Kong does best in manufacturing operations that use a minimum of land per worker (e.g., printing, clothing, watches) by locating these in multistory buildings. Canada produces agricultural and manufactured products that require lots of land per worker, such as wheat and automobiles. On the one hand, Germany, a country with a vast amount of capital relative to its population, excels at chemical production, which requires capital intensity. On the other hand, Bangladesh, a country with abundant labor relative to capital, excels at apparel production, which is labor intensive.

Source: (Left) Roberthardinq/Alamy Stock Photo; (Right) Mamunur Rashid/Alamy Stock Photo

▲ Harvesting rice is capital intensive in Japan (left), where labor rates are high. It is labor intensive in Bangladesh (right), where labor rates are low.

Production factors, such as land and labor, are not homogeneous.

A Deeper Observation Factor proportions theory assumes that production factors are homogeneous, so tests to substantiate the theory have been mixed.[15] Neither land nor labor is homogeneous. Land varies in its arability and productivity. Labor varies by skill level because of training and education differences that require capital expenditures. These expenditures do not show up in traditional capital measurements, which include only plant and equipment values. When the factor proportions theory accounts for capital invested to train people, the factor endowment theory explains many trade patterns.[16] For example, because high-income countries employ a higher proportion of highly educated employees (e.g., scientists and engineers) than do developing economies, they depend on an abundance of highly trained human resources in the production that they export. Low-income countries, though, show a high dependence on less-skilled labor in their exports.[17]

Companies may substitute capital for labor, depending on the cost of each.

Process Technology Factor proportions analysis becomes more complicated when the same product can be created by different methods, such as with labor versus capital intensity. The following photos show rice harvesting in Bangladesh, where many manual laborers are employed, versus Japan, where mechanized methods require few workers. In the final analysis, the optimum location of production depends on comparing the cost in each locale based on the type of production that minimizes costs there.

Countries with bigger markets depend more on producing products requiring larger production runs.

Not all products lend themselves to such trade-offs in production methods. Some require huge amounts of fixed capital and long production runs to spread the fixed capital costs over more output units. These usually are located in countries with large markets.[18] However, companies may locate long production runs in small countries if they are able to export from them.[19] In industries where long production runs reduce unit costs substantially, companies tend to locate production in only a few countries, using these locations to export. Where long production runs are less important, we find a greater prevalence of multiple production units scattered around the world in different countries so as to minimize transportation costs.

In addition, high R&D expenditures create high up-front fixed costs. Therefore, a technologically intensive company from a nation with a small market may need to sell more abroad than a company in a large domestic market. It may, in turn, pull resources from other domestic industries and companies, which leads to more national specialization than one finds in a larger country.[20]

Most new products originate in developed countries.

Product Technology Manufacturing is the largest sector in world trade, and competitiveness depends largely on technology to develop new products and processes, which, in turn, depends on a large number of highly educated people and a large amount of capital to invest in R&D. Because developed countries have an abundance of these features, they originate most new products and account for most manufacturing output and trade. Developing countries depend much more on the production of primary products; thus, they depend more on natural advantage.

WITH WHOM DO COUNTRIES TRADE?

Country similarity and distance play important roles in determining trading partners.

Developed countries trade primarily with each other because they
- produce and consume more,
- emphasize technical breakthroughs in different industrial sectors.

Country-Similarity Theory The **country-similarity theory** says that companies create new products in response to market conditions in their home market. They then turn to markets they see as most similar to what they are accustomed, especially those markets where consumers have comparable levels of per capita income.[21]

Specialization and Acquired Advantage In order to export, a company must provide consumers abroad with an advantage over what they could buy from their domestic producers. Trade occurs because companies in a given country spend more on R&D in some sectors than in others, thus leading to countries' specialization and acquired advantage. Germany, for instance, is traditionally strong in machinery and equipment, Switzerland in pharmaceutical products, and Denmark in food products.[22] Even developing countries gain advantages through specialization in very narrow product segments. Bangladesh has succeeded in exporting shirts, trousers, and hats, but not bed linens or footballs, which Pakistan has successfully exported.[23]

Product differentiation causes countries to conduct two-way trade in seemingly similar products.

Product Differentiation Trade also occurs because *companies* differentiate products, thus creating two-way trade in seemingly similar products. The United States is both a major exporter and a major importer of tourist services, vehicles, and passenger aircraft because different firms from different countries have developed product variations with different appeals. For instance, both Boeing from the United States and Airbus from Europe produce large passenger jets, but airlines buy both companies' aircraft because their models differ in such features as capacity, flying range, fuel consumption, and perceived reliability.[24] As a result, Boeing and Airbus sell within their own and each other's home markets as well as in countries that produce no aircraft.

Trading partners are affected by
- cultural similarity,
- political relations between countries,
- distance.

CONCEPT CHECK

Chapter 2 shows that a company should expect fewer adjustments when moving to a country whose culture is close to that of its home base.

Cultural Similarity Importers and exporters perceive greater ease in doing business in countries that are culturally similar to their home country, such as those that speak a common language. Likewise, historic colonial relationships explain much of the trade between specific developed and developing economies. For instance, France's colonial history in Africa has given Air France an edge in serving the continent's international air passenger markets.[25] Importers and exporters find it easier to continue business ties than to develop new distribution arrangements in countries where they are less experienced.

Political Relationships and Economic Agreements Trade is also affected—both negatively and positively—by political relationships and economic agreements among countries. Witness the political animosity between Israel and most other Middle Eastern countries that has diminished their mutual trade for about six decades. An example of trade encouragement is the agreement among many European countries to remove all trade barriers with each other, thereby causing a greater share of the countries' total trade to be conducted with each other.

The Effects of Distance Although no single factor fully explains specific pairs of trading partners, the geographic distance between two countries is important inasmuch as transport costs increase with distance. However, distance is more important for homogeneous products than for differentiated products inasmuch as the former compete more on the basis of price.[26] In addition, analysis of cost differences must take into account the available transportation modes. Wine exports from Australia can reach the United Kingdom (UK) by container ship for about the same transport cost as wine exports to the UK from southern France because the latter have substantial overland and expensive transport.[27]

THE DYNAMICS OF EXPORT CAPABILITIES

6-4 Explain why a country's export capabilities are dynamic

We've alluded to the fact that trading patterns change due to such factors as political and economic relations among countries and the development of new product and process capabilities. We now discuss two theories that help explain how countries develop, maintain, and lose their competitive advantages.

PRODUCT LIFE CYCLE (PLC) THEORY

According to the PLC theory of trade, the production location for many products moves from one country to another depending on the stage in the product's life cycle.

The international **product life cycle (PLC) theory of trade** states that the production location of certain manufactured products shifts as they go through their life cycle. The cycle consists of four stages: *introduction, growth, maturity,* and *decline.*[28]

The introduction stage is marked by

- innovation in response to observed need,
- exporting by the innovative country,
- evolving product characteristics.

Product Introduction Most new products and process technologies originate in developed countries in response to companies' observation of nearby needs for them.[29] Once a company creates a new product, theoretically it can manufacture it anywhere in the world. In practice, however, during this *product introduction stage,* it generally produces domestically to obtain rapid market feedback and save on transport costs to its predominantly domestic market. Production is apt to be more labor-intensive than in later PLC stages because more labor-saving machinery may be introduced only when sales begin to expand rapidly and the product becomes highly standardized. At this point the highly skilled and educated labor in high-income countries is usually cost efficient despite its high compensation because of its adeptness on nonstandardized production. Even if its cost is somewhat higher than production in a developing country, many consumers are willing to pay a high price for new products rather than wait for future price reductions.

Growth is characterized by

- increases in exports by the innovating country,
- more competition,
- increased capital intensity,
- some foreign production.

Growth Sales growth attracts competitors to the market, particularly in other developed countries where firms have technology to replicate the innovating company's product. Let's say the innovator is in the United States, and a competitor is in Japan. The Japanese production is sold mainly in Japan because:

1. The growing Japanese demand does not allow for much attention to other markets.
2. Japanese producers stay occupied in developing product variations for Japanese consumers.
3. Japanese costs may still be high because of production start-up problems.

Global sales growth creates an incentive for companies to develop labor-saving process technology, but this incentive is partly offset because competitors are differentiating their products, especially to fit the needs of different countries' consumers. Thus the capital intensity, though growing, is less than will come later. The original producing country will increase its exports, especially to developing countries, but will lose certain key export markets where local production commences.

Maturity is characterized by

- a decline in exports from the innovating country,
- more product standardization,
- more capital intensity,
- increased competitiveness of price,
- production start-ups in emerging economies.

Maturity In the *maturity stage,* worldwide demand begins to level off, although growing perhaps in some countries and declining in others. Typically, there is a shakeout of producers, more standardized production, and increased importance of price as a competitive weapon. Increased capital-intensive production reduces per-unit cost, thus creating even more demand in developing economies. Because markets and technologies are widespread, the innovating country no longer commands a production advantage, thus its exports decrease as foreign production replaces it. Shifting production to developing countries is advantageous because firms can employ less skilled and less expensive labor efficiently for standardized (capital-intensive) production.

Decline is characterized by

- a concentration of production in developing countries,
- an innovating country becoming a net importer.

Decline As a product moves into the *decline stage,* those factors occurring during the maturity stage continue to evolve. The markets in developed countries decline more rapidly than those in developing economies as demand among affluent customers becomes saturated and because those customers want ever newer products. By this time, market and cost factors dictate that almost all production is in developing economies. They export to the declining or small-niche markets in the developed world. In other words, the country in which the innovation first emerged—and was exported from—then becomes the importer.

Verification and Limitations of PLC Theory Empirical evidence verifies the PLC theory for many products, such as ballpoint pens and hand calculators. They were first produced in a single developed country and sold at a high price; then, production shifted to multiple developed country locations to serve those local markets. Today, most production is in developing countries, and prices have declined.

Not all products conform to the dynamics of the PLC.

However, types of products abound for which production locations usually do not shift. Such exceptions include the following:

- Products with high transport costs (non-tradable goods) that may have to be produced close to the market, thus never becoming significant exports.
- Products that, because of very rapid innovation, have extremely short life cycles, making it impossible to reduce costs by moving production from one country to another. Some fashion items fit this category.
- Luxury products for which cost is of little concern to the consumer. In fact, production in a developing country may cause consumers to perceive the product as less luxurious.
- Products for which a company can use a differentiation strategy, perhaps through advertising, to maintain consumer demand without competing on the basis of price.
- Products that require specialized technical personnel to locate near production so as to continually move the products into their next generation of models. This seems to explain the long-term U.S. dominance of medical equipment production and German dominance in rotary printing presses.

Regardless of product, the current trend is for international companies to introduce new products at home and abroad almost simultaneously. In other words, instead of merely observing needs within their domestic markets, companies develop products and services for observable worldwide market segments. In so doing, they choose an initial production location (which may or may not be in the innovating company's home market) that will minimize costs for serving markets in multiple countries.

According to the diamond of national competitive advantage theory, companies' development and maintenance of internationally competitive products depends on favorable

- demand conditions,
- factor conditions,
- related and supporting industries,
- firm strategy, structure, and rivalry.

THE DIAMOND OF NATIONAL COMPETITIVE ADVANTAGE

Why have countries developed and sustained different competitive advantages? The **diamond of national competitive advantage** is a theory showing four features as important for competitive superiority: demand conditions; factor conditions; related and supporting industries; and firm strategy, structure, and rivalry[30] (see Figure 6.4).

We have discussed these conditions in the context of other trade theories, but how they combine affects the development and continued existence of competitive advantages. The framework of the theory, therefore, is a useful tool for understanding how and where globally competitive companies develop and sustain themselves.

FIGURE 6.4 The Diamond of National Competitive Advantage

The interaction of these conditions must usually be favorable if an industry in a country is to develop and sustain itself. The theory was developed with domestic conditions in mind, but globalization results in favorable conditions that may come from anywhere.

Source: Based on Michael E. Porter, "The Competitive Advantage of Nations," *Harvard Business Review*, 68:2 (March–April 1990).

Facets of the Diamond Usually, all four conditions need to be favorable for an industry within a country to attain and maintain global supremacy.

Demand Conditions Both PLC theory and country-similarity theory show that new products (or industries) usually arise from companies' observation of need or demand, which has traditionally been in their home countries, where they start production. This was the case for the Italian ceramic tile industry after World War II: In a postwar housing boom, consumers wanted cool floors (which tile would provide) because of the hot Italian climate.

Factor Conditions Recall natural advantage within the absolute advantage and factor proportions theories. Wood was expensive, and most production factors (skilled labor, capital, technology, and equipment) for producing tile were available within Italy on favorable terms.

Related and Supporting Industries Tile production needed enamels and glazes. Had these not been available nearby, as they were in the case of Italy, costs would have increased too much. Recall, for instance, the importance of transport costs in our discussions of the theory of country size, assumptions of specialization, and factors limiting the PLC theory.

Firm Strategy, Structure, and Rivalry The combination of three features—demand, factor conditions, and related and supporting industries—influenced companies' ability to successfully initiate ceramic tile production in postwar Italy. The ability of the companies to sustain a competitive advantage required favorable circumstances for the fourth feature: *firm strategy, structure,* and *rivalry.*

Barriers to market entry were low in the tile industry (some companies started up with as few as three employees), and hundreds of companies initiated production. Rivalry became intense as companies tried to serve increasingly sophisticated Italian consumers. These circumstances forced breakthroughs in both product and process technologies, which gave the Italian producers advantages over foreign firms and enabled them to gain the largest global share of tile exports.

Domestic existence of all conditions

- does not guarantee an industry will develop,
- is not necessary with globalization.

Limitations of the Diamond of National Advantage Theory The existence of the four favorable national conditions does not guarantee that a flourishing industry will develop. Entrepreneurs may face favorable conditions for many different lines of business. In fact, comparative advantage theory holds that resource limitations may cause a country's firms to avoid competing in some industries despite having an absolute advantage. For instance, Swiss conditions would seem to have favored success if companies in Switzerland had become players in the personal computer industry. However, doing so might have lessened protection of Swiss global positions in such product lines as watches and scientific instruments as companies downsized innovation in those industries by moving their highly skilled people into developing a new industry.

A second limitation concerns the growth of globalization. The industries on which this theory is premised grew when companies' access to competitive capabilities was much more domestically focused. We can see how globalization affects each of the four conditions:

1. Observations of foreign or foreign-plus-domestic demand conditions have spurred much of the recent Asian export growth. In fact, such Japanese companies as Uniden and Fujitech target their sales almost entirely to foreign markets.[31]
2. Companies and countries do not depend entirely on domestic factor conditions. For example, capital and managers are now internationally mobile, and companies may depend on foreign locations for portions of their production.
3. If related and supporting industries are not available locally, materials and components are now more easily brought in from abroad because of transportation advancements and relaxed import restrictions. In fact, many MNEs now assemble products with parts supplied from a variety of countries.
4. Companies react not only to domestic rivals but also to foreign-based rivals at home and abroad. Thus the prior domestic absence of any of the four conditions from the diamond may not inhibit companies and industries from gaining these conditions and becoming globally competitive.

Using the Diamond for Transformation By expanding the diamond of national advantage theory to include changes brought about by globalization, we can see its validity for countries' economic policies. In our opening case, Taiwan diversified its economy from agricultural products to modern high-tech products by satisfying the market entry conditions of the diamond. This transformation could not have occurred had Taiwanese authorities looked only at what was available within their own borders. In Taiwan itself, there was (and still is) insufficient demand for the high-tech products it now produces, such as microchips and medical devices; good transportation, however, makes efficient export possible. Similarly, the country initially lacked some of the factor conditions necessary for producing high-tech products, especially trained personnel. Eventually, though, it altered its educational system so that human resource development fit production needs. It also allowed companies to bring in foreign managers and technicians to fill personnel gaps. Finally, it developed local factors and competition, such as by attracting high-tech companies to ensure a vibrant competitive environment. Thus, understanding and having the necessary conditions to be globally competitive is important, but these conditions are neither static nor purely domestic.

THE THEORY AND MAJOR EFFECTS OF FACTOR MOBILITY

6-5 Summarize the reasons for and major effects of international factor movements

We have already noted that major trade theories assume that production resources are not mobile between countries. However, land and natural resources are really the only truly immobile factors of production. Increasingly, labor, capital, and technology are becoming more mobile internationally. **Factor mobility theory** focuses on why production factors move, the effects of that movement on transforming countries' factor endowments, and the impact of international factor mobility on trade.

POINT

Should Nations Use Strategic Trade Policies?

A **strategic trade policy**, or **industrial policy**, is one in which a government identifies target industries to develop to be internationally competitive.

YES If you're a country that wants to compete in today's globalized business environment (and you have to), you must develop and maintain some industries that will be internationally competitive. Those industries must grow and earn sufficient revenues to keep your domestic economy growing at least as well as other countries are performing.

A government's role is rarely neutral. The government may claim that its economic policies don't affect the performance of specific domestic industries on the world stage, but a lot of those policies are bound to have precisely that effect. Who will argue that U.S. efforts to "improve agricultural productivity" and "enhance defense capabilities" have nothing to do with the fact that the United States does a healthy business in the export of farm and aerospace products?

Moreover, just about every government policy designed to help one industry will have a negative effect on another. European airlines complain (with some

COUNTERPOINT

Should Nations Use Strategic Trade Policies?

NO Of course, countries should try to become most competitive in the industries that promise the best returns and have the most potential for going global. Obviously, they're the ones most likely to add value to the national economy. However, strategic trade policy is not the best way to achieve this goal.

I'll make a concession: Under limited circumstances a targeting program will work, particularly for small countries such as Taiwan. Because Taiwan's GDP amounts to just a little more than the value of Walmart's annual sales, parties involved can manageably work together to reach mutually beneficial agreements with minimal frustration. But in a large economy? Impossible.

However, it's debatable just how much Taiwan's economic success is due to strategic trade policy and how much goes back to conditions that existed before the government began involving itself in foreign trade. During the era of Japanese occupation, Taiwan's infrastructure, literacy, and school attendance improved markedly so that its environment for becoming internationally competitive was well established. Further, when justification) that European government support for high-speed rail traffic deprives them of the revenue they need to compete with U.S. overseas carriers, which don't have much to worry about from railroad passenger traffic at home. In other words, national policymakers everywhere face trade-offs. So if every government policy will help one party while hurting another, why shouldn't a country's practices call for taking special care of the industries that will likely give it its best competitive advantage?

Executing such a plan can be pretty simple. First, target a growth industry and figure out what factors make it potentially competitive. Next, identify your country's likely competitive advantages (and make sure you know why you have them). Finally, develop a little synergy between the strong points you've uncovered during both processes: Target the resources needed to support the industries that fit best with your country's advantages.

A strategic trade policy is particularly effective if you're a developing country. Why? Because you've probably already decided that (1) you need to integrate yourself into the global economy and (2) you need to figure out the best way to excel in the international game. If other countries support high-potential start-ups and you don't, your new industries will be disadvantaged.[32] But you need to remember that simply opening up your borders to foreign competition doesn't necessarily mean that domestic producers will have an easier time competing either abroad or at home.

When you do this, foreign competitors may have considerable advantages over homegrown companies you're trying to foster. They've had a head start that's allowed them to develop not only certain efficiencies but cozy relations with everybody in the international distribution channel. Moreover, no matter how promising your targeted industries may be, or how carefully you've tried to match up your industries with your competitive advantages, as a developing country your businesses probably lack the technology and marketing skills they'll need to compete. So, why not help them?[33]

This brings us back to why strategic trade policy is your optimal choice. Your government must protect your local industries—say, by helping them get the skills and technology they'll need. You could also focus your efforts on attracting foreign investment by companies that have the marketing and technical skills you need; that's one good way to bring in the kind of production you need. It also wouldn't hurt to extend incentives within the industries you're counting on.

Want some evidence that strategic trade policy is effective in helping developing nations go global? Look at South Korea, which not only managed to attract companies with experience in consumer-electronics production but eventually emerged as a global competitor by building on imported technologies and targeting technical education to become both a competitive and technical leader.[34] By the same token, we have ample evidence that laissez-faire often doesn't work in developing countries. In sub-Saharan

it instituted its import substitution policies, these policies were not really targeting industries to be internationally competitive.

An alternative is for a country to focus on conditions affecting its attractiveness as a competitive location in general instead of targeting specific industries. In other words, a government can alter conditions affecting, say, factor proportions, efficiency, and innovation by upgrading production factors—cultivating human skills, moving to new levels of infrastructure, encouraging consumers to demand higher-quality products, and promoting an overall competitive environment—for any industry interested in doing business within its borders.

Let's turn to your comments about sub-Saharan Africa. I'll even make another concession: Inefficiency from political bureaucracy is indeed a way of life in much of the area, and there's no reason to expect that it will go away any time soon.[38] But what if we looked at things from another perspective? Rather than trying to focus on a specific industry in, say, the global high-tech universe, wouldn't all these bureaucratic agencies and ministries find it more constructive to review (and enforce) their own laws; take steps to stabilize their populations; rectify their most glaring economic, social, and gender inequities; and support entrepreneurial activity in the informal sectors of their economies? Wouldn't they find it more positive to foster an environment of trust—one in which, say, the government helps cut transaction costs so local firms will be willing to work with other companies, domestic and foreign, to acquire a little of the knowledge and a few of the resources they need to compete?[39] Again, instead of picking and haggling over special industries, wouldn't they be better advised to improve the investment environment in which, after all, everybody will ultimately have to operate anyway?

At this point, I might as well take the offensive in this debate. Strategic trade policies typically result in no more than small payoffs—primarily because most governments find difficulty in identifying and targeting the right industries.[40] What if a country targets an industry in which global demand never quite lives up to expectations? That's what happened to the United Kingdom and France when they got together to underwrite supersonic passenger planes. Or what if the domestic companies in a targeted industry simply fall short of being competitive? That's what happened when Thailand decided to support the steel business.[41] And even in your example of China, previous industrial policies targeting semiconductors and automobiles have not produced competitive industries.[42]

What if too many nations target the same global industries, thereby committing themselves to excessive competition and inadequate returns?[43] What if two countries compete to support the same industry, as happened when both Brazil and Canada decided

Africa, for example, government institutions are so deeply rooted that it's almost impossible for anyone—either individuals or multinationals—to make a move without getting entangled in the bureaucratic undergrowth.[35] One reason for China's economic success is its industrial and trade policy. Its 2015 policy, "Made in China 2025," specified 10 sectors that are the focus of planning, which includes targets for domestic and global market share.[36]

Moreover, because no single political institution in developing countries has much in the way of resources, all are better off focusing their collective efforts on specific industries that have some potential for international competitiveness; otherwise, what you have is a bunch of under-resourced agencies and ministries aiming at markets scattered all over the economic landscape.[37]

to produce regional jets in the same hemisphere?[44] Finally, what if a country successfully targets an industry only to find unexpected conditions? Should it stay the course by reacting to various pressures, such as the pressure to support employment in a distressed industry?[45]

Finally, even if a government can identify a future growth industry in which a domestic firm is likely to succeed—a very big if—it doesn't follow that a company deserves public assistance. History recommends that nations permit their entrepreneurs to do what they do best: take risks that don't jeopardize whole sectors of the economy. The upshot will probably be the same as always: Some will fail, but the successful ones will survive and thrive competitively.

Currently, one of the biggest changes underway concerns relative population numbers. Presently, 46 percent of the world's population lives in countries, mainly developed ones, where the fertility rates are below the population replacement rate.[46] These countries are also encountering a higher portion of people at a postretirement age along with a higher portion who are entering the workforce at a later age because of extended education. This leaves a smaller percentage of residents in their workforces. Further, the aging of the population is expected to require more workers in order to care for illnesses.[47] Concomitantly, many countries, primarily the developing ones, are experiencing rapid population growth. Nine countries are expected to account for half of the world's population increase, with India and Nigeria leading the pack. India is projected to overtake China as the world's most populous country around 2027, and the population of sub-Saharan Africa is expected to double by 2050.[48] High population growth means there are more young people looking for employment, and jobs in these countries are typically difficult to find.

Even with increases in productivity, countries experiencing low population growth will need more immigrants to help provide for their nonemployed populations, and countries with high population growth are in a position to supply them. Japan is an example of a country with a low birth rate and an aging population that has reformed its immigration policies to permit more foreign workers in its economy.[49] After a longstanding taboo on immigration, the Japanese government introduced a visa program for foreign workers, particularly for the restaurant, agriculture, and nursing sectors. Most come from developing countries in Asia, such as Vietnam and the Philippines.

Population changes are important in understanding and predicting changes in export production and import market locations. At the same time, mobility of people, capital, and technology affects trade and relative competitive positions.

WHY PRODUCTION FACTORS MOVE

People and capital move internationally to

- gain more income,
- flee adverse political situations.

People Movement of people across borders has become physically easier over time. Of course, some people travel to other countries as tourists, students, and retirees; however, this does not affect factor endowments because these travelers do not work in the destination countries. But as movement has become physically easier, migration has become bureaucratically more difficult.[50] To live and work abroad, people must get immigration papers and work permits, which most countries provide sparingly. Migrants must also incur high relocation costs, and they may have to learn another language and adjust to a different culture away from their customary support groups. Despite such barriers, people do endure hardships and risks to move to other countries, and there are now 270 million people who live outside the country where they are born. The largest populations outside their homelands are Indians, Mexicans, Russians, and Chinese, each with more than 10 million people.[51]

Migration was the major engine of globalization during the late nineteenth and early twentieth centuries, and at present it is important again. A person who lives outside their native country is known as an **expatriate.** About 3.5 percent of the world's population has migrated to another country. Because movement of people is spread unevenly, expatriate populations are much greater in some countries than in others (e.g., 29.6 percent of the population in Australia and less than 1 percent in Mexico). The foreign-born population in the United States is 13.6 percent.[52]

Of the people who go abroad to work, some move permanently, some temporarily. On the one hand, some people immigrate to another country, become citizens, and plan to reside there for the rest of their lives. On the other hand, some enter a country on temporary work permits, usually for short periods. For instance, most workers in the United Arab Emirates are there on temporary work permits.[53] In addition, MNEs may assign employees to work abroad for periods ranging from a few days to several years (usually to a place where they also transfer capital). In many cases, workers leave their families behind in the hopes of returning home after saving enough money while working in the foreign country. Some move legally, others illegally (undocumented)—that is to say they lack government permission to enter or work.

Motives About 90 percent of the people who move to another country do so largely for economic reasons, such as Indonesian laborers working in Malaysia. Migrants who move to higher-income countries earn three to six times more than they did at home. This is good for economic growth, and by one estimate global output would double if everyone who wanted to migrate could do so.[54]

About 10 percent of migrants move for political reasons—for example, because of persecution or war dangers, in which case they are known as **refugees**—and usually become part of the labor pool where they live. It is not surprising that most refugees emanate from war-torn countries—recently many from Syria, Afghanistan, South Sudan, The Democratic Republic of the Congo—and mainly go to nearby countries. Recently, the largest recipients have been Turkey, Pakistan, and Iran.[55] In addition, there are about 10 million people who have no citizenship, most of whom are seeking some country to give them rights as citizens.[56]

Sometimes it is difficult to distinguish between economic and political motives for international mobility because poor economic conditions often parallel poor political conditions. In recent years, hundreds of thousands of Syrians fled the civil war in their country; however, the fact that many have returned after not finding work may indicate that their motive was economic.

Capital Capital also moves across borders. When we think of factor endowments, capital is the physical plant and equipment, such as the factory buildings, offices, machinery, and computers that are used to produce goods and services. Equipment and some other physical capital can move across borders through exports and imports. Buildings may "move" across borders through trade in building materials. Either way, the relocation of physical capital is associated with international lending and borrowing or else it would simply be trade. Typically, the capital movement is in fact viewed from the monetary (lending and borrowing) aspect, and from this perspective capital is a very mobile production factor.

As an example, consider BMW's factory in the United States. BMW, the German MNE that produces luxury automobiles and motorcycles, built a plant in South Carolina to produce automobiles for the U.S. market as well as for exporting from the U.S. The amount BMW spent on the investment is a movement of capital from Germany to the U.S. We see the additional physical capital – in the form of the plant and equipment – in the U.S., but this would not have been possible without borrowing financial capital from Germany. The plant adds to the productive capacity of the U.S., but the owners of the plant are German so this is a foreign direct investment. The U.S. has in fact relied extensively on foreign direct investment in the U.S. for several decades.

Relocation of capital by MNEs is only one type of capital movement. There are also portfolio investments, which involve buying and selling corporate stocks and bonds across borders. At the point of initial offering, a corporation selling stocks or bonds to foreigners (whether individuals, investment funds, or other companies) directly enables the movement of financial capital from foreign countries to increase physical capital investment at home.

(Subsequent sales and purchases of these stocks and bonds represent changes in ownership, but do not affect the physical investment.) The banking sector also plays an important role in cross-border lending and borrowing, as when U.S. banks take deposits from foreigners and subsequently lend domestically. These forms of capital movement focus on the financial flows, but in all cases they enable additional investment in production resources that would not be possible with the prevailing level of domestic savings. From the financial perspective, investors can transfer capital by wire instantaneously at a low cost, so these forms of capital are more mobile than direct investment because there are active markets for buying foreign holdings and selling them when investors want to transfer the capital back home.

CONCEPT CHECK

Chapter 3 defines political risk as the threat that decisions or events in a country will reduce the profitability of an investment.

Motives As with the movement of people, capital moves to another country primarily for economic reasons, such as when an investor expects a higher rate of return abroad than at home. In our example of BMW, the rate of return on the investment in South Carolina must have been higher than the rate of return in Germany in order to justify the deployment of capital abroad. Taxation of the returns may play a role as well; an otherwise low pre-tax rate of return will be more appealing when taxes are lower, since corporations care about after-tax rates of return. Capital movement may also occur because of political considerations. Capital may move out of a country to avoid high political risk and will move into a country with low political risk, often referred to as a **safe haven** for investment.

EFFECTS OF FACTOR MOVEMENTS

Factor movements alter factor endowments.

Neither international capital nor population mobility is a new occurrence. For example, had it not been for historical mass immigration, Australia, Canada, and the United States would have greatly reduced populations today. Further, many immigrants brought human capital with them, thus adding to the base of skills that enabled those countries to be newly competitive in an array of products they might otherwise have imported. Finally, these same countries received foreign capital to develop infrastructure and natural resources, which further altered their competitive structures and international trade.

What Happens When People Move? We have already indicated that migration is good for growth, and as a result there currently may not be enough of it. However, immigration is controversial in many countries, and some people think there is already too much.

The United States is an example of a country whose recent immigration is largely concentrated at the high and low ends of human skills. Over a third of all people with doctoral degrees in the United States are foreign-born. Immigrants with entrepreneurial skills have been important in American business; 43 percent of the 500 largest U.S. companies are reported to be founded or co-founded by immigrants or their children.[57] At the other end, much recent U.S. immigration has been made up of low-skilled workers. At both extremes, the United States has had shortages of native-born workers, which has been partially alleviated through immigration.

Inward migration has been controversial in the United States and many other countries because of perceptions that it puts downward pressure on domestic workers' wages and that some immigrants may be taking jobs from local citizens. There is scant evidence on this, however, and most economists think the impact is quite small. This is partly because immigration stimulates demand, and this allows native citizens to move into better jobs.[58] Nevertheless, there are additional controversies because countries receiving migrants incur costs by providing social services and acculturating people to a new language and society. There is also a backlash against immigration for fear that some immigrants, particularly illegal (undocumented) immigrants, are a source of crime or terrorist activity.

Another controversial issue is the effect of outward migration on countries. On the one hand, countries lose potentially productive resources when educated people leave—a situation known as a **brain drain**. On the other hand, many of these people are now sending remittances back, which often amount to more than they would have earned if they worked at home. Remittances are now more than 10 percent of GDP in 28 countries, and are more than 30 percent in Haiti, Tajikistan, and Tonga.[59]

There is also evidence that the outward movement and remittances of people leads to an increase in start-up companies and capital in their home countries. Further, the emigrants learn abroad, transfer ideas back home, use remitted capital to start businesses in their native lands, and export to countries with which they have developed connections abroad.[60]

What Happens When Capital Moves? Movement of capital is usually less controversial than movement of people, but still has consequences. We have primarily referenced long-term capital movements that support productive investments, but some capital movement is short-term, perhaps simply chasing higher interest rates or expected stock returns. These short-term capital inflows and outflows might be considered destabilizing to the financial system and the economy if they create volatility or uncertainty. It is in fact difficult to fund long-term capital investments with short-term lending from abroad because the lending might be withdrawn abruptly.

Even long-term capital movements have their critics. Reconsider the BMW plant in South Carolina. The investment may be good for German capital owners, but it deprives Germany of additional jobs in the auto industry. The jobs instead are for U.S. citizens, but the laborers are working for foreign owners who may not consider U.S. national interests when making business decisions. The foreign owners may owe more allegiance to their home country than to their host, and the United States may have less control and autonomy in the economy. Domestic capital may also be threatened; the construction of BMW's new plant likely lowered the rate of return on capital invested by U.S. automakers, such as Ford and GM. Indeed, industries in many countries try to keep foreign capital out in order to maintain high rates of return on the domestic capital.

Some investments also involve access to advanced technology developed in the United States, and foreign ownership of the technology may raise concerns about national security. For this reason, foreign investments in the United States are subject to approval from the Committee on Foreign Investment in the United States (CFIUS). The U.S. Congress expanded CFIUS's authority in 2018 and required mandatory disclosure of acquisitions by investors. Recently, CFIUS has denied several potential investments in the semiconductor industry by multinationals from China because of concerns for national security.[61]

THE RELATIONSHIP BETWEEN TRADE AND FACTOR MOBILITY

6-6 Assess the relationship between foreign trade and international factor mobility

Factor movement is an alternative to trade that may or may not be a more efficient use of resources.[62] Let's see how international factor mobility can affect trade.

SUBSTITUTION

There are pressures for the most abundant factors to move to areas of scarcity.

When the factor proportions vary widely among countries, pressures exist for the abundant factors to move to countries with greater scarcity, where they can command a better return. If permitted, many in the labor pool where workers are unemployed or poorly paid go to countries that have full employment and higher wages. They receive higher wages not only because of the greater scarcity, but also because capital-rich countries have invested in machinery and infrastructure that make the imported laborers more productive than in their home countries.

Of course, as discussed in the section on factor endowment theory, the ratio of land (an immobile factor) to people also influences the movement of labor. Russia has a low population density and the most unfarmed arable land of any country. Next door is China with the highest population and little available unfarmed land. About 400,000 Chinese are now working on Russian farms, and much of the output is shipped to China.[63]

Similarly, capital tends to move away from countries in which it is abundant to those in which it is scarce (e.g., Mexico getting capital from the United States, which gets labor from Mexico).[64] If finished goods and production factors were both free to move internationally, the comparative costs of transferring goods versus factors would determine production location. Let's look at a hypothetical example of supplying the United States with tomatoes. Because U.S. labor to cultivate and pick tomatoes is costly, U.S. capital might move to Mexico to set up tomato production, which is then exported to the United States. Or Mexican labor might move to the United States to work in tomato production. The comparative cost of moving either workers or tomatoes will determine whether trade or factor mobility is used to minimize costs.

In some cases, the inability to gain sufficient access to foreign production factors may stimulate efficient methods of substitution, such as the development of alternatives for traditional production methods.[65] For example, at one time U.S. tomato growers in California depended almost entirely on Mexican temporary workers under what was known as the *bracero program*. Since the termination of this program, the California tomato harvests have quadrupled, while mechanization has replaced 72 percent of the number of workers.

However, not all harvesting jobs can be mechanized. Because cantaloupes ripen at different times, pickers go through a cantaloupe field about 10 times. A robot would have to be able to distinguish colors so as to leave green cantaloupes behind.[66] However, advancement of robots using cameras that distinguish ripeness foretell the diminished need for future agricultural laborers.[67] At the same time, many other jobs that defy mechanization—such as bussing tables at restaurants and changing beds in hotels—are largely filled by unskilled immigrants in developed countries.

COMPLEMENTARITY

Factor mobility through foreign investment often stimulates trade because of

- the need for components,
- the parent company's ability to sell complementary products,
- the need for equipment for subsidiaries.

Our tomato example for the United States and Mexico illustrates that factor movements may substitute for or stimulate trade. Companies' investments abroad often stimulate exports from their home countries. In fact, MNEs account for 80 percent of global exports, such as among their parents and subsidiaries or to independent companies.[68]

Many exports would not occur without foreign investments, partly because a company may export equipment as part of the investment. Or, domestic operating units may export materials and components to their foreign facilities for use in a finished product, such as Coca-Cola's exports of concentrate to its bottling facilities abroad. Finally, a company's foreign facility may produce part of the product line while serving as sales agent for exports of its parent's other products.

CONCEPT CHECK

Chapter 2 emphasizes societal differences in trust along with strength in family ties, especially as it affects trust. Higher trust reduces the cost of business transactions.

Finally, immigration enhances trade by creating ethnic enclaves of networks that link immigrants with their native countries. The enclaves serve as niche markets for imports from their native countries (e.g., early U.S. soy sauce imports sold mainly to Asian-Americans). The ethnic networks also embody product and country-specific knowledge that aids exporting to immigrants' birth-countries. This is more important when a network is from a low-trust culture, especially one that also values family ties strongly. Most people from such a culture have more trust for people they know better, which leads them first to prefer business within the family, next with close friends, etc. Conducting business with people from another country is well down the list of trusted people. But the ethnic network offers an alternative, allowing people from low-trust cultures to deal abroad with others whose language and responses are similar to their home-country experiences. Without this network, they need more time to overcome the perceived risk brought about by lack of knowledge and low trust of potential business partners. Thus potential importers and exporters are more willing to trade when they are part of the ethnic network.[69]

LOOKING TO THE FUTURE Scenarios That May Change Trade Patterns

When countries have few restrictions on foreign trade and factor mobility, companies have greater latitude in reducing operating costs. For example, fewer trade restrictions give them opportunities to gain economies of scale by servicing markets in more than one country from a single base of production. Fewer factor movement restrictions allow them to combine factors for more efficient production. However, government trade and immigration restrictions vary among countries, over time, and under different circumstances.

Nevertheless, it's probably safe to say that trade restrictions have been diminishing, primarily because of the economic gains that countries foresee through freer trade. Further, restrictions on the movement of capital and technology have become freer, but whether restrictions on the movement of people are freer is questionable.

There are uncertainties as to whether the trend toward the freer movement of trade and production factors will continue. Groups worldwide question whether the economic benefits of more open economies outweigh some of the costs, both economic and noneconomic. Although the next chapter discusses government influence on trade in detail, it is useful at this point to understand the overall evolution of protectionist sentiment.

One key issue is the trade between developed and developing economies. As trade barriers are being lowered, some developing economies with very low wage rates are growing economically more rapidly than developed countries. Concomitantly, as companies shift production to developing economies, they displace jobs at home. These displaced workers need to find new jobs. But it is uncertain how quickly new jobs will replace old ones and how much developed countries will tolerate employment displacement and job shifts. If they become intolerant, they may enact protectionist measures that would stifle trade.

Another key issue is the future of factor endowments. If present trends continue, relationships among land, labor, and capital will continue to evolve. For example, the population growth rate is expected to be much higher in developing economies than in developed ones, which could result in continued shifts of labor-intensive production to developing economies and pressures on the developed countries to accept more immigrants.

Urbanization will likely grow faster in developing than in developed countries, which are already heavily urbanized. Considerable evidence indicates that productivity rises with urbanization because firms can more likely find people with the exact skills they need, because there are economies in moving supplies and finished products, and because knowledge flows more easily from one company and industry to another. Thus we might expect higher growth in some developing countries due to their pace of urbanization. Such growth should also help them account for a larger share of world trade.

At the same time, on the one hand the finite supply of natural resources may lead to price increases for these resources, even though oversupplies have often depressed prices. The limited supply may work to the advantage of developing economies because their supplies have been less fully exploited. On the other hand, technology to find and extract natural resources, such as fracking to secure natural gas from shale, may shift supply locations and lessen price rises.

We will probably see the continued trend toward a more finely tuned specialization of production among countries to take advantage of specific conditions. Although part of this will be due to wage and skill differences, other factors are important as well. For instance, country differences in property rights protection may influence businesses to locate more of their technologically intensive activities within countries that offer more protection. Or they may disperse portions of production to different countries in order to hinder potential competitors from gaining the full picture needed to pirate their products and processes.

Four interrelated factors are worth monitoring because they could cause product trade to become relatively less significant in the future:

1. As economies grow, efficiencies of multiple production locations also grow because they can all gain sufficient economies of scale. This may allow country-by-country production to replace trade in many cases. For example, most automobile producers have moved into China and Thailand—or plan to do so—as a result of those countries' growing market size.
2. Flexible, small-scale production methods, especially those using robotics and digital technologies, may enable even small countries to produce many goods efficiently for their own consumption, thus eliminating the need to import them. For example, before the development of efficient mini-mills that can produce steel on a small scale, steel production took larger capital outlays that needed enormous markets. Similarly, consumers' demand for ever more differentiated products largely negates the cost advantages of long production runs, thus making smaller scale manufacturing close to markets more advantageous.[70]
3. Output from and research on 3-D printers are increasing expeditiously. We already see production of such final products as medical implants, jewelry, lampshades, car parts, and mobile phones. Now there is research using 3-D printers for making molds, tools, and dyes. There have been notable breakthroughs, such as the printing of a footbridge, prefabricated sections of buildings, and the replica of an automobile.[71] As this technology develops, products can be fabricated efficiently where they are used rather than traded from one country to another. However, there will still be a need to trade production-grade materials as inputs to the printers.
4. Services are growing more rapidly than products as a global portion of production and consumption. Part of this change involves technology, such as substituting digitized products like music and reading material for traditionally manufactured products. Thus, one buys the right to copy (a service sale) from anywhere in the world with no need to ship products. Consequently, product trade may become a less important part of countries' total trade.

CASE

Ecuador: A Rosy Export Future?[72]

Rose is a rose is a rose is a rose
—*Gertrude Stein, "Sacred Emily" from* Geography and Play *(1922)*

Stein intended her line to illustrate what a word can invoke. Given the many uses of "rose" throughout the ages, the word brings a nearly unique image and emotion to each of us. It has been a name for daughters, an adornment for a garden or vase, a representation of a deceased versus living mother on Mother's Day, a mark of love on Valentine's Day, an ingredient for perfume and medicine, a confetti of strewn petals, and even the symbol of opposing armies during England's War of the Roses.

Some Global Changes

Although growers have sold roses for centuries, their perishability (they should usually be sold within three to five days of being cut) prevented extensive export before there was timely, dependable, and economical air service. Today, roses compose about half the $9.0 billion cut-flower export industry. Developing countries, many without significant domestic cut-flower markets, have accounted for most recent export growth. The world's largest exporter is the Netherlands, followed by Colombia, Ecuador, and Kenya. Given that consumers purchase roses as discretions rather than as necessities, most exports are to high-income countries. Given the need to reach markets quickly and inexpensively, most exports are regional—Kenya sends most of its flowers to Europe, Taiwan to Japan, and Colombia and Ecuador to the United States. However, chilling technology may soon allow cut flowers to be sent in containers on ships.

In addition to feasible air service, other logistical improvements have speeded the connection between growers and consumers. Take, for example, flower imports into the United States. About 80 percent of the annual market enters by air through Miami, which has more than 50 wholesalers and importers. These flowers, mainly from Colombia and Ecuador, are packaged where they are cut and air freighted the same day. The packaging often includes address labels and tracking information so as to avoid the costly and time-consuming process of re-packaging for transshipment. On arrival in Miami, the roses are placed at once in refrigerated warehouses, where U.S. government customs and agriculture inspectors clear shipments by spot-checking packages to ascertain their invoice accuracy and absence of insects.

Of course, long before the growth in export markets, many countries produced flowers for nearby sale, and some are still domestically focused. China and India have larger land areas under flower cultivation than any other countries, but their quality is insufficient to compete much internationally. Japan, the world's second-largest cut-flower market, has purchasing power, but it fills most demand with domestic production. However, in many other countries, imports have largely displaced domestic output. For instance, the United States now imports more than twice the value of its domestic flower production.

Ecuadoran Advantages

Developing countries have a labor cost advantage in the rose market because production is very labor-intensive at almost every stage—planting, fertilizing, fumigating, pruning, removing thorns, assembling by size and rose variety, and packaging. Although Ecuador has this overall advantage, it has a labor cost disadvantage with Colombia, its main competition, because its monthly minimum wage is almost $100 more. Further, its transport cost for roses to the United States averages 20–30 percent more than Colombia's. However, Ecuador has almost unique advantages in rose cultivation.

Because the equator runs through the country, the sun is almost directly overhead throughout the year, which speeds growth and allows for year-round temperature consistency. It grows roses at high altitudes (averaging about 2000 meters, or 6561 feet) that provide the very cool nights that are ideal. Seventy percent are grown north of the capital of Quito, and 30 percent to the south. These areas obtain water from the mineral-rich melting snow of the Andes. The result is that Ecuadoran roses have very large buds, stems up to a meter in length, vivid colors, and extended vase life. The growers sell them at about a one-third price premium above Colombian exported roses. In addition, because Ecuadoran growing areas have less rainfall variation than those in Colombia, they enjoy a lower climatic risk. Nevertheless, damage from weather conditions, particularly wind and rain, is an uncertainty for growers everywhere. In addition, the growing area south of Quito, because of its higher altitude, can produce more premium roses (bigger buds and longer stems), but it is subject to a greater risk of frost than the area to the north.

Market Structure

Ecuador's cut-flower exports, of which 73 percent are roses, have become very important to its economy, employing over 100,000 people directly and many more in supporting industries. Its rose farms are typically owned by individual families, who engage in a mixture of cooperation and competition. They cooperate through a producers' association, Expoflores, to negotiate better airline carriage rates and find means to improve production methods; they compete vigorously with each other for customers abroad; and it is

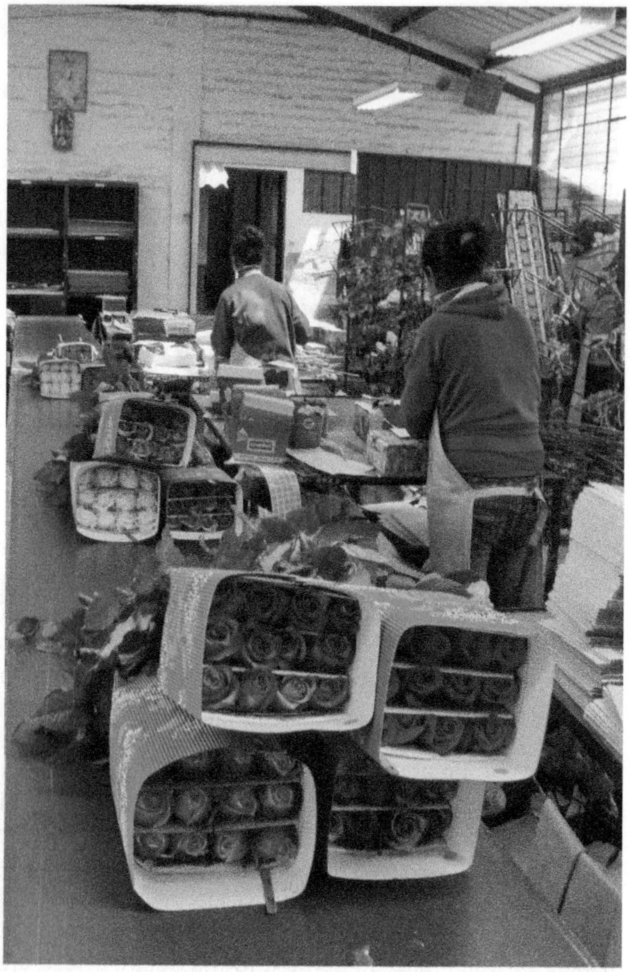
Source: Angela N. Perryman/Shutterstock

Roses on a conveyor belt at a rose farm in Tabacundo, Ecuador, bound for export

common for them to sell below cost if they are short of cash and have excess supplies that might otherwise perish.

For Ecuador's largest market, the United States, growers sell to both importers and wholesalers. The importers sell to large customers, such as wholesalers, mass-market retailers (including grocery chains), and hotels. Wholesalers, in turn, sell to mass-market retailers or florists, who then sell to final consumers. The farms have been trying to sell more directly to wholesalers in order to capture some of the margin in sales between importers and wholesalers; however, too much effort to do so could jeopardize their existing sales to the importers on whom they depend. Given final distribution fragmentation, it is impractical for farmers to sell directly to retailers abroad.

Sales to importers and wholesalers are generally highly personalized, handled via verbal agreement rather than written contract, and dependent on trust. In most instances, there is a buyers' market for cut flowers, so exporters seek to develop confidence and trust among buyers to help secure repeat sales. For instance, if a farm cannot supply what it has promised, perhaps due to adverse weather conditions, it will typically try to buy supplies from other producers in order to fulfill its commitment and build buyer confidence. Negotiations take place largely via e-mail, but exporters make occasional visits to importers and wholesalers to help cement personal relationships. Contacts, both in person and via e-mail, also help the growers plan the quantity of future production by date and rose variety. Growers generally extend credit to the importers and wholesalers; however, if importers do not pay as agreed, then exporters require payment by letter of credit in future sales. Sales are f.o.b. Quito, which means that growers keep title only until the roses are loaded on the aircraft; thus, they do not have legal responsibility if the roses arrive damaged or no longer fresh. (They are responsible for damage caused by disease and for sending a different variety of rose than was ordered.) However, the personal relationship in transactions means that importers, wholesalers, and growers work out responsibility in such circumstances. Although wholesalers and importers try to maintain high quality on roses sold to final consumers, there is an underground market for older and damaged roses that is difficult to control.

Fluctuations in Demand

Planning rose production is difficult because of demand changes during business cycles, during periods of the year, and by variety of rose. This planning is further complicated by unforeseen supply situations.

The demand for roses, especially the high-end market for Ecuador's large, long-stemmed varieties, has been particularly sensitive to income changes in importing countries. For instance, a global economic recession caused the value of Ecuador's cut-rose exports to fall 42 percent between 2007 and 2009, but export sales recovered nearly to the 2007 level by 2012. With the 2014 fall in oil prices, Ecuador's exports to oil-dependent-Russia (Ecuador's second-largest market) fell 30 percent in value. The decreases occurred as consumers bought fewer flowers of any kind, replaced some rose purchases by buying less expensive flowers, and switched in part to less premium roses. The demand change was most noticeable through florists' sales, which depend more on the most expensive roses; mass-market sales of mixed flower bouquets held up fairly well.

Demand during the calendar year changes substantially in both volume and rose type. The biggest spike in sales by far is for red roses on Valentine's Day. Accounting for 25 to 30 percent of Ecuadoran rose exports, they are primarily office gifts and must usually be presented on February 14. (When Valentine's Day falls on the weekend rather than on a weekday, sales drop substantially.) Since the growth period for a rose stem is between 90 and 100 days, the farms must keep clipping stems so that they start growing and then mature on the right date for shipment. However, this 10-day margin between 90 and 100 days is due to uncontrollable weather conditions. With more sunlight, the roses mature faster; with colder weather, they mature slower. Farms can warm growing areas artificially (at a cost). Slowing down maturity when temperatures rise is even more costly inasmuch as agronomists must paint rose encasements with mud or cover entire greenhouses with black fabric. The second-biggest spike is for Mother's Day, but the demand is spread among different colors of roses. During the whole month of June, demand increases again because it is a big month for weddings and the demand is primarily for cream-colored roses. During the rest of the year, the export demand is fairly steady in both volume and color of rose, and growers try to get standing orders to assure steady sales. However, growers must make decisions on how much effort to put into production for the high-demand periods versus the remainder of the year. Further, they must make these decisions without knowing what other growers are doing, which could mean over- or under-supply at any given time.

Roses vary by such characteristics as color, fragrance, size, stem length, and the way they open. In fact, there are about 6,500 varieties of roses, and a farm cannot grow them all. The variety per farm depends largely on the farm's size. Hoja Verde, one of the largest Ecuadoran producers, grows over 400 rose varieties, whereas a more typical Ecuadoran rose farm, such as Grupo Vegaflor, grows about 60. Regardless of farm size, its managers must estimate what the market will demand in order to choose which varieties to grow, how much area to allocate to each, and when to bring different quantities to maturity. Of course, growers depend largely on a few fairly standard but distinct roses for which there is demand throughout the year and in ongoing years. Despite its dependence on standard roses from year to year, the industry also depends on innovation. Growers are pressured, like producers in a fashion industry, to sell new varieties each year. Rose breeders, almost all in developed countries, such as Rosen Tantau in Germany and E. G. Hills in the United States, develop new rose varieties that they promote to distributors. Rose growers must then predict the success of new varieties in order to choose which to grow. In turn, growers pay a fixed licensing fee to the breeders for the rights to grow the new varieties and use their names.

Another factor affecting the rose market is the emergence of demand for fair-trade products, including cut flowers, from developing countries. For instance, TransFair, a not-for-profit organization, certifies whether flowers are grown by using techniques promoting the environment and providing sufficient benefits to workers and communities. Once certified, the flowers sell for about a 10 percent premium, which is used for the workers and community. While reliable figures are unavailable on the size of this market, some estimates put it as high as 10 percent of the rose export market. As of 2011, less than 10 percent of Ecuadoran rose farms had been certified.

Present and Future Market

Our discussion implies that Ecuadoran rose growers could benefit by having consumers treat flowers as a less expendable purchase, choose roses over other flowers, develop a preference for Ecuadoran roses, increase rose buying during nonpeak periods, and better align their rose partiality with the varieties that growers have chosen to produce. However, the growers presently have little influence on final consumers and must therefore depend on distributors to promote those final sales. In fact, many florists advertise through various media, and a quick perusal of the Internet indicates that some specifically promote Ecuadoran roses. Thus, for growers to increase exports they must convince importers and wholesalers to promote final demand, such as through retailers, for the differentiated Ecuadoran premium-priced roses. This is difficult because the number of players (growers, importers, wholesalers, and retailers) is so large and fragmented that no single player at any point in the distribution chain has much influence on final consumers.

Many Ecuadoran growers are putting more emphasis on some countries than on others. Although Ecuador exports roses to more than 90 countries, its sales are highly concentrated in the United States and Russia, which account for a bit over 60 percent of its export market. These two countries are also the largest final consumer markets for imported cut roses. Ecuador and Colombia dominate the rose export sales to these countries. Colombian roses dominate the U.S. import market, and Ecuadoran roses dominate the Russian import market. Observers believe this discrepancy in market share between the two leading markets is due to Russian consumers' preference for long-stemmed roses, whereas the U.S. mass-market preference is for shorter and less expensive roses sold in supermarkets.

Ecuador and Colombia together dominate the export sale of cut roses to some other markets as well, such as Canada and Spain, but these markets are small compared to the United States and Russia. Thus, there is a question of the existence of some fairly untapped markets. Some Ecuadoran growers are considering the Middle East as a possibility for sales expansion as air service improves. Other growers believe that most future growth must come from traditional export locations, either through increasing total rose sales in those locations or by picking up market share from Colombian and other countries' producers. At any rate, whether Ecuador's future cut-rose export sales will be rosy or not seems to have nothing to do with its production ability. Rather, it will depend partly on foreign demand (i.e., the penchant of consumers in other countries for buying its roses). It will depend also on foreign competition (i.e., East African countries, such as Kenya, Zimbabwe, and Uganda are presently in the process of increasing their output).

QUESTIONS

6-3 Look back in Chapter 1 to the factors in increased globalization and explain which have influenced the growth of world trade in cut roses and why.

6-4 Think back to the external institutional conditions (cultural, legal-political, and economic) discussed in Chapters 2 through 4 and discuss how these have affected and might affect future demands for Ecuadoran cut roses.

6-5 There are a number of ways Ecuadoran growers might increase demand for their cut roses. Among these are (a) to try to get more consumers to move up-market by buying premium roses, (b) to promote more rose demand for a different special day (e.g., roses account for a small percentage of U.S. flower sales for Christmas/Hanukkah, Thanksgiving, and Easter/Passover), and (c) to promote sales in relatively untapped markets, such as the Middle East. Compare these and any other alternatives you can think of.

6-6 Some countries have found success by promoting the nationality of their products, such as the Juan Valdez campaign for Colombian coffee. Discuss the viability of a national campaign to promote Ecuadoran roses abroad.

CHAPTER 7
Governmental Influence on Trade

OBJECTIVES

After studying this chapter, you should be able to

7-1 Recognize the conflicting outcomes of trade protectionism

7-2 Assess governments' economic rationales and outcome uncertainties with international trade intervention

7-3 Assess governments' noneconomic rationales and outcome uncertainties with international trade intervention

7-4 Describe the major instruments of trade control

7-5 Understand how companies deal with import competition

Charity begins at home.

—English proverb

Source: bamboofox/Alamy Stock Photo

▲ Workers filleting pangasius catfish in a seafood factory in the Mekong delta of Vietnam.

CASE

The U.S.–Vietnamese Catfish Dispute[1]

Catfish, long a part of the U.S. Deep South diet, is the fourth most consumed seafood or fish product in the United States. The industry is centered (accounting for 89 percent of its 2017 production) in poor areas of two states—Alabama and Mississippi. At its height, it employed about 10,000 people. However, U.S. per capita consumption of fish and seafood has been decreasing (by 4 percent between 2004 and 2017). Further, catfish imports from Vietnam have taken a larger share of the U.S. market (20 percent in 2005 versus 75 percent in 2013), and U.S. production has fallen. Vietnam's industry is also centered in one of its poorer areas, the Mekong Delta. (The opening photo shows a seafood factory in southern Vietnam.) The Vietnamese industry employs about 1 million people and accounts for about 2 percent of Vietnam's economy. The changing competitive situation has spurred the U.S. catfish industry to seek means to limit the importation of Vietnamese catfish. (Map 7.1 shows the production areas in the two countries.)

THE RISE OF AQUACULTURE

During most of history, marine life grew faster than humans could consume it. However, during the last half century, overfishing has led to many species not being fully replenished, a situation caused by population growth and technology that enables locating and landing fish like never before. One factor countering the overfishing has been the rise in aquaculture, or "fish farming," of which the U.S. and Vietnam industries have been a part. In other words, rather than being caught in the wild in nets or hooked on fish line, most catfish are grown in ponds and harvested when they grow to a certain size. In turn, catfish have ceased to be traditional scavengers; instead, they are fed corn and soybean feed, a change publicized by U.S. catfish growers as they promote sales to consumers who do not want to eat scavenger fish.

THE VIETNAMESE ADVANTAGE

The U.S. catfish industry developed largely by converting lands that would no longer grow much cotton, but are high in clay content and hold pumped-in water very well. Meanwhile Vietnam has some competitive advantages that enable it to export to the United States. Its winterless climate permits the fish to grow faster. One of its species, the tra, can surface to breathe air; thus enabling the fish to grow in greater density. Vietnam's lack of restrictions (unlike the United States) on the discharge of fishpond waters into rivers also allows for a greater production density. Finally, its lower labor rates are an important factor for filleting and freezing the fish.

THE U.S. INDUSTRY FIGHTS BACK

Changing Names Alarmed by market losses, U.S. catfish growers' first defense was to convince Congress to disallow Vietnamese imports to be called "catfish." Because Vietnamese fish were of a different variety (from about 3,000 catfish varieties found all over the world) than those farmed in the United States, the Vietnamese varieties had to be imported as swai, tra, basa, or pangasius. The U.S. producers reasoned that consumers were not likely to buy some strange-sounding and unknown fish in lieu of catfish. However, the name change did not prevent Vietnamese inroads. One of the problems was that few U.S. locales have truth-in-menu laws. Thus, the names for swai, tra, basa, and pangasius were changed on menus and grocery labels to be "catfish," a more expensive grouper, or just plain "fish." Clearly, the U.S. catfish producers needed a different means to stifle the imports.

In the meantime, the U.S. industry's profits diminished because of increased costs for corn and soybean feed. In order to raise prices and increase demand, an association representing catfish growers,

MAP 7.1 Areas of Major U.S. and Vietnam Catfish Production

Catfish production for both the United States and Vietnam are near deltas of major rivers, the Mississippi and the Mekong respectively. Both areas have a great deal of poverty.

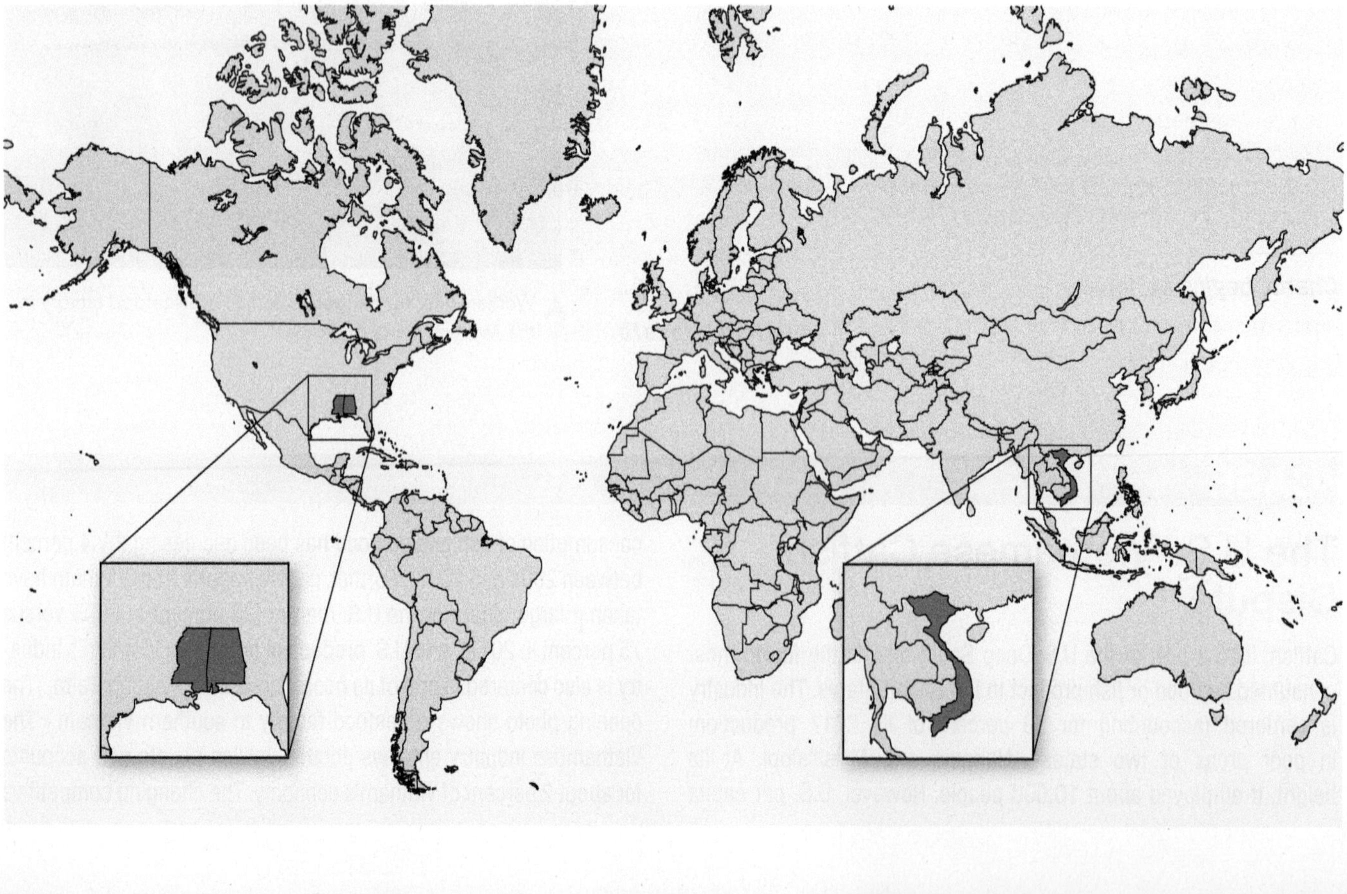

the Catfish Institute, is now promoting a premium catfish with a different name—delacata. Basically, the name "catfish" has a negative connotation for many people, and the Institute noted how name changing had recently helped sales of other previously unpopular fish (e.g., the slimehead became the "orange roughy" and the Patagonian toothfish became "Chilean sea bass"). It is too early to tell if the change-of-name strategy will work.

Unfair Competition: Dumping Because the U.S. industry was losing jobs and sales, it petitioned for increased taxes on the imported Vietnamese fish, claiming that they were being sold below the cost of production (dumping). Given that Vietnam is a command economy, it was difficult to establish what the true production costs were; however, these were estimated on the basis of Bangladesh production costs, and antidumping taxes (tariffs) of 64 percent were placed on imports of the fish. Later, the industry succeeded in having estimates based on higher Indonesian costs.

Health Arguments Despite the higher prices, the Vietnamese fish have taken an increasing share of the U.S. market. However, in 2007, the U.S. catfish industry seemed to have found salvation when about 39,000 U.S. dogs and cats were sickened or killed after consuming imported Chinese pet food. This led to a negative attitude toward imported food products in general, especially seafood originating anywhere in Asia. The U.S. catfish farmers responded quickly. First, they publicly implied that imported fish may be contaminated, such as through publicity saying, "U.S. farm-raised catfish: Safety you can trust." The Catfish Institute convinced several states to require country-of-origin labeling on food and menus by advocating that consumers have the right to know whether the fish and seafood they buy could be contaminated. The Institute has followed up with videos showing unsanitary areas where Vietnamese catfish are cultivated. However, studies on changes in consumer purchases indicate that these measures have had no effect on demand.

Second, catfish farmers lobbied to increase inspections of fish from Vietnam. Their congressional representatives pointed out that U.S. seafood inspection is of only 2 percent of the imports, whereas the European Union inspection is of about 20 percent. They were successful at burying a provision deep in the 2008 farm bill, which called for the U.S. Department of Agriculture (USDA)—rather than the Food and Drug Administration (FDA)—to be in charge of catfish safety. All other fish are regulated by the FDA, making catfish a deviation from the usual regulatory structure. The result of the transfer was that safety requirements and inspections became more intense. Beginning in 2017, the Vietnamese government was required to prove that their inspections were just as rigorous as the U.S. ones (via periodic USDA audits). The USDA also placed inspectors at all ports receiving foreign catfish.

OPPOSITION IN THE U.S.

As with most regulatory changes, there has been opposition to the protection of the U.S. catfish industry, mainly along five lines:

1. Although the farm bill's inspection requirement was ostensibly to protect the health of American consumers, it singled out only catfish-like species without any evidence that these posed more danger than other types of imported fish.
2. The cost of the catfish inspection program is high (e.g., Vietnam exports about 500 tons of catfish to the United States per month), and critics charge that it is wasteful spending.
3. Vietnam is a fast-growing economy with a large population, and U.S. exports to Vietnam amounted to $10.4 billion in 2017. U.S. catfish import restrictions could jeopardize U.S export sales to Vietnam. Vietnam has threatened to take retaliatory action by buying less U.S. beef and agriculture products, for example.
4. Economic conflicts between the U.S. and Vietnam could deteriorate political relations between the two.
5. Finally, some parts of the U.S. catfish industry are having difficulty complying with the new USDA requirements and would like to return regulatory authority to the FDC. In particular, the requirements are much more costly for fishermen catching wild catfish than for farmed catfish.

VIETNAM FIGHTS BACK

Vietnamese producers long complained that the U.S. inspection requirements were onerous, and even the U.S. Government Accountability Office concluded that the USDA program was unnecessary and not based on science. In February 2018, Vietnam filed a dispute at the World Trade Organization (WTO) claiming that the U.S. program discriminates against foreign catfish producers, because U.S. catfish farmers largely met the standards already, and no other types of fish face the same degree of scrutiny. (Chapter 8 discusses the WTO's dispute mechanisms further.) If Vietnam were to win at the WTO, the win may negate the protective catfish measures, but also weaken U.S. efforts to persuade other countries to reduce their trade barriers.

An adage says that if you give a person a fish, they will eat for a day. If you teach them to fish, they will eat for a lifetime. However, the U.S.–Vietnamese catfish controversy illustrates that knowing how to fish is insufficient in international competition. One also needs to know how to influence and maneuver through a maze of government regulations that affect competition.

QUESTIONS

7-1 List the advantages and disadvantages for the U.S. protection of its catfish industry.

7-2 As you read through the chapter, list the protective measures (instruments) the United States has *not* used to protect its catfish industry. Briefly explain why each would or would not be successful.

CONFLICTING OUTCOMES OF TRADE PROTECTIONISM

7-1 Recognize the conflicting outcomes of trade protectionism

At some point, you may be an employee or shareholder in a company whose performance or survival depends on governmental trade policies. These may affect foreign producers' ability to compete in your home market or your company's ability to operate abroad. Collectively, governmental actions to influence international trade are known as **protectionism**.

Restrictions, such as those illustrated in the opening case, are common inasmuch as all countries regulate the flow of goods and services across their borders. Figure 7.1 illustrates the institutions that pressure governments to regulate trade and the subsequent effect on business competitiveness. This chapter reviews the economic and noneconomic rationales for trade protectionism, the major forms of trade controls, and how companies deal with import competition.

Countries seek to influence trade and respond to their economic, social, and political objectives.

Despite free-trade benefits, governments intervene in trade to attain economic, social, or political objectives. Officials enact trade policies that they reason will have the best chance to benefit their nation and its citizens—and, in some cases, their personal political longevity. Their decisions are complicated because outcomes are uncertain and affect groups of their citizens differently.

CONCEPT CHECK

Chapter 6 demonstrates how specialization and free trade can increase output, but here we point out that protectionist policies, although sometimes warranted, can lead to conflicting outcomes.

THE ROLE OF STAKEHOLDERS

Proposals on trade regulations often spark fierce debate among people who believe they will be affected—the so-called *stakeholders.* Of course, those most directly affected are apt to speak out, such as workers, owners, suppliers, and local politicians whose livelihoods depend on the actions taken. Displaced workers may see themselves as unemployed for the long term or forced to take new jobs in new industries, perhaps even in new towns at lower wages. People threatened in this way tend to voice their views often and loudly.

Stakeholders most affected by trade regulations push hardest for trade rules favorable to them.

In contrast, consumer stakeholders typically buy the best product they can find for the lowest price, often without knowing or caring about its origin. They frequently don't realize how much retail prices rise in aggregate because of import restrictions. Nor do they take much notice, since the retail price rises are typically spread out among many people over time and entail a small increase for individual purchases. Despite high visibility, U.S. tariffs imposed in 2018—on steel and aluminum, imports from China, and a few other targets—are estimated to cost consumers approximately $22 billion,[2] or $67 per person. Even if U.S. consumers realized that import restrictions cause them to pay more, they would not likely band together to lobby for removal of the restrictions. In effect, their potential gains would be too low in comparison with their efforts.

FIGURE 7.1 Institutional Factors Affecting the Flow of Goods and Services

In response to a variety of institutional factors (i.e., cultural, political/legal, and economic), governments enact measures designed to either enhance or restrict international trade flows. These measures invariably affect the competitive environment in which companies operate internationally. To an extent, of course, the converse is also true: Companies influence government trade policies that affect their institutions.

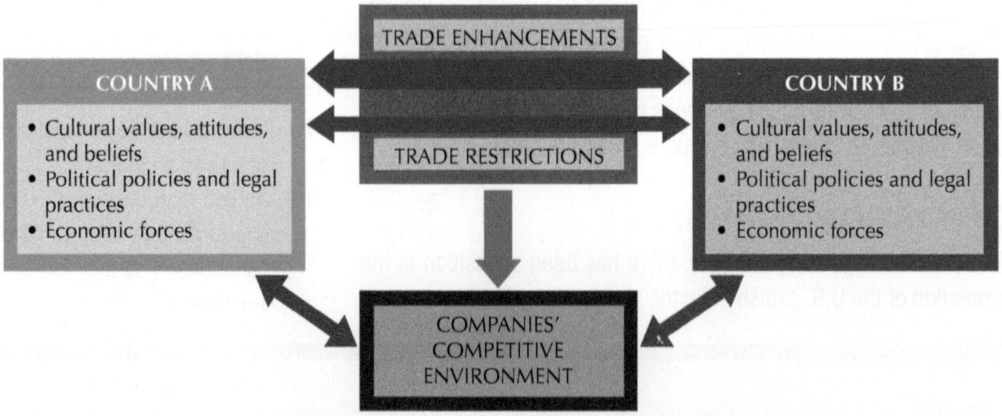

ECONOMIC RATIONALES FOR GOVERNMENTAL TRADE INTERVENTION AND OUTCOME UNCERTAINTIES

7-2 Assess governments' economic rationales and outcome uncertainties with international trade intervention

Governments intervene in international trade for either economic or noneconomic reasons, as shown in Table 7.1. Let's begin by analyzing some leading *economic rationales.*

FIGHTING UNEMPLOYMENT

The unemployed can form an effective pressure group for import restrictions.

Probably no pressure group is more effective than the unemployed; no other group has more time and incentive to protest publicly and contact government representatives. Import-displaced workers are often the least able to find alternative work, especially if large numbers are concentrated in small company towns where there are few alternative employment opportunities.[3] When they do, they generally earn less than before.[4] Moreover, they often need to spend their unemployment benefits to survive in the short term, and they put off retraining because they hope to be recalled to their old jobs. Further, many workers, especially older ones, lack the needed educational background to gain required skills. Or they train for jobs that do not materialize.

Import restrictions to create domestic employment

- may lead to retaliation by other countries,
- affect large and small economies differently,
- reduce import handling jobs,
- may decrease jobs in another industry,
- may decrease export jobs because of lower incomes abroad.

What's Wrong with Full Employment as an Economic Objective? Nothing! However, gaining jobs by limiting imports may not fully work as expected. Even if jobs are gained, the costs may be high and must be borne by someone. For example, one study indicated that tariffs on imported washing machines imposed in 2018 created 1,800 new jobs in the United States, but at the cost of about $817,000 per job, paid for by U.S. consumers through higher prices.[5] But there are other consequences as well.

The Prospect of Retaliation When restricting imports to create jobs, foreign countries losing those jobs may retaliate with their own restrictions. Our opening case addressed the concern that Vietnam would respond to more U.S. catfish import restrictions by buying fewer U.S. agricultural products. Thus, unemployment would merely shift from one sector to another.

However, large trading countries are more important in the retaliation process. For instance, China would have more power to retaliate than, say, Mauritius, to U.S. limits on imports. After the United States put tariffs on $50 billion of Chinese imports in mid-2018, China retaliated by putting tariffs on imports of U.S. soybeans, America's biggest farm export. This disrupted the global market as China began importing from Brazil; prices for U.S. soybeans plummeted and prices for Brazilian ones skyrocketed. A small importer of soybeans would not have been able to cause such an extensive disruption. The market shift will probably be long-lasting, as China seeks to diversify away from reliance on the United States.[6]

Other Limits on Employment Gaining jobs by limiting imports has the following additional limitations:

1. Fewer imports mean fewer import-handling jobs, such as those in the container-shipping industry, the clearance of goods through customs, and the distribution of the imports.

TABLE 7.1 Why Governments Intervene in Trade

Economic Rationales	Noneconomic Rationales
Fighting unemployment	Maintaining essential industries
Protecting infant industries	Promoting acceptable practices abroad
Promoting industrialization	Maintaining or extending spheres of influence
Improving comparative positions	Preserving national culture

2. Given the global complexity of production, import restrictions on one industry cause higher input costs for other industries, thus making them less competitive.[7] For example, U.S. import restrictions on steel raise input costs in the U.S. automobile and farm equipment industries.
3. Imports stimulate exports, though less directly, by increasing foreign income, which foreign consumers then spend partially on new imports. Thus, restricting earnings abroad has some negative effect on domestic earnings and employment.

Analyzing Trade-Offs Analysis of net changes in employment cannot capture the price of distress suffered by people who lose their jobs through import competition. Nor is it easy for working people to understand that their economic gains through lower prices from freer trade may exceed their higher taxes to support unemployment or welfare benefits for those who lose jobs.

In summary, many groups call for protectionism to increase or protect employment. However, evidence suggests that employment is better dealt with through fiscal and monetary policies.

PROTECTING "INFANT INDUSTRIES"

The infant-industry argument says that production becomes more competitive over time because of
- increased economies of scale,
- greater worker efficiency.

The **infant-industry argument** holds that a government should shield an emerging industry from foreign competition by guaranteeing it a large share of the domestic market until it can compete on its own.

Underlying Assumptions The infant-industry argument presumes that early operating costs within a newly producing country may be too high to compete in world markets and that sufficient cost reductions will occur over time. Therefore, protection for fledgling companies enables them to gain economies of scale and higher productivity through worker experience.

CONCEPT CHECK

The Point-Counterpoint discussion in Chapter 6 emphasizes governmental problems determining what industries to support in a strategic trade policy and the difficulty of removing the support if the industries do not become globally competitive.

Risks in Designating Industries However, production costs may never fall enough to create internationally competitive products. Inherently, there are problems.

Determining Probability of Success First, governments must identify those industries that have a high probability of success, and this is hard. For example, governmental protection worked for the Brazilian automobile industry, but not for the Malaysian one. Second, the security of government import protection may deter managers from adopting the cost and quality measures needed to compete. Third, if a protected industry fails to become globally competitive, its affected stakeholders may successfully prevent the imports that benefit consumers.

Possible costs of import restrictions include higher prices and higher taxes. Such costs should be compared with those of unemployment.

Who Should Bear the Cost? Even if policymakers choose the right industries, some economic segment must absorb the high early cost before domestic production becomes internationally viable. This burden may fall on consumers who pay higher prices for the protected products or on taxpayers who pay for subsidies. When taxes go for subsidies, governments may be less able to spend to improve overall competitiveness, such as on education and infrastructure. Finally, why rely on governmental assistance? Many entrepreneurs have endured early losses to achieve future competitiveness.

DEVELOPING AN INDUSTRIAL BASE

Countries seek protection to promote industrialization because that type of production
- can use surplus agricultural workers more easily,
- brings in investment funds,
- diversifies the economy,
- brings faster growth than primary products do.

Since the industrial revolution, countries increasing their industrial bases grew their employment and economies more rapidly. This observation led to protectionist arguments to spur local industrialization. These arguments have been based on the following assumptions:

1. Surplus workers can increase manufacturing output more easily than agricultural output.
2. Import restrictions lead to foreign investment inflows, which provide jobs in manufacturing.
3. Diversification of the economy will reduce dependence on agricultural products and raw materials, which have volatile prices.

4. Markets for industrial products grow faster than markets for both agricultural and raw material commodities.

In the sections that follow, we review each of these assumptions.

Surplus Workers Disguised unemployment is high in rural areas of many developing countries, where many people effectively contribute little, if anything, to agricultural production. Consequently, they can move into the industrial sector without significantly reducing agricultural output. This **industrialization argument** presumes that, although a country may develop an inefficient and non-globally competitive industrial sector, it will achieve economic growth by enabling the unemployed and underemployed to work in industry.[8]

When a country shifts from agriculture to industry
- output may increase if the agricultural workers produced little before,
- demands on social and political services in cities may increase,
- development possibilities in the agricultural sector may be overlooked,
- industrial jobs may not be forthcoming.

Shifting people out of agriculture, however, can create problems:

1. The underemployed in rural areas may lose the safety net of their extended families, while many migrating to urban areas cannot find suitable jobs, housing, and social services. For example, although millions of Chinese have moved to cities to find jobs, many have not prospered through the move.[9]
2. Improved agricultural practices may be a better means of achieving economic success than a drastic shift to industry. Many developed countries continue to profit from exports of agricultural products and maintain high per capita income with a mix of industrial and efficient agricultural production.
3. Most past manufacturing was performed by relatively unskilled workers and at a time when this output's proportion of global output and growth exceeded those in other sectors (e.g., agriculture, raw materials, and services). Thus, there were ample opportunities in factories for the unskilled labor force who were "fresh off the farm." However, this situation has changed and is known as *premature industrialization*. Manufacturing employment has been falling as a portion of total global employment because technology is replacing the need for many workers, especially unskilled ones. Although there are growing employment opportunities in the service sector, people lacking much education are forced into low-paying service jobs.[10]

If import restrictions keep out foreign-made goods, foreign companies may invest to produce in the restricted area.

Investment Inflows Import restrictions, applied to spur industrialization, also may increase FDI, which provides capital, technology, and jobs. Barred from exporting to an attractive foreign market, foreign companies may transfer manufacturing to that country to avoid the loss of a lucrative or potential market.

Although prices for commodities fluctuate markedly, a shift to production of manufactures creates competitive risk.

Diversification Export prices of many commodities, such as oil and coffee, fluctuate markedly because of weather and technology affecting supply or business cycles affecting demand, thus wreaking havoc on economies that depend on their export. Because many developing countries rely on only one or a few commodities, they are caught in a feast-or-famine cycle, as it were: able to afford foreign luxuries one year but unable to find the funds for essential equipment's replacement parts the next. However, a greater dependence on manufacturing does not guarantee diversification of export earnings. The population of many developing economies is small; a move to manufacturing may shift dependence from one or two agricultural commodities to one or two manufactured products, which face competitive risks and potential obsolescence.

Terms of trade may deteriorate because
- demand for primary products grows more slowly than manufactured ones,
- production cost savings for primary products will be passed on to consumers.

Growth in Manufactured Goods The quantity of imports that a given quantity of a country's exports can buy—say, how many bananas Country A must sell to purchase one refrigerator from Country B—is the **terms of trade**. Historically, except for short periods, the prices of commodities have not risen as fast as those of finished products.[11] Over time, therefore, it takes more low-priced primary products to buy the same amount of high-priced manufactured goods.

Why? First, the quantity of primary products demanded does not rise as rapidly as manufactured products and services, due partly to consumers' spending a lower percentage of income on food as their incomes rise and partly to raw-material-saving technologies. Second, because commodities are hard to differentiate, they usually must compete on price, whereas the prices of manufactured products can stay high because competition is based more on differentiation.

Industrialization emphasizes either

- products to sell domestically or
- products to export.

Import Substitution and Export-Led Development Traditionally, developing countries fostered industrialization by promoting **import substitution**—restricting imports to boost local production of products they would otherwise import. In contrast, some countries, such as Taiwan and South Korea, have achieved rapid economic growth by promoting the development of industries with export potential, an approach known as **export-led development**. In reality, it's not easy to distinguish between import substitution and export-led development. Industrialization may result initially in import substitution, yet export development of the same products may be feasible later.

IMPROVING COMPARATIVE ECONOMIC POSITIONS

Nations monitor their absolute economic situations and compare their performance to other countries. Among their many practices to improve their relative positions, four stand out: making balance-of-trade adjustments, gaining comparable access to foreign markets, using restrictions as a bargaining tool, and influencing prices.

Balance-of-Trade Adjustments A trade deficit influences reductions in a nation's exchange reserves—the funds that help purchase priority foreign goods and maintain the trustworthiness of its currency. So balance-of-trade deficits may cause a government to act to reduce imports or encourage exports. Two options that can affect its competitive position broadly are:

1. Depreciating or devaluing its currency, which makes basically all of its products cheaper in relation to foreign products
2. Relying on fiscal and monetary policy to bring about lower price increases in general than those in other countries

Both of these options take time. Furthermore, they aren't selective; for instance, they make both foreign essentials and foreign luxury products more expensive. Thus, a country may use protection instead to affect only certain products. Doing so is really a stopgap measure to gain time to address the fundamental competitive situation—the perceived quality, quantity, characteristics, and prices of products—that is causing its residents to buy more abroad than they are selling.

If domestic producers have less access to foreign markets than foreign producers have to their market, they may be disadvantaged but:

- restricting foreign entry may disadvantage domestic consumers,
- negotiating equal market access for each product is impractical.

Comparable Access or "Fairness" The **comparable access argument** holds that industries are entitled to the same access to foreign markets as foreign industries have to theirs. The issue is that tariffs are not reciprocal. For example, the U.S. tariff rate on automobiles is 2.5 percent, but the EU's tariff is 4 times that and India's is 10 times. This helps explain why automobile exports from the EU to the U.S. are triple the amount going in the other direction, and why the U.S. is India's third-largest market for automobiles but giant India is a tiny market for U.S. producers.[12] Economic theory supports the idea of equal access when substantial production cost decreases result from economies of scale. Companies that lack equal access to a competitor's market will be relatively disadvantaged in gaining enough sales to be cost-competitive.[13]

Comparable access is also presented as "fairness." For instance, the U.S. government permits foreign financial service firms to operate in the United States, but only if their home governments allow U.S. financial service firms equivalent market access. There are, however, at least two practical reasons for rejecting the idea of fairness:

1. Tit-for-tat market access can lead to restrictions that may deny one's own consumers lower prices.
2. Governmental negotiation and monitoring of separate agreements for each of the thousands of different products and services that might be traded would simply be impractical.

Import Restrictions as a Bargaining Tool The threat or imposition of import restrictions may persuade other countries to lower their import barriers or not raise them. The danger is that each country then escalates its restrictions instead, creating, in effect, a trade war that negatively impacts all their economies. Using restrictions successfully as a bargaining tool requires very careful product targeting by considering the following criteria:

- *Believability:* Either the country has access to alternative sources for the product or its consumers are willing to do without it. The EU successfully retaliated against U.S. import restrictions on clothing by threatening to impose trade restrictions on U.S.-grown soybeans when Brazil had a surplus.

Successful countries' threats to levy trade restrictions to coerce other countries to change their policies

- must be believable,
- involve products important to the other countries.

- *Importance:* Exports of the restricted product must be significant to influential parties in the producer country. This consideration was emphasized when the United States placed restrictions on imported steel. The EU threatened to restrict apple and orange imports, which would hurt producers in Washington and Florida. Given the importance of these two states in a close presidential election, apple and orange stakeholders quickly convinced the United States to remove the steel import restrictions.

Export restrictions may

- raise world prices,
- require more controls to prevent smuggling,
- be ineffective for digital products,
- lead to product substitution or new ways to produce the product,
- keep domestic prices down by increasing domestic supply,
- give producers less incentive to increase output.

Export Restrictions Countries that hold a near-monopoly of certain resources sometimes limit their international sale in an effort to raise prices abroad. However, this policy often encourages smuggling (such as occurs with emeralds and diamonds), the development of technology (such as synthetic rubber in place of natural rubber), or different means to produce the same product (such as caviar from farm-grown rather than wild sturgeons).[14] Export controls are especially ineffective for digital products because they are so easily copied abroad.

A country may also limit exports of a product that is in short supply worldwide to favor domestic consumers. During COVID-19, at least 75 countries restricted exports of critical medical supplies. For example, Germany restricted exports of surgical face masks to neighboring countries in order to keep them at home.[15] Despite the global emergency and Germany's commitment to free trade within the European Union, Germany's government paid more attention to its national emergency and prevented masks from going where the need may have been greater. (COVID-19 was more severe in Italy and Spain in the spring of 2020.)

Typically, a greater supply drops domestic prices beneath foreign ones. Russia and Argentina have pursued this strategy by limiting exports of food products; India has limited cotton exports to increase supplies for its textile industry; and the United States has curtailed crude-oil exports. Confronted with rising prices for rice during COVID-19, Vietnam, Cambodia, and Myanmar restricted exports.[16] However, favoring domestic consumers disfavors domestic producers, so they have less incentive to maintain production when prices are low.

Affecting Import Prices Import restrictions may aim either to raise or lower prices.

Prevention of Foreign Monopolies There is fear that foreign producers will price their exports so artificially low that they will drive producers out of business in the importing country. If they succeed, there are two potential adverse consequences for the importing economy:

CONCEPT CHECK

Discussion of neomercantilism in Chapter 6 explains that countries may attempt to shift their economic and social problems abroad.

1. The foreign country may be shifting its unemployment abroad by subsidizing the sales.
2. If there are high entry barriers, surviving foreign producers may be able to charge exorbitant prices. However, for most products competition is so widespread that no country or company can reach such a dominant position. For example, low import prices have eliminated most U.S. production of consumer electronics; still, the United States has some of the world's lowest consumer electronics prices because so many companies make them in so many countries.

Dumping

- may be used to introduce a new product,
- may cause higher prices or subsidies in the exporting country,
- is hard to prove.

Prevention of Dumping Exporting below cost or below home-country price is called **dumping**. Most countries restrict imports of dumped products, but enforcement usually occurs only if the imported product disrupts domestic production; otherwise host-country consumers get the benefit of lower prices and don't complain. While exporting countries may encourage dumping to improve employment, companies may dump products to introduce them and build a market abroad. Essentially, a low entry price encourages consumers to sample the foreign brand—after which they can charge a higher price to make a profit.

Companies can afford to dump products if they are subsidized or if they can charge high prices in their home market. Ironically, exporting-country consumers or taxpayers seldom realize that they are paying for foreign consumers' lower prices. An industry that believes it's competing against dumped products may appeal to its government to restrict the imports. However, determining a foreign company's cost or even its domestic price to middlemen is difficult because of limited access to its accounting records, fluctuations in exchange rates, and the passage of products through layers of distribution before reaching the end consumer. Nevertheless, industries do manage to succeed (e.g., U.S. steelmakers' curtailment of Korean steel pipes).[17] However, critics claim that governments allegedly limit imports arbitrarily through antidumping restrictions and are slow to dispose of the restrictions if pricing situations change. Companies caught by antidumping restrictions often lose the export market they labored to build.

An optimum tariff's success
- shifts revenue to an importing country,
- is difficult to predict,
- may cause lower worker income in developing countries.

Invoking the Optimum Tariff **Optimum-tariff theory** addresses whether a foreign producer lowers export prices when an importing country places a tax on its products. If this occurs, benefits accrue to the importing country.

Let's examine a hypothetical situation. Assume an exporter has costs of $500 per unit and is selling abroad for $700. With the imposition of a 10 percent tax on the imported price, the exporter may choose to lower its price to $636.36 per unit, which, with a 10 percent tax of $63.64, would keep the price at $700 in the foreign market. The exporter may feel that a foreign market price higher than $700 would result in lost sales and that a profit of $136.36 per unit instead of the previous $200 is better than no profit at all. Consequently, an amount of $63.64 per unit has shifted to the importing country.

As long as the foreign producer lowers its price by any amount, some revenue shifts to the importing country. There are many examples of products whose prices did not rise as much as the amount of the imposed tariff. After U.S. tariffs on steel were imposed in 2018, foreign producers dropped their prices and U.S. customers paid only about half the tariff.[18] Similarly, purveyors of luxury products have narrowed profit margins in Brazil to help offset import levies and sales taxes.[19] However, predicting when, where, and which exporters will voluntarily reduce their profit margins is imprecise. When the United States introduced tariffs on imports of Chinese goods in 2018, there was a suggestion that China would pay the tariffs by lowering prices on exports. However, there were no immediate signs that prices fell when the tariffs went into effect, and a comprehensive assessment allowing for delayed impacts suggests that China is not paying the tariffs, instead passing 100 percent on to U.S. consumers.[20] Further, a criticism of the optimum tariff is that developing country exporters reduce payment to their workers rather than absorbing the full impact through a lower profit margin, thus sometimes causing severe hardships.[21]

NONECONOMIC RATIONALES FOR GOVERNMENTAL TRADE INTERVENTION AND OUTCOME UNCERTAINTIES

7-3 Assess governments' noneconomic rationales and outcome uncertainties with international trade intervention

Although noneconomic arguments are used to influence trade, many of these also have economic undertones and consequences. However, let's look at the major noneconomic rationales:

- Maintaining essential industries (especially defense)
- Promoting acceptable practices abroad
- Maintaining or extending spheres of influence
- Preserving national culture

MAINTAINING ESSENTIAL INDUSTRIES

In protecting essential industries, countries must
- determine which ones are essential,
- consider costs and alternatives,
- consider political and economic consequences.

Under the **essential-industry argument** nations apply trade restrictions to protect crucial domestic industries so that they are not dependent on foreign supplies during hostile political periods. For example, the United States subsidizes domestic silicon production so that its computer-chip makers need not depend on foreign suppliers. Because of nationalism, defense needs have much appeal in rallying support for import barriers. The rationale for the 2018 U.S. tariffs on steel and aluminum was to protect national security. In some cases, countries also prevent foreign companies from acquiring domestic companies needed for national security; the United States does this through the Committee on Foreign Investment in the United States (CFIUS). However, in times of real (or perceived) crisis or military emergency, almost any product could be deemed essential.

The essential-industry argument should not be (but frequently is) accepted without a careful evaluation of costs, real needs, and alternatives. Once given, protection is hard to remove, even when the rationale for protection no longer exists. For instance, the United States subsidized mohair producers for more than 20 years after mohair was no longer essential for military uniforms.[22]

In addition, governments buy and stockpile supplies of essential raw materials that might be in future short supply. For example, the United States stockpiles rare-earth elements because China controls most output and because the military needs them for weapons, jet engines, high-powered magnets, and other gear.[23]

PROMOTING ACCEPTABLE PRACTICES ABROAD

Trade limitations may be used to compel a foreign country to amend an objectionable practice.

Governments limit exports, even to friendly countries, of strategic goods that might fall into the hands of potential enemies. They also limit exports and imports to compel a foreign country to change some objectionable policy or capability. The rationale is to weaken the foreign country's economy by decreasing its foreign sales and by limiting its access to needed products, thus coercing it to amend its practices on some issue such as human rights, environmental protection, military activities, and production of harmful products. Trade limitations are often combined with other economic pressures and incentives such as restricting access to bank accounts and cutting off or increasing foreign aid.

The effectiveness of trade sanctions depends on the sanctioned country's inability to retaliate effectively, secure alternative markets and supplies, and develop a production capability of its own. Our Point-Counterpoint section discusses the pros and cons of sanctions.

POINT

Should Governments Impose Trade Sanctions?

YES Let's face it: We're now living in a global society where actions in one country can spill over and affect people all over the world. For instance, the development of a nuclear arsenal in one nation can escalate the damage that terrorists can do elsewhere. The failure of a country to protect endangered species can have long-term effects on the whole world's environment. We simply can't sit back and let things happen elsewhere that will come back to haunt us.

At the same time, some pretty dastardly things occur in some countries that most of the world community would like to see stopped: human trafficking for forced prostitution, child slaves to harvest crops, political prisoners given near-starvation diets, to name a few. Even if we can't stop such occurrences, we have a moral responsibility not to participate even if it costs us. I may get some economic benefits by buying from criminals, and I may not stop their activity by withholding my business; however, I refuse to deal with them because, in effect, that makes me a criminal's associate.

Although not all trade sanctions have been successful, many have at least been influential in achieving their objectives. These included UN sanctions against Rhodesia (now Zimbabwe), U.K. and U.S. sanctions against the Amin government of Uganda, and Indian sanctions against Nepal.[24] Sanctions against Myanmar helped bring the country to such economic disaster

COUNTERPOINT

Should Governments Impose Trade Sanctions?

NO Every time I turn around, I see governments imposing a new sanction. Some of these cause law-abiding companies to lose revenue that took years to develop. For one, there is a chance of retaliation. Trade sanctions on Russia after its annexation of Crimea were costly to Norwegian fish exporters because Russia turned to Chile.[28] Thus, the trade sanctions aimed at hurting the Russian government ended up hurting non-Russian companies even though they'd never engaged in any objectionable behavior.

Besides, I really question whether these sanctions even work. When the United States was maintaining its 20-year trade embargo on Vietnam, Vietnamese consumers could still buy U.S. products such as Coca-Cola, Kodak film, and Apple computers through other countries that did not enforce the sanctions.[29] The more than 50-year trade embargo with Cuba weakened over time and became ineffective as countries ceased their trade suppression. Oil embargoes against South Africa, because of its racial policies, merely spurred South African companies to become leaders in converting coal to oil.[30]

Even if trade sanctions succeed at weakening the targeted countries' economies, who really suffers? You can bet that the political leaders will still get whatever they need, so innocent people bear the costs of sanctions. This occurred in Iran, where there were widespread reports of deaths because of sanction-induced shortages of medicine.[31] Moreover, the people adversely affected usually blame their suffering not on their internal regime that its military leaders decided democracy was a better route to take.[25] Sanctions against Iran helped terminate Iran's nuclear program, and pressure on Brazil led to greatly reduced cutting of Amazon forests.[26] Further, even if sanctions do not completely change behavior, they may force countries not to escalate their unacceptable practices.[27]

Finally, when a nation breaks international agreements or acts in unpopular ways, what courses of action can other nations take? Between 1827 and World War I, nations mounted 21 blockades, but these are now considered too dangerous. Military force has also been used, for example, during the overthrow of the Hussein regime in Iraq, but such measures have little global support. Thus, nations may take such punitive actions as withholding diplomatic recognition, boycotting athletic and cultural events, seizing the other country's foreign property, and eliminating foreign aid and loans. These may be ineffective in and of themselves without the addition of trade sanctions.

but on the countries imposing the sanctions. Despots are very good at manipulating public opinion.[32]

In addition, critics of sanctioning point to import restrictions that are not fully effective because they aim too much at curtailing supply rather than demand, such as U.S. actions aiming to curtail the production of opiates abroad rather than efforts to restrain U.S. demand. In another example, many countries restrict ivory imports so that countries (mainly African) will limit ivory supplies by protecting elephants.[33] However, although restrictions may have slowed elephant slaughter, poaching still continues (in the five years between 2010 and 2015, Tanzania and Mozambique lost 60 and 48 percent of their elephants respectively) because of high demand for ivory.[34] The photo below shows seized ivory ready to be destroyed.

Finally, governments sometimes seem to impose trade sanctions based on one issue rather than on a country's overall record. For instance, some critics have suggested using trade policies to press Brazil to restrict the cutting of Amazon forests, even though its overall environmental record—particularly its limitation of adverse exhaust emissions by converting automobile engines to use methanol instead of gasoline—is quite good.

MAINTAINING OR EXTENDING SPHERES OF INFLUENCE

Governments use trade to support their spheres of influence—giving aid and credits to, and encouraging imports from, countries that join a political alliance or vote a preferred way within international bodies. For example, the EU and 78 states from Africa, the Caribbean, and the Pacific participate in the Cotonou Agreement that formalizes an array of economic and political ties and economic issues.

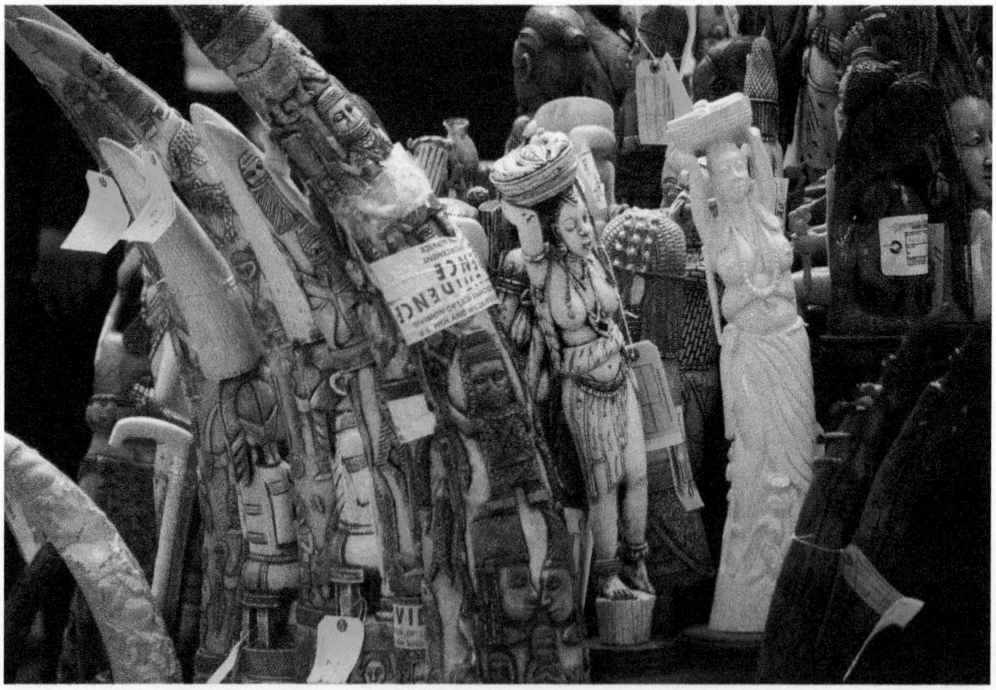

Seized ivory, ready to be crushed, in Times Square, New York City. ▶

Source: Wendy Hapgood/Shutterstock

PRESERVING NATIONAL CULTURE

CONCEPT CHECK

Chapter 2 observes that a primary function of culture is that it supports a nation's sense of its uniqueness and integrity.

To help sustain a collective identity that sets their citizens apart from other nationalities, governments prohibit exports of art and historical items deemed to be part of their national heritage. In addition, they limit imports that may either conflict with or replace their dominant values. The relevance of culture has been confirmed through several UNESCO conventions aimed at preserving cultural diversity, and the concern has been largely focused, but not entirely, on media (print, visual, and audio).[35] For instance, many countries, such as Canada and Australia, require levels of national content in media.[36] Japan, South Korea, and China maintained for many years an almost total ban on rice imports, largely because rice farming has been a historically cohesive force in each nation.[37] In 2017, East African countries raised tariffs on imports of used clothing and shoes so high that such imports are essentially prohibited; Rwanda justified the tariff partly by saying that wearing hand-me-downs compromises the dignity of Rwandans.[38]

MAJOR INSTRUMENTS OF TRADE CONTROL

7-4 Describe the major instruments of trade control

In seeking to influence exports or imports, governments' choice of trade-control instrument is crucial because each may incite different responses from domestic and foreign groups. One way to understand these instruments is by distinguishing between those that directly influence export or import *prices* and those that directly limit the *amount* of a good that can be traded. Let's review these instruments.

TARIFFS: DIRECT PRICE INFLUENCES

Tariffs may be levied

- on goods entering, leaving, or passing through a country;
- for protection or revenue;
- on a per-unit basis, a value basis, or both.

Tariff barriers directly affect prices, and *nontariff barriers* may directly affect either price or quantity. A **tariff** (also called a **duty**) is a tax levied on a good shipped internationally. That is, governments charge a tariff on a good when it crosses an official boundary—whether it be that of a nation or a group of nations that have agreed to impose a common tariff on goods crossing the boundary of their bloc. A tariff assessed on a per-unit basis is a **specific duty**, on a percentage of the item's value an **ad valorem duty**, and on both a **compound duty**.

Tariffs collected by the exporting country are called **export tariffs**; if they're collected by a country through which the goods pass, they're **transit tariffs**; if they're collected by importing countries, they're **import tariffs**. Because import tariffs are by far the most common, we discuss them in some detail.

Import Tariffs Unless foreign producers lower prices by the same amount (discussed earlier in the chapter), import tariffs raise the price of imported goods by taxing them, thereby giving domestically produced goods a relative price advantage. Although consumers are often unaware of the cost increase from tariffs on imports, they learn very quickly when encountering duty-free shops in international airports and at cruise ship stopovers. (See the following photo.)

Tariffs as Sources of Revenue Tariffs generate government revenue, but revenue is of little importance to developed countries because collection costs usually exceed the yield.[39] In the United States, tariff revenue runs around one percent of federal revenue, and even the high tariffs imposed in 2018 on imports from China increased revenues to just two percent. In many developing countries, though, they are a major source of revenue because they are often more easily collected than income taxes. The Bahamas, Botswana, Jamaica, and Namibia all derive more than 30 percent of government revenue from tariffs. Although tariffs are most commonly collected on imports, some countries charge export tariffs on raw materials. Transit tariffs were once a major source of countries' revenue, but governmental agreements have nearly abolished them.

A duty-free shop at Suvarnabhumi Airport, one of two international airports serving Bangkok, Thailand.

Source: Song_about_summer/Shutterstock

Developing countries argue that their processed portion of commodities have higher tariffs than the published rates.

The Effective Tariff Controversy Raw materials (say, coffee beans) from developing countries frequently enter developed countries duty-free; however, if they are processed (say, instant coffee), developed countries then assign an import tariff. Because an ad valorem tariff is based on the total value of the product (say, 10 percent on a $5 jar of instant coffee), the raw materials and the processing combined (say, $2.50 for the coffee beans and $2.50 for the processing) pay the tariff ($0.50). Developing countries have argued that the **effective tariff** on the manufactured portion turns out to be higher than the published tariff rate (the coffee processing is effectively charged 20 percent). This anomaly further challenges developing countries to find export markets for products that use their raw materials.

NONTARIFF BARRIERS: DIRECT PRICE INFLUENCES

Now that we've shown how tariffs raise prices, let's discuss other ways that governments alter product prices to affect their trade.

Governmental subsidies may help companies be competitive,

- but there is little agreement on what a subsidy is,
- but agricultural subsidies are difficult to dismantle,
- especially to overcome market imperfections because they are least controversial.

Subsidies **Subsidies** offer direct assistance to companies to boost their competitiveness. Although this definition is straightforward, disagreement on what constitutes a subsidy causes trade frictions. In essence, not everyone agrees that companies are being subsidized just because they lose money, nor that all types of government loans or grants are subsidies. One long-running controversy involves commercial aircraft. Airbus Industrie and the EU claim that the U.S. national and state governments subsidize Boeing through R&D contracts for military aircraft that also have commercial applications and through the granting of incentives to influence their location decisions. Further, because the U.S. Ex-Im Bank offers loan guarantees to foreign buyers, Delta Air Lines has argued that this gives non-U.S. airlines an advantage not available to U.S. airlines.[40] Meanwhile, Boeing and the U.S. government claim that the EU subsidizes Airbus Industrie through low-interest government loans.[41]

An area that may well raise future questions about subsidies is governmental support to shore up floundering companies and industries, especially during global recessions. For instance, governments have bailed out banks, granted generous consumer loans to support their auto companies, eliminated taxes on their companies' export earnings, and invested in an ownership share of key companies. In turn, these actions alter international competitiveness.[42]

Agricultural Subsidies The one area in which everyone agrees that subsidies exist is agriculture, especially in developed countries. The official reason is that food supplies are too critical to be left to chance. Although subsidies lead to surplus production, they are argued to be preferable to the risk of food shortages. Further, to counter overproduction, the United States pays additional subsidies to farmers so that they do not produce as much.[43] However, this official reason does not explain agricultural subsidies for nonfood products, such as U.S. cotton subsidies that Brazil claims to disadvantage its competitiveness.[44]

The strength of agricultural interests is also important. Within Japan, the United States, and the EU, rural areas have a disproportionately high representation in government decision-making. For instance, Japanese rural interests have been able to force a 778 percent tariff on rice.[45] In the United States, there is one senator per 300,000 people in Vermont (a state with a 68 percent rural population) and one senator per 19 million in California (which is 93 percent urban). Agriculture accounts for 38 percent of the EU budget even though it composes only 7 percent of GDP.[46] The result is that internal politics effectively prevent the dismantling of such instruments as price supports for farmers, government agencies to improve agricultural productivity, and low-interest loans to farmers.

What is the effect? Although some developing countries, such as India, are also major agricultural subsidizers, many are deprived from fully serving the developed markets with competitive agricultural products. Further, much surplus production from developed countries is exported at very low prices, thus distorting trade and further disadvantaging developing countries' production.[47]

Overcoming Market Imperfections Most countries offer potential exporters many business development services, such as market information, trade expositions, and foreign contacts. This type of subsidization is less contentious than tariffs because the actions seek to overcome, rather than create, market imperfections. Further, collecting and disseminating information widely is less costly than if each potential exporter were to work individually.

Tied Aid and Loans When governments require foreign aid and loan recipients to spend the funds in the donor country, a situation known as *tied aid* or *tied loans,* some otherwise noncompetitive output can compete abroad. For instance, tied aid helps win large contracts for infrastructure, such as telecommunications, railways, and electric power projects.

However, tied aid and loans sometimes require the recipient to use output and suppliers that may not be the best. They may also slow the advancement of local suppliers in developing countries. These concerns led OECD members to untie financial aid to developing countries.[48] However, China is using tied aid for nearly all its foreign infrastructure projects.[49]

Because it is difficult for customs officials to determine the honesty of import invoices,

- valuation procedures have been developed,
- they may restate the value,
- they may question the origin of and product-classification of imports.

Customs Valuation Import tariff assessments depend on the product, price, and origin—which tempts exporters and importers to declare these wrongly to pay a lower duty and tempts governments to declare wrongly as a protectionist measure.

What Is the Import Worth? Most countries have agreed to use import invoice information unless customs doubt its authenticity. Agents must then appraise on the basis of the value of identical or similar goods arriving at about the same time.[50] Customs must appraise similarly when goods enter for lease rather than purchase because there is no invoice. Critics, especially companies and governmental authorities from exporting countries, complain that agents in importing countries too often use discretionary power to levy higher duties, such as on Philippine cigarettes imported into Thailand.[51]

What Is the Product? Misclassifying a product (by accident or intentionally) is an easy way to change its corresponding tariff. Administering more than 13,000 categories of products (with new products coming onto the market all the time) means a customs agent must use discretion to determine, say, if silicon chips should be considered "integrated circuits for computers" or "a form of chemical silicon." In our opening case, we saw the controversy over whether the Vietnamese fish are catfish or whether they are swai, basa, tra, or pangasius. The differences among products in tariff schedules are also minute. For example, the U.S. tariffs on athletic footwear are different from those on sports footwear, and these are subcategorized by whether the sole overlaps the upper part of the shoe or not. Each type of accessory and reinforcement of the shoes' uppers is a different category.

Although classification differences may seem trivial, the disparity in duties may cost or save companies millions of dollars. Some contentious examples include whether the French company Agatec's laser leveling device would be used primarily indoors or outdoors,[52] whether Marvel's X-Men Wolverines were toys or dolls, and whether sport utility vehicles—such as the Suzuki Samurai and the Land Rover—were cars or trucks.

Where Does the Product Originate? Because of different trade agreements, customs must determine products' origins. For example, red meat products may involve animals born in one country, raised in a second, and slaughtered in a third. U.S. Customs requires traders to provide details on these stages of production, thus adding documentation costs above those for meat products of a 100 percent U.S. origin.[53] Officials have also uncovered many instances of product transshipment and document falsification to avoid or lessen restrictions. For instance, U.S. Customs fined Staples, OfficeMax, and Target for mislabeling the country of origin of pencils in order to avoid paying antidumping duties assessed on Chinese imports.[54]

Other Direct-Price Influences Countries use other practices to affect import prices, including special fees (such as for consular and customs clearance and documentation), requirements that customs deposits be placed in advance of shipment, and minimum price levels at which goods can be sold after they have cleared customs.

NONTARIFF BARRIERS: QUANTITY CONTROLS

Governments' regulations and practices affect the quantity of imports and exports directly. Let's take a look at the various forms these typically take.

A quota may
- be on imports or exports,
- set the total amount to be traded,
- allocate amounts by country,
- be negotiated as a voluntary export restraint (VER),
- prohibit all trade when it is an embargo.

Quotas A **quota** limits the quantity of a product that can be imported or exported in a given time frame, typically per year. *Import quotas* normally raise prices because they (1) limit supplies and (2) provide little incentive to use price competition to increase sales. A notable difference between tariffs and quotas is their effect on revenues. Tariffs generate revenue for the government. Quotas generate revenue only for those companies that obtain and sell a portion of the intentionally limited supply of the product at prices higher than what competitive prices would be. Sometimes governments allocate quotas among countries based on political or market conditions.

To circumvent quotas, companies sometimes convert the product into one for which there is no quota. For instance, the United States maintains sugar import quotas that result in its sugar prices averaging more than the world market price. As a result, some U.S. candy producers have moved plants to Mexico and Canada where they can buy lower-cost sugar and import the candy duty-free to the United States.[55]

A country may establish *export quotas* to provide domestic consumers a sufficient supply of goods at a low price, to prevent depletion of natural resources, or to attempt to raise prices abroad by restricting supply.

Voluntary Export Restraints A **voluntary export restraint (VER)** is a quota variation whereby, essentially, Country A asks Country B to voluntarily reduce its companies' exports to Country A. For instance, the United States and Mexico agreed on a VER dealing with Mexican tomato exports.[56] The term *voluntarily* is misleading; typically, either Country B agrees to reduce its exports or else Country A may impose tougher trade restrictions. Procedurally, VERs have unique advantages. They are much easier to switch off than an import quota, and the appearance of a "voluntary" choice by a particular country to constrain its shipments can do less damage to political relations than an import quota.

Embargoes A specific type of quota that prohibits all trade is an **embargo**. As with quotas, a country or group of countries may place embargoes on either imports or exports, on particular products regardless of origin or destination, on specific products with certain countries, or on all products with given countries. Governments impose embargoes in an effort to use economic means to achieve political goals, thus they are a type of trade sanction which we discuss in our Point-Counterpoint section.

Through "buy local" rules
- government purchases give preference to domestically made goods,
- governments sometimes legislate a percentage of domestic content.

"Buy Local" Legislation *Buy local legislation* sets rules whereby governments give preference to domestic production in their purchases. Given the enormity of government sectors in most economies, this preference can be substantial. Sometimes governments, such as the U.S. government, specify a domestic content restriction—that is, a certain percentage of the product must be of domestic origin.[57] Sometimes governments favor domestic producers through price mechanisms, such as permitting an agency to buy a foreign-made product only if the price is a predetermined margin below that of a domestic competitor. Sometimes governments favor domestic purchases indirectly, such as the U.S. prohibition of foreign Medicare payments for elderly Americans except in emergency situations—a regulation that limits U.S. foreign purchases in the fast-growing area of medical tourism.

Other types of trade barriers include

- arbitrary standards;
- importing, exporting, and currency licensing;
- administrative delays;
- reciprocal requirements;
- restrictions on services.

Standards and Labels Countries can devise classification, labeling, and testing standards to allow the sale of domestic products while obstructing foreign-made ones. Consider product labels. The requirement that companies indicate products' origins informs consumers who may prefer buying domestic products. In our opening case, we saw that the U.S. catfish industry sought country-of-origin labeling on fish. Countries also may dictate that companies place content information on their packaging that differs from what is required elsewhere. These technicalities may seem trivial, but they add to a firm's costs, particularly if the labels must be translated for different export markets. In addition, raw materials, components, design, and labor increasingly come from many countries, so most products today are of such mixed origin that they are difficult to sort out.

The professed purpose of standards is to protect safety or health, but some companies argue they are just a means to protect domestic producers. For example, some U.S. and Canadian producers have contended that EU regulations and labeling requirements on genetically engineered corn and canola oil are merely means to keep out the products until their own technology catches up.[58] In another case, the U.S. Food and Drug Administration appeared more likely to reject incoming shipments of food from developing countries (such as avocados from Mexico) during the financial crisis of 2008. Although purportedly to protect the U.S. food supply, the financial crisis probably did not cause the quality of imports to deteriorate, so it is more likely that the crisis made the protection of domestic growers more valuable.[59] Similarly, following U.S. publicity about contaminated Chinese foods, China retaliated by upping its rejection of foodstuffs from the United States, citing contamination with drugs and salmonella.[60]

In reality, there's no way of knowing to what extent products are kept out of countries for legitimate safety and health reasons versus arbitrarily protecting domestic production. Rejecting shipments for health and safety reasons, particularly those from developing countries, may cause a negative image for the exporting countries' other products, causing them to lose sales and lower their export prices.[61]

Licensing Requirements Countries may require that importers or exporters secure an **import or export license** before trade is permitted. A company may have to submit samples to government authorities to obtain such a license. The procedure can restrict imports or exports directly by denying permission or indirectly because of the cost, time, and uncertainty involved.

A **foreign exchange control** requires an importer to apply to a government agency to secure the foreign currency to pay for the product. As with an import license, failure to grant the exchange, not to mention the time and expense of completing forms and awaiting replies, obstructs foreign trade.

Administrative Delays Closely akin to licensing requirements are administrative customs delays that may be caused by intention or inefficiency. In either case, they create uncertainty and raise the cost of carrying inventory. Intentional delays may occur not only to protect domestic producers, but also for political reasons. Japanese companies reported such delays in China after Japan and China clashed over ownership of islands in the East China Sea.[62]

Reciprocal Requirements Importing countries sometimes require that whole or partial payment be made to exporters in merchandise rather than fully in currency, a transaction known as barter trade. The World Trade Organization estimates that 15 percent of world trade involves some type of barter.[63]

Countertrade In **countertrade** or **offsets**, a government in the importing country requires the exporter to provide it with additional economic benefits such as jobs or technology as part of the transaction. Critics in exporting countries contend that large defense contractors, by participating in these arrangements, shift purchases from smaller domestic contractors to those in foreign countries, thus weakening these domestic suppliers and the exporting country's future defense capabilities.[64]

Problems for Exporters Reciprocal requirements necessitate that exporters assess the value and find markets for goods outside their expertise, engage in complicated operating arrangements, and undertake activities outside their proficiency. Raytheon, which makes such products as missiles and radar systems, had to undertake shrimp farming to gain a Saudi Arabian contract.[65] All things being equal, companies avoid these transactions. However, some have developed competencies in these types of arrangements in order to gain competitive advantages. Others rely on specialized companies that handle barter transactions.

Four main reasons why trade in services is restricted are

- essentiality,
- preference for not-for-profit operations,
- different professional standards,
- immigration.

Restrictions on Services Service is the fastest-growing sector in international trade. In deciding whether to restrict service trade, countries typically consider four factors: *essentiality, not-for-profit preference, standards,* and *immigration.*

Essentiality Governments sometimes prohibit private companies, foreign or domestic, from operating in some sectors because they feel the services are essential and provide social stability. In other cases, they set price controls or subsidize government-owned service organizations that create disincentives for foreign private participation. Some essential services in which foreign firms might be excluded are media, communications, banking, utilities, and domestic transport.

Not-for-Profit Services Mail, education, and hospital health services are often not-for-profit sectors in which few foreign firms compete. When a government privatizes these industries, it customarily prefers local ownership and control.

Standards Some services require face-to-face interaction between professionals and clients, and governments limit entry into many of them to ensure practice by qualified personnel. The licensing requirements include such professionals as accountants, actuaries, architects, electricians, engineers, gemologists, hairstylists, lawyers, medical personnel, real estate brokers, and teachers.

At present, there is little reciprocal recognition in licensing because countries' occupational standards and requirements differ substantially. Thus an accounting or legal firm from one country faces obstacles in another, even to serve its domestic clients' needs. The firm must hire professionals within each foreign country or else have its domestic professionals earn certification abroad. The latter option is problematic because of having to take examinations and learn new materials, sometimes in a foreign language. There also may be lengthy prerequisites for taking an examination, such as internships, time in residency, and coursework at a local university.

CONCEPT CHECK

In discussing "Factor Mobility" in Chapter 6, we explain the increasing reliance on people as an internationally mobile production factor and that countries hand out immigration papers only sparingly.

Immigration Satisfying the standards of a particular country is no guarantee that a foreigner can then work there. In addition, governmental regulations often require an organization—domestic or foreign—to search extensively for qualified personnel locally before it can even apply for work permits for personnel it would like to bring in from abroad.

HOW COMPANIES DEAL WITH IMPORT COMPETITION

7-5 Understand how companies deal with import competition

When facing import competition, companies can

- move abroad or find foreign supplies,
- seek other market niches,
- make domestic output competitive,
- try to get protection.

When companies are threatened by import competition, they have several options, four of which stand out:

1. Move operations to another country.
2. Concentrate on market niches that attract less international competition.
3. Adopt internal innovations, such as greater efficiency or superior products.
4. Try to get governmental protection.

Each option entails costs and risks; therefore, different companies make different choices. For example, competition from Japanese imports spurred the U.S. automobile industry to move some production abroad (such as subcontracting with foreign suppliers for parts), develop niche markets through the sale of minivan and sport utility vehicles (SUVs) that initially had less international competition, and adopt innovations such as lean production techniques to improve efficiency and product quality. They also successfully sought VERs from Japan, and General Motors and Chrysler eventually received substantial government funding to survive.

Granted, these methods are not realistic for every industry or company. Companies may lack the resources to shift their own production or find suppliers abroad. They may not be able to identify more innovative or profitable product niches. Even if they do, foreign competitors may quickly emulate them. In such situations, companies often ask their governments to restrict imports or open export markets.

CONVINCING DECISION-MAKERS

Governments cannot try to help every company that faces tough international competition. Likewise, helping one industry may hurt another. Thus, as a manager, you may propose or oppose a particular protectionist measure. Inevitably, the burden falls on you and your company to convince officials that your situation warrants particular policies. You must identify the key decision-makers and convince them by using the economic and noneconomic arguments presented in this chapter. You must also put forward the types of restrictive mechanisms most likely to help your situation and convey to public officials that voters and stakeholders support your position.[66]

A company improves the odds of success if it can ally most, if not all, domestic companies in its industry. Otherwise, officials may feel that its problems are due to its specific inefficiencies rather than the general trade challenges. Similarly, involving stakeholders, such as taxpayers and local merchants, can help. Finally, it can lobby decision-makers and endorse the political candidates who are sympathetic to its situation.

PREPARING FOR CHANGES IN THE COMPETITIVE ENVIRONMENT

Companies take different approaches to deal with changes in the international competitive environment. Frequently, their attitudes toward protectionism are a function of the investments they have made to implement their international strategy. Those that depend on freer trade and/or have integrated their production and supply chains among countries tend to oppose protectionism. In contrast, those with single or multi-domestic production facilities, such as a plant in Japan to serve the Japanese market and a plant in Taiwan to serve the Taiwanese market, tend to support protectionism.

Companies also differ in their confidence to compete against imports. Thus when companies recommend protection for their industries, typically one or more companies in that industry oppose it. The opposition usually comes from companies with commanding competitive advantages in terms of scale economies, supplier relationships, or differentiated products. Thus, they reason that not only can they successfully battle international rivals, they also stand to gain even more as their weaker domestic competitors fail to do so.[67]

LOOKING TO THE FUTURE Dynamics and Complexity of Future World Trade

When trade restrictions change, there are winners and losers among countries, companies, and workers. So it's probably safe to say that we'll see mixtures of pushes for freer trade and greater protection.

In addition, consumers' gains from freer trade may be at the expense of some companies and workers—people who see themselves as big losers. They are not apt to lose without a struggle; they'll garner as much support for protection as they can, and they may win. The support may well come from alliances that cross national borders, such as clothing companies in various developing nations uniting to push importing countries to enact quota agreements to protect their export markets against Chinese and Indian competition. Thus, if you are a manager in an industry that may be affected by changes in governmental protection, you must watch closely to predict how the evolving politics may affect your own situation.

Finally, the international regulatory situation is becoming more, rather than less, complex—a situation that challenges companies to find the best locations in which to produce. These complexities include new products that challenge the task of tariff classification, Internet services that create new channels of foreign competition, and heightened concerns about terrorism and product safety that compound considerations of what can be traded and with whom.

CASE

Should U.S. Imports of Prescription Drugs from Canada Be Widened?[68]

During the 50-year period through 2016, the U.S. life expectancy at birth for males and females increased by 9.3 and 7.3 years respectively. Although there were multiple reasons for this increase, the development and availability of pharmaceuticals was a significant one. Despite the gains, there has been growing concern about U.S. life expectancy *relative* to other countries (i.e., ranking only 31st in the world). In turn, this gap has led to greater scrutiny of medical services and costs, including pharmaceuticals. On one hand, the U.S. per capita spending on both health care and pharmaceuticals is the world's highest. On the other hand, U.S. pharmaceutical expenses have been rising faster than incomes, and the portion paid by workers has been rising faster than the portion paid by health plans. A Kaiser Family Foundation/*New York Times* survey found that about a quarter of Americans between 18 and 64 had trouble paying medical bills during 2015. Further, anecdotes illustrate that some people are not filling their prescriptions because they have insufficient funds.

U.S. Import Regulations

There are different ways to categorize pharmaceuticals, such as those approved for U.S. sale versus those that are not, and those that have current patented brand names versus those that are generic because they are off-patent. Although there have been numerous proposals to deal with U.S. pharmaceutical imports, we examine one type from one source—prescribed brand-name drugs that are approved for U.S. sales and sold in Canada. In essence, the issues for each category of drugs are different and controversial. For instance, in the United States, the Food and Drug Administration (FDA) is charged with assuring the safety and efficacy of drugs. It does not accept foreign clinical findings for a new drug's approval. However, critics claim not only that the nonacceptance, say from Germany or Switzerland, is misguided, but that the policy also delays U.S. patients' treatment with the latest advancements.

Since 1987, with the passage of the Prescription Drug Marketing Act, only pharmaceutical manufacturers may import their products into the United States. At the same time, these manufacturers sell the same medicines abroad, often at a lower price than in the United States. The lower foreign price has occurred partially because of market conditions and partly because foreign governments, such as in Canada, have negotiated maximum retail prices. In contrast, U.S. law prohibits the federal or a state government from negotiating drug prices. In many cases, the drugs sold in Canada are actually produced and exported from the United States or from a U.S. company's foreign facility that distributes to multiple countries. For example, the same Pfizer factory in Ireland exports its Lipitor pills to both Canada and the United States. Because non-manufacturers, such as pharmacy chains, are prohibited from importing prescription drugs, they cannot buy the cheaper product in Canada and export it to the United States. Thus, pharmaceutical companies can basically set their U.S. prices. In effect, U.S. consumers are subsidizing the purchase of medicines by consumers in other countries.

Although U.S. pharmaceutical companies have an overall record of maintaining justifiable prices, some recent incidents demonstrated the risk of excessive price increases of essential drugs when there is little or no domestic competition. Valeant Pharmaceuticals purchased the cardiac drug Nitropress, and immediately tripled the price. Turing Pharmaceuticals acquired and then raised the price overnight of an off-patent pill (Daraprim) from $13.50 to $750. Turing could do this because Daraprim had no good substitute, was essential for serving a small clientele, and had little short-term likelihood of U.S. competition inasmuch as the cost and time necessary to gain U.S. approval for sales were high. Daraprim was sold widely abroad—such as in India for five cents a pill and in the United Kingdom for $1.50— but it was illegal to import it. Subsequent inquiries have turned up other examples of "price gouging" for other medicines (e.g., Nitroprusside's price jumping from $44 to $830 a vial).

This discussion does not imply that the United States imports no pharmaceuticals from abroad. In fact, the United States imports more than any other country, $96.6 billion in 2017, which was $42.6 billion more than Germany, the next-largest importer. Further, busloads of elderly people have long gone regularly to Canada to import drugs into the United States for personal use. This importation is illegal, but it is almost always overlooked. The only permissible individual U.S. drug importation—and generally for no more than a three-month supply—is when a patient has a serious condition for which no effective treatment or commercialization is available within the United States.

Price Comparisons

Most assessments conclude that Canadian prescription drugs may cost 40–60 percent less at the retail level than in the United States. However, comparing overall prices is a problem because prices and sales volumes per drug vary substantially. This hinders predictions of what consumers might save by having access to drugs sold in Canada. First, U.S. per capita drug expenditures are highly skewed because about a third of the market value is to treat chronic illnesses that serve only about 1–2 percent of patients. Second, almost 80 percent of U.S. volume sales are for generic products, which account for only 28 percent of the market value. Third, U.S. pharmacy drug prices vary substantially. Fourth, drugmakers have list prices, but these are seldom what individual consumers pay because prices vary among insurance companies and between people with and without insurance. In the final analysis, if U.S. consumers were allowed to import their drug supplies, they would have to identify appropriate domestic prices for each medication and then individually compare them with dispensers in Canada.

U.S. consumers with medical insurance, however, are usually more interested in their co-pays than in the prices insurance companies pay for medications. If their co-pays are less than buying in Canada, there is no personal incentive to buy there. However, this comparison overlooks the cost to the system. By buying at higher U.S. prices than in Canada, U.S. pharmacies and health insurance companies incur higher costs that get passed on to their customers in the form of insurance costs.

Safety and Counterfeits

One argument for why the United States should not import prescription drugs from Canada is because the FDA cannot regulate their safety. The FDA assesses drug safety and efficacy, such as by evaluating new drugs' ability to combat health problems without unacceptable side effects. It also evaluates generics through an "abbreviated new drug application (ANDA)" when competitors want to produce and market a patent-expired drug. This approval is based largely on assessment that the manufacturer can and will produce a medicine with exactly the same attributes as the original. We are largely omitting generic drugs in our analysis because their U.S. prices have been going down to the point that they are generally lower than in Canada, thus they are not a significant issue in the import question.

The Prescription Drug Marketing Act attempted to strengthen an already closed distribution system by putting more responsibility on supply chain participants through requiring maintenance of records for each sale as drugs moved from manufacturer to final consumer. Pursuant to this, the FDA has claimed that there are insufficient resources to halt the shipment of illicit drugs (e.g., medicines arrive by mail and within mislabled shipments from abroad). Further, they cannot adequately check outlets abroad that produce and distribute pharmaceuticals. For instance, in an operation at three U.S. airports, virtually all Internet-ordered shipments (supposedly from Canadian pharmacies) were checked. The FDA found that 85 percent came from 27 other countries. In turn, a large portion of these were unsafe or inadequate to treat the intended illness.

Recouping Development Costs

Pharmaceutical firms may incur hundreds of millions of dollars in development costs before a new drug is approved for the market. In addition, many of their research projects reach dead-ends because their approaches do not work or because a competitor usurps the market by entering first. There is no argument that these development costs need to be recouped. But how?

Under the present system, high U.S. prices bear the burden of recovering developmental costs. Why not charge the same prices everywhere so that the burden is spread? In effect, the system abroad does not permit this, particularly

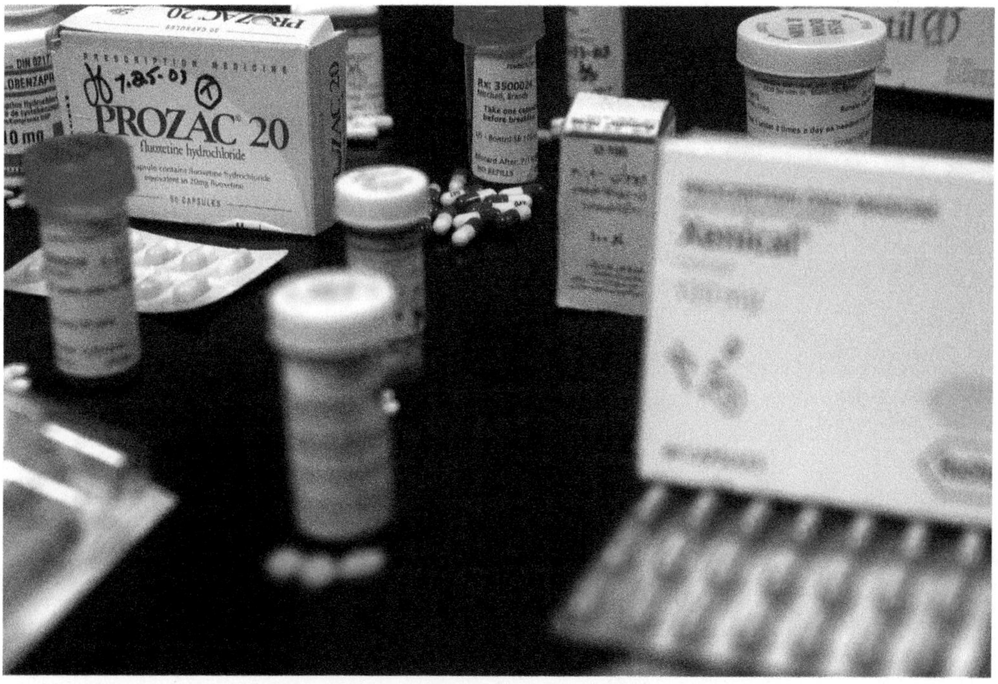

Drugs ordered online from international pharmacies. ▶

Source: Richard Levine/Alamy Stock Photo

as governments negotiate prices and put ceilings on them. Some states, such as Florida, where there is a large retired population, would like to use the system as a means to reduce high drug prices by importing drugs from countries where prices are low. In response, the U.S. Department of Health and Human Services recently proposed a regulation that would allow states to import brand-name prescription pills from Canada by working with pharmacies and wholesalers under federal oversight. In 2020, an executive order from the U.S. president initiated a rule-making process to speed imports of drugs from Canada. U.S. pharmaceutical companies claim that they will have to greatly reduce their research budgets if they lose the ability to charge high U.S. prices in the inception phase of their new drugs. Importing from Canada (or elsewhere) will counter this ability. Plus, Canada is concerned about the effects of the change, fearing that its own drug supply will be reduced by exports to the United States.

Many suggestions and proposals have been made for lowering prescriptions' costs, such as by extending the life of patents and allowing imports to come in from anywhere. Any of these are nearly unique in that they respond to domestic pressures to reduce costs rather than to pressures by producers abroad who wish to gain a greater share of the U.S. market.

QUESTIONS

7-3 Should the United States legalize the importation of lower-cost pharmaceuticals? If so, should this apply to individual consumers, pharmacies, or other entities?

7-4 If the United States were to permit importation of lower-cost pharmaceuticals from abroad, should this importation apply to all foreign countries or a limited number? If a limited number, which should they be and why?

7-5 If the United States were to permit importation of lower-cost pharmaceuticals from Canada, what safeguards should be enacted to help assure the safety and efficacy of the imports?

7-6 If the United States were to permit importation of lower-cost pharmaceuticals from abroad, should this apply to all pharmaceuticals or just to some? If just to some, what criteria should be used?

7-7 If pharmacies were allowed to import less costly drugs from abroad, should regulations be put into effect to pass on some/all cost savings to consumers? If so, what should they be?

7-8 Consumers seldom propose the reduction of import restrictions to lower their costs. Why has this occurred for pharmaceuticals and not for other products?

CHAPTER 8
Cross-National Cooperation and Agreements

OBJECTIVES

After studying this chapter, you should be able to

8-1 Define the three major types of international economic integration

8-2 Explain what the World Trade Organization is and how it is working to reduce trade barriers on a global basis

8-3 Summarize the major benefits of regional economic integration

8-4 Compare and contrast different regional trading groups

8-5 Describe the forces that affect the prices of commodities and their impact on commodity agreements

Marrying is easy, but housekeeping is hard.

—German proverb

Source: Belle Vue/Alamy Stock Photo

▲ Toyota's hybrid electric Yaris in France, where it was manufactured.

CASE

Toyota's European Drive[1]

Anna Kessler put the key into the ignition of her brand-new Toyota Yaris, started the engine, and began to navigate her way home from work through the crowded streets of Berlin, Germany. Having owned the car for just over a week, she was already satisfied with her decision. She liked the car's distinctive European look, the generous warranty it had come with, and its low fuel consumption. The name, Yaris, even has a European flare since it is derived from "Charis," the Greek goddess of charm and beauty.

Her decision the previous week marked the first time Anna had ever owned a vehicle manufactured by an Asian company; in fact, it was the first time she had considered one. When she had made her last car purchase, the thought of buying a car from Toyota—then known for its lackluster designs, limited options, and seven-month-long waiting lists—had not even entered her mind. However, as she was researching different vehicles, she found that Toyota had ranked the highest in several categories in a recent quality survey and that the Yaris had achieved an outstanding four-star Euro NCAP safety rating, which led her to investigate the car more thoroughly.

With her purchase, Anna became another one of the millions of Toyota vehicle owners located around the globe. Toyota, the largest auto manufacturing company in the world, sells vehicles in 170 countries and regions, has 54 manufacturing companies in 28 countries and regions outside of Japan, and has R&D facilities worldwide. In Europe Toyota has manufacturing facilities in 10 countries, including France where the Yaris is manufactured. It also has R&D facilities in Belgium, the U.K., Germany, and France.

So why has it taken Toyota so long to crack into the competitive European market, and why are European companies only now beginning to feel the pressure from Asian manufacturers? Many analysts have pointed to an agreement between the Japanese government and the European Community (predecessor to the European Union) in which the two negotiated a quota each year for the number of Japanese cars imported into Europe. The quota amounts agreed upon each year depended on such factors as the level of consumer demand and sales growth in the region and were fixed at 11 percent of the European market.

The arrangement was set up to allow European carmakers to become more competitive as the EC made the transition to a common market; prior to this, each country had its own import and registration restrictions on Japanese cars. Italy, for example, limited the number of imported Japanese vehicles to 3,000, while France kept them at a 3 percent share of its market. Britain, Spain, and Portugal imposed similar restrictions. This policy goes back to the end of World War II when the Japanese government asked the European automakers to curtail exports to Japan to help the nation rebuild its industry. The Europeans reciprocated by limiting the access of Japanese autos to their market. At the time, that wasn't a problem. However, when the Japanese auto companies became export conscious, they wanted access to the European markets. The quota system helped protect the domestic industry.

Under the new system, these countries had to abandon their individual policies, but French carmakers fought to include an 80 percent local-content rule and an allowance to export 500,000 cars a year to Japan, five times the then-current level. In the end, the EC disregarded these additional requests, and in the first year of the agreement, 1.089 million Japanese cars could be imported.

The quota, however, also fixed separate caps for each participating country and then divided this amount among the Japanese automakers according to their historical market shares. The caps essentially prevented the Japanese from being able to transfer their excess imports from countries where their quotas weren't being met to ones where they were unable to meet demand due to having already reached the maximum limits. It was primarily for this reason that they never actually met their quota for the EC; during the seven years the quota system was in effect, Toyota was held to a 2 to 3 percent market share in most EU countries.

Although the system seemed to be having the desired effect, even some French auto officials admitted that the eventual opening of the market was inevitable. One noted, "Can we put off change for years? Officially, yes. But honestly, I don't think so." That statement proved prophetic when the EU lifted the import quota in 1999 and made it easier for Japanese auto manufacturers to expand distribution and sign up dealers. Although this move did not necessarily cause the Japanese to flood the European market with their products, it did open the way for them to invest more heavily in design and manufacturing facilities in the EU, to broaden the range of products they marketed there, and to customize their offerings to better appeal to European tastes.

Toyota responded to the drop in barriers by introducing a new strategy of designing vehicles targeted specifically at European customers. This involved setting up a European Design and Development center in southern France and allowing design teams across the globe to compete for projects. The Yaris, Toyota's best-selling vehicle in the EU, was designed by a Greek and was the first to be developed within the region. It subsequently was named Car of the Year in both Europe and Japan. As another key element of its European strategy, Toyota set up additional production centers in the region.

The collapse of the auto industry in Europe has been hard on all manufacturers, which is one reason for Toyota's investment in Russia. In addition, Japanese competitors continue to open facilities in the Eastern bloc countries that are now members of the EU. As noted above, Toyota has already set up state-of-the-art production plants in the Czech Republic and Poland. Because of the elimination of internal tariffs in the EU, Toyota can manufacture automobiles and parts anywhere within Europe and ship them to all markets duty-free. Riding on its success in Europe in the mid-2000s and its growth internationally, Toyota had ambitious goals for the future. However, Europe is now considered a mature market, which makes it less attractive than the emerging markets, including China. Toyota has only 5 percent of the European market, well behind market leader VW with 24.2 percent.

Toyota is continuing its push to increase its share of the European market by restructuring its Brussels-based European division, including transferring more decision-making power from Japan, and focusing on the values of European consumers. This includes placing renewed focus on hybrid technology in Europe, in which the company still retains a comparative advantage over its global rivals. In 2012, Toyota introduced a hybrid engine for the Yaris, giving potential Yaris customers access to hybrid technology, such as the hybrid electric Yaris model in the opening photo. But, Toyota faces steep R&D challenges as the future of automobiles moves to electric cars and self-driving technology.

QUESTIONS

8-1 Why did the Europeans try to protect their auto industry from Japanese imports, and do you think this was fair to European consumers?

8-2 What has Toyota done to be more successful in Europe, and why do you think it hasn't been more successful? What else can it do?

FORMS OF ECONOMIC INTEGRATION

8-1 Define the three major types of international economic integration

CONCEPT CHECK

Recall from Chapter 6 (page 169) our discussion of the ways in which the mobility of capital, technology, and people affect a country's trade and the relative competitive positions of domestic firms and industries. Imbalances in the mobility of factors of production are often addressed in strategies for cross-national integration.

Approaches to economic integration—political and economic agreements among countries in which preference is given to member countries—may be

- bilateral,
- regional,
- global.

In the mid- to late 1940s, many nations decided that if they were going to emerge from the wreckage of World War II and promote economic growth and stability within their borders, they would have to assist—and get assistance from—nearby countries. How do nations and regions combine forces to give and gain the assistance they need to prosper together?

Economic integration is a term used to describe the political and monetary agreements among nations and world regions in which preference is given to member countries. There are three major ways to approach such agreements:

- **Global integration**—Countries from all over the world decide to cooperate through the World Trade Organization (WTO)
- **Bilateral integration**—Two countries decide to cooperate more closely together, usually in the form of tariff reductions
- **Regional integration**—A group of countries located in the same geographic proximity decide to cooperate, as with the European Union

Trade groups, whether global, bilateral, or regional, are an important influence on MNE strategies. They can define the size of the regional market and the rules under which a company must operate. In fact, an increase in market size is their single most important reason for existing.[2] A company in the initial stages of foreign expansion must be aware of how the groups encompass countries with good manufacturing locations or market opportunities. Recall from our opening case that Toyota has been able to find success in Europe by taking advantage of changes in EU policy that allow it to adjust its design and production strategies to meet the unique needs of European consumers. Similarly, in the ending case we'll see how NAFTA affected Walmart's expansion into Mexico and Central America. Thus, as a company expands internationally, it must change its operating strategies to continually benefit from these alliances.

MNEs are interested in regional trade groups because they tend to be regional as well. Although MNEs operate worldwide, they usually generate a large percentage of their revenues in their home regions.[3] Additional research has shown that a 1 percent increase in physical distance results in a 1 percent decrease in trade and that a common border between two countries is likely to increase trade flows by 80 percent. This provides further evidence that firms are likely to generate a reasonably high percent of revenues from their home regions.[4] However, companies that sell in their own region are also interested in trade agreements with other regions. That is because some of the largest markets in the world, such as China, may be far away from the MNE's home country and/or not have a common border.

THE WORLD TRADE ORGANIZATION—GLOBAL INTEGRATION

8-2 Explain what the World Trade Organization is and how it is working to reduce trade barriers on a global basis

CONCEPT CHECK

In Chapter 7 (page 187), we define a tariff as the most common type of trade control and describe it as a "tax" that governments levy on goods shipped internationally. Here we emphasize the fact that tariff barriers affect the prices of goods that cross national borders.

GATT: PREDECESSOR TO THE WTO

In 1947, 23 countries formed the **General Agreement on Tariffs and Trade (GATT)** under the auspices of the United Nations to abolish quotas and reduce tariffs. By the time the WTO replaced GATT in 1995, 125 nations had become members. Many believe that GATT's contribution to trade liberalization enabled the expansion of world trade in the second half of the twentieth century.

Trade Without Discrimination The fundamental principle of GATT was that each member nation must open its markets equally to every other member nation. This principle of "trade without discrimination" was embodied in GATT's **most-favored-nation (MFN) clause**—

once a country and its trading partners had agreed to reduce a tariff, that tariff cut was automatically extended to every other member country, irrespective of whether the country was a signatory to the agreement.

Over time, GATT grappled with the issue of nontariff barriers in terms of industrial standards, government procurement, subsidies and countervailing duties (duties in response to another country's protectionist measures), licensing, and customs valuation. In each area, GATT members agreed to apply the same product standards for imports as for domestically produced goods, treat bids by foreign companies on a nondiscriminatory basis for most large contracts, prohibit export subsidies except on agricultural products, simplify licensing procedures that permit the importation of foreign-made goods, and use a uniform procedure to value imports when assessing duties on them.

Then GATT slowly ran into problems. Its success led some governments to devise craftier methods of trade protection. World trade grew more complex, and trade in services—not covered by GATT rules—grew more important. Procedurally, GATT's institutional structure and its dispute-settlement system seemed increasingly overextended. Moreover, it could not enforce compliance with agreements. These market trends and organizational challenges made trade agreements harder to work out. Restoring an effective means for trade liberalization led officials to create the **World Trade Organization (WTO)** in 1995.

CONCEPT CHECK

In Chapter 7 (pages 178 and 188), we explain that, in principle, no country allows an unregulated flow of goods and services across its borders; rather, governments routinely influence the flow of imports and exports. We also observe that governments directly or indirectly subsidize domestic industries to help them compete with foreign producers, whether at home or abroad. (In Chapter 1, we list the motivations for governments to engage in cross-national agreements—indeed, to cooperate at all.)

CONCEPT CHECK

In discussing "Nontariff Barriers" as instruments of trade control in Chapter 7 (page 188), we include subsidies, which we describe as direct government payments made to domestic companies, either to compensate them for losses incurred from selling abroad or to make it more profitable for them to sell overseas.

WHAT DOES THE WTO DO?

The WTO adopted the principles and trade agreements reached under the auspices of GATT but expanded its mission to include trade in services, investment, intellectual property, sanitary measures, plant health, agriculture, and textiles, as well as technical barriers to trade. Its 164 members collectively account for most of the world trade, and an additional 22 countries have applied for membership. The entire membership makes significant decisions by consensus. However, there are provisions for a majority vote in the event of a nondecision by member countries. Agreements then must be ratified by the governments of the member nations, which can be politically challenging.

The World Trade Organization is the major body for

- reciprocal trade negotiations,
- enforcement of trade agreements.

Most Favored Nation The WTO continued the MFN clause of GATT, which implies that member countries should trade without discrimination, basically giving foreign products "national treatment." Although the WTO restricts this privilege to official members, some exceptions are allowed, especially for developing countries or countries that are part of a regional or bilateral trading group.

Dispute Settlement One function of the WTO that is garnering growing attention is the organization's dispute settlement mechanism, in which countries may bring charges of unfair trade practices to a WTO panel, and accused countries may appeal. There are time limits on all stages of deliberations, and the WTO's rulings are binding. If an offending country fails to comply with the panel's judgment, its trading partners have the right to compensation. If this penalty is ineffective, then the offending country's trading partners have the right to impose countervailing sanctions. However, the effectiveness of this system is under serious debate, given the ambiguity and time-consuming nature of certain cases.

CONCEPT CHECK

In Chapter 7 (page 178), we show how the imposition of import restrictions can be used as a means of persuading other countries to lower import barriers. Here we point out that the same practice can also be used to punish nations whose policies fail to comply with provisions of the WTO or other agreements.

REGIONAL ECONOMIC INTEGRATION

8-3 Summarize the major benefits of regional economic integration

BILATERAL AGREEMENTS

Bilateral agreements can be between two individual countries or may involve one country dealing with a group of other countries.

Even though bilateral trade agreements are simpler than trying to forge a deal with the WTO, no trade agreement is easy. An example of a bilateral agreement is the trade negotiations between the United States and China precipitated by the potential levy of duties against China for unfair trade practices. These negotiations have resulted in ups and downs in the stock markets worldwide, but in 2020, a bilateral agreement was finally signed. However,

$370 billion of tariffs remained against China, and this agreement was only the first of several expected to take place to resolve trade differences.

Regional trade agreements—integration confined to a region and involving more than two countries.

Regional trade agreements are reciprocal pacts between two or more partners that range from bilateral treaties to larger regional groups of countries. Some of the best-known RTAs are the European Union; the U.S.-Mexico-Canada Agreement (USMCA), formerly the North American Free Trade Agreement or NAFTA; and the ASEAN (Association of Southeast Asian Nations) Free Trade Area (AFTA).

GEOGRAPHY MATTERS

CONCEPT CHECK

In discussing geographic distance in Chapter 6 (page 159), we observe that because greater distances ordinarily mean higher transportation costs, geographic proximity usually encourages trade cooperation. In the same chapter, we explain country similarity theory by showing that once a company has developed a new product in response to conditions in its home market, it will probably try to export the product to those markets that it regards as most like its own.

It's logical that most trade groups contain countries in the same area of the world. Neighboring nations tend to ally for several reasons:

- The distances that goods need to travel are short.
- Consumers' tastes are likely to be similar, and distribution channels can easily be established.

Neighboring countries may have common histories and interests, and they may be more willing to coordinate their policies than non-neighbors.[5] Even though geographic proximity is a major factor leading to RTAs, this is not the case for all agreements. India has a number of trade agreements with most of the countries in its region, but also with Finland, Japan, and Korea; Germany exports and imports about 58 percent of its merchandise to other EU members; Switzerland, which is not a member of the EU but has a trade agreement with it, shares more than half its exports and imports with EU countries; and USMCA includes Mexico and Canada, both of which share a common border with the United States. The Canada–Israel RTA, on the other hand, is not based on geographic proximity, nor is the U.S.–Korea FTA, as well as the current trade agreement with the U.S. and China.

Geographic proximity is an important reason for economic integration.

Geography matters for several reasons in the case of RTAs. Neighboring countries often share a common history, language, culture, and currency. Unless the countries are at war with each other, they have usually developed trading ties already. Proximity reduces transportation costs, thereby making traded products cheaper in general. In fact, as physical distance between two countries increases by 1 percent, international trade drops by 1.1 percent. On the other hand, trade is likely to rise by 80 percent between countries with a common border, 200 percent with a common language (such as English between Canada and the United States), and 340 percent with a common currency (such as the euro for countries in the EU that have adopted it). Another strong incentive for geographically close countries to establish an RTA is that trade among bloc members is likely to rise by 330 percent once an agreement is established.[6]

Major types of economic integration:

- Free trade area—no internal tariffs.
- Customs union—no internal tariffs plus common external tariffs.
- Common market—customs union plus factor mobility, etc.

As noted earlier, the major reason to establish a regional trade group is to increase market size. There are two basic types of RTAs from the standpoint of tariff policies; however, many agreements (especially agreements involving the United States) go beyond the liberalization of tariffs to include areas such as services, foreign direct investment, labor reform, and intellectual property. In the case of the bilateral agreement with China, there is a strong focus on Chinese subsidies to state-owned companies, and the protection of intellectual property. From the standpoint of tariff reduction, the two main types of agreements are free trade agreements and customs unions.

- *Free Trade Agreement (FTA)* The goal of an FTA is to abolish all tariffs between member countries and was the original objective of the WTO. It usually begins modestly by eliminating them on goods that already have low tariffs, and there is usually an implementation period during which all tariffs are eliminated on all products included in the agreement. Moreover, each member country maintains its own external tariffs against non-FTA countries.
- *Customs Union* In addition to eliminating internal tariffs, member countries levy a common external tariff on goods being imported from nonmembers in order to establish a customs union. For example, when the EU was organized in 1957, it began to remove internal tariffs among member states, but in 1967 it eliminated the remaining internal tariffs and established a common external tariff, meaning that goods shipped into one

member country from abroad are free from tariffs in the rest of the member countries. Now the EU negotiates as one region in the WTO and other regional and bilateral agreements rather than as separate countries.

Regional integration has social, cultural, political, and economic effects.

Static effects of integration—the shifting of resources from inefficient to efficient companies as trade barriers fall.

Dynamic effects of integration—the overall growth in the market and the impact on a company caused by expanding production and by the company's ability to achieve greater economies of scale.

Common Market Beyond the reduction of tariffs and nontariff barriers, countries can enhance their cooperation in a variety of other ways. The EU also allows free mobility of production factors such as labor and capital. This means that labor, for example, is generally free to work in any country in the common market without restriction. Adding free mobility of production factors to a customs union results in a **common market**. In addition, the EU has harmonized its monetary policies through the creation of a common currency, complete with a central bank. This level of cooperation creates a degree of political integration among member countries, which means they lose some of their sovereignty.

THE EFFECTS OF INTEGRATION

Regional economic integration can affect member countries in social, cultural, political, and economic ways. Initially, however, our focus is on its economic rationale. As we noted in Chapter 6, the imposition of tariff and nontariff barriers disrupts the free flow of goods, affecting resource allocation.

CONCEPT CHECK

In Chapter 6 (page 152), we define comparative advantage as the theory that global efficiency gains may result from trade if a country specializes in those products it can produce more efficiently than other products (regardless of whether other countries can produce the same products even more efficiently).

Static and Dynamic Effects Regional economic integration reduces or eliminates those barriers for member countries, producing both *static* and *dynamic effects.* **Static effects** are the shifting of resources from inefficient to efficient companies as trade barriers fall. **Dynamic effects** are the overall growth in the market and the impact on a company caused by expanding production and by its ability to achieve greater economies of scale. Figure 8.1 shows how RTAs result in static and dynamic effects on trade and investment flows.

Static effects may develop when either of two conditions occurs:

Trade creation—production shifts to more efficient producers for reasons of comparative advantage.

1. *Trade Creation:* Production shifts to more efficient producers for reasons of comparative advantage, allowing consumers access to more goods at lower prices than would have been possible without integration. Companies protected in their domestic markets

FIGURE 8.1 Impact of Free Trade Agreements

When economic integration reduces or eliminates trade barriers, the effects on the nations involved may be either *static* or *dynamic*. *Static effects* apply primarily to trade barriers themselves—for member countries they go down, and for nonmembers they go up. *Dynamic effects*, on the other hand, apply to economic changes affecting the newly structured market—not only does the market expand, but so do local companies, which take advantage of the larger market.

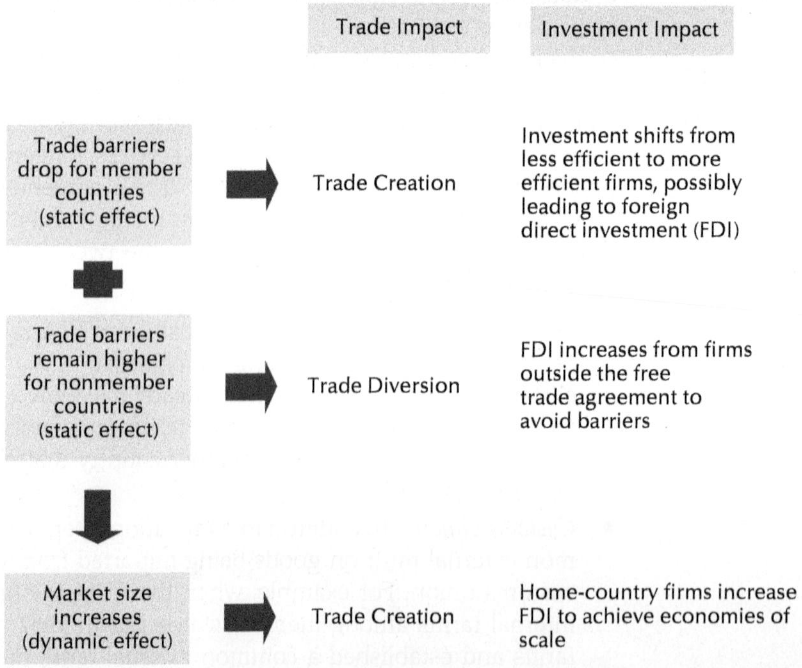

face real problems when the barriers are eliminated, and they attempt to compete with more efficient producers. The strategic implication is that companies that were unable to export to another country—even though they might be more efficient than producers there—are now able to export when the barriers come down, creating more demand for their products and less for the protected ones. Investment also might shift to countries that are more efficient or that have a comparative advantage in one or more factors of production.

Trade diversion—trade shifts to countries in the group at the expense of trade with countries not in the group.

2. *Trade Diversion:* Trade shifts to countries in the group at the expense of trade with other countries, even though the nonmember companies might be more efficient in the absence of trade barriers.

Economies of scale—the average cost per unit falls as the number of units produced rises; occurs in regional integration because of the growth in the market size.

Economies of Scale Dynamic effects of integration occur when trade barriers come down and markets grow. Because of that growth, companies can increase their production, which will result in lower costs per unit—a phenomenon we call **economies of scale**. Companies can produce more cheaply, which is good because they must become more efficient to survive. This could result in more trade between the member countries (trade creation) or an increase in investment in the region by local or foreign companies as the market grows.

Increased Competition Another important effect of an RTA is greater efficiency due to increased competition. Many MNEs in Europe have attempted to grow through mergers and acquisitions to achieve the size necessary to compete in the larger market. Companies in Mexico were forced to become more competitive with the passage of NAFTA due to competition from Canadian and U.S. companies, preparing them to be more competitive as NAFTA was replaced with USMCA. This could result in investment shifting from less efficient to more efficient companies, or it could result in existing companies becoming more efficient.

MAJOR REGIONAL TRADING GROUPS

8-4 Compare and contrast different regional trading groups

MNEs are interested in regional trading groups for their markets, sources of raw materials, and production locations. The larger and richer the new market, the more likely it is to attract the attention of the major investor countries and companies. In addition, it is important to understand how the reduction of tariffs and other barriers improves access to countries in the region. Table 8.1 compares the GDP and population of three regional trade groups to give you an idea of how different they are in size. Pick just one country in each group, such as Ireland in the EU, Canada in NAFTA, and Vietnam in ASEAN, and notice how small their national market would be compared with how big their market opportunities are in their regional trade group.

The European Union:

- Changed from the European Economic Community to the European Community to the European Union
- The largest and most successful regional trade group
- Free trade of goods, services, capital, and people
- Common external tariff
- Common currency

THE EUROPEAN UNION

The second largest by population and most comprehensive regional economic group is the **European Union (EU)**. It began by gradually abolishing internal tariffs but eventually established an external tariff while integrating in other ways such as facilitating the free movement

TABLE 8.1 Comparative Statistics by Trade Group

	Population in Millions (2018)	GDP Trillions of $ (2018)
European Union (EU)	446.835	15.913
United States-Mexico-Canada Agreement (USMCA)	490.417	23.478
ASEAN Free Trade Area (AFTA)	647.016	2.922

Source: Based on information from http://data.worldbank.org/ (accessed on February 1, 2020); http://www.asean.org/ (accessed on February 4, 2020); https://europa.eu/european-union/about-eu/figures/living_en (accessed on February 1, 2020).

For comparative purposes, the population and GDP data for the EU does not include the United Kingdom, which left the EU on February 1, 2020.

TABLE 8.2 European Union Milestones

From its inception in 1957, the EU has been moving toward complete economic integration. The initial six members were Belgium, Germany, France, Italy, Luxembourg, and the Netherlands.

1959	The first steps are taken in the progressive abolition of customs duties and quotas within the EEC (European Economic Community). The European Coal and Steel Community established in 1951 gave way to a broader vision of economic integration.
1960	The Stockholm Convention establishes the European Free Trade Association (EFTA) as a free trade alternative to the EU, now comprised of Iceland, Norway, Liechtenstein, and Switzerland.
1961	The first regulation on free movement of workers within the EEC comes into force.
1962	The Common Agricultural Policy is adopted.
1966	Agreement is reached on a value-added tax (VAT) system; a treaty merging the Executives of the European Communities comes into force; and the EEC changes its name to European Community (EC).
1967	All remaining internal tariffs are eliminated, and a common external tariff is imposed.
1973	Denmark, Ireland, and the United Kingdom become members 7, 8, and 9 of the EC.
1981	Greece becomes the 10th member of the EC.
1986	Spain and Portugal become the 11th and the 12th members of the EC.
1992	Agreement to change the EC to the European Union is adopted in 1992 and implemented in 1993.
1995	Austria, Finland, and Sweden become the 13th, 14th, and 15th members.
1996	An EU summit names the 11 countries that will join the European single currency with all EU countries joining except the UK, Sweden, Denmark (by their choice), and Greece (not ready, but later adopted in 2001).
1999	The euro, the single European currency, comes into effect (January 1, 1999). Coins and notes enter circulation on January 1, 2002.
2004–2016	Cyprus, Czechia, Estonia, Hungary, Latvia, Lithuania, Malta, Poland, Slovakia, and Slovenia are admitted in 2004. Bulgaria and Romania are admitted in 2007, and Croatia is the most recent country admitted in 2016.
2020	The United Kingdom left the EU on February 1, 2020.

Source: Europa, "The History of the European Union," at http://europa.eu/about-eu/index_en.htm (accessed February 4, 2020).

of workers, establishing a common agricultural policy, and agreeing on a value-added tax system. The formation of the European Parliament and the establishment of a common currency, the euro, make the EU the most ambitious of all the regional trade groups.[7] Table 8.2 summarizes its key milestones, whileMap 8.1 identifies its members and other key European groups.

CONCEPT CHECK

In Chapter 6 (page 156), we discuss the theory of country size, which holds that large countries usually depend less on trade than small countries. The same principle tends to be true of economic blocs, and here we point out that regional integration is one way to achieve the size necessary to reduce members' dependence on trade.

Predecessors Because of the economic and human destruction left by World War II, European political leaders realized that greater cooperation among their countries would help speed up recovery. Many organizations were formed, including the European Economic Community (EEC), which eventually emerged as the organization that would bring together the countries of Europe into one of the most powerful trading blocs in the world. Several other countries, including the United Kingdom, formed the European Free Trade Association (EFTA) with the limited goal of eliminating internal tariffs. But most of those countries eventually became part of the EU. Those that have decided not to leave EFTA (Iceland, Liechtenstein, Norway, and Switzerland) still have a free trade agreement with each other. All but Switzerland are part of the European Economic Area, which provides them access to the "four freedoms" of the EU: the free movement of goods, services, persons, and capital. However, it does not include other areas of cooperation, such as a customs union and monetary union.[8] It remains to be seen what will happen to the United Kingdom in terms of trade relationships.

European Free Trade Association—FTA involving Iceland, Liechtenstein, Norway, and Switzerland, with close ties to the EU.

Organizational Structure The EU encompasses many governing bodies, among which are the European Commission, European Council, European Parliament, European Court of Justice, and European Central Bank.[9]

To be successful in Europe, MNEs need to understand the EU's governance process, just as they need to understand the governance process of each individual European country in which they invest or do business. These institutions set parameters within which companies must operate, so management needs to understand the institutions and how they make decisions that could affect corporate strategy. This is because even though all member countries are part of the same trade agreement, there are still individual differences that need to be understood and planned for.

MAP 8.1 European Trade and Economic Integration

Although the 27-member EU is easily the dominant trading bloc in Europe, it's not the only one. Founded in 1960, the four-member European Free Trade Association (EFTA) also maintains joint free trade agreements with several other countries. The European Economic Area (EEA) unites the EU, Iceland, Liechtenstein, and Norway into an internal market. Switzerland is not part of the EEA.

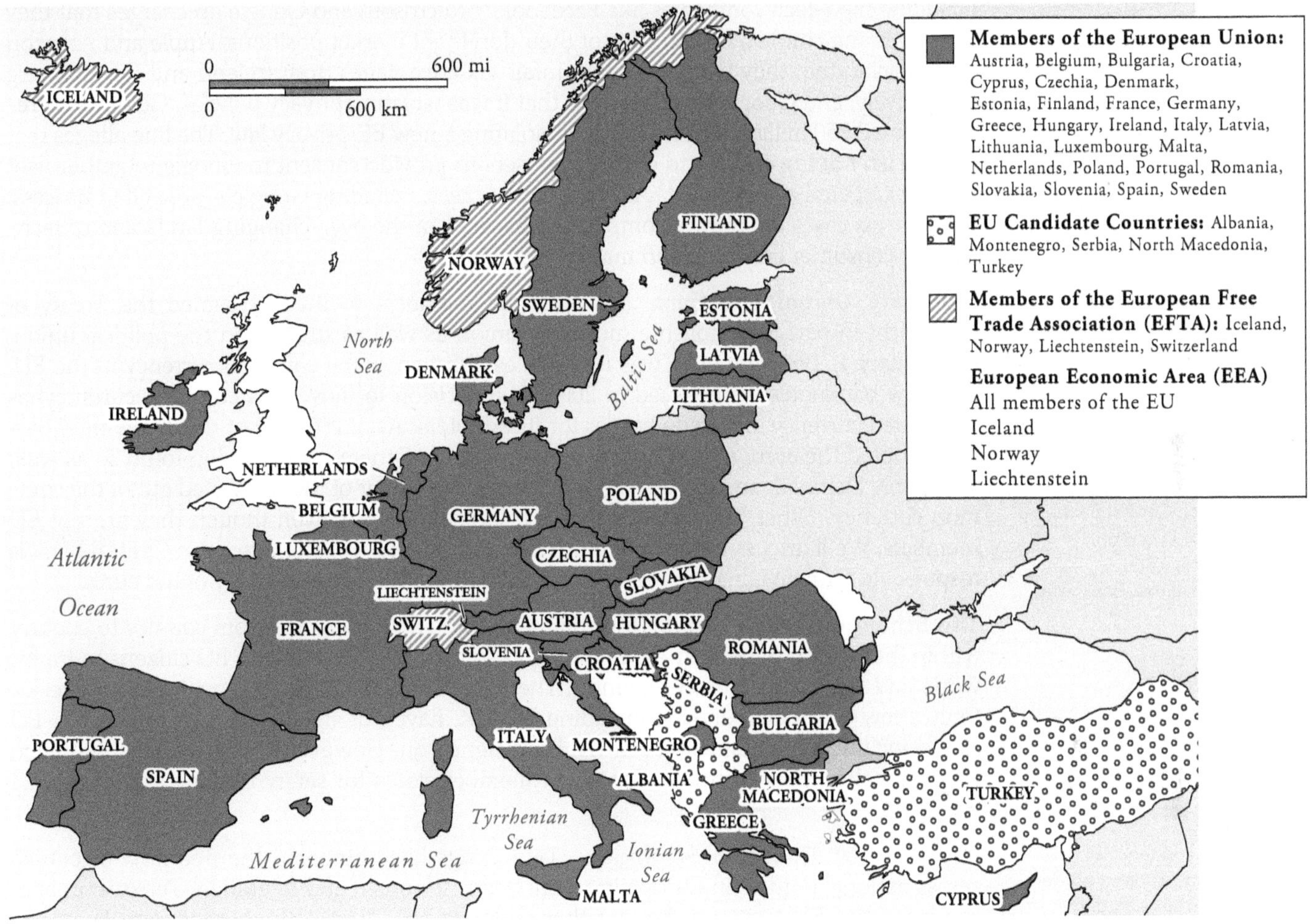

The European Commission provides political leadership, drafts laws, and runs the various daily programs of the EU.

Key Governing Bodies The **European Commission** provides the EU's political leadership and direction. It is composed of commissioners nominated by each member government and approved by the European Parliament for five-year terms of office. The president of the commission is nominated by the member governments and approved by the European Parliament. The commissioners run the different programs of the EU on a day-to-day basis rather than serve as representatives of their respective governments. The commission drafts laws that it submits to the European Parliament and the Council of the European Union.

The Council of the European Union is composed of the heads of state of each member country, the President of the European Commission, and the High Representative for Foreign Affairs and Security Policy.

The **European Council** is comprised of the heads of state of each member country, the President of the Commission, and the High Representative for Foreign Affairs and Security Policy. The Council meets quarterly and is responsible at the highest level for the general direction of the EU, especially but not exclusively for foreign affairs and the security of the EU. The Council also nominates and appoints members of the European Central Bank and the European Commission. However, the Council cannot pass laws.

The three major responsibilities of the European Parliament are legislative power, control over the budget, and supervision of executive decisions.

The **European Parliament** is composed of 705 members from all member nations; they are elected every five years, and membership is based on country population. Its three major responsibilities are legislative power, control over the budget, and supervision of executive decisions. Members are grouped by political affiliation (such as Christian Democrats, greens, etc.) rather than by nationality. The commission presents community legislation to the Parliament, which must approve the legislation before it is submitted to the council for adoption.[10]

The **Court of Justice** ensures consistent interpretation and application of EU treaties. Member states, EC institutions, and individuals and companies may bring cases to the Court,

The European Court of Justice ensures consistent interpretation and application of EU treaties.

which serves as an appeals court for individuals, firms, and organizations fined by the commission for infringing treaty law.[11]

Antitrust Investigations The EU has been very aggressive in enforcing antitrust laws,, including high-tech companies like Facebook,[12] Microsoft, and Google on charges that they were harming competitors because of their dominant market positions, Apple and Amazon on suspicion that they were receiving unfair tax advantages from Ireland and Luxembourg respectively, and Google on allegations that it was violating privacy policies. Google was recently fined €50 million ($57 million) for violating a new EU privacy law. The fine alleges that Google isn't doing enough to encourage users to provide consent to Google to gather user data for targeted advertising.[13] Although most cases, including Google's, are still in process, the non-tax cases are always complicated because of the ever-changing landscape of technology, consumer behavior, and market demand.[14]

The Treaty of Maastricht sought to foster political union and monetary union.

The euro

- is a common currency in Europe,
- is administered by the European Central Bank,
- was established on January 1, 1999,
- resulted in new banknotes in 2002.

Monetary Union: The Euro In 1992, the members of the EU signed the Treaty of Maastricht in part to establish a monetary union as well as strengthen the political union. On January 1, 1999, the **euro** was formally established as the common currency in the EU, and new banknotes were issued in 2002. The decision to move to a common currencyhas eliminated currency as a trade barrier for its adopters. As of 2020, 19 of the 27 EU members had adopted the euro, also known as the euro zone. Others are preparing to do so as well, while only Denmark and the UK (now no longer a member of the EU) opted out of the common currency. Other European countries also use the euro, even though they are not EU members. We'll discuss the euro in more detail in Chapter 10. The European Central Bank is responsible for managing the monetary policy of the EU and the stability of the euro.

The Schengen Area In order to facilitate the free flow of people from country to country within the EU, the Schengen Agreement was signed in 1990, allowing EU citizens to travel, work, and live in any member country. The agreement also does away with border checks. Only a few member countries, including the UK, have not signed on, but several non-EU states, including all members of EFTA, have signed on. However, countries have tightened the external borders with non-Schengen member states for safety reasons and in case of emergencies.[15]

Migration and terrorism are threatening the open borders that are at the heart of the Schengen Agreement.

Migration: A Threat to Schengen Two things have hindered the free flow of people across national borders in Europe in recent years: terrorism and migration. Terrorist attacks in France and Belgium and the fear that migrants would cross the border from France to Belgium forced Belgium to partly suspend passport-free travel to Belgium from France; large numbers of migrants from Syria and other countries who were living in camps close to the Belgian border were trying to move into Belgium.[16] The fear is that although Europe has always been open to refugees, especially political refugees, the crisis in Syria resulted in a massive flow of people to Europe in greater numbers than at any time since World War II. It happened so fast that the EU was not prepared. Refugees streamed from Syria to Turkey to Greece and then elsewhere in Europe. The EU worked with Turkey to convince them to keep the Syrian refugees there and even promised financial support and help in completing their entrance into the EU if they would harbor more of the refugees. However, the refugees continued to flow into Greece where an economy with over 20 percent unemployment and a financial crisis was hard pressed to accept and keep all the Syrian refugees.[17] As world leaders tried to figure out a way to solve the political crisis in Syria, Europe was trying to solve the refugee crisis. Solutions ranging from making borders more difficult to cross to sealing borders are among the options that have been considered. Clearly solving the migration crisis is important; otherwise the idea of open borders in Europe will be a major casualty, not only causing irreparable damage to the idea of open borders but also slowing and harming cross-border commerce. And simply closing the borders could result in a serious humanitarian crisis.[18]

The EU expanded from 15 to 25 countries in 2004 with countries from mostly Central and Eastern Europe. Romania and Bulgaria were admitted in 2007 and Croatia in 2013, bringing the number to 27, after the loss the UK.

Expansion One of the EU's major challenges is expansion. Official candidates for future membership currently include Albania, Montenegro, North Macedonia, Serbia, and Turkey. Turkey is an interesting candidate since it straddles Europe and Asia, is 99.8 percent Muslim (mostly Sunni), and has a large population of 75.9 million people, second only to Germany with 80.89 million people. It has a strong manufacturing base and strong trade ties with

Europe. As noted above, it may also be a key to help the EU come to grips with the humanitarian crisis with the Syrian refugees. Given its proximity to the Syrian border, Turkey is in a unique position to help assimilate Syrian refugees with temporary work visas and then facilitate their return to Syria when political conditions stabilize there. However, the political turmoil in Turkey is causing serious problems that will jeopardize its admission into the EU.

Bilateral Agreements In addition to reducing trade barriers for member countries, the EU has signed numerous bilateral free trade agreements with other countries outside the region. Since the EU negotiates with other countries as one entity, its trade talks are considered bilateral, even though all member states benefit from the results of the talks. The benefit to the other party to the agreement is that they get access to 27 countries when they sign the agreement.

CONCEPT CHECK

In Chapter 6 (page 156), we point out that in countries where labor is abundant compared to capital, many workers (not surprisingly) tend to be either unemployed or poorly paid. If permitted, they will migrate to countries that enjoy full employment and higher wages—a form of factor mobility that governments in the latter group of countries often restrict.

The Transatlantic Trade and Investment Partnership (T-TIP) One of the more intriguing potential agreements involves the United States and the EU. Even though tariffs between the two superpowers are already low (the United States and the EU have the world's largest trading relationship and account for nearly half of the world's economic output), the new agreement would eliminate the remaining tariffs, boost trade between the regions, and aid in harmonizing product standards between them. U.S. labor unions would be more willing to support such an agreement because of the region's similar labor and environmental standards and because an agreement could result in billions of dollars in yearly growth and thousands of jobs.[19]

As the United States and the EU began negotiations in 2013, however, several challenges began to arise. The French, backed by the European Parliament, want to continue providing subsidies and quotas to support its film and music industries and thus exclude the cultural industries from any future trade talks. On the other side, U.S. farmers are very upset about European agricultural safety standards and view them as protectionist. Obviously, any agreement will be difficult to reach, despite the hope for expanding economic growth in the regions.[20] As discussions continued in 2018–2019, other issues arose. The United States threatened tariffs on European automobiles, and the Europeans wanted to keep agriculture off the table because of the powerful agricultural industry in Europe, especially in France.[21] In addition, France adopted a tax on U.S. digital products, creating even greater stress. In 2019, the EU declared that T-TIP was obsolete and no longer relevant, even though the EU and United States were continuing to try to resolve trade issues.[22]

Implications of the EU for corporate strategy:

- Companies need to determine where to produce products.
- Companies need to determine what their entry strategy will be.
- Companies need to balance the commonness of the EU with national differences.

How to Do Business with the EU: Implications for Corporate Strategy The EU is a tremendous market in terms of both population and income—one that companies cannot ignore. It is also a good example of how geographic proximity and the removal of trade barriers can influence trade. More than half the merchandise exports and imports of EU countries are intrazonal trade. That is far better than other regional or even bilateral trade agreements. Again, geographic proximity, a common currency for most of the member countries, and the length of time the EU has been in existence are key reasons why the intrazonal trade is so high.

Doing business in the EU can influence corporate strategy, especially for outside MNEs, in three ways:

1. *Determining where to produce.* One strategy is to produce in a central location in Europe to minimize transportation costs and the time it takes to move products from one country to another. However, the highest costs are in central Europe. As we saw in our opening case, for instance, manufacturing wages in the German auto industry were much higher than the lower wages among Eastern European members. That's why Toyota opted to set up operations in lower-wage countries such as Czechia and Poland.
2. *Determining whether to grow through new investments, expanding existing investments, or joint ventures and mergers.* When Toyota initially set up its manufacturing platform in Europe, it entered into a joint venture with PSA Peugeot-Citroën to build a new factory in Czechia in order to take advantage of the European carmaker's supplier network. The market is still considered fragmented and inefficient compared with the United States, so most experts feel that mergers, takeovers, and spinoffs must continue in Europe, and U.S. companies are buying European companies to gain a market presence and to get rid of competition.

3. *Balancing "common" denominators with national differences.* There are wider national differences in the EU due to language and history. But there are also widely different growth rates, although that varies from year to year. Also, slow economic growth since 2008 means that nobody is growing very fast. In recent years, for example, economic growth in Southern Europe, especially Greece, Cyprus, Italy, and Spain, has been in negative territory, Germany and France have been positive but relatively flat, and Ireland has been relatively robust.

A good example of adapting business strategies to Europe is Toyota. In terms of products, Toyota is busy designing a European car, but for which Europe? Tastes and preferences—not to mention climate—vary greatly between northern and southern Europe. Toyota, however, is attempting to use production location and design to facilitate a pan-European strategy.

Companies will always struggle with the degree to which they develop a European strategy versus different national strategies inside Europe. Despite the challenges, there are many opportunities for companies to expand their markets and sources of supply as the EU grows and encompasses more of Europe.

THE U.S.-MEXICO-CANADA AGREEMENT (USMCA)

The North American Free Trade Agreement

- includes Canada, the United States, and Mexico;
- went into effect on January 1, 1994;
- involves free trade in goods, services, and investment;
- is a large trading bloc but includes countries of different sizes and wealth.

Various forms of mutual economic cooperation have historically existed between the United States and Canada, such as the Canada–U.S. Free Trade Agreement of 1989, which eliminated all tariffs on bilateral trade. In February 1991, Prior to the passage of the USMCA in 2020, Mexico approached the United States to establish a free trade agreement. Canada was included in the formal negotiations, and the resulting **North American Free Trade Agreement (NAFTA)** became effective on January 1, 1994. Although USMCA replaces the NAFTA agreement, many of the reasons for the two agreements are the same. USMCA changed some of the features of NAFTA and added others, but it is good to understand the basic idea behind NAFTA in order to understand USMCA.

NAFTA rationale:

- U.S.–Canadian trade is the largest bilateral trade in the world.
- The United States is Mexico's and Canada's largest trading partner.

Why NAFTA? NAFTA has a logical rationale in terms of both geographic location and trading importance. Although Canadian–Mexican trade was not significant when the agreement was signed, the United States had key trade relationships with each of them. In fact, the one between the United States and Canada is the largest in the world, not including the 27-member EU. As Table 8.1 indicates, NAFTA is a powerful trading bloc with a combined population and GDP greater than the 27-member EU. What is significant, especially when compared with the EU, is the tremendous size of the U.S. economy compared to those of its neighbors, whereas there is no such dominant country in the EU. Canada generates a slightly higher GDP than does Mexico but with a smaller population. In addition, Mexico's population is growing faster than that of Canada.

USMCA calls for the elimination of tariff and nontariff barriers, the harmonization of trade rules, the liberalization of restrictions on services and foreign investment, the enforcement of intellectual property rights, and a dispute settlement process.

Mexico made significant strides in tariff reduction after joining GATT in 1986, when its tariffs averaged 100 percent. Since January 1, 2008, all tariffs and quotas were eliminated on U.S. exports to Canada and Mexico, making it far easier to establish a regional free trade agreement. Unlike the EU, NAFTA was a free trade agreement in goods and services rather than a customs union or a common market, and there is no common currency. That has continued with USMCA. However, USMCA extends far beyond reductions in tariff and nontariff barriers to include provisions for digital trade, financial services, investment, intellectual property, labor, the environment, and a strong dispute resolution mechanism.

Static and Dynamic Effects USMCA illustrates the static and dynamic effects of economic integration. For example, Canadian and U.S. consumers benefit from lower-cost agricultural products from Mexico, a *static* effect of economic liberalization. U.S. producers also benefit from the large and growing Mexican market, which has a huge appetite for U.S. products—a *dynamic* effect.

USMCA is a good example of trade diversion; some U.S. trade with and investment in Asia has been diverted to Mexico.

Trade Diversion USMCA is also a good example of trade diversion. Prior to the NAFTA agreement, many U.S. and Canadian companies had established manufacturing facilities in Asia to take advantage of low-cost labor. IBM, for example, was making computer parts in Singapore. After NAFTA, Mexico became a good option for those companies, and in five years IBM boosted exports from Mexico to the United States from $350 million to $2 billion.

Companies from non-NAFTA countries began investing in Mexico to take advantage of NAFTA's access to the United States and Canada, especially in the auto industry.

Rules of origin—goods and services must originate in North America to get access to lower tariffs.

Rules of Origin and Regional Content Two important components of USMCA are rules of origin and regional content. Because it is a free trade agreement and not a customs union, each country sets its own tariffs to the rest of the world. Thus, to protect goods from being transshipped from China to the United States via Mexico, for example, measures had to be included to identify the origin of any product passing from one USMCA country to another member country.

Rules of Origin "Rules of origin" ensure that only goods that have been the subject of substantial economic activity within the free trade area are eligible for the more liberal tariff conditions created by USMCA. One of the objectives of the United States was to increase the amount of regional content to qualify for duty-free access and to come closer to leveling the playing field of wages to take away the incentive for companies to shift all of their production from a higher-wage to a lower-wage country.

Regional content:

- The percentage of value that must be from North America for the product to be considered North American in terms of country of origin.
- Regional content under USMCA was raised from 62.5 percent under NAFTA to 75 percent or autos.

Regional Value Content Requirement One aspect of rules of origin refers to the Regional Value Content requirement. Although the regional value content varies from industry to industry, a good example is the auto industry. Under USMCA, regional content for light vehicles was raised from 62.5 percent under NAFTA to 75 percent. A new provision called Local Value Content (LVC) was added to put upward pressure on Mexican wages by requiring that 40–45 percent of auto content must come from workers earning at least $16 per hour.[23] This is approximately three times higher than the minimum wage in Mexico.

Labor and Enforcement Provisions In addition to the discussion on wages above, there was a strong push by the United States to include stronger rights for workers, with the ability to see if the provisions outlined in the agreement were carried out. Among other things, all three countries had to agree to accept ILO labor practices, and workers had to be represented at collective bargaining agreements. To ensure that the labor mandates were followed, an inspection and arbitration process was established that includes representatives of all three countries.

A major challenge to NAFTA is illegal immigration.

CONCEPT CHECK

As you'll recall from Chapter 7 (page 192), trade restrictions may diminish export capabilities and induce companies to locate some production in countries imposing the restrictions; the absence of trade barriers gives them more flexibility not only in deciding where to locate production but also in determining how to service different markets.

Immigration A major challenge to NAFTA that will continue to be an issue with USMCA is immigration. As trade in agriculture increased with the advent of NAFTA, more than a million farm jobs disappeared in Mexico due to U.S. competition. Many of these farmers ended up as undocumented workers in the United States, sending home more money in wire transfers (see the opening case in Chapter 9) than Mexico receives in FDI. Rapid economic growth in the United States compared with Mexico in the 1990s also resulted in a rise in migration from Mexico to the United States. However, that has now changed due to smaller families and a stronger economy in Mexico. During the period 2009–2014, more Mexicans returned to Mexico from the United States than migrated to the United States from Mexico. A major factor in their decision to return was reunification with their families.[24] The bigger issue is the flood of immigrants from Central America due to crime, poverty, and those seeking asylum from their home countries. This is not dissimilar to the refugee situation in the European Union.

Rationalization of Production One of the predictions made when NAFTA was signed was that companies would look at NAFTA as one big regional market, allowing them to rationalize production, products, financing, and the like. That has largely happened in several industries, especially in automotive products and electronics. Each NAFTA member ships more automotive products, based on specialized production, to the other two countries than any other manufactured goods. Rationalization of automotive production has taken place for years in the United States and Canada, but Mexico is a recent entrant, attracting auto manufacturing from all over the world, not just the United States. NAFTA's rules of origin have forced European and Asian automakers to bring in parts suppliers and set up assembly operations in Mexico. U.S. auto companies are shifting more of their production from the United States to Mexico, and the same is true for non-NAFTA companies, such as VW and Toyota. Mexico is the seventh largest passenger vehicle manufacturer and the fifth largest auto parts manufacturer in the world. Seventy-seven percent of Mexico's auto production is exported, the majority going to the United States.[25] It will be interesting to monitor investment and cross border supply chains as affected by the new regional content and Labor Value Content rules in USMCA.

Mexico as a Consumer Market An additional benefit is that Canadian and U.S. companies have realized that Mexico is a consumer market rather than just a production location. Initially, the excitement over the country for U.S. and Canadian firms was the low-wage environment. However, as Mexican income continues to rise—which it must do as more investment enters and more of its companies export production—demand is rising for foreign products.

REGIONAL ECONOMIC INTEGRATION IN THE AMERICAS

The regional groups in Latin and South America are a mixture of common markets, customs unions, and free trade agreements. In addition, individual countries have also entered into free trade agreements with other countries inside and outside of Latin and South America, so it is important to know which agreements exist as you enter into business in different countries. If you look at Maps 8.2 and 8.3, you'll see six major regional economic groups in North and South America, excluding USMCA. Central America and the Caribbean are part of North America, and the major trade groups in those two areas are the Caribbean Community (CARICOM), the Central American Common Market (CACM), and the Central American Free Trade Agreement (CAFTA-DR). CAFTA-DR includes the members of CACM but also Honduras and the Dominican Republic, along with the United States. The two major groups in South America are the Andean Community (CAN) and the Southern Common Market (Mercosur). The Andean Community is a customs union, whereas Mercosur is set up to be a common market.

The major reason for these different collaborative groups is market size. The post–World War II strategy of import substitution to resolve balance-of-payments problems in much of Latin America was doomed because of the region's small national markets. Therefore, some form of economic cooperation was needed to enlarge the potential market size so that Latin American companies could achieve economies of scale and be more competitive worldwide.

Caricom The **Caribbean Community (CARICOM)** is working hard to establish an EU-style form of collaboration, complete with full movement of goods and services, the right of establishment, a common external tariff, free movement of capital and labor,

MAP 8.2 Economic Integration in Central America and the Caribbean

Throughout Central America and the Caribbean, the focus on economic integration has shifted from the concept of the *free trade agreement* (whose goal is the abolition of trade barriers among members) to that of the *common market* (which calls for internal factor mobility as well as the abolition of internal trade barriers). The proposed structure of the Caribbean Community and Common Market (CARICOM) is modeled on that of the EU.

MAP 8.3 Latin American Economic Integration

a common trade policy, and so on. It is officially classified by the WTO as an Economic Integration Agreement. Many of these initiatives have come about through an initiative called the CARICOM Single Market and Economy (CSME). In addition to the 15 members of CARICOM, there are five associate members in the region.

CONCEPT CHECK

In Chapter 6 (page 156), we observe that little of the trade of low-income countries is conducted with other low-income countries. Generally, emerging economies rely heavily on trade with high-income countries, typically exporting primary and labor-intensive products in exchange for new and technologically advanced products.

Mercosur is a customs union among Argentina, Brazil, Paraguay, and Uruguay.

The Challenge Export Reliance Countries in Latin America and the Caribbean rely heavily on countries outside the region for trade. For example, Jamaica, a member of CARICOM, exports 49.3 percent of its merchandise to the United States and 18 percent to the EU. Although Trinidad and Tobago is the third major exporter of merchandise to Jamaica, no other member is significant as either a destination or a source for its exports. The same could be said for most of Latin America. The United States and EU represent significant markets for most of its countries.

The Southern Common Market (Mercosur in Spanish and Mercosul in Portuguese)

The major trade group in South America is **Mercosur**, which was established in 1991 by Brazil, Argentina, Paraguay, and Uruguay. Its major goal is to become a customs union with free trade within the bloc and a common external tariff. Mercosur is classified as a customs union by the WTO for trade in goods and as an economic integration agreement for trade in services. Mercosur is significant because of its size: a population of 251 million and a GDP of $2.9 trillion. It generates 75 percent of South America's GDP, making it the third-largest trading bloc in the world in terms of GDP after the EU and NAFTA. However it is a very fractious group of countries with political, economic, and ethical issues. It had admitted Venezuela to the group, but in 2017 they suspended Venezuela indefinitely because of political and economic problems there. In addition, there is a major problem with refugees fleeing Venezuela for Brazil and other countries.

Pacific Alliance Although other countries in Latin America have explored trade agreements with Mercosur, the problems identified above led to the creation in 2012 of the **Pacific Alliance**, comprising Mexico, Colombia, Peru, and Chile. These countries refer to themselves as more hospitable to trade and investment due to their adherence to democracy and the rule of law rather than the more populist and protectionist philosophies of other countries in CAN and Mercosur.[26] Having borders with the Pacific also means that they are trying to be a bridge between Latin America and the Asia–Pacific region, which makes sense given their dynamic and market-oriented economies.[27] In addition, they have a combined GDP of $1.8 trillion, second only to MERCOSUR.

The Andean Community is one of the original regional economic groups but has not been successful in achieving its original goals. The Pacific Alliance includes Mexico, Chile, and two members of the Andean Community.

Andean Community (CAN) Although the **Andean Community (CAN)** is not as significant economically as Mercosur or the Pacific Alliance, CAN has been around since 1969, and it is the second most important official regional group in South America. The Pacific Alliance is larger in terms of GDP, but Mexico is not in South America. The focus of CAN has shifted from one of isolationism and statism (placing economic control in the hands of the state—the central government) to being open to foreign trade and investment. Colombia and Peru, two of the founding members of CAN, have changed significantly in recent years and entered into bilateral trade agreements with the United States, solidifying their move to greater openness in comparison with other members of CAN. As noted above, they also have decided to join the Pacific Alliance.

REGIONAL ECONOMIC INTEGRATION IN ASIA

There are several RTAs in Asia as recognized by the WTO and several significant trade initiatives in process, creating an alphabet soup in Asia. Of the officially approved RTAs, the most important is the Association of Southeast Asian Nations/ASEAN Free Trade Area. As is the case in Latin America, regional integration in Asia has not been as successful as in Europe or North America because most of the countries in the region have relied on the United States, EU, and China for a significant percentage of their trade and investment.

Association of Southeast Asian Nations (ASEAN) Organized in 1967, **Association of South East Asian Nations (ASEAN)** is a comprehensive association that includes preferential trade as one of its many goals. This preferential trade agreement comprises Brunei Darussalam, Cambodia, Indonesia, Laos, Malaysia, Myanmar, the Philippines, Singapore, Thailand, and Vietnam (see Map 8.4). With a combined GDP of $2.922 trillion and an estimated population of 647.016 million people,[28] it is a significant organization.

MAP 8.4 The Association of Southeast Asian Nations

Although the total population of ASEAN countries is larger than that of either the EU or NAFTA, per capita GDP is considerably lower. Economic growth rates among ASEAN members, however, are among the highest in the world.

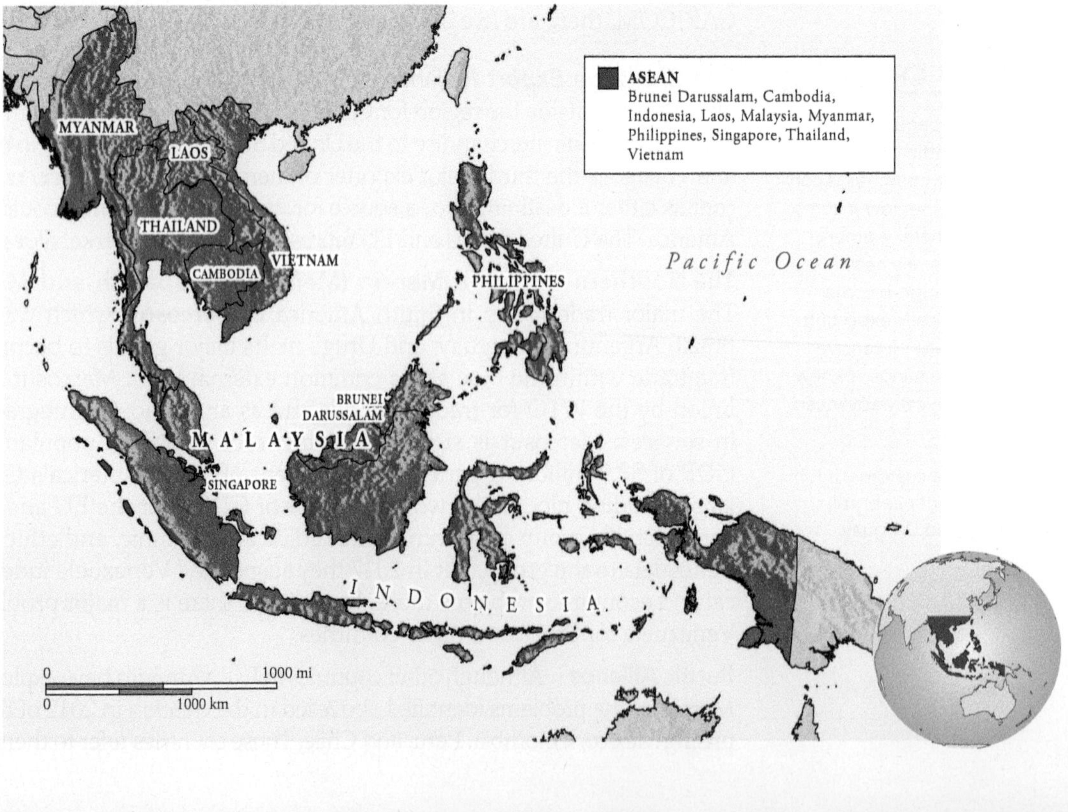

The ASEAN Free Trade Area is a successful trade agreement among countries in Southeast Asia.

ASEAN Free Trade Area On January 1, 1993, ASEAN officially formed the ASEAN Free Trade Area (AFTA) with the goal of cutting tariffs on all intrazonal trade to a maximum of 5 percent by January 1, 2008. The weaker ASEAN countries would be allowed to phase in their tariff reductions over a longer period. By 2018, most products traded among the AFTA countries were subject to duties from 0 to 5 percent, so AFTA has been successful in its objectives. Free trade is crucial to the member countries because their ratio of exports to GDP is almost 70 percent. The best achievement of AFTA is that it has reduced tariffs, attracted FDI, and turned the region into a huge network of production, leading to what some call "factory Asia."[29]

Although China is not a part of ASEAN, it is essential to ASEAN's future. China's working-age population was 998.3 million people at the end of 2017, which was a drop from the previous year, compared with over 300 million for the ASEAN countries. Although the average monthly wage for manufacturing workers is much higher in Singapore and Malaysia than in China, it is much lower in the other ASEAN countries. As wages continue to rise in China, there are opportunities for ASEAN countries to attract more FDI, but those countries need to work hard to improve their infrastructure, especially supply chain and manufacturing infrastructure.[30] These opportunities combined with China's competitive position are forcing ASEAN to work harder to strengthen the ties among member countries. In addition to the FTA, ASEAN finalized the establishment of the ASEAN Economic Community (AEC) in 2015, which the member countries hope will go beyond trade liberalization and help establish the region as a single market and production base, focusing on political and security issues as well as sociocultural problems.

In order to expand their influence throughout Asia, the ASEAN members are working together with six countries with whom they have a free trade agreement—Australia, China, India, Japan, Korea, and New Zealand—to move toward the creation of a Regional Comprehensive Economic Partnership (RCEP) that will be based on principles of a free trade agreement rather than a comprehensive common market.

APEC comprises 21 countries that border the Pacific Rim; progress toward free trade is hampered by size and geographic distance between member countries and by the lack of a treaty.

Asia Pacific Economic Cooperation (APEC) Formed in November 1989 to promote multilateral economic cooperation in trade and investment in the Pacific Rim,[31] **Asia Pacific Economic Cooperation (APEC)** is composed of 21 countries that border both Asia and the Americas. All but three members of AFTA are members of APEC, plus Canada, the United States, Mexico, Peru, and Chile in the Americas; Australia and New Zealand; and China, Japan, Korea, Russia, and Chinese Taipei. It is a large and powerful organization that is a forum for the discussion of a wide range of activities related to trade and investment, security, energy, sustainability, anticorruption, and transparency, among other things. However, it is not an RTA as defined by the WTO and does not show up on that list of RTAs. The sheer size of APEC is what sets it apart: 2.8 billion people, 59 percent of global GDP, and 49 percent of world trade.

Trans-Pacific Partnership (TPP) The **Trans-Pacific Partnership (TPP)** was initiated by the United States to spur economic growth and create jobs, and it involved Australia, Brunei, Canada, Chile, Japan, Malaysia, Mexico, New Zealand, Peru, Singapore, the United States, and Vietnam. The formation of the initiative was announced in 2011, and the agreement was concluded in October 2015 and signed by the trade ministers in February 2016. However, the U.S. government pulled out of the TPP for political reasons, and it looked as if it were dead. In spite of that, Japan and the remaining 10 members of TPP moved forward and created the Comprehensive and Progressive Agreement for Trans-Pacific Partnership, also known as CPTP, TPP11, or TPP-11. TPP-11 is moving forward with the same structure as the original agreement, and additional countries are looking to join.[32] In spite of the fact that the United States pulled out of TPP, some of the trade rules were incorporated in USMCA.

REGIONAL ECONOMIC INTEGRATION IN AFRICA

There are several African trade groups, but they rely more on their former colonial powers and other developed markets for trade than they do on each other.

Africa is truly the new frontier, with 49 countries in sub-Saharan Africa, and 54 in total. The estimated population of sub-Saharan Africa was 1.078 billion people in early 2019, growing at 2.7 percent annually.[33] However, it is difficult to verify the actual population in each country. The UN keeps revising its estimates of population growth in Africa, but the latest estimates are that sub-Saharan Africa's population will double to 2.5 billion in 2050, up from

1.2 billion people in 2015, with Nigeria having a population of 400 million, up from around 200 million in 2019. In 2015, only China and India had more than 400 million people. Not only is Africa's population large, but it is growing faster than most regions of the world as life expectancy has gone up from 37 years in 1955 to 60 years in 2015. Families are still large as fertility rates are among the highest in the world and infant mortality has dropped.[34] Africa has the fastest-expanding labor force in the world and is expected to surpass China and India in working-age population by 2040.[35]

From the standpoint of regional integration, however, Africa is complicated because of the large number of countries on the continent with multiple ethnic groups and languages and the fact that there are three regional monetary unions and 17 trade blocs. On Map 8.5, we have selected only four of the trade blocs to illustrate the situation in Africa. The problem is that African countries have been struggling to establish a political identity, and the different trade groups have political as well as economic underpinnings. In addition, there are different rules in each group. The key to continued growth in Africa is the reduction of risk as conflicts drop and peace improves. Nearly all 54 countries in Africa belong to more than one trade agreement. Africa's trade with the rest of the world has been more significant

MAP 8.5 Regional Integration in Africa

Although most African nations are members of more than one regional trade group, the total amount of trade among members remains relatively small. African nations tend to rely heavily on trading relationships with countries elsewhere in the world—notably with former colonial and other industrialized nations.

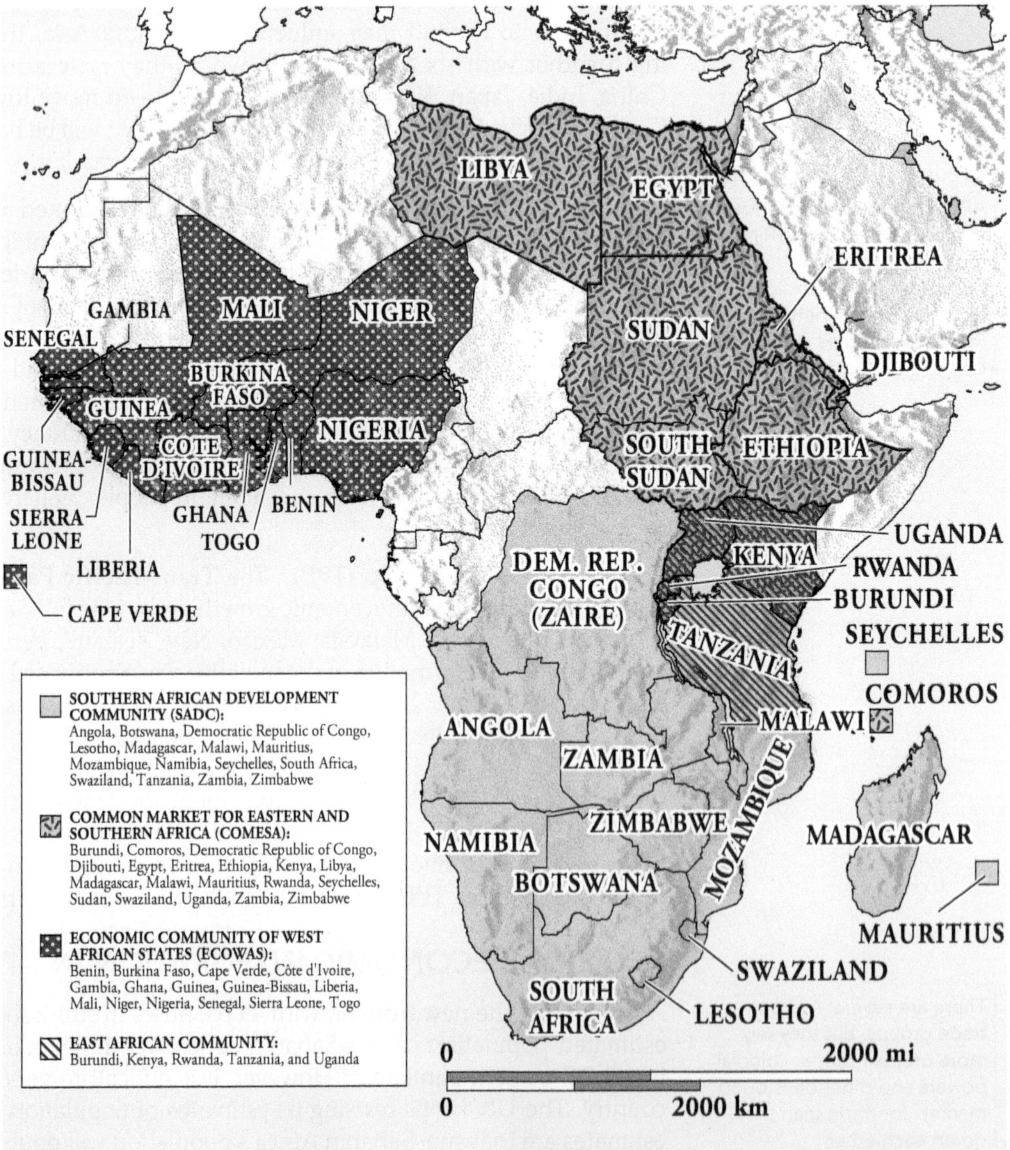

than intrazonal trade within Africa. Initially, trade was dependent on former colonial powers, and then the United States became Africa's largest trading partner. Most recently, however, China has surpassed the United States as the major trade partner with African countries, especially as they have increased investments in oil and minerals.[36]

To illustrate the challenges of economic integration in Africa, ECOWAS is a customs union, but there are lots of exceptions and there has not been a lot of progress on free movement of people, goods, and transportation. The lack of intrazonal trade is generally because most countries rely on export of commodities to developed countries, especially former colonial powers, and they have little else to trade with each other. As a result, they resort to protecting local industry rather than increasing intrazonal trade. The markets, with the notable exception of South Africa, are relatively small and undeveloped, making trade liberalization a relatively minor contributor to economic growth in the region. The East African Community is successful because it only includes five neighboring countries, so it is easier to resolve trade differences, and it has been successful in several joint infrastructure projects. A relatively new agreement was signed in 2015, creating the Tripartite Free Trade Area, which covers 26 African countries that are members of SADC, EAC, and COMESA, and it may be the first step in establishing free trade rules that will allow the countries to expand markets and establish more effective global value chains.[37] These countries represent 50 percent of Africa's GDP and 56 percent of its population.[38]

POINT

Is Regional Economic Integration a Good Idea?

YES A regional free trade agreement among a small group of countries is easy to establish and monitor, unlike the broader agreements of the WTO. It provides a larger market area, which will increase economies of scale and open investment opportunities. An example is USMCA, which only involves three countries, with the United States having a common border with both of the others. Since NAFTA is not a customs union, each country is free to set up bilateral trade agreements with other countries. The other extreme, however, is the European Union. From a trade perspective, the EU includes both a free trade agreement and a customs union.

The EU, unlike NAFTA and most other regional groups, has gone far beyond trade by establishing a common currency, a European Central Bank, a European parliament, and an extensive bureaucracy that is trying its best to bring the region ever closer together. Countries are willing to give up sovereignty in order to receive the economic benefits of being part of a larger community. The advantage of this more extensive approach is that large and small nations in Europe can work together to solve common problems, including migration, security, and economic turmoil. Because of its longevity, the EU has seen its intrazonal trade rise to nearly 50 percent, which is much higher than other regional groups.

Another good example of the positive benefits of regional economic groups is the Dominican Republic-Central American Free Trade Agreement, which links the United States together with six other countries—Costa Rica, Dominican Republic, El Salvador, Guatemala,

COUNTERPOINT

Is Regional Economic Integration a Good Idea?

NO The ongoing battle between the United Kingdom and the rest of the EU, known as Brexit, raises a number of challenges with regional integration. The UK was not one of the original members of the EU, and it decided not to adopt the Euro as its currency, being one of only two member countries (the other being Denmark) that negotiated to opt out of the Eurozone. In some cases, a negative of regional integration is when a country is small relative to other members and thus wields little power. But there is a difference between a free trade agreement and economic integration. A free trade agreement enhances trade but does not compromise sovereignty as much as regional integration at the level of the EU. In 2016, the UK held a referendum on whether to stay or leave the EU, known as "Brexit." In a voter turnout of an amazing 72 percent, Brexit was approved by 52 percent to 48 percent, with 17 million Britons voting to leave the EU.[40]

Those in favor of staying in were the Labour Party, the Liberal Democrats, and business and trade unions, as well as the Brits who lived in London, Scotland, and Northern Ireland. Many Brits who voted against Brexit feared the unknown and possible economic disaster. There didn't seem to be a good alternative to membership in the EU, so why leave? They were worried that if the UK left the EU, they would have to renegotiate all trade and investment relationships with EU countries and who knows what they would have ended up with. There was also a fear that if the UK left the EU, Scottish nationalists, who were not euro skeptics, might resurrect their desire to break away from the UK and join the EU on their own.[41]

Honduras, and Nicaragua. The FTA holds enormous benefits for its signatories: opening the door for increased trade between the United States and the region; stimulating economic growth in the region by encouraging FDI and offering shorter international supply chains; and encouraging economic and political reform in an area historically plagued by Marxism, dictatorships, and civil wars.

The United States has free trade agreements in force with 20 countries, including the members of CAFTA-DR and USMCA. One of the biggest benefits for the United States is reciprocal tariff treatment from the other nations. Due to temporary trade-preference programs and other regional agreements, 80 percent of the products from at least five Central American nations already enter the United States duty-free. Prior to signing the agreement, U.S. manufactured exports were subject to tariffs that averaged 30 to 100 percent higher than those faced by Central American exports when entering the United States.[39] CAFTA-DR allows the Central American nations to maintain these favorable gains, but it also leaves the playing field open for the United States to benefit similarly by reducing restrictions on 80 percent of U.S. consumer and industrial exports to the region.

There were lots of reasons to support Brexit. As noted, the UK was not one of the original six members of the EU, and it never did want to join the common Eurozone. The free flow of labor and open borders are critical to the EU. This seems like a good idea for aging countries that need younger workers, but the increase of migrants from war-torn Syria caused serious political tensions in the UK. Should they continue to have open borders and the risk of escalating social costs? It is hard to reject the EU mandate of the free flow of labor and still be a member of the EU.

A major problem of the EU is the broad diversity of political, cultural, and language forces. Of course, all countries must deal with these differences in normal trading relationships, but the problem with the EU and other regional trade groups is that these factors become more complicated with expansion, and it is harder to find a common ground to solve problems.

A major argument for Brexit is the loss of sovereignty from being a member of the EU. Since the goal of the EU is to keep bringing countries closer together, it is obvious that there will be an increasing loss of sovereignty. But Brexit forces in the UK are particularly concerned about the centralization of power in Brussels, which has affected many aspects of life. The forces leading to Brexit are extreme since they could lead to a powerful country leaving a powerful regional economic alliance, but they are the same forces at the heart of the negotiations of any potential regional economic alliance. For the UK to leave the EU, it had to officially notify the other member countries, which then initiated a complex process to establish the nature of a Brexit. Since the vote, the British government has been trying to negotiate a departure from the EU. This was finally settled on December 12, 2019, when the Conservative Party won a substantial majority in Parliament and the Prime Minister, Boris Johnson, declared that the UK would effectively leave the EU by the end of 2020. The first step occurred at midnight, January 31, 2020, when the UK formally left the EU, However, they had until the end of 2020 to work out the details, especially the development of a new free trade agreement between the UK and EU. In the meantime, they still have trade relationships and commitments that will be in force until they finish negotiations with the EU at the end of 2020. The EU now has 27 instead of 28 members, and in many ways, the UK is considered an outsider with no voting power in EU affairs. As it develops plans with the EU for trade relationships, it will begin negotiating trade deals with other countries, such as Canada and the United States. It will be interesting to see what happens.

THE UNITED NATIONS AND OTHER NGOS

The United Nations The first form of cooperation worth exploring is the United Nations, which was established in 1945 in response to the devastation of World War II to promote international peace and security and to help solve global problems in such diverse areas as

The historic "yes" vote for Brexit in 2016 was followed up by the announcement of Prime Minister Boris Johnson after elections in December 2019 that the UK would definitely leave the EU on February 1, 2020, with final details to be resolved by the end of 2020 after extensive negotiations between the UK and the EU.

Source: FGC/Shutterstock

economic development, antiterrorism, and humanitarian actions. If the UN performs its responsibilities, it should improve the environment in which MNEs operate around the world, reducing risk and providing greater opportunities.

The UN was established in 1945 following World War II to promote international peace and security. It deals with economic development, antiterrorism, and humanitarian movements.

Organization and Membership The UN family of organizations is too large to list, but it includes the WTO, the International Monetary Fund, and the World Bank (the latter two discussed in subsequent chapters). These organizations are all part of the Economic and Social Council, one of six principal organs of the UN System, which also includes the General Assembly, the Security Council, and the International Court of Justice.

The UN has 193 member states represented in the General Assembly, including 15 that compose the Security Council. There are five permanent members of the Security Council—China, France, the Russian Federation, the United Kingdom, and the United States—and 10 other members elected by the General Assembly to serve two-year terms.[42]

UNCTAD was established to help developing countries participate in international trade.

UNCTAD The **United Nations Conference on Trade and Development (UNCTAD)**, is the main UN organization dealing with globalization and development strategies, trade in goods and services, commodities, investment and enterprise development, and trade logistics and human resource development. As a result, it is of greatest importance to companies doing business internationally.[43]

NGOs—private nonprofit institutions that are independent of the government.

Nongovernmental Organizations (NGOs)

Nongovernmental, nonprofit voluntary organizations are all lumped under the category of NGOs: private institutions that are independent of any government. The UN is an intergovernmental organization and thus not an NGO. Some NGOs operate only within the confines of a specific country, whereas others are international in scope. Some NGOs target activities of MNCs whereas others, such as Medicins Sans Frontieres, are global in scope and are concerned with alleviating poverty and global health issues. One of the functions of UNCTAD is to work with NGOs in helping shape policies and activities related to concerns of developing countries. NGOs perform an important role in bringing potential abuses to light and tend to be very narrowly focused, usually on a specific issue (e.g., Transparency International discussed in Chapter 5).

COMMODITY AGREEMENTS

8-5 Describe the forces that affect the prices of commodities and their impact on commodity agreements

The attempts of countries to stabilize commodity prices through producer alliances and commodity agreements have been largely unsuccessful.

Commodities refer to raw materials or primary products, such as metals or agricultural products. Primary commodity exports—such as crude petroleum, natural gas, copper, iron ore, tobacco, coffee, cocoa, tea, and sugar—are still important to developing countries. Out of 189 countries tracked by UNCTAD, 102 (54 percent) generated at least 60 percent of their exports from commodities, and they are concentrated in the developing countries. This is especially true of sub-Saharan Africa where 89 percent of the countries are commodity dependent. Without greater diversity of exports, these countries are especially influenced by commodity price shocks and volatility, factors over which they have little control.[44]

COMMODITIES AND THE WORLD ECONOMY

CONCEPT CHECK

Commodities often represent natural advantages, which we define in Chapter 6 (page 151) as advantages in production resulting from climatic conditions, access to certain natural resources, or availability of certain labor forces.

Both long-term trends and short-term fluctuations in commodity prices have important consequences for the world economy. On the demand side, commodity markets play an important role in industrial countries, transmitting business cycle disturbances to the rest of the economy and affecting the growth rate of prices. On the supply side, as noted above, primary products account for a significant portion of the GDP and exports of many commodity-producing countries.

CONSUMERS AND PRODUCERS

CONCEPT CHECK

Remember from Chapter 6 (pages 155–156) the fact that lower-income countries depend much more on the production of primary products than do wealthier nations; consequently, they depend more heavily on natural advantage as opposed to the kinds of acquired advantage that involve more advanced technologies and processes.

For many years, countries tried to band together as producer alliances or joint producer/consumer alliances to try to stabilize commodity prices. However, these efforts—apart from OPEC, which we discuss below—have not been very successful. UNCTAD established a Special Unit on Commodities to attempt to deal with the issues facing developing countries because of high dependence on commodities, especially agricultural commodities, for export revenues. Given such reliance, UNCTAD is concerned that it will be impossible to resolve poverty issues, especially in Africa, without dealing with fluctuating commodity prices.

The most important international commodity organizations and bodies, such as the International Cocoa Organization and the International Copper Study Group, take part in UN-led discussions to help commodity-dependent countries establish effective policies and strategies. However, each one, such as the International Coffee Organization (ICO), has its own organizational structure independent of the UN. The ICO is composed of 42 coffee-exporting nations—all of them developing countries—and 8 importing nations, most of which are developed countries, although the entire EU is considered one country. ICO members are responsible for over 98 percent of the world's coffee exports and 67 percent of the world's coffee consumption.

Many commodity agreements now exist for the purpose of

- discussing issues,
- disseminating information,
- improving product safety.

Whereas many of the original commodity agreements were designed to influence price through a variety of market-interfering mechanisms, most of the existing ones have been established to discuss issues, disseminate information, improve product safety, and so on. Very little can be done outside of market forces to influence price. The ICO, for example, helps fund projects for coffee-growing nations to combat pests and diseases and to expand coffee consumption through promotion efforts. Coffee consumption varies a lot from country to country, so the promotion efforts supported by ICO are designed to increase per capita consumption in low-consuming countries.

For many years, commodity prices fluctuated but did not increase dramatically. In the decade of the 2000s, however, global economic growth pulled them up. China was growing so fast that it was pulling most commodity prices up, leading to trade agreements between China and many commodity-producing countries, as well as substantial foreign investment. Global economic crises from 2009 to 2020, including the COVID-19 epidemic in 2020, however, caused a significant contraction in commodity prices, which had a negative impact on the economies of the commodity-producing countries.

THE ORGANIZATION OF THE PETROLEUM EXPORTING COUNTRIES (OPEC)

OPEC is a producers' alliance in oil that has been successful in using quotas to keep oil prices high.

Although OPEC supplies oil and natural gas, it's important to understand that the world is dependent on the following main sources of energy: oil (31.1 percent), coal (28.9 percent), natural gas (21.4 percent), and everything else (hydroelectric, nuclear, and renewables, 18.6 percent). In terms of crude oil, OPEC is an important player.

The **Organization of the Petroleum Exporting Countries (OPEC)** is an example of a producer cartel that relies on quotas to influence prices. It is a group of 13 oil-producing countries that have significant control over supply and band together to control output and price. Its members include Algeria, Angola, Ecuador, Indonesia, Iran, Iraq, Kuwait, Libya, Nigeria, Qatar, Saudi Arabia, the United Arab Emirates, and Venezuela. Several of the largest oil-producing countries, including the United States, Russia, and China, are not members of OPEC. In 2019, the United States became the largest oil producer in the world, followed by Saudi Arabia, and for the first time since 1953 became a net oil and gas exporter.

Price Controls and Politics OPEC controls prices by establishing production quotas on member countries. Saudi Arabia has historically performed the role of the dominant supplier in influencing supply and price. Periodically OPEC oil ministers gather together to determine the quota for each country based on estimates of supply and demand. Politics is also an important dimension of the deliberations. OPEC member countries with large populations need large oil revenues to fund government programs. As a result, they are tempted to exceed their export quotas to generate more revenues.

Output and Exports OPEC has 81.9 percent of the world's crude oil reserves, with the Middle East containing 65.3 percent of OPEC's total reserves. Therefore, OPEC can have a strong influence on the oil market, especially if it decides to reduce or increase its level of production.[45]

Sometimes OPEC policies work; sometimes they don't. In addition, events beyond its control can influence prices. The rapidly escalating price of crude oil prior to the global economic crisis was a mixture of rising demand worldwide (especially in China), political instability in the Middle East, and a shortage of refining capacity, caused in part by environmental rules in some countries that preclude the building of new refineries. The fall in prices was due to drop in global economic growth and a reduction in demand for oil.

The downside of high oil prices for OPEC:

- Producers investing in countries outside of OPEC
- Complication of balancing social, political, and economic objectives

The Downside of High Prices Keeping oil prices high has some downside for OPEC. Competition from non-OPEC countries rises because the revenues accruing to the competitors are higher. Because some OPEC countries are putting up roadblocks to production, major producers like BP, ExxonMobil, and Shell are investing heavily in areas like the Caspian Basin, the Gulf of Mexico, and Angola and are trying to enter areas like the Russian Federation. High prices also attract competition from nonconventional oil, (such as oil shale, oil sands, and biofuels, and nuclear energy.Unfortunately for the oil industry, the COVID-19 pandamic has devastated demand and pushed down oil prices to incredibly low levels.

LOOKING TO THE FUTURE Will the WTO Overcome Bilateral and Regional Integration Efforts?

Will regional integration be the wave of the future, or will the World Trade Organization become the focus of global economic integration? Or will bilateral trade deals take the place of both regional and global (WTO) trade efforts? The WTO's objective is to reduce barriers to trade in goods, services, and investment. Regional groups attempt to do that and more. Bilateral deals are the same, but they can sometimes be more successful because you only have two countries trying to come to an agreement. Although the EU has introduced a common currency and is increasing the degree of cooperation in areas such as security and foreign policy, the WTO will likely never engage in those issues. Regional integration deals with the specific problems facing member countries, whereas the WTO needs to be concerned about all countries in the world.

However, regional integration (or even a series of bilateral agreements) might help the WTO achieve its objectives in three major ways. Regional integration:

1. can lead to liberalization of issues not covered by the WTO.

2. is more flexible, given that it typically involves fewer countries with similar conditions and objectives.
3. locks in liberalization, especially in developing countries.

As we have seen in this chapter, no trade agreement is easy or perfect. The WTO has serious challenges due to its size. Regional agreements like USMCA, the EU, ASEAN, and others have many different challenges as well. In cases of USMCA and Mercosur, one dominant country in each (the United States and Brazil, respectively) implies that the balance of power among the member countries is not equal. The EU has its own challenges due to enlargement; the debt crises of several member countries, especially Greece; inward migration from Syria and other countries; and the loss of the UK as a member.

Regional integration in Africa may improve, in spite of the vast size of the continent and the fact that so many countries have common borders with countries that are involved in different regional economic groups. Africa is flush with natural resources and will be a favorite trading partner of resource-hungry China as the Chinese and global economies recover. In addition, greater peace and stability in Africa and the rise in working-age population will make the continent an interesting place in which to invest and a potential source for consumer growth. However, Africa will struggle with dependence on commodities for their exports.

Asian integration, primarily in APEC and the Comprehensive Trans-Pacific Partnership (CPTPP or TPP-11), will pick up steam as the economies of East and Southeast Asia continue to open and as they collaborate to meet the challenge of China. TPP-11, however, has to deal with possible new entrants and their existing trade relationships with countries outside of TPP-11.

CASE

Walmart Goes South[46]

In 2020, Mexico's top retail chains were trying to figure out how to compete with Walmex, the Walmart of Mexico. With the change from NAFTA to USMCA, things have become even more challenging. Since Walmart's aggressive entry into the Mexican food and staples retail market, local retail chains, such as Comerci, Gigante, and Soriana, have found it increasingly difficult to remain competitive. Walmart's strong operating presence and low prices since NAFTA's lifting of tariffs have put pressure on other retail chains, and now their management must determine how to compete against Walmart.

Mexico's retail sector has benefited greatly from the increasing trade liberalization the government has been pushing. After decades of protectionism, Mexico joined GATT in 1986 to help open its economy to new markets. In 1990, with Mexico's economy on the upswing and additional free trade negotiations with the United States and Canada taking place, the founder of Walmart met with the president of Cifra, Mexico's leading retail store. Their meeting resulted in a 50/50 joint venture in the opening in 1991 of Mexico's first Sam's Club, a subsidiary of Walmart, in Mexico City.

It took only a couple of months after the opening to prove the store's success—it was breaking all the U.S. records for Sam's Club. The JV evolved to incorporate all new stores, and by 1997, Walmart could purchase enough shares to have a controlling interest in Cifra. In 2000, the name changed to Walmart de México, S.A. de C.V., and the ticker symbol to WALMEX.

Prior to 1990, Walmart had never made moves to enter Mexico or any country other than the United States. Once it started growing in Mexico, management created the Walmart International Division in 1993. By 2020, Walmart had expanded to 27 countries outside the United States through new-store construction and acquisitions. With growth stalling in the United States, Walmart is looking to international expansion. It currently has more than 11,300 retail units worldwide, operating under 58 banners in 27 countries, and e-commerce websites in 10 countries. In spite of its challenges in some markets, Walmart has flourished in Canada and, most notably, in Mexico. Walmart's operations in Canada began in 1994 with the acquisition of 122 Woolco stores. It now has more than 400 Walmart stores and enjoys strong partnerships with Canadian suppliers. In Mexico, Walmart operates 2,449 units, including Sam's Clubs, Bodegas (discount stores), Walmart Supercenters, and Superamas (grocery stores), and it has become the largest food and staples retailer in the country, followed by Organizacion Soriana.

Given its hit-and-miss success rate on the international scene, it is natural to wonder how much of Walmart's triumph in Canada and Mexico has stemmed from its internal processes, international strategies, and geographic proximity and how much can be attributed to the close economic ties shared by the United States with the two countries through NAFTA.

Walmart's Competitive Advantage

Much of Walmart's international success comes from the tested practices on which the U.S. division bases its success. Walmart is known for the slogan "Every Day Low Prices," which is the core of their value proposition. It has expanded that internally to "Every Day Low Costs" to inspire employees to spend company money wisely and work hard to lower costs. Because of its sheer size and

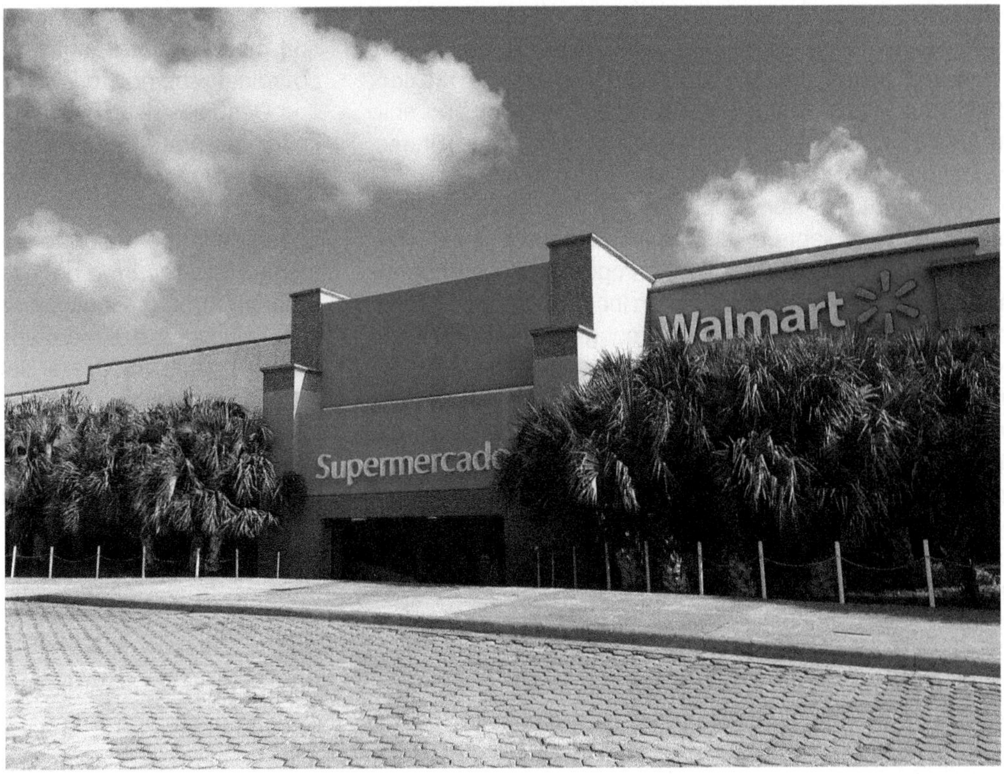

Walmart's Supermercado (Supermarket) store in Playa Del Carmen, Mexico, one of Walmart's 2,449 retail stores in Mexico.

Source: Phortun/Shutterstock

volume of purchases, Walmart can negotiate with suppliers to drop prices to agreeable levels.

The company also works closely with suppliers on inventory levels using an advanced information system that informs suppliers when purchases have been made and when Walmart will be ordering more merchandise. Suppliers can then plan production runs more accurately, thus reducing production costs, which results in cost savings for Walmart and passes on the savings to the consumer as lower prices.

Walmart also has a unique distribution system that reduces expenses. It builds super warehouses known as Distribution Centers (DCs) in central locations that receive most of the merchandise sold in Walmart stores. It sorts and moves the merchandise via a complex system of bar codes, then its inventory information system directs transport to the various stores using its company-owned fleet or a partner. The central distribution center helps Walmart negotiate lower prices with its suppliers because of the large purchasing volumes. These strategies have resulted in great success for the company. And it even uses the second most powerful computer in the world—behind the Pentagon's—to run its logistics.

Walmart in Mexico

Prior to the passage of NAFTA, Walmart faced some challenges as it expanded into Mexico. One of the biggest was import charges on many of the goods sold in its stores, which prevented it from being able to offer its "Every Day Low Prices."

Unsure of local demand, Walmart stocked its shelves with items like ice skates, fishing tackle, and riding lawnmowers—all unpopular items in Mexico. Rather than informing headquarters that they wouldn't need those items, local managers heavily discounted the items, only to have the automatic inventory system reorder them when the first batch sold. Walmart also encountered logistics problems due to poor roads and the scarcity of delivery trucks. Yet another problem was culture clashes between the Arkansas executives and the local Mexican managers.

Some of these problems were solved by trial and error, but the emergence of NAFTA in 1994 helped solve most of them. Among other things, NAFTA reduced tariffs on American goods sold to Mexico from 10 to 3 percent. Prior to NAFTA, Walmart was not much of a threat to companies like Comerci, Gigante, and Soriana, Mexico's top retailers at the time. But once the agreement was signed, the barriers fell, and Walmart was on a level playing field with its competitors—which was all it needed to become number one. However, the retail sector in Mexico is the second most competitive sector of the economy behind auto parts, so Walmart has had its work cut out for it to remain competitive against local Mexican retail chains and other foreign retailers, such as U.S.-based Costco and French-based Carrefour, which sold its outlets to Mexican competitor Chendrauí in 2005.

Since the passage of NAFTA, Mexico has invested significantly in public and private infrastructure, which has helped Walmart to improve the efficiencies in its distribution network. The signing of NAFTA also opened the gates wider to foreign investment in the country. Walmart was paying huge import fees on goods shipped to Mexico from areas like Europe and Asia. Foreign companies knew that if they built manufacturing plants in Mexico, they could keep costs low with Mexican labor and ship to NAFTA's free trade zone—Mexico, the United States, or Canada.

As companies from Japan and China began to build manufacturing plants in Mexico, Walmart could buy their products without paying the high import tariffs. NAFTA resulted in better suppliers due to an increase in competition, competitiveness, and efficiency among companies in order to gain the trust of their clients. Suppliers have invested in being more productive in order to be more competitive, while at the same time gaining greater access to better materials and technologies in the region. Better suppliers also increased the variety of products available to consumers with wider price ranges, which allowed Walmart to offer customers better savings and thus increase their purchasing power. NAFTA also helped Mexico achieve greater economic growth and lower rates of inflation, again adding to the purchasing power of consumers.

Soriana and other retailers have combated Walmart's tactics by lowering their own prices, and Soriana even has flyers in its stores that compare prices from their stores and Walmart's, but on many items, they can't get the prices as low. Walmart's negotiating power with its suppliers is large enough that it can get the better deal. Also, most of Mexico's retailers have priced goods differently. They were used to putting certain items on sale or at deep discount, a strategy known as "high and low," rather than lowering all prices. Though they have been trying to adjust their pricing structure to match Walmart's, they are still frustrated with Walmart's continued cost cutting.

Walmart's Expansion into Central America

Walmart also made two significant changes in its operations in Mexico. First, Walmart de Mexico purchased Walmart Centroamerica in 2009, which included Costa Rica, El Salvador, Guatemala, Honduras, and Nicaragua. One thing that facilitated that acquisition was the fact that Mexico, in addition to being a NAFTA member, signed free trade agreements with 49 countries around the world, including several in Central America. This meant that they could gain access to even more products and suppliers. Walmart worked with thousands of suppliers throughout Mexico and Central America, with more than 60 percent of their supplier base in Mexico composed of SMEs (small- and medium-sized entities). They were also able to better coordinate the network of 14 distribution centers in Mexico and Central America. As a result, Walmart de Mexico (also known as WALMEX) changed its name to Walmart Mexico & Central America (or Walmart de Mexico y Centroamérica).

Second, Walmart established a multi-format operations approach in the region to address different consumer segments. This occurred not only in Mexico but also in Central America through Bodegas and discount stores, hypermarkets, clubs, and supermarkets. Two different store concepts it established are Bodega Aurrera and Superama, both supermarket stores aimed at different demographics. In addition, Walmart has entered the eCommerce area aggressively. It also learned things in Mexico to help target the Hispanic community in the United States by opening a Latin-themed warehouse store in Houston, Texas, called Más, a spinoff of Sam's Club. In addition, Walmart imported products from Mexico for its stores in the United States for the Hispanic community.

Impact of USMCA on the Future of Walmart

In order to help boost the manufacturing wages in Mexico, at least 40 percent of the regional content must come from workers earning at least $16 per hour, a significant increase in Mexican wages. On the one hand, that will increase the earning power of manufacturing workers, but on the other, there may be pressure on other companies like Walmart to raise wages as well. Another impact has to do with digital trade. The agreement strengthens the protection of intellectual property and digital trade, including the ability to transfer data across borders and to limit civil liability on internet platforms. Given Walmart's strong integrated supply chain and its growth in e-commerce, this new provision in USMCA should be a big boost to business.

QUESTIONS

8-3 How much of Walmart's success is due to NAFTA, and how much is due to Walmart's inherent competitive strategy? In other words, could any other U.S. retailer have the same success in Mexico post-NAFTA, or is Walmart a special case?

8-4 What can local Mexican retailers do to compete against Walmart?

8-5 How do you think the passage of USMCA will impact Walmart's strategy in Mexico?

CHAPTER 9

Global Foreign-Exchange Markets

OBJECTIVES

After studying this chapter, you should be able to

9-1 Define what foreign exchange is and who the major players are in the foreign-exchange market

9-2 Summarize the major characteristics of the foreign-exchange market

9-3 Compare and contrast spot, forward, options, and futures markets

9-4 Explain some of the major aspects of the foreign-exchange markets

9-5 Show how companies use foreign exchange to facilitate international trade

Another person's trade costs money.

—Portuguese proverb

Source: Claudine Klodien/Alamy Stock Photo

▲ Western Union Agency in India.

CASE

Going Down to the Wire in the Money-Transfer Market[1]

Long known as "the fastest way to send money," U.S.-based Western Union is the world leader of retail wire transfers—the electronic transfers of funds from one individual or financial institution to another. However, it is facing stiff competition from a variety of sources and is also struggling with a complex economic and political environment.

Western Union was started in 1851 when a group of businesspeople in Rochester, New York, formed the New York and Mississippi Valley Printing Telegraph Company. The name was changed to Western Union in 1861 when the first transcontinental telegraph line was completed. Western Union introduced its money-transfer service in 1871, and in 1989 it began offering the service outside North America. Today, more than 550,000 Western Union agent locations are found in over 200 countries and territories around the world, in addition to more than 100,000 ATMs and kiosks. Because of their global reach, they execute transactions in more than 130 currencies. Western Union operates C2C, B2C, and B2B, although 79 percent of its revenues are C2C (consumer to consumer).

Consumers have many different options when sending money through Western Union: in person, at an agent location, over the phone, or online; via cash, debit cards, or credit cards. And they can use the service at a variety of locations: an actual Western Union office, a grocery store, a post office—just about anywhere people go to transact business. To send money to, say, India or Mexico using a Western Union agent location, the customer fills out a "Send Money" form and gets a receipt, which includes a Money Transfer Control Number (MTCN) to give to the person receiving the funds. To retrieve the funds, the receiver then fills out a "Receive Money" form and presents the MTCN along with valid identification at a Western Union agent location.

CONVERTING CURRENCY

Transfer funds are converted into the foreign currency using an exchange rate set by Western Union. The fees for sending money are determined based on how much is sent, in what form (cash or debit/credit card), and where it is going. For example, sending $500 to Mexico from a convenience store in Washington DC costs $9.00. In this case, payment must be made in cash, the $9.00 fee is subtracted, and the recipient on the other end receives 9,284 Mexican pesos in cash, which is about 1.5 percent less than the going spot exchange rate. Part of Western Union's attractiveness is its speed—it can move cash from one location of the world to another in just minutes.

HOW MIGRATION DRIVES WESTERN UNION'S BUSINESS

From a business standpoint, it is interesting to think of migration corridors, such as the U.S.–Mexico corridor or the India–United Arab Emirates (primarily Dubai) corridor. The larger and more stable the corridor, the more important it is to have the availability of Western Union services on both ends. Migration is based on supply and demand. People generally migrate to other countries because of better economic opportunities, although the flow of immigrants from Syria to Europe is also a function of political unrest and security. The World Bank estimates that the top recipients of officially recorded remittances in this $500 billion annual market are India, China, Mexico, and the Philippines. Each of these countries has large numbers of people working abroad who are sending money home to their families. Relative to GDP, remittances are highest in Tonga (38.5 percent) and Haiti (34.3 percent).

Most of the migrant workers in the United States come from North America (which includes Canada and Mexico), Latin America, and the Caribbean. Most of Western Union's wire transfer business in the United States comes from Mexican immigrants who send part of their paychecks home to support their families. Mexico has historically ranked as the largest host country in Latin America for remittances, followed by Brazil. Remittances often exceed foreign direct investment and overseas aid as sources of foreign exchange. Before the drop in oil prices, annual remittance income passed tourism to become the second-largest source of foreign-exchange income in Mexico, after oil revenues.

COMPETITIVE FORCES

Competition from financial institutions such as banks has pressured Western Union to use better exchange rates. Profit margins in the money-transfer business can reach 30 percent, and many banks have started to offer their own money-transfer services in an attempt to take advantage of the continued expected growth of the foreign money-transfer industry.

This new onslaught of competition by banks has forced Western Union to cut its fees and offer new services, including a home-delivery service, where money is delivered directly to the recipient's door. Western Union is also moving into countries such as China and India to boost its market share. The increased competition has driven down remittance fees around the world. Western Union has also developed other delivery mechanisms, including online and mobile delivery.

In addition, Western Union is affected by currency forces since it is a dollar-based company and earns revenues in other currencies. When the dollar strengthens, its revenues from foreign earnings fall. A slowdown in economic growth worldwide means that some countries are not attractive for immigration due to the lack of good jobs. Terrorism has also forced countries to implement stronger immigration policies and tighten up controls on the movement of money that could be used to finance terrorism.

EXAMPLES FROM MEXICO AND DUBAI

Immigrant workers may complain about the high transfer fees and exchange-rate spread associated with Western Union, but many continue to use this service instead of the lower-cost method of remitting money through banks. For example, Mexico has a history of unstable currencies and widespread inflation, resulting in a traditional mistrust of banks. Other immigrants base their choice of how to remit money on word of mouth or convenience and location.

A major advantage of Western Union is its worldwide availability. For thousands of tiny villages, Western Union is the main link to the outside world. Coatetelco, a small village south of Mexico City, has no bank. Remittances—mostly from agricultural or construction workers in Georgia and the Carolinas—account for 90 percent of the villagers' incomes. Patricio, 49, says that at the end of each month he gets a call from his two sons, who are working in Georgia. They give him a code number, and he drives or rides his horse four miles to the nearest Western Union office, located in a government telegraph office, to pick up the $600 they spent $40 to wire to him. Less expensive remittance services are available at the nearby Banamex branch in Mazatepec, but so far Patricio and his neighbors are not willing to travel the eight miles to get there. Besides, he says, "we do not trust the banks, and they make everything more difficult." Fortunately, costs have dropped dramatically since Patricio first started receiving money from his sons in Georgia.

Dubai, one of the seven states in the United Arab Emirates (UAE), is an interesting point of comparison with Mexico. Although workers from India and Pakistan go to Dubai to work because of higher wages, they are actually recruited by companies in Dubai. Because of Dubai's relatively small local Emirati population (only 19 percent of the total population), there is no way the country could develop without foreign workers—skilled, semiskilled, and unskilled. India is the natural source of workers, with Mumbai only about 1,200 miles (1,900 km) away. Employees must have a permit to work in Dubai, typically for three years at a time. Workers can be sent home whenever their employers decide they are no longer needed. But these workers are critical for the growth of the local economies. They have increased the speed of urbanization, fast-tracked infrastructure and economic development, helped the GCC countries diversify from oil by constructing hotels and tourist attractions, and contributed to solid economic growth.

Western Union, with a deep understanding of the remittance markets, its ethnic marketing expertise, diversified presence and resulting closeness to customers, and its rapid growth in Dubai, has developed high and growing brand awareness there and has worked hard to develop products and messages that appeal to the customers. Dubai and the United States are different in terms of size and the demand for labor, while India and Mexico are different in terms of how and why they supply labor, but there is one constant: people need to move money, and that is where Western Union comes in.

QUESTIONS

9-1 The United Arab Emirates, of which Dubai is a member, is one of the Gulf Cooperation Council members. How does it compare with the other GCC countries in terms of total population and the nonimmigrant population as a percentage of total population? How important do you think migration and therefore capital remittances are for each of the countries in the GCC?

9-2 What forces are likely to have the greatest influence on Western Union's business in the future?

WHAT IS FOREIGN EXCHANGE, AND WHO ARE THE MAJOR PLAYERS IN THE MARKET?

9-1 Define what foreign exchange is and who the major players are in the foreign-exchange market

CONCEPT CHECK

Chapter 1 introduced the multinational enterprise (MNE) and emphasized that MNEs are firms that take a global approach to production and markets. Here we add that the need to deal with foreign exchange is one of the important factors in the environment in which MNEs must conduct business.

Foreign exchange (FX) is money denominated in the currency of another nation or group of nations.[2] The market in which such transactions take place is the **foreign-exchange market**. Foreign exchange can be in the form of cash, funds available on credit and debit cards, traveler's checks, bank deposits, or other short-term claims.[3] As an example, our opening case illustrates how Mexican immigrant workers in the United States often use Western Union to convert dollars to pesos and wire the pesos to offices in Mexico, where relatives can retrieve the cash.

Foreign exchange is money denominated in the currency of another nation or group of nations and an exchange rate is the price of a currency in terms of another.

An **exchange rate** is the price of a currency—specifically, the number of units of one currency that buy one unit of another currency. The number changes throughout the day. On January 1, 2020, €1 could purchase US$1.1221 (or $1 could purchase €0.8912).

The foreign-exchange market is made up of many different players. The **Bank for International Settlements (BIS)**, a financial organization centered in Basel, Switzerland, owned and controlled by 60 member central banks, divides the market into three major categories: *reporting dealers*, other *financial institutions*, and *nonfinancial institutions*.[4]

The Bank for International Settlements divides the foreign-exchange market into reporting dealers (also known as dealer banks or money center banks), other financial institutions, and nonfinancial institutions.

Reporting dealers, also known as *money center banks*, are large financial institutions that actively participate in local and global foreign-exchange and derivative markets. They are widely assumed to include the largest banks and financial institutions in terms of overall market share in foreign-exchange trading, such as Deutsche Bank, Citi, Barclays, UBS, JP Morgan, HSBC, Bank of America, and Goldman Sachs. Because of the volume of transactions that the money center banks engage in, reporting dealers influence price-setting and are the market makers.

The other financial institutions are not classified as reporting dealers. They include smaller local and regional commercial banks, investment banks and securities houses, hedge funds, pension funds, money market funds, currency funds, mutual funds, specialized foreign-exchange trading companies, and so forth. Western Union is a nonbanking financial institution that deals in foreign exchange. Nonfinancial customers comprise any counterparty other than those described above and include any nonfinancial end user, such as governments and companies. In the 2019 BIS Triennial Central Bank Survey of foreign-exchange market activity, 38 percent of the daily turnover was by reporting dealers, whereas 55 percent was by other financial institutions, and only 7 percent by nonfinancial customers.[5]

ASPECTS OF THE FOREIGN-EXCHANGE MARKET

9-2 Summarize the major characteristics of the foreign-exchange market

HOW TO TRADE FOREIGN EXCHANGE

Dealers can trade foreign exchange
- directly with customers,
- through voice brokers,
- through electronic brokerage systems,
- directly through interbanks.

Foreign exchange is traded using electronic methods (eTrading), customer direct, interbank direct, or voice broker. Recently, more than 50 percent of foreign-exchange trading volume was being executed by electronic means. Although connection by voice with a broker is still important for some types of transactions, high touch trades by voice (where the broker provides research and advice) is giving way to low touch voice (which involves a voice transaction combined with eTrading).[6] Different kinds of electronic methods are involved. One is an electronic broking system in which trades are matched up for foreign-exchange dealers using electronic systems such as EBS, Thomson Reuters, and Bloomberg. Another is an electronic trading system that is executed on a single-bank proprietary system or a multibank dealing system. Interbank direct refers to trades between dealer banks via telephone or direct electronic trading.

Foreign-exchange market:
- Over-the-counter (OTC) commercial and investment banks
- Securities exchanges

Electronic services provided for customers also furnish a great deal of market data, news, quotes, and statistics about different markets around the world. It is not uncommon for a trading room to have more than one electronic service and for traders to have different preferences within the same office. Bloomberg and Thomson Reuters provide market quotes from a large number of banks, so their quotes are close to the market consensus.

The foreign-exchange market has two major segments: the over-the-counter market (OTC) and the exchange-traded market. The OTC market is composed of commercial banks as just described, investment banks, and other financial institutions. The exchange-traded market comprises securities exchanges, such as the CME Group, NASDAQ, and Intercontinental Exchange (ICE), where certain types of foreign-exchange instruments, such as futures and options, are traded.

GLOBAL OTC FOREIGN-EXCHANGE INSTRUMENTS

The phrase "global OTC foreign-exchange instruments" refers to *spot transactions, outright forwards, FX swaps, currency swaps, currency options,* and other foreign-exchange products. These instruments are all traded in the markets mentioned above.

The spot rate is the exchange rate quoted for transactions that require delivery within two days.

- **Spot transactions** involve the exchange of currency for delivery in two business days after the day the transaction was made. For example, a bank would quote an exchange rate for a transaction on Monday, but delivery would take place on Thursday.[7] The rate at which the transaction is settled is the **spot rate**.

Outright forwards involve the exchange of currency beyond three days at a fixed exchange rate, known as the forward rate.

- **Outright forward transactions** involve the exchange of currency on a future date beyond two business days. It is the single purchase or sale of a currency for future delivery. The rate at which the transaction is settled is the **forward rate** and is a contractual obligation between the two parties. The forward transaction will be settled at the forward rate no matter what the actual spot rate is at the time of settlement.

An FX swap is a simultaneous spot and forward transaction.

- In an **FX swap**, one currency is traded for another on one date and then swapped back later. Most often, the first or short leg of an FX swap is a spot transaction and the second or long leg a forward transaction. Let's say IBM receives a dividend in British pounds from its subsidiary in the United Kingdom but has no use for British pounds until it has to pay a UK supplier in 30 days. It would rather have dollars now than hold on to the pounds for a month. IBM could enter into an FX swap in which it sells the pounds for dollars to a dealer in the spot market at the spot rate and agrees to buy pounds for dollars from the dealer in 30 days at the forward rate.

Currency swaps, options, and futures contracts are other forms of transactions in foreign exchange.

- **Currency swaps** trade interest-bearing financial instruments (such as loans and bonds) and involve the exchange of principal and interest payments.
- **Options** are the right, but not the obligation, to trade foreign currency in the future.
- A **futures contract** is an agreement between two parties to buy or sell a particular currency at a particular price on a particular future date, as specified in a standardized contract to all participants in a currency futures exchange rather than over the counter.

FX swaps remain the dominant category of instruments with 47 percent of the market, closely followed by spot transactions with 33 percent. Outright forwards represent 14 percent, and options, currency swaps, and other transactions are only 6 percent of the market.[8]

SIZE, COMPOSITION, AND LOCATION OF THE FOREIGN-EXCHANGE MARKET

Before we examine the market instruments in more detail, let's look at the size, composition, and geographic location of the market. The BIS estimated in its 2019 survey of global foreign-exchange activity that daily foreign-exchange turnover was $6.6 trillion, an increase of 33 percent from the 2016 survey.

CONCEPT CHECK

The most widely traded currencies in the world are those issued by countries that enjoy high levels of political freedom (Chapter 3) and economic freedom (Chapter 4).

Using the U.S. Dollar on the Foreign-Exchange Market The U.S. dollar is the most important currency on the foreign-exchange market; in the latest BIS Survey, it was one side (buy or sell) of 88.3 percent of all foreign currency transactions worldwide, as Table 9.1 shows. (Numbers in the table are percentages and add up to 200 percent because there are two sides to each transaction.) Although the dollar, euro, yen, and pound sterling are the most widely traded currencies, the Chinese yuan is steadily growing in importance. In 2019, the yuan became the eighth most-traded currency, and it is expected to increase in importance as the Chinese financial system integrates with the global system.

Source: eye35.pix/Alamy Stock Photo

The financial district in London, known as "the City," handles 36.9 percent of the foreign exchange trading in the world.

TABLE 9.1 Global Foreign Exchange: Currency Distribution

The U.S. dollar is involved in 88.3 percent of all worldwide foreign exchange transactions

Currency	April 2004	April 2007	April 2010	April 2013	April 2016	April 2019
U.S. dollar	88.0	85.6	84.9	87.0	87.6	88.3
Euro	37.4	37.0	39.0	33.4	31.4	32.3
Japanese yen	20.8	17.2	19.0	23.0	21.6	16.8
British pound	16.5	14.9	12.9	11.8	12.8	12.8
Australian dollar	6.0	6.6	7.6	8.6	6.9	6.8
Canadian dollar	4.2	4.3	5.3	4.6	5.1	5.0
Swiss franc	6.0	6.8	6.3	5.2	4.8	5.0
Chinese yuan	0.1	0.5	0.9	2.2	4.0	4.3
All others	21.0	27.1	24.1	24.2	25.8	28.7

Source: Based on Bank for International Settlements, *Triennial Central Bank Survey: Foreign Exchange Turnover in April 2019* (Basel, Switzerland: BIS, September 2019): 10.

There are five major reasons why the dollar is so widely traded:

1. It's an investment currency in many capital markets.
2. It's a reserve currency held by many central banks.
3. It's a transaction currency in many international commodity markets.
4. It's an invoice currency in many contracts.
5. It's an intervention currency employed by monetary authorities in market operations to influence their own exchange rates.

The U.S. dollar is an important vehicle for foreign-exchange transactions between any two countries. Let's say a Mexican company importing products from a Korean exporter converts Mexican pesos into dollars and sends them to the Korean exporter, who converts them into Korean won. Thus, the dollar has one leg on both sides of the transaction—in Mexico and in Korea. Why? One reason is that the Korean exporter might have no need for pesos but can use dollars for a variety of reasons. Or the Mexican importer might have trouble getting won at a good exchange rate if the Mexican banks are not carrying won balances. However, the banks undoubtedly carry dollar balances, so the importer might have easy access to the dollars. Thus, the dollar greatly simplifies life for a foreign bank because the bank doesn't have to carry balances in many different currencies.

The dollar, the most traded currency in the world, is part of the top eight currency pairs: the dollar/euro and the dollar/yen are the top two.

Frequently Traded Currency Pairs Another way to consider foreign currency trades is to look at the most frequently traded currency pairs. The top eight pairs in the 2019 BIS Survey involve the U.S. dollar, with the top two being euro/dollar (EUR/USD)—24.0 percent of the total—and dollar/yen (USD/JPY).[9] Because of the importance of the U.S. dollar in foreign-exchange trade, the exchange rate between two currencies other than the dollar—for example, the exchange rate between the euro and the Brazilian real—is known as a **cross rate**.

The euro is in two of the top ten currency pairs: against the dollar and the British pound. However, the euro is also important for other currencies in the EU that are not part of the monetary union as well as non-EU countries in Europe, such as Turkey.

The biggest market for foreign exchange is London, followed by New York and Singapore.

Given that the dollar is the most widely traded currency in the world, you'd expect the biggest market for foreign-exchange trading to be in the United States. As Figure 9.1 illustrates, however, the biggest by far is in the United Kingdom. The five largest centers for foreign-exchange trading (the United Kingdom, the United States, Singapore, Hong Kong, and Japan) account for 77 percent of the total average daily turnover. The U.K. market is so dominant that more dollars are traded in London than in New York.[10]

FIGURE 9.1 Foreign-Exchange Markets: Geographical Distribution, April 2019

The United Kingdom handles 43.1 percent of all world foreign-exchange activity (compared to just 16.5 percent by the United States). Location is a big factor in the United Kingdom's popularity: London is close to all the capital markets of Europe, and its time zone makes it convenient for making trades in both the U.S. and Asian markets.

Source: Based on Bank for International Settlements, *Triennial Central Bank Survey: Foreign Exchange Turnover in April 2016* (Basel, Switzerland: BIS, December 2016: 14).

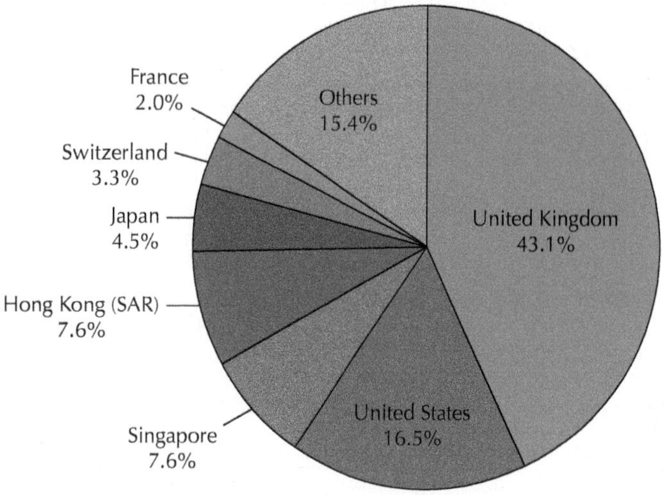

FOREIGN-EXCHANGE TRADES AND TIME ZONES

If the U.S. dollar is the most widely traded currency in the world, why is London so important as a trading center? There are two major reasons. First, London is close to the major capital markets in Europe and is a strong international financial center where many domestic and foreign financial institutions operate. Thus, its geographic location relative to significant global economic activity is key.

Second, London is positioned in a unique way because of its time zone. As Map 9.1 shows, noon in London is 7:00 A.M. in New York and evening in Asia. The London market opens toward the end of the trading day in Asia and is going strong as the New York foreign-exchange market opens up. Thus, the city straddles both of the other major world markets.

Figure 9.2 indicates when trading occurs in each location based on New York time. Because of overlapping time zones, the times of greatest foreign-exchange activity are when Tokyo and London are both open, a period of about two hours, when it is 3:00–5:00 A.M. in New York. The next period of greatest foreign-exchange activity is when New York opens and London is still in full swing, from 8:00 A.M. until 1:00 P.M. New York time. However, London has already been open and active for four hours before New York opens, so New York foreign-exchange traders usually start early so as not to miss the activity in London.

Key foreign-exchange terms:

- Bid—the rate at which traders buy foreign exchange.
- Offer—the rate at which traders sell foreign exchange.
- Spread—the difference between bid and offer rates.
- American terms, or direct quote—the number of dollars per unit of foreign currency.
- European terms, or indirect quote—the number of units of foreign currency per dollar.

MAJOR FOREIGN-EXCHANGE MARKETS

9-3 Compare and contrast spot, forward, options, and futures markets

THE SPOT MARKET

Rates are quoted by foreign-exchange dealers. The **bid (buy) rate** is the price at which the dealer is willing to buy foreign currency; the **offer (sell) rate** is the price at which the dealer is willing to sell foreign currency. The difference between the bid and offer rates is the dealer's profit margin.

Direct and Indirect Quotes Let's look at an example of how a bid and offer might work. The rate a dealer quoted for the British pound on February 12, 2020, was \$1.2964/66.[11] This

MAP 9.1 International Trade Zones and the Single World Market

The world's communication networks are now so good that we can talk of a single world market. It starts in a small way in New Zealand at around 9:00 A.M., just in time to catch the tail end of the previous night's market in New York. Two or three hours later, Tokyo opens, followed an hour later by Hong Kong, then half an hour later by Singapore. By now, with the Far East market in full swing, the focus moves to the Near and Middle East. Mumbai opens two hours after Singapore, followed after an hour and a half by Abu Dhabi and Athens. At this stage, trading in the Far and Middle East is usually thin as dealers wait to see how Europe will trade. Paris and Frankfurt open an hour ahead of London, and by this time Tokyo is starting to close down, so the European market can judge the Japanese market. By lunchtime in London, New York is starting to open up, and as Europe closes down, positions can be passed westward. Midday in New York, trading tends to be quiet because there is nowhere to pass a position to. The San Francisco market, three hours behind New York, is effectively a satellite of the New York market, although very small positions can be passed on to New Zealand banks.

Source: Based on Julian Walmsley, *The Foreign Exchange Handbook* (New York: John Wiley, 1983): 7–8. Reprinted by permission of John Wiley & Sons, Inc. Some information taken from David Crystal, ed., *The Cambridge Factfinders*, 3rd ed. (New York: Cambridge University Press, 1998): 440.

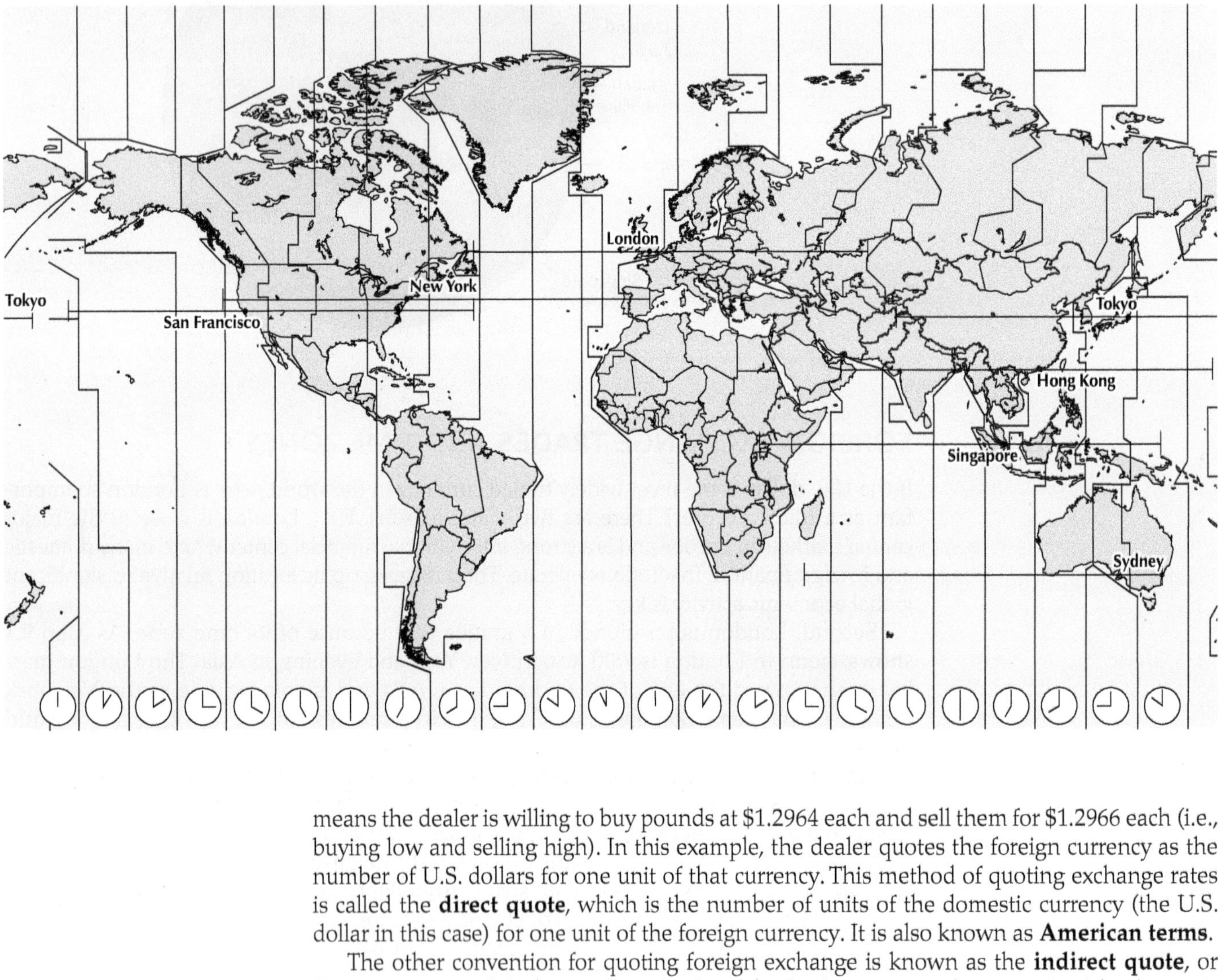

means the dealer is willing to buy pounds at \$1.2964 each and sell them for \$1.2966 each (i.e., buying low and selling high). In this example, the dealer quotes the foreign currency as the number of U.S. dollars for one unit of that currency. This method of quoting exchange rates is called the **direct quote**, which is the number of units of the domestic currency (the U.S. dollar in this case) for one unit of the foreign currency. It is also known as **American terms**.

The other convention for quoting foreign exchange is known as the **indirect quote**, or **European terms**. It is the number of units of the foreign currency for one unit of the domestic

FIGURE 9.2 Overlapping Time Zones and Foreign Exchange Trades

Although foreign exchange is traded 24 hours a day, most of the trading activity occurs when the major foreign-exchange markets, especially London and New York, are open.

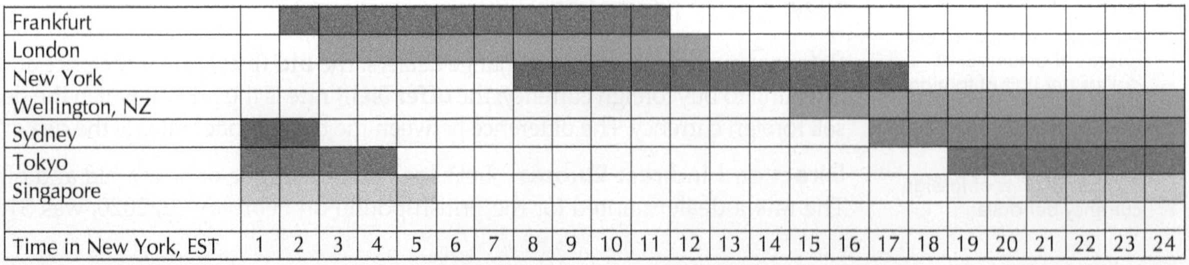
Frankfurt
London
New York
Wellington, NZ
Sydney
Tokyo
Singapore
Time in New York, EST
1 2 3 4 5 6 7 8 9 10 11 12 13 14 15 16 17 18 19 20 21 22 23 24

currency. On February 20, 2020, the indirect quote for the pound was £0.7713, which is the number of British pounds per U.S. dollar.

Base and Term Currencies When dealers quote currencies to their customers, they always quote the **base currency** (the denominator) first, followed by the **terms currency** (the numerator). A quote for USD/JPY (also shown as USDJPY) means the dollar is the base currency and the yen is the terms currency (the number of Japanese yen for one U.S. dollar). If you know the dollar/yen quote, you can divide that rate into 1 to get the yen/dollar quote. In other words, the exchange rate in American terms (the direct quote) is the reciprocal or inverse of the exchange rate in European terms (the indirect quote). For example, on February 12, 2020, the indirect quote for Japanese yen (USD/JPY) was ¥110.01 for one dollar. The reciprocal would be 1/¥110.01=$0.00909.

In a dollar/yen quote, the dollar is the denominator, the yen the numerator. By tracking changes in the exchange rate, managers can determine whether the base currency is strengthening or weakening. For example, on April 1, 2015, the dollar/yen rate was ¥119.75/$1.00, compared with ¥110.01/$1.00. As the numerator decreases, the base currency (the dollar) is weakening. Conversely, the terms currency (the yen) is strengthening.

There are many ways to get exchange rate quotes, including online and print media. Because most currencies constantly fluctuate in value, it is possible to get up-to-the-second quotes from providers like Reuters, Bloomberg, and oanda.com. Quotes are also available from online and printed media such as *The Wall Street Journal* or *Financial Times.*

Interbank Transactions The spot rates provided by *The Wall Street Journal* are the selling rates for **interbank transactions** of $1 million and more. Retail transactions—those between banks and companies or individuals—provide fewer foreign currency units per dollar than interbank transactions.

FORWARDS

The forward rate is the rate quoted for transactions that call for delivery after two business days.

As noted earlier, the spot market is for foreign-exchange transactions that occur within two business days. But in some transactions, a seller extends credit to the buyer for a period longer than that. For example, a Japanese exporter of consumer electronics might sell television sets to a U.S. importer with immediate delivery but payment due in 30 days. The U.S. importer is obligated to pay in yen in 30 days and may enter into a contract with a currency dealer to deliver the yen at a forward rate—the rate quoted today for future delivery.

In addition to the spot rates for each currency, foreign-exchange traders can provide forward rates for most currencies. The most widely traded are the euro, the Japanese yen, the British pound, and the Australian dollar due to their market liquidity. Although forward rates are available for different dates in the future, the more exotic the currency, the more difficult it is to get a forward quote out too far in the future, and the greater the difference is likely to be between the forward rate and the spot rate.

A forward discount exists when the forward rate is weaker than the spot rate.

Forward Discounts and Premiums The difference between the spot and forward rates is either the **forward discount** or the **forward premium**. In order to explain how to compute and interpret the premium or discount, let's use the direct rate between the U.S. dollar and the Swiss franc from the perspective of a U.S. trader—in this case, the number of dollars per franc. If the forward rate for the Swiss franc is greater than the spot rate, the franc would get more dollars in the future, so it would be trading at a premium. If the forward rate is less than the spot rate, the franc would be selling at a discount since it would get less dollars in the future. Assume the spot rate for the Swiss franc is $1.0784 and the six-month forward rate is $1.0808. The premium or discount would be computed as follows:

$$\frac{\$\ 1.0808 - 1.0784}{1.0784} \times \frac{12}{6} = .00445 \times 100 \text{ or } 0.45\%$$

A premium exists when the forward rate is stronger than the spot rate.

The premium is annualized by multiplying the difference between the spot and forward rates by 12 months divided by the number of months forward—6 months, in this example. Then you multiply the results by 100 to put them in percentage terms. Because the forward rate is greater than the spot rate, the Swiss franc is selling at a premium in the forward market by 0.45 percent above the spot rate. During this particular period of time, interest rates in the United States and Switzerland are very close to each other, so the premium is also quite low. During periods of greater divergence in interest rates, the premium or discount could be much larger. In 2007, for example, the franc was selling at a 2.5 percent premium in the six-month forward market.

OPTIONS

An option is the right, but not the obligation, to trade a foreign currency at a specific exchange rate.

An option is the *right,* but not the *obligation,* to buy or sell a foreign currency within a certain time period or on a specific date at a specific exchange rate. It can be purchased OTC from a commercial or investment bank or on an exchange. For example, a U.S. company purchases an OTC option from a commercial or investment bank to buy 1,000,000 Japanese yen at ¥85 per US$ ($0.011765 per yen)—or $11,765. The writer of the option will charge the company a fee for writing it. The more likely the option is to benefit the company, the higher the fee. The rate of ¥85 is called the *strike price* for the option; the fee or cost is called the *premium.* On the date when the option is set to expire, the company can look at the spot rate and compare it with the strike price to see what the better exchange rate is. If the spot rate were ¥90 per US$ ($0.01111 per yen)—or $11,111—it would not exercise the option because buying yen at the spot rate would cost less than buying them at the option rate. However, if the spot rate at that time were ¥80 per US$ ($0.0125 per yen)—or $12,500—the company would exercise the option because buying at the option rate would cost less than at the spot rate. The option gives the company flexibility because it can walk away from the option if the strike price is not a good price. In the case of a forward contract, the cost is usually cheaper than the cost for an option, but the company cannot walk away from the contract. So a forward contract is cheaper but less flexible.

The above example is for a simple, or *vanilla,* option. However, exotic or structured options are used more widely to hedge exposure, especially by European companies. The idea behind them is to provide an option product that meets a company's risk profile and tolerance and results in a premium that is as close to zero as possible. The writer of the option can still make money on the structured option, but if the option is set up effectively, the company buying it won't have to write out a big check for the premium.

FUTURES

A futures contract specifies an exchange rate in advance of the actual exchange of currency, but cannot be tailored to suit a company's needs the way a forward contract can.

A foreign currency futures contract resembles a forward contract insofar as it specifies an exchange rate some time in advance of the actual exchange of currency. However, futures are traded on an exchange, not OTC. Instead of working with a bank or other financial institution, companies work with exchange brokers when purchasing futures contracts. A forward contract is tailored to the amount and time frame the company needs, whereas a futures contract is for a standardized amount and maturity date. Forward contracts are generally more valuable to a company, although futures contracts offer more liquidity and can be extinguished before maturity. Further, futures may be useful to speculators and small companies that cannot enter into forwards.

THE FOREIGN-EXCHANGE TRADING PROCESS

9-4 Explain some of the major aspects of the foreign-exchange markets

When a company sells goods or services to a foreign customer and receives foreign currency, it needs to convert it into the domestic currency. When importing, the company needs to convert domestic to foreign currency to pay the foreign supplier. This conversion usually takes place between the company and its bank.

Sometimes foreign-exchange services are provided by the large money center banks, such as Citi or HSBC, to corporate clients. For mid-market and smaller local companies, services are provided by the local banks who establish correspondent relationships with the larger

FIGURE 9.3 The Foreign-Exchange Trading Process

U.S. Company A received euros in payment for goods and wants to sell them for dollars. To make the exchange, the company contacts a local financial institution or goes directly to a money center bank.

On the other hand, perhaps U.S. Company A expects to receive euros as a future payment. To protect against fluctuations in the exchange rate, it wants to arrange to sell euros in the future. It could choose a forward or a swap, and the path would be similar to an exchange today – through financial institutions.

Finally, either Company A or Company B could choose to convert by such means as an option or a futures contract—in which case the trade could be made by an options and/or futures exchange, either directly or through a broker.

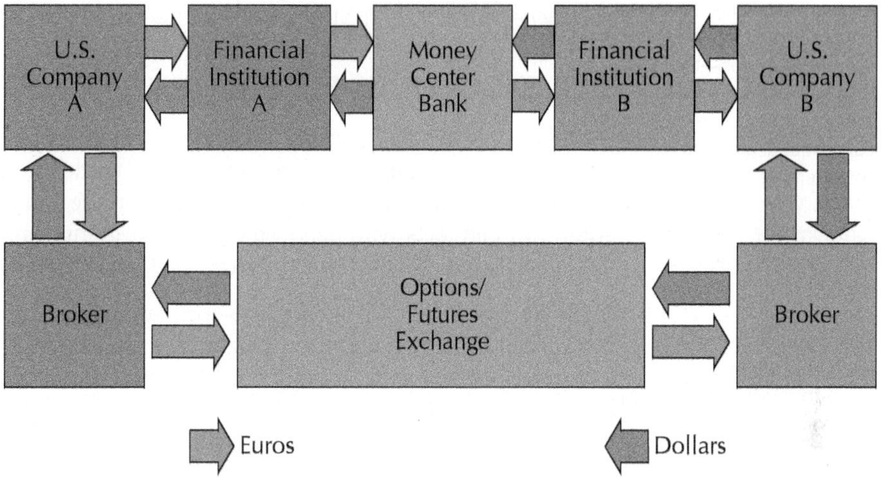

money center banks. The left side of Figure 9.3 shows what happens when U.S. Company A needs to sell euros for dollars. This situation could arise when A receives payment in euros from a German importer. The right side of the figure shows what happens when B needs to buy euros with dollars, which could happen when a company has to pay euros to a German supplier. In either case, the U.S. company would contact its bank for help in converting the currency. If it is a large MNE, such as a *Fortune* 500 firm in the United States or a *Fortune* Global 500 company, it will probably deal directly with a money center bank and not worry about another financial institution. Smaller companies would probably work through Financial Institution A or B (a local or regional bank), which operates through a money center bank to make the trade.

What happens if U.S. Company A is going to receive euros *in the future*? Because it cannot convert in the spot market until it receives the euros, it can consider a forward, swap, option, or futures contract to protect itself until the currency is finally delivered. Financial Institution A can do a forward, swap, or option contract for Company A. However, Company A can also consider an option or futures contract on one of the exchanges, such as the CME Group. The same is true for Company B, which will need euros in the future.

BANKS AND EXCHANGES

At one time, only the big money center banks could deal directly in foreign exchange. Regional banks had to rely on them to execute trades on behalf of their clients. The emergence of electronic trading has changed that. Now even the regional banks can hook up to Bloomberg, Thomson Reuters, or EBS and deal directly in the interbank market or through brokers. Despite this, the greatest volume of foreign-exchange activity takes place with the big money center banks. Because of their reach and volume, they are the ones that set the prices in global trading of foreign exchange.

The top banks in the interbank market are chosen because of their location, expertise in major and specific currencies, and ability to deal in different financial instruments.

Top Foreign-Exchange Dealers There is more to servicing customers in the foreign-exchange market than size alone. Each year, *Euromoney* magazine surveys treasurers, traders, and investors worldwide to identify their favorite banks and the leading dealers in the interbank market. The criteria include transaction volumes and quality of services, their location, the capability of handling major and exotic currencies, their offering of derivatives, and their research and consulting capabilities.[12]

CONCEPT CHECK

Chapter 12 explains why companies establish and maintain effective value chains—frameworks for dividing value-creating activities into separate processes. A reliable value chain permits a firm to focus on its core competencies—the unique skills or knowledge that make it better at something than its competitors. Because managing currencies and cross-trades is typically not among a firm's core competencies, its bankers are key components of its value chain.

Major exchanges that deal in foreign currency derivatives are the CME Group, NASDAQ, and NYSE:ICE.

Given the differing capabilities, large companies may use several banks to deal in foreign exchange, selecting those that specialize in specific geographic areas, instruments, or currencies. At one time, for example, AT&T used Citi for its broad geographic spread and wide coverage of different currencies, Deutsche Bank for euros, Swiss Bank Corporation (now Union Bank of Switzerland) for Swiss francs, NatWest Bank (now part of the Royal Bank of Scotland) for British pounds, and Goldman Sachs for derivatives. Based on the criteria mentioned above, the major banks that deal in foreign exchange worldwide in the 2019 *Euromoney* survey are JPMorgan, Deutsche Bank, Citi, XTX Markets, and UBS.[13]

TOP EXCHANGES FOR TRADING FOREIGN EXCHANGE

In addition to the OTC market, foreign-exchange instruments, mostly options and futures, are traded on commodities exchanges. In the OTC market, companies work directly with their banks to enter into forward and options contracts. On the commodities exchanges, buyers and sellers enter into contracts with each other without going through banks. Three of the best-known exchanges are the **CME Group, NASDAQ,** and **NYSE:ICE (Intercontinental Exchange).**

CME Group The CME Group was formed on July 9, 2007, as a merger between the Chicago Mercantile Exchange and the Chicago Board of Trade. Until approximately 2015, CME operated via open outcry: Traders stood in a pit and called out prices and quantities. Although some open outcry options markets remain in Chicago, more than 80 percent of CME's trading is now electronic. The CME Group handles nearly 5 billion contracts annually across a wide range of commodities, including more than 50 types of foreign-exchange futures and more than 200 types of foreign-exchange options.[14] Contracts are available for the dollar against a variety of currencies as well as cross-trades, such as the euro against the Australian dollar. CME uses three electronic trading platforms to trade different commodities, including currencies: CME Globex, DME Direct, and CME ClearPort.

NASDAQ Prior to 2008, the Philadelphia Stock Exchange was one of the pioneers in trading currency options. In July 2008, it merged with NASDAQ OMX, and in 2014, the name was changed to NASDAQ. It trades options in seven currencies—the Australian dollar, British pound, Canadian dollar, euro, Swiss franc, New Zealand dollar, and Japanese yen.

NYSE:ICE In 2013, Intercontinental Exchange (ICE) purchased NYSE Euronext, forming NYSE:ICE. The combined company is a giant in futures and options. ICE Futures US offers cross-trades in a number of currencies through ICE's futures contracts on key currency pairs traded in the interbank market through an electronic trading platform.[15]

HOW COMPANIES USE FOREIGN EXCHANGE

9-5 Show how companies use foreign exchange to facilitate international trade

Companies enter the foreign-exchange market to facilitate their regular business transactions and/or to speculate. Their treasury departments are responsible for establishing policies for trading currency and for managing banking relationships to make the trades. From a business standpoint, a company, first of all, trades foreign exchange for exports/imports and the buying or selling of goods and services.

When Boeing sells a 787 Dreamliner commercial airplane to LATAM, the largest airline in South America, it has to be concerned about the currency in which it will be paid and how it will receive payment. In this case, the sale is probably denominated in dollars, so Boeing will not have to worry about the foreign-exchange market (nor, in theory, will its employees). However, LATAM will have to worry about the market. Where will it come up with the dollars, and how will it pay Boeing?

CASH FLOW ASPECTS OF IMPORTS AND EXPORTS

When a company must move money to pay for purchases, or receives money from sales, it has choices as to the documents it can use, the currency of denomination, and the degree of protection it can ask for. Although transactions can be settled with cash in advance, it is more common to use a commercial bill of exchange or letter of credit.

With a draft or commercial bill of exchange, one party directs another party to make payment.

Commercial Bill of Exchange An individual or a company that pays a bill in a domestic setting can pay cash, but checks are typically used—often electronically transmitted. The check is also known as a **draft (or commercial bill of exchange)**. A draft is an instrument in which one party (the *drawer*) directs another party (the *drawee*) to make a payment. The drawee can be either a company, like the importer, or a bank. In the latter case, the draft would be considered a bank draft.

A sight draft requires payment to be made when it is presented. A time draft permits payment to be made after the date when it is presented.

Documentary drafts and documentary letters of credit are used to protect both the buyer and the seller. They require that payment be made based on the presentation of documents conveying the title, and they leave an audit trail identifying the parties to the transactions. If the exporter requests payment to be made immediately, the draft is called a **sight draft**. If the payment is to be made later—say, 30 days after delivery—the instrument is called a **time draft**.

A letter of credit obligates the buyer's bank to honor a draft presented to it and assume payment; a credit relationship exists between the importer and the importer's bank.

Letter of Credit With a bill of exchange, it is always possible that the importer will not be able to make payment to the exporter at the agreed-upon time. A **letter of credit (L/C)**, however, obligates the buyer's bank in the importing country to honor a draft presented to it, provided the draft is accompanied by the prescribed documents. Of course, the exporter still needs to be sure the bank's credit is valid as well, since the L/C could be a forgery issued by a nonexistent bank. Even with the bank's added security, the exporter still needs to rely on the importer's credit because of possible discrepancies that could arise in the transaction. The L/C could be denominated in the currency of either party. If it is in the importer's currency, the exporter will still have to convert the foreign exchange into its currency through its commercial bank.

Although a letter of credit is more secure than a documentary draft alone, there are still risks. For the L/C to be valid, all of the conditions described in the documents must be adhered to. For example, if the L/C states that the goods will be shipped in five packages, it will not be valid if they are shipped in four or six packages. It is important to understand the conditions of the documents, as well as counterparty risk. Although a forged L/C is an obvious danger, the global financial crisis exposed counterparty risk when banks did not have sufficient capital to stand behind their L/Cs. In addition, letters of credit are irrevocable, which means they cannot be canceled or changed in any way without the consent of all parties to the transaction.

Confirmed Letter of Credit A letter of credit transaction may include a confirming bank in addition to the parties mentioned previously. A **confirmed letter of credit** thus adds the obligation of an additional bank—sometimes in the exporter's home country, sometimes in a third country—to pay the exporter. It rarely happens that the exporter establishes the confirming relationship. Usually, the opening bank seeks the confirmation of the L/C with a bank with which it already has a credit relationship.

OTHER FINANCIAL FLOWS

Companies may have to deal in foreign exchange for other reasons. For example, if a U.S. company has a subsidiary in the United Kingdom that sends a dividend to the parent company in British pounds, the parent company has to enter the foreign-exchange market to convert pounds to dollars. If it lends dollars to the British subsidiary, the subsidiary has to convert them into pounds. When paying principal and interest back to the parent company, it has to convert pounds into dollars.

Speculators take positions in foreign-exchange markets and other capital markets to earn a profit.

Speculation Companies sometimes deal in foreign exchange for profit. This is especially true for some banks and all hedge funds. But sometimes corporate treasury departments see their foreign-exchange operations as profit centers and also buy and sell foreign exchange with the objective of earning profits.

Investors can use foreign-exchange transactions to speculate for profit or to protect against risk. Speculation is the buying or selling of a commodity—in this case, foreign currency—that has both an element of risk and a chance of great profit. Assume that a hedge fund buys euros in anticipation that the euro will strengthen against other currencies. If it does, the investor earns a profit; if it weakens, the investor incurs a loss. Speculators are important in the foreign-exchange market because they spot trends and try to take advantage of them. They can create demand for a currency by purchasing it in the market, or they can create a supply by selling. However, speculation is also a very risky business. In recent years, the advent of eTrading has attracted a lot of day traders in foreign exchange. The problem is that day traders rarely make money speculating in exchange rates. Forecasting currency movements is a risky business.

Arbitrage is the buying and selling of foreign currencies at a profit due to price discrepancies.

Arbitrage One type of profit-seeking activity is **arbitrage**, which is the purchase of foreign currency on one market for immediate resale on another market (in a different country) to profit from a price discrepancy. For example, a dealer might sell U.S. dollars for Swiss francs in the United States, then Swiss francs for British pounds in Switzerland, then the British pounds for U.S. dollars back in the United States, with the goal of ending up with more dollars.

Here's how the process might work: Assume the dealer converts 100 dollars into 150 Swiss francs when the exchange rate is 1.5 francs per dollar. The dealer then converts the 150 francs into 70 British pounds at an exchange rate of 0.467 pounds per franc and finally converts the pounds into 125 dollars at an exchange rate of 0.56 pounds per dollar. In this case, arbitrage yields $125 from the initial sale of $100. Given the transparency of exchange rate quotes globally, it is difficult to make a lot of money on arbitrage, but it is possible for an investor who has a lot of money and can move quickly.

Interest arbitrage involves investing in interest-bearing instruments in foreign exchange in an effort to earn a profit due to interest rate differentials.

Interest arbitrage is the investing in debt instruments, such as bonds, in different countries. A dealer might invest $1,000 in the United States for 90 days, or convert $1,000 into British pounds, invest the money in the United Kingdom for 90 days, then convert the pounds back into dollars using a forward contract it negotiated at the time of the investment. The investor would pick the alternative that would yield the highest return at the end of 90 days. Given the efficiency of the forward market, arbitrage profits are possible only for investors with unique opportunities.

POINT

Is It OK to Speculate on Currency?

YES People trade in foreign exchange for a number of reasons, and one of them is speculation, which is not illegal or necessarily bad. Just as stockbrokers invest people's money to try to earn a return higher than the market average; foreign currency traders invest people's money in foreign exchange to make a profit for the investors. Speculation is merely taking a position on a currency in order to profit from market trends.

Electronic trading has made it easier for a variety of investors to speculate in foreign exchange. Hedge funds are an important source of this foreign-exchange speculation. However, the transparency in trading has driven the smaller players out of the market and allowed the large institutions and traders to earn profits on small margins that require large volumes of transactions. Hedge funds generally deal in minimum investments that are quite large, so the hedge fund managers that trade in foreign exchange trade in very large volumes. They might make long-term bets on a currency based on macroeconomic conditions, or they might try to balance off buy-and-sell strategies in currencies so that one side offers protection against the other. In either case, the hedge fund manager is

COUNTERPOINT

Is It OK to Speculate on Currency?

NO It depends on whose money you are using to speculate, whether the speculation is supposed to benefit the institution or the trader, and if positions and gains and losses are accurately reported. There are plenty of opportunities for a trader, whether in foreign exchange or securities, to make money illegally or contrary to company policy. The culture of individual traders trying to make money off trading foreign exchange or other securities, combined with lax controls in financial institutions, contributes greatly to these scandals.

One of the most publicized events in the derivatives markets in recent years involved 28-year-old Nicholas Leeson and the 233-year-old British bank Barings PLC. Leeson, a dealer for Barings, went to Singapore in the early 1990s to help resolve some of the bank's problems. Within a year, he was promoted to chief dealer, with responsibility for trading securities and booking the settlements. This meant that there were no checks and balances on his trading actions, thus opening the door to fraud.

In 1994, Leeson bought stock index futures on the Singapore International Monetary Exchange, or SIMEX, on the assumption that the Tokyo stock market would rise. Most dealers watching his feverish trading activity assumed Barings had a large client that he was trading for. It turns out, however, that he was using the bank's money to speculate. Because the Japanese economy betting on the future position of a currency to earn money for the investors in the fund.

Political and economic conditions outside the speculators' control can quickly turn profits to losses. Currencies are inherently unstable. Consider the problems of the U.S. dollar in 2007 and 2008, when it was quite weak against the euro and the yen. What should hedge fund managers do? They might expect the dollar to continue to weaken. But what if it strengthens? Or they might think the dollar has reached its floor and is ready for a rise, which would argue that the managers should buy dollars. But when will it rise and by how much? By mid-March 2008, the dollar had declined by 15 percent in the prior 12 months; 2 months later, many experts felt it had reached a low point and expected it to rise. This was based on market expectations that interest rate cuts by the Fed were expected to stop and that the credit crisis was beginning to soften. Now the speculators had to decide what to do with those expectations. Sometimes speculators can buy a currency on the basis of good economic fundamentals, or they can sell currency because they feel that governments are following poor economic policies. In late 2012, the Japanese economy was very weak, but the yen was strong. As the new Japanese government announced that it was considering policies to weaken the yen, many hedge funds jumped into the market and sold yen, helping to push down the value. At what point do they feel that the yen has fallen enough and that it will rise again? As long as markets are free and information is available, traders ought to be able to make some money on their predictions of the future. There is even a good argument that speculators help keep governments honest by betting in directions they feel reflect political and economic fundamentals.

The key is that currency speculation is a different way to invest money and allows investors to diversify their portfolios from traditional stocks and bonds. Just as foreign exchange can be traded for speculative purposes, trading in shares is also speculation. Even though we call such trades "investments," they are just another form of speculation.

was recovering, it made sense to assume the market would continue to rise, thus generating more profits for Leeson and Barings. Unfortunately, something happened that nobody could predict—the January 17, 1995, earthquake that hit the port city of Kobe.

As a result of the devastation and uncertainty, the market fell, and Leeson had to come up with cash to cover the margin call on the futures contract. A margin is a deposit made as security for a financial transaction that is otherwise financed on credit. When the price of an instrument changes and the margin rises, the exchange "calls" the increased margin from the other party—in this case, Leeson.

However, Leeson soon ran out of cash from Barings and had to come up with more. One approach he used was to write options contracts and use the premium he collected on the contracts to cover his margin call. Unfortunately, he was using Barings' funds to cover positions he was taking for himself, not for clients, and he also forged documents to cover his transactions.

As the Tokyo stock market continued to plunge, Leeson fell further and further behind and eventually fled the country, later to be caught and returned to Singapore for trial and prison. Barings estimated that Leeson generated losses in excess of $1 billion, and the bank eventually was purchased by Dutch bank ING.[16]

In 2012, Bruno Iksil, nicknamed the London Whale because of the large positions he was taking in derivatives trades, engaged in a trading strategy that cost JP Morgan Chase $6.2 billion in losses, far exceeding Leeson's losses. Iksil, a French citizen, was working for an investment unit of JP Morgan Chase in London, and he executed a trading strategy that he claimed was "initiated, approved, mandated, and monitored" by his supervisors. Although four regulators in two countries investigated the case, it was decided to drop charges against him. He supposedly alerted everyone internally about the concerns with the trading strategy and increasing exposure, and someone had to shoulder the blame. Iksil, his boss, and his subordinate were all fired, and JP Morgan Chase paid over $6 billion in fines for fraudulently hiding the amount of the losses and using improper valuation procedures. Speculation is the name of the game, but the key is to make sure regulatory oversight is followed carefully. It's one thing to lose money, and it's another thing to hide the losses.[17]

LOOKING TO THE FUTURE Where Are Foreign-Exchange Markets Headed?

Significant strides have been made and will continue to be made in the development of foreign-exchange markets. The speed at which transactions are processed and information transmitted globally will certainly lead to greater efficiencies and more opportunities for foreign-exchange trading. The impact on companies is that trading costs should come down and companies should have faster access to more currencies.

The Rise of the Yuan

Although the dollar will continue to be the major player in the foreign-exchange market in terms of the total transactions as well as the top currency pairs, the euro and yen will continue to be strong. However, the big change in the future will be the increasing usage of the yuan in global transactions, especially for countries that trade with China. The yuan can only be successful as a major player in the global foreign-exchange market as it becomes more accepted as a reserve currency that countries have confidence in. For that, the yuan will need further liberalization to reduce control by the government and increase the role of market participants. The sheer size of the Chinese economy and the efforts of the Chinese government to move the yuan closer to becoming a global currency will help the yuan become more accepted as a major player in the foreign-exchange market.

Presently, London and New York are the major financial centers for trading currencies. As the yuan increases in importance, it will be interesting to see how much Singapore and Hong Kong will increase in importance, and whether or not Shanghai will increase in importance. Currencies from emerging markets are in trouble and will continue to be so until the global economy exhibits stable growth. Many of these currencies, such as the Brazilian real, are tied to the strength of the Chinese economy. However, Brazil is also suffering from a serious economic contraction that will be a drag for the foreseeable future.

Technological Developments

Technological developments may not cause the foreign-exchange broker to disappear entirely, but they will certainly cause foreign-exchange trades to be executed more quickly and cheaply. The advent of technology clearly has caused the market to shift from phone trades to electronic trades.[18]

Cryptocurrencies

In 2009, Bitcoin was launched as one of the world's first cryptocurrencies, also known as virtual or digital currencies. Although more than 1,600 other virtual currencies have been launched, Bitcoin is still number one—but Ethereum is gaining ground. These digital currencies are based on a blockchain in which every transaction is recorded publicly. Programmers write the software behind the currencies, and "miners" use computers to mint the digital currency. It is estimated that there are around $188 billion of Bitcoin outstanding, compared with $29 billion in Ethereum, and both systems are supported by thousands of computers or nodes.

Bitcoin and other cryptocurrencies are small compared with foreign-exchange markets, but there is substantial interest in these as possible supra-national currencies not affiliated with central banks. Some bankers are anticipating that the dollar will face intense competition as the world's reserve currency.[19] Facebook, Inc., is launching a digital currency, known as Libra, which utilizes blockchain technology. The original plan to base the libra token on a basket of five currencies met resistance from central banks, so the project is being scaled back and will proceed in stages. The blockchain concept is also being considered by banks and corporations for certain types of transactions, and JP Morgan announced in 2019 that it would be creating its own cryptocurrency. Bitcoin and Ethereum, therefore, are looking at different ways to use their digital currencies for legitimate transactions while at the same time working to get regulatory approval and protect their blockchains from illegal activities, including financing terrorism.[20]

CASE

Do Yuan to Buy Some Renminbi?[21]

On November 30, 2015, the International Monetary Fund announced that the Chinese yuan, also known as the renminbi (RMB or "people's currency"), would join the U.S. dollar, the euro, the British pound, and the yen in the basket of reserve currencies known as SDRs, or Special Drawing Rights. Inclusion became effective October 1, 2016. This recognition of the yuan is due to China's increasing dominance in the global economy and its moves in recent years to liberalize its financial markets. However, what does all of this mean to China and the rest of the world, and will China continue down the road to liberalization of its currency and other financial markets?

A Little History

In the currency markets, the sign for the yuan is ¥ (the same symbol used for the Japanese yen) and the code is CNY. On January 7, 1994, the Chinese government, after debating what to do with its currency, decided to fix the value to the U.S. dollar at a rate of ¥8.690 per dollar. This was easy to do, given that currency trading was controlled by the Chinese government and not allowed offshore. In 2004, Hong Kong residents were allowed to exchange local Hong Kong dollars for yuan in a first move to allow some limited trading offshore. By early 2005, the yuan was trading at a fixed rate of ¥8.2665 per U.S. dollar. But pressure began to build in 2005 as both the European Union and the United States faced strong competition from imports from China as well as from Chinese exports to developing markets.

When China fixed the value of its currency in 1994, the country was not considered a major economic powerhouse. Then things began to change. By 1999, China was the largest country in the world in population, and in 2003 it was the sixth-largest in the world in GDP, exceeded only by the United States, Japan, Germany, the United Kingdom, and France. It was also growing faster than any of the top five countries. In the decade of the 1990s, China grew by an annual average of 9.5 percent and was above 8 percent every year in the first half of the 2000s.

Because of China's low manufacturing wages, it was exporting far more to the United States than it was importing. In 2004, it had a trade surplus of $155 billion with the United States, compared with a surplus of only $86 billion with the EU. However, between 2002 and 2004, China's surplus with the EU doubled, while growing by a little over one-half with the United States. Also during that time, there were capital controls on the flow of yuan in and out of China, so there was a tremendous inflow of yuan into the banking sector in China with no real way to move the money offshore. That meant that banks could lend money at very low interest rates, fueling a real estate boom. Also, China had to do something with its building reserves. Initially it invested huge sums of money in U.S. treasury bills, helping to fund the growing U.S. budget deficit. Then it began encouraging foreign direct investment, especially in natural resources around the world.

However, the competitive pressure of China in Asia was not the same. Because most Asian currencies were also locked onto the dollar, the yuan traded in a narrow range against those currencies. Most of the Asian countries were using China as a new market for their products, and they were not anxious to have anything upset the Chinese economy and reduce demand for their products.

Critics from the United States and EU argued that the yuan was undervalued by 15 to 40 percent and the Chinese government needed to free the currency and allow it to seek a market level. The pressures for and against change were both political and economic. The U.S. government had been working with the Chinese for an extended period of time to get them to revalue their currency, but the Chinese government had found plenty of excuses not to do that.

Political Pressures in China

China had its own political pressures. For one thing, a lot of people had been moving currency there in anticipation of a revaluation of the yuan, which was creating inflationary pressures. The Chinese government was forced to buy the dollars and issue yuan-denominated bonds as a way of "sterilizing" the currency—taking it off the market to reduce the pressures. The government was not very excited about revaluing the yuan and rewarding the speculators, so it kept saying it would not announce if, when, or how much the revaluation would be. It also did not want to revalue under pressure from foreign governments lest it appear to be bowing under pressure from abroad.

China also has serious problems with employment. Even though its billion-plus population grows at only 1 percent annually, it adds the equivalent of a new country the size of Ecuador or Guatemala every year. China needs to add enough jobs to keep up with its population growth and displaced workers from its agricultural sector and state-owned firms. That means adding 15 to 20 million new jobs per year, or about 1.25 million per month.

The Advent of the Currency Basket

Given these pressures, China took an historic step on July 21, 2005, and de-linked the yuan from its decade-old peg to the U.S. dollar in favor of a currency basket containing 11 currencies. Although the dollar has been the dominant currency in determining the value of the yuan, there are periods of time when some Asian currencies have also shown themselves to be influential. The currency basket was largely dominated by the dollar, euro, yen, and South Korean won—currencies that were selected because of their impact on China's foreign trade, investment, and foreign debt.

The People's Bank of China (PBOC, the country's central bank) decides a central parity rate daily and then allows a trading band on either side of the decided point. Before the peg was de-linked, the yuan was kept around ¥8.2665; immediately afterward, it rose to ¥8.1011, an increase of 2 percent. The PBOC responded to the pressures by the international community to strengthen the yuan and move closer to a flexible currency regime by widening the trading band, on May 18, 2007, from 0.3 percent to 0.5 percent on either side of the fixed rate. Obviously, that small difference allowed little room for traders.

Playing It SAFE

Until the yuan began its ascent against the U.S. dollar, it was very easy to deal in foreign exchange in China because the rate was fixed against the dollar. It doesn't take a lot of judgment for a trader to operate in a fixed-rate world. The exchange rate is managed by the State Administration of Foreign Exchange (SAFE), which is closely linked to the PBOC. SAFE is responsible for establishing foreign-exchange trading guidelines as well as for managing China's foreign-exchange reserves. A major concern of the PBOC is that China's financial infrastructure might not be capable of trading foreign exchange in a free market.

SAFE was moving to change that. When the PBOC made the decision to loosen up the value of the yuan in 2005, it opted to allow banks in Shanghai to trade and quote prices in eight currency pairs, including the dollar-sterling and euro-yen. Prior to that, licensed banks were only allowed to trade the yuan against four currencies: the U.S. dollar, the Hong Kong dollar, the euro, and the yen. Shanghai was being positioned as the financial center of China. However, all the trades were at fixed rates, and they did not involve trades in non-yuan currency pairs. SAFE also decided to open up trading to seven international banks (HSBC, Citigroup, Deutsche Bank, ABN AMRO, ING, Royal Bank of Scotland, and Bank of Montreal) and two domestic banks (Bank of China and CITIC Industrial Bank).

Fast-Forward

The global financial crisis forced the Chinese government to return the yuan to a peg against the U.S. dollar from July 2008 until June 2010, during which time the United States and China were embroiled in a war of words over the value of the currency. The United States wanted the Chinese to allow their currency to continue to rise to help solve the trade imbalance, and the Chinese wanted the United States to get its economy under control and stabilize the value of the dollar, which had been falling in value against most other currencies. China was even calling for the creation of a new reserve asset to take the place of the dollar in the global economy. Why was China so worried about the dollar's value? Because most of its reserves—the largest in the world at more than $3 trillion, fed largely by its huge trade surpluses—are in U.S. dollars. The last thing China wanted was to have all of its dollar reserves losing value in the global economy.

China's Economic Challenges

By the end of 2010, not only had China replaced Japan as the second-largest country in the world in terms of GDP, it was closing fast on the United States. In addition, China surpassed Germany and the United States as the largest exporter in the world, which meant that it was continuing to generate large foreign-exchange assets that were exposed to losses in value as the dollar fell against other world currencies.

China, however, had its own set of problems, irrespective of what was going on in the West. When it decided to let the yuan gradually rise against the dollar in June 2010, the result was a 3.6 percent appreciation by the end of 2010. However, inflation was rising in China faster than in the United States, so Chinese exports were becoming increasingly expensive. The rise in the currency compounded the loss in competitive position brought on by the rise in inflation. Powerful Chinese exporters were very upset with the idea that the government might free up the currency and accelerate their competitive challenges. Because of inflation, Chinese workers were increasingly unhappy with their working conditions, and they began to demonstrate, sometimes violently. As workers pushed for higher wages, manufacturers faced even greater cost pressures. With general inflation, higher wages, and the possibility of an even more expensive yuan, manufacturers were being forced to move further inland to find cheaper labor, or even move abroad. Many U.S. manufacturers began moving manufacturing back to the United States or to cheaper Asian countries.

Improvement of the Trading Infrastructure

In the meantime, the PBOC announced in 2009 that it was going to allow companies in Shanghai and four other major cities to settle foreign trade in yuan instead of dollars. If Chinese companies can get more exporters and importers to settle their obligations in yuan instead of dollars, they can save a lot of transaction fees and the yuan will gradually increase in importance.

Even though China wants to make Shanghai its financial center, a lot of yuan transactions occur in Hong Kong. For a while, it was the only place outside of mainland China allowed to set up yuan bank accounts. Hong Kong is China's testing ground for the liberalization of currency trading.

The PBOC permitted HSBC and the Bank of East Asia to issue yuan-denominated bonds in Hong Kong in 2007, allowing Hong Kong to increase in importance as an offshore financial center for yuan trading. As banks and companies issue bonds and securities in yuan, the amount of yuan in circulation outside China will steadily grow. In October 2010, ICAP PLC and Thomson Reuters began to trade yuan on their electronic-trading platforms and announced that they were working with banks in the United States and Europe to use their platforms to trade yuan. Before this, banks in Hong Kong were trading yuan with each other OTC or through brokers. The use of the electronic platform promises to increase transparency and traffic.

The offshore market in Hong Kong grew and soon became larger than the onshore market in mainland China. The fixed exchange rate set by SAFE is the most important rate for the onshore market, and the market in mainland China is far more tightly controlled than the offshore market. Even though major money center banks such as HSBC are allowed to trade currency in China, their volume dwarfs that of the large Chinese banks. As those banks gain greater expertise in global trades, they will become even more significant outside of China. As capital controls in China are loosened, the international banks will also have to ramp up their presence there to compete with the huge Chinese banks that are now starting to get involved in the global foreign-exchange trading game.

The 2015 Reform

As China moved closer to the yuan being accepted as a global currency, it widened the trading band around the fixed rate, first to 1 percent in 2012 and then to 2 percent

The Beijing headquarters of the People's Bank of China, the Central Bank of the People's Republic of China

Source: Guenter Fischer/imageBROKER/Alamy Stock Photo

in 2014. The PBOC allowed the yuan to appreciate against a basket of currencies by more than 30 percent, and by 10 percent alone from mid-2014 to mid-2015. The IMF concluded that the yuan changed from being undervalued to "roughly appropriate," although that is disputed by the United States. The government was also moving to allow foreign investors greater access to Chinese securities and make it easier for Chinese to invest abroad. The yuan was still not freely convertible, but a number of central banks began using yuan as reserve assets.

In August 2015, the PBOC announced a new fixing mechanism that moved the exchange rate regime toward a managed float. Instead of setting the daily fixed rate close to the previous day's rate as had been done, the new fix would take the previous day's close only as the starting point. This was important because the yuan had been closing near the (weak) edge of the band from the currency basket. The PBOC also simultaneously allowed the biggest devaluation of the yuan in two decades in order to rekindle economic growth. The PBOC said it was doing this to show that the yuan was more flexible and that it could move both up and down. Every morning, the PBOC sets the value of the yuan, and the feeling is that the devaluation gives the market more freedom in setting rates. However, the devaluation resulted in many Chinese companies paying off foreign debts for fear that more devaluations would occur, and investors switched out of yuan to dollars and other currencies. This forced the bank to spend over $100 billion in August 2015 to support the yuan.

In addition, 2015 saw more non-Chinese banks start using yuan. More than 1000 banks in 100 countries were using yuan for payments with China and Hong Kong, up more than 20 percent compared with 2013. Although Hong Kong is still the major trading center for yuan transactions, London, Singapore, and New York are now top centers as well. Several central banks have entered into swap agreements with China, including the Bank of England and the European Central Bank.

The 2015 reform of the exchange regime has undergone some changes, but is largely intact. The PBOC returned to a currency basket system between February 2016 and May 2017, first using a basket containing 13 currencies that was published in December 2015, and then using an expanded basket of 24 currencies in January 2017. Since then, management of the yuan has been a mix of the currency-basket and managed-float approaches, and the yuan has been stable against the 24-currency basket. The PBOC still has more than $3 trillion in foreign-exchange reserves and is prepared to intervene to maintain the yuan within 2 percent of the daily fixed rate but has not had to do that. And there are still political problems from the regime: the U.S. Treasury declared China a currency manipulator in August 2019 after the yuan broke through the symbolic threshold of 7 per dollar and the PBOC set the daily fixed rate at 7.13. The designation requires the U.S. administration to work with the IMF to eliminate any unfair advantage, but the U.S. dropped the designation in January 2020 after China agreed to make changes.

What's Next?

The yuan will continue to progress toward a flexible exchange rate regime. In spite of the current moves, however, the yuan is still not widely accepted, especially by consumers. In London, for example, the yuan represents only 1.6 percent of daily currency turnover. Chinese tourists can't use yuan for daily transactions, whereas the U.S. dollar and euro are freely accepted. London is trying to attract more yuan deposits, but banks there trail Hong Kong and Singapore by a significant margin. Even though Canada and the U.K. have set up yuan-clearing hubs in Toronto and London, the United States is still lagging behind. Part of that is because U.S. companies can still use dollars to settle transactions with Chinese companies, so they don't see a big demand to use yuan. But the United States will have to take the yuan seriously.

As the renminbi moves closer to being a global currency, China will achieve greater control over global decisions that used to be made by the countries with global reserve currencies. On the other hand, China will lose control over its ability to manage its economy and control its capital flows. It will also have to be more transparent in its financial dealings. Also, to be accepted as a global currency, it will need legal, political, and institutional reforms that will inspire confidence of foreign investors. Is it ready to do that?

QUESTIONS

9-3 Why is it important for the Chinese yuan to become a major world currency? What are the risks for China?

9-4 What role do foreign banks like HSBC and electronic platforms like Thomson Reuters and ICAP play in helping the yuan move closer to becoming a global currency?

9-5 Why is the yuan being used more widely in global business transactions? Do you think it will ever replace the dollar or the euro? Why or why not?

CHAPTER 10

The Determination of Exchange Rates

OBJECTIVES

After studying this chapter, you should be able to

10-1 Describe the International Monetary Fund and its role in exchange rate markets

10-2 Discuss the major exchange-rate arrangements that countries use

10-3 Identify the major determinants of exchange rates

10-4 Show how managers try to forecast exchange-rate movements

10-5 Examine how exchange-rate movements influence business decisions

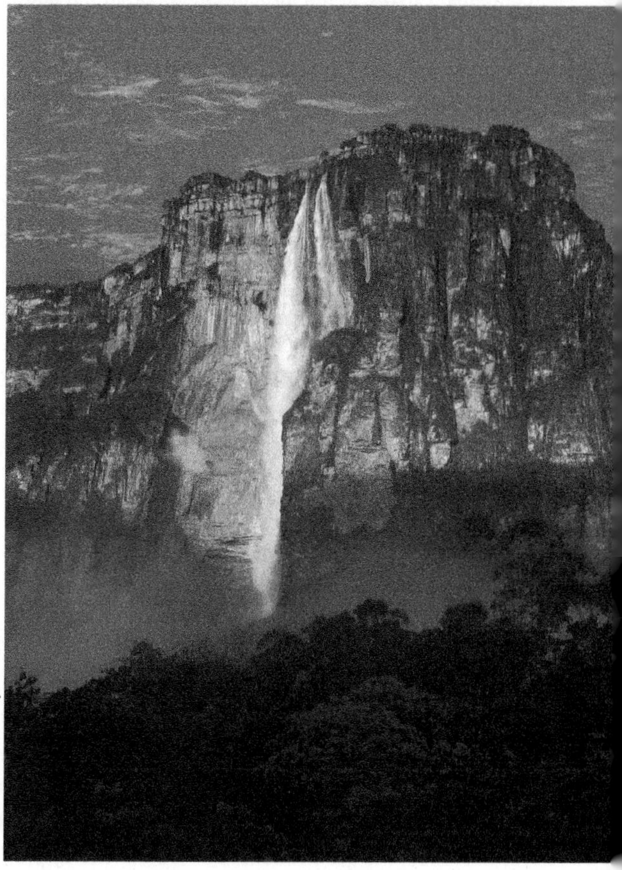

Source: Dim_dok/Alamy Stock Photo

▲ Dawn at Angel Falls, the world's highest uninterrupted waterfall. The 807-meter (2,648-foot) drop is symbolic of the precipitous fall of the Venezuelan bolívar.

One that has no money has no friends.

—Arabian proverb

CASE

Venezuela's Rapidly Changing Currency[1]

Angel Falls in Venezuela is the world's highest uninterrupted waterfall. The 807-meter drop (2,648 feet) is symbolic of the steep fall of the Venezuelan bolívar in the past few years. In 2014, 100 billion bolívares was worth \$15.9 billion, but by 2020 its value plunged to less than 2 cents at the official exchange rate. Just as the mist rises from the floor of the falls, inflation is rising as well. In 2015 when inflation in the developing countries was 5.7 percent, inflation in Venezuela was 159.1 percent, the highest in the world by far. In 2016, inflation rose to 800 percent, and by 2017 it reached 2,616 percent. And it didn't stop there. By 2018 inflation was estimated to be 80,000 percent, and by 2019 economists were quoting numbers in the range of 1,000,000 and 2,000,000 percent. That may not be quite the record of Zimbabwe, which hit 80 billion percent in November 2008, but Zimbabwe figured it out and got inflation under control, at least for a few years.

The bolívar, named after Simón Bolívar, a Venezuelan military leader who was instrumental in South America's revolutions against the Spanish empire in the early 1800s, wasn't always so weak. In 1934, the bolívar (then known as the VEB) was fixed at 3.914 per U.S. dollar, and three years later, it strengthened to 3.18 per dollar. For the next 40 years, the VEB was one of the strongest and most internationally recognized currencies in the region.

The key to the Venezuelan economy is oil. A founding member of OPEC, Venezuela has the world's largest oil reserves. Its state-run oil company, PdVSA, is the largest enterprise in the country. Venezuela has historically been one of the world's top five oil-exporting countries, and it relies on the shipment of crude oil for nearly all its export revenues and a majority of its government's revenue.

Oil and the bolivar are in a symbiotic relationship. In 1983, the VEB was devalued, partially because of the drop in oil prices in the early to mid-1970s. The currency continued to slide, and oil prices took a big hit in the early 2000s as the terrorist attacks on September 11, 2001, led to a slowdown in the global economy. Then strikes in 2002 at PdVSA cut production. In 1998, Venezuela produced 3.5 million barrels of oil per day, but by 2003 output fell to 2.3 million barrels per day. The drop in production and softening of oil prices forced the government to further devalue the VEB to 1600 VEB per dollar in 2003, and foreign-exchange controls were instituted to limit capital flight.

SHORTAGES, CONTROLS, AND NEW CURRENCIES

Hugo Chavez, the president of Venezuela from 1999 to 2013, implemented a program of nationalism, a centralized economy, a strong military, and a focus on social programs for the poor, the basis of his political support. His programs, known as *chavismo*, resulted in huge budget deficits that led to extensive external borrowing as well as a reliance on oil revenues to fund government programs. As oil revenues fell, the government financed deficits by printing more bolívares.

On March 7, 2007, Chavez announced that the currency would have three zeros dropped from the value so that the rate would be 1:1000, and the currency would be renamed the bolívar fuerte or VEF on January 1, 2008. Along with the devaluation of the currency, Chavez instituted foreign-exchange controls. On January 8, 2010, he devalued the currency from 2.15 to 2.60 VEF/$ for some imports and 4.30 for other imports. On April 11, 2011, he changed the VEF to 4.30 per dollar for all imports. The VEF was locked onto the U.S. dollar at a fixed rate known as a conventional peg, and it was not allowed to freely float. However, Chavez retained the right to devalue the VEF if he wanted to.

After Chavez died in 2013, his successor, Nicolás Maduro, continued with *chavismo*. However, that was just before a plunge in oil prices. Shortages began to mount in Venezuela. Russia went through a similar transformation when *perestroika* was instituted in mid-1980s: prices were controlled and shortages were the norm. The joke in Russia was that if you saw a line, you waited in it; when you got to the front of the line, you bought whatever was available; if you didn't need it, someone in your family did. Subsidies on everything from rice to gas to rural homes may seem to make life easier, but it's making things worse. Shortages in everything from pharmaceuticals and medical supplies to toilet paper to diapers have led to the creation of a thriving black market. One woman described how she bought a bag of washing powder for 400 VEF (when the controlled price was actually VEF 32), and she sold it for 600 VEF. Even though this is illegal, it is the norm. Sometimes companies get around the price controls by changing the nature of the product. For example, if they add garlic to rice, they sell it as garlic rice and avoid the price controls on rice. This happens all over the world where there are price controls. You change the ingredients or you change the size of the package.

In February 2015, the VEF was devalued to 6.3 per dollar for most essential imports. Some imports, such as auto parts, could convert currency at an intermediate rate of 12 VEF per dollar, and a free rate, which was about 50 VEF per dollar. The free rate replaced the third tier exchange rate that existed previously. In 2016, President Maduro adjusted the VEF again, this time to 10 per dollar. However, the government adopted a second rate, which allowed it to float against the dollar but was managed by the government and not freely floating. Unfortunately, this also resulted in a black market for the currency. Instead of the fixed rate of 10 VEF per dollar, the black market rate at times was as high as 1,150 VEF per dollar.

Despite the monetary reform, the economy continued to contract. Oil production in 2018 fell to 1.5 million barrels per day, down from 2.8 five years earlier. According to the IMF, gross domestic product fell 50 percent between 2013 and 2018. Venezuela needed another new currency. In March 2018, President Maduro announced the creation of the new bolívar soberano, VES, which would replace the VEF by chopping off three zeros beginning in June. However, implementation delays postponed the introduction of the new currency until August, and by then inflation was so high that the government decided to chop off five zeros rather than three. The VES was also supposedly pegged to a cryptocurrency controlled by the Government of Venezuela, the petro, which itself was supposedly backed by the country's oil reserves; however, there isn't much transparency about this arrangement, and details have not been furnished to markets. One thing we know, unfortunately, is that the introduction of the new currency did not end the inflation. By early 2019, economists estimated that the annual inflation rate reached two million percent!

IS DOLLARIZATION THE SOLUTION?

Obviously, many of Venezuela's problems could be solved with a return to high oil prices. However, that will take too long to alleviate the serious pain being inflicted on the Venezuelan economy. Riots at the end of April 2016 due to power and water cuts and shortages in food and medical imports led to petitions to recall President Maduro. By 2019, over 3 million people (10 percent of the country's total) had the fled the country as refugees. The United States, along with other countries in the region, extended humanitarian assistance. With the economy in collapse, the bolívar became increasing useless. Venezuela risked not having enough bills to circulate in the economy. It doesn't print its own bills but has them printed by companies in France, Britain, and Canada, among others. Even the supply of printed money is subject to shortages. To tame the crisis, in 2020 the government began allowing U.S. dollars to circulate freely alongside the VES, enabling businesses to conduct operations using the dollar.

Chavez said that he would never dollarize the economy, meaning that he would never replace his currency with the U.S. dollar, but he pegged the value of the bolívar to the U.S. dollar. That is mostly because oil is priced in dollars. And while the bolívar is pegged to the dollar, Venezuela has the flexibility to devalue against the dollar if it chooses to do so. That allows it to inflate the currency at will. But there are countries that have successfully replaced their currency with the dollar as their legal tender. Panama did so when it gained independence from Colombia over a century ago. Two other countries in Latin America have adopted the dollar as their currency more recently.

In 1994, the government of El Salvador decided to peg its currency, the colón, to the U.S. dollar. In 2001, it did away with the peg and the colón altogether and adopted the dollar as the national currency, thus completing the transition to dollarization. El Salvador is now one of 13 countries that have entered into an exchange arrangement in which they do not have their own currency; 7 of the 13 use the U.S. dollar. By switching to the dollar, Salvadoran companies and the government gained access to cheaper interest rates because the move eliminated, or at least reduced, the risk of devaluation, thereby infusing more confidence in foreign banks to lend to the country. Corporate borrowing rates in El Salvador are among the lowest in Latin America, and consumer credit rose as the lower rates made it more attractive to borrow.

Ecuador tied its currency to the dollar in 2000. When Ecuador decided to dollarize its economy, the president was in the midst of a political crisis and the announcement was totally unexpected. In 1999, the country's consumer price inflation was 52.2 percent, the highest in Latin America at the time. Until February 1999, the central bank had maintained a crawling peg exchange-rate system. However, pressure on the currency forced the central bank to leave the peg and allow the currency to float freely, upon which it promptly devalued by 65 percent. Finally, the president of Ecuador realized that the best thing to do was dollarize the exchange-rate system. Initially, Ecuador continued to use the sucre, but within a year, it decided to drop the sucre and use the dollar as its currency.

A World Bank official, discussing the rationale for Ecuador's decision, noted that "most countries have a large amount of their debt in dollars, maintain a large percent of their reserves abroad in dollars, and write contracts indexed to the dollar." Moreover, Ecuador, a member of OPEC, generates most of its foreign-exchange earnings from oil, which is also priced in dollars. In some respects, Venezuela is similar to Ecuador in its reliance on oil.

QUESTIONS

10-1 Do you think Venezuela should drop its currency, the VES, and adopt the U.S. dollar? Why or why not?

10-2 If Venezuela does not replace the VES with the dollar, what do you think will happen to the Venezuelan economy, inflation, and the exchange rate?

CONCEPT CHECK

Recall that Chapter 9 discusses the foreign-exchange market, the ways in which currencies are quoted and traded, and the various instruments through which foreign exchange may be traded. This chapter shifts our focus to the ways in which currency values are determined, considering especially the roles of governments and the vagaries of the market.

As we learned in Chapter 9, an exchange rate represents the number of units of one currency needed to acquire one unit of another. Although this definition seems simple, managers must understand how markets and governments set an exchange rate and what causes it to change. Such understanding can help them anticipate exchange-rate changes and make decisions about business factors that are sensitive to those changes, such as the sourcing of raw materials and components, the placement of manufacturing and assembly, and the choice of final markets.

THE INTERNATIONAL MONETARY FUND

10-1 Describe the International Monetary Fund and its role in exchange rate markets

In 1944, toward the close of World War II, the major Allied governments met in Bretton Woods, New Hampshire, to determine what was needed to bring economic stability and growth to the postwar world. As a result of those meetings, the **International Monetary Fund (IMF)** came into official existence on December 27, 1945, with the goal of promoting exchange-rate stability and facilitating the international flow of currencies. The IMF began financial operations on March 1, 1947.[2]

ORIGIN AND OBJECTIVES

Twenty-nine countries initially signed the IMF agreement; there were 189 member countries as of January 1, 2020.[3] The fundamental mission of the IMF is to:

CONCEPT CHECK

Chapter 8 reports on the establishment of the United Nations and the subsequent creation of a number of UN satellite organizations, including the IMF. Today, the IMF is in a position to influence economic policy among UN-member nations.

- Foster global monetary cooperation,
- Secure financial stability,
- Facilitate international trade,
- Promote high employment and sustainable economic growth, and
- Reduce poverty around the world.[4]

Through a process of surveillance, the IMF monitors the global economy as well as the economies of individual countries and advises on needed policy adjustments. In addition to surveillance, it provides technical assistance—mainly to low- and middle-income countries—and makes loans to countries with balance-of-payments problems.

The Bretton Woods Agreement established a par value, or benchmark value, for each currency initially quoted in terms of gold and the U.S. dollar.

Bretton Woods and the Principle of Par Value The **Bretton Woods Agreement** established a system of fixed exchange rates under which each IMF member country set a **par value** for its currency based on gold and the U.S. dollar. Because the value of the dollar was fixed at $35 per ounce of gold, the par value would be the same whether gold or the dollar was used as the basis. This par value became a benchmark by which each country's currency was valued against others. Currencies were allowed to vary within 1 percent of their par value (extended to 2.25 percent in December 1971), depending on supply and demand. Additional moves from, and formal changes in, par value were possible with IMF approval. As we see later, par values were eliminated when the IMF moved to greater exchange-rate flexibility.

Because of the U.S. dollar's strength during the 1940s and 1950s and its large reserves in monetary gold, currencies of IMF member countries were denominated in terms of gold and U.S. dollars. By 1947, the United States held 70 percent of the world's official gold reserves, so governments bought and sold dollars rather than gold. The understanding, though not set in stone, was that the United States would redeem dollars for gold. The dollar became the world benchmark for trading currency and has remained so, in spite of the move away from fixed rates to flexible exchange rates.

THE IMF TODAY

The IMF quota—the sum of the total assessment to each country—becomes a pool of money that the IMF can draw on to lend to other countries. It forms the basis for the voting power of each country—the higher its individual quota, the more votes a country has.

The Quota System When a country joins the IMF, it contributes a certain sum of money, called a *quota*, broadly based on its relative size in the global economy. The IMF can draw on this pool of money to lend to countries, and it uses the quota as the basis of how much a country can borrow from the Fund. It is also the basis on which the IMF allocates special drawing rights (SDRs). Moreover, the quota determines the voting rights of the individual members. The largest quotas are held by the United States (17.45 percent), Japan (6.48 percent), China (6.41 percent), and Germany (5.60 percent). On December 15, 2010, the Board of Governors of the IMF approved a package of reforms that would double the total quotas to SDR 476.8 (about $750 billion at current exchange rates at the time) and shift more of the quota shares to dynamic emerging markets and developing countries. According to the realignment, the United States would still have the largest quota, but the four BRIC countries would be among the 10 largest shareholders in the Fund.[5]

The SDR is

- an international reserve asset given to each country to help increase its reserves,
- the unit of account in which the IMF keeps its financial records.

Special Drawing Rights (SDRs) To help increase international reserves, the IMF created the **special drawing right (SDR)** in 1969 to help reinforce the fixed exchange-rate system that existed at that time. To support its currency in foreign-exchange markets, a country could use only U.S. dollars or gold to buy currency. The SDR is an international reserve asset created to supplement members' official holdings of gold, foreign exchange, and IMF reserve positions. However, the collapse of the Bretton Woods system, the move to floating exchange rates by most of the major currencies, and the growth of global capital markets as a source of funds for governments lessened the need for SDRs. The SDR also serves as the IMF's *unit of account*—the unit in which the IMF keeps its records—and can be used for IMF transactions and operations.

Currencies making up the SDR basket are the U.S. dollar, the euro, the Chinese renminbi, the Japanese yen, and the British pound. The Chinese renminbi (yuan) was added in 2016.

Since October 1, 2016, the value of the SDR has been based on five currencies. The currencies and their weights are: 42 percent for the U.S. dollar, 31 percent for the euro, 11 percent for the Chinese renminbi, 8 percent for the Japanese yen, and 8 percent for the British pound. The Chinese renminbi had not been part of the SDR basket prior to October 1, 2016, and its inclusion was designed to recognize China's importance in the world economy. The weight of the dollar remained unchanged at the time the renminbi was added, but the weights of the other three currencies fell to make room for the renminbi.[6]

THE ROLE OF THE IMF IN GLOBAL FINANCIAL CRISES

An important responsibility of the IMF is to monitor and assess vulnerabilities of the economic and financial policies of member countries in relation to domestic and global stability. Where necessary, the IMF can provide precautionary credit lines to countries that are in distress. The IMF increased lending to member countries during the global financial crisis beginning in 2008 and used its expertise to recommend policy solutions and reforms. During the COVID-19 pandemic of 2020, it announced that it was ready to use its entire $1 trillion lending authority to support its members and the global economy. These loans are short-term emergency assistance loans, and in order to receive a loan, a country has to ensure that it will follow sound fiscal and monetary policies as determined jointly with the IMF staff.[7]

Mozambique has major economic problems, and it was relying on medium- and long-term loans from commercial banks and the World Bank, a multilateral UN-based lending organization that is close to, but separate from the IMF. The IMF had also been working with Mozambique on short-term relief on the assumption that they were accurately disclosing their external debt position. When it was revealed that the government had borrowed far more money than had been disclosed to the IMF, the World Bank and others scaled back their support until after the IMF could complete a study on Mozambique's risk and vulnerability. This is important because donors and other lenders rely on IMF information when determining where and how much to give to emerging markets.[8]

EVOLUTION TO FLOATING EXCHANGE RATES

The IMF's system was initially one of fixed exchange rates. Because the U.S. dollar was the cornerstone of the international monetary system, its value remained constant with respect to the value of gold. Other countries could change the value of their currency against gold and the dollar, but the value of the dollar remained fixed.

Exchange-rate flexibility was widened in 1971 from 1 percent to 2.25 percent from par value.

The Smithsonian Agreement On August 15, 1971, as the U.S. balance-of-trade deficit continued to enlarge, U.S. President Richard Nixon announced that the United States would no longer trade dollars for gold unless other industrial countries agreed to support a restructuring of the international monetary system. That resulted in the **Smithsonian Agreement** in December 1971. The agreement resulted in:

- An 8 percent devaluation of the dollar (an official drop in the value of the dollar against gold)
- A revaluation of some other currencies (an official increase in the value of each currency against gold)
- A widening of exchange-rate flexibility (from 1 to 2.25 percent on either side of par value)

This effort did not last, however. World currency markets remained unsteady during 1972, and the dollar was devalued again by 10 percent in early 1973 (the year of the Arab oil embargo and the start of fast-rising oil prices and global inflation). Major currencies began to float against each other, relying on the market to determine their value. The period from 1972 to 1981 led to the end of the Bretton Woods system and the move to flexible exchange rates.

The Jamaica Agreement of 1976 resulted in greater exchange-rate flexibility and eliminated the use of par values.

The Jamaica Agreement Because the Bretton Woods Agreement was based on a system of fixed exchange rates and par values, the IMF had to change its rules to accommodate floating exchange rates. The **Jamaica Agreement** of 1976 amended the original rules to eliminate the concept of par values and permit greater exchange-rate flexibility.

EXCHANGE-RATE ARRANGEMENTS

10-2 Discuss the major exchange-rate arrangements that countries use

The IMF surveillance and consultation programs are designed to monitor exchange-rate policies of countries and to see if they are acting openly and responsibly in exchange-rate policies.

To foster greater flexibility, the IMF permits countries to select and maintain an exchange-rate arrangement of their choice, provided they communicate their decision to the IMF. The formal decision of a country to adopt a particular exchange-rate mechanism is called a *de jure* system. In addition, the IMF surveillance program determines the *de facto* or actual exchange-rate system that a country uses.

The IMF consults annually with countries to see if they are acting openly and responsibly in their exchange-rate policies. Each year, each country notifies the IMF of the arrangement it will use, and the IMF uses information provided by the country and evidence of how the country acts in the market to place it in a specific category. Table 10.1 identifies the different exchange-rate arrangements that countries have adopted.

THREE CHOICES: HARD PEG, SOFT PEG, OR FLOATING

The IMF requires countries to identify how they base their exchange-rate policy—hard peg, soft peg, or flexible.

The IMF classifies currencies into one of three broad categories, moving from the least to the most flexible. Each category is subdivided into other categories as described below. If they have adopted a hard peg (12.5 percent of the total), they lock their value onto something and don't change. If they have adopted a soft peg (46.4 percent), they are pretty rigid but not as rigid as the hard peg. If they have adopted a floating arrangement (34.4 percent), their value is based on supply and demand. Some countries are not classified.[9]

HARD PEG

Countries can adopt another currency in place of their own, as is the case with Ecuador.

There are two possibilities for countries that adopt a hard peg. The first, called *dollarization,* can occur when a country does not have its own currency but has adopted the U.S. dollar (or possibly the euro) as its currency. Ecuador has been fully dollarized since 2001, and six additional countries are currently dollarized. Three countries have adopted the euro even though they are not officially part of the Eurozone. And other countries are discussed as candidates for dollarization, including Argentina.[10]

The second example of the hard peg is a *currency board,* which is separate from a country's central bank. It is responsible for issuing domestic currency, typically anchored to a

TABLE 10.1 Exchange Rate Arrangements, April 2018

	Percent*	Number
Hard Peg	12.5	24
Soft Peg	46.4	89
Floating	34.4	66
Residual	6.8	13
Total	100.1	192

*Includes 189 member countries plus 3 territories

Source: Based on International Monetary Fund, *Annual Report on Exchange Arrangements and Exchange Restrictions*, 2018 (Washington, DC, IMF, April 2019, p. 5–8).

Another form of a hard peg is a currency board.

foreign currency. Unless the currency board has deposits on hand in the foreign currency, it cannot issue more domestic currency. Eleven countries now have currency boards, of which eight are anchored to the U.S. dollar.[11] Hong Kong is a good example, having maintained 100 percent backing of the Hong Kong dollar with U.S. dollars since 1983. Even though the HK dollar is locked onto the U.S. dollar (at a fixed rate of HK$7.80 per U.S. dollar), it moves up and down against other currencies since the U.S. dollar is a freely floating currency.

SOFT PEG

There are many different kinds of soft pegs, but the most common is a conventional fixed-peg arrangement.

There are several different types of soft pegs, but most countries in this category (43 out of 89) have adopted a *conventional peg,* whereby a country pegs its currency to another currency or basket of currencies and allows the exchange rate to vary plus or minus 1 percent from that value.[12] Most countries use the U.S. dollar and the euro to anchor their pegs. In the other soft peg categories, the degree of flexibility increases, but the IMF determines that the currencies are not floating.

FLOATING

Floating exchange-rate regimes include floating and freely floating.

Currencies considered to be in floating arrangements are either floating (35 countries) or free floating (31 countries). Floating currencies are those that generally change according to market forces but may be subject to market intervention with no predetermined direction in which the currency should move. Free floating currencies are subject to intervention only in exceptional circumstances. The major trading currencies, including the U.S. dollar, the Japanese yen, the British pound, and the euro, are freely floating currencies. Brazil and India, two of the BRIC countries, are considered to have floating currencies.

THE EURO

CONCEPT CHECK

Each commitment to greater economic cooperation represents a step in the direction of regional integration, a form of economic integration we defined in Chapter 8 as the elimination of economic discrimination among geographically related nations. Here we emphasize that the EU has introduced a common currency to its already-existing internal free trade agreement and common external tariff policy.

One of the most ambitious examples of a freely floating arrangement that resulted in countries giving up their own currency to create a new one is the euro. Not content with the economic integration envisaged in the Single European Act, the EU nations signed the Treaty of Maastricht in 1992, which set steps to accomplish two goals: political union and monetary union. To replace each national currency with a single European currency, the countries first had to converge their economic policies.

The European Monetary System and the European Monetary Union Monetary unity in Europe did not occur overnight. The roots of the system began in 1979, when the **European Monetary System (EMS)** was set up as a means of creating exchange-rate stability within the European Community (EC). A series of exchange-rate relationships linked the currencies of most members through a parity grid. As the countries narrowed the fluctuations in their exchange rates, the stage was set for replacing the EMS with the Exchange Rate Mechanism (ERM) and full monetary union.

According to the Treaty of Maastricht, countries had to meet certain criteria to comply with the ERM and be part of the **European Monetary Union (EMU).** Termed the "Stability and Growth Pact," the criteria outlined in the treaty are:

The criteria that are part of the Stability and Growth Pact include measures of deficits, debt, inflation, interest rates, and exchange-rate stability.

- Annual government deficit must not exceed 3 percent of GDP,
- Total outstanding government debt must not exceed 60 percent of GDP,
- Rate of inflation must remain within 1.5 percent of the three best-performing EU countries,
- Average nominal long-term interest rate must be within 2 percent of the average rate in the three countries with the lowest inflation rates,
- Exchange-rate stability must be maintained, meaning that for at least two years the country concerned has kept within the "normal" fluctuation margins of the European Exchange Rate Mechanism.[13]

CONCEPT CHECK

Chapter 12 will point out that when a country initiates a comprehensive policy change over which businesses (whether domestic or foreign) have no control, they should reexamine each link in their value chains—the collective activities required to move products from materials purchasing through operations to final distribution. Here we observe that a change in a nation's exchange-rate regime is just one of the changes in economic conditions that foreign firms can't control.

19 of 27 members of the EU are members of the Eurozone. Denmark has opted out of the Eurozone, and the other members are working to qualify for the Eurozone.

The European Central Bank sets monetary policy for the adopters of the euro.

As of February 29, 2020, 19 members of the EU were officially in the Eurozone, one had opted out (Denmark), and 7 were still preparing to join the Eurozone. The ERM requires countries to have a maximum budget deficit of 3 percent of GDP and public debt 60 percent of GDP. However, the economic crisis of 2008 created problems for countries. For example, Greece's public debt is 181.9 percent of GDP, Italy's is 131.5 percent, and France's is 97.0 percent. Rather than levy major sanctions against these and other members of the Eurozone, there is an attempt to work with them to get them back into compliance.

The euro is administered by the **European Central Bank (ECB)**. The ECB has been responsible for setting monetary policy and managing the exchange-rate system for all of Europe since January 1, 1999. Because the ECB is independent of the political process, it can focus on its mandate of controlling inflation. Of course, different economies are growing at different rates in Europe, and it is difficult to have one monetary policy that fits all. Because of slow economic growth in the EU, the ECB recently adopted a policy of negative interest rates and quantitative easing (printing euros to purchase government debt). Although a popular strategy among the southern European countries that were struggling with high unemployment and budget problems, it was less popular in countries like Germany and the Netherlands where the population was getting very low returns on their savings. But the president of the ECB could see no reason to raise interest rates when economic growth was so slow.[14]

The Euro and the Global Financial Crisis During the financial crisis of 2008, the euro fell because investors were pulling money out of stocks and putting it into safe-haven currencies such as the Japanese yen and the U.S. dollar. When the stock markets recovered, the dollar fell in value and the euro rose. At the time, interest rates were higher in Europe than in the United States, so the euro was perceived to be an investment asset whose value was greater than the dollar. As interest rates fell in the major industrial countries to help stimulate their economies, the interest rate differential disappeared, and currency values began to reflect other factors, such as the perceived strength in their relative economies. This was not helpful to the euro since the European economies were in serious financial trouble.

The role of the European Central Bank is to protect the euro against inflation. However, the weakness in European economies, especially countries like Greece, Italy, and Spain, forced the ECB to use monetary stimulus to attempt to boost economic growth. The hardest hit has been Greece. Because of Greece's large sovereign debt and weak economic growth, it has been difficult for Greece to make debt payments to external creditors. As a result, the European Central Bank teamed up with the IMF and the European Commission, nicknamed the "troika," to help increase financial liquidity and to pressure Greece to solve its budget problems. The ECB's main mandate to control inflation expanded to include increasing liquidity when they approved a European stability mechanism that would enable them to lend to struggling countries that met certain conditions. The idea was to allow the fund to buy bonds from troubled Eurozone governments to keep interest rates low. However, the concern in Europe is that if the ECB purchases bonds that default, the individual governments would be stuck with the bill, which means that taxpayers from the entire EU, especially powerful Germany, could be the ones to pay for Greek debt. Obviously, that is not a politically popular situation.

POINT

Should Africa Develop a Common Currency?

YES So far, we've looked at the success of the EU in initiating a common currency. But what about Africa, the continent of some of the world's fastest-growing frontier economies? The success of the euro and the deep economic and political problems in Africa have caused many experts to wonder whether the continent should attempt to develop one common currency with a central bank to set monetary policy.[15] In 2003, the Association of African Central Bank Governors of the African Union (AU)

COUNTERPOINT

Should Africa Develop a Common Currency?

NO There is no way the countries of Africa will ever establish a common currency, even though the African Union hopes to do so. The institutional framework in the individual African nations is simply not ready. Few of the individual central banks are independent of the political process, so they often have to stimulate the economy to respond to political pressures. If the process is not managed properly and the currency is subject to frequent devaluation, there will be no pride in announced it would work to create a common currency by 2021, but more recently this target has been postponed. This would benefit Africa by hastening economic integration in a continent that desperately needs to increase market size to achieve more trade and greater economies of scale. A common currency would lower transaction costs and make it easier to engage in intra-continent trade.

Africa has several degrees of economic cooperation already, including two forms of currency cooperation that are classified by the IMF as conventional pegs tied to the euro:

1. The Economic and Monetary Community for Central Africa (CAEMC), including Cameroon, Central African Republic, Chad, Republic of Congo, Equatorial Guinea, and Gabon
2. The West African Economic and Monetary Union (WAEMU), including Benin, Burkina Faso, Côte d'Ivoire, Guinea-Bissau, Mali, Niger, Senegal, and Togo

Both monetary unions are part of the CFA franc zone. Their respective currencies are the Central African CFA franc and the West African CFA franc. The French treasury guarantees the full convertibility of both currencies.[16] WAEMU recently began working with France on reforms to the arrangement, and wants to rename the currency the "eco," a reference to the Economic Community of West African States (ECOWAS), of which WAEMU member countries are a part. Leaders of the 15 ECOWAS nations announced an agreement in June 2019 to adopt a common currency for the entire region.[17]

In addition to the two regional monetary unions, there is also a Common Monetary Area in which Namibia, Lesotho, and Swaziland peg their currency to the South African rand within the Southern African Customs Union. Africa also has several existing regional economic communities: Arab Maghreb Union, Common Market for Eastern and Southern Africa, Economic Community of Central African States, Economic Community of West African States (ECOWAS), East African Community, and Southern African Development Community. These groups are working hard to reduce trade barriers and increase trade among member countries, so all they would have to do is combine into one large African economic union, form a central bank, and establish a common monetary policy like the EU has. The East African Community Council of Ministers announced in 2013 that it planned to establish an East African Bank to facilitate the development of a common currency within 10 years, but that assumes the countries can resolve issues of differences in GDP, currencies, and institutions.[18]

A major advantage of establishing a central bank and common currency for Africa is that institutions in each nation will have to improve, and the central bank may be able to insulate the monetary policy from political pressures, which often create inflationary pressures and subsequent devaluations.

the region or clout on the international stage. The only two regional economic groups that are successful at this point have adopted the euro as their reference point, and the French treasury is backing up their currencies, so it is acting as if it is the central bank. Even the plan to adopt a common currency for ECOWAS has run into friction between the francophone WAEMU countries and the Anglophone countries (Ghana, Nigeria, Gambia, Liberia, and Sierra Leone) that advocate different arrangements.[19]

Further, each country will have to give up monetary sovereignty and rely on other measures—such as labor mobility, wage and price flexibility, and fiscal transfers—to weather shocks. Even though there is good labor mobility in Africa, it is difficult to imagine that the African countries will be able to transfer tax revenues from country to country to help stimulate growth. In addition, it is difficult to transfer goods among the different countries in Africa because of transportation problems.

The establishment of the euro in the EU was a monumental task that took years, following a successful customs union and a gradual tightening of the ERM in Europe. For Africa to establish a common currency there must first be closer economic integration. Thus, it is important to be patient and give Africa a chance to move forward. Maybe one way to move to a common currency is to strengthen the existing regional monetary unions and then gradually open them up to neighboring countries until there are a few huge monetary unions. These can then discuss ways to link together into a common African currency.

DETERMINING EXCHANGE RATES

10-3 Identify the major determinants of exchange rates

A lot of different factors cause exchange rates to adjust. The exchange-rate regimes described earlier in the chapter are either fixed (hard peg or soft peg) or floating, with fixed rates varying in terms of how fixed they are and floating rates varying in terms of how much they actually float. However, currencies change in different ways depending on the type of regime.

NONINTERVENTION: CURRENCY IN A FLOATING-RATE WORLD

Demand for a country's currency is a function of the demand for that country's goods and services and financial assets.

Currencies that freely float respond to supply and demand conditions. This concept can be illustrated using a two-country model involving the United States and Japan. Figure 10.1 shows the equilibrium exchange rate in the market and then a movement to a new equilibrium level as the market changes. The demand for yen in this example is a function of U.S. demand for Japanese goods and services, such as automobiles, and yen-denominated financial assets, such as securities.

The supply of yen is a function of Japanese demand for U.S. goods and services and dollar-denominated financial assets. Initially, this supply of and demand for yen meet at the equilibrium exchange rate e_0 (for example, 0.00926 dollar per yen, or 108 yen per dollar) and the quantity of yen Q_1.

Assume that Japanese consumers' demand for U.S. goods and services drops because of, say, high U.S. inflation. This lessening demand would result in a reduced supply of yen in the foreign-exchange market, causing the supply curve to shift to S'. Simultaneously, the rising prices of U.S. goods might lead to an increase in American consumers' demand for Japanese goods and services, which in turn would lead to an increase in demand for yen in the market, causing the demand curve to shift to D', and finally to an increase in the quantity of yen and in the exchange rate.

The new equilibrium exchange rate would be at e_1 (for example, 0.00943 dollar per yen, or 106 yen per dollar). From a dollar standpoint, the higher demand for Japanese goods would increase the supply of dollars as more consumers tried to trade their dollars for yen, and the reduced demand for U.S. goods would result in a drop in demand for dollars, causing a reduction in the dollar's value against the yen.

FIGURE 10.1 The Equilibrium Exchange Rate and How It Moves

If inflation in the United States is higher than in Japan, U.S. consumers will want more Japanese goods and services and Japanese consumers will want fewer U.S. goods and services. As a result, the demand for the Japanese yen will go up, but the supply will go down, and the yen will appreciate from e_0 to e_1. What if Japan wants to keep the dollar/yen exchange rate at e_0? It can sell the quantity $(Q_3 - Q_2)$ of yen for dollars.

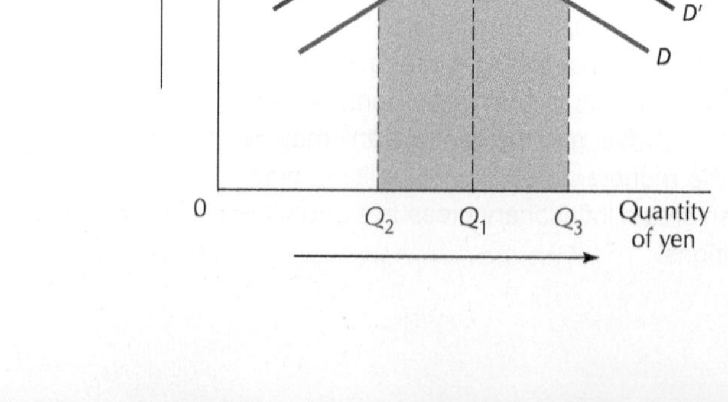

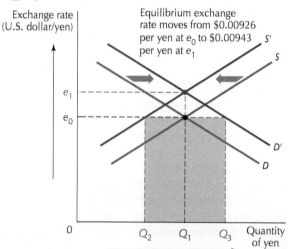

INTERVENTION: CURRENCY IN A FIXED-RATE OR MANAGED FLOATING-RATE WORLD

In the preceding example, Japanese and U.S. authorities allowed supply and demand to determine the values of the yen and dollar. However, the United States and Japan could decide to manage their exchange rates. Although both currencies are independently floating, their respective governments could intervene in the market. The U.S. government might not want its currency to weaken because its companies and consumers would have to pay more for Japanese products, which would lead to more inflationary pressure in the United States. Or the Japanese government might not want the yen to strengthen because it would mean unemployment in its export industries. Let's examine the role of central banks in this process.

Central banks control policies that affect the value of currencies; the Federal Reserve Bank of New York is responsible for foreign-exchange market operationsin the United States.

The Role of Central Banks Each country has a central bank responsible for the policies affecting the value of its currency, although countries with independent currency boards use them to control the currency value. In the United States, the New York Federal Reserve Bank, in close coordination with and representing the Federal Reserve System of 12 regional banks and the U.S. Treasury, is responsible for intervening in foreign-exchange markets to achieve dollar exchange-rate policy objectives and counter disorderly conditions in foreign-exchange markets. The U.S. Treasury is responsible for setting exchange-rate policy, whereas the Fed is the central bank and is responsible for executing foreign-exchange intervention. Further, the New York Fed serves as a fiscal agent in the United States for foreign central banks and official international financial organizations.[20]

In the European Union, the European Central Bank coordinates the activities of each member country's central bank, such as the Bundesbank in Germany, to establish a common monetary policy in Europe, much as the Fed does in the United States.

Central bank reserve assets are kept in three major forms: gold, foreign-exchange reserves, and IMF-related assets. Foreign exchange is 90 percent of reserve assets worldwide.

Central Bank Reserve Assets Central banks hold foreign currencies in what is known as **international reserves**. These reserve assets are kept in three major forms: foreign-exchange reserves, IMF-related assets (including SDRs), and gold. Foreign exchange composes over 90 percent of total reserves worldwide. In third quarter 2019, the U.S. dollar represented 62 percent of total foreign-exchange reserves, followed by the euro at 20 percent, the Japanese yen at 6 percent, and the British pound at 4 percent.[21] The countries with the most foreign-exchange reserves are China, Japan, Europe (the Eurozone), and Switzerland.

Having strong central bank reserve assets is essential to a country's fiscal strength. When the financial crises in Asia, Russia, and South America hit in the late 1990s, very few countries had strong central bank reserve assets. As a result, they had to borrow a lot of U.S. dollars, which turned out to be devastating when they finally had to devalue their currencies. Since 2000, however, the picture has changed. Due to strong commodity prices, expanding exports, and restraint in incurring dollar debt, many of those same countries have strengthened their financial position by increasing their reserves.

Central banks intervene in currency markets by buying and selling currency to affect its price.

How Central Banks Intervene in the Market A central bank can intervene in currency markets in several ways. The U.S. Fed, for example, can use foreign currencies to buy dollars when the dollar is weak, or sell dollars for foreign currency when the dollar is strong. Central banks may coordinate actions with other central banks, make policy statements to influence markets, and intervene to reverse, resist, or support a market trend.

Different Attitudes Toward Intervention Government policies change over time, depending on economic conditions and the attitude of the prevailing administration in power, irrespective of whether the currency is considered to be freely floating.

The global financial crisis roiled foreign-exchange markets and forced many central banks to intervene to support their currencies. Many emerging-economy central banks have been active in foreign exchange markets ever since the crisis, as they seek to improve liquidity and stability in the markets.[22] During the crisis, Switzerland placed a cap on its exchange rate against the euro and kept it in place for 3½ years. It eliminated the cap in January 2015 because it was concerned about the stability of the euro, coupled with the problems of falling energy prices and a rising dollar. Removal of the cap caused a rapid rise in the Swiss franc against the euro.[23]

Challenges with Intervention In general, it is very difficult, if not impossible, for intervention to have a lasting effect on the value of a currency. Given the daily volume of foreign-exchange transactions, no one government can move the market unless its movements can change market psychology. Intervention may temporarily halt a slide, but the country cannot force the market to move in a direction it doesn't want to go, at least for the long run.

BLACK MARKETS

A black market approximates a price based on supply and demand for a currency instead of a government-controlled price.

In many of the countries that do not allow their currencies to float according to market forces, a **black market** can parallel the official market and yet be aligned more closely with the forces of supply and demand. The less flexible a country's exchange-rate arrangement, the more likely there will be a thriving black (or parallel) market, which exists when people are willing to pay more than the official rate for hard currencies, such as dollars and euros. In order for such a market to work, the government must control access to foreign exchange so it can control the price of its currency. The opening case on Venezuela demonstrated how the black market in currency existed because of an artificial exchange rate set by the government.

In 2009 when Zimbabwe was in a financial crisis, the government issued a $100 trillion banknote that was worth about US$5 on the black market. Prices were doubling every day, and food and fuel were in short supply. The currency was so worthless that most trades in Zimbabwe were in U.S. dollars or the South African rand. That led the country to convert to the use of dollars in place of its own currency, officially demonetizing the Zimbabwean dollar and adopting the U.S. dollar as legal tender in 2015.[24] In 2016, Zimbabwe issued a new currency, referenced as "bond notes," at the time pegged 1:1 to the U.S. dollar. By early 2020, however, the new currency (with the new name "RTGS dollar") was trading in the official market at approximately 16.85 per dollar. On the black market, it traded at 23 per dollar, a premium of 36.5 percent. Turmoil continued and in mid-2020 the official exchange rate hit 66 Zimbabwean dollars per U.S. dollar, but the black market premium persisted in the range of 29 to 52 percent.[25]

FOREIGN-EXCHANGE CONVERTIBILITY AND CONTROLS

Fully convertible currencies are those that the government allows both residents and nonresidents to purchase in unlimited amounts. In contrast, some countries with fixed exchange rates control access to their currencies.

Black market foreign exchange ▶ trading in Harare, Zimbabwe, in July 2018. The Zimbabwe "bond notes" are shown at the left.

Source: Aaron Ufumeli/EPA-EFE/Shutterstock

A hard currency is a currency that is usually fully convertible and strong or relatively stable in value in comparison with other currencies.

A soft currency, also called a weak currency, is one that is usually not fully convertible.

Hard and Soft Currencies **Hard currencies**—such as the U.S. dollar, euro, British pound, and Japanese yen—are those that are fully convertible. Highly liquid and relatively stable in value over a short period of time, they are generally accepted worldwide as payment for goods and services. They are also desirable assets. Currencies that are not fully convertible, or **soft currencies**, have just the opposite characteristics: they are very unstable in value, not very liquid, and not widely accepted as payment for goods and services. A major reason why countries restrict convertibility of their currencies is that they are short on foreign-exchange reserves and try to use them for essential transactions.

Most countries today have *nonresident* (or *external*) *convertibility*, meaning that foreigners can convert their currency into the local currency and back. Tourists generally have no problems doing this, although sometimes countries put restrictions or conditions on trade from the local currency back to the hard currency when tourists leave the country.

Controlling Convertibility To conserve scarce foreign exchange, some governments impose exchange restrictions on companies or individuals who want to exchange money.

Licenses Government licenses fix the exchange rate by requiring all recipients, exporters, and others who receive foreign currency to sell it to its central bank at the official buying rate. The bank then rations the foreign currency it acquires by selling it at fixed rates to those needing to make payment abroad for essential goods. An importer may purchase foreign exchange only if it has obtained an import license for the goods in question.

In a multiple exchange-rate system, a government sets different exchange rates for different types of transactions.

Multiple Exchange Rates Another way governments control foreign-exchange convertibility is by establishing more than one exchange rate. This restrictive measure is called a **multiple exchange-rate system**. The government determines which kinds of transactions are to be conducted at which exchange rates. Countries with multiple rates often have a floating rate for luxury goods and financial flows, such as dividends, and a fixed, usually lower rate for other trade transactions such as imports of essential commodities and semi-manufactured goods. The opening case on Venezuela illustrated how the government used multiple exchange rates. The IMF reported that out of 192 countries, only 12 use dual exchange rates and 9 use multiple rates.[26]

Import Deposits Another form of foreign-exchange convertibility control is the **advance import deposit**. In this case, the government tightens the issue of import licenses and requires importers to make a deposit with the central bank—often for as long as one year and interest-free—covering the full price of manufactured goods they would purchase from abroad.

Quantity Controls Governments may also limit the amount of exchange through quantity controls, which often apply to tourism. A quantity control limits the amount of currency a local resident can purchase from the bank for foreign travel.

EXCHANGE RATES AND PURCHASING POWER PARITY

Exchange rates have relationships to other macroeconomic variables. The first relationship we examine is the one between prices and exchange rates.

Purchasing Power Parity (PPP) The PPP exchange rate is the rate at which the currency of one country would have to be converted into that of another country to buy the same amount of goods and services in each country.[27] Examining the difference between the PPP exchange rate and the market exchange rate helps us understand how trade relations might be affected.

The "Big Mac Index" An illustration of the PPP theory is the "Big Mac index" of currencies used by *The Economist* each year. Since 1986, the British periodical *The Economist* has used the price of a Big Mac to estimate the exchange rate between the dollar and another currency.[28] Because the Big Mac is sold in more than 36,000 McDonald's restaurants in more than 100 countries every day, it is easy to use it to compare prices. PPP would suggest that the exchange rate should leave hamburgers costing the same in the United States as abroad. However, the Big Mac sometimes costs more and sometimes less, demonstrating how far currencies are under- or overvalued against the dollar.

The Big Mac price in U.S. dollars is found by converting the local currency price into dollars at the current exchange rate. Using data from 2019, a Big Mac costs $5.58 in the United States, while in China it costs ¥20.9. Converting ¥20.9 into dollars at the actual exchange rate of ¥6.85/$, we find that the dollar equivalent of a Big Mac in China is $3.05. The implied PPP of the dollar shows what the exchange rate *should* be if the price in dollars equals the price in the local currency. If we continue with China as the example, dividing ¥20.9 by US$5.58 (the prices in China and the United States) gives ¥3.75 per dollar, which is what the exchange rate should be for a Big Mac to cost the same in the two countries. We can then calculate how much the currency is under- or overvalued. For the Chinese yuan, $(3.75 - 6.85)/6.85 = -0.453$, so the yuan is undervalued against the dollar by 45.3 percent.

In fact, most currencies were undervalued against the dollar in 2019, so it was harder for U.S. companies to export during this period of the strong dollar. Conversely, it was easier for companies outside of the United States to export to the United States. However, these relationships change as the dollar weakens against other currencies.[29]

The Big Mac index, also known as "McParity," has both supporters and detractors. Although it is an easy way to see how PPP works, the index includes only one product, the Big Mac, rather than a basket of commodities. The IMF goes to great lengths to identify a basket of goods that makes sense when determining its PPP index.[30]

The PPP exchange rate is the rate at which the currency of one country would have to be converted into that of another country to buy the same amount of goods and services.

The value of the Big Mac index is in understanding that price differences are not sustainable in the long run. Exchange rates will eventually have to equalize price differences more closely, or the law of supply and demand will take over. Of course, nobody is going to import Big Macs from China to the United States because they are so cheap. But if Big Macs are cheap, so are other products, and trade flows could be influenced by price differences.

A variation of the PPP theory considers inflation rates. In our example of Big Mac prices, suppose the Chinese yuan exchange rate achieves the PPP equilibrium at ¥3.75/$. If prices of Big Macs then change, there is a new PPP equilibrium. Suppose the price in China rises to 23.0 yuan, representing 10 percent inflation, while the price in the U.S. does not change (zero inflation). The new equilibrium would be ¥4.12/$, a depreciation of approximately 10 percent for the Chinese yuan. PPP thus specifies that the country with the higher inflation rate should have a weakening currency, and the country with a low inflation rate should have a strengthening currency.

EXCHANGE RATES AND INTEREST RATES

Although prices are important medium-term influences on exchange rates, interest rates are also important. Interest rate differentials, however, have both short-term and long-term components to them. In the short term, exchange rates are strongly influenced by interest rates. When the U.S. Federal Reserve Bank raised interest rates on December 16, 2015, the first time in nearly a decade, the result was hot money flowing into the United States to take advantage of the slightly higher interest rate. In early 2015, even before the rise in U.S. interest rates, money was flowing out of Europe at a rapid pace because of differences in interest rate policies, which also pushed down the euro against the dollar by 22 percent in less than a year. Investors were moving cash based on future expectations.[31]

In the long term, however, there is a strong relationship between inflation, interest rates, and exchange rates. To understand this, we need to examine two key finance theories: the *Fisher Effect* and the *International Fisher Effect*. The first links inflation and interest rates, while the second links interest rates and exchange rates.

The nominal interest rate is the real interest rate plus inflation. Because the real interest rate should be the same in every country, the country with the higher interest rate should have higher inflation.

The Fisher Effect The **Fisher Effect** is the theory that the nominal interest rate in a country (*r*, the actual monetary interest rate earned on an investment) is determined by the real interest rate (*R*, the nominal rate less inflation) and the inflation rate (*i*) as follows:

$$(1 + r) = (1 + R)(1 + i) \text{ or } r = (1 + R)(1 + i) - 1$$

According to this theory, if the real interest rate is 5 percent, the U.S. inflation rate 2.9 percent, and the Japanese inflation rate 1.5 percent, then the nominal interest rates for the United States and Japan are computed as follows:

$$r_{US} = (1.05)(1.029) - 1 = 0.08045, \text{ or } 8.045\%$$

$$r_j = (1.05)(1.015) - 1 = 0.06575, \text{ or } 6.575\%$$

Thus, the difference between U.S. and Japanese interest rates is a function of the difference between their inflation rates. If inflation rates were 1.5 percent in both countries (zero differential) but interest rates were 8.045 percent in the United States and 6.575 percent in Japan, investors would place their money in the United States, where they could get the higher real return.

The IFE implies that the currency of the country with the lower interest rate will strengthen in the future.

The International Fisher Effect The bridge from interest rates to exchange rates can be explained by the **International Fisher Effect (IFE)**, the theory that the interest-rate differential reflects expectations of future changes in the spot exchange rate. For example, if nominal interest rates in the United States are higher than those in Japan, IFE predicts that the dollar's value should fall in the future by that interest-rate differential, which would be an indication of a weakening, or depreciation, of the dollar. That is because the interest-rate differential is based on differences in inflation rates, as we discussed earlier. The previous discussion on PPP also demonstrates that the country with the higher inflation should have a weakening currency. Thus, the country with the higher interest rate (and the higher inflation) should have a weakening currency.

Of course, these issues cover the long run, but anything can happen in the short run. During periods of general price stability, a country that raises its interest rates is likely to attract capital and see its currency rise in value due to the increased demand. However, if the reason for the increase in interest rates is that inflation is higher than that of its major trading partners, the currency will eventually weaken until inflation cools down.

OTHER FACTORS IN EXCHANGE-RATE DETERMINATION

Exchange-rate movements are also influenced by investors' appetite for risk versus their appetite for safety.

Confidence: Flight to Safety Versus Flight to Risk Various other factors can affect currency values. One not to be dismissed lightly is confidence: In times of turmoil, people prefer to hold currencies that are considered safe. During the COVID-19 pandemic in 2020, investors fled to the safety of the U.S. dollar and dumped the currencies of emerging markets. The dollar appreciated and emerging market currencies depreciated even as interest rates in the United States declined and those in emerging markets rose.[32] When the banking crisis in Cyprus unfolded in March of 2013, investors moved money out of euros (the currency in Cyprus) and invested in U.S. dollars (a flight to safety) because of concerns over the effect of the crisis on the rest of Europe, which already had a fragile banking sector.

On the other hand, sometimes the appetite for risk (which implies greater returns) is more important than safety. In early 2016, the dollar began to fall as oil prices stabilized and increased, and investors began to look at investments in emerging markets like Brazil, which caused their exchange rates to rise against the dollar. Clearly, the flight to risk outweighed the flight to safety.

FORECASTING EXCHANGE-RATE MOVEMENTS

10-4 Show how managers try to forecast exchange-rate movements

FUNDAMENTAL AND TECHNICAL FORECASTING

Fundamental forecasting uses economic variables to predict future exchange rates.

Managers can forecast exchange rates by using either of two approaches: fundamental or technical. **Fundamental forecasting** uses economic variables to predict future rates. The data can be plugged into an econometric model or evaluated on a more subjective basis.

Technical forecasting uses past trends in exchange-rate movements to spot future trends.

Technical forecasting uses past trends in exchange rates themselves to spot future trends. Technical forecasters, or *chartists*, assume that if current exchange rates reflect all facts in the market, then under similar circumstances future rates will follow the same patterns.[33] However, research has shown that, except in the very short run, past exchange rates are not an accurate predictor of future ones. According to this theory, then, exchange-rate movements are a random walk, implying they cannot be predicted.[34]

Dealing with Biases Some biases exist that can skew forecasts:

- Overreaction to unexpected and dramatic news events;
- Illusory correlation—that is, the tendency to see correlations or associations in data that are not statistically present but are expected to occur on the basis of prior beliefs;
- Focusing on a particular subset of information at the expense of the overall set of information;
- Insufficient adjustment for subjective matters, such as market volatility;
- The inability to learn from one's past mistakes, such as poor trading decisions;
- Overconfidence in one's ability to forecast currencies accurately.[35]

Managers need to be concerned with the timing, magnitude, and direction of an exchange-rate movement.

Good treasurers develop their own forecasts of what will happen to a particular currency and use fundamental or technical predictions of outside forecasters to corroborate them. Doing this helps them determine whether they are considering important factors and whether they need to revise their forecasts in light of outside analysis.

Timing, Direction, and Magnitude Forecasting includes predicting the timing, direction, and magnitude of an exchange-rate change or movement. For countries whose currencies are not freely floating, the timing is often a political decision and not easy to predict. And though the direction of a change can probably be predicted, the magnitude is difficult to forecast. So, not only is it difficult to predict what will happen to currencies, it is equally difficult to use those predictions to forecast profits and establish operating strategies.

FUNDAMENTAL FACTORS TO MONITOR

Key factors to monitor include the institutional setting, market fundamentals, confidence factors, current circumstances, and technical analysis.

For freely fluctuating currencies, the law of supply and demand determines market value. Your ability to forecast exchange rates depends on your time horizon. In general, the best predictors of future exchange rates are interest rates for short-term movements, inflation for medium-term movements, and current account balances for long-term movements.[36] Given that even those countries whose currencies are freely floating are concerned about the value of their currencies, managers can monitor the same factors the governments follow to try to make a prediction:

- *Institutional Setting*
  - Does the currency float, or is it managed—and if so, is it pegged to another currency, to a basket, or to some other standard?
  - What are the intervention practices? Are they credible? Sustainable?
- *Market Fundamentals*
  - Does the currency appear undervalued or overvalued in terms of PPP, balance of payments, foreign-exchange reserves, or other factors?
  - What is the cyclical situation in terms of employment, growth, savings, investment, and inflation?
  - What are the prospects for government monetary, fiscal, and debt policy?
- *Confidence Factors*
  - What are market views and expectations with respect to the political environment, as well as to the credibility of the government and central bank?
- *Current Circumstances*
  - Are there national or international incidents in the news, possible crises or emergencies, or governmental or other important meetings coming up?

- *Technical Analyses*
  - What trends do the charts show? Are there signs of trend reversals?
  - At what rates do there appear to be important buy and sell orders? Are they balanced? Is the market overbought? Oversold?
  - What is the thinking and what are the expectations of other market players and analysts?[37]

We have already discussed interest rates and inflation, but what about current account balances? A current account surplus means that a country exports more than it imports and is building foreign-exchange reserves from the countries that are buying its goods and services. For the long term, the expectation is that the currency of that country will strengthen vis-à-vis its trading partners. Conversely, a current account deficit means that a country imports more than it exports and is building up debt abroad as it struggles to find the foreign exchange to pay for its imports. In that case, the long-term expectation is that the currency will weaken vis-à-vis its trading partners.

BUSINESS IMPLICATIONS OF EXCHANGE-RATE CHANGES

10-5 Examine how exchange-rate movements influence business decisions

As we will see in the closing case, exchange-rate changes can dramatically affect operating strategies as well as translated overseas profits.

MARKETING DECISIONS

Marketing managers watch exchange rates because changes can affect demand for a company's products at home and abroad. For example, in 2013, as the Indian rupee plunged in value against the U.S. dollar, Indian small importers were in trouble because they didn't have the financial strength to deal with the currency fluctuations. In most cases, they had to pay their suppliers in U.S. dollars; when the rupee fell, they had to come up with more rupees to convert into dollars to pay the suppliers, and they were struggling to do so.[38] On the other side, U.S. exporters struggled with a strong dollar as the prices in local currencies rose during a time when economic growth abroad was weak in the first place.

Companies might locate production in a weak-currency country because

- initial investment there is relatively cheap,
- such a country is a good base for inexpensive exportation.

PRODUCTION DECISIONS

Exchange-rate changes can also affect the location of production, although it will be only one of many variables companies consider. A manufacturer in a country where wages and operating expenses are high might be tempted to relocate production to a country with a currency that is rapidly losing value. The company's home currency would buy lots of the weak currency, making the company's initial investment cheap. Further, goods manufactured in that country would be relatively low-cost in world markets.

Exchange rates can influence the sourcing of financial resources, the cross-border remittance of funds, and the reporting of financial results.

FINANCIAL DECISIONS

Exchange rates can affect financial decisions primarily in sourcing financial resources, remitting funds across national borders, and reporting financial results. For example, a company might be tempted to borrow money in currencies that are depreciating. However, recall that interest-rate differentials often compensate for exchange-rate changes: depreciating currencies have higher interest rates.

In deciding about cross-border financial flows, a company would want to convert local currency into its own home-country currency when the foreign currency is strong so it can maximize its return. However, countries often have currency controls or limits on remittance of funds, making it difficult for MNEs to do so.

Finally, exchange-rate changes can influence the reporting of financial results. For example, Procter & Gamble generates 65 percent of its revenues outside the United States.

CONCEPT CHECK

Chapter 19 will explain how companies factor in foreign exchange in preparing financial statements, show how exchange rates influence financial flows, and describe some of the strategies that companies enlist to protect themselves against exchange-rate risk.

Because of the strong dollar in 2015, P&G found that its revenues and earnings generated in weaker currencies were lower when translated back into dollars than if the dollar were stable or a little weaker. On the other hand, sales and earnings in a strong currency result in higher profits when translated back into dollars.[39]

LOOKING TO THE FUTURE Changes in the Relative Strength of Global Currencies

The international monetary system has undergone considerable change since the early 1970s, when the dollar was devalued the first time. New countries have been born with the breakup of the Soviet empire, and with them have come new currencies. In addition, China has come of age.

The world has come out of the global financial crisis, but is still weak. Inflation is relatively low, and so are interest rates. In some cases, rates are below zero, which was unthinkable not too many years ago. Deflation is a greater concern than inflaton. Oil prices are low, which adds to low levels of inflation. Estimated global growth in GDP was only 3.0 percent in 2019, and in China it was only 6.1 percent—the fifth consecutive year in which it was below 7.0 percent after 24 years above it.[40] Because of slow economic growth, many countries are having budget crises that are affecting their ability to service debt.

Although the U.S. dollar is the main reserve asset used by central banks, the Chinese RMB is gaining steam. However, the three key determinants of the reserve status of a currency are size, stability, and liquidity.[41] Will the RMB ever replace the dollar as the chief reserve asset, or will they share power? Or will there be three reserve assets—the dollar, the RMB, and the euro? And will the yen be part of that picture?

The RMB suffers in all three areas: size (although the Chinese economy is formidable), stability, and liquidity. The financial institutions in China are still very weak, even though they are improving. Although the RMB became part of the SDR basket in 2016 and thus eligible to be a reserve asset, it has been struggling. China has the largest foreign-exchange reserves in the world, exceeding $3 trillion in 2020. However, the RMB is not a freely floating currency. In spite of that, there has been a large outflow of RMB from China for several reasons. One is that the People's Bank of China has been trying to support the RMB by using its foreign-exchange reserves. In January 2016 alone, it used $100 billion in reserves to defend the RMB.[42] Will the government continue to support the RMB and further drain its foreign currency reserves? It largely resisted large-scale intervention to support the RMB, and by 2018 China tightened capital controls to help stabilize the RMB.[43] This simply made the RMB even less freely floating.

The euro is a strong currency and represents the second-largest amount of allocated reserves behind the dollar. The major challenge of the euro is that its member countries are fragmented with numerous internal problems, such as Greek debt. In addition, Britain, one of the strongest countries in Europe, never adopted the euro, and left the European Union in 2020.

CASE

Welcome to the World of Sony—Unless the Falling Yen Rises (or Falls) Again[44]

For three consecutive years from 2012 to 2015, the yen was falling against the U.S. dollar, and this was good for Sony. The reason is that stronger revenues and earnings from abroad translate into more yen. In addition, the weaker yen helped Sony in export markets. However, in early 2016 the yen began to strengthen against the dollar from ¥123 in November 2015 to ¥120 at the end of 2015, to ¥112.4 on March 31, 2016, the close of Sony's fiscal year. Sony ended the year posting a 1.3 percent decline in sales and operating revenue. Whereas Toyota disclosed in August 2015 that the weaker yen was fueling its profits, in the first quarter of 2016 it changed its tune and noted that the stronger yen was going to hurt. Toyota ended the fiscal year on March 31, 2016 with a modest increase in revenue (4.3 percent) as sales quantity fell (3.2 percent) from the year before. By June 2016, the yen strengthened further, to ¥100 per dollar. After weakening during the remainder of 2016, reaching ¥118 by December, the yen traded in a range of ¥105 to ¥115 well into 2020. What will the future bring for Sony and other Japanese companies?

The Past

Before attacking the future, let's look at the past, especially from the perspective of the Japanese yen. In the post–World War II years, the yen was extremely weak against the dollar, trading at ¥357.65 in 1970. At that time, in 1946, the Tokyo Tsushin Kogyo Corporation was founded, officially becoming known as Sony Corporation in 1958, the year its stock was first listed on the Tokyo Stock Exchange. It also became the first Japanese company to list American Depositary Receipts (ADRs) on the New York Stock Exchange in 1961, finally listing its own shares in September 1970.

In those early years of operation, Sony had the luxury of operating in a currency that was not only weak against the dollar, but also highly controlled by the government. Japanese foreign-exchange policies favored companies and industries that the government wanted to succeed, especially in export markets. With a cheap yen, it was easy for companies to expand exports rapidly.

The First Endaka

From its 1970 high, the yen steadily strengthened until 1985, when it *really* shot up in value. Due to economic problems in the United States, the dollar began to fall during the latter part of 1985, and the yen ended the year at ¥200 per dollar (as the number of yen per dollar falls, the dollar gets weaker and the yen gets stronger). By the latter part of 1986, it was trading at ¥150, a steep rise from its historical highs. The Japanese called this strengthening of the yen *endaka,* which literally translates "high yen." *Endaka* resulted in serious problems for Japanese exporters and potential pain for the entire Japanese economy, which depended heavily on international trade. However, one advantage of *endaka* was that imports were cheaper, and Japan relied heavily on imports of virtually all commodities. Thus its input costs fell, even as it found its export prices rising.

The strong yen was due primarily to a strong Japanese economy, large trade surpluses, and the largest foreign-exchange reserves in the world. In addition, Japan had low unemployment, low interest rates, and low inflation. But cracks began to show in its economy. A combination of a drop in the stock market, a rise in inflation, and a real estate bubble hurt the economy and confidence in the yen. Since the interest rates in the United States were higher, investors pulled money out of Japan and put it into U.S. dollars to take advantage of higher returns. This drop in demand for yen and rise in demand for dollars pushed up the value of the dollar against the yen, and the yen closed out 1989 at ¥143.45, from ¥125.85 only a year earlier.

Both the United States and Japan were worried about inflation in the early 1990s, and they tried to coordinate exchange-rate policies, but the United States didn't want to push down the value of the dollar too much and lose its own fight against inflation. The two nations tried to get the central banks of Germany, the United Kingdom, and other countries to intervene in the markets and sell their currencies for yen in order to strengthen it. But there wasn't much they could do to move the market given that interest rates were driving market psychology.

In the ensuing years, many factors influenced the yen/dollar exchange rate, including a weak U.S. economy (favoring a drop in interest rates), the Persian Gulf War (which favored the dollar as a safe-haven currency), a rise in Japanese interest rates relative to U.S. interest rates, and a lack of agreement among G8 countries in 1993 about whether the yen was too weak or about right.

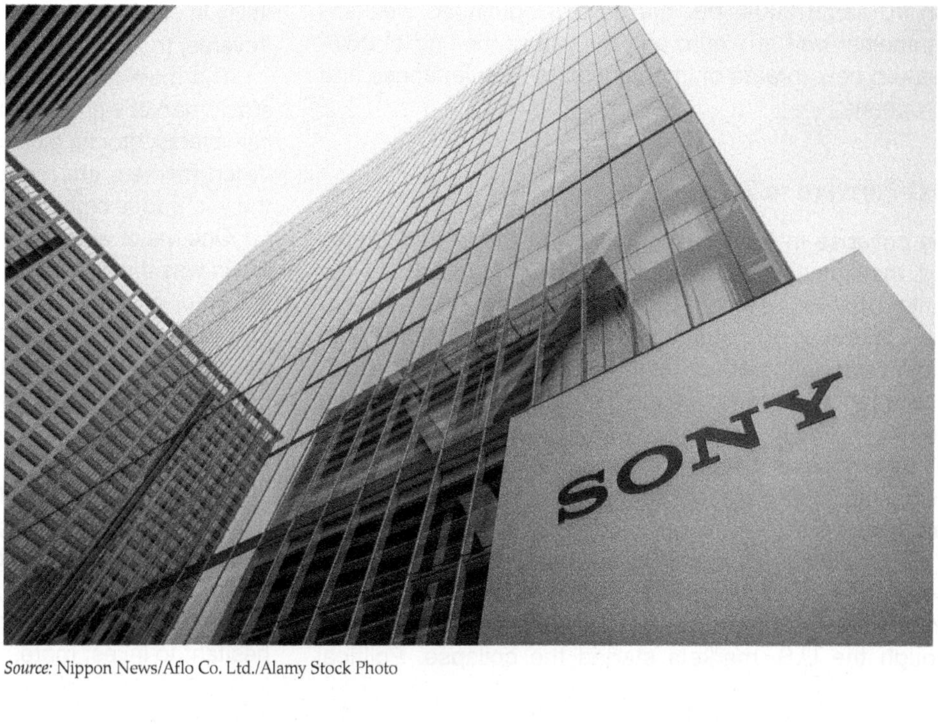

The Sony Corporation's global ▶ headquarters in downtown Tokyo, Japan.

Source: Nippon News/Aflo Co. Ltd./Alamy Stock Photo

A Second Endaka

As if one *endaka* were not enough, a second one hit in 1995, when the yen rose to ¥80.63 per dollar. As they did with the first *endaka,* Japanese companies looked for ways to cut costs and remain competitive. During that period, the Japanese economy was in a recession, so the Bank of Japan cut interest rates to stimulate demand, and the yen fell against the dollar, favoring exporters once again.

Competitive Pressures

During these decades of currency swings, Sony kept moving along as one of the premier companies in the world in consumer electronics, games, music, and movies. Its wide array of product innovations earned it a premium in the market; then competition began to step in. Korean companies like Samsung began to produce cheaper products that rose in quality as each year went by, and Samsung began to develop its own reputation for innovation in electronics. In addition, Samsung and other foreign competitors began setting up plants offshore, especially in China, to improve their cost advantage even more. Some of Sony's Japanese competitors, including Toshiba and Panasonic, reduced their exposure to a strong yen by moving plants overseas to countries like Indonesia and the Philippines and by increasing the dollar-based imports of parts.

From the beginning of 2003 until the end of 2004, the dollar continued to weaken against both the euro and the yen. In an attempt to strengthen the dollar, the Japanese central bank spent a record 20 trillion yen in 2003 and 10 trillion yen in the first two months of 2004. Despite such efforts, the yen rose 11 percent against the dollar in 2003 and continued to strengthen through 2004. The Japanese finance ministry stopped its foreign-exchange intervention in March 2004, but the dollar's continued weakening against both the euro and the yen at the end of 2004 sparked new threats of intervention by the Japanese and Europeans.

Fast-Forward to 2008

The collapse in the housing market in the United States and the ensuing credit crisis in 2007, followed by the bankruptcy of Lehman Brothers and the U.S. government takeover of global insurer AIG in September 2008, had a devastating effect on the global economy. The U.S. stock market crashed, followed by similar crashes around the world, and investors pulled funds out of risky emerging markets and placed them in safe-haven assets. As a result, the euro dropped against the U.S. dollar and the Japanese yen.

Why did this happen? In the case of the U.S. dollar, the market reaction was a standard flight to safety—which often happens when global events get scary—even though the U.S. markets started the collapse. Political stability and the size of the economy tend to make the United States an attractive place for investment. Thus, the fear factor seemed to be a critical vote for the dollar during the crisis. This was a short-term phenomenon, however, and was eventually replaced by economic fundamentals.

During the crisis, the dollar vacillated depending on what news was most important. When the crisis was the news, the dollar was strong. When the news favored a recovery of the U.S. economy, money flowed into equity markets in the United States and abroad seeking higher returns, causing the dollar to drop in value. With the slowdown in the U.S. economy, export-dominated countries, especially emerging markets, were expected to suffer. Also, the credit crisis the United States was going through was expected to expand to other countries. One interesting effect of the crisis was that the euro tended to be very sensitive to the U.S. stock market. When the market was falling, so was the euro. When the market began to recover, so did the euro. The euro is obviously a strong and important currency, but it lacks a strong central government that can coordinate a response to economic crisis. The European Central Bank can influence interest rates, but that's about all.

What about the yen? Interestingly enough, the yen also became a safe-haven currency during the crisis, along with the dollar. At the time, the yen was Asia's most important currency because Japan had the second-highest foreign-exchange reserves in the region and the world (just after China) and because the yen is a freely convertible currency with high market liquidity, as well as an important trading currency. Also, with Japanese interest rates so low, many investors were borrowing in yen and investing their proceeds abroad to get access to higher returns, a practice called the *carry trade*. When the crisis hit, the money quickly left the emerging markets and returned to Japan. When volatility in currency markets went up, investors would unwind (reverse) their carry trades; this gave strength to the yen.

The markets also demonstrated that the yen and U.S. stock market were inversely related. When markets are less risk averse, stocks gain in value and the yen drops in value. When markets are more risk averse, stock prices fall and the yen trades higher.

One major effect of the strong yen and the global slowdown was the sharp drop in exports from Japan. In January 2009, for example, exports dropped 49 percent compared to a year earlier. As exporters found their sales falling, they cut orders from their suppliers, so there was a ripple effect in the Japanese economy, affecting both production and employment. These events caused a sharp contraction in Japan as GDP fell 12.1 percent in the fourth quarter of 2008 compared to a year earlier, and many experts felt that Japan was going through its worst recession since World War II. Deflation was also affecting the Japanese economy again, and consumers were delaying purchases hoping that prices would continue to fall, while companies were hesitant to invest more.

2011: The Year of Tragedy

The earthquake and tsunami that struck Japan on March 11, 2011, were devastating in terms of lives lost and overall human tragedy. In addition, there was a great deal of uncertainty over damage to nuclear reactors and disruption to the global supply chain. (Consider that Japanese factories produce about 25 percent of the world's semiconductors and 40 percent of electronic components.) Plants in affected areas were shut down due to property damage, power outages, and a transportation infrastructure that ground to a halt.

What happened to the Japanese yen during this crisis? Conventional wisdom would say that the yen should fall against the dollar, but it actually rose in value. After the quake, there was a massive inflow of capital as the Japanese liquidated investments (made with cheap Japanese money) in emerging markets (where returns are high, another example of carry trade). In addition, many Japanese companies brought money back to the country at the end of the fiscal year (March 31), so the need for capital resulted in a tremendous inflow of it, causing the yen to rise in value.

A Reversal of Fortunes—Abenomics

Just when things looked bleak due to the strong yen and weak demand in Europe and China, in November 2012 Japan elected a new prime minister, Shinzo Abe, who decided to fight deflation and a weak domestic economy through loose monetary, fiscal, and structural policies. For most of 2012, the yen had been trading below ¥80/US$, but by the end of 2012 it was trading at 85.96; by May 6, 2013, it was at 99.10 and falling. At the end of the first quarter of 2013, Sony doubled its annual profit estimates due partly to the falling yen. And the yen kept falling, to ¥105 by the end of 2013, and to ¥120 by the end of 2014. In July 2015, it reached its low at ¥123.94.

If the strong yen made it difficult for exporters to sell abroad and weakened foreign earnings, the weak yen was just the opposite. Exporters like Sony, Toyota, and Panasonic were ecstatic about the weaker yen (which had fallen by more than 20 percent since Abe took office) and the opportunity to expand their sales abroad. The full extent of their ability to take advantage of the weaker yen still depended on economic recovery in the United States, Europe, and China, but at least the currency wasn't an additional weight on their competitive position.

What Does All This Mean to Sony?

Now we are in 2020 where the yen reversed years of weakness against the dollar but finally stabilized in a range of ¥105 – ¥115 per dollar. Although strong relative to 2015 when it was ¥123/US$, it is still weaker than where it had been in 2011, trading below ¥80/US$. In FY 2019 Sony generated 30.0 percent of its sales in Japan, 22.9 percent in the United States, 21.5 percent in Europe, 10.5 percent in Asia/Pacific (including India, South Korea, Oceania, Thailand, and Malaysia), 8.9 percent in China, and 6.3 percent elsewhere. Thus, the company was well diversified geographically.

Sony's production of electronics products was done 60 percent in-house and 40 percent outsourced. Of the in-house production, 35 percent was done in Japan, of which 75 percent was exported; 40 percent was manufactured in China, of which 75 percent was exported; 5 percent was manufactured in the United States and Europe for local consumption; and the rest was manufactured in other parts of Asia, of which 65 percent was exported to the Americas, Japan, Europe, and China, and the rest was sold in local markets. What is interesting about the location of sales and manufacturing is that there are multiple kinds of exposure to exchange rates.

The strong yen was hurting Sony's financial statements. As Sony translates U.S. dollar or euro financial statements into yen, net assets and earnings are worth less in yen, dragging down Sony's consolidated results. The only way to offset this drop is to sell more and improve profit margins, both of which are hard to do in a slow global economy. From a cash-flow point of view, Sony's operations abroad are remitting dividends back to Japan, but they are worth less yen as the dollar and euro weaken against it. One silver lining is that the purchasing power of the yen rises as it strengthens compared to other currencies, so everything Sony imports into Japan for its manufacturing is cheaper. The same would be true for anything manufactured outside Japan, thus reducing costs and hopefully increasing margins. As long as Sony is invoicing its exports in dollars to customers worldwide, it needs to match the dollar revenues with dollar expenses through investing more in the United States or in other countries in Asia, like Taiwan, where components are cheaper and where Sony can invoice its purchases in dollars.

QUESTIONS

10-3 Why do you think it is important for Sony to manufacture more products in the United States and Europe and to also buy more from suppliers in other countries in Asia?

10-4 What are the major forces that affected the Japanese yen over the years? What factors do you think are important to monitor as you try to forecast what will happen to the value of the yen in the future?

CHAPTER 11
Global Capital Markets

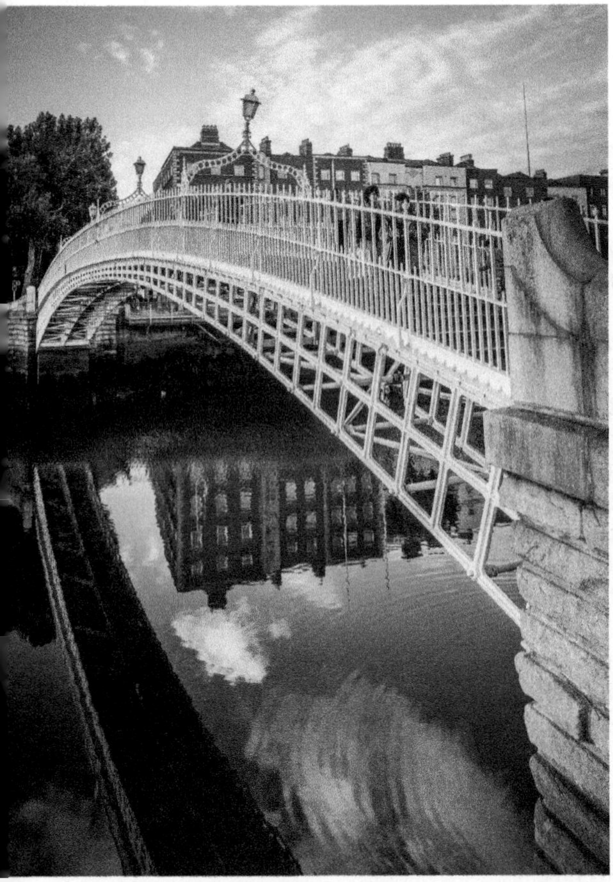

Source: Benoit Daoust/Shutterstock

Pedestrian bridge in Dublin, Ireland. ▲

OBJECTIVES

After studying this chapter, you should be able to

11-1 Describe the finance function of an MNE in a global context

11-2 Define leverage and how it affects the choice of capital structure

11-3 Explain the different ways to access capital internationally

11-4 Summarize how foreign source income is taxed

11-5 Analyze how offshore financial centers provide financing opportunities for MNEs

To have money is a good thing; to have a say over the money is even better.

—Yiddish proverb

CASE

Tax Wars: Pfizer Versus the U.S. Government[1]

In 2014, Pfizer, the U.S.-based pharmaceutical company, began looking at Allergan, the pharma headquartered in Ireland, for a possible merger. From one perspective, the deal made sense. Pfizer needed to expand its portfolio of new drugs, and Allergan had some high-profile drugs, like Botox. From another perspective, Allergan's headquarters were located in Ireland, where the corporate tax rate is 12.5 percent, compared with the 35 percent U.S. corporate tax rate (39 percent for combined federal and local taxes), the highest in the world. If the merger went though and Pfizer was able to move its corporate headquarters to Ireland, it stood to significantly reduce its corporate tax liability and therefore free up more cash for its equity shareholders and for reinvestment into the development of new drugs.

TAX INVERSIONS

Pfizer and Allergan were caught in a war of words and phrases, like serial inverters, earnings-stripping, stuffing, cherry-picking, and the best of them all, skinny down. But let's go back a few years to when tax inversions really took hold because of high U.S. corporate tax rates and the inability of Congress to make any progress on comprehensive tax reform. It's easy to see the difference in corporate tax rates between the United States and Ireland, but the rates were 30.18 percent in Germany, 20 percent in the U.K., 25 percent in the Netherlands, 21.5 percent in Switzerland, and 26.7 percent in Canada. However, tax loopholes in the U.S. tax code allow the 50 biggest MNCs to reduce their effective tax rate to 24 percent compared to 35 percent for their European counterparts. In order to reduce the U.S. corporate tax rate to be comparable with its European counterparts, comprehensive tax reform also needed to take place.

Burger King, a U.S.-based company that was owned by 3G Capital Partners LP, a Brazilian private equity firm, was part of one of the first high-profile tax inversions that created tensions on both sides of the Canadian border, but for different reasons. In 2014, Burger King decided to merge with Tim Hortons, a coffee-and-doughnuts chain started in Canada. Burger King's goal was to complete the merger with Tim Hortons, move the corporate headquarters to Canada, and change the name to Restaurant Brands International. In the process, it would save $117 million dollars in U.S. taxes since it would never have to pay U.S. taxes on foreign profits it holds offshore. Of course, Burger King announced that it was driven by growth opportunities, not tax savings, by completing the inversion. On the Canadian side, the concern was that Canada was losing another one of its corporate icons, Canada's largest coffee-shop chain with a market cap about the same size as Burger King. In spite of Burger King being called "unpatriotic" by the U.S. government for completing the tax inversion, it has since proven its prediction that growth, not just taxes, was the foundation of the merger. 3G Partners is now expanding its new Tim Hortons business in the United States, creating more American jobs as well as creating more wealth for Tim Hortons.

In the absence of tax reform, enterprising U.S. companies discovered tax inversion as a way to reduce their tax liability. Using Pfizer as an example, Pfizer would merge with Allergan and adopt Ireland as its tax domicile. Since the new firm would not be a U.S. company, it would not be subject to U.S. corporate income taxes. It could then use its tax savings to pay dividends to shareholders and use the excess cash for global expansion. It is estimated that since 2012, there have been at least 20 such tax inversions, including Burger King and Tim Hortons, and many others were moving in that direction.

THE FIGHT AGAINST TAX INVERSIONS

The fight against inversions was taken up by the U.S. Treasury, not Congress. The problem with Congress was that the Democrats and Republicans couldn't agree on comprehensive tax reform, so there wasn't much incentive to take on one isolated issue. However, the Treasury was looking for money anywhere it could find it to fund government programs. In addition, there was a broader concern that U.S. companies wanted to have all the benefits of the United States without paying the taxes. As noted by the U.S. Treasury Secretary leading the fight against tax inversions, "These firms involved in these transactions still expect to benefit from their business location in the United States, with our protection of intellectual property rights, our support of research and development, our investment climate and our infrastructure, as funded by various levels of government. But these firms are attempting to avoid paying taxes here, notwithstanding the benefits they gain from being located in the United States."

In September 2014, the Treasury Department announced its first set of rules to try to discourage tax inversions. The rules would prohibit companies from using offshore profits to finance the inversion deals. While President Obama said there is no substitute for Congressional action, and one senator on the Senate Finance Committee said that "any solution that permanently addresses inversions must be legislated by Congress," it was clear that Congress would not be part of the solution and that the Treasury Department would make the rules.

THE FINAL BATTLE

In spite of the rules announced in 2014, Pfizer and Allergan moved ahead in their plans to merge and for Pfizer to move its corporate headquarters to Dublin. If successful, it would have been the largest inversion yet. The $151 billion would also have been the largest merger in 15 years, as well as the largest corporate inversion. Pfizer's CEO maintained that the reason for the inversion wasn't just to save taxes. He maintained that some of Pfizer's biggest global rivals, GlaxoSmithKline and AstraZeneca of Britain and Novartis of Switzerland, are at a distinct advantage because of their lower tax rates, which puts them at an advantage over Pfizer in acquiring other companies. The merger would give each company access to new technologies and would allow Pfizer the size and product diversity it needs to split the company into two parts—one emphasizing faster-growing, innovative drugs and the other for more mature products that have to compete with generics.

However, tax issues are not insignificant. Not only was Pfizer interested in the tax benefits from the inversion, but it also had over $74 billion in profits kept overseas that would be subject to U.S. tax if brought back to the United States. If Pfizer became an Irish company, it would no longer have to worry about that. A merger between Pfizer and Allergan would probably not have been an issue for U.S. regulators from a competitive standpoint. However, the Treasury Department has a different mandate than the Justice Department's Antitrust Division and the Federal Trade Commission. The issue for them is not a loss of competition; it's a loss of tax revenues. The real question was, if the U.S. government eliminated the possibility of a tax inversion, would the merger still go through?

In 2016, the Treasury Department slammed the door shut on certain tax inversions, or at least made it more difficult for them, in a series of regulations aimed directly at Pfizer. The 300-page ruling included as its centerpiece the acquisitions of "serial inverters," when determining whether a company is a foreign company. In the case of Pfizer and Allergan, Pfizer would have to own between 50 and 60 percent of the combined company in order to obtain full benefits from the inversion. When the last three years of Allergan's acquisitions were eliminated, Allergan shareholders would have held only 20 percent of the shares, with Pfizer owning 80 percent. That meant that the merged company would be subject to U.S. tax and would not be a foreign company. A second change was the elimination of "earnings stripping" where the inversion company would lend money to its U.S. subsidiaries, allowing the subsidiaries to claim the interest paid as a tax deduction, thus lowering U.S. taxes. The interest earned by the inverted company would be considered taxable income but at the lower rate in the inversion country.

What about the merger? After the new regulations were announced in April 2016, Pfizer and Allergan followed up with their own announcement that the merger would no longer make sense. Who won the war? Obviously the U.S. government felt like it won since it eliminated another case of tax inversion. Congress didn't win, because it wasn't part of the decision.

What about tax reform? Comprehensive changes in the U.S. tax law came in 2017 in the Tax Cuts and Jobs Act. With both houses of Congress controlled by the Republicans, and with strong support from President Trump, the United States enacted the most significant tax reforms since 1986. The U.S. corporate tax rate was reduced from 35 to 21 percent, making it closer to the global average, although it is still high compared to Ireland. Furthermore, the U.S. changed its laws on the taxation of foreign source income so that MNCs no longer pay tax on most foreign income and can freely repatriate earnings. Together these provisions reduce the incentives for corporate tax inversions – and hopefully make U.S. MNCs more competitive globally.

QUESTIONS

11-1 In the case of Allergan and Pfizer, there are two sovereign powers in play: Ireland and the United States. Why was Ireland interested in letting the inversion take place, and why was the U.S. government against the inversion? Is the decision by the United States a direct affront to the sovereignty of Ireland?

11-2 In what ways are tax inversions beneficial to both the United States and the host country of the inversion?

THE FINANCE FUNCTION

11-1 Describe the finance function of an MNE in a global context

CONCEPT CHECK

Chapter 19 will discuss how the corporate controller reports to the CFO and is responsible for accounting and managing foreign-exchange exposure. Chapter 15 will show how the expansion of the MNE through FDI and other entry strategies requires financial resources that must be managed by the CFO.

The role of the chief financial officer (CFO) and the financial management is to create and maintain economic value by maximizing shareholder wealth—the market value of existing shareholders' common stock.[2] The management activities related to cash flows can be divided into three major areas:

- Make financing decisions—especially regarding capital structure (the proper mix of debt and equity) and long-term financing (selecting, issuing, and managing long-term debt and equity capital, including location—home country or elsewhere—and currency—home or foreign)
- Make investment decisions—typically in the context of capital budgeting
- Manage short-term capital needs—the MNE's currency assets and liabilities (cash, receivables, marketable securities, inventory, trade receivables and payables, and short-term bank debt)

The corporate finance function acquires and allocates financial resources among the company's activities. The key functions are

- making financing decisions,
- making investment decisions,
- managing short-term capital needs.

THE ROLE OF THE CFO

The CFO acquires financial resources—either internally or from external sources—at the lowest possible cost, and allocates them among the company's activities and projects. The CFO's job is more complex in a global environment than in the domestic setting because of such forces as foreign-exchange risk, currency flows and restrictions, political risk, different tax rates and laws determining taxable income, and regulations on access to capital in different markets.

CONCEPT CHECK

The *treasurer* is responsible for controlling the company's cash payments and the related financial functions, both domestic and foreign. The treasurer's functions fall under the overall responsibility of the chief financial officer (or the VP of finance), as we'll describe in Chapter 19.

The rest of this chapter examines the following areas:

1. Corporate capital structure
2. Global capital markets
3. Taxation of foreign-source income and influence on capital markets
4. Offshore financing, offshore financial centers, and tax havens

CAPITAL STRUCTURE

11-2 Define leverage and how it affects the choice of capital structure

A CFO must determine the company's *capital structure* — the proper mix between long-term debt and equity. Many companies start off with an initial investment and then grow through internally generated funds. However, when those sources are inadequate to fund continued growth into new markets, the CFO's office must decide the proper debt/equity mix.

LEVERAGING WITH DEBT FINANCING

Leverage is the degree to which a firm funds the growth of business by debt.

The degree to which a firm funds the growth of business by debt is known as **leverage**. The degree to which companies use leverage instead of *equity capital*—known as stocks or shares—varies throughout the world. Country-specific factors are a more essential determinant of a firm's capital structure than any others because a firm tends to follow the financing trends in its own country and within its particular industry there. Leveraging is often perceived as the most cost-effective route to capitalization because the interest that companies pay on debt is a tax-deductible expense in most countries, whereas the dividends paid to investors are not.

When Is Leveraging *Not* the Best Option? Leveraging is not always the best approach in all countries, for two major reasons. First, excessive reliance on long-term debt raises financial risk and thus requires a higher return for investors. This was evident in Europe during the global financial crisis as companies and governments tried to raise capital through bond issues, and they either had to offer high interest rates to attract investors or they had difficulty getting any investors at all. Second, foreign subsidiaries of an MNE may have limited access to local capital markets, making it difficult for the MNE to rely on debt to fund asset acquisition.[3]

FACTORS AFFECTING THE CHOICE OF CAPITAL STRUCTURE

Choice of capital structure depends on tax rates, degree of development of local equity markets, and creditor rights.

A recent and extensive study on leverage of 36,767 firms in 39 countries over a 15-year period shows that the financing choices available to a company depend on many factors, both unique to the firm itself as well as the environment in which they operate.[4] The authors found that the most important determinants in capital structure are a country's legal and taxation system, the level of corruption, and the preferences of capital suppliers (banks and pension funds). Where tax differences are critical, firms tend to use more debt since they can deduct interest expense and therefore lower their tax liability. However, that is not as significant as other factors. Firms in corrupt countries tend to use more debt, especially short-term debt, to fund operations. Firms in common law countries, such as the United States, the United Kingdom, Canada, etc., use less leverage and more long-term debt, and firms in countries with an explicit bankruptcy code have higher leverage and more long-term debt. When examining the median leverage ratio (in this case being defined as total debt over the market value of the firm), firms in developing countries tend to have the highest amount of leverage. The most highly leveraged countries are Korea, Indonesia, Brazil, Portugal, and Pakistan. Firms in developed countries tend to be in the lower end of the leverage spectrum. The countries with the lowest leverage are Australia, South Africa, Canada, the United States, Turkey (an outlier), and the United Kingdom.[5] Firms that rely excessively on leverage often are in countries with less active securities markets, as opposed to those that rely less on debt, which are often in countries with large, active, and liquid stock markets.

MNEs tend to use debt in countries with relatively high tax rates and a high degree of corruption. Also, capital structure of foreign subsidiaries tends to be more sensitive to local conditions.

A separate study of the capital structure of U.S.-based MNEs' foreign affiliates found that local tax rates strongly influenced the debt-to-equity ratios. Although the firm as a whole might have a debt-to-equity ratio based on U.S. capital-market expectations, its foreign affiliates have to be sensitive to local conditions. The study noted:

> Ten percent higher local tax rates are associated with 2.8 percent higher debt/asset ratios, with internal borrowing particularly sensitive to taxes. Multinational affiliates are financed with less external debt in countries with underdeveloped capital markets or weak creditor rights, reflecting significantly higher local borrowing costs.

Instrumental variable analysis indicates that greater borrowing from parent companies substitutes for three-quarters of reduced external borrowing induced by capital market conditions. Multinational firms appear to employ internal capital markets opportunistically to overcome imperfections in external capital markets.[6]

Debt and Exchange Rates The global financial crisis of 2007–2009 highlighted foreign-exchange risk. Leading up to the crisis, many Asian companies borrowed in dollars at relatively low interest rates. But when the dollar rose in value, the companies couldn't generate enough cash to convert into dollars to pay off their debts.

A similar phenomenon occurred in Iceland, a country with its own currency (the krona). The Central Bank of Iceland kept interest rates high, attracting lots of foreign investment and keeping the krona strong. People's standards of living, among the highest in the world, were supported by the strong currency and the ability to import products. They sustained their high consumption by financing houses and other purchases through borrowing in euros when interest rates were low. When the global crisis hit in 2007–2009, however, the krona plunged in value, the banks failed, and firms as well as consumers could not afford to service their debts. Sourcing debt in a currency with a lower interest rate seemed like a good idea, but the lower foreign interest rates were replaced by exchange-rate risk.[7]

Regulatory Risk A second factor that affects local borrowing is regulatory risk. Regulatory reform has complicated access to debt financing. As noted below, bonds are a great way for companies to raise capital for operations. However, companies also rely heavily on bank financing, and the failure of banks during the global financial crisis and resulting impact on the global economy has made countries very nervous about the financial stability of banks. The Basel Committee on Banking Supervision, which is a part of the Bank for International Settlements and comprises some of the world's top regulators and central bankers, has worked hard to put together rules to ensure that banks will be able to withstand future economic crises. The basic idea is to set standards for stronger capital positions and increased liquidity. The most recent agreement is called Basel III; it is designed to strengthen regulation, supervision, and risk management of the banking sector.[8] On the one hand, the world should be better off as banks comply with Basel III and increase their capital positions, but on the other hand, higher capital requirements also mean lower funds available to lend to companies that might not be able to raise capital by issuing bonds or listing stock on an exchange.

GLOBAL CAPITAL MARKETS

11-3 Explain the different ways to access capital internationally

Two major sources of funds external to the MNE's normal operations are debt markets and equity markets.

Companies have many ways of raising capital to fund operations, including debt and equity sources as well as domestic and international sources. Initially, we'll examine sources of debt financing. As an example, Nu Skin Enterprises, a U.S. company that specializes in personal care products and nutritional supplements, sells products in more than 50 international markets, and Japan was initially its most important international market. Recently, Nu Skin entered into a Japanese yen-denominated credit term loan facility for 6.6 billion yen at 2.3 percent variable interest rate. Nu Skin uses revenues in Japanese yen to pay off the debt in yen, which helps eliminate the foreign-exchange risk. In addition to the long-term debt in yen, Nu Skin also has a revolving line of credit in yen, which is classified as short-term since it pays off the funds over a relatively short time. Many firms like Nu Skin use banks in the local markets as an important source of financing.[9]

EUROCURRENCIES AND THE EUROCURRENCY MARKET

A Eurocurrency is any currency outside its country of origin, but it is primarily dollars banked outside the United States.

The **Eurocurrency market** is an important source of debt financing to complement what MNEs can find in their domestic markets. A **Eurocurrency** or *offshore currency,* is any currency banked outside its country of origin.

The Eurodollar market is the most significant Eurocurrency market. A **Eurodollar** is a deposit in U.S. dollars in a bank outside the United States. Most Eurodollar deposits are held in London, but they could be held anywhere outside the United States, such as the Bahamas, the Cayman Islands, etc. A major advantage of the Eurodollar market is that it is outside the control of national banking regulators. The Eurodollar market started with the deposit of U.S. dollars in London banks during the Cold War by the Soviet Union to avoid the possibility that their accounts could be frozen in the United States. As other currencies entered the offshore market, the broader "Eurocurrency" name was adopted for market use, although the market tends to use the name of the specific currency, such as *Euroyen* or *Eurosterling*. Eurodollars constitute a majority of the Eurocurrency market. Dollars held by foreigners on deposit in the United States are not Eurodollars, but dollars held at branches of U.S. or other banks outside the United States are.

There are several sources of Eurocurrencies, including governments, banks, and companies that have excess amounts of cash that they want to deposit in offshore locations.

Major Sources of Eurocurrencies There are four major sources of Eurocurrencies:

- Foreign governments or individuals who want to hold dollars outside the United States
- Multinational enterprises that have cash in excess of current needs
- European banks with foreign currency in excess of current needs
- Countries, such as China, that have large foreign-exchange reserves

Characteristics of the Eurocurrency Market The Eurocurrency market is a wholesale (companies and other institutions) rather than a retail market (individuals), so transactions are very large. Public borrowers such as governments, central banks, and public-sector corporations are the major players. Since the late 1990s, however, London banks have shifted to using nonbank customers for Eurodollar transactions, partly because of the introduction of the euro and consolidation in the banking sector.[10]

Eurocredits are loans with a maturity of one to five years. Syndicated loans involve several banks.

The Eurocurrency market is both short- and medium-term. Short-term borrowing is composed of maturities less than one year. Anything from one to five years is considered a **Eurocredit**, which may be a loan, a line of credit, or another form of medium- and long-term credit. This would include **syndication**, in which several banks pool resources to extend credit to a borrower and spread the risk. Short-term borrowings, called euro commercial paper, are unsecured loans issued by a bank or corporation in the offshore money market and typically in a currency that is different from the corporation's domestic currency. For example, a German company can issue eurocommercial paper in London, denominated in U.S. dollars. Maturities are less than one year.

Interest Rates in the Eurocurrency Market A major attraction of the Eurocurrency market is the difference in interest rates compared to those in domestic markets. Domestic rates are a function of the monetary policies adopted by the central banks of each country. The rate a company must pay to get loans or issue bonds depends not only on benchmark rates but also its creditworthiness. The better the creditworthiness, the lower the rate compared to other borrowers. Because of the large transactions and the lack of controls and their attendant costs, Eurocurrency deposits tend to yield more than domestic deposits do, and loans tend to be cheaper than in domestic markets.

ICE Libor is an interest rate on five different currencies for seven different maturities, the most common of which is the three-month Eurodollar rate.

London Interbank Offered Rate Traditionally, loans are made at a certain percentage above the **London Interbank Offered Rate (Libor)**, which is a short-term interest rate for loans between banks priced in London. Until recently, the British Bankers' Association published Libor rates in 10 currencies and 15 different maturities based on rates submitted by 18 different banks, reflecting the rates at which banks can borrow from each other.[11] However, in 2012, a scandal broke out in London over how Libor was set. There were rumors that bankers were collaborating to fix the rates, and since then, tens of billions of dollars in fines have been levied against the worst offenders. In 2014, the responsibility for setting Libor shifted to the Intercontinental Exchange or ICE. Now the ICE Benchmark Administration is responsible for setting interest rates for five currencies in seven different maturities from overnight to one year. The most common ICE Libor rate is the three-month U.S. dollar rate. ICE Libor is the benchmark interest rate for more than $260 trillion of wholesale and retail financial products, including a variety of debt instruments such as corporate bonds, mortgages, credit cards, etc.[12] More recently, a group of global banks has been working with U.S. and European regulators to come up with replacements for Libor. Until that happens, ICE Libor is still the standard.[13]

INTERNATIONAL BONDS

The United States has the largest domestic bond market in the world, and the bond market exceeds the stock market in size.

Many countries have active bond markets available to domestic and foreign investors. The global bond market in 2018 totals $103 trillion, more than equity markets totaling $75 trillion.[14] The United States is the largest market in the world for bonds, with $41 trillion outstanding, bigger than the U.S. stock market with $30 trillion.[15] The next-largest market is the EU (excluding the UK), with $22 trillion in bonds and $8 trillion in stocks. Bonds are used by governments, financial institutions, and corporations, with corporate issues being the smallest segment.[16]

One reason the bond (and stock) markets in the United States are so influential is because the companies of continental Europe have traditionally relied on banks for finance. However, that began to change due to the economic crisis in Europe and the drop in available bank funding. In addition, emerging markets are increasingly turning to the bond market for funding and now constitute about 14 percent of the market worldwide.[17]

MNEs can use their domestic bond market to raise capital in the local currency, and the bonds can be sold to both domestic and foreign buyers. The bond market in Europe is interesting. Since the countries in the Eurozone use the same currency, a German firm could issue a bond denominated in euros and have it be a domestic bond and a Eurobond. If it's listed in Germany, it would be considered a domestic bond. If it's listed in London, it would be a Eurobond. When the European Central Bank announced that it would start buying corporate bonds of European companies as part of its quantitative easing strategy, bonds suddenly became cheaper for European companies to issue, thus opening up more possibilities for European firms to issue bonds.[18]

There are three types of international bonds: foreign bonds, Eurobonds, and global bonds. The international bond market is primarily a wholesale market in which bond holders are usually institutional investors while issuers are large companies, governments, and international organizations.

A foreign bond is one sold outside the country of the borrower but denominated in the currency of the country of issue.

Foreign Bonds **Foreign bonds** are sold outside the borrower's country but denominated in the currency of the country of issue. A French company floating a bond issue in London in pounds sterling would be issuing a foreign bond.

A Eurobond is a bond issue sold in a currency other than that of the country of issue.

Eurobonds A **Eurobond** is usually underwritten (placed in the market for the borrower) by a syndicate of banks from different countries and sold in a currency other than that of the country of issue. A French company issuing a bond in London, denominated in U.S. dollars, is an example of a Eurobond.

A global bond is a Eurobond which is issued in several locations at the same time.

Global Bond A global bond is issued outside the country where the currency is denominated, such as a U.S. dollar bond issued outside the United States, in multiple locations. For example, it could be a dollar bond issued by a U.S. company in London, Paris, Frankfurt, and Hong Kong. The goal is to get access to investors in multiple locations, sometimes in countries where the MNE is doing business or considering doing business.

Rising in importance are "dim sum" bonds, which are offshore bonds denominated in Chinese yuan. Although Chinese companies are issuing bonds in China that are available to foreign investors, capital outflow restrictions by the Chinese government are increasing the risk of raising capital in China.[19] However, the bonds' popularity rises as China looks for a way to capitalize on its immense foreign-exchange reserves. Foreign investors who want to buy debt denominated in Chinese yuan can purchase dim sum bonds, which are typically issued in Hong Kong.[20]

What's So Attractive About the International Bond Market? The international bond market is a desirable place to borrow money. For one thing, it allows a company to diversify its funding sources from the local banks and the domestic bond market and borrow in maturities that might not be available in the domestic markets. It also tends to be less expensive than local bond markets and attracts investors from around the world.

U.S. firms first issued Eurobonds in 1963 as a means of avoiding U.S. tax and disclosure regulations. They're typically issued in denominations of $5,000 or $10,000, pay interest annually, are held in bearer form, and are traded over the counter (OTC), most frequently in London.[21] Any investor who holds a bearer bond is entitled to receive the principal and interest payments. In contrast, for a registered bond, which is more typical in the United States, the investor is required to be registered as the bond's owner to receive payments. The secrecy of a bearer bond also makes the Eurobonds more attractive.

For example, Gazprom, Russia's largest company, uses the Eurobond market extensively. In 2016, it issued a 500 million Swiss franc Eurobond maturing in November 2018 at a yield of 4.625 percent. The main purchasers of these Eurobonds were private banks managing the savings of wealthy individuals, whereas Eurodollar bonds are typically acquired by institutional investors. Approximately 39.4 percent of the bonds were bought by Swiss investors, 34.1 percent by Russian investors, and the rest by other European investors. Private banks and wealth management firms bought 58.6 percent of the bonds.[22]

GLOBAL EQUITY MARKETS

Another source of financing is *equity securities*, whereby an investor takes an ownership position in return for shares of stock in the company and the promises of capital gains and dividends. A company that wants to raise equity capital to fund operations may work with private investors who want to take an equity interest in the company rather than just loan money to the company. Or it might work with investment banks to raise equity capital by going to a stock market. If the company wants to issue on a stock exchange, it has to decide if it wants to raise capital in its domestic market or abroad.

A Sovereign Wealth Fund is a state-owned investment fund that generates its resources from a variety of sources, with oil being the main source for many SWFs.

Sovereign wealth funds (SWFs) are also an important source of capital. An SWF is a state-owned investment fund that generates its resources from a variety of places, including revenues from the exports of natural resources such as oil.[23] The top five SWFs in terms of assets are the Norway Government Pension Fund Global, the China Investment Corporation, the Abu Dhabi Investment Authority, the Kuwait Investment Authority, and the Hong Kong Monetary Authority Investment Portfolio. Four of the top 10 funds are based on oil revenues.[24] The funds, which are professionally managed, can invest in specific projects or stock markets. For example, Invest AD (the Abu Dhabi Investment Company) is one of the SWFs in the UAE, with a primary role of investing in the Middle East and Emerging Africa and providing investment opportunities to third-party clients. Its officers scour the capital markets in the region to find stocks to invest in, and it has developed several funds, including the Emerging Africa Fund and the GCC (Gulf Cooperation Council) Focus Fund. When SWFs invest in specific projects, they operate more like a venture capital firm. When they invest in stock markets, one of the strategies of Invest AD, they are not providing new capital but are taking advantage of shares already listed on stock markets.

An IPO is the first sale of stock by a company to the public. It may be in the issuer's home country or in another country.

MNEs raise new capital in the equity capital market through an Initial Public Offering, or IPO, by listing shares on a stock exchange, either in their home country or in another country. An example of the former is the 2012 IPO by U.S.-based Facebook when it raised $16 billion in the United States. However, the largest IPO was on September 14, 2014, when e-commerce giant Alibaba Group of China raised $21.8 billion in an IPO issued in the United States. Although Alibaba could have issued the IPO in China or Hong Kong, it decided to go after funds in the U.S. market instead.[25] The closing case in this chapter discusses more features of the Alibaba IPO.

The three largest stock markets in the world are in New York (with two markets) and Tokyo, with the U.S. markets controlling 40 percent of the world's stock market capitalization.

The Size of Global Stock Markets The total **market capitalization** of the world's 83 stock exchanges is $92.6 trillion in January 2020, up from 79.6 trillion in January 2019. Map 11.1 identifies the 10 largest stock markets in the high-income countries and top-10 largest stock markets in emerging countries in terms of domestic market capitalization (total number of shares of stock listed multiplied by market price per share). The numbers in Map 11.1 represent each specific stock market rather than all of the markets in the country. The three largest stock markets in the world are the New York Stock Exchange, Nasdaq-US, and the Japan Exchange Group, closely followed by the Shanghai Stock Exchange in China.

Major sources of influence on global stock markets are oil prices, growth in the global economy, weakness in the Chinese economy, and interest rates.

Political and Economic Forces and Trends in Global Stock Markets During the past few years, global markets have been in turmoil, and that will continue to be the case. There are several factors that are affecting markets, although the forces change from year to year and aren't always consistent. In the first place, when oil prices began dropping, so did the stock markets. When oil prices began to rise, so did the markets. One possible explanation is that rising prices resulted from increased demand and possibly a recovery in economic growth.[26] Second, weakness in the global economy hurts markets in general and causes money to flee to safety rather than gamble on returns from risk.[27] Third, China has been a huge force. When

MAP 11.1 Global Stock Exchanges: Market Capitalizations, January 2020

Data (in billions of dollars) reflects domestic market capitalization of the top 10 exchanges in high-income countries and the top 10 emerging markets.

Source: Based on World Federation of Exchanges, https://focus.world-exchanges.org/issue/february-2020/market-statistics (accessed March 2, 2020).

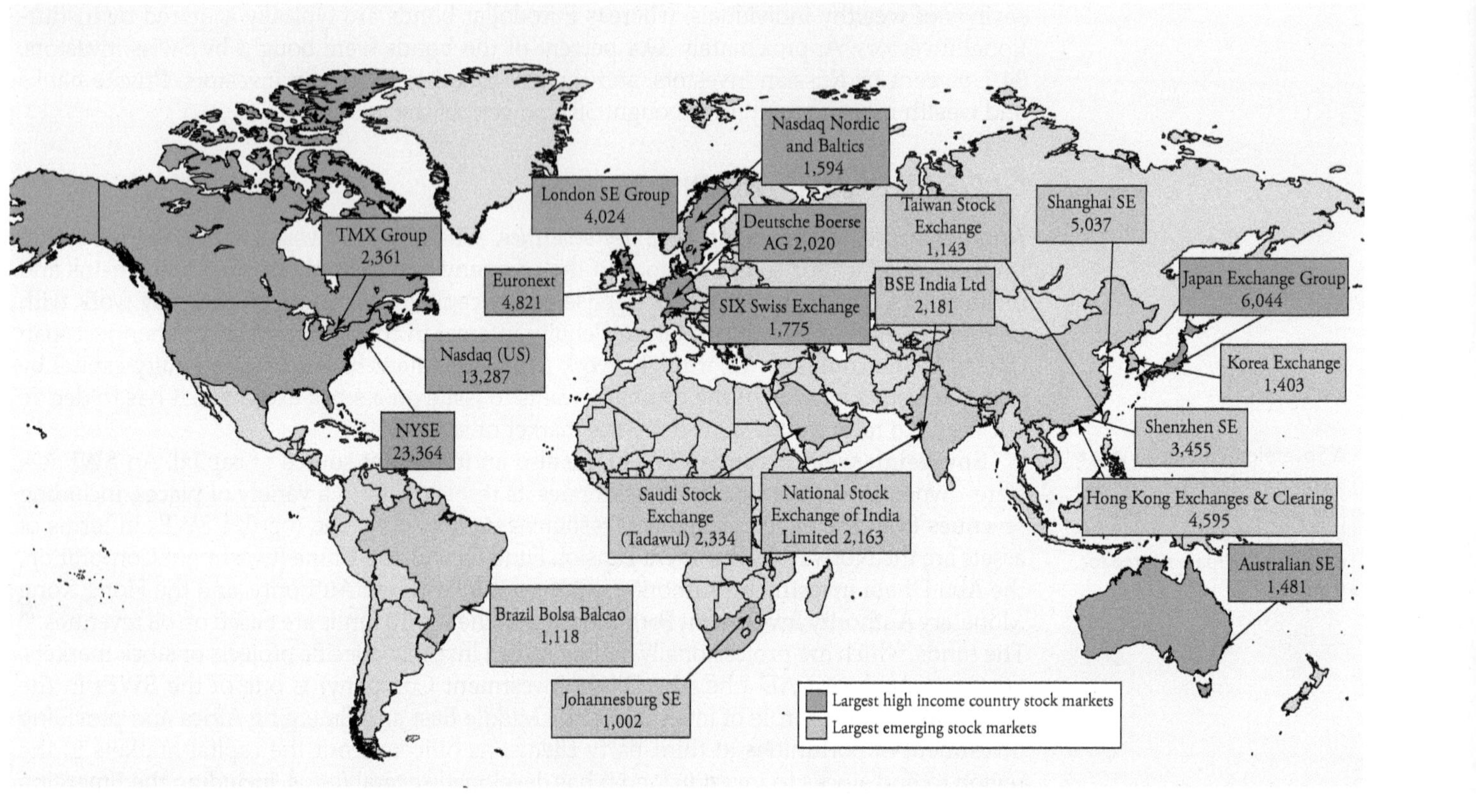

the Chinese economy began slowing, the impact was felt all over the world, from the drop in demand in commodities to the resulting drop in commodity prices. When China devalued the yuan, the ripple effect was felt worldwide and equity markets fell.[28] Fourth, uncertainty in interest rates created uncertainty in markets. When the U.S. economy was weak, interest rates were low, but when it looked like economic activity was heating up, interest rates were predicted to rise. This caused a drop in the U.S. stock market, the largest in the world. On the other hand, as emerging markets reduced interest rates, investment money began to flood into the emerging markets on the bet that their economies would grow and provide higher returns than in the weaker industrial markets.

An interesting example is Europe. In 2016, investors were pulling money out of Europe at a rapid rate. This was due largely to concerns about an unstable political situation in Europe, low interest rates (thus low returns on many investments), weak banks, and a broader European economy that continued to be weak. That was in sharp contrast to 2015 when it looked like Europe had recovered from the debt crisis of 2010–2012.[29] It is clear that to understand trends in stock markets, it is important to understand trends in political and economic forces worldwide and that forces in countries or regions often vary.

Euroequities are shares listed on stock exchanges in countries outside the home country of the issuing company.

The Rise of the Euroequity Market Besides domestic markets, there is also the **euroequity market**, the market for shares sold outside the boundaries of the issuing firm's home country. A euroequity IPO occurs when a company's shares are made available internationally rather than just in the country where the company is based.[30] An example is the 2016 IPO by Line Corporation, a Japanese messaging-app operator, which raised over $1 billion by simultaneously offering 13 million shares on the Tokyo Stock Exchange and 22 million on the New York Stock Exchange.[31] This is a euroequity IPO even though it was issued in Japan and the United States and not in Europe.

More generally, an MNE will list its existing shares on multiple stock markets in a process called cross-listing. For example, 3M's common stock trades on the New York Stock Exchange and on the SIX Swiss Exchange, where its shares trade in Swiss francs.[32]

The Trend Toward Delisting The trend of listing on more than one exchange began to reverse somewhat as more and more companies reduced the number of exchanges on which their stocks were listed. In 2019, Procter & Gamble, the U.S. MNC that trades on the New York Stock Exchange, delisted from the Euronext Paris exchange due to low trading volumes, high costs, and administrative requirements.[33] Companies pay annual fees to list on exchanges, so if trading is light they can save money by removing the listing. Another reason for delisting is increased regulation, often cited as a reason for companies delisting from the U.S. exchanges (e.g., due to the Sarbanes–Oxley Act). In addition, investors are finding that the best price for stocks is usually in the home market of the company in which they are investing.

Most foreign companies that list on the U.S. stock exchanges do so through American Depositary Receipts, which are financial documents that represent specified number of shares in the foreign company.

American Depositary Receipts In 2019, 508 foreign companies or 22.6 percent of the total listings on the NYSE[34] were made through an **American Depositary Receipt (ADR)**, a negotiable certificate issued by a bank in the United States to represent underlying shares of a foreign corporation's stock held in trust at a custodian bank in the foreign country. ADRs are traded like stock shares, with each one representing some number of shares of the underlying stock. For example, Toyota has listed ADRs on the NYSE since 1999 at a rate of two common Toyota shares per ADR. Toyota sponsors a facility operated by the Bank of New York. In addition to the NYSE and the Tokyo Stock Exchange, Toyota also lists its ADRs on the London Stock Exchange.

TAXATION OF FOREIGN-SOURCE INCOME

11-4 Summarize how foreign source income is taxed

Gaining access to capital is about more than interest rates and stock exchange listing requirements. Tax planning is a crucial responsibility for a CFO because taxes can profoundly affect profitability and cash flow. This is especially true in international business. As complex as domestic taxation seems, it is child's play compared to the intricacies of international taxation. The international tax specialist must be familiar with both the home country's tax policy on foreign operations and the tax laws of each country in which the MNE operates.

Taxation has a strong impact on several decisions:

- Location of operations
- Choice of operating form, such as export or import, licensing agreement, or overseas investment
- Legal form of the new enterprise, such as branch or subsidiary
- Possible facilities in tax-haven countries to raise capital and manage cash
- Method of financing, such as internal or external sourcing, and debt or equity
- Capital budgeting
- Method of setting transfer prices

INTERNATIONAL TAX PRACTICES

Differences in tax practices around the world often cause headaches for MNEs. Lack of familiarity with laws and customs can create confusion. In some countries, tax laws are loosely enforced. In others, taxes may generally be negotiated between the tax collector and the taxpayer—if they are ever paid at all. In still others, they must be rigidly followed.

With a value-added tax, each company pays a percentage of the value added to a product at each stage of the business process.

Differences in Types of Taxes Countries differ in terms of the types of taxes they have (income versus excise), the tax rates applied to income, the determination of taxable income, and the treatment of foreign-source income. Although we focus in this section on corporate income taxes, excise taxes are another important source of income to governments. The value-added tax (VAT) is an example of an excise tax used in Europe as well as other parts of the world, including China. It is a percentage levied on products at the point of sale in every stage of the value chain, and is included in the final price of the product rather than added to the price at the final point of sale, as is the case with the sales tax in the United States. There are many other excise taxes, and the large number of taxes in some countries, like Brazil, is very confusing to both local and foreign investors.

Differences in Generally Accepted Accounting Principles (GAAP) Variations among countries in **GAAP (Generally Accepted Accounting Principles)** can lead to differences in determining taxable income. In countries where tax laws allow firms to depreciate assets faster than accounting standards allow but where the firms must use the same standards for tax and book accounting, higher depreciation expenses result in lower income and therefore lower taxes. Revenue recognition is also an important issue. Some countries tax income from worldwide revenues of MNEs, whereas others only recognize income from revenues generated in the domestic environment.

Differences in Tax Rates Corporate tax rates also vary from country to country. As noted in the opening case, the corporate tax rate was 12.5 percent in Ireland and 35 percent in the United States when Pfizer was considering the issue of tax inversion. As part of the 2017 Tax Cuts and Jobs Act, the United States lowered the corporate tax rate to 21 percent beginning in 2018. This is still higher than Ireland, but there are a few countries that have even higher rates. However, tax rates vary depending on whether the rate includes a combined central government and sub-central government, such as federal and state taxes in the United States. According to one report, the United States now has a combined statutory tax rate of 25.89 percent, the 84th highest of 218 economies in the world.[35]

In the separate entity approach, governments tax each taxable entity when it earns income.

Two Approaches to Corporate Taxation Taxation of corporate income is accomplished through one of two approaches in most countries: the *separate entity approach* (also known as the *classical approach*) or the *integrated system approach*.

Separate Entity Approach In the separate entity approach, which the United States uses, each separate unit—company or individual—is taxed when it earns income. For example, a corporation is taxed on its earnings, while stockholders are taxed on the distribution of earnings (dividends). The result can be double taxation.

An integrated system tries to avoid double taxation of corporate income through tax credits or split tax rates.

Integrated System Approach Many other developed countries use an integrated system to eliminate double taxation. Australia and New Zealand, for example, give a dividend credit to shareholders to shelter them from double taxation. This means that when shareholders report the dividends in their taxable income, they also get a credit for taxes paid on that income by the company that issued the dividend. That keeps the shareholders from paying tax on the dividend because the company has already done so.

Germany used to have a split-rate system with two different tax rates on corporate earnings: one on retained earnings and one on distributed earnings. However, they abolished it in 2001 and adopted a classical system with an overall lower corporate tax rate on earnings of 15 percent (15.285 percent including the solidarity surcharge to help with the reunification with East Germany) plus a municipal trade tax ranging from 14 to 17 percent, resulting in an effective tax rate of 30 and 33 percent.[36]

Differences in Taxing Foreign-Source Income Taxation of foreign-source income also depends on the country where the parent company is domiciled. Sometimes, countries tax MNEs on their worldwide income and give them credits for foreign corporate income taxes paid. This is referred to as the "worldwide method." More commonly, countries now tax MNEs only on their domestic income, which is referred to as the "territorial system." The 2017 Tax Cuts and Jobs Act in the United States switched the method of taxing U.S. multinationals from the worldwide system to the territorial system. Thus, the United States no longer taxes foreign-source income of U.S. multinationals, but the new law also limits MNCs' ability to move profits out of the United States to low-tax jurisdictions (as discussed below).

TAXING BRANCHES AND SUBSIDIARIES

In order to innovate and expand, companies need to gain access to capital, both debt and equity, from home-country capital markets or markets abroad. However, companies can also raise capital through minimizing their tax liability worldwide so that they can use internally generated cash to expand. To illustrate how this is done, let's look at how U.S.-based companies pay taxes on earnings from a *foreign branch* and a *foreign subsidiary*.

Foreign branch income (or loss) is directly included in the parent's taxable income.

The Foreign Branch A foreign branch is an extension of the parent company rather than an enterprise incorporated in a foreign country. Any income the branch generates is taxable immediately to the parent, whether or not cash is remitted by the branch to the parent as a distribution of earnings. However, if the branch suffers a loss, the parent is allowed to deduct that loss from its taxable income, reducing its overall tax liability.

The Foreign Subsidiary Whereas a branch is a legal extension of a parent company, a foreign corporation is an independent legal entity set up (incorporated) in a country according to that country's laws of incorporation. When an MNE purchases a foreign corporation or sets up a new one in a foreign country, it is called a *subsidiary* of the parent. Income earned by the subsidiary is either reinvested in the subsidiary or remitted as a dividend to the parent company.

Tax deferral means that income is not taxed until it is remitted to the parent company as a dividend.

Foreign income is either taxable to the parent or tax-deferred—that is, it is not taxed until it is remitted as a dividend to the parent. Which tax status applies depends on whether the foreign subsidiary is a *controlled foreign corporation (CFC)*—a technical term in the U.S. tax code—and whether the income is active or passive. This is a relatively unique concept for U.S. companies since most countries only tax income earned in their countries and do not tax foreign source income.

In a CFC, U.S. shareholders hold more than 50 percent of the voting stock.

The Controlled Foreign Corporation A **controlled foreign corporation (CFC)**, from the standpoint of the U.S. tax code, is any foreign company in which more than 50 percent of its voting stock is held by "U.S. shareholders," which are U.S. citizens or companies that each hold 10 percent or more of the CFC's voting stock. Any foreign subsidiary of an MNE would automatically be considered a CFC from the standpoint of the tax code. However, a joint venture company abroad that is partly owned by the U.S.-based MNE and partly by local investors might not be a CFC if the U.S. MNE does not own more than 50 percent of the JV's stock.

To qualify as a *controlled foreign corporation (CFC)*, more than 50 percent of a company's voting shares must be held by U.S. shareholders. A *U.S. shareholder* must be a U.S. person or company holding at least 10 percent of the corporation's voting shares. Assume three scenarios: foreign corporation A has one U.S. shareholder who owns 100 percent of the shares. Foreign Corporation B has four shareholders. One owns 45 percent of the shares, one owns 10 percent, one owns 20 percent, and one owns 25 percent. Foreign corporation C has four shareholders. One owns 30 percent, one owns 10 percent, two each own 8 percent, and one, a non-U.S. person, owns 44 percent. Which of these are CFCs? A definitely is. B is because all of the shareholders are U.S. persons who own at least 10 percent of the shares. C is not, because two U.S. persons own at least 10 percent of the shares, and they only own a total of 40 percent.

When former U.S.-based company Enron set up its shell companies in tax-haven countries, it was careful not to own more than 50 percent of the stock so that it could avoid having to include the debt in those operations in its consolidated income.[37]

Active income is derived from the direct conduct of a trade or business. Passive income is usually derived from operations in a tax-haven country.

Active Versus Passive Income If a foreign subsidiary qualifies as a CFC, the U.S. tax law requires the U.S. investor to classify the foreign-source income as *active* or *passive income.* **Active income** is derived from the direct conduct of a trade or business, such as from sales of products manufactured in the foreign country. **Passive income**, or **Subpart F income** because it is specifically defined in Subpart F of the U.S. Internal Revenue Code, comes from sources other than those connected with the direct conduct of a trade or business, generally in tax-haven countries, and includes the following:

- *Holding company income*—income primarily from dividends, interest, rents, royalties, and gains on sale of stocks.
- *Sales income*—income from foreign sales corporations that are separately incorporated from their manufacturing operations. The product of such entities is manufactured and sold for use outside the CFC's country of incorporation, and the CFC has not performed significant operations on the product.
- *Service income*—income from the performance of technical, managerial, or similar services for a company in the same corporate family as the CFC and outside the country in which the CFC resides.

The 2017 tax reform in the United States makes an effort to expand the taxation of passive income. To reduce incentives for shifting profits out of the United States by using intellectual property, the tax law introduces Global Intangible Low Tax Income, or GILTI. The intent is to tax foreign income earned from intangible assets such as patents, trademarks, and copyrights held abroad. Previously, ownership of such intangible assets may have been transferred to an MNC's foreign subsidiaries in order to avoid paying taxes on rents and royalties collected. Often, the parent is paying rents and royalties to foreign subsidiaries as a means of shifting profits to low-tax jurisdictions. Effective in 2018, the income is subject to the GILTI tax, and this may reduce the incentives to transfer ownership of intellectual property abroad.

However, the GILTI tax itself is only a rough attempt to tax income on intangible assets in low-tax jurisdictions. In reality, GILTI is simply a new category of foreign-source income, and an additional tax on high income in low-tax countries based on a complex calculation. The tax is calculated as the total active income earned by a foreign subsidiary that exceeds 10 percent of the firm's depreciable tangible property; then the corporation can generally deduct 50 percent of the GILTI and claim a foreign tax credit for 80 percent of foreign taxes paid. Through this complicated formula, the result is that the effective U.S. tax rate on GILTI is as high as 10.5 percent in a country without a corporate income tax, and the tax is zero in any country with a 13.125 percent tax or higher.[38] Once again, the GILTI is only the amount of income over 10 percent of the firm's physical assets. Some elements of the new tax are still being worked out, but this scheme is expected to have the effect of adding an extra tax to highly profitable subsidiaries operating in low-tax countries.

Passive income and GILTI often derive from the activities of subsidiaries in so-called "tax-haven" countries such as the Bahamas, the Cayman Islands, and Panama. The tax-haven subsidiary may act as an investment company, a sales agent or distributor, an agent for the parent in licensing agreements, or a holding company of stock in other foreign subsidiaries that are called *grandchild*—or *second-tier*—*subsidiaries.* This setup is illustrated in Figure 11.1. In the role of a holding company, its purpose is to concentrate cash from the parent's foreign operations into the low-tax country and use the cash for global expansion.

Determining a Foreign Affiliate's Income Figure 11.2 illustrates how the tax status of a foreign affiliate's income is determined. All non-CFC income—active and passive—earned by the foreign corporation is deferred until remitted as a dividend to the U.S. shareholder (the parent company, in this example). In contrast, a CFC's active income is non-taxable to the parent, but its passive income is taxable immediately to the parent as soon as the CFC earns it, subject to some limitations and exceptions. The CFC must also calculate Global Intangible Low-Tax Income (GILTI) and pay taxes if owed. If a foreign branch earns income, it is immediately taxable to the parent company, whether it is active or passive.

FIGURE 11.1 The Tax-Haven Subsidiary as Holding Company

A U.S. company has established a *tax-haven subsidiary* as a *holding company* in an offshore location. As such, the offshore subsidiary owns shares in three foreign subsidiaries called *grandchild subsidiaries*. The offshore holding company generates *holding company income*, which is recorded by the U.S. parent company as *passive income*.

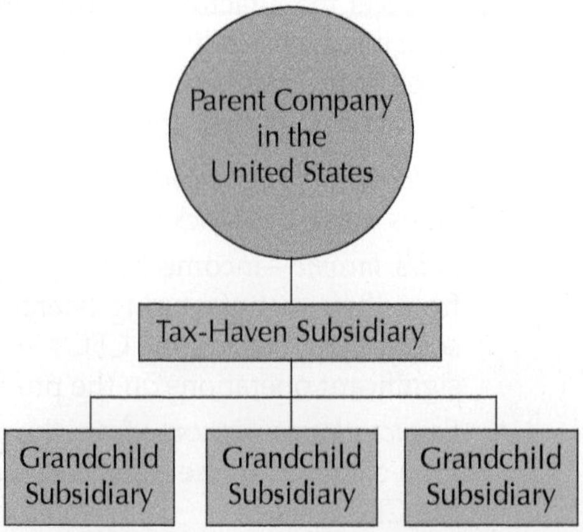

FIGURE 11.2 The Tax Status of U.S.-Owned Foreign Affiliates

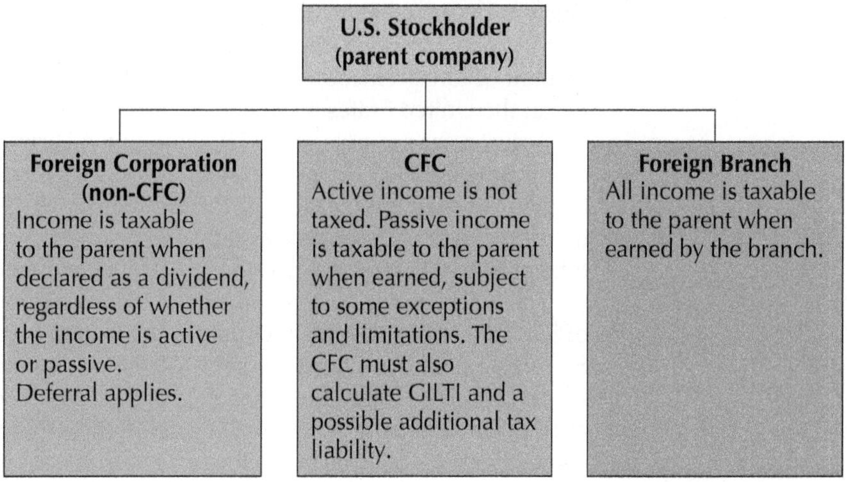

U.S. Stockholder (parent company)
Foreign Corporation (non-CFC)
Income is taxable to the parent when declared as a dividend, regardless of whether the income is active or passive.
Deferral applies.
CFC
Active income is not taxed. Passive income is taxable to the parent when earned, subject to some exceptions and limitations. The CFC must also calculate GILTI and a possible additional tax liability.
Foreign Branch
All income is taxable to the parent when earned by the branch.

TRANSFER PRICES

A transfer price is a price on goods and services one member of a corporate family sells to another.

A major tax challenge as well as an impediment to performance evaluation is the extensive use of transfer prices in international operations. A **transfer price** is a price on goods and services one member of a corporate family sells to another. Because the price is between related entities, it is not necessarily an **arm's-length price**—that is, a price between two companies that do not have an ownership interest in each other. The assumption is that an arm's-length price is more likely than a transfer price to reflect the market accurately.

Transfer Prices and Taxation Companies establish arbitrary transfer prices primarily because of differences in taxation between countries. For example, if the corporate tax rate is higher in the parent company's country than in the subsidiary's country, the parent could set a low transfer price on products it sells to the subsidiary to keep taxable profits low in its country and high in the subsidiary's country. The parent could also set a high transfer price on products sold to it by the subsidiary.

The OECD is very concerned about the ways in which companies manipulate transfer prices to minimize their tax liability worldwide. For this reason, the OECD Centre for Tax Policy and Administration meets periodically to discuss the adoption of sound transfer pricing policies (along with a wide range of other tax issues). The OECD issued guidelines on transfer pricing in 1979 and updated the policies in 1995 to provide guidance on different transfer methods that could be used and how to tell if a transfer between independent firms is similar to a transfer within a group. To avoid transfer-price manipulation, it recommends determining the tax liability in each country by applying an arm's-length price, and it has issued guidelines on the matter. Additional OECD policy revisions have been published since 1995 and continue to be published periodically.[39]

Companies can get into disputes with different tax jurisdictions over transfer pricing policies. GlaxoSmithKline (GSK), the British pharmaceutical company, settled a transfer pricing dispute with the U.S. Internal Revenue Service in 2006 by paying $3.1 billion in federal, state, and local taxes and interest—slightly less than the $5 billion the IRS was seeking and nearly half of GSK's operating cash flow. The IRS contends that GSK charged its U.S. affiliate too little for marketing services provided by the affiliate, which meant that U.S. earnings were low, resulting in lower taxes collected in the United States. The dispute arose over whether GSK should have paid for the marketing services at cost or at the price it would have paid an independent third party. These are complex issues that leave companies open to significant financial risks if they don't price services or products correctly.[40]

DOUBLE TAXATION AND TAX CREDITS

A tax credit is a dollar-for-dollar reduction of tax liability and must coincide with the recognition of income.

Every country has a sovereign right to levy taxes on all income, which could result in double taxation if both the home and host country tax the income. Under U.S. tax law, a U.S. MNE gets a credit for income taxes paid to a foreign government when the same income is taxable in the United States. For example, when a U.S. parent recognizes foreign-source income (such as the passive income discussed above) in its taxable income, it must pay U.S. tax on that income. However, the IRS allows the parent company to reduce its tax liability by the amount of foreign income tax already paid. It is limited by the amount it would have had to pay in the United States on that income.

Assume, for example, that U.S. Company A earns $100,000 of foreign-source income and that it pays $20,000 (20 percent tax rate) on that income in the foreign jurisdiction. If that income is considered taxable in the United States, Company A would have to pay $21,000 in income taxes (21 percent tax rate). In the absence of a tax credit, Company A would pay a total of $41,000 in income tax on the $100,000 of income, a 41 percent tax rate.

The IRS, however, allows Company A to take credits for foreign taxes paid, up to a maximum of $21,000—what it would have paid in the United States if the income had been earned there. Since Company A's subsidiary paid $20,000 in foreign income tax (a 20 percent tax rate), it would be able to claim the entire $20,000 as a credit because it was less than the U.S. liability of $21,000. Company A will pay a total of $21,000 in corporate income tax on its foreign-source income—$20,000 to the foreign government and $1,000 to the U.S. government.

The purpose of tax treaties is to prevent double taxation or to provide remedies when it occurs.

Tax Treaties: Eliminating Double Taxation The primary purpose of tax treaties is to prevent international double taxation or to provide remedies when it occurs. The United States is an active participant in 77 different tax treaties involving 58 different countries.[41] The general pattern between two treaty countries is to grant reciprocal deductions on dividend withholding and to exempt royalties—and sometimes interest payments—from any withholding tax.

The United States has a domestic withholding tax of 30 percent for dividends, interest, and royalties for owners of U.S. securities issued in countries with which it has no tax treaty. When a tax treaty is in effect, the U.S. rate on dividends is generally reduced to 5 to 15 percent, and the tax on interest and royalties is either eliminated or reduced to 5 to 10 percent. The rate varies by country, however.

DODGING TAXES

Two things will always be true: governments will always try to figure out how to collect as much in taxes as they can and companies (and individuals) will try to avoid paying as much in taxes as they can. The challenge is that some countries provide tax incentives to attract investment, and these incentives can help MNEs lower their overall tax liability. Take Google, for example, a U.S.-based company that operates worldwide. Google established its European headquarters in Ireland where the corporate tax rate is 12.5 percent, as mentioned elsewhere in the chapter, and has its customers who buy advertising on Google's search engine sign contracts with its Irish subsidiary rather than in the country where they reside. Thus Google generates revenues across Europe but pays taxes in Ireland rather than in the other countries whose tax rates are substantially higher. To reduce their tax liability even more, Google runs some of its royalty payments through a subsidiary in Bermuda, where there are no corporate income or withholding taxes.[42] The EU is now forcing MNEs to pay tax in the countries where their sales are generated rather than in low-tax countries like Ireland.

There are many reasons why companies locate in Ireland, such as cheap workers and a business-friendly environment, but the low corporate tax rate is not insignificant. To attract more knowledge-based firms, Ireland announced a 6.25 percent tax rate on revenue generated from patents and other intellectual property developed in Ireland.[43] In some ways, this avoids the criticism that MNEs develop their R&D outside of Ireland but collect royalties in low-tax Ireland.

One advantage that MNEs have is that it may be hard for a country to figure out its own tax policy, but it is almost impossible for countries to come up with one global tax policy that everyone can agree on. As a result, companies do the best they can to exploit the differences. The EU is even fighting over differences in tax policies from country to country. Luxembourg and the Netherlands, in addition to Ireland, are criticized by the European Commission, which is trying to eliminate different tax policies as tools to attract investments from MNEs. And the United States is also getting involved in the criticism of the EU because U.S. tax treaties are made with individual countries, not the EU as a whole. They worry that the European Commission is bullying individual countries that have set their own tax policies.

OFFSHORE FINANCING AND OFFSHORE FINANCIAL CENTERS

11-5 Analyze how offshore financial centers provide financing opportunities for MNEs

Offshore financing is the provision of financial services by banks and other agents to nonresidents.

Companies are partly able to reduce their tax liabilities because of tax-haven countries and the ability to use them for a variety of offshore activities. **Offshore financing** is the provision of financial services by banks and other agents to nonresidents. In its simplest form, this involves borrowing money from and lending to the nonresidents.[44] A good example of legitimate offshore financing is the use of the Eurodollar market. A U.S. company can raise Eurodollars in London by working with a bank to issue bonds or syndicate a loan. Or it could float Eurobonds in Bermuda where there are no withholding taxes on interest, which is more beneficial to the investor.

WHAT IS AN OFC?

Offshore financial centers (OFCs) are cities or countries that provide large amounts of funds in currencies other than their own.

Offshore financial centers (OFCs) are cities or countries that provide large amounts of funds in currencies other than their own and are used as locations in which to raise and accumulate cash. Usually, the financial transactions are conducted in currencies other than that of the country and are thus the centers for the Eurocurrency market. An OFC could be defined as any financial center where offshore activity takes place, but a more practical definition is a center where the bulk of financial activity is offshore on both sides of the balance sheet, the transactions are initiated elsewhere, and the majority of the institutions involved are controlled by nonresidents.[45]

CONCEPT CHECK

Chapter 5 introduced the OECD in discussing the OECD Anti-Bribery Convention. The OECD is also concerned about a broader range of activities that involve cross-border operations. The OECD's earlier Guidelines for MNEs, which came out in 1976, includes a code of conduct for MNEs engaged in cross-border operations. Because offshore financing is conducive to such misbehavior as tax avoidance, the OECD and several other multilateral organizations have made efforts to strengthen ethical practices in offshore transactions.

Characteristics of OFCs The markets in these centers tend to be regulated differently—and usually more flexibly—than domestic markets. The centers provide an alternative, (usually) cheaper source of funding for MNEs so the latter don't have to rely strictly on their own national markets. Offshore financial centers have one or more of the following characteristics:

- A large foreign-currency (Eurocurrency) market for deposits and loans (in London, say)
- A market that functions as a large net supplier of funds to the world financial markets (such as in Switzerland)
- A market that functions as an intermediary or pass-through for international loan funds (e.g., the Bahamas and the Cayman Islands)
- Economic and political stability
- An efficient and experienced financial community
- Good communications and support services
- An official regulatory climate favorable to the financial industry, in the sense that it protects investors without unduly restricting financial institutions[46]

However, the OECD prefers to differentiate between well and poorly regulated financial centers rather than offshore and onshore.[47]

Operational Versus Booking Centers *Operational centers* have extensive banking activities involving short-term financial transactions; *booking centers* have little actual banking activity taking place but transactions are recorded to take advantage of secrecy and low (or no) taxes. In the latter case, individuals may deposit money offshore to hide it from their home-country tax authorities, either because the money is earned and/or to be used illegally—such as in the drug trade or to finance terrorist activities—or because the individual or company does not want to pay tax. London is an example of an operational center; the Cayman Islands is an example of a booking center.

OFCs offer low or zero taxation, moderate or light financial regulation, and banking secrecy and anonymity.

OFCs as "Tax Havens" A major concern with OFCs is the tax avoidance dimension of their activities. The OECD has been working closely with the major OFCs to ensure that they are engaged in legal activity. It uses the following key factors in identifying tax havens: (1) no or only nominal taxes, (2) lack of effective exchange of information (especially bank secrecy), (3) lack of transparency, and (4) no substantial activities.[48] Although not trying to tell the

Panama City, Panama, a location often considered a leading tax haven.

Source: GTS Productions/Shutterstock

sovereign countries what their tax rates should be, the OECD is trying to eliminate harmful tax practices in these four areas:

1. The regime imposes low or no taxes on the relevant income (from geographically mobile financial and other service activities).
2. The regime is ring fenced (i.e., separated) from the domestic economy.
3. The regime lacks transparency; for example, the details of it or its application are not apparent, or there is inadequate regulatory supervision or financial disclosure.
4. There is no effective exchange of information with respect to the regime.[49]

Obviously, there is a lot of overlap in these definitions. In a 2009 report, the OECD identified 28 tax-haven countries and 10 other financial centers that were moving to adopt their standards for good tax behavior, while no national jurisdictions were reported that had not committed to the internationally accepted tax standard. That is pretty significant progress.[50] The OECD is trying to reduce harmful tax practices through improved translation and disclosure. Putting the spotlight on countries seems to be the best approach.

POINT

Should Offshore Financial Centers and Aggressive Tax Practices Be Eliminated?

YES The problem with OFCs is that they operate in a shroud of secrecy that allows companies to establish operations there for illegal and unethical purposes. In 2016, the so-called Panama Papers, a treasure trove of an estimated 11.5 million internal documents of a firm in Panama called Mossack Fonseca, were obtained by German newspapers and shared with others worldwide, including the *New York Times*. The papers showed how

COUNTERPOINT

Should Offshore Financial Centers and Aggressive Tax Practices Be Eliminated?

NO OFCs are an efficient way for companies to use their financial resources more effectively. They are good locations for establishing finance subsidiaries that can raise capital for the parent company or its subsidiaries. And they allow the finance subsidiaries to take advantage of lower borrowing costs and tax rates.

Not all types of tax-minimization activities are illegal because the companies are still subject to home- and

Mossack Fonseca helped wealthy clients evade U.S. taxes in very creative ways. Mossack Fonseca set up over 2,800 companies for at least 2,400 U.S. clients in the British Virgin Islands, Panama, and the Seychelles, among other tax-haven countries. However, this scandal was worldwide. The prime minister of Iceland, who was named in the papers, even resigned because of the appearance of impropriety. Not all of the transactions were considered illegal, but several people have been indicted for their activities. A former prime minister of Pakistan was convicted and sentenced to prison. U.S. officials indicted four participants in late 2018, and it's probably just a matter of time before more people face charges.[51]

As another example, Italian company Parmalat set up three shell companies based in the Caribbean to capture cash. The companies allegedly sold Parmalat products, and Parmalat sent them fake invoices and charged costs and fees to make the sales look legitimate. It would then write out a credit note for the amount the subsidiaries supposedly owed and take that to banks to raise money. Given the location of the subsidiaries, you would think the banks would have been suspicious, but Parmalat got away with these activities.

Off-balance-sheet financing was also used to hide debts at Parmalat. The company transferred over half of its liabilities to the books of small subsidiaries based in offshore tax havens such as the Cayman Islands. This allowed it to present a healthy balance sheet and a profitable income statement to investors and creditors by hiding large amounts of debt, understating interest expenses (thus overstating income), and overstating revenues for false bookings. Parmalat's actual debt was nearly double the amount disclosed to outsiders.

Terrorists and drug dealers also use OFCs to launder money. When the U.S. government went after the money of Osama bin Laden, it went after OFCs notorious for their secrecy. When a bank in the Bahamas refused to open its books to U.S. government investigators, the United States cut the bank off from the world's wire transfer systems. Within two hours, the bank changed policies.[52] Standard Chartered plc, a British bank, was fined $340 million for violating U.S. money-laundering laws involving an illegal scheme to hide more than 60,000 transactions worth $250 billion for Iranian clients.[53] These kinds of activities must stop.

host-country laws and tax regulations. It is true that some transactions may be illegal, but most are not. The key to policing truly illegal activities, such as hiding drug money or engaging in corporate fraud like the Parmalat case, is to improve transparency and reporting.

Why shouldn't countries have the opportunity to attract business by offering tax-haven status to MNEs? Many don't have other visible means of generating resources. They are too small to set up manufacturing operations, have too small a population base to offer low-cost labor, and don't have natural resources they can sell. So what can they do? Companies and individuals need places to bank their wealth or raise capital, so the OFCs have decided to use the theory of factor proportions (discussed in Chapter 6) and develop the banking and financial infrastructure necessary to attract wealth. As long as they establish banking, privacy, and taxation laws that attract money, they should be allowed to do so. The Cayman Islands attract a lot of tourism, but the territory is also one of the world's biggest financial centers, and one of the most secretive as well. It has worked hard to crack down on money laundering so it can use its financial expertise in legal ways to help companies and individuals.[54]

OFCs don't rely on taxation to fund huge government expenditures because they don't have a large military budget or significant welfare costs. Is there anything wrong with not collecting large amounts of taxes? Some countries are upset that OFCs offer a tax-free environment for revenues generated offshore, but that's their business. Nobody should force them to collect higher taxes just because the high-tax countries are at a disadvantage in attracting banking and finance. If countries want to charge high taxes on financial transactions, let them do so, but don't force the OFCs to play their game.

Even the chairwoman of the British Public Accounts Committee, in complaining about the tax policies of MNEs like Google, Amazon, and Starbucks, admitted that they are probably not doing anything illegal; she was accusing them of being immoral.[55]

QUESTION

You can order a book from Amazon in the UK using a British website (amazon.co.uk) and receive it from a British warehouse through the British Royal Mail. However, you will be paying an Amazon subsidiary set up in Luxembourg, which offers more favorable tax conditions than the UK. Is Amazon illegal, immoral, both, or neither for having a subsidiary in Luxembourg to minimize its tax bill?

LOOKING TO THE FUTURE — The Growth of Capital Markets and the Drive by Governments to Reform Corporate Taxes

Global capital markets are in disarray largely because of unstable macroeconomic forces—weak economic growth, low interest rates, low prices on commodities, and political instability. Stock markets are very volatile as they rise and fall with changing economic news. With low oil prices, many of the sovereign wealth funds don't have the resources to invest in companies or take advantage of IPOs. In spite of this, companies are scouring the world in search of cheap capital. Because of low interest rates in Europe, there will be continued interest by corporate and sovereign buyers to issue bonds as a way to capture investment capital. The stock and bond markets will be increasingly important as banks deal with their own financial problems and increased regulations to protect against default.

Emerging markets can be great places to invest if their economies begin to recover. However, investments in emerging markets will continue to be a flight to risk, assuming that the unstable global economy doesn't favor the flight to safety in places like Japan, the United States, and Switzerland. China is in deep trouble and will continue to be so for several years because of mountains of debt and weak economic growth.

The competition for global capital will be fierce as companies are forced to shift funding from banks that are under great financial stress to issuing stocks and bonds as a way to grow and expand. In addition, stock markets will continue to compete with each other to attract companies that are looking for a place to raise capital. Mergers of stock markets to reduce costs and expand their market potential will continue to be the wave of the future, barring regulatory concerns.

Another source of cash to MNEs will continue to be tax minimization schemes. However, the OECD countries are working hard to close tax loopholes used by MNEs as they expand abroad. On the other hand, there will be tension between those countries trying to close the loopholes and countries using loopholes to attract investment. The recent tax reform in the United States may ignite efforts to reform tax laws and reduce tax rates in other countries. It is safe to say that governments will continue to push for ways to increase their tax base, and companies will continue to react to the changing tax environment to find new ways to reduce their tax burden.

The OECD, the IMF, and the EU are three institutions that will help countries narrow their tax differences and crack down on the transfer of money for illegal purposes. Although illegal financial transfers have occurred for years, drug trafficking and the financing of terrorist activities have created a more urgent need to reform the global financial system. As governments attempt to institute tax reforms, they will have to perform a delicate balancing act of raising revenue without stifling innovation and competitiveness, in the process reducing incentives for companies to look for tax havens.

CASE

Open Sesame: Alibaba Isn't Poor Anymore[56]

The poor woodcutter in *One Thousand and One Nights*, Ali Baba, discovered riches hidden in a cave to which access was granted with the phrase "open sesame." Like the poor woodcutter, Alibaba Group discovered riches when it said "open sesame" to the New York Stock Exchange (NYSE) and listed its shares for the first time in September 2014. Alibaba Group, named after the poor woodcutter in the story (who is also featured in the Alibaba corporate logo), is China's largest e-commerce company. In 2014, it needed capital and a mechanism to allow owners of the privately held firm to realize their investment gains. The initial public offering (IPO) is on record as one of the world's largest, raising $25 billion for Alibaba in a listing that valued the company at $179 billion.

At the time, only three IPOs raised more than $20 billion for their firms, and all had taken place on the Stock Exchange of Hong Kong (SEHK). The Agricultural Bank of China raised $22.1 billion in 2010; the Industrial and Commercial Bank of China raised $21.9 billion in 2006; and AIA raised $20.5 billion in 2010. Why would Alibaba come to the NYSE rather than the nearby SEHK? This question is especially intriguing since Alibaba was not well known in the U.S. market at the time.

Who Is Alibaba?

Alibaba, based in Hangzhou, China, is the largest e-commerce company in China and likely the largest in the world. Incorporated in 1999, it is involved in a variety of internet businesses, most notably online retail sites. Taobao Marketplace is a commercial site similar to eBay in the United States. Tmall is an online marketplace for name-brand retailers. Juhuasuan is a daily deals site similar to Groupon. The company is also associated with a financial technology application called AliPay, which is similar to PayPal. Other investments include online video, mobile messaging, and cloud computing.

Although it is often called the "Amazon of China" in the West, there are significant differences in their business models. Alibaba is a marketplace where merchants, small and large, sell their goods. Hence, Alibaba does not sell and ship items to customers itself. Alibaba makes money from merchants' search ads on its website and by charging commissions on some transactions, respectively a bit like Google and eBay. In 2013, Alibaba handled approximately $248 billion in transactions. It reported revenues of $7.95 billion and net income of $3.56 billion, for an astonishing profit margin of 45 percent.

The IPO

Alibaba's founder, Jack Ma, had already raised capital from external sources. Japan's SoftBank made a $20 million investment in 2000 and owned 34 percent of Alibaba at the time of the IPO. Yahoo, the U.S. internet company, paid $1 billion for a 40 percent stake in 2005. After a sale of half the shares back to Alibaba in 2012 for $7.6 billion, Yahoo still owned approximately 20 percent of Alibaba at the time of the IPO. The rest of the firm's shares were in the hands of the founder (who alone owned 8.9% of the company), other insiders, and a consortium of investors that purchased a stake in 2011.

In 2014, the timing seemed right for an IPO. Stock prices were relatively high and Alibaba was at the historical height of its success and poised for even more. The IPO would enable Alibaba to generate additional capital. Moreover, it would provide an opportunity for its owners to monetize their investments. Yahoo, in particular, was under pressure from its shareholders to harvest some of the gains in its Alibaba position. In May, Alibaba filed paperwork in the United States to sell stock to the public for the first time. Because Alibaba raised capital, it was required to disclose an extensive amount of financial and non-financial information about itself. It released a detailed prospectus, a formal document that provides information about an investment offering to help investors make more informed investment decisions. The prospectus indicated that the use of the proceeds was intended for "general corporate purposes," suggesting that the capital was not associated with any specific new projects, and may be a mechanism to liquidate some ownership shares.

The prospectus listed a set of lead underwriters that read like a "Who's Who" of Wall Street: Credit Suisse, Deutsche Bank, Goldman Sachs, JPMorgan Chase, Morgan Stanley, and Citigroup. The investment banks competed for months to take a slice of the pie, not just for the fees to be collected but for the possibility of selling more services to Alibaba in the future. In fact, Alibaba was expected to pay IPO fees well *below* the norm because of the competition among banks. Each of the banks had a specific role. Credit Suisse and Morgan Stanley took the lead preparing the prospectus, JPMorgan and Goldman worked on structuring the offer and worked with existing shareholders, and Deutsche Bank and Goldman lead the legal due diligence. Three prominent investment banks were notably absent from the party: Bank of America Merrill Lynch, UBS, and Barclays were missing because they were working on an upcoming IPO for an Alibaba competitor.

Alibaba chose to list on the New York Stock Exchange, adopting the ticker symbol "BABA." Since it is a foreign firm, its shares trade as American Depository Receipts (ADRs). Citibank is the depositary bank for the ADRs. This means that Citibank holds the underlying ordinary shares through its local custodian in China and issues 368,122,000 ADRs on the NYSE, each representing one ordinary share of the company. The shares represent about 14.9% of the ownership of Alibaba.

The IPO was priced at $68 per share on September 18, 2014, and Alibaba raised $21.8 billion. Trading on the NYSE began on September 19, and shares rose to $92.70, a 36 percent jump. The IPO was very well received in the marketplace! The company exercised an option to sell additional shares at the $68 IPO price, boosting the total amount raised to $25 billion. It was able to do this due to a "greenshoe" option, which allows IPO underwriters to buy additional company shares at the IPO price in order to satisfy more investor demand.

Investors welcomed the stock because it gives them (especially U.S. investors) a direct way to hold exposure to China's booming technology industry. Its biggest rival in China is Tencent, but Tencent's shares are not available in the United States. Trading on the SEHK since 2004, investors in the United States would have to make arrangements to purchase Tencent shares in Hong Kong, and that is more difficult than purchasing ADRs at home.

The success of the IPO made Alibaba's owners very rich. SoftBank's $20 million investment ballooned to a value of $58 billion at the time of the IPO, although it chose not to sell shares. Yahoo, on the other hand, became the largest seller of shares in Alibaba's IPO, even eclipsing the shares offered directly by the company. Yahoo received more than $9.5 billion for the sale of 140.4 million shares – approximately one-fourth of its ownership position. And Jack Ma, who built the company from humble beginnings in his Hangzhou apartment, collected more than $1 billion. Despite the sale of shares to the public, most Alibaba shares remain in the hands of three owners: SoftBank Group holds 29.11% of shares; Yahoo owns 14.95%; and Jack Ma owns 7.00%.

Alibaba's IPO no longer retains the record as the world's largest. The Saudi Arabian Oil Company's IPO in 2019 raised $29.4 billion for the state oil company. Saudi Aramco, as the company is colloquially known, listed on Saudi Arabia's Tadawul Exchange. This location limited its appeal to international investors and the shares were marketed mainly to local investors.

The third largest IPO was by Japan's SoftBank Group itself, which raised $23.5 billion in 2018. It listed on the Tokyo Stock Exchange.

Why Is a Chinese Company Listing on a U.S. Exchange?

Notably, Alibaba chose to list on the New York Stock Exchange instead of a Chinese Stock exchange, such as the Shanghai Stock Exchange, the Shenzhen Stock Exchange, or the Hong Kong Stock Exchange. Financial markets are becoming more globally oriented every year, so Alibaba was not limited to choosing a Chinese stock exchange—or any other Asian exchange—for its listing. The NYSE has in fact been courting foreign firms for decades and now has 514 non-U.S. issuers listed.

There are many reasons foreign firms list on exchanges in the United States. First, they often want access to the broad pool of investors in the U.S. market, which includes not only U.S. investors but many foreign investors from around the world. Shares listed on mainland Chinese markets are much more difficult for foreign investors to acquire, so Alibaba ruled out the Shanghai and Shenzhen markets fairly quickly. Listing in the United States is usually not feasible for firms without visibility in the United States, but although Alibaba was not well known in the market, the appetite for exposure to China and its internet market was strong. As a result, Alibaba likely reached more investors globally by listing in the world's largest economy than it would have by listing in the mainland Chinese markets, and this was probably important for what was the world's largest IPO at the time.

A related reason firms list on U.S. exchanges is that they value the liquidity of U.S. markets, where shares can change hands relatively easily, quickly, and cheaply. This is important for firms with large shareholders who are potentially interested in exiting the investment. For Alibaba, the liquidity of the NYSE will make it easier for SoftBank, Yahoo, and the founders to sell their shares in the future.

Finally, firms from emerging markets such as China often list in the United States because they want to align themselves with financial markets in advanced countries, where institutions are stronger than they are in their home countries. This requires more information transparency from the firms, but the association with strong investor protection may have benefits later, such as when the firms want to undertake mergers and acquisitions. At the time of the listing, Alibaba's founder focused on this element when he said, "What we raised today is not money, it's the trust. It's the responsibilities that we have."

An Alibaba listing on the SEHK would have provided approximately the same access to global investors, ongoing liquidity, and strong institutions such as investor protection, and Alibaba would have been much better known closer to home. Why then did Alibaba choose New York over Hong Kong? In Alibaba's case, there was an important additional reason why the company chose the NYSE. The company wanted a dual-class share structure, which would alter the control of the company vis-à-vis ownership. In particular, Jack Ma and his management team wanted to retain complete control, so they created a governance structure in which Alibaba Partnership (at the time, 28 executives in the Alibaba Group) elects a majority of the Board of Directors. Since the partnership owns a minority position (just 14 percent of the outstanding stock at the time), the arrangement gives them disproportionately large influence over the 11-member board. The class of shares held by Alibaba executives thus carries more voting rights than ordinary shares do. SoftBank, which held 34.4 percent of shares at the time, was permitted just one director, and Yahoo with 22.6 percent was not permitted any at all.

Not all stock exchanges permit a divergence of voting rights from ownership. Such dual-class structures are not unusual among companies listed on the NYSE, and have in

Open Sesame: Alibaba marked its initial public offering (IPO) at the New York Stock Exchange on September 19, 2014.

Source: Christopher Penler/Shutterstock

fact been used by other internet firms like Facebook, Google, and Groupon to allow founders to retain control. The availability of this governance structure in New York was a major attraction for Alibaba compared to Hong Kong, because the SEHK required firms to follow a "one share, one vote" principle and thus disallowed dual-class structures altogether. Perhaps not surprisingly, the SEHK subsequently changed its rules in 2018 to allow dual-class structures. Alibaba then took advantage of the changes and raised $12.9 billion in a secondary listing of its shares on the HKSE in 2019. At the time of the 2014 IPO, however, Alibaba was forced to look outside China for its dual-class IPO location, and when it said "open sesame," the NYSE—and the United States markets more generally—opened the door.

QUESTIONS

11-3 Do you agree with the decision to list an IPO, or should Alibaba have borrowed more money, possibly floating a Eurobond in London or elsewhere?

11-4 What do you feel are the best justifications for Alibaba to issue the IPO in New York? Are there any downsides to their decision to list in New York?

11-5 What is the impact to existing shareholders of diluting Alibaba's ownership, and is this a model that other companies can be expected to follow?

11-6 What do you think Alibaba's future is in the United States?

CHAPTER 12

The Strategy of International Business

Source: TonyV3112/Shutterstock

OBJECTIVES

After studying this chapter, you should be able to

12-1 Explain the idea of strategy in the MNE

12-2 Profile how executives make strategy

12-3 Analyze resources, capabilities, and competencies

12-4 Assess approaches to create value

12-5 Diagram the features and functions of the value chain

12-6 Compare global integration and local responsiveness

12-7 Distinguish the types of strategies used by MNEs

Vision without action is a daydream. Action without vision is a nightmare.

—Japanese proverb

CASE

Zara's Disruptive Vision: Data-Driven Fast Fashion[1]

The everyday ordinariness of clothing belies its significance in the global market. Apparel and textile is one of the largest industries in the world. It employs countless millions and generates more than $3 trillion in transactions.[2] Its activities are vast in scale and scope: design, branding, fiber production, fabric cutting, assembly, finishing work, logistics, merchandising, and marketing functions circle the world. Traditionally, big retailers drive the market, determining what to make, where to make it, how to distribute it, and how to sell it. Operationally, global apparel companies and national retailers outsource apparel production via global brokers, such as 3PL Center, GlobalTranz, or Li & Fung. The latter, for instance, supplies billions of pieces of apparel to department stores, hypermarkets, specialty stores, and e-commerce sites worldwide.

It owns no fabric mills, no sewing machines, and no clothing factories. Rather, Li & Fung's 22,000 employees in 250 offices in 40 nations manage the supply chains of many of the world's biggest retailers and brands.[3]

Historically, the typical garment maker is a small-scale, labor-intensive operation, usually located in a low-wage country that employs a few to a few dozen workers. There, workers make specific pieces of apparel, often in a narrow range of sizes and colors, which global brokers then integrate with the output of hundreds of other such companies that span dozens of countries. As more companies in more countries make more specialized products (i.e., one factory makes zippers, one makes linings, one makes buttons, and so on), global brokers perform as cross-border intermediaries and supervise the logistics and assembly of components into finished goods. Ultimately, these goods are distributed to apparel retailers worldwide.

The dynamics of ever-changing fashion relentlessly pressure apparel retailers to have the right style in the right sizes in the right quantities at the right time for the right price. In turn, they press global brokers to improve coordination among the many players. By planning collections closer to the selling season, testing the market, placing small initial orders, and reordering more frequently, retailers can reduce forecasting errors and avoid the dreaded "death by inventory." Industry wisdom and historic practice spurred apparel firms, no matter how big or small, to choose a "sliver" of an activity (i.e., make zippers, manage logistics, focus on retail) instead of trying to create value across multiple slivers. Effectively, the global apparel industry pressed firms to see strategy in terms of "do what you do best and outsource the rest."

CHANGING MARKETS, CHANGING OPPORTUNITIES

Steadily, globalization resets the global apparel industry. Fewer barriers, better logistics, and improving technologies create paths to disrupt industry standards. That is, rather than accepting the determinism of industry structure, some managers bet on revolutionary visions and radical missions.[4] A compelling example is the compression of cycle times in the apparel-buyer chain. Traditionally, moving a garment from designer to factories to brokers to shippers to shops takes approximately six months—three to design a new collection and another three to make, ship, and stock it. Now, a few companies, notably H&M, Topshop, and Uniqlo, have cut the cycle to three to five months.

One, Zara, has slashed the cycle to a phenomenal two weeks. Zara's vision of data-driven fast fashion, by outrightly rejecting sacred rules about strategy and success in the apparel industry, has disrupted long-running principles and practices.[5] For instance, unlike its rivals, Zara makes most of what it sells, shuns advertising, avoids sales, and directs distribution. These choices, once seen as heresies, have propelled Zara to the world's leading apparel company and made its founder, Amancio Ortega, one of the world's wealthiest person with a fortune of more than $75 billion.[6]

THE VISION OF FAST FASHION

In 1975, Señor Ortega opened a small clothing shop, Zara, in the small town of Arteixo, in a remote corner of Spain, far, faraway from the fashion capitals of New York, London, Paris, Milan, and Tokyo.[7] From its humble beginnings, today there are more than 2,250 Zara storefronts strategically located in premier spots in 96 countries.[8] In the beginning, Señor Ortega had a compelling vision: "Give customers what they want, and get it to them faster than anyone else."[9] Over the years, Zara's founding vision has held true, and today anchors its mission: "satisfying the desires of our customers . . . we plan to continuously innovate our business to improve your experience. We promise to provide new designs for quality materials that are affordable."[10] Others offer clever spins, characterizing Zara's vision as "Armani at moderate prices," or "Banana Republic priced like Old Navy."[11] No matter the nuance, Zara's vision of data-driven fast fashion anchors its strategy to integrate cutting-edge systems, state-of-the-art technology, efficient production, smart logistics, and alluring distribution that designs, makes, moves, and sells sophisticated, yet affordable, apparel.

BUILDING A STRATEGY OF FAST FASHION

Disrupting a global industry requires radically rethinking what customers want, how you make and market it, and how you make money doing so. Zara, in starting and sustaining the data-driven, fast fashion revolution, translates its vision into a practical strategy through a range of ingenious choices in acquiring resources, developing capabilities, and creating competencies. Separately and collectively, these sustain Zara's competitiveness.

Resources

Making and selling fast fashion calls for integrated manufacturing systems, logistic know-how, and retail locations. Progressively, Zara has developed world-class resources in each.

Manufacturing Zara, as does virtually every other apparel firm, sources finished garments, like generic t-shirts, slips, and the like, from suppliers in Europe, Africa, and Asia. Unlike its rivals, Zara also employs thousands who staff its factories circling Arteixo to make more than half of its fashion garments.[12] Zara's production prowess stems from Señor Ortega's insight that exploiting short-lived fashion trends requires speedy designs and quick distribution—which, operationally, means making items close to home in order to get them quickly to customers around the world. Hence, Zara makes millions of its most time- and fashion-sensitive products in its own state-of-the-art factories on its own schedule.

Logistics Garments flow through Zara's distribution center in Arteixo—more than the size of 90 football fields—or smaller satellite centers in Brazil and Mexico. In Arteixo, garments travel along 24 miles (about 200 km) of underground monorails that link its 11 factories within a 10 mile (16 km) radius of its headquarters, known as "The Cube." Along the way, they are swiftly sorted by carousels in carousels capable of processing 45,000 folded garments per hour. Zara ships more than million items per week to its stores in 96 countries. Custom orders reach its stores in Europe, the Middle East, and much of the United States in 24 hours, and 48 hours for Asia and Latin America.[13]

Retail Sites If there is marketing at Zara, it's done via high-profile real estate. "We invest in prime locations. We place great care in the presentation of our storefronts. That is how we project our image," explained Director Luis Blanc. Zara's stores command high-profile slots in premier shopping venues such as the Champs-Elysées in Paris, Regent Street in London, Fifth Avenue in New York, and Nanjing Road in Shanghai. The opening photo, for example, showcases Zara's flagship storefront in Beijing. Its location strategy creates interesting tensions. Noted a consultant, "Prada wants to be next to Gucci, Gucci wants to be next to Prada. The retail strategy for luxury brands is to try to keep as far away from the likes of Zara. Zara's strategy is to get as close to them as possible."[14]

Capabilities

Building factories and opening shops set the firm's resources. Managers' insight in how best to bundle them to complete an activity in a way that is integrative, consistent, and productive creates capabilities. Expectedly, Zara shines in translating ordinary resources, such as factories and shops, into formidable capabilities.

Design Zara's designers gather data from store managers, industry publications, TV, films, and Internet sites and social medial streams. Its trend spotters focus on university campuses and nightclubs. Its slaves-to-fashion staff snaps photos at couture shows and posts them to headquarters. There, designers sift the data, quickly converting the latest looks into affordable fashion for the masses. Zara often translates a fashion trend from a catwalk in Paris to a blouse or ensemble ready for sale in Shanghai in as little as two weeks; its rivals, notably Gap and H&M, take months to do the same. For example, when Madonna played a series of concerts in Spain, teenage girls arrived at her final show sporting a Zara knockoff of the outfit that she had worn during her first show. Zara's real-time sense of what people want to wear lets it tap the convergence of fashion and taste across national boundaries. It does not adapt products to a particular country's preferences but looks to standardize its designs for the global market. Executives reason that offering affordable, quality garments with a hip vibe, by effectively offering customers a hard-to-resist value proposition, globalizes fashion preferences.

Scarcity and Scenery Attractive stores, both inside and out, are vital to Zara's mystique. Explains Luis Blanc, "We want our clients to enter a beautiful store where they are offered the latest fashions. We want our customers to understand that if they like something, they must buy it now because it won't be in the shops the following week. It is all about creating a climate of scarcity and opportunity."[15] Fitting in with fancy neighbors, like Prada and Gucci, requires that Zara put its best face forward. Its designers roam the globe, adjusting window displays, testing store ambience, and rethinking arrangement schemes. Just as layouts are always changing, so too is the inventory mix. Zara rejects the idea of conventional spring and fall clothing collections in favor of "live collections" that are designed, manufactured, and sold almost as quickly as customers' fleeting tastes—few styles linger more than a few weeks.[16]

Promotion Zara's product policy emphasizes reasonable quality, affordability, and high fashion. It has little use for advertising or promotion. Founder Amancio Ortega saw advertising as a "pointless distraction"; he himself has never given an interview and rarely allows his photo taken.[17] Zara spends just less than half a percent of sales on advertising, compared with 3 to 4 percent for its rivals. It avoids flashy campaigns, relying instead on word-of mouth among loyal shoppers. Like Señor Ortega, it does not promote itself; it leaves that to thrilled customers.

Competencies

Just as bright managers combine resources into capabilities, they then transform them into competencies. Somewhat difficult to pinpoint, one can think of a competency as the special knowledge, skill, or ability that a firm uses to connects its resources and capabilities. The resulting synthesis sets and sustains its ability to create superior value for its customers.

Flexibility Zara quickly turns around the latest, greatest fashion—many items you see in its stores didn't exist a few weeks earlier. Explains Director Marcos Lopez, "The key driver in our stores is the right fashion. Price is important, but it comes second."[18] Zara aggressively prices its products, and adjusts pricing for the international market, making customers in foreign markets bear the costs of shipping products from Spain. Likewise, if the product line fails to excite customers, Zara can "scrap an entire production line if it is not selling. We can dye collections in new colors, and we can create a new fashion line in days."[19] Integrating new ideas and new designs into reasonably priced, high-fashion garments that are available worldwide within weeks is an awfully hard objective. Zara's insight in blending its resources and capabilities successfully develops a value-creating, hard-to-copy competency—perhaps best seen in its rivals' struggles to do to the same.

Fashion-Tech Zara's stores, besides presenting its face to the world, function as grassroots marketing agents. Networked stores feed sales data and customer requests (the latter helping to localize otherwise globally standardized products) to headquarters in Arteixo. At the center of the Zara-web, physically and symbolically, is "The Cube," the gleaming central command of the company. Here, designers, analysts, and planners bundle and blend resources and capabilities, experimenting with ways to leverage real-time data into real-time fashions. Designers, for instance, simulate product presentation and positioning (even testing the acoustics of the in-store soundtrack) on its "Fashion Street," a Potemkinesque strip of mock storefronts that mimic the layout of its strategically significant storefronts around the world. Constant and continual refinement of resources and capabilities fortifies Zara's competencies.

Clothes Shopping as an Exciting Adventure The timeliness of its offerings, aura of exclusiveness, captivating in-store ambience, and positive word of mouth, fed by rapid product turnover, leverages Zara's resources and capabilities. Loyal shoppers learn which days of the week the latest, greatest fashions are delivered—so-called "Z-days"—and shop accordingly. Zara fuels the frenzy with small shipments—say, three or four dresses in a particular style—to a store. Small shipments make for sparsely stocked shelves. Moreover, products have a display limit of one month. Rapid turnover does the rest: even though consumers visit Zara frequently, when they return, things look different. The CEO of the National Retail Federation, reflecting on Z-days, rapid turnover, and sparse inventory, marveled, "It's like you walk into a new store every two weeks."[20]

MOVING ONWARD

The first Zara shop opened its doors in 1975 in Arteixo. Today, there are more than 2,200 outlets and, on average, a new one opens every few days. The elegant clarity of Zara's vision, mission, and strategy, translated into a compelling mix of resources, capabilities, and competencies, drives its stunning success. Significantly, Zara's choice to be great rejected the long-established strategic standards of the global apparel industry. Currently, no other apparel company comes close to designing, making, moving, and selling fashion as speedily as Zara. Its success leaves rivals with less time to figure out how to better configure and coordinate their operations. Some stay in the game, such as H&M, while others fall further behind, notably Gap. Ultimately, struggling rivals must follow Zara's strategic lead—if they don't, warns analysts, they won't stay in business.

QUESTIONS

12-1 Evaluate how Zara translates its "Give customers what they want, get it to them faster than anyone else" into its day-to-day operations.

12-2 Assess the difficulty a competitor, such as Gap, faces recreating the resources, capabilities, and competencies that define Zara.

STRATEGY IN THE MNE

12-1 Explain the idea of strategy in the MNE

Evolving customer preferences, innovative competitors, changing market structures, new tech-platforms and shifting institutional contexts create opportunities and threats. The job of the strategist is identifying the implications of these, along with many others, to which products to make, where to make them, where to sell them, how to compete, and, all the while, earn a profit. Doing so, as we'll see in this and subsequent chapters, centers on how managers assess and enter foreign markets, make investments, form alliances, and organize activities. Then, given these choices, we profile how managers implement marketing, manufacturing, supply, accounting, finance, and human resource programs to run operations worldwide.

Superior performance requires managers plan for the opportunities and threats in the global business environment.

For the strategist in the MNE, the global marketplace is often too much of a good thing. The World Bank identifies 217 discrete economic environments in the world today—189 countries and 28 economies with populations of more than 30,000. The former include countries that most are familiar with, such as Australia, China, France, Indonesia, and so on. The set of 28 includes some that many have likely heard of, such as Bermuda or Macau, but also others that many have not, such as the Isle of Man or Vanuatu.[21] No matter the designation, managers scan these markets, evaluating events and trends in formulating and implementing the ideal value-creating strategy.

Strategy is an integrated and coordinated set of choices and commitments that reflects the company's present situation, identifies the direction it should go, and determines how it will get there.

The scale and scope of opportunities and threats spanning 217 markets can overwhelm analysis. Complicating matters is ever-present resource scarcity. The reality of never enough time, talent, and capital means managers, at some point, must make big decisions: which opportunities to pursue, which to pass, and then, based on the targeted products and markets, what actions to take. These tasks focus our attention on the idea of strategy.

In principle, **strategy** is an integrated set of choices and commitments that supports and sustains an MNE's competitiveness. It defines and communicates an MNE's plan on how it will use its resources, capabilities, and competencies to compete anywhere and everywhere (see Figure 12.1). Strategy maps an MNE's plan to create value, for itself and its stakeholders. Strategy specifies what an MNE will do and, just as importantly, what it will not do. Strategy calls on managers to deal with the questions and complexities that follow from cross-checking opportunities with competencies, assessing competitive threats, and setting

FIGURE 12.1 The Role of Strategy in IB

An MNE's operating environment includes physical, institutional, political, economic, cultural, market, monetary, and competitive factors. Making sense of those is the domain of strategy. Beginning with conceptualizing a vision and mission and moving through to performance outcomes, the idea of strategy is robust, varied, and fascinating.

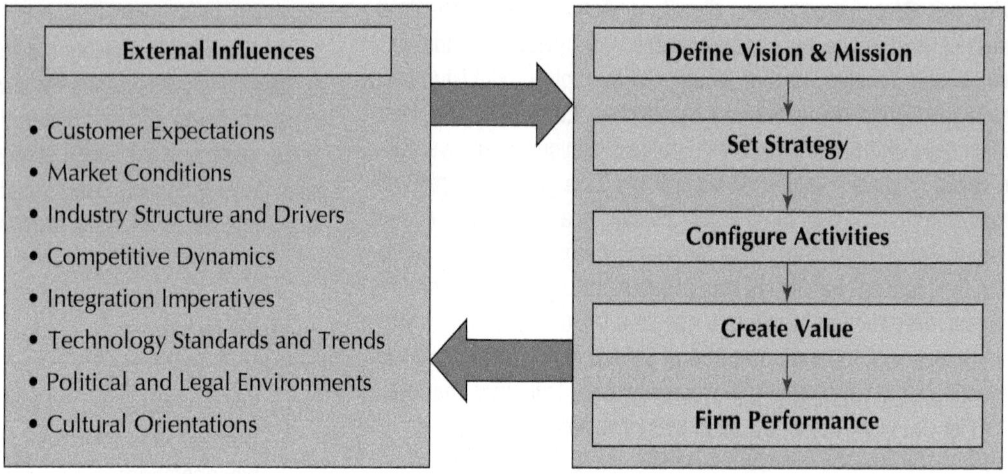

and sustaining superior performance. As tough as all that sounds, the track record of MNEs confirms that managers consistently make it happen, devising strategies that develop endlessly ingenious ways to build productive and profitable enterprises.[22]

GETTING STARTED: VISION AND MISSION

Vision is the idealization of an MNE's aspiration. Its mission declares what it is going to do, how it is going to do so, who it is going to do that for, and what value will it create in doing so.

Strategy starts with a vision and a mission. The MNE's **vision**, a future-oriented declaration of its purpose and aspirations, outlines its broad ambitions. It communicates to stakeholders, notably employees, stockholders, governments, partners, suppliers, customers, and society, what the MNE is and where it is going. The MNE's **mission** complements its vision. Whereas a vision statement inspires people to dream, a mission statement inspires them to action. It communicates what the MNE is going to do, how it is going to do that, who it is going to do that for, and what value will it create in doing so. Put differently, the vision statement conveys inspirational, motivational aspirations whereas the mission statement specifies the path the enterprise will take to attain them. Combined, an MNE's vision and mission define its purpose, values, goals, and direction.

Table 12.1 profiles the vision and mission statements of various MNEs. Each conveys how executives worldwide use these tools. Some, such as Google and IKEA, communicate a message in clear, simple, and precise language. Others, like Microsoft and Disney, take a more aspirational approach, appealing to the boundless spirit of humanity to set goals, identify direction, and inspire performance. Finally, some like Facebook and Infosys have comparatively straightforward declarations. No matter the scale or scope, a company's vision and mission statements guide management's thinking on strategic issues, promote buy-in, outline performance standards, and guide employee action. They also serve an external purpose, communicating with customers, suppliers, and partners as well as courting public support. Likewise, they give investors and analysts a perspective to interpret an MNE's choices. Most importantly, MNEs with easily understood and collectively shared vision and mission typically outperform those without them.[23]

Rhetoric to Reality Translating the lofty rhetoric of an MNE's vision and mission into relevant programs and realistic performance standards, one can imagine, is tough. Increasing the challenge for the typical MNE is the fact that its vision and mission statements must work in many businesses run by many different people operating in many different environments. Nestlé, for instance, has operations in 190 countries, relies on 413 factories in 85 countries, manages more than 2,000 brands, and has 308,000 employees—its transcendent vision of "Good Food, Good Life" expresses a universal aspiration. Likewise, the 340,000 employees of Toyota make vehicles in 67 factories spanning 29 countries and then sell them in more than

TABLE 12.1 Vision and Mission Statements, Leading MNEs

Company	Vision Statement	Mission Statement
Amazon	To be Earth's most customer-centric company, where customers can find and discover anything they might want to buy online.	We strive to offer our customers the lowest possible prices, the best available selection, and the utmost convenience.
Disney	To make people happy.	Be one of the world's leading producers and providers of entertainment and information, using its portfolio of brands to differentiate its content, services and consumer products.
Facebook	People use Facebook to stay connected with friends and family, to discover what's going on in the world, and to share and express what matters to them."	To give people the power to share and make the world more open and connected.
Google	To provide access to the world's information in one click.	To organize the world's information and make it universally accessible and useful
IKEA	To create a better everyday life for the many people of the world.	Offer a wide range of well-designed, functional home furnishing products at prices so low that as many people as possible will be able to afford them.
Infosys	To help our clients meet their goals through our people, services and solutions	Providing the people, services and solutions our clients need to meet their information technology challenges and business goals.
Microsoft	Help people and businesses throughout the world realize their full potential.	Empower people through great software anytime, anyplace, and on any device.
Nestlé	Good Food, Good Life	Provide food that is a source of nourishment and satisfaction, but also pleasure, health, happiness, and peace of mind.

170 countries—its vision of "leading the way to the future of mobility, enriching lives around the world with the safest and most responsible ways of moving people" anchors its strategy. Lastly, Vodafone's 98,996 employees direct telecom networks in 25 countries and work with partners in 47 more to provide telecom and IT services to clients in 150 countries—its mission "to enrich our customer's lives through the unique power of mobile communication" organizes its efforts. Hence, Nestlé, Toyota, and Vodafone, like other MNEs, look to their vision and mission statements to help everyone, from headquarters to the front lines, work purposefully toward common goals.

MOVING ONWARD: STRATEGIC PLANNING

An MNE systematizes the ideals that anchor its vision and mission to improve the consistency of interpretation and action. For instance, converting the vision of "Good Food, Good Life" to consistent, integrated day-to-day actions is a big step. **Strategic planning** is a powerful tool to do so. It converts ideals into reasonable challenges, testable propositions, action programs, and measurable outcomes. Done well, strategic planning promotes a collective understanding about how the world works and how the MNE will navigate it.[24] Toyota's vision quest to "lead the future of mobility. . ." is immensely broad and open to endless interpretation. Toyota deflects these threats by anchoring its strategic planning in its so-called "Toyota Way." This codification of how Toyota gets things done guides how managers define issues and make decisions.[25]

Strategic planning is a comprehensive process that determines how the firm can best achieve its vision and mission.

The discipline of strategic planning sets a rigorous decision-making framework. Its purpose—formalizing the actions that an MNE takes to achieve its vision and mission—has several benefits. Strategic planning organizes how managers deal with the routine as well as the unusual so that they can resolve situations in those ways that support the company's vision and mission. It promotes consensus on outcomes, harmonizes standards of interpretation, socializes managers to think longer-term, stipulates success standards, and increases confidence in the business's direction. Each and all are fundamental facets of an effective, high-performance strategy.

Managers use various frameworks to organize strategic planning. No absolute standard prevails. Again, think of the different challenges, considerations, and circumstances facing Nestlé, Toyota, or Vodafone as each, respectively, develops the optimal strategy to compete in the global "good food," "future of mobility," or "unique power of mobile communication"

TABLE 12.2 Strategic Planning: Outlooks and Issues

- Analyze strengths and weaknesses
- Assess opportunities and threats
- Assess strengths and weaknesses
- Estimate customers' expectations and competitors' positioning
- Evaluate the mix of resources, capabilities, and competencies
- Formalize programs, policies, and tactics
- Identify potential product markets
- Institute adaptive and learning systems to enable feedback loops
- Monitor thresholds and adjust standards given change in performance, rivals, or markets
- Pinpoint pathways that outperform rivals
- Profile the preferences of targeted customer segments
- Set clear, concise, and compelling objectives

markets. Undeniably, overlaps exist, but so too do differences. For instance, some situations call for creative, entrepreneurial perspectives while others encourage incremental, deliberate approaches. Ultimately, each looks to strategic planning to institute the interpretive logic that optimizes decision-making. Table 12.2 highlights outlooks and issues that organize strategic planning.

MAKING SENSE TO MAKE STRATEGY

12-2 Profile how executives make strategy

CONCEPT CHECK

In Chapter 3, we used the dichotomy between democracy and totalitarianism to assess political freedom. In Chapter 4, the principles of the command, market, and mixed economies helped assess economic freedom. This chapter does the same, highlighting the perspectives managers use to assess strategy.

The complexity of the global business environment can easily overtax strategic planning. Think of, for a moment, the planning challenges facing Nestlé, Toyota, or Vodafone. A recurring problem, given the vast scale and scope of global operations, is overanalyzing a situation to the point that a decision is never made, or, in effect, "analysis paralysis." Consider, for instance, the typical sorts of question that face strategic planners in the MNE: How should we set global standards? When does local responsiveness make sense? Should we make products here, there, or everywhere? How do we fund operations? How might host governments challenge our choices? Can our suppliers support our plans? What makes for effective marketing tools? What kind of people should we hire to run operations? Answering these, along with many similar questions, is tough for one market. It's challenging, to say the least, for planners evaluating say, 2, 20, or even 200 markets.

Preempting analysis paralysis spurs managers to integrate sensemaking perspectives into strategic planning. Sensemaking involves studying all sorts of issues, such as shifting markets, evolving regulations, competitors' actions, and consumer behaviors, to determine how economics, politics, culture, technology, trade, and industry influence the MNE's plans. Sensemaking converts these complexities into explanations that provide a springboard for action.[26] These insights help strategic planners determine the catalysts of success and the causes of failure. Managers apply a range of sensemaking perspectives. No standard governs which perspective is used in which situation. Currently, one commonly sees variations of the Industrial Organization and the Resource-Based Views.

Industrial Organization (IO) The **industrial organization (IO)** outlook sets the external environment as the primary determinant of an MNE's strategy. It emphasizes the determinism of industry structure given the thesis that its characteristics directly influence the potential profitability of an MNE's strategy. Characteristics are varied, including basic conditions such as location effects and demand elasticity; structural characteristics, such as barriers to entry and diversification; firm conduct aspects, such as mergers and acquisition, advertising, and investments; and government policy factors, such as protectionism, regulation, and taxation. Planners frame their interpretation in terms of how these characteristics influence the interaction among the suppliers of inputs, buyers of outputs, substitute products, potential for new entrants, and rivalry among competing firms.

The IO model holds that markets tend toward perfect competition—e.g., many firms with small market shares are price takers, sell identical products, and freely enter and exit the industry; buyers understand product features and competitors' prices; and risk-adjusted rates of return are constant. Consequently, in situations of high profits, new companies enter and compete based on better or cheaper products. Expanding supply then lowers industry profits. Facing declining profitability, some firms exit and fewer firms enter. Over time, a market's tendency toward perfect competition means that no firm or industry consistently outperforms others, no matter the innovativeness of a particular company or the imperfections within a particular industry.

Resource Based View (RBV) In reality, some industries are, and persistently remain, far from perfectly competitive. In these settings, proprietary advantages, high-entry barriers, or oligopolistic dynamics, for instance, produce market imperfections. Consequently, some MNEs earn above-average, risk-adjusted returns, while others in the same industry underperform. In this context, industry structure shapes, but does not determine a firm's performance.[27]

These sorts of situations spotlight an alternative sensemaking perspective. Rather than the structure of the industry, managers' insight in terms of acquiring resources, organizing capabilities, and developing competencies determines success. The RBV, also referred to as the 'Great by Choice' view, highlights the power of bright managers and their keen sense of devising a strategy that is difficult, if not impossible, to imitate. In contrast to the industry determinism of the IO model, the RBV holds that "Greatness is not a function of circumstance. Greatness, it turns out, is largely a matter of conscious choice."[28] Executives look internally to set and sustain competitive advantage instead of, as the IO view advocates, optimizing positioning given the structure of the industry.

Think of, for example, the ingenuity of Amazon's digital platform, LVMH's luxury goods portfolio, Zara's vision of affordable fast fashion, Apples tech-media mix, Tata's industrial scope, or Google's search expertise.[29] Rather than emphasizing elements of industry structure, managers anchor strategic planning process in a sensemaking perspective that engages tools such as BHAGs (Big Hairy Audacious Goals), Tyranny of the "OR," Genius of the "AND," Level 5 Leadership, or the Hedgehog Concept. Certainly, industry structure matters, but some MNEs thrive because of their executives' inventive insights in bundling resources, capabilities, and competencies.[30]

THE ROLE OF RESOURCES, CAPABILITIES, AND COMPETENCIES

12-3 Analyze resources, capabilities, and competencies

Both the IO and RBV perspectives focus strategic planning on articulating where the MNE is going and the actions it must take to get there. Granted, each has a different orientation—IO focuses sensemaking in terms of an MNE's external environment whereas the RBV centers on an MNE's internal setup. Still, each highlights the importance of resources, capabilities, and competencies to support its competitiveness.

Resources drive the production of goods and services that are sold to customers. Resources of the sort seen in Table 12.3 develop the firm's productive capacity. Resources are controlled by the MNE and are largely inaccessible to customers; these include manufacturing systems, technological expertise, and information systems. For example, Zara's manufacturing and logistics operations represent some of its resources. Its retail units are resources as well and, yes, they are accessible to customers, but only partially and on a regulated basis.

Collectively, resources represent the stocks of available factors that managers bundle into **capabilities**. Managers' insight in organizing resources to perform in configurations that are integrative, consistent, and productive creates capabilities that are unique to the firm. As such, capabilities reflect how well an MNE effectively manages its resources. Although not directly used in the production process, capabilities directly support productive operations. Capabilities are found throughout the firm, as suggested in Table 12.4. Again, Zara developed robust capabilities by cleverly managing its resources in market

TABLE 12.3 Resources of the Firm: Specification and Profile

Resources are available factors that are owned or controlled by the firm. Here are common types of tangible and intangible resources.

Type	Specification	Example
Tangible	Physical resources that are observable and measurable. In theory, are available to any company. In reality, constraints complicate acquisition and replication.	• Creditworthiness • Distribution Network • Employees Skills • Property Portfolio • Scale of Manufacturing Facilities • Scope of Service System • Sophistication of Technology Systems
Intangible	Resources that lack physical form. Often embedded in the principles, practices, and processes that comprise an MNE's culture, knowledge, expertise, or relationships with customers.	• Brand Recognition • Corporate Goodwill • Decision-Making Process • Executive Skills • Foreign Exchange Risk Expertise • Intellectual Property • Stakeholder Management

intelligence, design creativity, manufacturing flexibility, and logistic efficiency to sense, design, make, move, and sell affordable, cutting-edge fashion.

Managers bundle resources and capabilities to create competencies.

Just as bright managers combine resources into capabilities, they also convert resources and capabilities into **competencies**. Difficult to define precisely, competencies are the unique, inimitable knowledge, skill, or ability that, in synthesizing links between resources and capabilities, sets and sustains an MNE's competitiveness. Think of, for example, Zara's blend of high tech and high fashion or, for that matter, Apple's eye for design and delivery, the elegance of Google's search algorithm, Walmart's sophisticated information-management and product-distribution systems, Honda's mastery of engine mechanics, or Nestlé's marketing finesse.[31]

Competencies emerge over time—managers accumulate resources, combine them into capabilities, and convert them into competencies. The challenge of accumulation, combination, and conversion makes competencies the "crown jewels" of a company. With them, an MNE outperforms rivals. Without them, an MNE struggles. The fact that rivals find it difficult, if not impossible, to copy an MNE's competencies makes them the basis for superior, sustainable competitive advantage.

TABLE 12.4 Capabilities of the Firm: Specification and Profile

Capabilities are the nontransferable, firm-specific bundles of an MNE's resource. Here we see leading types.

Functional Orientation	Capability
Decision-Making	Insightfully interpreting strategic choices and consequences.
Design	Capacity to translate insights into products and processes.
Distribution	Mastering supply chain logistics to support design and delivery efficiency
Management Information Systems	Operationalizing platforms that translate big data analytics into decision-making tools.
Manufacturing	Devising assembly line layouts that maximize efficiency.
Marketing	Promoting brand recognition that inspires customer loyalty.
Product Technology	Developing a product portfolio that leverages proprietary technology.
Research & Development	Designing innovative products and processes.

THE QUEST TO CREATE VALUE

12-4 Assess approaches to create value

Value measures a firm's capability of selling what it makes for more than the costs incurred in making it.

Fundamentally, strategy is doing what others are doing, but doing it more efficiently, or doing something no one else can do, and doing it effectively. Successfully done, an MNE creates superior value by then selling products rivals find too costly to imitate or cannot duplicate. In either scenario, a company successfully creates value while rivals scramble for solutions.

Regarding the idea of value, one can define it in various ways, including economic, market, pro forma, social, book, insurance, use, par, or replacement. One can also define value from different perspectives, such as that of customers, employees, stakeholders, or shareholders. We follow convention and define **value** in economic terms, specifying it as the difference between the cost of making a product and the price that customers are willing to pay for it. An MNE that sells its product for more than the costs incurred to make it generates profits, and hence, creates value.[32] The greater its ability to make and sell products that exceed customers' value expectations, the higher the price it can charge, and the more value it creates. Consider, for instance, the iPhone 11 Pro Max. Technically, each unit costs approximately $490.50 in parts and labor. Apple adds value through a strategy of cool design, ingenious features, extensive support, and captivating marketing. Ultimately, Apple sold the iPhone 11 for $999, and after royalty expenses and licensing fees, generated $400 in gross profit.[33]

Strategy specifies an MNE's compelling value proposition (why a customer should buy its goods or use its services) as well as specifies its targeted markets (those customers for whom it creates goods or services). This analysis, whether done on a city-by-city, country-by-country, continent-by-continent, or worldwide basis, compels managers to make and sell products that exceed customers' value expectations. In broad terms, an MNE can create value by perfecting processes and products to do things more efficiently than others, thereby making products for lower costs than can competitors—the strategy of cost leadership. Or, it can create value by effectively doing something rivals cannot match, thereby making products for which consumers pay a premium price—the strategy of differentiation. Lastly, it can insightfully combine these two approaches—the strategy of integrated cost leadership-differentiation—and offer a cost-efficient, uniquely-effective product.

THE COST LEADERSHIP STRATEGY

The cost leadership strategy aims to make a product at a given level of quality for a cost below that offered by rivals.

The MNE implementing a cost leadership strategy aims to make a product at the lowest cost, relative to those offered by rivals, that appeals to the largest number of potential customers. Minimizing cost requires maximizing efficiency. This mandate requires exploiting scale, learning, and **location economies**. As a rule, the greater the quantity of a product made, the lower its per-unit fixed cost, given that the firm allocates fixed costs over more units of output. Consequently, the **cost leadership strategy** spurs selling standardized goods or services to the broadest customer segment; standardization is imperative given that customization increases costs. Singular focus on maximizing efficiency leads executives to acquire resources and develop capabilities that reduce absolute cost, but more importantly, costs relative to rivals. Common methods include product innovations, such as frugal designs or enhanced materials, or process innovations, such as lean production or Six Sigma programs.

One routinely sees the cost leadership strategy in scale-sensitive industries, such as the airline, steel, mortgage, large appliances, consumer credit, streaming, online education, and package delivery markets. MNEs such as Southwest Airlines, UPS, Haier, Thai Union Frozen, Citigroup, 2U, ArcelorMittal, Cemex, Ranbaxy Laboratories, Netflix, Virgin Mobile, and Foxconn apply it. Many emerging market companies apply the cost leadership strategy, outperforming rivals by combining state support, growing scientific and technological sophistication, efficient manufacturing, inexpensive labor, and expanding distribution.

The cost leadership strategy has several risks, including

- disruptive technologies change efficiency standard
- customer's needs change
- cheaper, better products from rivals

Risk of the Cost Leadership Strategy The cost leadership strategy requires single-minded focus on standardizing processes and products. However, disruptions, incremental or transformational, can change customers' expectations or bolster competitors' competencies, thereby obsolescing the MNE's otherwise efficiently configured system. Likewise, the relentless quest to lower costs may blind managers to market trends. For instance, a classic example is Henry Ford's vision to "put a car in the front of every house" and mission to make the lowest-cost car, the Model A; these outlooks led to the infamous strategy that "Any customer can have a car painted any color that he wants—so long as it is black."[34] General Motors successfully exploited this outlook, making a comparably priced car that was available in assorted colors. Today, one sees similar contests in smartphones and allied consumer electronics.

Similarly, disruptive innovations trigger secular shifts that displace established market leaders' precisely engineered systems. For example, Walmart's vision of offering everyday low prices depends on the finely honed integration of its retail network resources, global supply chain capabilities, and executive competencies. Increasingly, online retailers, by disrupting the traditional dynamic of the in-store shopping experience, challenge Walmart's low-cost leadership. Amazon's improving capability to offer competing, if not the same, products at an equivalent, if not lower, price, threatens the sustainability of Walmart's cost leadership. Similarly, success inspires emulation, and rivals invariably study the cost leader, assessing its innovative ways and then tweaking their operations. Hence, Wal-Mart acquired Jet in the United States and Flipkart in India, both fast-growing online retailers, to challenge Amazon.

THE DIFFERENTIATION STRATEGY

The differentiation strategy champions developing products that customers value and that rivals find hard, if not impossible, to match.

An MNE implements a **differentiation strategy** when it aims to do something no other firm can do, and, besides doing it, do it effectively. Like the cost leadership strategy, the differentiation strategy is an integrated set of choices to make a good or provide a service. Unlike the cost leadership strategy, the differentiation strategy requires designing and delivering products that customers see as different in ways that are important to them—and thus are willing to pay a premium price. The differentiation strategy pushes managers to champion continuous innovation, not relentlessly reduce costs, as the basis for sustainable competitiveness. It compels developing resources, capabilities, and competencies that rivals find hard, if not impossible, to match. For instance, think of the sleek design of an Apple iPhone, the engineering sophistication of a Lexus sedan, the customer service at Ritz-Carlton, or the appeal of Coca-Cola's secret formula.

Approaches to differentiation are many, including cool design, extreme performance, speedy innovation, responsive service, high prestige, trendy novelty, or chic style. The differentiation strategy is typically seen in terms of high-profile products in high-margin markets—from haute couture to high-tech. Still, differentiation dynamics play elsewhere. MNEs try to differentiate commodities, such as milk, aspirin, DRAM chips, gasoline, cellphone plans, or debit cards, based on features customers value more than just low price. In either case, selling a product at a price that exceeds the cost of creating its unique attributes helps the MNE outperform its rivals. Interestingly, the cost leadership strategy's fixation on reducing cost ultimately hits hard boundaries, such as the price of inputs, physics of materials, or capacity for service. In contrast, anything a firm can do to produce value that no one else can do quite as effectively creates a virtually infinite basis for differentiation. Think of, for example, the powerful appeal of prominent brands, like Apple, Nike, Louis Vuitton, or Mercedes-Benz, to loyal fans.

The differentiation strategy has several risks, including

- changing customers' expectations,
- customers no longer see sufficient value justifying the price premium,
- a rival introduces a higher-performing alternative.

Risks of the Differentiation Strategy The ever-present threat to the differentiation strategy is shifting customer behavior that provokes resistance to the higher price of a product. This is particularly compelling if a rival offers an alternative that provides more value, real or perceived, for the same or lower price. This threat is salient in emerging and developing markets, where cost-conscious customers are especially value conscious. For example, Apple has adjusted its preferred premium pricing strategy in emerging markets, notably India, to compete with far cheaper, full-function smartphones. Originally, it charged 52,370 rupees ($735) for the iPhone 7; after sales struggled, Apple cut its price 39,900 rupees ($560). Meanwhile, India's best-selling smartphone, the Redmi 6A made by Xiaomi, sells for 5,999 rupees ($84); Keep in mind, also, that the real per capita income in India is approximately $7,100. The price-performance gap results in Apple's less than 1 percent share of India's booming smartphone market; in comparison, it has a 39 percent market share in the United States.[35]

An ongoing threat to the differentiation strategy is the risk that today's innovation is tomorrow's trash. The presence of enterprising rivals worldwide makes sustaining the basis of differentiation a never-ending challenge. Innovations conceived in Germany quickly diffuse to rivals in Brazil, the United States, and China. Companies that compete in terms of the differentiation strategy, as the former CEO of IBM explained, must tirelessly determine "what will cause work to move to me? On what basis will I differentiate and compete?"[36]

THE INTEGRATED COST LEADERSHIP-DIFFERENTIATION STRATEGY

In principle, the asymmetric demands of cost leadership and differentiation make it difficult to pursue both simultaneously. It is difficult to blend the discipline of efficiency, the imperative of cost leadership, with the flexibility of effectiveness, the imperative of differentiation. In practice, some MNEs do, ingeniously developing value propositions that offer low-cost, high-performance products. Zara, for instance, essentially implementing a vision of "Armani at moderate prices," turns cool ideas into competitively priced, hot fashions. Huawei, likewise, delivers high-performance-competitively priced smartphones, replete with impressive features that customers see offering greater value, relative to price, than alternatives. Lastly, Target, targeting higher-income, fashion-conscious, yet price-sensitive customers, implements its integrated strategy of "Expect More. Pay Less" that "delivers greater convenience, increased savings and a more personalized shopping experience."[37]

The cost leadership champions improving cost control whereas the differentiation strategy advocates continual innovation. The **integrated cost leadership-differentiation strategy** targets both objectives. Effectively implemented, it provides customers with relatively lower-cost products that also have differentiated features. Zara, Lexus, and Target, for example, use an integrated cost leadership-differentiation strategy to design products and processes with unique aspects, make them efficiently, and sell them effectively. Successful implementation requires an MNE adapt quickly to change to support differentiation while continually optimizing efficiency to sustain competitiveness.

Risks of the Integrated Cost Leadership-Differentiation Strategy Efficiently producing unique products that customers see offering compelling value that justifies a premium price is endlessly challenging. It requires managing a symbiosis of resources, capabilities, and competencies to develop mutually beneficial relationships that reconcile the asymmetric standards of efficiency and effectiveness. Some MNEs get "caught in the middle," falling short of optimizing production or sufficiently differentiating. Trapped between competing goals, their cost structure neither supports compulsory low prices nor delivers acceptable distinctiveness.

POINT

Is Strategic Planning Productive?

YES Strategic planning, goes the story, was once like playing chess. The board, the players, and the moves were well defined, the pace of play permitted deliberative movement, and surprises were few and far between. Indeed, one needs only recall the infamous "3-6-3" rule in banking a couple of generations ago: bankers gave 3 percent interest on depositors' accounts, lent depositors money at 6 percent interest, and then hit the golf links at 3 P.M.[38] Today, the global business environment, turbocharged by innumerable factors, makes the game far more complex. Technology, both routine and disruptive, resets efficiency frontiers and market boundaries. Competitors, both established and emerging, reinvent systems of production and distribution as well as experiment with entirely new business models. Governments,

COUNTERPOINT

Is Strategic Planning Productive?

NO The productivity of strategic planning rests on an appealing, yet fundamentally dubious, thesis: strategy is a science with immutable laws that, by reliably guiding decision-making toward optimal outcomes, lets bright strategists imagine bright plans that build bright futures. In reality, the complex dynamics of the global marketplace means strategic planning works in theory, but struggles in practice. More pointedly, after more than 40 years of empirical study, an equivocal relationship between strategic planning and firm performance persists.[40]

Persistent Problems

Notwithstanding managers' best intentions to map the future, they continually run into the problem that the both democratic and authoritarian, change the rules of the game. Making sense of situations and acquiring resources, developing capabilities, and creating competencies is tough. Strategic planning makes it possible.

Framing Questions

Strategic planning pushes managers to break free of day-to-day routines, look toward the horizon, and ask and answer big questions. Determining goals and mapping optimal paths pinpoints the potential of a business and links vision to actions. Setting systematic criteria and imposing rigorous analytics, by organizing the chaos of the global business environment, helps managers set standards, formalize objectives, formulate strategies, and specify actions. Besides that, the planning process frames and facilitates coordination, communication, and learning. Promoting conversations among executives about the future of the MNE and the resources, capabilities, and competencies required to reach it fortifies decision-making.

Pushing Proactivity

Strategic planning improves the flexibility to change as markets change. Few contest the importance of proactive executives, but, still, "analysis paralysis" is a recurring problem. Planning pushes managers to get on with it, asking big as well as small questions. Purposeful debate optimally repositions resources as well as gauges the urgency to reset or reverse commitments. Instituting strategic planning with an eye toward improving flexibility prior to disruptions sensitizes managers to identify options.

Improving Outcomes

Strategic planning supports higher performance and improved competitiveness. Systematically clarifying opportunities and threats invariably improves decision-making. Planning pays off by integrating interpretation and organizing analysis across multiple markets in multiple countries. Performance effects do not vary significantly between different industry groups. Some evidence indicates a positive and direct relationship—the more the firm plans, the better it performs.[39]

Overcoming Difficulties

Unquestionably, as the Counterpoint explains, the complexity of mapping markets means that strategic planning hits difficulties. Ironically, its shortcomings follow from its strengths. Planning imposes an analytical discipline that frames how managers assess markets. Acceptable for similar markets (say, moving from the United States to Canada), this perspective may struggle to adjust analytics for dissimilar markets (say, moving from China to Chile). In theory, anchoring analysis in terms of the orderly progression of systematic planning procedures helps managers formulate optimal strategies. Still, as with any objective future famously does not cooperate with brilliant visions, insightful missions, and prudent plans. Consider the less than inspiring record of firms that consistently invest great effort into strategic planning, namely those comprising the Standard & Poor's 500 Index (S&P 500).[41] The average time a company spends in the S&P 500 index has declined from 61 years in 1958 to about 14 years today, an average of 22 companies are replaced annually, and more than half of the companies included in the S&P 500 index in 2000 no longer exist.[42] Similarly, up to 90 percent of ventures fail shortly after start-up; venture-capital firms see more than 80 percent of their investments fail; more than 80 percent of equity mutual funds consistently underperform the S&P 500; the average business model life span has fallen from about 15 years to less than 5 over the past 50 years; and more than 75 percent of mergers and acquisitions never pay off.[43] Many companies committed to rigorous, objective, systematic planning processes, rather than reaping great success, struggle to survive.

Deficiencies and Deceptions

Skeptics point to planning's fundamental limit: the delusion that a comprehensive strategic planning process, anchored in countless hours assessing strengths, weaknesses, opportunities, and threats, improves short-term competitiveness and fortifies long-term sustainability. Notwithstanding best intentions, strategic planning falls prey to deficiencies and deceptions. It confuses the superficial trappings of rigor and discipline with grand storytelling. It muddles managers' ability to think critically about the nature of success in business—including vastly underestimating the power of plain old good luck.[44] Inevitably, planning devolves into glorified soothsaying that erodes the effectiveness of decision-making.[45] Then, in the off chance that planning generates a genuine insight, it often runs into implementation problems—plans poorly connected to vague action steps that are just as likely to be a day late and a dollar short. Interestingly, the COVID-19 pandemic highlighted that leaders can make decisions with imperfect information, pivoting operations and reallocating resources swiftly with imperfect information.

Disruptive Dynamism

Difficult under stable conditions, these tendencies prove damaging given the extreme sorts of changes we see in IB. Disruptions here, surprises there, and occasionally, really big surprises such as COVID-19, make for uncertainties everywhere. New players, new products, new processes, periodically turbocharged by radical events that create "unknown unknowns," create endless complexities and contingencies. Terrestrially, expansion in once peripheral, but now core markets (such as China, India, Indonesia) resets performance standards. Some model, managers must deflect linear thinking that misinterprets markets and misdirects decision-making.

Organizing Disorder
Enterprising executives, recognizing the messiness of internal conditions and external circumstances, stress-test their planning process. Brainstorming identifies "what-if" situations that test the planning model before committing to a course of action. Managers incorporate elements of scenario analysis, rooted maps, and contingency planning. In the former they assess alternative futures, interpreting likely outcomes of various operating strategies and industry conditions. Rooted maps help leaders enhance their intuition about opportunities and threats in the global market. Finally, contingency planning helps managers estimate the effect of potential disruptions and devise preemptive strategies.

A Productive Path
Ultimately, performance records of leading MNEs worldwide show that tried-and-true strategic planning processes productively equip managers to deal with the messy, ill-structured realities of IB. Strategic planning, by enforcing rigorous, disciplined, systematic decision-making, supports successfully expanding into familiar markets as well as venturing into new zones.

400-midsize emerging-market cities, many unfamiliar in the West (e.g., Sanaa, Ouagadougou, Chittagong, Kinshasa), will produce about 40 percent of global growth over the next 15 years. Today's market revolution spans the globe, includes far more people in far more countries, and represents the biggest change in the history of capitalism. Digitally, the ever-evolving Internet, adapting and adjusting to algorithms and artificial intelligence, opens never before seen options. Already, digital processes are the most powerful force for globalization in history.[46] Indeed, say some, whatever the Internet touches, it transforms in ways that reset analytics and defy prediction. The upshot is that no matter how sensitive their strategic compass, executives struggle to plan in the face of minor as well as momentous dynamism.[47]

Delusions and Biases
Ultimately, managers intent on overlaying logical rules of cause and effect on erratic markets delude themselves that strategic planning is an effective decision-making process. Strategic planning struggles given intractable biases—from generalizing halo effects, confusing correlation and causality, and connecting only the winning dots, to name just a few of the many.[48] Then, as before, impressive plans fall short of performance targets.

ORGANIZING VALUE CREATION: THE VALUE CHAIN

12-5 Diagram the features and functions of the value chain

An MNE sets and sustains its competitive advantage when the value it creates, whether through cost leadership, differentiation, or a combination, is greater than the costs it incurs to do so. In practical terms, an MNE faces issues, opportunities, and constraints in designing, making, moving, selling, and servicing products. Each activity imposes costs that influence value creation. Just as strategic planning helps managers develop their strategy, **value chain** analysis helps them assess how different activities create value.

Value-chain analysis helps managers understand the performance of resources and capabilities, the context of competencies, and the drivers of value creation.

Value chain analysis frames the evaluation of an MNE's strengths and weaknesses. It guides managers' breakdown of the components and determinants of the internal cost structure. Diagramming the firm's value chain models the linkage of resources, capabilities and competencies to the cost leadership, differentiation, or integrated strategy options. In the case of cost leadership, it models the potential of resources and capabilities to streamline activities. In the case of differentiation, it highlights activities that support outperforming rivals in providing the latest, greatest products. In the case of the integrated mix, it helps reconcile the efficiency–effectiveness dialectic. Lastly, value chain analysis guides estimating rivals' cost structures and, thus, their relative competitiveness.

The value chain is the set of linked activities the company performs to design, make, market, distribute, and support a product.

The systemic perspective of value chain analysis deconstructs the abstraction of creating value into an easily understood, step-by-step model. This sequence specifies the value that is created as a product moves from conception in R&D through sourcing materials, organizing manufacturing, supervising logistics, applying marketing, and providing servicing. Value chain analysis maps the productivity of each functional activity, pinpointing how resources, capabilities, and competencies improve efficiency or boost effectiveness. Figure 12.2 maps the activities that comprise the value chain. Figure 12.3 profiles their characteristics.

FIGURE 12.2 Visualizing the Value Chain

The value chain is made up of primary activities that reflect classical business functions and managerial orientations. The value chain also specifies support activities, representing day-to-day tasks, which help implement the primary activities. Support activities apply to all primary activities, as we see in their run along the breadth of the value chain.

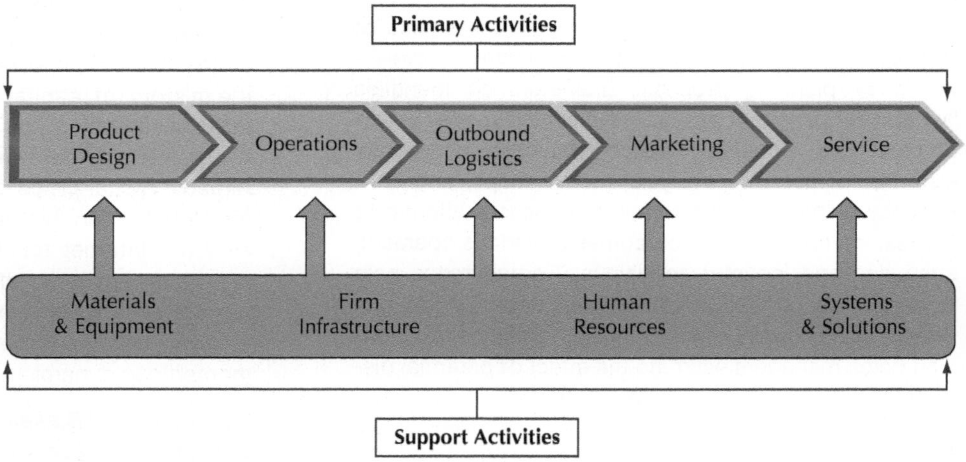

Primary activities represent the core business functions that make and move products. Their sequence follows from that of designing a product, building the operations that make it, and onward through the tasks of logistics, marketing, distribution, and service. Primary activities reflect classic business activities and managerial orientations. Thus, they carry functional labels such as operations or marketing. Figure 12.2 also identifies secondary processes called **support activities.** These represent the infrastructure of the firm, identifying the activities that support working the primary activities. Human resources, for example, are needed for each primary activity, from warehousing materials to directing production to shipping products to serving customers.

FIGURE 12.3 Specifying the Value Chain

The primary and support activities of the value chain identify the steps an MNE takes to create value. By disaggregating activities into discrete responsibilities, as we see here, the value chain provides managers a powerful tool to plan strategically.

The Value Chain	Primary Activities	Product Design	Design the functions, features, and aesthetics of the product or process.
		Operations	Convert inputs into a finished product in terms of sourcing components, arrange supply chains, configure plant location, and optimize manufacturing processes.
		Outbound Logistics	Move finished product from operations to wholesalers, retailers, or end-consumers. Deal with distribution channels, inventory management, warehousing, and transportation logistics.
		Marketing	Inform buyers and consumers about products and services, develop a sales force, devise packaging schemes, define the brand, and devise promotions.
		Service	Service customers with installation support, after-sales assistance, training, and maintenance.
	Support Activities	Materials & Equipment	Manage the procurement, transportation, storage, and distribution of materials and equipment necessary to conduct the primary activities.
		Human Resource Management	Recruit, develop, motivate, compensate, and retain workers.
		Systems & Solutions	Manage information processing, oversee information systems, and integrate technology platforms.
		Infrastructure	Classic overhead functions, like accounting, finance, legal, safety and security, and quality control.

CONFIGURING THE VALUE CHAIN

Value-chain analysis helps managers evaluate their cost structure and identify how their activities create value.

An MNE's option to go anywhere in the world to perform a primary or support activity gives it tremendous choice of location. How an MNE distributes value activities around the world is the matter of **configuration**—essentially, the task of deciding which activity to do where. Besides the option to sell in the 217 markets that comprise the global business environment, the MNE has the option to install operations in each. For example, Nestlé operates 447 factories in 86 countries whereas Toyota runs 70 factories in 29 countries. Rather than happenstance, the decision to open a factory here, but not there, reflects their strategic planners' interpretation of global opportunities and local threats.

Location economies influence how an MNE concentrates or disperses value activities.

The option to go anywhere to do anything pushes an MNE to configure its value chain to exploit **location advantages**. Locating primary and support activities operations in productive places optimizes the MNE's competitive positioning. In theory, a whole range from a **concentrated configuration** (the MNE performs all value-chain activities in one location) to a **dispersed configuration** (the MNE performs different value-chain activities in different locations) exists. So, suppose a single market provides the lowest-cost, highest-productivity environment for all activities. An MNE could then concentrate its value chain there and serve its global market through exports. For instance, nearly all of the world's iPhones are made in China, at Iphone City in Zhengzhou and by Pegatron near Shanghai. Concentrating production enables Apple to achieve powerful design, production, and supply chain efficiencies.[49] Conversely, a dispersed value chain makes sense when some activities cost less in country X, others cost less in country Y, and still others less in country Z. So, if the best industrial designers are in Taiwan, the company bases R&D there. If the most productive labor force is in Vietnam, that's where it builds its plants. If the most creative minds are in Denmark, it develops its advertising campaign there. Recently, the COVID-19 pandemic highlighted the value a dispersed value chain. The pandemic showed that concentrating supply chains, great went things go well, can collapse quickly into bottlenecks, shortages, and stoppages. As COVID-19 reset life, Apple's China-centric manufacturing strategy led to costly and complicated disruptions. In recourse, Apple, like other MNEs with concentrated value chains, evaluated dispersing value activities in multiple parts of the world. [50]

CONCEPT CHECK

The profile "Scenarios That May Change Trade Patterns" in Chapter 6 notes technological innovations can diminish international trade due to the efficiency and ease of manufacturing goods nearer to customers. Similarly, 3-D printing introduces revolutionary production technologies. Besides resetting the economics of manufacturing, it changes how we interpret location advantages.

Determining which activities to concentrate and which to disperse follows from the fact that different environmental conditions means costs differ in different locations. Labor, capital, and resources costs are traditional determinants of location advantages. The MNE pursuing a low-cost leadership strategy with a labor-intensive production process, for instance, is sensitive to the supply, cost, and productivity of workers and targets locations that optimize those factors. Other moderators include political risks, trade zones, cluster effects, environmental regulations, logistic connections, and infrastructure (see Table 12.5). Increasingly, trends in digitalization moderate locations' advantages, and, hence, MNE's configuration choices.[51] Our *Looking to the Future* profile looks at these trends and finds they signal a brave new world that challenges how we interpret location advantages.

CONCEPT CHECK

In discussing "Elements of the Economic Environment" in Chapter 4, we note labor costs and productivity are key concerns for MNEs. In Chapter 6, we discuss theories to explain the relative trade performance of different countries. Here, we reiterate that location economies directly moderate how MNEs configure value activities.

Economies of Scale Selling globally, rather than only locally, superbly positions an MNE to achieve economies of scale. Specifically, an MNE captures economies of scale in terms of size, output, or scale of operation. Increasing output lets it distribute fixed costs across a higher number of units, thereby systematically decreasing per-unit cost. More precisely, long production runs of the sort that serve a large global, rather than small local, market lower per-unit costs as marginal production cost decreases while cumulative output increases. Exploiting scale effects is a powerful driver of productivity and profitability. It's an enduring explanation of value chain configurations in IB.

An MNE implementing the cost leadership strategy sees efficiency as the foundation of its competitiveness. Hence, it captures available scale economies by concentrating its value activities among a few, large-scale plants. A minimum efficient-sized factory for making integrated circuits, for instance, costs several billion dollars. As a result, Intel, the world's largest semiconductor chipmaker, supplies customers worldwide from 15 fabrication plants located in four countries—11 in the United States, three in Ireland, two in Israel, and one in China and Ireland. Certainly, Intel could opt for smaller plants in more countries. The reduced productivity of dispersed, small-scale manufacturing activities would suboptimize scale efficiencies, thereby inflating its operating costs and diminishing its capacity to create value.

TABLE 12.5 Locating Value Activities: Key Moderators

Given expanding terrestrial and digital options, managers figuring out "where to go to do what and how" consider a range of moderators.

Dimension	Influence
Business Environment Quality	MNEs configure value chains to enter, or avoid, a country given its business environment. Countries improve their location economies by reducing capital requirements for start-ups, streamlining property registration, expediting regulatory review, and liberalizing labor regulations. Opportunistic governments recruit foreign investors, promising business-friendly markets that offer flexible operating requirements, lower tax rates, cheap financing, and responsive public policies.
Cluster Effects	Competing, complementary, interdependent firms and industries that do business with each other and share overlapping needs for talent, technology, and infrastructure increasingly operate in close geographic proximity, namely clusters (e.g., New York City for global finance or Baden-Württemberg for cars). Vibrant clusters attract related vendors, service providers, investors, analysts, skilled workers, trade association members, and consultants.
Digitalization	Growing use of digital technologies to reset business models and access new value-creating opportunities compels companies to seek markets that support increasingly sophisticated digital activities.
Innovation Context	Host governments build knowledge-intensive, tech-enabled business environments. Leveraging technologies, expanding human capacities, streamlining organizational capabilities, and improving institutional responsiveness develops locations that leverage knowledge into innovations.
Labor Costs	Differences in wage rates, worker productivity, and workplace regulations mean that the labor cost of doing the same thing varies from country to country. MNEs configure value chains to exploit these differentials.
Logistics	Logistics, namely procuring, transporting, transhipment, and storing products, connect value-chain activities. Depending on the product, logistics adds a little to a lot to its landed cost. Hence, MNEs configure the location of value activities to optimize logistics economics.
Political Risk	Distributing value activities across nations exposes an MNE to political risk, namely the chance that local decisions, events, or conditions will cause it to lose some or all of the value of its investment or accept a lower-than-projected rate of return. Political risks differ from market to market; some countries are less risky than others, given fair legal systems, stable institutions, and the rule of law.

The improving functionality of 3-D printing foreshadows a radical reset in our idea of the scale, scope, and location of "factories" in the future. ▶

Source: Alexander Kirch/123RF

Generally, exploiting economies of scale effects is less pressing for an MNE implementing a differentiation strategy. Yes, price matters, but less so than other features of the product such as its image, positioning, or exclusivity. Still, it too must find ways to offset the **liability of foreignness**—specifically, the additional costs an MNE operating outside its home country incurs above those experienced by a local firm. If its differentiation strategy limits manufacturing options, it can target other elements of the value chain, such as managerial (leveraging executive expertise), financial (obtaining lower-interest rates when borrowing from banks), marketing (spreading advertising costs over a broader range of media markets), or technological (taking advantage of returns to scale in information processing).[52]

The Risks of Configuration Choices Configuration decisions face the risks of unpredictable market change. Disruptions, such as a regime change, material shortages, labor unrest, currency instability, or periodic "black swan" can quickly convert an efficient location into a costly one. Apple, for example, has long relied on two Foxconn factories in Zhengzhou, China for most of its iPhone production. COVID-19 in China quickly slowed production at both and threatened ongoing deliveries. Likewise, following yet another disruption, Jack Welch, former CEO of General Electric (GE), thought the best location for GE factories was a mobile platform, explaining, "Ideally, you'd have every plant you own on a barge, to move with currencies and changes in the economy."[53] The impracticality of an armada of barges ferrying factories through the seas requires that managers monitor markets trends. Planning tools, such as scenario analysis and contingency assessments, help managers estimate the implication of shifting location advantages to configuration choices.

LOOKING TO THE FUTURE Digits, Widgets, and Changing Location Advantages

Since business began, location advantages have influenced how companies configure value activities. Searching for raw materials, seeking productive, low-cost labor, arbitraging taxes and tariffs, and the like push MNEs to travel the world, continually seeking optimal locations. Making products there yet moving products here required an expansive, often expensive logistics matrix. Today, in a bit of understatement, "the times they are a changin." Revolutionary developments in digitalization, robots, and 3-D printers spur radically rethinking the implication of location advantages to configuring value activities.

Digitization

The representation of an object, image, sound, document, or signal into a series of numbers digitizes it. MNEs digitize products like software, music, and books, as well as services like application processing, financial consolidation, and legal assistance. Jacked into the network, MNEs move more products anywhere in the world at negligible cost and complication. The flexibility to locate digital activities virtually anywhere, particularly as the Internet expands, influences where and how MNEs do what. Options unavailable a generation ago—say, X-rays taken in Boston, but read in Bangkok—are now commonplace. Distance, historically represented in terms of geographic space, is now measured in terms of electronic time in the "cloud."

Ongoing improvements in digitization signal continuing disruption. Once, many activities could be done in a few specialized places. For instance, due diligence processes in mergers and acquisitions largely took place in New York City or London given the corresponding concentration of value activities such as regulatory registration or evaluation. Digitization disperses these activities. Indeed, it has created a new global model for financial services, unleashing disruptive innovations that change the gameboard. Arguably, we have never seen disruption of this magnitude in history. Companies respond in kind, rethinking the location of value activities. Some see digitization "creating a second economy that's vast, automatic, and invisible—thereby bringing the biggest change since the Industrial Revolution."[54]

Similar trends, for instance, disrupt location effects in the legal field. India's legal outsourcing industry is growing from an experimental enterprise to a mainstream part of the global business of law. Staff at Pangea3 and Cobra Legal Solutions do the routine work traditionally assigned to enterprising junior lawyers in the United States, but at a fraction of the cost. Moreover, amendments to the U.S. Federal Rules of Civil Procedure expand discovery to include electronic documents, such as e-mails, instant messages, and voice mails. E-discovery further incents offshoring legal work to productive providers. Add it all up, and legal outsourcing "is not a blip . . . it is a big historical movement."[55]

Going forward, the narrowing **digital divide**—the gap between those with regular access to connected digital technologies and those without—plugs more people into the matrix. Accordingly, changing location economies changes MNE's configuration choices. The diffusion of lower-priced technology to people worldwide means that fewer spots remain off the grid. As newly-wired folks connect with counterparts worldwide, they develop

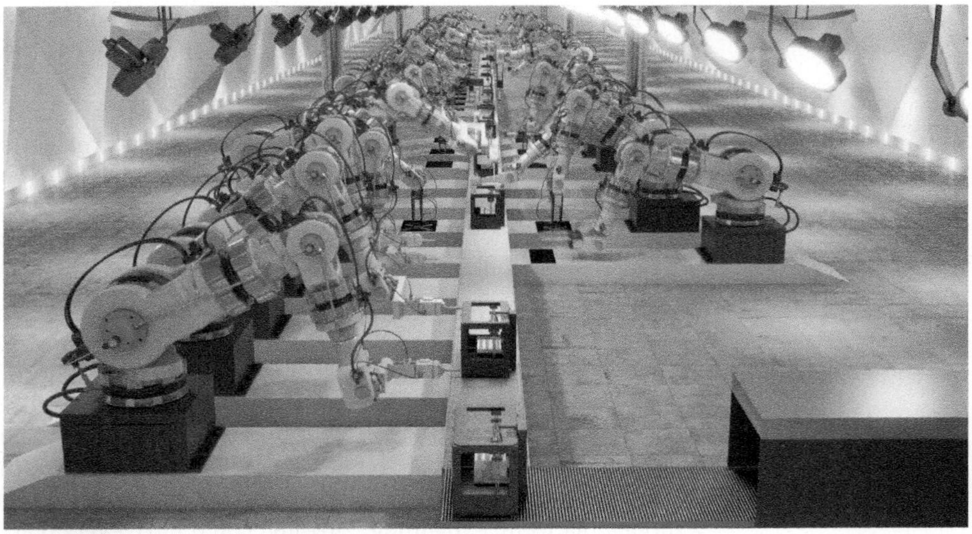

One wonders, considering the rise of robots in workplaces worldwide, how unfolding tech trends will reset our understanding of strategy in the global business environment.

Source: U3d/Shutterstock

proficiencies with technology platforms. Consequently, MNEs rethink configuration options to tap emerging capabilities.

The Rise of Robots

Widgets, technically small, mechanical devices, sound benign. In the context of the rise of robots and the expansion of 3-D printing, the idea of widgets takes on an entirely new meaning. The rise of robots threatens to disrupt much of what we know about configuring activities. Location decisions, originally made based on hand labor, later based on assembly lines manned by humans, increasingly follow the promise of robots getting the job done. In your daily life, think of the implications of ATMs, self-checkout, and driverless vehicles.

Consider that the Philips Electronics factory in Zhuhai, China, employs hundreds of workers who work old-school, using hand tools to assemble electric shavers. Meanwhile, 128 robots do the same work, making the same product at a sister factory in the Netherlands. The Dutch factory has several dozen workers per shift, about a tenth as many as the Zhuhai plant. Still, it out produces its Chinese counterpart.[56] Elsewhere, fear of rising wages drives others to do the same. Foxconn, the maker of "all things Apple," has factories filled with tens of thousands of workers but looks to install more than a million robots. In 2018, China's factories installed 154,032 industrial robots, up more than 70 percent from 2016, and more than Europe and the United States combined.[57]

Change is not limited to manufacturing. In distribution warehouses, increasingly agile robots store, pick, and pack goods far more adeptly than people. In journalism, robot writers generate hundreds of millions of news reports annually—more than all human journalists in the world—at an increasingly diminishing cost.[58] In accountancy, forecasters see computer systems replacing the bulk of tax preparers, bookkeepers, budget analysts, loan officers, accountants, and auditors.[59] Machines' ability to do things faster, cheaper, and capably anywhere, anytime makes them more productive than humans in a growing number of applications. Says the founder of robot builder Industrial Perception, "We're on the cusp of completely changing manufacturing and distribution. I think it's not as singular an event, but it will ultimately have as big an impact as the Internet."[60]

Robots in the form of 3-D printing add fascinating angles to future location decisions. Building big factories in low-cost labor markets to mass-produce standardized goods, long a determinant of factory locations, slowly becomes secondary to smaller-scale, 3-D printer–equipped facilities that enable "mass customization." The capacity of 3-D printers to efficiently make smaller batches of a wider variety of goods supports scenarios where products are made on-site, in real time, and tailored to a customer's precise specification. Increasingly, 3-D printing, powered by improving software and ingenious materials, supports small-scale factories "manned" by maker-bots located anywhere and everywhere in the world. The COVID-19 pandemic has made this already-attractive option even more so; for instance, an Italian hospital rapidly exhausting its supply of critical valves for reanimation devices and facing broken supply chains was able to begin 3-D printing valves on-site to save the day.[61] Given the advantages of proximity to customers, likely down the street and, one day, in your home rather than in foreign factories, 3-D printing is a game-changer.

Implications

Digits and widgets push managers to increasingly question long-sacred strategic principles, such as "Exploit location advantages," "Maximize production runs," "Minimize unit-labor costs," or "Go big or go home." Locating value

TABLE 12.6 The Expanding Lexicon of Locations

The option to configure value activities expand in scale and scope. Once, discussion revolved around the issue of offshoring. Now, trends in digitization and automation, shifting location effects, intellectual property protection, and improving customer responsiveness expand interpretation. Consequently, the interpretation of "shoring" evolves.

Form of "Shoring"	Characteristic
Homeshoring	Home-based staff handle activities that had previously been offshored to foreign locations.
Nearshoring	A less aggressive form of offshoring whereby an MNE transfers an activity to a neighboring or nearby country.
Offshoring	Relocating a value activity to a different country that either remains within or moves outside the MNE
Onshoring	Relocating a business process or work unit to a productive, lower-cost location in the home country.
Reshoring	Returning an activity from the foreign location to the country where the work had originally been done.

activities based not on the availability of land, labor, or materials, but on connectivity, robotics, and automation, lets MNEs rethink how to configure operations.[62]

We already see production activities that had been moved to low-cost labor locations now reshoring to developed countries and, in the process, expanding the notions of locations (see Table 12.6). Nearly half of U.S.-based manufacturing executives at companies with sales greater than $10 billion are planning to, or are considering, returning production to the United States from China—and this was before the COVID-19 pandemic radically changed the game. As COVID-19 tested the world, companies across 12 global sectors in North America, Europe, and Asia-Pacific (ex-China) announced plans to reshore activities, signaling the first reversal in the multidecade offshoring trend.[63] Amplifying this tectonic shift is the growing share of the goods that the United States imports from China in transport, computer-fabricated metals, and machinery industries that will soon be made with robots and 3-D printers. Already, we see consequences, with the United States reporting record-breaking FDI since 2015, and notching the rank of the top destination for FDI in the world in 2018.[64] These trends, unfolding worldwide, herald a widget-led, digitally fueled revolution that likely resets our ideas and interpretation of location advantage.

GLOBAL INTEGRATION VERSUS LOCAL RESPONSIVENESS

12-6 Compare global integration and local responsiveness

Global integration standardizes worldwide activities to maximize efficiency, whereas local responsiveness adapts local activities to optimize effectiveness.

Competing in the global market puts an MNE on the horns of a dilemma: should it single-mindedly standardize products and processes and resolutely exploit location effects to maximize operational efficiencies? Doing so endorses the idea of **global integration**. Or, should it adapt products and processes to the unique situations in each market to maximize operational effectiveness? Doing so endorses the idea of **local responsiveness**. Table 12.7 lists motivations for each. The perpetual tug-of-war between the standardization of global integration versus the customization of local responsiveness influences an MNE's ideal bundle of resources, capabilities, and competencies. Maximizing integration imposes far different imperatives than optimizing differentiation. Few MNEs operate in an industry where either imperative indisputably predominates. Rather, most MNEs, given the particularities of their vision, mission, and objectives, navigate their competing demands.

Consider Nestlé's situation. Its vision, "Good Food, Good Life," anchors its mission to provide food that is a source of nourishment and satisfaction, but also pleasure, health, happiness, and peace of mind. These ideals, although universal in theory, differ in practice from market-to-market given that local habits, cultural traditions, and social norms shape the standards of preferred, palatable food. Moreover, food inputs are generally commodities, production has limited scale potential, distribution is costly given low value-to-weight ratios, and promotion is best done locally given differentiated tastes, regulations, rivals, and retail channels. Hence, Nestlé's designers, regulatory specialists, and consumer care

TABLE 12.7 Objectives of Global Integration and Local Responsiveness

Objectives for Global Integration	Objectives for Local Responsiveness
Accelerate consumers' quest to maximize purchasing power.	Accommodate differences in distribution channels and service systems
Build a global image with universal message	Adjust products and processes to the digital divide
Capitalize on converging consumer preferences and universal needs	Adjust to local political, economic, and cultural circumstances
Directly engage global competitors	Build local goodwill by supporting national agenda
Exploit cross-national connections instituted by transnational organizations	Customize products and process to local preferences to optimize scale, experience, and learning effects
Exploit location effects	Directly engage local competitors
Leverage expanding cross-national connectivity	Increase sensitivity to new product and process options
Maximize productivity of resources, capabilities, and competencies	Promote a local profile to placate national stakeholders
Provide uniform service to all customers	Respond to historical or geographic imperatives
Respond to the ongoing globalization of markets	Satisfy host government requirements and regulations
Source materials and inputs globally	Tailor marketing message to local ideals
Standardize products and processes to maximize scale, experience, and learning effects	Tap local resources, capabilities, and competencies

representatives apply a local outlook to customize its activities so that it responds effectively to the differentiated situations in the 190 markets in which it sells its products.

Global integration combines differentiated parts into a standardized whole. Local responsiveness disaggregates the standardized whole into differentiated parts.

CONCEPT CHECK

As seen in Chapter 4, fast-growing emerging economies spur big changes in IB. Here, we observe that one of these changes moves companies to assess operating in different environments with a keen eye toward leveraging global innovations in local markets.

Offsetting the costs imposed by its liability of foreignness, however, requires Nestlé standardize some activities, such as information systems, brand names, advertising message, and packaging processes, which overlap across countries. Attaining, efficiencies in those "global" activities enables Nestlé to attain cost advantages that are unavailable to local rivals and, therefore, offsets expense the latter do not incur. To that end, Nestlé looks to its 5,000-plus scientists, engineers, and nutritionists who staff its network of 34 R&D facilities to set global standards for safe products of the highest quality that support its vision. Granted, the leadership of Nestlé would prefer to do the same thing, the same way, everywhere—strategic planning would be easier, operations would run smoother, and complications would be fewer. However, pressures to respond locally mean it cannot. Consequently, Nestlé, like many MNEs, manages the conflicting pressures of global integration and local responsiveness by standardizing some activities worldwide while customizing others to local situations.

Reconciling the competing imperatives of integration and responsiveness calls on managers to navigate a range of issues, constraints, and concerns. Strategic planning, in framing analysis and developing scenarios, helps managers assess the implications to resources, capabilities, and competencies. As a rule, planners monitor multiple aspects of the environment. Key concerns center on assessing the potential for standardization, interpreting consumer behavior, and assessing the agendas of institutional agents.

THE POTENTIAL FOR STANDARDIZATION

The greater the potential to standardize value activities, the greater the importance of global integration to an MNE's competitiveness. Proponents hold that doing the same thing, the same way, everywhere, has immense potential, given the growing degree to which the "experience of everyday life is becoming standardized around the world."[65] Inexorably, goes the reasoning, people worldwide consume an increasing number of products, from high-touch t-shirts from Zara to high-tech smartphones from Samsung, increasingly in the same way. The stronger this tendency, the greater the opportunity to concentrate value chains to make low-cost, high-quality products that differ little, if any, in features and functionality. Successfully doing so enables offering consumers anywhere and everywhere a compelling value proposition.

The logic of standardization is straightforward. Repeatedly doing the same thing the same way, by maximizing economies of scale, creates efficiencies that reduce costs without sacrificing quality. Efficiencies emerge across the value chain. An MNE, for example, can streamline product designs to rationalize assembly, negotiate quantity discounts on material purchases, rationalize materials management, and optimize outbound logistics. It also realizes efficiencies in other value activities: R&D benefits by leveraging a common design platform, advertising benefits by communicating a universal message, and distribution benefits by streamlining channels.

The convergence of national markets, standardization of preferences, and efficiency imperatives push MNEs to integrate activities.

Our opening case profiles the power of standardization to create compelling competitive advantage in the global apparel industry. Zara saw that standardizing its product offerings supported longer production runs in centralized plants that translated into lower unit costs. This, in turn, enables it to offer attractive fashion at reasonable prices that neutralize stubborn local preferences. Relatedly, its global network, supported by its state-of-the-art logistics, gave customers worldwide real-time access to the newest, coolest fashion trends. Manufacturing standardized products for global markets, therefore, lets Zara leverage its investment in design, manufacturing, distribution, and retail activities. The resulting efficiencies, in turn, support making high-quality, competitively priced products that, by offering compelling value to customers worldwide, repower the cycle. Ultimately, Zara's insight made it the premier apparel retailer in the world.

THE CONTEXT OF CONSUMER BEHAVIOR

Responding to local customers' behavior pushes MNEs to customize products and processes. In absolute terms, adaptation reduces the efficiencies of standardization, thereby increasing the liability of foreignness, inflating operational costs, and reducing value creation. Hence, MNEs oppose adapting operations unnecessarily. Still, local imperatives often compel them to do so. Differing cultural, political, legal, and economic circumstances create business conditions that press the MNE to customize products and processes. Some differences surrender to the allure of higher-quality, lower-cost products—think of worldwide demand for an Apple iPhone, Starbucks latte, or Instagram stream. In these sorts of situations, the appeal of the standardized products dominates local consumer preferences.

CONCEPT CHECK

Chapter 2 notes that globalization spurs a variety of managerial approaches. Similarly, Chapters 3 and 4 emphasize that MNEs invariably encounter different political, legal, and economic practices. Likewise, here we highlight that global imperatives and local constraints shape planning in the MNE.

Other differences, however, press MNEs to tailor products and processes. *Ceteris paribus*, consumers prefer products that are sensitive to their lifestyle. Examples include designing and making products that local customers prefer (e.g., large cars in the United States, smaller cars in Europe, still smaller cars in emerging markets), tailoring channel structures to buyer preferences (e.g., web content in South Korea, print and media promotion in France, personal selling in Brazil), modifying product features for local tastes (e.g., light coffee roasts in Germany and Scandinavia; dark coffee roasts in Italy and Spain; coffee flavored with spices, like cinnamon, lemongrass, or cloves, in Ethiopia and India), and adapting marketing practices to consumption patterns (e.g., large package sizes in Australia, smaller sizes in Japan, single-unit sizes in poorer countries). In these sorts of situations, local preferences and circumstances often trump global standards.

Standardization advocates dismiss the call to customize. Instead, they argue that expanding connections across borders steadily converges consumer behaviors. Ultimately, they predict, everyone, everywhere will consume the same things, the same way. As Steve Jobs observed during his travels to Turkey, "All day I had looked at young people in Istanbul. They were all drinking what every other kid in the world drinks, and they were wearing clothes that look like they were bought at the Gap, and they were all using cell phones like kids everywhere else. It hit me that, for young people, the whole world is the same now."[66] Localization advocates argue otherwise, countering that about one percent of the world's physical mail crosses borders, less than two percent of calling minutes are international, and a quarter of Internet traffic crosses national borders.[67] Likewise, just 329 brands are recognized by consumers in eight or more countries; only 16 percent of all brands are recognized in two or more countries.[68] Furthermore, most people live their entire lives within one country, supporting local production and consumption of goods and sustaining local politics, history, culture, and identity. Localism, not globalism, is the lifestyle of many people in many countries.

Differences in local consumers' behaviors endure due to cultural predisposition, historical legacy, and latent nationalism.

MNEs facing stubborn variation in consumer preferences across countries, therefore, adapt products and processes to local circumstances.[69] Certainly, expanding connectivity encourages consumer behaviors that weaken buy-local outlooks. Nevertheless, differences endure due to market structures, cultural outlooks, historical legacies, and latent nationalism. Responding to different preferences in different markets presses

MNEs to adapt products and processes. Then, optimizing, rather than maximizing, standardization offsets the liability of foreignness.

THE AGENDA OF INSTITUTIONAL AGENTS

Opportunities for standardization endorses global integration whereas divergent consumer behaviors endorse local responsiveness. A third factor, the agendas of institutional agents, can, at different times, support each. Transnational institutions, such as the G20, AIIB, IMF, WTO, and World Bank, progressively build an integrated, densely connected global business environment. Systematically integrating nations opens their markets to international trade and foreign investment, thereby creating greater potential for MNEs to build, expand, and run globally integrated operations. Presently, for instance, 164 nations are members of the WTO, the regulator of the rules of world trade. Membership requires a nation replace its local regulations with global standards. Likewise, the members of the G20, a mix of the world's largest established and emerging economies, regularly meet to expand cross-national integration. The fact that the G20 collectively produce 85 percent of the global gross domestic product makes its policies and practices powerful tools of integration.

As transnational institutions standardize the rules of the globalization game, so to speak, MNEs more easily standardize the methods of play. Expanding cross-national connectivity along with progressive trade liberalization enables MNEs to configure value activities in optimal locations without forsaking access to markets worldwide. Hence, business-process outsourcing firms in India, robot builders in Germany, solar-panel makers in China, or chip architects in Taiwan can design value chains that maximize efficiency without sacrificing access to consumers in other countries.

The G20 bring together the governments and central bank governors from 19 countries and the European Union to share perspectives and develop consensus.

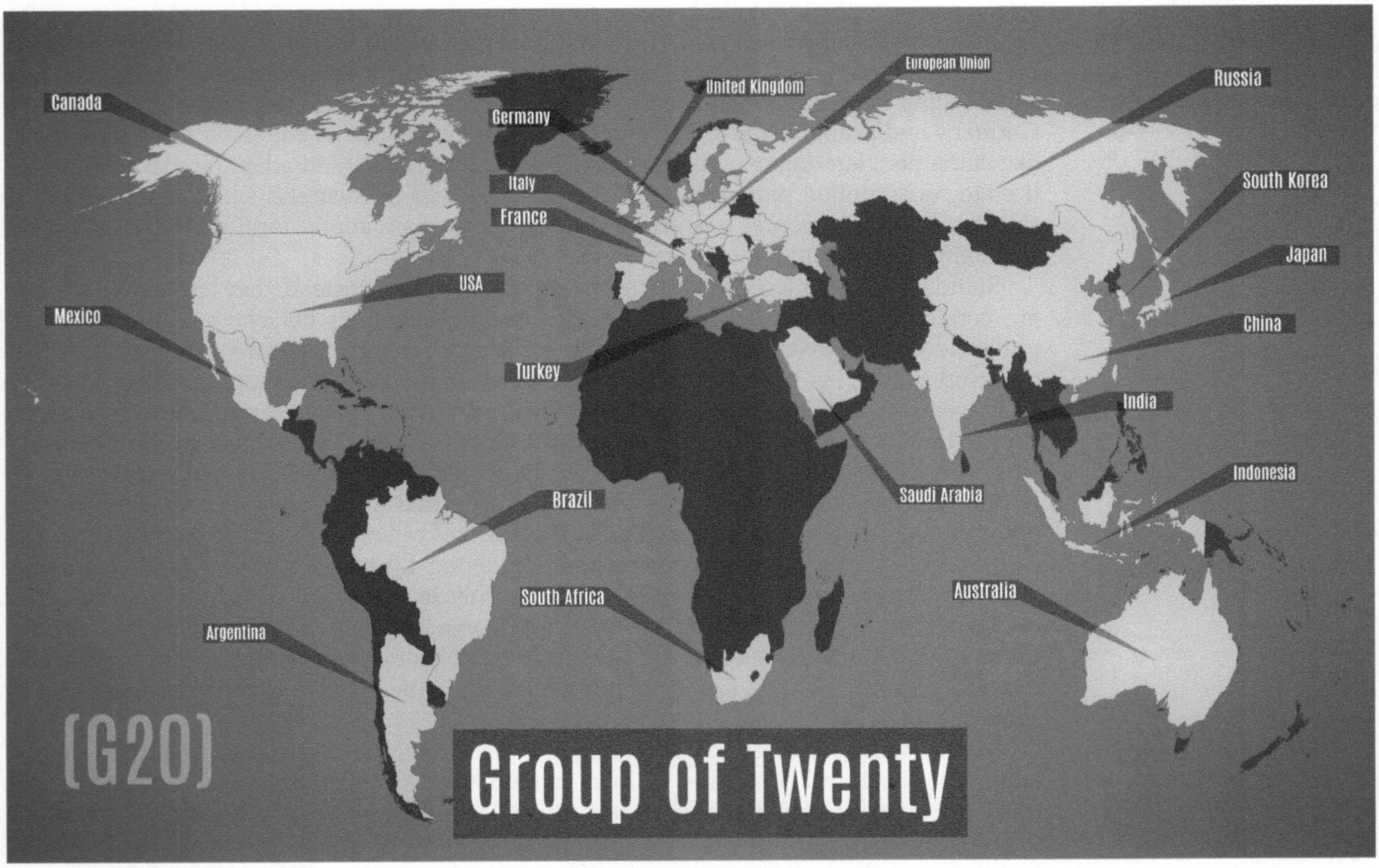

Source: Art1980/123RF

CONCEPT CHECK

Chapter 8 profiles movements in national markets toward regional trade agreements. Chapter 10 highlights the cross-national integration of capital markets. These trends, by standardizing key aspects of the global market, support the standardization of products and processes. Increasing standardization, in turn, supports concentrating value chains.

On the other hand, institutional agents, particularly host governments, often advocate, if not mandate, MNEs adapt operations to local circumstances. In general, different countries take different paths to develop fiscal, monetary, and market regulations. Some champion economic freedom, others constrain it. Some advocate openness, others endorse autarky. Nationalist policies spur MNEs to localize value activities or else forsake sales, if not access. Routine pressures for local responsiveness, for example, require pharmaceutical MNEs to disperse value activities to meet host governments' mandate that clinical testing, certification procedures, pricing policies, and marketing practices comply with local regulations. In these sorts of situations, an MNE trades global efficiency for local access, choices that require adapting resources, capabilities, and competencies to support dispersed value chains.

MNEs often face extraordinary pressures for local responsiveness. Brazil, for instance levies a 30 percent tax increase on imported cars with less than 65 percent local content. Likewise, it requires foreign energy firms to spend one percent of gross revenue on local R&D. Thailand's Alien Occupation Act reserves many architecture and engineering services jobs for Thai nationals. Uber's international expansion has hit speed bumps; in Paris and Madrid, protests mobilize public opposition, while in Frankfurt and London, officials mull stricter regulations to compel responsiveness. Consequently, host-country policies on, say, local content standards, buy-national policies, trade protectionism, hiring regulations, and currency repatriation, often require an MNE localize value activities or else forsake market access.

GLOBAL INTEGRATION AND LOCAL RESPONSIVENESS: MAPPING THEIR INTERACTION

Operating internationally calls for configuring and coordinating operations in ways that reconcile the competing demands of global integration and local responsiveness. The **Integration-Responsiveness (IR) Grid** provides a straightforward framework to organize analysis (see Figure 12.4). Procedurally, it positions an industry in the quadrant that represents its sensitivity to each imperative. As such, it provides executives a straightforward framework to improve strategic planning.

The IR Grid relates the global and local pressures that influence an MNE's strategy.

Strong pressures to respond locally, but low pressures to integrate globally—the lower-right quadrant of the IR Grid—encourage adapting value activities to host-country conditions. In this context, an MNE that operates in an industry with distinctive cultural sensitivities sees higher returns from local responsiveness and fewer benefits from global integration. Alternatively, an MNE experiencing high pressure to integrate globally but slight pressure for local responsiveness—the upper-left quadrant of the IR Grid—uses standardization to support the cost leadership strategy. It then exploits location effects and maximizes scale economies to provide consumers worldwide, who share universal needs, competitively priced, acceptably standardized products. Flat-panel displays, for instance, are vital components in a range of products; few consumers care much where they are made, as long as they are competitively priced and perform as promised. Thus, manufacturers, like LG Philips, Chi Mie Optoelectronics, and Samsung, concentrate value activities in economically superior locations that then supply the world.

CONCEPT CHECK

Globalization, though powerful, is not inevitable. Chapters 3 and 4 developed this thesis by noting that political and economic freedoms are constantly in flux. Similarly, both buy-local and pro-national campaigns pressure companies to localize value activities.

A third class of MNEs compete in industries that simultaneously impose powerful demands for local responsiveness and strong pressures for global integration. We find these industries in the center zone of the IR Grid. MNEs operating in salient national sectors, such as telecommunications, defense, information technology, automobiles, pharmaceuticals, and financial services, face differentiated customer preferences, market structures, regulatory codes, and institutional settings. Still, investment requirements, scale economies, and experience effects set high productivity thresholds. Configuring and coordinating value activities to resolve this dilemma is difficult. MNEs like Dentsu, China Mobile, Vodafone, or Infosys must develop complex configuration formats that support an intricate integrated cost leadership-differentiation strategy.

In summary, the IR Grid helps managers map their strategic options given prevailing pressures for global integration and local responsiveness in their industry.[70] It proves useful to making sense of competitive situations, helping to frame analytics as well as providing tools to track rivals' moves in terms of cost structures, institutional dynamics, and consumer preferences. It clarifies how industry structure sets the context, strategy specifies the end, and managers configure operations to mediate the two.

FIGURE 12.4 The Integration-Responsiveness Grid

Each strategy archetype embodies a unique concept of value creation that reflects its resolution of the asymmetric pressure for global integration versus local responsiveness. The Integration-Responsiveness Grid maps this relationship, highlighting the interaction between each pressure that confronts an MNE in an industry. As such, it helps managers interpret the competing imperatives.

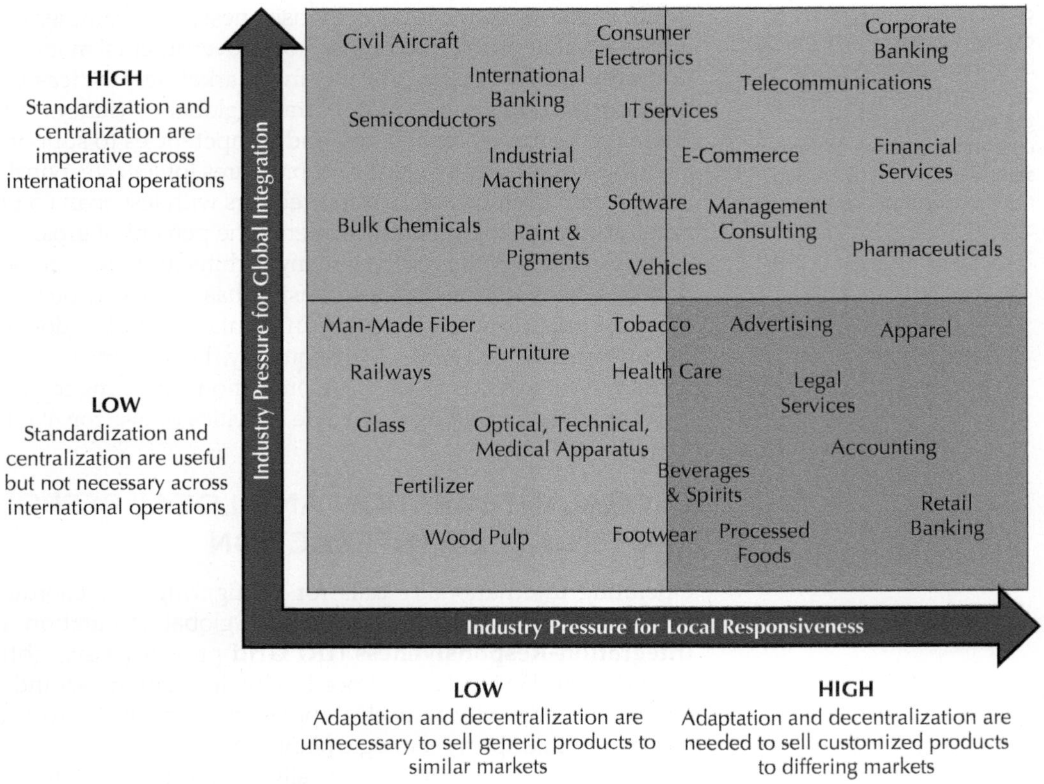

INTERNATIONAL CORPORATE-LEVEL STRATEGIES

12-7 Distinguish the types of strategies used by MNEs

Earlier, we profiled business-level strategies—namely, the cost leadership, differentiation, and integrated cost leadership-differentiation strategies. These ideas explain how a company competes in a given market, such as Apple in the United States, Nestlé and Switzerland, or Toyota in Japan. Going international, by diversifying an MNE's operation from a single nation to multiple nations, introduces the idea of a corporate-level strategy. This idea helps us make sense of how managers unite the individual parts of the MNE, whether spanning 2 to 217 markets, into a cohesive, coherent whole. Apple, for example, implements a differentiation strategy in its home market, the United States. As Apple expands into foreign markets, it aspires to apply the same business strategy in each additional market. Doing so consistently supports its vision and mission and productively uses its unique bundle of resources, capabilities, and competencies. Still, navigating different pressures across different countries creates questions and complications As Apple expands strategic planning from one to many nations, it must set its corporate-level strategy to manage those issues, such as the respective decision-making roles of headquarters and subsidiaries, which span multiple markets.

Similarly, think of the executives at Nestlé headquarters in Vevey, Switzerland, directing 447 factories in 86 countries to make products that are then sold in 197 countries. Or, likewise, Toyota's leaders in Toyota City, Japan, overseeing 70 factories in 29 countries making vehicles that are then sold and serviced in more than 170 countries. The leaders of Nestlé and Toyota, as do their counterparts at Apple and other MNEs, organize worldwide operation with a corporate-level strategy that helps everyone, no matter where they are or what they are doing, support the MNE's strategy. Absent this unifying logic, workers worldwide may make decisions that support different, even contradictory, strategies, thereby undermining the collective success of the global enterprise. Moreover, think again of the operational scope of Apple, Nestlé and Toyota. Their global span imposes costs and complications beyond those operating in a single market—the so-called liability of foreignness. HQ executives, surveying their far-flung operations, develop a corporate strategy to specify how they will leverage ownership, location, and internalization advantages to generate the value that offsets the additional expenses of international operations.

Against this backdrop, a **corporate-level strategy** is the set of actions taken by an MNE to manage its business across nations. More precisely, the corporate-level strategy (1) articulates how managers plan to reconcile global integration and local responsiveness in ways that support the MNE's vision and mission, (2) stipulates how managers will integrate the MNE's various parts into a strategic whole, and (3) specifies the decision-making role that headquarters and subsidiaries take doing so. Moving from theory to the practices of MNEs directs our attention to the international, localization, global standardization, and transnational strategies. Table 12.8 profiles the principles and practices of each while Figure 12.5 highlights their linkage to the I-R Grid.

TABLE 12.8 Characteristics of the Strategy Types Used by MNEs

The strategy gamut of "international-localization-global-transnational" anchors IB theory. Each archetype profiles how an MNE reconciles the dynamic tensions of global integration versus local responsiveness. Managers, mindful of industry structure, influence of insightful choices, and drivers of value creation, trade off the benefits and constraints of the archetypes in optimizing their strategic choice.

	International Strategy	Localization Strategy	Global Strategy	Transnational Strategy
Orientation	Leverage home-country resources, capabilities, and competencies into superior competitive positions abroad.	Customize resources, capabilities, and competencies to national differences in customer behavior, industry characteristics, government regulation, and market context.	Target universal needs or wants that support selling standardized products worldwide. Emphasize volume, cost minimization, and efficiency.	Simultaneously manages the tensions of global integration and local differentiation in ways that leverage specialized knowledge and promote worldwide learning.
Value Chain Configuration	Concentrated; value activities are set and directed by headquarters.	Dispersed; subsidiaries command discretion to adapt value activities.	Concentrated; value activities exploit location economies.	Concentrated to tap location economies. Dispersed, subject to minimum efficiency standards, to meet local preferences.
Decision-Making Outlook	Centralization as HQ retains control of resources and capabilities to apply, regulate, and protect competencies.	Decentralization as subsidiaries operate quasi-independently, tailoring activities to local circumstances.	Centralization as HQ directs activity to maximize standardization, enforce consistency, regulate the global matrix of inputs and outputs, and contain costs.	Simultaneous goals of integration and responsiveness calls for sharing decision-making between headquarters or subsidiaries.
Key Advantage	Directly transfers expertise from headquarters to international units.	Reduced need for central support to manage local activities. Sensitivity to local preferences.	Make low-cost, high-quality, standardized products that differ little, but appeal to consumers worldwide.	Supports efficiency, compels effectiveness, and leverages learning that drives innovations through units worldwide.
Key Disadvantage	Centralizing decision-making in the home country can misread local innovations.	Encourages "mini-me" phenomenon that replicates value activities across subsidiaries. Fuels accountability and allegiance conflicts.	Reduced learning opportunities given the dominance of the global standard.	Elaborate decision-making mechanisms integrate dispersed operations. Difficult to configure, tough to coordinate, and prone to performance shortfalls.
IR Grid Positioning	Low to moderate pressure for global integration and national responsiveness.	Low pressure for global integration. High pressure for national responsiveness.	High pressure for global integration. Low to mid-pressure for national responsiveness.	High pressure for global integration. High pressure for national responsiveness.
Examples	Google, P&G, Nucor, Harley Davidson, Baidu, Apple, Tesco, Facebook, Carrefour.	Unilever, Nestlé, McDonald's, Johnson & Johnson, Pfizer, Embraer, Ranbaxy.	Toyota, Canon, Haier, Caterpillar, Cemex, Infosys, Walmart, great by choice, Haier, American Express, Cisco.	GE, Tata, Zara, IBM, SAP.

FIGURE 12.5 The Integration-Responsiveness Grid: Organizing Interpretation of Corporate Level Strategy

Applying the organizing logic of the IR Grid to the different corporate level strategies highlights their key features.

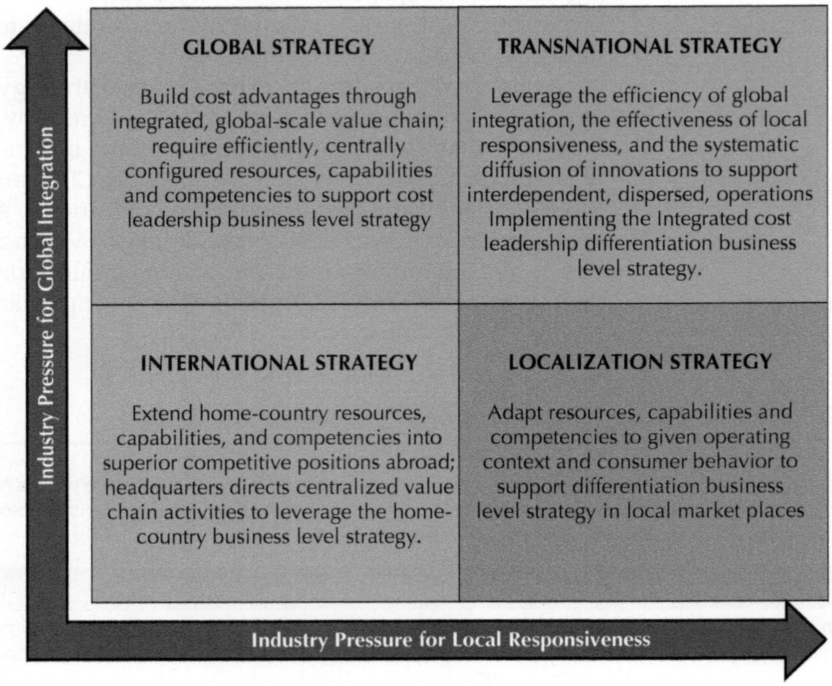

THE INTERNATIONAL STRATEGY

MNEs that compete in industries with low pressures for global integration and local responsiveness (the lower-left quadrant of the IR Grid) have the flexibility to sell products designed for their home market, with minimal, if any, customization for foreign markets. Moreover, they often face few, if any, rivals that offer a competitive product. In addition, their superior competitive position creates the flexibility to arbitrage location effects. Given this scenario, managers implement the **international strategy**.

The international strategy directly transfers a company's strategic outlook and orientation, as practiced in the home-country headquarters, to foreign markets without much, if any, adaptation. Ultimate control of the company's resources, capabilities, and core competencies resides with headquarters given senior executives' superior understanding of their optimal bundling. The testing ground of new ideas is the home market, not foreign countries. Headquarters, in its role as overseer of global operations, makes the decisions that the troops running the local subsidiaries then implement. This outlook gives local managers limited authority to adapt plans, processes, or products. MNEs implementing an international strategy include Airbus, Apple, Google, and Huawei.

Google, for example, centralizes strategic planning at the Googleplex, its headquarter complex in Mountain View, California—all the big decisions are made there. Certainly, Google decentralizes some elements of its marketing mix to local subsidiaries in order to respond to unique situations. Still, executives in the Googleplex safeguard the search algorithms and platform systems that anchor its competitive advantage. Planners in the Googleplex direct product development and set business processes for overseas operations. Hence, headquarters transfers principles, practices, and processes to foreign operations. It does not, however, transfer control. In strategic calls, the Googleplex rules.

Advantages The international strategy works well when an MNE's products or processes competitively speak to a universal customer preference—and, most critically, where they do not exist locally, or if they do, are less efficiently made or less effectively delivered. Again, think of Alibaba, Boeing, or Google operating overseas; no matter the market, it offers an appealing option that transcends product preferences or price elasticities. Each MNE's products, by setting the global standard, benefits from few rivals (the result of superior competitiveness), moderate operational costs (the efficiency of direct product transfer), and high profits (the yield of international leverage).

Limitations Headquarters' confidence in the superior competitiveness of its unique blend of capabilities, resources, and competencies discourages local adaptation. Initially, this outlook does not carry high risks. But, as an MNE expands its global operations, a one-way view of the world may miss opportunities or misread risks. Moreover, robust performance continues as long as foreign rivals scramble futilely. Companies worldwide, especially those in emerging economies, are reinventing systems of production and distribution, experimenting with new business models, and resetting the standards of innovation. Hence, an unexpectedly enterprising competitor may disrupt industry structure or market dynamics. Google, for example, faces adept local rivals in China, Russia, India, and South Korea—Baidu, Yandex, 123Khoj, and Naver, respectively—whose native sensitivities to local search tendencies position them in significant markets.[71] The centralization ethos of the international strategy, consequently, can struggle interpreting local threats.

THE LOCALIZATION STRATEGY

Some MNEs face high pressure to respond locally, but low pressure to integrate globally (the lower-right quadrant of the IR Grid). Cultural, political, legal, and economic conditions in foreign markets often push, if not require, MNEs to customize products and processes. Granted, managers prefer not, given the resulting increases in costs and complications. Failure to do so in the face of strident local pressures typically results in low sales, weak competitiveness, and eventual exit. Hence, MNEs in this sort of situation, like J&J, McDonald's, Nestlé, or HSBC, adopt a **localization strategy**, orienting their vision and mission, and plans to customize products and processes.

In terms of strategic planning, the localization strategy encourages decentralized decision-making—that way, local subsidiaries can adapt value activities to local circumstances. National subsidiaries, not global headquarters, take the lead in configuring the resources, capabilities, and competencies needed to design, make, and sell products that respond to preferences, practices, and the mélange of politics, law, and culture in the local market. At J&J, for example, headquarters recognizes that health-care regulations and patient care standards vary across countries. The scale and scope of differences preclude universal planning from headquarters. Optimizing global performance requires that J&J let its 250 business units worldwide behave like innovative, entrepreneurial firms, directing strategic planning and organizing value activities to fit local circumstances.[72]

CONCEPT CHECK

Chapter 4 profiles the idea of state capitalism, Chapter 6 discussed the economic rationales for governmental trade intervention, and Chapter 8 notes how trade agreements shape markets. These situations explain that state intervention into the market reduces the freedom that MNEs have to pursue the efficiencies of global integration. Alternatively, state intervention also benefits those MNEs that stress local responsiveness.

Advantages The localization strategy superbly speaks to the unique features of consumer preferences, business situations, and market context found in a particular country. Consider Starbucks, which began internationalizing operations in 1996 and now has nearly 31,200 outlets in 80 countries. It expands by adapting its blend of coffee, aesthetics, and aura to local preferences. Boosting performance in Europe, for example, relies on edgy architecture, including chandeliers and stages for poetry readings, to lure customers socialized to a high-touch café culture. In contrast, Starbucks runs more than 174 outlets in India through a 50/50 joint venture with Tata Global Beverages. These outlets sell coffee from beans grown and roasted in-country, brewing a distinctive Indian blend. It adapts its menus to Indian tastes, adding local dishes to the menu in each city.[73] Likewise, Starbucks taps the expertise of its joint venture partner to design outlets that, besides engaging historical architecture and ideals, includes aspects of the local culture.

The localization strategy gives the MNE's local units a distinctive advantage against in-country competitors who lack the benefits provided by a typically resource-rich parent company. Industries of the sort found in the lower-right corner of the IR Grid, such as food, health care, and retail banking, historically have local companies that operate nationally. Although competitive, many cannot match the pools of resources, capabilities, and competencies found in successful MNEs. For example, J&J's headquarters configures and coordinates global activities that support local units in order to then leverage its world-class research, executive, financial, marketing, and logistics competencies. Hence, the localization strategy helps subsidiaries build competitive positions in local markets on the strength of the parent's global advantages; this is crucial to offset the costs imposed by the liability of foreignness. Efficiently customizing products and process from market to market in the face of high pressures for adaptation, if headquarters aims to direct activity, however, is costly and complicated. Offsetting the liability of foreignness as well as providing a competitively priced alternative to local products, however, requires an MNE to optimize productivity.

The localization strategy, by encouraging operational overlap, increases overhead expenses.

Limitations Localization requires replicating value activities from subsidiary to subsidiary. Essentially, an MNE implementing the localization strategy builds "mini-me" units around the world. Customizing products or processes requires adapting resource and capabilities, thereby reducing efficiency along the value chain. Different product designs necessitate different materials, smaller markets make for shorter production runs, different channel structures call for dissimilar distribution formats, and divergent technology platforms complicate information exchange. Hence, the localization strategy is especially practical for the MNE competing in largely price-inelastic businesses.

Likewise, localization promotes management styles and value chains that differ from market to market. Allocating authority to local decision-makers can, over time, develop powerful subsidiaries. Eventually, some may opt to ignore headquarters' lead, instead maintaining that the unique features of their situation warrant a different, even contradictory, vision and mission. Left to their own devices, they may then adopt a strategy that, by nullifying the potential scale effects of cross-subsidiary integration, escalates costs. Moreover, if a subsidiary evolves into a virtual stand-alone operation, resource and power dynamics may neutralize headquarters' authority. Ensuing conflict over visions, mission, and plans blunts competitiveness.

GLOBAL STRATEGY

MNEs competing in industries of the sort found in the upper-left quadrant of the IR Grid face high pressures for global integration yet low pressures for local responsiveness. Industry effects press these firms to adopt a **global strategy** that is keenly sensitive to the economics of efficiency, advantages of standardization, and imperative of integration. Productivity pressures push an MNE to, ideally, be the cost leader or, minimally, be competitive with the industry pacesetter. Competitive positioning depends on exploiting potential scale economies, experience effects, and location advantages. Operationally, an MNE concentrates value activities in a few, ideal locations, standardizes products to enable long production runs, and rationalizes marketing to support aggressive pricing and direct distribution.

A global strategy champions worldwide standardization of value activities.

The global strategy has stark implications to value-chain design. Units operate in favorable locations that maximize productivity—e.g., a shoe factory in Vietnam, an auto-parts maker in China, a service call center in the Philippines. Value activities need not take place in the same location; a fully optimized global value chain locates an activity in the most efficient locale. IBM, for instance, supports its Asian value chain with HR specialists in Manila, accounts receivable experts in Shanghai, accountants in Kuala Lumpur, and procurement officers in Shenzhen.[74] Headquarters directs decision-making by standardizing practices and processes. Still, relentless cost pressures from rivals require that headquarters regularly raise productivity thresholds.

For some products, notably commodities, the global strategy is essentially the only profitable option. Commodities serve a universal need (think of gasoline, DRAM chips, steel, aspirin, debit cards, sugar, and so on). Consumer preferences in different countries, if not identical, are similar. Choosing between basically identical products (i.e., Company X's gasoline versus Company Y's gasoline) makes price a key point of competitiveness. The global strategy is not restricted to commodity markets. The globalization of markets encourages MNEs like Zara in apparel, IKEA in home furnishings, or LVMH in luxury goods to standardize features of historically differentiated products, manufacture them on a global scale, market them with a global brand, and sell them through focused distribution channels. Unquestionably, cross-national differences in consumer preferences exist, but they necessitate minor customization.

The global strategy positions MNEs to respond to a powerful trend in consumer behavior. Specifically, customers will forsake their preference to buy local and, instead, purchase a foreign-made product—provided it is a higher-quality, competitively priced, substitute. Driving this trend is the outlook that no matter the society, money exhibits three inalienable features: it is hard to acquire (one typically must work for it), transient (it is quickly used), and scarce in supply (no matter the amount, it inevitably seems too little). Consequently, consumers worldwide pursue a common quest: maximize utility by buying the highest-quality product for the lowest possible price.[75] Ultimately, goes this reasoning, economically rational consumers disregard a product's national origin, buying a foreign-made product rather than a local substitute, when it delivers superior value. The sweep and scope of technology intensifies this tendency. Consumer preferences converge as connections proliferate across countries. The shrinking digital divide exposes more people to common media, thereby promoting universal consumption ideals, and, in turn, standardizing consumer behaviors. Ultimately, consumers' disposition to discount nationalism in the quest for a product offering superior value girds the global strategy.

CONCEPT CHECK

Previous chapters highlight the growing potential and performance of emerging economies, such as China, India, and the Philippines. Fast-rising MNEs in these countries develop product and process innovations to ingeniously engineer goods and services. These innovations push western MNEs to rethink the economics of value creation.

Advantages The global strategy directly responds to the ongoing integration of national markets. Institutional developments progressively reduce the trade frictions and investment restrictions that had historically constrained mobility. Increasingly, MNEs more easily configure efficient production networks given growing ease to move anything, anywhere. Improving opportunities to achieve economies of scale, leverage experience effects, and exploit location economies enable the global strategy to produce increasingly higher-quality, lower cost products; this, in turn, offers products whose superior value proposition overcomes the appeal of local substitutes in national markets. Combined, institutional developments as well as changing consumer behaviors supports the progressive globalization of markets. Ongoing integration expands opportunities for managers to translate resources and capabilities into competencies that leverage the global strategy. Lastly, a key advantage of the global strategy is it's clarity of vision and discipline of mission; single-minded focus on improving efficiency imposes an absolute logic on strategic planning.

Limitations The extreme cost sensitivity of the global strategy leaves MNEs little latitude to customize processes or products to local conditions; each change creates differences that reduce efficiency. Hence, an MNE's success is a function of the validity of the "one type product fits all customers' needs worldwide" thesis. A single bet on a single approach for the global market is risky. Disruptive change can turn the laser focus of a globally-tuned value chain into a maladapted delusion. The fallout of the global financial crisis, for example, saw big banks such as Citibank, Royal Bank of Scotland, and Fortis foiled by their previously high-performance global strategies. Despite leadership in global capital markets, the crisis and ensuing demand for local responsiveness turned many of their strengths into liabilities. Finally, concentrating value activities in a few productivity-maximizing locations exposes the MNE to a host of risks, such as political change, legal manipulations, trade conflicts, and exchange-rate instability.

TRANSNATIONAL STRATEGY

The quest to maximize efficiencies through cost leadership while, at the same time, maximizing effectiveness via differentiation is difficult. Each strategy imposes requirements that run counter to others. The asymmetric demands of maximizing efficiencies through cost leadership and effectiveness via differentiation make it difficult to pursue both simultaneously. Still, some companies, like Target or Zara, successfully implement an integrated cost leadership-differentiation business-level strategy. The corporate-level analogue, the **transnational strategy**, takes this idea globally.[76]

The transnational strategy targets the efficiency of global integration, the effectiveness of local responsiveness, and the systematic diffusion of innovations.

The MNEs operating in the sort of industries we see in the upper-right quadrant of the IR Grid, notably, airlines, financial services, or e-commerce, simultaneously integrate globally to reduce costs as well as adapt to national circumstances to appease local stakeholders. Resolution requires managers standardize some activities while differentiating others. Choosing to optimize both objectives, rather than maximize one, reduces efficiency and caps effectiveness. Offsetting high costs, given the ever-present liability of foreignness, requires that an MNE develop firm-specific resources, capabilities, and competencies that create hard-to-copy advantages. Hence, the transnational strategy champions interactive global learning. It pushes managers to leverage local insights learned meeting "particularizing tendencies" by diffusing them worldwide to meet "universalizing tendencies."[77] Systematically diffusing local insights from one locale to others enables the transnational strategy to optimize local effectiveness and global efficiency.

The transnational strategy does not centralize authority in headquarters or decentralize it to local units. Instead, its advocates communication and collaboration between idea generators and idea adopters, no matter where each resides. Implementing the transnational strategy requires a sophisticated value chain that simultaneously supports integration, responsiveness, and learning. Managers configure value activities, ideally satisfying minimum efficiency standards, on a country-to-country basis given prevailing cultural, political, legal, and economic conditions. Location choices are biased toward neither concentration nor dispersal. Rather, they balance the universalizing tendencies that endorse global integration with the particularizing tendencies that push local responsiveness. Successfully implementing the transnational strategy opens opportunities to optimize productivity, create value, and sustain competitiveness "glocally."

The transnational strategy reconciles global integration and local responsiveness in ways that leverage the MNE's competencies throughout worldwide operations.

Advantages Some see the transnational strategy ideally suited to optimally respond to the emerging requirements of the global business environment. Charging strategic planners to gain location economies and experience effects without sacrificing the flexibility to customize processes and products pushes for an innovative mix of resources, capabilities, and competencies. The transnational strategy is keen to the payoff of multidirectional knowledge exchange between units. Essentially, as we saw in the opening profile of Zara, strategic planners presume that neither headquarters nor local subsidiaries know best, but collectively they develop 'glocal' innovations that help each reconcile imperatives of both. Validating the vitality of learning throughout the MNE's global network helps managers make sense of optimizing headquarters' resources and local subsidiaries' capabilities given particularizing and universalizing tendencies.

The transnational strategy is difficult to implement in practice, given the challenges of complicated agendas, high costs, and cognitive limits.

Limitations The transnational strategy is tough to direct, difficult to configure, and prone to shortfalls. Reconciling integration and responsiveness pressures, further complicated by the necessity to generate knowledge locally but diffuse it worldwide, can overwhelm the best-intentioned MNEs. Simultaneously developing integration and differentiation advantages requires ingeniously converting resources and capabilities into competencies that support a broad cross-section of value activities. Developing a network mindset among executives, installing the requisite communication network, and navigating the ambiguity of multi-criteria decision makes strategic planning challenging. The complexity of the transnational strategy means an MNE may fall short of sufficiently integrating global activities and/or differentiating local operations—essentially, getting stuck in the dreaded "middle" where costs run too high and responsiveness runs too low.

CASE

The Multinational Enterprise of the Future: Leading Scenarios

Evolving workflows, changing technologies, and shifting markets intensify globalization trends. MNEs respond in kind, rethinking visions, clarifying missions, adjusting strategies, and reconfiguring value chains to compete in the brave new world. Forecasts of accelerating change due to digitization, frugal innovations, robotic cells, and activist transnational institutions, among others, spur MNEs to identify the ideal path to bundle resources, capabilities, and competencies. Let's look at some high-concept forecasts of the MNE of the future.

The Globally Integrated Enterprise

The evolutionary perspective sees MNEs responding systematically to the steadily unfolding imperatives of globalization. As policies and practices progressively connect countries, MNEs similarly respond, progressively integrating their international operations. The former CEO of IBM has a provocative take. Reflecting on IBM's evolution, he contends that it has passed through three strategic phases, each fitting the prevailing circumstances and collectively foreshadowing the MNE of the future.

First, there was the nineteenth-century "international model, whereby the company was headquartered both physically and mentally in its home country; it sold goods, when it was so inclined, through a scattering of overseas sales offices."[78] Headquarters focused on business activities in its home country and configured international operations with little input from overseas units. As such, it used an international strategy to engage a world composed of erratically connected countries.

Phase two of the evolution ushered in the classic multinational firm of the late twentieth century. Echoing the localization strategy, this phase saw HQ build smaller versions of itself abroad to respond to highly differentiated markets.

Steadily, the expanding connection among countries, by supporting concentrated value chains geared toward exploiting location economies and scale economies, highlighted the inefficient economics of the "mini-me" option.[79] Steadily, escalating redundancy costs—each country essentially ran a stand-alone operation—grew unacceptable given intensifying competition.

The third phase, the "globally integrated enterprise," speaks to the dawn of globality in which "business flows in every direction. Companies have no centers. The idea of foreignness is foreign. Commerce swirls and market dominance shifts."[80] Competing with everyone from everywhere for everything requires putting investments, people, and work anywhere in the world "based on the right cost, the right skills and the right business environment [with] work flow[ing] to the places where it will be done . . . most efficiently and to the highest quality."[81] Earlier models saw configuration and coordination barriers constrain knowledge flows, production opportunities, and organizational options. Now, like the Internet, the globally integrated enterprise designs its strategy, configures its activities, and coordinates its processes to connect everything, everywhere.

The Metanational

In the future, goes this scenario, world-class operational efficiency will no longer determine an MNE's competitive advantage. Nor will an MNE build superior competitiveness from unique features of its home country or, for that matter, from a set of national subsidiaries. Rather, success will go to those who move from designing multinational operations to synthesizing metanational competencies.

The metanational seeks unique ideas, activities, and insights that complement its existing operations as well as create new leverage points. It expands its mission from selling stuff worldwide to mining the treasure trove of ideas, resources, and capabilities that emerge anywhere and everywhere. It scans the world, identifying and interpreting the untapped potential of the specialized knowledge that lies latent in unique market situations. Exploiting these opportunities positions managers to "build a new kind of competitive advantage by discovering, accessing, mobilizing, and leveraging knowledge from many locations around the world."[82]

Metanationals, goes the theory, orient strategic planning to:

- *Prospect* for and access untapped technologies and unidentified consumer trends.
- *Leverage* globally the specialized knowledge scattered throughout local subsidiaries.
- *Mobilize* fragmented knowledge to generate innovations that produce, market, and deliver value globally.
- *Apply* superior project management skills across teams to foster a strong collaborative culture.[83]

Which sorts of MNEs aspire to be a metanational? Generally, those facing pressures for global integration and local responsiveness yet seeing opportunities in prospecting, leveraging, mobilizing, and applying knowledge that is fragmented across countries. Finding ways to integrate fragmentation sets the metanational up for the big time. Until recently, the metanational option attracted few companies. Communication and collaboration barriers complicated sharing knowledge. Moreover, national differences posed problems. Today, environmental conditions, institutional agendas, and technology trends, by easing sensing, mobilizing, and operationalizing knowledge, steadily open the era of the metanational.[84]

MNEs, like Shiseido, ARM, McDonald's, STMicroelectronics, Procter & Gamble, SAP, and Tata, are emergent metanationals, able to convert local insights into global innovations. Consider McDonald's in Russia. It has more than 700 outlets and plans to add hundreds more, given that Russia is one of its fastest-growing and most-profitable markets. In metanational style, McDonald's leveraged its Russian experiences worldwide to develop new competencies; notably, it began its worldwide pushback against coffee chains by tapping knowledge it developed with test runs in Russia. It opened McCafés there in 2003, fine-tuned its espresso-style drinks, and then successfully moved the concept to the United States in 2009 and, from there, to the world.[85]

The Micro-Multinational

The future frontier for the MNE is set by the matter of size, say others. Historically, MNEs were colossi that straddled the globe. Today, the number of MNEs grows worldwide, but the average size is falling—many firms operating internationally employ fewer than 250 folks and, in many cases, some count just a handful. This anomaly signals the era of so-called micro-multinationals: nimble, small firms that are born global, operating internationally from day one. Unlike their bigger counterparts that expanded internationally by gradually entering new markets, micro-multinationals go global immediately. They go where they wish, typically following the circuit paths of the Internet, but always targeting markets with plentiful customers and innovative environments. The born-global does not see international markets as a refuge when sales slow at home. Rather, it begins with the belief that the domestic market is just one of the many opportunities in the world.

The micro-multinational's distinctive break from the past follows from its global focus at start-up. Folks who found born-global firms often have a strong international orientation gained from living or studying abroad. Take SoundCloud, a Swedish audio-sharing web service. Its cofounders—one born in England and one in Sweden—were previously knowledgeable enough about the German and U.S. markets to move into both within months of starting up.[86] Other startups, like Airobotics of Israel, maker of the "Swiss Army Knife of drones," develop compelling technical solutions.[87] Akin to the idea "build a better mousetrap, and the world will beat a path to your door," they have customers worldwide from the get-go. Often, too, we see a seasoned executive, motivated by an entrepreneurial vision and aware of a worldwide market niche, leave a large MNE and launch a firm that goes global from day one.[88] For instance, Zoom Video Communication provides remote teleconferencing services using cloud computing technologies. It began when a lead engineer from Cisco Systems, an early adopter of video conferencing, saw expanding opportunities worldwide. He left Cisco, launched his startup, and, within a few months, registered more than one million users worldwide.[89]

Increasingly, the micro-multinational moves from theory to practice precisely because circumstances let it do so. The ongoing globalization of markets, marked by trade liberalization, growing demand for specialized products, and improving technologies, enables born-globals to implement their vision cheaply and quickly. Clever folks exploit these changes, ingeniously leveraging platforms to develop and deliver innovations in niche markets that span the world.

The Glorecalized MNE

Advocates of regionalization endorse the awkward term **Glorecalization** as the next step in the evolution of the MNE.[90] Glorecalization, a portmanteau of **Glo**balization-**Re**gionalization-Lo**calization**, champions a global vision and customized local mission through a value chain configured to exploit location economies within a regional market. Essentially, rather than "think global, act local," the glorecalized MNE opts to "go global, think regionally, act local." It configures neither a global nor local system, but rather a regional network that, given the size of the regional market, enables it to achieve the requisite efficiencies to support competitive positioning. Correspondingly operating within the context of a well-defined region, where geographically proximate countries share political, economic, and cultural characteristics, enables it to optimize local effectiveness. Various conditions support the glorecalized MNE. First and foremost, the institutional structure, regulatory framework, and system integration of regional trade blocs (e.g., AU, ASEAN, CARICOM, EU, OBOR, and USMCA) create sustainable sanctuaries.

The European Union, for example, unites 27 countries and creates a common "home" for 445 million who share similar outlooks, overlapping national interests, and convergent consumption preferences. Efficient flows of people, capital, information, products, and processes throughout the EU streamline how an MNE acquires resources, develops capabilities, and crafts competencies. Similarly, regionalizing production exploits location effects and scale economies, but without sacrificing the flexibility to adapt goods and services. China's One Belt, One Road (OBOR) Initiative might prove to be the ultimate market frontier for the Glorecalized MNE. This plan progressively integrates, via an expanding network of roads, pipelines, railways, seaways, ports, power plants, digital networks, and cultural centers, countries in Asia, Africa, Europe, and Oceania. Combined, these nations include 70 percent of the world's population, 45 percent of current global GDP, and more than 90 national economies. If successful, the scale and scope of the OBOR market offers the well-positioned glorecalized MNE a robust gameboard.

The Digi-Corp

The digi-corp, a form unimaginable a generation ago, is increasingly a reality today.[91] The digi-corp does not organize products, consumers, or markets to reflect or respect the geography set by quaint lines on a map. Instead, the digital connectivity of the Internet, not national borders, defines its operational boundaries. Facebook, for instance, exists physically in its California headquarters, but its workforce of about 45,000 runs a company that serves more than 2.25 billion "customers" in nearly 200 nations through a website interface translated into more than 100 languages.

Digi-corps develop competencies that help them react in real time to changes in customers, markets, and environments. They engage perspectives and strategies that bias value chains toward virtuality to link resources, capabilities, and competencies within dynamic digital networks that encircle the globe. For instance, Nike and Reebok own no plants, instead relying on contract manufacturers to make and distribute their products. Apple, Cisco, and Qualcomm do the same, outsourcing production to third-party manufacturers, like Pegatron, TSMC, and Foxconn; each then does what each does best. Though nominally independent, communications and collaboration systems integrate agents into the network, thereby creating virtual capabilities. Nike, for example, focuses on increasing value creation by leveraging its competencies in design and marketing, confident in its manufacturers' expertise to adjust product mixes as consumer behavior evolves.

The digi-corp builds on crowdsourcing, swarm intelligence, and artificial intelligence to tap the collective insight developed in self-organizing systems that are remotely executing, global, always on, and endlessly configurable. It, in collaboration with partners, operates in the infinity of cyberspace. Many of these agents were, just a generation earlier, far off the global grid. Now, innovations enact a techno-utopia that connects everyone to the "evolving nervous system of civilization."[92] The digi-corp, built to engage strategies that learn, evolve, and transform, has the outlook and orientation to navigate the workplace of the future.

Make the Call

Indisputably, calling the MNE of the future is more speculation than stipulation. No matter the standard that ultimately emerges, we expect it will showcase the historic markers of companies that are built to last: a down-to-earth, pragmatic, committed-to-excellence framework run by bright people who articulate an insightful vision, practical mission, and clever strategy that changes the game.[93] Still, we watch, tracking the contenders, waiting to see whose performance ultimately sets the standard.

QUESTIONS

12-3 You have a choice to work for a globally integrated enterprise, a metanational, a glorecalized, a micro-multinational, or a digi-corp. Which would you choose? Why?

12-4 Looking out over the next decade, estimate the likely standards of how the "typical" MNE will create value. In your opinion, which form of MNE from this set seems best positioned for this scenario? Why?

12-5 The MNE of the future, in whatever form it takes, will face pressures for global integration and local responsiveness. In your opinion, which form of MNE from this set seems best positioned to reconcile that challenge?

CHAPTER 13
Country Evaluation and Selection

Source: Jack Young-Places/Alamy Stock Photo

A Burger King restaurant at the base of the Great Wall of China at Mutianyu. ▲

OBJECTIVES

After studying this chapter, you should be able to

13-1 Elaborate on the significance of location in IB operations

13-2 Illustrate why comparing countries through scanning is important and how it connects to final location choices

13-3 Discern major opportunity and risk variables and how to prioritize and relate them when deciding whether and where to expand abroad

13-4 Summarize the sources and shortcomings of comparative country information

13-5 Explain alternative considerations and means for companies to allocate resources among countries

13-6 Recognize why companies make noncomparative decisions when choosing where to operate abroad

The place to get top speed out of a horse is not the place where you can get top speed out of a canoe.

—African (Hausa) proverb

CASE

Burger King®[1]

Burger King is the world's largest flame-broiled fast-food hamburger chain. The chapter's opening photo shows one of its restaurants in China, the country with the most Burger Kings outside of the U.S. and Canada. Figure 13.1 shows Burger King's four geographic divisions in terms of the number of restaurants.

A BIT OF HISTORY

Starting out as Insta-Burger King in 1954, the company grew to five restaurants in the next five years. In 1959, with its name shortened to Burger King, it began domestic franchising. Beginning in the early 1960s the company expanded internationally to the Bahamas and Puerto Rico. Then it entered Europe, Asia, and Latin America in the 1970s.

Since 1967, Burger King has at times been publicly owned, a division of other companies, a holding company owned by private equity firms, and a privately owned company. In fact, over a 20-year period it had seven different parents and corporate structures. The years of transformed ownership caused changes in emphasis, and its interests have sometimes been secondary to those of its parent company. Nevertheless, some of its international moves turned out to be highly successful, and a few did not. It entered and then retreated from operations in such countries as Colombia, France, Israel, Japan, and Oman. (It has reentered some of these.) Many of Burger King's early international forays came about either because someone in another country initiated it or because a corporate manager was familiar with a particular country and thought it would offer opportunities. Its retreats have occurred because of low cash flow and because of having entered markets too small to support the necessary infrastructure, such as slaughterhouse and beef-grinding facilities.

FIGURE 13.1 Regional Emphasis of Burger King

Based on data for 2018 from Restaurant Brands International's investor day presentation, May 15, 2019.

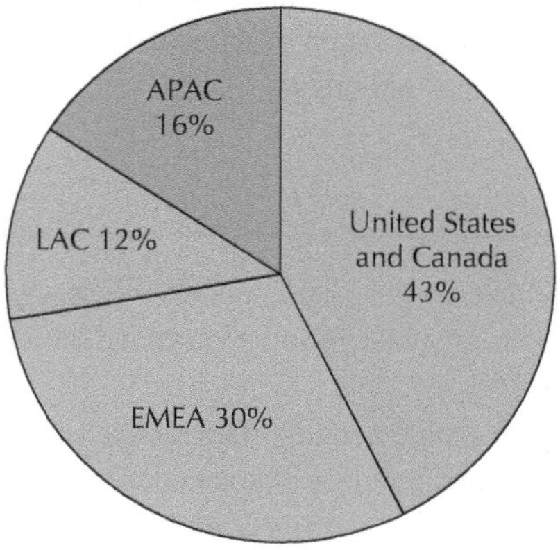

Over time, Burger King has taken a more systematic approach toward restaurant expansion. It still sees substantial U.S. growth opportunities but considers it to be a more mature market than other countries. Nearly all of the growth in the number of Burger King restaurants since 2010 has occurred outside the U.S. and Canada. In seeking new places to enter, Burger King looks most favorably at countries with large populations (especially young people), high beef consumption, availability of capital for franchisees, a safe pro-business environment, growth in shopping centers, and availability of a potential franchisee with experience and resources. Recently its model has been to grant franchise rights by pairing a private equity firm with an experienced restaurant operator in a joint venture (JV). In some cases, Burger King has become the third party in the JV without committing capital to it.

Overall, Burger King expanded abroad later than its primary rival, McDonald's. On the one hand, later entry is a drawback in very small markets due to an inadequate number of suppliers, such as only one slaughterhouse whose owners may be unwilling to work with more than one customer. On the other hand, its later entry into larger markets allows Burger King to benefit from earlier entrants' creation of product demand and a supply infrastructure. In Latin America and the Caribbean, McDonald's and Burger King compete in almost all countries and territories, with Burger King currently leading in the number of restaurants in about half of those markets.

Burger King's Latin America and Caribbean group has many sparsely populated countries (e.g., the Cayman Islands, Aruba, and Saint Lucia) in which Burger King developed a presence long before entering more abundantly populated countries such as China, Russia, and South Africa. The reason is largely due to its headquarters location in Miami, which is often called "the capital of Latin America." Because so many people from that region go to or through Miami, the Burger King reputation spilled over there early on, which simplified gaining brand recognition and acceptance. Further, Miami's nearness to Latin America and the Caribbean enhances the ability of Burger King's executives and franchisees to visit each other.

REENTERING COLOMBIA AND FRANCE

Colombia

Burger King entered Colombia in the early 1980s but departed because of Colombian royalty expatriation restrictions and prolonged economic and political turmoil. By the time Burger King reentered the country in 2008, the cities were safe for people to go out to eat, the peso was strong, families had disposable income to eat out, and all the major cities had large new shopping centers with food courts. Although incomes were unevenly distributed, the richest 20 percent of the population (almost 9 million people) had a per capita expenditure in 2007 of over US$17,000. In addition, Burger King was able to sign franchise rights with two well-established and experienced companies. By 2019, there were 20 Burger King restaurants operating throughout Colombia.

France

Burger King entered France in 1979, departed in 2001, and reentered in 2013. When entering, Quick (a Belgian fast-food operator) and McDonald's were already well established there. Burger King's British parent, Grand Metropolitan, also owned Wimpy, a chain of U.K. hamburger restaurants, and required Burger King to absorb the chain. This sapped resources needed for French expansion. When Burger King left the French market, it had grown to only 16 restaurants there, whereas McDonald's had about 450.

When reentering France, Burger King was determined to put in enough effort to compete. By 2015, it grew to 50 restaurants and in 2016 it acquired Quick, which had about 500 restaurants. Those in France were rebranded as Burger King; whereas those in Belgium and Luxembourg maintain the Quick brand. The number of Burger Kings in France reached approximately 300 by 2020.

THE BRICS

The possibilities in the BRIC countries are too great to ignore. Burger King opened its first Brazilian and Chinese restaurants in 2004. While Burger King has had success in both these countries, it has been able to expand much faster in the former due largely to its recognition advantage in Brazil. A half million Brazilians fly into Florida each year, where Burger King's restaurants abound. In addition, about 300,000 Brazilians live in South Florida, most of whom maintain contact with relatives and friends back home.

In China, Burger King encountered laws requiring it either to form a JV with a Chinese firm or own and operate two or more stores for at least a year before starting franchise operations. The company chose the latter alternative, which delayed its start of franchising. After doing so, finding potential franchisees with sufficient financial and restaurant capabilities was difficult, particularly since the franchise concept was rather new to China. (Some of its competitors, mainly Yum! Brands and McDonald's, made joint venture investments and expanded with owned stores.) In 2012 Burger King entered a three-partner JV to serve the Chinese market. One partner, the Carpesian Capital Group, is a global private equity company specializing in developing country investments. The other is the Korduglu family from Turkey, which is Burger King's largest non-U.S. franchisee. The number of Burger King restaurants in China surpassed 1,000 in 2018.

In 2010 Burger King entered Russia, an attractive country not only because of its large population and growth potential, but also because of integration possibilities with operations in Eastern Europe. Indeed, Burger King entered Slovenia in 2011 and now depends on supplies from the Russian operation. In addition, concluding the essentiality of finding the right franchisee, Burger King's managers spent over a year getting to know the eventual franchisee, who owns a chain of about 200 Russian coffee shops. Although the franchise has resulted in growth in Moscow and St. Petersburg, the franchise formed a JV with Russia's VTB Capital in 2013 to gain resources needed to expand outside those cities.

In 2014 India became Burger King's 100th operating country. It partnered with Everstone Capital, a private equity firm that also holds controlling interest in India's largest restaurant group. India's fast-food segment has recently been growing at 26 percent per annum. Because of the large number of vegetarians in India, Burger King has delegated much of the menu selection to its partner. At the same time, it has done extensive market research to develop a vegetarian menu to accompany its nonvegetarian one. With under 200 restaurants, Burger King has a much smaller presence in India than in the other BRICs (which each have more than 600), but the company identifies it as one of its top five growth markets.

THE FUTURE

Until recently, Burger King's growth in its U.S. and Canada region lagged its growth elsewhere. To counter McDonald's faster growth in breakfast sales, Burger King merged in 2014 with Tim Hortons, a Canadian coffee and doughnuts chain with about 4,500 (almost all franchised) restaurants. The combined company now operates as Restaurant Brands International. In 2017, it pursued growth through the acquisition of Popeyes Louisiana Kitchen, a fried chicken chain with 2,600 locations worldwide.

In 2018, Burger King opened over 1,000 restaurants worldwide—more than its bigger rival, McDonald's. It also became more aggressive about modernizing restaurants and introducing new products. New investments are designed to help Burger King catch up to its competitors in updating restaurants with digital menu boards, self-order kiosks, and sleek design. A plant-protein patty is being introduced to make the hamburger chain more appealing to younger generations. The fact that some of its competitors have expanded abroad much more than Burger King may indicate that it has untapped international potential. Burger King's management, however, faces a number of questions regarding location priorities; such questions challenge managers in any company with international operations.

QUESTIONS

13-1 Discuss the risks that an international company such as Burger King would have by operating abroad rather than just domestically.

13-2 How has Burger King's headquarters location influenced its international expansion? Has this location strengthened or weakened its global competitive position?

THE IMPORTANCE OF LOCATION

13-1 Elaborate on the significance of location in IB operations

Companies lack resources to take advantage of all international opportunities.

The adage that "location, location, and location" are the three most important factors for business success rings true for IB. The world has more than 200 countries, each offering distinct opportunities and risks. Thus, some locations fit companies' capabilities and strategies better than others. By comparing the external environment with a company's objectives and capabilities, managers might ask: Where can we best leverage our existing competencies? And where can we best sustain, improve, or extend our competencies? Because companies have limited resources, they must be careful in choosing among countries when making the following decisions:

1. The location of sales, production, and administrative and auxiliary services, such as R&D
2. The sequence for entering different countries
3. The portion of resources and efforts to allocate to each country where they operate

Companies need to
- determine the order of country entry,
- allocate resources among countries.

Committing human, technical, and financial resources to one locale may mean forgoing or delaying projects elsewhere. In actuality, a company may first set a strategy of domestic versus international emphasis, such as General Electric's objective of making 60 percent of its sales internationally.[2] Afterward, a company may sequence its entry by country or region. Once operating in multiple countries, it must allocate efforts among them. This chapter emphasizes the country decision process.[3] Taking time to pick and emphasize the more outstanding locations affects firms' ability to gain and sustain competitive advantage.[4]

In choosing geographic sites, a company must decide
- where to sell,
- where to produce.

The choice of country for sales may or may not coincide with the choice of country to produce. On the one hand, they may be the same, particularly if transport costs or government regulations require production in the countries where you sell. Many service industries, such as restaurants (like Burger King), construction, and retailing, must locate most production facilities near their foreign customers.

On the other hand, large-scale capital-intensive production technology favors producing in only a few countries and exporting to others, such as with automobiles and steel. Further, production locations are complex, such as sourcing raw materials and components from different countries and dividing operating functions among countries (e.g., headquarters in one, a call center in another, an R&D facility in still another, and so on).

Location flexibility is essential because conditions change. A company must respond to new opportunities and withdraw from less profitable ones. There is no one-size-fits-all theory for picking operating locations because product lines, competitive positions, resources, and strategies make each company unique.[5] Moreover, hiring the right people to analyze country differences and implement company operations is critical. Highly skilled managers can sometimes compensate for location deficiencies, and poor managers can sometimes cause poor performance in the best locations. Having skilled management in the most appropriate locations, however, is the best possible combination. Figure 13.2 shows the major steps IB managers should take in making location decisions. The following discussion examines those steps in depth.

COMPARING COUNTRIES THROUGH SCANNING

13-2 Illustrate why comparing countries through scanning is important and how it connects to final location choices

Managers use **scanning** techniques to examine countries on broad indicators of opportunities and risks.[6] Scanning compares many countries using information that is readily available, inexpensive, and fairly comparable with the goal of identifying the most promising locations.

WHY IS SCANNING IMPORTANT?

Without scanning, a company may examine too many or too few possibilities.

Scanning is like seeding widely and then weeding out; it is useful insofar as a company might otherwise consider too few or too many possibilities. Comparison among countries, however, is not always practical. We discuss the topic of when noncomparative decisions are appropriate later in the chapter.

FIGURE 13.2 The Location Decision Process

Location, location, location: Committing resources to a foreign location may entail risky trade-offs—say, forgoing or abandoning projects elsewhere. The start of the decision-making process is essentially twofold: examining the external environments of proposed locations and comparing each of them with the company's objectives and capabilities.

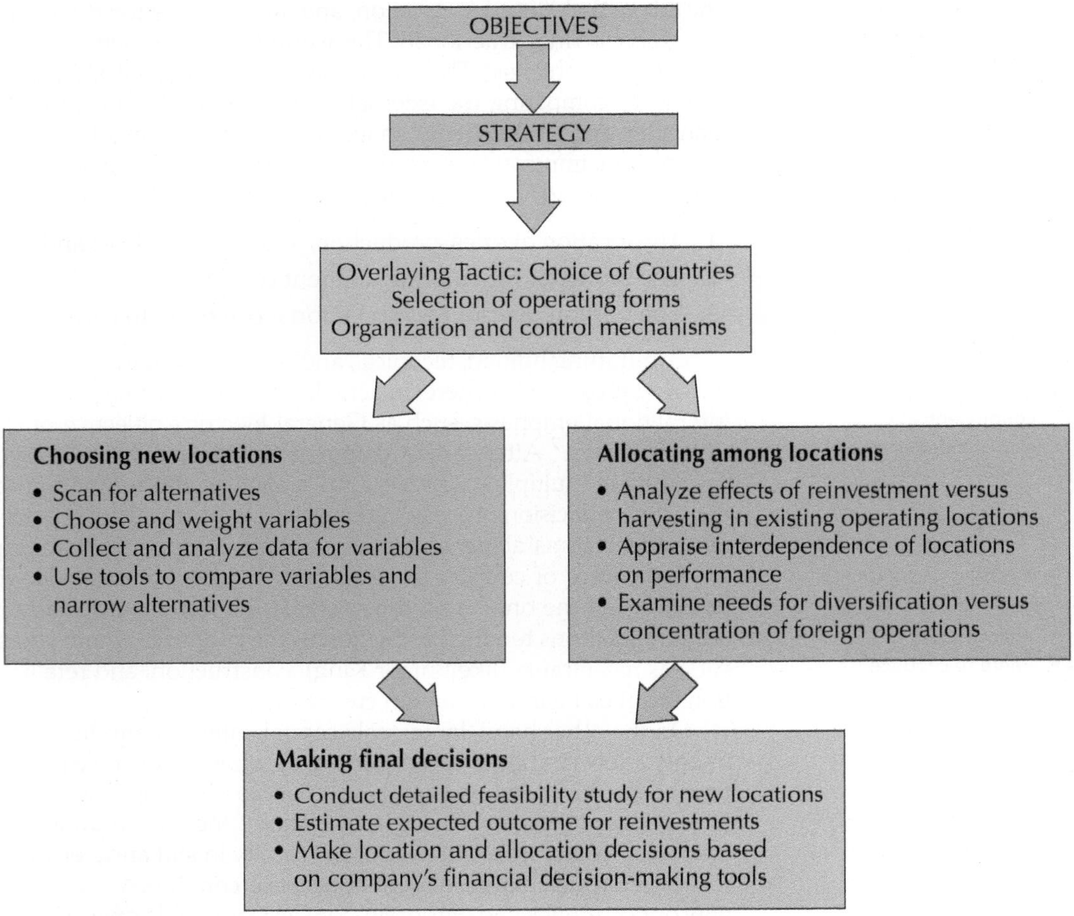

SCANNING VERSUS DETAILED ANALYSIS

Scanning utilizes "yes" or "no" questions, direct statistics, indirect indicators, and qualitative assessment.

Step 1: Scanning In scanning, managers examine many countries broadly in order to narrow detailed analysis and travel to only a few highly promising ones. They analyze publicly available information and communicate with experienced people on conditions that could significantly affect the success and fit for their business. Because managers use fairly easy-to-find information, they may consider a large group of countries, such as all those within a global region.

Information gathered at this point may be of four types:

1. *Yes or no questions:* For a question like "Does the country allow 100 percent ownership of foreign direct investments?" the answer is "yes" or "no."
2. *Direct statistics:* For a question such as "What is the highest marginal tax rate on corporate earnings?" direct information is available from tax schedules.
3. *Indirect indicators:* For a question such as "What are the potential sales for my product?" estimates must use indirect indicators, such as those based on per capita GDP and population size.
4. *Qualitative assessment:* For a question akin to "What will be the future political leaders' philosophy about IB?" a qualitative assessment is necessary based on different opinions and indirect indicators.

On-site visits follow scanning and are part of the final location decision process.

Step 2: Detailed Analysis Once narrowing the number of countries, managers need to compare them in greater detail. Unless they are satisfied to outsource all their production and sales, they almost always need to go on location to collect and evaluate more specific information.

Let's say that managers need to decide where best to emphasize sales. They will likely need to visit the shortlisted countries to observe the market and visit with distributors. Or let's say managers need to decide where best to locate production. If outsourcing, they may want to inspect potential contractors' facilities. If planning to own facilities themselves, they will need to collect such specific on-site information as availability and cost of land and supplies.

Intel's manufacturing expansion into Latin America illustrates this process. Intel used scanning to limit visits to a few Latin American countries. The follow-up visits sought much more detailed information—even the availability of suitable housing, medical services, and food products for the personnel Intel would need to transfer. The visitors were also able to gain qualitative information, such as impressions of the welcome they might get from government officials and business leaders.

Managers' country familiarity—the sense of knowing and understanding a target country when considering foreign market entry—is an important element of country selection.[7] Managers' international experience—from travel, language proficiency, or living or working abroad—is also important. Unfortunately, the more time and money companies invest in examining an alternative, the more likely they are to accept it regardless of its merits—a situation known as **escalation of commitment**. A feasibility study should have clear-cut decision points, whereby managers can discontinue the commitment before they invest too much.

OPPORTUNITY AND RISK VARIABLES

13-3 Discern major opportunity and risk variables and how to prioritize and relate them when deciding whether and where to expand abroad

Companies may simplify the scanning of research by first eliminating countries with conditions unacceptable to them.

Managers should first identify country conditions they will not accept. Companies differ in what these conditions are, such as prohibitions of 100 percent foreign ownership or the common use of child labor in hazardous jobs. By eliminating countries with unacceptable conditions, they simplify the task of scanning. Companies then need to consider opportunity and risk indicators that could significantly affect their success or failure. Keep in mind that some conditions may be viewed by one company as an opportunity but by another as a risk. We discuss a sample of these below.

OPPORTUNITIES: SALES EXPANSION

Expectation of a large market and sales growth are probably a potential location's major attractions.

Sales expansion is probably companies' most motivating factor for IB engagement because managers assume that more sales will lead to more profits.

Managers would like to have country sales figures for what they want to sell, but such information may be unavailable, especially if they want to introduce a new product. In such instances, they can estimate sales potential roughly by examining what has happened to sales for a similar or complementary product, such as projecting potential 3-D television sales based on past sales for HD units. They can also use economic and demographic data to project sales potential, the most common of which are a combination of income and population size.

Of course, you should examine indicators related directly to your products. If you're trying to sell luxury products, GDP per capita may tell you very little. Instead, you need to know how many people have income above a certain level. If you are trying to reach a youth market or an elderly market, total population figures will not help you as much figures on the number of people by age category. Moreover, although your product or service may not appeal to the average customer, you may seek out niches. Guatemalan-based Pollo Campero identified countries and then cities with large Central American populations, which led it to enter the United States by going first to Los Angeles.[8]

Companies must consider variables other than income and population when estimating potential demand for their products in different countries.

Examining Economic and Demographic Variables Some primary considerations when examining economic and demographic variables are listed below:

- Obsolescence and leapfrogging of products. Demand estimation in one country based on occurrence in others should take into account that emerging economy consumers do not necessarily follow the same patterns as those in higher-income countries. Chinese consumers have largely leapfrogged landline telephones by going from phoneless to cell phones.[9]
- Demand for necessities versus discretionary products. People buy necessities, such as food, before making discretionary purchases; thus, the cost of necessities influences the demand for optional ones. For example, expenditures on food in Japan are high because food is expensive and work habits promote eating out, thus food purchases displace some discretionary purchases.
- Substitution. Consumers may substitute certain products or services differently in one country than in other countries. In India, increased gasoline prices relative to diesel prices forced companies such as Suzuki, Toyota, and General Motors to alter their mix of vehicle production to include a higher portion of diesel-powered cars.[10] In Venezuela, an economic downturn caused a huge switch from traditionally popular expensive Scotch whisky to rum, which was less expensive.[11]
- Income inequality. Where income inequality is high, the per capita GDP figures are less meaningful. Many people have little to spend, while many others have substantial spending money. For example, high income inequality has resulted in a very small middle class in most sub-Saharan African countries.[12]
- Cultural factors and taste. Although cultural factors affect overall country sales for certain products, such as Hindu restrictions on meat in India, one needs to examine cultural subsegments. There is a large market for Indian meat sales among people who are neither Hindu nor vegetarian.
- Existence of trading blocs. A country's small population and GDP obscure its potential if it is in a regional trading bloc.[13] For instance, Uruguay has a small domestic market, but its production has duty-free access to other countries in Mercosur unless countries leave the bloc.

CONCEPT CHECK

Chapter 8 explains that when trade barriers come down within a regional bloc, the size of the market available to small member nations typically increases quite dramatically.

Although managers cannot project potential demand perfectly, they can make workable estimates that help them narrow detailed studies to a reasonable number.

OPPORTUNITIES: RESOURCE ACQUISITION

When undertaking IB to secure resources (e.g., labor, raw materials, knowledge), companies are limited to those locales that likely have what they want, such as securing petroleum only where there are prospective reserves. Even among these countries, some offer better opportunities than others (e.g., petroleum cost variations from extraction, transportation, and taxes). When considering cost differences, a particular resource may be overriding for specific industries or companies, such as sugar for candy companies or low-cost water power for aluminum companies.

Costs—especially labor costs—are an important factor in companies' production-location decisions.

Cost Considerations A company's total cost is made up of numerous sub-costs, many of which are industry- or company-specific. Nevertheless, several of the factors affecting these sub-costs—*labor, infrastructure, external connections,* and *government incentives*—apply to a large cross-section of companies.

Labor Although capital intensity, especially through the use of robotics, is growing in most industries, labor cost remains important for most companies. Scanning allows companies to examine such factors as labor market size, minimum and ongoing wages, required and customary fringe benefits, education levels, and unemployment rates. These help in comparing labor cost, skills, and availability. Analyses should also include likely changes, such as cost increases in China that have been making such countries as Myanmar and Mexico more attractive.[14]

CONCEPT CHECK

Chapter 6 shows that, in applying factor proportions theory to locate production, a company needs to consider that factors of production are not homogeneous. It also shows that new technologies can change optimal production locations.

Neither labor nor companies' needs are homogeneous. Consider call centers, for example. U.S. and French companies have different language needs (English and French respectively), which have led many U.S. companies to the Philippines and French companies to Senegal. Or, take the desire to acquire R&D personnel as opposed to inexpensive manufacturing labor. Figures on the number of science and engineering graduates have given a rough idea of where needed skills are available and have influenced companies to set up R&D facilities in China, Hungary, India, and Israel.[15]

Entering a country with a shortage of required labor skills will require MNEs to train, redesign production, or add supervision—all of which are expensive. Keep in mind also that a country's wage rates (and education) may differ by sector and region and may change because of emigration and health conditions.

Note also that when companies move into emerging economies because of low labor-wages, their advantages may be short-lived for one or more of three reasons:

- Competitors follow leaders into low-wage areas.
- There is little first-mover advantage for this type of production migration.
- The costs may rise quickly as a result of pressure on wage or exchange rates.

Infrastructure problems add to operating costs.

Infrastructure Poor internal infrastructure escalates costs. Consider Nigeria where employees spend extra hours commuting for work on congested roads, which decreases their productivity. Many companies, such as Cadbury and Nestlé, use their own costly power generators because of erratic publicly provided power so as to prevent assembly line stoppages and spoilage of food products. Because phone reception is often unreliable, they must send people out to visit customers and suppliers. Delivery of goods must again face the congestion on inferior roads.[16]

The need to integrate operations among countries influences location decisions.

External Connections IB requires diverse levels of cross-national integration, all of which incur time and costs. At a minimum, headquarters personnel visit foreign locations to support control efforts. Further, companies need a smooth flow of shipments as they import and export among their facilities in different countries. Because distance roughly correlates with time and cost, a geographically isolated country like New Zealand does not fit as easily into a company's global integration strategy as one located near the headquarters or various suppliers.[17] Relatedly, countries with few trade restrictions and efficient customs offer advantages of reduced tariff costs and shorter clearance times.[18]

Government practices may increase or decrease companies' costs.

Governmental Incentives and Disincentives Governments promote inward foreign investment to create jobs, enhance competitiveness, and improve trade balances. They do so through ads, investment missions, and foreign consular activities. In addition, many provide incentives that cut investors' costs, such as lower taxes, employee training, loan guarantees, low-interest loans, exemption of import duties, and subsidized energy and transportation. For example, the European Structural Funds program has helped finance projects for such companies as Coca-Cola, Fiat, and GlaxoSmithKline.[19] Incentives and entry conditions, however, often depend on company–government negotiations (i.e., how much each needs and offers the other). When a company wants limited resources, such as prime areas for building beach resorts, governments are in a strong bargaining position when ceding rights to a foreign firm.[20] When companies have hard-to-duplicate assets, such as unique technology, access to foreign markets, and well-known global brands, they are in a strong position.

CONCEPT CHECK

Chapter 3 details country differences in red tape (i.e., the time and steps necessary to start-up, operate, and close down businesses).

Companies prefer operating in countries where red tape and corruption are minimal and where legal transparency and law enforcement are high.[21] In contrast, when managers must spend excessive time to satisfy government agencies on taxes, labor conditions, environmental compliance, and other matters because of uncertainty about the legal consequences of their actions, they take time away from their primary responsibility of overseeing production and sales.[22]

Poor protection of intellectual property rights is a double-edged sword. On the one hand, international companies might relinquish technology to competitors where protection is poor. On the other hand, these locations may enable international companies to more easily gain access to competitors' technologies.[23]

RISKS

Company decisions should weigh opportunity against risk. For example, a company may forgo the country with the highest sales potential or the cheapest assets because decision-makers perceive that risks are too high. In this section we examine four types of risks: political, foreign exchange, natural disaster, and competitive.

Factors to Consider in Analyzing Risk Keep in mind several factors as we discuss specific types of risk:

Estimation of risk varies because of different perceptions, company situations, product lines, and operating forms.

1. *Companies differ in their approaches to risk.* Managers vary in their perceptions of what is risky, how tolerant they are of taking risk, the returns they expect, and the portion of their assets they are willing to put at risk.[24]
2. *One company's risk may be another's opportunity.* For example, companies offering security solutions (e.g., alarm systems, guard services, insurance, and armaments) may find their biggest sales opportunities where other companies find only risks. Companies offering risk-assessment services do better when the perception of risk increases.[25]
3. *Companies may reduce their risks by means other than avoiding locations,* such as by insuring. But all these options incur costs.
4. *There are trade-offs among risks.* Avoiding a country where, say, political risk is high may leave a company more vulnerable to competitive risk if another company earns good profits there.
5. *Risks may occur for suppliers and within suppliers' supply chains.* Companies thus need to examine the complex external dependencies and vulnerabilities of its suppliers.[26]

CONCEPT CHECK

Chapter 3 explains that political risk is the possibility that political decisions, events, or conditions will reduce investors' value or force them to accept lower-than-projected profits.

Political Risk Changes in political leaders' opinions and policies, civil disorder, and animosity between the host and other countries, particularly the firm's home country, may lead to a company's loss of or damage to property, disruption of operations, and adjustment to changes in operating rules. For example, Unilever encountered foreign executives' refusal to work in Pakistan because of security concerns; Chiquita Brands had to pay Colombian revolutionaries to protect its employees there; Owens-Illinois's investments were nationalized in Venezuela; Marriott's Indonesian hotel was bombed; and Coca-Cola's Angolan services required police to protect its trucks and telephone services.

Managers use three approaches to predict political risk: *analyzing past patterns, evaluating opinions,* and *examining potentially risky social and economic conditions.*

To predict political risk, companies can

- analyze past patterns,
- get a cross-section of opinions,
- examine unsatisfactory social and economic conditions.

Analyzing Past Patterns Predicting political risk based on past patterns is problematic because situations may change. Moreover, a country's overall political situation masks differences within countries and for different firms. For example, unrest may be limited geographically, such as Slovenia's avoidance of damage during Yugoslavia's civil war. Nationalizations have generally been highly selective, primarily affecting only operations with a visibly widespread effect on the country because of their size or monopoly position. Further, state-owned MNEs from countries with strong ties to the host country appear to be less subject to expropriation risk.[27]

Property damage or asset takeover does not necessarily cause investors a full loss. First, insurance may cover damage. Second, most nationalizations have begun with formal declarations of intent and have followed with legal processes to determine the foreign investor's compensation, such as the settlement between Venezuela and Holcim.[28] (Past settlements serve as indicators of likely compensation.) In addition to the settlement value, there may be side agreements that affect the adequacy (or lack thereof) of compensation. For example, the former investor may continue to manage an operation for a fee and receive output at a favorable price.

Evaluating Opinions Because influential people may sway future political events, managers should evaluate statements by political spearheads to determine their philosophies on private business, foreign business relations, means of effecting economic changes, and feelings toward given foreign countries. They should also access polls showing different leaders' likelihood of gaining political office. Opinions from a cross-section of embassy officials, foreign and local businesspeople, journalists, academicians, middle-level local government authorities, and labor leaders often reveal their attitudes, which often reflect current and future political conditions. These opinions may be gathered through publications and conversations or, if the firm is already operating within a country, through reports from its managers working therein.

Examining Social and Economic Conditions Unrest may occur if population segments have unmet social and economic aspirations. Frustrated groups may disrupt business by calling general strikes, destroying property and supply lines, and causing the downfall of

Anti-government protesters in Algiers, Algeria, in 2019.

Source: Farouk Batiche/dpa picture alliance/Alamy Stock Photo

government leaders. For example, anti-government protests in Algeria, shown in the photo below, disrupted ExxonMobil's plans to develop a natural gas field in 2019.[29] And political leaders sometimes harness support by blaming problems on foreigners and foreign companies, which could lead to boycotts, property damage, expropriation, or changes in operating rules. Thus, the examination of social and economic conditions in relation to aspirations helps companies foresee deteriorating political situations.

Foreign-Exchange Risk Let's examine two types of risk: exchange-rate changes and immobility of funds. In both, companies should consider current situations along with conditions that can lead to changes.

CONCEPT CHECK

Chapter 10 discusses some of the causes of exchange-rate changes and explains methods of forecasting exchange-rate movements.

Exchange-Rate Changes The change in foreign currency value is a two-edged sword, depending on whether you are going abroad to seek sales or resources. Let's say a U.S. company exports to India; deterioration in the Indian rupee's value makes the exports less competitive because it takes more rupees to buy them. If it produces within India to serve the Indian market, its competitiveness within India will likely change insignificantly, but its rupee profits will buy fewer U.S. dollars to bring back to the United States. If, however, it is seeking resources from India, such as Indian personnel to staff a call center, a fall in the rupee value lowers the dollar cost.

Companies may accept a lower return in order to move their financial resources more easily.

Immobility of Funds When a company exports to or invests in a foreign country, it prefers international mobility of its sales receipts, earnings, and capital there. Without the mobility, many firms either forgo operations or expect a higher rate of return there than elsewhere. Simply, their liquidity preference results from their needs or desires to make near-term payments, such as for dividends, unexpected contingencies (such as stockpiling materials before a threatened strike), and shifting of funds to possibly more profitable opportunities.[30]

CONCEPT CHECK

Chapter 10 reviews the methods countries use to control currency convertibility in order to conserve scarce foreign exchange.

A greater facility to access funds is affected by active capital markets and an absence of governmental exchange controls. An active capital market, particularly a stock market, helps a company sell its assets, especially if it wishes to sell a portion of ownership on a local exchange or dispose of its operations. An absence of exchange controls enables companies to convert their local currencies. Thus, it's not surprising that companies prefer operations in countries with strong and convertible currencies.

Natural disasters and debilitating diseases upset operations and are spread unevenly around the world.

Natural Disaster Risk Adverse "mother nature" catastrophes and widespread debilitating diseases have existed throughout history, but their relationship to choosing optimal IB locations has emerged only recently as comparative data have become more obtainable.

"Mother Nature" Catastrophes Each year, hundreds of millions of people are exposed to risks from earthquakes, cyclones, flooding, drought, volcanic eruptions, rising ocean levels, mudslides, and tornados. These disasters upset markets, infrastructure, and production while damaging companies' property, injuring their personnel, and increasing their insurance costs. They also play havoc with global supplies; the Japanese earthquake-induced tsunami in 2011 disrupted the world auto industry's production by creating auto parts shortages.[31]

These events are spread unevenly. Parts of Asia are heavily exposed to earthquakes; some African countries are most vulnerable to drought. Exposure, however, must be examined alongside countries' abilities to cope. Although only 11 percent of people exposed to such disasters are in the world's poorest nations, those nations account for 55 percent of the deaths because so much of their population live in poor housing and lack adequate medical assistance. Likewise, their rural-to-urban migration is largely to dangerous mountainsides, ravines, and low-elevation areas ill-equipped to deal with earthquakes, mudslides, and cyclones. Map 13.1 shows the most and least vulnerable countries, taking into account both their potential exposure and their coping abilities.

Debilitating Diseases The World Health Organization (WHO), a specialized agency of the United Nations, has developed global atlases of infectious diseases,[32] many of which occur where medical facilities are weakest because of the diseases' association with poverty. They are also associated with catastrophic events, such as cholera and malaria outbreaks after flooding, and tend to follow geographic patterns. For example, malaria kills about 2 million people a year, mainly in Africa.

The incapacitating effects of disease have an impact on several facets of business operations. For example, during the West African Ebola outbreak, the financial performance of many Sierra Leone firms declined in tandem with economic deterioration from the reduced workforce. In turn, international firms with Sierra Leone clients, such as KPMG, saw weakened

MAP 13.1 The 20 Countries at Highest and Lowest Risk from Natural Disasters

The calculations are based on a combination of exposure (number of people exposed or threatened by earthquakes, storms, floods, droughts, and sea level rise), susceptibility (infrastructure, housing conditions, nutrition, poverty and dependencies, and economic capacity and distribution), and coping and adaptive capacities.

Source: Based on data from United Nations University Institute for Environmental and Human Society, *World Risk Report 2016*, 64–66.

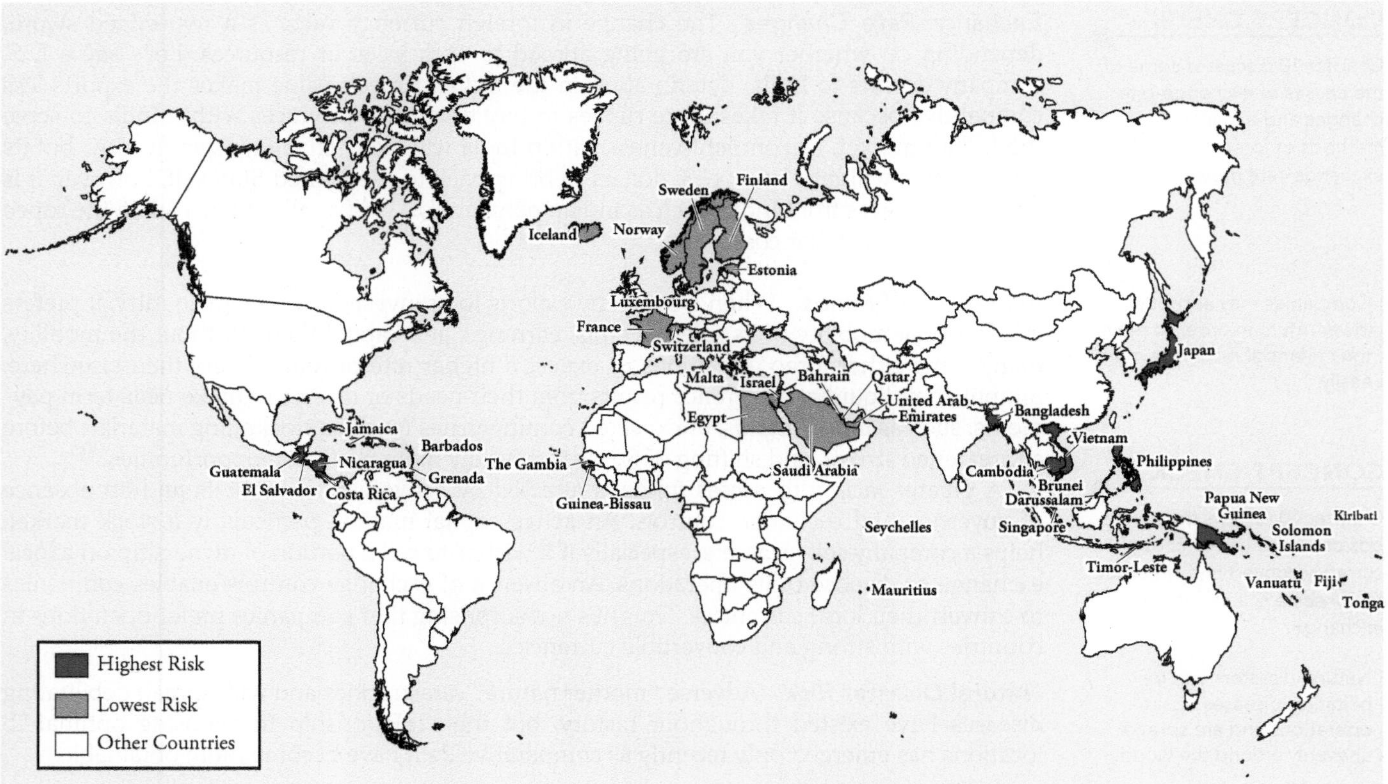

sales.[33] During the Zika crisis in Latin America and the Caribbean, many companies, such as Kimberly-Clark, set up costly education programs for employees in affected areas to educate them regarding how to protect against the virus.[34] At the same time, companies faced new ethical and legal decisions, such as whether to advise employees about dangers of pregnancies. Further, because of both Ebola and Zika, companies decreased business travel to distressed areas, thus hindering their buying programs and oversight of subsidiaries there.[35]

The WHO, as the lead agency responsible for public health internationally, is the body with the authority to declare a global pandemic, as it did in 2020 for COVID-19. This pandemic disrupted business everywhere in the world, but nevertheless has implications for choosing international business locations. The origin of the virus in China, and some early missteps dealing with it, might suggest that risks are higher and international business would avoid China in the future. However, China's developed hospital system and draconian policy response were effective in containing the spread of the virus nationally, albeit with significant economic cost. In contrast, most developing countries suffered from poor health systems and some advanced nations struggled with the policy response, while bearing high economic costs as well.[36] The episode illustrates that MNEs need to take health institutions and policy into account when choosing foreign locations.

Competitive Risk Factors affecting companies' competitive positions through location decisions include: *compatibility for companies' operations, diversification of locations, following competitors or customers,* and *heading off competitors.*

Companies are highly attracted to countries that

- share the same language,
- have institutions similar to those in their home countries,
- are located nearby.

Compatibility for Companies' Operations Because companies encounter less familiar environments abroad than at home, their operating risks are normally higher abroad. Thus, managers initially prefer to operate where they perceive conditions to be more similar to their home country—provided, of course, that the location also offers sufficient opportunities.[37] In fact, MNEs have a lower survival rate than local companies for many years after they begin operations, a situation known as the *liability of foreignness.*[38]

CONCEPT CHECK

Chapter 2 observes that a company usually expects fewer differences—and must make fewer adjustments—when moving to culturally similar countries. Chapter 6 explains that country similarity helps support patterns of trading partners.

This perception of similarity helps explain why more U.S. companies put earlier and greater emphasis on Canada and the United Kingdom than is indicated by the opportunity and risk variables discussed so far. In short, managers feel more comfortable doing business where the per capita GDP is comparable and where there is a similar language, culture, and legal system.[39] Following early entries, companies also find usefulness in creating an expansion pattern that allows a portfolio of countries to work interdependently.[40]

Similarity also occurs among adjacent nations because of the ease of travel and communications among them. For example, marketing programs in one country often result in product awareness elsewhere, particularly in an adjacent country, an occurrence known as a **spillover effect**. For example, U.S. television ads regularly reach Canadians, making it easier for U.S. firms to do business there.

CONCEPT CHECK

Chapter 6 shows that a positive historical relationship, especially between a former colonizer and its former colonies, helps explain trade patterns.

Positive historical home and host countries' ties also help explain companies' location preferences because companies perceive lower risk therein.[41] A company may also reduce risk by choosing countries where it can employ products, plant sizes, and practices familiar to its managers and which are crucial for its competitive advantage. For instance, Blockbuster failed in Germany partially because of laws preventing stores from being open during evening hours and on Sundays and holidays—popular times for last-minute impulse video rentals.[42]

In terms of location strategies, some options are to go

- first to a few versus many foreign countries,
- to similar versus dissimilar countries,
- to places to prevent competitors from gaining advantages,
- into markets that competitors have not entered versus where there are clusters of competitors.

Diversification of Locations Operating in economically diverse countries whose business cycles are not highly interrelated may enable companies to smooth their sales and profits, which, in turn, is an advantage in raising funds.[43] They may further guard against the effects of currency value changes by locating in countries whose exchange rates are not closely correlated with each other.[44] These diversifications are in many ways opposite to what we just discussed about advantages of operating in countries similar to the home country. Thus management must weigh the importance of one type of risk reduction versus the other.

Given the growth in product complexity, technology content, and companies' product specialization, there is a need to tap knowledge emanating from multiple companies. At the same time, such knowledge may be country-specific because of long-term country dominance in some industries. Thus, there is a need to tap knowledge in different countries. Although knowledge flows internationally and from one organization to another, MNEs enhance their speed of access to it by having foreign subsidiaries that serve as information access points in source countries.[45]

CONCEPT CHECK

Chapter 6 explains how countries' traditional specialization has led to long-term production advantages over other countries.

Following Competitors or Customers Managers may purposely crowd a market to prevent competitors from gaining advantages there that they can use to improve their positions elsewhere—a situation known as **oligopolistic reaction**.[46] In other words, a company's location decision is made on the basis of a competitor's action rather than on location-based characteristics such as the cost of labor or market size and growth. It looks at performance *relative* to that of competitors rather than on its *absolute* performance.

At the same time, companies may gain absolute performance advantages by locating where competitors are. First, they may follow competitors that have performed the costly task of evaluating locations and building market acceptance for a particular type of product, thus getting a so-called free ride. Second, clusters of competitors (known as agglomerations) attract multiple suppliers, personnel with specialized skills, and buyers who want to compare a number of product and service options in a single trip. In agglomeration, a company also gains better access to information about new developments because it has frequent contact with its competitors' personnel, customers, and suppliers.[47] For example, the Indian state of Gujarat has emerged as the world's largest center for cutting and polishing diamonds, handling 90 percent of the global market. More than 5,000 firms employ hundreds of thousands of skilled workers.[48] The photo below shows a workshop in the city of Surat.

Agglomeration by nationality occurs when firms from the same home country, regardless of industry, cluster in a location. The cluster provides expatriate employees with a more familiar environment to live and work. This gathering, however, may shield MNEs from interactions with competitors from elsewhere, thus delaying their ability to innovate and adapt.[49]

Following customers into a foreign market may secure sales with them and help secure relationships in their home market. For example, Bridgestone Tires followed one of its Japanese customers, Toyota, into the United States. First, its track record with Toyota gave it an advantage over other tire companies in the U.S. market. Second, if another tire manufacturer were to develop a strong U.S. relationship with Toyota, it might use this to undermine Bridgestone's sales to Toyota in Japan.

Heading Off or Avoiding Competition Companies may seek competitive advantage by (1) being the first to go into a foreign country, (2) avoiding country entry where competition is strong, and (3) moving quickly by whatever operating mode into as many markets as possible. We now discuss each of these.

First, being first into a country enables a firm to more easily gain the best partners, best locations, and best suppliers—a strategy known as a **first-mover advantage**. This strategy may also support attaining strong relations with the government, such as Volkswagen did in China and Lockheed in Russia.[50]

Workers in a diamond workshop in Surat, India, part of the agglomeration that handles 90 percent of the world's cutting and polishing.

Source: David Gee 4/Alamy Stock Photo

Second, a company may try to avoid significant competition, especially if competitors are much larger. PriceSmart, a U.S.-based discount operator, has all its warehouse stores outside the United States and has succeeded by targeting locations in Central America, the Caribbean, and Asia that seemed too small to attract early entry of competitors like Walmart, Carrefour, and Tesco.[51] However, its Central American success has drawn Walmart into that market.

Third, moving as quickly as possible by whatever operating mode into many markets is advantageous within an industry with very rapidly changing technology. In other words, waiting to enter a country increases the risk of competitors' superseding one's technology and securing markets with it. As we discuss later in the "Geographic Diversification Versus Concentration" section, however, there are other considerations for entering markets quickly or slowly.

ANALYZING AND RELATING THE OPPORTUNITY AND RISK VARIABLES

Teams comprising people from different functional areas are useful in choosing and rating indicators of countries' opportunity and risk.

After companies have completed the data collection for their scanning process, they must scrutinize that data to prioritize among countries. Using a team of people from different functions—marketing, finance, etc.—will more likely uncover the best fits with companies' resources and objectives. Dividing data collection based on team-members' functional expertise (e.g., having the finance member examine all the countries' foreign exchange situations, or having the accounting member examine tax rates) allows for more uniform analysis of data across the spectrum of countries. (If responsibility is divided, instead, by having each member examine a subsection of countries in their entirety, there is a risk that optimistic members will rate their countries more favorably than will pessimistic members, thus diminishing the equivalence of the assignment.)

Grids are tools that

- may depict acceptable or unacceptable country conditions,
- rank countries by important variables.

Obviously, the team will consider some conditions as more important than others, say that political risk is more important than natural disaster risk. Thus some variables need to be weighted more heavily than others. Two common tools to help at this stage are *grids* and *matrices*. We now illustrate each of these with abbreviated and simple examples.

Grids Table 13.1 is a simplified example of a grid with information placed into three categories: (1) acceptable/unacceptable conditions, (2) opportunity indicators, and (3) risk indicators. Note

TABLE 13.1 Simplified Country Comparison Grid

This table is merely an example. In reality, a company chooses the variables and countries to consider (usually many more than this table demonstrates) and weights some variables as more important than others. Here managers eliminate Country I because the company will go only where 100 percent foreign ownership is allowed. Country II is the most attractive because it's regarded as having high opportunity and low risk. (With a larger number of scanned countries, several should end up with these characteristics and become the ones for detailed analysis.) Country III offers low opportunity and risk, and Country IV has high opportunity and risk. (One of these may be chosen for further analysis, depending on the company's tolerance for risk.) Country V is eliminated because of having low opportunity and high risk.

Country Variable	Weight	I	II	III	IV	V
1. Acceptable (A), Unacceptable (U)						
Allows 100% foreign ownership	–	U	A	A	A	A
2. Opportunity						
a. Sales potential	0–5	–	4	3	3	3
b. Labor conditions	0–3	–	3	1	2	2
c. Infrastructure	0–2	–	2	1	2	2
d. Ease of external integration	0–4	–	3	2	4	1
e. Possibility of governmental incentives	0–3	–	2	1	3	1
f. Tax rate	0–2	–	2	1	2	0
Total	–	–	16	9	16	9
3. Risk (lower number = preferred rating)						
a. Political	0–4	–	2	1	3	2
b. Foreign exchange	0–3	–	1	0	3	3
c. Natural disaster	0–4	–	0	0	4	3
d. Competitive	0–2	–	0	1	2	2
Total	–	–	3	2	12	10

in this example that country I can be immediately eliminated because the company will go only where it can take 100 percent ownership. Although, in this example, sales potential is given more weight than infrastructure as an opportunity indicator and political is given more weight than competitive as a risk indicator, different companies will choose indicators and weight them differently. Table 13.1's description shows how this exercise helps managers choose countries for a more detailed analysis.

With an opportunity–risk matrix, a company can decide on factors to consider and compare them.

Matrices To more clearly show the opportunity/risk relationship, managers can plot values on a matrix such as the one shown as Figure 13.3. The plotting of this type of matrix also allows a company to make a more precise distinction in weighting and comparing variables.

But how can managers plot values on such a matrix? As in the case of grids, they must determine unacceptable factors so as to eliminate countries from consideration and choose indicators for their companies' risk and opportunity. Then, they weight them to reflect their importance. For instance, using the same risk factors as we used for the grid explanation, they might give 35 percent (0.35) of the weight to political risk, 30 percent (0.30) to foreign-exchange risk, 20 percent (0.2) to natural disaster risk, and 15 percent (0.15) to competitive risk, for a total allocation of 100 percent. They would then rate each country on a scale, such as from 1 to 10 for each variable, with 10 indicating the best score (note that more than one country may have the same score), and multiply each variable by the weight they allocate to it. If they rate Country A as 8 on the political risk variable, they would multiply 8 by 0.35 (the weight they assign to expropriation) for a score of 2.8. They would then sum all of Country A's risk-variable scores to place it on the risk axis, and similarly plot the location of Country A on the opportunity axis.

But how might managers come up with a score of 8 for a country's political risk? They would likely divide the maximum score of 10 into subcategories, such as expropriation, civil unrest, relationship with the company's home government, and likelihood of negative regulatory changes. They might even weight these subcategories before totaling them to secure the score for political risk. They would do similarly for each of their variables.

Once managers plot each country's values on the matrix, they may sometimes have to choose between a country with high risk and high opportunity and another with low risk and low opportunity, thus making a decision based on their tolerance for risk. Further,

FIGURE 13.3 Opportunity–Risk Matrix

Countries E and F are the most desirable because they boast a combination of a high level of opportunity and a low level of risk. But what if the decision came down to Countries A and B? The level of opportunity in Country A may not be as high as a company would like, but the low level of risk may be attractive. Country B, however, promises a high level of opportunities but also threatens a high level of risk. A decision between Countries A and B will probably take the firm's risk tolerance into consideration.

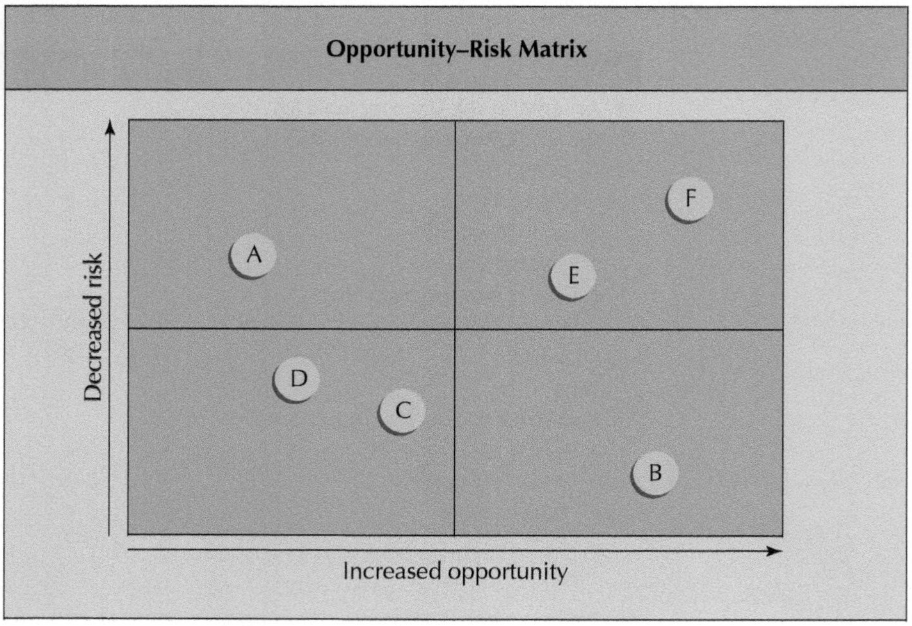

although A, B, C, and D are less appealing than E and F in Figure 13.3, the company may nevertheless find opportunities in A, B, C, and D—perhaps licensing or shared-ownership arrangements—without necessarily making a large commitment.

A key element of this kind of matrix, and one that managers do not always include in practice, is the projection of where countries will be in the future, or at least the *direction* in which they are expected to move. Such a projection is obviously useful, but the farther one forecasts into the future, the less certain the projection.

SOURCES AND SHORTCOMINGS OF COMPARATIVE COUNTRY INFORMATION

13-4 Summarize the sources and shortcomings of comparative country information

Information is needed at all levels of control. Companies should compare the cost of information with its value.

Companies undertake business research to reduce uncertainties and to assess performance. Our emphasis here is on information to aid in choosing a location. Because managers can seldom get all the information they want, they should compare information costs with the probable payoff it will generate in revenue gains or cost savings.

SOME PROBLEMS WITH RESEARCH RESULTS AND DATA

Information inaccuracies result from

- difficulty in collecting and analyzing data,
- purposefully misleading data, exclusion of nonmarket and illegal activity.

Because of the lack, obsolescence, and inaccuracy of data on many countries, research can be problematic. Let's discuss the two basic problems: inaccuracy and noncomparability.

Inaccuracy Six basic reasons why reported information may be inaccurate are:

1. *Governmental resources may limit accurate data collection.* Countries' resources may limit budgets for data collection, the latest computer hardware, software, and training programs (e.g., they may give priority, for example, to spending on health and literacy programs rather than on measuring health and literacy rates).
2. *Governments must depend on estimates and revisions.* Although both are important, there is a trade-off between accuracy and timeliness of data. Estimates, for example of countries' GDP growth, are initially made without the full range of sample returns so as to honor timeliness. But then revisions (sometimes several) are necessary to improve accuracy as more sample information is available. For example, the United States once revised its GDP downward by an amount about the size of Sri Lanka's total output.[52]
3. *Governments may omit or purposely publish misleading information.* Government researchers sometimes publish false or purposely deceptive information designed to mislead their superiors, the country's rank and file, or companies and institutions abroad. For instance, Venezuela suspended release of data on mosquito-borne diseases, GDP, and balance of payments to prevent the public from receiving bad news.[53]
4. *Respondents may give false information to data collectors.* Mistrust of data usage may lead respondents to answer questions falsely, particularly if questions probe financial details or anything else that respondents either consider private or to be used by government authorities against them.
5. *Official data may include only legal and reported market activities.* Nationally reported income figures seldom include illegal income from such activities as the drug trade or cash transactions to avoid tax payments. EU countries have begun estimating these within their GDPs, but they admit that the math can be fuzzy.[54]
6. *Questionable methodology may be used.* Inaccuracies may occur because of methods used to collect and analyze information. For instance, by using two different methods (both generally acceptable) to estimate Chinese consumption, there was a difference of more than the entire GDP of Australia.[55]

CONCEPT CHECK

Chapter 2 explains that false responses hinder accuracy when comparing cultures.

Problems in information comparability arise from

- differences in definitions and base years,
- distortions in currency values.

Noncomparability Countries do not necessarily publish reports for the same time periods or at the same time as each other. So a company must extrapolate in order to estimate how countries compare. Countries also differ in accounting rules and how they define items, such as family income, literacy, and FDI. Activities taking place outside the market economy, such as within the home, do not show up in income figures. Because people in developing countries are more prone to produce for their own consumption (growing vegetables, preparing meals at home, sewing clothes, cutting hair, and so on), developing countries' official income figures tend to understate economic levels.

Further, exchange rates must be used to convert countries' financial data to a common currency, usually U.S. dollars. Although 10 percent appreciation of the Japanese yen in relation to the U.S. dollar results in a 10 percent increase in the dollar value of Japanese per capita GDP, it does not mean the Japanese are suddenly 10 percent richer. Because Japanese use about 85 percent of their income to make purchases in yen within Japan, they have little additional purchasing power for 85 percent of what they buy.

EXTERNAL SOURCES OF INFORMATION

Information sources differ by cost and detail.

Companies need information for making good location decisions. Chances are, at least for scanning purposes, the Internet will be the source for most of the information. Some of the information there is free, and some requires payment. Apart from the Internet, the most costly sources are marketing research and consulting companies, but their advantage is that they can target more closely what companies want. Some of the major Internet sources are prepared by service companies (e.g., banks, transportation agencies, accounting firms), government agencies (e.g., the U.S. Department of Commerce, CIA), international organizations (e.g., the UN, the WTO, the IMF, the OECD, and the EU), and trade associations. In any case, it is wise to know how sources generate their information and, in the case of those offering advice (e.g., a risk-assessment company), what their past success rates have been.

INTERNALLY GENERATED DATA

MNEs may have to collect much information themselves, sometimes simply by observing keenly and asking many questions. During visits to countries, investigators can see, for example, what kind of merchandise is available, determine who is buying and where, and uncover hidden competition—such as seamstress-made clothes in homes versus ready-made clothing in stores. They might also discover that surreptitiously sold contraband is a competitive factor in the market.

Companies may also seek out information from companies already experienced in the country. Limited Brands, for example, met with Apple's managers in China to ascertain experiences they encountered during entry.[56]

POINT

Should Companies Operate in and Send Employees to Violent Areas?

YES Where there's risk, there are usually rewards. Companies should not shun areas with violence. Businesspeople have always taken risks, and employees have always gone to dangerous areas. As far back as the seventeenth century, immigrants to what are now the United States, India, and Australia encountered disease and hostile native populations. Had companies and immigrants not taken chances, the world would be far less developed today.

Violence is only one type of risk. Although we lack historical data, most locations are probably safer today. Disease is still a bigger danger than violence, but medical advances against a number of historic killers (polio,

COUNTERPOINT

Should Companies Operate in and Send Employees to Violent Areas?

NO We're no longer concerned simply with being caught in the crossfire between opposing factions. Antiglobalization groups want international publicity, and they target MNEs' personnel and facilities so that they'll leave or pay ransoms. Still others are against foreigners or people of another religion, regardless of their aims. Such groups have killed staff members from Médecins sans Frontières and the Red Cross who were abroad to treat sick and injured people.[57]

At the same time, getting caught in the crossfire has become a bigger risk. Arms trafficking has risen and has lowered prices not only to revolutionaries but also measles, smallpox, tuberculosis, etc.) have reduced that risk, while evacuation in case of a real emergency is much faster.

But let's assume that we decide to avoid countries with the potential for violence against our facilities and employees. Is there any such place? To answer this question, you need to consider an array of indicators that include overall crime and murder rates, terrorism, kidnapping, and political violence. Because so many occurrences go unreported, statistics are unreliable. Further, situations change quickly, such as the sudden outbreak of violence in Syria. Opinions from so-called risk experts are conflicting. Finally, countries that we think of as safe—France, Belgium, the United States—have had recent fatal violence.

Some industries don't have the luxury of avoiding violent countries. For example, oil companies have to go where there is a high likelihood of finding oil. Most of the credible alternatives—the Middle East, West Africa, the Central Asian former Soviet republics, and Colombia—have had recent bombings, kidnappings, or organized crime. If companies didn't go to these places, they'd be out of business.

In effect, we'll keep operating anywhere there are opportunities. If a place seems physically risky, we'll take whatever precautions we can. We'll share intelligence reports, put people through safety training courses (there are plenty of these available now), and take security actions abroad. And perhaps we won't transfer spouses and children to the "risky" areas so we don't have to be on top of what is happening with as many people.

to drug and alien smugglers and money launderers.[58] MNEs can't help being visible and thus vulnerable.

In essence, if MNEs operate where risk of violence is great, they put their personnel in danger. Even if no violence comes to them, they endure stress that negatively affects their performance.[59] Although local personnel may be at a lesser risk of, say, kidnapping, experience shows that they too are not immune. Further, MNEs must send personnel to areas where they operate. Some go as managers or technicians on long assignments; others go short-term to audit books, ensure control, and offer staff support. The dangers are not inconsequential. There are thousands of reported kidnappings per year as well as countless unreported ones. Many of these target foreign workers and their families.

It's simply unethical to put employees in such situations. Of course, they are not forced to go to dangerous places, and firms can get enough people to work there. Experience, however, shows there are three types of people who want or are willing to work in such areas, and none are ideal. First are those who simply want the high compensation and big insurance policies, some of whom are experienced in military or undercover activities. They tend to be highly independent and hard to control. Second are the naïve who don't understand the danger and are difficult to safeguard through training and security activities. Third are the thrill seekers who find that adrenaline is like an addictive drug; they are most at risk because of the thrill of danger and their reluctance to leave when situations worsen.[60]

High risk to individuals is indicative of a political situation out of control—a harbinger of additional risks that may occur through governmental changes, falls in consumer confidence, and a general malaise that damages revenues and operating regulations. This is not the kind of country in which to conduct operations.

ALLOCATING RESOURCES AMONG LOCATIONS

13-5 Explain alternative considerations and means for companies to allocate resources among countries

We now examine three complementary strategies for international expansion: alternative gradual commitments, geographic diversification versus concentration, and reinvestment versus harvesting.

Companies may reduce risks from the liability of foreignness by

- going first to countries with characteristics similar to those of their home countries,
- having experienced intermediaries handle operations for them,
- operating in formats requiring commitment of fewer resources abroad,
- moving initially to one or a few, rather than many, foreign countries.

ALTERNATIVE GRADUAL COMMITMENTS

As we've discussed, liability of foreignness influences companies to minimize risk by favoring operations in countries similar to their own. Nevertheless, Figure 13.4 illustrates alternative expansion patterns for minimizing this risk. The farther a company moves from the center on any axis, the deeper its international commitment. A company does not necessarily move at the same speed along each axis, however. In fact, it may jump over some of the steps. A slow movement along one axis may free up resources and lower risk, which then allows faster expansion along another.

Let's examine Figure 13.4 more closely. Axis A shows that companies may move gradually from a purely domestic focus to one encompassing operations in countries similar to, and

FIGURE 13.4 Patterns of Internationalization

The farther a company moves outward along any of the axes (A, B, C, D), the deeper its international commitment. Most companies move at different speeds along different axes.

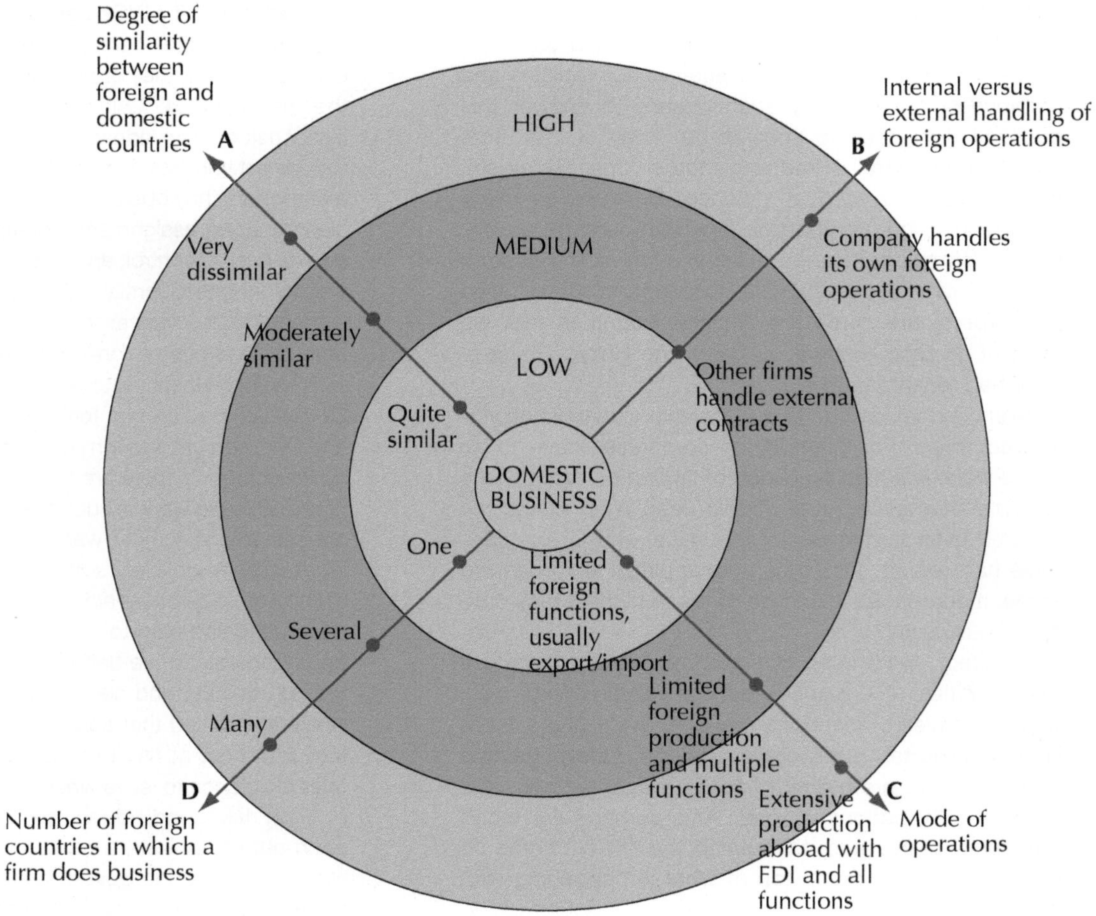

then dissimilar to one's own country. An alternative, however, when moving quickly along the A axis (and even jumping the intermediate step) is to move slowly along the B axis.

The B axis shows that a company may use intermediaries—especially ones that already know how to operate in a dissimilar foreign market—to handle operations abroad during early stages of international expansion. Doing so minimizes the resources the company puts at risk abroad and, thus, its degree of liability of foreignness. A related example is the international expansion of some high-tech companies from emerging economies. Rather than first targeting nearby countries with characteristics similar to their home markets, these companies have gone to high-income countries while relying heavily on intermediaries and foreign acquisitions to utilize personnel who know the markets they are targeting. Over time, however, a company may want to move farther out on the B axis by handling the operations with its own staff. This is because, by learning more about foreign operations, it perceives them as less risky than at the onset, and it realizes that its growth in business may justify the inclusion of internal capabilities, such as a department to handle foreign sales or purchases.

Axis C illustrates companies' beginning IB by importing or exporting, forms that require the placement of few company resources abroad. Again, as a company gains experience it might commit capital, personnel, and technology abroad by making a direct investment.

Axis D shows that companies can move internationally one country at a time, which keeps them from being overwhelmed by learning about many countries all at once. As we discuss in the next section, however, there may be operational reasons to move to a number of countries almost simultaneously.

GEOGRAPHIC DIVERSIFICATION VERSUS CONCENTRATION

Strategies for ultimately reaching a high level of commitment in many countries are

- diversification—go to many fast and then build up slowly in each,
- concentration—go to one or a few and build up fast before going to others,
- a hybrid of the two.

Ultimately, a company may gain a sizable presence in most countries; however, there are different paths to that position. Although any move abroad means some geographic diversification, the term **diversification strategy** in the context of IB location describes a company's rapid movement into many foreign markets, gradually increasing its commitment within each one. A company can do this, say, through an initial liberal licensing policy that enables widespread expansion, followed by increasing involvement that takes on activities it first contracted to other companies.

At the other extreme, with a **concentration strategy**, the company will first move to only one or a few foreign countries, not going elsewhere until it develops a very strong involvement and competitive position. There are, of course, hybrids of the two strategies—for example, moving rapidly to most markets but increasing commitment in only a few.[61] We now outline reasons for using one strategy versus the other.

1. *Need for Rapid Growth in Country* Within industries requiring a high entry cost because of capital-intensive technology or mass marketing, companies may lack resources enabling them to enter many countries simultaneously, thus a concentration strategy is usually preferred. Similarly, if country markets are all growing rapidly, companies may need to invest heavily in each to build and maintain a threshold market share, thus straining resources if simultaneously entering a large number of countries.[62]
2. *Competitive Lead Time* We have discussed that in cases where technology obsolesces rapidly, companies need to enter many markets quickly before competitors usurp their advantages, thus being in situations that favor a diversification strategy. Born-global companies are particularly prone to follow diversification strategies because so many of them depend on new and quickly obsolescing technologies that require fast market penetration.[63]
3. *Need for Product, Communication, and Distribution Adaptation* When companies must tailor their products and operating methods for each country they enter, they incur additional costs. They may need to follow a concentration strategy to minimize the costs of entering multiple countries simultaneously.
4. *Program Control Requirements* The more a company wants to control its operations in a foreign country, such as because of fear that a partner will become a competitor, the more favorable a concentration strategy is. This is because the company will need to use more of its resources to maintain that control, such as by taking a larger percentage of ownership in the operation.

REINVESTMENT VERSUS HARVESTING

So far, we've discussed the sequencing of country entry. Once operating abroad, a company must evaluate how much effort to allocate to each location. With successful FDI, the company earns money that it may remit to headquarters or reinvest to increase the investment value. If the investment returns are inadequate, however, the company may consider transferring capital and diverting efforts elsewhere.

A company may have to make new commitments in a locale to maintain its competitiveness.

Reinvestment Decisions Once committed to a given locale, a company may need to reinvest its earnings there. The failure to expand might result in not attaining its target growth objectives. Moreover, headquarters management may delegate certain investment decisions to experienced foreign subsidiary managers because they believe that subsidiary management is the best judge of what the operation needs.

Companies must decide how to get out of operations if

- they no longer fit their overall strategy,
- there are better alternative opportunities.

Harvesting Companies commonly reduce commitments in some countries because they have poorer performance prospects than do others—a process known as **harvesting** (or **divesting**). Burger King, for example, sold off underperforming operations in Korea and Slovakia so as to have funds for more promising ventures in the Chinese and Russian markets. There are other reasons as well. Dana sold its UK facility to use funds to concentrate on developing different automotive technologies.[64] Goodyear sold its Indonesian rubber plantation because of its decision to stop producing rubber.[65]

Evidence suggests that companies might benefit by planning divestments better and by developing divestment specialists. Companies have tended to wait too long before divesting, instead trying expensive means, usually suggested by subsidiary managers, to improve performance. After all, these managers' performance evaluations typically depend heavily on growth in their areas of responsibility, but they have no such incentive to propose divestments.[66]

A company may divest by a sale or closure of facilities, usually preferring a sale because it receives some compensation. If it considers divesting because of a country's well-publicized political or economic situation, it may find few potential buyers except at very low prices. In such situations, it may try to delay divestment, hoping that the situation will improve.

A company cannot always simply abandon an investment either, and leaving may take years. Governments frequently require performance contracts, such as substantial severance packages to employees that make a loss from divestment greater than the direct investment's net value. Further, many MNEs fear adverse international publicity as well as difficulty in reentering a market if they do not sever relations with a foreign government on amicable terms.

NONCOMPARATIVE LOCATION DECISIONS

13-6 Recognize why companies make noncomparative decisions when choosing where to operate abroad

Most companies examine proposals one at a time and accept them if they meet minimum-threshold criteria,

- because unforeseen opportunities give little time to make decisions,
- because of difficulty incorporating global performance into single-country analyses.

One might expect companies to maintain a storehouse of ranked foreign operating proposals, undertaking the best, second best, etc. until they could make no further commitments, but this is usually not the case. They make **go-no-go decisions** by examining one opportunity at a time and pursuing it if it meets some threshold criteria. Three factors inhibit companies from comparing investment opportunities: time, the interrelation of operations on global performance, and cost.

To begin with, companies sometimes need to respond quickly to prospects they had not anticipated, such as unsolicited proposals to sell abroad, to enter a joint venture, or sign a licensing contract. In fact, many companies initiate export activity passively—that is, foreign companies approach them to be suppliers. Similarly, undertakings may be one-time opportunities because a government or another company solicits bids, requests collaboration, or changes rules to encourage competition and foreign acquisitions, such as Mexico did for telecommunications.[67] Moving fast enables a company to acquire the best assets. Further, there may be a chance to buy properties that another company divests.

Another factor inhibiting comparison is the interdependence of country operations. Profit figures from individual operations may obscure the real impact on overall company performance. For example, placing a production facility abroad may either increase or reduce exports from the home country. Moreover, headquarters may have to incur additional costs to oversee the foreign facility, particularly if it coordinates the movement of components between the home and foreign countries. These costs are difficult to estimate and to allocate among the different countries. Further, a supplier's dealings with a global customer may cause it to suboptimize profits in one country in order to satisfy the customer in a second country. Finally, interdependence occurs because much of the sales and purchases of foreign subsidiaries are among units of the same parent company. The prices the company charges on these transactions will affect the relative profitability of one country's unit compared to another's.

Clearly, companies cannot afford to conduct very many feasibility studies simultaneously. Even if they can, the studies are apt to be in various stages of completion at any given time. Can the company afford to hold off on making a decision about a study that has been completed? Probably not. Waiting would likely invalidate much of the completed data, thus necessitating added expense and further delays to update it.

LOOKING TO THE FUTURE Conditions That May Cause Prime Locations to Change

Future sales- and resource-seeking opportunities and risks may shift among countries because of a variety of demographic, sociocultural, political-legal, technological, and economic occurrences. We will concentrate here on population changes and where people can and will prefer to work.

Where Will Markets Grow?

Chapter 6 discusses how demographers expect a slowing in the growth of global population, with some countries experiencing declining populations and the most robust growth in developing economies, particularly those in sub-Saharan Africa. These trends will reduce the percentage of people living in currently developed countries. Given the importance of population size for sales potential, these changes, if they materialize, will be profound.

Further, because the world's population will continue to age and people will pursue education for more years, the share of what we now consider the working-age population should fall for developed countries and increase in many developing ones. Because there is a positive relationship between the proportional size of the working-age population and per capita GDP, the growth in per capita GDP should be higher in today's developing economies than in today's developed countries unless we redefine working age.[68] If these demographic changes occur, they will affect the location of both markets and labor forces.

Where Will People Work?

An intriguing possibility is the near-officeless headquarters for international companies. Technology may permit more people to work from anywhere as they e-mail and teleconference with their colleagues, customers, and suppliers. In fact, they can live anywhere in the world and work from their homes, as is already occurring in some professions. If people can work from home, however, they may situate their homes where they want to live rather than near their employers. Highly creative, innovative, self-motivated people can usually get permission to live in almost any country of the world.

A leading researcher on urbanization and planning has shown that beginning at least as early as the Roman Empire these types of people have been drawn to certain cities that were innovation centers. This attraction is due to people's desire to improve through interchange with others like themselves—like "a very bright class in a school or a college. They all try to score off each other and do better." Thus, if he's correct, the brightest minds may work more at home but still need face-to-face interaction with their colleagues.[69] The continued attraction of young technical people to places like Silicon Valley seems to confirm this viewpoint.[70] The researcher further suggests that these people will be drawn to the same places that attract tourists.

These arguments are provocative, particularly because we now have technology to allow people to communicate without traveling as much. Yet the continued increase in business travel shows that there is still a need for face-to-face interaction.

Concomitantly, another view is that in leading Western societies the elite, made up of intellectuals and highly educated people, is increasingly using its capability to delay and block new technologies. If successful, their efforts will result in the emergence of different countries at the forefront of technological development and acceptance.[71]

CASE

Amazon.com[72]

Amazon.com, Inc. seeks to be Earth's most customer-centric company. Since its founding in a garage in Seattle, Washington, in 1994, Amazon has achieved remarkable success in the United States as an online retailing and technology company. It now occupies a campus in downtown Seattle; the photo below shows the plant-filled spheres at its headquarters. Amazon's international expansion is well underway, but many analysts don't see success abroad. Although international revenues from online storefronts outside North America amount to 28 percent of total revenues, the segment is not profitable. This calls into question Amazon's country selection strategy.

The Rise of Amazon in the United States

Amazon began as an online bookstore, competing effectively against brick-and-mortar bookstores by offering larger selection and low delivery charges. The company went public in 1997, and that year recorded $148 million in sales. The next year it began selling music CDs, DVDs, and videos. In 1998, it also made its first foreign investment. Over time, Amazon introduced more products and expanded into more countries. But it wasn't until 2003 that Amazon posted a profit, as Amazon spent heavily to capture markets in a strategy called "Get Big Fast."

Growth continued at a rapid pace. In 2007, Amazon introduced its Kindle device for electronic editions of books, and it quickly became popular in the United States.

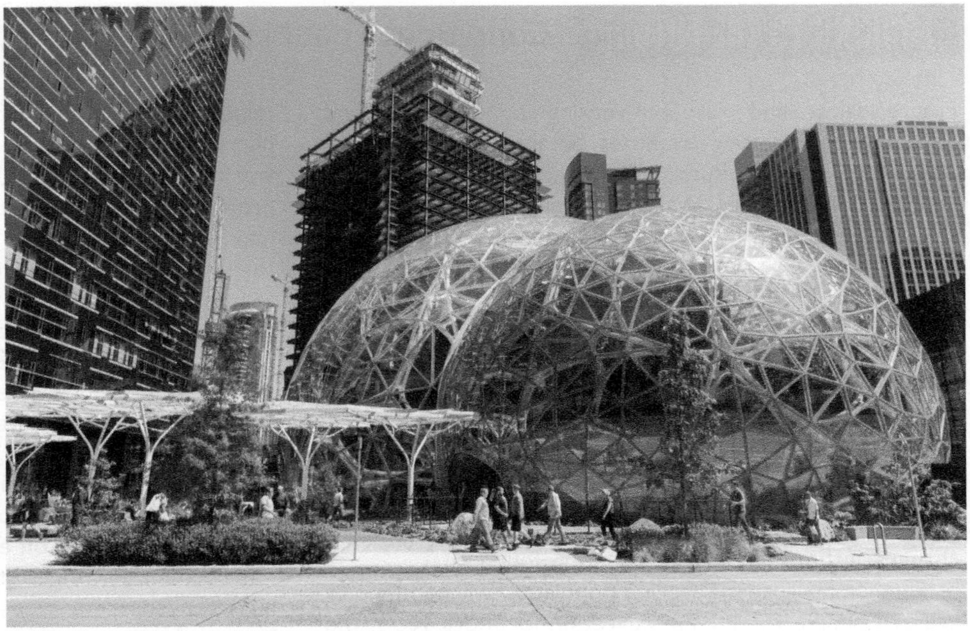

The world headquarters of Amazon in Seattle, Washington.

Source: Richard Theis/Alamy Stock Photo

By 2018 its sales reached $233 billion, for a compound annual growth rate of 42 percent over its 21-year history (partly aided by its acquisition of Whole Foods grocery). It has also been expanding internationally, taking products successful in the U.S. market into new countries, and supporting new geographies and new languages. The Kindle, for example, was fully developed as an English-only device through three generations of product before it was capable of supporting other languages. Today, Amazon operates 17 localized online storefronts, as shown in Map 13.2.

Major Country Selection Criteria

After its first year as a publicly traded company, Amazon indicated that it would undertake international expansion over time. The retail industry was transforming into a technology business, in which there are large economies of scale. There was potential for products developed in one market to be introduced across many others. But a number of offerings depend on expensive infrastructure and differentiation by geography.

MAP 13.2 Localized Online Storefronts and Date of Establishment

Source: Based on data from https://en.wikipedia.org/wiki/Amazon_(company) and Amazon annual reports.

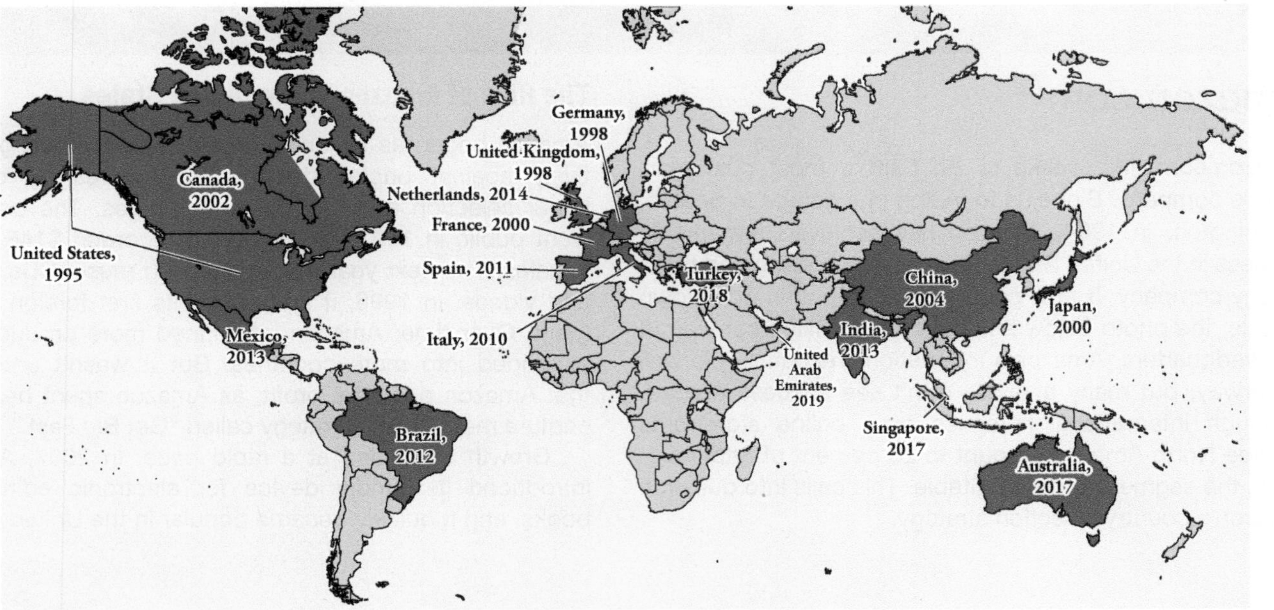

While looking for opportunities, Amazon also focused on the risks involved. Although it had been shipping to more than 150 countries from its U.S. website, it did not equate that with expertise operating abroad. It admitted that it had very limited experience in sourcing, marketing, and distributing products internationally and in developing localized versions of its website and other systems. It warned investors that there was no assurance that international efforts would be successful. It also highlighted international business risks, including unexpected changes in regulatory requirements, export and import restrictions, tariffs and other trade barriers, difficulties in staffing and managing foreign operations, longer payment cycles, political instability, fluctuations in currency exchange rates, seasonal reductions in business activity in other parts of the world, and potentially adverse tax consequences.

Amazon developed an approach to country selection that balanced opportunities and risks. Retail sales are dependent on market size, so it was natural for Amazon to consider the largest countries. It articulated the three main criteria for country selection as population, size of the economy, and density of internet use. In 1998, the top five economies were the United States, Japan, Germany, France, and the United Kingdom, in that order. Amazon needed to balance the potential market size and economies of scale with the risks involved, including ones associated with lack of familiarity with culture and methods of doing business in foreign countries.

Initial Foreign Expansion: The United Kingdom, Germany, France, and Japan

Amazon's first foreign subsidiaries came in April 1998, when it acquired internet companies in the United Kingdom and Germany. The two countries are similar to the United States, with comparable per capita income levels and a shared Anglo-Saxon heritage, so Amazon would feel comfortable operating in them. U.S.-based managers could easily travel to oversee the operations. Amazon established a UK headquarters and distribution center in Slough, England. The German subsidiary's headquarters and distribution center were established in Regensburg, and additional German editorial and marketing offices were located in Munich.

Amazon relaunched the acquired internet companies as www.amazon.co.uk and www.amazon.de by the end of 1998. The websites had the same look, feel, and functionality as the U.S. website, but offered content, products, and services tailored to the local market, along with pricing in the local currencies. The United Kingdom was a relatively easy first step because of the language, but www.amazon.de was presented in German. Amazon became the number one online bookseller in both of these markets. In 1999, Amazon claimed that it was well positioned to be a leading global retailer, and announced that there would be further international expansion in the coming year.

Amazon entered two new countries in 2000: France and Japan. This completed its coverage of the top five economies in the world. Amazon was able to avoid setting up a customer service center in France by leveraging its German and UK centers, but it did establish a fulfillment center in Orleans.

The expansion to Japan was more ambitious because Japanese customs are so different from those of the United States and Europe. The population, however, is technologically sophisticated and accustomed to using the internet. Japan is a big market, and aggregate book sales in 2000 were actually larger than in the U.S. market despite the much smaller population. Most booksellers were small, so Amazon sensed an opportunity, and www.amazon.jp quickly became the leading online bookseller in Japan.

Despite subsequent expansion throughout the world, Germany, the United Kingdom, and Japan represent a majority of international sales. In 2018, Germany accounted for $19.9 billion, and the United Kingdom and Japan represented $14.5 billion and $13.8 billion, respectively. Together, this is 66 percent of its $72.7 billion in international sales. Despite this, analysts don't necessarily regard Amazon as successful in Europe and Japan. In Europe, it is the biggest e-commerce website (with 22 percent of the market), but success has been elusive in the apparel and footwear business. Local websites offer more fashionable brands, more aesthetic presentation, and superior browsing experiences. In Japan, Amazon now trails a local e-commerce rival, Rakuten.

Amazon in Alibaba's Den

After a relatively easy expansion into Canada in 2002, Amazon knew that it needed to go after large emerging markets. By 2004, China was the sixth largest economy in the world, even larger than Italy and Spain, and was growing rapidly. A local internet site, Alibaba, was establishing a dominant market position, and many analysts wondered if Amazon would compete. Alibaba understood Chinese culture and was already close to customers and knew what appealed to them. Other e-commerce services were also growing in China.

Amazon entered China by acquiring Joyo.com for $75 million. Although incorporated in the British Virgin Islands, the company operated an internet retail website in China, www.joyo.com.cn. Amazon eventually relaunched it as www.amazon.cn. Although this was similar to expansion strategies in Europe, the business model that worked elsewhere simply didn't work in China. Amazon failed to anticipate the need for more local customization. It did not recruit talented locals, and made too many decisions in Seattle. China, with considerable government protectionism, technology restrictions, and regulatory scrutiny, is also a tough market for foreign companies. After more than a decade in the country, Amazon had less than 1 percent of the e-commerce market. Analysts were not expecting Amazon to gain any meaningful share of the market, and in 2019 it gave up on China.

More BRICs: Amazon near the Amazon and the Battlefield of India

After the problems it had in China, Amazon was criticized as lacking a global strategy, especially compared to other technology giants like Apple. It added two more European countries, Italy in 2010 and Spain in 2011, the eighth and twelfth largest economies respectively. Amazon knew it needed to go back to the BRICs. In 2011, Brazil was the sixth largest economy, and Russia and India were ninth and tenth.

Amazon chose Brazil as its first foreign subsidiary in Latin America in 2012 (even before Mexico, which it entered in 2013). It began by selling books, e-readers, and streaming videos, and then expanded to other products. But late entry meant it faced local competition from an e-commerce website already familiar to Brazilian consumers, and there were several smaller competitors as well. Furthermore, Amazon had challenges navigating Brazil's poor infrastructure, lower levels of automation, and Brazilian bureaucracy. It still faces a steep learning curve for doing business in Brazil and is struggling to catch up.

Amazon entered India in 2013 and announced a $5 billion investment in 2014. In sheer numbers, India had the third largest number of internet users in the world (after the United States and China). Amazon established a large research and development center in Bangalore, second only to the one in the United States, and is undertaking more localization in order to get closer to the consumer. Amazon also faces new challenges, however. For example, regulations prevent it from owning inventory directly, and differences in financial infrastructure require new payment options. But more importantly, Amazon's large investment set up a battle with Alibaba, which announced plans to invest even more. Further, in 2018 it lost a bidding war with Walmart to acquire a controlling stake in Flipkart, an Indian e-commerce firm (built by two Amazon alumni) that dominates the market.

A Change in Country Selection Strategy?

By 2013, Amazon had subsidiaries in nine of the 10 largest economies (Russia being the exception). It was also starting to be criticized for spreading itself too thin. Amazon's expansion continued, but in a relatively slow, deliberate way, more characteristic of a risk-averse investor than an aggressive titan. The strategy in fact seemed to change, becoming less focused on penetrating the largest markets first. Amazon entered the Netherlands in 2014. Given its experience in Europe, the entry was low-risk, but Amazon passed over several larger countries: Russia, Australia, South Korea, and Indonesia. Amazon did expand to Australia in 2017.

In 2017, Amazon also entered Singapore, a small economy, thirty-fifth in size globally. It doesn't make sense as a market on its own. It has, however, excellent infrastructure, high population density, high internet penetration, and is routinely ranked as a top investment climate. Singapore also has potential as a regional base due to its membership in the Association of Southeast Asian Nations (ASEAN); Indonesia is the largest economy in the group, and analysts think Singapore might provide a springboard into it. Thus, Amazon's country selection strategy may be shifting focus to smaller but stronger geographies. In a familiar refrain, however, Amazon faces stiff competition in Southeast Asia from Alibaba, which has already invested there heavily.

Subsequent expansion shows similar selectivity of location. In 2017, Amazon acquired an e-commerce corporation in the United Arab Emirates and relaunched it under its own name in 2019. It also launched a portal for Turkey in 2018.

The Future

Many analysts point out that Amazon's future growth is tied to international expansion, but also that there are significant international risks that might limit success. With high international growth comes high expenditure, and the international expansion has not been profitable. In 2018, expenses outside North America exceeded revenues and created a $2.1 billion loss. Amazon's usual strategy of heavy spending to gain control of the market may not work abroad. One thing for sure is that the selection of countries will play a role in its overall corporate performance. Where will Amazon go next? And will it get out of the underperforming countries?

QUESTIONS

13-3 What advantages and disadvantages would Amazon likely have when compared with domestic e-commerce websites where it operates?

13-4 Evaluate the reasons for following a geographic concentration versus a diversification strategy as they apply to large e-commerce retailers such as Amazon.

13-5 Do you think Amazon should enter Russia?

CHAPTER 14
Export and Import

OBJECTIVES

After studying this chapter, you should be able to

14-1 Explain the principles and practices of exporting

14-2 Distinguish the motivations and methods of exporting

14-3 Understand the startup and expansion of exporting

14-4 Explain the principles and practices of importing

14-5 Distinguish the motivations and methods of importing

14-6 Describe the problems and pitfalls that challenge international traders

14-7 Identify the resources and assistance that help international traders

14-8 Define the standards of an export plan

14-9 Distinguish the principles and practices of countertrade

When one is prepared, difficulties do not come.

—Ethiopian proverb

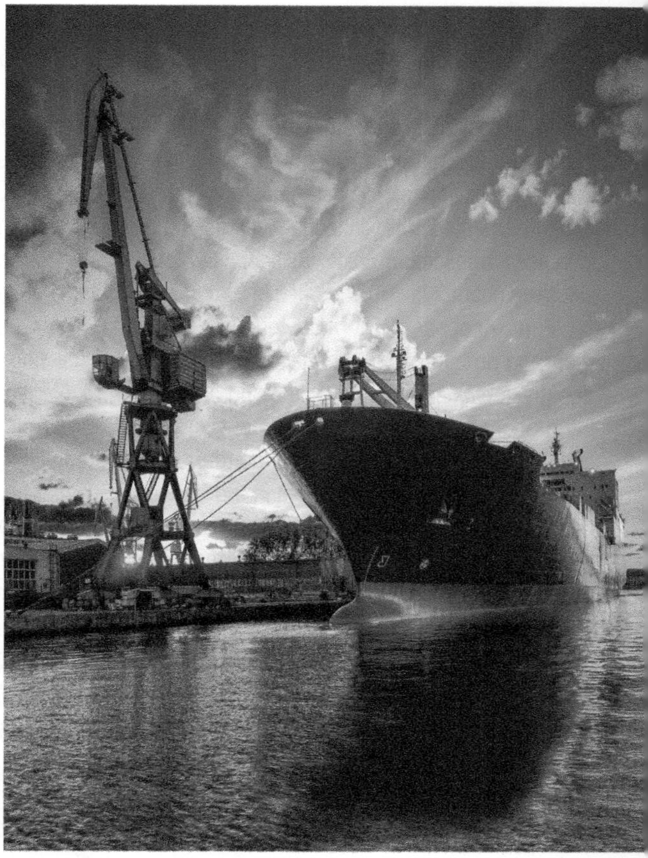

Source: Nightman1965/Shutterstock

▲ Here we see export in action, as a cargo ship prepares to depart port.

CASE

SpinCent: The Decision to Export

There were 287,314 U.S. exporters, accounting for $1.3 trillion in exports of goods.[1] Some 7,000 of these, such as Caterpillar, Boeing, Exxon Mobil, Johnson & Johnson, Coca-Cola, and Intel, annually generate about two-third of the total value of exports from the United States. Their smallest shipments are often larger than the largest shipments of smaller companies. Indeed, the top 20 exporting companies accounted for just over 20 percent of the total export value. Still, some 280,000 small and medium-size enterprises (SMEs)—specifically, companies with fewer than 500 workers—account for 98 percent of all U.S. exporters. One such SME is SpinCent of Pennsylvania.[2]

SpinCent manufactures laboratory and industrial centrifuges. Companies in chemical, pharmaceutical, food, environmental, and mining industries use them to spin a substance into high-speed rotation around a fixed axis, thereby moving heavy elements to the bottom, lighter objects toward the top, and liquid in between.

SpinCent's 65 employees—53 assembly technicians, eight product and process engineers, and four managers—operate out of its 120,000-square-foot facility in suburban Philadelphia.

SpinCent began operations with the vision to provide premium centrifuges that inspire absolute confidence and deliver superior performance. Its patented spin technology anchors a full line of automatic and manual centrifuges recognized for quality and value. To this day, management believes it builds "centrifuges for which there simply are no equals."

TO EXPORT OR NOT TO EXPORT: THAT IS THE QUESTION

From startup, SpinCent approached export passively. Its international sales often resulted from other U.S. firms' orders that were set for export, occasional sale leads gathered at industry trade shows, or an unsolicited order from a foreign buyer. Higher prices and fees meant that its occasional export sale generated high gross margins. Sometime, unexpected complications, such as customs or credit problems, increased transaction costs. Still, SpinCent's net margins on export sales ran about 20 to 30 percent higher than that for its domestic sales.

Paul Knepper, CEO and founder, conceded that, early on, recurring problems had diminished his interest in exporting. Consequently, it was not long before he and his team were skeptical about international sales. Early efforts spent too much time on unfocused searching or solving odd situations rather than strategically growing markets. Too, serving customers in the United States had kept SpinCent quite busy; developing export markets stretched its resources. Moreover, ongoing difficulties confirmed that going international poses tough challenges, especially in terms of competing with seasoned exporters from Germany and Japan.

Still, as time passed, domestic problems raised concerns about SpinCent's ongoing productivity and profitability. The shrinking U.S. manufacturing sector slowed SpinCent's growth. Meanwhile, some of its customers had begun importing cheaper, lower-end centrifuges, thereby intensifying price competition. Paul knew the day of reckoning was at hand: SpinCent must (1) focus on the domestic market and exploit every possible efficiency to sustain productivity given falling domestic demand and growing import competition or (2) expand aggressively into exporting, looking to fast-growing overseas markets to fuel performance. Ultimately, Paul conceded, these market trends forced his hand. The slow-moving deindustrialization of the United States, forecast to continue for years, would steadily reduce domestic demand. Meanwhile, quickly industrializing emerging economies, particularly in Asia, signaled rich opportunities. Hence, Paul accepted that SpinCent must export to protect margins and sustain its competitive position.

ASIA CALLS

Big market trends signaled big opportunities in Asia. "Companies were starting up everywhere and seemingly overnight," observed Paul. Pro-market reform and accelerating industrialization throughout Asia developed more and more companies that used the types of centrifuges made by SpinCent. Unlike the United States, which was in the mature part of the product life cycle, emerging economies looked set to grow, and grow fast, for years.

GETTING STARTED

New to the idea of the Asian market, Paul sought help on accessing the large, diverse region—technically, 48 countries spanning 17 million square miles, and home to 4.2 billion who speak nearly 2,300 languages, comprise Asia. Paul feared flying solo would prove risky and expensive. Moreover, he was not looking to generate a single-shot export burst. Rather, he wanted to build long-term relationships with up and coming companies. Hence, Paul reasoned, his first challenge was finding competent and trustworthy distributors who could develop, make,

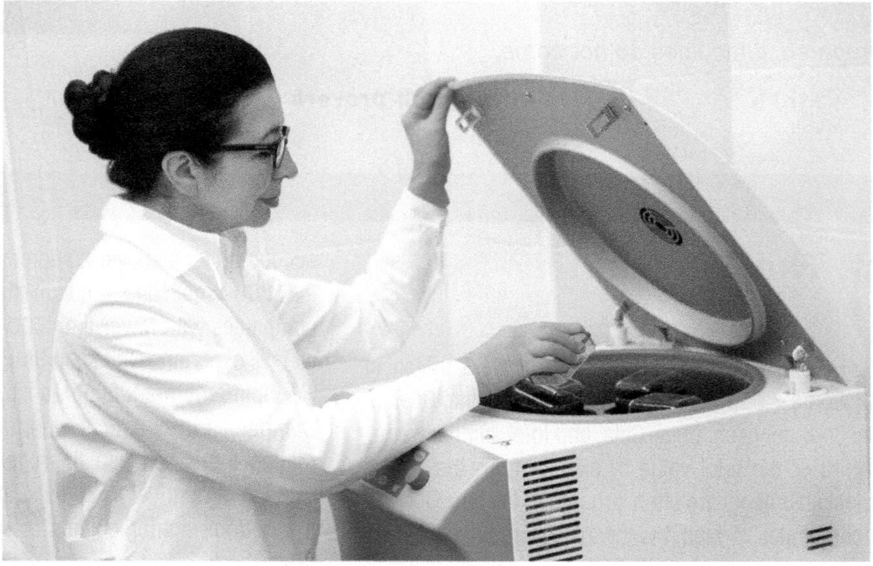

A scientist using centrifuge machine technology equipment. ▶

Source: Nestor Rizhniak/Shutterstock

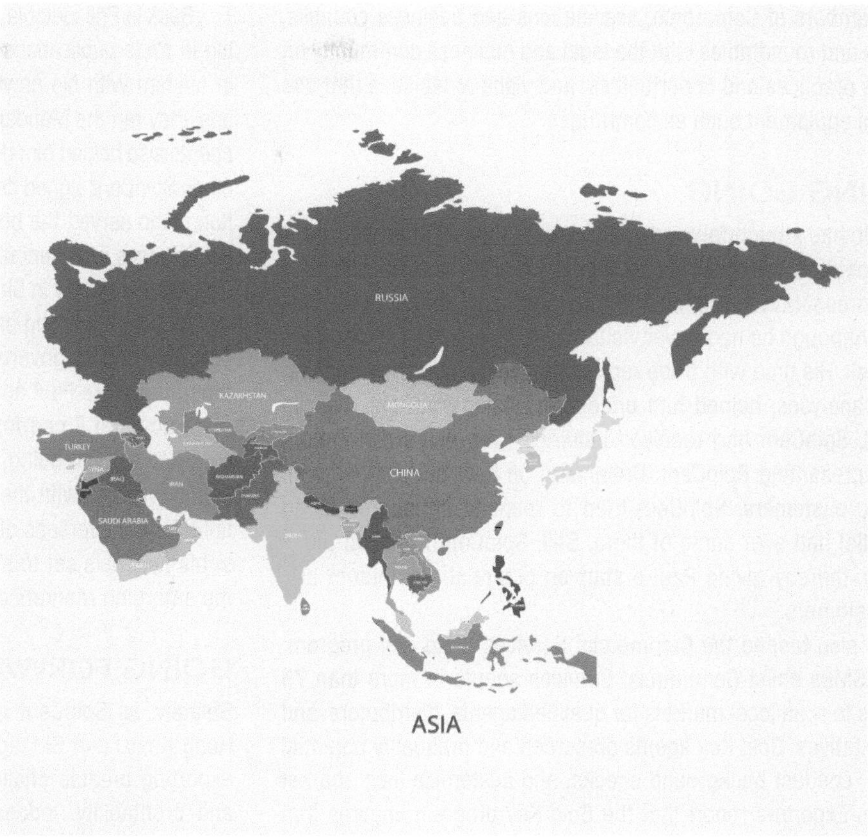

Countries that constitute the Asian Market. ▶

Source: Okili77/Shutterstock

and service local sales. "We were looking for a long-term partner and not a quick export sale," he explained. "The right partner for SpinCent needed to be as confident and competent about the product as we are, and able to promote, educate, and serve consumers in their respective territories." The key, he added, was partnering with credible, respected firms. On the flip side, he acknowledged that SpinCent had to convince potential agents that partnering with it made long-term sense.

Paul began by seeking information on potential distributors, verifying their reputation and resources. A few of the company's earlier export transactions, for instance, had run into problems with agents who struggled financially. As Paul warned, "Getting paid is a huge part of running a business, and unless a company has the right payment policies in place with the right partners, small disagreements quickly became big problems."

GETTING HELP

Mindful of these issues, Paul attended a trade seminar sponsored by the U.S. Commercial Service's Export Assistance Center of Philadelphia. This group is one of the 106 domestic offices of the U.S. Commercial Service. This federal agency's mission is to help companies get started in exporting or, for those already active, diversify sales to new markets. Since exports promote economic growth, government agencies offer extensive assistance, such as trade seminars, market research, training programs, and financial planning. Trade officials encourage SMEs like SpinCent, seeing them as the primary beneficiaries of export assistance programs. Given that 60 percent or so of all SME exporters posted sales to only one foreign market, many could boost performance by entering just one or two others. Expanding SMEs' market horizons through trade seminars, official reasoned, bolstered their confidence to do so.

That day, a session reported market profiles and trade reports on emerging economies of Asia. Taking his seat, Paul couldn't help but wonder about opportunities and risks. Sure, he conceded, big projections about big markets always sounded great. However, he had seen hype like this come back to bite, not to mention the horror stories he'd heard of the problems and pitfalls of exporting. Indeed, he reflected, a key reason for attending was reconciling his unease about the trade-off between opportunities and risks.

After a full morning of profiles and presentations, Paul believed Asian markets held far more potential than problems. He learned quite a bit about Asia, as well as some of the procedures and technicalities of exporting. Still, his unfamiliarity with Asian business practicalities, compounded by the lack of local sales representatives, bothered him. Filling in these blanks, he concluded, called for some on-the-ground research. So, before leaving, he spoke to Commercial Service agents and signed-on to join a 10-day trade mission, along with various officials and businesspeople, that was heading to Hong Kong, Philippines, Taiwan, and Vietnam in three weeks. This trip would set him up with one-to-one meetings with local executives and officials, networking events with guests from local Chambers of Commerce, associations and business councils, briefings and roundtables with the legal and business community on business practices and opportunities, and visits to facilities that use industrial equipment such as centrifuges.

GETTING GOING

Paul's trip had straightforward goals: assess market potential, identify competitors, get a sense of reasonable price points, recruit local sales representatives and distributors, and begin mapping key obstacles. Although he had never visited Asia, he believed he had prepared well. His time with trade representatives, along with studying country analyses, helped him understand Asian markets. Also, in the past, SpinCent had received inquiries from Asian distributors about representing SpinCent. Depending on how busy it was with domestic customers, SpinCent tried to respond although nothing substantial had ever come of them. Still, SpinCent has filed these contacts, thereby giving Paul a start on potential distributors and likely customers.

Paul also tapped the Commercial Services' Gold Key program; it helps SMEs enlist Commercial Services agents in more than 75 countries to scan local markets for qualified agents, distributors, and representatives. Gold Key agents prescreen and prequalify potential partners, conduct background checks, and customize local market research. Exporters report that the Gold Key program ensures that when a firm adds a partner to its network, it is a respected local company.

Thinking back to his days as a Boy Scout, Paul believed that he honored the maxim: "Be Prepared." With a briefcase full of brochures, a laptop loaded with profiles of his product line, and the sense of doing something potentially great, he headed to Asia. Over the next 10 days he ran hard, interviewing potential agents, chatting with likely customers, scouting competitors' offerings, test calling their service support, consulting with freight forwarders and logistics companies, and visiting trade officials and customs agencies.

ASIA CALLS, SPINCENT ANSWERS

On the flight home, exhausted but charged, Paul realized that he must rethink his doubts about exporting. Unquestionably, there were risks. The opportunities, however, far exceeded them. Now, he knew, exporting was no longer an option—it was an imperative. Fortifying his commitment, Paul noted, were the newly signed distributors in the Philippines and Taiwan as well as promising sales leads there and in Hong Kong.

Back in Philadelphia, Paul tested Asian markets a bit more, advertising in trade publications as well as running banner ads on trade sites in tandem with his newly signed distributors (he handled the English ads, they ran the Mandarin and Filipino versions). Commercial Services agents also helped him develop an export plan. Soon, his hard work paid off as SpinCent signed its largest overseas partner, a distributor in Hong Kong who served the booming Chinese market. Meanwhile, Commercial Services representatives generated more sales leads, and SpinCent signed a distributor in Singapore and evaluated options in Australia.

Allied with strong partners, SpinCent continues tapping the support provided by government agencies. The more he has dealt with them, the more Paul appreciates a friend's advice: "Let the government do what it can for you. It is resource rich, eager to help, and set up to get you going." Now, with an export plan in hand, Paul has begun working with the Export-Import Bank to secure financing options for his overseas distributors and customers. And, with a gleam in his eye, he's set to attend a U.S. Commercial Service's profile of the emerging markets of sub-Saharan Africa.

GOING FORWARD

Steadily, as SpinCent gains experience in Taiwan, the Philippines, Hong Kong, and Singapore, it looks onward and upward. Although exporting creates challenges, it helps SpinCent boost productivity and profitability. Indeed, overseas sales had generated a steady stream of business during recent economic downturns; rivals who had not diversified via exports struggled. Too, exporting helps SpinCent leverage its proprietary centrifuge technology.

All in all, reflects Knepper, his experiences had straightforward lessons: "If you are thinking about exporting internationally, do it. Get going, do your homework, tap low-cost resources, participate in trade missions, and build relationships. Always verify your potential business partners. Get as much information as you can. Stress-test your assumptions; the wrong guess costs you time and money. Above all, no matter the problems that you'll run into, stay committed. All of these seem tough, but they only cost pennies on the dollar while their returns can be huge."

QUESTIONS

14-1 Identify two challenges that SpinCent overcame in developing its export activity. Describe how it overcame them.

14-2 Based on its Asian experiences, map a sequence to guide SpinCent's export expansion to sub-Saharan Africa.

Exports and imports have always been an important facet of the global economy. Expanding consumer demand, growing cross-national connections, and broadening multilateral agreements progressively open more markets, thereby increasing the ease of international trade. Consequently, exporting and importing are among the fastest-growing economic activities in IB. Figure 14.1 shows that the sum of exports and imports of goods and services, in terms

FIGURE 14.1 World Trade as a Percent of World GDP, 1960–2018[3]

Source: The World Bank Indicators, Trade (% of GDP), retrieved February 15, 2020.

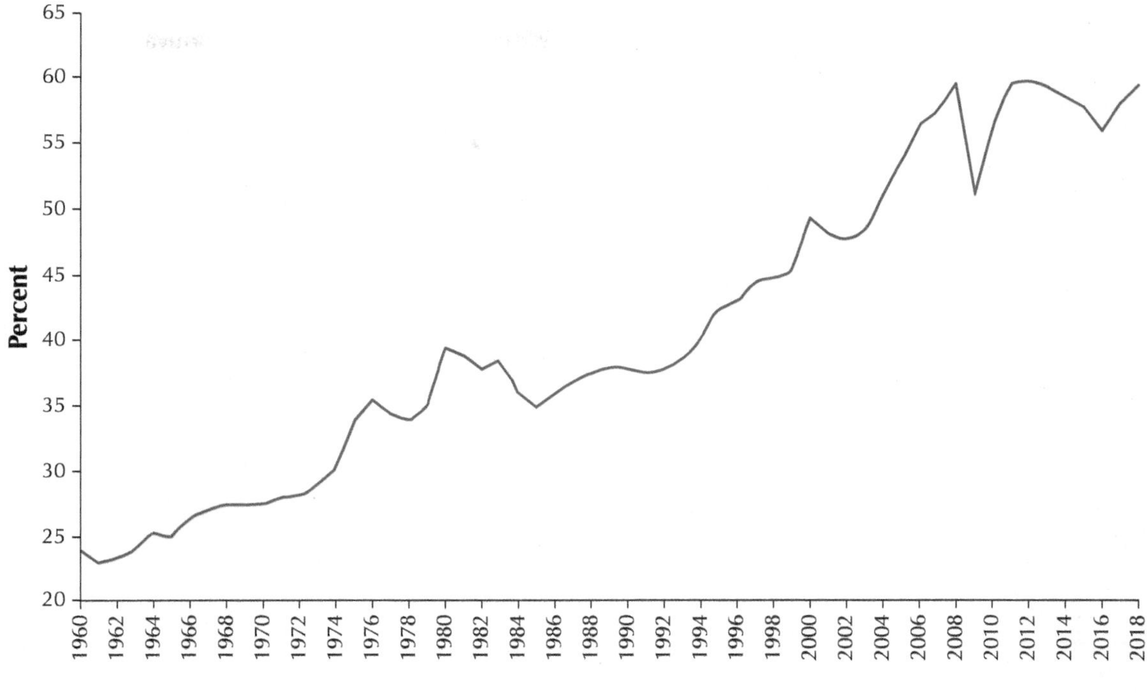

of its share of global gross domestic product, has grown over the past 50-plus years. Despite periodic ups and downs, the dominant trend in international trade, as a share of global business activity, has been steady expansion.

Earlier chapters report that companies engage in IB through several modes. The choice a company makes in, say, choosing exporting or importing rather than licensing, franchising, joint ventures, or FDI, follows from its analysis of market factors as well as its unique mix of resources, capabilities, and competencies (see Figure 14.2). Export and import, for a range

FIGURE 14.2 Factors Influencing Export and Import Operations

Assessing export and import directs attention to the environmental and operational factors that influence options, opportunities, practices, and performance.

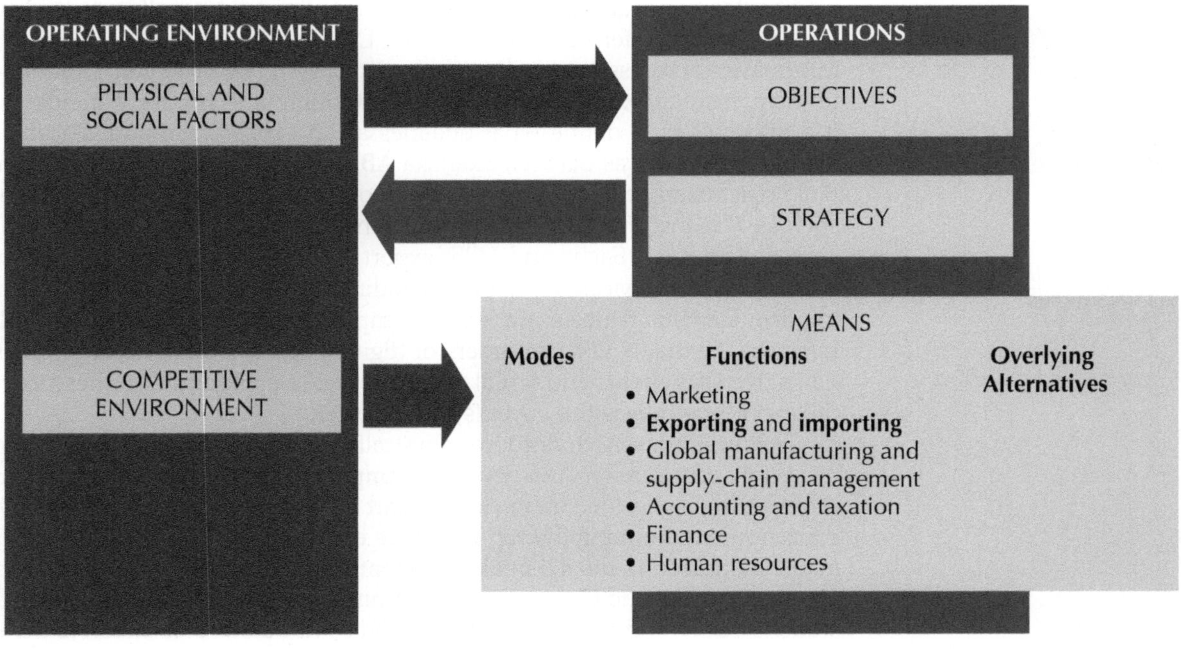

of reasons that we cover in this chapter, are consistently the most common modes of IB. Hence, although the terms may strike some as rather ordinary, exporting and importing are predominant aspects of IB. International trade, effectively the collective movement of imports and exports, is a major part of the global economy, a critical driver of nations' economic performance, and a strategic choice for companies of all sizes worldwide.

Exporting sends products to another country; importing brings products in from another country.

The enduring utility of export and import follows from their key advantages. Both are, relative to the other modes of international entry and operations, straightforward and low-cost. Both impose the least business risk and require relatively low-resource commitment. Moreover, international trade helps companies, from the smallest to the largest, expand sales, increase profits, and diversify risk. In practical terms, international trade effectively deals with the simple fact that the vast majority of people live outside your home country. In the case of Japan, an export powerhouse, nearly 99 percent of potential consumers live outside it and, by the way, they command more than 95 percent of the world's purchasing power. Therefore, a Japanese company selling domestically can reach a maximum of some 126 million consumers; selling internationally reaches 7.5 billion more. In sum, international trade presents opportunities to enterprising companies. Likewise, it also exposes them to risks. Still, as this chapter shows, there are useful approaches to interpret options. Furthermore, companies' successes as well as failures identify tried-and-true methods to optimize performance.

EXPORTING: PRINCIPLES AND PRACTICES

14-1 Explain the principles and practices of exporting

CONCEPT CHECK

Chapter 1's profile "Why Companies Engage in IB" identified three objectives: expanding sales, acquiring resources, and minimizing risk. To achieve one or more of these objectives, companies choose from various "IB Operating Modes." Among these modes, exporting and importing are the most popular modes, especially among small and medium-sized enterprises (SMEs).

Exporting is the sale of products produced by a firm based in one country to customers that reside in another country. The idea of a merchandise export is straightforward. These are tangible goods, such as machinery, soybeans, cloth, computer chips, and gasoline, that are sent *out* of one country and brought *into* another country. For example, the German carmaker BMW sending automobiles made in Munich to customers in Cambodia means BMW is the exporter and its Cambodian customers are the importers. Because we see, touch, and weigh these physical goods, they are sometimes called *visible* exports.

Expectedly, leading exports differ from country to country. For example, in the United States, the top three merchandise export product groups are food beverage and feeds, crude oil, fuel and other petroleum products, and civilian aircraft and aircraft engines. In China, they are electrical machinery, machinery including computers, and furniture, bedding, lighting, science, and prefab buildings. In Germany, they are machinery, including computers, vehicles, and electrical machinery. Globally, the world's top three export product categories are electrical machinery and equipment, mineral fuels including oil, and machinery including computers.[4]

Service exports are intangible products—one can't really see things such things and, hence, they are referred to as *invisibles*. Leading types of service exports include financial, information, professional, scientific, and technical services; telecommunication; travel and tourism; insurance; transportation; and entertainment. The hazy standards of a service make it a bit tougher to define what qualifies as an export or import. For instance, engineering contractors—such as Bechtel, Skanska AB, or Kajima—export services when they construct buildings, roads, utilities, airports, or seaports in a foreign country. Management consultants, such as McKinsey & Company, export when they advise foreign clients. Investment banks, such as Goldman Sachs and UBS, export when they help a foreign client navigate capital markets. Also, services are exported indirectly, for example, when the Japanese advertising firm Dentsu creates a marketing campaign for Sony that is then used outside of Japan. Likewise, Hydraulx VFX, designers of digital effects of all sorts, exports its services when it helps overseas clients add visual effects to videos and games. In these examples, the seller is the exporter whereas the buyer is the importer.

Technically, a service need not physically leave a country to qualify as an export. Rather, it need only earn foreign currency. For example, you may not think of the foreign national students sitting alongside you in class as part of your country's export strategy. However, higher education ranks among the top 10 service exports for several nations. The United States hosts about 1.1 million of the 4.6 million international students enrolled worldwide; next up are the United Kingdom and China. Tuition, fees, and living expenses paid by U.S.-hosted international students supported nearly 400,000 jobs and contributed $39.6 billion to the U.S. economy.[5]

Expectedly, leading service exports differ from country to country. For example, in the United States, the top three service exports product groups are public transportation, computer business services, and royalty licensing fees. In China, they are miscellaneous business services, travel, and transport. In the United Kingdom, they are miscellaneous business services, financial services, and travel. Globally, the top three are travel, miscellaneous business services, and transport.[6]

WHO ARE EXPORTERS?

Types of exporters include:
- sporadic exporter
- regular exporter.

Many companies evaluate export options, reasoning it will expand sales, improve productivity, and boost profits. In reality, few move from evaluation to action. Among those that do, some do far more than the others. Recurring patterns identify the following types.

Sporadic Exporter This company takes a passive approach to international trade—it neither avoids nor pursues export but responds opportunistically. Generally, a sporadic exporter focuses on its domestic market but, as the occasion arises, fills an unsolicited order from a foreign buyer.[7] Sporadic exporters understand the basics of the export process but, for any number of reasons, assign it a low priority. Think of, for example, SpinCent's trade activities prior to Mr. Knepper's realization of the importance of export. Until then, it filled the occasional export order, seeing it as a sporadic event, not a promising platform.

Regular Exporter This type pursues export sales as a productive, profitable, and strategic activity. A regular exporter looks to international markets for growth, invests resources to expand trading activities, and proactively responds to export signals. It is experienced with the technicalities of international trade, understanding the importance of finding the right partners, creating an export plan, and knowing where to look for help. Again, think of SpinCent's redirection following Mr. Knepper's realization—encouraged by his chats with Commercial Service agents and travels to Asia—that exporting was worth his time and effort. Each step demystified aspects of the experience, steadily supporting his progression from a sporadic to regular exporter.

Non-Exporter Technically not an exporter, it helps to understand the idea of the non-exporter precisely because there are so many; the 290,000 exporters in the United States, for example, are five percent of the nearly 5.6 million employer firms in that nation. This type is generally disinterested in international trade and, for any number of reasons, has little to no familiarity with exporting. In many cases, this orientation is practical. Many firms focus on their domestic market precisely because they make goods or provide services that do not travel well to foreign markets—think of, for example, the local law firm or beauty spa. Nonetheless, many firms qualify as non-exporters. Yes, they make products that customers elsewhere use, but disregard exporting for various reasons, such as benign indifference, insufficient resources, or apprehension about the challenge of going international.

THE MATTER OF ADVANTAGES

The decision to go international, in whatever mode, is a defining stage in a company's evolution. Done well, big success follows. Done poorly, big problems result. Hence, managers study options, determining which offers the greatest opportunity with the lowest risk. Earlier materials profiled modes that firms consider, such as licensing, joint venture, alliances, or FDI. They also profiled the influence of ownership, location, and internalization advantages on a firm's optimal entry mode into foreign markets. Here, we apply these discussions to the export decision.

Ownership advantages of the company, location advantages of the market, and internalization advantages from controlling transactions shape how firms enter foreign markets.

Ownership Advantages Chapter 12 explained how managers bundle resources and capabilities to develop competencies that, in creating the firm's competitive advantage, influence if and how it enters foreign markets. For instance, SpinCent capitalized on its ownership advantages by leveraging its core competency in designing, manufacturing, and servicing centrifugal equipment. These advantages, "owned" by SpinCent due to its proprietary technology and specialized expertise, influenced its export decision. Safeguarding its intellectual property pushed SpinCent to find trustworthy distributors. Companies with weak ownership advantages, anticipating tough struggles with foreign rivals, especially if their product is easily counterfeited, typically disregard export.

Resource-constrained or risk-averse companies that have strong ownership advantages often enter foreign markets through export.

Location Advantages The combination of high opportunity and low risk in foreign markets creates favorable export options. Stable markets with many consumers increase the odds that someone wants your product. Hence, stable markets, such as that seen in Canada, Japan, or Germany, attract exporters. Steadily, high-potential emerging economics, like China, India, Indonesia, and Malaysia, attract aspiring and experienced traders. Although they pose greater risks, their greater potential offers compelling incentives. Again, SpinCent saw the accelerating industrialization of Asian markets creating favorable locations marked by strong demand and pro-business policies.

Internalization Advantages Notwithstanding the virtues of perfect markets, companies often operate in imperfect markets. Imperfections follow from a number of factors that contribute to transaction inefficiencies and general uncertainties caused by arbitrary regulation, unfair competition, or incomplete information. Companies often respond to market imperfections by internalizing market processes. That is, a firm opts to conducts transactions within its internal organization, rather than through arm's-length transactions in the imperfect external market. Migrating activities into the company reduces the risks as well as exploits gaps resulting from imperfections. Internalizing activities, for instance, defends competencies within the context of the company rather than licensing it to firms in markets that poorly enforce intellectual property rights.

Again, SpinCent could have bypassed exporting, instead opting to license its proprietary centrifuge technology to Asian manufacturers. While inexpensive in the short term, this choice could prove costly over the long haul as SpinCent might then inadvertently help less scrupulous licensees develop into rivals. Chapter 3's profile of the rule of man as the basis of law, a legal orientation commonly found in Asian markets, highlighted the corresponding poor protection of intellectual property. This sort of market imperfection leads a company to internalize activities in order to safeguard its core competencies, an outlook that encourages exporting.

CHARACTERISTICS OF EXPORTERS

CONCEPT CHECK

The complexity posed by cross-national differences in cultural, political, legal, and economic environments creates a "liability of foreignness." This idea holds that foreign companies, because of their poorer familiarity with local conditions, incur additional costs. In theory, the liability of foreignness makes IB activity too expensive. In practice, companies offset this liability by capitalizing on their unique advantages through the optimal mode of international business.

The mission to promote international trade spurs public officials to identify the characteristics of successful exporters. Pinpointing important attributes helps agencies improve export promotion programs. General characteristics of successful exporters include ordinary as well as extraordinary aspects. Regarding the former, they are successful in their domestic market, have insightful business plan with a track record of effectiveness, and make unique products. Regarding extraordinary, they are more willing to invest resources, namely time, people, and capital, without return for while, cautiously gambling on eventual success. Clarifying these characteristics, with an eye toward identifying the correlates and causes of successful exporting, success often begins by assessing the influence of firm size.[8]

The trading activities of big versus small companies has interesting relationships with export activity. Large MNEs like Samsung, Boeing, Audi, and Foxconn are big exporters. Their ownership, location, and internalization advantages help them identify markets, leverage competencies, and manage risks. The difficulty of these tasks leads many to conclude that export is best left to big companies. This inference does have face validity. The largest companies routinely account for the lion's share of exporting worldwide. In the United States, the 500 biggest firms accounted for nearly 60 percent of total export value, the 250 biggest accounted for more than half, the 100 biggest contributed just under one-third, and the top 20 accounted for a fifth.[9]

Nevertheless, many see great export potential in **small and medium-sized enterprises (SMEs)**—those firms that, by definition, have fewer than 500 employees. In the United States, for example, SMEs are 97 percent of all exporters and importers and generate a third of the total trade value; moreover, 91,860 of the companies that exported in 2016 did not export in 2015.[10] This situation is found worldwide as approximately two-thirds of exporters and importers report fewer than 20 employees. China's 38 million SMEs, for instance, account for nearly 99 percent of all Chinese companies and generate more than 60 percent of its exports.[11] So, while big companies are the biggest exporters, many SMEs are active exporters, and many anticipate expanding activity expanding activity.

A Moderator, Not a Determinant Firm size helps explain who exports. It does not, however, determine who exports. SpinCent, a typical SME, marshaled resources, found help, and made exporting a part of its strategy. Its size, however, did not determine its decision to export. Consistently, research reports that, rather than firm size, characteristics such as competencies, competitive prices, efficient production, executive leadership, and effective marketing, better predict a firm's export activity.

In Sweden, for instance, production efficiency was the best predictor of companies' export activity; those firms with higher productivity targeted foreign markets while those with lower productivity focused on domestic customers. In China, labor costs, R&D advantages, and state ownership better predicted Chinese SMEs' export activity than did their size. Likewise, high-performing Taiwanese firms, no matter how large or small, were more likely to become exporters than low-performing firms.[12] Similarly, firm competencies, not size, better explained Canadian companies' export propensity, the number of countries they exported to, and their export intensity (the ratio of a firm's revenue from its export sales to its total revenue). In East Africa, worker productivity, industrialization, foreign direct investment, and exchange rates influenced companies' export performance.[13] Finally, top management's favorable perception of exports, based on its anticipated contribution to growth and profits, shaped exporting in British companies.[14]

A firm's characteristics moderate its export activity. Size matters, but often management commitment, productivity, innovativeness, and cost structure matter more.

In summary, firm size, as a proxy for resources and resiliency, influences a company's inclination to initiate or escalate exporting. Often, other features matter as much, if not a bit more. For example, Texas-based Coffee & More, a small company selling premium coffee and related products, looked to boost growth through export. As its CEO reasoned, "People thought we were cutting our throats by exporting, and I admit we had our own doubts. However, we knew the customer base for our product outside the United States was large, and so was the potential for success. Perseverance and commitment paid off. Now international exporting has become an integral part of the company."[15]

EXPORTING: MOTIVATION AND METHODS

14-2 Distinguish the motivations and methods of exporting

Why companies do, or do not, export is an ongoing fascination. Analysis studies the influence of external circumstances (e.g., consumer trends, market size, proximity of countries, geographical linkages, or government regulations) and internal motivators (e.g., resources, capabilities, competencies, risk affinity, intellectual rights, scale potential, or strategic vision). Companies that are capital and research intensive, such as those making pharmaceuticals, industrial machinery, or automobiles, export products to amortize the steep costs of research and development. Others in less capital-intensive enterprise, such as apparel, food, or consumer goods, export to serve universal needs or leverage powerful brand names. Those in the realm of "invisible services," such as advertisers, lawyers, and consultants, export to meet clients' overseas needs; often, they must follow clients abroad or risk losing them to rivals. Aspects like industry and risk preference also shape the decision. In the former, smaller firms may export to counter the industry leader's local advantage whereas, in the latter, some opt to export, rather than directly invest abroad, given their risk thresholds.

Exporting helps companies all types of companies

- increase profitability,
- improve productivity,
- diversify risk.

The study of export scenarios identifies many motivators. Fortunately, it also identifies common themes. Fundamentally, the export decision centers on the matters of profitability, productivity, and diversification.

PROFITABILITY

Exporting opens opportunities to increase profits. Dental equipment maker Aseptico, for instance, was first approached by international distributors at trade shows more than 40 years ago. Today, it exports to more than 125 countries. Thinking back on the journey, its Director of International Sales explained that "[t]he U.S. is only so big and there's great potential in the global marketplace to increase our bottom line." Likewise, explained the Director of Business Development for Certified Worldwide, "By not exporting, we were not tapping our full sales potential—sort of like leaving money on the table."[16]

Often, companies sell their products for higher prices abroad than at home. Foreign markets may lack competitive alternatives. Or, they may be in different stages of the product's life cycle. Mature products at home often face price competition, whereas growth stages in foreign markets support premium prices. Also, exporting enables a firm to expand its sales frontier. Though not quite decisive for firms in large markets, such as the United States, accessing bigger markets is a make-or-break factor for those in smaller markets, such as South Korea or Switzerland.

PRODUCTIVITY

CONCEPT CHECK

The improving efficiencies of international trade boost the appeal of export and import. Chapters 7 and 8 note the liberalization of the cross-border movement of resources and the development of services that support trade make export and import more practical to more companies. Likewise, Chapters 9, 10, and 11 profile the progressive integration of financial markets that supports IB in general and export and import specifically.

Exporting helps companies improve productivity, creating options to use scarce resources, such as capital and labor, more efficiently. Productivity is often linked to increasing economies of scale; i.e., making more units of a product, by spreading costs over a larger volume, improves productivity and, as a result, reduces costs. Exporting also improves productivity by inspiring all sorts of innovations. The U.S. International Trade Commission, for instance, reports that the skills developed navigating international trade helps exporters outperform those that do not. Besides more than doubling the total revenue of their non-exporting counterparts, their revenue per employee, a rough measure of labor productivity, was more than 70 percent higher than for exporters.[17]

Research reports a "dynamic virtuous cycle" between export and innovation in which each positively reinforces the other.[18] Exporters often run into ideas and practices that are absent in their domestic market. New questions and different ideas spark learning, thereby helping managers improve process effectiveness and product quality. Ingenuity, in turn, boosts productivity, thereby opening more export options. When Mississippi-based Domes International, maker of inexpensive housing, decided to expand internationally, it headed to India. Early experiences spurred innovations that improved its business practices and, in turn, fortified its competitiveness. Its CEO explained, "There's no doubt that Domes International is a better company as a result of our experience in India. We are much more flexible and innovative. The client wanted a less expensive structure, so we went back to our labs and came up with an insulation solution that met their needs. Now we use these discoveries to improve core products and to offer more variations. We are much more confident going into new situations—listening, adapting, and finding the best solution."[19]

DIVERSIFICATION

Exporting diversifies activities, thereby fortifying a firm's adaptability to business cycles and disruptive innovations. Exports, besides boosting growth and powering profits, has spillover benefits. The Office of International Trade for the U.S. Small Business Administration found that "companies that export are more resilient, and they are more likely to stay in business."[20] Beside growing sales, creating more jobs, and paying employees higher wages, U.S. exporters are less likely to go out of business than non-exporters. Serving customers in different markets reduces a firm's vulnerability to the loss of a local buyer while safeguarding its bargaining power with suppliers. Different growth rates in different markets enable an exporter to use strong sales in one country to offset weak sales in another. SpinCent, for example, saw export markets in faster growing Asia as a means to reduce overdependence on the slowing U.S. economy.

The shift in economic power from the West to the East is often portrayed as a threat to established countries. Alternatively, it signals opportunities to diversify activities by exporting to faster-growing, increasingly prosperous emerging economies.[21] The industrial and infrastructure ambitions of emerging economies push them to import tools and technologies from firms in many established countries. In fact, imports into emerging economies have grown twice as fast as those into established nations over the past decade.[22] The United States, for instance, saw 30 percent of its export go to emerging markets in 1990; by 2019, more than 60 percent did. Projections that Asia-Pacific is on track to top 50 percent of global GDP by 2040 and drive 40 percent of the world's consumption will accelerate this trend.[23]

EXPORT: STARTUP AND EXPANSION

14-3 Understand the startup and expansion of exporting

Two views of export shape interpretation: the deliberate, sequential dynamic of incremental internationalization and the instant internationalization of the born-global.

Research studies how, when, and why a company initiates and develops exporting. Reports cover a lot of territory, evaluating the influence of managerial attitudes, product features, organizational resources, firm strategy, competitive circumstances, market trends, technology platforms, public policy, and so on. Although there is some consensus, wide-ranging interpretations persist. Indeed, as far back as 1991, research identified more than 700 variables as credible drivers of the decisions to initiate or expand exporting.[24] Currently, the **incremental internationalization** and the born-global perspectives integrate interpretations.

INCREMENTAL INTERNATIONALIZATION

This view, introduced in the 1970s, sees physical distance, cultural outlooks, and market circumstances fundamentally shaping how a company engages and expands exporting.[25] Specifically, export activity follows a sequential process that sees a company sell initially to geographically and psychologically proximate countries. From there, it methodically expands, systematically exporting to more distant and dissimilar countries. So, for example, a U.S. company would initiate export by looking first toward Canada and Mexico and, if successful, next to the European Union, and then onward to the world. Likewise, a Swiss exporter would look to Europe, then the Americas, and on to Asia and Africa.

Expanding Experiences Initially, companies find it easier and less risky to trade with customers in countries that share geographic, cultural, linguistic, political, and legal commonalities. As one would expect, trading with folks in similar markets—so-called natural trade partners, such as Germany and Austria or Canada and the United States—who speak the same or similar languages, share historical legacies, and endorse similar legal principles, reduce otherwise tough entry and operating challenges.[26] Trade data confirm the influence of geographic proximity; two countries will engage in 42 percent more trade with each other if they share a common language than if they do not, 47 percent more if both countries belong to a trading bloc such as the European Union, 114 percent more if they share a common currency, and 188 percent more if they have a common colonial past.[27]

Progressively gaining experience in successfully dealing with increasingly dissimilar markets encourages managers to expand their international horizon.

The experiential dynamic of incremental internationalization is straightforward. Initial success trading in similar foreign markets, by developing managers' confidence along with the firm's resources, capabilities, and competencies, reduces perceived uncertainties and encourages expanding exporting to different places. Practically, the firm's country-by-country export expansion path follows a learning process through which managers' improving knowledge of and growing experience in progressively dissimilar foreign markets develop the confidence to export to countries that share fewer commonalities and are farther afield. Essentially, as the company exports more, managers' sees challenges decreasing and opportunities increasing. Consider the experiences of Analytical Graphics of Pennsylvania, a manufacturer of software applications that support space, defense, and intelligence missions. It began exporting in the late 1990s, targeting opportunities in Europe. Progressively, success encouraged management to pursue export opportunities in Japan and South Korea. Expanding experience with Asian business culture led it to open a sales office in Singapore to coordinate its expanding regional sales.[28]

Popular Paths The interaction of managers' experiential learning and the features of increasingly dissimilar countries results in common expansion scenarios. SMEs in the United States, for example, typically export first to Canada or Mexico, then move on to Europe, and eventually countries in South America, Oceania, Asia, Africa, and the Middle East.[29] Conversely, an SME in Vietnam, Thailand, or Malaysia would follow a different path, exporting first to countries in Southeast Asia, moving on to greater Asia, and then, as business practices improved based on lessons learned, looking to the United States, Europe, Middle East, and Africa.

THE BORN-GLOBAL PHENOMENON

The international entrepreneurship literature reports that some firms initiate exporting as a born-global (also known as an instant international, micronational, or international new venture). Rather than methodically engaging a sequence of exporting to progressively dissimilar markets, the born-global steps onto the world stage immediately upon, or soon after, its founding. It regards the home as just one of many opportunities in the world and, from the get go, looks to export to anyone, anywhere.[30]

Born-globals, owing to their executives' international orientation and improving technological options, begin trading internationally at inception.

We find born-globals worldwide, in markets big and small, emerging and established. A common characteristic is their executives' international focus. Logitech, the Swiss-based maker of computer devices like mice, keyboards, and speakers, was founded by a Swiss and an Italian who met while studying in the United States. Logitech began exporting products worldwide soon after start-up.[31] Similar examples indicate that folks who start born-globals have a strong international orientation owing to insights gained from living or studying abroad. Often, too, we see a seasoned executive, aware of a worldwide market niche, leave her employer, and launch a born-global.[32] For instance, Zoom Video Communication provides remote teleconferencing services using cloud computing technologies. It began when a lead engineer from Cisco Systems, an early adopter of video conferencing, saw expanding opportunities worldwide. He left Cisco, launched his startup and, within a few months, registered more than one million users worldwide.[33]

Digitalization as a Driver The born-global phenomenon largely follows the ongoing globalization of markets, improving trade liberalization, and growing worldwide demand for specialized products. Most decisively, changing times change the game whereby improving digital communication and logistics technologies let's one easily access immense opportunities. Digital processes and platforms reset the economics of doing business across borders, decreasing the cost of international interactions and transactions. Markets and user communities with global scale emerge, providing the born-global with efficient means to reach many customers. Hence, managers of born-globals internationalize quickly precisely because environmental circumstances let them quickly do so. Technological advances along with expanding, cross-national linkages enable managers to implement bold visions, efficiently delivering innovations to customers spanning the world.

Consider the moves of Zady, a New York–based online retailer of clothing, accessories, and household goods that prides itself as a provider of high-quality products that had been manufactured in ways explicitly mindful of environmental and labor standards. Soon after startup, Zady saw growing website traffic from Canada, France, Japan, and the United Kingdom. Zady then enlisted Borderfree, the global e-commerce subsidiary of Pitney Bowes, to manage its international shopping experience, including site localization, multicurrency pricing, payment processing, fraud management, customs clearance, and global logistics. Zady's products were soon available, via its website supported by Borderfree, to shoppers in 220 countries and territories who use 74 currencies.[34]

CONCEPT CHECK

Change in the structure and dynamics of IB endorses new and novel standards. Various trends, such as emerging economies and digital globalization, challenge conventional theories. Consequently, we study trends, such as those shaping incremental internationalization and the born-global phenomenon, to assess the direction and momentum of change.

Likewise, Evertek Computer, a U.S. SME started in 1990, quickly began exporting and now has customers in more than 100 countries. Its sells refurbished computers and parts, for which worldwide demand is booming because buyers, particularly poorer ones, don't need the latest, greatest, costliest tech. "They want cheap," explains Evertek's international sales manager, "The firm's business model," he adds, "matches these folks with those who want to sell their used personal computer equipment."[35] At first glance, liquidating tech-equipment seems an unlikely basis for successful exporting. Also, Evertek does not command the intimidating ownership advantages that usually support exporting. However, the international orientation of its top management creates a powerful driver and highlights a key aspect of born-globals. That is, the sales director's enthusiasm for IB symbolizes the firm's vision of the value of exporting anywhere and everywhere: "For me," he explains, "it started with being curious about the world. I enjoy learning about other cultures and respecting people who have a different background than mine."[36] Then, speaking like a true born-global, he adds, "We're thriving. The world is shrinking, and it's getting easier and less expensive to do business on a global basis."[37]

THE INFLUENCE OF TIME AND PLACE

Neither the incremental-international nor the born-global perspective definitively represent how companies initiate and expand exporting. Unquestionably, each credibly interprets elements of the export process. For instance, U.S. companies' exports travel to 233 countries and territories around the world.[38] Many paths reflect long-running trade relationships, such as that between the United States and Canada. Others reflect newer links, such as the United States and Kyrgyzstan. The scale and scope of this export universe support scenarios in which companies progressively developed the resources, capabilities, and competencies to service more markets (the incremental-internationalization perspective) and reach faraway markets with greater ease and immediacy (the born- global view).

Trends indicate increasing interaction between the incremental-international and born-global perspectives.

Going forward, we anticipate stronger interaction between the incremental internationalization and born-global approaches. A generation ago, going global involved navigating slow-acting trade officials directing slow-moving flows between tough-to-understand markets that differed on countless regulations and routines. Hence, incremental, market-by-market export expansion was not only feasible, it was arguably the only practical option.[39] Now, e-commerce tools and platforms, like Alibaba and Amazon, immediately give small start-ups global reach, letting them efficiently connect with customers and suppliers worldwide. The closing case for this chapter profiles the role of Alibaba, an e-commerce powerhouse, in this transformation.

More than 3.5 billion people have connections on social media and nearly a billion participate in cross-border e-commerce.[40] Expanding cross-national linkages, supported by improving digital systems, position born-globals to open options for clever business models that reach consumers everywhere and anywhere. Too, those inclined toward incremental expansion find the Internet enables cheap, easy, and effective means to analyze and access dissimilar markets. Hence, their progressive expansion to dissimilar markets fits the incremental internationalization view, whereas the acceleration of this process fits the born-global perspective.

THE WILDCARD OF SERENDIPITY

Exporters are often proactive decision-makers. Sometimes, however, serendipity—making fortunate discoveries by accident—initiates export activity.

It's appealing to depict export initiation and expansion, whether done incrementally or immediately, as a purposeful strategy designed and delivered by proactive executives. However, reports tell of accidental exporters who, responding to happenstance, unexpectedly but successfully begin trading internationally. Essentially, some companies start exporting because of fortuitous events rather than purposeful intent. Perhaps the most common trigger is the surprising arrival of an unsolicited order from a foreign buyer. Others include a new hire that has connections to foreign markets, an international contact made at an industry conference, awareness created unintentionally by a social media influencer, or travel abroad that alerts one to opportunities. Unquestionably, hard work and talent are necessary, but not always sufficient, for successful exporting. Sometimes, luck, or rather, **serendipity**—making fortunate discoveries by accident— plays a pivotal part.[41]

Edward Cutler is such a case. He is the owner and founder of Pennsylvania-based Squigle, a unique brand of toothpaste for people who cannot tolerate the chemicals found in mass-produced varieties. Upon launching Squigle, Mr. Cutler exclusively focused on the U.S. market. Internet posters spread word of his product, and Squigle soon received inquiries from Canada, France, Turkey, and elsewhere. One customer, a canker-sore sufferer in England, was so enthusiastic that he began importing Squigle into England. This was good news for Mr. Cutler, letting him expand at little cost and negligible risk. Now he is eager to export more, explaining, "We're looking to sell overseas for the same reason the big companies do: Most of the world's population lies outside the United States."[42]

Similarly, Vellus is a small Ohio-based company that makes a high-end pet grooming products. It began its export odyssey when a Taiwanese businessperson, after trying its customized shampoos, bought $25,000 worth of the company's products to sell in Taiwan.

Buyers and sellers convene in tradeshows, namely exhibitions for companies in a specific industry to showcase and demonstrate their latest offerings. Serendipitous contacts and chats often create export opportunities.

Source: Adriano Castelli/Shutterstock

Soon, word spread from show to show on the global canine circuit. Recounted Vellus's CEO, "I started receiving calls from people around the world who would hear of our products at dog shows and ask organizers how they could get in touch with me to buy our products."[43] Initially triggered by serendipity, but then developed through its competencies, Vellus exports to more than 30 countries.

APPROACHES TO EXPORTING

Granted, export sounds straightforward: "make it, sell it, pack it, ship it." This holds true for many trades. Many sorts, however, are tougher to accomplish. Generally, the ease or, for that matter, the difficulty of export transactions shapes how a company chooses to serve its foreign customers. As we now see, there are several options.

Exporting directly involves independent representatives, distributors, or retailers outside of the exporter's home country.

Direct Exporting In this mode, the company directly sells its product to the end user in a foreign market. Or, it can sell it via an intermediary, such as a sale representative, distributor, or foreign retailer, who then sells it to local customers. In either case **direct exporting** requires a company manage the export process. It must mind making, moving, marketing, and monetizing the product. Direct exporting requires executive commitment and company resources to get the show started and then to sustain activity.

Indirect exports are products sold to an intermediary in the home market, which then exports those products to end users in other countries.

Indirect Exporting Some companies prefer to do what they do best and outsource the rest. In this scenario, they make the product and then enlist independent distributors, agents, or export management companies to supervise their exports. Technically, a company sells its products to an independent intermediary in the domestic market, which then exports the product to its foreign agents, who then sells it to the end consumer. This process qualifies as **indirect exporting** whereby an exporter makes its product (do what they do best), but relies on an intermediary to supervise marketing, terms of sale, packaging, distribution, and credit and collection procedures (the activities they do best).

Operationally, this is a relatively stress-free method. Explained Edward Cutler, maker of Squigle toothpaste, "It is just easier to deal with distributors. We prefer to deal in master shippers of 144 tubes. We don't have to do anything then but slap a label on it."[44] However, unlike direct exporting, where the company handles all the work and retains all the profits, the fact that indirect exporting requires that a company hire an intermediary reduces its profits. Moreover, indirect exporting also imposes strategic costs, constraining developing relationships with end users; direct experience with customers often identifies options and opportunities.

The intersection of retail and globalization trends makes indirect exporting increasingly practical, especially for SMEs. Global retailers, such as Walmart, Carrefour, Amazon, and Ahold, easily move products from exporters to customers. Think of, for example, a headphone manufacturer in Vietnam who supplies Walmart International with a product that Walmart then sells worldwide through its many storefronts. Likewise, tens of thousands of Chinese companies easily access foreign markets via Amazon's and Alibaba's platforms. Though not as lucrative as direct exporting, indirect exporting imposes fewer demands. Too, it is often a transition phase whereby an occasional exporter gains insights into foreign markets that support its later expansion.

Service companies often export their product indirectly rather than directly. Technically, an indirect service export results when a non-exporting firm provides services to another company that ultimately exports its products abroad. An indirect service export on the part of, say, a Swedish accounting firm, occurs when it prepares the books of a Swedish company that exports to foreign markets. We commonly see indirect services exports with professional and business services in accounting, advertising, consulting, and legal domains. It's also common in other industries, including audiovisual providers to film and television studios whose media are viewed overseas, or a hedge fund that sells shares to foreign investors through a wealth management advisor.

Passively Filling Orders from Domestic Buyers Who Then Export the Product In this mode, a company supplies an input to other firms who then use it as a component in making a product that they then export. Essentially, Buyer Alpha contacts Supplier Omega, submits an order for a particular components, takes delivery, and uses it as an input into making its product, which it then exports. From the perspective of Supplier Omega, these sorts of international sales are indistinguishable from domestic sales. Often, Supplier Omega is unaware, or does not necessarily care, that its product has been exported.

WHICH APPROACH WHEN?

Several factors shape an SME's preferred approach to export, notably its mix of ownership, location, and internalization advantages.

Ceteris paribus, no export approach is intrinsically superior. At the broadest level, a company's ownership, location, and internalization advantages determine the optimal approach. Protecting ownership advantages, for example, endorses exporting directly. SpinCent, for example, saw direct selling as the best means to retain control of its ownership advantages. Similarly, top management's experience as well as company resources and capabilities endorse some choices while discouraging others. A regular exporter is more likely to export directly whereas a sporadic one looks to easier, indirect methods.

The various export approaches are not mutually exclusive. Firms often engage different approaches to export different products to different markets. A Canadian company may export directly to similar markets such as the United States and Britain, but then use indirect methods to export to dissimilar markets in Asia or Africa. For example, Analytical Graphics, which began exporting in the late 1990s, has expanded sales into 13 countries, serving them through a mix of methods. It uses direct exporting in Canada and the United Kingdom, and indirect exporting via reseller partners in Japan, South Korea, India, Russia, and Brazil.[45]

CONCEPT CHECK

The Internet influences political change, improves the operations of foreign-exchange markets, and changes the location economies that, in turn, influence how companies configure their value chains. Similarly, the Internet reshapes export and import activity by opening new markets, supporting new strategies, and providing new tools.

Technology influences the relative merits of the different approaches. The Internet makes direct exporting increasingly efficient and effective. It provides immediate, low-cost access that lets regular exporters, particularly born-globals, more easily access more markets. In addition, expanding e-commerce tools helps companies, both big and small, overcome capital and infrastructure limitations. Some exporters use extranets to communicate with buyers around the world. Others open online shops to export directly. Our closing case looks at how electronic magic at Alibaba, the world's largest business-to-business online marketplace, helps SMEs connect with customers. Twenty years ago, firm resources, communication channels, and trade logistics mattered immensely if you were a SME in Argentina trying to reach markets in Europe. Today, due to Alibaba and similarly organized platforms, they matter far less.

Lastly, firm size matters a bit. Generally, large MNEs export directly via their foreign units, while SMEs often export directly or indirectly. Regarding the former, large companies report that 40 percent of their exports were related-party trade—that is, a transaction between two parties that are connected by a preexisting relationship, such as a subsidiary-to-subsidiary transfer. Alternatively, approximately half of SMEs' exports are direct (e.g., produced by the exporting SME immediately before export) while the other half are indirect (e.g., supplied by the SME to other companies, such as a wholesaler, that then export it).[46]

POINT

Exporting E-waste: A Just Solution?

YES Exporting is always and everywhere a win-win scenario. The more companies trade, the more they create opportunity, improve productivity, boost profitability, and diversify activities. Likewise, exporting helps countries generate jobs, accelerate innovation, and raises living standards. In broader terms, it promotes connections among countries that improve foreign relations and stabilize international affairs.

Despite these virtues, some contend there is a dark side of exporting, namely the trade of hazardous waste in the form of obsolete tech equipment. E-waste—trash

COUNTERPOINT

Exporting E-waste: A Just Solution?

NO In principle, we fully agree that reusing, reducing, refurbishing, and recycling is beneficial. And, yes, exporting the electronic detritus of our tech-saturated lives promotes productive recycling as well as spurs local development. Still, exporting e-waste does not always mean you're doing the right thing. Often, it cruelly exploits desperate people, arbitrages lax regulations, and poisons minds, bodies, and souls.

As the Director of the Basel Action Network explains, "The dirty little secret is that when you take [your electronic waste] to a recycler, instead of throwing it composed of computers, monitors, electronics, game consoles, hard drives, television, smartphones, and similar sorts of items—inexorably increases as the Information Age rolls on. Yes, the world trashes hundreds of millions of electronic components, generating million of tons of e-waste.[47] Some is recycled locally, but most gets exported, and of that, most goes to depots and dumps in developing countries in Africa and Asia. The never-ending parade of newer, cooler, faster, shinier devices that, by replacing their predecessors and then eventually being replaced themselves, will increase e-waste nearly 500 percent over the next decade.[48]

Where Does E-waste Go? Where to put all this e-trash is a tough question. Many countries ban outright dumping in local landfills. This legislation means that disposing e-waste products, when possible, in any given country can quickly become prohibitively expensive. In contrast, e-waste regularly sold to processor soon ends up in Africa and Asia—where it will be recycled, reused, or dumped.[49] Low costs are a result of abundant labor, different environmental regulations, and expanding capacity. Plus, sporadic opposition reduces processing expenses and enterprising folks seeking work dampen community objections.

Benefits for All Exporting e-waste is an efficient solution to an escalating problem. Recycling sustains resources and safeguards the environment. In developing countries, industries have sprung up to recycle computers, monitors, circuit boards, game consoles, scanners, printers, routers, cell phones, network cards, and on, and on, and on. These businesses create opportunities in places where jobs are hard to find and difficult to sustain.

Many struggling communities have converted their superior location economics into vital jobs, income, and prosperity. For example, one finds thousands of small businesses employing tens of thousands of workers at ground zero of the e-waste trade: Guiyu, China. Previously subsistence farmers and fishermen, residents now process the tens of truckloads of e-waste that arrive daily.[50] Mexico has similar spots, where folks wait for the never-ending parade of 18-wheelers full of spent tech to cross the U.S.–Mexican border. Notwithstanding the dangerous, dirty work of recycling, people living near the Acumuladores de Jalisco plant find opportunity. As one worker explained, "There are not many other jobs around here."[51]

Exporting e-waste helps entrepreneurs in developing countries create value by recovering, recycling, refurbishing, and reusing scarce resources. Copper, a valuable commodity, can represent nearly 20 percent of a smartphone's total weight. Atul Maheshwar, owner of a recycling depot in India, says of U.S. exports, "If your country keeps sending us the material, our business will be good."[52] On that note, the raw materials contained in e-waste were worth in a trashcan, about 80 percent of that material, very quickly, finds itself on a container ship going to a country like China, Nigeria, India, Vietnam, Pakistan—where very dirty things happen to it."[57] Adds the chief executive of RSR, "We're shipping hazardous waste to a neighbor ill-equipped to process it, and we're doing it legally, turning our heads, and pretending it's not a problem."[58] Growing exports of hazardous waste encourage dangerous and deadly recycling practices in many developing countries. Going forward, exports will only increase, always a step behind the never-ending waves of new tech powered by the fuel of planned obsolescence.

A Witch's Brew Many developing countries lack the regulatory codes or disposal infrastructure to safeguard against common dangers. Locals use makeshift methods that, besides being illegal in the United States and European Union, expose workers to a witch's brew of toxins. For example, some e-waste contains trace amounts of precious metals like gold and silver. Extracting them encourages cash-strapped, loosely regulated recyclers to use unsafe, open-air incineration methods. Burning electronic parts to separate these metals from plastic coatings releases hazardous chemicals. Snagging that elusive sliver of silver unleashes a mixture of more than a thousand toxic chemicals, including lead, barium, mercury, flame-retardants, cadmium, acids, plastics, and chlorinated and brominated compounds. Air quality suffers as "circuit boards are burned after acid washing, spewing deadly smoke and exposing workers and people living around these facilities."[59] Once local scrap shops finish scavenging equipment, the trash goes into public landfills, the acid runoff flows into groundwater, and the noxious fumes follow the wind—all mercilessly contaminating the environment.

Benign Inhumanity Hard to believe, but Madhumita Dutta of Toxics-Link Delhi argues that these eco-costs are less disturbing than the "appalling" working conditions in recycling facilities "Everything from dismantling the computer to pulling out parts of the circuit boards to acid-washing boards to recover copper is done with bare hands without any protective gear or face protection." Rare is the worksite that follows safe disposal practices. Workers and society, to say nothing of environmental sustainability, suffer. What, then, of the premise of charity—that is, sending electronic components from countries where they have little use to countries where they can support education, development, and civil society? Critics shred this straw man, asserting that amoral companies donate obsolete equipment to dodge high recycling expenses. "Too often, justifications of 'building bridges over the digital divide' are used as excuses to obscure and ignore the fact that roughly $61 billion in 2016, greater than the gross domestic product of more than 135 countries.[53]

In addition, some of the e-waste exports shipped to poor communities worldwide helps improve the local standard of living. Scrap Computers, a recycler in Phoenix, claims that virtually every component of old electronic devices is reusable. Old televisions turn into fish tanks in Malaysia, while silicon shortage creates demand for old monitors elsewhere. "There's no such thing as a third-world landfill," another explains. "If you were to put an old computer on the street, it would be taken apart for the parts."[54] Similarly, the director of BMP Recycling says, "We don't send junk—we only send the materials that they are looking for."[55]

The Moral Choice Exporting hazardous waste helps MNEs practice social responsibility. Samsung, Dell, and Mitsubishi, among others, increasingly take cradle-to-grave responsibility for their products. Various initiatives institute collaboration among manufacturers, retailers, collectors, recyclers, nongovernmental organizations, and government agencies. ERI, the leading recycler of electronic waste in the United States, recycles more than a billion pounds of electronic devices annually. Too, it has an international network in 46 countries managing more than 100 vetted and certified facilities. Allied organizations, such as the Institute of Recycling Industries, the Recycling Leadership Council, and the 3R Initiative, have recycled billions these bridges double as toxic waste pipelines," argued one critic.[60]

Institutional Gaps Consumers and companies must take responsibility for the hazardous materials they use to enable their lives and sustain their profitability.[61] Certainly, some companies have moved in this direction, sponsoring green campaigns to recycle e-waste. Progress has been slow, however. Even today, just 20 percent of the world's e-waste is collected and delivered to registered recyclers; where the rest goes is largely unknown.[62] Environmentalists advocate tougher standards to monitor, control, and certify cross-border shipments. Then again, presumed solutions can lead to unintended problems. Most states in the United States require companies take responsibility for recycling electronic equipment. This policy has curtailed the export of e-waste to developing countries—but only of the more valuable components. Consequently, processors cherry-pick valuable pieces, urban mining for silver, gold, and palladium, then ship the remaining trash, the worst of the worst, to desperate folks eking out a living.[63]

Whom to Turn To? Many endorse stronger enforcement of the Basel Convention on the Transboundary Movement of Hazardous Wastes and their Disposal, a United Nations treaty that regulates the generation, management, movements, and disposal of hazardous waste. It advocates aggressive measures, including

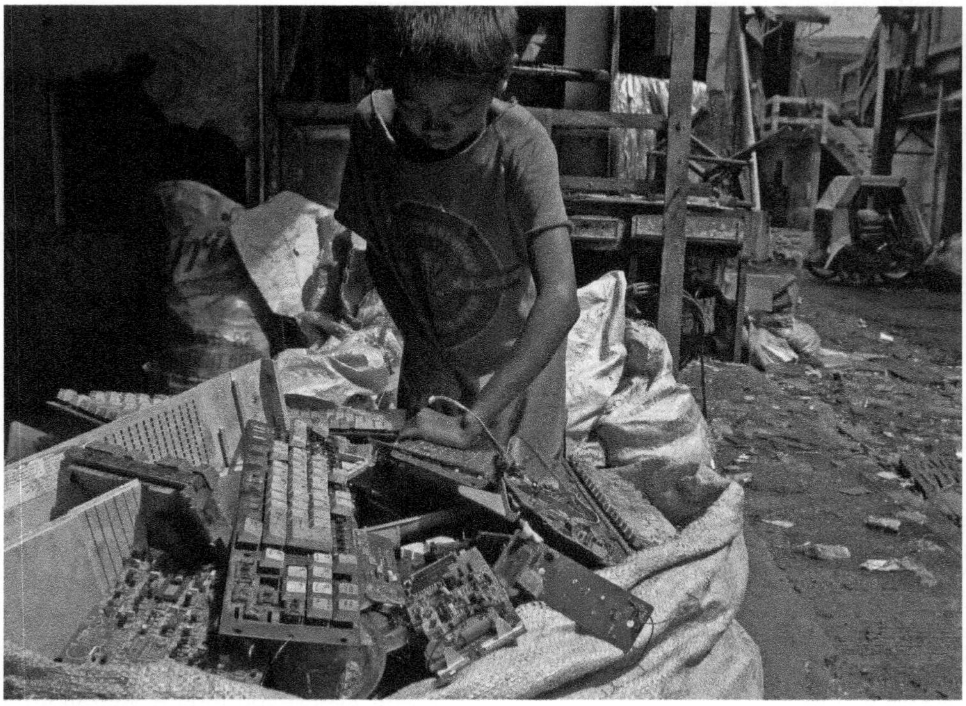

Here we see an enterprising child working at a grassroots e-recycling facility. Although these materials are junk to many, scavenging and selling useful parts creates value for him, his community, and the world.

Source: Enrique Soriano-Silverlens/ZUMA Press/Newscom

Here we see a frightful wasteland near Lagos, Nigeria. Notwithstanding the toxic threats of this witch's brew, desperation spurs people to scavenge for anything of value.

Source: n86/ZUMA Press/Newscom

of pounds of waste.[56] Elsewhere, regulation spurs laggards to go green.

An Optimal Solution Certainly, callous consumers and dishonorable companies dump useless, toxic e-waste around the world. And, yes, some of it pollutes landfills, poisons waterways, and fouls the air. Overall, though, exporting e-waste works for consumers, communities, companies, and countries. E-waste exports, argue optimists, feed a circular economy whereby refurbished, reused, or recycled materials improve resource usage and support a sustainable future. Ultimately, when one gets down to it, exporting e-waste is the optimal solution to a tough problem. The U.S. Environmental Protection Agency, for example, concedes that inappropriate practices mark e-waste disposal, but suggests stopping its export is impractical. For those in wealthier countries, it resolves an otherwise irresolvable problem. For those in poor countries, it provides a path to prosperity. For all, it's part of the price of our digital existence.

an international ban on the export of all toxic waste, no matter whether for recovery, recycling, reuse, or final disposal.[64] As of 2020, 187 states and the European Union are parties to the treaty. The United States signed it in 1990, but has not ratified it, thereby not legally bound by its terms. Progress protecting humanity, while slow, continues. Meanwhile though, many people in many places sacrifice utopian takes for dystopian fates.

IMPORTING: PRINCIPLES AND PRACTICES

14-4 Explain the principles and practices of importing

Together, imports and exports are the foundation of international trade.

Importing, along with exporting, are the foundation of international trade. Exporting, as we saw earlier, is sending goods or services to another country for sale. In contrast, **importing** is the purchase of a good or service by a buyer in Country X—the importer—from a seller in Country Y—the exporter. Effectively, importing is the reverse of exporting. Goods imports are straightforward: Samsung's shipment of a smartphone made in Seoul, for example, to a buyer in Montreal registers as an import for Canada and, correspondingly, an export for South Korea. Both terms, export and import, by the way, derive their root "port" from the fact that goods historically entered or exited a country via a seaport.

Expectedly, the leading merchandise imports differ from country to country. For example, in the United States, the top three merchandise import product groups are machinery, including computers, electrical machinery, and vehicles. In Brazil, they are mineral fuels including oil, electrical machinery, and machinery, including computers. In Taiwan, they are mineral fuels, including oil, iron/steel, and organic chemicals. Globally, the world's top three export product categories are crude oil, integrated circuits and micro assemblies, and cars.[65]

Service imports, given their "invisibility," take various forms. Services provided by German banks to Swiss customers qualify as service imports for Switzerland. Similarly, when Lloyd's of London writes an insurance policy for a client in Saudi Arabia, trade authorities in Saudi Arabia record an import. The import of services has subtle characteristics. For example, the installation of nuclear power equipment in Poland by French firm Areva, even though it results in a tangible, visible facility, qualifies as a service import for Poland. The standard to keep in mind is that a service import is any transaction that (1) does not result in ownership and (2) is rendered by nonresidents to residents.[66]

CHARACTERISTICS OF IMPORTERS

A service import is a service transaction that does not result in ownership and is rendered by nonresidents to residents.

Wide-ranging research has assessed many characteristics of exporters. Importers generally receive less attention largely because governments encourage exports but discourage imports. Recall, that the balance of trade is the difference between the value of a country's exports and imports for a given period. Technically, a trade deficit results when a country's imports exceed its exports. A chronic trade deficit negatively affects employment, economic growth, and stability within a country. Understandably, governments are keenly sensitive to these threats and encourage studying and supporting exporting activity.

Nonetheless, the general characteristics of exporters overlap with those of importers. For instance, importers are likely to be exporters, and these firms account for the bulk of the world's exports and imports. In the United States, for instance, out of the 287,314 exporting companies and 211,335 importing companies, 85,324 companies both imported and exported.[67] So, as does an exporter, so too does an importer develop international activities given its mix of ownership, localization, and internalization advantages. Likewise, importers exhibit incremental and born-global characteristics. Lastly, firm size, efficiency, innovation, and management commitment similarly moderate an importer's trading activity.

Historically, importers traded relatively few products with relatively few developing countries.[68] Essentially, the bulk of imports tended toward opportunism or arbitrage (i.e., cheap oil in Saudi Arabia became expensive oil in the Germany). Fast-growing economies, such as the Philippines, Peru, Nigeria, and Indonesia, accelerate and alter this relationship. These countries produce more goods and services that outperform, in price and function, local choices in many markets. They also provide higher-end products that once were the exclusive province of local companies in the developed markets. For example, once European manufacturers like Nokia and Ericsson dominated the global smartphone market. Now, it's Samsung, from South Korea, and Xiaomi and Huawei, from China. Likewise, think of German and Japanese companies now importing business process services from Indian MNEs like Infosys and Cognizant. Finally, globalization supports differentiated supply chains with more links that cross more markets; expansive supply chains, in turn, expand the scale and scope of import and export transactions.

IMPORTING: MOTIVATION AND METHODS

14-5 Distinguish the motivations and methods of importing

Several reasons motivate importing:

- Specialization of labor
- Global rivalry
- Local unavailability
- Diversification
- Top management's outlook

Numerous factors spur a firm to start and sustain importing. Research highlights the significance of high-quality products, price elasticity, reliable logistics, and local market imperfections. These factors, singly and collectively, spur importers to scan foreign markets in search of lower-priced, higher-quality, or locally-unavailable products. This situation inevitably raises the question: Why do these anomalies exist? Absent these gaps, there is little need to import or, for that matter, export. Other parts of the text, particularly materials in Chapters 6 and 12, speak to this issue. For our purposes, the following conditions clarify key motivations to import.

IMPORT DRIVERS

The specialization of labor is a powerful tool to improve productivity. It benefits the import potential and performance of SMEs and large firms.

Specialization of Labor Managers usually divide a production process into a sequence of separate yet interdependent steps. They then assign workers to discrete steps so that one worker does one task, another does another task, and so on—think of the structure of the profile of the value chain framework in Chapter 12. This sort of specialization of labor organizes the workplace to achieve available economies of scale (i.e., the inverse relationship between the quantity produced and per-unit fixed costs) as well as location economics (i.e., different wage rates and material costs across countries). The resulting efficiencies reduce costs, thereby enabling a company to offer higher-quality products at lower prices to consumers locally and abroad. Sales to the latter, naturally, qualify as imports. For instance, Nike buys shoes manufactured by companies in several Asian countries; conditions in their business environments enable local companies to make higher quality shoes for lower cost. Nike finds it impossible to manufacture the same products in its home market, sell them for a reasonable price, and still make a profit. As a result, it profitably exports shoes made in Asian factories and imports them into other markets worldwide.

Input Optimization Companies import goods from foreign suppliers to lower costs. Always important, it is imperative in industries where competitive rivalry imposes stiff cost pressures, such as we see in telecommunications, industrial machinery, and business services. Many companies, such as car makers, import thousands of parts produced in factories around the world to centralized manufacturing centers. Likewise, financial service providers routinely rely on back-office support or customer call-centers in foreign markets. In both cases, from making cars to taking calls, companies look to imports to access low cost inputs.

Local Unavailability A primary benefit of import, declares the WTO, is expanding the scope of available goods and services in local markets. Importing helps local markets expand the variety of their offerings, providing consumers with products that are otherwise unavailable or are superior substitutes. Practically, think of the seasonal consequence of geography to trade flows; Canada imports bananas from tropical climates because of its unsuitable climate; absent imports, Canadians would not enjoy fresh bananas.

Diversification Importers, like exporters, access international markets to develop options to diversify risks. Diversification via importing lets a company find higher quality, lower cost products, thereby making it less vulnerable to the dictates of a local supplier or the vagaries of business cycles. For example, customers of South Korean steelmakers, such as automobile companies, diversify their purchases to include Chinese, European, and Indian suppliers. Developing alternative suppliers reduces the consequence of local supply shortages or unilateral price hikes by steelmakers; this sort of diversification encourages imports.

TYPES OF IMPORTERS

There are three general types of importers:

- Optimizers
- Opportunism
- Arbitrageurs

Importers process a wide range of goods and services in mass markets, such as apparel or food, as well as niche segments, such as medical devices or legal discovery. No matter the product or market, one sees three broad types of importers.

Optimizers This type of importer taps foreign providers to optimize, in terms of price or quality, the inputs fed into its supply chain. Essentially, a company scours the globe for optimal inputs, then directs them to its various production points—much as Fiat Chrysler does, extensively relying on Chinese auto parts makers to supply its Serbian plant that manufactures Fiat 500L's that are then sold globally. Its factories then assemble inputs into finished goods that are then imported by markets worldwide. Logically, the flow of inputs and finished goods from country to country, besides representing imports, also qualifies as exports.

Opportunism This type of importer looks for products worldwide that it can import and profitably sell to local citizens. It identifies imperfections in the local marketplace, whether real (customers prefer higher-quality or lower-cost options) or perceived (the outlook that foreign products are superior to local substitutes). It then opportunistically exploits gaps by finding, buying, transporting, and distributing those products from foreign suppliers to local customers. To considerable degree, the specific product is secondary. Rather, the game is using import channels to fill gaps in the local marketplace profitably.

In principle, arbitrage is the simultaneous buying and selling of the same product in different markets to exploit differences in price.

Arbitrageurs According to the law of one price, a product sold in one market should sell for the same price in another—after controlling for currency effects, transportation costs, and trade regulations.[69] In practice, the price of the same product can vary significantly from country to country due to market imperfections that result from government regulations, trade inefficiencies, political risks, and other factors. These imperfections, by creating supply gaps, create the basis for import arbitrage.

For example, an enterprising firm in one country looks elsewhere for locally unavailable products, and then imports and sells them. For example, the release of the latest, greatest iPhone once triggered a consumer frenzy, including scalpers aiming to exploit a temporary market gap given that it was available only in the United States for the first several weeks. Demand in other countries created compelling opportunities. Buyers in China, for instance, hired shoppers in Los Angeles, Chicago, and New York to buy iPhones that they then express shipped to Beijing, Chengdu, or Shanghai, where they were then marked up twice or thrice more.[70] Eventually, once Apple sold the "latest, greatest" iPhone directly in China, through its local retail outlets and licensed resellers, the arbitrage gap closed, and imports faded.

EXPORTING AND IMPORTING: PROBLEMS AND PITFALLS

14-6 Describe the problems and pitfalls that challenge international traders

CONCEPT CHECK

As straightforward as the concept of exporting may seem on the surface, whether you are a born-global entrepreneur or an established MNE, it has many challenges. Behavioral barriers routinely complicate managing international activities. Political and legal codes pose pitfalls, government regulation influence trade relationships, and foreign exchange instruments necessitate financial sophistication.

Indisputably, export and import offer all sorts of benefits, including sales growth, risk diversification, strategic positioning, and so on. Some firms find these compelling and expand outlook and operations to sell to the big, bold world. Others, seeing overwhelming difficulty in the problems and pitfalls of international trading, forsake the option. The types, characteristics, and impact of barriers that impede exporting and importing run the gamut. Track records, surveys, and horror stories identify many obstacles that deter international trading. Table 14.1 profiles key concerns.

OPERATIONS MANAGEMENT

Traders regularly complain about optimizing transportation and logistics, weak foreign market connections, difficulties matching foreign rivals' price-to-quality standards, mapping market channels, promotion tactics, and consumer behavior, and tailoring after-sales service programs. Non-exporters express greater anxiety about these marketing uncertainties, particularly when they benchmark them against the comparatively easier demands in their home markets. In addition, shifting economics opens markets in places where new sorts of market structures and consumer behaviors pose new challenges. Going from the United States to Canada is one thing; going from the United States to Turkmenistan, Zambia, or Kosovo, for example, is entirely another.

Historically, exports and imports were arm's-length, ship-it-and-forget-it transactions. Contact with customers relied on documents either faxed or express mailed. This situation created advantageous time lags with which to manage questions and complaints. Now,

TABLE 14.1 Common Barriers to Trade[71]

Operations	Navigating language and culture, preferences for local goods/services, distribution channels, logistics expenses, product adaptation pressures, different service norms
Strategic	Top management commitment, IB expertise, staff flexibility, lower profitability, difficulty developing sales, finding trustworthy partners, IPR protection
Financial	Difficulty receiving/processing payments, different taxation regimes, obtaining trade credits, funding working capital, currency fluctuations, exchange controls
Governmental	Home and foreign trade regulations, complex tariffs schedules, non-tariff barriers, inadequate public support programs, buy national codes
Documentation	Custom procedures, homeland security regulations, export-import forms, permit and licensing arrangements, fees and charges

buyers, irrespective of time zones, easily, directly contact vendors via e-mail, SMS, or video-calls. The resulting rise in customers' real-time service expectations diminishes the appeal of international trade to some. "The new notch in the bar for us is the requests from our customers for additional services beyond the port of delivery," said the materials manager of Seco/Warwick, a manufacturer of heat-treating equipment. "In previous years, I would be responsible for cost, insurance, and freight (CIF) to the port of import, but now I'm often tasked with all aspects of delivery to the customer's plant location. Now we're often involved in the installation and start-up of the equipment, so we have service engineers and cranes waiting for the on-time delivery."[72] Customer management concerns particularly challenge SMEs. Their focus on specialized segments prompts them to apply niche strategies. Customers' increasing expectations push them to customize services in ways that can overwhelm their resources.[73]

STRATEGIC MANAGEMENT

International traders study the structure and conduct of target foreign markets, aiming to see where their strategy works, and just as importantly, where it does not. Making sense of requirements, rivals, and regulations drive the export decision. The steady expansion of international trade indicates that enterprising managers consistently find paths to leverage resources, capabilities, and competencies into successful exporting. Think back, for example, to our opening profile of SpinCent. Fear of misinterpreting export markets led its CEO to hire local agents and distributors as well as consult with trade officials, both at home and overseas.

More pointedly, consider the saga of San Diego–based Iron Fist Brewing Company. It began with the vision to make the best hand-crafted beer in the world. Success locally meant that Iron Fist benignly disregarded export options—until a chance meeting with an agent of the U.S. Commercial Service.[74] Its interest piqued, Iron Fist worked with its local office, leveraging its expertise to deal with international beer importers. Now, Iron Fist sells its beer in Australia, Canada, Finland, Hong Kong, Mexico, and Norway, and has hired workers to manage its export expansion.

Management characteristics, especially executives' international outlook and entrepreneurial orientation, influence interpretation of the strategic methods of export and import activity. Companies, particularly SMEs, typically focus on their domestic rather than foreign markets. In the United States, for instance, SMEs compose 97 percent of all exporters, yet less than one percent of all SMEs export. Of those that do, nearly two-thirds export to just one foreign market.[75] Asked why, managers explain that their preference for the familiarity of the home market often offsets overseas interests. Although many acknowledge the benefits of internationalization, they see its riskiness and demands countering their preferred strategy. Difficulties run the gamut, from complicated documentation, confusing cultural differences, different business practices, and just the lack of time to deal with the contingencies of export. Individually and collectively, these barriers pose big difficulties to all sorts of traders.

Rare is the firm that has the flexibility, resources, and inclination to adjust its preferred strategy for business standards in target markets. As a result, management often emphasizes domestic sales, duly noting the ambition to export down the road. Recall Paul Knepper's original outlook at SpinCent; at best, he was a sporadic exporter who saw risks outweighing rewards. Eventually, productivity, profitability, and diversification concerns led him to reconsider. From then on, ownership advantages, support from public agencies, and trustworthy distributors fortified his strategic positioning.

FINANCIAL MANAGEMENT

SMEs regularly rate financial constraints as the most daunting barrier to trading internationally.

Financial constraints pose tough complications to international traders. A survey of 978 SMEs asked their perceptions of trade barriers—the greatest problem was the shortage of working capital to finance exports.[76] Financial concerns, such as payments and taxation, consistently challenge manufacturing and services companies. Completing international sales often requires helping foreign customers secure credit, whether in the form of trade credits, government-financed support, or bank guarantees. Firms accustomed to offering financing in terms of the traditional 30- or 60-day trade-credit cycle in the United States dislike managing the longer payment terms customary in some markets.[77] Cycles in some countries stretch to 90 days or more; while advantageous to the importer in terms of cash flow and cost, it is a riskier arrangement for an exporter. Similarly, traders object to obtaining expensive protection against nonpayment by customers, inflated transaction fees, and differences in regulatory and legal frameworks. Managing these problems involves currency and credit processes that call for sophisticated expertise. Hence, some traders reason that export or import offers low profitability given higher costs and financial risks, both of which are aggravated by fluctuating exchange rates.

GOVERNMENT REGULATION

Research identifies a range of internal and external factors that influence export and import activity. Many are incentives that encourage companies to go international.[78] Still, many are barriers that discourage expansion. Especially daunting are the rules that regulate trade. The success of the WTO, the transnational organization whose mission is to expand international trade, has made it easier worldwide. Still, government regulations, in terms of standards, security, and protection, confound exporters and importers.

Standards SME run into problems complying with product and process standards that governments specify to ensure they do not represent harm or hazards to consumers.[79] New Jersey–based Spectra Colors, manufacturer and distributor of high-quality, customized dyes and colorants, runs into problems because import regulations differ from one country to the next. "In Europe, REACH regulations (Registration, Evaluation, and Authorization of Chemicals) have caused us lengthy delays and expense," said Spectra's business manager.[80] Occasionally, shipments to various markets require government clearance. Refusals come easily to officials facing product constraints at home or political tension abroad. REACH disproportionately affects SME exporters, given staff and resource constraints to ensure compliance. Other countries, such as Canada, China, Japan, Switzerland, Taiwan, and Turkey are developing regulations that mimic REACH. Similar situations emerge elsewhere. Exporters of medical devices routinely face regulations that require extensive clinical data. Many countries, including Australia, Canada, China, certain EU member states, Japan, and the United States, require firms institute an ISO-certified quality management system. Companies, particularly SMEs, often struggle to obtain and maintain certification.

CONCEPT CHECK

"Legal Issues Facing International Companies," profiled in Chapter 3, notes how a country's legal system significantly influences decision-making in IB. Chapter 7 shows how governments influence import flows with instruments of trade control. Here, we add revenue collection and homeland security to the long list of moderators.

Homeland Security The policies and practices that ensure a safe and secure homeland inevitably limit business freedom. In the United States, for instance, security issues constrain the efficiency of international trade. The logistics manager at Schott North America explained that the real danger to international trade these days is not tariffs; rather, it's "that your containers are stuck down at the terminal in New York [harbor] waiting for inspection" by radiation detection instruments before being allowed to enter the United States.[81] Considering that more than 11 million containers annually enter the 328 official ports of entry in the United States, persistent security concerns pose ongoing difficulties. Similarly, moving goods across borders takes far longer today given expanding security procedures: processing a truckload of goods across the Canadian–American border, for instance, takes three times as long as it did pre–September 11, 2001.

Governments work toward common standards, adopting similar screening methods and harmonizing security measures. The U.S. Customs and Border Patrol implemented the Container Security Initiative (CSI); it negotiates bilateral cargo security agreements with trading partners to set procedures for inspecting high-risk maritime cargo containers before they are loaded aboard vessels bound for the United States. Currently, CSI operates in North America, Europe, Asia, Africa, the Middle East, and Latin and Central America seaports. Likewise, looking to streamline the way air cargo is cleared before uplift onto an aircraft, Australia and the United Kingdom instituted "Known Consignor" schemes. These allow authorized logistics groups to accept goods from self-certified businesses, who then supervise scanning shipments in high-security depots, in order to expedite processing air cargo.[82]

Labor Policies Governments, understandably sensitive to domestic situations, actively protect workers from displacement due to imports. In terms of "visible" merchandise, tariff barriers are a common defense. In terms of "invisible" services, governments often apply indirect nontariff barriers. Professional service providers, such as the sort found in the engineering, legal, finance, and entertainment sectors, regularly send employees abroad to perform contracted services. In Malaysia, however, foreign engineers cannot work on building projects unless the hiring company convinces the Malaysian Board of Engineers that a Malaysian engineer cannot do the job.[83] It's tougher in Thailand—its Alien Occupation Act reserves architecture and engineering services jobs for Thai nationals.[84] India restricts the right to practice law to persons who are both Indian citizens and on the advocates' roll in the relevant Indian state. Furthermore, to qualify as an advocate, candidates must be either an Indian citizen or a citizen of a country that allows Indian nationals to practice law on a reciprocal basis, hold a degree from a university recognized by the Bar Council of India, and be at least 21 years of age.[85] Similar situations in Brazil, Bahrain, Philippines, and Hong Kong, to name just a few, challenge the legal firm with international ambitions.

TRADE DOCUMENTATION

Governments require international traders to thoroughly document trade transactions.

A battery of documents regulates international trade; Table 14.2 profiles prominent types. Many concerns motivate a government to monitor export activities, including tracking transactions, collecting tariffs, and safeguarding national security. Inevitably, the burden of documenting transactions falls upon the trader. Customs regulations, though overlapping, invariably differ across countries. Tariff classifications, value declarations, and duty management pose complications. Homeland security expands regulations given that protecting citizens, infrastructure, and territory requires more, not less, information.[86] Navigating these obstacles requires that traders manage the document flow that tracks, certifies, and legalizes transactions.

Missing or inaccurate trade documents boost costs, disrupt schedules, or halt the transaction. Difficulties often follow from the incorrect use of International Commercial Terms, or **Incoterms**. Exporters may misclassify their products in terms of the tariff schedule of the country of destination. Goods that arrive with commercial invoice descriptions that do not

TABLE 14.2 Types of Export Documents

Here we have a sample of the forms that exporters complete to comply with U.S. Customs and Border Protection and Homeland Security.

Type	Specification
Bill of Lading	A receipt for goods delivered to the common carrier for transportation, a contract for services rendered by the carrier, and a document of title. The customer usually needs the original as proof of ownership before assuming title.
Certificate of Origin	Reports the product's origination and is usually validated by locally designated agency, such as a Chamber of Commerce. It helps customs officials determine the appropriate tariff schedule.
Commercial Invoice	A bill for the goods from the buyer to seller describing the goods, buyer/seller addresses, and delivery and payment terms. Governments use it to determine the value of goods when assessing customs duties.
Consular Invoice	Invoice certifying a shipment of goods and shows information such as the consignor, consignee, and value of the shipment; its submission to the consul, or often embassy, of the receiving country earns it its title.
Electronic Export Information (EEI)	The most common export document, it requires an exporter declare key elements of the transaction, such as the involved parties, dates, ultimate consignee, forwarding agent, ultimate destination, and loading pier. Provides vital trade statistics and enables export control.
Export-Packing List	Itemizes the material in each individual package, indicates the type of package, and is attached to the outside of the package. Used by the shipper and customs officials to verify the cargo.
Pro Forma Invoice	A document from the exporter to the importer that outlines the selling terms, price, and delivery as if the goods had shipped. If the importer accepts the terms and conditions, it sends a purchase order and arranges for payment. At that point, the exporter issues a commercial invoice.

match those of the importing country's tariff classification are registered under a catchall description, such as "machinery, other." Besides slowing the transaction, imprecise descriptions can incur higher duty charges.

Importers face similar, yet also different, difficulties. Some importers receive products prior to purchasing them—that is, they take the title of ownership before payment, then wait to see if the shipment arrives as contracted. Its arrival in-country requires the importer navigate various offices and agencies to settle accounts, register the title, pay duty charges, and arrange delivery. The required documents vary by country. Typically, customs agencies require an importer to provide an entry manifest, bill of lading, commercial invoice, valuation statement, and packing list before releasing the shipment.

IMPORTING AND EXPORTING: RESOURCES AND ASSISTANCE

14-7 Identify the resources and assistance that help international traders

CONCEPT CHECK

Parts I and II of the text note that IB creates jobs, generates income, and raises living standards. Parts II and III profile how governments use regulation to shape trade relationships. Here, we observe that governments provide programs to improve the efficiency of exporting and importing.

Globalization encourages companies, both big and small, to expand their market frontiers. Liberalizing markets and opening borders increase the options and opportunities for trade. Historically, big companies outperformed their smaller counterparts. Their commanding ownership and internalization advantages supported aggressive expansion. Many SMEs lack the competencies and connections to pursue international trade ambitiously. These constraints might not matter greatly in some places, but in others, they are decisive. Quite simply, there is wide variability in the ease of exporting and importing among countries (see Table 14.3).

In some countries, trading is easy. For example, several of the top 10 countries on the ease-of-trading list are European. Trading across Europe, for instance, has become progressively seamless due to the ongoing integration efforts of the European Union. Free trade pacts in other parts of the world have similar effects, such as USCMA easing and expediting trade among Canada, Mexico, and the United States. In contrast, trading is harder elsewhere. Irregular customs practices in African and South Asian markets routinely hamper exports and imports. Moving from port to port in these markets finds a hodgepodge of hazy regulations that can veer toward illegality. One Zambian trader noted, "My cargo of copper wire was held up in Durban, South Africa, for a week. The port authorities required proof that the wooden pallets on which the wire was loaded were free of pests. After some days, the Ministry of Agriculture's inspector checked that the wood was fumigated—for a $100 fee."[87] No matter the locale, importing requires understanding customs regulations, knowing how to navigate goods through border control, assigning appropriate customs duties, and completing procedures accurately.

TABLE 14.3 Where Trading Is Easy—and Where It's Not

Here, we see those countries that lead and lag the world in making export and import easy. These rankings reflect a country's performance in terms of the time and cost (excluding tariffs) of documentary compliance, border compliance, and domestic transport of a standardized cargo of goods by sea transport. Key indicators include the number of documents customs requires traders to complete and the length of time and overall cost required to complete a transaction.

Easiest	Rank	Hardest	Rank
Croatia	1	Iraq	181
Denmark	2	Tanzania	182
France	3	Congo, Republic	183
Hungary	4	Liberia	184
Italy	5	Sudan	185
Luxembourg	6	Cameroon	186
Poland	7	Congo, DR	187
Romania	8	Venezuela	188
Slovenia	9	Yemen	189
Spain	10	Eritrea	1909

Source: "Trading across Borders | Topic Analysis," Doing Business, World Bank Group.[88]

PUBLIC AGENCIES

Firms often find themselves in situations where third-party assistance influences the productivity and profitability of their international activities. They can enlist aid from various public or private agents.

Public officials support export given its macroeconomic and microeconomic benefits. In terms of the former, exporting helps countries generate jobs, build foreign-exchange reserves, improve the balance of trade, develop foreign relationships, and raise living standards. In the United States, for example, exports and imports supported more than 10 million jobs; effectively, each billion dollars of trade supports nearly 6,000 jobs.[89] From a microeconomic perspective, exporting helps firms leverage competencies, improve financial performance, diversify risk, and fortify competitive positioning. New markets open paths to higher productivity and profitability. Consequently, officials universally regard exports and imports as drivers of development. Expectedly, governments assist potential and active exporters, offering trade counseling, market intelligence, business matchmaking, and commercial diplomacy. To a lesser degree, given the regulations stipulated in cross-national trade agreements, they support the ambitions of importers.

Agents and Services In the United States, companies can start at the nearest Commercial Service office, the trade promotion arm of the U.S. Department of Commerce's International Trade Administration. In Japan, one contacts the Japan External Trade Organization (JETRO), while executives in the United Kingdom consult the UK Trade and Investment. As do similar agents elsewhere, these units promote trade and investment, particularly helping SMEs start up and sustain export. In terms of the U.S. Commercial Services, its representatives in more than 100 U.S. cities and 70 countries help U.S. companies target markets, organize operations, and navigate pitfalls.

In the United States, as in most countries, public agencies help firms initiate and develop exports and imports.

Public agencies offer a wide range of benefits, running from procedural to strategic. Explained the Director of International Sales of Aseptico, "Exporting can be very different from selling products in the U.S. The language, culture and competition are different. It is not as straightforward as selling domestically." Aseptico tapped the resources of U.S. Commercial Service to identify overseas opportunities, create an export strategy, and connect with potential foreign partners. Added the director, "I greatly appreciate the collaborative relationship we have with the U.S. Commercial Service. They have provided us with expert advice to enable us to continue our sales expansion worldwide."[90]

Likewise, U.S. companies look to the International Trade Administration (ITA) for negotiation expertise and commercial diplomacy to resolve trade complications. Remember, imports replace local production; labor pressures often spur public officials to institute import barriers. The ITA, here and elsewhere, works with government officials and, as needed, the WTO Technical Barriers to Trade Committee, to promote fair trade. U.S. government agencies offer information on the practicalities and insight on the technicalities of exporting. Its official gateway, www.export.gov, offers robust resources. Companies also tap personal help at export centers run by the Commerce Department, ITA, and the Small Business Administration. These agencies promote trade and investment, help companies compete at home and abroad, find international partners, and advocate fair trade. Similarly, local government offices run export financing programs, including pre- and post-shipment working-capital loans and guarantees, accounts receivable financing, and export insurance.

CONCEPT CHECK

Assessing foreign markets, navigating regulations, mastering foreign-exchange, and complying with homeland security, just a few of the steps one must take to operate internationally, are doable, but not easily. Consequently, some companies look to the sophisticated knowledge of international trade intermediaries to get going quicker.

PRIVATE AGENTS

Companies routinely enlist private agents to help navigate international trade. Prominent types include export intermediaries, freight forwarders, customs brokers, World Trade Centers, and international banks. These agents offer an operationally easier and less risky approach to export than going alone.[91] Their expertise provides skills and advantages that companies, especially SMEs, may lack. Likewise, they help manage regulations, duties, insurance, and transportation issues.

Trade intermediaries are third parties that provide exporters a variety of services.

Export Management Company (EMC) An EMC, by acting as the international trade arm of a company, helps firms overcoming otherwise intimidating start-up barriers. It often acts as the unofficial marketing department, generating orders, organizing distribution channels, and developing promotions. Likewise, it verifies credit information, confirms foreign accounts and payment terms, and even uses a SME's letterhead in communicating with foreign sales representatives. An EMC oversees trade documents, schedules transportation, and arranges patent and trademark protection.[92] It can expedite resolutions and, if needed, represent its client in customs investigations.

Many EMCs are entrepreneurial ventures that specialize by product, function, or market area.

EMCs operate on a contractual basis, providing exclusive representation in a formally defined market. Contracts customarily specify pricing, credit, and financial policies, promotional services, and method of payment. An EMC might operate on a commission basis, except in situations where it takes title to the merchandise. Similarly, it charges fees for other services. It usually concentrates on complementary and noncompetitive products from assorted companies in order to gain efficiencies through marketing a broad product line. Although versatile, EMCs are not a panacea. Some EMCs have limited resources and may struggle to warehouse products or finance sales.

The United States exempts ETCs from antitrust provisions, thereby permitting competitors to combine forces in foreign markets.

Export Trading Company (ETC) In 1982, the United States passed the Export Trading Company Act. It allows U.S. firms to collaborate with each other to improve efficiency, and, in turn, compete more effectively in export markets. Exemption from U.S. antitrust laws allows a company to coordinate overseas activities with its domestic rivals. They can legally work together to share expertise, streamline systems, reduce transport costs, boost negotiating power, and fill larger orders. An ETC differs from an EMC in that it operates based on demand rather than supply. Operationally, an ETC brings buyers and sellers together, functioning as a trade matchmaker. It creates value by determining foreign customers' preferences, identifying domestic suppliers, and facilitating transactions. Rather than representing a single manufacturer, an ETC works with many. Operating as independent distributors, they avoid carrying inventory in their own name or performing post-sales service.

Freight Forwarders Popularly known as the "travel agent of cargo," **freight forwarders** are the largest export/import intermediary in terms of the value and weight of products shipped internationally.[93] One sometimes see these agents referred to as Logistics Services, a term borrowed from the military given its expertise in the timely delivery of freight from one place to another. Operationally, upon finalizing a foreign sale, an exporter hires a freight forwarder to arrange the fastest, cheapest transportation method. Often, freight forwarders look to the pack mules of globalization, namely immense container ships that transport nearly 90 percent of cargo worldwide—and, in the process, fundamentally shape international trade.[94]

ETCs operate based on demand rather than supply. They identify suppliers who can fill orders in overseas markets.

Balancing the constraints of space, speed, and cost, a freight forwarder identifies the optimal path to move a shipment from the manufacturer to an air, land, or ocean terminal, supervises clearing customs, and schedules delivery to the foreign buyer. A freight forwarder also can arrange pre-shipping storage, verifies creditworthiness, obtains export licenses, pays consular fees, processes documentation, and prepares manifests. It may also advise on packing and labeling, transportation insurance, repacking of shipments damaged en route, and warehousing products. It does not take ownership title or act as a sales representative—those tasks fall in the realm of an EMC or ETC. Generally, freight forwarders offer fewer services than those agents.

Container ships, of the sort seen here, are the steady, sure-sailing movers of imports and exports. Pound for pound, they are the most efficient means of moving goods.

Source: hxdbzxy/123RF

A freight forwarder specializes in moving goods from sellers to buyers.

Freight forwarders are particularly important when the cost or timing of delivery can make or break a deal. Advised the Director of Certified Worldwide, "seek out your local Commercial Service office and find a freight forwarder, interview different freight forwarders, and remember that the company chosen will be responsible for shipping your product."[95] A freight forwarder usually charges the exporter a percentage of the shipment value, plus a minimum charge depending on the number of services provided. Most companies, especially SMEs, find international logistics costly and complex. Freight forwarders' expertise enables them to secure cost-effective transportation.

A 3PL is a trade intermediary that applies sophisticated technologies and systems to supervise trade logistics.

Third-Party Logistics (3PLs) A **3PL** is a third party in logistics and supply-chain management business that directs part or all of a business' distribution and fulfillment services; it is a fast-growing force in international trade. Like freight forwarders, 3PLs move cargo across global markets. Unlike freight forwarders, 3PLs collaborate with manufacturers, shippers, and retailers to assume responsibilities for transportation, warehousing, cross-docking, inventory management, packaging, and freight forwarding. 3PLs, such as Mohawk Global Logistics, UPS, or FedEx, simplify the complexities of logistics and supply chain management through end-to-end solutions in transportation, customs brokerage, insurance, and most everything else needed to move cargo across the globe on time, cheaply, and worry-free. Think of, for instance, your last UPS experience; just as you did, a company relies on a 3PL to transport its product, hiring it to manage the process. 3PLs consolidate billing inclusive of all transportation, customs brokerage, duties, taxes, and package delivery services. Finally, they handle product returns, warranty claims, parts exchanges, and reverse logistics.

Expanding globalization and trade liberalization accelerate the growth of 3PLs.[96] They are particularly helpful to the born-global company. Rather than building its own logistics operation, it need only tap the services of a 3PL. Big companies also benefit: nearly every *Fortune 100* company uses 3PLs to optimize logistics.[97] 3PLs have been growing at the expense of freight forwarders. In response, the latter expands its historical role as the travel agents of cargo to provide additional logistics services. Maersk and CMA CGM SA, for example, are expanding beyond port-to-port operations to manage the flow of goods deeper into the supply chains of international manufacturers and retailers. Maersk, for example, aims to become the "FedEx of the oceans." It is leveraging its proprietary "Pit Stop" app along with digital platforms and blockchain technologies to deliver containers to customers like Tesco and Carrefour as efficiently as parcel carriers deliver packages to homes.[98]

A customs broker helps an importer navigate the regulations imposed by customs agencies. It helps importers in matters of

- valuation,
- qualification,
- deferment,
- liability.

Customs Brokers Trading internationally requires familiarity with customs regulations, understanding how to clear goods through customs, determining the appropriate customs codes, and satisfying a battery of regulations. The United States, for example, has more than 17,000 unique classification code numbers in its Harmonized Tariff Schedule; the latter provides the applicable tariff rates and statistical categories for all merchandise imported into the United States. Approximately 60 percent of code classifications are open to

Source: Travel media/Shutterstock

As do markets, so too do export and import activities increasingly integrate into tightly networked systems.

interpretation—that is, a product fits more than one category. Often, it is an art form to determine the tariff classification that minimizes duty assessment. Likewise, importing requires expertise to sort through these processes. The required documentation is extensive, involving calculating and paying taxes, duties, and managing communications with authorities. Not every company commands these proficiencies. Consequently, some hire a **customs broker**.

The Costs and Constraints of Private Agents Expectedly, private intermediaries charge for their services. Many variables influence fees. For freight forwarders, the mode of transport, distance, destination, weight, volume, value, contract type, handling requirements, and security requirements influence charges. Expanding the degree of collaboration and interdependence, as is the case with hiring a 3PL or an EMC, changes the fee structure. 3PLs often charge upfront costs based on the complexity of planning and development of material handling, operational and information systems, and implementation of the proposed system. Similarly, ETCs and EMCs operate on (1) a commission rate ranging from 10 percent for consumer goods to 15 percent or more for industrial products, (2) a buy-sell basis that asks for a firm's best home-country discount plus an extra discount for a product that is marked up when sold abroad, and/or (3) contributions for special events such as exhibiting products in a foreign trade show or advance payments for promotion.

Enlisting the support of a trade intermediary requires the trader surrender some degree of operational control.

Hiring a trade intermediary requires an exporter relinquish some control of shipping, product positioning, price policies, promotion materials, delivery schedules, or customer service. Depending on the contract, the intermediary oversees some to all of these matters. The intent to retain control leads some traders to use intermediaries less extensively. Like any make-versus-buy dilemma, companies balance their control preference relative to the demands of managing the activity.[99]

Supportive governments, fading language barriers, tightening connections, harmonizing regulations, and improving electronic exchange steadily diminish the appeal of fee-based trade agents. Besides the mechanics of trade transactions getting easier, companies have more confidence and improving competencies to manage them. In response, private intermediaries innovate and upgrade their services. Some focus on transporting high-value products within the context of a single industry to select markets, rather than shipping bulk and commodity products worldwide. Others improve industry expertise to boost effectiveness, whereas others sponsor multiple product lines to optimize efficiency. Agents see these sorts of innovations, by moving SMEs into foreign markets faster, justifying their fees.

RECONCILING OPPORTUNITY AND CHALLENGE: AN EXPORT PLAN

14-8 Define the standards of an export plan

Going international imposes many demands that, collectively, influence

- resource allocation,
- executive effectiveness,
- operational flexibility,
- financial stability,
- decision-making.

Beginning with identifying attractive markets and moving onward through negotiating an international sale to shipping and receiving products, an exporter/importer manages an array of manufacturing, marketing, financial, logistic, and regulatory responsibilities. At times, some activities press more than others, such as financial worries prior to shipment or, following delivery, service concerns. The decision to engage or escalate these activities, given their implication to profitability, is consequential. Successful exporters, citing the notion that "companies don't plan to fail, they fail to plan," develop an **export plan**.

An export plan prioritizes markets, formalizes top management buy-in, organizes trade activities, and forecasts business scenarios. The process of defining objectives, sequencing tactics, and setting timelines pushes the firm to assess resources, develop competencies, assign responsibilities, and stipulate controls. A rigorous export plan helps executives track performance and make real-time course corrections. It defines a company's intent to leverage resources and manage constraints in initiating and developing export activity. At first glance, compiling an export plan may appear daunting. It need only be just a few pages to start; inevitably it expands as it evolves. Table 14.4 identifies useful questions to frame the planning process.

Success Factors Managers report that developing an export plan in a transparent, collaborative process improves its effectiveness. By no means does that guarantee success. Strategic

TABLE 14.4 Improving the Effectiveness of the Export Planning Process

Strategic planning is a challenging but rewarding process. Considering the following sorts of questions throughout the process improves analysis:

- Is exporting consistent with our vision and mission?
- Do we see ourselves as sporadic or regular exporters?
- Would our resources be better utilized in developing our domestic businesses?
- Will exporting put excessive demands on management, production, finance, and marketing?
- Does exporting leverage our ownership advantages?
- Do our internalization advantages support export activity?
- Do targeted export markets offer location advantages?
- Does exporting fit our current mix of resources, capabilities, and competencies?
- What is the relative price performance of competitive products?
- How much will it cost to transport our products?
- What is the best mix of public and private assistance?
- How do we incorporate public and/or private support into planning?

planning in any context is challenging, especially when one must abandon the familiarity of domestic routines for the contingencies of international trade. External validation goes a long way toward confirming choices. More practically, a well-specified plan is a precondition for export financing assistance from public agencies.

Successful exporters note that consulting government agencies and third-party intermediates helps clarify opportunities and preempt problems. Noted the CEO of Coffee & More, "My advice to other companies considering exporting is to go for it, but be smart and do your homework first. Educate yourself and use your local U.S. Commercial Service office."[100] Added the Manager of International Operations at Analytical Graphics, "Don't just strike out on your own; take advantage of the U.S. Commercial Service. They are familiar with the ways of doing business in your market destination and know how U.S. companies can succeed there. It's saved us valuable time and resources."[101]

Last, like yin and yang, import and export are complementary opposites within the greater whole of international trade. Strategic and practical aspects of the export process mirror those of the import process. Changing the terminology from "export" to "import" does not require changing the structure of the plan. Rather, companies adjust their analytics and interpret events from the relevant perspective.

LOOKING TO THE FUTURE Technology Transforms International Trade

The transaction costs of international trade steadily decrease. Advances in transportation and communications systems, by making it easier and cheaper to trade, expedite exporting and importing. The Internet helps individuals engage each other easily and quickly. Online filing of cargo manifests, customs documents, and transit forms eases logistics. Customs software that works in Hamburg or Sydney is also used in Hong Kong and Long Beach. More parties, including shippers, transit depots, and customs agents, along with the buyer and seller, directly monitor trade flows. All in all, greater flexibility and improving efficiency let companies engage an expanding range of export and import options.

The evolving technology of trade redefine how companies, both big and small, connect with foreign buyers and sellers. Historically, big companies reaped the biggest rewards. Their superior resources, capabilities, and competencies enabled them to handle the big-time complexity of managing goods, funds, and information. Now, the technology of trade offers game changing benefits to smaller companies. Improving online, software, and logistics platforms provide powerful tools that blur the distinction between the big, global giant and the small, neighborhood start-up. In fact, it has become harder to tell the difference between an SME operating on a shoestring budget and its larger, richer counterpart.

Online Platforms

Increasingly, companies use online technologies to start and expand exporting. They rely on the Internet to gather information, source inputs, find suppliers, finance transactions, and advertise products. Many companies build virtual value chains, running trade transactions from start to finish without ever leaving their hometown. The Internet gives potential and active traders seemingly infinite resources.

They browse government data, online catalogs, business-to-business exchanges, electronic trade boards, consumer surveys, social media, trade journals, and virtual trade shows to find a product to import or a market for their export.

The emergence of country-specific portals and web exchanges accelerates this trend. Replicating the dynamics of consumer-to-consumer e-commerce, several sites offer online bazaars. Here, traders lay their wares on the digital carpet and haggle with potential buyers from the four corners of the earth. For instance, potential importers looking for products from India can check out www.trade-india.com; those focusing on Europe need only visit www.bizeurope.com to tap into high-quality trade boards. One can also shop the world at tradekey.com, alibaba.com, or go4worldbusiness.com to find, connect, and trade.

Online platforms provide many services to traders, such as export training, cyber-trade infrastructures, international special exhibitions, virtual trade shows, and trade strategies. In principle, they share a common vision: connect sellers here to buyers there. In practice, they provide powerful business-to-business tools that improve the mechanics of trade, creating flexible and dynamic platforms that let buyers and sellers of everything from bamboo toothpicks to crawler bulldozers find each other, negotiate the terms of trade, and seal the deal.

Increasingly, as SMEs worldwide gain Internet access, they use online platforms to build their export businesses. Besides introducing mom-and-pop shops throughout the world to each other, online platforms open a vast and largely uncharted small-business hinterland. Many of these SMEs were long the unseen production sites of the global economy, trading within the context of global supply chains directed by large MNEs. Now, going online independently plugs them into the matrix, letting them go straight to buyers.

Software Platforms

A burst of business software in the past few years has revolutionized what SMEs are able to accomplish internationally.[102] Collaborative software lets entrepreneurial exporters with single-digit headcounts wheel and deal with foreign vendors without traveling the world. Evertek Computer Corporation, a U.S. SME, has capitalized on software innovations to build e-commerce websites and portals that expand its market frontier. Within a year of purchasing BuyUSA.com, an Internet-based program from the U.S. Commerce Department that identifies buyers worldwide, Evertek began selling in 10 new countries, with single purchases reaching up to $75,000. In 2010, it reported exports to 105 countries. Today, Evertek serves customers, principally via the web, in more than 200 countries.

SMEs use innovative programs to manage overseas factories with tools that once were reserved for big MNEs. California-based Global Manufacturing Network, for instance, coordinates production of industrial devices among a network of independent factories in greater China. Customers, who provide parts and subassemblies, subcontract to Global Manufacturing Network to then coordinate production scheduling, quality control, and delivery logistics. Making it all work taps on-demand, scalable enterprise software to track orders, monitor build rates, and manage network flows.

Logistics Platforms

Improving logistics help SMEs move products more cheaply and easily to more places. High-tech, low-cost shipping services rob big firms of a long-running advantage. Now, the no-name, one-person exporter down the street from you, because of its big-name shipping partner that spans the globe, arguably has many of the same logistics capabilities commanded by a large MNE—but with a fraction of the overhead. SMEs increasingly have as much, if not a bit more, logistic flexibility. Unlike big companies that rely on in-house systems, SMEs arbitrage solutions from freight forwarders to 3PLs—think of the ease of using FedEx or UPS, for example. The small international trader can hire these sorts of intermediaries to warehouse, truck, ship, fly, and deliver goods from factories in Asia to customers in Europe—all the while never taking physical possession of the goods.

Great progress has been made, but big moves lie ahead. 3Pls and freight forwarders are on digital quests to leverage new methods, such as artificial intelligence and blockchain technology, to move goods more efficiently. Improving cargo-management platforms guide orders from ship to shore and then to overland delivery to the ultimate customer. All the time, logistics platform generate data on costs, payments, clearance, destinations, and delivery.[103]

The Great Leveling

Improving online, software, market, and logistics platforms, by improving the technology of buying and selling, level the playing field of international trade. The combination of ubiquitous Internet connections and cheap cloud computing makes it easier to export and import. Big and small companies respond, confident that tech-tools help them resolve problems, avoid pitfalls, and capture opportunities. SMEs, in particular, prosper from the improving technology of trade. Perhaps most significantly, technology decouples the issues of size and capability. Observed the CEO of China Manufacturing, "Our customers can't really tell how big we are. In a way, it's irrelevant. What matters is that we can get the job done."[104]

COUNTERTRADE

14-9 Distinguish the principles and practices of countertrade

Currency or credit—easy, fast, and direct—are the preferred payment options for international trade transactions. Sometimes, though, companies face the harsh reality that a buyer cannot pay in cash because the home country's currency is nonconvertible or the nation holds scant reserves, has insufficient credit, or imposes strict currency controls. Consequently, if they aim to trade, they must resort to other means.

Consider the following transactions. Coca-Cola traded its syrup for cheese from the Soviet Union, oranges from Egypt, tomato paste from Turkey, beer from Poland, and soft drink bottles from Hungary. Malaysia swapped palm oil for fertilizer and machinery with North Korea, Cuba, and Russia and negotiated similar deals with Morocco, Jordan, Syria, and Iran. Thailand, the world's largest exporter of rice, uses rice-for-oil deals with Middle Eastern countries. Boeing exchanged ten 747s for 34 million barrels of Saudi Arabian oil. Chinese companies agreed to build a coal mine, a power station, and a dam in Zimbabwe, with revenue from the mine being used to repay the loan. These sorts of trades fall under the umbrella term *countertrade*. Technically, transactions that use limited or no currency or credit qualify as a countertrade. Table 14.5 identifies its common forms.

Countertrade is an umbrella term for several sorts of trade transactions, such as barter or offset, in which the seller accepts goods or services, rather than currency or credit, as payment.

Inconsistent disclosure hinders estimating the global volume of countertrade. Secretive government-to-government deals and disguised transactions are not unusual. Estimates generally peg countertrade transactions under ten percent of world trade, which was approximately $19.5 trillion in 2018.[105] Countertrade generally increases as countries experience economic difficulties. Boom-bust market dynamics, particularly in commodity markets, makes it an enduring feature of international trade.

COSTS

Although effective, countertrade is an inefficient way to do business. Understandably, companies prefer straightforward cash or credit to settle a transaction. That sort of deal requires merely consulting foreign-exchange tables to set transaction terms. In contrast, countertrade requires buyers and sellers assess nonmarket factors to set the value of the trade, negotiating some standards such as how many tons of rice for how many tractors. Negotiating the exchange rate is not the only hurdle. Goods may be of poor quality, packaged poorly, or difficult to service. Consequently, countertrade deals are prone to price, financing, and quality problems. Ultimately, countertrade and its variations test free market forces with indirect protectionism and price-fixing.

CONCEPT CHECK

Recall our discussions of poverty in Chapters 4 and 5. Here, we point out that shortages of resources affect individuals as well as nations. Some countries struggle to acquire the foreign reserves needed to purchase products from other nations. If unsuccessful, they often turn to countertrade.

BENEFITS

Countertrade is often unavoidable for companies that want to do business with buyers who have limited or no access to cash or credit. Companies and countries in tough binds use it to generate jobs, manage foreign-exchange reserves, and develop trade relationships.

TABLE 14.5 Common Forms of Countertrade

Barter	Products are exchanged directly for products of equal value without the use of cash or credit.
Buyback	A supplier of capital or equipment agrees to accept future output generated by the investment as payment. The exporter of equipment to a chemical plant, for instance, may be repaid with output from the factory to whose owner it "sold" the equipment.
Offset	An exporter sells products for cash and then helps the importer find opportunities to earn hard currency for payment. One often sees offsets with big-ticket deals.
Switch or Swap Trading	One company sells to another its obligation to purchase something in a foreign country. Typically, the arrangement involves switching the documentation and destination of merchandise while it's in transit.
Counter-purchase	A company sells products to a foreign country, promising to make a future purchase of a specific product made in that country.

Countertrade helps countries reduce their need to borrow working capital and give them access to companies' technological skills and marketing expertise. Companies also benefit: countertrade helps them resolve bad debts, repatriate blocked funds, and build relationships. Accepting countertrade signals a seller's good faith and flexibility, often positioning it to gain preferential market access in the future.

CASE

Alibaba: Redefining Export Pathways, Platforms, and Performance

E-commerce, by changing the way companies around the world do business, makes trading easier, cheaper, and more profitable.[106] Before the Internet, tracking down a product to import, or finding customers to export to, was daunting for the typical company. Most relied on occasional trade shows and expensive, time-consuming foreign travels to identify possible products or assess potential markets. Certainly, traders could tap local embassies or trade consulates to support export promotion or provide import assistance. Although sounding straightforward, in practice they typically proved cumbersome. Consequently, international trade was largely limited to big companies that could afford to attend trade shows, translate brochures, travel internationally, hire intermediaries, and supervise the many activities that are part and parcel of exporting and importing.

Today, the Internet gives SMEs cost-effective means to manage these demands. It makes information on any conceivable product from virtually any market readily and inexpensively accessible. Spearheading this transformation is Alibaba, a Chinese Internet company that began as an e-commerce platform in 1999. Then, explained its founder, Jack Ma, it aimed to make trading cheaper, faster, and easier. Headquartered in Hangzhou, about a two-hour drive south of Shanghai, Alibaba began operations with the goal of getting big by staying small. Jack Ma believes that his target customers are SMEs, not MNEs, or, in his words, "shrimps," not "whales." Given powerful tech trends in trade, Alibaba's vision has expanded; it now aims to "foster the development of an open, coordinated, prosperous e-commerce ecosystem" that links buyers and sellers of goods within a sprawling, systemically integrated network of traditional business functions, like advertising, marketing, logistics, and finance, and emerging ones, such as affiliate marketing, product recommenders, and social media influencers.[107]

Designing and Delivering the Ecosystem

Currently, Alibaba is the world's largest online business-to-business marketplace. It reaches Internet users in more than 240 countries and territories, and connects tens of millions of merchants to more than two billion consumers. Its e-platform supports an interactive community where buyers meet sellers, chatting, negotiating, and trading. Running an online global trade fair, Alibaba enables "shrimps" with import and export ambition but tight budgets to easily reach the global market. Alibaba provides an array of business management software, digital infrastructure services, logistics payment

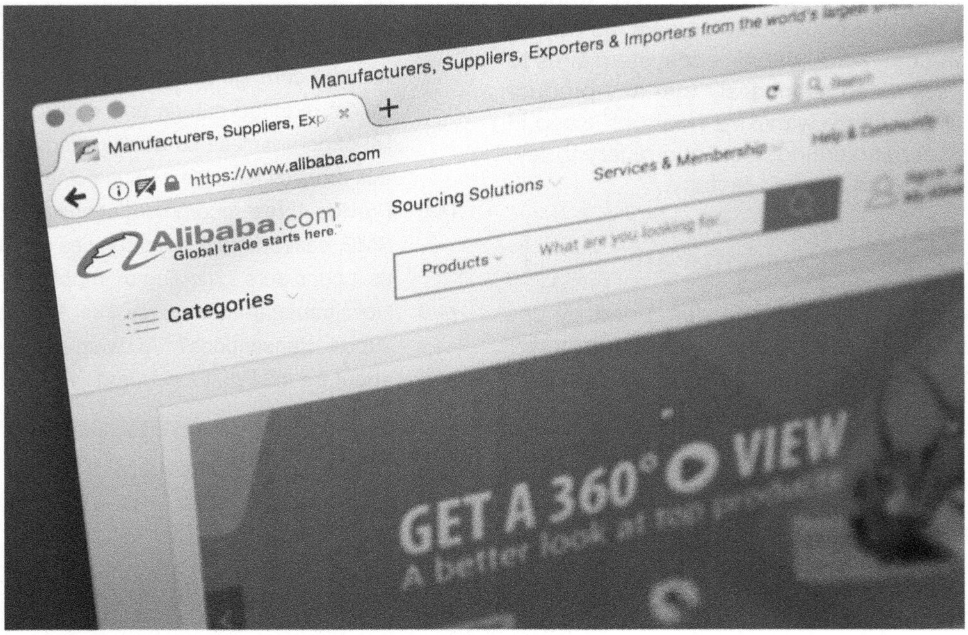

Source: chrisdorney/Shutterstock

processing, and export-related services. Effectively, Alibaba rolls into one big ecosystem a global, data-driven network of sellers, marketers, service providers, logistics companies, and manufacturers. Indeed, it's helpful to think of Alibaba as an eclectic mix of Amazon, eBay, PayPal, Google, UPS, along with a host of functions performed by wholesalers, shipping, 3PLs, and consumer financial services.

Many Alibaba users are SMEs that span the globe, from rural areas to large cities, in countries such as Kyrgyzstan, Sierra Leone, and Peru. Few are glamorous and high-tech; many are low-tech firms making labor-intensive, scale-insensitive products. However, Alibaba provides a rich repertoire of tools to expand their market reach, run their operations, and grow their business. An SME, working from even the smallest apartment anywhere in the world, can conceivably build a global business in the realm of the Alibaba ecosystem.

Here to There in 72 Hours

The mechanics of Alibaba are straightforward: Importers around the world request bids from suppliers for a mind-boggling array of goods—from cookware to poker chips, washing machines to surgical scissors. Alibaba organizes more than a thousand product categories, each with many subcategories, and offers new channels to trade services. For example, the classic garage inventor, no matter where in the world, can design a product and then use Alibaba to find manufacturers to make, package, and ship it to customers worldwide.

Operationally, buyers use Alibaba to find potential suppliers, thereby eliminating the need to hire a local representative to negotiate with manufacturers. So, for example, an enterprising company in Argentina looking to buy 5, or 50, or 500, or 5000, or whatever, iPhones cases can visit Alibaba.com, search among suppliers, compare terms of trade, contact the preferred vendor, negotiate the specifics, and set the deal in motion. Said the cofounder of meetchina.com, a similar e-commerce site, "We want to make buying 1,000 bicycles from China as easy as buying a book from Amazon.com."[108] Alibaba's ecosystem aims to do precisely that, working so seamlessly that any product can reach any buyer anywhere within 72 hours.[109] Keep in mind that while this scenario sounds sort of ordinary today, a generation ago it was a far-fetched fantasy.

Trust and Transparency

As a rule, importers worry about being defrauded by unknown suppliers. More practically, how does an importer in Buenos Aires find a trustworthy supplier in Guangzhou? Recall from our opening case SpinCent's concern on getting paid; if that confidence is missing, trade grinds to a stop. As sites like Alibaba inject more transparency into trade, buyers worry less about fraud. Alibaba suppliers, like those on similar e-commerce sites, post profiles of their performance. Buyers then access these, as well as the independent reports and references, to verify their status. These data let the importer in Argentina crosscheck the credibility of potential trade partners.

The Brave New World of Export and Import

The moves of Alibaba, or for that matter those by Amazon in the United States or Flipkart in India, signal the ongoing revolution of trade technology. On one level, their expanding ecosystems digitally transform the economy in straightforward, yet also surprising, ways. Yes, they have improved the efficiencies of existing trade systems. Looking forward, they will likely transform trading systems with innovations from artificial intelligence, cloud computing, blockchains, quantum computing, and the internet-of-things. Add it all up, and today's ecosystem is likely just a primitive version of tomorrow's network.

Never before has the cost of going international been so low, never before has the task been so straightforward, and never before has the opportunity been so global. Companies, big and small, intent on starting or expanding international trade, react in kind, thinking and rethinking on how best to play in the brave new world of export and import.

QUESTIONS

14-3 Do you think most international trade might eventually take place through websites like Alibaba.com? How might that influence your interest in importing and exporting?

14-4 Identify a product you would like to import. Visit www.alibaba.com, go to the advanced search field, and enter it. Select required criteria and click on "Search." Review the list of companies that qualify. Find a suitable seller. Analyze this process for ease and usefulness.

14-5 Provide three recommendations that you would offer an SME, based on the opportunities and limitations of Alibaba, as it considers exporting or importing.

14-6 How transparent do sites like Alibaba.com make import-export transactions? To what degree would you worry about fraud? What safeguards would you seek?

CHAPTER 15

Direct Investment and Collaborative Strategies

OBJECTIVES

After studying this chapter, you should be able to

15-1 Comprehend why export and import may not suffice for companies' achievement of IB objectives

15-2 Explain why and how companies make wholly owned foreign direct investments

15-3 Ascertain why companies collaborate in international markets

15-4 Compare and contrast modes of and considerations for selecting an international collaborative arrangement

15-5 Grasp major reasons why IB collaborative arrangements fail or succeed

If you can't beat them, join them.

—American proverb

Source: Eden Breitz/Alamy Stock Photo

▲ Entry to Meliá Hotel in Berlin, Germany.

CASE

Meliá Hotels International[1]

—Fidel León-Darder and Cristina Villar[2]

God bless the inventor of sleep.

(Miguel de Cervantes Saavedra, *Don Quijote de la Mancha*)

Li Feng arrived in London after a 13-hour flight from Beijing, her first company trip since completing her MBA and her first time outside China. Upon entering her room at the Meliá White House, she felt too exhausted to do much more than shower and enjoy her room. (The quote from Don Quijote was certainly applicable.) However, her excitement kept her from sleeping right away. So she perused the hotel directory by her bedside and was surprised to read that her hotel belonged to a Spanish company with more than 300 hotels all over the world. The photos showed attractive hotels, ranging from those in big cities (primarily to serve businesspeople) to others on pristine beaches (primarily to serve vacationers).

She was also intrigued by a small picture of Gabriel Escarré, who founded the chain in 1956. At only 21, he leased his first hotel in Majorca (Mallorca), Spain, with only his savings and the expertise he gained from his job at a travel agency. Li Feng fell asleep and dreamed of vacationing in a Meliá beach resort, but she awoke curious as to how Mr. Escarré had built Meliá's position in the global hospitality industry. For the next five days, she worked long hours, squeezed in a little sightseeing, and then returned to Beijing. Despite jet lag, she worked the next day. In her spare time she did some research on Meliá. What she learned is described below. (The chapter's opening photo shows a Meliá Hotel in Berlin.)

GROWTH IN SPAIN

That Gabriel Escarré's first hotel was in Majorca is not surprising because most entrepreneurs begin in familiar surroundings. His timing was good—European incomes were rising and package tours for sun-loving tourists were gaining popularity. Most important, Escarré exhibited both a knack for hotel management and a motivation to expand. He grew by acquiring other properties in Spain's Balearic and Canary Islands, branding them first as Hoteles Mallorquines, later as Hoteles Sol, still later to Sol-Meliá, which many people still call it, and finally to Meliá Hotels International in 2011. The early hotels aimed sales at beach-seeking tourists. In 1982, three years before its first foreign entry, the company began diversifying with urban hotels targeted to business travelers.

In 1984, the company rebranded hotels as Sol and bought 32 hotels from a Spanish chain, Hotasa, which expanded the company into more Spanish cities. Three years later, Sol acquired Meliá from Paretti, an Italian group, which led to further client-based diversification—most Sol Hotels were three- and four-star beach properties, whereas most Meliá's were four- or five-star urban hotels. In 2000, Meliá merged with another Spanish hotel chain, TRYP, thus adding 45 hotels in Spain. Meliá is now the largest hotel operator in Spain, and Spain is the largest location for Meliá.

INTERNATIONAL EXPANSION

Although Meliá has 43 percent of its hotels in Spain, international has been growing more rapidly. Some international expansion has come from acquisitions. The TRYP agreement included eight leased arrangements in Tunisia and three management contracts in Cuba. Meliá has used its 1999 purchase of the White House in London and the 2007 acquisition of the Innside Inns in Germany to bolster its European urban presence. (Map 15.1 shows the 2018 regional breakdown of Meliá's hotels.)

Having acquired experience and expertise within Spain, the firm's first start-up abroad was a joint venture for the Meliá Bali in Indonesia. This start-up was long and complicated, involving difficulty in finding local suppliers. There were also logistics and import problems in sending materials from Majorca. Soon after, the

MAP 15.1 Meliá's Geographic Spread of Operations

Source: Meliá Hotels 2018 Integrated Consolidated Management Report, pp. 17–18.

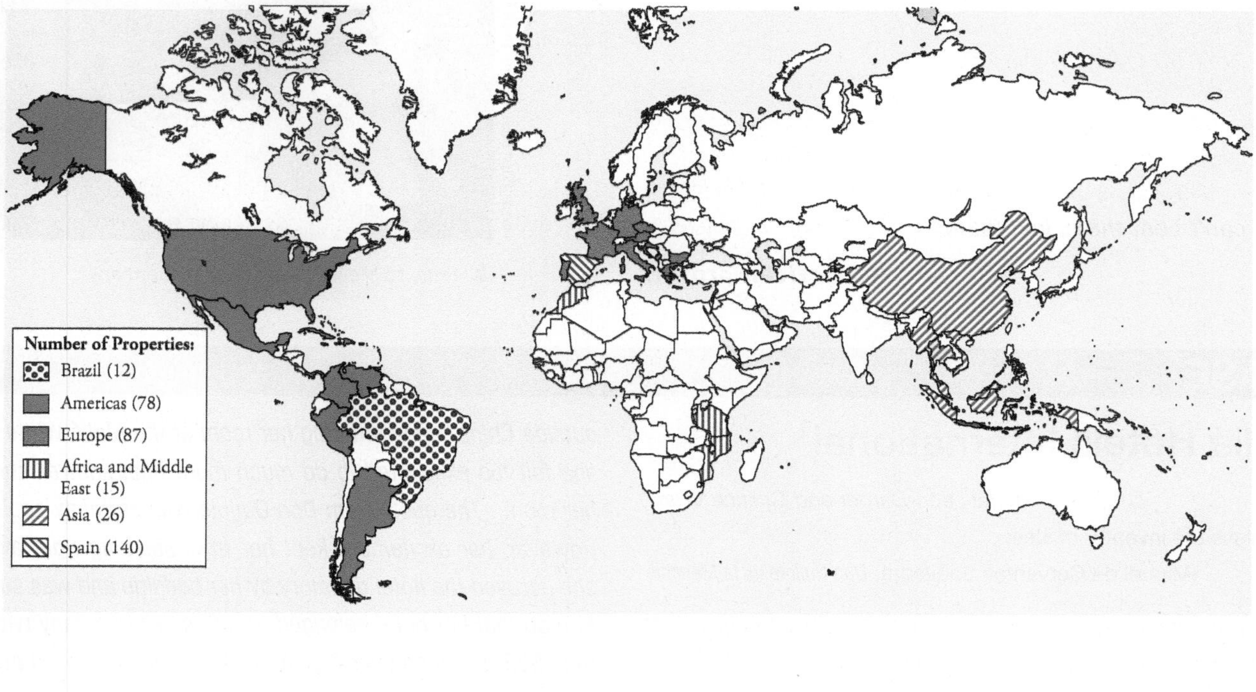

company focused on Latin America and eventually on other areas. Let's examine some major international forays that demonstrate different modes of operations.

Cuba

Meliá works in 34 hotels in Cuba. Yet the company has no ownership in hotels there because Cuba's centralized economy disallows full ownership by foreign hotel groups. Thus, Meliá has had to establish an agreement with a public agency, Cubanacán, which owns the properties while Meliá has a contract to manage them.

Operating in Cuba slowed Meliá's access to the U.S. market because the U.S. government maintained restrictions on companies doing business with Cuba, such as on those managing expropriated assets once owned by U.S. citizens. Meliá had to prove that the hotels it managed were not expropriated from U.S. citizens before it could enter the U.S. market, where it currently operates.

China

Despite more than 25 years of international expansion, Meliá's Asian expansion has been slow. In 2009, Meliá signed a 10-year contract renewable for 10 more to manage The Gran Meliá Shanghai. This became the first Spanish-branded hotel in China, even though the country had long been an important growth market for many non-Spanish international hotel chains, such as Hyatt, Marriott, Radisson, and China's largest hotel chain, Jin Jiang. This anomaly is not due to Spanish hotel chains' unawareness of the Chinese market potential; indeed, many projects were developed to conquer the market as much as 10 years earlier. However, the unsuccessful experience of Spain's Barceló Hotels discouraged other Spanish hotel chains from carrying out Chinese operations.

Barceló, one of Meliá's main competitors, reached an agreement in 2000 with a Chinese state-owned company to manage the Shanghai International Convention Center & Hotel. Surprisingly, after operating eight months and bringing the hotel back into profitability within six, the owners unilaterally terminated the contract by stating that the results were inadequate. Although Barceló won a two-year court battle on breach of contract and received some compensation, the affair left Spanish hoteliers with a bitter aftertaste and the suspicion that Chinese government partners would break agreements once they learned enough from their foreign partners.

Meliá's Chinese entry was facilitated by its favorable 20-year relationship with Cubanacán, which shares the Shanghai hotel ownership with the Chinese company Xintian (Suntime). Still, getting the deal was not easy; it took more than five years from the time talks began to the hotel's opening. Further, from almost the beginning, there was friction between Meliá and the hotel's owners, which led to cancellation of the agreement in 2013. The hotel is now operated by the Swiss chain, Kempinski.

During the period of friction, Meliá began seeking other means of growth in China. In 2011 it opened a representative office in Shanghai in order to boost its brand image and broaden its alliances within China. Subsequently, Meliá announced comanagement plans with Jin Jiang and Greenland, a Chinese real estate company. The plans provide for management sharing in six hotels, of which each partner had previously managed three. This allows the Chinese partners to extend their operations into three hotels—one each in Germany, Spain, and France—in exchange for Meliá's comanagement of hotels in three Chinese cities. The partners share knowledge and best practices as well as integrate and develop training, information, and booking systems.

Relationship with Wyndham

Meliá's motivation for a 2010 agreement with Wyndham was largely to facilitate North American expansion by using Wyndham's knowledge of that market and reputation with developers who are potential hotel investors. (Wyndham is one of the world's largest hospitality companies and hotel franchisors, with 7700 hotels and 15 brands in 75 countries.) Through the agreement, Meliá sold its TRYP brand to Wyndham, but sold no real estate. The hotels in the transaction were re-branded as TRYP by Wyndham. Meliá became the franchisee for all the hotels using the TRYP by Wyndham brand for a 20-year period. Wyndham gained by increasing its reservations offerings for a mid-market brand in Europe and Latin America, even though the same hotels are also included in Meliá's reservation system. Of the hotels in the 2010 agreement, Meliá maintains business through a combination of ownership, leases, management contracts, and re-franchises to other parties. Subsequently, TRYP by Wyndham has opened hotels in 21 countries.

INTERNATIONAL HOTEL OPERATING MODES

The hotel industry is included in the so-called "soft services" sector because production and consumption cannot be separated. There is usually a need to adapt operations locally—tourist clientele usually want an ambiance that resembles their perceptions of the foreign country, but at the same time, they expect a similar threshold level of service and amenities wherever a hotel brand operates.

The industry presents some unique characteristics, such as high investment costs and the possibility of separating ownership and management through contractual operating modes. Thus, firms have a wide range of feasible operating modes, especially management by third parties for all or a part of necessary hotel services.

To classify hotel operating modes, it is necessary to look at a chain's degree of exercised control over the foreign operation. This control involves four non–mutually exclusive dimensions:

1. The daily operation of the hotel (e.g., the hiring and scheduling of personnel and the securement of supplies).
2. Physical assets (primarily property ownership and the maintenance thereof).
3. Organizational routines and tacit elements of the company, such as the culture and systems to gain both efficiency and effectiveness.
4. Codified assets, such as the brand and reservations system.

The responsibility for controlling these elements may lie with the international hotel chain or with contractual parties, depending on the operational mode used. The capital contribution for each of the above four dimensions may be categorized as controlling ownership (usually direct investment), shared ownership (usually equity joint ventures, though non-equity joint ventures also exist, such as the one between Meliá and Jin Jiang to comanage hotels in Europe and China), and no ownership (licensing, management contracts, turn-key operations, franchising, and leasing).

Operating modes can be combined. For instance, for the TRYP by Wyndham brand, Meliá has owned some hotels, paid a franchise fee to Wyndham for using the brand name, and depended both on its own and Wyndham's reservation systems. In some other cases, it has no property ownership and is paid for managing the operation. The former Gran Meliá Shanghai is a joint venture between Chinese and Cuban organizations that, in turn, granted a management contract to Meliá (and subsequently to Kempinski) for day-to-day operations and signed a franchise contract to use its name and reservations services.

In partnering with other companies, regardless of operating mode, one increases the chance of developing competitors because partners may gain access to critical and core resources, especially knowledge. Thus, Meliá, like other companies, seeks ways to prevent partners' opportunistic behavior. Meliá's main control is over its codified resources, especially brands and reservations system, which are protected legally and which Meliá does not cede to other companies. Meliá has developed the recognition and reputation of its brands over decades, so new brands cannot easily overcome its advantage. The codified resources are tied closely as well to Meliá's tacit resources because the value of the brands is dependent on clients' hotel experience, and both physical resources and human behavior influence their opinions. Competitors can easily copy the physical resources if they have enough money. However, the human behavior is harder to emulate because learning must take place on a person-to-person basis (tacitly). Such learning in hotel operations is substantial—everything from greeting guests to making beds to assuring the flow of supplies—and affects efficiency and reputation. Over time, the actions become the essence of the company's culture.

MELIÁ'S EVOLVING OPERATING MODES

As we have seen, Meliá has made and continues to make use of various operating modes. However, it has not always had discretion in choosing a mode. When Gabriel Escarré established his first hotels, he had no track record to entice other hotel owners to pay him to manage their facilities or use his brand name and reservations system. He developed a positive reputation through his successful expansion over nearly 30 years in Spain before moving internationally.

Nevertheless, most of Meliá's early international growth resulted from acquisitions, such as its purchase of the Spanish chain TRYP that already had foreign operations and of Innside Inns in Germany. The success of these ventures built Meliá's reputation as a quality hotel operator, allowing it to keep expanding its hotel portfolio with shared or no capital investment, including growth in countries that place restrictions on foreign ownership.

Why grow? There are economies in handling larger hotel portfolios because of the clout and logistics in dealing with suppliers and the spreading of reservation and training system costs over more properties. There are also marketing advantages because potential customers are more familiar with the larger chains.

MELIÁ NOW AND IN THE FUTURE

Currently, Meliá Hotels International comprises strong brands such as Meliá, Gran Meliá, ME by Meliá, Paradisus, Innside by Meliá, TRYP by Wyndham, Sol Hotels, and Club Meliá. The maintenance of different brands is important because of existing brand recognition and value when Meliá made acquisitions. Nevertheless, Meliá is linking that recognition with its name (hence Innside by Meliá and Meliá White House). In fact, the company includes "Meliá" in almost all its brands because the name has long been associated with luxury hotels and thus brings a certain cachet. Additional brand linkage comes from handling all of them in the same reservations system (currently 37percent of its beds are sold directly to customers through the corporate website). Further, the different brands are aimed at different market niches.

In recent expansion, such as in Africa and the Middle East, Meliá has used alliances with local or international partners. Typically, the partners develop and own the properties while Meliá participates in the design and the subsequent management of the new hotels. In the United States, Meliá has signed long-term lease agreements with property owners that guarantee a source of income to the owners. In these agreements the developer assumes the risk associated with the ownership while Meliá assumes the operational risks. Overall, Meliá has been moving from ownership to non-ownership operating modes. (See Table 15.1.)

Meliá's reservation system has benefitted its operations in countries with high inflation and problems of currency conversion and repatriation, such as in Venezuela. This system allows it to receive payments in hard currency from people who reserve over the Internet.

TABLE 15.1 Meliá's Evolution of Operating Modes

Operating Mode/Period	1985–1995	1996–2005	2006–2015	2016–2018
Leasing	1.56	8.68	16.67	17.00
Franchise	10.94	13.24	8.97	15.00
Management Contracts	76.56	62.56	57.69	67.00
Ownership (FDI)*	10.94	15.53	16.67	1.00
Total	100.00	100.00	100.00	100.00

*Includes wholly and partially owned

Meliá expects more international growth by entering additional countries and adding hotels in those where it now operates. It has also indicated an interest in linking with brands held by other companies, such as the Hard Rock Café and Flintstones. Its ambitions seem too great to do everything alone. And it might not want to, even if it has the capital resources, where it perceives the operating environment to be too different from its European (especially Spanish) experience. Thus, the use of non-equity operations is the crux of Meliá's future.

As part of its growth strategy in high-potential markets, Meliá has recently entered several African and Middle Eastern countries and has indicated an interest in others by focusing on both the leisure and business traveler. In Asia, it has doubled its presence in recent years and has announced agreements in new countries such as Mongolia and Myanmar. In Latin America, recent growth has been carried out through the TRYP by Wyndham brand in Brazil, which has wide experience in that market.

In 2018 more than two thirds of Meliá's new operations were via management contracts, followed by leasing and franchise agreements. Thus, the use of nonequity operations supported by its low capital inputs is the crux of plans for Meliá's future. Its strategic plan in 2020 calls for 95 percent of new projects to be outside Spain, most of which will be in emerging economies. The firm expects to consolidate major tourist destinations such as the United States, Latin America, and the Caribbean. In Europe, Meliá plans to reinforce its presence in major European cities by adding new brands to its current portfolio. Meliá aims to increase expansion in Africa and the Middle East, and it expects hotels there to become international benchmarks of excellence, such as ME Dubai. In Latin America, recent growth has been carried out through the TRYP by Wyndham brand in Brazil, which has wide experience in that market. Meliá plans for Asia Pacific and China to maintain growth through agreements in new countries such as Mongolia and Myanmar, thus making this region's size to be very similar to that of the Caribbean.

Fast-forwarding to nearly a year since Li Feng returned to Beijing, we find that she has worked almost nonstop and has taken no more trips. Contractually, physically, and emotionally she is ready for a vacation. She looks back at the hotel directory she brought from London and focuses on a picture showing a hotel half hidden among the foliage in front of a white sand beach and turquoise waters. "Who knows," she thought, "maybe I should forget my laptop and spend some time in such a beautiful place."

QUESTIONS

15-1 Explain the advantages for Meliá to own its hotels versus managing them for other organizations.

15-2 Discuss the advantages and risks for Meliá in its non-equity joint venture with Jin Jiang.

To tap foreign market opportunities, firms may

- not be able to depend entirely on home-country production,
- rely on most types of operating modes,
- combine different operating modes for their foreign production.

Figure 15.1 shows that companies choose operating modes/forms to seek fulfillment of their international objectives by carrying out their strategies. These are sometimes called *entry strategies*, however, we prefer to call them *operating modes* because companies frequently enter with one and later change to another. Chapter 14 examined exporting and importing—the preferred and most common IB modes. But compelling factors can make these modes impractical. Thus companies may depend, instead, on foreign production, which they may own in whole or in part, develop or acquire it, and/or use some type of collaborative agreement with another company.

Figure 15.2 shows the types of operating modes associated with each of these options, categorized by whether the company's IB activity involves foreign production and, if so, whether the company owns equity in the foreign production or depends on a collaborating company to own the equity. Experienced MNEs commonly use a variety of operating modes, selecting them according to company capabilities, specific product, and foreign operating characteristics. The modes may also be combined, such as Meliá's contract in the opening case to manage a Shanghai hotel jointly owned by Chinese and Cuban organizations. This chapter first examines why exporting/importing may not suffice, thus leading to foreign production.

FIGURE 15.1 Factors Affecting Operating Modes in IB

Companies may conduct IB operations independently or in collaboration with other companies. The choice will be determined both by external factors in the firm's operating environment (such as legal requirements, perception of risks, and availability of desirable partners) and by internal factors that include its capabilities, objectives, and strategies.

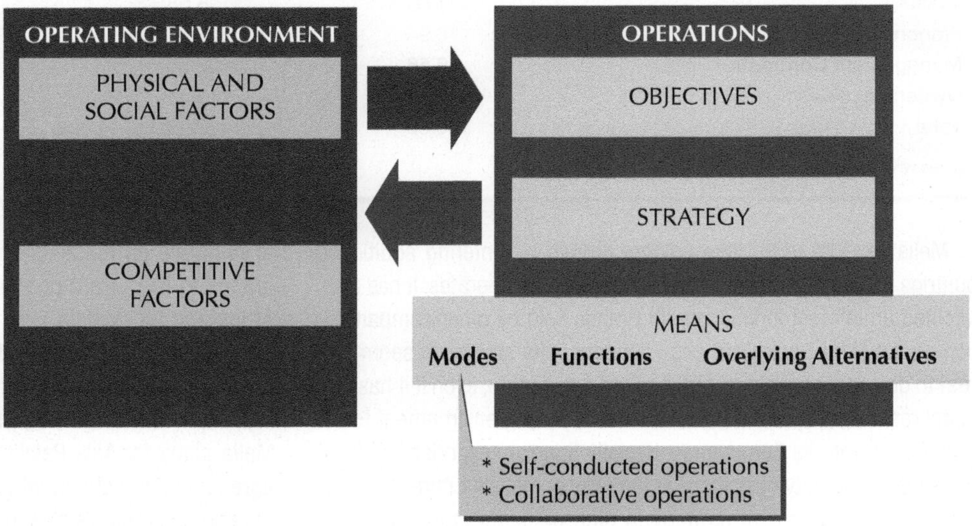

WHY EXPORT AND IMPORT MAY NOT SUFFICE

15-1 Comprehend why export and import may not suffice for companies' achievement of IB objectives

Companies may find more advantages to locate production in foreign countries than export to them. The advantages occur under six conditions:

1. When production abroad is cheaper than at home
2. When transportation costs are too high for moving goods or services internationally
3. When companies lack domestic capacity
4. When products and services need to be altered substantially to gain sufficient consumer demand abroad
5. When governments inhibit the import of foreign products
6. When buyers prefer products originating from a particular country

FIGURE 15.2 Foreign Expansions: Alternative Operating Modes

A firm may choose to operate globally either through equity arrangements (e.g., wholly owned operations or joint ventures) or through non-equity arrangements (e.g., licensing). Exporting operations are from production in the home country, while all other modes entail production in foreign locations. The modes listed in the lavender area at the bottom right are collaborative arrangements. Note that, in any given location, a firm can conduct operations in multiple modes.

*Joint ventures may also be non-equity, but equity joint ventures are by far the more common.

PRODUCTION OWNERSHIP	PRODUCTION LOCATION Home country	 Foreign country
Equity arrangements	a. Exporting	a. Wholly owned operations b. Partially owned with remainder widely held c. Joint ventures* d. Equity alliances
Non-equity arrangements		a. Licensing b. Franchising c. Management contracts d. Turnkey operations

WHEN IT'S CHEAPER TO PRODUCE ABROAD

Although companies may offer products or services desired by consumers abroad, producing them in their home markets may be too expensive. For example, Turkey has been a growing market for automobiles. However, it is generally less expensive to produce the vehicles in Turkey than to export them there because the country's skilled laborers and sophisticated engineers cost less and are willing to work more days per year and longer hours per day than workers in many home countries. Thus, some automakers and parts suppliers have established Turkish production to serve that market.[3]

WHEN TRANSPORTATION COSTS TOO MUCH

CONCEPT CHECK

In Chapter 6 (page 155), we explain the concept of nontradable goods—products and services that are seldom practical to export because of high transportation costs.

Transportation costs make some products and services impractical to export. Generally, these costs increase with distance. The higher they are relative to production costs, the harder for companies to develop viable export markets. For instance, the international transportation cost for a soft drink is usually a high percentage of the production cost, so a sales price would have to be too high to develop much of an export market. However, products such as watches have low transportation costs relative to production costs, so watch manufacturers lose few sales through exporting. The result is that companies such as Rolex and Seiko export watches from Switzerland and Japan, respectively, into the markets where they sell them.

WHEN DOMESTIC CAPACITY ISN'T ENOUGH

Excess home-country capacity
- usually favors exporting rather than direct investment,
- may lead to competitive exports because of declining unit costs.

A company with excess capacity may export effectively as long as the excess exists. In fact, its average cost of production per unit usually falls as it uses more of its capacity, such as by selling abroad, because of spreading fixed costs over more sales units. But this cost decrease continues only as long as there is unused capacity. Volkswagen, for instance, located its first plant to build the new Beetle at its Mexican facilities, which served global markets. When demand pushed that plant toward capacity, Volkswagen built a second plant in Europe to serve the markets there, thus freeing Mexican capacity to serve nearby markets while reducing transport costs for European sales.[4]

WHEN PRODUCTS AND SERVICES NEED ALTERING

Product alterations for foreign markets
- require additional investment,
- may lead to foreign production of the products.

Altering products to gain sufficient sales in a foreign market requires firms to make an additional investment, such as adding an assembly line to put automobile steering wheels on the right as well as on the left. As long as they must make an investment to run an added assembly line, they may place it near the market they wish to serve.

The more a product must be altered for foreign markets, the more likely some production will shift abroad. Whirlpool finds that most U.S. washing machine demand is for top-loading, large-capacity units using 110 electrical voltage, whereas most European demand is for smaller capacity front-loaders using 220 volts.[5] Given the differences in preference, Whirlpool produces in both the United States and Europe.

WHEN TRADE RESTRICTIONS HINDER IMPORTS

CONCEPT CHECK

In Chapter 8 (pages 202–203), we explain why governments are reciprocally reducing trade restrictions. Nevertheless, exporters still face regulatory restrictions, of which some encourage them to produce abroad.

Despite reductions in import barriers, many barriers still exist. As a result, companies may need to produce in a foreign country if they are to sell there. For instance, many auto companies manufacture or assemble in India because of its high duty on fully built imported cars.[6]

Managers must view import barriers along with other factors, such as the market size of the country imposing the barriers and the needed scale of production technology. For example, import trade restrictions have been highly influential in enticing automobile producers to locate in Brazil's large market. Similar restrictions by Central American countries have been ineffective because of their small markets. However, Central American import barriers on products requiring lower amounts of capital investment for production, such as pharmaceuticals, have successfully enticed direct investment because these industries can be efficient with smaller-scale technologies and markets.

Regional or bilateral trade agreements may also attract direct investment because they create expanded markets that may justify larger scale production.

WHEN COUNTRY OF ORIGIN BECOMES AN ISSUE

Consumers sometimes prefer goods produced in certain countries because of

- nationalism,
- a belief that these products are better,
- a fear that foreign-made goods may not be delivered on time.

Consumers' preference to buy goods from certain countries (perhaps preferring domestic products because of nationalism) constrain production location choices.[7] They may also believe goods from certain countries are superior, like German cars and Italian fashion.[8] They may further fear that service and replacement parts for imported products will be more difficult to obtain. As a result, Australia and the United States are two countries that require country-of-origin labels on many products so that consumers may include this information when making their buying decisions.[9] Finally, companies using just-in-time manufacturing systems favor nearby suppliers who can deliver quickly and reliably. In any of these cases, companies may find advantages in placing production near to where their output will best be accepted.

WHY AND HOW DO COMPANIES MAKE WHOLLY OWNED FDI

15-2 Explain why and how companies make wholly owned foreign direct investments

In situations where exporting is not feasible and companies, nevertheless, wish to tap foreign opportunities, they may choose to hold equity in operations abroad or contract other companies to produce or provide services on their behalf. In this section, we discuss the reasons and methods for these two alternatives. Note that Figure 15.2 distinguishes equity versus non-equity operations as well as wholly owned operations versus partially owned operations abroad.

REASONS FOR WHOLLY OWNED FOREIGN DIRECT INVESTMENT

Generally, the greater percentage of equity a company has, the greater its ability to control decisions. However, if the remainder of equity is widely held, a company may sometimes be able to effectively control with even a minority interest. Nevertheless, because governments often protect minority owners, a company may be unable to control if it lacks 100 percent ownership. The desire for control through wholly owned FDI has four explanations: *market failure, internalization theory, appropriability theory,* and *freedom to pursue global objectives.*

Market Failure Collaboration is appealing as an operating mode because a firm may reduce its liability of foreignness if it teams with a company well versed in a host country's environments and institutions. But this works only if an environmentally knowledgeable potential associate is also adequately equipped to deal efficiently with the entry company's technology and is willing to partner on acceptable terms.[10] Otherwise there is a market failure in finding an acceptable collaborator. The entering company must manage the activities itself within its own management structure (known as an *internal hierarchy*) if it perceives that it has sufficient operating advantages to overcome its liability of foreignness.

Internalization **Internalization** is control through self-handling of operations.[11] The concept comes from *transactions cost theory,* which holds that companies should seek the lower cost between self-handling of operations and contracting another party to do so for them. Self-handling may reduce costs for the following four reasons:

1. *Different operating units within the same company are likely to share a common corporate culture, which expedites communications.* Executives have concluded that a lack of trust, common terminology, and common knowledge are major obstacles to successful collaboration.[12]
2. *The company can use its own managers, who understand and are committed to carry out its objectives.* When GE acquired a controlling interest in the Hungarian company Tungsram, it was able to expedite control and changes because it put GE managers in key positions.[13]

3. *The company can avoid protracted negotiations with another company on such matters as partner responsibilities and how each will be compensated for contributions.* Otherwise negotiations may go on for years, with no guarantee that agreements will be reached.[14]
4. *The company can avoid possible enforcement problems.* Such companies as L'Occitane and Burberry's had to fight licensed manufacturers from selling production overruns to non-prestige distributors, which cheapened their brand images.[15]

Companies may want control through FDI to lessen the chance of improving competitors' capabilities.

Appropriability The explanation for denying rivals access to resources is the **appropriability theory**.[16] Companies are reluctant to transfer vital resources—capital, patents, trademarks, and management know-how—to another organization for fear of their competitive position being undermined. The fear of turning over strategically important know-how has led Germany's Faber-Castell to manufacture abroad only where it can own its factories.[17] Nevertheless, this does not imply that ownership is the only mechanism to avoid appropriability.[18] Nor does this imply that no transfer of know-how to another firm takes place. In fact, such transfer improves suppliers' efficiency, and companies use formal and informal mechanisms to speed and improve the comprehension of transferred knowledge.[19] At the same time, companies are less concerned about appropriability of non-strategic than of strategic resources. For instance, Coca-Cola collaborates with partners all over the world, but it steadfastly refuses to collaborate in concentrate production because its formula is too critical to the company's competitive viability.

CONCEPT CHECK

In Chapter 12 (pages 305–307), we explain the difference between a global and a local responsiveness strategy.

Freedom to Pursue a Global Strategy A wholly owned foreign operation permits a company to more easily participate in a global strategy. For instance, a U.S. company owning 100 percent of its Brazilian operation might be able to take actions that, although suboptimizing Brazilian performance, could deal more effectively with competitors and customers globally, such as by decreasing prices to an industrial customer in Brazil to gain that customer's business in Germany. Or it might standardize its product to gain global cost savings even though this loses some sales in Brazil. But if the company shared ownership in Brazil, its partners would balk at such practices.

ACQUISITION VERSUS GREENFIELD

Companies acquire FDI by transferring abroad financial and/or other tangible or intangible assets. They can either acquire an interest in an existing operation or make a greenfield (start-up) investment. The reasons for each are discussed below.

The advantages of acquiring an existing operation include

- gaining vital resources that are otherwise hard to develop,
- making financing easier at times,
- adding no further capacity to the market,
- avoiding start-up problems.

Acquisition A company may invest abroad via acquisition to obtain some vital resource that may otherwise be slow or difficult to secure.[20] Let's say a company acquires knowledgeable personnel that it cannot easily hire at a good price on its own[21]—or perhaps it could hire them, but lacks experience in managing them effectively. For instance, some Russian companies with good scientific inventions and innovative products have expanded internationally to acquire management that is experienced in transforming innovation into successful product sales.[22] Acquisitions also allow a company to gain an existing organization that has experience in coordinating functions such as product development, production, and marketing.

In addition, a company may gain goodwill, brand identification, and access to distribution. Recently, much Chinese investment in the United States has been by acquisition, seemingly because of Chinese companies' desire to secure well-known brand names that will help them sell.[23]

There are also financial considerations. First, a company depending substantially on local financing may find local capital suppliers more willing to put money into a known ongoing operation than to invest in a new facility owned by a less familiar foreign enterprise. Second, a company may be able to buy facilities, particularly those of a poorly performing operation, for less than the cost of new operations when it perceives a capability of turning the poor performance around. For example, Brazil's José Batista Sobrinho (JBS), the world's largest meat company, bought U.S. companies Swift and Pilgrim's Pride at opportunistically low prices because they were in financial trouble.[24] Third, if a market does not justify added capacity, acquisition enables a firm to avoid the risk of depressed prices through overcapacity.

Finally, by buying a company, an investor avoids start-up inefficiencies and gets an immediate cash flow rather than tying up funds during construction and early operations.

Companies may choose greenfield expansion if

- host governments discourage acquisitions,
- it is easier to finance,
- available acquisitions are performing poorly,
- personnel in acquiring and acquired firms may not work well together.

Making Greenfield Investments Foreign companies may face local roadblocks to acquisitions. For example, host governments may want more competitors in the market because of fearing market dominance. In addition, a foreign company may find that development banks prefer to finance new operations because they create new jobs.

Acquisitions often don't succeed.[25] First, a potential acquisition may be performing poorly, thus the reasons for the poor performance may make it difficult to turn around. It may have personnel and labor relations problems, ill will toward its products and brands, and inefficient or poorly located facilities. Second, managers in the acquiring and acquired companies may not work well together because of different management styles and organizational cultures or because of conflicts over decision-making authority.[26] For instance, after acquiring IBM's PC division, Lenovo had to overcome cultural differences between its Chinese and U.S. managers (e.g., the former thought the Americans talked even when having nothing to say, and the latter disapproved of publicly shaming latecomers to meetings).[27]

Leasing We saw in our opening case that Meliá operates extensively by leasing hotels. This mode is much like an acquisition, but one that forgoes the need to invest. While common in the hospitality industry, it is not common in others. Although companies in other industries might lease certain assets abroad—computers, vehicles, buildings, aircraft—such arrangements are quite different from leasing an entire operating facility.

WHY COMPANIES COLLABORATE

15-3 Ascertain why companies collaborate in international markets

Companies collaborate (use alliances that are often called *strategic alliances*) abroad for much of the same reasons they do so domestically. However, there are some reasons specific to international operations. Figure 15.3 shows both the general and internationally specific reasons for collaborative arrangements, which we now discuss.

GENERAL MOTIVES FOR COLLABORATIVE ARRANGEMENTS

Both domestically and internationally, companies collaborate to spread and reduce costs, enable them to specialize in their competencies, avoid competition, secure vertical and horizontal links, and gain knowledge.

FIGURE 15.3 Collaborative Arrangements and International Objectives

A company may enter into an international collaborative arrangement for the same reasons that it does so domestically (e.g., to spread costs). In other cases, it may enter into a collaborative arrangement to meet objectives that are specific to its foreign-expansion strategies (e.g., to diversify geographically).

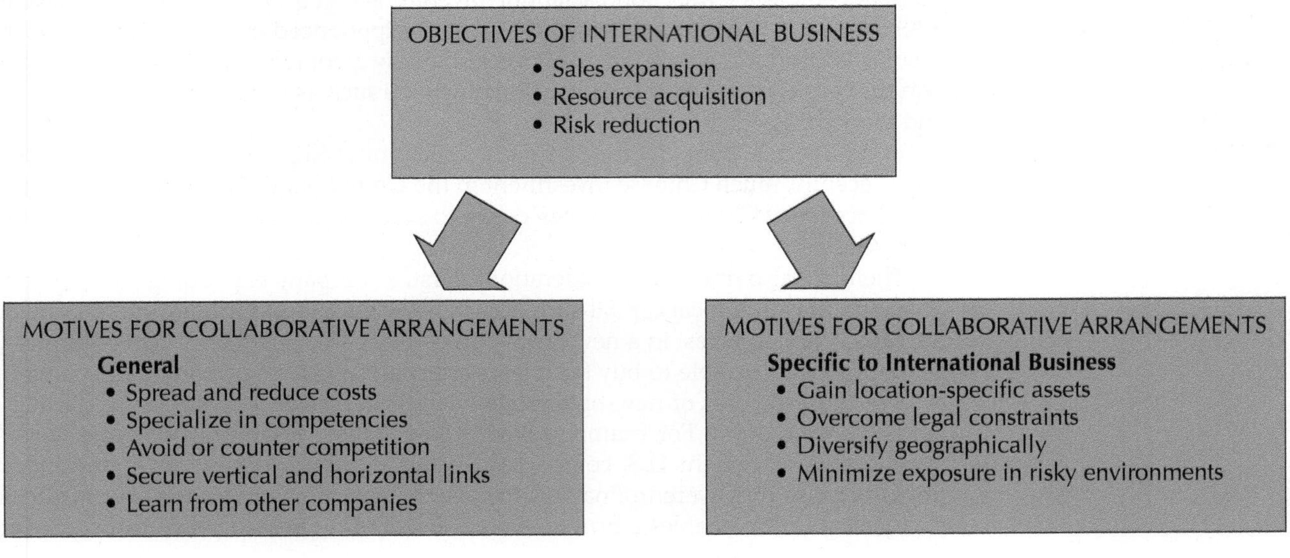

OBJECTIVES OF INTERNATIONAL BUSINESS
• Sales expansion
• Resource acquisition
• Risk reduction
MOTIVES FOR COLLABORATIVE ARRANGEMENTS
General
• Spread and reduce costs
• Specialize in competencies
• Avoid or counter competition
• Secure vertical and horizontal links
• Learn from other companies
MOTIVES FOR COLLABORATIVE ARRANGEMENTS
Specific to International Business
• Gain location-specific assets
• Overcome legal constraints
• Diversify geographically
• Minimize exposure in risky environments

Sometimes it's cheaper to get another company to handle work, especially
- at small volume,
- when the other company has excess capacity.

To Spread and Reduce Costs Producing and selling incur fixed costs. At a small volume of business, contracting to another firm rather than self-handling may be cheaper because of spreading the fixed costs to more than one company. Further, this can prevent the company entering a foreign market from having to incur fixed costs and longer delays for start-up and receipt of cash flows.

Companies may lack resources to "go it alone"—especially small and young ones.[28] By pooling efforts, they may be able to undertake activities that otherwise would be beyond their means. But large companies may also benefit when the cost of development and/or investment is very high. Disney's theme park in Hong Kong cost so much to develop that Disney and the Hong Kong government share ownership and expenses.[29]

One of the fastest collaborative growth areas has been for projects too large, both in capital and technical-resource needs, for any single firm to handle, such as new aircraft and communication systems. From such an arrangement's inception, different firms (sometimes from different countries) take on the cost and risk of developing different components. Then a lead company buys the components from the companies. A good example is development of the Boeing 787 aircraft, which involved companies from around the globe.

Granting asset or operating rights to another company can yield income when the asset or function does not fit the yielding company's strategic priority based on its competencies.

To Specialize in Competencies The **resource-based view** of the firm holds that each company has a unique combination of competencies. A company may improve its performance by concentrating on those activities that best fit its competencies, depending on other firms to supply it with products, services, or support activities in which it is less competent. However, a collaborative arrangement has a limited time frame, which may allow a company to exploit a particular product, asset, or technology at a later date if its core competencies change.

By banding together, companies may move faster, raise profits, and fight larger competitors.

To Avoid or Counter Competition When markets are too small to accommodate many competitors, companies may band together so as not to compete. Companies may also combine resources to combat competitors (e.g., Sony and Samsung combined resources to move faster in the development of LCD technology).[30] Or they may simply collude to raise everyone's profits. For example, Canpotex, a group of Canadian companies accounting for more than a quarter of the world's potash market, joined together so as not to compete on export sales.[31] (Only a few countries take substantial actions against the collusion of competitors.)[32]

Allying to gain vertical and horizontal links may enable companies to fill competency gaps, reduce costs, and deal more effectively with customers and suppliers.

To Secure Vertical and Horizontal Links Vertical integration provides potential cost savings as well as supply and sales assurances. However, companies may lack competences or resources necessary to own and manage the full value chain of activities, thus they ally themselves with other companies to handle their gaps. Horizontal links may provide economies of scope in distribution, such as by offering a full line of products, such as increasing the sales per fixed cost of customer visits. For example, in many parts of the world Avon representatives market such products as books and crayons in addition to the company's cosmetics fare. An example of gains from both vertical and horizontal links involves a group of small and medium-sized Argentine furniture manufacturers. By allying horizontally, they pool resources to gain manufacturing efficiencies. By allying vertically, they deal more effectively in securing sales and supplies abroad.[33]

A company can improve its competence by learning from partners.

To Gain Knowledge Many companies pursue collaborative arrangements to learn about a partner's technology, operating methods, or home market so as to improve their competitiveness.[34] Sometimes each partner can learn from the other, a motive driving joint ventures between U.S. and European winemakers—such as the Opus One Winery by Constellation Brands' Robert Mondavi from the United States and Baron Philippe de Rothschild from France that combined old world and new world wine styles.[35]

INTERNATIONAL MOTIVES FOR COLLABORATIVE ARRANGEMENTS

In this section, we continue discussing why companies enter into collaborative arrangements, covering those reasons that apply only to international operations. Reasons include gaining location-specific assets, overcoming legal constraints, diversifying geographically, and minimizing risk exposure.

Local companies may more easily access competitively important country-specific knowledge than foreign companies can.

To Gain Location-Specific Assets Cultural, political, competitive, and economic differences among countries create barriers for firms operating abroad. Those ill-equipped to handle the differences may seek help through collaboration with local firms. When Walmart first entered the Japanese market on its own, it gave up after having disappointing sales. It returned later with a Japanese partner, Seiyu, which was more familiar with Japanese tastes and rules for opening new stores. In fact, most foreign companies in Japan need to collaborate with Japanese firms that can help in securing distribution and a competent workforce—two assets that are difficult for MNEs to gain on their own there.

Legal factors may
- prohibit certain operating forms, such as wholly owned foreign facilities,
- favor locally owned firms.

To Overcome Governmental Constraints Recall from the opening case that in centrally planned economies (e.g., China and Cuba) Meliá cannot own its hotels, so it must collaborate with local organizations. In addition, nearly all countries limit foreign ownership in some sectors. India, for example, sets maximum foreign percentage ownership in an array of industries.[36]

Government procurement policies also sometimes lead to collaboration because they favor bids that include national companies. For instance, Taiwan does this with purchases by the state enterprise monopoly, Taiwan Power (Tai Power).[37]

Collaboration may hinder nonassociated companies from pirating an asset.

Protecting Assets Many countries provide little protection for intellectual property rights such as trademarks, patents, and copyrights unless authorities are prodded consistently. On one hand, companies are more likely to transfer rights to countries with strong protection.[38] On the other hand, some rights can be seized abroad, especially trademarks, even though a company has not purposely transferred them. To prevent pirating of these proprietary assets, companies sometimes collaborate with local companies, which can more effectively monitor the local market and deal with authorities.

For instance, some countries provide protection only if the internationally registered asset is exploited locally within a specified period. If not, then the first organization that does so gains the right to it. In some cases, local citizens, known as *trademark squatters*, register rights to the not-yet-exploited trademarks, then negotiate a transfer to the original owners when they do try to enter the market. One Russian company registered over 300 foreign trademarks, including that of Starbucks. Foreign companies then have to pay to regain their rights or go through lengthy and expensive court proceedings.[39] Or they may enter under a different name. Burger King sells under the Hungry Jack brand in Australia for this reason.[40]

CONCEPT CHECK

In Chapter 13 (page 339), we explained the differences between and reasons for pursuit of a geographic diversification versus concentration strategy.

To Diversify Geographically For a company wishing to diversify geographically, collaboration offers a faster initial means of entering multiple markets because other companies contribute part of the resources. Arrangements will be less appealing for companies that have ample resources for such extension.

Collaborative arrangements reduce risk by allowing for greater asset-spreading among countries.

To Minimize Risk Exposure A way to lessen a company's international political and economic risk is to minimize its assets located abroad. This may be possible through collaboration because other organizations provide part of the assets. Further, if the company's foreign assets are spread among countries, there is less risk because of lower chance that they will all encounter similar adversity at the same time.

Local partners may also be effective at thwarting governmental takeover of assets. Further, partnerships with other foreign companies, especially from different countries, may inhibit host governments' takeovers or enactment of discriminatory measures because each can elicit support from its home government.

FORMS OF AND CHOICE OF COLLABORATIVE ARRANGEMENTS

15-4 Compare and contrast modes of and considerations for selecting an international collaborative arrangement

CONCEPT CHECK

In Chapter 1 (page 17), we defined the different forms of collaborative arrangements.

Now that we have discussed reasons for collaborating in IB, we shall first discuss some factors to consider when choosing among collaborative forms, also known as alliances. Then we shall describe each of the forms.

SOME CONSIDERATIONS IN CHOOSING A FORM

Each operating mode brings both advantages and disadvantages.

Trade-Offs and Limitations Recall from Figure 15.2 that foreign operating modes differ in the amount of resources a company commits and the proportion of the resources it locates abroad. In this respect, keep in mind that there are *trade-offs.* A decision, let's say, to take no ownership abroad, such as by licensing another company to handle foreign production, may reduce exposure to political risk. However, learning about that environment will be slow, delaying (perhaps permanently) the ability to reap the full profits from producing and selling the product abroad.

Companies have a wider choice of operating mode when they hold unique and needed capabilities.

Furthermore, a company may be limited in entering a market with the operating mode it prefers. Governmental actions and potential partners have a great deal to say. However, if a company has a desired, unique, difficult-to-duplicate resource, it is in a much better position to choose its preferred operating form and to increase its compensation therein.

Terms differ for alliances depending on their purposes, whether they extend cooperation vertically or horizontally, and whether they involve competitors.

What's the Purpose?: Alliance Types Alliances vary by companies' objectives and by where they place them in their value chains. These variances have led to terms that describe different types. *Scale alliances* aim to provide efficiency for partners by pooling similar operations, such as airlines have done by combining their lounges. In a *link alliance,* firms use their partners' complementary resources to expand into a new business.[41] Nokia did this to develop and market cellular phones.[42] A *vertical alliance* connects firms in different links of their value chains, such as a food franchiser with a franchisee. A *horizontal alliance,* such as the Mexican joint venture between Mercedes and Infiniti, enables each partner to extend its product offerings (in this case, a new compact car) on the same level of the value chain.[43] **Coopetition**, such as the Mercedes-Infiniti example, refers to collaboration while competing (i.e., although these partners are closely collaborating at every development stage, their end products will be different and competitive with each other).[44]

Companies' experience and assets in a foreign country influence their choices of operating mode when introducing new products or businesses.

Prior Company Expansion Each time a company adds products or businesses that it wishes to internationalize, it must decide on an operating form. If it already has operations (especially wholly owned ones) in a foreign country, some of the advantages of collaboration are no longer as important. It knows how to operate within that country and may have excess plant or human resource capacity it can use for new production or sales. At the same time, companies' performance experience (especially recent experience) with particular operating modes influences their choice of entry modes.[45] However, much depends on the compatibility between existing foreign operations and the new ones the company is planning abroad. The more the similarity, the more that existing ones will influence decisions.

Collaboration in foreign operations implies less control and a sharing of profits.

Compensation Collaboration also implies sharing revenues and knowledge—an important consideration when profit potentials are high. How to divide revenue is not clear-cut because many variables influence the outcome. Certainly, the bargaining power of the collaborative partners is important in any agreement, but such factors as government mandates, partners' perception of risk, and competitive constraints are all important.[46] Further, the mode of collaboration guides normal practices. As we discuss the different modes, we will introduce some of these practices.

POINT

Should Countries Limit Foreign Control of Key Industries?

YES I believe they should, because a key industry affects a very large segment of the economy by virtue of its size or influence on other sectors. I'm not talking about either foreign control of small investments or noncontrolling interest in large investments. If countries need foreign firms' resources—technology,

COUNTERPOINT

Should Countries Limit Foreign Control of Key Industries?

NO The passionate arguments against foreign control of key industries don't convince me that such control leads to corporate decisions that are any different from those local companies would make. Nor do they convince me that limits on foreign ownership are in the best interests of people in host countries.

capital, export markets, branded products, and so on—they can get them by requiring collaborations without ceding control to foreigners. In turn, the foreign companies can still achieve their objectives without control, such as gaining access to markets through collaboration.

Of course each country should and does define key industries. For instance, the United States prohibits foreign control of television and radio stations and domestic transportation because of security concerns. Canada limits foreign control of sectors that are sensitive to maintenance of its culture. Chile prohibits foreign investment in its economically dominant copper industry because of negative experiences with past foreign control therein.

The rationale for protecting key industries is supported by history, which shows that home governments have used powerful companies to influence policies in the foreign countries where they operate. During colonial periods, firms such as Levant and the British East India Company often acted as the political arm of their home governments.

More recently, governments, especially the United States, have pressured their companies to leave certain areas and to prohibit their subsidiaries from doing business with certain countries, even though the prohibition is counter to the interests of the countries where the subsidiaries were located.[47]

At the same time, some companies are so powerful that they can influence their home-country governments to intercede on their behalf. Probably the most famous example was United Fruit Company (UFC) in so-called banana republics, which persuaded the United States to overthrow governments to protect its investments. Miguel Angel Asturias, a Nobel laureate in literature, referred to UFC's head as the "Green Pope" who "lifts a finger and a ship starts or stops. He says a word and a republic is bought. He sneezes and a president . . . falls. . . . He rubs his behind on a chair and a revolution breaks out."[48]

Whenever a company is controlled from abroad, its decisions can be made abroad. Such control means that corporate management abroad can decide such factors as personnel staffing, export prices, and the retention and payout of profits. These decisions might cause different rates of expansion than would occur with local control as well as possible plant closings, sometimes with subsequent employment disruption.

Finally, by withholding resources or allowing strikes, MNEs may affect other local industries adversely. In essence, the MNE looks after its global interests, which may not coincide with what is best for an operation in a given country.

Certainly, companies make strategic global decisions at headquarters, but typically they depend on a good deal of local advice beforehand. Further, MNEs staff their foreign subsidiaries mainly with nationals of the countries where they operate, and these nationals make most routine decisions.

Regardless of the decision-makers' or companies' nationalities, managers decide based on what they think is best for their firms' business, rather than based on some home-country or local socioeconomic agenda. At the same time, their decisions have to adhere to local laws and consider the views of their local stakeholders. Of course, MNEs sometimes make locally unpopular decisions, but so do local companies. In the meantime, governments can and do enact laws that apply to both local and international companies, and these laws can ensure that companies act in the so-called local interest.

Although preventing foreign control of key industries may be well intentioned, the resultant local control may lead to the protection of inefficient performance. Further, the key-industry argument appeals to emotions rather than reason. That's why arguments in the United States for security make little sense on close examination. Although foreign propaganda through foreign ownership of radio and television stations is the rationale for ownership restrictions, there are no such restrictions on foreign ownership of U.S. newspapers, magazines, and material appearing on the Internet. (Is this because people who read newspapers, magazines, and Internet articles are presumed to be less swayed by propaganda?) The protection of U.S. domestic transportation for security reasons is a sham, just to protect domestic firms and their national employees, such as the shipbuilding industry and maritime employees. For instance, U.S. merchant flagships must employ only U.S. citizens as crews because of ships' vulnerability to bombs in U.S. waters, but foreign flag carriers (such as cruise ships) regularly use U.S. ports, while foreigners can join the U.S. Navy.

The banana-republic arguments are outdated and go back to **dependencia theory**, which holds that emerging economies have practically no power in their dealings with MNEs.[49] More recent **bargaining school theory** states that the terms of a foreign investor's operations depend on how much the investor and host country need each other.[50] In effect, companies need countries because of their markets and resources, while countries need MNEs because of their technology, capital, access to foreign markets, and expertise. Through a bargaining process, they come to an agreement or contract that stipulates what the MNE can and cannot do.

I completely disagree that either countries or companies can necessarily gain the same through collaborative agreements as through FDI. Although collaborative agreements are often preferable, there are company and country advantages from foreign-controlled operations. For example, with wholly owned operations, companies are less concerned about developing competitors, so they are more willing to transfer essential and valuable technology abroad.[51]

LICENSING

Licensing agreements may be
- exclusive or nonexclusive,
- used for patents, copyrights, trademarks, and other intangible property.

The rights for use of intangible property/assets may be for an *exclusive license* (the licensor can give rights to no other company for the asset over a specified geographic area for a specified period of time) or a nonexclusive one.

The U.S. Internal Revenue Service classifies intangible property into five categories:

1. Patents, inventions, formulas, processes, designs, patterns
2. Copyrights for literary, musical, or artistic compositions
3. Trademarks, trade names, brand names
4. Franchises, licenses, contracts
5. Methods, programs, procedures, systems

Usually, the licensor is obliged to furnish sufficient information and assistance, and the licensee is obliged to exploit the rights effectively and pay compensation to the licensor.

The motive for licensing is often economic, such as to gain faster start-up, lower costs, or access to additional resources.

Major Motives for Licensing A product or process may affect only part of a company's business, and then only for a limited time. In such a situation, the company may foresee insufficient sales to warrant establishing or continuing its own manufacturing and sales facilities. Meanwhile, a licensee may be able to produce and sell at a low cost and within a short start-up time.

For industries in which technological changes are frequent and affect many products, companies in various countries often exchange technology or other intangible property rather than compete with each other on every product in every market—an arrangement known as **cross-licensing**. An example is Google (U.S.) and Samsung (Korea) entering a cross-licensing agreement for access to each other's patents.[52]

Payment Considerations The amount and type of payment for licensing arrangements vary, as each contract is negotiated on its own merits. For instance, the value to the licensee will be greater if perceived potential sales are high. These depend, in turn, on such factors as the size of the sales territory and the longevity of the asset's market value.

Putting a Price on Intangible Assets Valuing partners' contributions and rewards is complex and negotiable. Companies commonly agree on a "front-end" payment to cover technology transfer costs. Licensors of technology do this because there is usually more involved than simply transferring *explicit* knowledge, such as through documents. The move requires the transfer of *tacit* knowledge, such as through engineering, consultation, and adaptation. To understand the difference between the two, think of giving a novice cook only a recipe for a chicken pot pie (explicit knowledge) versus going with the novice cook to choose a chicken, feel and smell produce, and work together on chopping ingredients and rolling out dough (tacit knowledge). Of course, the license of some assets, such as copyrights or brand names, has much lower transfer costs.

Intangible assets may be old or new, obsolete or still in use in the home market when a company licenses them. Many companies transfer rights to assets at an early or even a developmental stage so products hit different markets simultaneously. This is important when selling to the same industrial customers in different countries and when global advertising campaigns can be effective. On one hand, a licensee may be willing to pay more for a new intangible asset because it may have a longer useful life. On the other hand, a licensee may be willing to pay less because of its untested market value.

Licensing to subsidiaries is common because of parent and subsidiary legal separation and the potential effect on taxes.

Licensing to Subsidiaries Although we think of licensing among unassociated companies, companies commonly license to their foreign-owned operations. One reason is that operations abroad, even if 100 percent owned by the parent, are usually subsidiaries, which are legally separate companies. As such, taxes may differ depending on whether funds transferred to the parent are in the form of dividends versus royalties. When a company owns less than 100 percent, a separate licensing arrangement also helps compensate the licensor for contributions beyond capital and managerial resources.

FRANCHISING

Franchising includes providing an intangible asset (usually a trademark) and a continual infusion of necessary assets.

In franchising, a specialized form of licensing, the parties act almost as a vertically integrated company because they are interdependent and each creates part of the product or service that ultimately reaches the consumer.

Many types of products, companies, and countries participate in franchising.

Today, franchising is mostly associated with U.S. fast-food operations, although many international franchisors are from other countries and in many other sectors, such as Meliá's hotel franchises discussed in the opening case. To illustrate how diverse franchising can be, consider the Danish company Cryos International, which franchises human sperm and egg banks in many countries.

Franchisors once depended on trade shows and costly foreign travel to promote their expansion. While such methods are still important, especially for young and fairly unknown franchising operations, the Internet gives companies another channel to exchange information.

Franchise Organization A franchisor may deal directly with individual franchisees abroad or set up a *master franchise* that has rights to open outlets on its own or to develop subfranchisees in the country or region. Subfranchisees pay royalties to the master franchisee, which then remits payments to the franchisor. Companies are most apt to use a master franchise system when they are not confident about evaluating potential individual franchisees and when their direct oversight and control would be too expensive.[53]

Franchisors face a dilemma:

- Inadequacy of local supplies may hamper global product uniformity.
- The more global standardization, the less acceptance in the foreign country.
- The more adjustment to the foreign country, the less the franchisor is needed.

Operational Modifications Franchising success generally depends on product and service standardization, high identification through promotion, and effective cost controls. The latter two are pretty straightforward, but transferring the home country's product and service, especially for food franchising, is often difficult, first, because of local supplies. McDonald's, for instance, had to build a plant to make hamburger buns in the United Kingdom, while in Thailand it had to help farmers develop potato production.[54] Second, foreign country taste preferences may differ from those in the home country—even within regions of large countries. However, the more adjustments made for the host consumers' different tastes, the less a franchisor has to offer a potential franchisee.

MANAGEMENT CONTRACTS

Foreign management contracts are used primarily when the foreign company can manage better than the owners.

An organization may pay for managerial assistance under a management contract when it believes another can manage its operation more efficiently than it can, usually because the contractor has industry-specific capabilities. Such contracts are common when host governments want foreign expertise, but do not want foreign ownership. In turn, the management company receives income without having to make a capital investment. For example, contracts are popular in the hotel industry. (Recall the Meliá case.) In essence, host-country real estate owners may have good hotel locations, but know little about running a hotel. At the same time, many hotel chains prefer management contracts because they perceive too much risk from property ownership abroad.[55]

TURNKEY OPERATIONS

Turnkey operations are

- most commonly performed by industrial-equipment, construction, and consulting companies,
- often performed for a governmental agency.

Companies handling turnkey operations are usually industrial-equipment manufacturers, construction companies, or consulting firms. Manufacturers also sometimes provide turnkey services when they are disallowed to invest. The customer for a turnkey operation is often a governmental agency. Recently, most large projects have been in those developing countries that are moving rapidly toward infrastructure development and industrialization.

Turnkey operations generally differ from other IB collaborations because they

- may be so large,
- depend on top-level governmental contacts,
- are often in very remote areas.

Contracting to Scale One characteristic setting turnkey business apart from most other IB operations is the size of most contracts, frequently for many billions of dollars. This means that a few very large companies—such as Vinci (France), Bechtel (U.S.), and Hochtief (Germany)—account for a significant market share. Recently, several Chinese firms have become major players. Some projects are so large that a consortium of turnkey operators handle them, such as for the Panama Canal's additional wider channel, led by Spain's Sacyr Vallehermoso. Often, smaller firms serve either as subcontractors for primary turnkey suppliers or specialize in a particular sector, such as the handling of hazardous waste.

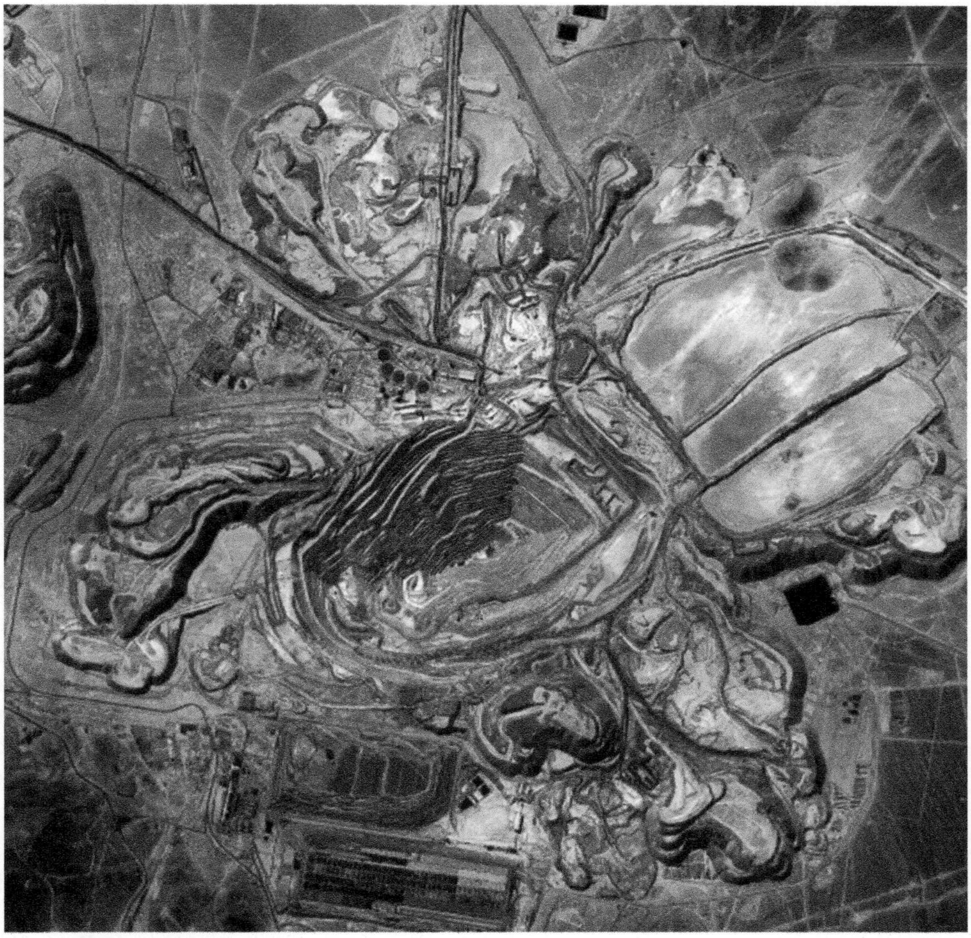

Aerial view of a Chilean copper mine built by Bechtel through a turnkey contract high in the Andes mountains.

Source: DigitalGlobe via Getty Images

Making Contacts The nature of these contracts places importance on hiring executives with top-level governmental contacts abroad, as well as on ceremony and building goodwill, such as opening a facility on a country's national holiday or getting a head of state to inaugurate a facility. Although public relations is important to gain contracts, other factors—price, financing, managerial and technological quality, experience, and reputation—are necessary to sell contracts of such magnitude.

Marshaling Resources Many turnkey contracts are in remote areas, necessitating massive housing construction and importation of personnel. Projects may involve building an entire infrastructure under the most adverse conditions, such as Bechtel's complex for Minera Escondida high in the Chilean Andes (see the adjacent photo) and connected by a 112-mile pipeline to a desalinization plant at the Pacific Ocean side of the Atacama Desert. So turnkey operators must have expertise in hiring people willing to work in remote areas for extended periods and in transporting and using supplies under very difficult conditions.

If a company has a unique capability, such as the latest refining technology, it will have little competition. As the production process becomes known, however, competition increases. Companies from developed countries have moved largely toward projects involving high technology, whereas those from such countries as China, India, Korea, and Turkey can compete better for conventional projects requiring low labor costs. The Chinese companies, China State Construction Engineering and Shanghai Construction Group, have worked on subway systems in Iran and Saudi Arabia, a railway line in Nigeria, a tourist complex in the Bahamas, an oil pipeline in Sudan, and office buildings in the United States.

JOINT VENTURES (JVs)

Joint venture ownership may vary by type of participants and the portion of ownership they hold.

Although usually thought of as 50/50 companies, JVs may nonetheless involve more than two companies and ones in which a partner owns more than 50 percent. For example, Flagship Ventures (U.S.), AstraZeneca (U.K.-Sweden), Nestlé Health Science (Switzerland), and Bayer CropScience (Germany) have joined together to develop health-care innovations.[56] When more than two organizations participate, the venture is sometimes called a **consortium**.

Possible Combinations Examples of the many combinations of JV partnerships include:

- Two companies from the same country joining together in a foreign market (e.g., NEC and Mitsubishi [Japan] in the United Kingdom)
- A foreign company joining with a local company (e.g., Barrick [Canada] and Zijin Mining Group in China)
- Companies from two or more countries establishing a joint venture in a third country (e.g., Mercedes-Benz [Germany] and Nissan [Japan] in Mexico)
- A private company and a local government forming a joint venture, or *mixed venture* (e.g., Mitsubishi [Japan] with the government-owned Exportadora de Sal in Mexico)
- A private company joining a government-owned company in a third country (e.g., BP Amoco [private British-U.S.] and Eni [government-owned Italian] in Egypt)

The more companies in the JV or any alliance, the more complex its management.

Development of the Boeing 787 (the Dreamliner) and the Airbus A380 were joint efforts among numerous companies from several countries.[57] The projects were difficult to control, and a delay or performance hitch by any participating company delayed the others and caused project problems. Figure 15.4 shows that as a company increases the number of partners and decreases its portion of equity, its ability to control that operation decreases.

EQUITY ALLIANCES

Equity alliances help solidify collaboration.

An **equity alliance** is a collaborative arrangement in which at least one of the companies takes an ownership position (almost always minority) in the other(s). For instance, the Port of Antwerp (Belgium) took a minority position in Essar Ports (India) when the two signed a

FIGURE 15.4 Collaborative Strategy and Complexity of Control

The more equity a firm puts into a collaborative arrangement, the more control it will likely have over the foreign operations conducted under the arrangement. Note that non-equity arrangements typically entail at least one and often several partners.

Source: Based on Shaker Zahra and Galal Elhagrasey, "Strategic Management of International Joint Ventures," *European Management Journal* 12:1 (March 1994): 83–93. Reprinted with permission of Elsevier.

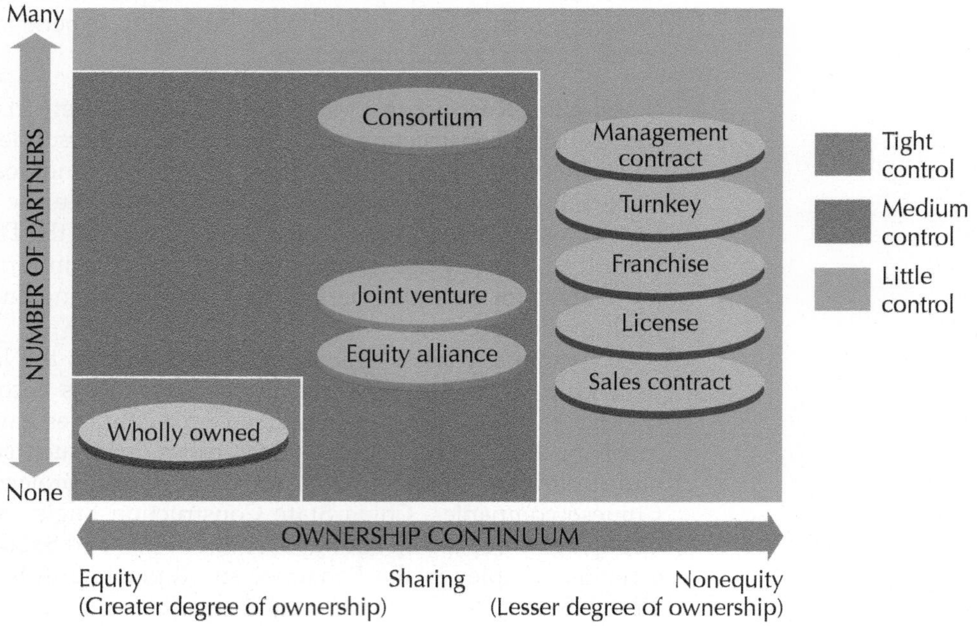

long-term alliance to mutually improve quality and productivity.[58] In some cases, each party takes an ownership in the other, such as occurred with Panama-based Copa and Colombia-based AeroRepublic (airlines).[59]

The purpose of the equity ownership is to solidify a collaborating contract, such as a supplier–buyer contract, so that it is more difficult to break—particularly if the ownership is large enough for the investing company to secure a board membership.

WHY COLLABORATIVE ARRANGEMENTS FAIL OR SUCCEED

15-5 Grasp major reasons why IB collaborative arrangements fail or succeed

All collaborative arrangement parties must be satisfied with performance; otherwise, the arrangement may fail.

REASONS FOR FAILURE

Situations change that lead partners to renegotiate in terms of objectives, responsibilities, ownership, performance criteria, or management structure. Despite renegotiation to restructure, many agreements break down because at least one partner becomes dissatisfied. Frequently, a partner buys out the other's interest and the operation continues as a wholly owned entity. In other breakups, companies agree to dissolve the arrangement.

The major strains on the arrangements are due to five factors:

- Relative importance to partners
- Divergent objectives
- Control problems
- Comparative contributions and appropriations
- Differences in culture

Partners' uneven attention to a collaborative arrangement is often due to their disparate sizes.

Relative Importance Partners may give uneven management attention to a collaborative arrangement. If things go wrong, the more active partner blames the less active partner for its lack of attention, while the latter blames the former for making poor decisions. Disparity in partners' sizes may cause a difference in attention. For example, a smaller partner may take more interest in the venture because it is using a larger portion of its resources therein.

Further, the smaller firm may be disadvantaged in fighting its bigger partner legally. For example, Igen, a small U.S. firm, licensed its technology to Boehringer Mannheim of Germany, whose sales were more than 100 times greater. When the two companies disagreed over royalty payments, Igen had to fight four years and spend the equivalent of a year's sales on legal fees before winning a settlement.[60] This example is unusual, however, because few small firms can or will fight a much larger company so effectively.

As partners' capabilities and strategies evolve, their collaborative objectives may change.

Divergent Objectives Partners' initial complementary objectives may evolve differently as a result of competitive forces and product dynamics. Thus, a partner may no longer perceive collaboration to be in its best interest. For instance, IBM partnered with Toshiba, but later it shifted its product line. At that point, it required a type of monitor with which Toshiba lacked expertise.[61] Further, one partner may want to reinvest earnings for growth while the other wants to receive dividends. Or one partner may want to expand the product line and sales territory while the other may see this as competition with its wholly owned operations (a point of disagreement between BP and its Russian partner, TNK).[62] If one partner wants to sell or buy from the venture, the other may disagree with the price.

"Who's in charge?" plagues collaboration despite all parties being held responsible.

Questions of Control Sharing assets with another company may generate confusion over control. Such confusion is rife with gray areas and may cause anxiety among employees. In a proposed JV between Merrill Lynch and UFJ, a Japanese senior manager queried, "Who is going to be in charge—a Japanese, an American, or both?"[63] Moreover, when companies license their logos and trademarks for use on products they do not make, they may lack the ability to discern and control quality. Pierre Cardin's licensing of its label for hundreds of products—from clothing to clocks to toilets—led to some poor-quality goods that hurt the image of the high-quality ones.[64]

In collaborative arrangements, even though control is ceded to one of the partners, both may be held responsible for problems. In a joint venture to make baby formula between the Israeli company Remedia and the German firm Humana Milchunion, Humana Milchunion's removal of vitamin B1 from the formula concentrate led to the deaths of three infants.[65] Remedia was jointly responsible even though it had not been notified of the removal.

If one partner perceives that the other is contributing too little or taking out too much, the collaboration may weaken.

Comparative Contributions and Appropriations Partners' relative capabilities may change, thus one partner may no longer contribute as much as was expected initially. In addition, one partner may suspect that the other is taking more from the operation than it is (particularly knowledge-based assets or key JV personnel). To counteract this appropriability, the suspicious firm may withhold information, eventually weakening the operation. In fact, there are many examples of companies "going it alone" after they no longer needed their partners—particularly if the purpose of the collaboration was to gain knowledge.

Differences in country and company cultures may cause one partner to be satisfied and the other dissatisfied.

Culture Clashes Both national and company cultural differences can affect the relationship between partners.

Differences in Country Cultures Managers and companies are affected by their national cultures, and collaborative arrangements bring them directly together. Although studies relating the longevity of joint ventures to partners' national cultural distance is inconclusive,[66] specific cultural characteristics can create dissention. For instance, preferences may vary in the method, timing, and frequency with which companies report on performance and whether they evaluate primarily on the operations' effect on shareholders or on stakeholders in general.[67] These differences may mean that one partner is satisfied while the other is not. Such a clash led to the dissolution of a joint venture between Danone and its Chinese government-owned partner because the latter put employment maximization ahead of efficiencies and profits.[68]

Trust is another factor. There are national differences that influence interactions with foreign partners. In fact, some companies don't like to collaborate with those of very different cultures.[69] Nevertheless, JVs from culturally distant countries can thrive when partners learn to deal with each other's differences.[70]

CONCEPT CHECK

In Chapter 2 (page 39), we discussed differences in trust among national cultures and explained that in high-trust cultures, the cost of doing business tends to be lower.

Differences in Company Cultures Similar company cultures aid companies' ability to communicate and transfer knowledge to each other, whereas collaborations can experience problems when these cultures differ.[71] For example, the joint venture between Japan's ANA and Malaysia's AirAsia broke up as the former wished to emphasize its culture of "meticulous service," whereas the latter had a culture of cutting costs.[72] One partner may be accustomed to internal managerial promotions while the other opens its searches to outsiders. One may use a participatory management style and the other an authoritarian style. One may be entrepreneurial, the other risk-averse. This is why many companies delay JV collaboration until they have had long-term positive experiences with each other, such as through distributorship or licensing arrangements which involve lower levels of commitment. In fact, there is evidence that a gradual increase in commitment, such as developing an alliance with a company before acquiring it, is a means of improving performance.[73] Of course, as with marriage, a good prior relationship between two companies does not guarantee a good match in a joint venture.[74]

HELPING COLLABORATIVE OPERATIONS SUCCEED

Despite our discussion on problems and failures of collaborative operations, we do not mean to imply that there are no success stories. There are. The JV between Xerox (U.S.) and Rank (U.K.) is a case in point: not only has it performed well for decades, it even has a JV in Japan with Fuji Photo, which has also performed well.

Aside from awareness of and adjustment to the pitfalls we have discussed, the following considerations help assure success when choosing among and managing operating forms:

- Fitting modes to country differences
- Finding and evaluating partners

- Negotiating agreements: The question of secrecy
- Controlling through contracts and trust
- Evaluating continually
- Adjusting the internal organization

Fitting Modes to Country Differences Country conditions influence the operating forms that best suit companies' IB operations. To begin with, regulations (such as prohibitions on 100 percent foreign-owned FDI) and opportunity differences (such as economic growth rates) mesh differently with companies' capabilities and strategies. Thus, choosing the best operating form for each country helps companies succeed.

Companies should make their highest commitments in terms of operating modes where markets are most attractive and best fit their competences and strategies.

A company should ordinarily commit more of its IB resources to those markets that are most attractive and fit best with its strategies and competence. The choice of operating mode directly affects this resource allocation inasmuch as different modes commit different levels of resources and different portions of those resources abroad. Figure 15.5 illustrates a matrix relating country attractiveness, a company's competitive strength per country, and operating forms. Step one in Figure 15.5 is for a company to evaluate countries' general attractiveness (such as high, medium, or low) irrespective of the company's fit with that country. Step 2 is to assess the company's competitive strength to fulfill its objectives (high, medium, or low) for each of the countries. By using results from the two steps to plot each country within the six sectors of the matrix, one has a visual description of preferred mode per country.

CONCEPT CHECK

In Chapter 13 (pages 333–335), we discussed how risk and opportunity differ among countries and how (pages 337–338) the choice of operating mode may reduce a company's risk.

Although such a matrix may serve to guide decision-making, managers must use it with caution. First, separating the attractiveness of a country from a company's position is often difficult; the country may seem attractive because it fits with the company. Second, some of the recommended actions take a defeatist attitude toward competitive capability. Many companies have built competitive strength in markets where they initially were weak competitively.

Finding and Evaluating Potential Partners Contracting with a satisfactory partner is significant for success in collaborative agreements. Managers can identify potential partners by monitoring journals, attending technical conferences, developing links with academic institutions—even through social acquaintances.[75]

Partner pairing should depend on mutual assessment of each other's resources, motivation, and compatibility.

FIGURE 15.5 Country Attractiveness/Company Strength Matrix

In a given scenario, a country in the upper left-hand corner may be a company's most attractive operating location. Why? Because its market is attractive and is compatible with the company's greatest competitive strength. Thus it favors the highest level of commitment (e.g., establishing a wholly owned subsidiary). A country in the upper right-hand corner also boasts an attractive market but poses a problem for a company whose competitive strengths don't quite match the opportunity (perhaps it has no experience in this particular market). It needn't forgo the opportunity, but it will probably prefer a joint venture or some other form of collaborative operation. Situations in the lowest areas may, nevertheless, offer opportunities with lower commitments. Finally, note that because everything is subject to change—both a company's capabilities and the features of a country's market—firms should be dynamic in their approach to potential operating modes.

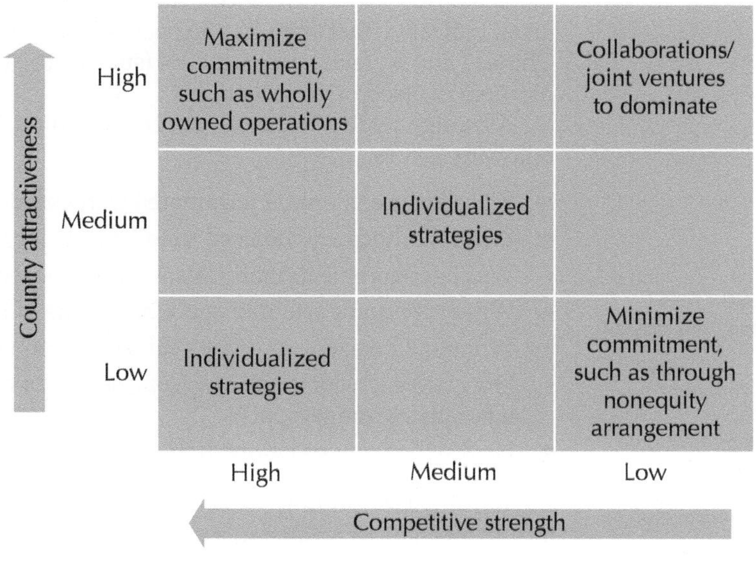

A company must evaluate potential partners' resources, motivation, and compatibility. Potential partners' proven ability to handle similar types of collaboration is a key professional qualification. A good track record may indicate trustworthiness that could lessen the need for expensive control mechanisms to carry out interests.

At the same time that you are looking for and evaluating potential partners, those potential partners are doing the same. You can boost your visibility and partnership potential through trade fair attendance, brochures, websites, and contacts in the potential collaboration locale. If you are new to foreign operations and to collaboration, you have no track record and you may have to negotiate harder and make more concessions.

In technology agreements,

- sellers do not want to give information before assuring an agreement can be reached,
- buyers want to evaluate information before committing to an agreement,
- the contract terms may be considered proprietary.

Negotiating the Arrangement: The Question of Secrecy Numerous collaborative arrangements involve technology transfers. Because the value of many technologies would diminish if they were widely used or understood, technology owners have historically insisted on including contract provisions whereby recipients will not divulge such information. Some have also held onto the ownership and production of specific components so recipients would not have full knowledge of the product or the capability to produce an exact copy.

Often companies want to sell techniques they have not yet completed, much less commercialized. A buyer is reluctant to buy what it has not seen, but a seller that shows the work in process to the potential buyer risks divulging the technology. For these and other reasons, it is common to set up pre-arrangement agreements that protect all parties.

A controversial negotiation area is the secrecy surrounding the financial terms of arrangements. In some countries, for example, licensing contracts must be approved by governmental agencies, which may consult their counterparts in other countries about similar agreements in order to improve their negotiating position. Many MNEs object, believing that contract terms between two companies are proprietary information with competitive importance. Further, market conditions usually require very different terms in different countries.

Although both trust and contracts have control limitations, there are provisions that should be included in any collaborative agreement.

Controlling Through Contracts and Trust The ceding of asset rights to another company entails some loss of control over the asset transferred. This creates two concerns—the partner's performance and the partner's integrity so as not to act opportunistically.[76] A host of potential problems must be settled as well as possible by setting mutual goals and spelling out all expectations in a contract, but not everything can be included this way. Further, national culture influences how much a partner wants to cover in a contract. Thus, the parties need to develop sufficient rapport so that common sense plays a part in running the operation.[77] Once operating, partners can also build trust through actions.[78] So, if parties from cultures with similar levels of trust come together, they can more likely agree on what must be incorporated in detailed contractual arrangements and what must be left to trust.[79]

Partnering with a firm that highly values its reputation is probably a plus as well, inasmuch as it may prefer to settle differences quietly rather than having them exposed in the press. Frank communications may help determine potential partners' underlying expectations, which may otherwise come as a surprise. For instance, a study of Chinese and Russian firms indicated that they had expected their foreign partners to deal much more with the Chinese and Russian governments (such as to alleviate bribery payments) than their foreign partners realized or actually did.[80]

Although contracts cannot cover everything, their provisions should at least address the following issues:

- Will the agreement be terminated if the parties don't adhere to the directives?
- What methods will be used to test for quality?
- What geographic limitations should be placed on an asset's use?
- Which company will manage which parts of the operation outlined in the agreement?
- What will be each company's future commitments?
- How will each company buy from, sell to, or otherwise use assets that result from the collaborative arrangement?
- How will revenues be divided?

When collaborating with another company, managers must

- continue to monitor performance,
- assess whether to change the form of operations,
- develop competency in managing a portfolio of collaborations.

Evaluating Continually Contracting with a capable and compatible partner is necessary but insufficient to ensure success. An agreement, once operational, must be run effectively.

Management should estimate potential sales and costs, determine whether the arrangement is meeting quality standards, assess if goals are being met, and evaluate whether partners are performing satisfactorily. In this respect, the relationship among partners may evolve positively or negatively, thus necessitating operational changes or even the termination of an agreement.

In addition to continually assessing partners' performance, a company must periodically assess the relative value of the type of collaboration, such as whether to replace a licensing agreement with a joint venture. Such modifications may be warranted because of changes in resources and strategies as well as external conditions such as host-country political and economic situations.

The evolution to a different operating mode may

- be the result of experience,
- create organizational tensions.

Adjusting Within the Internal Organization As companies enter into and grow their international collaborative arrangements, they gain competencies. As they change operating modes, they encounter pressures necessitating organizational adjustments. These include organizational application of what they have learned and the need to alter group and individual evaluations as operating forms change.

Learning and Its Applications Evidence suggests that companies' collaborative performance improves with experience. However, improvement is most associated with similar types of collaborations, such as applying what a firm has learned from JV operations in one country to JVs in another country.[81] With experience, companies choose partners better and improve synergies with them. Thus, as a company's collaborations increase, it should develop competency in managing the portfolio of arrangements so that it applies what it learns in one situation to others.[82] Nevertheless, companies may not necessarily replicate their past successes.[83] This is because, although they learn more about specific operation modes (such as licensing), they still must learn about new partners and the attributes of the new countries they enter.[84]

Pressures from Switching Collaborative Modes Changes in operating mode, such as from serving a foreign market through exports to that of producing abroad, cause some individuals to gain and others to lose responsibilities. For example, the size of home country marketing and manufacturing divisions may shrink, thus disadvantaging people who lose responsibilities if bonuses and promotions are based largely on their sales or profits. Given that lower performance is due to decisions outside their control, companies will need to revise performance evaluations.

LOOKING TO THE FUTURE Growth in Project Size and Complexity

More than a half century ago, John Kenneth Galbraith wrote that the era of cheap invention was over: "because development is costly, it follows that it can be carried out only by a firm that has the resources associated with considerable size."[85] The statement seems prophetic in terms of the estimated cost to bring a new commercial aircraft to market, eliminate death from diseases, develop defenses against unfriendly countries and terrorists, guard against cyberspace intrusions, and develop means to counteract adverse effects of climate change. However, Galbraith's conclusion overlooks several factors.

First, can firms reach the "considerable size" to solve the problems just mentioned? This is doubtful. Some of the largest companies in the world are in the auto industry, but they are finding that they have to work with each other (e.g., Toyota with BMW, to meet ever-stricter rules on carbon-dioxide emissions).[86] Further, governments constrain mergers and acquisitions because of antitrust concerns, thus inhibiting companies' growth.

Second, can companies internalize the breadth of technology necessary to solve these big problems? This is also doubtful. A recent catchphrase in strategy is to do what you do best and outsource the rest. Thus large companies' breadth of unrelated technology has been receding rather than growing. Consequently, we are apt to see more horizontal and vertical linkages among firms from many industries in many countries. On the downside, some evidence indicates that collaborations slow the speed of innovation because firms consider internalization and appropriation factors.[87]

If we see greater horizontal and vertical linkages, will these linkages be traditional? Some will probably not be. For instance, in recent years, some of the fastest-growing start-ups, such as Uber and Airbnb, have been companies that link with outsiders who provide most of the investment. Thus, collaboration will probably increase, but it will involve new forms and may attack more than the big developments that Galbraith envisioned.

At the same time, most product development is much more modest than required to unravel the gigantic projects. Concomitantly, although business strategists have advised companies for some time to specialize on what they do best (which fosters collaboration), there is growing evidence that many customers prefer to deal with one rather than multiple suppliers. The result, especially in emerging economies, may be the return in popularity of conglomerates.[88] In other words, because companies may find few other companies therein with necessary resources to collaborate, they are likely to expand both vertically and horizontally to serve the needs of their markets. Nevertheless, they likely lack all the product- and market-specific resources to go it alone if they move internationally, especially if national differences dictate operating changes on a country-to-country basis. Thus we may see them embracing more collaboration as they move abroad.

Collaborative arrangements will bring both opportunities and problems as MNEs move simultaneously to new countries and to contractual arrangements with new companies. Differences must be overcome in a number of areas:

- Country cultures that may cause partners to obtain and evaluate information differently
- National disparities in governmental policies, institutions, and industry structures that constrain companies from using operating forms they would prefer
- Distinct underlying ideologies and values affecting corporate cultures and practices that strain relationships
- Different strategic directions resulting from partners' interests that cause disagreement over objectives and contributions
- Diverse management styles and organizational structures that cause partners to interact ineffectively[89]

CASE

The oneworld Airline Alliance[90]

The airline industry is almost unique in that its need to form collaborative arrangements has been important almost from the start of international air travel because of cost, regulatory, and competitive factors. In recent years, this need has accelerated.

In effect, the airlines' performance has been squeezed. First, costs have become uncertain, particularly due to fluctuations in oil prices. Second, there is a need for greater security. In addition to airport passenger-security checks, airlines must provide advanced passenger information to governmental agencies and work with freight forwarders and supply-chain operators to ensure the safety of cargo shipments on passenger aircraft. Third, a long-term trend toward greater price competition has hindered airlines' ability to pass on increased costs to passengers—a situation exacerbated by discount airlines and customers' ability to search for lower fares on the Internet. Fourth, at this writing the COVID-19 pandemic has caused a sharp decrease in airline travel and uncertainty about when this trend might change.

Although growth in international passenger travel has largely spurred globalization, no airline has sufficient finances or aircraft to serve the whole world. Yet passengers are traveling the whole world and want airline connections that will minimize both distances and connecting times at airports while offering reasonable assurance of reaching destinations with checked luggage more or less on schedule. Thus, airlines have increasingly worked together to provide more seamless experiences for passengers and to cut costs.

This discussion, however, should not imply that all cost cuts necessitate collaboration. Airlines have implemented cost-saving changes that cover the gamut from ticket purchase to arrival at destination. Online purchases of electronic tickets have largely replaced airlines' need to pay travel agency commissions and to issue and maintain costly inventories of paper tickets. Self-service check-in at airports reduces the need for agents. On board, especially on short flights, less is included in the price of a basic ticket, such as generous leg space between rows of seats, food, pillows, and headphones.

A Bit of History: Changing Government Regulations

Historically, governments played a major role in airline ownership. Many government-owned airlines were monopolies within their domestic markets, money losers, and recipients of government subsidies. However, although some airlines remain subsidized, there has been a subsequent move toward privatization.

What Governments Can Regulate

Despite the move toward privatization, governments still regulate airlines and agree on restrictions and rights largely through reciprocal agreements. Specifically, they control:

- Which foreign carriers have landing rights
- Which airports and aircraft the carriers can use
- The frequency of flights
- Whether foreign carriers can fly beyond the country (for instance, whether a Spanish airline Iberia, after flying from Spain to the United States, can then fly from the United States to Panama)

- Overflight privileges
- Fares airlines can charge

Several notable regulatory changes have occurred in recent years. First, the U.S. domestic market has been deregulated, which means that any approved U.S. carrier can fly any U.S. domestic route in any frequency while charging what the market will bear. Deregulation has forced many U.S. airlines out of business because of competition, but new ones keep emerging. Second, similar deregulation within Europe influenced the demise of some airlines, but, like the United States, new airlines are emerging. Third, several open-skies agreements permit any airline from countries in an agreement to fly from any city in one signatory area to any city in the other signatory area. Further, these flights have no restrictions on capacity, frequency, or type of aircraft. For instance, an open-skies agreement between the United States and Japan spurred American Airlines (AA) to begin previously unapproved service between New York and Haneda International Airport. Fourth, European countries have permitted cross-national acquisitions, such as German Lufthansa's acquisition of Swiss International Airlines.

Why Governments Protect Airlines

These factors influence governments' protection of their airlines:

1. Countries believe they can save money by maintaining small air forces and relying on domestic airlines in times of unusual air transport needs (e.g., the U.S. government using U.S. commercial carriers to help carry troops to and from Afghanistan).
2. Public opinion favors spending at home. The public sees, for example, the requirement that government employees fly on national airlines as foreign-exchange savings.
3. Airlines are a source of national pride, and aircraft (sporting their national flags) symbolize a country's sovereignty and technical competence. This national identification has become less important, but it still persuades some developing countries.

Regulatory Obstacles to Expansion

Even if airlines had the financial capacity to expand everywhere in the world, national regulations would limit this expansion. With few exceptions, airlines cannot fly on lucrative domestic routes in foreign countries. For example, Japan Airlines (JAL) cannot compete on the New York to Los Angeles route, nor can AA fly between Tokyo and Nagoya. These restrictions prevent airlines from developing domestic routes abroad to feed into their international routes (e.g., JAL has no U.S. domestic flights into Chicago to connect to its Chicago–Tokyo flights, but AA does). Further, the U.S. government limits foreign ownership in a U.S. airline to 25 percent of voting stock.

Finally, airlines usually cannot service pairs of foreign countries. AA cannot fly between Brazil and South Africa because those governments give landing rights on such routes only to Brazilian and South African airlines. To avoid these restrictions, airlines must ally themselves with carriers from other countries.

Collaboration Examples Related to Motives

Cost Factors

Certain airlines have always dominated certain airports, thereby amassing critical capabilities in them, such as baggage handlers and aircraft-handling equipment. Sharing these capabilities with other airlines may spread costs. For example, British Airways (BA) has long handled passenger check-in, baggage loading, and maintenance for a number of other airlines at London's Heathrow Airport.

The high cost of maintenance and reservations systems has led to JVs involving multiple airlines from multiple countries, such as ownership in the Galileo reservation system. Actually, the reservations systems are motivated by more than cost savings, inasmuch as the pooling of resources provides customers with better service.

Connecting Flights

Given that governments restrict routes, airlines have long had agreements whereby passengers can transfer from one to another with a through ticket. However, people tend to select from among the first routings that show up on computer screens, and routings from one airline to another often appear on screens after those involving only one airline. Further, when passengers see that they must change airlines, they worry more about making those connections across great distances within ever-larger airports. To help avoid this worry, airlines have agreed to *code sharing*—a procedure whereby the same flight may have a designation for more than one carrier. For instance, the same flight operated by Iberia from Miami to Madrid is also listed as AA, Finnair, and BA flights. Hence, AA passengers originating in, say, Tampa and connecting at Miami may worry less about the connection because they see themselves on the same airline all the way. However, they may still need to go from one departure section to another to make the plane-change. In such a situation, airlines must adhere to a longer minimum connecting time when showing a through/connecting flight.

The oneworld Alliance

At this writing the oneworld Alliance comprises 15 core airlines: AA, BA, Cathay Pacific, Fiji Airlines, Finnair, Iberia, Japan Airlines (JAL), LATAM, Malaysia Airlines, Qantas, QATAR, Royal Air Maroc, Royal Jordanian, S7 Airlines, and SriLankan Airlines in addition to affiliates of this core group. oneworld competes largely with two other alliances: Star and SkyTeam. Airlines in these alliances cooperate on various programs, such as allowing passengers to earn credits for free or upgraded travel on any one of them. In the case of oneworld, all members flying into Narita Airport in Tokyo have moved into terminal 2, which shortens legal connecting times among them. They also advertise their affiliation; you may have seen aircraft painted with the airline's name and logo along with the oneworld name. These alliances allow for considerable cooperation, such as code-sharing; however, U.S. antitrust regulations (unless given immunity) prohibit their members from coordinating routes, schedules, and prices.

Antitrust Immunity

AA has received antitrust immunity that allows it to cooperate more in both a joint venture across the Atlantic and one across the Pacific. In both cases, the agreements allow representatives from each airline to jointly manage capacity, sell and promote space on flights operated by each other, divide revenues, and schedule connecting flights. The major thrusts for these ventures are to cut operating costs by better controlling capacity, to avoid disruptive price competition, and to improve scheduling so that there are more and better departure times and connections for passengers.

The Transatlantic Joint Venture

Three airlines—AA, BA, and Iberia—have a combined network of over 400 destinations in over 100 countries and account for more than 6,000 daily departures. When their JV and antitrust immunity were approved, they collectively had 48 different routes between Europe and North America that included 22 North American and 13 European cities. Of these 48 routes, they competed directly on only 9.

Since these airlines entered this JV, they have been able to coordinate schedules better for the convenience of passengers. For instance, whereas AA and BA used to have flights leaving between New York-JKF and London-Heathrow within minutes of each other, they have been able to coordinate departure times so that the flights leave approximately one hour apart. This gives passengers more options in finding a departure time convenient to them and allows for more connecting flight alternatives in either direction. Further, the participating airlines can now designate their own flight numbers on domestic connections when they connect to transatlantic destinations. For instance, Iberia shows one of its routes as San Diego to Madrid, even though both the San Diego–Chicago and Chicago–Madrid flights are operated by AA.

Because of dual or multiple designations and the sharing of revenue, more than one airline's sales force is trying to fill seats on the same route. The result is boosted sales, which allows the JV members to offer new routes—nonstop service between Chicago and Helsinki and between New York and Budapest have come about since the JV's formation.

The AA–JAL Joint Venture

JAL is also a large airline, serving 80 cities in 20 countries and territories. Its joint venture with AA has the same advantages and objectives as the JV across the Atlantic. Some changes since inaugurating the JV are notable. By altering each company's flight times between Chicago O'Hare and Tokyo Narita and tweaking schedules of connecting flights in both cities, many more passengers can make connections within two hours. For instance, 22 more flights from 20 more departure cities can make such connections for travel from O'Hare to Narita. Map 15.2 shows the joint AA–JAL routes and illustrates that flights between Honolulu and Japan are not included in the agreement.

JAL moved its O'Hare flights from the international terminal to be adjacent to AA. Meanwhile, AA moved its Japanese offices to JAL's headquarters building in Tokyo, a move that eases communications between the two airlines. Both are helping each other with cultural questions, such as JAL aiding AA with public address announcements in Japanese to make them more meaningful to Japanese passengers. Meanwhile, the airlines have greatly increased code sharing between them, especially to points beyond gateway cities, such as showing both AA and JAL as airlines between Tokyo and Salt Lake City and as both an AA and JAL flight beyond Tokyo to JAL-served cities such as Hanoi.

Why Not a Merger or an Acquisition?

To begin with, government regulations such as ownership requirements would prevent a merger or acquisition between U.S. and non-U.S. carriers. Even if they didn't, fusing companies together creates daunting problems, even for domestic mergers and acquisitions. To complete the merger between AA and US Airways, the companies had to combine different operating and compensation systems between their respective pilots' unions. US Airways transatlantic routes had to interface with AA's agreements with BA and Iberia. US Airways had to sever its membership in the Star Alliance, and AA and US Airways had to combine their accrued frequent flyer passenger points.

The Advantages of JVs

In the JVs, each company keeps its own identity and operates independently except for the coordination of the transoceanic routes. In addition, each airline in the JVs and within oneworld has developed its own culture and brand to appeal to its own nationality. BA is still strongest with British passengers, JAL with Japanese passengers, etc. By keeping separate identities, despite sharing flights, the member airlines can capitalize on the differences. Nevertheless, natural extensions are possible by strengthening collaboration, such as having check-in counters worldwide that handle all oneworld passengers and combining more airport lounges as a cost-saving measure. It is probably safe to say that future cooperation will strengthen rather than weaken among oneworld members.

MAP 15.2 American Airlines and Japan Airlines: Transpacific Routes

Note that the joint activity involves only flights from mainland North America into East Asia.

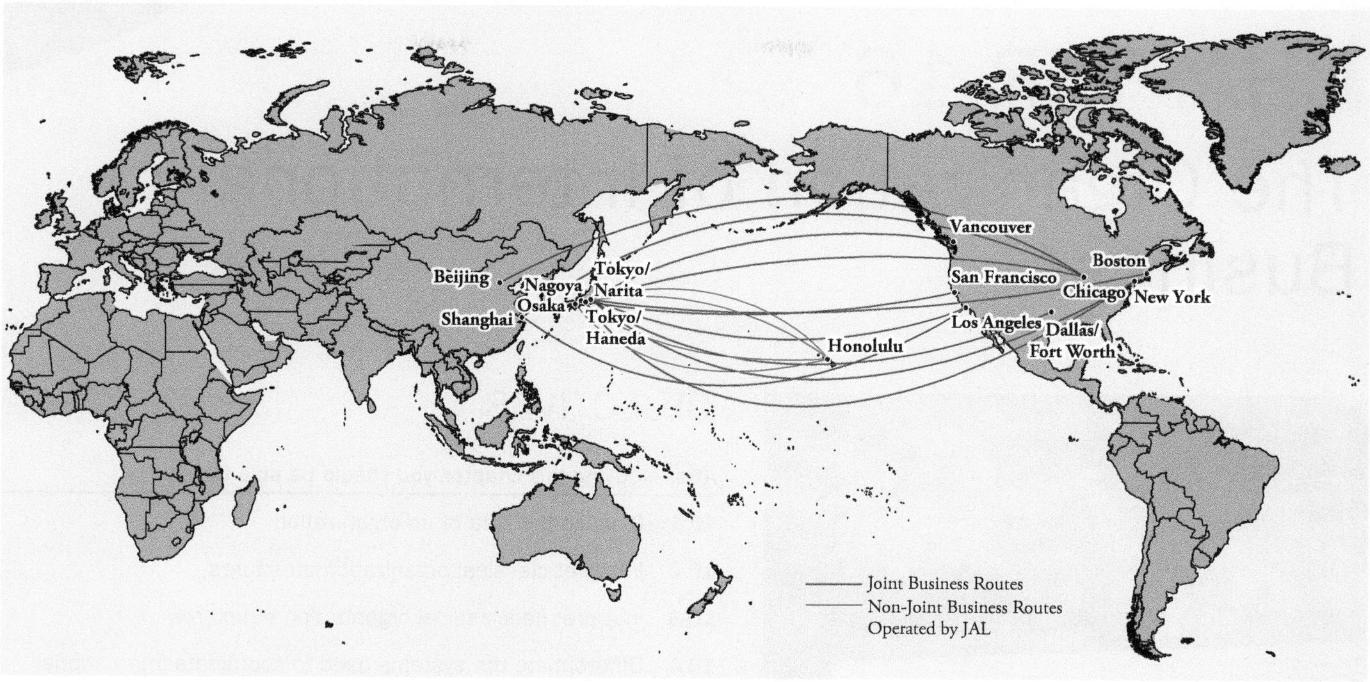

QUESTIONS

15-3 Companies within the oneworld, Star, and Sky Team alliances have also engaged in major mergers and acquisitions (M&A): American and US Air (oneworld), Delta and Northwest (Sky Team), and Continental and United (Star). What are the advantages and disadvantages of M&A versus non-equity alliances in this industry?

15-4 Some airlines, such as Southwest, have survived as niche players without extensive international connections. Can they continue this strategy?

15-5 Why should an airline not be able to establish service anywhere in the world simply by demonstrating that it can and will comply with the local labor and business laws of the host country?

15-6 The U.S. law limiting foreign ownership of U.S. airlines to no more than 25 percent of voting shares was enacted in 1938. Is this law an anachronism, or are there valid reasons for having it today?

15-7 Many airlines have sometimes been no more than marginally profitable. Is this such a vital industry that governments should intervene to guarantee survival? If so, how?

CHAPTER 16

The Organization of International Business

Source: Daniel Sullivan

W. L. Gore & Associates paper mill in Newark, Delaware. ▲

OBJECTIVES

After studying this chapter, you should be able to

16-1 Discuss the idea of an organization

16-2 Interpret classical organization structures

16-3 Interpret neoclassical organization structures

16-4 Differentiate the systems used to coordinate international activities

16-5 Differentiate the systems used to control international activities

16-6 Explain the principle and practices of organizational culture

Words have no wings, but they can fly many thousands of miles.

—South Korean proverb

CASE

Organizing Global Operations: The "Gore Way"

Since 1958, W. L. Gore & Associates (hereafter Gore) has found ways to convert the versatile polymer polytetrafluoroethylene (PTFE) and related fluoropolymers into pioneering products that are used in all sorts of ways by all sorts of people to do all sorts of jobs.[1] Best known for its waterproof, breathable, high-performance GORE-TEX® fabric, Gore's product portfolio includes medical devices, pharmaceutical processing, consumer products, cables and cable assemblies, fibers, sealants, industrial components, and aerospace electronics. Its ingenuity and imagination have earned it more than 5,500 patents in a wide range of fields, including electronics, medical devices, and polymer processing. Given its unique stature, some point to Gore as the "the world's most innovative company."[2]

Notwithstanding its discoveries, many contend that Gore's supreme invention is setting and sustaining a stunningly effective global organization.[3] Reports confirmed something special goes on. It consistently ranks as a "Great Place to Work" and a "100 Best Companies to Work For." Globally, Gore gains accolades. Its units in China, France, Germany, Italy, Spain, and Sweden have been named one of the respective nation's best workplaces. Likewise, nearly 3,000 MNEs worldwide participated in the 2017 Great Place to Work® review. Assessment centered on issues of mutual trust, esprit de corps and camaraderie, and workplace supportiveness. Gore placed among the top 15 "World's Best Multinational Workplaces."[4]

Gore employs some 10,500 "Associates," (the official designation of its employees). They staff research labs, manufacturing facilities, and sales offices in more than 25 countries. Gore, headquartered in Newark, Delaware, is one of the 200 largest privately held companies in the United States; it reported more than $3.7 billion in sales in 2019. Members of the Gore family, along with its Associates, via the company's stock plan, own the company. Gore prefers this mode of private ownership, believing that people put in the position of an owner, not a worker, take the long-term view.

ENVISIONING THE GORE WAY

Wilbert L. (Bill) Gore and his wife, Genevieve, cofounded W. L. Gore & Associates on January 1, 1958. Startup began upon Bill leaving his successful career as a DuPont research chemist to pursue opportunities for fluorocarbon polymers. While at DuPont, Bill had worked on several small task forces that he believed were especially effective in solving problems. Meaningful interactions in small groups, he noted, helped him get to know his colleagues and appreciate their capabilities in ways that are hard, if not near impossible, in a multilevel hierarchical organization.

These formative experiences inspired Bill to build an organization where workers could come together in small teams to get things done—or, as he put it, "make money and have fun doing so." As Bill explained, "One of the objectives that I had in starting our own enterprise was to try and apply the task-force kind of organization to a business enterprise. In the task-force operation, there were no titles, and the interaction was one-on-one within the team." This vision set and has sustained an organization that puts into play innovative, influential ideas on enterprise, accountability, authority, and shared ownership of success.[5] Or, in company shorthand, it instituted the "Gore Way."

THE GORE WAY

Philosophically opposed to the customary chain of command found in a top-down organization, Bill Gore rejected the principles and practices of the classical hierarchy. He objected to working in a regimented organization that promoted elitism, ranking people or groups above others according to authority or status. Instead, just as he had experienced in his small team work, he believed in the virtues of a flat organization whereby everyone could freely talk with anyone, no matter their role or rank. Making this happen, he figured, meant eliminating obstacles to connection, communication, and collaboration. Hence, no one in his company, not even Bill himself, had a title like boss, supervisor, manager, director, controller, etc.[6] Everyone was and, to this day, is an "Associate." As an aside, Gore's opposition to boxing in either an individual or an idea anchors the symbolism of its corporate logo. Its largely obtuse triangle has three key vertices; the one toward the furthest left represents the past, the one midway represents the present, and the one that has broken through the box represents the future.

In 1976, Bill Gore set forth his manifesto, "*The Lattice Organization—A Philosophy of Enterprise.*" It articulates the Gore Way, advocating a flat, network-like structure that rejects the standard that one person (the boss) should specify who others (workers) may talk to and work with.[7] As Bill Gore reasoned, "A lattice organization is

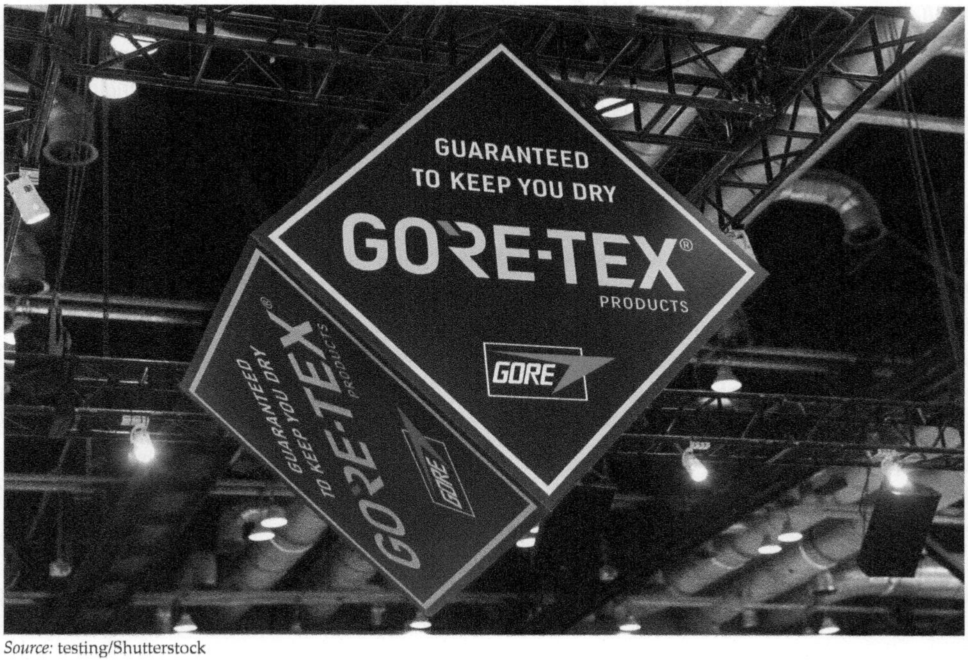

Logo, W. L. Gore & Associates. ▶

Source: testing/Shutterstock

one that involves direct transactions, self-commitment, natural leadership, and lacks assigned or assumed authority . . . Every successful organization has a lattice organization that underlies the façade of authoritarian hierarchy. It is through these lattice organizations that things get done, and most of us delight in going around the formal procedures and doing things the straightforward and easy way." Operationally, Associates "own" the team-based, non-hierarchical workplace that rejects conventional structural formats to encourage personal initiative, removes the chain of command to promote connections and collaborations, and resets channels of communication from a priori specification to natural emergence.

Translating the lattice organization from theory to practice institutes an interlaced system of relationships among Gore's Associates. Operationally, leaders attract team members based on their proven effectiveness in getting things done, and Associates, based on their read of opportunities and colleagues, self-organize into multifunctional teams—meritocracy, not aristocracy, determines leaders. Associates have a say in choosing what they work on, aligning their talents and interests with business needs. Associates create value that supports business goals—and their fellow Associates, by directly assessing each other, corroborate their performance.[8] Liberated from a rigid bureaucracy, Associates make decisions based on knowledge and initiative rather than seniority and titles. Success translates into the workplace credibility to define and drive projects. Gore's lattice organization frees the flow of information and enables the sorts of personal communications that encourages productive collaboration—and, as report after report indicates, makes for a great workplace.

No matter where in the world, no matter what an Associate works on, the Gore Way champions entrepreneurial innovation. Notwithstanding considerable personal autonomy, Associates stay mindful of Bill Gore's four basic guiding principles: (1) Fairness to each other and everyone with whom we come in contact; (2) Freedom to encourage, help, and allow other Associates to grow in knowledge, skill, and scope of responsibility; (3) The ability to make one's own commitments and keep them; and (4) Consulting other Associates before undertaking actions that could impact the reputation of the company.[9] Add it all up, suggest some analysts, and Gore translates communication and collaboration, within a context of meritocracy, into an "innovation democracy."[10]

SUSTAINING THE GORE WAY

A vibrant element of the Gore Way is its organizational culture. Intentionally humanistic, its foundational belief holds that the innate motivation of each Associate, given the opportunity and incented as an owner, drives one and all to stretch toward their full potential. To that end, Associates collectively commit to foster a safe and healthy work environment in which they develop their talents, enjoy their work, and responsibly direct their activities—again, as founder Bill Gore declared, "The objective of the Enterprise is to make money and have fun doing so."[11] Gore continues championing that cause—and, the results indicate, it pays off. Associates find ingenious ways to meet customers' need through innovative products.

The norms and values shared by Associates help facilitate coordination and control. Crucially, the goal to work collectively, even while retaining individuality, endorses informal integrative mechanisms. Explained Gore's former CEO, "We take great pride in our culture and recognize the very important role it plays in driving business success. By fostering an environment where people feel motivated, engaged, and passionate about the work they do, we are better able to tap into our potential and create innovative products that truly make a difference in the world."[12] A leader of a company-wide culture initiative adds that, "Our global teams bring together the best knowledge by collaborating across the enterprise to take on opportunities where we can make the biggest impact. Our strongly embedded values, passionate Associates, and winning teams are instrumental to creating a rewarding environment and great experiences for our customers. This is our culture in action."[13]

Certainly, one wonders how these principles and practices can organize the work of 10,500 Associates that run 50 facilities spanning more than 25 countries. Gore's commitment to keeping units small and informal plays a vital role. Gore prefers that a physical facility house no more than a few hundred Associates. Given Bill Gore's vision, the company believed that crossing that threshold, no matter whether in the United States, Germany, or China, insidiously turns decision-making from "we decided" to "they decided." Unguarded, those tendencies set a company on the path to hierarchy, bureaucracy, control, and coercion. Similarly, Gore prefers opening a subsidiary, rather than acquiring an existing company, when entering a new market. It reasons that it's easier to set and sustain its vision and values in a new enterprise rather than transforming the legacy mindsets that linger after an acquisition.

CHANGING FOR CHANGING TIMES

Continuing growth, fueled by expanding internationalization, has spurred Gore to formalize some elements of its organization. Today, it has a CEO, several product divisions, numerous product-focused business units, and the usual business support functions.[14] Coordinating far-flung global operations means Associates use the latest, greatest technology. Teams regularly convene, physically and virtually, to plan, assess gaps, and fortify the relationships that anchor the Gore Way.[15] Still, at its core, Gore has little hierarchy. Multidisciplinary teams, freed from layers of supervisory "management," protect the innovative spirit of individuals that power the company's entrepreneurialism.

Echoing its lattice structure, Gore configures its facilities into clusters, like the dozen units located in Arizona or the multiple units interspersed throughout the Delaware Valley. Multiple interdependent sites, rather than one large facility, means people meet and mingle. Then, within a cluster, Gore promotes cross-functional collaboration by having R&D specialists, engineers, marketers, chemists, and machinists work in the same plant or on the same campus. Emblematic of its approach, Gore's headquarters remains simple and humble: several low-rise buildings in the Delaware countryside that collectively house a panorama of people. Outside many of its facilities, one finds a volleyball court, picnic areas, horseshoe pits, and other areas that promote teamwork, fun, and camaraderie. Unofficially the company's official sport, volleyball is unique because players rotate through every position, unlike, say, in baseball or football, where players specialize in a single slot.

Going forward, Associates look to meld the Gore Way with the expanding opportunities of globalization, to say nothing of the revolutionary options created by increasingly robust connection, communication, and collaboration technologies. Explained an enterprise leader, "Twenty or thirty years ago, markets in different parts of the world were still somewhat distinct and isolated from one another. At that time, we could have pretty much the entire global business team for a particular market niche located in a building. Today, as our markets become more global in nature, we are increasingly seeing the need to support our customers with global virtual teams.[16] Managing these changes questioned the evolution of Gore's organization. Answering them had big implications. Gore's 60-plus years of insight and adaptation signaled that, come what may, its Associates would develop ingenious organizational solutions that sustain the Gore Way.

QUESTIONS

16-1 The World Economic Forum, noting that the world of work is changing, emphasizes the importance of complex problem-solving, critical thinking, creativity, and dealing with ambiguity to effective executive performance. Estimate how these skills would support your performance as an Associate at W. L. Gore.

16-2 Identify two reasons that encourage you to work for W. L. Gore. Then, identify two that discourage you. Based on these, what would you decide to do?

Designing an **organization** that adeptly runs activities worldwide, all the while ingeniously reconciling the competing pressures for global integration and local differentiation, is an enduring challenge for MNEs. Moving from ambition to action requires managers organize how work gets done, how to coordinate differentiated activities, how to apply controls when plans go awry, and how to institute values that set and sustain a common cause among employees. Everywhere and anywhere, from the largest to the smallest MNEs, executives face these questions. Bright, astute choices optimally configure the workflow, effectively coordinate decision making, and support a unifying *esprit de corps*.

Hence, the idea of an organization refers to the activities that managers engage to build the structure, systems, and culture needed to implement a strategy. These simple sounding yet infinitely complex topics are the crux of organizing an MNE. This chapter profiles how managers make it all come together, a feat requiring they map the structure that organizes who does what job, design the systems that gets and keeps everyone moving, and set the culture that sustains the enterprise (see Figure 16.1). When effectively done, managers convert strategic ambitions into outstanding performance.

FIGURE 16.1 Factors Affecting Organizing Operations

Managers arranges the roles, responsibilities, and relationships that constitute an organization in order to implement the chosen strategy within the general context of the external environment.

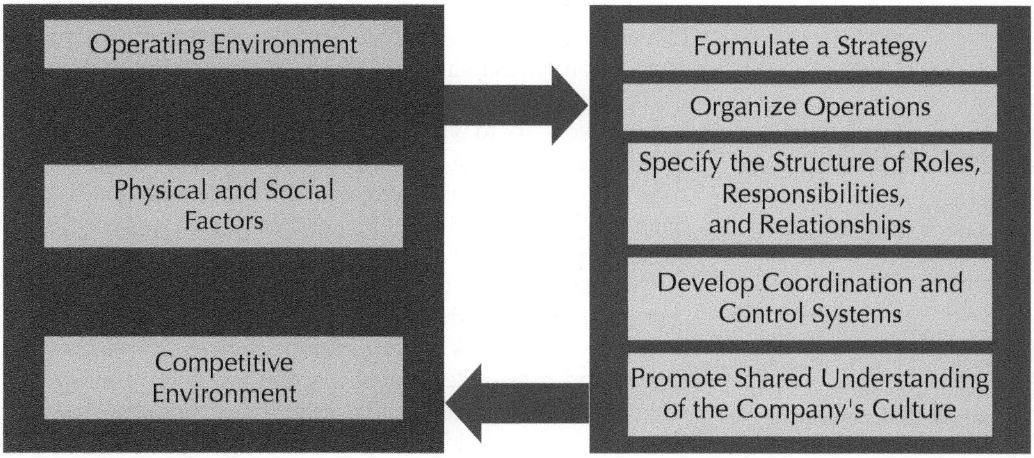

THE IDEA OF AN ORGANIZATION

16-1 Discuss the idea of an organization

Chapter 12 explained that an MNE develops a vision and mission that it then translates into its strategy. Converting its lofty ambitions into practical outcomes calls on managers to institute an organization that supports the requisite roles, relationships, and responsibilities. Instituting this organization calls for making decisions, big and small, on who does what, where, and why. These issues put into play matters, to name just a few, of coordination, control, accountability, automation, identity, communication, collaboration, differentiation, and integration. Set well, executives get the organization moving, confident that it focuses attention on the strategic priorities and critical operations of each business unit, region, and product. As this chapter profiles, powerful perspectives and practical tools help executives set the structure, systems, and culture of the organization to do precisely that.

Organization in any context is challenging. It's particularly so in IB given the many questions, contingencies, and anomalies that managers run into when arranging operations to navigate a diversity of cultural, political, and economic environments. A survey of 300 executives at 17 major global companies, for example, found that despite their best efforts, about only half believed that their organization created clear accountability, purposeful direction, and decision-making clarity.[17] Moreover, the average large firm reorganizes operations every 2 to 3 years, and each iteration takes up to 18 months.[18] Lastly, reorganizations are costly and disruptive; HSBC, struggling with falling profitability, is "remodelling" its global banking operations and, in the process, eliminating 35,000 jobs, shedding $100 billion in assets, and cutting goodwill by $7.3 billion.[19] Nonetheless, as this chapter develops, executives apply helpful perspectives that make sense of the way that work gets done.

An MNE's organization reflects its
- market circumstances,
- strategic choice,
- value chain configuration,
- administrative legacy,
- executive preferences.

Everywhere and always, MNEs optimize the configuration of structure, systems, and values to build, as we'll see in our closing case, what Johnson & Johnson (J&J) calls a "magical" organization. Different MNEs apply different approaches to create magic. Some, like Nestlé in Switzerland, Cemex in Mexico, Toyota in Japan, Infosys in India, and Walmart in the United States, apply and refine classical hierarchical formats. Walmart, for example, relies upon a tried-and-true international division, headquartered in Arkansas, to oversee the 700,000 associates staffing more than 5,900 outlets spanning 26 countries and who serve more than 100 million customers every week in ringing up $2.3 billion in sales.[20] Walmart, as does Nestlé, Infosys, Toyota, and Cemex, fine-tunes its classical organization, process-mapping activities to rationalize the work environment and improve system standards. Reengineering workflows, streamlining decision making, specifying information flows, tightening planning sequences, and preventing duplication are key tools.

Others, like Oticon in Sweden, IBM in the United States, Belcorp of Peru, Grupo Empresarial Antioqueño of Colombia, Mitsui of Japan, and Li & Fung in Hong Kong, employ neoclassical heterarchial formats. Li & Fung, the world's largest sourcing and logistics company, supplies billions of pieces of apparel to department stores, hypermarkets, specialty stores, and e-commerce sites worldwide. However, it owns no fabric mills, no sewing machines, and no clothing factories. Rather, Li & Fung's 22,000 employees in 250 offices spanning 40 nations work with more than 15,000 suppliers that make virtually any and all sort of apparel items.[21] Likewise, IBM's transition to a "globally integrated enterprise" aims to put investments, people, and work anywhere in the world based on the optimal mix of costs, skills, and location effects. Explained IBM's vice president of global strategy, "Instead of taking people to where the work is, you take work to where the people are."[22] New, sometimes radically different, workflows for IBM, as for Li & Fung, Oticon, Gore, and Mitsu, mandate swapping the command-and-control code of the classical hierarchy with the coordinating and collaborating ethos of the neoclassical heterarchy. Cross-functional task forces, knowledge webs, flat structures, virtual formats, and social networking are key tools to optimize an organization.

CONCEPT CHECK

Designing an organization's structure requires fitting it to conditions in the external environment. These conditions involve, among many others, legal regulations on ownership structures, degree of economic freedom, location economics, and expectations of alliance partners.

No matter the outlook, whether classical or neoclassical, managers configure, coordinate, and combine units that span anywhere from a couple of to a couple of hundred countries. Invariably, managers make different choices in how best to organize, determining whether this option maximizes global integration, determining whether that option improves local responsiveness, or magically, identifying options that ingeniously do both. Ideally, this chapter would provide the precise blueprint to make a magical organization. Sadly, it does not—the topic, as you likely suspect, is far too complicated to simply specify. Rather, we profiles how managers in all sorts of situations cleverly organize a company's structure, systems, and culture to optimize the way work gets done, here, there, and everywhere.

CLASSICAL ORGANIZATION STRUCTURES

16-2 Interpret classical organization structures

In the early twentieth century, companies responded to the emerging technologies of railroads, telephone, and telegraph by adopting then unusual organizational ideas.[23] The global titans of the day, such as General Motors, Matsushita, Phillips, Sears, General Electric, and DuPont, developed hierarchical structures, reasoning that this then-novel organizational format would best implement the novel strategies that had been made possible by then emerging technologies. Succeeding generations of managers refined the hierarchical design, better determining who did what job, who made which decision, who worked in which unit, who reported to whom, and who told whom what to do. The output of these analyses, codified in the "lines and boxes" that represent a company's structure, instituted a hierarchical system of command, control, constraint, and contract. It directed the efforts and ensured the compliance of workers worldwide.[24]

Structure is the formal arrangement of jobs that specifies roles, responsibilities, and relationships.

This formal arrangement of roles, responsibilities, and relationships represents an **organization structure**. Operationally, managers configure the elements of the company's workflow into a schematic of lines and boxes that assigns authority, roles, duties, and relationships that collectively constitute its organization structure. These decisions, notwithstanding their seeming straightforwardness, often determine the success of a company.[25] Earlier, we saw how this process plays at W. L. Gore & Associates in terms of instituting its lattice structure. Likewise, executives of J&J see its thoughtfully-crafted, adroitly-sustained decentralized structure as the bedrock of its magical organization. Similarly, as we saw in Chapter 12, Zara's CEO says its structure fundamentally anchors its competitiveness. Innovatively combining vertical integration, tech-choreographed coordination, just-in-time manufacturing, finely-engineered logistics, and state-of-the-art merchandising poses tough challenges to its rivals. Zara's structure, by ingeniously arranging jobs, roles, rules, and responsibilities, organizes its workflows to implement its hard-to-beat strategy.

Designing an organization typically begins by determining the ideal structure for arranging individuals and units in order to implement the MNE's strategy—indeed, a long-running thesis in management theory holds that "structure follows strategy."[26] Does the MNE's strategy, for instance, champion global integration or local adaptation? In the former, centralized decision-making is crucial, while, in the latter, decentralized decision-making is decisive. Operationally, does the MNE's strategy led it to concentrate value activities in a few nations or disperse them across many countries? Concentration requires precise controls, whereas dispersal calls for flexible systems. Complicating matters is the general context of IB. Organizing domestically lets one reasonably treat technology level, cultural orientation, and workplace practices as constants. Organizing internationally requires treating them as variables, with potentially extreme variation from country to country.

Differentiation means that the company is composed of different units that work on different tasks with different degrees of authority.

Collectively, these sorts of circumstances endorse the usefulness of some forms of structure, while rejecting others. Making sense of the strategy-structure situation forces a cascade of decisions. Managers begin by resolving (1) the degree of **vertical differentiation**—deciding who has what authority to make which decision; and (2) the degree of **horizontal differentiation**—specifying which people in which units do which jobs.

CONCEPT CHECK

International business is marked by recurring dialectics; for example, global versus local, democracy versus totalitarianism, economic freedom versus state capitalism, free versus fair trade, or standardization versus adaptation. Here we add another, namely, centralization versus decentralization.

VERTICAL DIFFERENTIATION

No matter the mix of markets, products, or ambitions, MNEs face competing calls for global integration and local responsiveness. Inevitably, questions run the gamut: Who should decide to close a factory in Country Alpha or open one in Country Omega? Does only headquarters decide whom to hire and fire, both at home and overseas? How often and in what format do foreign subsidiaries report to headquarters? Running a global enterprise, from the small born-global to the large MNE, expectedly, faces an endless stream of these sorts of decisions.

In classical terms, managers design the company's structure to reconcile these sorts of questions. They create and configure the "boxes and lines" of their structure to specify who has the authority to make what decision—indeed, one can think of stage one of organizing in terms of determining who makes what decision among different units doing different jobs in different places. If the plan is to make most decisions headquarters' call, then managers differentiate the structure to implement that outlook. Alternatively, if the plan is to have local subsidiaries makes those calls, then, again, managers differentiate the structure to transfer authority to local units. Managers implement their preferred outlook by vertically differentiating structure in terms of the **centralization** (how high up) versus the **decentralization** (how low down) of decision-making.

Operationally, high-vertical differentiation institutes a "top-down" structure in which the CEO set the strategy and direct the middle management, supervisors, and rank-and-file workers to "get it done." The clear chain of command. no matter the "length" of the chain, means everyone understands who makes decisions and who is responsible for which tasks. Generally, a top-down structure works in those companies whose strategy requires a multi-level hierarchy to discipline decision making, maximize efficiency, and impose order. Alternatively, low-vertical differentiation institutes a flat, "bottom-up" structure that grants employees at all levels the authority to makes decisions that matter. The CEO shares guidance and sets guardrails that help workers use their knowledge, skills, and abilities to "build a better way, every day."

Generally, decisions made above the subsidiary level signify centralization, whereas those made at or below that level signify decentralization. Operationally, a centralized structure concentrates decision-making authority among the executives who staff the top levels of the MNE. A decentralized structure pushes decision-making authority down to the folks on the front lines in operating units. Resolving the tension between centralization versus decentralization, as seen in Table 16.1, sets different objectives, advocates different principles, and implements different practices.

TABLE 16.1 The Principles and Practices of Centralization and Decentralization

Centralization	Decentralization
Premise	**Premise**
• Decisions should be made by senior managers who have superior expertise and broader experiences. • Effective configuration and coordination of the value chain requires that headquarters direct local activities. • Centralized decision-making ensures local operations support the MNE's vision and mission.	• Decisions should be made by managers closest to customers. • Effective configuration and coordination of the value chain requires adaptation by local managers. • Success achieving local objectives anchors global performance.
Advantages	**Advantages**
• Ensures decisions support objectives. • Retain authority with HQ to regulate change. • Preempts duplicating activities. • Reduces the risk lower-level managers make strategic errors. • Simplifies coordinating activities • Promotes consistent relationships with stakeholders.	• Managers that directly deal with customers, competitors, officials, and markets make decisions. • Encourages lower-level managers to behave entrepreneurially. • Improves the allegiance and accountability of frontline employees. • Links subsidiary managers' choices directly to performance.
Disadvantages	**Disadvantages**
• Requires that top executives monitor and manage multiple activities. • Discourages initiative among lower-level employees. • Demoralizes lower-level employees who must wait to be told what to do. • Information flows "top-down," thereby preempting bottom-up innovations.	• Risks subunits making counterproductive decisions. • Subsidiaries champion local interests at the expense of global performance. • Slows the company's response to global innovations. • Information flows "bottom-up," thereby obstructing top-down innovations.
Factors Encouraging Centralization	**Factors Encouraging Decentralization**
• Environment and industry conditions push for worldwide uniformity of products, methods, and policies. • Interdependent subsidiaries share activities, segments, and rivals. • Strategy calls for exploiting location economics globally. • Lower-level managers are less experienced decision-makers than upper-level executives. • Decisions are important and downside risk is great.	• Environment and industry conditions require adapting products and policies. • Local production fully exploits location affects. • Lower-level managers are effective decision-makers. • Speed and flexibility drive performance. • Little need to develop managers for positions elsewhere in the world. • Supports rapid expansion into new markets. • Goal to develop executive talent at the local level.

Structure Follows Strategy The choice of centralization versus decentralization is not an either–or proposition. In principle, decision-making should occur at the level of those who are most directly affected by its outcome and have the most direct knowledge of the situation. So, for example, some activities spur centralized decision-making, such as configuring value activities worldwide to exploit location economies or rationalize production systems. Likewise, other activities encourage decentralized decision-making, such as adapting product packaging or negotiating with local officials. Again, in the context of the "structure follows strategy" thesis, the requirements of the MNE's strategy determine its ideal structure and, by extension, how managers balance centralization versus decentralization.

Centralization is the degree to which high-level managers, usually above the country level, make strategic decisions and delegate them to lower levels for implementation.

An MNE implementing an international strategy, for instance, centralizes most decision-making. Recall from Chapter 12 that the international strategy transfers a company's strategic outlook and orientation to foreign markets. Ultimate control of the company's resources, capabilities, and core competencies resides with headquarters given senior executives' superior understanding of their optimal bundling. Headquarters, in its role as overseer of global operations, makes the decisions that the troops running the local subsidiaries then implement. For example, Google, given its international strategy, centralizes strategic planning at the Googleplex in Mountain View, California—all the big decisions are made there. Google decentralizes some elements of its marketing mix to local subsidiaries in order to respond to unique situations. Still, the Googleplex ultimately rules.

Decentralization is the degree to which lower-level managers, usually at or below the country level, make and implement strategic decisions.

Alternatively, the MNE implementing a localization strategy decentralizes authority to the troops in the field, reasoning that those closest to the customer have a better understanding than far-removed generals. In this scenario, an MNE, such as J&J, reasons it optimizes performance by forsaking centralized control in favor of decentralized decision-making that supports the entrepreneurially minded folks who run the local subsidiaries.

Technology, Balance, and Globality Technology increasingly alters the calculus of who should have the authority to make which decision. It makes immediately available information and interactions that a generation ago seemed impossible, thereby shaping organizations in ways we never imagined. ERP, e-mail, VoIP, and teleconferencing let executives at headquarters and subsidiaries track global conditions and local performance in real time. Not long ago, each relied upon reports that slowly traveled up and down the chain of command. Economical, off-the-shelf platforms, such as Skype, TelePresence, or Zoom, make the magic of being in many places simultaneously happen effortlessly. The click of a mouse let's one connect with anyone, anywhere, anytime. Looking down the road, automation along with artificial intelligence will radically reconfigure organizations, enabling less hierarchy, greater autonomy, better flexibility, and more collaboration.[27] Ultimately, MNEs fine-tune organizations for the tech-powered **globality** in which "business flows in every direction. Companies have no centers. The idea of foreignness is foreign."[28] Increasing ease to work with anyone from everywhere requires intricately balancing centralizing this decision with and decentralizing that responsibility.

HORIZONTAL DIFFERENTIATION

Vertical differentiation deals with the chain of command that runs from the "top to the bottom" of the organization. Horizontal differentiation deals with the separate tasks or skills that run "sideways" in the organization.

Vertically speaking, MNEs run from the top (the CEO) to the bottom (the entry-level worker)—this shows up in the long series of boxes, from the high to the low, that make up a multilevel hierarchy. Horizontally speaking, MNEs also run sideways from activity to activity, such as business functions like research, production, marketing, and finance. Horizontal differentiation involves assigning specific tasks to specific people in specific activities.

Organizing tasks horizontally makes manageable the typically broad scale and scope of international operations. Technically, an MNE horizontally differentiates its structure to (1) specify the set of tasks that must be done by each group; (2) specify who does what by dividing those tasks among the different groups, whether in terms of business units, divisions, subsidiaries, departments, committees, teams, jobs, and individuals; and (3) stipulates superior and subordinate relationships within each group to set accountability.

Operationally, high-horizontal differentiation institutes a more elaborate structure of multiple units with shared authority and overlapping responsibilities. Decision making requires more communication and coordination. Alternatively, low-horizontal differentiation institutes a straightforward, streamlined structure of fewer, different units.

A classical structure applies explicit vertical and horizontal differentiation to organize the workplace.

In theory, managers can horizontally differentiate a structure in terms of function, process, product, service, geography, or client. For an MNE, the standards of function, product, geography, or some combination have traditionally dominated. Horizontally differentiating based on business activity anchors the functional structure. Doing so based on product or geography installs a divisional structure. Doing so based on a combination results in a matrix or mixed structure. The long-running use of these formats by MNEs designates them as **classical structures**. This characterization does suggests they are relics. Rather, it signifies their prevalent use over the past century by many companies in many industries in many countries. Currently, as many have, many MNEs use classical structures to specify the roles, responsibilities, and relationships that institute their structure.[29]

THE FUNCTIONAL STRUCTURE

Functional structures

- group people based on similar skills, expertise, and outlooks,
- apply vertical differentiation to centralize decision-making,
- work well in a stable environment that supports continuous operations.

The **functional structure**, as depicted in Figure 16.2, organizes the company's operations by business functions (i.e., production people work with production people, marketing people work with marketing people, finance people work with finance people). Each group's responsibility for its function worldwide sets precise roles and relationships.

Arranging the structure so that like-minded folks work together creates powerful points of expertise. Specialized experience supports incisive decision-making. The clear mandate, precise roles, and standardized routines in a functional structure, by centralizing decision-making, contribute to high levels of vertical differentiation. MNEs that institute it commonly see maximizing global integration, in order to configure resources, standardize capabilities, and leverage competencies, as more important than optimizing local responsiveness.

Drawbacks The often-extreme vertical differentiation found in the functional structure, represented by a multi-layered chain of command, can bureaucratize decision-making. Likewise, horizontally differentiating people and processes by business function—i.e., finance folks work with finance books, IT folks work with IT folks—puts boundaries on developing cross-functional knowledge-generating and decision-making relationships. Consequently, coordinating different functional units, in response to a market disruption or strategic change, can prove difficult. Adjusting if not resetting operations for the consequences of the COVID-19 pandemic, for example, tested the vitality of functional organizations. As the chain of command is overtaken by events, people start to pull in multiple directions, or they stop pulling, reasoning it's better to hunker down, and let someone else make a decision. Then again, absent crisis mode, the functional format can fuel zero-sum battles for control

FIGURE 16.2 The Functional Structure

Executives institute a functional structure to set precise roles, rules, and responsibilities that, in turn, leverage specialized expertise, streamline decision-making, and improve efficiency.

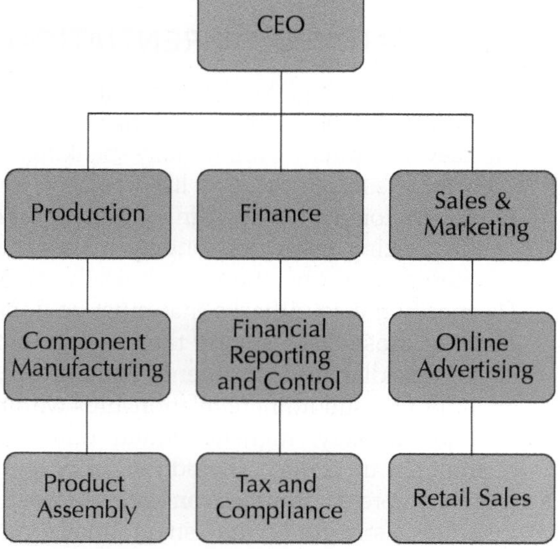

among divisions, groups, and people—e.g., production versus marketing versus finance. The goal of maximizing power in a compartmentalized hierarchy fuels turf battles that hinder collaboration.

DIVISIONAL STRUCTURES

Divisional structures

- divide the workplace in terms of product, service, or geography,
- have autonomous divisions that are accountable for assigned activities,
- fit the organizational demands of the MNE that manages differentiated activities.

The **divisional structure** follows from executives' choice to organize work in terms of the products they make, services they provide, or the places they sell. That is, the MNE can organize in terms of product (e.g., medical devices, pharmaceutical processing, consumer products, industrial components, and aerospace electronics for a consumer products firm), services (e.g., retail, commercial, investing, and asset management for a bank), or markets (e.g., North America, Europe, Africa, and Asia for a geographically diversified company). Each division is relatively autonomous, is directly accountable for its assigned activities, and typically manages its own planning processes. Divisional structures institute less vertical differentiation and more horizontal differentiation in order to decentralize decision-making.

An international division

- creates a critical mass of international expertise,
- competes with powerful domestic divisions for resources,
- fits the demands of the MNE that generates most sales in a single nation.

International Division An MNE institutes an international division structure when its international activities are a relatively small share of its total business. In this situation, the domestic divisions supervise the home market, while the international division takes responsibility for the less strategic foreign sector (see Figure 16.3). Segregating domestic and international activity enables consolidating personnel within a dedicated division. Organizing folks in a stand-alone international division allows people to make decisions more quickly, find ways to collaborate more directly, and challenge one another more credibly. Ultimately, goes the reasoning, organizational proximity promotes the crucial knowledge-generating and decision-making relationships that better interpret the unique needs of international markets.

Historically, U.S. MNEs have found the international division appealing, given that the scale of their home market usually far exceeds their overseas activity. Likewise, it is a popular choice for Japanese, Korean, and Chinese firms, as well as emerging market MNEs, given the size of their home markets along with concerns optimizing early stages of international activity. It finds less use among European MNEs, given the small size of their domestic markets relative to their international activity.

Drawbacks Dividing an MNE into domestic-international divisions can fan "us versus them" tensions. Managers in the larger, powerful domestic division may deemphasize supporting the international division, seeing it as a sidelight to the big show in the home market. Conflict between domestic and international units often obstructs sharing

FIGURE 16.3 The International Division

Executives institute an international division structure by organizing its international operations into a self-contained, relatively autonomous unit.

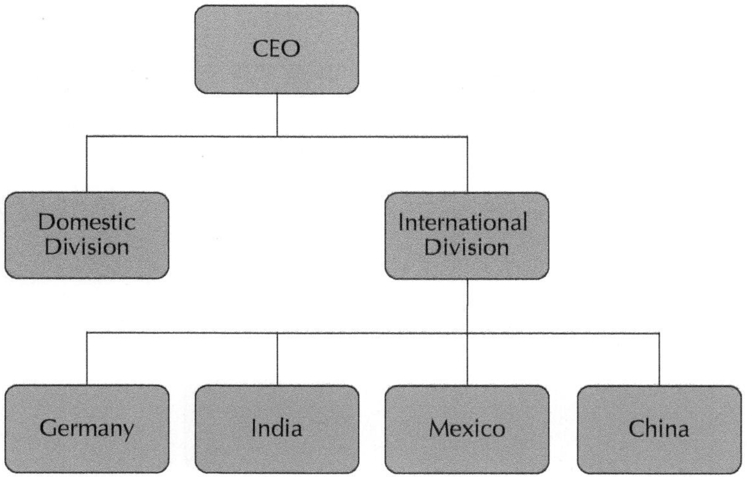

competencies, leveraging best practices, and integrating decision-making. Unguarded, ongoing tension can block cross-division connections, communication, and collaboration, thereby weakening global performance.

Worldwide Product Division The product division format is the most widely-used structure among MNEs worldwide. Its prevalence follows from the fact that many MNEs make and sell a broad portfolio of related products based on overlapping competencies in multiple markets (see Figure 16.4). Overlapping product activities in multiple markets opens opportunities to integrate activities that optimize global efficiencies.

Gore's structure, for example, sets four product divisions: electronics, fabrics, industrial, and medical. Each division serves different industries, but each makes and sells products worldwide based on Gore's proprietary PTFE expertise. The electronics product division, for example, makes PTFE-based high-performance cables and assemblies. Alternatively, the fabrics division makes PFTE-based materials for the outdoor clothing, military, law-enforcement, and fire protection markets. Effectively, Gore relies on the product division structure to exploit similarities and achieve synergies across markets.

Drawbacks The autonomy of different product divisions, particularly in a diversified MNE, challenges coordinating practices, exchanging ideas, and leveraging resources. Communication and collaboration more easily take place within, not across, product divisions, especially when some divisions are much larger, more profitable, or command a higher profile. Likewise, the global outlook that dominates decision-making in a product division can struggle adapting to local market contingencies. Self-contained, quasi-autonomous product divisions might make decisions inefficiently; this is compounded by the fact that different subsidiaries within different product divisions, often within the same country, report to different executives at headquarters.

At one point, for instance, Nestlé's various product divisions had configured more than 500 factories in nearly 90 countries to make products carrying one of some 8,000 brands.

FIGURE 16.4 The Worldwide Product Division

Executives institute a worldwide product division structure by organizing activities that support specific products within a self-contained, relatively autonomous unit that configures and coordinates activities worldwide.

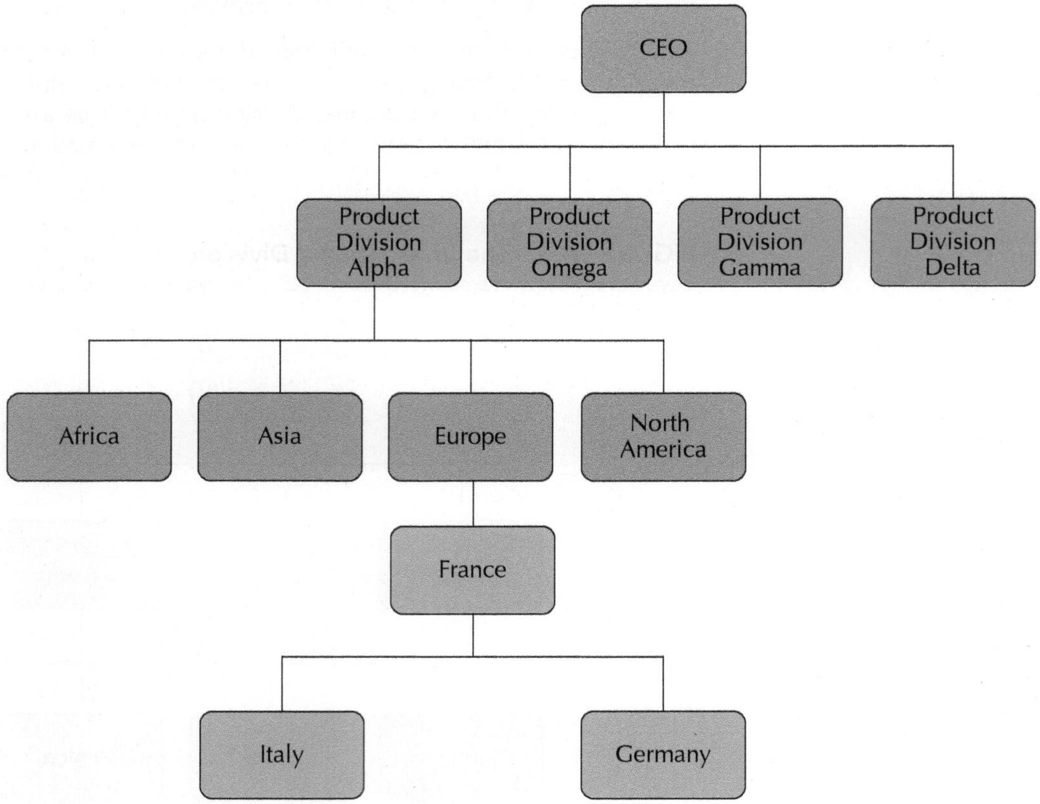

FIGURE 16.5 The Worldwide Area Division

Executives institute a worldwide area division structure by organizing the various activities within a geographic area. Each area division then configures and coordinates activities in its assigned territory.

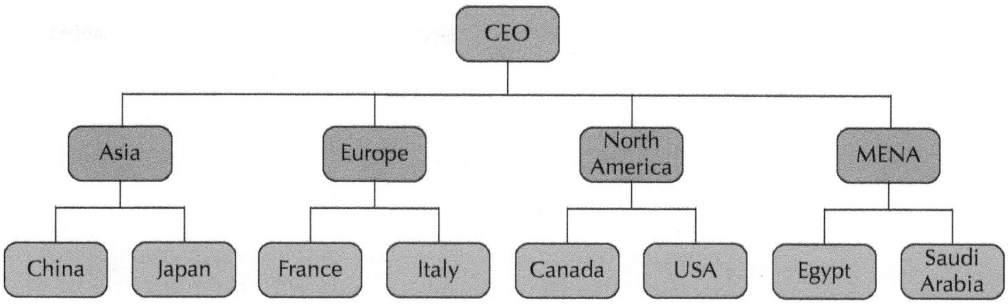

Headquarters in Switzerland struggled to determine the costs of the raw materials that its factories purchased from suppliers. In an extreme case, Nestlé's 40 U.S. factories procured raw materials independently. Lack of cross-division coordination, compounded by the fact that Nestlé's product divisions then used five different e-mail systems, meant that its U.S. factories, affiliated with different product divisions, unwittingly paid more than 20 different prices for vanilla extract to the same supplier.[30]

Geographic divisions fit the demands of MNEs who have extensive international operations that are distributed across many countries.

Worldwide Area Division An MNE institutes the worldwide area division, as depicted in Figure 16.5, when its sales are not dominated by a single country, including its home market, but are distributed across multiple markets. In this case, an MNE horizontally differentiates activities by geography, setting Division Alpha responsible for region/country A, Division Beta in charge of region/country B, and so on. Contrary to the product division's orientation to the global market, the area division focuses on specific needs in specific regions or countries. Geography is the common criterion for an area division. Still, in some cases, cultural similarity, economic conditions, business prospects, or regional integration moderates it.

Historically, European MNEs preferred the area structure. Based in small countries, many generated most revenues in foreign markets. Hence, they expanded into bigger markets, relying upon their version of the area division in the form of the so-called "mother-daughter" structure—in which foreign subsidiaries report straight to corporate headquarters.[31] The predominant of one market, such as the United States, or proximity of several smaller markets, such as the Middle East/North Africa, similarly encouraged organizing by area. For example, Swiss-based Nestlé organizes its food and beverage business geographies by disaggregating the globe into Zones EMENA (Europe, Middle East, and North Africa), Americas, and Asia/Oceania/Africa. Countries within an area are geographically contiguous and share cultural, linguistic, historical, political, and economic characteristics. Hence, Nestlé sees its area divisions facilitating coordination and collaboration among units within the region, accommodating new, contiguous markets, and promoting broader executive development.

The different economic and political realities between established and emerging economies increasingly spur executives to fine-tune their interpretation of a geographic area. Once small in scale and scope, markets in Asia, Africa, and South America have greater potential than many established countries; MNEs adjust their structures accordingly. For example, the rising importance of China and Eastern Europe led Nike to reset its four-region structure into six areas: North America, Western Europe, Eastern/Central Europe, Japan, Greater China, and Emerging Markets. Nike also announced that China and Eastern/Central Europe would operate separately from the others. Their growing share of the company's total sales, comparatively faster growth rates, and superior long-term potential called for different degrees of vertical and horizontal differentiation. Likewise, London-headquartered HSBC, Europe's largest bank with operations in 64 countries, is reconfiguring its organization to focus more on Asia and the Middle East, while winding down operations in slower-growing Europe and the United States.[32]

The geographic division structure is commonly used by MNEs pursuing localization strategies—as seen in Nike's and HSBC reorganization to better respond to shifting markets. The decentralization of the area structure—North America tends to North America, Europe tends to Europe, and so on—gives local managers more authority to adapt value activities within their zone. As Nike explained, "We are confident these changes will best position us for future growth. . . This model allows our global categories to connect directly with consumers at the local level."[33] Still, integration objectives typically push headquarters to retain strategic and financial authority.

Historically West-centric MNEs rethink the horizontal differentiation of their structures given fast-growing emerging markets. For example, Panasonic adjusted its worldwide area structure given its sales trends in emerging versus established markets. It had organized its area format in terms of the conventional zones of North America, Europe, and Asia. Now, given the equatorial proximity of many emerging economies, Panasonic differentiated its structure by organizing in terms of temperature and tropical climate zones—longitude, not latitude, mattered more. Executives in Brazil, who previously directly collaborated with colleagues in Chile, swap ideas with counterparts in Malaysia, who previously had coordinated with colleagues in Japan.[34]

Administrative legacies, executive preference, or legal constraints lead some firms to make smaller adjustments. Rather than the reposition entire divisions, some locate key functions in high-priority markets: finance and tax may go to Singapore, as Dell did, while global procurement goes to Shenzhen, as Walmart chose.[35] Similarly, P&G moved the headquarters of its global skin, cosmetics, and personal-care unit from Cincinnati to Singapore while Philips Electronics moved the headquarters of its domestic appliances business from Eindhoven to Shanghai.

Drawbacks Conducting similar organizational activities in several places increases administrative inefficiency. Each area division essentially builds a "mini-me" operation, replete with its own full-scale organization, to make and sell products in its assigned territory. Replication, besides being expensive, complicates integration. Some MNEs accept this inefficiency as the unavoidable, yet acceptable, cost of differentiating activities. Rather than a structural deficiency, the quest to boost local responsiveness, they reason, inevitably requires replicating activities. Managers then look to minimize expenses elsewhere in the organization. Popular options include coordination and control systems that optimize information flows and adopting automation and artificial intelligence systems to run rote ordinary tasks. IBM, for example, reports that artificial intelligence has replaced 30 percent of its HR staff and can predict with 95 percent accuracy which workers are about to quit—and advise HR to step in with skills training, education, job promotions, and raises before they do.[36]

THE MATRIX STRUCTURE

A matrix organization

- institutes overlap among functional and divisional forms,
- gives functional, product, and geographic groups a common focus,
- has dual-reporting relationships rather than a single line of command,
- fits the demands of MNEs that cannot easily reconcile competing market pressures.

The worldwide product division structure centralizes decision-making to improve operational efficiencies in order to optimize global integration. Alternatively, the worldwide area structure decentralizes decision-making to improve operational effectiveness in order to optimize local responsiveness. The MNE implementing a global strategy, in the quest to maximize worldwide integration, would opt for the former, while an MNE implementing a localization strategy, given its quest to maximize local responsiveness, would opt for the latter. As we saw in Chapter 12, some MNEs implement the transnational strategy, developing a value proposition that simultaneously reconciles globalization and localization pressure points. Organizing the resulting workflow encourages instituting a **matrix structure** (see Figure 16.6).

Typically, the matrix structure horizontally differentiates the MNE along two dimensions. Interlacing decision-making across different divisions, say product and area, theoretically integrates units that are sensitive to competing pressures. Requiring managers from different divisions to negotiate mutually agreeable plans, goes the reasoning, infuses each perspective into decision-making, thereby reconciling integration and responsiveness pressures. Since the matrix structure assigns equivalent authority to the product and area managers, they must work together to set responsibilities, coordinate resources, and share rewards.[37] Not surprisingly, a matrix structure requires frequent interaction between and across divisions. Hence, a successful matrix structure requires wide-ranging coordinating mechanisms and collaboration routines, driven by folks in the field, but monitored and, as needed, reconciled at headquarters.

FIGURE 16.6 The Matrix Structure

Executives institute a matrix structure by organizing a dual relationship among different divisions to integrate decision-making in order to simultaneously represent globalization and localization views.

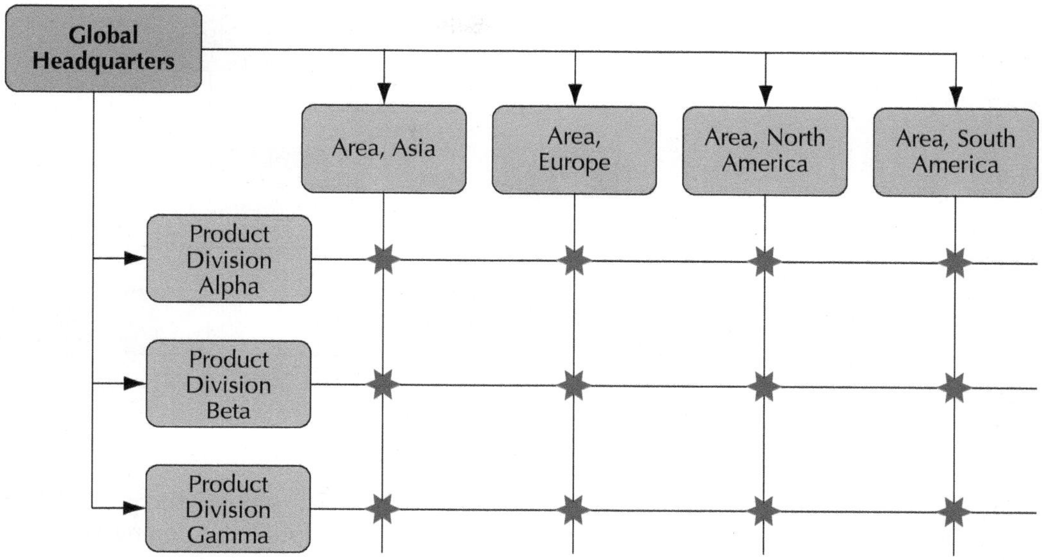

Typically, one sees two-dimensional matrix structures—say product and market or function and product. A three-dimensional matrix structure blending product, area, and function is possible, but difficult. In 2013, for example, Procter & Gamble configured its global organization in terms of a three-way matrix comprised of its Global Business Units, Sales and Marketing Operations, and Corporate & Global Business Services. Procter & Gamble aimed to exploit its global scale, minimize redundancies, and leverage functions throughout its 3-D matrix in ways, management reason, that better supported its increasingly sophisticated global strategy.

Drawbacks In principle, the matrix structure promotes cross-divisional communication and multifunctional collaboration. In practice, office politics fans competition for resources and rewards. Unchecked, gamesmanship threatens collaboration, thereby short-circuiting the knowledge-generating and decision-making relationships that had originally motivated its adoption. Likewise, coordination challenges often escalate. ABB, the automation and power-technology giant, organized a matrix of sectors and countries that divided itself into more than 5,000 profit centers. Early success soon gave way to growing difficulties organizing communication among units, some that advocated product imperatives, others that championed area perspectives. Communication and collaboration difficulties were complicated by all sorts of problems, including the fact that different units' different preferences meant that, at one point, ABB had 576 enterprise-resource-planning systems in play—systems that, ironically, had promised to integrate plans and present a unified view to facilitate better decisions.[38]

Persistent problems coordinating responsibilities and resources have led MNEs to question the matrix structure's practical usefulness.

Fundamentally, a matrix structure institutes a dual hierarchy—that is, there are two bosses, say, one representing products, the other area. This situation violates the **unity-of-command principle** that an unbroken chain of command should run from CEO to the entry-level employee. Assigning one worker two bosses, by blurring lines of responsibility, creates conflicting command and nebulous accountability. The CEO of Dow Chemical, an early adopter of the matrix structure, explained, "We were an organization that was matrixed and depended on teamwork, but there was no one in charge. When things went well, we didn't know whom to reward; and when things went poorly, we didn't know whom to blame."[39] Proctor & Gamble conceded the same, noting that its three-dimensional matrix confused accountability and slowed decision making. Its CEO similarly explained there were too many people involved in the decision-making process, and the resulting "thicket" meant that no one singularly owned a decision, particularly when it went wrong. Hence, in 2019, Proctor & Gamble abandoned its three-dimensional matrix and shifted to six sector business units, within a worldwide product structure, in order to institute the autonomy needed to act quickly while also holding people accountable.[40]

FIGURE 16.7 The Mixed Structure

Executives institute a structure that mixes various formats to organize work for difference across business due to varying sales trends, industry conditions, market situations, or environmental circumstances.

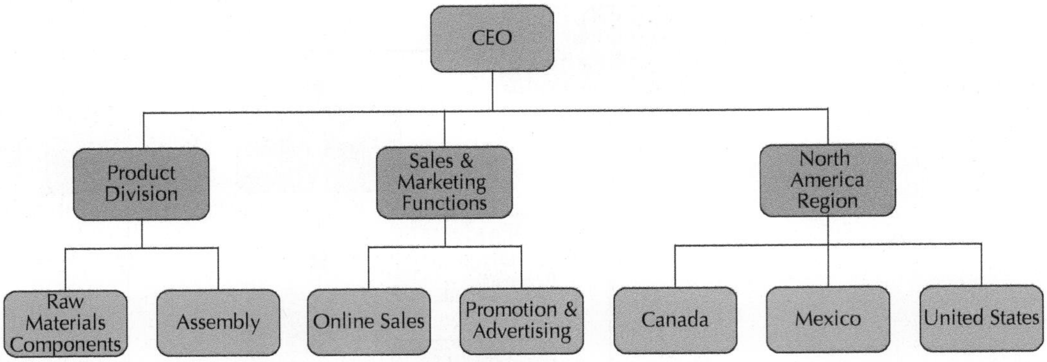

THE MIXED STRUCTURE

Few MNEs set a structure that neatly applies the precise characteristics of a functional, divisional, or matrix structure. Unquestionably, many would—if they could. In reality, sales trends, industry conditions, market situations, or environmental circumstances often prevent instituting a superior single organizational model. R&D-intensive companies, like Toyota or Siemens, open research centers in emerging economies and then must integrate them with units in established markets. Firms extracting natural resources, like ExxonMobil or Vale, must adapt to evolving, often disruptive, regulatory situations. Consumer-oriented firms, like Henkel or Shishido, face conflicting imperatives to customize their businesses to local needs while maintaining consistent global processes. Despite preference for structural consistency, organizing for differing conditions leads some MNEs to institute a **mixed structure** that combines features of the functional, geographic, and product formats (see Figure 16.7).

The mixed structure does not signify indecisiveness, but a practical solution. Depending upon circumstances, for example, a geographic format is optimal for Area A, but a functional structure fits for business activity in Area B. Nike, for example, installed vertical and horizontal arrangements in China and Eastern/Central Europe that did not fit its activities in North America, Western Europe, and Japan. Likewise, Dell Computers horizontally differentiated its Asian headquarters in Singapore by business function, aiming to improve its regional financial, operational, and tax efficiency. Nestlé organizes most of its food and beverage business in terms of geographies (Areas EMENA, Americas, and Asia/Oceania/Africa) but runs some products globally (e.g., Nestlé Waters, Nestlé Nutrition, Nespresso). Toyota's structure mixes product, geography, and functional orientations; one division takes charge of its established markets in North America, Europe, and Japan, one oversees emerging markets in China and Latin America, one runs its Lexus brand, and the last directs the development and production of vehicle components.

CONCEPT CHECK

Discussion of the "Types of Economic Systems" in Chapter 4 noted that a mixed economy combines some of the characteristics of a free market with features of command systems. A mixed organizational structure reflects a similar choice to sacrifice purity for practicality.

NEOCLASSICAL STRUCTURES

16-3 Interpret neoclassical organization structures

This text identifies a panorama of conditions that lead MNEs to develop increasingly sophisticated strategies. Correspondingly, given the thesis that "structure follow strategy," they must look to institute commensurately sophisticated structures. In established markets, automation and artificial intelligence, within the broader context of digitalization, steadily ushers in the workplace of the future. Technology, by making information and interactions immediately available, enables shaping organizations in ways we never imagined. In emerging economies, improving infrastructure, accelerating growth, and expanding demand creates immense opportunities to rethink who does what job, why and where. Organizing this workflow requires different modes of communication and collaboration to connect the increasingly interdependent people working in increasingly different places.

Technology, by making information and interactions immediately available, enables shaping organizations in ways we never imagined.

Some see the hierarchical architecture of classical structures increasingly struggling to support the demands of novel, tech-intensive strategies. Its advantages of maximizing command, control, coercion, and compliance often deteriorate into complexity, bureaucracy, conformity, and inflexibility. Analysts conclude that the "models and frameworks that shaped our leading organizations from the end of the second world war through the conclusion of the cold war are clearly obsolete in this new era of e-business, perpetual innovation, and global competition."[41] The Chairperson of Lego, maker of premium plastic construction toys, in the face of falling sales, momentum, and productivity, concedes as much, lamenting that "[w]e have built an increasingly complex organization . . . with too many layers and overlapping functions that could lead to stagnation or decline."[42] Likewise, Procter & Gamble, facing flagging performance, reasoned it must create a simpler, more efficient organization that inspires initiative and innovation.

Classical structures emphasize the principles of command and control. Neoclassical structures emphasize the principles of coordinate and collaborate.

MNEs facing these sorts of situations rethink traditional approaches to horizontal and vertical differentiation.[43] They seek formats that promote relationships, expand communication, and support collaboration. They seek formats that give greater clarity and simplicity to employees, which unlocks their productivity and performance. They seek formats that create flexibility and entrepreneurialism, and encourage faster decisions by motivating employees to act not as workers, but as owners. These concerns and ambitions direct executives attention to **neoclassical structures**.

In principle, neoclassicalism advocates thinking about an organization as a social system in order to understand how human behavior fundamentally shapes its performance. In absolute terms, neoclassical structures serve the same purpose as their classical counterparts: they stipulate how an MNE arranges its workplace, organizes decision-making, and assigns authority, accountability, roles, and responsibilities. However, neoclassical structures do so in ways that differ radically. Notably, they move organization design from stipulating the boundaries that precisely specify a hierarchy to developing the **boundarylessness** that loosely arranges a heterarchy.

Changing Circumstances Neoclassical structures speak to the emerging conduct and context of employees' jobs, whether done at the biggest headquarters or the smallest subsidiary, given 24/7 connectivity, shifting global workflows, and the influence of automation and artificial intelligence. Change in the nature of work is changing the nature of international management. Historically, the higher one's level in the hierarchy, the more one knew about the various jobs in the company. Hence, a generation ago, MNEs relied on elite executives to make the big decisions that were then delegated to workers worldwide. The technologies of that day meant that information was hard to acquire, tough to process, and difficult to distribute; senior executives were best positioned to develop and drive the company's strategy.

Today that thesis is increasingly debatable, and, at MNEs like Gore, as you saw in the opening case, and J&J, as you'll see in the closing case, arguably dubious. Historically, the folks running local subsidiaries were far removed from the global drama. That no longer holds. Real-time access to information, facilitated by cheap, powerful telecommunications, closes the global–local gap. The growing supply of bright, motivated workers everywhere, not just in a few cities in a few countries, means work can be done well, anywhere. Consequently, there are far fewer jobs that senior executives can script or that subsidiary managers cannot do. Big change in the workplace triggers big change in the organization of the workplace. This change highlights the idea, appeal, and utility of neoclassical structures.

CONCEPT CHECK

"The Forces Driving Globalization and IB," profiled in Chapter 1, explains that market drivers such as expanded technology, liberalized trade, and increased cross-national cooperation reset the interpretation of IB. Recognizing these changes as opportunities moves MNEs to experiment with neoclassical structures that reset the interpretation of vertical and horizontal differentiation.

THE CHALLENGE OF BOUNDARIES

In the context of an organization, **boundaries** are (1) the vertical divisions that separate employees into specific slots in the hierarchy; each is marked by marked by formal superior–subordinate relationship and (2) the horizontal divisions that follow from having specific employees do specific jobs in specific units. In a classical structure, vertically and horizontally differentiating the workflow sets standards, imposes order, disciplines decisions, and determines accountability. Each specification, by definition, institutes a boundary among roles, relationships, and responsibilities. Think of, for example, the schematic of boxes and lines

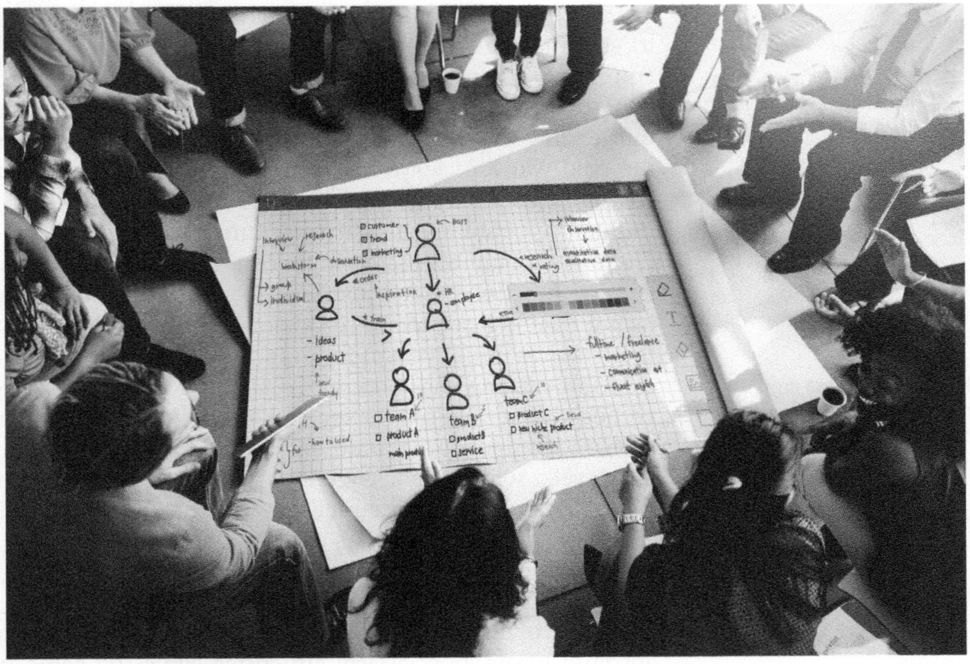

Discussion, debating, and deciding who does what with whom in a neoclassical context.

Source: Rawpixel.com/Shutterstock

shown in Figures 16.2 through 16.7; each 'box' demarcates the boundaries that segregate the people who run the various functions, markets, and products, each 'line' stipulates the path of information, communication, and decision-making.

The boundaries that establish the command-and-control format of classical structures, by instituting divisions between people, often slow communication, discourage collaboration, create rigidities, and bureaucratize decision-making. Sony's CEO, for example, blamed poor performance not on the wrong strategy, but the reality that rivalry and conflict between its differentiated businesses obstructed individual effort and collective effectiveness.[44] Removing the boundaries that block communication, slow coordination, and hinder collaboration among divisions, he added, repositioned Sony to better respond to its expanding diversity of markets, customers, and rivals. As did Sony, so too do other MNEs, developing sophisticated structures to implement sophisticated strategies, apply the principles of the neoclassical structure.

THE QUEST FOR BOUNDARYLESSNESS

Boundaries and, more importantly, how to preempt them, direct attention to neoclassical structure. This format questions setting boundaries between vertical ranks and roles, between horizontal units in different functions, products, and areas, and between the firm and its suppliers, distributors, partners, strategic allies, and customers. GE's performance elaborate the idea; directing it far-flung global operations led former CEO Jack Welch to experiment with progressively flatter structures. He aimed to build an organization that eliminated the vertical and horizontal boundaries that put barriers between company, managers, customers, suppliers, and stakeholders. As Welch explained, "The simplest definition of what we are trying to create—what our objective is—is a boundaryless company, a company where the artificial barriers and walls people are forever building around themselves or each other—for status, security, or to keep change away—are demolished and everyone has access to the same information, everyone pulls in the same direction, and everyone shares in the rewards of winning—in the soul as well as in the wallet."[45]

Boundarylessness follows from eliminating vertical, horizontal, and external boundaries that constrain information, relationships, and initiative.

In the boundarylessness of a neoclassical structure, value lies not in how much you know, but how much you know how to find. Getting things going requires recruiting, motivating, rewarding and retaining bright people, wiring them into loosely connected networks that self-organize and self-govern, maximizing information flows that provoke more learning, and minimizing infrastructure to get rid of anything that gets in the way of people exchanging ideas. Speed, flexibility, productivity, and empowerment are the objectives—typically advantageous, but especially so when crises, like the COVID-19 pandemic, push MNEs to pivot operations and reallocate resources swiftly. Now, in this model, managers forsake controlling things, keeping them in channels, and building boundaries between functions and ranks. Now, as leaders, they challenge and contest in order to share ideas from anywhere.

Making Moves Radical then, the vision of boundarylessness is less so today. Gore's lattice structure and its egalitarian workplace philosophy, for instance, exemplify its principles and practices. More precisely, the Gore Way sees the hierarchy suppressing creativity and innovation. Gore downplays organizational charts, chains of command, preset channels, and job titles. Instead, its lattice structure encourages Associates to share, not control information. Rather than a few telling the many what to do, its multifunctional teams self-organize around opportunities. Collaboration compels communication, and high-performance validates leaders. "We work hard at maximizing individual potential, maintaining an emphasis on product integrity, and cultivating an environment where creativity can flourish," explained Gore's former CEO. She added, "A fundamental belief in our people and their abilities continues to be the key to our success, even as we expand globally."[46] The task is, then, instituting the structure that gives workers the incentive and authority to make decisions.

Cisco set off on similar adventures. Asked why, Cisco's CEO replied that he really had no choice. He needed a structure that would react quickly to new opportunities, develop entire solutions rather than one-shot fixes, and help Cisco "become a globally integrated company by making it easier for executives from all around the world to weigh in."[47] Going forward, he expects cheaper, easier technology will move more MNEs from the classical standards of command and control to the neoclassical ideals of coordinate and collaborate. Tesla, fearful of the consequences of growing from a flexible startup to a rigid hierarchy, radically reset itself. It flattened its structure to improve communication, thinned management levels, accelerated feedback loops, and improved transparency—all the sorts of things that set and sustain boundaries that, explained its CEO, threaten "the success of our mission."[48] Likewise, Procter & Gamble abandoned its once revolutionary three-dimensional matrix structure in favor of a far less boundary-based sector business unit structure; announcing the change, its CEO reported, "We believe this is the most important organizational change we've made in the last 20 years" that, by simplifying operations, improves autonomy and accountability.[49] Finally, even the most hierarchical chain of command, the United States military, adopted neoclassical elements of decentralized decision-making in order to help defeat Al Qaeda's Iraqi-based forces.[50]

Key Features Neoclassical structures emphasize lateral decision processes, horizontal linkages, and extensive collaboration. Key features include self-organizing and self-governing agents. Flexibility encourages entrepreneurial rather than bureaucratic decision-making. Cross-partner linkages emphasize transactional efficiency, but also advocate mutually beneficial relationships. Unlike classical structures, in which the formal attributes of managers (i.e., title, location, number of direct reports, levels from the CEO) matter most, neoclassical structures make the managers' relationships with others matter more. So called *'laissez faire'* leaders provide guidance and guardrails. In sum, neoclassical structure spurs people to share rather than control information, collaborate rather than compete, promote rather than suppress innovation, cultivate rather than command relationships, engage rather than resist change, and make rather than take decisions. These sorts of moves, whether taking place at Gore, Cisco, Tesla, or P&G, among others, signal the transformation of "Organization Man" into "Network Person."

THE NETWORK STRUCTURE

A network structure is a flatter, less-hierarchical format that decentralizes decision making to promote connections, communications, and collaboration among agents, both internal and external to the firm.

The **network structure** exemplifies principles of a neoclassical structure. It optimally arranges roles, relationships, and responsibilities in a patterned flow of activity that coordinates activities and configures resources (see Figure 16.8).[51] Connecting people, products, and processes into a flat, horizontally differentiated structure decentralizes decision-making. Communication channels maximize the connections that energize collaboration. Coordination and control systems set, regulate, and integrate the interactions among members, the latter motivated by common goals and specific objectives. How one creates

FIGURE 16.8 A Network Structure

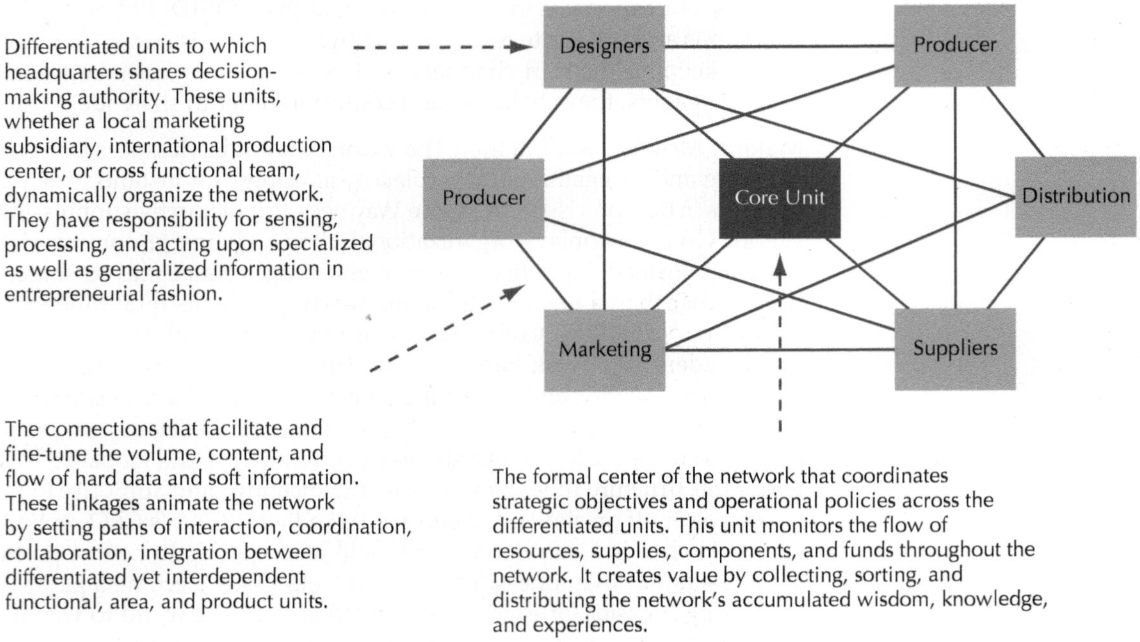
Designers
Producer
Producer
Core Unit
Distribution
Marketing
Suppliers
Differentiated units to which headquarters shares decision-making authority. These units, whether a local marketing subsidiary, international production center, or cross functional team, dynamically organize the network. They have responsibility for sensing, processing, and acting upon specialized as well as generalized information in entrepreneurial fashion.
The connections that facilitate and fine-tune the volume, content, and flow of hard data and soft information. These linkages animate the network by setting paths of interaction, coordination, collaboration, integration between differentiated yet interdependent functional, area, and product units.
The formal center of the network that coordinates strategic objectives and operational policies across the differentiated units. This unit monitors the flow of resources, supplies, components, and funds throughout the network. It creates value by collecting, sorting, and distributing the network's accumulated wisdom, knowledge, and experiences.

and shares knowledge, not the capacity to control it, sets standards.[52] As Bill Gore reasoned in *The Lattice Organization—A Philosophy of Enterprise,* "A lattice organization is one that involves direct transactions, self-commitment, natural leadership, and lacks assigned or assumed authority." As such, it rejects the standard that one person (the boss) should specify who others (workers) may talk to and work with.[53]

The organizational center of the network does what it does best and outsources the rest—that is, it leverages ownership advantages and competencies and, where it has none, collaborates with those firms that do.[54] For example, Apple, Qualcomm, and Cisco concentrate on value creation in R&D, design, or marketing. They then contract world-class manufacturers, like Pegatron, Foxconn, Kyocera, or Yue Yuen Industrial, to make their products. Operationally, cross-partner arrangements share production, distribution, and service resources.

CONCEPT CHECK

The notion of a network shapes discussions of IB: Chapter 1, for instance, notes the idea, of connectivity and expanding cross-national infrastructure links, Chapter 7 describes trade networks arranged by the WTO, Chapter 9 discusses financial networks in global capital markets, and Chapter 15 profiles how MNEs network with partners through collaborative alliances.

MNEs worldwide use various forms of the network structure.

The latest, greatest communication systems, cloud computing, social media, and teleconferencing tools, increasingly turbocharged with automation and artificial intelligence, support coordination and expedite collaboration in the network structure. IBM, for example, employs clerks in Shanghai to process accounts receivables, specialists in Manila to oversee human resources, accountants in Kuala Lumpur to keep the books, buyers in Shenzhen to procure components, and customer specialists in Brisbane to run its help desk. Each unit, responding to IBM's quest to move work to places where it will be done most efficiently and to the highest quality, manages projects that arise throughout the global market.[55] Customers, meanwhile, care less where work is done provided the results satisfy contract specifications.

Networks Aren't New The network structure, while sounding newfangled, is not unprecedented. Gore, as we saw in our opening case, launched its lattice structure in the 1950s. Likewise, Japanese MNEs have long used the so-called *keiretsu* format, an integrated collective of nominally independent companies in which each owns a share of the others.[56] *Keiretsus* rely on personal relationships among the companies' executives. Sometimes the network is vertical, such as the *seisan keiretsu,* a manufacturing system in which managers connect the factors of production of a certain product (e.g., Toyota and its parts suppliers), or the *ryūtsū keiretsu,* a distribution network that links storage facilities, transportation systems, and customers (e.g., Suzuken in medical supplies). Or, the network is horizontal, like a *kigyō shūdan,* a diversified business group that links

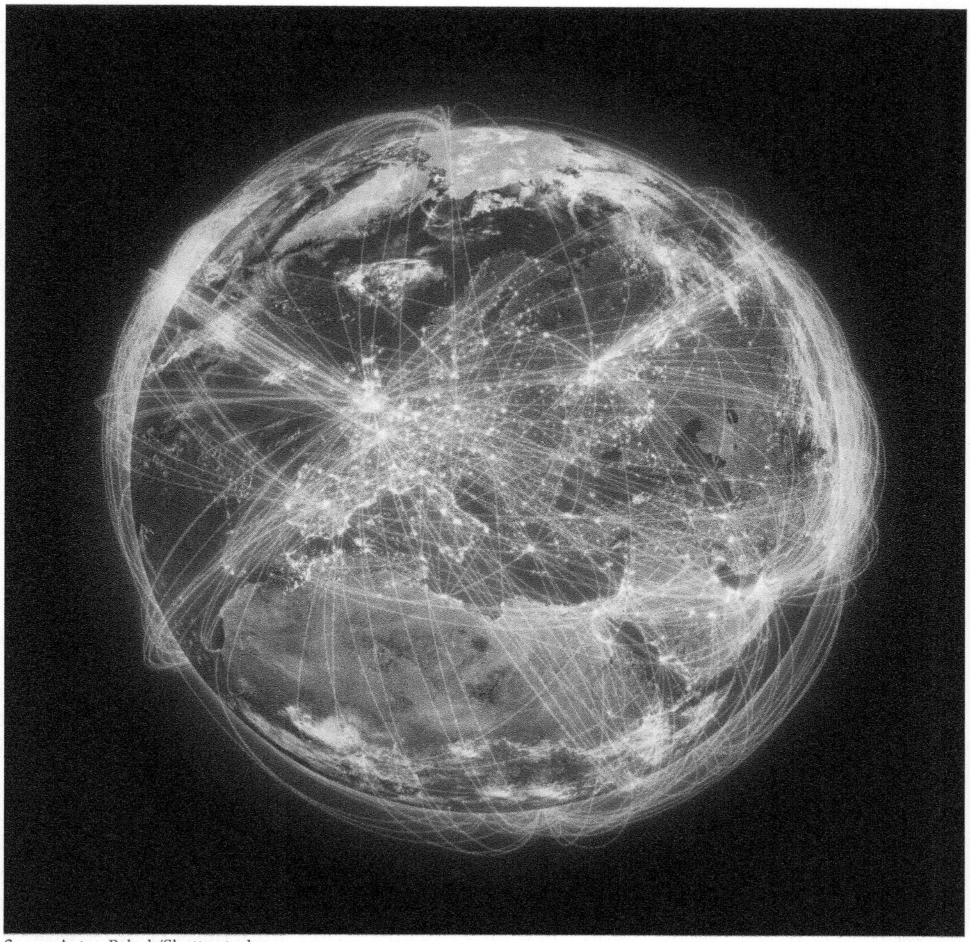

Source: Anton Balazh/Shutterstock

Networks are marked by extensive connections and seemingly chaotic, but purposeful links. This network, set by air routes among key nodes in the Caribbean and Central and North America, depicts fundamental principles.

companies across related and different industries. At its center is a *sogo shosha* (trading company), like Mitsubishi, or a financial institution, like Sumitomo. In both vertical and horizontal *keiretsus*, the network center configures production, coordinates marketing, and regulates financing among allied units.

South Korean companies like Samsung, LG, or Hyundai share characteristics of the *keiretsu* in their *chaebol* format. These large industrial conglomerate, typically run by an owner or family, consists of many diversified affiliates; the ten main *chaebols*, for example, list more than 600 affiliated companies.[57] Currently, several dozen South Korean family-controlled corporate groups qualify as *chaebols*. The extended family network organizes the connections that constitute the *chaebol*. German firms, such as Deutsche Bank, are similarly intertwined, but no formal term describes the format. Like their Japanese counterparts, its various groups have extensive, self-sustaining connections. Unlike the Japanese, they formalize central control. MNEs elsewhere exhibit elements of these formats, including IKEA, Scania, Virgin Group, Cisco, and Grupo Empresarial Antioqueño.[58]

THE VIRTUAL STRUCTURE

A virtual organization is an agile arrangement among partners that e flexibly adapts to change.

Digital platforms progressively makes the **virtual structure** a practical neoclassical option. The ubiquity of mobile devices, the vast pools of workers and customers worldwide, and the increasing ease of managing information to make efficient matches support virtual strategies that, in turn, require a virtual structure. This format centers on individuals or enterprises organizing around a shared set of resource-sharing rules and conditions. It extensively uses technology to sustain and expand connections. The virtual structure "works across space, time, and organizational boundaries with links strengthened by webs of communication technologies."[59] Instead of command and control, the virtual structure uses associations, agreements, and alliances to organize otherwise independent workers. Deemphasizing formal rules, responsibilities, and procedures promotes informal communication that deemphasizes hierarchical boundaries. Improving technologies support coordination among people working from different locations, making it easier to cultivate relationships, acquire resources, and develop capabilities. Market mechanisms, such as contracts, formalize relationships. Strong performers replace poor performers.

Analysts point to MNEs like British Telecom, Reuters Holdings, Corning, and Aventis exhibiting aspects of a virtual structure—each institutes elements of a loosely connected, cloud-based, dynamic organization that champions the coordination, collaboration, and control ethos of virtuality. More adventurous forms are found in firms such as Airbnb, Deliveroo, Uber, or Upwork, whose virtual platforms match workers with customers; the growing online gig or sharing economy, whereby freelancers, contractors, and temporary workers connect with buyers, inspires ongoing innovations. The film industry provides an extreme model of a virtual structure. Worldwide, approximately 60,000 films are made annually by many "employees," who, as free agents move from project to project, applying their skills (i.e., directing, acting, talent search, animation, costuming, and set design) as contracted. Temporary arrangements let them organize, disband, and reorganize as projects start and stop.[60] In all types, command-and-control gives way to connect and collaborate.

NEOCLASSICAL STRUCTURES: PRACTICAL PROBLEMS

Neoclassical structures, like their classical counterparts, inevitably face practical difficulties. As dynamic structures, they require adaptive reconfiguration and responsive coordination.[61] Organizing something that continually evolves is tough. Gore, for example, worries that the intricacies of its workplace may prove too socially complex as well as physically wearisome. Cisco struggles to manage teams amid its ongoing acquisitions and divestures. Nokia's consensus-seeking leaders promoted *esprit de corps* among its loosely bounded units; that, though, did not stop the company's gradual collapse.

More pointedly, IKEA, seeing its sales falling as the retail landscape transformed at a scale and pace never seen before, launched its most dramatic restructuring ever—'Organization for Growth' (O4G). It slashed thousands of jobs to cut red tape and speed decision making in repositioning for an emergent "multichannel world" and escalating "customer-centric" standards. A year later, conceded its CEO, O4G had worsened the working environment, unexpectedly eroding teamwork, communication, flexibility, and initiative. IKEA then launched a "positive people movement" program, given that, "We cannot change the past, but we can shape our future . . . We are in the middle of creating a whole new IKEA together."[62]

Some firms devise means to preempt these threats. Srijan, an Indian digital transformation company, lets employees monitor coworkers' compensation. Zappos's organizational chart changes several times a day, but is available real-time online and workers can check coworkers' evolving roles and responsibilities. SumAll, as does Zappos, institutes a corporate constitution that formalizes the rights of individuals and teams to participate in decision-making. The jury is still out on their effectiveness. Some note that the egalitarianism of neoclassical formats works well organizing small firms, but struggles in larger ones. Likewise, boundary-busting could prove detrimental in knowledge-intensive firms, like McKinsey or Google, that already find it difficult measuring individual productivity.[63]

Lastly, some executives champion self-organization to the troops but, when push comes to shove, they pull rank, take charge, and direct the show. Recurring gaps between the principle of boundarylessness and workplace practices fans motivation problems. Hidden hierarchies arise as workers forsake management's visionary rhetoric and organize around the day-to-day reality of rules, rewards, and punishments.[64] Said one observer, "I've been inside a lot of companies that espouse flat organizational structures and self-management. But when you really start looking at how things actually work, you find that there is in fact a hierarchy—just one that is not explicit."[65]

POINT

The Hierarchical Structure: The Superior Format

YES The superior way to organize an MNE is a ongoing debate. The classical hierarchy, we argue, is the enduring foundation for how MNEs optimally arrange the roles, responsibilities, and relationships of its structure for a simple reason—its explicit vertical and horizontal differentiation identifies, as we see in Figure 16.9, who's who in the organization. Doing so sets a clear chain of command and precisely assigns tasks. It streamlines rules, routines, policies, and procedures. It organizes planning, coordination, and control systems. As Frederick Taylor, arguably the first management consulting, noted in his 1895 manifesto, *The Principles of Scientific Management*, "In the past the man has been first; in the future the system must be first."[66] Today, we know the system as the hierarchical structure.

An advocate of the hierarchy, Harold Geneen of ITT, argued correctly that it "makes people as predictable and controllable as the capital resources that they're responsible for."[67] Discipline lets managers specify roles, determine accountability, and minimize uncertainty. These strengths have rightly made the hierarchical organization the *sine qua non* of professional management since the early twentieth century. Given the strong preference for this format in countries, such as India and China, it continues as the standard in the twenty-first century. While

COUNTERPOINT

The Hierarchical Structure: The Superior Format

NO Although imperfect, history helps interpret the present and predict the future. Think back to the early 1900s, when emerging technologies, by radically resetting workflows, rightly signaled the superiority of the then-heretical hierarchy. A generation later, debate was over, and the hierarchy prevailed and predominated. We see the same today, as emerging technologies endorse new structural heresies that make for interesting debate, but again, in a generation or so, will be moot. Over the next decade, automation and artificial intelligence technologies, by enabling immediate information in interactions, will radically reset the workplace. Expanding digital infrastructures allows MNEs to organize their activities in new ways, letting them efficiently diffuse information and effectively integrate its flows. Before, organizations relied on managers to control things, keep them in channels, build boundaries between functions and ranks, stay within company walls—all part and parcel of the hierarchical organization. Now the progressive practicality of non-hierarchical structures, or alternatively, heterarchial structures, calls for leaders who draw the best ideas from anywhere, whether the factory floor, other businesses, other companies, or other countries, to create unique, high-spirited, entrepreneurial enterprise.

FIGURE 16.9 A Classical Hierarchy

Although simplistic, this depiction communicates the organizing logic of a hierarchy—different people of different rank at different levels do different jobs. The top-down flow highlights the idea of vertical differentiation while the various shades of folks speak to horizontal differentiation.

Source: Paperboat/Shutterstock

neoclassical structures may gain converts here or there, we see many companies whose lofty leader, many rungs removed from the factory floor, commands and controls activity through a hierarchical structure.

Ongoing Refinements Contemporary technological, regulatory, and competitive trends, we agree, have interesting implications for organizing a company—immediate information and interactions are game changers. Unquestionably, as environments evolve, so too must companies' strategies and structures. However, the Counterpoint's call to discard the tried, tested, and true principles of the hierarchy in favor of the new-fangled heterarchy strikes us as reckless. Yes, gaps emerge in the hierarchy, creating temporary uncertainties. Managers need only reengineer processes to fill them. Powerful programs, like Total Quality Control, Six Sigma, and the Balanced Scorecard, turbocharged by artificial intelligence and automation, effectively do so. Fine-tuning workplace arrangements through these sorts of methods equips the MNE to organize its workplace.[68]

What then, you may wonder, do we think of the neoclassical alternatives championed in the Counterpoint? Quite honestly, we see radical tinkering as exhibiting commendable courage but questionable judgment given the harsh realities organizing international operations. Success centers on methods with successful track records, not the wistfulness of a brave new world powered by gimmicky social networking tools.

The Crux of Change Unquestionably, the tried-and-true classical hierarchy has virtues. Nevertheless, market trends spotlight its limits. It organizes workplace activities and information flows in ways that thwart integration—an expanding challenge as work is increasingly "unbundled" and "rebundled" as it travels the world. Even when turbocharged with matrix overlays and mixed adjustments, the hierarchy slows relationships, blurs accountability, and complicates collaboration.[70] McKinsey & Company, for example, reports that struggling MNEs' reliance on traditional organization formats imposes a steep penalty. By leashing employees' motivation, stifling adaptation, and squelching entrepreneurialism, hierarchies impede common cause, erode relationships, and discourage innovation.[71] So, just as a century earlier, today astute executives break free of the shackles of the status quo, building organizations that leverage the expanding waves of information flowing in, through, and out of the MNE.

The Heterarchy Looking around today one sees examples of networks, virtual organizations, lattice structures, flat formats, and further afield, the helix and holacracy formats.[72] These neoclassical forms exhibit features of a heterarchy: namely, "a large-scale, self-organizing community that sets free unusually high degrees of energy and engagement."[73] The heterarchy is a constellation of actors and relationships that follow from the interactions of technology, knowledge, social relations, administrative routines, and legal ties. It is "infinitely large, never balanced, never optimal and has unique perspectives for all members."[74] As seen in Figure 16.10, agents connect to

FIGURE 16.10 A Neoclassical Heterarchy

This depiction of a heterarchy, again simplistic, highlights key features. A network of connections replaces precise ranks and divisions. Communication, coordination, and collaboration links, aided and abetted by technology, integrate equivalent, interdependent executives.

Source: Paperboat/Shutterstock

Leading Indicator Google, we submit, exemplifies running a hierarchy that respects the past but engages the future. Google organizes its senior executives and work groups by business function, with the largest functions represented by engineering, product management, and marketing divisions. Despite the founders' description of Google as engineering-centric, they see virtue in chaos by design. Insiders' tales of orderly disorder, purposeful disarray, and certain uncertainty signal its plans to thrive on the edge of controlled chaos, all the while firmly anchored in the functional order of a classical hierarchy.

Rather than retreat to the hierarchical conventions commonly found in iconic engineering-centric companies, such as DuPont and General Motors in earlier times, Google stretches its hierarchy as much as possible. Asked why, Larry Page, Google's co-founder, CEO, and unofficial thought leader, explained, "I want to run a company where we are moving too quickly and doing too much, not being too cautious and doing too little. If we don't have any of these mistakes, we're just not taking enough risk."[69]

others through direct and indirect channels. "Information flows along multiple and intermediate paths; this allows for multiple and overlapping points at which information can be sorted and interpreted. It makes it possible to process an abundance of information effectively."[75] By remedying the bias toward bureaucratic boundaries, it provides the framework to build a truly integrated enterprise.

The Tools Automation and artificial intelligence progressively reset the workplace, making the rote and mundane tasks of running a company the responsibility of the machines, while liberating workers to solve complex, creative tasks. Estimates say over half of the work activities that currently exist today will not be needed within a generation or two; moreover, many remaining tasks will be automated.[76] Meanwhile, technologies of all sorts promote greater collaboration, increasingly and easily enabling more team-based setups and agile ways of working. The resulting efficiency and effectiveness of heterarchial decision-making, much as the hierarchy did a century ago, signals the dawn of a new age.

The Test Inexorably, the standards of organization shift. The precision of vertical and horizontal differentiation gives way to loosely-coupled, less-bounded neoclassical formats.[77] Moreover, it's over-optimistic to think that one need merely mend a struggling hierarchy with organizational band-aids, such as Six Sigma or the Balanced Scorecard. Certainly useful, they increasingly far short of fixing an anachronistic structure. Explained an analyst, "today's big companies do very little to enhance the productivity of their professionals. In fact, their vertically oriented organizational structures, retrofitted with ad hoc and matrix overlays, nearly always make professional work more complex and inefficient."[78]

Andy Grove, once CEO of Intel, explains how the apparent chaos of the heterarchy will likely reset the presumed order of the hierarchy. A structure must encourage and energize constructive confrontation in ways that let workers agree and disagree, but, ultimately, commit to the same goals. The challenge, he advises, is developing a structure that will "let chaos reign and then rein in chaos."[79] In our view, the neoclassical heterarchy, not the classical hierarchy, provides the principles and practices to do precisely that.

COORDINATION SYSTEMS

16-4 Differentiate the systems used to coordinate international activities

An MNE's strategy determines how it configures its resources, capabilities, and competencies. Making its configuration perform requires, as you just saw, setting a structure, and as you'll see now, coordinating how people and processes work in it. One way to engage these ideas is to think of an MNE specifying a structure that puts units (pieces) atop the global game board. For various reasons, it places its R&D piece in Sweden, factory piece in Vietnam, logistics piece in the United States, marketing piece in Brazil, and service piece in Malaysia. Once it arranges this structure of pieces atop the global gameboard, executives specify how these pieces link to and relate with each other. Doing so requires developing **coordination systems** that synchronize, integrate, and regulate the activities of the pieces of its organization. Technically, coordination ranges from nonexistent (each piece is independent) to comprehensive (all pieces are interdependent).

Evolving markets and dynamic industries push MNEs to devise sophisticated strategies. Pioneering plans to configure value activities require commensurately innovative coordination methods. Coordinating activities requires adeptly moving ideas, materials, people, and capital. For example, IBM, GE, Microsoft, and Accenture opened R&D facilities in India, reasoning that the productivity of the local technical community coupled with the unique local outlook of frugal innovation offered promising points of value creation. Breakthroughs at GE's Technology Center in Bengaluru, owing to agile coordination systems, spread to GE's operations in Hungary, Brazil, China, the United States, and onward. In one instance, GE's Indian center developed a low-cost electrocardiograph machine for rural healthcare. Coordination links diffused it elsewhere, and soon GE's German and U.S. subsidiaries began selling it.[80]

Improving communications systems, made faster by cheaper voice, video, and data options, help link more people doing more processes in more places. Still, MNEs run into problems due to time zones, differing languages, and ambiguous interactions. Picture, for a moment, the MNE whose resources, capabilities, and competencies span the globe. Products flow from mines in South Africa and Chile to assembly operations in Mexico and India to customers worldwide. Each transfer, from mines to depots to plants to ships to warehouses to storefronts, creates links that require coordination. Toss into the mix multiple time zones, multiple languages, and multiple cultures, and the potential for mishaps escalates. Coordination systems minimize mishaps by synchronizing rules, responsibilities, and relationships that link the 'pieces' that make up the organization. Therefore, organizing activities, whether the structural format is classical or neoclassical, requires managers develop coordination systems to integrate differentiated units. Today, prevalent coordination systems center on the ideas of standardization, planning, or mutual adjustment.

COORDINATION BY STANDARDIZATION

Standardizing rules and routines to compel consistency has a straightforward mandate: do the same thing, the same way, everywhere. **Coordination by standardization** attains this goal by specifying the way employees do their jobs, work with one another, and deal with customers. Aspects range from the mundane (i.e., dress and decorum requirements stipulated in employee manuals) to the strategic (i.e., decision-making heuristics, protocols for entering new markets). Asked why it standardizes its processes and procedures worldwide, Starbucks notes the need to standardize the aesthetics, aura, and performance of its coffee shop concept in its nearly 31,000 locations spanning the globe— i.e., Starbucks in Seattle is interchangeable with Starbucks in Sydney is interchangeable with Starbucks in Santiago.[81] Coordination by standardization, by precisely specifying workplace standards and workflow scripts, achieves this goal.

CONCEPT CHECK

Earlier discussion of the "Rise and Application of Technology" in Chapter 1 notes that technology fosters new ways of communicating among worldwide operations. New technologies enable MNEs to experiment with options, many of them unprecedented, to coordinate dispersed value activities.

Coordination by standardization

- sets universal rules and procedures that apply to units worldwide,
- enforces consistency of activities among dispersed units.

Coordination by standardization is ideally suited for the MNE implementing an international or global strategy. Each strategy's imperative of consistency worldwide advocates standardizing activities. For an international strategy, transferring, applying, and protecting competencies requires tight, precise regulation. The global strategy typically runs densely linked, interdependent activities that has little slack for deviations. Clear lines of accountability, centralized decision-making, and codified knowledge prescribes who, when, why, and how one does a job. Resources and components, for instance, are needed at specific plants at specific times. Standardizing the methods of coordination, such as the format for processing information and administering logistics, preempts irregularities.

Efficient operations depends on effective links between interconnected activities that spur workers to meet precise schedules—no matter where they are in the world. Standardizing coordination, notably, reduces the disruptive influence of national cultures in the workplace. A unit in a monochronic culture, for instance, likely sees deadlines as hard promises while its counterpart in a polychronic culture likely sees them as general guidelines. Coordination by standardization synchronizes how each interpret time in the workplace. Similarly, an MNE with factories in Mexico and Japan that manufacture the same product, but, because of cultural legacies and location economics, apply different production approaches. The Mexican factory uses a traditional assembly-line system because of inexpensive local labor, patchy transportation infrastructure, and a high marginal cost of technology. The Japanese factory, in contrast, uses a lean production system due to local labor competency, manufacturing expertise, efficient logistics, and high warehouse expense. Coordination by standardization, in synchronizing their activities, harmonizes different orientations.

Challenges Differences in industry conduct and legal regulation complicate, if not obstruct, coordination by standardization. Rarely do preferred standards fit every situation in every unit in every country. Workplace rules on, say, who one can hire and fire, can differ dramatically from country to country, thereby preventing standardizing operating policies. Some MNEs, especially those uniquely differentiating their structure, as does HSBC in reorienting operations toward emerging economies, decentralize authority to let those subsidiaries adapt activities to local conditions. Ultimately, adjusting this policy rule or changing that procedure diminishes the consistency of coordination by standardization.

COORDINATION BY PLAN

Coordination by plan requires that interdependent units meet common deadlines and objectives.

Applying objectives, guidelines, and schedules to link people and processes implements **coordination by plan**. Generally, plans set success factors, specify expectations, assign accountability, and formalize deadlines. They regulate how units accept, adopt, and, where legitimate, adjust activities. Plans identify participating managers and programs and set format, sequence, and timing. Unlike coordination by standardization, coordination by plan allows managers of interdependent units to mutually adjust plans—provided they still hit targets set by headquarters. Put differently, whereas coordination by standardization maximizes operational efficiency, coordination by plan optimizes organizational effectiveness.

Improving technologies boost the practicality of coordination by plan by increasing the ease of analyzing, exchanging, and synthesizing information. Faster travel, expanding exchange options, and robust teleconferencing technologies overcome long-running barriers. The historic bane of IB has been the necessity of visiting faraway colleagues, partners, and customers, often at a moment's notice, high expense, and considerable effort. Now, teleconferencing creates the magical ability to be in many places at once.

Innovative management methods help out as well. Six Sigma, a rigorous and disciplined planning process, uses data and statistical analysis to coordinate practices and systems. Companies worldwide use similar programs, such as Activity Based Costing, Balanced Scorecard, and Total Quality Management. Likewise, MNEs apply other methods. Some locate international and domestic personnel in proximity to each other—say, by mixing folks from different divisions in the same building—to promote personal networks that facilitate communication and collaboration. Others build cross-national teams of people with different responsibilities to bridge gaps.[82] Dutch banking group ING, for example, organized 350 nine-person, multidisciplinary, co-located "squads" that focused on a specific client-related objective. Squads with overlapping missions then form tribes, typically not exceeding 15 individuals that coordinate priorities. Resetting the workplace for a new workflow helped ING accelerate its innovations in mobile banking.[83]

CONCEPT CHECK

No matter the coordination system adopted by an MNE, none are immune to the complications posed by national cultures. Different national cultures differently influence the social, workplace, political, legal, and economic contexts. Differences in cultural conditions, introduced in our Chapter 2 profile of "Major Behavioral Practices Affecting Business," shape a company's choice of coordination system.

Challenges Notwithstanding a plan's brilliance, the unexpected is ever-present; think of, for example, the aphorism, "the best-laid plans of mice and men often go awry." Market changes, government regulations, mergers and acquisitions, and black swan events like the COVID-19 pandemic, to name just a few, trigger disruptions. Adjusting objectives and schedules then requires dense communication among distinct groups spanning multiple borders. Problems escalate quickly given the scale and scope of multinational operations. For example, consider Red Hat's Global Support Services; it solves technical problems facing users of its intricate software products. Red Hat's support engineers and account managers work from 16 countries, support 3,600 coworkers in 65 offices distributed across 35 countries and provide round-the-clock customer service in 9 languages.[84] Synchronizing these activities is an ongoing challenge. Similarly, cultural differences routinely pose complications. Coworkers differ in their orientations toward time, trust, exchange, accountability, and allegiance.[85] Units anchored in individualistic cultures may disagree over information sharing or task responsibilities with their collectivist counterparts; ensuing uncertainty muddles coordination. Absent rules regulating relationships, cultural divergence confuses cross-national exchange.

COORDINATION BY MUTUAL ADJUSTMENT

Coordination by mutual adjustment depends on managers interacting extensively with counterparts.

Some MNEs coordinate people and processes with a personal touch, socially engineering their systems to cultivate relationships among workers that, in turn, promote connections, communication, and collaboration. Rather than rules and routines in the context of standardization, or objectives and schedules in the context of planning, they rely on social networking outlooks and methods in the context of **coordination by mutual adjustment**. Promoting knowledge-generating and decision-making relationships among coworkers, goes the reasoning, builds the sophisticated systems needed to support sophisticated strategies.

Coordination by mutual adjustment taps various methods, especially cross-national, cross-functional, and cross-business teams. Charged to collaborate, these teams share viewpoints and champion cooperative efforts. Similarly, MNEs rotate managers among various units, reasoning that cultivating relationships and expanding networks busts boundaries. In addition, rotation across divisional, business, or functional lines weakens insular thinking and reinforces knowledge sharing. As such, coordination by adjustment is philosophically and practically compatible with neoclassical structures.[86]

Consider 3M's 8,000 scientists in its 100-plus applied engineering laboratories and customer technical centers spanning more than 50 countries worldwide. The abstraction of the scientific process along with the complexity of product development are intrinsically challenging. 3M sees networking bright, independent-minded knowledge workers, distributed across far-flung units, requires robust, personal, and frequent interactions in order to exchange ideas, coordinate programs, and integrate activities.

Nearly 70 years ago, 3M's R&D community launched 'Tech Forum' to promote the sorts of connections and communication that anchor coordination by mutual adjustment. Key tools include a Technical Council, which includes the heads of the major labs, that meets monthly in order to cultivate the relationships that support mutual adjustment.[87] Likewise, Gore relies on similar sorts of coordination methods. Associates regularly hold meetings during which scientists, engineers, and analysts share ideas. Reflecting on the process, an enterprise leader explained, "we put a lot of effort into trying to make sure that we connect informally and formally across a lot of boundaries."[88] Pulling this off makes for a dramatic payoff for a company; research reports that improving the quality of decision-making generates 2.5 times higher growth, two times higher profit, and 30 percent higher return on invested capital.[89]

Challenges Coordination by mutual adjustment imposes tough organizational demands. The personalized dynamic of coordination by mutual adjustment resets the official trappings set by formal roles, status, and power. The dynamics of social networks blur positional relationships among superiors, colleagues, and subordinates. Coordination by standardization or plan, in contrast, recognizes and reinforces vertical and horizontal differentiation. Hence, coordination by mutual adjustment puts big demands on senior executives; it requires resetting executives' roles from telling people what to do to facilitating their success. Operationally, the scale and scope of the typical MNE poses tough logistical obstacles. Typical geographic circumstances, for example, mean teams must meet from early morning through late evening to accommodate various time zones. It is not unusual, over the course of the day, for a manager in the United States to teleconference with folks in Asia at 2 a.m., colleagues in Western Europe at 9 a.m., and coworkers and then South America at 3 p.m. Senior executives participating in a few, and often many, coordination teams may have teleconferences around the clock. Often, decision-making slows as views adjust and readjust. Managers' commitment may waver as some tire of ongoing negotiations. Looking forward, digital platforms, particularly social networking modes, promise solutions.

CONTROL SYSTEMS

16-5 Differentiate the systems used to control international activities

A key function of management is making sure workers are doing what must be done. If not, and schedules are slipping and productivity is sliding, then managers step in and correct problems. **Control systems**, the methods and means of problem correction, are part of a well-designed organization. Managers apply them to compare performance to plans, identify gaps, and impose adjustments. Similarly, control systems regulate executive efforts, resource allocation, and self-interest. They directly complement coordination processes and structural designs. Prominent control systems include bureaucratic, market, and clan.

CONCEPT CHECK

"Guidelines for Cultural Adjustment," profiled in Chapter 2, notes that managers deal with differences in the ways in which colleagues and subordinates, especially those with distinct cultural outlooks, respond when it comes to issues like task motivation, relationship preferences, and workplace behavior. Here we observe that, to accommodate these differences, MNEs mind cultural orientations when setting coordination systems.

Control systems are policies and procedures that command, direct, or regulate workplace behavior.

BUREAUCRATIC CONTROL

Using explicit rules and routines to govern activities institutes **bureaucratic control**. It supports operations that lend themselves to universal rules and exact scripts and, importantly, fits workplaces where rules regiment behaviors. It complements programs like Six Sigma or Total Quality Management. Bureaucratic controls partition authority and accountability, thereby stipulating roles and relationships. The scale and scope of global operations, executives report, means rules and regulations can vary unintentionally across cultures and countries. Bureaucratic controls reduce this problem.[90] Moreover, trust between people in an organization often declines as geographic distance increases. Western Europeans, for instance, trust citizens of their own country twice as much as they trust people from neighboring countries; they place less trust in people farther away.[91] Standardizing rules helps diminish this tendency. Hence, bureaucratic control shares organizing principles with coordination by standardization and supports classical structures.

Bureaucratic control emphasizes organizational authority and relies on rules and regulations.

MARKET CONTROL

Market control uses external market mechanisms to set standards that regulate performance.

Establishing performance benchmarks with external market mechanisms, such as profitability or market share, installs **market control**. Objective standards, not subjective interpretations, control activities. Relying on market standards creates universal metrics that work in all countries (e.g., we measure market share the same way, everywhere). Hence, market control metrics simplify tracking performance across different units in different countries. The objective indicators of market control help executives precisely track a subsidiary's performance. Control systems escalate when a unit deviates from benchmarks—say, a drop in market share. Market controls are particularly useful when executives decentralize decision-making. For instance, MNEs such as Nestlé and Nike decentralize some authority to local subsidiaries. The home office typically supports subsidiaries with technical, financial, administrative, and legal resources, and waits for superior results. If not forthcoming, control systems activate and senior executives step in. The principles of market control overlap with those of coordination by plan and fit the principles of the classical and knowledge-generating structures.

CLAN CONTROL

Clan control uses shared values and ideals to regulate employee behavior.

Clan control relies on values, beliefs, shared norms, and informal relationships to regulate employee behaviors. It aims to socialize employees to identify with the MNE's vision and mission as they go about their day-to-day routines, thereby allowing less vigilant supervision. Clan control is challenging in an MNE. Instituting a unifying vision spanning a dispersed, diverse workforce inevitably conflicts with some employees' values and norms. Still, there are renowned clan control systems, such as J&J Credo, the Toyota Way, Matsushita's Seven Spiritual Values, and the Gore Way. Clan control shares organizing principles with coordination by mutual adjustment and supports neoclassical structures.

CONCEPT CHECK

Chapter 12 explains that MNEs face various obstacles building communication channels among value activities. Not long ago, inefficient transportation and expensive communications hindered efforts to coordinate global activities. Today, improving social networking tools make clan control an increasingly practical option.

CONTROL METHODS

A generation ago, the costs of travel, data exchange, and communication technologies endorsed certain sorts of control methods. Improving economics, courtesy of expanding infrastructures and digital technologies, make control cheaper, faster, and easier. This process reduces the productivity of some tools, boosts the usefulness of others, and creates new options. Presently, MNEs support their control system with the following sorts of tools.

Reports The intricacies of IB make reports a vital control method. Frequent, accurate, and real-time reports help managers allocate resources and monitor performance. Endlessly expanding data flows call for sophisticated information technologies. The global diffusion of standardized software packages, often in the form of enterprise resource planning (ERP) platforms, from SAP, Oracle, Microsoft, and Red Hat, organize many report systems. Standardizing the format worldwide, by leveraging corporate management's familiarity, improves the real-time performance of reporting controls.

CONCEPT CHECK

In discussing measures for "Degrees of Cultural Differences" in Chapter 2, we explain how different attitudes toward cultural distance and different responses to culture shock frustrate the efforts of managers to coordinate value activities that span diverse cultural environments. Managers use control measures to fortify the organization.

Visiting Subsidiaries Boundaries limit the usefulness of data analytics. Senior executives, especially those applying coordination by adjustment and clan control, fortify control by visiting subsidiaries. Face-to-face meetings, formal budget reviews, and planning seminars clarify responsibilities. Old-school subsidiary visits, awash with strategizing and socializing, promote communication between headquarters and local managers. Increasingly, technologies expand managers' options. Teleconferencing help MNEs reduce travel, save time, boost productivity, and tighten controls. Cisco, for instance, averages several thousand teleconferences a week. Besides cutting its annual travel budget by more than half, teleconferencing significantly increased "face time" among managers.[92]

Information Systems Digital platforms, by expediting information exchange, provide useful control methods. MNEs use ERP systems to monitor activities, such as product planning, parts purchasing, maintaining inventories, customer service, and order fulfillment. Electronic transactions boost efficiency by streamlining exchanges among links in the value chain. In larger markets, this interface is prevalent among manufacturers and their first-tier suppliers, such as the relationship between Costco and Procter & Gamble in United States or Carrefour and Nestle in Europe. Many MNEs set the open-source language protocol of the Internet as the global standard. The increasing simplicity, generality, and usability of information exchange over digital platforms spurs global standards. Still, managers face challenges acquiring information, notably reconciling the cost of that information compared to its value and difficulties to triage the irrelevant.

WHICH CONTROL SYSTEM WHEN?

Like most decisions in IB, there are few hard and fast rules about which control system when. MNEs that have grown organically, moving from startup to global enterprise, like Starbucks, often operate relatively consistently across countries and, given a standardized business model, prefer bureaucratic controls. Alternatively, MNEs that have grown through acquisitions, joint ventures, or alliances, like J&J, find it hard to tightly integrate different units and, hence, emphasize market and clan controls.[93]

Generally, as structure follows strategy, so too do control methods. MNEs following a global strategy prefer market controls, given that they can apply standard, objective benchmarks to evaluate performance in any market. Alternatively, transnational companies find value in clan control. The necessity of open exchange among geographically diffuse workers encourages control based on common values and norms. Still, in any strategic scenario, managers adjust control systems for contingencies posed by the dynamic tensions of global integration and local responsiveness.

Likewise, implementing sophisticated strategies requires managers craft commensurately sophisticated control methods that reflect the different operating circumstances facing different units. Consequently, few MNEs rely on a single control method. J&J and Gore, for instance, blends aspects of market and clan control. Certainly, both would prefer the clarity of a single system. Both make adjustments given the contingencies imposed by their structure, coordination approach, and, as we now see, organizational culture.

ORGANIZATIONAL CULTURE

16-6 Explain the principle and practices of organizational culture

Organizational culture refers to the ideologies, symbols, and core values that employees, no matter their location in the MNE's worldwide operations, regard as legitimate.

Having profiled the roles played by structure and systems in organizing an MNE, we turn to the final design element: its culture. In theory, one can profile the idea of organizational culture from an applied perspective, specifying it as the way things are done in an MNE and evaluating how workers organize around rules, rewards, and punishments. Alternatively, we could adopt a philosophical view and assess how organizational culture, as an embedded set of shared values and normative principles, guides actions and sanctions behaviors within the MNE. We integrate these perspectives and define **organizational culture** as the coherent, consistent system of workplace norms and idealized values that describe the goals and endorse the practice shared by employees worldwide. This system legitimates standards, endorses common beliefs about how the world works, and frames how workers make decisions, take actions, and sustain common cause.

A KEY PIECE OF THE PERFORMANCE PUZZLE

Analyses and anecdotes of performance indicate that building a resourceful organization is a challenging balancing act: an MNE must find ways to inspire employees worldwide to develop and apply ideas but then ensure their actions support its strategy. Few MNEs strike and sustain this balance solely by designing the structure, coordination, and control systems. Rather, they look to their organizational culture to complete the trick. On this point, Jack Welch, one-time CEO of GE, advised that "In real life, strategy is actually very straightforward. You pick a general direction and implement like hell. . . . But objectives don't get you there. Values do."[94] The matter of values focuses attention on the matter of organizational culture.

An organization's culture, by endorsing workplace values, shapes the behavior patterns of current workers as well as new hires.

Assessment of strategic successes and failures spotlights the performance implications of organizational culture. Executives see it as a powerful tool to shape how workers do their job, how executives integrate decision-making, and how individuals make decisions that collectively implements the strategy. Research confirms a powerful link between an MNE's organizational culture and its success. Key facets of an MNE's culture, such as its values and principles, nature of the work climate, and traditions and ethical standards, always and everywhere influence its performance.[95]

Sophisticated Strategy, Sophisticated Culture Implementing increasingly sophisticated strategies in increasingly different places requires increasingly sophisticated organizational cultures. The growth of global business changes MNEs' opportunities and options. Markets once predominant, like the United States, Japan, and Germany, transition to new positions. Markets once on the periphery, such as China, Indonesia, and Nigeria, move toward center stage. Four hundred midsized emerging-market cities, many unfamiliar in the West, such as Ghaziabad, Chittagong, Sanaa, Kano, and Bamako, will generate about 40 percent of global growth over the next 15 years.[96]

MNEs respond by redeploying operations and engaging strategies that, in turn, create intricate workflow patterns. Coordinating and controlling these activities requires more robust organizations than MNEs have traditionally developed. Most emerging markets are far, both physically as well as psychologically, from more familiar markets in Europe and North America. For instance, managers moving from established to emerging markets, say from Germany to Turkmenistan, Japan to Rwanda, or Canada to Cambodia, must prepare for unique sets of cultural, political, and economic issues. If neglected, these issues quickly complicate organizing operations.[97] Consequently, expanding to increasingly diverse markets with increasingly diverse workplaces, especially for those with a traditionally Western-centric outlook, calls for improving the flexibility and versatility of an organization. Done well, the MNE aligns decision making, no matter by who or where, so that the right things get done in the right way.

CONCEPT CHECK

The accelerating performance of emerging economies indicates an "inflection point" at which old strategic patterns give way to new. Our discussion of different national perspectives on value creation in Chapter 12 argues that such problems challenge coordinating increasingly sophisticated value chains devised to support new business models. Evidence indicates that developing a supportive organizational culture provides managers a powerful tool.

Culture Is Key Managing the evolving configurations of resources, capabilities, and competencies escalate demands on an MNE's structure and systems. Aligning perceptions and processes, particularly when an MNE decentralized decision making to people closest to customers, partners, and communities, can quickly overwhelm structures and systems. The track record of success and failure show that executives have low odds of successfully meeting those demands without a supportive organizational culture. Poorly understood, partially shared cultural values impose boundaries that distort the communication and collaboration that gird coordination and control systems.

Certainly, MNEs could opt to ignore values and norms, instead applying constraints, controls, and contracts to compel employees to do their job. Granted, the notion that "beatings will continue until morale improves" may boost short-term performance. Understandably, improving the fit between an MNE's culture and its strategy has proven a more powerful driver of superior performance.[98]

THE POWER OF COMMON CAUSE

Successful MNEs develop a culture that inspires in their employees the engagement and enthusiasm beyond that justified solely by economic rewards.[99] Certainly, pay motivates performance. An effective culture, however, inspires workers to identify with the company's vision, invest in their job, and collaborate open-mindedly, all the while lessening the need to regulate their behaviors with elaborate structures and systems.[100] Culture's capacity to power individual performance beyond that motivated by monetary incentives puts the onus on executives to build a company that people do not want to merely work for, but aspire to belong to. Effectively, employees no longer check in to get a check. Rather, the organization's culture inspires vision-led and principle-driven identification.[101]

Competitive changes and performance expectations steadily alter the social contract between high-performance workers and MNEs. Security, pay, and benefits matter, but workers increasingly expect to directly participate in decision-making, devising solutions to unique problems, and receiving challenging assignments. Furthermore, many work with digital systems to create value of astonishing variety, problem solving, and intellectual content. "Controlling" workers charged with reasoning or problem-solving tasks is problematic; the bright, self-motivating, self-organizing people who staff these sorts of slots generally oppose direct supervision. Whether "knowledge workers" or the "creative class," these individuals aim to behave as if they are the CEO.[102]

The fit between a worker's outlook and the norms and values that anchor the company's organizational culture is a powerful determinant of performance and commitment. Google's worries about brain drain to rivals, for instance, led it to identify why people quit; it found that executives left for another company not for higher pay, but when they more directly identified with its vision.[103] Losing talent is always a problem, but it is increasingly significant as companies rely more on strategic capabilities that are embodied in individuals. If disgruntled or simply bored, those folks easily walk out the door.

The shared meaning and beliefs that shape how employees interpret information, make decisions, and implement actions define an organization's culture.

Sharing Values, Shaping Interpretation The shared values that enact an organization's culture, goes the reasoning, influence what employees perceive, how they interpret, and how they respond to their world. Convergent cultural values ease the exchange of ideas, thereby improving communication, coordination, and collaboration. J&J, for example, anchors its vision of value creation in the principles of its Credo. This manifesto unequivocally champions the values that embody J&J's responsibilities to its stakeholders worldwide. No matter the decision, the Credo helps workers define, analyze, and resolve in in ways that support J&J's strategy. Likewise, a robust organization culture provides a powerful tonic for workplace problems. IKEA, facing employees opposed to its radical reorganization, launched a "positive people movement" focusing on "fostering leadership and development that reflects IKEA's culture and values . . . to creating a whole new IKEA together."[104]

Good to Great A vibrant organizational culture helps explain why some companies make the leap from good to great and, likewise, why others do not.[105] Unquestionably, product development, marketing ingenuity, and financial stewardship moderate progress. Research finds that attaining greatness depends on a culture of unwavering faith and passion, rigorous discipline and focus, clearly communicated and practiced core values and timeless principles, strong work ethics, and finding and promoting people with the right outlook.[106] Great companies purposefully promote an integrated system of overarching values, perspectives, and practices—much as J&J does with its Credo, Toyota with its Toyota Way, and Gore with the Gore Way—in order to give employees a consistent way to relate to their jobs, to each other, to customers, to shareholders, and to stakeholders. Perhaps most decisively, it legitimates the company's vision in the eyes of employees worldwide.

DEVELOPING AN ORGANIZATIONAL CULTURE

MNEs proactively develop their organizational culture, just as they purposefully design their structure and systems.

Historically, uncertainty about the dynamic of social engineering led managers to adopt a benign perspective, letting the organization's culture organically emerge and naturally evolve. Information and advice on "how things work around here" spread by word-of-mouth on the factory floor or during coffee-break chats. Today, MNEs proactively manage their culture's emergence and evolution.[107] Organizing a globally integrated enterprise, for example, calls for extensive coordination and collaboration among workers. The importance and intricacies of setting and sustaining common values among employees worldwide turn attention to how an MNE develops, diffuses, and sustains its organizational culture. The overlapping practices of cultural exemplars, notably Gore, J&J, Google, Infosys, and Toyota, highlight the importance of hiring, rewarding, and promoting people who support the MNE's vision and then "walk the talk," in implementing its mission. Leading through example, they promote socialization processes and communication practices that diffuse as well as fortify the idealized values and norms.

Key features of a company's organization culture include
- values and principles of management,
- work climate and atmosphere,
- logics of "how we do things around here,"
- traditions and legacies,
- ethical outlooks.

The values and norms of managers, especially those from culturally dissimilar countries, often differ.[108] Furthermore, many workers, especially those in markets far removed from the home office, have slight exposure to the behaviors of senior managers. Even on the standards of the MNE's strategy, a far more objective concept than the values and norms of its organizational culture, executives struggle to unify understanding. Just half of the executives in a cross-section of MNEs, for instance, believed that they communicated their strategy clearly to their workers worldwide.[109] Rather than relying on chance encounters among employees to develop common cause, MNEs proactively set and sustain their idealized organizational culture with various methods.

Setting the System Instituting common cause encourages managers to arrange closer contact among managers from different countries to unify values. Consensus depends on coworkers sharing common values, rather than coerced compliance through coordination routines or control systems. Cross-national teams are a prevalent method.[110] MNEs also rotate executives from headquarters and subsidiaries throughout global units. Wipro, an Indian technology company, employs 54,000 people in 35 countries, more than 11,000 of whom work for units outside of India and more than 90 percent of whom are Indian. Explained the chief executive of global programs, "We sprinkle Indians in new markets to help seed and set up the culture and intensity."[111] Others endorse focused methods. Leadership development programs commonly thrust managers from different businesses and different parts of the world into situations where they challenge and clarify the company's culture.

Hiring people from around the world expands the mix of nationalities and ethnicities. Organizing engineers in Bengaluru to collaborate with folks in Seattle makes compelling economic sense. Preempting a Tower of Babel requires socializing the mix of people to the sensitivities and skills that are needed to navigate multifunctional, multicultural, multinational teams. Tempting as it is to rely upon happenstance to manage the process, benign neglect is risky. Rather, managers proactively set the system.

Sustaining the System Instead of letting the organization's culture emerge naturally, many managers do as they do with structure and systems: proactively develop the system of shared values that supports the MNE's vision and mission. Reflected Gore's former CEO, "we take great pride in our culture and recognize the very important role it plays in driving business success. By fostering an environment where people feel motivated, engaged, and passionate about the work they do, we are better able to tap into our potential and create innovative products that truly make a difference in the world."[112]

Toyota relies on its Technical Skills Academy, essentially its corporate university, to fortify its organizational culture as well as anchor its next generation of leadership in it. Some sessions teach factory controls and assembly procedures, others develop management skills, but all share principles and practices of the "Toyota Way."[113] Familiarizing employees with its renowned outlook and orientation, top management believes, helps them base decisions on a "philosophical sense of purpose, to think long term, to have a process for solving problems, to add value to the organization by developing its people, and to recognize that continuously solving root problems drives organizational learning."[114]

Toyota posts graduates to its offices worldwide, acting as missionaries who evangelize the Toyota Way. Long a fundamental feature of the company, the Toyota Way steadily plays a bigger part in developing its culture. Expanding international operations, particularly into emerging economies, worried management that the Toyota Way was losing influence. When Toyota was primarily Japan-centric, it relied upon informal socializing to sustain it. Explained the director of the Toyota Institute, "Before, when everyone was Japanese, we didn't have to make these things explicit . . . Now we have to set the Toyota Way down on paper and teach it."[115]

Increasingly, MNEs turn to proprietary corporate universities to promote their organizational culture. Worldwide, more than a thousand companies have opened universities over the past decade. By region, they are steadily expanding in the United States, thriving in Europe, and accelerating in Asia. The number of U.S. corporate universities grew from around 400 in 1993, to 2,000 in 2001, to nearly 4,000 today. Prominent MNEs, including Apple, Walt Disney, Infosys, General Electric, J.P. Morgan Chase, and SAP, run one.[116] Besides skills development, these units profile the principles and practices that anchor the organizational culture. The vice president of Unisys University explains that getting people into the classroom aligns employee development with the company's strategy and fortifies their identification with its culture. Likewise, Toyota relies on its Toyota Institute in Toyota City, Japan, along with its centers in Thailand and the United States, to socialize workers worldwide with its core values, thereby harmonizing its organizational culture throughout its far-flung operations.

LOOKING TO THE FUTURE Changing Times, Changing Skills, and Changing Organizations

The invention of the telephone and telegraph, by expanding connections and improving communication, reset the workplace in the early twentieth century. At the time, corporations responded with organizations that reflected the organizing logic of these technologies. We see the same processes in play today. The Internet, by radically redefining how we organize information in interactions, pushes managers to rethink their assumptions of how they arrange roles and responsibilities in the workplace

Incongruously, the Internet has no formal structure, no board of directors, and no official administrator. Its self-organizing and self-regulating capabilities prompt rethinking conventional notions of design, coordination, and control. Alternatively, contemporary global juggernauts like Tencent, Facebook, Amazon, Flipkart, Airbnb, Yandex, Alibaba, PayPal, Uber, and Baidu were organizational pipedreams a generation ago. Therefore, just as novel strategies called for innovative organizations in the early 1900s, so too do we see similar circumstances today. Arguably, given the ongoing procession of stunningly powerful technologies, so too will be the approaches, tools, and methods of organizing the MNE of the future.

Tools in Play

Already, we see evidence of digitization, in the form of advanced analytics, automation, and artificial intelligence, radically resetting the ways and means through which workers work and leaders lead. Moreover, the party is just getting started. Whereas consumers have largely gone digital, the digitization of jobs is still in the early stages.[117] IBM's artificial intelligence systems, for instance, anchors it "predictive attrition" software; it has saved $300 million by identifying which of its roughly 350,000 workers are on the verge of quitting. Explains the CEO, since implementing the system, IBM has reduced headcounts in its global HR department by 30 percent. Moreover, artificial intelligence systems have other benefits; she added that "We found manager surveys were not accurate. Managers are subjective in ratings. We can infer and be more accurate from data."[118] If the present is a valid predictor, then the only constraint on the workplace of the future is our imagination.

Consider, for example, wearable workplace technology, where we pin on sociometric badges or plug-in instant language translator earbuds. In the former, the badges track your interactions and social behaviors with co-workers whereas in the latter, plugging in the appropriate earbud means you effortlessly communicate with anyone speaking any language.[119] Although bizarre to many, millennial workers see it as just another part of the game. Collectively, these and many other tools will continue digitizing the workplace and, in turn, require a radical rethink of structure, coordination, control, and culture.

How might you, looking to start or accelerate your career, prepare for the organizations of the future? The CEO of IBM has direct advice for you: "If you have a skill that is not needed for the future and is abundant in the market and does not fit a strategy my company needs, you are not in a good square to stay inside of."[120] The World Economic Forum has some recommendations. It sampled executives from leading global employers on what the future held for the employment, skills, and workforce strategy. Unsurprisingly, all agreed that developments will transform the way we live and the way we work. Data suggest that executives respond in kind, transforming their organizations and, hence, transforming the standards of who they hire, and likewise who they fire.

Currently, the report advises enterprising individuals to improve their complex problem-solving, critical thinking, and creativity. Other skills, such as people management, emotional intelligence, judgment and decision-making, and cognitive flexibility matter too. The tsunami of new products, new processes, new technology, and new ways of working will push people to tackle complex problems, think critically about them, and create ingenious solutions. Indisputably, the organization of the future must evolve to support them.

CASE

Building a Magical Organization at Johnson & Johnson[121]

The typical bio-pharmaceutical MNE, such as Novartis, Gilead Sciences, and Amgen, emphasizes global integration. This imperative follows from the steep product development costs and potential scale economies—developing a new prescription medicine that gains marketing approval, which approximately 12 percent of cases do, costs $2.6 billion and spans several years.[122] Offsetting this expense as well as leveraging the opportunity encourages global integration. However, bio-pharmaceutical MNEs must respond to local market conditions, obtaining government approval for its product in various countries as well as establishing sales, support, and distribution systems that meet local healthcare standards. Achieving these outcomes, besides authorizing its local operations, anchors its customer responsiveness. Consequently, headquarters and subsidiaries each play crucial roles in implementing strategy, the former sensitizing decision-making toward global efficiencies, the latter emphasizing local effectiveness. Building an organization that can meet this mission is tough. One standout that does is Johnson & Johnson (J&J).

From its start in 1886, J&J has evolved into the most broadly based, highly valued bio-pharmaceutical company in the world. Headquartered in New Brunswick, New Jersey, J&J has more than 134,000 workers that staff some 260 operating units in 60 countries. Nearly 60 percent of its $85 billion in sales occurs outside the United States and is transacted in more than 175 countries. Its diversified portfolio of anti-infective, cardiovascular, dermatology, immunology, and oncology products rests on tens of thousands of U.S. and foreign patents. Some, though, believe the intricacy of J&J's organization, in terms of its decentralized structure, sophisticated coordination and control systems, and Credo-based culture, explain its superior performance.

The "Magic of Decentralization"

Decentralized management is the heart of J&J's worldwide area structure. It empowers managers who are closest to customers and competitors to make decisions. As J&J says, it aims to be big and small all at once, building its global reach from the integration of its many small units. Rather than the standard, "safer" *modus operandi* whereby locals collect data, send it up the hierarchy to folks at headquarters who make the call, who then pass it back down, J&J moves decision making to the front lines. An operating unit acts as it believes is best given its read of local conditions. It performs as its own business, entrepreneurial in character, and aware that success begins by anticipating local customers' needs and delivering solutions.

Decentralization, explained a former CEO, "gives people a sense of ownership and control—and the freedom to act more rapidly."[123] His successor, concurred, adding that reducing bureaucracy, liberating initiative, and rewarding enterprise—the hallmarks of a decentralized organization—are the wellspring of the "magic around J&J."[124] Decentralizing decision-making from headquarters to the front lines, J&J reasons, helps a large, globe-spanning MNE capture the vibrancy typically found in a small enterprise.

Certainly, a classical command-and-control hierarchy has benefits. Still, J&J believes it ruins the magic that flows from entrepreneurialism, customer-centricity, and agile decision-making. Ultimately, executives concluded that meeting the mandates of a decentralized organization—shortening chains of command, increasing spans of responsibilities, and breaking down boundaries—gives everyone a strong sense of ownership of action and accountability for outcomes. These outlooks make the managers running J&J's operating units intensely competitive, both with each other as well as rivals. Furthermore, managers who control their destiny are inspired to innovate, translating ideas into new products and insights into better processes. Backstopping their efforts are the deep pools of resources and capabilities that one finds in a large, successful MNE.

J&J's successful decentralization attracted talented and motivated people. The authority to make decisions encourages them to dream big dreams, keen to test ideas, and sharpen their skills. While often found in small companies, these sorts of entrepreneurial outlooks are rare in large, diversified, globe-straddling companies. As such, instituting these outlooks positions J&J to magically blend a global outlook with local entrepreneurialism.

The primacy of decentralization influences J&J's international expansion. J&J enters markets by adding subsidiaries through investment, alliance, or acquisition. New units do not fear being overrun by legions of expatriates, directed by home-office generals, looking to clone headquarters into another "mini-me" subsidiary. With few exceptions, host-country folks direct local subsidiaries—indeed, executives pointed out that "companies love to be acquired by J&J because they don't mess with you."[125] Granted, headquarters negotiates stiff performance targets. Then it steps aside, supporting subsidiaries as needed, expecting superior results, and ready to intervene if shortfalls show. Steadily, as market and industry trends have connected countries, headquarters increasingly relies on coordination and control systems to ensure that subsidiaries maximize local responsiveness while optimizing global performance.

Herding 260 Strategic Business Units

Decentralization enables J&J to rely on people who understand how it creates value, are familiar with its competencies, and are culturally and physically positioned to respond to local needs. However, decentralization inevitably slows diffusing corporate programs and policies throughout global operations. As one executive explained, trying to synchronize 260 SBUs, each confident in the importance of its local imperatives, is much like trying to herd 260 cats into an organized group. Still, given the importance of leveraging global integration to offset the higher costs of conducting business internationally, headquarters installs coordination and control systems. Too, when reasonable, J&J institutes measures and methods that standardize processes across subsidiaries.

Preserving the magic of decentralization, however sensitizes managers to guard against excessive command-and-control. System changes, therefore, are mindful of the coordinate and cultivate outlook of planning and mutual adjustment processes. Communication channels cut across the organization, helping far-flung units integrate ideas. Self-directed councils—for research, engineering, and operations, among others—meet regularly to swap ideas. Headquarters negotiates planning formats, schedules mandatory reports, tracks interim results, and formally reviews budgets. Senior executives push a global perspective into local decision-making and, likewise, local objectives influence global discussions.

Inconsistent market development and duplicated efforts fan friction between headquarters and subsidiaries. Tempting as it is to adopt a policy of benevolent tyranny, J&J's proud legacy encourages otherwise. Pressures to integrate operations due to market trends, competitors' moves, and improving automation and artificial intelligence push J&J to centralize some activities and tighten coordination control systems. These changes, while understood, are not entirely welcome. Some local units resist integration, arguing that global standards poorly fit their unique circumstances.

Senior executives acknowledge these concerns and reiterate their commitment to decentralization and agile systems. They argue, however, that leveraging competencies, as well as capturing location and scale effects, means that when J&J rolls out a key product or process, country operations worldwide roll with it. To this end, J&J sets standards for issues common to all operating units, such as finance, science and technology, government affairs, and quality management. Executives install centralized reporting processes for key business functions, including manufacturing and quality control. Centrally managing common support activities, reasoned senior executives, frees operating units to focus on their day-to-day performance.

Culture and the Credo

Structure and systems, even when optimally designed and performing well, only take you so far. Jack Welch, former CEO of General Electric, noted that, ultimately, "Objectives don't get you there, values do." In the context, J&J relies on its powerful, profound organizational culture— instituted in "Our Credo"—to sustain its magical organization.

Conceived in 1943 by Robert Wood Johnson, company chair from 1932 to 1963, this one-page ethical code of conduct declares how J&J fulfills its responsibilities. But J&J notes, "Our Credo is more than just a moral compass. We believe it's a recipe for business success. The fact that J&J is one of only a handful of companies that have flourished through more than a century of change is proof of that." J&J's "Credo" is the "glue that binds this company together."[126]

Senior executives evangelize the Credo so that all 134,000 employees understand it, believe it, and live it. The Credo, chiseled into the wall of J&J's New Jersey headquarters, is officially displayed in more than 800 facilities worldwide. No matter where you are in the world of J&J, the Credo is there with you, always evident in the reception lobby, hanging in conference rooms, and posted in offices.

The Credo specifies who and what to care about and in what order. It declares that the "first responsibility is to the doctors, nurses, patients, mothers, and fathers who use our products and services." It addresses the communities where J&J operates and the roles and duties of employees. Notably, shareholders come last, long after customers, suppliers, and distributors. It declares that shareholders will get a reasonable return if other stakeholders are treated fairly. Collectively, executives proclaim that "Our Credo underscores J&J's personal responsibility to put the needs of the people we serve first. It liberates our passion and deepens our commitment to delivering meaningful health innovations."[127]

Despite its direct message, executives worry that differing outlooks in different markets might blur how its workers worldwide interpret the Credo. Thus, it has been translated into dozens of languages and dialects, from Arabic to Vietnamese. Interestingly, the English version contains 342 words. Translating it into different languages is a bit challenging—the Romanian version has 415 words, while the Chinese version runs 607. At one point, J&J compiled local versions of the Credo from 65 countries into a document. Many see it symbolizing that 'Our Credo,' no matter where or how expressed, fundamentally unites J&J into a global organization. Officially, it declares, "Our Credo looks different from country to country. But no matter what the language, its enduring principles remind us of the values that make up the character of J&J. It is a heritage of enormous importance and a legacy we honor."[128]

J&J periodically surveys employees on how well the Credo fits their world. 'Credo Surveys' rate how J&J meets its responsibilities while 'Credo Challenges' assess its fit with changing times. Shortcomings trigger review. J&J has modernized aspects given concern about environmental sustainability and societal change regarding work-life balance. Regarding the latter, for example, in 1987, "fathers" was added to accompany "mothers" in the opening passage. Fundamentally, as evidenced by the rare need for revision, management believes its founding spirit transcends time and place.[129]

Our Credo

We believe our first responsibility is to the patients, doctors and nurses, to mothers and fathers and all others who use our products and services. In meeting their needs everything we do must be of high quality. We must constantly strive to provide value, reduce our costs and maintain reasonable prices. Customers' orders must be serviced promptly and accurately. Our business partners must have an opportunity to make a fair profit.

We are responsible to our employees who work with us throughout the world. We must provide an inclusive work environment where each person must be considered as an individual. We must respect their diversity and dignity and recognize their merit. They must have a sense of security, fulfillment and purpose in their jobs. Compensation must be fair and adequate and working conditions clean, orderly and safe. We must support the health and well-being of our employees and help them fulfill their family and other personal responsibilities. Employees must feel free to make suggestions and complaints. There must be equal opportunity for employment, development and advancement for those qualified. We must provide highly capable leaders and their actions must be just and ethical.

We are responsible to the communities in which we live and work and to the world community as well. We must help people be healthier by supporting better access and care in more places around the world. We must be good citizens — support good works and charities, better health and education, and bear our fair share of taxes. We must maintain in good order the property we are privileged to use, protecting the environment and natural resources.

Our final responsibility is to our stockholders. Business must make a sound profit. We must experiment with new ideas. Research must be carried on, innovative programs developed, investments made for the future and mistakes paid for. New equipment must be purchased, new facilities provided and new products launched. Reserves must be created to provide for adverse times. When we operate according to these principles, the stockholders should realize a fair return.

Johnson & Johnson

Attaining the Holy Grail

J&J's accomplishments and accolades, earned by developing, adjusting, and improving its structure, systems, and culture, have built an organization that confidently leverages bright ideas, proposed by anyone, from anywhere. Ingeniously blending the autonomy of decentralization, intricacies of coordination and control systems, and clarity of its Credo institutes a magical organization. Employees can then capitalize on their initiative, develop their capabilities, enrich their perspectives, and quite possibly change the game. In so doing, J&J arguably attains the Holy Grail of multinational organization.

QUESTIONS

16-3 Profile the perspective that you think best explains how J&J makes its structure, systems, and culture work.

16-4 Given the choice, would you rather work in J&J's corporate headquarters in New Jersey, United States, or, alternatively, in a local subsidiary in an overseas market? Why?

16-5 The World Economic Forum emphasizes the importance of complex problem-solving, critical thinking, and creativity to effective executive performance. Estimate how these skills would make you an outstanding performer if you were working for J&J.

CHAPTER 17
Marketing Globally

Source: Sorbis/Shutterstock

Hilfiger storefront in Seoul, Korea. ▲

OBJECTIVES

After studying this chapter, you should be able to

17-1 Classify international marketing strategies in terms of marketing orientations, segmentation, and targeting

17-2 Discuss the pros and cons of country adaptation versus global standardization of products

17-3 Describe pricing complexities when selling in foreign markets

17-4 Recognize the pros and cons of using uniform promotional marketing practices among countries

17-5 Explain the different branding strategies companies may employ internationally

17-6 Discern major practices and complications of international distribution

17-7 Illustrate how gap analysis can help in managing the international marketing mix

Markets have customs and communes have traditions.

—Vietnamese proverb

CASE

Tommy Hilfiger[1]

For it's Tommy this, an' Tommy that

—"Tommy" by Rudyard Kipling from *Department Duties: Barrack Room Ballads* (1890), United States Book Company, New York.

Mark Twain said, "The finest clothing is a person's skin, but, of course, society demands more than this." Tommy Hilfiger, a notable international clothing brand, exemplifies efforts to respond to these demands. Its 2017 retail sales were nearly $4 billion, with over half coming from abroad. Europe, to which it began its push in 1997, accounts for the largest portion of international sales, and China is the fastest-growing area. (The opening photo shows one of its stores in Seoul, Korea.) As the company moved internationally, it learned that applying every U.S. marketing strategy abroad did not work because country markets are very different. Our discussion centers on contrasting Hilfiger's U.S. and foreign (mainly European) operations.

PRODUCT

The Hilfiger brand's early success was largely due to two men: U.S. designer Tommy Hilfiger and Indian clothing magnate Mohan Murjani. Murjani sought Hilfiger as a designer for a new brand of clothing by offering a line of slightly less preppy and less expensive clothes than those offered by Ralph Lauren to attract a young mass-appeal audience. From the start, Hilfiger clothes have been casual, of good quality, and distinctive enough in color and shape (along with their red, white, and blue logos) that the public can usually distinguish them from those of competitors. Nevertheless, this is an industry in which product lines must evolve. Maintaining that "fashion brands have to reinvent themselves," Hilfiger has gone from preppy to urban and back again. It has also recently reintroduced retro designs from the 1980s and 1990s because millennials missed them the first time around and now demand them.

In addition, Hilfiger has encountered some different national preferences. To accommodate European tastes, new collections include gender neutral clothing and bags. Hilfiger has added wool sweaters, adjusted to the European partiality for slimmer-looking jeans and smaller shirt logos, and created a line of added-luxury items, such as leather jackets and cashmere sweaters for the Italian market. It also developed brighter colors for Italy, tartans and plaids for Japan, and sleeker designs for Chile.

During the late twentieth and early twenty-first centuries, Hilfiger's U.S. sales fell each year, apparently because its product lines had become faddish (e.g., baggy jeans and large logos on clothing) and no longer compatible with its established image. This led to discounting, compromising on quality, and a lower brand image. Meanwhile, the autonomously operated European division refused to go along with the United States' faddish moves, and its sales grew in tandem with U.S. decreases.

In response, Hilfiger set up a European design staff that led to more harmonization in its U.S. and European products, a more upmarket move, and a turnaround of its U.S. performance.

PRICING

Whereas the early U.S. pricing strategy was to sell a shirt for $79 that looks like an $89 shirt, Hilfiger learned that its brand cachet warranted selling a shirt in Europe for $99 that looks like a $150 shirt. For instance, in Germany, its largest European market, customers don't mind paying $50 more than the highest-priced men's Hilfiger shirts in the United States, but they want them in higher-quality cotton. In addition, European department store margins can be 50 percent to 100 percent higher than those in the United States, thus impacting price differences.

PROMOTION AND BRANDING

Hilfiger's promotion and branding have been much intertwined. At the company's inception, there were two primary needs: to convince stores to stock a new brand and to convince customers to want it. Although the first year's (1985) ad budget was quite small for an unknown brand in a mass consumer market, the ads were aimed strictly at getting Tommy Hilfiger's name known. These ads were in leading magazines and newspapers, along with a billboard in New York's Times Square. They showed no clothes or models. Instead, they included Hilfiger's face, the logo for the clothes, and words describing Hilfiger as being on a par with such well-known designers as Ralph Lauren, Perry Ellis, and Calvin Klein.

The bizarre ads resulted in free publicity through newspapers around the world and quips on popular late-night TV shows. The publicity showed an eclectic group of celebrities—Bill Clinton, the Prince of Wales, Elton John, and Snoop Dogg—wearing Hilfiger clothes. This fed into Hilfiger's image; thus the company's brand was quickly known nationally and internationally. Soon, surveys revealed that the public thought of Hilfiger as one of the four or five most important U.S. designers. And the logo-loving public rushed to buy the brand, especially young managers who were eager to be seen in upscale sportswear during the newly popular "casual Friday" workdays.

Hilfiger's European acceptance was not as quick as it expected. Because Europeans tend to see France and Italy as the upscale fashion centers, Hilfiger initially encountered some negative reactions to being a U.S. upscale brand. However, Hilfiger has since played up its Americanism, and the perception that the brand and price are a step below the pure luxury brands has successfully helped its European sales find a niche.

Hilfiger has used celebrity advertising, such as Beyoncé, Rafael Nadal, and Zendaya. The company has used "delebs" (dead celebrities), such as Grace Kelly and James Dean. To help advertise its children's clothes, Disney artists have drawn Pluto and other Disney characters wearing the line. However, aside from celebrities, Hilfiger learned that the type of models it uses to sell successfully in the United States may not work well in Europe. For example, its models for men's underwear in Europe, including those on point-of-purchase package displays, must be thinner and less muscular than those in the United States. Hilfiger also found that its average European consumer was older than that in the United States, so it dropped the Tommy Jeans name in some countries because it sounded too much like a teen product.

Advertising has been a cornerstone of Hilfiger's success, depending on multimedia campaigns that include indoor and outdoor print placements, digital and social media promotions, and webisodes.

DISTRIBUTION

Early on, Hilfiger relied mainly on wholesaling to about 1,800 U.S. department stores, many of which contained stand-alone Hilfiger departments. It has avoided chains considered more low-end, though it does sell its outdated stock to discount chains T. J. Maxx and Marshalls. However, in 2007, Hilfiger gave Macy's exclusive rights to sell its sportswear lines. Although Macy's has about 800 stores, the move required Hilfiger to pull sales from other department stores, such as Dillard's.

Distribution is perhaps the biggest difference Hilfiger found when entering Europe. Because of the company's U.S. department stores success, it put an early European emphasis on such department stores as Galeries Lafayette in France and El Corte Inglés in Spain. However, Hilfiger found the European market to be one of fragmentation (sending small amounts to small stores that carry select pieces) as opposed to the U.S. market's concentration (sending a lot to department stores). European operational costs are about three times those in the United States because of this more fragmented sales system.

Hilfiger has inaugurated large flagship stores in prime locations within large markets, such as in New York City, Paris, and Tokyo. These stores not only make sales, but also demonstrate the variety of Hilfiger merchandise. Non-U.S. stores are decorated to emphasize an American image, while simultaneously connecting the United States to the host country, such as including a poster of a U.S. magazine with the Eiffel Tower on the cover in the Paris store. By locating in prestige areas, Hilfiger promotes an aura of having high-end products, yet its aim is to be a high-margin brand with prices a notch lower than luxury brands. Nevertheless, this concept did not work in London, where Hilfiger opened and closed its Bond Street store within a year. In effect, Hilfiger overpromoted to retailers and underpromoted to final consumers. Thus, too much merchandise was in stores, which forced them to get rid of excess inventory. Further, a cheap lookalike brand called Tommy Sport confused consumers, tarnished Hilfiger's image, and forced the company to buy it out.

Writers as far back as Homer, Erasmus, and Shakespeare indicated the importance of clothing and appearance to success. Hilfiger, while making and selling clothes, has succeeded in convincing customers that its merchandise will help boost (or make) their positions.

QUESTIONS

17-1 The chapter explains five international marketing orientations. Which one most applies to Tommy Hilfiger? Explain why.

17-2 The chapter explains five elements in the marketing mix (product, price, promotion, brand, and distribution). In which of these have Tommy Hilfiger's operating practices been the most standardized globally? Explain why this has been possible and desirable.

INTERNATIONAL MARKETING STRATEGIES: ORIENTATIONS, SEGMENTATION, AND TARGETING

17-1 Classify international marketing strategies in terms of marketing orientations, segmentation, and targeting

Although marketing principles are global, companies may need to apply them differently abroad.

Marketing brings revenue, without which a firm cannot survive. Similar principles apply globally (i.e., a company must have desirable products and services, tell people about them, and offer them at appropriate prices at consumers' favored locations). However, companies may apply these principles differently abroad, such as by customizing products to correspond with local preferences. Hilfiger's experience in the opening case emphasizes the need to find the right balance between the benefits of local responsiveness and the efficiency gains of standardization.

CONCEPT CHECK

In Chapter 12 (pages 305–308), we describe the strategies of global integration versus local responsiveness and explain how a company can save money by standardizing many of its policies and practices.

Although international marketing approaches should be compatible with companies' overall aims and strategies, they need not standardize every practice for every product where they sell. For instance, market differences may call for pursuing cost leadership through standardization in some countries and more costly differentiation in others. A mass-market orientation may be appropriate in one country and a focused strategy in another. Finally, the degree of global standardization versus national responsiveness may vary within the marketing mix, such as standardizing the product as much as possible while promoting it differently among countries.

Figure 17.1 shows marketing's place in IB.

As we first discuss the orientations that commonly describe companies' marketing strategies, keep in mind that they are not entirely mutually exclusive. We emphasize product policy in our discussion because it is central to a firm's strategy, whereas the other elements in the marketing mix are supportive to it.[2]

MARKETING ORIENTATIONS

Five common marketing orientations can be applied around the world: *production, sales, customer, strategic marketing,* and *social marketing.* Each is discussed below.

Under certain circumstances, the assumptions that consumers simply want lower prices or higher quality are valid.

Production Orientation In this orientation, managers concentrate on production by assuming that customers simply want products with lower prices, higher quality, or whatever they sell domestically. Although this approach has largely gone out of vogue, it is used internationally for certain cases (as described in the following sections).

FIGURE 17.1 Marketing as a Means of Pursuing an International Strategy

Recall that we used Figure 15.1 to introduce the various modes and means by which a company can pursue its international objectives and strategy. Among those means we included functions, and here we focus on one of the most important of those functions: *marketing.*

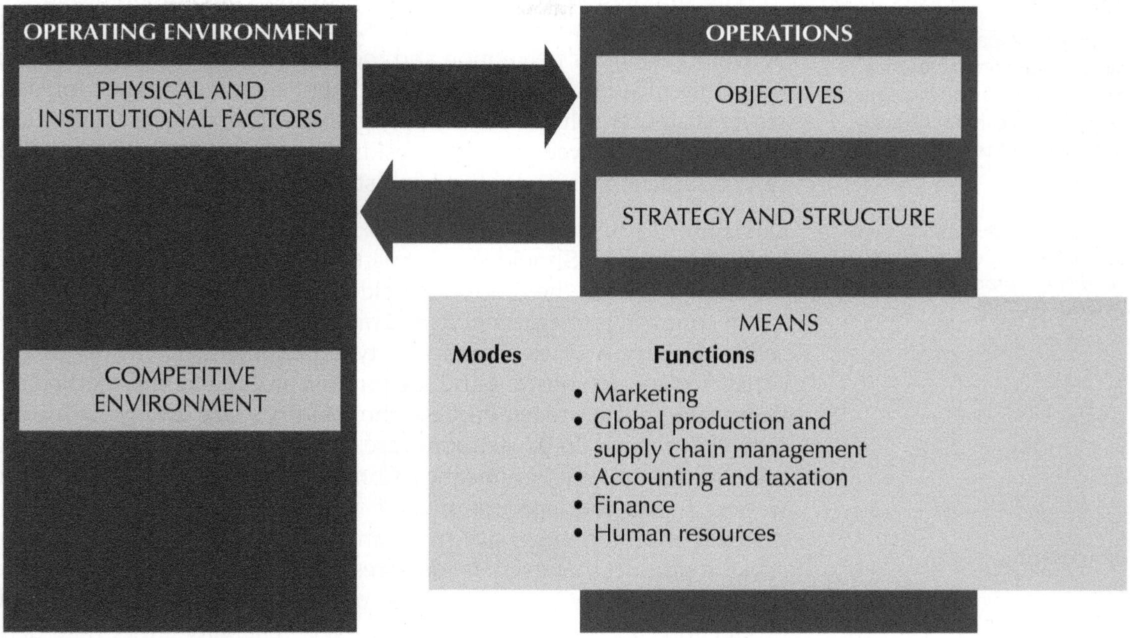

CONCEPT CHECK

In Chapter 7 (page 181), we explain that commodity prices generally rise less than manufacturers' prices, partially because of differentiation difficulty. Here, we demonstrate success in differentiation.

Commodity Sales Companies sell many undifferentiated commodities primarily on the basis of price because of universal demand. However, even for commodities, companies have sometimes had positive international sales results through differentiation that builds favorable consumer perceptions, such as with the Chiquita brand of bananas. In addition, oil producers, such as Saudi Aramco and Motiva, have bought branded gasoline refiners and distributors to extend operations in their value chains and help them sell an otherwise undifferentiated product. Commodity producers also put effort into business-to-business marketing by providing innovative financing and ensuring timely, high-quality supplies.

Passive Exports Many companies export passively by filling unsolicited foreign requests and adapting their products very little, if at all. This suffices for companies that view foreign sales simply as a means to dispose of excess inventory they can't reasonably sell domestically. In fact, if they cover fixed costs through domestic sales, they can quote lower export prices to liquidate inventories without disrupting their domestic markets.

Passive sales also occur when foreign buyers seek new products.

Serving niche markets abroad may forgo the need to be nationally responsive.

Foreign-Market Segments or Niches A company may aim a product at a large share of its domestic market and then find a few consumers abroad who will also buy it. Inca Kola, a major soft drink brand in Peru, has only niche markets abroad, primarily among people who consumed it in Peru. However, a niche market abroad may become a mass market, as is the case with Mexico's Corona beer.

Similarly, a company may sell in countries with minimal market potential and little competition from firms that adapt to local market preferences, particularly in small developing nations. In effect, the market size does not justify the alteration expense—for instance, not changing plugs on electrical products to fit local sockets, which local purchasers must convert.

The unaltered product may have appeal at home and abroad because of

- globally similar demand,
- spillover in product information from its home country,
- foreign and domestic input in development.

Sales Orientation In a sales orientation, a company sells abroad what it sells domestically by assuming that consumers are sufficiently similar. Hilfiger launches much of its children's collection simultaneously in multiple countries this way.[3] Similarly, some products need no international adaptation, such as razor blades, aircraft, and cat food. For others, however, a company may succeed best with a sales orientation by selling to culturally similar countries with a great deal of spillover in product information, such as between the United States and Canada.[4]

CONCEPT CHECK

In Chapter 2 (page 29), we discuss that companies may gain competitive advantages by nurturing cultural diversity, such as within teams.

This orientation differs from the production orientation because of its active rather than passive approach to promoting sales. However, failures may occur because of a mismatch between managers' perception and the reality of what will be accepted abroad.[5] To help alleviate this mismatch, product development teams composed of different nationalities can create customer solutions that apply globally from the start.[6] Additionally, a strong information exchange between foreign subsidiaries and headquarters can help develop products that can be sufficiently standardized and still fit the needs of consumers in different countries.[7]

A customer orientation takes geographic areas as given and seeks products to sell there.

Customer Orientation In a *sales orientation*, management is usually guided by answers to such questions as: Should the company send some exports abroad? Where can it sell more of product X? That is, the product is held constant and the sales location is varied.

In contrast, management in a *customer orientation* asks: What and how can the company sell in country A or to a particular type of consumer? In this case, the country or type of consumer is held constant and the product and marketing method vary. An MNE may most likely take this approach because the country's size and growth potential or the consumer type is attractive. In an extreme case, it would move to completely different products—an uncommon strategy. For instance, Compañía Chilena de Fósforos, a Chilean match producer, wanted to tap the Japanese market because of its growth and size. However, because its matches were too expensive in Japan, it successfully entered the market by making chopsticks, a product that used its forest resources and wood-processing capabilities.[8]

Business-to-business suppliers may be concerned primarily with promoting their production capabilities, prices, and delivery reliability rather than determining what will sell in foreign markets. Instead, they depend on other companies to give them product specifications. For example, Hong Kong's Yue Yuen Industrial is the world's largest branded-footwear manufacturer, making athletic shoes to the specifications of companies such as Nike, New Balance, and Adidas.

The most common product strategy is to adapt by degree.

Strategic Marketing Orientation Companies committed to continual foreign sales usually adopt a strategy that combines production, sales, and customer orientations. They customize to accommodate foreign customers so as not to lose too many sales to aggressive competitors while, at the same time, considering their own competencies so as not to deviate too much from what they do well. Thus, they rely on product variations. Hermès, known for its luxury silk products, has introduced limited edition luxury silk saris for the Indian market.[9] Thus, Hermès uses its competency in prestige design clothing to produce something that fits the unique Indian market. Such personal care firms as Procter & Gamble and Henkel have altered their cosmetics' content by eliminating pork derivatives and alcohol on sales to the Islamic (Halal) market.[10]

Companies consider the effects on all stakeholders when producing and selling their products.

Social Marketing Orientation Companies with social marketing orientations pay close attention to the potential environmental, health, social, and work-related problems that may arise when selling or making their products. Such groups as consumer associations, political parties, labor unions, and NGOs are becoming more globally aware—and vocal. Because they can quell demand when they believe a product somehow violates their concept of social responsibility, companies must consider how a product is made, purchased, used, and discarded. Such considerations led Coca-Cola to use returnable glass containers for Argentina and Brazil.

CONCEPT CHECK

Chapter 5 (page 126) illustrated the problem in trading off the interests of diverse stakeholders.

SEGMENTING AND TARGETING MARKETS

Companies must decide on their target markets, which may include segments that exist in more than one country.

Seldom can a company convince virtually an entire population to consume its product. Thus, based on the orientations just discussed, companies must segment markets for their products and services and then decide which to target and how. The most common way to do this is through demographics, such as income, age, gender, ethnicity, religion, or a combination of factors. Companies may further refine these segments by adding psychographics (attitudes, values, lifestyles). Internationally, segmentation and targeting may take place at a global or country level.[11]

By Global Segment A firm may identify some global segments that transcend countries.[12] For instance, Red Bull targets a global, athletically minded, young-adult market.[13] Ferrari targets high-net-worth individuals who want exclusivity.[14] Thus, each country may have some people within the same segment, but the proportional and actual size of the segment will vary by country.

CONCEPT CHECK

Chapter 13 (page 326) describes the importance of demographics in selecting countries for operations, and much of these data are valid in marketing decisions.

By Country Let's say a company decides to go to the Canadian market. It may modify its global segmentation to fit Canadian nuances, for example by including regional ethnic differences such as Quebec's and British Columbia's French and Chinese speakers, respectively. It must decide whether to target one or multiple segments there, whether to use the same marketing mix to sell to all segments, whether to tailor the products separately to each segment, and whether to vary the promotion and distribution separately as well. The company may also compare these Canadian segments with those in other countries in order to gain possible economies through standardization that serves market segments that cut across countries.

Mixing the Marketing Mix A company may hold one or more elements of its marketing functions—prices, promotion, branding, and distribution— constant while altering the others. For instance, Chanel aims its cosmetics sales at a segment that transcends national boundaries. It uses branding, promotion, pricing, and distribution globally, but adapts the cosmetics to local ethnic and climatic norms.[15]

Mass Markets Versus Niche Markets At the same time, most companies have multiple products and product variations that appeal to different segments; thus, they must decide which to introduce abroad and whether to target them to mass markets or niche segments. For example, General Motors aims at most income levels in the United States with models ranging in price from its Chevrolet Spark through its Cadillac Escalade SUV, but it entered China by aiming only at a high-income segment—first with Buicks and later with Cadillacs.

Because the percentage of people who fall into any segment varies among countries, a niche market in one country may be a mass market in another. An MNE may be content to accept a combination of mass and niche markets; however, if it wishes to appeal to mass markets everywhere, it may need to change elements in its marketing program.

PRODUCT POLICIES: COUNTRY ADAPTATION VERSUS GLOBAL STANDARDIZATION

17-2 Discuss the pros and cons of country adaptation versus global standardization of products

Although cost is a compelling reason to globally standardize any part of a company's marketing mix, product standardization generally gains the biggest savings.[16] Nevertheless, product adaptations are common.

WHY FIRMS ADAPT PRODUCTS

Companies have legal, cultural, and economic reasons for adapting their products to fit the customers' needs in different countries.

Direct and indirect legal factors are usually related to safety, health, and environmental protection.

Legal Considerations Obviously, explicit legal requirements, usually meant to protect consumers, cause companies to customize products for foreign markets. If they don't comply with the law, they won't be allowed to sell. Pharmaceuticals and foods are particularly subject to regulations concerning purity, testing, and labeling, while automobiles must conform to diverse safety, pollution, and fuel-economy standards.

When standards (such as for safety) differ among countries, firms may either conform to the minimum standards of each country or make and sell products fabricated to the highest country standard everywhere. Managers must consider cost along with public opinion by having lower standards in some countries. Critics have complained, for example, about companies' sales—especially in developing countries—of such products as toys, automobiles, contraceptives, and pharmaceuticals that did not meet safety or quality standards elsewhere.

Labeling Requirements One of the more cumbersome product alterations concerns laws on labeling, such as for origin, ingredients, and warnings. Labeling differences on food products include their bioengineered content and whether they are organic or fair traded. Countries have varying warning requirements and methods, such as for cigarettes; Australia requires all companies to put them in the same drab dark brown packs and to use standardized lettering for their brand names.[17]

Environmental-Protection Regulations Another problem concerns laws that protect the environment, such as Denmark's requirement for a refundable deposit on certain metal, glass, and plastic containers. Other countries restrict the volume of packaging materials to save resources and decrease trash. There are also differences in national requirements as to whether packaging materials must be recycled, incinerated, or composted.

Indirect Legal Considerations Indirect legal requirements also affect product content or demand. In some nations, companies cannot easily import certain raw materials or components, forcing them to construct a product with local substitutes that may modify the final result. Laws, such as high taxes on heavy automobiles, also shift companies' sales to smaller models, thus indirectly altering demand for tire sizes and grades of gasoline.

Although some global product standardization would eliminate wasteful alterations, there is resistance because

- a changeover would be costly,
- people are familiar with the "old."

Issues of Standardization Countries' legal differences require firms to incur costly product adjustments. Although governments have reached agreements to standardize some product characteristics (technical standards on mobile phones, bar codes to identify products), other products (railroad gauges, power supplies) continue to vary. A global standard has usually resulted from companies wanting to emulate a dominant producer, such as making blades to fit Gillette razors.

In reality, there is both consumer and economic resistance to global standardization—such as the U.S. reluctance to adapt to the metric system. Economically, a changeover would be costlier than simply educating people and relabeling. Containers would have to be redesigned and production retooled so that sizes would be in even numbers. Even for new products or those still under development, companies and countries are slow to reach agreement because they want to protect the investments they've already made. At best, international standards will come very slowly.

Examination of cultural differences may pinpoint possible product problems.

Cultural Considerations Religious differences obviously limit the standardization of product offerings globally, such as the limitation of pork product sales by food franchises in Islamic countries. These franchises, such as McDonald's and Burger King, also add items to fit local tastes, such as squid oil on buns in Japan.[18] However, cultural differences affecting product demand may not be so easily discerned. Toyota failed to sell enough pickup trucks in the United States until it redesigned the interior with enough headroom for drivers to wear cowboy hats. Home Depot left the Chinese market after it could not overcome consumers' preference for hiring people to do jobs rather than embracing the do-it-yourself concept.[19] International food marketers substantially alter ingredients (especially fat, sodium, and sugar) to fit local tastes and requirements, such as Kellogg's All-Bran bar having more salt in the United States than in Mexico.

Economic Considerations

Personal incomes and infrastructures affect product demand, thus firms may

- aim product variations at different income levels,
- tailor products to compensate for infrastructure differences.

Income Level and Distribution In countries with many low income consumers, companies may sell to them differently. For instance, in Peru, Unilever sells deodorants in aerosol cans to more affluent consumers, and it sells cream sachet in small containers to those with lower incomes.[20] Diageo and SABMiller have lowered beer prices to low-income consumers in several African countries by brewing with local ingredients, such as yams, and convincing governmental authorities to remove excise taxes because of the agricultural jobs created by the ingredient change.[21] When segmenting sales by economic levels, a company may need to distinguish its products by giving them different brand names, such as what Procter & Gamble does in China with both a Duracell and a Nanfu brand of batteries.[22]

Infrastructure Poor infrastructure may also require product alterations, such as making them to withstand rough terrain and utility outages. Whirlpool sells washing machine models in remote areas of India with rat guards to protect hoses, extra-strong parts to survive transportation on potholed roads, and heavy-duty wiring to cope with electrical ebbs and surges.[23] Japan has adapted its excellent infrastructure to crowded conditions and high land prices, which limits sales of some large foreign automobile models (i.e., they are too wide to fit into elevators that carry cars to parking areas on upper floors or to make narrow turns on back streets).

ALTERATION COSTS

The cost of product alterations should be compared with their expected sales generation.

Some product alterations, such as the labeling of packages, are cheaper than others, such as designing a different car model. Further, some will increase sales more than others, thus potential costs versus sales generation should be evaluated for each type of change.[24] However, even packaging changes may necessitate costly research if the aim is to help build a certain product image. For example, packaging can partially sway consumers' purchase decisions, but the image needed to do this may differ by target market.[25]

MNEs can compromise between products' uniformity and diversity by standardizing them a great deal while altering some characteristics. Whirlpool does this by putting the same basic mechanical parts in all its refrigerators while changing such features as doors and shelves for different countries.[26]

THE PRODUCT LINE: EXTENT AND MIX

Broadening the product line may gain distribution economies, but not all of a company's line has sales appeal everywhere.

When a firm introduces multiple products abroad, the percentage share of sales for each commonly differs from the shares in its home country. For instance, a tire manufacturer may sell all its car tire sizes everywhere, but the share for each size depends on sales of different automobile models in each market. Cultural factors may also be important. Most of Nike's specialty sports shoes have sold well in China, but its running shoes have not. Why not? Running in China has been associated with unpopular school exercise programs and with people being chased.[27]

In many cases, not all of an MNE's multiple products can generate sufficient sales to justify the cost of penetrating each market with each product. Even if they can, the company might offer only a portion of its product line, perhaps as an entry strategy or because distributors have limited space and high inventory costs when handling a very broad product line. Walmart's Canadian stores, for instance, have only 20 percent of the merchandise variety available in its U.S. stores.[28]

Sales and Cost Considerations In reaching product-line decisions, managers should consider the sales and cost of having a large versus a small family of products. Sometimes a firm must produce and sell a wide variety of products to gain distribution with large retailers. Further, if the sales per retailer are small, fixed distribution costs may cause delivery costs per sales unit to be high. In such a case, the company can broaden the product line it distributes, either by introducing a larger family of its products or by grouping sales of several manufacturers.

INTERNATIONAL PRICING COMPLEXITIES

17-3 Describe pricing complexities when selling in foreign markets

A price must be low enough to gain sales but high enough to guarantee the flow of funds required to cover expenses and make sufficient profits to achieve long-term competitive viability.

POTENTIAL OBSTACLES IN INTERNATIONAL PRICING

Pricing is more complex internationally than domestically, and we'll now examine the major reasons.

Government Intervention Every country has laws that affect prices. Minimum prices are usually set to prevent companies from eliminating competitors and gaining monopoly positions. Maximum prices are usually set so that poor consumers can buy products and services.

Some nationalities simply like certain products more and are willing to pay more for them.

Market Diversity Country-to-country variations in demand and competition create natural segments and differences in pricing possibilities. In terms of culture, a seafood company would sell few sea urchins or tuna eyeballs in the United States at any price, but it can export them to Japan at a high price, where they are considered delicacies. In terms of competition, the more there is, the less discretion a firm has in setting its prices.

Country-of-origin stereotypes also affect pricing possibilities. For example, exporters in developing economies are characterized by limited resources that negatively affect their ability to market in developed countries.[29] Further, they must often compete primarily through low prices because of negative perceptions about some of their products' quality. The danger is that a lower price may weaken the product image even further.

Diversity in buying on credit affects sales, especially through impulse buying.[30] For example, the average consumers in some countries, such as Japan, are less willing to undertake debt (e.g., they have a feeling of insecurity when incurring debt) than consumers in other countries, such as the United States. In the former, it is harder to generate sales by offering credit.

CONCEPT CHECK

In Chapter 14 (pages 370–373), we discuss the importance of export intermediaries and the process of indirect selling (page 358) through independent companies that facilitate international trade.

Export Price Escalation If standard markups occur within distribution channels, lengthening the channels or adding expenses somewhere in the system will further raise the price to the consumer by more than incremental transport and duty costs—a situation known as *export price escalation.* Figure 17.2 shows price escalation in export sales.

There are two main implications of price escalation. Seemingly exportable products may turn out to be noncompetitive abroad if companies in the value chain use cost-plus pricing—which many do. To become competitive in exporting, a company may have to sell its product to intermediaries at a lower price or convince intermediaries to lower their margins to lessen the amount of escalation.

Export prices generally rise by more than incremental transport and duty costs, thus exporters may have to lower margins to make sales.

Fluctuations in Currency Value For companies accustomed to operating with one relatively stable currency, pricing in highly volatile currencies can be extremely troublesome. Managers should price to ensure the company enough funds to replenish its inventory and still make a profit. Otherwise, it may be making a "paper profit" while liquidating itself—that is, what shows on paper as a profit may result from the failure to adjust for inflation while the merchandise is in stock.

CONCEPT CHECK

In Chapter 10 (pages 248–249), we point out why foreign-exchange values fluctuate, and in Chapter 13 (page 329), we describe how fluctuations affect companies' operations either positively or negatively.

Two other pricing problems occur because of inflationary conditions:

1. The receipt of funds in a foreign currency that, when converted, buy less of the company's own currency than had been expected
2. The frequent readjustment of prices necessary to compensate for continual cost increases

In the first case, the company sometimes can specify within sales contracts an equivalency in some hard currency. For example, a U.S. firm's sale to a company in Argentina may specify that payment be made in dollars or in pesos at an equivalent price in terms of dollars at the time payment is made.

FIGURE 17.2 Why Cost-Plus Pricing Pushes Up Prices

Let's say that a product is being exported from Country A and imported into Country B. Let's also say that both the producer/exporter and the importer/distributor tack on 50 percent markups to the prices they pay for the product. If you add in the costs of transport and tariffs, the product is substantially more expensive in Country B than in Country A—perhaps too expensive to be sold competitively.

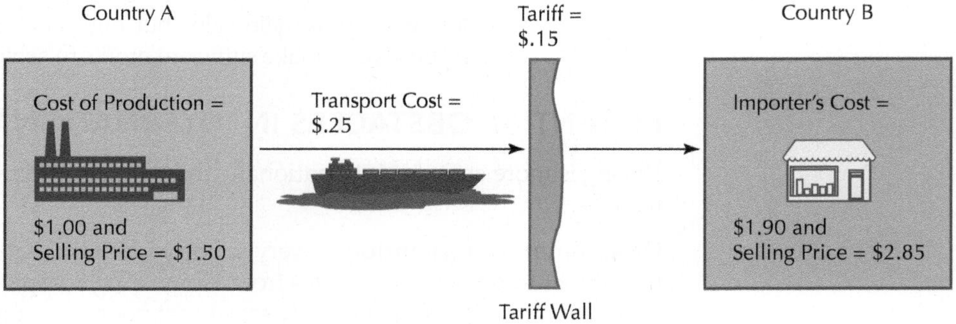

In the second case, frequent price increases may hamper the ability to quote prices very far in advance in the currency that is losing value. Further, it would be difficult to make vending-machine sales because of having to recalibrate machines and come up with coins or tokens that correspond to the new prices. Another alternative is to change the product's quality, which few firms are willing to do, or its size, which is what Coca-Cola did to its canned soft-drinks in Hong Kong when aluminum prices rose.[31]

Currency-value changes also affect pricing decisions for any product that has potential foreign competition. For example, when the U.S. dollar is strong, companies can sell non-U.S.-made goods more cheaply in the United States because their prices in dollars decrease. In such a situation, U.S. producers may have to accept a lower profit margin to be competitive. When the dollar is weak, however, producers in foreign countries may have to adjust their margins downward.

When companies' prices are significantly different among countries, consumers are tempted to buy in the cheapest country.

The Gray Market The **gray market**, or **product diversion**, is the selling and handling of goods through unofficial distributors, thus enabling the unofficial ones to import cheaper supplies from abroad to compete against official ones. Such unauthorized selling can undermine the longer-term viability of the distributorship system, induce a company's operations in different countries to compete with each other, and prevent companies from charging what the market will bear in each country. However, transport costs as a percentage of product costs are important in determining whether product diversion is feasible. When they are high, such as for ice cream, large-scale movements across borders are impractical. But for many other products, the movements are practical. Traditionally, for example, publishers sold texts at substantially different prices in different countries, but the U.S. Supreme Court ruled on the legality of buying lower-priced textbooks abroad to resell in the United States. In essence, maintaining large price differences among countries has become more difficult as consumers have gained access to more global price information and more access to buying abroad because of lower trade barriers.

Fixed Versus Variable Pricing MNEs often negotiate their prices with producers and distributors in other countries. Small firms, especially those from developing countries, frequently give price concessions too quickly, limiting their ability to negotiate on a range of marketing factors that affect their costs:

There are country-to-country differences in

- whether prices are fixed or bargained,
- where bargaining occurs,
- what products' prices are bargained.

- Discounts for quantity or repeat orders
- Deadlines that increase production or transportation costs
- Credit and payment terms
- Service
- Supply of promotional materials
- Training of sales personnel or customers

Some people, regardless of culture, avoid price negotiation even when they know they may gain economically by doing so.[32] In essence, many people fear being perceived as too aggressive or too poor. Or, they may not want to take the time, preferring to develop long-term relationships that bargaining might upset. Regardless of cause, there is a substantial variation among countries in whether, where, and for what products consumers bargain in order to settle on an agreed price. In the United States, consumers commonly bargain for automobiles, real estate, and large orders of industrial supplies but not for grocery items. However, some auto dealerships sell only on a fixed-price basis, while bargaining for smaller items is growing as buyers more easily obtain alternative prices through the Internet. In contrast, consumers in most developing countries commonly bargain for both large and small items, but more routinely in traditional markets than in retail stores.[33]

Markets' dominant companies have strong negotiating power.

Supplier Relations Dominant companies with clout can get suppliers to offer lower prices, thereby gaining cost advantages over competitors. But they may lack this ability when entering foreign markets because of not dominating the market there. Walmart, Tesco, and Carrefour have such clout in their respective domestic markets (U.S, UK, and France), but they have been hard pressed to gain the same advantage when entering the others' home markets.

The Internet is also causing more companies to compete for the same business, especially for sales of largely undifferentiated products. Thus, many industrial buyers are claiming large price decreases through Internet buying. However, sellers can improve their positions by negotiating and by combining the Internet with face-to-face interaction.[34]

SHOULD PROMOTION DIFFER AMONG COUNTRIES?

17-4 Recognize the pros and cons of using uniform promotional marketing practices among countries

Promotion is the presentation of messages intended to help sell a product or service. The types and direction of messages and the methods of presentation may be extremely diverse, depending on the company, product, and country of operation.

THE PUSH–PULL MIX

Promotion may be **push**, which uses direct selling techniques, or **pull**, which relies on mass media. Most companies use combinations of both. For each product in each country, a company must determine the mix between push and pull within its total promotional budget.

Factors in Push–Pull Decisions Several factors help determine the mix of push and pull:

- Type of distribution system
- Cost and availability of media to reach target markets
- Consumer attitudes toward sources of information
- Price of the product compared to incomes

Push is more likely when

- self-service is not predominant,
- advertising is restricted,
- product price is a high portion of income.

Generally, the more tightly controlled the distribution system, the more likely a company is to emphasize a push strategy to distributors because a greater effort is needed to get them to handle a product. This is true where most distributors can carry few brands because they are small, thereby forcing companies to concentrate on making their goods available.

Also affecting the push–pull mix is the amount of contact between salespeople and consumers. In a self-service situation, in which customers have few or no salespeople to turn to for opinions on products, it is more important for the company to use a pull strategy by advertising through mass media or at the point of purchase.

Finally, consumers react to word-of-mouth opinions, especially where uncertainty avoidance is high.[35] To enhance word-of-mouth opinions, companies need to persuade existing customers that their purchases have been of high quality and at reasonable prices, such as by providing after-sales support and service. Social media platforms are rapidly becoming more important in conveying independent experiences for products and services because they allow users to interact, such as by rating their recent hotel stays and sharing information about their experiences.

CONCEPT CHECK

In Chapter 2 (page 39), we discuss the cultural concept of uncertainty avoidance.

SOME PROBLEMS IN INTERNATIONAL PROMOTION

Diverse national environments create varied promotional challenges. For example, over half of China's population is rural, many are poor, and many lack access to traditional media to view advertisements. Thus, PC makers such as Lenovo and Hewlett Packard have promoted in rural areas, such as in local markets, by providing variety shows and films to demonstrate their products.[36] In rural Nigeria, Kuwait's Mobile Telecommunications Company first tried direct marketing, but found its salespeople facing too many dangers. The company then turned successfully to small shop owners—tailors, retailers, etc.—and established a mini-franchise system with them.[37]

In many areas, government regulations pose additional barriers, such as in Scandinavia where television cannot broadcast commercials aimed at children. In China, ads cannot interrupt dramas, thus they are all bunched together between shows, which companies claim make the ads less effective. Other countries may put legal constraints on what a company says. For instance, the United States allows pharmaceutical firms to advertise prescription drugs for physical symptoms, such as erectile dysfunction, in television ads and tell viewers to ask their physicians about a particular brand, such as Viagra or Cialis. However, Pfizer's and Eli Lilly's European ads simply tell TV viewers, without mentioning their brands, to talk with their physicians about their problems.[38]

Finally, when a product's price compared to consumer income is high, consumers usually want more time and information before making a decision. In these situations, information is best conveyed in a personal selling situation that fosters two-way communication. Thus, in developing economies MNEs will often use push strategies for more products because of lower incomes.

Advantages of standardized advertising include
- some cost savings,
- better quality at the country level,
- a common image globally,
- rapid entry into different countries.

Advertising Standardization: Pro and Con Standardizing advertising among countries reduces costs by avoiding duplication of preparation, may improve the quality at the local level (because local agencies may lack expertise), prevents internationally mobile consumers from being confused by different images, and speeds the entry of products into different countries.

However, globally standardized advertising usually refers to *similarity* among markets rather than being *identical*. For example, Red Bull's ad campaigns are similar in that they focus on sports, but the sports differ among countries.[39] Standardization typically involves using the same ad agency globally. By doing this, MNEs such as Colgate and Tambrands can quickly introduce good ideas from one market into others without legal and ethical problems that could arise over agency copying. Other companies, like Procter & Gamble, prefer to use more than one agency to promote competition and to cover one agency's weak spots by drawing on another's strong points.

Finally, the issue of standardization in advertising raises problems in a few other areas—namely, *translation, legality,* and *message needs.*

CONCEPT CHECK

In Chapter 2 (pages 41–42), we emphasize the problems in translating messages and the role of nonverbal communications (pages 42–43) in conveying messages.

Translation Selling in a country with a different language necessitates translation unless the advertiser tries to communicate an aura of foreignness. Because voice dubbing of TV ads creates sound tracks that never quite correspond to lip movements, companies usually turn to voice or print overlays of commercials in which actors do not speak.

Another type of advertisement dubbing involves product and brand placement in books, movies, and television shows, especially those that are widely distributed internationally. First, some countries limit product placement of certain products, such as India of cigarettes. Second, some brands may not be available everywhere. In the latter case, technology may reduce the problem. For instance, *Spider-Man 2* had Cadbury Schweppes's Dr. Pepper logo on a refrigerator for U.S. screenings and PepsiCo's Mirinda logo in Europe.[40]

On the surface, translating a message would seem easy. However, some messages, particularly plays on words, don't translate—even between countries that have the same language. Sometimes an acceptable word or direct translation in one place has a nuance that is offensive, misleading, or meaningless in another. An additional issue lies in choosing the language when a country has more than one. For instance, many companies use Creole in Haiti to reach the general population but French to reach the upper class.

Differences in nations' values have led to advertising differences among them.

Legality The legality of advertisements varies mainly because of diverse national views on consumer and competitive protection, civil rights promotion, standards of morality and behavior, and nationalism. For example, there are products that some societies view as being in such bad taste that restricting their advertising is necessary.[41]

Effective promotional messages may be different among countries because of
- cultural factors,
- economic levels of target markets,
- stages of products in their life cycles.

In terms of consumer protection, policies differ on the amount of deception permitted and what can be advertised to children. Mexico, for example, limits using TV advertisement of products high in sugar content directed at children.[42] The United Kingdom and the United States allow direct comparisons with competitive brands, while the Philippines prohibits them. Only a few countries regulate sexism in advertising. Elsewhere, governments restrict ads that might prompt misbehavior or law-breaking (such as promoting automobile speeds that exceed the speed limit), as well as those that show barely clad women.[43]

Message Needs An advertising theme may not be appropriate everywhere because of country differences in consumers' product awareness and perception, the people who make the purchasing decision, and what appeals are most important. At one time fewer Italians owned dishwashers than would be expected from Italian income levels because of a belief that buying for the sake of convenience reduces cleanliness; hence, a group of dishwasher manufacturers teamed up to advertise that dishwashers clean better because they use hotter water.[44] Because of economic differences, Home Depot promotes its U.S. stores by appealing to hobbyists, whereas in Mexico it promotes the cost savings for do-it-yourselfers.[45]

The reaction to messages may also vary. Leo Burnett Worldwide produced a public service ad to promote breast exams that showed an attractive woman being admired in a low-cut sundress. The voice-over message said, "If only women paid as much attention to their breasts as men do." Japanese viewers found this a humorous way to draw attention to breast cancer, whereas French viewers found it offensive because cancer should not be viewed humorously.[46] Given the increase in television and Internet transmissions that reach audiences in multiple countries, advertisers must find common themes and messages that will appeal to potential consumers everywhere their ads are viewed.

Countries may differ in either the shape or the length of a product's life cycle. Thus, a product facing declining sales in one country may have growing or sustained sales in another. Consider cars: They are a mature product in Western Europe, in the late growth stage in South Korea, and in the early growth stage in India. At the mature stage, automobile companies must emphasize characteristics that encourage people to replace their still-functional cars, such as lifestyle, speed, and accessories. In the early growth stage, they need to appeal to first-time buyers who worry more about cost, so they emphasize fuel consumption and price.[47]

The growth in products' online availability through the Internet creates promotional and distributional opportunities and challenges.

The Internet Estimates vary widely on the current and future number of worldwide online households and the electronic commerce generated through online sales, but Internet ads may now account for about a quarter of advertising business.[48] The Internet has done more in recent years than any other innovation to alter international promotion. Through e-commerce, customers worldwide can quickly compare prices from different distributors, which drives prices down. Through the growing use of social media, they can obtain better information to compare the quality and reliability of products and distributors.

Opportunities There are certainly many international e-commerce success stories. These include promotion for direct sales as well as information to pre-sell and inform shoppers where they may buy the products. One such success story is the New Zealand prefab housing company Tristyle International, for which about 95 percent of sales are export and 40 percent are through the Internet.[49] Another is Lee Hung Fat Garment Factory of Hong Kong and Bangladesh. It flashes pictures of merchandise samples to apparel companies abroad that tinker with and return them so that it produces exactly what they want. For some products and services, such as airline tickets, hotel space, and music, the Internet has largely replaced traditional sales methods. But even here, companies may need to adapt to country differences, such as providing access through various languages.[50]

Problems Global Internet sales are not without glitches. A company wanting to reach global markets may need to supplement its Internet sales with other means of promotion and distribution, which can be very expensive. Further, a switch to Internet sales may risk upsetting existing distributors and, if unsuccessful, hamper future sales.[51]

On the Internet, an MNE cannot as easily differentiate its marketing program for each country in which it sells even if it channels customers to local sites. In many instances, the same web ads and prices reach customers everywhere, even though different appeals and prices for different countries might yield more sales and profits. Making direct sales over the Internet requires expeditious delivery, which may require warehouses and service facilities abroad. Finally, the MNE's Internet ads and prices must comply with the laws of each country of sales. This is problematic because of the web's global reach. Clearly, although the Internet creates opportunities for companies to sell internationally, it also creates challenges for them.

INTERNATIONAL BRANDING STRATEGIES

17-5 Explain the different branding strategies companies may employ internationally

A *brand* is an identifying mark for products or services. If it is legally registered, it is a trademark. A brand gives a product or service instant recognition and may save promotional costs. Because companies have spent heavily in the past to create brand awareness, many brands are worth billions of dollars and are the most valuable assets firms possess.[52] (The photo below demonstrates the preponderance of branded trademarks that come from all over the world.) From a consumer standpoint, a brand conveys a perception of whether firms will deliver what they promise; however, the importance is more crucial in countries with strong cultural characteristics of uncertainty avoidance.[53]

Keep in mind that a company may use the same brand globally while altering the brand image for different markets. For example, individualistic cultures offer greater advantages in creating an image of innovativeness than collectivist cultures. However, within the latter, images of social responsibility apparently contribute more to brand commitment than in the former.[54]

GLOBAL BRAND VERSUS LOCAL BRANDS

International marketers must decide whether to adopt a global brand or use different brands for different countries.

Using the same brand name globally
- helps develop a common image,
- may increase consumers' demand if they think global products are better,
- is hampered by language differences,
- has a drawback in the case of acquisitions.

Advantages of a Global Brand Some companies, such as Apple, use the same brands and logos for most of their products around the world. This helps develop a global image, especially for customers who travel internationally. In addition, there is evidence that the use of global brands helps identify companies as global players, which many consumers view more favorably.[55] Other companies, such as Nestlé, associate many of their products under the same family of brands, such as Nestea and Nescafé, to share the positive perception of the Nestlé name.

Some Problems with Global Brands A number of problems are inherent in using global brands.

Language A brand name may carry a different association in another language. GM renamed its Buick LaCrosse to Allure in Canada after discovering, through a pre-entry focus group, that the word was slang in Quebec for masturbation.[56] Coca-Cola uses global

Source: Onurhazar/Shutterstock

You probably recognize most of this sample of trademarks.

branding wherever possible, but given that the word *diet* in Diet Coke had a connotation of illness in Germany and Italy, the brand became Coca-Cola Light outside the United States.

Pronunciation presents other problems, since a foreign language may lack some of the sounds of a brand name, or give it a different meaning. Marcel Bich dropped the *h* from his name when branding Bic pens because of fearing mispronunciation in English. Microsoft's search engine Bing became Biying in China so that it sounded like the word for "seek and ye shall find" instead of "illness."

When alphabets use pictograms, such as in China, brands should both look and sound appealing. Thus, MNEs should ensure not only that the translation of their names is pronounced roughly the same in Mandarin or Cantonese Chinese as elsewhere but also that the brand name is meaningful in pictograms. Tide became Tai-zi in Mandarin, which means "gets rid of dirt."[57] Companies seek names and prices using symbols considered lucky in China, such as one with eight strokes in it and displayed in red rather than blue.[58]

Brand Acquisition Much international expansion is through acquisitions of companies with established brands, such as Bimbo's Sara Lee of various Brazilian coffee roasters. Although Sara Lee became the coffee-market leader in Brazil, stretching the promotional budget over many brands has been challenging.[59] Overall, the proportion of local to global brands is declining; however, companies lose the recognition and goodwill of strong local brands if they displace them.[60] Similarly, having a combination of global and local brands that appeal to different segments can sometimes be advantageous, such as those used for Anheuser-Busch InBev's beers.[61]

Images of products are affected by where they are made.

Country-of-Origin Images Consumers have limited knowledge of the nationality of most brands, and they often misclassify the production origins.[62] Such confusion is compounded with the increased mixed source of the components that make up products. In addition, both the country of origin and the brand images interact so that a positive brand image can help overcome a negative country-of-origin image.[63] Nevertheless, many consumers are influenced by their emotional affinity toward certain countries; their affinity affects their images of certain countries and buying decisions based on where products are made.[64]

When the country of origin affects consumers' opinion of a product,

- a positive brand image may help overcome a negative country-of-origin image,
- these opinions can change over time.

But purchase decisions based on product origins are complex, depending on such factors as type of product, the economic level of and nearness of the producing country, consumers' national culture (such as effects of individualism versus collectivism), and consumers personalities (such as how materialistic they are).[65] Despite the complexity, companies may play up positive and play down negative country-of-origin images. For example, because many Japanese believe that clothing made abroad is superior to clothing made in Japan, Burberry has created separate labels for its products made in Japan and the United Kingdom. South African wineries, La Motte and Leopard's Leap, have a wine brand, L'Huguenot, for the Chinese market because the French-sounding name is perceived positively by Chinese consumers.[66]

Still, images can change. For many years various Korean firms sold abroad only under private labels or in contract with foreign companies. On the one hand, some of these, such as Samsung, now emphasize their own trade names and Korean product quality. On the other hand, the Korean LG Group, best known for its Gold Star brand, has introduced a line of high-end appliances with a European-sounding name, LG Tromm.[67]

Locational Origin of Names One ongoing international legal debate concerns product names associated with location. The EU protects the names of many European products based on location names, such as Roquefort and Feta cheeses, Parma ham, and Chianti wine.[68] It has also pushed for protection against the foreign use of regulated names associated with wines, such as *clos, chateau, tawny, noble, ruby,* and *vintage.*[69]

If a brand name is used for a class of product, a company may lose its trademark.

Generic and Near-Generic Names Companies want their brands to become household words, but not so much that they become *generic* (commonly used for a class of product), in which case competitors can use the names to call their products. In the United States, the brand names Xerox and Kleenex are nearly synonymous with copiers and facial tissue, but they have nevertheless remained proprietary brands. Some other names that were once proprietary—cellophane, linoleum, Cornish hens—are now generic.

In this context, companies sometimes face differences among countries that may either stimulate or frustrate their sales. For example, *aspirin* and *Swiss Army knives* are proprietary names in Europe but generic in the United States—a situation that impairs European export sales of those products to the United States, since U.S. companies can produce them.

POINT

Should Home Governments Regulate Their Companies' Marketing in Developing Countries?

YES MNEs advertise, promote, and sell products in developing markets that their home countries have banned. If they've made a decision not to sell these products domestically because of their dangers or ethical implications, they have a moral obligation to prevent the same consequences abroad. This statement may smack of extraterritoriality, but let's face it: Too many consumers in developing countries lack the education and reliable information to make intelligent decisions about products, and/or they are saddled with corrupt political leaders who don't look after their interests. We must ensure that they spend on upright needs rather than on wants engendered by MNEs' clever promotion programs. If developed countries don't regulate to protect consumers in developing countries, who will?

Companies also export or market products that don't meet quality standards at home or that are potentially dangerous. Take DDT: It's so dangerous to the environment that all developed countries banned its use, but some developed country firms continue to market DDT that is produced in countries that have not banned it. Or consider battery recycling: Developed countries have pretty strict and expensive antipollution requirements to prevent lead poisoning, which shows up only after slow, cumulative ingestion through the years. So now companies export the batteries to developing countries that have either weak or weakly enforced pollution laws.[70]

With the World Health Organization (WHO) estimating that tobacco is the leading cause of preventable death in the world, we have also attempted to limit tobacco use through warning labels and ads, restrictions on sales to minors, and smoking bans in certain public areas. While tobacco use has been declining in developed countries, it is burgeoning in developing ones, especially those in Africa, where tobacco companies have increased their promotions.[71] Similarly, as publicity has caused a decrease in U.S. sales of sugary drinks, such as Tang, companies have upped their marketing and sales in developing countries.[72]

MNEs also pay too little attention to the needs of consumers in developing markets. Instead, they primarily create products suitable to the wants of wealthier consumers who can afford them, but these products are

COUNTERPOINT

Should Home Governments Regulate Their Companies' Marketing in Developing Countries?

NO The answer here is education rather than limiting people's choices by regulating MNEs. In fact, there are many examples of behavior change in both consumers and governments when they learn the facts. For example, antismoking radio and television ads in a three-country African study showed a decrease in propensity to smoke.[76]

Your argument that products banned at home should not be sold abroad assumes that the home government knows best. For example, much of the research on the effects of pesticides and herbicides is conducted by the companies producing them, thus their results may be highly selective.[77] Further, there are different scientific opinions. For example, the EU produces many pesticides and chemicals that are banned for EU usage, but are allowed to be used in the United States.[78] Further, differences may reflect variations in a difference in what is considered moral rather than a problem of creating physical danger. For instance, some countries have banned the sale of the morning-after pill RU-486 on moral grounds. But to ban sales in other countries that accept a different morality would smack of cultural imperialism.

Conditions between rich and poor countries are sometimes so different that they need different regulations. Take your example of DDT sales. Developing countries are aware of DDT's adverse long-term effect on the environment, but in the short term many of them face mosquito crises that cause Zika, dengue, chikungunya, and malaria.[79] When South Africa was persuaded to ban the use of DDT and turned instead to a different pesticide, the number of new malaria cases tripled in four years; renewing DDT spraying brought that number down again.[80] Until there is a better solution for mosquito controls, DDT bans may do more harm than good. Certainly, if one government has found a product dangerous, it should pass on this information to other governments; in terms of DDT and toxic materials exports, this is already being done.

Yes, tobacco companies are promoting more heavily in developing countries. Keep in mind, though, that a good part of that promotion is for smokeless tobacco products, which are safer than cigarettes and can help smokers stop.[81] In fact, Philip Morris is developing a product that will produce an aerosol without the combustion that causes most harm.[82] Nevertheless, if MNEs' home governments were to limit their companies' sales or promotion often superfluous for low-income consumers, to whom MNEs introduce and promote them heavily. Thus, the poor end up buying products they don't need instead of spending their money on nutritional and health items. Bottled water, sold mainly in plastic bottles by such companies as Nestlé, Danone, Coca-Cola, and PepsiCo, is an example. It is often no better than tap water (in fact, it often is tap water), but it sells for 10,000 times more in bottles that are thrown out and take 1,000 years to biodegrade.

Finally, MNEs spend little to create products to fit the needs of developing countries. Consider that little of the global health research budget is spent on diseases that account for most of the global disease burden—mainly those that largely bypass developed countries.[73] Instead of spending heavily on life-threatening illnesses like malaria, Chagas disease, and sleeping sickness, they spend on lifestyle treatments, such as penile erectile dysfunction and baldness. Although Ebola had long plagued African countries, pharmaceutical companies spent little to develop a vaccine until there was danger of its spread to developed countries.[74] The U.S. Food and Drug Administration (FDA) did institute an incentive—faster approval of potential "blockbuster drugs"—for pharmaceutical companies that research previously neglected diseases. However, there is skepticism about whether faster approval is enough of an incentive.[75] Surely we can find the regulatory means to force companies to meet real needs in the developing world rather than concentrating on selling dangerous and superfluous products there.

of tobacco abroad, developing countries' citizens would still be able to buy cigarettes. Many developing countries have indigenous tobacco companies, some of which are even government-owned, such as in Thailand. How far can we go to try to protect people? Obesity, considered a growing health problem in the developed world, is being attacked through education—the same way we should attack problems in developing countries. I can't imagine a widespread rationing or banning of sugars, fats, and carbohydrates. Certainly, products such as soft drinks and bottled water seem superfluous when people are ill-nourished and in poor health. But the lack of access to sanitary water is one of the world's biggest health problems, which the sale of soft drinks and bottled water are helping in the short term. In a longer term, Coca-Cola is working to distribute small-scale purifying systems to mitigate the problem.[83] Moreover, there is no clear-cut means of drawing a line between people who can and can't afford these so-called superfluous products.

Companies do alter products to fit the needs of poor people—everything from less expensive packages to less expensive products. The pharmaceutical firms you criticized for not attacking low-income health needs spend heavily to find solutions to diseases that attack all people regardless of their locations, such as cancer, diabetes, and the COVID-19 virus. In fact, they have seen, and expect to see, huge prescription drug growth in emerging markets.[84] However, they must recoup their expenses if they are to survive, so they concentrate on drugs for which they can be paid. Governmental research centers and nonprofit foundations are better candidates for solving the developing countries' health problems. Some are working jointly with pharmaceutical firms to find solutions, while the National Institutes of Health (NIH) in the United States has instituted a program to find treatments for some of the 6,800 diseases for which there is likely insufficient revenue to recoup research expenditures.[85]

DISTRIBUTION PRACTICES AND COMPLICATIONS

17-6 Discern major practices and complications of international distribution

A company will not likely reach its sales potential unless its products are conveniently available. **Distribution** is the course—physical path or legal title—that goods take between production and consumption. This section discusses distributional differences and conditions within foreign countries.

DECIDING WHETHER TO STANDARDIZE

Distribution is difficult to standardize globally. Each country has its own distribution system, which is difficult to modify because of its intertwinement with the country's cultural, economic, and legal environments. In fact, most companies take a country's distribution system as a given and try to adapt to it. Although there are some large multinational distributors, such as Arrow and Grainger, wholesalers and retailers have generally lagged manufacturers' and

Because distribution reflects different country environments,

- it may vary substantially among countries,
- it is difficult to change.

service companies' entries into foreign markets because of difficulty in breaking into these systems. Nevertheless, many retailers have more recently moved successfully abroad.

Some factors that influence countries' retail distribution include citizens' attitudes toward owning their own store, the cost of paying retail workers, legislation restricting store sizes and operating hours, laws on chain stores and individually owned stores, the trust owners have in employees, the efficacy of delivery systems, the quality of the infrastructure system, and the financial ability to carry large inventories. An example should illustrate how widespread differences are. Compare grocery distribution in Hong Kong with the United States: the average Hong Kong food stores carry a higher proportion of fresh goods, are smaller, sell less per customer, and are closer to each other, which means that companies selling canned, boxed, or frozen foods in Hong Kong encounter less demand per store, have to make smaller deliveries, and have a harder time fighting for shelf space.

At the same time, a company's system of distribution may give it strategic advantages not easily copied by competitors, such as Avon's direct sales through independent reps and Amazon.com's through the Internet. Even these companies have had to adjust to national nuances. For instance, Avon does a thriving mail-order business in Japan because of the popularity of that distribution, has beauty counters in China because of regulations on house-to-house sales, has franchise centers in the Philippines because of infrastructure inefficiencies, and has beauty centers in Argentina because many customers want services when they purchase cosmetics.

INTERNALIZATION OR NOT?

Should companies handle their own distribution? Or should they contract other companies to do it for them?

Sales Volume and Cost When sales volume is low, a company usually must rely on external distributors to be more economical. As sales grow, it may handle some distribution itself to gain more control. However, such internalization may still be difficult for small firms that lack necessary resources.

A company may enter a market gradually by limiting geographic coverage.

Nevertheless, companies may limit early distribution costs if they are able to sell regionally before moving nationally. Many products and markets lend themselves to this sort of gradual development. For example, many foreign companies enter the Chinese market by first going to Beijing, Shanghai, and Guanghou, then to provincial capitals, then to other large cities, and finally to smaller cities. Often, geographic barriers and poor internal transportation systems divide countries into very distinct markets. In fact, within developing countries most wealth and potential sales may lie in a few large metropolitan areas.

Factors Favoring Internalization Circumstances conducive to internalization include not only high sales volume but also the following factors:

- When a product has the characteristic of high price, high technology, or the need for complex after-sales servicing (such as aircraft), the company will probably have to deal directly with the buyer, but may simultaneously use a distributor to identify sales leads.
- When the company deals with global customers, especially business-to-business (such as an auto-parts manufacturer selling original equipment to the same automakers in multiple countries), sales may go directly to the global customer.
- When the company's main competitive advantage is its distribution methods, it may control distribution abroad, such as Avon's direct selling through independent representatives.

DISTRIBUTION PARTNERSHIP

If a company wishes to use a distributor abroad, it can usually compare a number of potential alternatives. While trying to find the best distributors, it must also convince them to handle its products.

Which Distributors Are Best Qualified? The choice of international distributor depends on the same criteria as for domestic options. These criteria include the distributor's financial strength, its good connections, the extent of its other business commitments, its current situation (e.g., personnel, facilities, and equipment), and its reputation as an honest performer.

Distributors choose which companies and products to handle. Companies

- may need to give incentives,
- may use successful products as bait for new ones,
- must convince distributors that product and company are viable.

Promoting to Potential Distributors Companies must evaluate potential distributors, but distributors must choose which companies and products to represent and emphasize. Wholesalers and retailers alike have limited storage facilities, display space, money for inventories, and transportation and personnel to move and sell merchandise, so they try to carry only those products with the greatest profit potential.

In seeking to enter a foreign market, a company may find that distributors there are tied into exclusive arrangements with manufacturers that impede new competitive entries. For example, in Japan many manufacturers have arrangements with thousands of distributors to sell only their products. Even if arrangements are not exclusive, existing distributors may already be handling similar products, thus being reluctant to deal with a new company. In such a situation, an entering company may need to offer effective handling incentives (higher profit margins, after-sales servicing, promotional support, and so on). In the end, however, incentives will be of little use unless the distributors believe the company is reliable and its products viable.

DISTRIBUTION CHALLENGES AND OPPORTUNITIES

Although international distribution involves many challenges and opportunities, the following discussion highlights two: the need for after-sales service, and some often overlooked cost advantages and disadvantages.

Confidence in securing replacement parts and service are important for sales, especially for imported products.

How Reliable Is After-Sales Service? Consumers are reluctant to buy products that may require future replacement parts and service unless they feel confident that these will be readily available in good quality and at reasonable prices. This reluctance is especially keen for imported products because of concerns that distance and customs clearance will delay needed replacement parts. For fairly mature products, there are usually multiple service companies locally to which consumers can turn in case of problems. However, for products encompassing new technology, especially complex and expensive products, producers may face the downside of having to invest in or develop service centers. Nevertheless, the upside is that earnings from sales of parts and after-sales service may sometimes exceed those of the original product.

The question of after-sales service is especially important for the growing number of technologically oriented entrepreneurial companies from developing countries. Many face multiple problems in selling abroad because they are young, small, fairly unknown, perhaps suffering negative country-of-origin effects, and often assumed to be laggards in technological development.[86]

Hidden Distribution Costs and Gains Several factors often contribute to country differences in distribution costs.

CONCEPT CHECK

In Chapter 13 (page 327), we illustrate how poor infrastructure hampers distribution.

Infrastructure Conditions Where roads and warehousing facilities are in bad condition, getting goods to consumers quickly, cheaply, and with minimum damage or loss is challenging. For example, Nigeria has no rail links to its ports, has fallen behind in road construction, and has poor connections between big and small cities.[87]

Distribution costs increase when there is

- poor infrastructure,
- many levels in the distribution system,
- inefficient retail distribution,
- inadequate carrying of inventory by retailers.

Levels in the Distribution System Where there are multitiered wholesalers that sell to each other (e.g., national wholesalers sell to regional ones, which sell to local ones, and so on) before the product reaches the retail level, each intermediary adds a markup and prices escalate. For example, Japan, though changing rapidly, has many more levels of distribution than, say, France and the United States.

Retail Inefficiencies Where low labor costs and owners' distrust of nonfamily members cause counter- rather than self-service displays, there is less productivity in serving customers. (In fact, some retailers require payment to a cashier before customers receive the merchandise.) On the one hand, the additional personnel add to retailing costs, and the added time people must be in the store means fewer people served in the given space. On the other hand, if clients spend more time in one store, they have less time to compare offerings in other stores.[88] In addition, many retailers (mainly in developing economies) lack equipment that improves the efficiency of handling customers and controls, such as electronic scanners and payment systems linked to inventory-control records and to credit-card companies.

CONCEPT CHECK

In Chapter 2 (pages 36 and 39), we describe societies in which people tend to distrust people outside their families.

Man bringing eggs on a bicycle to markets in Kathmandu, Nepal.

Source: ImageBROKER/Alamy Stock Photo

Costs rise where governments restrict retailers from using more productive distribution practices. For example, France, Germany, and Japan have laws protecting small retailers, effectively limiting the efficiencies that large retail establishments can bring to sales. Most countries have patchwork systems that limit days or hours of operations because of religious and national commemoration observances or protection of employees from having to work late at night or on weekends. Although these systems serve social purposes, they limit retailers from covering the fixed cost of their space over more hours, and they usually pass costs on to consumers.

Inventory Stock Outs Where most retail establishments are small, there is little space to store inventory. Wholesalers must incur the cost of making small deliveries to many more establishments, sometimes visiting each retailer more frequently to avoid stock outages. However, these latter costs may be diminished through labor and transport cost savings that result from low-paid delivery personnel who may carry small quantities of merchandise on bicycles or by foot. (The preceding photo shows delivery by bicycle in Nepal.) Further, the retailers themselves incur lower costs because their inventory-carrying costs are low compared to sales.[89]

GAP ANALYSIS: A TOOL FOR HELPING TO MANAGE THE INTERNATIONAL MARKETING MIX

17-7 Illustrate how gap analysis can help in managing the international marketing mix

Emphasis in the marketing mix

- should be on the functions that account for major lost sales,
- may differ by country,
- may combine needs from different countries.

Although every element in the marketing mix—product, price, promotion, brand, and distribution—is important, the relative importance of one versus another may vary from product to product, place to place, and over time.

A company should calculate how well it is doing in each country, how it might do better, and how to gain synergy among marketing activities in different countries. One such tool is **gap analysis**, whereby a company estimates potential sales for a given type of product and compares how emphasis on different marketing mix elements can better help it serve prospective customers.[90]

The difference between total market potential and a company's sales is due to several types of gaps:

- *Usage*—collectively, all competitors sell less than the market potential
- *Product line*—the company lacks some product variations
- *Distribution*—the company misses coverage by geography or type of outlet
- *Competitive*—competitors' sales are not explained by product-line and distribution gaps

FIGURE 17.3 Gap Analysis

Why aren't sales as high as they could be? That's the question managers ask when they undertake gap analysis. The arrow at the top represents total sales potential for all competitors during a given period. The arrow at A indicates actual sales. Notice that there's a gap between the product's potential and actual sales—the so-called usage gap. But there are other gaps as well. The arrow bracketing points A and B, for example, designates all sales lost by the company to its competitors—the gap, that is, between what the company did sell and what it could have sold if, for a variety of reasons, it hadn't lost so many sales to competitors. Finally, remember that in the real world, gap sizes will fluctuate.

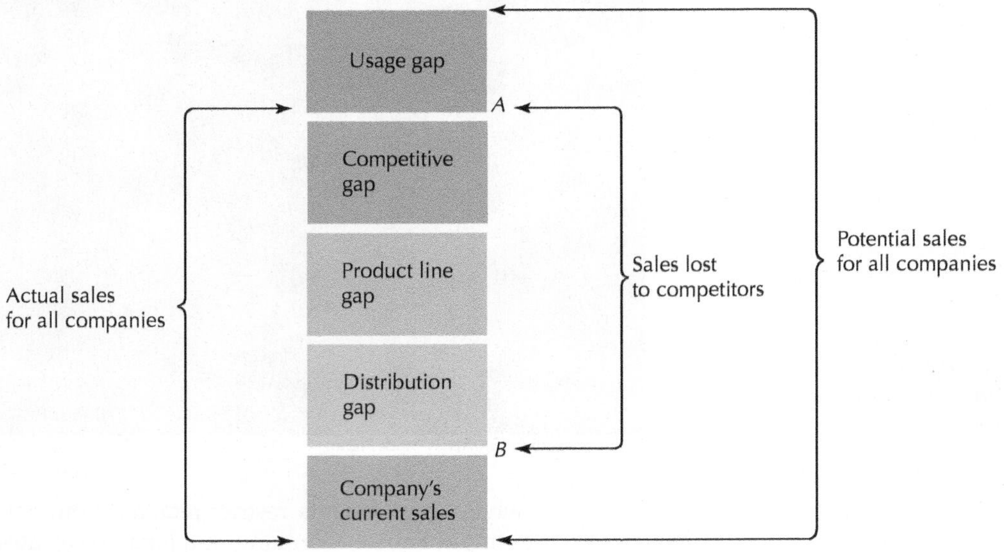

Figure 17.3 is a bar showing these four types of gaps. To construct such a bar, a company first needs to estimate the potential demand for all competitors in the country for a relevant period—say, for the next year or the next five years. This figure gives the height of the bar. Second, a company needs to estimate current sales by all competitors, which is point A. The space between point A and the top of the bar is a *usage gap,* meaning that this is the growth potential for all competitors in the market for the relevant period. Third, a company needs to plot its own current sales of the product, point B.

Finally, the company divides the difference between points A and B into types of gaps—distribution, product line, and competitive—based on its estimate of why sales are lost to competitors.

USAGE GAPS

Companies may have different-sized gaps in different markets. Large chocolate companies, for instance, have altered their marketing programs among countries because of this. In some markets, they have found less chocolate being consumed than expected on the basis of population and income levels. This has been the case in India, which has per capita consumption of less than one percent of that in Germany, although low incomes and the inability to use certain animal fats (thus affecting taste) contribute to India's low consumption. But it has been the world's fastest growth market in recent years. Why? Chocolate companies have developed small affordable chocolates to reach the masses, and they have promoted chocolate as a more hygienic and longer-lasting confection than alternative sweets.[91] Industry specialists estimate that in many developing economies, much of the population has never even tasted chocolate, leading companies to promote sales in those areas for chocolate in general rather than for their particular products.[92]

The U.S. market shows another type of usage gap. Nearly everyone in this market has tried most chocolate products, but per capita consumption has fallen because of concern about weight. Further, U.S. per capita consumption is much lower than in most European countries. Mars has concluded that the main reason for the different consumption is cultural (i.e., U.S. consumers usually take wine or flowers to dinner hosts, whereas Europeans usually take chocolates). To counter this, Mars has a U.S. campaign of "Share your favorites with your favorites" to promote taking chocolate to friends and joining with them to eat chocolate at movies. Earlier, Nestlé promoted chocolate as an energy source for the sports-minded to build U.S. demand for chocolate. However, building general consumption is most useful to the market leader. With Nestlé's U.S. chocolate sales below those of Mars and Hershey, it actually benefited its competitors during the short-lived campaign.

PRODUCT-LINE GAPS

Chocolate companies have also found that they have product-line gaps. Several have recently added sugar-free, high cocoa content, and fair-traded chocolate products to their repertoire. In addition, they have added such ingredients as bacon, chia, green tea, and quinoa to some of their offerings.[93] Godiva has introduced specialty products in China to compete with local companies that sell theme products for the Chinese Zodiac year and for the Mid-Autumn Festival.[94]

DISTRIBUTION AND COMPETITIVE GAPS

A company's products may be sold in too few places, creating a gap in distribution. To combat this, Ferrero Rocher has emphasized product placement in more mainstream outlets. There also may be competitive gaps—sales by competitors that cannot be explained by differences between product lines and distribution. That is, competitors are selling more because of their prices, advertising campaigns, goodwill, or any of a host of other factors. In markets where per capita chocolate consumption is high, companies exert most of their efforts in gaining sales at the expense of competitors. For instance, Switzerland has the world's highest per capita consumption of chocolate. In that market, such competitors as Migros, Lindt, and Nestlé's Cailler go head to head in creating images of better quality.[95]

AGGREGATING COUNTRIES' PROGRAMS

Although gap analysis prioritizes elements in the marketing mix within countries, it is also possible to use the tool by aggregating needs among countries. Let's say the product-line gap is too small in a single country to justify the expense of developing a specific new product, such as a low-calorie chocolate bar. Nevertheless, the combined market potential among several countries for this product may justify the product- and promotional-development costs. Thus, comparing the importance of the different elements within the marketing mix may help managers improve country-level performance along with enhancing synergy among the countries where they operate.

LOOKING TO THE FUTURE How Might International Market Segmentation Evolve?

Recall the discussion on how both demographics and psychographics affect market segmentation. How both of these will unfold in future years will likely affect international marketing. There are, of course, many more global trends that may affect future international marketing than we can possibly highlight (e.g., aging population, growing obesity, increasing use of social media); thus, the following discussion highlights only one key demographic and one key psychographic area.

Income Demographics

Most projections show growing disparities between the "haves" and "have-nots" in the foreseeable future, both within and among countries. Furthermore, because haves will be more educated and more connected to the Internet, they will be better able to search globally for lower prices. Therefore, globally, the disparate purchasing power of the affluent segment will be even more than indicated by incomes.[96]

As discretionary income increases, some luxury products will become more commonplace (partly because it will take less work time to purchase them), and seemingly dissimilar products and services (such as cars, travel, jewelry, and art) will compete with each other for the same discretionary spending. How does this affect demand? For example, Japan was the premier importer of luxury clothing during the 1980s and early 1990s, but competition from an array of other luxury services, such as spas and expensive restaurants, eroded those imports.[97] In addition, many Japanese consumers have moved down-market during Japan's stagnated economic growth, and there is speculation that they may not move up-market again when their economy becomes more robust. Nevertheless, because of better communications and rising educational levels of the haves, they will want more choices. However, market segments may not fall primarily along national lines. Rather, companies may depend more on identifying consumer niches that cut across country lines.

At the other extreme, because of the large number of poor people with little disposable income, companies will have opportunities to develop low-cost standardized products to fit the needs of the have-nots. In reality, low-income households collectively have considerable purchasing power and will likely spend mainly on basic housing, food, health care, education, communications, finance charges, and consumer goods.[98] Thus, companies will have conflicting opportunities: develop luxury to serve the haves and cut costs to serve the have-nots. Some producers are already responding to this market dichotomy. Frito-Lay calls it the "bifurcation" of the snack market and is emphasizing new products for the high and low ends, but not the middle.[99] The president of the Wine Academy of Spain pointed out this market split for wine sales in China. He indicated that there is no middle market; rather there is a high-end where people spend thousands of dollars per bottle as an investment or as an ostentatious drink and a low-end where people spend no more than the equivalent of a few dollars per bottle while buying in large containers.[100] Despite the growing proportions of haves and have-nots, demographers project that the actual numbers of people moving out of poverty levels and into middle-income levels will increase. This is largely because of population and income growth in a few low-income countries, especially in Asia. Such a shift raises questions: Will sales growth in poorer countries mainly be for products that are mature in industrial countries, such as many consumer electronics and household appliances? Or, will consumers in poorer countries leapfrog to newer products as they have done by bypassing landline phones and going directly to cellular ones?

Will National Markets Become Passé?

In addition to demographic differences in income, attitudinal differences affect demand in general as well as for particular types of products and services. Although global communications are reaching far-flung populations, different people react differently to them. At least three—not mutually exclusive—types of personality traits interact and affect how potential consumers react.[101] They exist in all countries (thus creating a segment that cuts across the globe), but the portion of people who are strongly influenced by one versus the other presently varies by country. How these factors evolve will likely have a profound influence on the future of international marketing.

The first of the traits is **materialism**, which refers to the importance of acquiring possessions as a means of self-satisfaction and happiness, as well as for the appearance of success. There is evidence of this trait's growth and spread. However, there is also evidence that people who have always been affluent may exhibit lower materialistic behaviors than those who have recently become affluent, the so-called *nouveau riche*. The second of these traits is **cosmopolitanism**, which refers to openness to the world. While there is debate on whether this is a learned or an inborn trait, some of the characteristics include comparing oneself with what is in the whole world rather than with what is local. Cosmopolitanists may actually seek out foreign products and services. The third of these traits is **consumer ethnocentrism**, which refers to a preference for local over global, such as seeking out local alternatives when buying products and services.

CASE

Grameen Danone Foods in Bangladesh[102]

—Professors Jon Jungbien Moon and John D. Daniels

In 1932, U.S. President Franklin D. Roosevelt referred to an impoverished person as "the forgotten man at the bottom [base] of the economic pyramid." Later, the term—shortened to "BoP"—became business jargon after publication in 2010 of *The Fortune at the Bottom of the Pyramid*.

Few places have more impoverished people than Bangladesh, even though the country has been one of the fastest growing in the world since 2004, with the average annual GDP growth rate of 6.5 percent. With 169 million people in 2019, its per capita GDP at PPP was $4753, with 22 percent of the population below the international poverty line of $1.90 per day.

Thus, Bangladesh has conditions that correlate closely with poverty: an adult illiteracy rate of 26 percent in 2018, a high incidence of infectious diseases, a poor infrastructure, high underemployment, crowded conditions (imagine half the U.S. population squeezed into the state of Iowa), and more than its share of natural disasters—especially periodic flooding—that impede development. In the face of these ominous conditions, two companies—the Grameen Foundation from Bangladesh and Groupe Danone from France—formed a joint venture (JV) social business to serve Bangladesh's BoP.

What Is a Social Business?

Mohammad Yunus, founder of the Grameen Bank in 1974 and winner of the Nobel Peace Prize in 2006, originated the social business concept, which aims to generate social benefit by creating sustainable businesses. The Grameen Danone Foods JV was established to make a profit but pay no dividends. All earnings are reinvested, except that investors may recoup their original capital input. Unlike NGOs, charities, and not-for-profit organizations, a social business must sustain itself by generating revenue competitively rather than receiving charitable contributions to carry on.

The Grameen Bank and Foundation

The Grameen Bank (GB) began when Yunus lent $27 to a group of indigent villagers who repaid the money even though he had required no collateral from them. This small beginning, contrary to Bangladeshi bank practices, led to GB's microfinancing program. It has competed primarily with usurious money lenders who charge as much as 10 percent interest per day. GB's typical rate of 20 percent per year may sound high, but Bangladesh has had an inflation rate of up to 8 percent, and GB supports many noninterest loans as well. Some banks outside Bangladesh, such as Citigroup and Deutsche Bank, have since used GB's example as a model.

Before GB, hardly any Bangladeshi loans went to women, and Yunus had to convince religious opposition that the Prophet Muhammad would have supported what he was doing. Today, about 97 percent of GB's loans go to women, and audits show a repayment rate of 98 percent. (Borrowers must repay a loan in order to get a new one.) GB uses repayments and interest to make additional loans and to support the Grameen Foundation's poverty-fighting projects. Its loans, which in 2017 came to almost $1.75 billion, have included initial financing for street vendors and construction of more than 700,000 houses. It provides more than 50,000 student loans and 27,000 scholarships per year. It has given noninterest loans to more than 77,000 beggars so they can sell trinkets during their house-to-house begging. The Foundation's activities have expanded into a variety of businesses, such as telephone service, solar power generation, and health care.

Groupe Danone

France's largest food company, Groupe Danone (spelled "Dannon" for the U.S. market), operates in four product divisions: dairy (world's largest, with Danone being almost a generic word for yogurt); bottled water (ranked second globally, including such brands as Evian and Volvic); baby food (second globally under the Blédine brand); and medical nutrition (largest in Europe). It operates worldwide and had 2018 sales of €24.6 billion ($28 billion). Before its JV with Grameen, it had no Bangladeshi operations. In fact, it aimed most of its products, such as its Activia and Actimel brands of yogurt, at higher-end consumers.

Why Invest in a Social Business?

Why would Danone, or anyone, want to invest in an operation that yields them no dividends or capital gains? Yunus contends that people are multidimensional and thus may desire more than economic gains for themselves. He points to business leaders (e.g., Carnegie, Gates, Rockefeller) who turned their attention to philanthropy after amassing large fortunes. Danone's JV participation fits this multidimensional vision. In fact, it has a history of socially responsible behavior, with a corporate mission "to bring health through food to as many people as possible." Nevertheless, Danone must generate profits, and its management must answer to shareholders. The Bangladeshi JV could offer several potential economic advantages.

Maturing of Traditional Markets

The demand for Danone's products has been maturing in wealthier countries, which have been Danone's traditional markets. Hence, its management has been shifting more emphasis to poorer countries. Between 1999 and 2010, the share of its sales coming from LDCs increased from 6 percent to 47 percent. Yet, even there its sales centered on affluent segments, about which its chairman, Frank Riboud, said, "It would be crazy to think only about the peak of the pyramid." Thus, Bangladesh could serve as a laboratory for learning about customers and ways of operating at the BoP.

Promoting LDC Growth

Critics complain that MNEs contribute to economic underdevelopment by pushing poor consumers to purchase superfluous products instead of nutritious food. In contrast, Danone's products are all healthful and sanitary. Although one company's successful marketing of such products is not likely to have a significant impact on development, it is a potential catalyst, which perhaps also leads to favorable publicity. Further, as BoP consumers move upward economically, they will have more to spend on other Danone products and may favor them because of their earlier experience. Riboud said, "When poverty is on the rise, my own growth prospects shrink. [This] means that combating poverty is good for my business."

Building Sales and Loyalty Abroad

Being perceived as socially responsible may improve business performance in various ways. However, there are an almost infinite number of competing ways to be socially responsible. The initial amount Danone invested in the JV was $500,000, a small outlay for a company of that size, and Danone stood to get the money back if the operation became sufficiently profitable. Moreover, the fact that it would become one of the first major corporations to invest in a social business could generate free positive publicity globally.

Preceding the Bangladeshi JV

At a 2005 lunch in Paris, Riboud asked Yunus what Danone might do to help the poor. When Yunus explained the social business concept, Riboud immediately said, "Let's do it," and the two shook hands on setting up their JV. Although this JV is one of the first social businesses established in partnership with a major MNE, Roosevelt's "forgotten man" was not completely forgotten in the interim. Many organizations have marketed to the BoP (most notably in India during the 1970s' heyday of the appropriate technology movement) with such devices as dung-powered stoves.

These experiences offer the following lessons for companies wishing to tap the BoP, especially with a nutritious product:

- **Price**—Low and stable prices help create and sustain sales, so companies gain an advantage by finding new means to cut and stabilize their own costs, which they then pass on to customers.

- **Product compatibility**—High nutrition at a low price alone is insufficient. Products must be compatible with the target markets' accustomed habits and visually appealing and flavorful to them. So it is vital to pick the right products and adapt them to local markets.
- **Education**—Within some countries the BoP is largely illiterate, has low access to popular media, and is unconvinced about cause-and-effect scientific relationships. Hence, it may be important to reach people in this segment by nontraditional means, convince them that changes from nutrition are important and take time, and convey information that they will believe.
- **Promotion**—Publicity prior to the start of sales is quite valuable, so the use of opinion leaders (those that the target market group accepts) is essential in developing credibility.
- **Competition**—Given efforts to help the poor, competition may come from government programs, not-for-profit organizations, and charities. Thus, companies need to outperform this competition or find means of working cooperatively with it.

Strategic Thrust and Orientation

After their 2005 Paris handshake, the JV began production in less than two years. The partners started with a small rural factory to serve only its surrounding poverty-stricken area. Given the JV's social objective, the partners agreed that product and production would be as green as possible. Even though the factory is the size of only one percent of Danone's standard factories elsewhere, it has the latest equipment, treatment of both incoming and outgoing water, and solar panels to generate renewable energy.

Product Policies

The introductory plant and two more built by 2015 make only yogurt, a product of high nutritional value for children. It relies on efficient small-scale production and nearby supplies of the main ingredient (milk).

Through market testing, Danone decided to sell a sweeter and thinner yogurt, drinkable directly from the container (subsequent market feedback led the JV to include spoons as well). It fortifies the yogurt with 30 percent of the daily need for vitamin A, zinc, and iodine, and it uses biodegradable technology so that containers can be converted to fertilizer.

Pricing

To keep costs and prices low, the plant uses mostly local ingredients, mainly from small suppliers such as farmers with only one or two cows, who collect and deliver milk in jugs (thus saving refrigeration and transportation costs). Because of fluctuating milk prices, the JV negotiated longer-term contracts with farmers to better stabilize prices; hence, the JV pays higher than market price sometimes and less at other times. Fixed sales costs are kept low by selling only on commission (about 20 percent to saleswomen and 80 percent to small local stores). To minimize saleswomen's commissions, the company successfully suggested their selling additional products during house-to-house visits. Personnel costs have been kept low since completion of its start-up phase by employing only Bangladeshis. Although the yogurt plant lacks scale economies, its unit costs are equivalent to Danone's larger plants elsewhere.

Promotion

Most promotion is word of mouth; however, one promotional event was noteworthy. Riboud arranged for the

Zidane, Riboud, and Yunus ▶ entering the national soccer stadium in Dhaka, Bangladesh.

Source: Durand Patrick/Abaca/Newscom

best-known Frenchman in Bangladesh, the soccer star Zinédine Zidane (Zizou), to visit the plant's opening, an event that made major headlines in newspapers throughout the country. While in Bangladesh, Zizou played with youth in the national stadium, signed the cornerstone of the plant, and contributed to instant national recognition for the new JV and its yogurt. (See the preceding photo showing the stadium entry of Zinedine Zidane, Franck Riboud, and Mouhammad Yunus.)

Branding

The JV name put Grameen first because of its high recognition. The yogurt brand is Shokti Doi, meaning "yogurt for power," and its symbol is a muscled lion that appears on the product and in ads. Lion-dressed mascots also visit youth areas to describe the value of eating yogurt.

Distribution

Bangladesh's high underemployment attracted more than enough women—mainly poor mothers from the target sales market—to work part time selling yogurt. However, the JV had to overcome a backlash similar to the one GB faced when lending to women; the complaint this time was about the impropriety of women going house-to-house. The next big task was to train the saleswomen on (1) the significance of selling yogurt other than to earn a commission and (2) the essentiality of the yogurt's quality and how to maintain it.

MAP 17.1 Grameen Danone Foods Joint Venture

Groupe Danone from France joined the Grameen Foundation to form a social business joint venture in Bangladesh. Subsequently, Group Danone learned about serving the base of the pyramid and has transformed this knowledge to help it operate in Indonesia and Senegal.

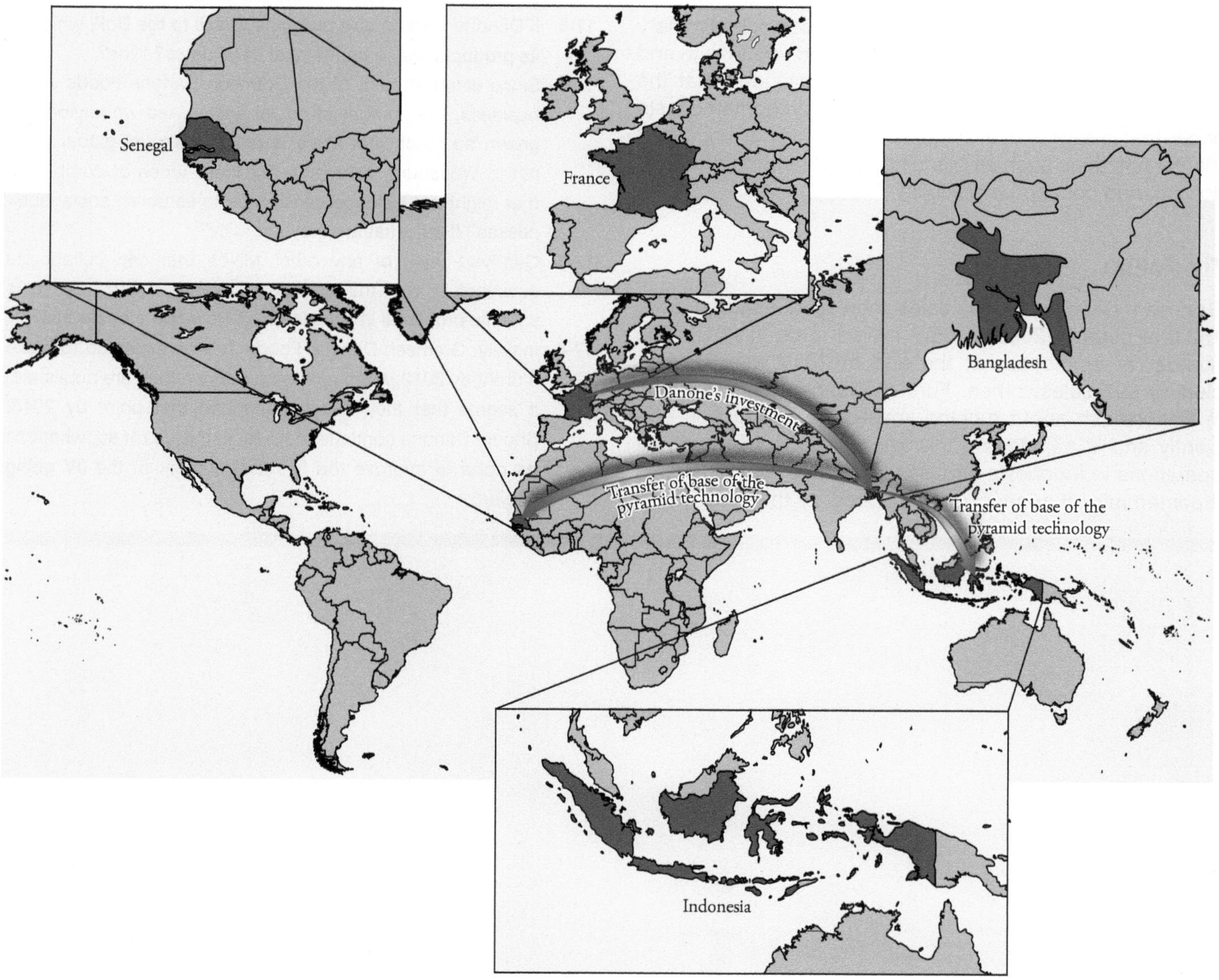

First, the significance for selling was primarily nourishment. The company engaged doctors who explained that children could regain any physical loss from previously deprived nutrition within 9 to 10 months by consuming only two cups of yogurt per week. Second, selling would help improve the economy by using suppliers who would then hire more people and spend within the community.

Maintaining yogurt quality was essential because few homes had refrigeration, and eating a spoiled product could cause illness and future sales losses. The company demonstrated to saleswomen how it makes yogurt, provided them with insulated bags, showed them how to use the bags properly, and stressed the need for them to carry only a minimum inventory to lessen the chance of spoilage.

Evaluation

Evaluating the JV's financial performance is straightforward; however, assessing its social effects is challenging. For this, the JV has hired a Swiss-based nutrition organization (GAIN) to develop, test, and validate its performance in terms of meeting the objectives for poor people. Preliminary findings compared children who consumed yogurt with and without micronutrient fortification and concluded that the former grew more in height. In addition, psychometric tests show that the former are significantly better at important mental functions such as planning, concentration, problem solving, and conceptual flexibility.

The Future

Grameen Danone Foods' sales increased steadily, from 150,000 cups in 2008 to 35.2 million cups in 2013. The number of employees at the end of 2013 was 976, including 697 saleswomen. Further, Danone learned much in Bangladesh about running small-scale production efficiently and is transferring this knowledge to help with its operations in Indonesia and Senegal. (Map 17.1 illustrates the international connections.) Inspired by this new model of collaboration, other major MNEs have been establishing social businesses with the Grameen Foundation (e.g., Intel developed software applications on handheld devices that test soil and provide fertilizer recommendations; UNIQLO designed and produced clothing lines in Bangladesh and opened 15 outlets; Veolia invested to make clean and safe water accessible to residents in the poorest parts of the country). Despite the publicity and promise of these high-profile collaborative ventures, however, Danone will need to evaluate how brand recognition and goodwill at the BoP can be harnessed for sales farther up the pyramid in order to expand to more affluent market segments.

QUESTIONS

17-3 What advantages might Danone receive from the Grameen Danone joint venture?

17-4 How much do you think Danone's decision to set up a social business was motivated by wanting to be socially responsible versus believing the move would help its performance? Does the answer to this make any difference?

17-5 If Danone were to add products to sell to the BoP, which of its products would be the best candidates? Why?

17-6 Since establishment of the Grameen Danone Foods social business, the number of social businesses worldwide has grown so much that there is now an annual global summit in Wolfsburg, Germany. Are there types of companies that might not be good candidates to establish social businesses? If so, what are they and why?

17-7 Can you think of any other MNEs that can collaborate successfully with the Grameen Foundation and help solve specific problems in Bangladesh? How can they do this?

17-8 Initially, Grameen Danone Foods JV was expected to make a profit by 2012. Although no official numbers are published, it seems that they had not reached that point by 2018. Should Danone continue to invest in this JV? If so, what can be done to improve the financial outlook of the JV going forward?

CHAPTER 18

Global Operations and Supply-Chain Management

OBJECTIVES

After studying this chapter, you should be able to

18-1 Define what is meant by global supply-chain management

18-2 Describe the different facets of global operations strategies

18-3 Show how global sourcing is an important aspect of global supply-chain and operations management

18-4 Explain how information technology is used in global operations and supply-chain management

18-5 Summarize how quality management is important in global operations and supply-chain management

A cheap thing doesn't lack defect, nor an expensive thing quality.

—Afghan proverb

Source: Street VJ/Shutterstock

▲ Apple Store in Shenzhen, China, one of over 500 retail locations worldwide, referred to by Apple as "a community gathering place," as customers relax at tables just outside of the store.

CASE

Apple's Global Supply Chain[1]

How long does it take to get an iPhone? In September 2012, Apple, at that time the largest consumer electronics company in the world and the largest company in the United States in market capitalization, formally announced the iPhone 5, the sixth generation of the iPhone and successor to the popular iPhone 4S. The hype over the new phone was so high that preorders swamped Apple's ability to get enough phones from its factory in Zhengzhou, a city in the north-central region of China. Mandy Xiao was living in Provo, Utah, at the time and wanted to get the phone by Christmas of 2012, so she ordered the phone directly from Apple.com on December 5.

The factory in Zhengzhou is actually owned by Taiwan-based Hon Hai Precision Industry Co. Ltd., also known as the Foxconn Technology Group. Given the Christmas rush and the fact that Zhengzhou was a little over 6,500 miles away, Mandy wasn't sure how long it would take to get her phone. But Apple's supply chain was fast. Mandy was able to track her phone's journey by UPS online from Zhengzhou to Incheon International Airport in Korea to Anchorage, Alaska, to her door in Provo, Utah—only two days after it was ordered. If you are going to compete today, you need to get the product to the consumer as soon as possible, and Apple excels at this, even when it's 6,500 miles away from the consumer. If Mandy were in the market today, she would be looking at an iPhone 11Pro and could buy it in an Apple Store in Salt Lake City, at retail outlets such as Best Buy, or through her cellphone provider. How the world has changed.

APPLE'S ORIGINS

Apple's initial supply chain was relatively simple. In 1976, Steve Jobs and Steve Wozniak ("Woz") sold their first product, the Apple I computer, out of the Jobs' family garage in Cupertino, California. Woz was the designer and Jobs ran the business in the up-and-coming microcomputer industry. Jobs and Woz had to design the product, develop the operating system that made it work, manufacture it, and market it. Large auto companies like Ford and GM had the same issues, but they invested significant resources into building massive manufacturing facilities to supply the market. Unlike the auto companies, the new Apple Computer company was not a major manufacturer of products, but primarily an assembler of components supplied by other companies. However, Apple was extremely successful with this new venture, although the cost of the computer was quite high (since the company was in its infancy), volumes were not very high, and competition was not very strong.

What really changed the game was the entry of IBM into the market. IBM knew that to beat Apple, it needed to drive down costs as low as possible. Initially, IBM was a large vertically integrated company that produced most of its parts and components itself within the United States. In the early 1980s, however, IBM realized that it needed to use external suppliers for key components in an effort to create a cheaper alternative to the Apple II computer, the successor to Jobs' and Woz's successful Apple I computer. Then IBM outsourced its operating system to Microsoft and its microprocessor to Intel, and the race was on. By taking a close look at the value chain, IBM was able to modularize the industry so that Microsoft, for example, could sell its operating system to any company that wanted to use it, and Intel could develop semiconductors for a wide range of products for many different companies. This allowed them to achieve even greater economies of scale.

APPLE'S ADAPTATION

Apple adapted in many different ways, as did the entire consumer electronics industry. Apple's strength was in the design of new products that consumers wanted. However, it realized that it had to go far beyond just computers. Rather than just stick with personal computers, it branched off into a variety of mobile communication and media devices, portable music players, software, and cloud storage. Its products include the Apple Watch, iPhone, iPad, Mac, iPod, and the Apple TV, and it designs and manufactures its own products. Apple always comes up with cool stuff, and it is being pushed by a variety of entrants in the market like Samsung. But it is still known for new ideas and new products—the strength of Steve Jobs and the organization he created before he died.

The big challenge is how to manufacture this wide range of products. A majority of Apple's supply chain, manufacturing and assembly operations are located outside of the United States, principally in Asia. In 2012, it announced that it was "reshoring" (also called onshoring) or bringing the manufacturing of some of its Macs back to the United States by investing $100 million in new facilities to assemble the computers. Even though Apple no longer manufactures its own components, it buys them from a variety of suppliers, what is also called supply chaining. Apple's decision to reshore some of its production is partly due to lower energy costs, rising wages in countries like China, a weaker U.S. dollar (at the time), quality control issues, and proximity to the large U.S. market. However, this is not a major shift in the way Apple manufactures all of its products.

THE RISE OF CONTRACT MANUFACTURING

Most of the components Apple uses come from multiple sources, but some are from single or limited sources, which can create supply problems. This is especially true when Apple uses some custom components that are not widely used in the industry but are used only for its products. In addition, Apple's search for reliable suppliers coincided with the emergence of Hon Hai Precision Industry Company, Ltd., widely known as Foxconn Technology Group. Foxconn was founded in Taiwan in 1976 by Terry Gou, about the same time Apple was founded. Gou began his company with a loan of $7,500 from his mother with a goal of increasing the affordability of electronics products by combining his expertise for mechanical and electrical parts with a low-cost solution. He started supplying parts to Atari and then traveled to the United States to develop relationships with U.S. companies. One of the companies that he won orders from was IBM. Gou arrived at just the right time. IBM's supply chain moved from being vertical to horizontal and from sourcing only domestically to sourcing internationally.

When Apple assembles products at its factory in Singapore, it is offshoring, meaning that it is moving a factory offshore from the United States to assemble products. The factory still belongs to Apple, but it may get parts and components from a variety of suppliers, mostly from Asia. Apple's relationship with Foxconn is different. As wages began to rise in Taiwan, many companies moved to the Philippines and Malaysia, but Foxconn invested in China, initially in Shenzhen but later in other cities where labor was plentiful and cheap. As it picked up more orders from abroad, it rose from a small company in Taiwan to the largest contract electronics manufacturer in the world, employing over 1 million people in China.

Although Foxconn supplies components to a variety of companies from all over the world, it is clear that Apple is its number-one customer. In fact, when concerns arose in the first few months of 2013 over Apple's first quarter results, shares of Hon Hai fell by 14 percent, with similar results for shares of other Apple suppliers. However, when the first-quarter results were released and Apple appeared to be doing just fine, the shares recovered their losses and posted gains. Such is the relationship between Apple and its suppliers.

When Tim Cook, the current CEO of Apple and successor to Steve Jobs, was brought into the company in 1997, he was asked by Jobs to clean up the manufacturing process. Manufacturing problems and excess inventory were a drag on corporate profits, cash flow, and therefore on funds available for investment in new products. As Cook worked to strengthen manufacturing, he developed strong supplier relations with companies throughout Asia, including Foxconn. The difference with Foxconn is that Apple was able to outsource the assembly of entire products to Foxconn instead of just sourcing components that Apple could assemble at its own facilities. Rather than manufacture the product through offshoring in Ireland or Singapore, Apple was able to outsource the entire production process to Foxconn as a contract manufacturer. Apple designed the product with very tight specifications and worked with Foxconn and their suppliers to roll out new products, but Foxconn was responsible for the manufacture and delivery of the product to Apple. Now nearly all of Apple's hardware products are manufactured by outsourcing partners located primarily in Asia. A significant amount of the manufacturing is currently performed by a small number of contract manufacturers, like Foxconn, in single locations. Some of these partners are sole-sourced suppliers of components and manufacturers of many of Apple's products.

Although Foxconn has become a very trusted contract manufacturer, Apple still has to work hard to make sure the quality of the product and components is exactly what it is looking for. It's one thing to control quality at your own assembly facilities, and it's quite another thing to make sure Foxconn's quality is high enough. Apple's strong relationship with Foxconn and other suppliers is the envy of the industry. However, contract manufacturing is not without its problems. News of Foxconn's problems with its employees at its facilities in China created PR problems for Apple. Workers were accusing Foxconn of forcing them to work long hours in poor conditions, and some employees even committed suicide by jumping from Foxconn buildings. As a result, Mr. Cook visited factories in China and insisted that Foxconn and other suppliers comply with Chinese labor laws and even higher international standards of worker safety. For its part, Foxconn is turning more to robotics in its plants, especially in dangerous and repetitive production lines, in many cases using its own robots called Foxbots. Apple became the first technology company to join the Fair Labor Association, and Apple began publishing the results of its audits on worker conditions in 2007. In 2018, Apple published the top 200 companies that supplied it with parts and other services used in manufacturing its products. The suppliers were primarily but not exclusively in Asia. In fact, Foxconn, Apple's dominant supplier, has agreed to build 5 manufacturing facilities in Sao Paulo, Brazil as well as investing in a facility in Wisconsin, USA. As will be discussed later in the chapter, the reliance on contract manufacturing in China was dealt a serious blow by COVID-19, which started in China and spread worldwide. Factory shutdowns in China created serious problems with Apple's global supply chain.

THE LAST PART OF THE SUPPLY CHAIN

In addition to designing and manufacturing good products, Apple needs to worry about marketing, the last part of the supply chain. When Mandy decided to buy her iPhone, she had lots of options. Apple sells its products worldwide through its retail stores, such as the one in the photo at the beginning of the chapter, cellular providers, and retailers such as Costco and Best Buy in the United States.

QUESTIONS

18-1 Although Apple's inbound logistics began with Apple controlling the assembly of its computers, it shifted to having suppliers acquire raw materials with contract manufacturers handling most of the production and assembly of final products. Why did they do this, and what are the major challenges Apple faces?

18-2 Foxconn, a major contract manufacturer for Apple, is by far the largest ODM/EMS (original design manufacturer/ Electronics Manufacturing Services) company in the world, dwarfing U.S.-based Flextronics, which is the major manufacturer and assembler of Samsung phones. In 2013, Foxconn announced it was opening manufacturing operations in the United States. In what way could this be either a plus or a minus for Apple, Inc.?

GLOBAL SUPPLY-CHAIN MANAGEMENT

18-1 Define what is meant by global supply-chain management

Supply chain—the coordination of materials, information, and funds from the initial raw-material supplier to the ultimate customer.

Most companies agree that effective supply-chain management is one of their most important tools in reducing costs and boosting revenue.[2] Our opening case on Apple illustrates dimensions of these supply-chain networks that link suppliers with manufacturers and customers. In the chapter, we will discuss the international dimensions of the global supply chain, focusing on the upstream processes of the purchasing function and supplier networks; operations strategy; the role of information technology in global supply-chain management; and quality management as it affects operations. The downstream process is covered primarily in Chapter 17.

Logistics (also called materials management)—that part of the supply-chain process that plans, implements, and controls the efficient, effective flow and storage of goods, services, and related information from the point of origin to the point of consumption in order to meet customers' requirements.

CONCEPT CHECK

On page 295 in Chapter 12, we explain value as the underlying principle of strategy, defining it as "the measure of a firm's capability to sell what it makes for more than the costs incurred to make it."

Compatibility—the degree of consistency between FDI decisions and a company's competitive strategy.

CONCEPT CHECK

In discussing the process of "The Quest to Create Value" on pages 295 and 296 in Chapter 12, we explain that a firm that aspires to a position of cost leadership strives to be the low-cost producer in an industry for a given level of quality. This strategy, we observe, means that the firm adopts one of two tactics, both of which must be compatible with the structure of its value chain: (1) earning a profit higher than industry rivals by selling products at average industry prices or (2) capturing market share by selling products at prices below the industry average.

CONCEPT CHECK

Recall from page 305 in Chapter 12 our extended discussion of "Global Integration Versus Local Responsiveness" as an issue in configuring and coordinating a firm's value chain. We then proceed to explain how efforts to resolve this issue may contribute to the formulation of a global strategy or a multi-domestic strategy for international operations. Here we analyze ways in which this same issue can put pressure on specific strategic decisions about the configuration of manufacturing facilities.[8]

WHAT IS SUPPLY-CHAIN MANAGEMENT?

As illustrated in Figure 18.1, the **supply chain** is the network that links together the different aspects of the value chain, from sourcing and procurement, to conversion through operations, to the final consumer.[3]

Supply-chain management refers to activities in the value chain that occur outside the company, whereas **operations management** (also known as **logistics management**) refers to internal activities. Suppliers can be part of the company's organizational structure, such as in a vertically integrated company, or they can be independent of it. For example, Foxconn, a contract manufacturer for Apple, has its own network of suppliers used in the manufacturing of Apple products in its factories in China. Suppliers can be located in the country where the manufacturing or assembly takes place, or they can be located elsewhere and ship materials to the final assembly facility or to an intermediate storage point. Manufacturing process output can be shipped directly to the customers or to a warehouse network and sold directly to the end consumer or to a distributor, wholesaler, or retailer, then on to the final consumer. As is the case in the supplier network, the output can be sold domestically or internationally.

Most MNEs have excelled in their ability to manage their supply-chain networks. One of the best examples is Spanish retailer Zara, which is discussed in Chapter 12. Companies we study in this chapter are considered part of a global network that links together designers, suppliers, subcontractors, manufacturers, and customers. The supply-chain network is quite broad, and its coordination takes place through interactions between firms in the network.[4]

GLOBAL SUPPLY-CHAIN AND OPERATIONS MANAGEMENT STRATEGIES

18-2 Describe the different facets of global operations strategies

Recall that Apple initially set up manufacturing facilities in China because of *location-specific advantages* (notably cheap labor and associated costs), choosing to enter the country through an agreement with Foxconn, its future contract manufacturer. This allowed Apple to focus on its *firm-specific assets* (innovation, product development, and marketing) and thus move away from vertical integration to become more effective by giving up more of the elements of the value chain to Foxconn.

Apple is not the only company to outsource manufacturing to others. Examples abound. Nike subcontracts its manufacturing, remaining basically a design and marketing firm.

FIGURE 18.1 An Integrated Global Supply Chain and Operations Strategy

Source: S. Thomas Foster, Scott Sampson, Cindy Wallin, and Scott Webb, *Managing Supply Chain and Operations: An Integrative Approach* (Pearson Education, Inc., 2016): 2.

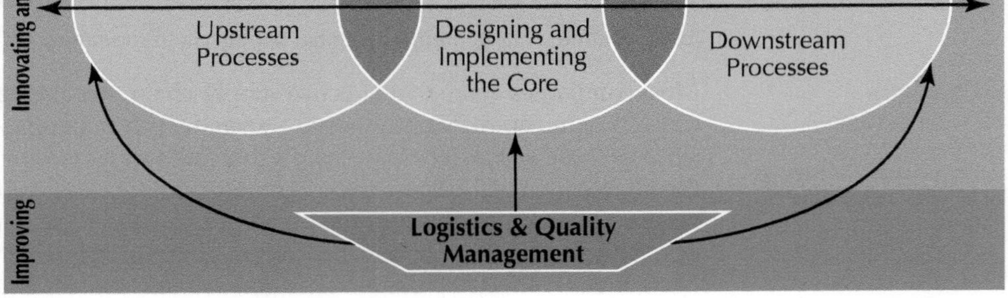

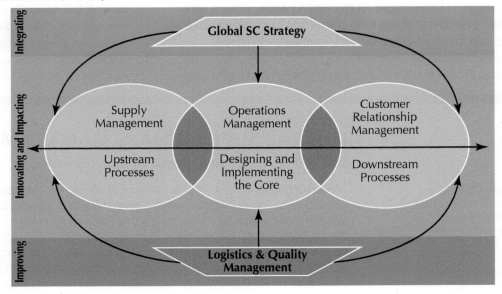

Rather than owning facilities in China to manufacture Barbie dolls, Mattel instead outsources the manufacturing to a Hong Kong–based company that invests in China.[5] As we note in Chapter 19, H&M purchases all of its fashion merchandise from external suppliers in Europe and Asia, rather than vertically integrating and establishing its own facilities.

OPERATIONS MANAGEMENT STRATEGY

One piece in the supply-chain strategy for both manufacturing and services is **operations**: the conversion of inputs into outputs. The success of a global operations strategy depends on four key factors: *compatibility, configuration, coordination,* and *control.*[6]

Compatibility Compatibility in this context is the degree of consistency between the foreign investment decision and the company's competitive strategy. Some companies such as Walmart adopt a low-cost strategy. Others, like Apple, have adopted a differentiation strategy where they design products that are relatively unique. Some factors that companies must consider as they align their overall strategy with operations are

- *Efficiency/cost*—reduction of operational costs
- *Dependability*—degree of trust in a company's products, its delivery, and its price promises
- *Quality*—performance reliability, good service, speed of delivery, and dependable product maintenance
- *Innovation*—ability to develop new products and ideas
- *Flexibility*—ability of the production process to make a variety of products and adjust the volume of output.[7] For example, Wall's makes ice cream in China, including the Magnum Bar and the Cornetto, which are global brands for Unilever, Wall's parent company. However, Wall's found that it can produce some of its global brands during the winter, when demand is down, and ship them to South Africa and Australia during their summer, enabling the use of excess production facilities and reducing costs in markets outside China.

Manufacturing Configuration In the global supply chain, suppliers transform raw materials into parts that make up the inputs that go into the conversion of parts into final products in the operations management phase. The discussion below focuses on the manufacturing configuration of a company like Ford Motor Company, which manufactures automobiles worldwide. MNEs must consider three basic configurations in establishing a global manufacturing strategy:

Manufacturing configuration:

- Centralized manufacturing in one country
- Manufacturing facilities in specific regions to service those regions
- Multi-domestic facilities in each country

- *Centralized Manufacturing*—There are several options with a centralized strategy. MNEs may centralize their manufacturing in one plant, usually their home market, which services the entire world. A second option is they may have several plants in one country that service the domestic and international markets. A third is that they have factories that focus on a particular product that is sold worldwide. Ford doesn't have just one factory that produces all models, but it has different factories that produce different models. For example, Ford will manufacture the Ford Focus in Germany and China, while the U.S. plant that was manufacturing the Focus will manufacture two other models.[9]
- *Regional Manufacturing*—Many companies use Asia as a regional hub for manufacturing. Hong Kong–based apparel maker, Tal Group,[10] is one of Asia's largest manufacturers and wholesalers of apparel for companies such as Giordano, Brooks Brothers, Banana Republic, and J. Crew. TGroup used to manufacture apparel exclusively in China, but rising labor costs forced them to open factories in Malaysia, Indonesia, Thailand, and Vietnam. It still employs 4,000 workers in China to make shirts, and it has several manufacturing facilities in the region.[11] It now has a production capacity of over 53 million pieces and employs over 25,000 employees in 11 factories.[12] In this case, Tal Group's regional manufacturing strategy allows it to service clients outside the region. BMW, Volkswagen AG, and Toyota Corporation have factories in the United States and Mexico to service clients in the North American region.[13] Most of the major auto manufacturers have set up manufacturing facilities in Mexico to service North America as well as other markets.[14]

- *Multi-Domestic Manufacturing*—As MNEs expand markets internationally, they may be forced to manufacture products in individual markets where they can be closer to consumers and meet individual needs. This is consistent with a multi-domestic strategy as discussed in Chapter 12.[15] This is the approach that Philips, the Dutch electronics company, used after World War II. Because there were barriers to entry in European countries, Philips had to manufacture on a country-by-country basis. As trade barriers dropped, they were able to rationalize their production in a regional manufacturing approach, but as the markets in the different countries grew, they found it made sense to have local manufacturing, even though there was a duplication of efforts.

Offshore manufacturing—any investment that takes place in a country other than the home country.

Offshoring, Nearshoring, and Onshoring Once a company decides to manufacture outside its home market, it is engaging in **offshore manufacturing**, as was the case when Apple set up manufacturing facilities in Singapore and Cork, Ireland. The main driver was cheap wages. As wages have continued to rise in China, companies moved to countries with even lower wages like Vietnam, Indonesia, and Thailand. Now, Africa is becoming popular as a low-wage destination.[16]

Nearshoring implies moving the supply chain closer to the home market, such as Mexico for U.S. firms or Prague for German firms.

Reshoring or onshoring means bringing back production to the home country from offshore locations.

However, some companies have modified their offshore strategy by **nearshoring** (e.g., GM moved some of its manufacturing operations to Mexico to be closer to the U.S. market). Lower wages in Mexico compared with U.S. wages, coupled with NAFTA and the ability to have a closely aligned supply chain, make it far more attractive to be located in Mexico than other markets that may have even cheaper wages but are farther from the U.S. market. Some MNEs have improved the efficiency of their operations so much that they have even moved back to their home countries, known as **reshoring** or **onshoring**. For example, Boeing announced that it was reshoring some of the parts production of its 777X plane and that it would reshore approximately 8,000 jobs in the next few years.[17]

Coordination is linking or integrating activities into a unified system.

Coordination and Control Coordination and control fit well together. *Coordination* is the linking or integrating of activities into a unified system.[18] The activities include everything along the global supply chain, from purchasing to warehousing to shipment. It is hard to coordinate supplier relations and logistics activities if those issues are not considered when the manufacturing configuration is set up.

CONCEPT CHECK

We discuss control on page 429 in Chapter 16 from the perspective of organization structure, coordination and control systems, and organizational culture. In explaining coordination and control systems, we explain that, regardless of its structure, the MNE must develop coordination and control mechanisms to prevent duplication of efforts, to coordinate resource allocation, and to ensure that company-wide operations benefit from ideas generated anywhere in the organization.

Once the company determines the manufacturing configuration it will use, it must adopt a control system to ensure that company strategies are carried out. *Control* can be the measuring of performance so a firm can respond appropriately to changing conditions. Another aspect of a control structure is the organizational structure, discussed in more detail in Chapter 16.

GLOBAL SOURCING

18-3 Show how global sourcing is an important aspect of global supply-chain and operations management

Control systems, such as organizational structure and performance measurement systems, ensure that managers implement company strategies.

Sourcing—the process of a firm having inputs supplied to it from outside suppliers (both domestic and foreign) for the production process.

Global **sourcing** is the first step in the process of materials management, which includes obtaining a supply of inputs used in the production process, inventory management, and transportation between suppliers, manufacturers, and customers. Global sourcing and production strategies can be better understood by taking a look at Figure 18.2, which illustrates the basic operating-environment choices (home country or any foreign country) by stage in the production process.

Although global sourcing is often linked with high-tech and complex processes such as automobile manufacturing, global sourcing affects even the low-cost products we use and consume every day. Take U.S.-based Sara Lee's whole-grain white bread. To make this bread, Sara Lee acquires ingredients from a variety of suppliers, nearly a third of which are located in foreign countries. Its guar gum, used to keep the bread moist, is a powder that comes from the guar plant seedpods grown in India. Calcium propionate, a powdery mold inhibitor that is manufactured in several countries, is sourced in the Netherlands. Honey, used as a natural sweetener, is purchased from suppliers in the United States, China, Vietnam, Brazil, Uruguay, India, Canada, Mexico, and Argentina. Sara Lee sources from several different countries besides the United States because the U.S. supply can often run short. Flour enrichments to

FIGURE 18.2 Global Sourcing and Production Strategies as Affected by Location and Stage of Production

When a company wants to *source* raw materials, parts, or components as a function of its global strategy, it's faced with some key decisions. It may, for example, decide to source components at home, assemble them abroad, and then export the final product to the home market, to foreign markets, or to both.

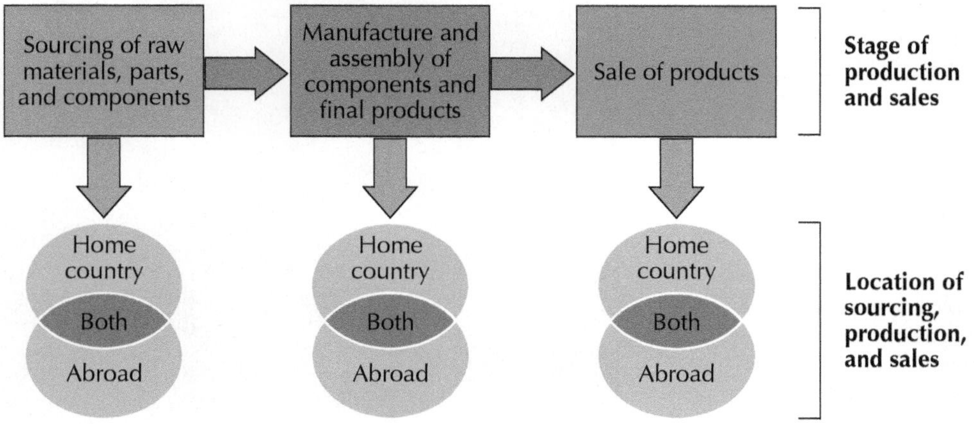

replenish the vitamins lost in the milling process come from China. Due to industry consolidation, suppliers of flour enrichments are limited. Beta-carotene, an artificial coloring used to provide color to the bread and crust, is sourced from Switzerland, though it is available in many countries. Vitamin D3 is sourced from China, while wheat gluten comes from several countries, including France, Poland, Russia, the Netherlands, and Australia.[19]

With its ingredient sources spread all over the globe, Sara Lee must manage its supply chain carefully to ensure timeliness, safety, and quality. So it has centralized its global ingredients purchasing by consolidating its previously scattered procurement operations into a single division known as the "nerve center" located at company headquarters. Purchasing specialists monitor weather patterns, commodity trends, and energy prices. They also communicate and work closely with Sara Lee's diverse base of suppliers—in some cases, even investing money in suppliers' operations to ensure that they are complying with U.S. food safety standards.[20]

Companies can manufacture parts internally or purchase them from external manufacturers.

On the sourcing side, a company can manufacture parts internally or purchase parts from external (unrelated) manufacturers. It can also assemble its own products internally or subcontract to external firms; the manufacture of parts and final assembly may take place in its home country, the country in which it is trying to sell the product, or a third country.[21]

The term sourcing is used in a variety of ways. **Outsourcing**, for instance, refers to a situation in which one company externalizes a process or function to another company. This most often occurs with the IT function but is also being used in other areas, such as research, service centers, and even accounting and tax functions. In addition to offshore manufacturing, another type of offshoring occurs when a company moves part of its business processes outside its home country but internalizes the function rather than outsourcing it to another firm. An example would be setting up its own R&D facilities in another country or, say, a U.S.-based public accounting firm setting up a branch of its tax practice in India. Outsourcing can be domestic or offshore. Sometimes the entire operations can be shipped offshore using talent hired in that location.

Supply chaining is a method of collaborating horizontally—among suppliers, retailers, and customers—to create value.

Contract manufacturers are companies like Foxconn that enter into a contract with the hiring company, such as Apple, to assume the entire manufacturing process.

Another way to look at outsourcing is **supply chaining** "which is a method of collaborating horizontally among suppliers, retailers, and customers to create value."[22] Zara, Walmart, and IKEA are three good examples of companies whose strategy is to engage in supply chaining with key suppliers from around the world to provide products for their customers. Supply chaining is slightly different from traditional outsourcing, which focuses more on a business process, but is far more extensive and complicated since it relates more directly to the final product sold to customers. Apple's use of Foxconn as a **contract manufacturer** for products such as the iPhone is technically supply chaining, although it is similar to outsourcing since the entire manufacturing process is being handled by Foxconn. In Figure 18.1, a contract manufacturer like Foxconn not only assumes the upstream processes, but it also takes on some of the operations management functions since it also does the assembly.

Many companies outsource to specialized call centers around the world. For example, call center employees in Monterrey, Mexico, may utilize their bilingual skills to work with customers in the United States or in Latin America.

Source: Cabeca de Marmare/Shutterstock

Using domestic sources for raw materials and components allows a company to avoid problems with language differences, distance, currency, politics, and tariffs, as well as other problems.

Sourcing in the home country enables companies to avoid numerous problems such as language differences, long distances, lengthy supply lines, exchange-rate fluctuations, wars and insurrections, strikes, politics, tariffs, and complex transportation channels. However, for many companies, domestic sources may be unavailable or more expensive than foreign sources. In Japan, foreign procurement is critical because nearly all of the raw materials used in the manufacturing process such as uranium, bauxite, nickel, crude oil, iron ore, copper, and coking coal are imported. Japanese trading companies came into being expressly to acquire the raw materials needed to fuel Japan's manufacturing.

WHY GLOBAL SOURCING?

Companies pursue global sourcing strategies for a number of reasons:

- To reduce costs through cheaper labor, laxer work rules, and lower land and facilities costs
- To improve quality
- To increase exposure to worldwide technology
- To improve the delivery-of-supplies process
- To strengthen the reliability of supply by supplementing domestic suppliers with foreign ones
- To gain access to materials that are only available abroad, possibly because of technical specifications or product capabilities
- To establish a presence in a foreign market
- To satisfy offset requirements
- To react to competitors' offshore sourcing practices[23]

These reasons are similar to the benefits to FDI discussed in Chapter 15. Whether the suppliers are company-owned or independent firms, MNEs can take advantage of the location-specific advantages in foreign countries.

In 2015, Abu Dhabi–owned Globalfoundries purchased from IBM a business that manufactured advanced microchips used in U.S. spy satellites, missiles, and combat jets. Globalfoundries has operations in Germany and Singapore in addition to IBM's former facilities in New York. One goal of the Pentagon was to globalize its supply chain in response to market trends and to reduce its costs. However, it still wanted the manufacture of the microchips to take place in New York until it could expand its supplier base. This is a good example of global sourcing in a unique business where cybersecurity is a real issue.[24]

In some ways, however, global sourcing is more expensive than domestic sourcing. For example, transportation and communications cost more. Given the longer length of supply lines, it often takes more time to get components from abroad, and lead times are less certain. This problem increases inventory carrying costs and makes it more difficult to get parts to the production site in time. If imported components come in with errors and need to be reworked, the cost per unit will rise, and some components may have to be shipped back to the supplier.

MAJOR SOURCING CONFIGURATIONS

Major outsourcing configurations include
- vertical integration,
- outsourcing through industrial clusters,
- other outsourcing.

Vertical Integration **Vertical integration** occurs when a company owns the entire supplier network, or at least a significant part of it as was the case with Apple before it began to use contract manufacturers. The company may have to purchase raw materials from outside suppliers, but it produces the most expensive parts itself. Integrating vertically can reduce transaction costs by internalizing the different levels in the value chain.[25]

Industrial Clusters Utilizing **industrial clusters** is an alternative way to reduce transportation and transaction costs. Under clustering, buyers and suppliers locate close to each other to facilitate doing business. For example, the growth in auto manufacturers in Mexico has drawn suppliers to Mexico so they can be closer to their clients. Silicon Valley is a cluster of software firms that are taking advantage of research out of Stanford University and other high-tech firms in the IT supply chain.

Keiretsus Japanese *keiretsus* are groups of independent companies that work together to manage the flow of goods and services along the entire value chain.[26] Toyota's highly coordinated supplier network is among the most successful and well known of the Japanese *keiretsus* and a good example of industrial clustering. It borders on vertical integration because parts suppliers tend to set up shop close to Toyota's assembly operations, and Toyota usually has an ownership interest in them. The trusted relationships among companies in the *keiretsu* allow the companies to work closely together from the design phase onward, often sharing proprietary technology but also allowing each other the first right of refusal when new technology is developed. Changes in its global markets and price pressures resulting from the high cost of steel and the strong yen forced Toyota to start looking beyond its closely knit supplier base in Japan by pressuring its *keiretsu* suppliers to benchmark against China's cheaper suppliers. If the suppliers can't achieve low enough pricing, Toyota will be forced to court suppliers outside Japan.[27] The keiretsu model may be changing a little to cope with globalization, but it is still significant in Japan.[28]

CONCEPT CHECK

As we explain on page 389 in Chapter 15, the resource-based view of the firm holds that every company has a unique combination of competencies. Here we suggest that make-or-buy decisions may depend on the extent to which a firm embraces this view, which may prompt it to concentrate internally on those activities that best fit its competencies while depending on other firms to supply products, services, or support activities for which it has lesser competency.

THE MAKE-OR-BUY DECISION

Make or buy—outsource or supply parts from internal production.

When it comes to production activities, MNE managers struggle with a *make-or-buy decision*: Which should be performed internally (make) and which could be subcontracted to independent companies (buy)? In the case of subcontracting, a company must also decide whether the activities should be carried out in the home market or abroad. This often involves developing a strategy that might be a combination of outsourcing, offshoring, and/or supply chaining.

If MNEs outsource parts instead of sourcing them from internal production, they need to determine the degree of involvement with suppliers.

In deciding whether to make or buy, MNEs can focus on those parts of production that are critical to the final product and that the MNE is particularly good at making. They can outsource parts when suppliers have a distinct comparative advantage, such as greater scale, lower cost structure, or stronger performance incentives. The MNE must determine the design and manufacturing capabilities of potential suppliers compared to its own capabilities. If the supplier has a clear advantage, management needs to decide what it would cost to catch up to the best suppliers and whether it would make sense to do so.

POINT

Should Firms Outsource Innovation?

YES A firm should outsource innovative processes if it can maintain focus and position itself effectively in the roiling high-tech and electronics industries. More and more companies are coming to realize the advantages of doing so. Suppliers are taking on such responsibilities as designing and manufacturing prototypes, converting them into workable products, upgrading mature products, conducting quality tests, putting together user manuals, and selecting parts vendors. In 2011, 94 percent of the laptops in the world were designed by a small number of Taiwan-based original design manufacturers (ODMs), although they were often produced in China. The biggest companies are Quanta, Compai, Wistron, and Foxconn. The companies they supply include HP, Lenovo, Apple, Dell, and Acer.[29] Even Boeing collaborated with an Indian company to develop software for its 787 Dreamliner jet.

Companies willing to outsource some R&D and technological designs can experience enormous cost savings. Although innovation is key to remaining competitive, more and more firms find that their internal R&D teams aren't producing results that justify the large investments in them. Thus, in the face of demanding customers and relentless competition that pressures margins, managers must find a way to reduce costs or increase R&D productivity.

Outsourcing is a viable solution. Companies can save millions by simply buying designs rather than developing them in-house. For instance, using a predesigned platform for cell phones can reduce the costs of developing them from scratch—which takes approximately $10 million and 150 engineers—by 70 percent. Furthermore, demands by retailers and customers as well as uncertain future market trends require developing a costly range of product models. Third-party developers are better equipped to handle such costs, spreading them over many buyers and possessing the expertise to develop a variety of models from a single basic design.

Outsourcing also helps get products to market faster, which is crucial where products become commodities in a matter of months. Hewlett-Packard claims that by working with partners and suppliers on designs, it now gets a new concept to the market in 60 percent less time. Critics worry that by outsourcing technology, companies are outsourcing their fonts of competitive advantage; still, outsourcing certain design and development processes allows firms to focus more on their true core competencies. Few, if any,

COUNTERPOINT

Should Firms Outsource Innovation?

NO When it comes to outsourcing R&D, design, and development work, how does a firm know where to draw the line? How does it determine what is core intellectual property and what is commodity technology? The truth is, outsourcing turns the former into the latter, which becomes available to most anyone. Look at Toshiba. By working with South Korean chipmakers to develop its DRAM memory chips, it allowed the technology behind these components to become commoditized and is now struggling to stay ahead.[31]

Competitive advantage often depends on trade secrets that set a firm apart from its rivals. Outsourcing innovation enhances the risk that it will pass on these proprietary technologies to suppliers and partners, thereby fostering new competitors. Because suppliers rarely cooperate solely with one customer, the R&D they do for one can easily be transferred to another. Such was the case for Japanese company Sharp, which worked closely with suppliers to develop a "sixth-generation" plant for making larger flat panels for televisions. Unfortunately, its suppliers also work closely with Sharp's rivals, many of them Taiwanese companies, and not long after the completion of the plant, these competitors were constructing their own "Gen-6" facilities. Sharp tried to protect itself by secretly rewriting software on some equipment and fixing machinery in-house rather than having suppliers do it. However, in 2012, Foxconn of Taiwan bought 10 percent of Sharp and one of its factories in Japan that manufactures LCD displays.[32] In 2016, Foxconn completed the takeover of Sharp by investing $3.5 billion in the company that produces screens for Apple products. Foxconn was hoping that the investment would solidify its relationship with Apple even more.[33]

Suppliers and partners might also take the information and technology that have been shared with them and become competitors themselves. After Motorola hired Taiwanese company BenQ Corp. to design and manufacture its mobile phones, BenQ began selling the phones under its own brand name in the highly competitive Chinese market, causing Motorola to terminate the contract. Even Foxconn is now competing with Apple by manufacturing a phone designed by the owner of Nokia. There is no implication that it is stealing Apple proprietary technology, however.[34]

In addition to giving rise to new competitors, outsourcing innovation may cause firms to lose their competitive edge and the desire to invest in innovation. Although some assert that outsourcing certain development and design work allows companies to focus more on new companies plan on completely eliminating their own R&D forces, and most insist they will continue with the more proprietary R&D work.

No one company can manage everything in-house. Even the chief technology officer of Nokia—a company that once prided itself on developing almost everything on its own—has stated, "Nobody can master it all." In fact, a recent survey of MNEs found that almost three-quarters of respondents believed they could boost innovation dramatically by collaborating with outsiders, even competitors.[30] The companies that will survive in the future are those able to efficiently and effectively control a network of partners and suppliers around the world.

innovative technologies, it more often prompts companies to decrease internal R&D investments and become lazy in their pursuit of future breakthroughs, relying too much on suppliers to do their work. Jim Andrew, senior vice president of Boston Consulting Group, warns, "If the innovation starts residing in the suppliers, you could incrementalize yourself to the point where there isn't much left."

High-tech and electronics firms that outsource their innovation processes risk losing the essence of their actual business, becoming mere marketing fronts for others. It also sends a bad message to investors, who might have difficulty finding intrinsic value in a company that owns little true intellectual property and whose profits from successful products are most likely being paid out in licensing fees to the companies that actually developed them.

Much has been made of manufacturing outsourcing in the past few decades, but outsourcing innovation poses a potentially greater threat to high-tech firms that see it as a shortcut to cost savings. Looking to immediate savings is shortsighted, and firms that do so will ultimately damage their competitive positions and lose viability as true industry players.[35]

QUESTION

Now that Apple purchases its iPhones and iPads from Foxconn, should it let Foxconn develop the new technology that goes in Apple's products so that it can focus more on marketing? Why or why not?

SUPPLIER RELATIONS

Supplier relationships are very important but sometimes complicated, especially for MNEs trying to manage them around the world. IKEA's global supply chain involves over 1,000 suppliers from around the world supplying products to 367 IKEA stores in 30 countries. Many of the suppliers have sub-suppliers, so IKEA established IWAY, a supplier Code of Conduct that focuses on a variety of issues, including energy and water sustainability, child labor, forced and bonded labor, and health and safety issues.[36] In addition, they conduct IWAY audits using a team of internal auditors and in some cases third-party auditors. Apple's supplier responsibility report is similar to that of IKEA, focusing on empowering workers, labor and human rights, health and safety, the environment, and accountability. In 2018, Apple conducted 770 supplier assessments using its own or third-party auditors, covering 93 percent of their supplier spends, 17 percent of which were first timers.[37] Most MNEs are very conscious about supplier relationships and how supplier activities reflect on their reputations.

CONFLICT MINERALS

Conflict minerals are certain minerals that come from warring areas, principally the eastern provinces of the Democratic Republic of the Congo, that generate revenues to fund conflicts.

A real challenge for U.S.-based MNEs is compliance with a provision in the Dodd–Frank Act that requires companies to disclose the use of certain minerals mined in war-torn or conflict areas, primarily in Africa. The minerals in question are known as G3T (gold, titanium, tungsten, and tin), mined from ore and extracted from Congo or nine surrounding countries. The objective of the provision is to stamp out militias in these countries that are funded by the sale of the minerals.[38] Since these minerals are important for consumer electronics, such as mobile phones, tablets, and laptops, companies like Apple, Microsoft, and Intel that have long supply lines are under scrutiny to determine if their suppliers are using conflict minerals. The companies have to show that they are using their best judgment to do country-of-origin tests with their suppliers, but most are stopping short of stating that they are conflict free. However, in its 2019 Supplier Responsibility report, Apple reports that any suppliers, mines, or smelters that don't follow its policies will be given a chance to correct practices, or they will be dropped from the supply chain. 100 percent of their smelters or refiners were audited by Apple or third-party auditors.[39] This is far better than a report by the U.S. Government Accountability Office, which did an investigation of the conflict minerals a few years prior to the reports by IKEA and Apple described above, and they found that most companies were unable to determine the source of their conflict minerals.[40]

THE PURCHASING FUNCTION

Global progression in the purchasing function:

- Domestic purchasing only
- Foreign buying based on need
- Foreign buying as part of a procurement strategy
- Integration of global procurement strategy

The purchasing agent is the link between a company's outsourcing decision and its supplier relationships. Just as companies go through stages of globalization, so does the purchasing agent's scope of responsibilities. Typically, purchasing goes through four phases before becoming "global":

1. Domestic purchasing only
2. Foreign buying based on need
3. Foreign buying as part of procurement strategy
4. Integration of global procurement strategy[41]

Phase 4 occurs when the company realizes the benefits that result from the integration and coordination of purchasing on a global basis and is most applicable to the MNE.

When purchasing becomes global, MNEs often face the centralize/decentralize dilemma. Should they allow each subsidiary to make every purchasing decision, or should they centralize all or some of them? The primary benefits of decentralization include increased control over purchases, better responsiveness to facility needs, and more effective use of local suppliers. The primary benefits of centralization are increased leverage with suppliers, better prices, eliminating administrative duplication, allowing purchasers to develop specialized knowledge in purchasing techniques, reducing the number of orders processed, and enabling purchasing to build solid supplier relationships.[42]

INFORMATION TECHNOLOGY AND GLOBAL SUPPLY-CHAIN MANAGEMENT

18-4 Explain how information technology is used in global operations and supply-chain management

A comprehensive supply-chain strategy is most effective with a strong commitment to information technology (IT), which aids in quick and efficient production, proficient inventory management, effective supplier communication, and customer satisfaction. In *The World is Flat*, Flattener #3 is workflow software.[43] Encompassing the standard protocols such as HTTP that allow computers to work with each other and business processes such as SAP, workflow software is critical for the supply-chain management process.

ELECTRONIC DATA INTERCHANGE (EDI)

A key to making the global supply chain work is a good information system.

EDI (electronic data interchange)—the electronic linkage of suppliers, customers, and third-party intermediaries to expedite documents and financial flows.

The key to making a global information system work is getting the relevant information in a timely manner. Apple, for example, has established a B2B (business to business) gateway that all of its suppliers are required to use, which basically allows suppliers to share electronic data with Apple. Many companies use **electronic data interchange (EDI)** to link suppliers, manufacturers, customers, and intermediaries, especially in the food-manufacturing and car-making industries, in which suppliers replenish in high volumes.

In a global context, EDI has been used to link exporters with customs to facilitate the quick processing of customs forms, thus speeding up cross-border deliveries. Walmart is known for its revolutionary use of EDI to connect its global suppliers to its inventory ordering system.[44]

ENTERPRISE RESOURCE PLANNING/MATERIAL REQUIREMENTS PLANNING

ERP (enterprise resource planning)—software that can link information flows from different parts of a business and from different geographic areas.

The next wave of technology affecting the global supply chain was the implementation of IT packages known as **enterprise resource planning (ERP)**. Companies such as Oracle, Baan, PeopleSoft, and German software giant SAP introduced software to integrate everything in the back office (the part of the business dealing with internal matters, as opposed to the front office, which deals with the customer). ERP is essential for bringing together the information inside the firm with information from different geographic areas, but its inability to link to the customer and take advantage of e-commerce has been a problem.

Material requirements planning (MRP)—computerized information system that addresses complex inventory situations and calculates the demand for parts from the production schedules of the companies that use the parts.

An extension of ERP is *material requirements planning* (MRP), a computerized information system that addresses complex inventory situations and calculates the demand for parts from the production schedules of the companies that use them. DENSO, the Japanese auto parts supplier for Toyota, uses MRP extensively to calculate the demand for parts from the production schedules of the non-Toyota companies it supplies.

RADIO FREQUENCY ID (RFID)

Radio frequency ID (RFID)—a system that labels products with an electronic tag, which stores and transmits information regarding the product's origin, destination, and quantity.

A newer wave has recently swept the technology scene in the form of *radio frequency ID (RFID),* a system that labels a product with an electronic tag that stores and transmits information on the product's origin, destination, and quantity. When electronic readers scan the tags by means of radio waves, the data can be rewritten or captured and sent to a computer-network database, which collects, organizes, stores, and moves the data—often in conjunction with an ERP system.

Such real-time information allows manufacturers, suppliers, and distributors to keep track of products and components throughout their manufacturing processes and transportation networks, resulting in greater efficiency and more visibility along the supply chain. The use of RFID in the Las Vegas airport to track luggage has resulted in more accurate sorting, better tracking, and fewer lost bags.[45] Walmart mandated that its top suppliers use RFID tags at the pallet level, predicting it could save billions of dollars for the entire retail industry through supply-chain efficiencies.[46] Apple even has an RFID app, which can be purchased on iTunes and downloaded to an iPhone or iPad, to display the location status of taggable items. In addition to supply chain management, one of the fastest areas of growth for RFID is health care management.[47]

CONCEPT CHECK

In discussing "Changing Times, Changing Skills, and Changing Organizations" on page 438 in Chapter 16, we observe that the Internet, which accelerates the spread of ideas throughout an organization, has created a new concept for organization structure. In other words, as a supremely efficient and effective means of organizing global knowledge, resources, and people, the Internet has inspired many people to imagine new ways of effectively organizing a company's resources (especially its people).

E-COMMERCE

E-commerce—the use of the Internet to join together suppliers with companies, and companies with customers.

A recent entrant in the technological wave linking together the parts of the global supply chain is **E-commerce**. Since Walmart moved its EDI-based infrastructure from traditional but expensive value-added networks (VANs) to the Internet, it has been good news for thousands of worldwide vendors. All of their transactions with Walmart are now web-based—a substantial cost savings for the MNE and its vendors.[48]

Extranets and Blockchains Companies with web-based systems usually establish an **extranet** for suppliers—a linkage to its information system via the Internet—so they can organize production and delivery of parts. Plugged into a company's customer database, the suppliers can keep track of changes in demand; plugged into the ordering process, they can track the progress of their orders from factory to doorstep.

Blockchain technology is the next wave of the utilization of technology in supply chain management linking together firms with their suppliers.

A future development in global supply chain management is the potential of utilizing blockchain technology, which is best known because of cryptocurrencies. However, companies such as Walmart are encouraging suppliers of green vegetables to develop an instant traceability of products. This occurred after an *e. Coli* outbreak of lettuce that Walmart was able to instantly trace because of its blockchain capabilities.[49]

"The Digital Divide" The challenge in global supply-chain management is that although some networks can be managed through the Internet, others—particularly in emerging markets—cannot because of the lack of technology or low Internet speeds. The use of the Internet varies by location and by industry. However, access to the Internet has grown in recent years. In December 2004, it was estimated that 12.7 percent of the global population was using the Internet compared with 56.1 percent by March 2019.[50] Access to the Internet through cell phones has made a big difference in the general population, and the use of social media, such as Facebook, with over 2.5 billion active users worldwide as of the 4th quarter 2019, [51] has provided another avenue for people to connect and shop online through the Internet.

The preceding discussion shows that IT can help companies manage their global supply chains, but it must be carefully integrated into their overall strategy. Because IT is highly technical as well as a support to a company's lines of business, it is often difficult to align it with company strategy. This is especially true in the international arena, where personnel in different countries may be accustomed to their own IT systems and may have difficulty adopting a global IT format that will allow them to achieve some economies of scale as well as fully integrate it in the overall strategy.

QUALITY

18-5 Summarize how quality management is important in global operations and supply-chain management

Quality—meeting or exceeding the expectations of a customer.

An important aspect of all levels of the global supply chain is quality management, for service firms as well as manufacturers. **Quality** can be defined here as meeting or exceeding customer expectations. More specifically, it is conformance to specifications, value, fitness for use, support (provided by the company), and psychological impressions (image).[52] Quality involves careful design of a product or service and ensuring that an organization's systems can consistently produce the design.[53] For example, no one wants to buy computer software that has a lot of bugs, but the need to get software to market quickly may mean speeding it there as soon as possible and correcting errors later. After two fatal airline crashes involving the popular Boeing 737 MAX plane, Boeing was struggling to complete a software fix so that it could have the planes certified to fly again. The glitch could have been part of a design failure of the aircraft.[54] The concern over quality makes a huge difference in the perceptions of customers, since many travelers were hesitant to fly on the 737 MAX until the problems were fixed.

In another example, Japan-based Takata Corporation manufactured motor vehicle seat belts, air bags, steering wheels, interior trims, and child restraint systems to major auto manufacturers worldwide. Although Honda was its largest customer, 14 Japanese, U.S., and European carmakers used its products. However, a major defect in Takata's air bags resulted in 10 deaths and over 100 injuries in the United States alone. Even though far more lives have been saved by the deployment of air bags during crashes, the deaths and injuries that resulted from defective air bags have resulted in the largest and most complex safety recall in U.S. history, in addition to similar recalls worldwide.[55] Finally, Tanaka declared bankruptcy in 2017 after it admitted that it had supplied more than 50 million defective airbags in the United States alone.

ZERO DEFECTS

Zero defects—the refusal to tolerate defects of any kind.

Quality also refers to **zero defects**, an idea perfected by Japanese manufacturers who refuse to tolerate flaws of any kind. Before this strong emphasis on getting rid of defects, many companies operated according to the premise of **acceptable quality level (AQL)**, which held that a few faulty products would be dealt with through repair facilities and service warranties. This type of manufacturing/operating environment required buffer inventories, rework stations, and expediting, with the goal of pushing through products as fast as possible and then dealing with the mistakes later. However, world-class companies prefer zero defects and they realize that taking quality seriously is the only way to beat the competition.[56]

Deming's suggestions on quality management encompass the idea that the responsibility for quality resides within the policies and practices of managers.

In the late 1970s, when Japanese companies began to seriously outpace those in the United States in achieving high-quality products and processes, a new emphasis was placed on actively managing the operations that affect quality. One contributor to this focus on quality management, and one of the people who trained the Japanese in quality was W. Edwards Deming. To espouse the idea that the responsibility for quality resides within the policies and practices of managers, Deming developed several suggestions on how companies could improve. His focus on quality was designed to reduce the variance in the manufacturing process through statistical control, design, and training and through the policies and practices of managers. He felt that higher quality would lead to lower costs and better acceptance by the consumer. His process for continuous improvement was to *plan* a process to correct problems, *do* or implement the plan, *check* to see how the improvements were progressing, and *act* to make sure the changes were permanent.

The emphasis on quality management has continued to provide a major source of competitive advantage and play a major role for companies across the globe. However, just as different countries possess different cultures, product preferences, and business practices, various regions of the world have approached the concept of quality management in various ways. The Japanese have long focused on lean production processes that eliminate waste and boost visibility, whereas the American approach has historically been more statistically based, and the Europeans have opted to concentrate more on quality standards.[57] These varying attitudes toward quality create a high level of complexity for MNEs with global operations. However, Japan's reputation for high quality has run into serious problems in recent years as some of the top companies in Japan, such as Nissan, Mitsubishi, and Kobe Steel, disclosed that they were falsifying quality inspections, covering up product faults and reporting false fuel-economy data (in the case of the auto companies). After Japan's bubble economy burst in the 1990s, manufacturing quality began to deteriorate. Quality-checking staffers were fired to cut costs, assembly-line workers were told to do quality checks themselves, and pressure to meet production deadlines and respond to foreign competition caused a deterioration in quality. The closed culture meant that factory workers were working to solve problems without including senior executives.[58]

LEAN MANUFACTURING AND TOTAL QUALITY MANAGEMENT (TQM)

CONCEPT CHECK

Compare the concept of employee involvement as it is characterized here with the idea of coordination by mutual adjustment, which we discuss on page 432 in Chapter 16. Both approaches to coordination signal a willingness to coordinate value activities through a range of informal mechanisms, including means by which employees are encouraged to engage one another in decisions about matters of mutual importance.

One reason why companies might hesitate when considering whether to source parts from foreign suppliers is because of *lean manufacturing*, the process of reducing waste in all areas of the supply chain.[59] This concept was popularized by Toyota and has been imitated worldwide. Because it relies on the efficiencies gained by reducing waste and defects, lean manufacturing is also closely tied to quality management.

Lean manufacturing—a productive system whose focus is on optimizing processes through the philosophy of continual improvement.

Total quality management (TQM) is a process that stresses three principles: *customer satisfaction, continuous improvement,* and *employee involvement.*[60] The goal is to eliminate all defects. TQM often focuses on benchmarking world-class standards, product and service design, process design, and purchasing.[61] The center of the entire process, however, is customer satisfaction, the achievement of which may raise production costs. In TQM, quality means the product is so good that the customer wouldn't think of buying from anyone else.

Total quality management (TQM)—a process that stresses customer satisfaction, employee involvement, and continuous improvement of quality. Its goal is to eliminate all defects.

TQM is a process of continuous improvement at every organizational level. It implies that the company is doing everything it can to achieve quality at every stage of the process. TQM does not use any specific production philosophy or require the use of other techniques, such as a just-in-time system for inventory delivery. Although benchmarking—determining the best processes used by the best companies—is an important part of TQM, it is not intended to be a goal. In essence, TQM means that a company will try to be better than the best.

Executives who have adopted the zero-defects philosophy of TQM claim that long-run production costs decline as defects decline. The continuous improvement process is also known as *kaizen,* which means identifying problems and enlisting employees at all levels to help eliminate those problems. The key is to make continuous improvement a part of every employee's daily work. However, the kaizen model failed for many Japanese companies that were hit with lawsuits and scandals in recent years due to a drop in quality. This included pressures on employees for a variety of reasons, including foreign competition, pressures to reduce costs, and the pressure to speed up deliveries. In addition, some companies, such as Kobe Steel, were found to fake quality certificates for products. In the ensuing investigations, it was determined that quality audits were being poorly conducted, leading to a drop in quality and an increase in defects, and that top management was out of touch with the factory floor.[62] An important element of lean manufacturing is just-in-time (JIT) inventory management, which focuses on "reducing inefficiency and unproductive time in the production process to improve continuously the process and the quality of the product

Just-in-time (JIT) approach to inventory management—a system that sources raw materials and parts just as they are needed in the manufacturing process.

or service."[63] The JIT system gets raw materials, parts, and components to the buyer "just in time" for use, sparing companies the cost of storing large inventories. However, the JIT system also relies on quality components, and as shown above, that has been a challenge for some companies.

JIT is what Dell hoped to accomplish in its Irish plant by having parts delivered just as they were to enter the production process and then go out the door to consumers as soon as the computers were built. However, the use of JIT means that parts must have few defects and must arrive on time. That is why companies need to develop solid supplier relationships to ensure good quality and delivery times if JIT is to work—and why industrial clustering is a popular way of linking more closely with suppliers.

Risks in Foreign Sourcing Foreign sourcing can create big risks for companies that use lean manufacturing and JIT because interruptions in the supply line can cause havoc. MNEs are becoming expert at meeting the requirements of JIT—ships that take two weeks to cross the Pacific docking within an hour of scheduled arrival, factories that are able to more easily fill small orders, and so on. However, because of distances alone, the supply chain is open to more problems and delays.[64] Uncertainties in trade agreements can also disrupt supply chains.

Many MNEs that have set up manufacturing and assembly facilities overseas to service local markets have practically forced their domestic parts suppliers to move overseas as well to allow them to continue with JIT manufacturing. That is why so many Japanese parts suppliers have moved to the United States and Mexico to be near their major customers.

A company's inventory management strategy determines the frequency of needed shipments. Since DENSO, one of Toyota's major suppliers, is very close to Toyota's assembly plants in Japan, JIT allows the DENSO components to arrive in a matter of a few minutes but no more than a few hours from when they are used.[65]

It is hard to combine foreign sourcing and JIT production without having safety stocks of inventory on hand, which defeats the concept of JIT.

Because JIT requires delivery just as the inventory is to be used, some concession must be made for inventory arriving from foreign suppliers. The less frequent the delivery, and the longer the supply line from international sources of supply, the more likely the need to develop backup stocks of inventory at the point of assembly or a warehouse close by, which increases storage costs but reduces the risk of shortages.

A *kanban* system facilitates JIT by using cards to control the flow of production through a factory.

The Kanban System One system pioneered by Toyota to facilitate its JIT strategies is the *kanban system,* named after the Japanese word for "card" or "visible record." Kanban cards are used to control the flow of production through a factory. In the system used by Toyota, components are shipped to a plant just before they need to go into production, where they are kept in a bin with an attached card identifying the quantity of items in the bin. When the assembly process begins, a production-order card signifies that a bin needs to be moved to the assembly line. When the bin is emptied, it is moved to a storage area and replaced with a full bin. The kanban card is then removed from the empty bin and is used to order a replacement from the supplier.

SIX SIGMA

Six Sigma—a quality control system aimed at eliminating defects, slashing product cycle times, and cutting costs across the board.

Six Sigma is an effective statistical approach to quality management developed by Motorola and popularized by General Electric. As a highly focused system of quality control that scrutinizes a company's entire production system, it aims to eliminate defects, slash product cycle times, and cut costs across the board. The system uses data and rigorous statistical analysis to identify "defects" in a process or product, reduce variability, and achieve as close to zero defects as possible.[66]

Since being introduced by Motorola in the 1980s, Six Sigma has been adopted by many MNEs, including GE, GlaxoSmithKline, Amazon, and Maersk. Although some have accused the program of diverting attention away from customers and squashing innovation, most of the 100 largest companies in the United States have embraced it.[67] Its main goal is defect reduction, and fewer defects should cause an improvement in yields, which should improve customer satisfaction and then lead to enhanced income. Given that Six Sigma is a metric designed to measure defects, some argue that it is most effective when used in conjunction with the Baldrige Criteria for Excellence or the European Quality Award.[68]

QUALITY STANDARDS

Levels of quality standards:
- General level—ISO 9000, Malcolm Baldrige National Quality Award
- Industry-specific level
- Company level

There are three different levels of quality standards: *general, industry-specific,* and *company-specific.* The first is a general standard, such as the Deming Award, which is presented to firms that demonstrate excellence in quality, or the Malcolm Baldrige National Quality Award, which is presented annually to companies that demonstrate quality strategies and achievements. However, even more important than awards is certification of quality.

General-Level Standards The **International Organization for Standardization (ISO)** in Geneva was formed in 1947 to facilitate the international coordination and unification of industrial standards. From the beginning, it has partnered with the IEC (International Electrotechnical Commission), which is the originator of global technical standards. It also collaborates with the International Telecommunications Union and the World Trade Organization. As an NGO, the ISO represents a network of standard setters in 164 countries and has established over 21,000 international quality standards.[69]

ISO 9000—a global set of quality standards intended to promote quality at every level of an organization.

ISO 14000—a quality standard concerned with environmental management.

ISO 9000 and ISO 14000 Even with more than 22,598 ISO standards, new ones are being published every year. The two main families of standards are ISO 9000, which describes the fundamentals of quality management systems, and ISO 14000, which addresses what the company does to improve its environmental performance. However, many different areas have ISO standards.

ISO 9000 is a set of universal standards for a quality assurance system that is accepted around the world. Applying uniformly to companies in any industry and of any size, it is intended to promote the idea of quality at every organizational level. Initially it was designed to harmonize technical norms within the EU. Now it is an important part of business operations throughout Europe. Under the ISO 9000 family of standards, companies must document how workers perform every function affecting quality and install mechanisms to ensure that they follow through on the documented routine. The documentation is generic and applicable to any organization that makes products or provides services. A major advantage of ISO 9000 is the documentation process, which not only requires workers to examine what they do to improve quality but also ensures continuity as workers change positions.

ISO certification entails a complex analysis of management systems and procedures, not just quality-control standards. Rather than judging the quality of a particular product, ISO evaluates the management of the manufacturing or service process according to the standards it has created in 20 domains, from purchasing to design to training. The operational principles of its management-system standards are: plan, do, check, and act (correct and improve plans), which is based on Deming's PDCA continuous improvement cycle. A company that wants to be ISO certified must fill out a report and submit to certification by a team of independent auditors. The process can be expensive and time-consuming, as each site of a company must be separately certified. The ISO 14000 family of standards is designed to help companies establish high-quality environmental standards in terms of air, water, and soil; ensure that environmental standards are followed; and develop products and services that are environmentally friendly.

Non-European companies operating in Europe need to become ISO certified in order to maintain access to that market.

U.S. companies that operate in Europe seek ISO certification to maintain access to its market. When DuPont lost a major European contract to an ISO-certified European company, it decided to become certified. By doing so, not only was it able to position itself better in Europe, it also benefited from the experience of going through the certification process and focusing on quality in and of itself. Some European companies are so committed to ISO that they will not do business with a certified company if its suppliers are not also ISO certified. They want to be sure that quality flows back to every level of the supply chain.

Industry-Specific Standards In addition to the general standards described earlier, there are industry-specific standards for quality, especially for suppliers to follow. Since ISO standards are relatively generic, some industries, such as the auto industry, have developed more specific ones to fit the industry. One such example is QS9000, which was initially required for any supplier of Ford and General Motors. However, it was eventually replaced by ISO/TS 16949:2009, which was more applicable to the auto industry. It is supposed to be used in conjunction with ISO 9001, and it defines the quality management system requirements for the design, development, production, installation, and service of automotive-related products.

Company-Specific Standards Individual companies also set their own standards for suppliers to meet if they are going to continue to supply them. Most large MNEs with large supply chains have set and published supply-chain standards, often in the context of a sustainability report. Apple's approach was noted above in the context of working with global suppliers. In the service sector, global public accounting firms, such as KPMG and PWC, have set high audit practices that it expects its affiliates around the world to use. This is always complicated since public accounting firms are an association of individual national partnerships operating under one name. However, the audit of a multinational client must be performed to high standards.

LOOKING TO THE FUTURE Uncertainty and the Global Supply Chain

Two competing ideas have been emphasized in this chapter: First, globalization has pushed companies to establish operations abroad or to outsource to foreign suppliers to reduce costs and be closer to markets; second, the longer the supply line, the greater the risk. Because of global political instability and an increase in terrorism, the risk of longer supply lines has increased dramatically. At any time, global political events could completely disrupt a well-organized supply chain and put a company at risk. This was demonstrated more recently in 2011 with the earthquake and tsunami in Japan.

A recent example is the outbreak of COVID-19, which started in China but has spread to other countries. The impact on China has greatly affected a number of companies with global supply chains, including Apple, Volkswagen AG, Fiat Chrysler Automobiles, as well as luxury brand companies whose sales are falling due to a lack of Chinese tourists. Fiat Chrysler had to temporarily halt auto production in Siberia because it couldn't get parts deliveries from China. Apple Inc. announced that it would not meet its first quarter 2020 revenue projections because of the virus. Most of Apple's products are manufactured in China through contract manufacturer Foxconn Technologies Group, which was having trouble reopening factories because of the lack of workers. Many were stranded in different parts of China while on the Lunar New Year holiday and not able to travel to the factories.[70]

As a supply chain stretches and uncertainty grows, companies have to become much better at scenario building so that viable contingencies are available. Maybe this means they will pursue more multi-domestic strategies to insulate their foreign operations from other countries and allow them to be more responsive to local consumers. However, as MNEs in the developed countries respond to competitive pressures to reduce costs, they will be forced to continue sourcing abroad, either in company-owned facilities or from third parties.

Any good firm must engage in scenario building to consider the "what-ifs." What if there is no secure air or ocean transportation available to move goods? What if the goods can move, but there are delays? What if terrorists begin to use the global supply chain of legitimate companies to contaminate products or move hazardous materials? What if another virus like COVID-19 turns into a complete global shutdown of supply chains? Obviously, many companies are considering diversification of their suppliers to reduce their reliance on China, but that is pretty complicated. That being said, it will be interesting to see how companies with diversified global supply chains respond to the challenges brought on by COVID-19, an unprecedented global health crisis. Clearly, the future appears much more complicated than current or past conditions, so let the manager beware. Escalating costs in China, the manufacturing floor of the world, are causing many firms to look to other countries for cheaper sources of supply as well as closer to home for their sourcing decisions.

CASE

Nokero: Lighting the World[71]

—*Manuel G. Serapio*

In June 2016, Steve Katsaros, founder and CEO of Nokero, was contemplating how to build on his company's accomplishments. Nokero, a marketer of solar light bulbs, has emerged as a successful born-global social enterprise. Since its establishment in 2010, Nokero had sold more than 1.4 million solar light bulbs to over 120 countries. The company has generated significant media attention. *CNN, The New York Times* (online), *The Washington Post, Fast Company, Popular Mechanics, Popular Science, The Denver Post*, and *Engadget*, to name just a few, have featured Nokero's story of doing well by doing good as a provider of environmentally friendly solar lighting to the world's poor. Katsaros himself has been recognized for his humanitarian work. In April 2013, he was awarded the U.S. Patent Office's Patent for Humanity Award.

Steve Katsaros, founder and CEO of Nokero, shows a group of children how his innovative solar light works.

Source: Courtesy of Steve Katsaros/Nokero

While Katsaros was very pleased with his company's overall performance to date, he was concerned with three fundamental questions. First, how should the company grow? Specifically, what market segments should the company focus on for profitable growth? Several opportunities had propelled Nokero's sales since its establishment. The company has sold tens of thousands of solar bulbs in small and sample order sales through the company's website from thousands of customers in North America and abroad. Additionally, Nokero has entered into distributorship or dealer agreements in several countries. Finally, governments, international agencies, and nongovernmental organizations have partnered with or approached Nokero on collaborative social programs relating to environmental sustainability, renewable energy, poverty alleviation, and disaster and relief projects. Katsaros wanted to make sure that Nokero explores the best pathways for growth in both the social enterprise sector and commercial channels.

Second, where should the company grow? Currently, Nokero has pursued an opportunistic sales approach. The company's major customers are in diverse and dispersed locations in Kenya, Ghana, South Africa, Fiji, Mexico, India, Indonesia, Nigeria, Haiti, and other markets. Although practical business sense may dictate that international new ventures like Nokero focus on a few markets at a time, Katsaros was hesitant to pursue this approach since it contradicted the company's social mission of reaching out to as many people as possible that could benefit from Nokero's solar light bulbs.

Third, how should Nokero manage its supply chain to support the company's growth? Katsaros understood that growth brings a number of challenges that require Nokero to address critical global supply-chain issues effectively. How can the company serve different markets and customer segments that are dispersed in many countries? How can Nokero bring down sourcing, manufacturing, and distribution costs to make the product more affordable to its customers? What should the company do to address the "last mile issue" of reaching customers in the most remote locations?

The Nokero Story

Identifying the Opportunity

Nokero (short for "No Kerosene") was established by Steve Katsaros in order to develop safe and environmentally friendly solar products that eliminated the need for harmful and polluting fuels used for light and heat around the world and that are affordable to the customers who need them. Katsaros saw a significant opportunity in developing a solar light product to replace kerosene and diesel lanterns. Katsaros described the opportunity as follows:

In many parts of the world, nonelectrified dwellings and workplaces are illuminated by kerosene or diesel lamps, candles or wood. There are electric options but most are expensive, or fragile, or don't have replaceable, rechargeable batteries.

According to the most recent data, more than 940 million people live without electricity. Of these, 591.05 million live in sub-Saharan Africa, and 254.91 million in South Asia. Many of these people live in remote areas and rely on kerosene and diesel-fueled lanterns for their lighting. By substituting solar light bulbs for kerosene lanterns, these people are able to recoup their purchase price within a period of 12 days to 2 months, depending on market forces. Moreover, the replacement of kerosene lanterns with solar light bulbs generates significant environmental and health benefits. Every solar light that replaces a kerosene lantern saves three-quarters of a ton of CO_2 emissions over the five-year lifetime of the product. According to the World Bank, daily exposure to emissions from kerosene lanterns is like smoking two packs of cigarettes per day.

Inventing the Solution: The N100, N200, and N233

Katsaros invented the first Nokero light bulb (the Nokero N100) on January 24, 2010, drawing a sketch of the idea on a notepad. Four days later, he filed a U.S. patent on the N100 that was eventually granted in February 2011. Production on the light bulb commenced in June 2010 and the newest model, the N233, was introduced in November 2016.

The Nokero solar light bulb is a small, lightweight, portable light, shaped like a light bulb for easy identification. The bulb hangs in the sun to charge and can be hung or laid on its side at night. A "pivot" feature allows users to swivel the solar panel toward the sun to maximize charge capability. The bulb can be swiveled at night to direct light where needed. The LED lights are enclosed in the shatter-resistant bulb, do not get hot, and produce an even light. (See the photo.)

The N233's brightness is 25 lumens on high illumination and 10 lumens on low illumination. The duration of light is 6–15 hours on one day's charge. While the brightness is not the same as traditional LED lighting, the N233's brightness is five times brighter than that of a kerosene lantern. The N233 is shatter- and rain-proof and built to last for five years.

Nokero sells the N233 in large-quantity orders (e.g., over 1,000 light bulbs) for about $8.00 (FOB China). Sample sales are priced between $15 and $20 (depending on shipping costs). In response to strong market feedback for a low-price starter version of the Nokero solar bulbs, Katsaros released a more basic version that sells for about half the price of the N233. In addition, Nokero products are available through Amazon, Sportsman's Warehouse, and eBay.

Building a Born-Global Company

A few weeks after developing the N100, Katsaros worked on Nokero's business model, package design, pricing, and manufacturing and distribution processes. In April 2010, he formed Nokero International Ltd., the operating company of Nokero.

The speed with which Nokero developed and manufactured the N100 and formed the business entity could be attributed to Katsaros' experience as an inventor and entrepreneur. He had previously licensed inventions to sports companies (e.g., Dynastar Skis, K2, and HaberVision) and built RevoPower, a motorized wheel for bicycles that gets 200 miles per gallon at 20 miles per hour. A BS Mechanical Engineering graduate from Purdue University, a Bard Center for Entrepreneurship (now the Jake Jabs Center for Entrepreneurship) certificate graduate recipient at the University of Colorado Denver, and a Collegiate Inventors Competition awardee, Katsaros is a patent agent registered with the U.S. Patent and Trademark Office, which has issued him several patents for his previous inventions.

From the start, Nokero was a "born-global company" with customers in different parts of the world, and

Source: Courtesy of Steve Katsaros/Nokero

co-owners and supplier partners in Hong Kong and China. Katsaros partnered with three Hong Kong–based entrepreneurs to form Nokero International Ltd. in Hong Kong. These partners, associates of Katsaros in previous businesses, provided start-up capital that represented a minority equity interest in Nokero and helped Katsaros find a strong and reliable factory supplier in China. Nokero also leveraged the HK partners' connections with the factory supplier to secure a trade financing line from the supplier. The HK partners manage Nokero's operations, including overseeing the supplier factory in China; filling large orders directly from the factory; maintaining an outsourced fulfillment center in Shenzhen, China, to supply small and sample sales from all over the world; and managing the company's supply chain.

Nokero's Chinese supplier is an established factory that has significant experience and scale in consumer electronics. In solar-powered consumer electronic products alone, the supplier produces more than 30 million pieces of solar products every year. The supplier's clients include Costco, Walmart, Home Depot, Lowe's, and other major retail customers in the United States and Europe. Nokero maintains its headquarters in Denver, Colorado, where the company oversees sales and marketing, business development, web-based sales, and overall administration of the business.

Creating Groundswell Support

Widespread and favorable coverage by traditional and social media outlets has been instrumental in getting the Nokero story out to as many people as possible. A key moment came with a six-minute daytime television segment featuring Katsaros and Nokero with Ali Velshi on the CNN show "The Big Eye." Not only did the coverage reach a global audience, it helped legitimize Nokero to those who were interested in solar lighting in general and Nokero's products in particular.

Nokero has benefited from dozens of stories by traditional print media and TV networks and hundreds of stories from new and social media, including sources from abroad such as *O Globo* (Brazil), *Sydney Times* (Australia), Air France, and Sudwestrundfunk (Germany). In a story entitled "A Solar Light Bulb May Light the Way," *The New York Times* noted that "Where Nokero's bulb appears to break ground is in its design; it is small enough to carry, self-contained, highly durable and features a replaceable battery." In another article, "The Power of Light," *The Denver Post* lauded the environmental, health, and safety benefits of Nokero's products and the social entrepreneurial aspects of the company's business model. These major stories resulted in a boost in traffic to Nokero's website and new orders for samples, as well as inquiries from prospective distributors.

Social media, particularly blogs, have been a powerful way for the company to create community groundswell support. In July 2010, an influential London businessman offered support to the company, an offer that led to an endorsement of Nokero's products by popular soccer star Didier Drogba. Social media have also been instrumental in creating awareness and mobilizing community participation in social initiatives championed by Nokero and other partners. For example, Nokero has partnered with Project C.U.R.E. on a buy-give program. Under this program, customers who buy a solar light bulb from Nokero can give a second light bulb to Project C.U.R.E. that the latter will distribute to people in need throughout the world.

Similarly, filmmaker Kurt Mann's organization, American Green, brought light bulbs to Haiti to help victims who have been devastated by the country's earthquake. Nokero and American Green have jointly set up a program, "The Gift of Light," for people to donate light bulbs to Haiti. Mann also filmed a short video during one of his recent visits to Haiti to document how Nokero's products have helped the people of Haiti and the world's poor by providing ready access to light. Nokero and third parties have used this video widely to help tell the company's story. Nokero has also been quick to respond to natural calamities, such as Typhoon Haiyan in the Philippines or Hurricane Sandy in the U.S. East Coast, by donating solar bulbs to victims, as well as instituting a program that led to the donation of these solar bulbs.

Growing the Business

Opportunities in Working with Governments and International Organizations

Several governments, international nongovernmental organizations, and international agencies have approached Katsaros and Nokero on a number of potential large-scale partnerships and projects. The governments of Mexico and Congo are pursuing the idea of buying Nokero's products for distribution to people in their respective countries who are earning less than $2 per day (i.e., bottom of the pyramid consumers) and do not have access to electricity. Through a partner in the Philippines, Nokero is exploring how best to provide its solar light bulbs to school children from poor families who still rely on kerosene lanterns. Nokero also partnered with the government of Indonesia to deliver solar lights to remote areas in Indonesia where it was difficult to set up complex power installations, providing power to 2.5 million people.

Nokero has also initiated discussions with international agencies, such as the United Nations, USAID, and various international foundations. While governments and international organization sales represent attractive opportunities for Nokero, they have posed three major challenges. First, the sales cycle in these organizations tends to be long and requires specialized skills and major business development resources. To address this challenge, Nokero has brought on board a consultant who is knowledgeable and has networked with these kinds of entities.

Second, the company would have to significantly scale production to fill larger orders from these governments. The governments that Nokero has been dealing with have talked about buying not thousands but *millions* of light bulbs. In addition, these governments are also likely to pressure Nokero to lower its price. Third, selling to these governments portends production and supply-chain challenges. Katsaros is also anticipating that governments that place large orders from Nokero would require the company to produce or assemble its products locally.

Opportunities in the Social Enterprise Sector

As previously mentioned, Nokero has been engaged in partnership programs with various social enterprises, such as Project C.U.R.E. (Commission on Urgent Relief and Equipment), Elephant Energy, Earthspark International, Shelterbox, Child Fund, and Power the World. As a case in point, Nokero and Project C.U.R.E. began the Lights for Life Campaign in 2010 whereby Nokero solar bulbs were added to the C.U.R.E. Kits for Kids (i.e., shoebox-sized kits of everyday health-care supplies, including bandages, antibiotic ointments, and insect repellent) and provided to parents who might not otherwise have access to an everyday medicine cabinet.

In contrast to working with governments and international organizations, partnerships with social enterprises entail a different set of challenges for Nokero. The programs championed by these partners are quite diverse, the customers that they serve are widely dispersed, and their order amounts tend to be smaller, although purchases are made more frequently. All of these considerations require different order and fulfillment mechanisms in Nokero's supply chain. While these processes may be more demanding, Katsaros is committed to working with micro-business and the social enterprise sector, since serving the people that these enterprises reach out to is at the core of Nokero's mission.

Opportunities in Commercial Channels

Nokero has driven sales through the commercial channel in two ways: through direct, web-based sales and through licensed distributors. Customers order directly through Nokero's website (Nokero.com) and pay using a credit card or an account through PayPal. Once an order is placed and payment is verified, the order is added to a sales spreadsheet and is exported nightly to Nokero's fulfillment center, which handles the order deliveries. Nokero fills order using Hong Kong Post or Singapore Post. The customer can then log on to Nokero's website to track the shipment of their package, usually with FedEx or UPS, and order history by entering the e-mail address that they used to place the order.

Since 2011, Nokero has been successful in selling tens of thousands of dollars of light bulbs to more than 120 countries through its website. Accordingly, one major opportunity that Katsaros sees in this channel is sales conversion (i.e., converting people who have placed sample orders to sign up as distributors). Nokero would like to put in place a strategy or process for such sales conversion other than a form on its website that invites people to apply to become distributors.

The company's largest customers are distributors, associations, and individuals that have ordered thousands of light bulbs, including Anzocare (South African Alternative Energy Association) and major individual distributors from India, Kenya, Zambia, Ghana, and Fiji. Additional distributors are in place in Afghanistan, Australia, Nigeria, Central America, Cote d'Ivoire, Mali, Burkina Faso, and Vietnam. Large commercial orders are filled directly from Nokero's factory in China via the port of Shenzhen, China. Nokero's outsourced fulfillment partner in Shenzhen, China, serves smaller orders.

Addressing Supply-Chain Issues

As previously mentioned, Katsaros understands that the success of Nokero's business hinges on its ability to address critical supply-chain issues. Katsaros and his Hong Kong partners must ensure that the company is ready to fill both large and concentrated orders from government and international organizations, as well as sample and small order sales from hundreds of customers that are geographically dispersed. At this point, Nokero needs to evaluate whether it should bring on board a second or third supplier that will support its major supplier partner in China. Moreover, it needs to evaluate the locations of the company's fulfillment centers.

In addition, Katsaros needs to address some operational issues related to supply-chain management. These include:

1. *Payments and Pricing of Shipping Charges.* Currently, customers who order through the website pay by credit card or PayPal. However, PayPal is not accepted in all countries, particularly in some markets that represent attractive markets for Nokero in Asia and Africa. In addition, determining the correct amount to charge for shipping has been a challenge since Nokero's fulfillment center does not provide a live feed with updated international pricing of shipping charges, and in general it is extremely difficult to reliably estimate the cost of shipping small orders to all the regions of the world.
2. *Order Tracking.* Tracking information usually stops once the package has left China (i.e., the Chinese factory location or fulfillment center in Shenzhen), making the tracking information limited and less useful.
3. *Timely Delivery.* Orders are filled and shipped in a timely manner from Nokero's factory and fulfillment center. However, the delivery process relies heavily on the timeliness and reliability of the postal system in the receiving country. In some instances, it has taken months for a sample or small order to be delivered to the customer.
4. *Last Mile Issue.* Often Nokero's customers are in remote locations that cannot be accessed by regular postal delivery. Even social enterprises and government organizations that partner with Nokero find it challenging to reach

international banking, and First Security had a trading room where they could provide foreign-exchange services and trade-related collections and payments for clients. With the merger, however, many of the more interesting businesses shifted to San Francisco, and the three could see the writing on the wall.

THE START-UP OF GPS

In 2002, with the help of some key investors, Manbeian, Langston, and Gibbons formed GPS Capital Markets Inc. Realizing there was a niche market in foreign exchange that was no longer being served in the Intermountain West, they struck out on their own with a business model they believed could be successful.

Bringing investors on board, particularly their large clients and brokers, was essential to their success because they needed the necessary credit backing and reputation to enter the wholesale market. Jason Langston noted that "90 percent of the transactions [we've] done in the past wouldn't have happened without these credible investors." However, GPS has been able to move beyond the help of its initial investors due to a strong working capital position.

TARGET MARKET AND CLIENT STRATEGY

To compete effectively in the market, GPS initially decided to target small and medium-sized companies (SMEs) and focus on serving those that had significant foreign-exchange needs, but not their own foreign-exchange team. They started out by providing the regular services that commercial banks offer, believing that their expertise and low overhead would help them outbid the larger banks for their business. At first, they offered traditional inbound and outbound payments—areas in which they excelled at First Security Bank. Such payments are the basic needs of firms that are going to receive, or are required to pay invoices in a different currency.

GPS, however, was finding it difficult to obtain clients. The first choice for most companies when it comes to foreign exchange is to use a commercial bank with which they already have a good relationship and which provides traditional banking services, including inbound and outbound payments. GPS has overcome this obstacle by visiting potential clients personally and building an open and transparent relationship. Travel to major market cities outside the Rocky Mountain region makes this more expensive, of course, but it has paid off because the advisers have developed relationships and obtained new clients. Some competitive advantages GPS has over the commercial banks are lower transaction costs, 100 percent transparency, and customizing solutions to satisfy customer needs.

Commercial banks have so many different departments and services that the foreign-exchange transactions tend to be more expensive in order to meet the overhead. Also, the banks look at foreign exchange as a potential area for earning a lot of money, so they price aggressively to build their profits. GPS is smaller and more specialized in the foreign-exchange market, so it can keep its costs low and pass on lower prices to companies.

Until the Internet brought more transparency to foreign-exchange markets, companies often didn't know how much banks or brokers were making on foreign-exchange transactions. GPS has adopted complete transparency with its clients, disclosing to them how much it will make on the deal.

While commercial banks want to sell standardized services—one size fits all—GPS focuses on satisfying the individual foreign-exchange needs of clients. Managers discuss needs and strategies with clients and come up with innovative solutions resulting in more satisfactory foreign-exchange transactions. These strategies have helped GPS grow significantly since its inception.

Thomson Reuters and Bloomberg play an important role in the business of GPS, with their powerful analytical tools, market information, real-time pricing, and a trading platform. In addition, the services are essential for trying to price more complex foreign-exchange products such as options. Despite the high cost of subscribing to these services, GPS decided to use both.

STRATEGIC MOVES

In order to keep growing, GPS has faced several challenges. The first is the range of services. If GPS had stuck with its initial goal of providing traditional foreign-exchange services, it would have opened itself up to significant competition with the banks and other market entrants. The key was to find ways to move clientele upstream with other value-added services, while the problem was to decide what areas to enter and where to find the expertise.

A second risk is its target market. Given the merger and acquisition activity in the United States, could GPS continue to maintain its client base, or would its clients get bought out by larger firms? If that were to happen, GPS would have to figure out how to sell its expertise to larger clients who had no experience or track record with them. However, as they examined their customer base, they realized that commercial banks were becoming more selective on their market segments, paying less attention to small and mid-market firms, a market space where GPS has a natural advantage.

A third risk is the government regulations. The regulatory environment of the foreign-exchange trade is intense and changes frequently, both in the United States and abroad. The Dodd–Frank Wall Street Reform and Consumer Protection Act was signed into law in the United States on July 21, 2010, with potentially significant ramifications to GPS's business in the foreign-currency derivatives market. In order to reduce risk, Dodd-Frank requires more capital, but that means the capital is tied up and not able to work efficiently for GPS. Another area of regulatory concern is Europe's push to ensure data integrity and data ownership. Another area of regulatory concern is cybersecurity, especially in the area of foreign exchange transactions where it is necessary to be able to identify the chain of a transaction from beginning to end.

THE GLOBAL FINANCIAL CRISIS: CHALLENGES AND OPPORTUNITIES

When the global economic crisis hit in 2008, it became obvious that *counterparty risk* was a real issue: the risk that the other party to an agreement—in this case, a money center bank entering into a foreign-exchange agreement—might default. Many of GPS's clients or potential clients became nervous as one major money center bank after another ran into problems in late 2008. Because GPS was on sound financial footing, many companies flocked to it to handle their foreign-exchange transactions, which caused a large spike in activity. In addition, GPS's lower rates were more attractive. As the global economy began to contract, investors realized how important it was to squeeze out any savings they could, which played right into the hands of GPS.

However, as soon as the U.S. Fed decided to bail out the banks and reduce the counterparty risk, many of GPS's new clients realized they needed to go back to the banks, given how tight credit was. GPS was able, however, to retain some of them.

EXPANDED SERVICES: A KEY TO FUTURE GROWTH

Al Manbeian and Ryan Gibbons are now the Managing Partners of GPS, and as they looked at their business, they realized that the key to their future was to develop a broader base of services to their clients. So they decided to focus on their strength—corporate foreign exchange—and provide expanded services in global business risk management. The general idea of trading currencies to satisfy their initial core business of import and export transactions was simple. Some transactions went beyond exports and imports and involved derivatives to protect against future risks. With their connection to Bloomberg and Reuters, they had the capabilities necessary to enter into any transaction the client needed.

Then, as they began to work with SME companies with operations around the world, they realized that many of these companies were spending a lot of money making trades. Analyzing the cash flows in different currencies, it was easy to see that as their clients' markets and the currencies in which they operated increased, they had to enter into more and more foreign-exchange transactions.

FXpert

GPS developed proprietary software called FXpert to help its clients monitor foreign-exchange flows and determine how to save money on transactions. FXpert, a secure online platform, allows clients to make FX payments through SWIFT, an electronic trading platform utilized in over 125 countries; manage balance sheet hedging, intercompany netting, balance reporting, and cash flow forecasting. After identifying the timing and nature of the cash flows through a specialized audit, a GPS financial adviser proposes an effective hedging solution that GPS can provide. The solution might be as simple as reducing the number of foreign-currency transactions or as complex as hedging some of the exposures using forwards, options, or futures contracts.

The global risk-management business also offers foreign accounts receivable reviews, worldwide business consultation on finance methods, dispute resolution in solving payment disputes, international loan packaging, and letters of credit. As it has developed these services, GPS has had to expand its expertise base to include an understanding of complex accounting rules on derivatives, complex financial hedging strategies, and software development.

ADDITIONAL STRATEGIC MOVES

Given the risky foreign-exchange environment, GPS has shifted some of its efforts to work as an agent or broker with clients' banks and use its proprietary software to find business solutions for clients to reduce foreign-exchange risks and lower the costs of trading foreign exchange. With its knowledge of the markets, GPS is able to negotiate with clients' banks to get the best possible exchange rate on a transaction and earn a little in the process.

In addition to technical expertise, GPS has developed a solid marketing strategy, continuing to focus on SMEs while expanding its client base by setting up additional offices in Los Angeles, Phoenix, Dallas, Atlanta, Charlotte, Waltham (Massachusetts), London, Sydney, and Melbourne. Entering London opened significant opportunities for GPS in the UK and the rest of Europe. Not only can it pick up new customers in Europe, it can also represent U.S. clients in Europe more effectively.

As GPS continues to expand, it must constantly refine its message. From a sales point of view, its managers need to make sure they understand what CFOs and treasurers need to know about the firm and what it has to offer. And they need to figure that out for the different regulatory environments in which GPS operates. In London they face competition that only offers traditional payments clearance, but it is nevertheless difficult even to get an audience with CFOs to explain how they can help in ways that go way beyond payments clearances to involve risk management in global capital markets.

QUESTIONS

19-1 What is the unique market niche for GPS, and what does it have to offer compared to larger banks and other financial institutions?

19-2 What do you think are the major obstacles to success for GPS in Europe and Australia?

THE CROSSROADS OF ACCOUNTING AND FINANCE

19-1 Explain the crossroads of accounting and finance

As noted in Chapter 11, the Chief Financial Officer (CFO) of a company is responsible for overseeing the financial activities of a company.[2] Working under the CFO, the accounting side of the business is managed by the controller who has responsibility for accounting-related

CONCEPT CHECK

We discussed **foreign currency exchange rates** and the ways in which they affect the operations of an MNE in Chapter 9 (pages 234–236). Here we explain the responsibilities of the CFO in overseeing a company's closely related financial and accounting functions. As we'll see, financial management deals with the effects of exchange rates on such financial-statement items as receivables and payables.

activities, providing management with relevant and reliable information, and preparing information for the external users of financial information. A good internal control system in a company leaves the accounting and reporting to the controller and the management of assets to the treasurer. You don't want to have the person who writes the checks also recording the checks. That's how money disappears.

Let's be honest. If you are not majoring in accounting or finance, why should you even be interested in this chapter? You might have struggled in your accounting and finance classes and were happy to be rid of them. But you need to realize that if you don't understand the international accounting and financial challenges of the company you work for, even at the most basic level, you may make poor decisions. Without accurate and current information from the controller, it is very difficult for the treasurer to manage the assets, such as cash, effectively. So we'll see in this chapter how the accounting and finance functions are closely related, with each relying on the other to fulfill its responsibilities. The actual and potential flow of assets across national boundaries complicates the finance and accounting functions. So MNEs must learn to cope with differing inflation rates, exchange-rate changes, currency controls, expropriation risks, customs duties, tax rates and methods of determining taxable income, levels of sophistication of local accounting personnel, and local as well as home-country reporting requirements.

WHAT ARE THE RESPONSIBILITIES OF THE CONTROLLER?

The controller is essential in providing information to financial decision-makers.

The controller of an MNE must be concerned about a range of issues dealing with corporate strategy utilizing accounting skills.

The role of the company controller is critical to providing useful and timely information to management and external stakeholders. If the shares of the company are traded on the stock market, the controller has to generate financial information that satisfies the reporting requirements of the stock market, based on the accounting standards that have to be used. If the company is an MNE and lists its shares on multiple stock exchanges, the controller has to generate financial information that satisfies the reporting requirements in different countries. In essence, the controller has to manage data based on financial information from all over the world and be able to generate myriad reports in different formats and different currencies. For internal purposes, the controller has to prepare specialized information that helps management to evaluate potential acquisitions abroad, dispose of a subsidiary or a division, manage cash flow, hedge currency and interest-rate risks, assist in tax planning, and make sure that processes and procedures are followed correctly through a strong internal control system.

DIFFERENCES IN FINANCIAL STATEMENTS INTERNATIONALLY

Both the form and the content of financial statements are different in different countries.

One problem an MNE faces is varying accounting standards and practices around the world. Financial statements among countries differ in form (or format) and content (or substance). As illustrated below, U.S. MNEs use the *balance format to prepare their balance sheets:*

$$\text{Assets} = \text{Liabilities} + \text{Shareholders' equity}$$

In the United States, the assets start with the most liquid assets, such as cash, accounts and notes receivable, and inventory, and then add long-term or fixed assets. These are funded by current liabilities, plus long-term debt, plus shareholders' equity. However, European companies are more likely to start with the least liquid assets (those that are harder to convert into cash quickly) followed by liquid assets. Swedish retailer H&M, which is the subject of the ending case in the chapter, uses the following format:

$$\text{Noncurrent assets} + \text{Current assets} = (\text{Shareholders' equity} + \text{Noncurrent liabilities} + \text{Current liabilities})$$

The balance sheet for British retailer Marks and Spencer uses the following format, which is very common among British firms:

$$\text{Noncurrent assets} + \text{Current assets} - \text{Current liabilities} - \text{Noncurrent liabilities} = \text{Total equity}$$

The British format illustrates how much total equity is left after assets are sold and liabilities are liquidated. No one format is better than another, but the logic in each country is often based on the format that the stock markets dictate. However, it is often confusing to see for the first time financial statement formats that are different what you are accustomed to in your own country.

DIFFERENCES IN THE CONTENT OF FINANCIAL INFORMATION

The types of financial information required in different countries can differ, while companies also have to consider who their audience is: Are they providing financial information only for the local market, or also for users from the broader global capital markets? Companies that list on stock exchanges usually provide several types of financial information, such as an income statement, a balance sheet, a statement of shareholders' equity, a cash-flow statement, and detailed footnotes, in their annual report. The depth of disclosure of information, especially in footnotes, is a major issue in terms of content. Providers of financial information for the broader investing community need to consider the following three factors:

Major reporting issues:
- Language
- Currency
- Underlying accounting standards on which the financial statements are based

1. Language
2. Currency
3. Underlying accounting standards on which the statements are based

Language Differences If companies are going to provide their annual reports in a language different from their home language, which language do they use? English tends to be the first choice of companies choosing to raise capital on multiple stock exchanges. For example, Sweden's H&M provides its annual reports in Swedish and English. German company Daimler provides information in English and German. In addition to language, companies have to deal with differences in terms. For example, U.S. companies use "inventory" to refer to what British firms call "stocks." However, U.S. firms use "stocks" to refer to "shares of stock," whereas British firms use "shares."

Major sources of influence on accounting are capital markets, the cultural and regulatory environments, global standards settings, and other users.

Currency Differences Companies around the world prepare their financial statements in different currencies—Daimler's are in euros, H&M's in Swedish kronor, Coca-Cola in U.S. dollars, and so on. So if you are trying to calculate financial results in dollars when the statements are in Swedish kronor, you have to figure out which exchange rate to use. Analysts often use the average exchange rate for the year for the income statement and the year-end exchange rate for the balance sheet. Sometimes companies provide information in their footnotes or elsewhere in the annual report on the impact of exchange rates on earnings, but exchange rates are so readily available that it is no problem to translate financial statements from one currency to another.

Underlying Accounting Standards A major hurdle in raising capital in different countries is dealing with widely varying accounting and disclosure requirements. Although this problem has decreased significantly in recent years as International Financial Reporting Standards (IFRS) are being adopted by more and more countries and their stock exchanges, some countries care more about those differences than others. Most countries, especially in Europe, also may apply one set of accounting standards for consolidated groups while using another set for the parent company in the group. In this situation, the individual companies must use local accounting standards that are usually tied to legal requirements and are the basis for tax accounting. Consolidated financial statements include financial information not only about the parent company but also for all of the subsidiaries within the corporate group. These consolidated statements are most oftenused for capital markets and not for tax purposes, and are prepared by a different set of standards, such as IFRS. U.S. companies do not have the same situation. They disclose only consolidated financial statements using U.S. accounting standards. Any differences that arise for U.S. companies because of tax requirements are reconciled in their consolidated financial statements.

CONCEPT CHECK

In discussing "Legal Issues Facing International Companies" on page 82 in Chapter 3, we survey the various ways in which local legal standards can affect the way foreign firms function on a day-to-day basis. Naturally, these standards include accounting standards, and here we emphasize that attitudes toward, and more importantly regulations concerning accounting practices vary widely from country to country.

FACTORS AFFECTING ACCOUNTING OBJECTIVES, STANDARDS, AND PRACTICES

19-2 Identify the major factors affecting the development of accounting objectives, standards, and practices

Figure 19.1 identifies some of the factors affecting the development of accounting standards and practices both domestically and internationally. Although all the factors shown are significant, their importance varies by country. Capital markets refer to equity and debt

FIGURE 19.1 Sources of Influence on Accounting Standards and Practices

Every aspect of the accounting process is influenced by a variety of internal and external factors, and they are all potentially important. The degree of importance will vary by country.

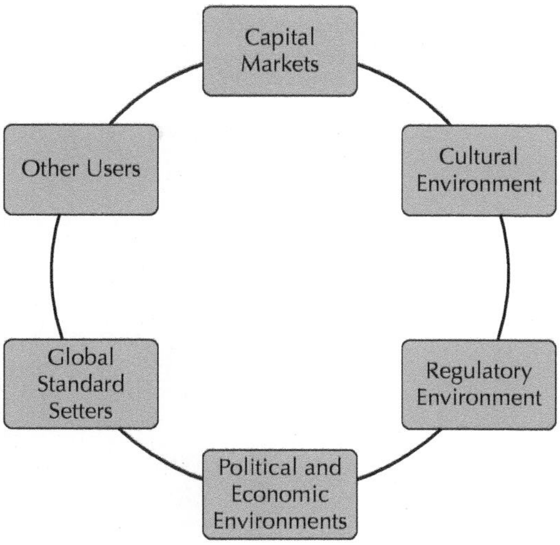

Culture influences measurement and disclosure practices:

- Measurement—how to value assets
- Disclosure—the presentation of information and discussion of results

markets. As noted in Chapter 11, lenders are considered to be bond holders, banks, and private equity funds. Equity market investors are influential in the United States and the United Kingdom, but creditors, primarily banks, have traditionally had more influence in Germany and Switzerland. That has changed over time, however, and companies that need large amounts of capital to expand have to rely more on capital markets to supplement what they can raise from banks.

As we will discuss in more detail below, cultural issues cut across all countries and strongly influence the development of accounting. The regulatory environment, including legal and tax systems, is very influential, especially in countries with historically weak stock markets. However, the regulatory environment is also influential on stock markets. Certain international factors also have weight, such as former colonial influence, foreign investment, and the influence of regional economic agreements (e.g., the EU).

CONCEPT CHECK

Chapter 2 is devoted to illustrating the many ways in which local culture shapes the environment in which international business is conducted from country to country. Here we point out that culture also affects differences in approaches to accounting systems and policies. In Chapter 2, we cite Geert Hofstede among the researchers who have studied national differences in managerial attitudes and preferences, and here we use applications of Hofstede's findings to studies of work-situation behavior as a means of shedding light on the effect of cultural differences on accounting standards and practices.

CULTURAL DIFFERENCES IN ACCOUNTING

The differences in measurement and disclosure practices among countries are of special interest to international investors. *Measurement* means how companies value assets, including inventory and fixed assets, whereas *disclosure* refers to how and what information companies provide and the level of detail and transparency.

Culture is discussed in great detail in Chapter 2, but much of the research on the interaction between culture and accounting is initially based on Hofstede's research on the structural elements of culture, particularly those that most strongly affect behavior in the work situations of organizations and institutions.[3] Hofstede's work was extended into the accounting area by Gray, which resulted in country classifications according to disclosure and measurement principles—specifically, secrecy/transparency and optimism/conservatism.[4]

Secrecy and transparency refer to the degree to which corporations disclose information to the public. Optimism and conservatism refer to the degree of caution companies display in valuing assets and recognizing income.

The Secrecy–Transparency/Optimism–Conservatism Matrix Figure 19.2 provides some historical context depicting the accounting practices of various groupings of countries within a matrix of the cultural values of secrecy–transparency and optimism–conservatism. With respect to accounting secrecy and transparency notice the degree to which one would expect companies to disclose information to the public. Historically, countries such as Germany, Switzerland, and Japan tended to rely on bank financing and have less disclosure (illustrating the cultural value of secrecy) than did the more transparent U.S. and British companies (Anglo-Saxon in Figure 19.2) due to their reliance on stock markets. The classification of countries in Figure 19.2 represents a point in time, and countries are always changing due to the increased importance of and demands by capital markets for more information and the influence of global accounting standards, such as IFRS. However, the importance of

FIGURE 19.2 A Disclosure/Assessment Matrix for National Accounting Systems

The vertical axis reflects practices according to transparency versus secrecy (the extent to which companies in a country disclose information to the public). The horizontal axis reflects accounting practices according to optimism versus conservatism (the degree of caution taken by companies when it comes to valuing assets and recognizing income). Note that, not surprisingly, transparency and optimism tend to go hand in hand, as do secrecy and conservatism.

Source: Based on Lee H. Radebaugh, Sidney J. Gray, and Ervin L. Black, *International Accounting and Multinational Enterprises*, 6th ed. (New York: John Wiley & Sons, 2002): 51.

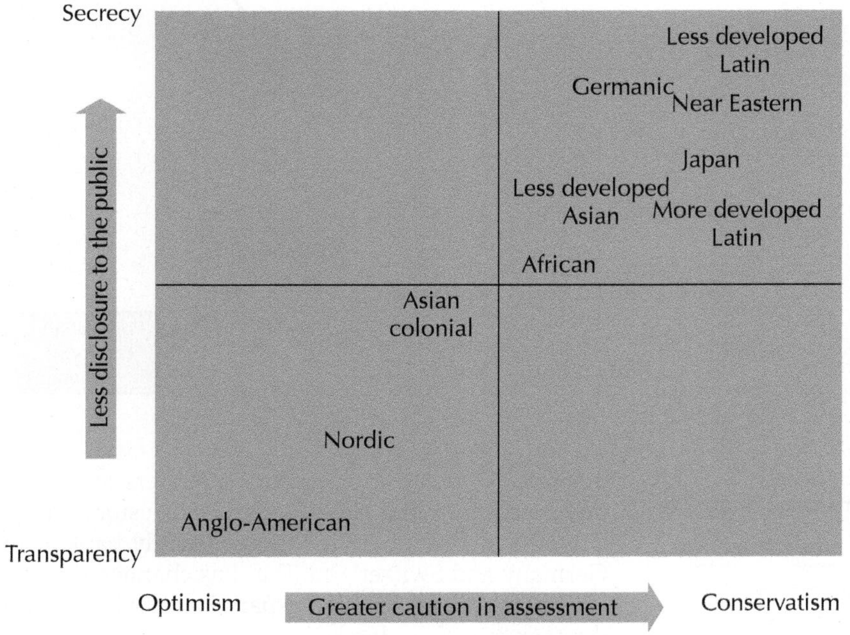

understanding how different countries were in terms of measurement and disclosure illustrates the complexity of moving everyone to one set of global accounting standards.

Optimism and conservatism (in an accounting sense, not political) are the degrees of caution that companies exhibit in valuing assets and recognizing income. The more conservative countries tend to understate assets and income, whereas optimistic countries tend to be more liberal in their recognition of income. Historically, banks have been a primary source of funding for companies in countries with weak capital markets, often accompanied by a strong influence on tax accounting.

As a result, those companies tend to be very conservative both when recording profits that keep them from paying taxes and when declaring dividends to pile up cash reserves to service their bank debts. However, as German MNCs in particular outgrew the ability of banks to provide the majority of their funding needs, they were forced to adopt accounting standards and reporting practices for their consolidated financial statements more in line with global capital markets, becoming less secret and more transparent. In contrast, U.S. and British companies are more optimistic and want to show earning power to impress and attract investors.

INTERNATIONAL STANDARDS AND GLOBAL CONVERGENCE

19-3 Describe international accounting standards and the process of global convergence

MUTUAL RECOGNITION VERSUS RECONCILIATION

British and U.S. companies are optimistic when recognizing income, whereas Japanese and continental European companies are more conservative.

Before the rise in importance of global capital markets and the move to a common set of accounting standards, it was common for many countries to apply the principle of **mutual recognition**, whereby a regulator, such as the German Stock Exchange, would accept financial statements provided in U.S. GAAP of a U.S. company wanting to list securities in Germany. Prior to the requirement in 2005 that EU companies provide financial statements prepared according to IFRS, some German companies such as Daimler and Deutsche Bank prepared their consolidated financial statements according to U.S. GAAP, as permitted at the time by German law. This made it easier for them to list on the New York Stock Exchange. However, they dropped this practice and moved to IFRS in 2007.

Major approaches to dealing with accounting and reporting differences:

- Mutual recognition
- Reconciliation to local accounting standards
- Issue financial statements according to IFRS
- Convergence to a common set of accounting standards

In general, the United States requires that non-U.S. and non-Canadian foreign private issuers provide financial information to the SEC prepared according to U.S. GAAP or IFRS as established by the International Accounting Standards Board. However, a foreign company that prefers to provide financial information according to their home-country accounting standards, must provide a statement of **reconciliation**. In this case, the company usually lists American Depositary Receipts (ADRs) on a U.S. exchange and then reconciles its financial statements prepared with home-country accounting standards with U.S. GAAP in a special statement called Form 20-F. This is the approach Daimler used before it adopted U.S. GAAP for its consolidated financial statements. Since 2007, however, the SEC permits foreign issuers to list without a reconciliation statement as long as their financial statements are prepared in accordance with full IFRS. In response, the EU announced in 2008 that it would allow U.S. firms to continue to list on EU stock markets using U.S. GAAP, given the progress of convergence and the fact that U.S. GAAP and IFRS are similar for most standards.[5]

Major forces leading to establishing global accounting standards:

- Investor orientation
- Global integration of capital markets
- MNEs' need for foreign capital
- Regional political and economic harmonization
- MNEs' desire to reduce accounting and reporting costs
- Convergence efforts of standards-setting bodies

Despite the many differences in accounting standards and practices around the world, a number of forces are leading to **convergence**:

- A movement to provide information compatible with the needs of investors
- The global integration of capital markets, which means easier and faster access to investment opportunities around the world and, therefore, the need for more comparable financial data
- The need of MNEs to raise capital outside their home-country capital markets while generating as few different financial statements as possible
- Regional political and economic harmonization, such as the efforts of the EU, which affect accounting as well as trade and investment issues
- Pressure from MNEs for more uniform standards to allow greater ease and reduced costs in general reporting in each country

THE FIRST STEPS IN ESTABLISHING IFRS

Established in 1973, the International Accounting Standards Committee (IASC) began working toward harmonizing standards by issuing a set of International Accounting Standards (IAS) that they hoped anyone in the world could use. Its original standards had a strong capital-markets focus so that they could be used worldwide to facilitate the free flow of capital. With such a goal, the IASC tended to lean more toward the capital market traditions of the United States and the United Kingdom rather than the legal- and tax-based systems of Germany and France. The early standards were often very superficial, with too many options to capture the support of everyone.

The International Organization of Securities Commissions accepted a core set of accounting standards issued by the IASB in which securities regulators can be confident.

The turning point in the significance of IAS came in 1995, when the **International Organization of Securities Commissions (IOSCO)** announced publicly it would endorse IAS if the IASC developed a set of core standards acceptable to it. IOSCO is significant because it comprises the regulators of most of the world's stock markets, including the SEC in the United States. In May 2000, the IASC completed a core set of standards acceptable to IOSCO, and securities market regulators began the process of convincing their standard setters to adopt these standards, called International Financial Reporting Standards (IFRS).

THE INTERNATIONAL ACCOUNTING STANDARDS BOARD

In March 2001, the IASC was reorganized into the International Accounting Standards Committee Foundation (now called the IFRS Foundation) with the **International Accounting Standards Board (IASB)** as the standard-setting body, taking over the standard-setting functions of the IASC.[6] The IASB is composed of 14 members who are standard setters, preparers, auditors, users, and academics with broad geographic representation from the Asia/Oceania region, Europe, the Americas, and Africa. One member is "at large" and is serving as the Vice-Chair of the IASB.[7]

International Financial Reporting Standards (IFRS) When the IASB was organized, all of the old standards from the IASC were adopted, and the Board began to review and upgrade each standard. Then the Board began to issue the new **International Financial Reporting Standards (IFRS)**; thus, when we use the term *IFRS*, we refer to the new standards as well as the old IAS.

The IASB is harmonizing accounting standards through issuing International Financial Reporting Standards (IFRS).

The objectives of the IFRS Foundation and the IASB include developing "a single set of high-quality, understandable, enforceable, and globally accepted international financial reporting standards (IFRSs) through its standard-setting body, the IASB, and [promoting] the use and rigorous application of those standards."[8] As of 2020, 144 out of a total of 166 countries and jurisdictions require the use of IFRS for domestic listed companies in their capital markets. Of the remaining countries and jurisdictions, some permit the use of IFRS or are moving toward the adoption of IFRS. The United States is one notable exception because it requires GAAP for financial reporting, although it allows foreign companies that list their securities on the U.S. stock exchanges to use IFRS.[9]

FASB and IASB are trying to converge their standards through removing differences in existing standards and engaging in joint projects to develop new standards.

The Relationship Between the FASB and the IASB The U.S. **Financial Accounting Standards Board (FASB)** and IASB have been working closely to achieve a convergence of accounting standards. In 2002, they issued the Norwalk Agreement, pledging their best efforts to remove individual differences between U.S. GAAP and IFRS and undertake joint projects to develop future standards.[10] Convergence implies a goal and a path to achieving it. The goal is to eliminate differences in accounting standards between FASB and the IASB. The convergence process (or path) takes several forms. Initially, the two boards identified standards that could easily be converged. Once these standards were converged, they decided to jointly develop new standards where existing standards were too far apart. Finally, they identified entirely new standards, which would be jointly developed.[11]

However, standard-setting in the United States depends on the cooperation of the Securities and Exchange Commission (SEC), whose mission is to "protect investors, maintain fair, orderly, and efficient markets, and facilitate capital formation."[12] Although the SEC does not set accounting standards, it empowers the FASB to do so because companies—both foreign and domestic—that want to raise capital in the United States must follow the SEC guidelines. Also, the SEC determines which accounting standards can be used by issuers on the U.S. stock exchanges as noted above. Convergence is complicated because it is both technical in terms of the quality of the standards as well as political.

The EU required adoption of IFRS in 2002, effective in 2005.

The European Response to Convergence The main body of financial reporting requirements for limited liability companies in the EU consists of two directives issued by the European Council. Thus, it is important to understand that IFRS and interpretations must be approved by the European Parliament and the European Council and adopted as an official regulation by the European Commission to have legal standing in the EU.[13] This illustrates the importance of the political process in IFRS adoption. Prior to the development of the IASB, the EU was working to harmonize reporting practices to better coordinate financial markets. To enhance that process, it supported the efforts of the IASB and, in the spring of 2002, directed its member countries to adopt IFRS by 2005. In the case of the EU, this meant that 7,000 publicly listed companies started using IFRS for their consolidated financial statements in 2005.[14] The two main reasons for the EU to push IFRS were to allow it to influence IASB standards and to avoid funding and developing a competing standard-setting body.[15] By working with the IASB, the EU would avoid relying on standards developed in the United States for capital market reporting. In one political decision, the EU suddenly made IFRS the most important set of accounting standards outside of standards issued by FASB in the United States.

Full application of IFRS in various countries and under various regulatory regimes is difficult to judge. The EU does not require companies to adhere to full IFRS, only those approved by the EU.

The EU has adopted most of the standards as written, but has "carved out" or suspended the standard on financial instruments due largely to political pressure from French banks. Thus the EU has its own version of IFRS, although the carve-out affects fewer than two dozen banks out of 8,000 listed companies in European markets.[16] As a result, European companies such as H&M, as described in the ending case, must state in their annual report that they apply IFRS "as adopted by the EU." That means that in the future, upon the EU's recommendation, its member companies can "opt out" or "carve out" certain standards, ending up with their own version of IFRS. Initial reactions of various parties to European firms' 2005 adoption of IFRS have been interesting. In fact, various interpretations and applications exist. Some firms use wide judgment in applying IFRS, while others use an adapted form with changes or alternative interpretations based on individual country accounting treatments.

POINT

Should U.S. Companies Be Allowed to Use IFRS?

YES A major issue for investors around the world is obtaining reliable, comparable financial-statement information for company evaluation and comparison. Creditors and other users also need this information for making well-informed decisions on a global basis. The IFRS Foundation views its standards as promoting transparency, accountability, and efficiency. As the composition of the business world has shifted from domestic economies to a global economy, the need for a single set of financial reporting standards has never been greater. IFRS are required for listed entities in 144 countries and territories, led by European Union, Canada, Australia, and New Zealand.

U.S. GAAP and IFRS are the two most recognized sets of standards today, and they are steadily becoming nearly identical to each other. The combined efforts of the IASB and the FASB in their convergence project have brought the two closer than ever before. The SEC currently allows foreign firms that list on U.S. exchanges to use IFRS for financial reporting and should allow U.S. firms as well. Not only would this make the United States more a part of the global economy, its companies could also raise more capital because investors in countries that use it would be more familiar and able to keep up with the single international set of standards.

U.S. investors would also benefit. They would become more familiar with the international standards and would feel more apt to invest in international companies. As the gap between IFRS and U.S. GAAP shrinks, the quality of the financial information presented under IFRS will not be lower than it has been under GAAP.

Many U.S. firms with international operations use IFRS abroad, so allowing IFRS to be used for U.S. reporting would reduce the costs of accounting for and reporting information to users. In addition, U.S. companies that acquire foreign companies that use IFRS would find it easier to use IFRS for all operations rather than convert the results of their acquired companies from IFRS to U.S. GAAP for reporting purposes.

COUNTERPOINT

Should U.S. Companies Be Allowed to Use IFRS?

NO It is unrealistic to assume that IFRS would be appropriate for the unique U.S. economic environment. As the largest economy in the world, with the largest and most sophisticated capital market, the United States should have the most stringent and transparent financial reporting standards in the world. Many companies around the globe continue to prepare their financial information in accordance with U.S. GAAP because it has historically been the world's most reliable set of standards, designed to present information that is both relevant and trustworthy. IFRS are far less comprehensive than GAAP, and the standards, though oriented to capital markets, cannot take into account specific issues important to U.S. capital markets. IFRS standards are less detailed and are not equipped to handle the accounting differences in different industries, which FASB deals with in the United States.

Allowing U.S. companies to use IFRS would impose tremendous costs on the nation's economy. Publicly traded firms would need trained employees proficient in IFRS application. U.S. accounting firms would be responsible for training their existing auditors in IFRS, hiring new employees and training them, or hiring existing IFRS experts. This training and/or hiring would impose tremendous burdens in both time and money on these firms, which would still be held responsible for meeting all the rigorous standards of the Public Company Accounting Oversight Board (PCAOB) and the Sarbanes–Oxley Act of 2002. Many contracts in the United States are based on U.S. GAAP, and it would be necessary to change nearly all of them to allow for the use of IFRS.

The differences between IFRS and U.S. GAAP, though narrowing, still exist. The standards are not directly comparable, which could mean trouble for investors who may have difficulty seeing the differences. Some of the newer IFRS standards are not consistent with GAAP, so there is unlikely to ever be convergence in those areas. In addition, multiple sets of IFRS seem to exist: (1) IFRS as issued by the IASB, (2) IFRS as adopted by the EU, and (3) IFRS as applied/adopted on an individual-country basis. How will investors ascertain which set is being used by various companies, and how will this information be comparable?

Just as politics enters into the adoption of IFRS in the EU, politics is important for U.S. GAAP. Since the SEC is a U.S. government entity whose five commissioners are appointed by the president,[17] it is impossible to believe that U.S. GAAP would be turned over to IFRS and the control of the IASB. Sovereignty, even over accounting, is not something the U.S. government would give up to an international organization over which it has some influence but not control.

TRANSACTIONS IN FOREIGN CURRENCIES

19-4 Demonstrate how companies account for foreign-currency transactions

When a company operates outside the domestic market, it must concern itself with the proper recording and subsequent accounting of assets, liabilities, revenues, and expenses that are measured or denominated in foreign currencies. These transactions can result from the purchase and sale of goods and services as well as the borrowing and lending of foreign currency.

RECORDING TRANSACTIONS

Anytime an importer has to pay for equipment or merchandise in a foreign currency, it must trade its own currency for that of the exporter to make the payment. Assume that Sundance Ski Lodge, a U.S. company, imports skis from a French supplier for €5,000 and agrees to pay in euros when the exchange rate is $1.4500/euro. Sundance records the following in its books:

Purchases	7,250	
Accounts payable		7,250
€ 5,000 @ 1.4500		

If Sundance pays immediately, there's no problem. But what happens if the exporter extends 30 days' credit to Sundance? If the rate changed to, say, $1.5000/euro by the time the payment was due, Sundance would record a final settlement as:

Accounts payable	7,250	
Foreign-exchange loss	250	
Cash		7,500

The merchandise stays at the original value of $7,250, but there is a difference between the dollar value of the account payable to the exporter ($7,250) and the actual number of dollars the importer must come up with to purchase the euros to pay the exporter ($7,500). The difference between the two accounts ($250) is the loss on foreign exchange and is recognized in the income statement.

Foreign-currency receivables and payables give rise to gains and losses whenever the exchange rate changes. Transaction gains and losses must be included in the income statement in the accounting period in which they arise.

The company that denominates the sale or purchase in the foreign currency (in this case, the importer) must recognize the gains and losses arising from foreign-currency transactions at the end of each accounting period. In the example here, assume that the end of the quarter has arrived and Sundance has still not paid the French exporter. The skis continue to be valued at $7,250, but the payable has to be updated to the new exchange rate of $1.5000/euro. The journal entry would be:

Foreign-exchange loss	250	
Accounts payable		250

The payable would now be worth $7,500. If settlement were made in the month following the end of the quarter and the exchange rate remained the same, the final entry would be:

Accounts payable	7,500	
Cash		7,500

If the U.S. company were an exporter and anticipated receiving foreign currency, the corresponding entries (using the same information as in the example here) would be:

Accounts receivable	7,250	
Sales		7,250
Cash	7,500	
Foreign-exchange gain		250
Accounts receivable		7,250

In this case, a gain results because the company received more cash than if it had collected its money immediately.

CORRECT PROCEDURES FOR U.S. COMPANIES

The FASB requires that U.S. companies report foreign-currency transactions at the original spot exchange rate and that subsequent gains and losses on foreign-currency receivables or payables be put on the income statement. The same procedure must be followed according to IFRS.

According to GAAP, U.S. companies must record the initial transaction at the spot exchange rate in effect on the transaction date and record receivables and payables on subsequent balance-sheet dates at the spot exchange rate on those dates. Any foreign-exchange gains and losses are recognized in the income statement in that period.[18] This is basically the same procedure required by the IASB as well as in IAS 21.[19]

TRANSLATING FOREIGN-CURRENCY FINANCIAL STATEMENTS

19-5 Determine how companies can translate foreign-currency financial statements

Translation—the process of restating foreign-currency financial statements.

Even though U.S.-based MNEs receive reports originally developed in a variety of different currencies, they eventually must end up with one set of financial statements in U.S. dollars to help management and investors understand their worldwide activities in a common currency. The process of restating foreign-currency financial statements into U.S. dollars is called **translation**. The combination of all of these translated financial statements into one is **consolidation**. The same concept exists for other countries, such as a British-based MNE that has to come up with a set of financial statements in British pounds. For the sake of illustration, we use a U.S.-based MNE.

Consolidation—the process of combining the translated financial statements of a parent and its subsidiaries into one set of financial statements.

Translation in the United States is a two-step process:

1. *Recast foreign-currency financial statements into statements consistent with U.S. GAAP.*
2. *Translate all foreign-currency amounts into U.S. dollars.* FASB Statement No. 52 describes how companies must translate their foreign-currency financial statements into dollars. All U.S. companies that list on a U.S. exchange must use Statement No. 52.

TRANSLATION METHODS

Statement No. 52 and IAS 21, the relevant translation standards issued by the FASB and the IASB, respectively, are basically the same in how they require MNEs to translate their foreign-currency financial statements into the currency of the parent's country. For simplicity's sake, we continue to use the example of a U.S.-based MNE that must translate its foreign-currency financial statements into U.S. dollars.

The functional currency is the currency of the primary economic environment in which the entity operates.

The temporal method applies when the parent's reporting currency is the functional currency.

The current-rate method applies when the local currency is the functional currency.

Two Methods: Current-Rate and Temporal Both standards allow companies to use either of two methods in the translation process: the **current-rate method** (called the *closing rate method* under IFRS) or the **temporal method**. The one the company chooses depends on the **functional currency** of the foreign operation, which is the currency of the primary economic environment in which that entity operates. Whichever method a company uses, it has to determine the proper exchange rate to translate the foreign-currency balances into U.S. dollars.

For example, one of Coca-Cola's largest operations outside the United States is in Japan. Its primary economic environment is Japan, and its functional currency is the Japanese yen. FASB identifies several factors that can help management determine the functional currency: cash flows, sales prices, sales market data, expenses, financing, and transactions with other entities within the corporate group. If the cash flows and expenses are primarily in the foreign operation's currency, that is the functional currency; if they are in the parent's currency, that is the functional currency.

If the functional currency (the Japanese yen in the case of Coca-Cola) is that of the local operating environment (Japan), the company must use the current-rate method, which provides that it translates all assets and liabilities at the current exchange rate, which is the spot exchange rate on the balance-sheet date. If Coca-Cola issues its balance sheet on December 31, the exchange rate it would use is the spot rate in Japanese yen on December 31. All income-statement items are translated at the average exchange rate, and owners' equity is translated at the rates in effect when the company issued capital stock and accumulated retained earnings. There are many ways to determine the average rate for the income statement, but Coca-Cola uses the monthly average exchange for each month.

FIGURE 19.3 Selecting a Translation Method

When an MNE receives reports from subsidiaries or branches located in different countries, the accounting department is faced with financial figures stated in different currencies. All foreign currency financial statements need to be translated in the currency of the parent company before preparing consolidated results. The functional currency, which may be either the currency of the economic environment in which the subsidiary or branch operates or the parent firm's currency, will determine the translation method that the company will use.

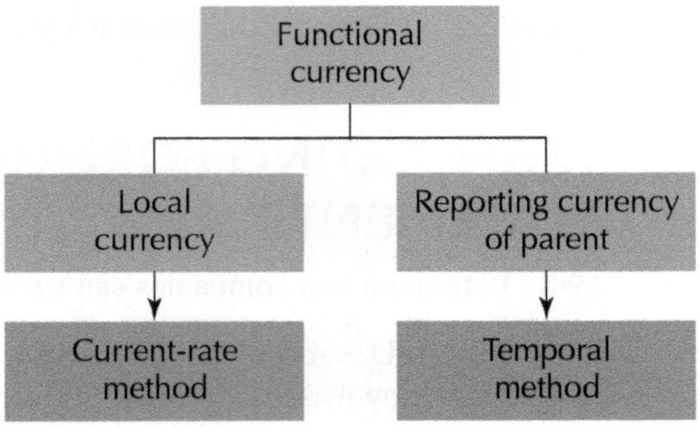

If the functional currency is the parent's currency, the MNE must use the temporal method, which provides that only monetary assets (cash, marketable securities, and receivables) and liabilities are translated at the current exchange rate. The company translates inventory, property, plants, and equipment at the historical exchange rates (the transaction rate in IASB terminology), which are the rates in effect when the assets were acquired. In general, the company translates most income-statement accounts at the average exchange rate, but it translates cost of goods sold and depreciation expense, as well as owners' equity, at the appropriate historical exchange rates.

Because companies can choose the translation method that's most appropriate for a particular foreign subsidiary, they don't have to pick just the temporal or the current-rate method. Coca-Cola faces this problem because it sells its products in over 200 countries and in 2019 used 70 different functional currencies in addition to the dollars.[20]

Figure 19.3 summarizes the selection of translation method, depending on the choice of functional currency. As in the preceding explanation, if the functional currency is the currency of the country where the foreign subsidiary is located, the current-rate method applies. If it is the reporting currency of the parent company, the temporal method applies. Why do you need to worry about this? By taking you through the translation process, you can understand better how foreign currency adjustments can impact a company's financial statements. That is more important than actually doing the calculations unless you are going to be an accountant responsible for preparing and disclosing the information.

The Translation Process Tables 19.1 and 19.2 show a balance sheet and income statement developed under both approaches to compare the differences in translation methods. In this simplified example, the beginning balance in retained earnings for both methods is assumed to be $40,000. The following exchange rates are used to perform the translation process in Tables 19.1 and 19.2:

- $1.5000—Historical exchange rate when fixed assets were acquired, and capital stock issued
- $1.6980—Current exchange rate on December 31, 2018
- $1.5617—Average exchange rate during 2019
- $1.5606—Exchange rate during which the ending inventory was acquired
- $1.5600—Historical exchange rate for cost of goods sold

Because the foreign currency was rising in value (strengthening) between the time the capital stock was issued ($1.5000) and the end of the year ($1.6980), the balance sheet reflects a positive accumulated translation adjustment under the current-rate method. This is consistent with the idea that net assets were gaining value in a strong currency.

An important financial indicator of a company's performance is earnings per share. Earnings is the same as Consolidated Net Income, as shown in the income statement in Table 19.2,

TABLE 19.1 Translating Foreign Currency: The Balance Sheet

		Temporal Method		Current-Rate Method	
	Foreign Currency	Rate	Dollars	Rate	Dollars
Cash	20,000	1.6980	33,960	1.6980	33,960
Accounts receivable	40,000	1.6980	67,920	1.6980	67,920
Inventories	40,000	1.5606	62,424	1.6980	67,920
Fixed assets	100,000	1.5000	150,000	1.6980	169,800
Accumulated depreciation	(20,000)	1.5000	(30,000)	1.6980	(33,960)
Total Assets	**180,000**		**284,304**		**305,640**
Accounts payable	30,000	1.6980	50,940	1.6980	50,940
Long-term debt	44,000	1.6980	74,712	1.6980	74,712
Capital stock	60,000	1.5000	90,000	1.5000	90,000
Retained earnings	46,000	*	68,652	*	89,988
Total Liabilities and Owners' Equity	**180,000**		**284,304**		**305,640**

**Retained earnings* is the U.S. dollar equivalent of all income earned in prior years retained in the business rather than distributed to shareholders plus this year's income. There is no single exchange rate used to translate retained earnings into dollars. It includes the beginning retained earnings balance plus Consolidated Net Income and Other Comprehensive Income, as explained below.

TABLE 19.2 Translating Foreign Currency: The Income Statement

		Temporal Method		Current-Rate Method	
	Foreign Currency	Rate	Dollars	Rate	Dollars
Sales	230,000	1.5617	359,191	1.5617	359,191
Expenses:					
Cost of goods sold	(110,000)	1.5600	(171,600)	1.5617	(171,787)
Depreciation	(10,000)	1.5000	(15,000)	1.5617	(15,617)
Other expenses	(80,000)	1.5617	(124,936)	1.5617	(124,936)
Taxes	(6,000)	1.5617	(9,370)	1.5617	(9,370)
Consolidated Net Income	**24,000**		**38,285**		**37,481**

which results from the normal operations of a company, but not foreign currency translation gains and losses, which are part of Other Comprehensive Income. The two equations below reflect the interaction between different aspects of income and retained earnings. OCI is the result of an accounting standard issued by FASB in 1997 and brings U.S. practice more closely in alignment with IFRS.

Consolidated Net Income + Other Comprehensive Income = Total Comprehensive Income [which seems a little confusing]

Beginning Retained Earnings + Total Comprehensive Net Income = Ending Retained Earnings

So how do we determine the amount of Other Comprehensive Income, which in this example only contains foreign currency translation losses? Using the accounting equation we discussed earlier in the chapter, total assets = liabilities + owners' equity (which includes capital stock and retained earnings). Using the data from the current rate method in Table 19.1 we can determine what the ending retained earnings balance should be as follows: 305,640 − 50,940 − 74,712 − 90,000 − (40,000 + 37,481) = 12,507. That plug figure is the amount of Other Comprehensive Income, which is added to Consolidated Net Income shown in the income statement in Table 19.2, resulting in Total Comprehensive Income of 37,481 + 12,507 = 49,988, the increase in retained earnings for the year. You can do the same calculation using the temporal method, and the result will be 284,304 − 50,940 − 74,712 − 90,000 − (40,000 + 38,285) = (9,633). In this case Total Comprehensive Income could end up being 38,285 − 9,633 = 28,652. Notice that the adjustment under the current rate method is positive, reflecting the increase in value of the foreign currency against the dollar, whereas the adjustment under the temporal method is negative since the nonmonetary assets (all assets except for cash and accounts receivable) and capital stock are recorded at weaker historical rates.

Under both the current rate method and the temporal method, translation gains and losses show up in Other Comprehensive Income rather than Comprehensive Net Income on the income statement. This is now consistent according to IFRS and FASB.

Disclosing Foreign-Exchange Gains and Losses Because of accounting rule changes in the United States, both U.S. GAAP and IFRS treat the recognition of translation gains and losses the same by making them a part of Other Comprehensive Income. Transactions gains and losses, which result from buying and selling goods and services denominated in a foreign currency, are recognized in Consolidated Net Income on the income statement.

INTERNATIONAL FINANCIAL ISSUES

19-6 List some of the key international finance functions

In Chapter 11, we examined the finance function from the standpoint of global capital markets. In this section, we will discuss some of the important treasury functions, including capital budgeting, cash flows and global cash management, and foreign-exchange risk management.

CAPITAL BUDGETING IN A GLOBAL CONTEXT

Capital budgeting—the process whereby MNEs determine which projects and countries will receive capital investment funds.

Capital budgeting is the technique that helps the MNE determine which projects and countries will receive its capital investment funds. The parent company must compare the net present value or internal rate of return of a potential foreign project with that of its other projects around the world to determine the best place to invest resources.

Methods of Capital Budgeting

Capital budgeting techniques:

- Payback period
- Net present value of a project
- Internal rate of return

Payback Period One approach to capital budgeting is to determine the **payback period** of a project, or the number of years required to recover the initial investment made. This is typically done by estimating the annual after-tax free cash flow from the investment, determining the present value of the future cash flow for each year, and then determining how many years it will take to recoup the initial investment.

Net Present Value A second approach is to determine the **net present value (NPV)** of a project, which is defined as follows:

$$\text{NPV} = \sum_{t=1}^{n} \frac{\text{FCF}_t}{(1 + k)^t} - \text{IO}$$

where FCF_t = the annual free cash flow in time period t

k = the appropriate discount rate; that is, the required rate of return or cost of capital

IO = the initial cash outlay

n = the project's expected life.

The required rate of return is the rate the company must get from the project to justify the cost of raising the initial investment or at least maintaining the value of its common stock. If the NPV is positive, the project is also considered positive. If the NPV is negative, the company should not enter into the project.

Internal Rate of Return A third approach is to compute the internal rate of return (IRR) of the project—the rate that equates the present value of future cash flows with the present value of the initial investment—and compare it with the required rate of return. If it is greater than the required rate of return, the investment is considered positive. However, the company then needs to compare the IRR with that of competing projects in other countries.

MNEs need to determine free cash flows based on cash-flow estimates and tax rates in different countries and an appropriate required rate of return adjusted for risk.

Several things are common about each of the methods. First, the firm needs to determine the free cash flows, which involves estimating those flows as well as bringing into the equation different tax rates from different countries. Second, in the case of both NPV and IRR, the company needs to determine what the required rate of return is.

Complications in Capital Budgeting Several aspects of capital budgeting are unique to foreign-project assessment:

- Parent cash flows (those from the project back to the parent in the parent's currency) must be distinguished from project cash flows (those in local currency from the sale of goods and services). Will the decision be based on one or both?
- Remittance of funds to the parent, such as dividends, interest on loans, and payment of intracompany receivables and payables, is affected by differing tax systems, legal and political constraints on the movement of funds, local business norms, and differences in how financial markets and institutions function. In addition, tax systems affect free cash flows on the project, irrespective of the remittance issue.
- Differing rates of inflation must be anticipated by both the parent and the subsidiary because of their importance in causing changes in competitive position and cash flows over time.
- The parent must consider the possibility of unanticipated exchange-rate changes because of their direct effects on the value of cash flows and their indirect effects on the foreign subsidiary's competitive position.
- The parent company must evaluate political risk in a target market because political events can drastically reduce the value or availability of expected cash flows.
- The terminal value (the value of the project at the end of the budgeting period) is difficult to estimate because potential purchasers from host, home, or third countries—or from the private or public sector—may have widely divergent perspectives on the project's value. The terminal value is critical in determining the total cash flows from the project. The total cash outlay is partially offset by the terminal value—the amount of cash the parent company can get from the subsidiary or project if it eventually sells.[21]

Determine different cash flow scenarios or adjust the hurdle rate (the minimum required rate of return for a project).

Because of all the forces listed here, it's very difficult to estimate future cash flows. There are two ways to deal with the variations in future cash flows. One is to set out several different scenarios and then determine the payback period, net present value, or internal rate of return of the project. The other less appropriate approach is to adjust the hurdle rate, which is the minimum required rate of return the project must achieve for it to receive capital. The adjustment is usually made by increasing the hurdle rate above its minimal level. This is easier than estimating cash flows, but it is also the easy way out.

Once the budget is complete, the MNE must examine both the return in local currency and the return to the parent in dollars from cash flows. Examining the return in local currency will give management a chance to compare the project with other investment alternatives in the country. However, cash flows to the parent are important, since dividends are paid to shareholders from those flows. If the MNE cannot generate a sufficient return to the parent in the parent's currency, it will eventually fall behind in its ability to pay shareholders and pay off corporate debt. Finally, the decision must be made in the strategic context of the investment, not just the financial context.

INTERNAL SOURCES OF FUNDS

Funds are working capital, or current assets minus current liabilities.

Although the term *funds* usually means "cash," it is used in a much broader sense in business and generally refers to working capital—that is, current assets minus current liabilities.[22] From a general perspective, funds come from the normal operations of a business (selling merchandise or services) as well as from financing activities, such as borrowing money, issuing bonds, or issuing shares. They are used to purchase fixed assets, pay employees, buy materials and supplies, and invest in marketable securities or long-term investments.

Sources of internal funds:

- Loans
- Investments through equity capital
- Intercompany receivables and payables
- Dividends

Cash Flows and the MNE Cash flows in an MNE are significantly more complex than for a company that operates in a strictly domestic environment. An MNE that wants to expand operations or needs additional capital can look not only to the domestic and international debt and equity markets but also to sources within itself. The complexity of its internal sources is magnified because of the number of its subsidiaries and the diverse environments in which they operate.

Figure 19.4 shows a parent company that has two foreign subsidiaries. All three may be increasing funds through normal operations that may be used on a company-wide basis,

FIGURE 19.4 How the MNE Handles Its Funds (I): Internal Funds

Funds consist of working capital that comes from normal business operations and that may be used to purchase assets and materials, to pay employees, and to make investments. If the company is an MNE, funds may come from either parent or subsidiary operations, or both, and can be used by the parent to support either its own operations or those of its subsidiaries.

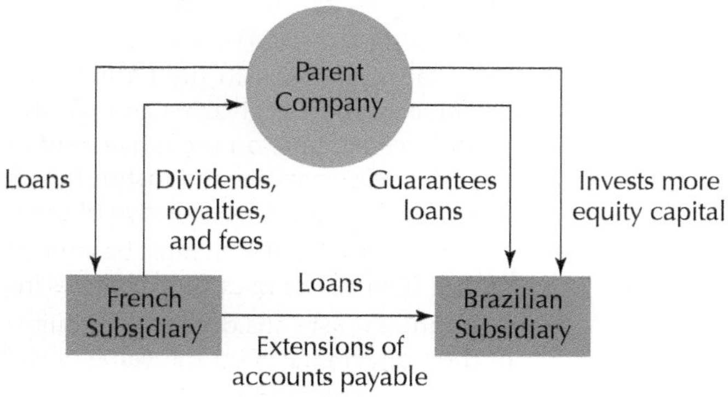

perhaps through loans. The parent can lend funds directly to one subsidiary or guarantee an outside loan to the other. Equity capital from the parent is another source of funds for the subsidiary.

Funds can also go from subsidiary to parent. A subsidiary could declare a dividend to the parent as a return on capital, or lend cash directly to it. If the subsidiary declared a dividend, the parent could lend the funds back. The dividend would not be tax deductible to the subsidiary, but it would be included as income to the parent, so the parent would have to pay tax on the dividend. If the subsidiary lent money to the parent, the interest paid by the parent would be tax deductible for the parent and taxable income for the subsidiary.

Merchandise, people, and financial flows can travel between subsidiaries, giving rise to receivables and payables. Companies can move money between and among related entities by paying quickly, or they can accumulate funds by deferring payment. They can also adjust the size of the payment by arbitrarily raising or lowering the price of intercompany transactions in comparison with the market price.

GLOBAL CASH MANAGEMENT

Managing cash effectively is a chief concern of the CFO, who must answer the following three questions:

1. What are the local and corporate system needs for cash?
2. How can the cash be withdrawn from subsidiaries and centralized?
3. Once the cash has been centralized, what should be done with it?

The cash manager, who reports to the treasurer, must collect and pay cash in the company's normal operational cycle and then deal with financial institutions. Before remitting any cash into the MNE's control center—whether at regional or headquarters level—the cash manager must first assess local cash needs through cash budgets and forecasts. Because the forecast projects the excess cash that will be available, the cash manager will know how much can be invested for short-term profits.

Cash budgets and forecasts are essential in assessing a company's cash needs. Dividends are a good source of intercompany transfers, but governments often restrict their free movement.

Once local cash needs are met, the cash manager must decide whether to allow the local manager to invest any excess cash or have it remitted to a central cash pool. If the cash is centralized, the manager must find a way to make the transfer. A cash dividend is the easiest way to distribute cash, but government restrictions may interfere. For example, foreign exchange controls may prevent the company from remitting as large a dividend as it would like. Cash can also be remitted through royalties, management fees, and repayment of principal and interest on loans.

Multilateral Netting An important cash-management strategy is **netting** cash flows internationally. For example, an MNE with operations in four European countries could

Brussels, Belgium, is the home ▶ of the Grand Palace and is a major cash management center for MNEs operating in Europe. Its low tax rates coupled with its prime location, political and economic stability, access to international banking and communications, and well-defined legal system make it ideal.

Source: Alpineguide/Alamy Stock Photo

Multilateral netting—the process of coordinating cash inflows and outflows among the subsidiaries so that only net cash is transferred, reducing transaction costs.

Netting requires sophisticated software and good banking relationships in different countries.

have several different intercompany cash transfers resulting from loans, the sale of goods, licensing agreements, and so forth. In the illustration in Figure 19.5, for example, there are no fewer than seven different transfers among four subsidiaries. As noted in the opening case, GPS Capital Markets Inc. provides specialized services for clients, including netting cash flows. One client, a large technology firm, was expanding internationally so rapidly that the growth was straining its capabilities to keep up. With hundreds of currency pairs and financial statements being generated in many different currencies and using several different functional currencies, the client was having a difficult time keeping up with the complexities. GPS realized it could save its client a lot of money by netting its transactions. Instead of having each entity around the world settle its transaction with every other entity, GPS helped the firm set up a multilateral netting system, as illustrated in Table 19.3 and Figure 19.6, that could reduce the number of times it had to exchange currency, thus reducing the cost of each transaction.

FIGURE 19.5 How the MNE Handles Its Funds (II): Multilateral Cash Flows

As the various subsidiaries of the MNE go about their business, cash can be transferred among them for a variety of reasons (e.g., in the form of loans or as proceeds from the sale of goods). Cash, of course, can flow in any direction, and if the MNE doesn't maintain some kind of cash-management center, each subsidiary must settle its accounts (receivables, payable, etc.) independently.

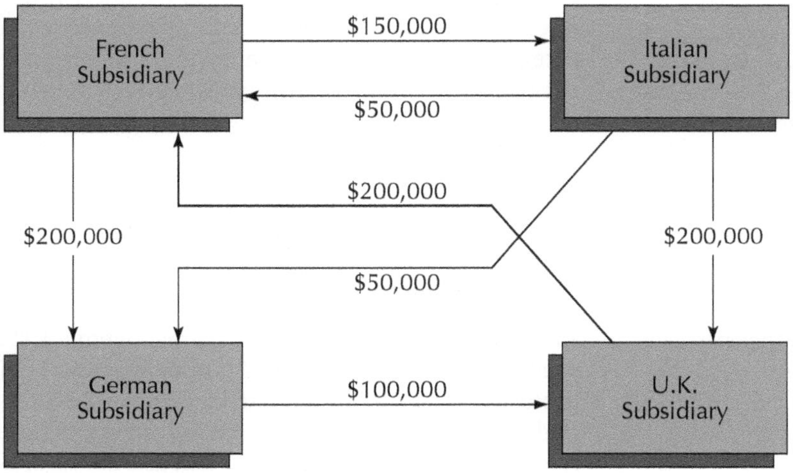

TABLE 19.3 How the MNE Handles Its Funds (III): Net Positions

Assume that these data are from the same MNE as the one introduced in Figure 19.5. Because the company has no cash-management center, *net positions*—the difference between *total receivables* and *total payables*—must be determined on a subsidiary-by-subsidiary basis.

Subsidiary	Total Receivables	Total Payables	Net Position
French	250,000	350,000	(100,000)
German	250,000	100,000	150,000
Italian	150,000	300,000	(150,000)
U.K.	300,000	200,000	100,000

FIGURE 19.6 How the MNE Handles Its Funds (IV): Multilateral Netting

Dissatisfied with the process represented in Figure 19.5, our MNE has now established a cash-management center—a *clearing account*—into which each subsidiary transfers its net cash. Naturally, the MNE may in turn distribute the total to support subsidiary operations.

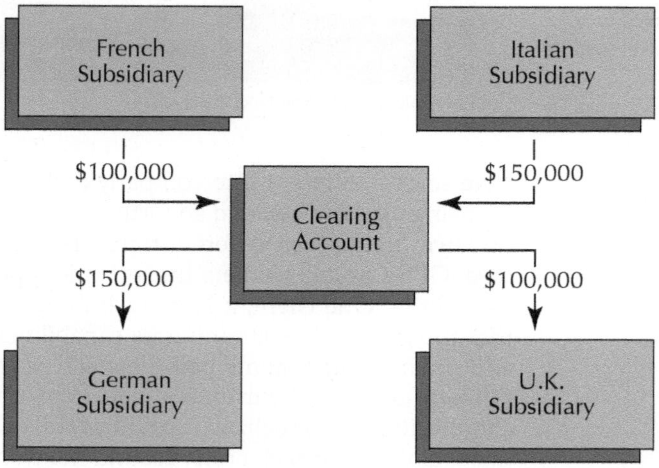

CONCEPT CHECK

In Chapter 9, we explain why it's important for MNEs to anticipate exchange-rate changes and make decisions about business activities that may be sensitive to those changes—decisions, for instance, about the sourcing of raw materials and components or the location of manufacturing and assembly facilities. We take up the same theme on page 329 in Chapter 13, where we cite exchange-rate movement as just one factor that can affect wages in a particular country—and thus any advantage in labor-cost differences that a company might hope to gain from locating operations in that country.

Table 19.3 identifies the total receivables, payables, and net position for each subsidiary. Rather than have each subsidiary settle its accounts independently with subsidiaries in other countries, many MNEs are establishing cash-management centers in one city (such as Brussels) to coordinate cash flows among subsidiaries from several countries.

Figure 19.6 illustrates how each subsidiary in a net payable position transfers funds to the central clearing account. The account manager then transfers funds to the accounts of the net receiver subsidiaries. In this example, only four transfers need to take place. The clearing account manager receives transaction information and computes the net position of each subsidiary at least monthly, then orchestrates the settlement process. The transfers take place in the payor's currency, and the foreign-exchange conversion takes place centrally. For netting to work, the company needs to match its cash needs with software that can track and transfer funds and with banking relationships that allow money to be moved among corporate entities.

FOREIGN-EXCHANGE RISK MANAGEMENT

19-7 Show how companies protect against foreign-exchange risk

As illustrated earlier, global cash-management strategy focuses on the flow of money for specific operating objectives. Another important objective of an MNE's financial strategy is to protect against the foreign-exchange risks of investing abroad. The strategies an MNE adopts to do this may mean the internal movement of funds as well as the use of one or more of the foreign-exchange instruments, such as options and forward contracts.

TYPES OF EXPOSURE

Three types of foreign-exchange exposure:

- Translation
- Transaction
- Economic or operational

If all exchange rates were fixed in relation to one another, there would be no foreign-exchange risk. However, rates are not fixed, and currency values change frequently. A change in the exchange rate can result in three different exposures for a company: *translation, transaction,* and *economic* or *operational.*

Translation exposure arises because the dollar value of the exposed asset or liability changes as the exchange rate changes.

Translation Exposure Foreign-currency financial statements are translated into the reporting currency of the parent company (assumed to be U.S. dollars for U.S. companies) so they can be combined with financial statements of other companies in the corporate group to form the consolidated financial statements. **Translation exposure** occurs because exposed accounts—those translated at the current exchange rate—either gain or lose value in dollars when the exchange rate changes.

Consider the example of a U.S. company with a subsidiary in Mexico. The subsidiary keeps its books in pesos, but it has to translate the financial statements into dollars so the parent can combine the results of the Mexican subsidiary with its operations from around the world. Assume the subsidiary has 900,000 pesos in the bank. So what is the effect of a change in the exchange rate on the dollar equivalent of the cash? If the exchange rate before the change was 18.5 pesos per dollar ($48,649) and the rate changes to 20 pesos per dollar (a weakening of the peso against the dollar), the cash would only be worth $45,000. The subsidiary still has pesos in the bank account, but the dollar equivalent of the peso has fallen, resulting in a loss. The gain or loss does not represent an actual cash flow effect because the pesos are only translated, not converted, into dollars. In addition, reported earnings can either rise or fall against the dollar because of the translation effect, which can affect other comprehensive income.

Transaction exposure arises when a transaction is denominated in a foreign currency and where the settlement gives rises to a cash flow gain or loss.

Transaction Exposure Denominating a transaction in a foreign currency gives rise to **transaction exposure** because the company has accounts receivable or payable in foreign currency that must be settled eventually. Consider the example of a U.S. exporter delivering merchandise to a British importer for $500,000 when the exchange rate is $1.9000 per pound (equivalent to £263,158). If the exporter were to receive payment in dollars, there would be no immediate effect to the exporter if the dollar/pound exchange rate changed. If payment were to be received in pounds, however, the exporter might incur a foreign-exchange gain or loss. If the exchange rate when the exporter receives the pounds from the importer falls to $1.8800, the exporter would only receive $494,737, which would be a loss of $5,263. In this case, because the pound is falling in value, the exporter would receive fewer dollars from the sale after the change in the exchange rate. This would be an actual cash flow loss to the exporter. This gain or loss does affect earnings and thus earnings per share.

Economic, or operating, exposure arises from the effects of exchange-rate changes on

- future cash flows,
- the sourcing of parts and components,
- the location of investments,
- the competitive position of the company in different markets.

Economic (or Operating) Exposure **Economic exposure (operating exposure)** is the potential for change in expected cash flows that arises from the pricing of products, the sourcing and cost of inputs, and the location of investments. Pricing strategies have both immediate and long-term effects on cash flows. In the example above, if the exporter decides to receive payment in dollars, the foreign-exchange risk would pass to the importer. However, the *importer* would have to come up with more pounds at the new exchange rate (£265,957) than at the original exchange rate. Now, the importer can either sell the product at the original price and not earn as much profit, or it can raise the price and hope that consumers will be willing to pay it. The *exporter,* however, also has two choices. It can continue to sell the merchandise at the same price, or it can lower it. If it lowers the price, it will incur a lower profit margin. If it continues to sell at the same price, the importer will have to pay more for the merchandise and then decide what to do.

Another economic-exposure decision involves how to make investment decisions. In 2011, Volkswagen AG decided to open a factory in the United States to take advantage of the strong euro versus the dollar. Because of the strength of the euro, Volkswagen had not been cost-competitive in the United States, and it realized that by opening a factory in Tennessee, it could take advantage of the strong euro as well as lower labor costs. Thus they were generating revenues in a weak currency and costs in a strong currency, severely affecting earnings. One of the economic solutions was to expand manufacturing operations in the United States to balance revenues and expenses in the same currency.[23]

EXPOSURE-MANAGEMENT STRATEGY

To protect assets from exchange-rate risk, management needs to
- define and measure exposure,
- establish a reporting system,
- adopt an overall policy on exposure management,
- formulate hedging strategies.

To adequately protect assets against the risks from translation, transaction, and economic exposure to exchange-rate fluctuations, management must do the following:

- Define and measure exposure
- Organize and implement a reporting system that monitors exposure and exchange-rate movements
- Adopt a policy assigning responsibility for minimizing—or hedging—exposure
- Formulate strategies for hedging exposure

All three types of exposure must be monitored and measured separately.

Define and Measure Exposure To develop a viable hedging strategy, an MNE must forecast the degree of exposure in each major currency in which it operates. Because the types differ, the actual exposure by currency must be tracked separately. For example, the firm should keep track of the translation exposure in Brazilian reals separately from the transaction exposure because it will result in an actual cash flow, whereas the translation exposure may not. Thus, the company generates one report for each type of exposure. It may also adopt different hedging strategies for the different types. Recall that GPS Capital Markets developed proprietary software, called FXpert, which not only conducts specialized audits of clients' foreign-exchange cash flows but proposes effective hedging strategies for improving them. Solutions may include such well-known hedging strategies as forwards, options, and futures contracts.

Exchange-rate movements are forecasted using in-house or external experts.

A key aspect of measuring exposure is forecasting exchange rates. A company should estimate and use ranges within which it expects a currency to vary over the forecasting period by developing in-house capabilities to monitor exchange rates or using economists who also try to obtain a consensus of exchange-rate movements from the banks they deal with. Their concern is to forecast the direction, magnitude, and timing of an exchange-rate change.

The reporting system should use both central control and input from foreign operations.

Organize and Implement a Reporting System Once the company has decided how to define and measure exposure and estimate future exchange rates, it must create a reporting system that will assist in protecting it against risk. To achieve this goal, substantial participation from foreign operations must be combined with effective central control.

Hedging strategies can be operational or financial.

Formulate Hedging Strategies Once a company has identified its level of exposure and determined which exposure is critical, it can hedge its position by adopting operational and/or financial strategies, each with cost-benefit as well as operational implications. The safest position is a balanced one in which exposed assets equal exposed liabilities.

Operational strategies include
- using local debt to balance local assets,
- taking advantage of leads and lags for intercompany payments.

Operational Hedging Strategies The use of debt to balance exposure is an interesting strategy. Many companies "borrow locally," especially in weak-currency countries, because that helps them avoid foreign-exchange risk from borrowing in a foreign currency and balances their exposed position in assets and earnings. One problem with this strategy is that, because interest rates in weak-currency countries tend to be high, there must be a trade-off between the cost of borrowing and the potential loss from exchange-rate variations.

Protecting against loss from transaction exposure becomes complex. In dealing with foreign customers, it is always safest for the company to denominate the transaction in its own currency to avoid any foreign-exchange exposure. The risk shifts to the foreign customer that has to come up with the company's currency. Or the company could denominate purchases in a weaker currency and sales in a stronger one. If forced to make purchases in a strong currency and sales in a weak one, it could resort to contractual measures such as forward contracts or options, or it could try to balance its inflows and outflows through astute sales and purchasing strategies.

A lead strategy means collecting or paying early. A lag strategy means collecting or paying late.

Leads and Lags Other operational strategies protect cash flows among related entities, such as a parent and subsidiaries. A **lead strategy** means either collecting foreign-currency receivables before they are due when the foreign currency is expected to weaken or paying foreign-currency payables before they are due when it is expected to strengthen. With a **lag strategy**, a company either delays collection of foreign-currency receivables if that currency is expected to strengthen, or delays payables when it is expected to weaken. In other words, a company usually leads into and lags out of a hard currency and leads out of and lags into a weak one.

Sometimes an operational strategy means shifting assets overseas to take advantage of currency changes. As mentioned earlier, when the euro strengthened against the U.S. dollar, VW shifted some of its manufacturing to the United States.

Forward contracts can establish a fixed exchange rate for future transactions.

Using Derivatives to Hedge Foreign-Exchange Risk In addition to the operational strategies just mentioned, a company may hedge exposure through *derivative* financial contracts such as forward contracts and options, with the most common hedge being a forward contract.

Consider a U.S. exporter selling goods to a British manufacturer for £1 million when the exchange rate is $1.9000 per £. If the exporter could collect the money right away and convert it into dollars, it would receive $1.9 million. However, if the exporter were not expected to receive payment for 90 days, it would be exposed to an exchange-rate change. One way to protect against this is to enter into a forward contract with a bank to deliver pounds and receive dollars at the forward rate of, say, $1.8500. In 90 days, the exporter would convert the pounds into dollars at $1.8500 and receive $1,850,000, which is less than it would have received at the initial spot rate. But if the pound had deteriorated even more in value, the exporter would still receive the $1.85 million. Also, the forward contract eliminates uncertainty.

Currency options can ensure access to foreign currency at a fixed exchange rate for a specific period of time.

A foreign-currency option is more flexible than a forward contract because it gives its purchaser the right, though not the obligation, to buy or sell a certain amount of foreign currency at a set exchange rate within a specified amount of time. In the same situation described above, the exporter would enter into an option contract with a trader to convert pounds into dollars at a certain exchange rate. For the cost of protection, the exporter pays a premium to the trader, which is like insurance. When the exporter receives the cash from the importer, it can decide whether to exercise the option. If the option gives it more money than the spot rate, the exporter will exercise the option. If not, it won't.

LOOKING TO THE FUTURE The Impact of Global Economic Forces on Accounting and Finance

The future of accounting is complicated. It is clear that more jurisdictions use IFRS than U.S. GAAP for external financial reporting. However, the United States is no closer to allowing IFRS to be used for U.S. companies listing on U.S. stock exchanges. A major reason is that GAAP is far more comprehensive than IFRS, both in depth and breadth. Also, it responds more to the background, needs, and regulatory requirements of U.S. capital markets than do IFRS. The SEC is trying to figure out how to make it easier for U.S. MNEs to report financial information, improve disclosure, simplify financial reporting, and move toward a single global accounting standard.[24] This sounds almost impossible. However, one possibility would be to "drop the reconciliation requirement, letting companies supplement their U.S. financial reports with ones filed with U.S. regulators using international standards." As noted by the director of global accounting for Ford Motor Company, "we are concerned that providing both international accounting standards and U.S. GAAP financial data could be complicated."[25] Complicated, yes; impossible, no.

An important aspect of financial reporting in the United States is an independent auditing profession that examines internal control processes and ensures the accuracy of the financial records of a firm. A major concern with IFRS is the enforceability of the standards by an independent accounting profession. Simply generating a set of accounting rules is not enough if the auditing profession in each country is not good enough to verify the accuracy of the financial information. The International Federation of Accountants has established an International Accounting Auditing Board, which is setting standards on auditing and control that could be used in any country, but there is far less pressure to adopt these standards than is the case for IFRS. One important contribution to the integrity of the financial markets in the United States is a strong auditing profession. This can be seen in recent cases brought by the SEC against Chinese firms that are listing on the NYSE. U.S.-based audit firms use local Chinese auditors to perform audits of Chinese companies that list on the NYSE as well as on the Chinese subsidiaries of U.S. MNEs.

The local Chinese audit firms would not provide documents to the SEC because Chinese law prohibited them from doing so. The SEC levied fines against the Big 4 PWC, Deloitte, KPMG, and E&Y and threatened to suspend the Chinese audit firms from auditing U.S.-traded Chinese companies.[26]

In order to appreciate the future of international finance, you just have to read the annual reports of global companies to see what they are worried about. In its 2018 annual report, H&M discusses many of its future challenges. Competition is getting stronger, putting pressure on H&M to adjust their business model to stay competitive. From a financial point of view, fluctuations in the foreign exchange markets will continue to wreak havoc. It is harder to forecast exchange rates to set realistic budgets and prepare effective capital budgets. In their report, they discuss the challenges of accounting for foreign operations as well as establishing effective hedging strategies. Companies like H&M will be forced to adopt better cash management and hedging strategies. This is where firms like GPS will be able to find a niche to help companies manage the future. Being successful on the accounting and finance side of a global company implies an understanding of global market forces as well as the technical side of accounting and finance.

CASE

H&M: The Challenges of Global Expansion and the Move to Adopt International Financial Reporting Standards[27]

Hennes & Mauritz AB (also known as H&M), the Swedish MNE that is a fashion trendsetter, has a stated goal "to give customers unbeatable value by offering fashion and quality at the best price." It doesn't own any factories, but rather outsources production to independent suppliers, primarily in Asia and Europe. H&M also rents space from international and local landlords rather than owning its own stores.

H&M is a major firm in the apparel retail market where fashion trends are critical and where goods move quickly. In this industry, the key buyers are consumers, the key suppliers are clothing manufacturers and wholesalers, designers are king, and a fast, well-organized supply chain is essential. Depending on the individual firm strategy, the apparel retail market doesn't have to be capital intensive, but the largest players in the industry are very international, both in retail footprint and suppliers. The biggest companies in the industry are U.S.-based The Gap, H&M, and Spain-based Industria de Diseno Textil, S.A. (Inditex), better known by its flagship brand, Zara. All three companies have different store brands: Gap, Banana Republic, Old Navy, and Athleta for The Gap; H&M, COS (collection of style), Monki, Weekday, H&M Home, Arket, Afound, and Cheap Monday

Swedish-based H&M places trendy stores in trendy locations. This store in Liverpool, England, is one of H&M's 5,000 stores in 74 markets.

Source: Julius Kielaitis/Alamy Stock Photo

for H&M; and Zara, Bershka, Pull and Bear, Massimo Dutti, Stradivarius, Oysho, Zara Home, and Uterque for Inditex.

Global Spread and Strategy

Both of H&M's competitors are very international. H&M operates about 5,000 stores in 74 markets, whereas The Gap operates 3,100 company stores and over 400 franchise stores in 90 countries, and Inditex operates in a network of over 7,000 stores in 96 countries. All three have a strong online presence as well.

Hennes & Mauritz AB started as a single women's wear store in Sweden in 1947. Today, H&M's business is much broader and currently includes the sales of clothing, accessories, footwear, cosmetics, and home textiles. Although H&M is known as one of Sweden's premier MNEs, in 2018 it generated 15.4 percent of its sales in Germany, 11.8 percent in the United States, and 5.4 percent in France. China was the next largest market, just above Sweden. But most of H&M's growth is outside the United States and Europe.

H&M and Zara have very different strategies. Zara delivers new products to its stores twice a week. Because of its highly organized supply chain, Zara takes only 10–15 days to go from design to the stores. Although it sources its apparel from around the world, it has adopted just-in-time manufacturing from the auto industry and established 14 highly automated Spanish factories where robots cut and dye fabrics, creating the unfinished "gray goods" that are the foundation for their final products. It then takes the gray goods and outsources them to a network of small shops in Portugal and Spain to do the finish work. Store managers are constantly sending updated information on consumer demand so that they can move to the next hot fashion. The rule at Zara is that if you see it in the store and you like it, you'd better buy it because as soon as it is gone, you'll never see it again. Veteran Zara consumers keep track of when new shipments come in so they can buy the latest stuff. H&M is trendy, but it outsources production to a network of over 800 suppliers, 60 percent of which are in Asia. It offers a main collection twice a year in the spring and the fall with several sub-collections that allow it to bring in new trendy items. Longer-lead-time items are produced in Asia, whereas short-lead-time items are manufactured in Europe.

Currently the second-largest apparel retailer behind Inditex, H&M Hennes & Mauritz has grown from 2,800 to 4,900 stores in the past six years, and it is still aggressively expanding, mostly outside the United States and Europe. Despite its global presence, H&M is listed on the Stockholm Stock Exchange, Nasdaq Stockholm. H&M adopted the EU's version of IFRS and presents its financial statements in both English and Swedish. The financial statements are reported in Swedish kronor, which also serve as its functional currency. Because the retail industry is less capital intensive, most companies have no need to list in any foreign stock exchanges. Inditex lists only on the stock exchanges throughout its home country, Spain, including Madrid, Barcelona, Bilbao, and Valencia. Consistent with domestic listings, The Gap, which was founded in the United States in 1969, is listed solely on the NYSE.

The ability to list solely in the country in which a company is domiciled can simplify the financial reporting process by avoiding the need to present financial statements that adhere to the accounting rules of multiple countries. Ericsson, another popular Swedish MNE, requires much more capital and is therefore listed on both the Stockholm exchange in Sweden as well as NASDAQ in the United States as American Depositary Receipts. As a result, Ericsson has had to accommodate multiple accounting bodies and become more transparent in its reports because of its desire to raise capital on foreign exchanges.

The Gap, H&M, and Inditex come from different accounting and regulatory environments. In its 201 annual report, H&M states that its consolidated accounts have been prepared in accordance with IFRS issued by the IASB and the interpretations provided by the IFRS Interpretations Committee. In addition, the IFRS that is used for its parent company reports are only those approved by the EU. Besides IFRS, H&M provides disclosures in accordance with the Swedish Financial Reporting Board's recommendation RFR 1. Both the parent company and consolidated balance sheets use the following format: fixed assets + current assets = equity + long term liabilities + current liabilities.

Given that Sweden is a member of the European Union, H&M was required to adopt IFRS as of 2005, which was a change from its past practices. Prior to that, H&M was using recommendations issued by the Swedish accounting standards setters, which were largely based in International Accounting Standards, so the consolidated reports of H&M were already pretty much adjusted to IAS. In preparation for the switch from Swedish GAAP to IFRS, H&M began a transition process in 2003 and 2004 that was intensified in 2005. In its 2005 annual report, H&M reported that the greatest impact of the change was because of financial instruments and hedge accounting. Under the new accounting standard, all derivatives had to be recognized at fair value, so H&M commented that reported profit was probably going to be more volatile than it was when gains and losses on hedges were deferred and recognized outside the balance sheet. That is exactly the volatility that the European, especially French, banks wanted to avoid, resulting in the EU carving out the treatment of derivatives.

Before the Changeover to IFRS

Prior to the move to IFRS in 2006, H&M reported its financial results in compliance with Swedish GAAP—a bit of a mixture between Anglo-American accounting, which is driven by the capital markets, and Germanic accounting, which is driven by bank financing and taxation. Swedish reporting tends to be a little more transparent than German accounting but less transparent than Anglo-American accounting.

Issues of Transparency

One reason why Swedish accounting has been less transparent is its orientation to creditors, government, and tax authorities. In addition, because the Swedish Stock Exchange has become a focal point for listings by Nordic companies, the influential Swedish accounting profession has pushed for consolidated accounts to represent the needs of shareholders, whereas the parent-company accounts have reflected Swedish legal requirements. Swedish accounting tends to be very conservative due to the importance of taxes to fund extensive social welfare programs and the tendency of the Swedish government to use tax policies to influence investment in areas deemed important to the government and its social objectives.

Sweden and the EU

Since Sweden entered the EU, its accounting has evolved to incorporate EU accounting directives and philosophies. The Swedish government established an Accounting Standards Board (BFN) in 1976 to recommend accounting principles that fit within the framework of the Company Law. The Swedish Financial Accounting Council (RR) was established in 1991 to take over the role of the accounting profession in making recommendations on accounting practices, especially with respect to how to prepare an annual report according to the Annual Accounts Act. Now the standards are set by the Swedish Financial Reporting Board.

The Swedish Stock Exchange has supported the efforts of the profession, even though their recommendations are voluntary and subject to the Company Law. However, the decision by the EU to require firms to use IFRS for consolidated financial statements takes precedence over everything.

Conversion Costs

H&M didn't provide much information about the cost of converting to IFRS in 2005, but Ericsson did. Ericsson provided more information because it was listing on NASDAQ in the United States as well the Swedish Stock Exchange, so it had to provide Form 20F reconciliation between Swedish and U.S. GAAP. Because of its higher level of disclosure, we find that Ericsson estimated that the conversion to IFRS in 2005 would result in net income being SKR 1.5 billion lower than it would have been under Swedish GAAP, and equity would have been SKR 5.7 billion lower. In addition, the recognition of cash on the balance sheet appears to be quite different under IFRS than it is under Swedish GAAP, with cash under IFRS being SEK46.1 billion less than cash under Swedish GAAP, whereas cash at the end of 2004 was the same under U.S. GAAP and IFRS.

Costs of implementing IFRS are difficult to gauge. Many countries implemented national regulations that attempted alignment with IFRS (e.g., Sweden). Thus costs of implementation may have been spread out over several years because companies knew that full IFRS implementation was drawing near. Ericsson's management notes the following in the 2004 annual report:

> Because Swedish GAAP, in recent years, has been adapted to IFRS to a high degree and as the rules for first time adopters allow certain exemptions from full retrospective restatements, the transition from Swedish GAAP to IFRS is expected to have a relatively limited effect on our financial statements. Furthermore, we believe the conversion to IFRS will align our reporting more closely with US GAAP.

For companies in many other European countries, however, the domestic regulators were slower to implement the change, so the change was more abrupt and painful. Countries with both parent-company and consolidated financial statements found that local regulations more attuned to domestic sources of capital held to the local environment, whereas consolidated financial statements had to adopt IFRS.

QUESTIONS

19-3 If an investor wants to compare the financial results of The Gap, Inditex, and H&M, what difference does it make that their financial statements are prepared according to different GAAP? Would you expect there to be a big difference between U.S. GAAP used by The Gap and IFRS as used by H&M and Inditex?

19-4 What type of IFRS did H&M decide to disclose in its financial statements in 2005? In 2018?

CHAPTER 20
International Human Resource Management

OBJECTIVES

After studying this chapter, you should be able to

20-1 Describe international human resource management
20-2 Distinguish the perspective of the expatriate
20-3 Differentiate the staffing frameworks used by MNEs
20-4 Describe expatriate selection
20-5 Appraise expatriate preparation
20-6 Profile expatriate compensation
20-7 Explain expatriate repatriation
20-8 Describe expatriate failure

A person does not seek luck; luck seeks the person.

—Turkish proverb

Source: Galina Peshkova/123RF

CASE

Globalizing Your Career

Companies have been moving people around for centuries, capturing the benefits of putting the right person into the right job at the right place at the right time at the right pay for the right stretch. Contemporary market trends, strategic imperatives, and executive performance standards intensify this task. Today, career success requires, at the least, sharpening your global awareness and, ideally, broadening your experiential knowledge of the ways that the business world works.

Globalization, by spurring trade, capital, and investment flows, expands the scope the scope of the hundreds of thousands of subsidiaries opening and operating in the 214 markets that compose the global business environment. Each unit, emerging and established, requires executives who command the knowledge, skills, and abilities to navigate economic complexities, cultural ambiguities, and political challenges, all the while maximizing the MNE's global efficiency and optimizing its local responsiveness. GE's former CEO explains that "A good global company does three things: It's a global sales company—meaning it's number one with customers all over the world, whether in Chicago or Paris or Tokyo. It's a global products company, with technologies, factories, and products made for the world, not just for a single region. And, most important, it's a global people company—a company that keeps getting better by capturing global markets and brains."[1] Hence, it's no surprise that the leading impact of a foreign assignment on an employee's career is increased likelihood of bigger, broader leadership activities.[2]

By no means must one immediately pack up, say good-bye, and head abroad. For those who do, fear not, as an international assignment has many benefits. Folks with international experience are better problem solvers and display sharper creativity. Moreover, the word is out: A Gallup World Poll reports that 1.1 billion people, or one-quarter of the earth's adults, want to move temporarily to another country to find a higher paying job and better career opportunities. Another 630 million aim to move abroad permanently.[3]

Even if your career plans anchor you to your home market, globalizing markets encourage globalizing your mindset. From Afghanistan to Zimbabwe, effective leadership increasingly calls for an openness to and awareness of differences across markets that, in turn, supports the propensity to synthesize integrative themes. "You have to have an intuitive sense of how the world works and how people behave," explained a vice president of A. T. Kearney.[4] Observed the CEO of Egon Zehender International, an executive search firm, "The world is getting smaller, and markets are getting bigger . . . we've always talked about the global executive, but the need to find managers who can be effective in many different settings is growing ever more urgent. In addition to looking for intelligence, specific skills, and technical insights, MNEs are also looking for executives who are comfortable on the world stage."[5] The CEO of ATT, Randall Stephenson, after a multiyear stint in Mexico, adds that "If you are going to serve a diverse market, you better have on your leadership team people who know those markets, and not just from a numerical, demographic standpoint, but people who have actually lived and breathed and operated in those markets."[6]

THE EXPATRIATE

MNEs routinely often send managers to live and work in another country to run their foreign operations. Some, such as W. L. Gore and Johnson & Johnson, send a few. Others, like Royal Dutch Shell and Wipro Technologies, send many. Unfortunately, few standards stipulate why, when, and where an MNE should use an expatriate (e.g., a person who works outside their home country). Moreover, ambiguities complicate selecting the right expatriates, developing the right predeparture programs, configuring the optimal support systems, designing the right compensation packages, setting the right stretch of time for the assignments, and determining the right way to reintegrate them into the home company when they complete their tour of duty.

The dividends of success and fallout of failure press MNEs to manage their human resources strategically. Honeywell, like many, begins developing candidates years before they might head abroad. It assesses candidates' knowledge, skills, and abilities and prescribes training paths that anticipate likely gaps. "We give them a horizon, a perspective, and, gradually, we tell them they are potentially on an international path," says Honeywell's VP of HR. "We want them to develop a cross-cultural intellect, what we call strategic accountability."[7] Honeywell might advise employees to network with experienced expatriates or improve their personal and professional resourcefulness. Nestlé leaves less to chance in developing its expatriate pipeline. High performers typically rotate through two stays at headquarters in Vevey, Switzerland; the first early in an executive's career and the second when reaching middle management. Finally, Schlumberger, the world's largest oilfield services provider, requires managers to rotate jobs every two to three years across business units and corporate functions; it expects its executives will spend more than half their career working outside their home countries.[8]

The pace of globalization, particularly for MNEs in emerging economies like China, India, Indonesia, and the Philippines, accelerates preparation. Some managers identify expatriate candidates upon hire. The director of global programs at India's Wipro Technologies notes, "A big part of our recruiting is telling people that they will get a chance to work abroad." This approach, he believes, improves the quality of new hires while fortifying the company's expatriate pipeline.[9]

NEW PLACES, NEW FACES, NEW WAYS

Figure 20.1 lists the benefits of working abroad. Enduring constants include improving job prospects, engaging new challenges, boosting

FIGURE 20.1 An International Assignment: Advantages and Benefits

Executives identify many benefits of their international assignments. Here we see leading personal and professional motivations.[10]

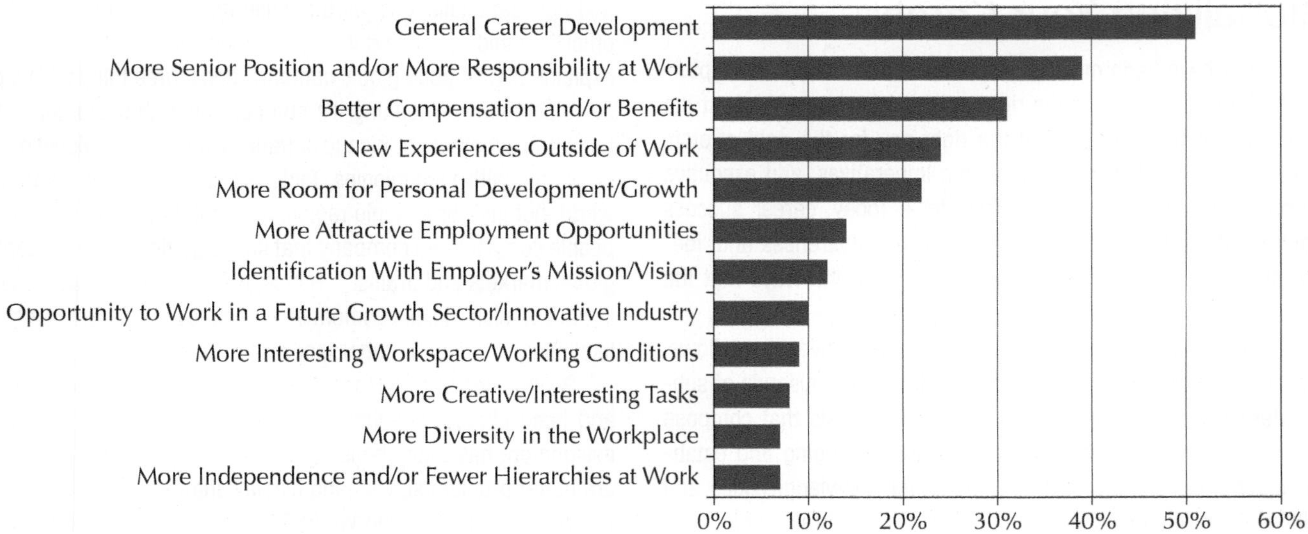

the quality of life, and increasing earning potential. Accomplished expatriates testify to the merits of the quest, describing how the experience changed their professional and personal identity. Many explain that working abroad pushed them, sometimes gently, sometimes harshly, to interpret situations differently. Galina Naumenko, of PwC Russia, says an international assignment "spurs global networking among employees, gives them an understanding of different cultures, and gets them thinking about alternative ways of approaching problems and solving them." Added the head of strategy for IBM's Growth Markets, "You get very different thinking if you sit in Shanghai or São Paulo or Dubai than if you sit in New York."[11]

Working internationally compels employees to develop broader management repertoires. Consider Joan Pattle, a Microsoft manager who worked at headquarters in Seattle before accepting a post as product leader in England. Her U.K. assignment came with wider responsibilities, as she explains: "At home, my job was very strictly defined. I basically had to know everything about managing a database. But when I got to London, I was also in charge of direct marketing and press relations. I was exposed to a much broader set of experiences."[12] Effectively, an expatriate assignment offers big-time opportunities to think outside the box since you are no longer in one box. Similarly, Laura Anderson, a spokesperson for Intel, explains that an assignment in Hong Kong expanded her horizons and increases her creativity. "For me," she concluded, "it was a tremendous growth experience."[13]

NEW PROBLEMS, NEW CHALLENGES

Notwithstanding the allure of adventure and rewards, working internationally is not for everyone. Difficulty adapting, no matter how strong the intent, explains nearly half of failed foreign assignments. Family problems, quality of life concerns, awkward socialization, and loneliness are enduring personal challenges. Operationally, cultural clashes, language difficulties, murky business practices, and safety hazards make for tough office situations. Recently, the COVID-19 pandemic dramatized the steep downside of a foreign posting; beside immediate health care concerns, difficulties returning home in the face of closed borders and travel bans added a new level of concern to those considering an international assignment. For many, these difficulties rule out anything beyond a short-term visit. Other problems arise when a company asks an executive to transfer to a second- or third-tier city in a less preferred location. Moving from paradise to the wastelands, besides being a tough sell, makes for a challenging experience.

The gap between life at home versus "over there" often fans professional, family, and personal problems. Expatriates can struggle making sense of the local milieu. Difficulty understanding and respecting differences, no matter how mundane, spiritual, or philosophical, cause expensive failures. To top it off, IB travel "is perhaps the most dangerous form of travel. Tourists wouldn't consider visiting a war zone, yet folks from oil, computer, pharmaceutical, agricultural, and telecom MNEs do it regularly."[14] Once there, merely frequenting high-profile hotels and restaurants is hazardous.

Finally, one does deal with subtle career politics and office positioning. While the intention to have an international career is positively associated with career adaptability and cultural intelligence, evidence indicates spending too little or too much time abroad can thwart promotion plans. This is particularly influential when assigned to a slot in a country that has high cultural and geographic distance from the head office.[15]

COMING HOME

Floating around the world are transpatriates, basically "expat lifers." Moving from assignment to assignment, whether with the same company or another, they plan never to return "home." Many, however, eventually do—they pack their bags, bid farewell to colleagues, board the plane, and return to a hero's welcome. A snap, right? Not so. In some cases, one gets everything but the big bash.

Repatriation—returning to one's country of origin—is tough but, data shows, doable. Tales of success confirm that career planning makes a big difference. Sanket Akerkar kept his U.S. network active while running Microsoft's India unit. During business trips to the United States, Mr. Akerkar stayed an extra day to network. Likewise, following a four-year assignment in Tokyo, Bryan Krueger returned to a promotion to president of Baxter North America. He had left for Tokyo without a guaranteed promotion upon return. While away, however, he tracked the goings-on at headquarters and visited every few months to sustain his network. As he explains, "I was definitely proactive. Anyone who is not, does himself a disservice. I made a conscious effort to stay in touch, and it paid off."[16] Likewise advises AsiaLink CEO Penny Burtt, "It is absolutely essential to stay in touch."[17]

Still, not all executives share victory tales. A survey of repatriated executives who successfully completed their international assignments found that more than a third held temporary posts three months after returning home. Nearly 80 percent saw their new job as a demotion. More than 60 percent felt they had too few opportunities to leverage their hard-earned international expertise. Some executives, for any number of reasons, accept this outcome. Others don't and move on—more than one-quarter of returning executives leave for another company ship within two years.[18]

RISK AND RETURN

The choice to work abroad has a high upside, but a steep downside. On balance, the allure of an international assignment regularly tips the scale. While overseas, an expatriate is well-paid, has big responsibilities, and commands high status. The adventure of living abroad makes an international career irresistible to some, effectively creating so-called "global nomads" along with expat lifers who travel from one assignment to the next. For example, after stints in Singapore and London, a Morgan Stanley expat in India reasoned, "I still don't want to go back to the United States. It's a big world—lots of things to see."[19]

Still, the risks of a career detour loom large. Some MNEs tout a foreign assignment as a meaningful experience that prepares managers for broader responsibilities—indeed, career development drives nearly a quarter of expat assignments.[20] As the reasoning goes, it improves skills and expertise, fosters cultural awareness, increases confidence in overcoming challenges, and enhances creativity through exposure to different ways of doing things. A neutral or negative career outcome, however, is not out of the question. As Tom Schiro of Deloitte & Touche observes, "Some MNEs just send somebody overseas and forget about them for two years."[21] Then, after returning, the company may be slow to reward successful experience with a bigger leadership role.

EMERGING STANDARDS

The expanding scale and scope of globalization triggers short supplies of talented executives. MNEs report difficulty finding skilled candidates, investing more time interviewing and hiring, and worrying about rivals poaching their high performers. Talent shortages only worsen. Manpower, a multinational human resource consulting firm, found that 34 percent of employers worldwide struggle to fill expatriate slots.[22] McKinsey & Company reports that most employers in leading markets, such as Brazil, Germany, India, Mexico, Saudi Arabia, Turkey, and the United States, struggle to hire skilled workers. Moreover, the world is short 40 million college-educated workers, meaning "there are far too few workers with the advanced skills needed to drive a high productivity economy."[23]

By changing the game, globalization also changes performance standards. Increasingly, MNEs regard international experience as the cornerstone of a high-impact career. Nearly 70 percent of the CEOs of the 100 largest European companies have completed a foreign assignment.[24] In the United States, 75 percent of the CEOs of the Fortune 100 spent at least two years working in a senior position overseas. Explained Procter & Gamble's HRM director, global awareness and experience are "ingredient[s] you must have if you aspire to be a global player in the long term.[25] P&G expects its leaders to be both innovative and worldly; they cannot rise to the top without running operations in a foreign market. Its German rival, Henkel, insists on the same, requiring executives to live in at least two different countries prior to promotion. Boyden, an executive search firm, notes that nearly three of every four clients request international experience when seeking C-suite executives or board members. Bluntly put, multinational experience is as essential as multifunctional and multiproduct experiences. Consequently, MNEs post high-potential executives overseas, giving them the opportunity to step up to the challenge, test their skills, and fine-tune their global mindset.

In summary, aspiring executives increasingly look abroad to move ahead. While perhaps over-hyped, personal ambition, environmental trends, market conditions, and workplace standards create situations where "the people with the top jobs in large corporations will have global exposure and ideally, international experience."[26]

QUESTIONS

20-1 Identify three compelling reasons to pursue an expatriate assignment.

20-2 Identity three key qualifications of a successful expatriate.

INTERNATIONAL HUMAN RESOURCE MANAGEMENT

20-1 Describe international human resource management

CONCEPT CHECK

Recall our discussion in Chapter 1 of "The Forces Driving Globalization and IB," in which we identify several factors that create connections among people worldwide. The convergence of cultures, politics, and markets diminishes the physical and psychic distances between countries. Here we suggest that this trend has begun to make the prospect of moving from one country to another a more attractive career plan.

Successful MNEs have great strategies, effective organizations, efficient supply chains, clever marketing, sharp financial systems, and the like. Ultimately, though, success is a function of the people who start and sustain operations here, there, and everywhere. The expanding IB web calls for executives who can manage interconnected operations across diverse markets. Putting the right person in the right job in the right place at the right time for the right compensation for the right stretch takes us to the front lines of IB. From launching new ventures, developing local expertise, filling skills gaps, setting technology platforms, diffusing the organizational culture, or rebuilding a failing unit, the star of the show is an executive. Indeed, any successful or, for that matter, struggling, activity has an executive at its core. Quite simply, the focal point of IB is an executive facing challenges that often lead to transformational opportunities. The contest between challenge and opportunity, the focus of this chapter, is the spirit of a career in IB.

IHRM is an umbrella term that refers to overseeing all things related to managing employees in the MNE.

International Human Resource Management (IHRM) shepherds an MNE's most valued assets—its people. IHRM develops policies and sets systems that improve individual productivity and collective performance. Opening and operating a business, whether a small-scale micronational or a vast multinational, requires finding people to implement the strategy, motivating them to perform well, upgrading their skills so they can move on to bigger challenges and, ultimately, retaining them. IHRM directs these functions, minding the staffing, training, evaluation, compensation, and retention given the requirements of the MNE's strategy. Functionally, IHRM performs many of the same activities as human resource management (HRM). Like HRM, IHRM manages recruitment, selection, performance measurement, compensation, training, industrial relations, career management, within the context of the company's strategy. However, IHRM differs significantly from its domestic counterpart in terms of the complexity associated with managing people across national boundaries. These issues direct extensive attention to the selection, preparation, support, compensation, and repatriation of the expatriate.

This chapter elaborates these issues, building on themes introduced in Chapter 12 and applied since to business functions and operating activities given the opportunities and challenges in the global business environment. We evaluate IHRM from the perspective that the successful MNE staffs its operations with skilled executives that are mission-led and principle-driven to leverage its strengths and managing its weaknesses, all the while reconciling the competing pressures of global integration and local responsiveness. This perspective emphasizes that IHRM activities perform best when managers link them to the MNE's strategy (see Figure 20.2).

IHRM is more difficult for the MNE than its domestic counterpart due to

- environmental differences,
- strategic contingencies,
- organizational challenges.

Unconditionally, managing human resources is more difficult in the MNE than its uninational counterpart. Besides dealing with situations in its home market, IHRM must adjust policies and programs for political, cultural, legal, and economic circumstances in foreign markets. Effective leadership styles and management practices, for example, often vary from country to country. Differences fan difficulties between people in different units—say, headquarters and local subsidiaries. Neglected, they can turn great managers at home into ineffective ones abroad. Consequently, IHRM continually evaluate how to staff international operations and fine-tune the mix of recruiting, preparation, support, compensation, and repatriation programs.

CONCEPT CHECK

A recurring theme of the text is the usefulness of instituting a strategic perspective. No matter if the issue involves political, legal, economic, or cultural dimensions, the quest for superior performance compels the MNE to interpret trends, opportunities, challenges, and consequences in terms of its strategy.

Inevitably, some ask why IHRM puts up with these difficulties. The short answer is that the megatrend of globalization demands it. The long answer is that, given the opportunities and challenges of globalization, successfully managing human resources creates value and fortifies competitiveness. Both answers highlight IHRM's mandate: Devise systems to develop and sustain a cadre of managers that lead the MNE to attain its strategy.

THE STRATEGIC ROLE OF IHRM

Anecdotes suggest, and research confirms, the powerful relationship between IHRM policies, executive expertise, and strategic performance. GE's former CEO, for example, sees global success as "truly about people, not about where the buildings are. You've got to develop people

FIGURE 20.2 Factors Influencing IHRM in IB

Successful MNEs consistently show that managing human resources, like managing finance, marketing, and supply chains, follows the requirements of the MNE's strategy. The key task centers on putting the right person in the right job in the right place at the right time for the right compensation for the right stretch—with the standard of "right" set by the MNE's strategy.

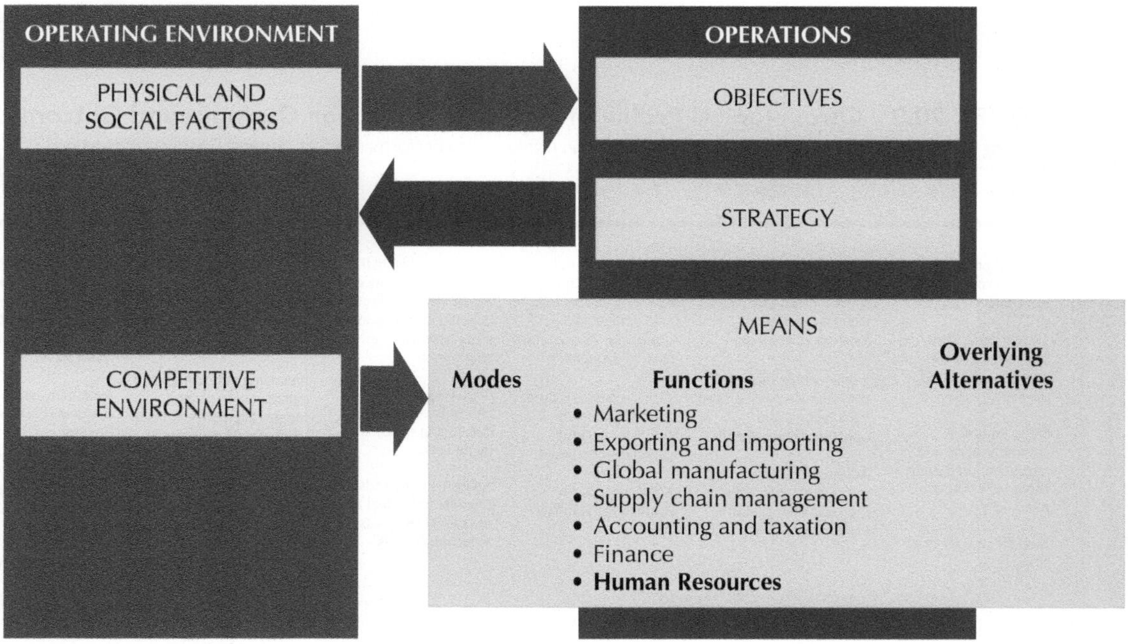

HRM policies that support the MNE's strategy generate high productivity and competitive advantage.

so they are prepared for leadership jobs and then promote them. That's the most effective way to become more global."[27] Ongoing study of MNEs in Asia, Europe, and the United States confirms that MNEs with superior human capital practices sustain high productivity, value creation, and competitive advantage. On average, they consistently create greater value than those with run-of-the-mill IHRM practices. Pulling this off makes for a dramatic payoff for a company; research reports that improving the quality of decision-making generates 2.5 times higher growth, two-times higher profit, and 30 percent higher return on invested capital.[28]

Improving understanding of the link between human resources and company performance tests the thesis that superior performance creates the resources that then enable an MNE to develop superior IHRM practices—that is, the notion that first comes success, then follows superior IHRM. Analysis indicates the reverse: Superior IHRM is a key determinant of a firm's performance. Furthermore, the interaction between an MNE's strategy and its IHRM practices accounts for more variation in performance than does IHRM in isolation. These relationships suggest IHRM is not a glorified euphemism for personnel management, concerned with administering routine workplace processes. Rather, IHRM is a performance driver, identifying, compensating, and retaining the executives that command the knowledge, skills, and abilities to direct the MNE.

Figure 20.3 puts this issue into broader perspective. Profiling the evolving outlooks and outcomes of expatriate management over the past 50 years shows the progression from practical to strategic interpretations. Early on, IHRM was typically a sidelight to the firm's domestic business; expats were selected opportunistically based on relevant experience. Then, functional expertise was seen as necessary and sufficient for high performance. The matters of outlook and orientation say, in terms of linguistics, cultural readiness, or leadership style, were largely left up to the individual. Presumably, the executive interested in an international career would monitor world events, travel abroad, and socialize with people of different ethnicities, cultures, and nationalities. Over time, performance records indicate that when eventually sent abroad, these sorts of managers progressively outperformed their less worldly counterparts. The variability in performance among expatriates led MNEs to expand preparation and support programs beyond optimizing technical capabilities.

Expanding IB activities pushed companies to amp up their game. IHRM steadily improved the assessment, selection, and organization of who ran overseas activities, applying operational, business, and market aspects to support the company's strategy. Steadily, understanding of the expat assignment grew sharper, selection of diverse candidates grew broader, and expertise integrating programs and policies grew sophisticated. As a result, IHRM progressively passed its acid test—today, approximately five percent of expats fail to complete their assignment. In the 1980s, expatriate failure was an big problem. Then nearly a third of American expatriates assigned to developed countries returned home early due to performance difficulties; the failure rate was twice that for those posted to less-hospitable countries.[29]

FIGURE 20.3 Chronological Profile of Expatriate Selection Outlooks and Outcomes

Profiling the evolving understanding of expatriate selection highlights key performance features and IHRM considerations.

Pre-1970

Informal processes govern expatriate selection.

Typical candidates are officials, diplomats, veterans, and world travelers.

Slow, expensive communication and transportation distances expatriates from the home office.

Men fill most if not all slots.

1970s

Singular focus on posting managers with technical skills and operational expertise to exploit location economies.

Home country nationals predominate given proven track records and operational experience.

Adjustment problems led to the early return of a third to half of posted expatriates.

1980s

Technical skills still dominates selection but expanding to find folks to build competitive subsidiaries that optimize location economics.

Efforts to reduce failure rates expand analysis to look at moderating workplace conditions.

Women are slowly included in candidate pools.

1990s

Accelerating globalization escalates importance of expatriates to improve operations and optimize cross-national supply chain links.

Improving selection effectiveness spurs developing systematic frameworks.

Assessment expands to consider individual and situational factors as well as technical skills.

2000s

Expatriates selection frameworks challenged by novel market situations in fast-growing emerging economies.

Improving information and transportation systems support alternative forms of international assignments.

Assessment emphasizes personal characteristics and family situation in order to improve effectiveness and reduce expatriate failure rates.

2010s

Growing supply of bright workers everywhere expands operations into more countries, opening more expat slots in more places.

Expatriate assignments progressively shorten in duration.

Women earn an increasing share of expatriate posts.

Expatriate failure rates drop to approximately five percent.

2020 Onward

Growing supply of bright executives everywhere expands pools of potential candidates.

Expatriate assignments progressively increase in strategic significance.

Increasing share of migrant and self-initiated expatriates.

Sophisticated software heuristics and programs enable HRM to apply algorithmic program; advances in artificial intelligence improve applications.

Expatriates in motion mark the ebb and flow of travelers worldwide.

Source: Rob Wilson/Shutterstock

flyer assignments." In all cases, IHRM more effectively recruits a broader cross-section of candidates given fewer restrictions imposed by family concerns and career planning.

Changing markets, growing cost consciousness, and evolving strategies reset notions of who is an expatriate—now we see growing interest in the young, the old, and the restless.

The Young, the Old, and the Restless Besides duration, who goes abroad also evolves. Traditionally, expatriates were mid- and upper-level executives sent overseas to fine-tune leadership skills and prepare for bigger and better things. Effectively, international assignments were career stepping-stones for the MNE's best and brightest. This mindset still prevails in many MNEs. Xerox and Bertelsmann, for instance, rotate rising stars through two- to four-year assignments; successfully passing this test makes one a C-level contender. Increasingly, IHRM expands expat searches to consider older employees, whose children have grown and whose spouses see an international assignment more positively, and younger employees, who are single, more mobile, and eager to experience life abroad. Reports indicate that 11 percent of expats were 20–29 years old, 31 percent were 30–39 years old, 30 percent were 40–49 years old, and 17 percent were 50-plus.[32] Moreover, the aging workforce in North America and Europe, as well as Asia and Latin America, within the context of the so-called silver revolution, steadily expand the growing proportion of older expatriates.[33]

MNEs trade performance track records for long-term potential when posting younger managers to international assignments.[34] Increasingly, one sees individuals who relocate on their own initiative and motivation to work abroad —these are commonly referred to a **self-initiated expatriates** (SIEs). Consider that a survey of 22,318 expats in over 100 countries found that just 12 percent has been asked by their employer to work abroad; 35 percent moved abroad to improve job prospects while 28 percent did so to seek a new challenge. This outlook is notably strong for millennials—98 percent rated career development/opportunities and 61 percent rated discovering new countries/cultures at the top motivation to take a foreign assignment. The Internet in general and social media in specific encourage SIEs, providing expanding information on and extolling the experience of international careers.[35]

University programs respond to as well as accelerate these trends. Schools worldwide internationalize their curricula, expand study-abroad options, offer joint degrees with foreign institutions, and recruit international students. Similarly, some students take the big plunge, heading abroad for college. The number of foreign students attending U.S. universities, for example, grew from 110,000 in 2001 to 524,000 in 2012, to 1,095,822 in 2019.[36] The reverse is evident too; Americans enroll in overseas programs, seeing foreign study as a gateway to an international career. Explained one attending ESADE in Barcelona, "If you look at the world today, at the state of business, you see that bridges are being built and borders broken down. I desired to focus on global business to expand both my knowledge and my network."[37] SIEs, heading abroad to pursue cultural, personal, and career experiences, refine interpretations.

CONCEPT CHECK

Chapter 12 reported that the search for superior competitive advantage pushes many MNEs to build globally integrated enterprises that implement increasingly sophisticated strategies. Consequently, they adjust their idea of an expatriate, fine-tuning the traditional notion of someone posted abroad for a lengthy tour as well as experimenting with novel formats that tinker with duration and design.

Expanding Scope of Women The gender dimension of expatriate selection evolves. Today, 1 of every 3 expatriates is female; in 1980, the ratio was 1 out of 20.[38] Since 2001, MNEs in the Asia–Pacific region have seen a 16-fold increase in women posted to international assignments, MNEs in North America have seen nearly a fourfold rise, and Europe has doubled its count. Reasoned an IHRM analyst, "Going on expatriate placements can be an important step on the career ladder, and women are increasingly interested in taking these assignments."[39] Research reports females executives, besides excelling in interpersonal interactions and adaptability, are equally effective as males in managing international assignments[40]

Growing Scope of Third-Country Nationals MNEs establish operations abroad in progressively dissimilar markets—say, from the United States to Canada to England to India to Singapore to China to Vietnam. The changing workflow of globalization elevates the role of third-country nationals, who often have the outlook, resourcefulness, and versatility to run operations in diverse locales. Longer term, the supply of skilled third-country nations expands, especially in emerging economies. China, for example, now has the world's largest education system, with enrollment growing from 7.4 million in 2000 to more than 45 million in 2019. Its higher education institutions graduate more than 8 million graduates annually—more than India and the United States and India combined—and is projected to grow by 300 percent until 2030.[41]

Western MNEs struggle to find executive talent in emerging markets at a pace that matches their expected growth. Executives from one set of MNEs reported that just 2 percent of their top 200 employees were based in Asian emerging markets; in the next few years, however, these markets will account for more than a third of total sales.[42] A popular solution designs short-term assignments that leverage the logistical flexibility and cultural versatility of third-country nationals. An executive living in Dubai, for instance, may spend Monday through Friday working in Mumbai, then return home via a 3-hour flight, for the weekend. Then, as the need arises for help in the MNE's Doha office, they change this commute.

"Fly In–Fly Out" mobility lets an MNE adroitly adapt its strategy, confident it has well-positioned exectives who can move in real time to make immediate changes. Data document the growing use of third-country nationals. A generation ago, most expatriates were selected from the executive pool in the MNE's home country. About 60 percent of international assignees relocated to or from the headquarters country; others relocated to or from a non-headquarters country.[43] Likewise, IHRM increasingly sources expatriates from new locations, recruiting mobile talent from non-traditional spots.

Reverse expats spend a predetermined amount of time at the company's home country operations before running emerging market operations.

Reverse Expatriates The rising importance of emerging markets refines our evolving ideas of expatriates. Historically, MNEs recruited executives in established markets, such as Germany and the United States, and assigned them to units in emerging markets, such as China or India. Now, talented executives from emerging economies—so-called **reverse-expats**—are posted straightaway to operations in established markets to speed their development. They spend anywhere from a few weeks to a year immersed in the home office before returning home—where they often supplant a traditionally defined, higher-paid, expatriate.

Bertelsmann, the German media giant, brings local managers to its corporate center, thrusting them into leadership situations where they compete for senior roles; the winners return with a keener strategic understanding and a network of like-minded high-performers. Some MNEs tweak this option. They recruit high-potential, foreign-born MBAs from Western universities and post them to, say, New York or London offices, before transferring them to emerging centers like Singapore, São Paulo, or Hong Kong.

THE ECONOMICS OF EXPATRIATES

Expats, if anything, are expensive—the disruption of changing countries calls for extraordinary compensation. Besides salary, relocation, taxation, housing, cost-of-living, and education allowances mean that an expat package runs two to three times an expat's annual pay. Furthermore, indirect expenses escalate as IHRM must oversee the special circumstances of predeparture training, relocation, family transitions, and repatriation. For example, an expat slot generates more paperwork than an equivalent domestic slot. Setting policies and systems to administer the complicated circumstances of expat assignments requires, on average, twice as many HR professionals than needed for a comparable non-expatriate executive slot.

Escalating cost concerns spur MNEs to emphasize commuter posts in lieu of longer-term international expatriate assignments.

Understandably, 70 percent of a worldwide sample of IHRM directors report ongoing efforts to reduce expat expenses.[44] Increasingly, IHRM focus on alternatives to the traditional, multiyear assignment, emphasizing short-term and commuter assignments. Rather than moving to foreign markets, executives travel far more often to far more places that lie farther from their home base. Currently, short-term posts (3 to 12 months) represent more than half of expat assignments.[45] Likewise, cost concerns accelerate deploying third-country nationals in place of parent-country executives. The latter often demands richer compensation packages, relocation allowances, and greater administrative support. Cost pressures encourage **localization**, whereby an expatriate retains the foreign assignment but accepts the status of a local hire and, correspondingly, a lower host-location salary. Some MNEs go with "expat-lite" slots that offer fewer monetary benefits without sacrificing opportunities for personal and career development.

Increasingly, IHRM adopts automation and artificial intelligence systems to improve the economics of expat management. Software platforms and predictive analytics, powered by ever-expanding data flows, perform ordinary administration as well as organize strategic aspects. IBM, for example, reports that its artificial intelligence system has replaced 30 percent of its HR staff and can predict with 95 percent accuracy which workers are about to quit and advise HR to step-in with skills training, education, job promotions and raises, before they do.[46] Improving technologies that expand workplace analytics and process control steadily improve the efficiency of managing expatriate programs—especially given that the most common challenges tracking assignment costs are multiple systems, insufficient technology, and inaccurate data. Expectedly, IHRM reports increasing demand of data, analytics, and benchmarks by senior management.[47]

THE ENDURING CONSTANT

Evolving trends in the global marketplace drive evolving ideas on staffing international operations. Still, there is an enduring constant: Running the hundreds of thousands of subsidiaries throughout the world requires a mix of talented, enterprising locals, parent-country, and third-country expats. So keen is demand that MNEs report ongoing shortages of expatriate talent for international assignments and, consequently, expand the pool to include candidates from all sorts from all sorts of places.[48] Throughout it all, IHRM aims to staff the right person in the right job in the right place at the right time for the right compensation for the right stretch. Success drives strategy and sustainability. Failure erodes careers and diminishes performance.

STAFFING FRAMEWORKS IN THE MNE

20-3 Differentiate the staffing frameworks used by MNEs

CONCEPT CHECK

Discussion of "Company and Management Orientations" in Chapter 2 (page 45) introduced the ideas of polycentrism, ethnocentrism, and geocentrism to describe how MNEs and their managers approach foreign cultures. Here, we reintroduce these terms, highlighting the ways these "attitudes or orientations" influence an MNE's staffing framework.

IHRM applies a **staffing framework** (a conceptual structure that helps solve complex issues) to organize expatriate policies and programs. A staffing framework identifies the optimal mix of local workers from the host nation, expatriates sent from the home country, and third-country nationals. Likewise, it makes sense of the trade-off between short versus long-term assignments. Most importantly, a staffing framework organizes the selection, training, duration, compensation, and repatriation guidelines in terms of the demands of the MNE's strategy. Recall from Chapter 16 that high performance requires the right organization, a task that, in turn, requires the right sorts of executives to run the show. In broad terms, IHRM applies an ethnocentric, polycentric, regiocentric, or geocentric staffing framework.

THE ETHNOCENTRIC FRAMEWORK

Ethnocentrism is the conviction that one's preferred policies and procedures are the superior way to manage anyone, anywhere.

Ethnocentrism occurs when one group sees itself atop a perceived social hierarchy. Hence, the **ethnocentric framework** signifies the belief that the management principles and business practices used by headquarters are superior to those used elsewhere. The proven success of the company's way of doing things, goes this reasoning, means there is little call to adapt people and processes to foreign markets. Thus, the MNE fills executive positions in foreign units with home-country nationals (i.e., a Japanese MNE fills its international slots with Japanese executives).

Advantages Home-office executives commonly explain there is no shortage of executive talent in a host country. Rather, the shortage is people with the right mix of operational expertise, industry experience, and fluency with the company's culture. Thus, staffing overseas slots with parent-country nationals has strategic, transfer, and socialization benefits.

Strategic Advantages A firm earns success in its home market by uniquely bundling resources and capabilities to create proprietary competencies. Success often leads a firm to see its way of doing business as the superior means of creating value. Likewise, it sees international success as dependent on doing the same things, the same way, elsewhere. Headquarters concludes that executives who have performed successfully at home will do the same overseas. Thus, they adopt an ethnocentric staffing framework and use home country nationals to fill expat slots. Likewise, the growing importance of protecting ownership advantages spurs an MNE to safeguard its competencies. With these strengths, the firm prospers; without them, the firm struggles. Many MNEs prefers entrusting control of the company's "crown jewels" to those who will best protect them: namely, trustworthy colleagues from the home country. Earlier discussion of intellectual property explained that legal safeguards deter, but do not prevent, theft. The ethnocentric framework fortifies defenses by posting reliable home-country executives to safeguard assets.

The ethnocentric framework fills key management positions with home-country nationals.

Transfer Advantages Regulating the transfer of an MNE's competencies is vital when they are difficult to articulate, specify, or standardize. For example, think of the challenge of codifying Apple's product-design and media expertise, Walmart's information-management and product-distribution systems, Ritz-Carlton's standards of service, or Honda's mastery of engine technology. An ethnocentric framework offsets this problem by posting home-country managers with technical knowledge and direct experience to local slots.

Socialization Advantages Expats from the home office, besides diffusing technical expertise and insight, also help socialize locals to the company's global outlook. Consider India's Wipro Technology, which has nearly 170,000 employees servicing over 900 of the *Fortune 1000* corporations with a presence in 175 countries. It uses more than 10,000 expats, most of whom are Indian, reasoning that they are best-prepared to spread the "Wipro Way." Explained its chief executive of global programs, "We sprinkle Indians in new markets to help seed and set up the culture and intensity."[49] The HSBC Group long epitomized this outlook. For generations, most top executives came from a tight-knit cadre of elite expatriates who, in circulating among foreign operations, proactively dispersed the "DNA of the organization."

Limitations MNEs have compelling rationales regarding relying on home-country nationals to run foreign operations. Yet, as the adage goes, vices are often virtues taken to extreme. The same applies to the ethnocentric framework. Difficulties arise on several counts.

Workplace Tensions Ethnocentric staffing policies often demotivate local workers. Posting parent-country nationals sends the message to subsidiary personnel that all the smart, capable people live within a 25-mile radius of the home-office headquarters. Unless an expatriate specifically transfers unique knowledge, local employees may resent someone they see as no more, perhaps even less, qualified than themselves. Unchecked, resentment can lower productivity and increase turnover as locals sense a glass ceiling capping their careers. For instance, Chinese executives' preference to work in a domestic, rather than a foreign, company has increased; data points to their sense of more upward mobility in local enterprises.

The ethnocentric staffing framework is vulnerable to problems arising from workplace, legal-political, and misreads and misfits tensions.

Legal-Political Tensions An ethnocentric staffing policy can prove legally difficult and politically impractical. National employment laws regulate, sometimes benignly, sometimes strictly, the use of expatriates in place of locals. Host governments, keen on developing their workforce, prefer that local business units hire locals. MNEs' plea that unique requirements prevent doing so often falls on deaf ears. If necessary, governments impose immigration laws that cap expats or workplace regulations that require local hires.

Misreads and Misfits Tensions Force-fitting foreign operations to mimic the standards of the home office risks pounding square pegs into circular slots. Certainly, an MNE can make its foreign operations mirror the outward appearance of its home-country headquarters. Assigning home-office executives to foreign operations, however, does not automatically create successful "mini-me" units. Consequently, an ethnocentric framework can post executives who inadvertently misread markets.

Early on, for example, Toyota aspired to sell a million cars annually year in China; early efforts fell short. Toyota conceded it had misread the Chinese market, notably offering cars priced too high with too little *daqi* (Chinese consumers' perception of road presence). Toyota's solution to its ongoing China problem, a reflection of its traditional ethnocentric staffing policy, complicated problems. Explained a senior Toyota executive, "Our way of beefing up operations in China is to bring in more people from Japan. We should be localizing our business here, promoting Chinese managers, and listening more attentively to Chinese consumers. But we don't."[50] Today, lessons learned have led Toyota to surpass its million-car mission.

THE POLYCENTRIC FRAMEWORK

The polycentric staffing framework looks to host-country nationals to manage local activities.

Polycentrism is the principle of organizing around different, but equivalently important political, social, or economic centers. Hence, the **polycentric staffing framework** acknowledges the business practices of foreign centers as philosophically and practically equivalent to those at home. Because business in the home country differs from that in foreign markets, and given the thesis of cross-national equivalency, IHRM adapts policies and programs to the host business environment. Thus, local executives are hired in the local market (e.g., home nationals staff home offices, Russians run Russian subsidiaries, Mexicans run Mexican subsidiaries, and so on). In rare cases where home-office executives are posted to foreign subsidiaries, the working assumption is that effectiveness requires immersion in the local environment.

Advantages Staffing foreign operations with locals has strategic, economic, and political advantages.

Strategic Advantages Proponents of polycentrism reason that local managers are superior performers given their sharper sense of local customers, markets, and institutions. Interviews of 300 senior executives at global companies, for instance, found that more than 60 percent believed locals better understood the local operating environment and customers' needs than did they.[51] As Microsoft's former COO explains, "You want people who know the local situation, its value system, the way work gets done, the way people use technology in that particular country, and who the key competitors are . . . If you send someone in fresh from a different region or country, they don't know those things."[52] Added Microsoft's chairman, "It sends the wrong message to have a foreigner come over to run things."[53]

Johnson & Johnson's (J&J) experiences spotlight related aspects. As a rule, locals run J&J's local subsidiaries. Each unit has substantial autonomy, commanding the freedom to act as it believes best given its read of the local market. Each unit performs as a small business, entrepreneurial in character and aware that success depends on its superior sense anticipating local customers' needs and delivering meaningful solutions. J&J's CEO explained that relying on locals to staff local operations "is a tremendous magnet for talent because it gives people room to grow and room to explore new ideas, thus developing their own skills and careers."[54] Likewise, fixing its Chinese market problems pushed Toyota to reset its IHRM policy, deemphasizing its traditional ethnocentric approach in favor of greater polycentricism. Explained a Toyota spokesperson, "We're promoting more local Chinese employees to management ranks and will continue to do so."[55]

Using host-country managers boosts local motivation and morale. Still, likely costs include gaps with global operations due to problems of autonomy and allegiance.

Economic Advantages A compelling motivation of the polycentric approach is its implications to expatriate economics. Hiring local managers eliminates the far higher expense of posting an expatriate. It is difficult to pinpoint the total cost of an expat assignment due to the range of relevant variables, including incentives, housing, relocation, taxation, and cost-of-living allowances. A general rule is that the total cost is two to three times the expat's annual compensation.

Political Advantages Host governments prefer polycentric approaches, seeing local managers as more inclined than expats to champion national interests over global objectives. Nationalist officials often require an MNE hire locals, imposing licensing requirements that prohibit certain sorts of expats, such as lawyers or accountants, as well as using visa regulations to limit the number of transfers—much as the United States, for example, does with its H-1B visa program. Besides neutralizing local pressures, the polycentric framework opens opportunities. Toyota, for instance, believes its Chinese managers better understand the intricacies of building relationships with the powerful Chinese Communist Party.

Limitations The polycentric approach, by effectively decentralizing authority to local subsidiaries, fans organizational tensions on several counts.

Autonomy and Allegiance Installing local executives in decision-making roles give them opportunities to develop their skills and build thriving operations. Success supports growing resource independence from the parent that can turn the local subsidiary into a quasi-autonomous unit. Unchecked, an MNE risks devolving into a federation of loosely connected, quasi-autonomous national operations that pay progressively less mind to headquarters. Likewise, dilemmas over allegiance emerge when host-country managers are loyal to local coworkers instead of their home-country colleagues. In theory, local managers balance the competing demands of making sense of events from a local and the home-office view. In practice, however, national concerns often take precedence given the immediacy of local pressures. Left to their own devices, local managers may respond to local circumstances in ways that complicate integration with global operations.

Motivation and Mobility Tensions There are few expatriate slots in the polycentric framework; again, host-country nationals manage local subsidiaries, parent-country nationals run corporate headquarters, and a select few move between countries. Locals' few opportunities to work outside their home country effectively cap their mobility. Consequently, local managers may see little incentive to study multinational business practices or identify ways to improve cross-national integration. The resulting single-country focus can isolate national subsidiaries as well as push enterprising executives, ambitious to work abroad, to look elsewhere.

THE REGIOCENTRIC STAFFING FRAMEWORK

The regiocentric staffing framework fills expat slots with executives that have the corresponding regional outlook and orientation and typically reside in the region.

Regionalism is the presumption of a common outlook and orientation that expresses an identity and shapes collective action within a defined region. Geographic proximity is a leading cause of regionalism, but other factors, such as political integration, shared language, common religion, are often the catalyst. More commonly, as profiled in Chapter 8, MNEs respond to cross-national cooperation and agreements that institute free-trade areas, customs unions, common markets, and economic unions. The European Union, for example, unites 27 countries and creates a common "home" for 445 million who share similar outlooks, overlapping national interests, and convergent consumption preferences. We see similar situations, for example, in the Caribbean Community, Association of Southeast Asian Nations, Southern African Development Community, the and the Economic Community of West African States, Asia-Pacific Economic Cooperation, Southern Common Market, and the United States-Mexico-Canada Agreement.

The flows of people, capital, information, products, and processes throughout an integrated region encourages staffing expat slots with executives that have the corresponding regional outlook and orientation; hence, the regiocentric staffing framework. Then, IHRM fills international assignments within a region with executives already residing in that region; candidates usually are home-country nationals (e.g., Nestlé, headquartered in Switzerland, assigning a Swiss executive to run its German unit) as well as third-country nationals (e.g., Nestlé assigning a German executive to run its French unit).

Advantages Staffing intra-regional units with "regio-pats" has strategic and proximity advantages.

Strategic Advantages Staffing expat slots within a region by folks who reside in the region develops cohesive, coherent interpretations of business activities and market situations and. Proximity, whether geographically, operationally, cognitively, and culturally, supports rapidly transferring ideas through the units that comprise the region. Navigating regional regulations on approvals, submissions, and government controls in, say, medical devices and pharmaceuticals, is easier done with regio-pats applying a regional perspective. Likewise, familiarity with customers and competitors, given overlapping cultural and linguistic practices, improves bundling resources, capabilities and competencies.

Proximity Advantages Managing human resources within a geographically proximate region supports all sorts of operational advantages. Flexpats, commuters, and gig-pats are compellingly practical options given the ease of traveling among neighboring countries. IHRM can then leverage a wider range of executive talent in that many intra-regional assignments do not require relocating—i.e., an executive that lives in Seoul but works Shanghai can easily move back-and-forth given the numerous, two-hour, daily flights. Then, to top it off, these sorts of assignments are less costly and impose fewer administrative complications. Other benefits follow from linguistic, cognitive, and cultural intersections; ultimately, goes the reasoning, improved communication improves collaboration that improves decision-making.

Limitations The focused domain of a regional operation can intensify organizational and interpersonal social dynamics. Unchecked, ordinary complications can escalate into charged complexities.

Position and Power Disaggregating the operations into regional zones directs regional units to focuses outlooks and orientations on regional matters at the expense of global integration. For example, the European Union is home to 445 million people, more than enough to support efficient and effective operations. Executives focusing on the unique needs of the immense European Union may overemphasize regional needs at the cost of poorly aligning with global objectives. Unchecked, expats may institute a regional decision-making process that runs counter to headquarters.

Legacies The rationale that folks that reside in a region share outlooks and orientations is appealing, but not necessarily realistic. For example, the scale and scope of integration that marks the EU certainly gives the appearance of unanimity; the Schengen Agreement, for instance, abolished national border checks among member nations. However, profound differences persist. For instance, the EU has 24 official languages; three, namely English, French, German, carry the higher status of procedural languages. Besides enabling communication, language also carries an immense range of cultural connotations and latent symbolism. So, tempting as it might be to think that expats from any of the 27 members of the EU can easily move among regional slots, all sorts of legacies pose problems to communication, and thus, collaboration. Differing cultural, social, political, and legal moderators among nations within a region similarly challenge the effectiveness of the regio-pat.

THE GEOCENTRIC STAFFING FRAMEWORK

The geocentric framework posts the most-qualified executives, regardless of nationality, to expatriate slots, regardless of location.

Geocentrism is a world-oriented set of attitudes and values that regards humanity as a single entity sharing universal outlooks and orientations. The **geocentric staffing framework** reasons that the best way, wherever discovered, works everywhere, whenever applied. As such, it sees the blunt split of home-, host-, and third-country managers as needless divisions. This charge pushes IHRM to develop executives, regardless of their original home or eventual host market, with the knowledge, skills, and abilities needed to get the job done. Reasoned the former CEO of GE, "It's more important to find the best people, wherever they may be, and develop them so that they can lead big businesses, wherever those may be."[56] Rather than the call for an executive to overcome the"liability of foreignness,"the critical limitation of the ethnocentric framework and the key motivation of the polycentric framework, the geocentric framework holds that an "asset of globalness" is the basis of outstanding executive performance.

Advantages The geocentric framework develops executives whose global mindset enables them to easily and effectively navigate cultures and countries.[57]

Strategic Advantages Geocentricity's advocacy of the value of globalness advocates expatriates command a global mindset in order to apply different outlooks, synthesize insightful interpretations, and collaborate productively. The geocentric expat effectively implement the global and, especially, transnational strategy, finding ways to exploit learning opportunities, transfer knowledge, and promote interaction. As the CEO of Schering-Plough explains, "Good ideas can come from anywhere . . . the more places you are, the more ideas you will get. And the more ideas you get, the more places you can sell them and the more competitive you will be. Managing in many places requires a willingness to accept good ideas no matter where they come from—which means having a global attitude."[58]

Performance Advantages Executives who identify with both their home and host cultures outperform those who identify only with one or with neither. Likewise, geocentric top teams are financial high performers, particularly those implementing ambitious global strategies with strong cross-cultural dimensions.[59] Promoting broader attitudes and values in the executive ranks promotes outlooks that bridge differences and promote collaboration. The geocentric expat withstands cultural myopia, improves team representativeness, and enhances market responsiveness.

Limitations The geocentric framework is tough to develop and costly to sustain. Professional and logistic complications test its effectiveness.

Professional Tensions Working in diverse groups takes on a different vibe than collaborating with like-minded folks from culturally proximate countries. Often, the mix of different perspectives generates creative breakthroughs. However, making sense of the various outlooks that potentially bear on a decision poses intricate challenges. Akin to the Tower of Babel, geocentrism can erode common cause as the clarity of the task is lost in a hodgepodge of dissimilar outlooks. Hence, difficulties emerge when an expat struggles to retain their professional identity.

The geocentric staffing framework is vulnerable to problems arising from professional and logistic tensions.

Logistics Tensions The geocentric framework imposes costly logistics. Exposing executives to different ideas in diverse places, given the quest to leverage the asset of globalness, is expensive. Compensation costs escalate when high-priced executives shift from country to country. The pay and prestige conferred on the geocentric vanguard can trigger resentment among the rank-and-file. The geocentric framework's preference for multiyear assignments, seen as necessary to expand a global mindset, runs up against pressure to reduce expenses via short-term posts and flexpatriate slots. Operationally, immigration laws and visa caps can hinder efficiently maneuvering executives among subsidiaries.

WHICH STAFFING FRAMEWORK WHEN?

Table 20.1 summarizes the ethnocentric, polycentric, regiocentric, and geocentric staffing frameworks. Fundamentally, expatriates are a critical strategic driver: they launch new ventures, build management expertise, fill local skills gaps, transfer technology, and diffuse organization culture. IHRM must optimize its staffing policies in terms of the executive requirements of the MNE's choice of strategy—whether international, localization, global, or transnational. Expectedly, different strategies impose different HR requirements. Hence, Table 20.1 applies a contingency perspective that fits each staffing framework to corresponding strategy.

TABLE 20.1 Frameworks to Staff International Operations: Principles and Practices

The assumptions, advantages, limitations, and strategic fit of the leading staffing frameworks run the gamut. IHRM, keen to the requirements of the MNE's strategy, applies the most appropriate staffing framework. As it does, it minds various opportunities and trade-offs.

Framework	Assumptions	Advantages	Limitations	Strategic Fit
Ethnocentric	• The leadership ideals, management values, and workplace practices of one's company are superior to those elsewhere. • Headquarters makes key decisions and foreign subsidiaries implement them.	• Leverages and protects core competencies. • Promotes executives' international outlook. • Fills local skills gaps. • Transfers principles and practices of the company's culture.	• Fans dissent and demotivation among locals. • Discourages cultural empathy. • Managers may misread local innovations. • Alienates locals who prefer national orientation.	International Strategy, given its quest to leverage and safeguard the company's resources, capabilities, and competencies in foreign markets.
Polycentric	• Headquarters develops a vision and mission that local units adapt. • Responds to differences between home and host countries. • Superior competitiveness requires understanding local customers, markets, and institutions in the host market.	• Respects the unique merits of the local environment. • Local hires demand less compensation. • Local managers holding top jobs attract, motivate, and retain local employees. • Appeases host governments that prefer locals who champion local goals.	• Complicates coordinating and controlling activities. • Isolates country operations that create agency dilemmas. • Reduces incentives among locals to engage a global perspective. • Promotes a single nation focus among local staff.	Localization Strategy, given its quest to maximize the local responsiveness of foreign operations by adapting people, products, and processes to local standards.
Regiocentric	• Disaggregates the global market into regions that share political, economic, social, and cultural linkages and legacies. • Organizes decision-making in terms of regional standards, outlooks, and orientations.	• Easier to staff operations within the region with like-minded individuals. • Supports short-term flexpatriate, gig, and commuter assignments.	• Encourages expats to privilege a regional over a global perspective. • Institutionalizes differences among different regions.	International and Localization Strategies, given that is supports streamlining international operations while improving responsiveness to national units in the region.
Geocentric	• All nations are equal and possess inalienable characteristics that are neither superior nor inferior. • Headquarters and subsidiaries collaborate to identify, transfer, and diffuse best practices. • Ideas and innovations are found anywhere and everywhere—provided one is open to insights.	• Adroitly deal with different people with different outlooks in different countries. • Leverages strategic scale and operational scope. • Promotes learning dynamics that develop, transfer, and leverage good ideas worldwide.	• Tough to develop, costly to run, hard to maintain. • Contrary to many countries' market development plans that champion local causes. • Difficult to find and fund qualified expatriates with a global mindset. • High status of global expats demotivates supporting players.	Global and Transnational Strategies, given the quest to optimize worldwide integration and local responsiveness.

CONCEPT CHECK

Chapters 2, 3, and 4 evaluated the environments—cultural, political, legal, and economic—that frame IB operations. The variability in each context prevents setting absolute standards for running international operations. Here, we observe the implications of that variability for selecting expatriates. General guidelines often take the place of absolute standards.

EXPATRIATE SELECTION

20-4 Describe expatriate selection

Certainly, outstanding expatriates emerge on their own—so much so that we see increasingly more self-initiated success stories. Still, the ongoing need to staff global operations requires IHRM abandon chance and systematically identify folks who are interested in an international assignment, prepare them for the adventure, devise ways to motivate them, post them to the appropriate job, and leverage their improved skills into their next assignment. Hence, IHRM progressively systematizes programs to perform these functions, starting with selection, and moving on through preparation, compensation, and repatriation. Nearly 80 percent of companies use formal tools to gauge candidates' leadership and cultural readiness to the assignment.[60] Screening executives to find those with the highest potential and greatest inclination for a foreign assignment is the focus of **expatriate selection** (see Figure 20.4).

FIGURE 20.4 Criteria for Identifying a Candidate for an Expatriate Assignment[61]

IHRM evaluates various aspects of a candidate's knowledge, skills, and abilities in order to identify those folks ready to head abroad.

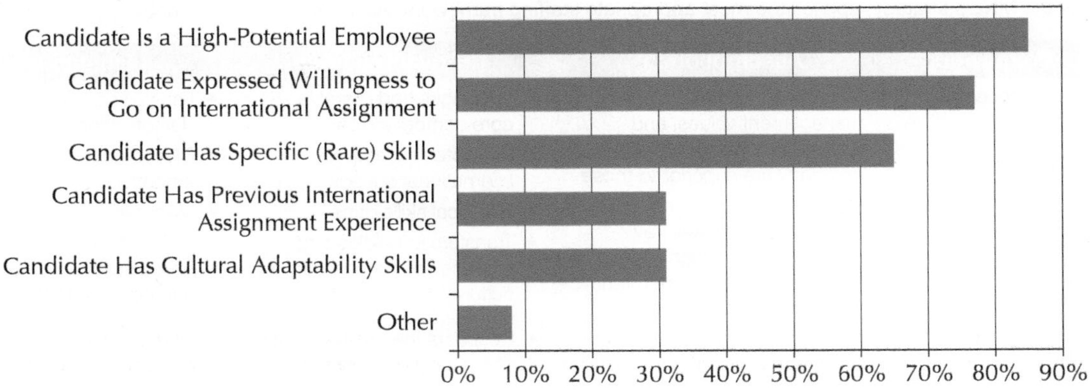

Generally, the challenge of expatriate selection is not finding candidates who are ready and willing to head abroad. Rather, it is identifying those who are also able. The complexity of running local operations defies precise metrics that reliably predict the performance of a potential expatriate. For example, most MNEs do not have a standard screening process to identify traits—such as resourcefulness and tolerance for ambiguity—that support successful performance. In recourse, IHRM may rely on hunch, sending someone who seems reasonably qualified. Failure, though, is expensive.

Avoiding this outcome, giving growing pressure to identify executives ready, willing, and able to go international, spurs IHRM to improve selection processes. Tests show assessing candidates' adaptability, resourcefulness, problem-solving, mindset, and tolerance for ambiguity help both the company and the candidate. For the company, it clarifies key success factors. For the candidate, it communicates the expectations of the job. Today, IHRM applies operational, cultural, cognitive, and personality measures, commensurate with its staffing framework, to screen candidates. Anecdotes and analysis emphasize the following categories.

TECHNICAL COMPETENCE

Technical competency and operational expertise are key determinants of executives posted to an expatriate slot.

An enduring selection criterion is an executive's technical expertise, as indicated by past job performance, and understanding of how to transfer it to the foreign unit. Implementing a software system, orchestrating a marketing campaign, or launching a new venture, for instance, often exceeds a subsidiary's competencies. Assigning a qualified expatriate transfers the necessary expertise. Consequently, filling a technical or managerial skills gap in a foreign subsidiary determines nearly half of the executives sent abroad.[62] The sorts of sophisticated expertise typically needed means candidates have practical experience. Relatedly, IHRM routinely screens candidates by consulting coworkers, thereby reinforcing the importance of operational expertise. Finally, outstanding technical competence is often seen as signifying the self-confidence needed to succeed abroad.

An ongoing debate in IHRM contests the relative importance of technical competence versus leadership and cultural readiness. Rather than the primacy of the former, some argue the latter should take precedence in the selection process. That is, instead of selecting the person who has the technical skills and assuming they can develop the necessary leadership and cultural skills, the reasoning goes, IHRM should identify behaviorally ready candidates and then confirm the requisite technical competencies. Still, IHRM routinely reports that filling a managerial or technical skills gap is the primary objective in more than half of international assignments. Moreover, given growing workplace diversity and cross-cultural connectivity, expats are typically more culturally ready than not; more than 80 percent of assignees adapt to the local environment.[63]

SELF-ORIENTATION

An expatriate assignment is marked by ambiguity, uncertainty, and risk. Thrust into challenging situations, an expat's effectiveness depends upon developing new knowledge, skills, and abilities. Facing ambiguities, one must organize interpretation and fortify decision-making. Tested by physical, emotional, and social stress, one must reconcile choices and consequences. Hence, one's self-orientation, in terms of motivation, reliance, and conscientiousness, help one start and move onward. HSBC's selection process uses tests, interviews, and exercises to gauge a candidate's capacity for self-orientation. Still, HSBC evaluates intangible indicators, such as ambition and resilience. Explained its CEO, "We don't look so much at what or where people have studied, but rather at their drive, initiative, cultural sensitivity, and readiness to see the world as their oyster. Whether they've studied classics, economics, history, or languages is irrelevant. What matters are the skills and qualities necessary to be good, well-rounded executives in a highly international institution operating in a diverse set of communities."[64]

OTHER-ORIENTATION

Orientation, both self and other, helps expats

- manage ambiguity, uncertainty, and risk,
- resolve physical, emotional and social stress,
- support effective communication,
- enhances interpersonal interactions.

Executives note that new situations in new settings test their values and outlooks. Understanding how colleagues, customers, and competitors in the local market see events, rather than criticizing dissimilar perspectives, supports strong performance. Interpreting events in ways that reject stereotypes, preconceptions, and unrealistic expectations enables an expat to adapt messages to listeners' outlooks. Effective communication, an element of other-orientation, helps one go far in IB. Likewise, other-orientation promotes cultural empathy. This outlook helps develop friendships with foreign nationals and encourages, no matter how rudimentary, speaking the local language. Other-orientation enhances one's interactions with people and, importantly, an understanding of why some went well while others did not. These are critical to negotiating, leading, and resolving conflict in the local workplace. The records of successful expats indicate that they did not recoil from cultural differences, criticizing locals for their choices. Rather, their other-orientation improved their communication, tolerance, and diplomacy.

RESOURCEFULNESS

Resourcefulness refers to a person's potential for

- self-maintenance
- situational flexibility,
- interpreting the immediate environment,
- developing productive workplace relationships.

Executives in foreign subsidiaries usually assume a broader range of leadership roles than counterparts running similar-size home-country operations.

The precise job descriptions found in the job bank of the home office inevitably give way to far broader profiles in foreign subsidiaries. Complicating matters is the fact that an expat usually lacks the battery of resources available at the home office. The call to do many jobs simultaneously requires an expat find ways to interpret how locals engage the workplace, make decisions, tolerate uncertainty, use power, and build consensus. In addition, expats confront different trade rules, investment regulations, and business practices. Resourcefulness enables insightful solutions to situations.

Fast-growing markets, for instance, have attracted many MNEs and, by extension, expatriates. For European MNEs, emerging Asia is farther away and more different, along multiple dimensions than, say, North America. Moving from a rule of law environment (where the rules governing business are objectives directives, as in Germany) into a rule of man setting (where the rules are seen more as flexible guidelines, as in China) creates difficulties. One expat noted that in the West, "everything is transparent. If you want to obtain a license to do something, you don't need to spend money bribing an official or hiring a go-between: You just download the form from the Internet and apply."[65] Trading the transparency of Germany for the translucence of China can prove daunting for those accustomed to traveling the straight and narrow. Resourcefulness, whether adapting to cultures, laws, or simply getting around town, shapes an expatriate's performance, and hence, shapes the selection process.

GLOBAL MINDSET

A global mindset helps expatriates see opportunities, not threats and complexities.

A **global mindset** is an increasingly important precondition as well as an outcome of expatriate success. In short, it is the openness to and awareness of interpersonal differences with the willingness and ability to identify similarities in order to enhance executive performance. A foreign assignment inevitably presents an expat with new challenges in new places with new people. Finding solutions often requires adjusting preferred methods to alternative approaches. A robust global mindset aids adjustment, equipping an expat to make sense of situations, engage players and processes, and cleverly respond with innovative solutions.[66]

McKinsey & Company confirm that technical competence anchors an expat's performance. Its data, however, indicate that some expatriates perform outstandingly given their global mindset. Specifically, "When you look behind the success stories of leading globalizers, you find MNEs that have learned how to think differently from the herd. They seek out different information, process it in a different way, come to different conclusions, and make different decisions. Where others see threats and complexity, they see opportunity. Where others see a barren landscape, they see a cornucopia of choices."[67] The ability to synthesize opportunities from challenges in new, different ways in new different markets highlights the growing importance of a global mindset.

EXPATRIATE PREPARATION AND SUPPORT

20-5 Appraise expatriate preparation

CONCEPT CHECK

Improving understanding of the intricacies of international business operations along with increasingly sophisticated IHRM programs has steadily reduced the rate of expatriate failure. Evidence confirms the importance of commanding a broad band of knowledge about institutions, markets, companies, and consumers.

Ideally, IHRM begins preparing an executive for an international assignment long before they are slated to go. Too, IHRM does not stop once the new job begins; support systems carry on. Often, circumstances prevent deliberative preparation. A foreign operation may be experiencing a technical meltdown, managerial impasse, or hostile takeover that requires headquarters immediately dispatch support. But, in a perfect world, IHRM can prepare and then support an executive for an international assignment.

Unquestionably, as reported in Figure 20.1, working abroad is often an inspiring experience. Still, expatriates run into difficulties that influence performance. Today, rare is the foreign assignment that fails because IHRM misjudged a candidate's technical qualification. An expat's poor performance often follows from poor preparation for the lows of the international assignment. Figure 20.5 identifies recurring stress points. Highlights, naturally, require little preparation. Stress points, however, do. Reestablishing a social life, overcoming loneliness, and connecting with family and friends top the list; indeed, family-related issues are regularly why international assignments fail. The challenge of building productive relationships with new, different colleagues, to say nothing of everyday interactions with host nationals, fans anxieties. These concerns show that improving cultural readiness

FIGURE 20.5 Leading Concerns of Expatriates Ahead of Moving to Their Foreign Assignment[68]

A foreign assignment is rich with opportunity yet, at the same time, fraught with challenges. Prior to heading abroad, executives worry about many issues. Anticipating and adjusting for the sorts of problems shown here improves the odds of a successful experience

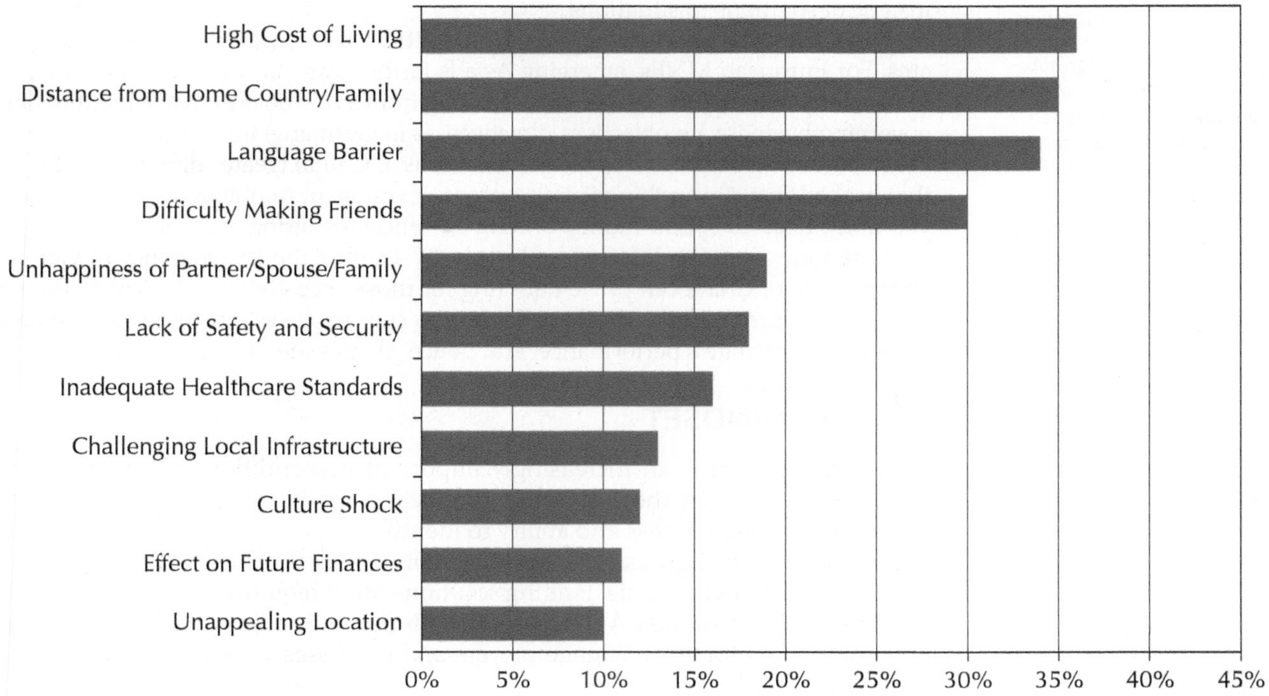

and interpersonal skills improves the odds of successful adjustment and, thus, a successful assignment. IHRM translates this imperative into a two-stage program: preparation prior to departure, and then, once in-country, ongoing support.

PRE-DEPARTURE PREPARATION PROGRAMS

Preparation programs transfer practical information about the host country as well as improve the expat's cultural readiness.

Host-country familiarization, cultural readiness, and socialization practices anchor most preparation programs. Profiles cover politics, laws, economics, workplace practices, business etiquette, logistics, and social norms. Instruction typically takes the form of roundtables, seminars, tutorials, videos, web activities, rooted maps, and readings. Collectively, these materials provide general area studies, market analysis, operational overviews, and workplace profiles. Time permitting, preparation includes cross-cultural training and rudimentary language lessons to help expatriates better navigate life in the host country. Cultural training clarifies how local ideas, attitudes, and beliefs influence workplace and social relations. These outlooks do not come naturally to all. Hence, preparing expats often requires helping them recognize gaps in their global mindset.

Culture shock is the anxiety and disorientation experienced when one moves into an unfamiliar culture.

Improving an expat's readiness helps immunize one to *culture shock*—a soon-after-arrival dissatisfaction with the host society, and in many cases, with the ways of the local office, that can deteriorate into homesickness, irritability, arrogance, and disdain.[69] Michelle Brown, for example, departed London for a job in Hong Kong, eagerly anticipating immersing herself in the new culture. The day-to-day practicalities of her new life, however, proved daunting. "I suppose I was quite naive, but Hong Kong was a complete culture shock," she says. "The humidity was insane, the smells made me ill, there was just so much to take in and not all of it pleasant."[70] Understanding the living and working environment boosts people's openness to and tolerance of foreign environments. Likewise, successfully navigating these pressures, reports show, makes expats more creative and entrepreneurial. Ongoing surveys report that more than 80 percent of expats see usefulness in cultural readiness preparation.[71]

IN-COUNTRY SUPPORT PROGRAMS

Once in-country, expatriates initially flow well in the workplace—colleagues share expertise and cut slack for the new guy. Ambiguous workplace situations eventually emerge that test the expat. IHRM often supports the expat via local mentorship, executive coaching, and virtual meetings that provide perspectives and resources. Increasingly, MNEs use web-based development programs, given that the expatriate can access them anywhere, anytime. Besides economical, their easy access provides convenient in-country reinforcement tools. Raytheon, takes it one step further, assigning an expat a support team that includes a sponsor, an in-country supervisor and an HR point of contact. The team participates in the expat's preparation, deployment and repatriation. Explained the VP of IHRM, "The support team is responsible for understanding the employee's assignment and career aspirations, and for engaging in regular communication and activities to help the employee fulfil development goals throughout their assignment."[72]

Key to successfully transitioning to a foreign assignment, beyond workplace adjustments, is mastering the new ways of the 3Ss—schooling, shopping, and socializing.

In terms of lifestyle, developing new routines in a different place is demanding. Expatriates, for instance, report big challenges arranging finances, health care, accommodations, and utilities in a host of locales, such as India, China, Brazil, Qatar, Russia, and Saudi Arabia. Notably easier, but still not the same as home, are South Africa, Canada, Thailand, and Australia.[73] Familiarizing expatriates and their families with host-country routines gives all a sense of the realities of daily life. The sooner they establish productive patterns of schooling, shopping, and socializing (to some, the "3Ss" of successful adjustment), the higher the odds of withstanding culture shock.

FAMILY MATTERS

Executives decline expatriate assignments for a variety of reasons, including career, compensation, and lifestyle concerns. All fall short of the influence of family and partner/spouse/children anxieties—executives cite those reasons nearly 60 percent of the time they decline a foreign assignment.[74] Furthermore, a persistent cause of poor performance is the struggles an expatriate's spouse and children experience adapting to their new home. The foreign assignment is stressful for the expatriate, but the transfer can overwhelm the family. Challenges follow from education concerns, lifestyle adjustments, and lingering regret about moving abroad.

Expats warn of a recurring dynamic. Abrupt separation from friends, family, and career isolates the spouse and children. Many then look for companionship and reassurance from the expatriate whose work responsibilities leave scant time to do so. Sometimes slowly, sometimes quickly, but almost always, family harmony suffers as stress escalates. Unchecked, the expat's work performance declines because, experiences indicate, if the family starts to unravel, the employee will likely too. Ultimately, family-related issues are the leading reason why expats fail at overseas assignments, nearly twice as influential as problems adapting to the location or poor candidate selection.[75]

Increasingly, expatriate preparation and support activities include the spouse and family members.

IHRM applies workarounds, such as including families in predeparture preparation, particularly destination familiarization and cultural readiness programs. Similarly, proliferating dual-career-track families lead IHRM to support spouses. Popular programs also include language training and career planning. Some offer allowances for spousal support, job possibilities, and volunteer options. Posting executives on short-term or commuter assignments, thereby avoiding uprooting families, helps circumvent these problems. Likewise, sending younger or older folks is productive. Younger candidates are likely single, seeking adventure, and open-minded. Alternatively, older candidates often have grown children, amenable partners, and a dash of wisdom.

POINT

English: Destined to Be the Global Language?

YES The use of English is greater than ever, and far more prevalent than any other language in the world—currently more than 2 billion people speak it. Inexorably, English performs as the lingua franca of the business world, providing a universal means for people to communicate and collaborate. When you get down to hard dollars, English rules. It accounts for a larger share of world output than that represented by the proportion of native speakers. Though it is the first language of roughly seven percent of the world's population, English speakers generate more than 40 percent of world output.

The Preferred Choice Situations in the European Union (EU), where more than half the population claims to be reasonably conversant in English, spotlight global trends. Among Europeans born circa 1950, English, French, and German are equally common. But 15- to 24-year-olds are five times more likely to speak English as a foreign language than either German or French. Add native speakers to those who have learned it, and some 60 percent of young Europeans speak English "well or very well."[76] Many envision improving their competency; more than 70 percent in a survey of 16,000 people living in the EU agreed, "Everybody should speak English." To that end, English is the working language of the European Union.[77]

We see similar trends elsewhere. India has the second-largest fluent English-speaking population, after the United States; it will capture the top rank within the decade. Hindi films, advertising billboards, and higher

COUNTERPOINT

English: Destined to Be the Global Language?

NO Learning a foreign language is an indisputably enriching experience that has life-changing and mind-altering benefits. Studying another society, through the prism of its language, clarifies one's understanding of the world as well as sense of self. The quest, and for many, struggle, to learn a foreign language opens new ways to think, do, and be

New Ways of Thinking Learning a foreign language changes the way you think, teaching you that there are other ways to express a concept, interpret an abstraction, and make sense of a situation.[86] Thinking differently, besides improving exchanges with stakeholders, sharpens business skills and expands global mindsets. Managers who learn a foreign language discover new ways to make innovative contributions. Research suggests that learning a foreign language makes you smarter. Bilingualism fortifies the brain's so-called executive function—basically, the command system that we use to plan, solve problems, and manage cognitively demanding tasks. Bilinguals demonstrate sharper sensitivity to environmental circumstances and show greater efficiency in solving problems. They sustain focus in the face of distractions, easily switch attention from one matter to another, and excel at organizing information.

Cultural Imperatives Language helps people build, understand, and express emotions, values, and intentions. A vibrant national language, besides defining and sustaining culture, fortifies nationalism. Rising education are in English. Most well-paying jobs in India require some English competency.[78] In China, state employees younger than 40 must master a minimum of 1,000 English phrases.[79] The prevalence of English throughout the Arab world fans worry about the decline of Arabic. American universities reflect these general trends as well. Although they are aggressively internationalizing their curricula, fewer universities require foreign language training—currently 37 percent versus 53 percent in 2001. Too, the share of university students enrolled in foreign language classes has dropped by half since 1960.[80]

The Default Choice Although English is not an official language in many countries, it is commonly taught as the second language. In the EU, 76 percent of schoolchildren study English, followed by French (32 percent), German (18 percent), and Spanish (8 percent). More than 90 percent study English in Malta, Austria, Spain, Italy, Cyprus, Poland, Croatia, and France.[81] More than a quarter billion students in China study English; some begin as young as two, but all by kindergarten. More than a fifth of Japanese five-year-olds study English conversation. Argentina requires students from the fourth grade through high school to study English two hours per week. Chile mandates public schools begin teaching English in the fifth grade.

Likewise, English is the language of choice in the classrooms of many African countries. Countries worldwide aim to become bilingual in English in the next decade or two in the belief that "it's the language for international teaching. English allows students to be able to come from anyplace in the world and for our students to go everywhere."[82] In sum, with 2 billion people speaking it and millions more studying it, we are witnessing the hegemony of English as the global lingua franca.

The Online Choice Expanding English usage gains from its predominance on the Internet. One can easily conduct business worldwide using the English interface of one's preferred browser. Heavyweight publications around the world, like *Der Spiegel, Al Jazeera*, and *China Daily*, offer English-language websites. The growing sophistication of translation software makes foreign language competency a moot point for those who prefer using their local language on the Internet. Nearly flawless simultaneous-translation devices are close at hand.[83]

Then again, online practices might change the notion of language. Rather than the phonetics or morphology of English, or for that matter, German or Mandarin, we'll master the semantics and syntax of Python, Java, or Ruby. The latter, forms of high-level programming languages, arguably better prepare people for a future in which digitalization is the foundation for nearly everything. Alibaba and Facebook serve more billions of customers in nearly 200 nations through websites that automatically translate more than 100 languages. Speaking a programming linguicide—the death of a language—spurs cultures and countries to protect their legacies. The death rate is accelerating: on average, every 14 days a language dies. By 2100, more than half of the 7,000 languages presently used will likely disappear.[87] Linguicide commonly follows from a community of speakers of the native language becoming bilingual in another language, then gradually shifting allegiance to the latter language until they no longer use the former.

Linguicide compels cultures to defend their language. Canada's Official Languages Act promotes and protects the equal status of French and English. France relies on its L'Académie française, its official authority on usage, vocabulary, and grammar, to prevent the Anglicization of French. Proliferating Arabizi—switching back and forth from Arabic to English—sparks concerns. Saudi Arabia prohibits using English to answer telephone calls in hotels, private companies, and government offices. Likewise, China's General Administration of Press and Publication sees the invasion of English words and abbreviations in Chinese texts as "abusing the language" and states that it "severely damages the standard and purity of the Chinese language and disrupts the harmonious and healthy language and cultural environment, causing negative social impacts."[88] China bans mixing foreign language phrases, such as English words or abbreviations like GDP (gross domestic product), CPI (consumer price index), or WTO (World Trade Organization), in Chinese publications. Lastly, deanglicization is a matter of national pride for some; India, for example, regarded Bombay as the corrupted English version of Mumbai and an unwanted legacy of British colonial rule. Hence, we now have Mumbai—and, for that matter, Kolkata, Bengaluru, and Chennai rather than Calcutta, Bangalore, and Madras.

New Networks Expats averse to learning a foreign language exclude themselves from influential networks, complicate relations with local officials, and slow socializing with workmates. Countries have different cultural and business expectations that one often deciphers by chitchatting in the local language. Working abroad is challenging; linguistic limitations worsen matters. As an expat recounted, her inability to speak Turkish made for a lonely stint in Istanbul—"You can't really mix with the locals or use local transportation because you can't read any of the signs."[89] Symbolically, the effort to speak the local language, no matter how poorly, sends a subtle but essential message: We are equal. Moreover, as anyone who has struggled to learn a foreign language knows, an unexpected benefit include a dose of humility.

New Requirements Eventually, foreign language competency will be a competitive necessity. The expanding international links and intercultural connections in a globalizing world make linguistic skills crucial for getting many jobs and accelerating careers. By the way, the language that solves the digital puzzle, rather than conversing with foreigners in their native tongues, may set the standard of linguistic competency in the context of digital globalization. As the director of government affairs of the Computing Research Association notes, "To be successful in the modern world, regardless of your occupation, requires a fluency in computers."[84]

The Only Choice MNEs respond in kind. Few employers rate foreign language competency as important to executive success; it regularly ranks well behind technical skills, leadership ability, and career development. Airbus, SAP, Lenovo, Honda, Daimler-Chrysler, Renault, Lufthansa, Rakuten, Aventis, Samsung, and Microsoft, to name a few, mandate English as the corporate language. Growing interest in programming languages, long considered arcane, changes standards. Finally, some say language skills ultimately are a misleading proxy of a global mindset. As one CEO explains, "I've met many people who speak three or four languages, yet still have a very narrow view of the world. At the same time, I've come across people who speak only English but have a real passion and curiosity about the world and who are very effective in different cultures."[85] Ultimately, sustaining a peaceful, prosperous global village requires people to communicate and collaborate—English, given its track record and progressive diffusion, is destined to do so.

notion that the spread of English competency worldwide means those who already speak it need not worry is dubious. Marketplace trends will likely punish, not privilege, English-only speakers. They steadily lose the advantages that once came with being among the small number of native Anglophones who spoke the language of business. Bilinguals or multilinguals increasingly match the skills of English monoglots, but also bring a broader perspective to the party. Officials have begun institutionalizing incentives. For instance, the EU's official language policy is "mother tongue plus two," whereby citizens are encouraged to learn two additional languages.

Which One? Ultimately, one wonders, which foreign language should I study? One has many choices, shaped by popularity, prevalence, and difficulty. Market trends clarify options for business players. Entrepreneurs may look around their hometown and go for fast-spreading languages such as Spanish, Chinese, or Arabic. Those looking abroad quickly sees jobs migrating from the established markets of the West, such as Germany, Japan, United States, to the emerging economies, such as Brazil, China, and India. As MNEs struggle to place executives in these high-growth markets, as well as hire local staff to communicate with foreign counterparts, proficiency in languages like Portuguese, Chinese, or Hindi opens opportunities.

EXPATRIATE COMPENSATION

20-6 Profile expatriate compensation

All things being equal, compensation determines the likelihood and success of an expatriate assignment. Pay too little, and people decline to go. Then, if they do go, resentment often proves demotivating and hastens an early return. Pay them too much, then costs escalate, returns fall short, and inequities fan dissension. Too, the higher the pay, the longer an expatriate assignment tends to last. Some managers, content to prolong a munificent lifestyle, are understandably less than eager to return home. Hence, IHRM must devise compensation plans that attract and motivate expatriates, but always mindful of their implication to the company's return on its investment.

Setting effective compensation systems that fairly reward executives require IHRM set differing pay levels, benefits, tax programs, and prerequisites. Should the MNE, for instance, pay executives in different countries according to the standards in each location? Or should it set pay for each position on a global basis? What sorts of allowances should it offer? How should it resolve the impact of different tax policies? Complicating matters is accommodating the different types of expatriates, such as long-term, short-term, commuter, flexpatriates, and third-country nationals. Finally, compensation policies fit the MNE's staffing framework, whether it is ethnocentric, polycentric, regiocentric, or geocentric.

Complicating matters is the relentless pressure on IHRM to economize the expense of an expatriate assignment. MNEs spend significant sums on an expatriate during a three-year assignment. Practically, posting a $250,000-a-year American executive from Atlanta to São Paulo overnight triples the cost to the employer. Moving to high-cost locales like Singapore, Luanda, or Zurich can suddenly make a million-dollar executive. Securing the move, along with safeguarding the return on the investment, requires IHRM negotiate a reasonable compensation plan. Several conditions shape the standards of reasonable.

- Setting compensation to "keep the expatriate whole," so that working abroad does not impose additional costs that diminish one's standard of living.
- Devising a package that convinces an executive and family to go abroad, reflects the assignment's responsibilities, and ensures that after-tax income does not fall.
- Setting plans that preserve pay equity among peers, promote parity among expatriates, and ensure compensation competes with packages offered by rivals.
- Designing compensation packages that reconcile the financial, tax, and legal differences between the home and host countries.

These are tough tasks. They expand with the scale and scope of the MNE's international operations. IHRM, through trial and error as well as astute analytics, meets the challenge through progressively improving compensation policies.

TYPES OF COMPENSATION PLANS

The most common approach to determining expatriate compensation is the balance sheet approach.

MNEs generally manage expatriate compensation with the **balance sheet approach**. This approach organizes compensation so that an expatriate has the same living standard in the foreign post as at home, no matter where the assignment is located. In the spirit of "keeping one whole," its fundamental principle is **equalization**: an expatriate should neither overly prosper nor unduly suffer from working abroad. The following methods implement variations of the balance sheet approach.

Variations of the balance sheet approach to expatriate compensation include

- home-based method
- headquarters-based method
- host-based method
- global market method

Home-Based Method This method bases expatriate compensation on the salary of a comparable job in the expat's home country, thereby preserving equity with home-country colleagues as well as simplifying the eventual return. Salary is set in the same manner as that for a domestic position, relying on job evaluation, competency assessment, market surveys, and incentives. It's the most prevalent compensation plan. Approximately 80 percent of MNEs apply it to short- and long-term assignments.[90]

Headquarters-Based Method This method sets the expatriate's salary in the terms of a comparable job in the city where the MNE has its headquarters. For example, if a Denver-headquartered MNE posts expats to its offices in London, Santiago, and Jakarta, it would give each executive a salary structured in terms of the going wage in Denver. This plan recognizes the disruption of a foreign assignment and helps expatriates live as they had in their home country. This plan eases moving an expatriate from a low- to a high-cost post.

Host-Based Method Sometimes called *destination pricing, going rate,* or *local-plus,* this method bases expatriate compensation on the pay standards in the foreign locale. IHRM starts by setting the expatriate's salary in terms of a local executive with similar responsibilities. The expat then negotiates additional compensation in the form of cost-of-living allowances, home-country benefits, taxation relief, and so on. The host-based method compensates expatriates, relative to the home- and headquarters-based methods, the least. Although not as beneficial to the expat, it reduces tension with the typically lower-paid, host-country colleagues.

"Keeping employees whole" requires IHRM nullify those features of an international assignment that negatively affect an expatriate's standard of living.

Global Market Method Variability in the types, conditions, and duration of expatriate assignments, from traditional to commuter to flexpatriate to gig, requires that IHRM tweak compensation methods. The global market approach views an international assignment as a continuous but irregular activity. It recognizes that an expatriate, in the context of a commuter, flex, or gig assignment, irregularly works for different durations in the same or, sometimes, different countries. Implementing this approach requires designing flexible systems and sophisticated performance tracking to "keep the expat whole."

COMPENSATION COMPONENTS

Expatriate compensation packages can include various payments, allowances, provisions, and reimbursements.

The home-, headquarters-, and host-, and global-market methods apply different goals and guidelines. Still, all expect an expat to negotiate the base salary along with various components like foreign-service premium, various allowances, fringe benefits, tax differentials, and benefits (see Table 20.2). The changing economics of expatriate assignments influences these components. Key points include:

TABLE 20.2 Components of Expatriate Compensation

Sending an executive on an international assignment imposes expensive logistics and considerable stress. IHRM tailors the various compensation components, given the location and duration of the post with an eye to keeping the expatriate whole. These sorts of components give HRM the flexibility to tailor pay plans to resolve special situations.

Dimension	Specification
Base Salary	An expat's base salary usually falls in the same range as that for a comparable job in the home country. It is paid either in the home-country currency or in the local currency.
Cost-of-Living	Ensures that expats don't suffer a decline in their standard of living due to the steep expense of a city (London or Lagos) or nation (Switzerland).
Foreign Service Premium	This cash incentive, a.k.a. mobility premium, compensates an individual for moving to a new country, living away from family and friends, dealing with the day-to-day challenges of the new culture, language, and workplace practices, and the reality of ultimately disrupting this life upon return. Long-term assignments often qualify for a mobility premium; short-term assignments rarely do.
Fringe Benefits	Various benefits supplement the expatriate's base salary, including health insurance, life coverage, education reimbursement, childcare assistance, and spouse support.
Hardship	Payment for an assignment in a difficult environment or dangerous location. A.k.a. combat pay, it offsets the costs of security systems, ransom insurance, crisis response safeguards, or threat management programs.
Housing	Allowance that enables the expatriate to replicate their accustomed standard of housing.
Tax Differentials	Varying tax policies require that MNEs adjust compensation so that expatriates' after-tax income does not suffer from the taxes incurred during the foreign assignment. Tax equalization is a costly component of expatriate compensation.

Assignment Type The growing use of commuters, flexpatriates, and gig-patriates the compensation calculus. Short-term assignments typically do not trigger a change in pay or benefits. Instead, the executive arranges per diem allowances for overseas activities.

Supply Dynamics More folks are willing to work most anywhere nowadays, motivated by career ambitions and personal quests. Some executives want to work abroad to turbocharge their career, whereas others want opportunities to expand their global mindset. In both cases, candidates see 'value' in aspects that offset lower pay. Consequently, many international assignments have moved from unique, munificent experiences to part of everyday operations. Foreign service premiums, likewise, have been phased out by many MNEs.

IHRM tailors allowances to help an expatriate offset the difficulties of

- different standards of living,
- replicating preferred housing,
- supporting a trailing spouse,
- extraordinary safety or security hardships.

Qualifying Locations Increasing globalization, by diffusing life-style standards, steadily reduces the number of hardship destinations. Certainly, some qualify on the basis of difficult climate, housing, crime, health care, or pollution conditions; expats assigned to such posts receive a hardship differential of between 10 and 35 percent of their salary. Still, IHRM reports decreasing hardship allowances for locales that are far more hospitable than they once were, such as Prague, Moscow, Shanghai, and Rio de Janeiro. Moreover, most MNEs with operations in Europe now treat the continent as if it were one country.

CONCEPT CHECK

The expanding scale and scope of globalization, driven by increasing physical and cybernetic connectivity, increasingly blur the idea of expatriates. Where once foreigners seemed exotic, today they seem almost commonplace. Consequently, there is less need to pay people premiums to go to business locations that are increasingly alike.

COMPENSATION COMPLICATIONS

Setting compensation in companies that use several types of expatriates in different types of locations expands analysis. IHRM, for instance, regularly resolves complications of the following sort.

Changing Standards The evolving dynamics of globalization require that IHRM fine-tune compensation methods. The home-based method, for example, was originally designed to compensate employees transferred from Western MNEs to slots throughout the world. Effectively, Western MNEs calibrated living indices and support allowances for moves from high-cost countries, such as England or the United States, to countries like Malaysia or Mexico. Difficulties emerge when the path reverses—say, transferring an executive from inexpensive Manila to costly San Francisco. Chinese expatriates, for example, generally do not enjoy lavish pay and benefits. China Unicom's managing director in Europe received his modest Chinese salary plus a small cost-of-living allowance during his foreign assignment. Combined, they totaled 30 percent of the local entry-level salary for his firm.[91] Hence, MNEs applying the balance sheet approach, particularly the home-based method, struggle to maintain pay equity and benefit consistency given the evolving locales of their international assignees.

MNEs struggle to equalize pay for the same type of job that is done by different people in different countries.

Consistency Concerns Systematizing pay and benefit programs while removing inconsistencies makes for fair and equitable compensation. Steadily, salaries for similar jobs vary less substantially among countries. Still, legal, cultural, and regulatory differences require tailoring performance-based pay by country and region. For instance, tax compliance poses ongoing disclosure requirements and accounting fees for expatriates who are U.S. citizens. Granted, the United States has treaties with more than 60 countries regarding the tax burden on American expatriates. Still, it is just one of two countries in the world, the other is Eritrea, that taxes its citizens regardless of where they live.[92]

Strategic Concerns An MNE applying an ethnocentric framework may have few expatriates today, but expanding internationalization complicates administering compensation packages run on a case-by-case basis. An MNEs applying a geocentric framework, alternatively, has expats of multiple nationalities that are moving from high- to low- or from low- to high-cost locations creates anomalies and exceptions. IHRM must determine if all managers who perform the same job, but in different locations, receive the same compensation. Extreme pay disparity among managers doing similar jobs saps co-workers' motivation. Organizing systems pushes IHRM to institutes standards.

EXPATRIATE REPATRIATION

20-7 Explain expatriate repatriation

IHRM directs a cycle of events: selection, preparation, compensation, support, and **repatriation**. The latter is the process of reintegrating an expatriate into the home company upon completion of the foreign assignment, intact, and in good spirits. Success at each stage in the sequence, not just early on, supports a self-sustaining cycle. Returning employees share their knowledge, experiences, and enthusiasm with colleagues. High-performing coworkers, realizing the rewards of an international assignment, look abroad.

Repatriation returns an expatriate to their home country.

Repatriation works for many returning expatriates; they report faster promotions, improved performance ratings, and increased compensation. Others, however, report careers stall, opportunities fade, and networks disappear. A survey of expatriates who had successfully completed their overseas assignments found that a third held temporary assignments three months after returning home. Some saw their new jobs as demotions that offered few opportunities to leverage their international expertise. Others report regrets coming home, complaining of struggles to have colleagues and company acknowledge their accomplishment.[93] Frustrated, former high flyers left for other companies—the long-term average switch is about 20 percent.[94] Still, spun differently, 80 percent of returning expats remain with their employer.

REPATRIATION CHALLENGES

IHRM, focused on boosting expat success rates, identifies recurring stress points. Consistently, job placement dominates concerns, followed by changes in personal finances and readjusting to life at home.

Repatriation can trigger work, financial, and social adjustment challenges.

Career Progression Pressed to pinpoint where repatriation breakdowns begin, IHRM target the difficulty of returning an expat to the right job. High performers who have worked abroad are less than thrilled to return to the same office and the same prospects. Others return home and see former peers promoted above them. Colleagues may question whether they've maintained cutting-edge skills during their all-expense-paid "vacation." Some may struggle to rejoin the office network, surprised by its changed culture. Resentment builds as a repatriate reasons that they have worked hard, taken one for the team, and deserve praise and promotion, but are casually neglected.

The principal cause of repatriation frustrations is finding the right job for the returning executive.

Going abroad often means leaving the power center for the periphery. As "out of sight overseas" deteriorates into "out of mind back home," repatriation difficulties emerge. This problem is compounded by the fact that most companies lack a formal repatriation strategy linked to career management, planning, and retention.[95] Hearing stories of stalled careers deters fast-track executives from considering an international assignment. Explains one executive, "MNEs station people abroad and then forget about them. If anything, advancement is even more difficult for the expat upon returning to headquarters, having missed out on opportunities to network with top management."[96] This situation plays havoc in business cultures, especially those anchored in collectivism, where face time with influential executives shapes promotions.

Reverse culture shock occurs when one experiences anxiety upon returning to one's own culture.

Changes in Personal Finances Returning home changes the expat's finances. Many enjoy rich benefits during an international assignment, living in exclusive neighborhoods, sending children to prestigious schools, employing domestic help, socializing with elites, and still saving a good amount. Returning home to a reasonable compensation plan with far fewer privileges can prove demoralizing.

CONCEPT CHECK

Chapter 4 notes that economic factors contribute to the changing profile of high-growth markets. Chapter 17 discusses new wrinkles in global manufacturing strategies and strategies in supply-chain management that respond to this changing profile. These trends lead some MNEs to preempt repatriation problems by changing their expatriate staffing policies to recruit locals to run local operations.

Personal Readjustment Return challenges repatriates to readjust to home life.[97] Difficulties emerge as they, and their families, experience reverse culture shock. Upon returning to the United States, one said, "I loved the culture so much in Peru. My feelings don't fit my own beliefs anymore. This is my home, but it doesn't make sense."[98] Depending on the length of the international assignment, repatriates may need to relearn what they once took for granted about hometown life. Meantime, children may struggle to fit into school, while spouses may feel isolated or out of touch with the career or friends they left behind.

MANAGING REPATRIATION

Repatriation dilemmas jam IHRM into difficult situations. An expat's office cannot sit vacant while they are posted abroad. Mergers, acquisitions, divestures, and restructurings, to name just a few, change a company's plans and, by extension, those it had for the expatriate. Likewise, permitting repatriated employees to bump their "replacements" on return solves one problem, but creates another. IHRM studies and solves repatriation complications precisely because the greater the difficulties that repatriates confront, the greater the difficulty in convincing others to accept international assignments. Hence, few dispute the importance of systematic repatriation programs.

Navigating repatriation requires a keen sense of its positive and negative aspects—before departure, while abroad, and especially before transitioning home.

IHRM routinely organizes workshops, appoints mentors, shares survival guides, and links return strategies to career management. Some find ways to create opportunities for the expatriate to utilize the international experience, providing official recognition, supporting the family's transition, and identifying more career options. IHRM integrate foreign assignments into career planning, developing oversight programs to safeguard the expat's career. Raytheon, for example, charges the expat's support team to help place the repat in a slot that aligns with their career aspirations and benefits from the international experience.[99] IHRM consistently advises that personal career management is vital to returning home triumphantly. Expats must manage the cycle, ideally through ongoing in-person and online networking. Passivity is hazardous given that repats report that networking is the most powerful tool to "stay in mind back home" while working abroad.

EXPATRIATE FAILURE

20-8 Describe expatriate failure

The best-laid plans, sadly, often go astray. Similarly, MNEs fall prey when they select their best and brightest executives, invest in their preparation, send them abroad, compensate them well, and watch them fail. Sometimes expatriate failure is the result of poor assignment planning, putting the wrong person in the wrong job at the wrong time with the wrong

FIGURE 20.6 Factors Most Commonly Responsible for Expat Assignments Not Going as Planned[100]

As is the expat position intrinsically diverse in expectations, outlook, and orientation, so too are the causes for failure. Individual, operational, environmental, and institutional factors play a part.

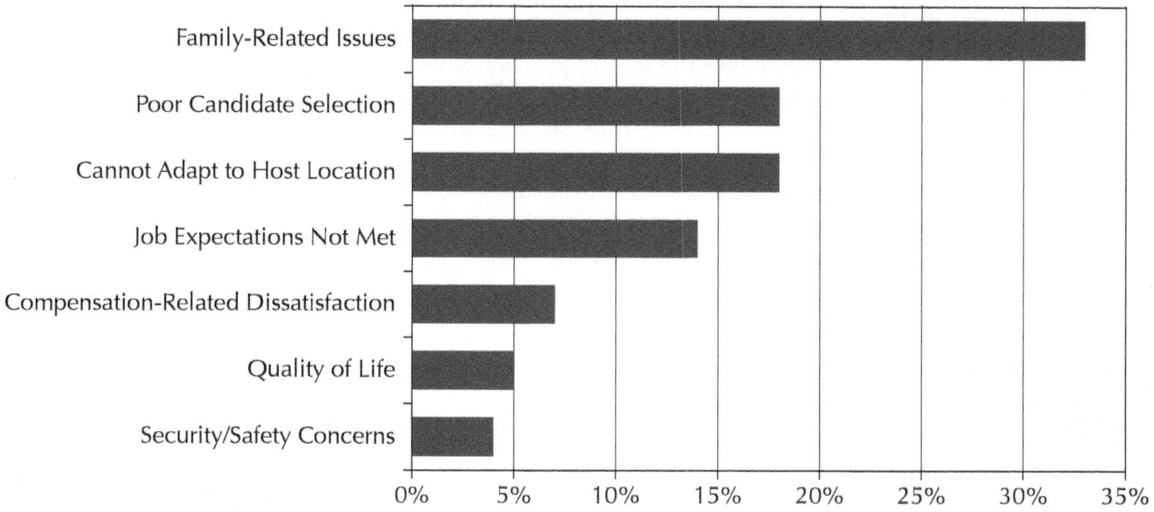

expectations. Other times it comes as a surprise, as personal circumstances disrupt what many saw as a sure thing. In either case, plans get twisted. **Expatriate failure**, narrowly defined, is a manager's premature return home due to poor performance. Broadly defined, it is the breakdown of IHRM's expatriate management systems.

The improving sophistication of expatriate selection processes has reduced the rate of expatriate failure.

In the 1980s, performance problems brought nearly a third of American expatriates assigned to advanced countries home early; the failure rate was twice that for those posted to less-hospitable countries. Today, approximately five percent of expats officially fail to complete their assignment. Figure 20.6 highlights leading causes. Worrisomely to IHRM is that many more—estimates run up to 25 percent—consider an early return but do not, given the negative connotations. Still, considering the option often reduces an expat's effectiveness. Difficulties adjusting to the host culture and quality of life, once commonplace concerns, are increasingly anomalies given improving cultural readiness and expanding global mindsets. Rather, increasingly, reconciling family issues, struggles to connect socially, and persistent loneliness are top reasons to return early; the latter two are notably daunting for millennials and Gen Zs.[101]

THE COSTS OF FAILURE

Expatriate failure is operationally costly, professionally detrimental, and personally stressful.

Declining failure rates testify to the improving sophistication of IHRM's talent to select, prep, and post the right individual to the right job. Certainly, the decline is cause for celebration. However, it does not signify mission accomplished. The financial and personal costs of failure, no matter how infrequent, are significant. Moreover, some worry about rising failure rates. Expansion into emerging economies puts expats into markets that test their resourcefulness to manage environments that are radically unlike their homes. Already, we see escalating difficulties. China and India, today's leading hotbeds of expat slots, top the list of locations with the highest failure rates.

Expat failure is costly. Direct costs often run as high as three times the expat's annual domestic salary plus the cost of relocation. Total financial costs are often eye-opening when one accounts for the expenses of selection, preparation, logistics, and then the resulting costs of lost productivity and damage control. An incalculable cost is the personal implications of professional failure to the formerly high-performing executive's self-confidence, corporate identity, and leadership potential. Finally, failure can impose severe hardship on the spouse and family.

THE WILDCARD

Going abroad calls for folks to navigate different environments marked by different norms, values, and behaviors. In theory, IHRM's screening processes identify those expatriates with the necessary technical qualification, conscientiousness, self-confidence, resourcefulness, cultural readiness, and global mindset. In some cases, notwithstanding noble intentions, some find the experience overwhelming. Sadly, early awareness of differences, as one might hear from an executive about to depart Boston for Bangkok, does not confirm the capacity to adapt to the odd, strange, and different. Notwithstanding the glamor and rewards, the expatriate lifestyle moves some beyond their comfort zone. Ensuing struggles can lead to nostalgia, culture shock, and loneliness. Then, no matter the degree of preparation, a sought-after adventure devolves into a depressing exile.

LOOKING TO THE FUTURE I'm Going Where? The Changing Geography of International Assignments

Increasingly, we see big changes in the geography of expatriate assignments and, more generally, professional paths. Western MNEs are reorienting their strategies toward countries that once were off the beaten path. A generation ago, expatriates, by and large, flocked to the premier business centers of the booming markets of Europe, North America, and Japan. Now, the rising importance of emerging economies, particularly in fast-growing Africa, Asia, and South America, leads them to open and expand operations there. Meanwhile, back in their home markets, Western MNEs downscale operations, reduce headcounts, and relocate activities to emerging markets.

Changing Configurations

As MNEs redraw battle lines, they redeploy their troops. In the 1990s, for example, U.S. companies added 4.4 million workers in the United States versus 2.7 million abroad. In contrast, during the 2000s they cut their workforces in the United States by nearly 3 million, while concurrently boosting employment overseas by 2.4 million. IBM, for instance, has steadily boosted its Indian headcount from a handful of folks in 1998 to approximately 130,000 today; it now employs more people in India than in the United States.[102]

Others similarly reorganize their executives, moving those that had worked in the West to business centers in the East. P&G moved the headquarters of its global skin, cosmetics, and personal-care unit from Cincinnati to Singapore while Philips Electronics moved the headquarters of its domestic appliances business from Eindhoven to Shanghai. Cisco combined all its emerging-markets activities into a single unit, "Cisco East" in Bengaluru, and transferred a high-ranking executive with the auspicious title of Chief Globalization Officer. Moreover, the pace of change accelerates—one set of MNEs reported that just 2 percent of their top 200 employees were located in Asian emerging markets that they expected would account for more than one-third of total sales.[103] Changing configurations, said one CEO, is brutally logical: "Today we go to Brazil, we go to China, we go to India, because that's where the customers are."[104]

Personal Ambitions and Professional Paths

The allure of emerging markets extends beyond companies. Graduates face slow-growing business and saturated executive markets in mature Western economies. Many see better chances getting promoted, to say nothing about starting a career, in Manila, Shanghai, Lagos, or Mumbai than in New York, Tokyo, Paris, or London. Explained one enterprising student, "A lot of my friends are going to Asia and Latin America to do their internships. It may be outside their comfort zone, but they see getting some experience there as helpful, since that's where many of the jobs will be."[105] Then again, let's not forget about the magnetic draw of working abroad to young people; a survey of 4,200 graduates in 44 countries found that 80 percent wanted to work internationally.[106]

Rather than patiently waiting, students jump-start the process and head straight to the markets they see powering the future. While compelling for graduates with cultural links to foreign locales as well as those with relevant language fluency, opportunity attracts those with less cultural experience and linguistic skills. Technologies, running the gamut from wearable tech (think cheap earbuds that enable real-time, multiple-language translation) to artificial intelligence (i.e., reframing the MNE as a boundless, pulsating network of humans and algorithms), will reset hiring requirements and promotion standards. Throw into the mix the high adventure of working internationally, along with the chance to bypass years spent in dues-paying entry-level jobs, and you have a powerful siren call for millennials and Gen Zs.

Full Speed Ahead

As sales, growth, labor, and executive opportunity migrate from the West to emerging economies, we anticipate a radical reset of the geography of expatriate assignments. Data confirms the trend is underway: China, Vietnam, the United Arab Emirates, Hong Kong, Thailand, Czechia, Qatar, India, and Singapore are leading destinations for expats. Not far behind are Thailand, Malaysia, Oman, Estonia, Kenya, and Nigeria. Finally, keep in mind that the flow is not one way. Emerging market MNEs increasingly look to their local talent to run operations in Western markets.

CASE

Tel-Comm-Tek: Selecting the Managing Director of Its Indian Subsidiary

In May 2020, Mark Hopkins, managing director of Tel-Comm-Tek India, a subsidiary of U.S.-based Tel-Comm-Tek (TCT), set this retirement for August 2020. Since, January 2016, Hopkins had directed the rising growth, market share, and profitability of the Indian operation. Upon his decision, the IHRM group at TCT Global, headquartered in Philadelphia, began searching for his replacement.

TCT manufactures office equipment, primarily photocopiers, laser printers, and document shredders, in 11 countries, which are then sold in 92 countries. It global strategy calls for HQ to tightly coordinate worldwide activities in order to manage costs, exploit locations effects, and optimize standardization. TCT entered India in 2012, initially relying on local agents to sell and service its imported products. Increasing sales led TCT to open a marketing subsidiary in New Delhi in 2016. TCT India's sales started slow, but are growing fast in tandem with the surging Indian economy. In 2019, TCT Global authorized opening a local manufacturing facility in India by March 2021.

Stunning Opportunities, Tough Constraints

Accelerating Growth

India is steadily developing into the world's next big economic power. In 2019, it became the fifth largest economy in the world, overtaking the United Kingdom and France. It is the fastest-growing trillion-dollar economy in the world, with an enormous population, favorable demographics, and tremendous catch-up prospects in infrastructure and consumption. These prospects spur MNEs to expand their Indian operations. For example, IBM, a long-time customer of TCT, has steadily boosted its Indian headcount from a handful of folks in 1998 to approximately 130,000 today, about one-third of its global workforce. Likewise, Infosys, a leading Indian IT company based in Bengaluru, and key TCT customer, has seen its employees grow from 36,000 employees in 2005 to 248,000 in 2019. Growing market demand anchors TCT forecasts that its Indian sales will surpass its U.S. sales by 2024.

Improving Infrastructure

The improving Indian logistics system encourages expanding TCT India's operational scope. Improving highways, railways, and ports steadily expand shipping options and improve transportation efficiencies. Management sees TCT India becoming a vital link in its global supply chain and, longer term, the hub of its growing Asian network.

Changing Political Economy

From 1947 through 1990, India had a centrally planned economy. Extensive market regulation was administered by an opaque bureaucracy that applied elaborate system of licenses, rules, and sometimes nefarious red tape that regulated opening and operating a business—so troublesome was the system that it gave rise to the notorious "License Raj" in which conflicted local government officials greatly complicated market activity. In 1991, a balance-of-payments crisis forced India's hand. The government began liberalizing the economy, scrapping regulations, and boosting investment, trade, and operating freedom. Its transition, an ongoing process, stabilized the economy and improves India's attractiveness. In the early 1990s, India's economic freedom score was just above 40 percent; in 2019, it was 55 percent. Likewise, the World Bank's Ease of Doing Business Index ranked India 133 in 2009, but 63 in 2019. Confidence in continuing market liberalization motivates TCT's expansion.

Pro-Labor Laws

Notwithstanding steady deregulation, India's labor laws impose constraints. India's Industrial Disputes Act requires a company employing 100 or more workers get the state's authorization before firing anyone, no matter how dire the situation. Permission typically hinges on extensive negotiations and settlements. Consequently, "companies think twice, 10 times, before they hire new people," said the CEO of India's Hero Group.[107] Other laws prohibit companies, for example, from letting manufacturing workers clock more than 54 hours of overtime in any three-month period—even if workers are willing.

Industry Regulations

Various laws, largely designed to protect the millions of small enterprises operating in scattered villages, restrict MNEs from competing in many Indian industries. High tariffs pose other challenges. Instituted to promote domestic production, they still apply to many imports. Minimizing tariff exposure spurs foreign manufacturers to make products locally.

Legal Legacies

Although a functioning democracy, corruption persists. In 2019, Transparency International ranked India 80 of 175 countries in terms of the misuse of public power for private benefit; it had ranked 87th a decade earlier.[108] Its legal system, though endorsing the rule of law, struggles with the problems posed by its vast bureaucracy—a legacy of its centrally planned economy and the infamous License Raj. Regulatory transparency has improved, but difficulties persist. Consequently, MNEs struggle to protect intellectual property rights.

Damn the Torpedoes, Full Speed Ahead

In May 2020, TCT began building a factory near Bengaluru, the center of India's Silicon Valley. The plant will make entry-level to high-end laser printers, with the first production run set for July 2020. Local shortages of quality components require initially sourcing inputs from Asian suppliers. Several of these inputs face high tariffs. Ultimately, TCT India plans to make these parts locally.

TCT India expects to hire 75 to 90 workers to run its assembly line. It anticipates no problems recruiting skilled labor, given demographic and educational circumstances. Millions regularly apply for the few thousand slots at prominent MNEs. Recently, more than 25 million applied for some 90,000 positions with India's state-run railways.[109] Similarly, when South Korean conglomerate LG staffed 458 assembly-line jobs at its Indian factory, it required applicants to have at least 15 years of education—that translates into high school and technical college certification. Preferring a young workforce, LG sought workers with some, but not much, previous experience. Ultimately, some 55,000 qualified for interviews.

TCT enlisted a Japanese engineering firm to supervise construction of its Bengaluru plant. TCT USA has transferred Gary Kent from his current post running its Texas laser printer factory to open and run the Indian facility. He jointly reports to TCT's U.S. headquarters as well as TCT India's managing director in New Delhi (the position made vacant by Mark Hopkins's retirement). Once the Indian factory is up and running, Mr. Kent will return to the United States. His replacement will be selected by the new managing director of TCT India.

Selecting the Managing Director of TCT India

TCT applies a geocentric staffing framework, mixing home-, host-, and third-country nationals to staff units worldwide. It routinely fills executive vacancies by promoting the best-qualified candidate from within the company. Senior management, most of whom have completed an expatriate assignment, believe that international experience is a key facet of leadership. Generally, TCT's expat selection criteria emphasizes technical competency and a global mindset. Unique circumstances in India highlighted the importance of resourcefulness and others orientation in order to navigate the ambiguity of interpersonal interactions, both within the company as well as within society.

IHRM folks at TCT USA charged its Asian Regional Office to select the Managing Director for TCT India. A committee, consisting of manufacturing, marketing, logistics, and administrative representatives of Indian, U.S., and Asian operations, convened to evaluate the following candidates. The broad scope of the position along with the diverse requirements of the Indian business context prevented stipulating precise job requirements. The committee applied the "Knowledge, Skills, Abilities" (KSA) framework to structure analysis, reasoning that the ideal candidate has broad strategic knowledge, skills evidencing the practical application of management principles, and abilities indicating an executive outlook as well as a global mindset.

The Candidates

Source: Shutterstock

▲ Atasi Das

- **Atasi Das:** Born in the United States, Das joined TCT nine years ago after earning her MBA from Columbia University. At 41, she has successfully moved between staff and line positions and assumed broader responsibilities in strategic planning. For two years, she was the assistant director of a midsized product group. Her performance regularly earns excellent ratings. Currently, she directs supply-chain logistics from TCT's Philadelphia headquarters. Upon joining TCT, she stated her goal was an international assignment, pointing to her undergraduate major in international business studies. She regularly reiterates interest in international opportunities, preferably with TCT but elsewhere if necessary. She speaks Hindi and is unmarried. Her parents, who live in the United States, are first-generation immigrants from India. Relatives reside in India's northern states, Kashmir and Punjab.

Source: EDHAR/Shutterstock

▲ Brett Harrison

- **Brett Harrison:** Harrison, 47, has spent 21 years with TCT, running both line activities and supervising staff centers. His superiors consider him a seasoned executive poised to move into upper-level management. For the past two years, he has worked in the

Singapore-based Asian Regional Office as director of strategic planning. He regularly tours TCT's Asian operations and, although only fluent in English, effectively navigates local business situations. He and his wife, along with their two teenage children, have travelled to India a couple of times and are somewhat familiar with its geography and customs. The Harrisons know other expats in Bengaluru. Mrs. Harrison works as the marketing director for the Singapore subsidiary of a Japanese pharmaceutical MNE; it currently exports to, but no operating unit, in India.

Source: Ajay Bhaskar/Shutterstock

▲ Jalan Bukit Seng

- **Jalan Bukit Seng:** Seng, 52, is the managing director of TCT's laser printer manufacturing plant in Malaysia. A citizen of Singapore, he has spent his career in Singapore or Malaysia. He regularly commutes to various TCT factories, helping to upgrade assembly systems and supervising equipment refits. He earned undergraduate and MBA degrees from the National University of Singapore and speaks Singapore's four official languages—Malay, English, Mandarin, and Tamil. His performance reviews are consistently positive, with a periodic ranking of excellent. Seng is unmarried but has family members in Singapore and Malaysia. Daily, direct flights between Singapore and Bengaluru run 4 hours and 20 minutes.

Source: Wong Yu Liang/Shutterstock

▲ Ravi Desai

- **Ravi Desai:** Currently an assistant managing director in TCT India, Desai oversees local market activity from TCT's office in New Delhi. A citizen of India, he has spent 14 years with TCT, primarily working in India, but also working, short-term, in the Japanese and Australian units as a flexpatriate. Now 37, he holds an MBA from the prestigious Indian Institute of Management. Performance reviews are outstanding and indicate strong leadership ability. He is married, has two children (ages 2 and 7), and speaks English and Hindi as well. His wife, also a native of India, neither works outside the home nor speaks English. The family regularly visits relatives throughout India.

Source: Ashwin/Shutterstock

▲ Saumitra Chakraborty

- **Saumitra Chakraborty:** At 36, Chakraborty is an executive assistant to the departing managing director in India. Like his officemate Ravi Desai, Saumitra is in the New Delhi office. He has held his current position since joining TCT India upon graduating from the University of Sydney, after studying at the University of Geneva in Switzerland. He consistently earns a job performance rating of superior in customer relationship management. He has increased TCT India's sales, largely owing to his social connections with prominent Indian families and government officials, along with his skillfulness in the ways of the Indian business environment; his father is a senior official in the Indian Ministry of Finance. Besides speaking India's main languages of English and Hindi, Chakraborty is the only candidate who speaks Kannada (the local language of Bengaluru). Currently, he lacks line experience.

Source: Andresr/Shutterstock

▲ Tom Wallace

- **Tom Wallace:** A 30-year veteran of TCT USA, Wallace has broad technical skills and sales experience. He worked with Gary Kent, the incoming Indian plant manager, on supply-chain projects in the United States. Although he has never worked abroad, he has regularly toured TCT's foreign operations. He recently expressed interest in an international assignment. His superiors typically rate his performance as excellent. Wallace is set to retire in seven years. He and his wife speak only English. They have three adult children who live with their families in the United States. Currently, Wallace manages a U.S. unit that is a little larger than the present size of TCT India. The merger of his unit with another TCT division will eliminate his current position in nine months.

Decision Time

Prepared with profiles of each candidate, the selection committee convened, ready for tough discussions and making a big decision. India's position and huge potential meant this was not the normal staffing call. Selecting the right person for this job is vital to supporting TCT's expansion in India as well as, ultimately, throughout Asia.

QUESTIONS

20-3 Identify the key advantage of each of the six candidates. Identify each candidate's key limitation. Then, rank-order the candidates, from most to least qualified, for the position of Managing Director of TCT India.

20-4 What operational and personal challenges might the person you recommend encounter if named managing director?

20-5 What steps would you recommend your preferred candidate take to manage those challenges?

20-6 Imagine TCT applied a polycentric staffing framework. Would that change your ranking of the candidates? Who now would be your preferred candidate?

20-7 Imagine TCT applied an ethnocentric staffing framework. Would that change your ranking of the candidates? Who now would be your preferred candidate?

20-8 Imagine TCT applied a regiocentric staffing framework. Would that change your ranking of the candidates? Who now would be your preferred candidate?

Endnotes

Chapter 1

1 *Sources include the following:* "Mr Putin's Awful Week," *The Economist* (December 14, 2019): 45; Rachel Axon, "Without Any Competitions, Olympic Athletes Feel Financial Squeeze as They Train for Tokyo Games," *USA Today*: n.p.; Ed Augustin, "Cuba Learns to Live Without Its Stars," *New York Times* (December 30, 2018): SP1+; "European Sports," *The Economist* (August 25, 2018): n.p.; "Cricket in Corfu," *The Economist* (September 15, 2018): 61; "Bigger Than Blatter," *The Economist* (June 6, 2015): 12; Andrew Zimbalist, *Circus Maximus: The Economic Gamble Behind Hosting the Olympics and the World Cup* (Washington: Brookings Institution Press, 2015); Binyamin Applebaum, "Globalization Under Attack," *New York Times* (April 2, 2015): A3; Stephanie Clifford and Matt Apuzzo, "U.S. Vows to Rid Global Soccer of Corruption," *New York Times* (May 28, 2015): A1+; CIES Football Observatory, "Monthly Report: Foreign Players in Teams" (February 9, 2016): n.p.; "The Swedish Model," *The Economist* (October 27, 2012): 56; Kim Daekwan, "The Global Impacts of World Event Sponsorships on Firm Market Performance: A Hierarchical Linear Modeling Approach," *Proceedings of the 54th Annual Meeting of the Academy of International Business* (Washington: June 30–July 3, 2012); Mike Esterl, "Olympics Sponsors Go for the Young," *Wall Street Journal* (July 3, 2012): B8; Harald Dolles and Sten Söderman, eds., *Sport as a Business: International Professional and Commercial Aspects* (Houndsmills, UK: Palgrave Macmillan, 2011); Mark Mulligan, "Football, Funding and MBAs," *Financial Times* (December 13, 2010): 11; Roger Blitz, "Sports Organisers Play High Stakes Games," *Financial Times* (September 29, 2010): 7; Jeremy Kahn, "N.B.A. in India, in Search of Fans and Players," *New York Times* (December 28, 2010): B13; Simon Kuper, "Lost in Translation," *Financial Times* (February 2–3, 2008): p. life & arts 2; Matthew Graham, "Nike Overtakes Adidas in Football Field," *Financial Times* (August 19, 2004): 19; L. Jon Wertheim, "The Whole World Is Watching," *Sports Illustrated* (June 14, 2004): 73–86; Jon Wertheim, "Hot Prospects in Cold Places," *Sports Illustrated* (June 21, 2004): 63–66; Grant Wahl, "Football vs. Fútbol," *Sports Illustrated* (July 5, 2004): 69–72; Grant Wahl, "On Safari for 7-Footers," *Sports Illustrated* (June 28, 2004): 70–73; Gregor Aisch, Kevin Quealy, and Rory Smith, "Where Athletes in the Premier League, the N.B.A. and Other Sports Leagues Come From, in 15 Charts," *The New York Times* (December 29, 2017): sec. The Upshot, www.nytimes.com/interactive/2017/12/29/upshot/internationalization-of-pro-sports-leagues-premier-league.html, www.nytimes.com/interactive/2017/12/29/upshot/internationalization-of-pro-sports-leagues-premier-league.html; TennisFansTV, "ATP Calendar 2018—All ATP Tournaments from the 2018," TennisFans.TV (blog), www.tennisfans.tv/atp-tour/ (accessed January 1, 2019); "National Sport," Wikipedia (December 14, 2018): https://en.wikipedia.org/w/index.php?title=National_sport&oldid=873768228; "Roger Federer Leaves Nike for Uniqlo in Blockbuster Deal," *Bloomberg* (July 2, 2018): www.bloomberg.com/news/articles/2018-07-02/roger-federer-leaves-nike-for-uniqlo-in-blockbuster-deal (accessed January 1, 2019); Smith, Rory, "Love the Club. Loathe the American Owner," *The New York Times* (January 20, 2018): sec. Sports, www.nytimes.com/2017/09/16/sports/soccer/premier-league-american-owners.html; "List of Sporting Scandals," Wikipedia (December 29, 2018): https://en.wikipedia.org/w/index.php?title=List_of_sporting_scandals&oldid=875922848

2 For a good discussion of the versatility of the term *globalization*, see Joyce S. Osland, "Broadening the Debate: The Pros and Cons of Globalization," *Journal of Management Inquiry* 10:2 (June 2003): 137–54.

3 Amy M. Thomas, "Brussels: The Chocolate Trail," *New York Times* (December 25, 2011): tr7 shows that the typical bonbon includes cacao from five different countries. Less than 75 percent of Ford's content originates in the United States; see Sue Callaway, "Cars Made in America? Chrysler, Ford No Longer Qualify," *Fortune* (June 29, 2015): n.p.

4 Greg Linden, Jason Dedrick, and Kenneth L. Kraemer, "We Estimate China Only Makes $8.46 from an iPhone—and That's Why Trump's Trade War Is Futile," *The Conversation*, http://theconversation.com/we-estimate-china-only-makes-8-46-from-an-iphone-and-thats-why-trumps-trade-war-is-futile-99258 (accessed January 1, 2019); Andrew Batson, "Not Really 'Made in China,'" *Wall Street Journal* (December 16, 2010): B1–B2. Incidentally, "the remaining $228.99 goes elsewhere. The U.S. and Japan each take a roughly $68 cut, Taiwan gets about $48, and a little under $17 goes to South Korea. And we estimate that about $283 of gross profit from the retail price—about $649 for a 32GB model when the phone debuted—goes straight to Apple's coffers."

5 Günther G. Schulze and Heinrich W. Ursprung, "Globalisation of the Economy and the Nation State," *The World Economy* 22:3 (May 1999): 295–352.

6 "Africa's Economy: Bulging in the Middle," *The Economist* (October 20, 2012): 43.

7 For example, see OECD, *Measuring Globalisation: OECD Economic Globalisation Indicators* (Paris: OECD, 2005); Pim Martens and Daniel Zywietz, "Rethinking Globalization: A Modified Globalization Index," *Journal of International Development* 18:3 (2006): 331–50; "The Globalization Index," *Foreign Policy* (November–December 2007): 68–76; M. Raab, M. Ruland, B. Schonberger, H. P. Blossfeld, D. Hofacker, S. Buchholz, et al., "GlobalIndex: A Sociological Approach to Globalization Measurement," *International Sociology* 23:4 (2008): 596–631; "KOF Globalization Index, 2011," http://globalization.kof.ethz.ch/ (accessed November 5, 2012).

8 "Biodegradable Plastic from Mushrooms," *Green Building Elements* (blog, March 27, 2015), https://greenbuildingelements.com/2015/03/27/biodegradable-plastic-from-mushrooms/; Gardiner Harris, "Tiny Bean, Crucial to Halliburton, Lifts India Farmers from Mud," *New York Times* (July 17, 2012): A1+; "The Tin Mines of Bangka Island," *Bloomberg* (August 26, 2015), www.bloomberg.com/news/photo-essays/2015-08-26/the-tin-mines-of-bangka-island. See also, "Mycelium and Sawdust-Based Biodegradable Material Could Replace Plastics," AZoM.com (July 10, 2018): www.azom.com/news.aspx?newsID=49312; "Mushrooms, Feathers Combine in Biodegradable Shoes," https://phys.org/news/2018-04-mushrooms-feathers-combine-biodegradable.html (accessed January 1, 2019).

9 "Rebirth of the Cool," *The Economist* (August 25, 2018): 10–11.

10 "Flight Prices: Prepare for Landing," *The Economist* (December 8, 2018): 85.

11 Dan McGraw, "The Foreign Invasion of the American Game," *The Village Voice* (May 28–June 3, 2003) (accessed June 4, 2007).

12 See Rodney C. Shrader, Benjamin M. Oviatt, and Patricia Phillips McDougall, "How New Ventures Exploit Trade-Offs Among International Risk Factors: Lessons for the Accelerated Internationalization of the 21st Century," *Academy of Management Journal* 43:6 (2000): 1227–47.

13 Mark Scott, "Companies Born in Europe, but Based on the Planet," *New York Times* (June 12, 2012): B7.

14 Alison Coleman, "The Tel Aviv Tech Start-ups to Watch in 2018," *Forbes*, www.forbes.com/sites/alisoncoleman/2018/03/06/the-tel-aviv-tech-start-ups-to-watch-in-2018/ (accessed January 2, 2019); Greg Nichols, "Swiss Army Knife of Drones Gets $28.5m in Funding," *ZDNet*, www.zdnet.com/article/swiss-army-knife-of-drones-gets-28-5m-in-funding/ (accessed January 2, 2019).

15 "Charlemagne: Coming off the Rails," *The Economist* (October 20, 2012): 51; "Railways Put China on a Belt and Road to Nowhere," *Bloomberg* (November 5, 2018), www.bloomberg.com/opinion/articles/2018-11-05/trans-asian-rail-puts-china-on-a-belt-and-road-to-nowhere; Hermesauto, "In Europe's East, a Border Town Strains under China's Silk Road Train Boom." *The Straits Times* (June 27, 2018), www.straitstimes.com/world/europe/in-europes-east-a-border-town-strains-under-chinas-silk-road-train-boom.

16 Landom Thomas, Jr., "Seeking Firewall Between Fed and World," *New York Times* (December 8, 2015): B1+, referring to criticism by Hélène Rey.

17 "G20 Information Centre," www.g20.utoronto.ca/ (accessed January 1, 2019); "G20 Osaka Summit 2019 Top Page," G20 Osaka Summit 2019, https://g20.org/en/ (accessed January 1, 2019); "G20." *Wikipedia* (January 1, 2019), https://en.wikipedia.org/w/index.php?title=G20&oldid=876253410.

18 For the cooperation on piracy, see "Malacca Buccaneers," *The Economist* (June 27, 2015): 34.

19 Alyssa Pagano, "Why Airlines Pay to Fly Over Other Countries," *Business Insider*, www.businessinsider.com/countries-charge-foreign-airlines-to-fly-through-airspace-travel-planes-international-flight-2017-9 (accessed January 1, 2019); "Overflight Fees," Template, www.faa.gov/air_traffic/international_aviation/overflight_fees/ (accessed January 1, 2019); Susan Carey, "Calculating Costs in the Clouds," *Wall Street Journal* (March 6, 2007): B1+.

20 John Glendall, "On the Coldest Continent, the Coolest Architecture," *New York Times* (January 7, 2020): D2.

21 Brad Plumer, "Outcomes Hazy for Countries That Tax Carbon Emissions," *New York Times* (April 5, 2019):B1+.

22 His views are discussed in Joellen Perry, "Nobel Laureates Say Globalization's Winners Should Aid Poor," *Wall Street Journal* (August 25, 2008): 2.

23 Lorraine Eden and Stefanie Lenway, "Introduction to the Symposium Multinationals: The Janus Face of Globalization," *Journal of International Business Studies* 32:3 (2001): 383–400.

24 For a discussion on the impact of international travel, see "Travelling Light," *The Economist* (August 29, 2015): 50.

25 Mark Piesing, "Cargo Ships Are the World's Worst Polluters, So How Can They Be Made to Go Green?," inews.co.uk (January 4, 2018), https://inews.co.uk/news/long-reads/cargo-container-shipping-carbon-pollution/; Victoria Heckstall, "Here's How Much Pollution Shipping Containers and Freight Trucks Cause," *Medium* (blog) (April 22, 2018), https://medium.com/@victoria27/heres-how-much-pollution-shipping-containers-and-freight-trucks-cause-b358cb034c70; Christopher DeMorro, "One Container Ship Pollutes as Much as 50 Million Cars" (June 3, 2009), http://gas2.org/2009/06/03/one-container-ship-pollutes-as-much-as-50-million-cars/ (accessed September 14, 2012).

26 On the question of absolute versus relative income gains, see Richard Easterlin, "Happiness, Growth, and Public Policy," *Economic Inquiry* 51:1 (January 2013): 1–15.

27 For an excellent discussion of the growing U.S. inequality from meritocracy see Matthew Stewart, "The 9.9 Percent Is the New American Aristocracy," *The Atlantic* (June 2018); A discussion that inequality is overstated is found in "Inequality Illusions," *The Economist* (November 30, 2019): 13–14.

28 His views are discussed in Joellen Perry, "Nobel Laureates Say Globalization's Winners Should Aid Poor," *Wall Street Journal* (August 25, 2008): 2.

29 "The Chinese Century Is Well under Way." *The Economist* (October 27, 2018), www.economist.com/graphic-detail/2018/10/27/the-chinese-century-is-well-under-way. "India Is on the Rise—But It Already Leads the World in These Sectors," World Economic Forum, www.weforum.org/agenda/2017/09/indias-rising-sectors/ (accessed January 1, 2019); "India to Become Fifth-Biggest Economy in 2019, Says Study," *The Financial Express* (blog) (December 20, 2018), www.financialexpress.com/economy/india-to-become-fifth-biggest-economy-in-2019-says-study/1419276/; Steve Lohr, "An Elder Challenges Outsourcing's Orthodoxy," *New York Times* (September 9, 2004): C1+; Paul A. Samuelson, "Where Ricardo and Mill Rebut and Confirm Arguments of Mainstream Economists Supporting Globalization," *Journal of Economic Perspectives* 18:3 (Summer 2004): 135–47.

30 An examination of this subject may be found in Arne Kalleberg, "Precarious Work, Insecure Workers: Employment Relations in Transition," *American Sociological Review* 74:1 (2009): 1–22.

31 "Trump Voters Were Motivated by Fear of Losing Their Status: Left Behind?," *The Economist (Online)* (April 27, 2018): n.p. discussing research by Diana Mutz.

32 Bernhard G. Gunter and Rolph van der Hoeven, "The Social Dimension of Globalization: A Review of the Literature," *International Labour Review* 143:1/2 (2004): 7–43.

33 Jagdish Bhagwati, "Anti-Globalization: Why?" *Journal of Policy Modeling* 26:4 (2004): 439–64.

34 Craig Karmin, "Offshoring Can Generate Jobs in the U.S.," *Wall Street Journal* (March 16, 2004): B1.

35 Keun Lee and Moosup Jung, "Overseas Factories, Domestic Employment, and Technological Hollowing Out: A Case Study of Samsung's Mobile Phone Business," *Review of World Economics* 151:3 (August 2015): 461–75.

36 Robert C. Feenstra and Gordon H. Hanson, "The Impact of Outsourcing and High-Technology Capital on Wages: Estimates for the United States, 1979–1990," *Quarterly Journal of Economics* 114:3 (1999): 907–40.

37 Alan S. Brown, "A Shift in Engineering Offshore," *Mechanical Engineering* 131:3 (2009): 24–29.

38 "An Internet of Airborne Things," *The Economist* (December 1, 2012): Monitor 3.

39 Paul Markille, "Cars on Autopilot," *The Economist* (The World in 2013 special issue): 152.

40 Carl Benedikt Frey and Michael A. Osborne, *The Future of Employment: How Susceptible Are Jobs to Computerization* (Oxford, UK: Oxford University Programme on the Impacts of Future Technology, 2013); Jeremy Bowles, "Chart of the Week: 54% of EU Jobs at Risk of Computerisation," blog post, Bruegel.org, July 24, 2014; Melanie Arntz, Terry Gregory, and Ulrich Zierahn, "The Risk of Automation for Jobs in OECD Countries," Organization for Economic Cooperation and Development, Working Paper 189, 2016; Aaron Smith and Janna Anderson, "AI, Robotics, and the Future of Jobs," Pew Research Center, August 6, 2014; Carl Benedict Frey and Michael Osborne, "The Future of Employment: How Susceptible Are Jobs to Computerisation?" Oxford University paper, September 17, 2013.

41 James Manyika, Susan Lund, Michael Chui, Macques Bughin, Jonathan Woetzel, Parul Batra, Ryan Ko, and Saurabh Sanghui, "Jobs Lost, Jobs Gained: Workforce Transitions in a Time of Automation," McKinsey Global Institute, December, 2017; Darrell M. West, "The Future of Work: Robots, AI, and Automation," Brookings Institution Press, 2018; Darrell M. West, "Will Robots and AI Take Your Job? The Economic and Political Consequences of Automation," *Brookings* (blog), April 18, 2018.

42 Lydia Bals, Anika Daum, and Wendy Tate, "From Offshoring to Rightshoring: Focus on the Backshoring Phenomenon," *AIB Insights* 15:4 (2015): 3–8.

43 "Compensation of Employees: Wages and Salary Accruals/Gross Domestic Product | FRED | St. Louis Fed," https://fred.stlouisfed.org/graph/?g=2Xa (accessed January 1, 2019); U.S. Bureau of Economic Analysis, "Corporate Profits After Tax (without IVA and CCAdj)," FRED, Federal Reserve Bank of St. Louis (January 1, 1946), https://fred.stlouisfed.org/series/CP; David H. Autor, "Why Are There Still So Many Jobs? The History and Future of Workplace Automation," *The Journal of Economic Perspectives*, 29:3 (Summer 2015): 3–30; and Tali Kristal, "Good Times, Bad Times: Postwar Labor's Share of National Income in Capitalist Democracies," *American Sociological Review* 75.5 (October 2010): 729–63.

44 "The Pay Gap between CEOs and Workers Is Much Worse Than You Realize," *Washington Post*, www.washingtonpost.com/news/wonk/wp/2014/09/25/the-pay-gap-between-ceos-and-workers-is-much-worse-than-you-realize/ (accessed January 1, 2019); "The Income Gap between Bosses and Workers Is Getting Even Bigger," *Washington Post*, www.washingtonpost.com/news/on-leadership/wp/2015/03/13/the-income-gap-between-bosses-and-workers-is-getting-even-bigger-worldwide/ (accessed January 1, 2019).

45 Deborah Solomon, "Federal Aid Does Little for Free Trade's Losers," *Wall Street Journal* (March 1, 2007): A1+.

46 Paul Windrum, Andreas Reinstaller, and Christopher Bull, "The Outsourcing Productivity Paradox: Total Outsourcing, Organisational Innovation, and Long Run Productivity Growth," *Journal of Evolutionary Economics* 19:2 (2009): 197–232; and Ryan Avent, "The Third Great Wave," *The Economist* (October 4, 2014): Special Report, The World Economy: 6.

47 US Census Bureau, Foreign Trade Division, "US Census Bureau Foreign Trade," www.census.gov/foreign-trade/Press-Release/edb/2017/index.html (accessed December 21, 2018); United States International Trade Association, Export Fact Sheet April 2015, www.trade.gov/press/press-releases/2015/export-factsheet-060315.pdf (accessed July 15, 2015).

48 Quora, "How Much Would An iPhone Cost If Apple Were Forced to Make It in America?" *Forbes*, www.forbes.com/sites/quora/2018/01/17/

how-much-would-an-iphone-cost-if-apple-were-forced-to-make-it-in-america/ (accessed January 1, 2019).

49 Heather Berry, "Leaders, Laggards, and the Pursuit of Foreign Knowledge," *Strategic Management Journal* 27 (2006): 151–68; and Jaeyong Song and Jongtae Shin, "The Paradox of Technological Capabilities: A Knowledge Sourcing from Host Countries of Overseas R&D Operations," *Journal of International Business Studies* 39:2 (2008): 291–303.

50 Smitha R. Nair, Mehmet Demirbag, and Kamel Mellahi, "Reverse Knowledge Transfer from Overseas Acquisitions: A Survey of Indian MNEs," *Management International Review* 55 (2015): 277–301.

51 Aaron Chatterji, ""Why Washington Has It Wrong," *Wall Street Journal* (November 12, 2012): R1+.

52 "Ships Take to Arctic Ocean as Sea Ice Melts," www.msnbc.com/id/39394645/ns/world_news-worldenvironment (accessed September 28, 2010).

53 Geoffrey M. Hodgson, "What Are Institutions?" *Journal of Economic Issues* XL: 1 (March 2006): 2; for a discussion on the measurement of institutional differences, see André van Hoorn and Robbert Maseland, "How Institutions Matter for International Business: Institutional Distance Effects vs Institutional Profile Effects," *Journal of International Business Studies* 47:3 (2016): 374–81.

54 Sam Anderson, "Home and Away," *New York Times Magazine* (August 23, 2015): 26–9; and Ed Agustin, "Cuba Learns to Live Without Its Stars," *New York Times* (December 30, 2018): SP1+.

55 Ronak Shah, "Top 10 Car Manufacturers in India: Know Car Makers Market Share in 2017," *The Financial Express* (blog) (January 11, 2018), www.financialexpress.com/auto/car-news/top-10-car-manufacturers-in-india-know-carmakers-market-share-in-2017/1011187/.

56 Paraq Khanna, *Connectography: Mapping the Future of Global Civilization* (New York: Random House: 2016).

57 David Wessel and Marcus Walker, "Good News for the Globe," *Wall Street Journal* (September 3, 2004): A7+.

58 Alan M. Rugman and Cecelia Brain, "Multinational Enterprises Are Regional, Not Global," *Multinational Business Review* 11:1 (2004): 3; and Alain Verbeke and Liena Kano, "An Internalization Theory Rationale for MNE Regional Strategy," *Multinational Business Review* 20:2 (2012): 135–52.

59 John Ralston Saul, "The Collapse of Globalism," *Harpers* (March 2004): 33–43; James Harding, "Globalisation's Children Strike Back," *Financial Times* (September 11, 2001): 4; Bob Davis, "Wealth of Nations," *Wall Street Journal* (March 29, 2004): A1; Harold James, *The End of Globalisation: Lessons from the Great Depression* (Cambridge, MA: Harvard University Press, 2001).

60 R. Andres Castaneda Aguilar, Tony Fujs, Christoph Lakner, Minh Cong Nguyen, and Espen Beer Prydz, "September 2019 Global Poverty Update from the World Bank," https://blogs.worldbank.org/opendata/september-2019-global-poverty-update-world-bank (accessed August 3, 2020); "Poverty in China," *Wikipedia* (December 23, 2018), https://en.wikipedia.org/w/index.php?title=Poverty_in_China&oldid=875103835; "Top 10 Facts About Poverty in China," The Borgen Project (February 24, 2018), https://borgenproject.org/top-10-facts-about-poverty-in-china/; "The Two Biggest Trends on Earth," *Axios*, https://www.axios.com/population-living-in-poverty-around-the-world-4e9a1682-8635-46f5-8c20-43264b765c5e.html (accessed January 1, 2019); Somini Sengupta, "Global Poverty Drops Sharply, But Gains are Uneven," *New York Times* (July 7, 2015): A4.

61 D. Ronen, "The Effect of Oil Price on Containership Speed and Fleet Size," *The Journal of the Operational Research Society* 62:1 (January 2011): 211–16.

62 On the schism between those who thrive in a globalized environment and those who don't, see Jagdish Bhagwati, "Anti-Globalization: Why?" *Journal of Policy Modeling* 26:4 (2004): 439–64; Roger Sugden and James R. Wilson, "Economic Globalisation: Dialectics, Conceptualisation and Choice," *Contributions to Political Economy* 24:1 (2005): 13–32; J. Ørstrøm Møller, "Wanted: A New Strategy for Globalization," *The Futurist* (January–February 2004): 20–22.

63 *Sources include the following:* We'd like to acknowledge the invaluable assistance of Brenda Yester, vice president of Carnival Cruise Lines. Other sources include Taylor Dolven, "The Virus Crisis," *Miami Herald* (May 17, 2020): 1A+; Taylor Dolven, "30 Million Passengers and 18 New Ships This Year. Will Cruising Continue to Grow?" *Miami Herald* (April 10, 2019): 26A; Taylor Dolven, "Judge Threatens to Block Carnival Ships from Docking at U.S. Ports Temporarily," *Miami Herald* (April 11, 2019): 21A; Hannah Sampson, "From Ships to Finance, Carnival's Woes Grow," *Miami Herald* (March 16, 2013): A1+; David McFadden, "World's Biggest Cruise Ships Drop Anchor in Caribbean, But Ship-to-Shore Feud Brews Over Cash," Associated Press (October 10, 2012): n.p.; Hannah Sampson, "Cruise Industry," *Miami Herald* (December 21, 2012): 10B+; Hester Plumridge, "Cruise Tragedy Takes Its Toll on Carnival," *Wall Street Journal* (January 17, 2012): C10; "Update: Japanese ECAs Credit Carnival's Cruise Ships," *Trade Finance* (February 2012): n.p.; Elliot Spagat, "Passengers Disembark 'Nightmare' Cruise Amid Cheers," www.msnbc.msn.com/id/40126918/ns/travel-cruise_travel?GT1=43001 (accessed November 11, 2010); "Cruise Market Watch," www.cruisemarketwatch.com/market-share/(accessesd December 16, 2012); "Cruise Ship Industry Statistics," www.statisticbrain.com/cruise-ship-industry-statistics/ (accessed December 16, 2012); "Holland America Line Adds Three New Segments to 2012 Grand Asia and Australia Voyage," *Marketing Weekly News* (July 14, 2012): 52; Pan Kwan Yuk, "Carnival Outlook Down on Discounts," *Financial Times* (March 25, 2009): 16; Tom Stieghorst, *McClatchy-Tribune Business News* (March 21, 2008): n.p.; "Carnival Cruise Lines; Carnival Experiencing Dramatic Increase on On-Line Shore Excursion Sales," *Entertainment & Travel* (March 26, 2008): 168; "The Wave Rolls On: Carnival Cruise Lines Reports Record Booking Week," *PR Newswire* (March 3, 2009): n.p.; Martha Brannigan, "Cruise Lines Aim for Wider Appeal," *Knight Ridder Tribune Business News* (March 14, 2007): 1; Cruise Lines International Association, "Cruise Industry Overview," Marketing Edition 2006, www.cruising.org/press/overview%202006.cfm (accessed May 9, 2007); Donald Urquhart, "Greed and Corruption Rooted in Flag of Convenience System," *The Business Times Singapore* (March 9, 2001): n.p.;

Chapter 2

1 We are particularly appreciative of personal insights given us by the following people in Saudi Arabia: Nora al Jundi, lecturer at Effat University; Omar Aljindi, consultant at Saudi Diyar Consultants; and Talah Tamimi, former executive at Saudi Investment General Authority. Additional sources include the following: Alan Rappeport, "Saudi Arabia's Sports Strategy," *New York Times* (December 3, 2019): B1+; Stanley Reed, "Saudis Bet on New Commodity: Tourism," *New York Times* (December 26, 2019): B1+; "Saudi Arabia: The Western Compound," americanbedu.com/2011/03/07/saudi-arabia-the-western-compound/ (accessed March 15, 2011); Abeer Allam, "Saudi Women Bridle at Business Rules," *Financial Times* (May 22, 2009): 4; Steve Jarvis, "Western-Style Research in the Middle East," *Marketing News* (April 29, 2002): International section, 37; Barbara Slavin, "U.S. Firms' Saudi Offices Face Manpower Issues," *USA Today* (May 13, 2002): 5A.

2 Patricia Faison Hewlin, "Authenticity on One's Own Terms," Chapter 6 in *Positive Organizing in a Global Society*, eds. Laura Morgan Roberts, Lynn Perry Wooten, and Martin N. Davidson (New York: Routledge, 2016): 53–8.

3 Robert J. Foster, "Making National Cultures in the National Acumen," *Annual Review of Anthropology* 20 (1991): 235–60, discusses the concept and ingredients of a national culture.

4 Helene Tenzer and Markus Pudelko, "Language Differences as Impediments to Shared Mental Model Formation in Multinational Teams," paper presented at the 54th Annual Meeting of the Academy of International Business (Washington, DC: June 30–July 3, 2012).

5 Jeanne Brett, Kristin Behfar, and Mary C. Kern, "Managing Multicultural Teams," *Harvard Business Review* 84 (November 2006): 84–91; Yaping Gong, "The Impact of Subsidiary Top Management Team National Diversity on Subsidiary Performance: Knowledge and Legitimacy Perspectives," *Management International Review* 46:6 (2006): 771–98; and Aida Hajro, Markus Pudelko, and Christina Gibson, "Multinational Teams: Cultural Differences, Interactions, Organizational Context, and Performance," paper presented at the 54th Annual Meeting of the Academy of International Business (Washington, DC: June 30–July 3, 2012).

6 Vas Taras, Pawel Bryla, Dan V. Caprar, Alfredo Jimenez, Peter Magnusson, and Riikka Sarala, "A Comparative Analysis of the Effects of Different Forms of Team Diversity on Global Virtual Team Performance," paper presented at the 54th Annual Meeting of the Academy of International Business (Washington, DC: June 30–July 3, 2012) and Christian Tröster and Daan van Knippenberg, "Leader Openness, Nationality Dissimilarity, and Voice in Multinational Management Teams," *Journal of International Business Studies* 43:6 (2012): 591–613.

7 Richard Gesteland, *Cross-Cultural Business Behavior* (Copenhagen: Copenhagen Business School Press, 2012).

8 David E. Brown, "Human Universals, Human Nature and Human Culture," *Daedalus* 133:4 (Fall 2004): 47–54.

9 Tomasz Lenartowicz and Kendall Roth, "The Selection of Key Informants in IB Cross-Cultural Studies," *Management International Review* 44:1 (2004): 23–51.

10 Four of the most significant are Geert Hofstede, *Cultures and Organizations: Software of the Mind* (New York: McGraw-Hill, 1997), which explores attitudes in 50 countries, primarily those concerning workplace relationships; Ronald Inglehart, Miguel Basañez, and Alejandro Moreno, *Human Values and Beliefs: A Cross-Cultural Sourcebook* (Ann Arbor: University of Michigan Press, 1998) analyzes political, religious, sexual, and economic norms in 43 countries; Robert J. House, Paul J. Hanges, Mansour Javidan, Peter W. Dorfman, and Vipin Gupta, eds., *Culture, Leadership, and Organizations* (Thousand Oaks, CA: Sage, 2004) examines leadership preferences in 59 countries; and S. Schwartz, "A Theory of Cultural Value Orientations: Explication and Applications," *Comparative Sociology* 5:2–3:(2006): 137–82.

11 Ben Casselman, "Risk-Averse Culture Infects U.S. Workers, Entrpreneurs," *Wall Street Journal* (June 3, 2013): A1+ shows how a variety of entrepreneurial indicators changed with the economy.

12 Patti Waldmeir, "Property Bubble Erodes China's Traditional Preference for Sons," *Financial Times* (November 2, 2010): 1.

13 Anne-Wil Harzing, Michelle Brown, Kathrin Köster, and Shuming Zhao, "Response Style Differences in Cross-National Research," *Management International Review* 52:3 (2012): 341–63.

14 Mary Lou Egan and Marc Bendick, Jr., "Combining Multicultural Management and Diversity into One Course on Cultural Competence," *Academy of Management Learning & Education* 7:3 (2008): 387–93; and Paul Brewer and Sunil Venaik, "National Culture versus Individual Culture: The Importance of the Ecological Fallacy," paper presented at the 54th Annual Meeting of the Academy of International Business (Washington, DC: June 30–July 3, 2012).

15 Geert Hofstede and Robert R. McCrae, "Personality and Culture Revisited: Linking Traits and Dimensions of Culture," *Cross-Cultural Research* 38:1 (February 2004): 52–88.

16 Irem Uz, "The Index of Cultural Tightness and Looseness Among 68 Countries," *Journal of Cross-Cultural Psychology* 46:3 (April 2015): 319–35; Michele Gelfand, Lisa Hisae Nishii, and Jana L. Raver, "On the Nature and Importance of Cultural Tightness-Looseness," *Cornell University CAHRS Working Paper Series 1-1* (2007).

17 Harry C. Triandis, "Dimensions of Cultural Variation as Parameters of Organizational Theories," *International Studies of Management and Organization* 12:4 (Winter 1982–1983): 143–44.

18 Choe Sang-Hun, "In Changing South Korea, Who Counts as 'Korean'?" *New York Times* (December 7, 2012): A10.

19 Terence Mughan, "Language and Languages: Moving from the Periphery to the Core," in *The Routledge Companion to Cross-Cultural Management*, eds. Nigel Holden, Snejina Michailova, and Susanne Tietze (New York: Routledge, 2015): 79–84.

20 "Nationalism of Small Differences," *The Economist* (August 25, 2018): 70.

21 "English Speaking Countries: Statistical Profile," http://www.nationmaster.com/country-info/groups/English-speaking (accessed February 6, 2016).

22 Robert Guest, "Anglosphere v Sinosphere," *The Economist: The World in 2020* special section on leaders (November 5, 2019): 19.

23 "A World of Languages," https://www.bing.com/search?q=a+world+of+languages&form=EDGSPH&mkt=en-us&httpsmsn=1&plvar=0&refig=7f850c0767d248f7bd4678c95a6bf966&PC=MSE1&sp=-1&pq=a+world+of+languages&sc=3-20&qs=n&sk=&cvid=7f850c0767d248f7bd4678c95a6bf966 (accessed April 15, 2019). Other statistics on languages are from the same source.

24 Yadong Luo and Oded Shenkar, "The Multinational Corporation as a Multilingual Community: Language and Organization in a Global Context," *Journal of International Business Studies* 37 (2006): 321–39; and Vesa Peltokorpi and Eero Vaara, "Language Policies and Practices in Wholly Owned Foreign Subsidiaries: A Recontextualization Perspective," *Journal of International Business Studies* 43 (2012): 808–33.

25 Jon Boone, "Native English Speakers Face Being Crowded Out of Market," *Financial Times* (February 15, 2006): 8; "The Golden Age of the Western Corporation May Be Coming to an End," *The Economist* (September 19, 2015): n.p. illustrates the faster growth of companies within emerging markets along with their proportional increase among *Fortune 500* companies.

26 Ariel Sabar, "Last Words," *Smithsonian* (February 2013): 31–34.

27 Inglehart et al., *Human Values and Beliefs*, 21.

28 Matthew Coy Mitchell, "Corporate Legitimacy across Cultural Contexts: Mapping the Cultural Schemata of Religio-Institutional Actors" (Columbia, SC: unpublished PhD dissertation, Moore School of Business Administration, 2010).

29 "When Culture Masks Communication: Japanese Corporate Practice," *Financial Times* (October 23, 2000): 10; Robert House et al., "Understanding Cultures and Implicit Leadership Theories across the Globe: An Introduction to Project GLOBE," *Journal of World Business* 37 (2002): 3–10.

30 Michael Segalla, "National Cultures, International Business," *Financial Times* (March 6, 1998): mastering global business section, 8–10.

31 Amartya Sen, *Development as Freedom* (Oxford: Oxford University Press, 1999): 192.

32 Fons Trompenaars, *Riding the Waves of Culture* (Burr Ridge, IL: Richard D. Irwin, 1994): 100–16.

33 "Putting the Malaise into Malaysia," *Asia Times Readers Forum*, forum.atimes.com/topic.asp?topic_ID=9002& whichpage=10 (accessed May 27, 2007); Thomas Fuller, "Malaysia Vote May Rule on Racial Divide," *New York Times* (April 4, 2013): A10.

34 Clara Chooi, "Poor English Skills, Race Quotas in Way of Malaysian Prosperity, Says ST," *The Malaysian Insider* (December 11, 2011): n.p. A downside of Malaysia's racial quota system has been an emigration of many of the best qualified Chinese-Malaysians. See "Race in Malaysia: Playing with Fire," *The Economist* (September 26, 2015): 38.

35 "Anti-Meritocracy in India, *The Economist* (January 12, 2019): 33.

36 "Black Women of Brazil" (November 20, 2011) www.blackwomenofbrazil.com/2011/11/ (accessed November 23, 2012); "Affirming a Divide," *The Economist* (January 28, 2012).

37 Information on a number of gender-related indices can be found in UN Human Development Report (2011). *Gender Inequality Index*, pp. 139–42. Available at hdr.undp.org/en/statistics/gii/ (accessed November 19, 2012). For a discussion of the relationship between gender gaps and a number of cultural values, see Andy Bertsch and Gillian Warner-Soderholm, "Updating Cross Cultural Management: Exploring the Relationships between Cultural Values and Gender Inequality Practices," paper presented at the 54th Annual Meeting of the Academy of International Business (Washington, DC: June 30–July 3, 2012).

38 Inglehart et al., *Human Values and Beliefs*, question V128.

39 Somini Sengupta, "Report Finds Most Nations Hinder Women," *New York Times* (September 10, 2015): A8.

40 Shaila Dewan and Robert Gebeloff, "More Men Enter Fields Dominated by Women." *New York Times* (May 21, 2012): A1+; Josh Mitchell, "Women Notch Progress," *Wall Street Journal* (December 5, 2012): A3, citing Census Bureau data that showed women composed about 10 percent of U.S. doctors in 1970, but 32 percent in 2010.

41 "Which European Country Has the Lowest Drinking Age?" (January 6, 2015), http://brilliantmaps.com/drinking-age-europe/ (accessed February 6, 2016).

42 "The Employers Forum on Age," *Legal: Europe*, at www.efa.org.uk/legal/europe.asp (accessed May 27, 2007); Cindy Wu, John J. Lawler, and Xiang Xi, "Overt Employment Discrimination in MNC Affiliates: Home-Country Cultural and Institutional Effects," *Journal of International Business Studies* 39:5 (2008): 772–94.

43 Inglehart et al., *Human Values and Beliefs*, question V129.

44 Francis Fukuyama, *Trust: The Social Virtues and the Creation of Prosperity* (New York: Free Press, 1995); Ana Paula Matias Gama and Jorge Manuel Mendes Galvão, "Performance, Valuation and Capital Structure: Survey of Family Firms," *Corporate Governance* 12:2 (2012): 199–214; "Spanish Business: Supersize Me," *The Economist* (February 21, 2015): 65.

45 For a good overview of the literature on the Protestant ethic, see Harold B. Jones Jr., "The Protestant Ethic: Weber's Model and the Empirical Literature," *Human Relations* 50:7 (1997): 757–86. For evidence that other religions have equal or higher work ethics, see Yavuz Fahir Zulfikar, "Do Muslims Believe More in Protestant Work Ethic Than Christians? Comparison of People with Different Religious Background Living in the US," *Journal of Business Ethics* 105:4 (Feb 2012): 489–502.

46 Luigi Guiso, Paola Sapienza, and Luigi Zingales, "People's Opium? Religion and Economic Attitudes," *Journal of Monetary Economics* 50:1 (2003): 225–38.

47 See, for example, David S. Landes, *The Wealth and Poverty of Nations* (New York: Norton, 1998).

48 Hamid Yeganeh, "An Investigation into the Cultural and Religious Determination of National Competitiveness," paper presented at the 54th Annual Meeting of the Academy of International Business (Washington, DC: June 30–July 3, 2012).

49 Triandis, "Dimensions of Cultural Variation as Parameters of Organizational Theories," 159–60.

50 Hofstede, *Cultures and Organizations.*

51 Abraham Maslow, *Motivation and Personality* (New York: Harper & Row, 1954).

52 F. Pichler and C. Wallace, "What Are the Reasons for Differences in Job Satisfaction across Europe?" *European Sociological Review* 25:5 (2009): 535–49.

53 Hofstede, *Cultures and Organizations* 49–78; House et al., *Culture, Leadership, and Organizations.*

54 Adam Grant, "Friends at Work? Not So Much," *New York Times* (September 6, 2015): Sunday Review 1+.

55 Hofstede, *Cultures and Organizations.*

56 Hofstede, *Cultures and Organizations.*

57 Inglehart et al., *Human Values and Beliefs,* question V94.

58 Srilata Zaheer and Akbar Zaheer, "Trust across Borders," *Journal of International Business Studies* 37:1 (2006): 21–29.

59 Miriam Muethal and Michael Harris Bond, "National Context and Individual Employees' Trust of the Out-Group: The Role of Societal Trust," *Journal of International Business Studies* 44:4 (2013): 312–33.

60 Walter Mischel, *The Marshmallow Test: Mastering Self-Control* (New York: Little, Brown & Company, 2014).

61 Examples in this section come from the GLOBE (Global Leadership and Organizational Behavior Effectiveness) project, *Journal of World Business* 37 (2002). See Szabo et al., "The Germanic Europe Cluster: Where Employees Have a Voice," 55–68; Bakacsi et al., "Eastern European Cluster: Tradition and Transition," 69–80; Jorge Correia Jesino, "Latin Europe Cluster: From South to North," 81–89.

62 Ping Ping Fu, Jeff Kennedy, Jasmine Tata, Gary Yukl, Michael Harris Bond, Tai-Kuang Peng, Ekkirala S. Srinivas, Jon P. Howell, Leonel Prieto, Paul Koopman, Jaap J. Boonstra, Selda Pasa, Marie-François Lacassagne, Hiro Higashide, and Adith Cheosakul, "The Impact of Societal Cultural Values and Individual Social Beliefs on the Perceived Effectiveness of Managerial Influence Strategies: A Meso Approach," *Journal of International Business Studies* 35:4 (2004): 284–304.

63 Shirley Wang, "The Science Behind Why We Love Ice Cream," *Wall Street Journal* (November 9, 2010): D1+; and Nicholas Wade, "Human Culture, an Evolutionary Force," *New York Times* (March 2, 2010): D1+.

64 Benjamin Lee Whorf, *Language, Thought and Reality* (New York: Wiley, 1956): 13 claimed there are more than 6,000 words. "How Many Words Are There for 'Camel' in Arabic?" *Arabglot* (November 11, 2011), http://www.arabglot.com/2011/02/how-many-words-are-there-for-camel-in.html (accessed November 23, 2012) found many fewer, but nevertheless many more than one would find in any other language.

65 Hyun-Jung Lee, Katsuhiko Yoshikawa, and Carol Reade, "Culture Under Strain? Leadership Challenges of Japanese Managers in the UK and China," paper presented at the 54th Annual Meeting of the Academy of International Business (Washington, DC: June 30–July 3, 2012).

66 "Getting from A to B," *The Economist* (September 20, 2014): 58.

67 Viviane A. Winkler and Ricarda B. Bouncken, "How Does Cultural Diversity in Global Innovation Teams Affect the Innovation Process?" *Engineering Management Journal* 23:4 (December 2011): 24–35.

68 Richard E. Nisbett et al., "Culture and Systems of Thought: Holistic Versus Analytic Cognition," *Psychological Review* 108:2 (April 2001): 291–310.

69 "Babel or Babble?: Machine Translation," *The Economist (Online)* (Jun 11, 2012).

70 Don Clark, "Hey, #@*% Amigo, Can You Translate the Word 'Gaffe'?" *Wall Street Journal* (July 8, 1996): B6.

71 Wenting Zhou, "Translation Errors Cause Disputes over Contract Terms," *McClatchy - Tribune Business News* [Washington] (March 23, 2012; accessed November 24, 2012).

72 Terry Mughan, "Culture and Management Crossing the Linguistic Rubicon," *Language and Intercultural Training* 13:1 (Spring 1993).

73 Manjeet Kripalani and Jay Greene, "Culture Clash," *Business Week* (February 14, 2005): 9.

74 Christina Hoag, "Slogan Could Offend Spanish Speakers," *Miami Herald* (March 8, 2005): C1+.

75 Much of the discussion on silent language is based on Edward T. Hall, "The Silent Language in Overseas Business," *Harvard Business Review* (May–June 1960). Hall identified five variables—time, space, things, friendships, and agreements—and was the first to use the term *silent language.*

76 Alberto Rubio Sanchez, Alejandro Pico, Lucette B. Comer, Purdue University, "Salespeople's Communication Competence: A Study of the Mexican Market," *Journal of Business & Economic Studies* 16:1 (Spring 2010): 1–18.

77 For an excellent explanation of four ways to view time, see Carol Saunders, Craig Van Slyke, and Douglas Vogel, "My Time or Yours? Managing Time Visions in Global Virtual Teams," *Academy of Management Executive* 18:1 (2004): 19–31. See also Lawrence A. Beer, "The Gas Pedal and the Brake: Toward a Global Balance of Diverging Cultural Determinants in Managerial Mindsets," *Thunderbird International Business Review* 45:3 (May–June 2003): 255–70.

78 Trompenaars, *Riding the Waves of Culture,* 130–31.

79 Vanessa Swales, "Supremacists Have Seized the O.K. Sign as Their Own," *New York Times* (December 16, 2019): A21.

80 Inglehart, *Human Values and Beliefs,* 16.

81 Amin Maalouf, *In the Name of Identity* (New York: Penguin Group, 2000): 26, asserts that people pinpoint the aspect of their identity that is most under threat.

82 Mary Yoko Brannen, "When Mickey Loses Face: Recontextualization, Semantic Fit, and the Semiotics of Foreignness," *Academy of Management Review* 29:4 (2004): 593–616.

83 Many food examples are given in "Overcoming the Yuck Factor," *The Economist* (January 11, 2020): 49–50.

84 Mary Yoko Brannen and Jane Salk, "Partnering across Borders: Negotiating Organizational Culture in a German-Japanese Joint Venture," *Human Relations* 53:4 (June 2000): 451–87; Baruch Shimoni and Harriet Bergman, "Managing in a Changing World: From Multiculturalism to Hybridization—The Production of Hybrid Management Culture in Israel, Thailand, and Mexico," *Academy of Management Perspectives* (August 2006): 76–89.

85 Geraldine Brooks, "Eritrea's Leaders Angle for Sea Change in Nation's Diet to Prove Fish Isn't Foul," *Wall Street Journal* (June 2, 1994): A10; M. Y. Teweldemedhin, "The Fish Industry in Eritrea: From Comparative to Competitive Advantage," *African Journal of Agricultural Research* 3:5 (May 2008): 327–33; "Taboo Food and Drink," *Wikipedia*, en.wikipedia.org/wiki/Taboo_food_and_drink (accessed November 26, 2012).

86 Patrick M. Reilly, "Pitfalls of Exporting Magazine Formulas," *Wall Street Journal* (July 24, 1995): B1; James Bandler and Matthew Karnitschnig, "Lost in Translation," *Wall Street Journal* (August 19, 2004): A1+.

87 John Tomlinson, *Globalization and Culture* (Chicago: University of Chicago Press, 1999).

88 Sam Schechner, "C'est What?: French TV in English," *Wall Street Journal* (November 21, 2012): B8; Ian Austen, "Crackdown in Quebec: 'Le Gap' Won't Do," *New York Times* (November 23, 2012): B1+; Maïa de la Baume, "Bid in France to Add Course in English Raises Fear for Language," *New York Times* (May 24, 2013): A10.

89 Nader Asgary and Alf H. Walle, "The Cultural Impact of Globalisation: Economic Activity and Social Change," *Cross Cultural Management* 9:3 (2000): 58–76; Tyler Cowen, *Creative Destruction: How Globalization Is Changing the World's Cultures* (Princeton, NJ: Princeton University Press, 2002): 128–52.

90 "Schumpeter: The Global Mexican," *The Economist* (October 27, 2012): 70.

91 Adrian Furnham and Stephen Bochner, *Culture Shock* (London: Methuen, 1986): 234.

92 Mzamo P. Mangaliso, "Building Competitive Advantage from Ubuntu: Management Lessons from South Africa," *Academy of Management Executive* 15:3 (August 2001): 23–34.

93 Gina Chon, "China Faces Unexpected Problem Drilling for Oil in Iraq—Farmers," *Wall Street Journal* (May 22, 2009): A6.

94 Sally Bowen, "People Power Keeps Peru's Investors in Check," *Financial Times* (February 6, 1998): 6.

95 Roberto P. Garcia, "Learning and Competitiveness in Mexico's Automotive Industry: The Relationship between Traditional and World-Class Plants in Multination Firm Subsidiaries," unpublished PhD dissertation (Ann Arbor, MI: University of Michigan, 1996).

96 Mary Yoko Brannen and Fiona Lee, "How Can the Organizational Literature Inform Psychology Research on Biculturalism?" in *The Handbook of Multicultural Identity: Basic and Applied Psychological Perspectives*, eds. V. Benet-Martinez and Y.Y. Hong (New York: Oxford University Press: 2014): 417–38.

97 Mary Yoko Brannen and David C. Thomas, "Bicultural Individuals in Organizations: Implications and Opportunity," *International Journal of Cross Cultural Management* 10:1 (2010): 5–16; and David C. Thomas, Mary Yoko Brannen, and Dominie Garcia, "Bicultural Individuals and Intercultural Effectiveness," *European Journal of Cross-Cultural Competence and Management* 1:4 (2010): 315–33.

98 Peter Capelli, Harbir Singh, Jitendra Singh, and Michael Useem, "The Indian Way, Lessons for the U.S.," *The Academy of Management Perspectives* 24:2 (May 2010): 6–24.

99 Neil Parmar, "Legalities: A Global Love Affair," *WSJ.Money* (Summer 2013): 12–13.

100 James Wilson and Quentin Peel, "Multicultural Attempts 'Failed,' Claims Merkel," *Financial Times* (October 18, 2010): 3.

101 *Sources include the following:* Creso M. Sá and Emma Sabzalieva, "The Politics of the Great Brain Race: Public Policy and International Student Recruitment in Australia, Canada, England and the USA," *High Education* 75:2 (February 2018): 231–253; Jillian Berman, "For U.S. Grad Students, Overseas Schools Beckon; The Price May Be Right. But Students First Need to Ask Themselves Some Hard Questions," *Wall Street Journal (Online)* (March 23, 2017), n.p.; Alex Vernon, Chris Moos, and Holly Loncarich, "Student Expectancy and Barriers to Study Abroad," *Academy of Educational Leadership Journal* 21:1 (2017): 1–9; Joshua E. Bienstock and Amr Swid, "International Students' Adjustment to U.S. Universities: Utilizing a Campus Mediation Approach," San Diego: *Proceedings of the American Society of Business and Behavioral Sciences* (March 2017), n.p.; Tamilla Curtis and John R. Ledgerwood, "Students' Motivations, Perceived Benefits and Constraints Towards Study Abroad and International Education Opportunities," *Journal of International Education in Business* 11:1 (2018): 63–78; Eric R. Terzuolo, "Worth the Trip? Debating the Value of Study Abroad/Ungar Replies," 95:5 (September/October 2016): 162–164; Paul M. Vaaler, "Immigrant Remittances and the Venture Investment Environment of Developing Countries," *Journal of International Business Studies* 42:9 (December 2011): 1121–49; Jim Russell, "Canada Is Dying," *Pacific Standard* (June 14, 2017) https://psmag.com/economics/canada-dying-70440 (accessed May 14, 2019).

102 H. Spencer-Oatey and D. Dauber, "How Internationalized Is Your University? From Structural Indicators to an Agenda for Integration." *Globalpad Working Papers* (2015). http://www.warwick.ac.uk/globalpadintercultural (accessed May 5, 2019).

103 J. Luo and D. Jamieson-Drake, "Examining the Educational Benefit of Interacting with International students." *Journal of International Students*, 3:2 (2013), 85–101.

104 D. Deardorff, "In Search of Intercultural Competence," *International Educator* (2004), NAFSA.

105 X. Zhang and M. Zhou, "Interventions to Promote Learners' Intercultural Competence: A Meta-Analysis." *International Journal of Intercultural Relations* 71 (2018) 31–47.

106 Op.cit, p. 43.

Chapter 3

1 *Sources include the following:* Michael Sylvester, "Flaming Hoops," *Corporate Counsel: Market Report China* (2004): 171; "A Survey of Business in China: A Disorderly Heaven," *The Economist* (March 20, 2004): 12; "Bulls in a China Shop," *The Economist* (March 20, 2004): 10; "*The Economist*, Country Briefings: China," https://econ.st/39c3KGi (accessed January 20, 2020); U.S. Department of State, Background Note: China, www.state.gov/r/pa/ei/bgn/18902.htm (accessed January 13, 2013); Central Intelligence Agency, *World Factbook*, www.cia.gov/library/publications/the-world-factbook/geos/ch.html (accessed January 12, 2019).

2 Richard McGregor, *The Party: The Secret World of China's Communist Rulers* (Harper Collins, 2010): 1.

3 Jinping Xi, *The Chinese Dream of the Great Rejuvenation of the Chinese Nation* (Foreign Languages Press, 2014).

4 "Foreign Investment in China: Even Harder Than It Looks," *The Economist* (September 16, 2010): 64.

5 "Chinese Negotiation: The Long Kiss Goodnight," https://bit.ly/2UafAw9 (accessed May 14, 2009).

6 "A Survey of Business in China: A Disorderly Heaven," *The Economist*, https://econ.st/3bibfwH (accessed March 24, 2011).

7 Ibid.

8 Zhenmin Wang, "The Developing Rule of Law in China," *Harvard Asia Quarterly*, 4, no. 4 (Autumn, 2000).

9 Personal Conversation, Daniel Sullivan and Kathy Stearman, Beijing (March 4, 2011).

10 Oded Shenkar, *The Chinese Century* (Upper Saddle River, NJ: Pearson Prentice Hall, 2006).

11 Counterfeiters Will Win the Trade War," Foreign Policy, https://bit.ly/3drDDP9 (accessed March 3, 2020).

12 Steven Weisman, "Before Visit to China, a Rebuke," *New York Times* (December 12, 2006): A-1.

13 "The World's Greatest Fakes," *60 Minutes*, quote by Dan Chow, https://cbsn.ws/2WCoMLM (accessed June 15, 2006).

14 "The Sincerest Form of Flattery," *The Economist* (April 4, 2007): 67.

15 The middle income trap emerges when a country make significant progress in reducing extreme poverty and experience structural change and growth but then find it difficult to make the climb from being a middle-income country to higher-income fully-developed status. The path from low income (about $5,000 per capita) to middle-income (about $10,000 per capita) is fairly straightforward and mostly involves reduced corruption, direct foreign investment and migration from the countryside to cities to pursue assembly-style jobs. The path from middle-income to high-income (about $20,000 per capita) is much more difficult and involves creation and deployment of high-technology and manufacture of high-value-added goods.

16 "Coronavirus and the Death of Xi's 'China Dream' | The Strategist" https://bit.ly/3991EqN; "Coronavirus Killed the 'China Dream' | The National Interest," https://bit.ly/2y2xcSg (all accessed March 23, 2020).

17 Political stability safeguards investment while uncertainty penalizes it. Daniel Kaufmann, Aart Kraay, and Massimo Mastruzzi, "Governance Matters IV: Governance Indicators for 1996–2004," *World Bank Policy Research Working Paper Series No. 3630* (May 2005).

18 "Business in Russia: Dancing with the Bear," *The Economist* (February 1, 2007): 23.

19 Ibid, Business in Russia: Dancing with the Bear.

20 "Putin Signs Law to Shut Down 'Undesirable' Foreign Organizations in Russia," https://bit.ly/2QDC1aY (accessed November 4, 2015); "Planet Plutocrat," *The Economist*, https://econ.st/33FvdiE (accessed November 4, 2015); "Corruption Perceptions Index—2014," www.transparency.org/cpi2014 (accessed November 4, 2015); "Crocodile Tears," *The Economist* (April 28, 2007):

44; Andrew Osborn,"Russia's Rule of Lawlessness," *Wall Street Journal*, https://on.wsj.com/3bhkVrl (accessed January 20, 2011); Corruption Perceptions Index 2012, https://bit.ly/2WzHLX7 (accessed January 15, 2013).
"Russia's Weakened Democratic Embrace," *Pew Global Attitudes Project*, https://pewrsr.ch/2J9Vmwy (accessed January 14, 2013);"Russia's Future: The Cracks Appear," *The Economist* (December 10, 2011): 13. Others, however, see Russia trapped in lawlessness and legal nihilism.

21 "Fragile States Index," *Wikipedia, the Free Encyclopaedia*, https://bit.ly/2WzOIra (accessed March 20, 2020).

22 Alan Ryan, *On Politics: A History of Political Thought from Herodotus to the Present* (London: Allen Lane, 2012).

23 Statement from the Declaration of Independence of the United States of America.

24 In Germany, before the adoption of liberal western economic ideas, its economic policy, called "Gemeinnutz geht vor Eigennutz," held that "the welfare of the nation takes precedence over the selfishness of the individuals," https://bit.ly/2QCjMTc (accessed, January 20, 2020).

25 "How China Contained the Coronavirus after Early Blunders - What Did China Do to Contain the Coronavirus? | The Economic Times," https://bit.ly/3bhsMFm; "Coronavirus: Government Must 'Promote Sense of Collectivism' in Order to Avoid Public Disorder | The Independent," https://bit.ly/2vHnJyQ (all accessed March 23, 2020).

26 Practically, the ideology of democracy anchors a political system that grants voters the power to alter the laws and structures of government, to make decisions (either directly or through representatives), and to participate directly in elections.

27 More specifically, a democracy accepts the legitimacy of (1) freedom of opinion, expression, press, religion, association, and access to information; (2) free, fair, and regular elections; (3) majority rule coupled with protection of individual and minority rights; and (4) subordination of government to the rule of law.

28 "Are Economic and Political Freedoms Interrelated? | Bruegel," https://bit.ly/397WdIt (accessed March 19, 2019).

29 The philosophy of Apple's founder Steve Jobs fit this outlook as well; he rejected the notion that individuals were rational, believing "consumers don't know what they want."

30 "China's Future: Rising Power, Anxious State," *The Economist* (June 25, 2011): 3; for example, bookstores in China stock works approved by the CCP.

31 "Iran: Police Use New Tactics to Confiscate Satellite Dishes," BBC News, https://bbc.in/2WHhMNH (accessed December 16, 2015).

32 Anne-Marie Brady, *Marketing Dictatorship: Propaganda and Thought Work in Contemporary China* (Lanham, MD: Rowman & Littlefield, 2007).

33 "The Long Arm of the State," *The Economist*, Special Report: China (June 25, 2011): 14.

34 "Fact Sheet: Communist Party Groups in Foreign Companies in China," *China Business Review*, https://bit.ly/2QCEUZL (accessed May 31, 2018).

35 Keith Brasher, "Solar Panel Maker Moves Work to China," NYTimes.com, https://nyti.ms/2QAWiho (accessed February 11, 2011).

36 "Chinese Politics and the WTO: No Change," *The Economist* (December 10, 2011): 46.

37 Extracted from Mission Statement, Freedom House, retrieved June 28, 2009, from www.freedomhouse.org/template.cfm?page=2. For example, classical liberal philosophy holds that freedom is the absence of coercion of one person by others; jurisprudence holds that one has the right to determine one's own actions autonomously; environmentalism advocates constraints on the use of ecosystems in any definition of freedom. Others take a more abstract approach, discussing notions of positive versus negative freedom (the right to fulfil one's own potential vs. freedom from restraints).

38 "New Periodic Report Looks into the Global State of Democracy—Democracy Without Borders," https://bit.ly/2Uw1RPd (accessed March 25, 2019).

39 Samuel P. Huntington, *The Third Wave: Democratization in the Late Twentieth Century* (Norman: University of Oklahoma Press, 1991).

40 Ronald Bailey, "Does Disease Cause Autocracy?" *Reason Magazine* (June 1, 2011).

41 Francis Fukuyama, *The End of History and the Last Man* (New York: Free Press, 1992).

42 "Freedom in the World 2018: Democracy in Crisis," https://bit.ly/2QDZ3hX (accessed January 26, 2019).

43 Arch Puddington, "Freedom in the World 2011: The Authoritarian Challenge to Democracy," *Freedom House*, https://bit.ly/2J6obKj (accessed April 21, 2011).

44 Arch Puddington, "Freedom in the World 2012," *Freedom House*, https://bit.ly/3aeyzvh (accessed January 15, 2013).

45 Ibid, "Freedom in the World 2018: Democracy in Crisis."

46 Adapted from "EIU Democracy Index 2018—World Democracy Report," https://bit.ly/2Ux7blu (accessed March 11, 2019).

47 "EIU Democracy Index 2018—World Democracy Report," https://bit.ly/2WCpw3w (accessed March 11, 2019).

48 John L. Thornton, "Long Time Coming - the Prospects for Democracy in China," *Foreign Affairs* 87 (2008): 2.

49 "Freedom in the World 2013: Middle East Gains Provoke Intensified Repression," *Freedom House*.

50 Julian Wucherpfennig, "Modernization and Democracy: Theories and Evidence Revisited," *Living Reviews in Democracy* (2009): 1.

51 "Dictatorships' GDPs 'greater than Economic Output of Democratic Nations for First Time in 120 Years,'" *Daily Mail Online*, http://dailym.ai/2ZjLHws (accessed May 19, 2020).

52 "On the People's Democratic Dictatorship," *Selected Works of Mao Tse-Tung*, https://bit.ly/2Uw25Wz (accessed January 15, 2013); Pushkar, "India Waits for Democracy with Benefits," *Asia Times Online*, https://bit.ly/3dw93ns (accessed January 16, 2013).

53 "Countries at the Crossroads," freedomhouse.org, https://bit.ly/3blSY1Q (accessed April 18, 2011).

54 Scott Shane, "America's Journeys with Strongmen," NYTimes.com, https://nyti.ms/398BZOH (accessed February 7, 2017).

55 "Democracy Index 2011," *Economist Intelligence Unit*, https://bit.ly/2UnV4Hu (accessed January 20, 2013).

56 "Can We Replace Politicians with Robots?," *IFLScience*, https://bit.ly/3baIXEu (accessed March 28, 2019).

57 Gallup, "Confidence in Institutions," Gallup.com, https://bit.ly/2vI3bX9 (accessed January 25, 2020).

58 ILO, "World of Work Report 2010: From One Crisis to the Next?" https://bit.ly/2UnVgGI (accessed February 7, 2011).

59 Kirk Hawkins, "Don't Try to Silence Populists – Listen to Them," *The Guardian*, https://bit.ly/2Ww8Me6 (accessed March 9, 2019).

60 "Democracy? Hu Needs It," *The Economist* (June 28, 2007): 44; "A Warning for Reformers," *The Economist* (November 17, 2007): 67.

61 "Xi Touts Communist Party as Defender of Confucius's Virtues," *New York Times*, https://nyti.ms/2WA51nV (accessed November 4, 2015).

62 "'I Am a True Democrat:' G-8 Interview with Vladimir Putin," *Spiegel Online*, https://bit.ly/3dlEhgK (accessed June 4, 2007).

63 E.g., "Brazil's President Lula Says G7 Nations No Longer Speak for the World," *The Telegraph* (March 16, 2009): A-1.

64 "Nigeria's Prospects: A Man and a Morass" *The Economist* (May 28, 2011): 24.

65 "Japan and China: Rattling the Supply Chains," *The Economist* (October 20, 201): 60.

66 "The 2010 Failed States Index," *Foreign Policy*, https://bit.ly/3agmRjO (accessed February 8, 2011).

67 "Coronavirus' Business Impact: Evolving Perspective | McKinsey," https://mck.co/2J6an2g (accessed March 23, 2020).

68 "Science: Getting in the Mood," *The Economist: The World in 2012* (November 17, 2012): 152.

69 Andrew Martin, "Turning Point for Suits over Chinese Drywall," *New York Times* (October 12, 2012): A-7.

70 "Russia: The Long Life of Homo Sovieticus," *The Economist* (December 10, 2011): 27–30; "Russian Politics: Fear and Loathing," *The Economist* (September 22, 2012): 60.

71 See Juriglobe World Legal Systems, www.juriglobe.ca/eng/.

72 *Stare decisis:* Latin, "to stand by that which is decided."

73 Denis Wiechman, Jerry Kendall, and Mohammad Azarian, "Islamic Law: Myths and Realities," https://bit.ly/2J6SqAz (accessed June 22, 2019).

74 "What Is Legality? Definition of Legality," *The Law Dictionary*, https://bit.ly/3bcA9hg (accessed October 19, 2012).

75 A. Kraay and M. Mastruzzi, "The Worldwide Governance Indicators: Methodology and Analytical Issues," https://bit.ly/3adAtw9 (accessed March 15, 2019).

76 Similarly, Thomas Paine wrote "in America, the law is king" in contrast to the view that the king was the law. *Common Sense*, https://bit.ly/2QDD6j2 (accessed March 26, 2011).

77 "Rule of Law Index," *World Justice Project,"* https://bit.ly/3acEa5o (accessed February 8, 2019).

78 Paul Collier, *Wars, Guns, and Votes: Democracy in Dangerous Places* (New York: HarperCollins, 2009). More pointedly, the rule of law is vital to a functioning democracy, given that, as John Locke warned some three centuries ago, "Wherever law ends, tyranny begins."

79 Alternatively, Thomas Jefferson reasoned, "Information is the currency of democracy." If so, then the satellite dish-covered exteriors we see worldwide play a crucial role.

80 "Revolution in the Arab World: The Twilight of the Dictators," *The Economist* (August 4, 2012): 73.

81 Richard McGregor, *The Party: The Secret World of China's Communist Rulers* (Harper Collins, 2010), Quote, He Weifang, p. 22.

82 Hernando De Soto, *The Mystery of Capital: Why Capitalism Triumphs in the West and Fails Everywhere Else* (Basic Books, 2000).

83 Louise Arbour, "The Rule of Law," *New York Times* (September 26, 2012): A-8; "Economics and the Rule of Law: Order in the Jungle," *The Economist* (March 13, 2008): 43–8.

84 Tom Friedman, "Our One-Party Democracy," *New York Times* (September 8, 2009): A-8.

85 Ibid., "Xi Touts Communist Party as Defender of Confucius's Virtues."

86 Ibid., "A Disorderly Heaven," *The Economist* (March 20, 2004): 75.

87 Ibid., "Russian Politics: Fear and Loathing."

88 Ibid., "Business in Russia: Dancing with the Bear.,"

89 "Belarus," *Freedom House,* https://bit.ly/2xh7Lfr, "Kazakhstan," *Freedom House,* https://bit.ly/3bovMjv, "Thailand," *Freedom House,* https://bit.ly/2Uw2OqL (all accessed January 16, 2020); Andrew Higgins, "Kazakhstan Gets New Leader, But Old System's Grip on Power Remains," *New York Times,* https://nyti.ms/3bgGEzK (accessed January 21, 2020).

90 "Big US Firms Shift Hiring Abroad," *Wall Street Journal* (April 19, 2011): B1.

91 "The World's New Growth Frontier: Midsize Cities in Emerging Markets," McKinsey & Company, https://mck.co/2Ux6eKd (accessed October 20, 2015).

92 Now, the more plausible scenario is one in which emerging economies may migrate from one basis of rule to another—that is, from rule of man to "rule by law" and its implicit notion that even the ruler is subject to the law.

93 Gardiner Harris, "India Backs Foreign Investment in Retailing," NYTimes.com, https://nyti.ms/2xljHwo (accessed January 17, 2013).

94 Geoff Lewis, "Who in the World Is Entrepreneurial?" *Fortune: Small Business* (June 1, 2007): 24.

95 A contract is a binding legal agreement that formalizes promises between parties, the breach of which triggers legal action.

96 "Economics Focus: The Himalayas of Hiring," *The Economist* (August 7, 2010): 76.

97 In the United States, the Internal Revenue Service requires reporting the sale of assets, payments to subcontractors, and termination of retirement plans.

98 "Three Years Later, India's Bankruptcy Reform Languishes in Courts," *Reuters,* https://reut.rs/2WA5GWr (accessed January 27, 2019).

99 "Lawmakers to U.S. Companies: Don't Buy Huawei, ZTE," *CNET News,* https://cnet.co/3bfQXnC (accessed January 17, 2013).

100 Duncan Fairgrieve and Geraint Howells, "Is Product Liability Still a Global Problem?" *Managerial Law* 49:1/2 (2007): 6–9.

101 "Lego: Bricks and Flicks," *The Economist* (May 7, 2011): 70.

102 "A High Cost to Developing Countries," *New York Times* (October 5, 1986).

103 Stephanie Clifford, "Recession? Knockoffs Go Down-Market," NYTimes.com, https://nyti.ms/3af74Su (accessed February 14, 2011).

104 Items commonly counterfeited include books, printer cartridges, music CDs, brake pads, DVDs, aircraft parts, cigarettes, wristwatches, razor blades, batteries, medicine, motorcycles, handbags, jewellery, automobiles, shampoo, pens, toys, wine, shoes, clothing, luggage, foods, beer, perfume, cleaning supplies, pharmaceuticals, and health-care supplies.

105 Stephanie Sutton, "EFCG: Counterfeit Medicines More Profitable than Heroin," https://bit.ly/2UssFA1 (accessed February 16, 2011).

106 Ibid.

107 "Statistics | IACC," https://bit.ly/2wxx6ld (accessed February 26, 2019); "Inside the Knockoff-Tennis-Shoe Factory," NYTimes.com (accessed February 14, 2011).

108 Owen Fletcher and Jason Dean, "Ballmer Decries Huge China Sales Holes," *Wall Street Journal* (May 27, 2011): A-1.

109 Ibid., Quote by Jonathan Erece, a trade enforcement coordinator for United States Protection.

110 "Fake Pharmaceuticals: Bad Medicine," *The Economist* (October 13, 2012): 74.

111 Ibid.

112 "Special 301 Report, *Office of the United States Trade Representative,"* https://bit.ly/33B7cZW (accessed February 24, 2013).

113 "Software Piracy Takes Toll on Global Scale," *Hack in the Box: Keeping Knowledge Free,* https://bit.ly/2Uw3tIL (accessed April 23, 2011).

114 "Microsoft Says Software Piracy Continues to Grow," *TG Daily,* https://bit.ly/3dlYLWR (accessed February 14, 2011).

115 View of Mr. Orhii reported in "Fake Pharmaceuticals: Bad Medicine," *The Economist* (October 13, 2012): 74.

116 Ibid., Microsoft Says Software Piracy Continues to Grow."

117 "Business in China and the West: A Tale of Two Expats," *The Economist* (December 29, 2010): 73.

118 "BSA | The Software Alliance," www.bsa.org/ (accessed January 12, 2020).

Chapter 4

1 Clyde V. Prestowitz, *Three Billion New Capitalists: The Great Shift of Wealth and Power to the East* (New York: Basic Books, 2006); Angus Maddison, *The World Economy, 1–2030 AD* (London: Oxford University Press, 2007); *The World Economy: Volume 1: A Millennial Perspective* (Paris: Development Centre, 2001); *Volume 2: Historical Statistics* (Paris: Development Centre, 2003); Parag Khanna, *The Future Is Asian* (Simon & Schuster, 2019); Joseph S. Nye, Jr., "The Rise and Fall of American Hegemony from Wilson to Trump," *International Affairs* 95, no. 1 (2019): 63–80; Boris Lee, "Assessing Made in China 2025, the US-China Trade War and Ways Going Forward" (2019), *CMC Senior Theses;* Colin Flint and Cuiping Zhu, "The Geopolitics of Connectivity, Cooperation, and Hegemonic Competition: The Belt and Road Initiative," *Geoforum* 99 (2019): 95–101.

2 "The World's Shifting Centre of Gravity," *The Economist* https://econ.st/3bjzAT2 (accessed June 28, 2012); "McKinsey: The World's Economic Center of Gravity from AD 1 To AD 2010," *Business Insider,* https://bit.ly/2xcwGAF (accessed December 30, 2015).

3 Martin Dewhurst, Jonathan Harris, and Suzanne Heywood, "The Global Company's Challenge," *McKinsey Quarterly,* https://bit.ly/2WyjErJ (accessed December 31, 2012).

4 We are currently experiencing roughly 10 times the economic acceleration of the Industrial Revolution, on more than 100 times the scale, resulting in an economic transformation that carries over 1,300 times the force of change.

5 Also see Angus Mattison, *The World Economy, 1-2001 AD; HS–8: The World Economy, 1–2001 AD,* https://bit.ly/2J9xY2e (accessed March 20, 2020).

6 "China Overtakes US as World's Largest Trading Country," *RT International,* https://bit.ly/2UrpatH (accessed March 9, 2019).

7 Clyde Prestowitz, "Three Billion New Capitalists," video transcript, *News Hour* (August 15, 2005), https://to.pbs.org/3bjzmva (accessed July 18, 2007).

8 "How Does the World Bank Classify Countries? – World Bank Data Help Desk," https://bit.ly/3966VіI(accessed March 3, 2019).

9 See, for example, Steven D. Levitt and Stephen J. Dubner, *Freakonomics* (New York: HarperCollins, 2009).

10 Nielsen, Lynge. "How to Classify Countries Based on Their Level of Development," *Social Indicators Research* 114, no. 3 (2013): 1087–1107.

11 "World Economic Outlook- GDP Based on PPP, Share of World," https://bit.ly/2xgNZAy (accessed March 6, 2019).

12 "Data - Country Classification," https://bit.ly/3dnp5zW (accessed January 22, 2020).

13 Quote, Jeffrey Sachs, "Commanding Heights: Jeffrey Sachs," *PBS,* https://to.pbs.org/2vHEMkv (accessed March 22, 2016).

14 Derek Thompson, "How Globalization Saved the World and Damned the West," *The Atlantic* (2019), https://bit.ly/2J9mQCe (accessed February 7, 2019).

15 "World Economic Outlook" (January, 2020), https://bit.ly/33BEatf (accessed January 22, 2020).

16 "The Next Billions: Unleashing Business Potential in Untapped Markets," *World Economic Forum* (January 2009): 44; C. K. Prahalad and S. L. Hart, "The Fortune at the Bottom of the Pyramid," *Strategy+Business* (2002) 26: 54–67.

17 Emerging-market status determined by "MSCI Index Country Membership," www.msci.com/emerging-markets and www.msci.com/market-classification, and "FTSE Benchmarks" (accessed March 3, 2019).

18 "World Economic Outlook (October 2018)—GDP Based on PPP, Share of World" https://bit.ly/2Uxuc7Q (accessed March 6, 2019).

19 "Emerging Markets: Group Statistics," https://bit.ly/2UsIu9V; "Stats for Country Grouping: High Income OECD Countries," https://bit.ly/3bmzb2d (accessed March 6, 2019).

20 Martin Dewhurst, Jonathan Harris, and Suzanne Heywood, "The Global Company's Challenge."

21 "Prosperity in Asia: The Intergenerational Dimensions," EABER, www.eaber.org/node/24815 (accessed December 13, 2015).

22 "Chart Focus: The World's Economic Center of Gravity Shifts," *McKinsey Quarterly*, https://bit.ly/3dorASi (accessed February 25, 2013).

23 William W. Beach and Marc A. Miles, "Explaining the Factors of the Index of Economic Freedom," *2005 Index of Economic Freedom*, https://herit.ag/2J3P5Cv (accessed August 14, 2006).

24 Quote extracted from *The Wealth of Nations.* Reported in "Executive Summary," Index of Economic Freedom, https://herit.ag/33KtmJm (accessed February 4, 2008).

25 Adapted from "Methodology," *2019 Index of Economic Freedom Book*, https://herit.ag/2y1O3oj, and "Country Rankings: World & Global Economy Rankings on Economic Freedom," https://herit.ag/3aeaKDR (accessed March 1, 2019).

26 "IMD World Competitiveness Centre," www.imd.org/wcc/ (accessed December 8, 2015).

27 "Index of Economic Freedom: Promoting Economic Opportunity and Prosperity by Country," www.heritage.org/index/ (accessed February 27, 2019); "Executive Highlights," *2019 Index of Economic Freedom Book*, https://herit.ag/2QCH6AB (accessed March 1, 2019).

28 "Doing Business 2020," *World Bank Group*, www.doingbusiness.org (accessed January 15, 2020).

29 The designations "developed" and "developing" are used for statistical convenience and do not convey a judgement about status or stage in the development process.

30 Anatole Kaletsky, *Capitalism 4.0: The Birth of a New Economy in the Aftermath of Crisis* (New York: Public Affairs, 2010).

31 "China | Data," https://bit.ly/3bmoFYv (accessed March 7, 2019).

32 "Q&A with Ian Bremmer on State Capitalism," *Foreign Affairs*, https://fam.ag/2QBZpWq (accessed April 13, 2011).

33 The state essentially prevents systemic distortions threatening the stability of the system and promoting societal welfare—or, as Marx prophesied, capitalism eventually is destroyed by its own contradictions.

34 Michael Wines, "Make No Mistake: In China, State-Run Firms Rule," *New York Times* (August 31, 2010): B-4.

35 "China's Future: Rising Power, Anxious State," *The Economist*, Special Report: China (June 25, 2011): 14.

36 Max Zenglein and Anna Holzmann. "Evolving Made in China 2025: China's Industrial Policy in the Quest for Global Tech Leadership," *MERICS Paper on China No* 8 (2019).

37 "Countries at the Crossroads," https://bit.ly/3ablgKN (accessed April 18, 2011).

38 Ian Bremmer, "State Capitalism and the Crisis," *McKinsey Quarterly* (July 2009): 4.

39 "Global Indicators Database: Country's Economic Situation (2015)," Pew Research Center, https://pewrsr.ch/3966ogI, and https://pewrsr.ch/2xjVlhu (accessed January 20, 2020).

40 Ian Bremmer, *The End of the Free Market: Who Wins the War Between States and Corporations?* (New York: Portfolio, 2010).

41 Adam Smith, "An Inquiry into the Nature and Causes of the Wealth of Nations, Book IV, Chapter IX," *Library of Economics and Liberty*, https://bit.ly/2U9PUQh (accessed December 8, 2015).

42 François Maniquet, "From Each According to His Ability, to Each According to His Needs, or (Even) More, If He Wishes," *Revue économique* 68, no. 1 (2017): 119–129.

43 Michael Todaro, *Economic Development*, 6th edition (Reading, MA: Addison Wesley, 1996): 705.

44 Regarding the informal, the *Economist* reported that "When Alan Greenspan was chairman of the Federal Reserve, he monitored several unusual measures. One favorite, supposedly, was sales of men's underwear, which are usually pretty constant, but drop in recessions when men replace them less often." See "Fast Food for Thought," *The Economist* (July 30, 2011): 12.

45 "GDP: One of the Great Inventions of the 20th Century," *Bureau of Economic Analysis*, https://bit.ly/2UwFDwR (accessed January 24, 2013).

46 Historically, GNI was referred to as gross national product. The definition and measurement of GNI and GNP are analogous, but institutions such as the World Bank and International Monetary Fund now use the term GNI.

47 See "On the Difference between GNP and GDP," *A (Budding) Sociologist's Commonplace Book*, https://bit.ly/2QSjB6L (accessed April 8, 2019).

48 "World Economic Outlook (October 2018)—Gross Domestic Product (GDP)," https://bit.ly/3bjeF2w (accessed January 15, 2020). Total Global Economy: $134,981.

49 "U.S. and World Population Clocks," POPClocks, retrieved January 23, 2020. Check www.census.gov/popclock/ for current statistics.

50 "GNI per Capita, Atlas Method (current US$)," *The World Bank*, https://bit.ly/33EBlrp (accessed March 27, 2019).

51 "Gasoline Prices around the World," GlobalPetrolPrices.com, www.globalpetrolprices.com/gasoline_prices/ (accessed January 20, 2020).

52 World Bank, 2013 Survey (Atlas methodology for GNI per capita). Typically, the prices of many goods are considered and weighted according to their importance in the economy of the country.

53 "Sex, Drugs and GDP: The Challenge of Measuring the Shadow Economy," WSJ.com, https://on.wsj.com/3blxjXx (accessed December 31, 2015).

54 OECD/ILO (2019), *Tackling Vulnerability in the Informal Economy*, Development Centre Studies, OECD Publishing, Paris.

55 A. T. Kearney, "Global Study Finds Nearly a Quarter of the World's Economy Is 'Off the Books,'" https://prn.to/2xgN2bs (accessed March 2, 2019).

56 "Changing the Scales," *The Economist* (August 23, 2014): 68–9; "How Nigeria's Economy Grew by 89 percent Overnight," *The Economist* (April 7, 2014): 56–7; Leandro Medina and Friedrich Schneider, "Shadow Economies Around the World: What Did We Learn Over the Last 20 Years?" (2018).

57 "British Shadow Economy Grown in Size," Institute of Economic Affairs, https://bit.ly/2wuR3ZJ (accessed March 14, 2019).

58 "Process of Preparation of the Environmental Perspective to the Year 2000 and Beyond," General Assembly Resolution 38/161, https://bit.ly/2UcX06W (accessed May 27, 2007).

59 Joseph Stiglitz, "Good Numbers Gone Bad: Why Relying on GDP as a Leading Economic Gauge Can Lead to Poor Decision-Making," *Fortune* (September 25, 2006): 45–9.

60 "Human Development Reports," http://hdr.undp.org/en/composite/HDI (accessed April 8, 2019).

61 "World Happiness Report 2018," *World Happiness Report*, http://worldhappiness.report/ed/2018/ (accessed March 8, 2019).

62 Roger Cohen, "The Happynomics of Life," NYTimes.com, nytimes.com/2011/03/13/opinion/13cohen.html?_r=1 (accessed April 27, 2011).

63 Eric Weiner, "The Happiest Places in the World," *Forbes* (April 23, 2008): 55.

64 "World Happiness Report 2019," http://worldhappiness.report/ (accessed March 26, 2019).

65 "World Happiness Report 2019."

66 "OECD Launches New Report on Measuring Well-Being – OECD," https://bit.ly/3dlh5PU (accessed March 3, 2019).

67 "Happy Planet Index," www.happyplanetindex.org/ (accessed April 8, 2019).

68 "World Bank Indicators, 2013," *The World Bank*, data.worldbank.org/data-catalog/world-development-indicators.

69 "Government v. Market in America: The Visible Hand," *The Economist* (May 28, 2009): 25–8.

70 "Thomas Hobbes: 'Solitary, Poor, Nasty, Brutish, and Short,'" *Yale University Press London Blog*, https://bit.ly/33BCPlW (accessed April 5, 2013).

71 E. Mishan, *The Costs of Economic Growth* (New York: Praeger, 1967).

72 Ibid.

73 Jerome Glenn, Theodore Gordon, and Elizabeth Florescu, *2009 State of the Future, The Millennium Project*, www.millenniumproject.org/millennium/sof2009.html (accessed May 15, 2011).

74 Technically, a score of zero implies perfect equality (everybody has the same income); a score of one implies perfect inequality (one person has all the income).

75 "Global Competitiveness Index," *World Economic Forum*, www.weforum.org/issues/global-competitiveness (accessed January 25, 2013).

76 "Global Competitiveness Report 2015–2016," *World Economic Forum*, http://reports.weforum.org/global-competitiveness-report-2015-2016/competitiveness-rankings/ (accessed December 8, 2015).

77 "IMD's 2020 World Competitiveness Ranking Revealed, Showing Strength of Small Economies." IMD Business School, /news/updates/IMD-2020-World-Competitiveness-Ranking-revealed/, accessed June 20, 2020.

78 "The Global Innovation Index 2012," www.globalinnovationindex.org/gii/ (accessed January 25, 2013).

79 "The Lottery of Life," *The Economist: The World in 2013* (November 21, 2012): 91.

80 *Sources*: The Global Competitiveness Report 2019, from https://bit.ly/2U8erW1; The World Competitiveness Ranking 2019, from https://bit.ly/3biTBZY; Global Innovation Index (GII) 2019, from https://bit.ly/2UsHPFt; Overall Best Countries Ranking, https://bit.ly/2Wz2V7H; Where-To-Be-Born" Index, https://bit.ly/2WBiUlG (all accessed January 15, 2020).

81 "World Economic Outlook (October 2018)—GDP Based on PPP, Share of World," www.imf.org/external/datamapper/PPPSH@WEO (accessed March 9, 2019).

82 "GDP Growth (Annual %)," *The World Bank*, http://data.worldbank.org/indicator/NY.GDP.MKTP.KD.ZG?order=wbapi_data_value_2014+wbapi_data_value+wbapi_data_value-last&sort=desc (accessed April 17, 2016).

83 Derek Thompson, "How Globalization Saved the World and Damned the West," *The Atlantic*, https://bit.ly/2UbzkzE (accessed February 7, 2019); James Manyika, Anu Madgavkar, Tilman Tacke, Sven Smit, Jonathan Woetzel, and Abdulla Abdulaal, The Social Contract in the 21st century, hello *McKinsey Global Institute*, February 2020; Dayana Yochim, "What's your net worth, and how do you compare to others?" *MarketWatch*, Retrieved January 23, 2020 from https://on.mktw.net/39a874A.

84 Elena Holodny, "The 5,000-Year History of Interest Rates Shows Just How Historically Low US Rates Still Are Right Now," *Business Insider*, https://bit.ly/2U8KjKf (accessed March 16, 2019).

85 "Negative Yields Mount Along with Europe's Problems – WSJ," https://on.wsj.com/2Ubsfzh (accessed March 9, 2019); Boungou, W. (2020). "Negative Interest Rates Policy and Banks' Risk-Taking: Empirical Evidence," *Economics Letters, 186*, 108760.

86 "What Is Helicopter Money?" World Economic Forum, www.weforum.org/agenda/2015/08/what-is-helicopter-money (accessed March 23, 2016).

87 "5 Ways of Understanding the Fourth Industrial Revolution," World Economic Forum, www.weforum.org/agenda/2015/11/5-ways-of-understanding-the-fourth-industrial-revolution/ (accessed February 1, 2016).

88 Quote by the founder of robot builder, Industrial Perception, reported in John Markoff, "New Wave of Deft Robots Is Changing Global Industry," *NYTimes.com*, https://nyti.ms/2xS8PXd (accessed February 25, 2013).

89 U.S. Bureau of Labor Statistics, Percent of Employment in Manufacturing in the United States, retrieved from FRED, Federal Reserve Bank of St. Louis; https://fred.stlouisfed.org/series/USAPEFANA (accessed January 29, 2020).

90 "Artificial Intelligence Meets the C-Suite," *McKinsey & Company*, www.mckinsey.com/business-functions/strategy-and-corporate-finance/our-insights/artificial-intelligence-meets-the-c-suite (accessed March 23, 2016).

91 "Nearly Half of US Jobs Could Be at Risk of Computerization, Oxford Martin School Study Shows," *Kurzweil Accelerating Intelligence*, www.kurzweilai.net/oms-working-paper-on-the-future-of-employment-how-susceptible-are-jobs-to-computerisation (accessed February 2, 2016).

92 "The Future of Jobs Report 2018." World Economic Forum, https://bit.ly/2wihVwd (accessed March 17, 2019).

Chapter 5

1 *Sources include the following:* Thomas Gryta and Ted Mann, "GE Powered the American Century – Then It Burned Out," www.wsj.com/articles/ge-powered-the-american-centurythen-it-burned-out-11544796010?mod=searchresults&page=1&pos=4. Appeared in the printed edition on December 14, 2018, as "Burned Out." General Electric Co. home page, at www.ge.com, especially the 2017 Annual Report in the section for investors and the ESG section (Environmental, Social, and Governance) (accessed February 19, 2019); Thomas Gryta, "GE Confronts Legacy of Bad Power Deals," *Wall Street Journal* (February 14, 2019), p. A1; Thomas Gryta, "GE Asserts Progress as Ills Persist," *Wall Street Journal* (February 1, 2019), B1; Alan Murray, "Business: Why Key Executives Are Warming to Legislation on Climate Change," *Wall Street Journal* (February 7, 2007): A10; Rachel Pulfer, "Gambling on Green," *Canadian Business* (April 24, 2006): 35; Kara Sissell, "Major Corporations Form Advocacy Group to Curb Climate Change," *Chemical Week* (January 31, 2007): 12; Neal St. Anthony, "'Green' Strategy Has GE Investor Seeing Red," *Minneapolis-St. Paul Star Tribune* (February 3, 2006): 1.

2 Pankaj Ghemawat, "Distance Still Matters: The Hard Reality of Global Expansion," *Harvard Business Review* (September 2001): 137–47.

3 Eduardo Porter, "Corporate Action on Social Problems Has Its Limits," *New York Times* (September 9, 2015): B1.

4 Bradley R. Agle, Thomas Donaldson, R. Edward Freeman, Michael C. Jensen, Ronald K. Mitchell, and Donna J. Wood, "Dialogue toward Superior Stakeholder Theory," *Business Ethics Quarterly* 18:2 (2008): 153–90.

5 John H. Dunning, "The Eclectic Paradigm of International Production: A Restatement and Some Possible Extensions," *Journal of International Business Studies*, 19:1 (1988): 1–32.

6 Mohsin Habib and Leon Zurawicki, "Corruption and Foreign Direct Investment," *Journal of International Business Studies* 33 (Summer 2002): 291–308.

7 Ravi Ramamurti, "The Obsolescing 'Bargaining Model'? MNE-Host Developing Country Relations Revisited," *Journal of International Business Studies* 32 (Spring 2001): 23.

8 "Global Apparel Manufacturing Industry Market Research Resport," IBIS World (August 2019), https://www.ibisworld.com/global/market-research-reports/global-apparel-manufacturing-industry/ (accessed January 24, 2020).

9 Maria Armental, "Ford Shakes Up South America Strategy," *Wall Street Journal* (February 20, 2019), B1.

10 Lawrence Kohlberg, "The Claim to Moral Adequacy of a Highest Stage of Moral Judgment," *Journal of Philosophy* 70 (1973): 630–46.

11 Richard T. DeGeorge, *Business Ethics*, 7th edition (Upper Saddle River, NJ, 2010): 22–4.

12 DeGeorge, *Business Ethics*, 39, 44.

13 Ibid., p. 39.

14 Alfred Marcus, *Business & Society: Ethics, Government, and the World Economy* (Homewood, IL: Irwin, 1996).

15 T. L. P. Tang, P. Sutarso, M. A. Ansari, et al., "Monetary Intelligence and Behavioral Economics: The Enron Effect—Love of Money, Corporate Ethical Values, Corruption Perceptions Index (CPI), and Dishonesty Across 31 Geopolitical Entities," *Journal of Business Ethics*, 148 (2018): 919.

16 David J. Vidal, *The Link between Corporate Citizenship and Financial Performance* (New York: Conference Board, 1999).

17 Trivia-Library.com, "Origins of Sayings—When in Rome, Do As the Romans Do" (accessed March 30, 2011), reproduced with permission from the People's Almanac series of books, 1975–1981 by David Wallechinsky & Irving Wallace.

18 See John M. Kline, *Ethics for International Business: Decision Making in a Global Political Economy* (London and New York: Routledge, 2005).

19 DeGeorge, *Business Ethics*, 33.

20 S. Prakash Sethi, "Standards for Corporate Conduct in the International Arena: Challenges and Opportunities for Multinational Corporations," *Business and Society Review* (Spring 2002): 20–39.

21 "The Ethics of Business," in "A Survey of Corporate Social Responsibility," *The Economist* (January 22, 2005): 20.

22 John R. Boatright, *Ethics and the Conduct of Business* (Upper Saddle River, NJ: Prentice Hall, 1993): 13–16.

23 Boatright, *Ethics and the Conduct of Business*, 16–18.

24 See A. M. Ali and I. H. Saiad, "Determinants of Economic Corruption," *Cato Journal* 22:3 (2003): 449–66; H. Park, "Determinants of Corruption: A Cross-National Analysis," *Multinational Business Review* 11:2 (2003): 29–48.

25 Transparency International, "How Do You Define Corruption?," www.transparency.org/what-is-corruption/ (accessed February 22, 2019).

26 Transparency International, "Bribe Payers Index Report," www.transparency.org/bpi2011/results (accessed February 10, 2015).

27 Chad Bray and Stanley Reed, "Petrobras of Brazil to Pay $2.95 Billion Over Corruption Scandal," *The New York Times* (January 3, 2018), online edition (accessed February 25, 2019).

28 www.theguardian.com/world/2015/sep/21/ex-treasurer-workers-party-sentenced-prison-petrobras-corruption-scandal and www.theguardian.com/business/2015/sep/27/rolls-royce-second-investigation-brazil-petrobas.

29 See The World Bank, *World Development Report 2002: Building Institutions for Markets*; M. Habib and L. Zurawicki, "Country-Level Investments and the Effect of Corruption—Some Empirical Evidence," *International Business Review* 10:6 (2001): 687–700.

30 S. Ghoshal and P. Moran,"Towards a Good Theory of Management,"in J. Birkinshaw and G. Piramal, eds., *Sumantra Ghoshal on Management: A Force for Good* (Upper Saddle River, NJ: Financial Times/Prentice Hall, 2005): 1–27.

31 Mark Pieth and Huguette Labelle,"Bribery in International Business: Making Sure That Bribes Don't Pay,"www.oecd.org/daf/anti-bribery/makingsurethatbribesdontpay.htm (accessed June 20, 2013).

32 *Progress Report 2015: Assessing Enforcement of the OECD Convention on Combating Bribery*, Transparency International, www.transparency.org/whatwedo/publication/exporting_corruption_progress_report_2015_assessing_enforcement_of_the_oecd (accessed February 10, 2016).

33 "Strengthening the Anti-Bribery Convention: Review of the 2009 OECD Anti-Bribery Convention,"Organization for Economic Cooperating and Development (OECD.org) (accessed February 25, 2019).

34 "EU Anti-Corruption Report: Report from the Commission to the Council and the European Parliament"(Brussels, European Commission, 3/2014 Com (2014) 38 Final).

35 Devlin Barrett, Christopher M. Matthews, and Aruna Viswanatha, "Charges Show U.S. Justice Department's Long Reach,"*Wall Street Journal* (May 28, 2015): A11.

36 David Child,"India Has the Worst Air Pollution: Report,"*AlJazeera* (March 5, 2019), www.aljazeera.com/news/2019/03/india-world-worst-air-pollution-report-190305151923982.html (accessed 27 January 2020).

37 "Choking on It," *The Economist* (December 5, 2015): 54.

38 John Carey, "Global Warming," *Businessweek* (August 16, 2004): 60–69.

39 "Green Light," *The Economist* (December 19, 2015): 89.

40 "Hope for the Trees," *The Economist* (December 19, 2015): 90.

41 Michelle Hackman, "Coal Fuels German Debate," *Wall Street Journal* (October 11, 2018), A18.

42 Rob Curran, "PG&E's Bankruptcy Highlights Blind Spots in Green Investing," *Wall Street Journal* (February 15, 2019):B5.

43 Danny Hakim, "VW Admits Cheating in U.S., But Says Its Practices Were Legal in Europe,"*New York Times* (January 22, 2016): B1.

44 Danny Hakim and Claire Barthelemy,"VW Fought Emissions Test Changes in Europe,"*New York Times* (December 2, 2015): B1.

45 Bill Vlasic, "Volkswagen Engineer Gets Prison in Diesel Cheating Case," *The New York Times* (August 25, 2017), www.nytimes.com/2017/08/25/business/volkswagen-engineer-prison-diesel-cheating.html (accessed February 27, 2019); Sonari Glinto and Rachel Gotbum,"Former Volkswagen CEO Indicted Over Testing Scandal,"National Public Radio (May 4, 2018), www.npr.org/sections/thetwo-way/2018/05/04/608374639/former-volkswagen-ceo-indicted-over-emission-testing-scandal (accessed February 27, 2019).

46 Danny Hakim and Jack Ewing,"Executive Had a Crucial Role as VW Struggled with Emissions,"*New York Times* (December 22, 2015): B1.

47 Ethical Trading Initiative, www.ethicaltrade.org (accessed February 27, 2019).

48 Ans Kolk and Rob van Tulder,"Child Labor and Multinational Conduct: A Comparison of International Business and Stakeholder Codes,"*Journal of Business Ethics* 36:3 (March 2002): 291–301.

49 International Labor Organization,"Global Estimates of Child Labour: Results and Trends 2012–2016 (International Labour Office, Geneva, Switzerland, 2017),"ILO.org (accessed February 27, 2019).

50 Ibid.

51 International Labour Organization,"Forced Labor, Modern Slavery, and Human Trafficking,"op. cit.

52 Edward Luce,"Ikea's Grown-Up Plan to Tackle Child Labour,"*Financial Times* (September 15, 2004): 7.

53 UNICEF's Corporate Partnerships: IKEA, www.unicef.org/corporate_partners/index_25092.html (accessed May 13, 2013).

54 www.globalreporting.org (accessed February 27, 2019).

55 Christopher Bartlett and Paul Beamish, *Transnational Management: Text, Cases, and Readings in Cross-Border Management*, 7th Edition (New York, NY: 2014): Chapter 8.

56 *Sources include the following:* "Our Goal in Ending the AIDS Epidemic by 2030," www.unaids.org/en (accessed on March 1, 2019; see various sections of the website on data and programs); angloamerican.com/sustainability/safety-and-health (accessed March 1, 2019); Alec Russell,"Answers to an AIDS Epidemic: New Initiatives to Help Infected Workers Mark a Big Shift in Attitude and Approach at Some of South Africa's Largest Companies,"*Financial Times* (October 4, 2007): 14; Mark Schoofs,"New Challenges in Fighting AIDS—Enlisting Multinationals in Battle,"*Wall Street Journal* (November 30, 2001): B1; James Lamont,"Anglo's Initiative,"*Financial Times* (August 8, 2002): 10;"Anglo American to Give Mineworkers AIDS Drugs Free,"*Wall Street Journal* (August 7, 2002): A13.

Chapter 6

1 Lichung Jen is Professor of Marketing within the Department of International Business, National Taiwan University.

2 For a good survey of mercantilism and the mercantilist era, see Gianni Vaggi, *A Concise History of Economic Thought: From Mercantilism to Monetarism* (New York: Palgrave Macmillan, 2002).

3 For reviews of the literature, see Jordan Shan and Fiona Sun,"On the Export-Led Growth Hypothesis for the Little Dragons: An Empirical Reinvestigation," *Atlantic Economic Review* 26:4 (1998): 353–71; George K. Zestos and Xiangnan Tao,"Trade and GDP Growth: Causal Relations in the United States and Canada,"*Southern Economic Journal* 68:4 (2002): 859–74.

4 For a good discussion of the history of free trade thought, see Leonard Gomes, *The Economics and Ideology of Free Trade: A Historical Review* (Cheltenham, UK: Edward Elgar, 2003).

5 "Year Round Production of Tomatoes in Iceland,"retrieved July 16, 2007, from www.freshplaza.com/news_detail.asp?id=3791;"The History of Wine Production in Brazil,"retrieved July 16, 2007, from www.brazilianwines.com/en/brazilie histoire.asp.

6 For simplicity's sake, both Smith and Ricardo originally assumed a simple world composed of only two countries and two commodities. Our example makes the same assumption. Now, although this simplification is unrealistic, it does not diminish the usefulness of either theory. Economists have applied the same reasoning to demonstrate efficiency advantages in multiproduct and multicountry trade relationships. Smith's seminal treatise remains abundantly in print; for a reliable recent edition, see *An Inquiry into the Nature and Causes of the Wealth of Nations* (Washington, DC: Regnery Publishing, 1998). Like Smith's *Wealth of Nations,* Ricardo's seminal work on comparative advantage, originally published in London in 1817, is continuously reprinted; see, for example, *On the Principles of Political Economy and Taxation* (Amherst, NY: Prometheus Books, 1996).

7 For a good discussion of this paradoxical thinking, see Paul R. Krugman,"What Do Undergraduates Need to Know about Trade?"*American Economic Review Papers and Proceedings* (May 1993): 23–26. For a discussion of some developing countries' views that monopolistic conditions keep them from gaining a fair share of gains from international trade, see A. P. Thirwell, *Growth and Development,* 6th ed. (London: Macmillan, 1999).

8 Thomas I. Palley,"Institutionalism and New Trade Theory: Rethinking Comparative Advantage and Trade Theory,"*Journal of Economic Issues* 42:1 (2008): 195–208.

9 Abhijit V. Banerjee and Esther Duflo, *Good Economics for Hard Times* (New York: PublicAffairs, 2019); see especially Chapter 2.

10 Murray Kemp,"Non-Competing Factor Groups and the Normative Propositions of Trade Theory,"*International Review of Economics and Finance* 17 (2008): 388–90.

11 Andrew Avery Herring, Roger Enrique Bonilla-Carríon, Rosilyne Mae Borland, and Kenneth Hailey Hill,"Differential Mortality Patterns Between Nicaraguan Immigrants and Native-Born Residents of Costa Rica,"*Immigrant Minority Health* 12 (2010): 33–42.

12 Gordon H. Hanson,"The Rise of Middle Kingdoms: Emerging Economies in Global Trade,"*The Journal of Economic Perspectives* 26:2 (Spring 2012): 41–64.

13 "Interiors: Why It's Better to Have a Coastline,"*The Economist* (May 9, 2015): 31.

14 Eli J. Heckscher, *Heckscher-Ohlin Trade Theory* (Cambridge, MA: MIT Press, 1991).

15 For a discussion of ways in which the theory does not fit the reality of trade, see Antoni Estevadeordal and Alan M. Taylor, "A Century of Missing Trade?" *The American Economic Review* 92:1 (2002): 383–93. For a study supporting the theory, see Yong-Seok Choi and Pravin Krishna, "The Factor Content of Bilateral Trade: An Empirical Test," *The Journal of Political Economy* 112:4 (2004): 887–915.

16 See, for example, Donald R. Davis and David E. Weinstein, "An Account of Global Factor Trade," *The American Economic Review* 91:5 (2001): 1423–53; Oner Guncavdi and Suat Kucukcifi, "Foreign Trade and Factor Intensity in an Open Developing Country: An Input-Output Analysis for Turkey," *Russian & East European Finance and Trade* 37:1 (2001): 75–88.

17 See, for example, P. Krugman and A. J. Venables, "Globalization and the Inequality of Nations," *Quarterly Journal of Economics* 110 (1995): 857–80.

18 See Paul Krugman, "Scale Economies, Product Differentiation, and the Patterns of Trade," *The American Economic Review* 70 (1980): 950–59; James Harrigan, "Estimation of Cross-Country Differences in Industry Production Functions," *Journal of International Economics* 47:2 (1999): 267–93.

19 Drusilla K. Brown and Robert M. Stern, "Measurement and Modeling of the Economic Effect of Trade and Investment Barriers in Services," *Title Review of International Economics* 9:2 (2001): 262–86, discuss the role of economies of scale and trade barriers.

20 See Gianmarco I. P. Ottaviano and Diego Puga, "Agglomeration in the Global Economy: A Survey of the 'New Economic Geography'," *The World Economy* 21:6 (1998): 707–31; Gianmarco I. P. Ottaviano, Takatoshi Tabuchi, and Jacques-François Thisse, "Agglomeration and Trade Revisited," *International Economic Review* 43:2 (2002): 409–35.

21 Stefan B. Linder, *An Essay on Trade Transformation* (New York: Wiley, 1961).

22 Dirk Pilat, "The Economic Impact of Technology," *The OECD Observer* 213 (August–September 1998): 5–8.

23 Anthony J. Venables, "Shifts in Economic Geography and Their Causes," *Economic Review—Federal Reserve Bank of Kansas City* 91:4 (2006): 61–85, referring to work by R. Hausmann and D. Rodrik, "Economic Development as Self Discovery" (2003), Harvard Kennedy School working paper.

24 Two discussions of intra-industry trade are: Don P. Clark, "Determinants of Intra-Industry Trade between the United States and Industrial Nations," *The International Trade Journal* 12:3 (Fall 1998): 345–62; H. Peter Gray, "Free International Economic Policy in a World of Schumpeter Goods," *The International Trade Journal* 12:3 (Fall 1998): 323–44.

25 Daniel Michaels, "Landing Rights," *Wall Street Journal* (April 30, 2002): A1+.

26 Lars Håkanson and Douglas Dow, "Markets and Networks in International Trade: On the Role of Distances in Globalization," *Management International Review* 52:6 (2012): 761–90.

27 Christopher A. Bartlett, "Global Wine Wars: New World Challenges Old," Harvard Business School Case 9-303-056 (July 21, 2003).

28 See Raymond Vernon, "International Investment and International Trade in the Product Life Cycle," *Quarterly Journal of Economics* 80 (May 1996): 190–207; David Dollar, "Technological Innovation, Capital Mobility, and the Product Cycle in North–South Trade," *American Economic Review* 76:1 (1986): 177–90.

29 This is true according to various indicators. See, for example, International Bank for Reconstruction and Development, "Science and Technology," *The World Development Indicators* (Washington, DC: International Bank for Reconstruction and Development, 2000): 300.

30 Michael E. Porter, "The Competitive Advantage of Nations," *Harvard Business Review* 68:4 (1990): 73–93.

31 Kiyohiko Ito and Vladimir Pucik, "R&D Spending, Domestic Competition, and Export Performance of Japanese Manufacturing Firms," *Strategic Management Journal* 14 (1993): 61–75.

32 Jeremy Wiesen, "The U.S. Needs Its Own Industrial Policy," *Wall Street Journal* (September 13, 2010): A19.

33 Hubert Schmitz, "Reducing Complexity in the Industrial Policy Debate," *Development Policy Review* 25:4 (2007): 417–28.

34 Ion Ignat Liviu-George and Andre Teofil Postolachi, "Theoretical Controversies on Strategic Trade Policy," *Economy Transdisciplinarity Cognition* 15:1 (2012): 300–7.

35 Sonny Nwankwo and Darlington Richards, "Institutional Paradigm and the Management of Transitions: A Sub-Saharan African Perspective," *International Journal of Social Economics* 1:1/2 (2004): 111.

36 "Biting the Bullet," *The Economist* (September 23, 2017): 65–66.

37 Jeffrey Sachs, "Institutions Matter, But Not Everything," *Finance and Development* (June 2003): 38–41.

38 Nwankwo and Richards, "Institutional Paradigm and the Management of Transitions," 111.

39 Andrés Rodríguez-Clare, "Clusters and Comparative Advantage: Implications for Industrial Policy," *Journal of Development Economics* 82 (2007): 43–57.

40 Paul Krugman and Alasdair M. Smith, eds., *Empirical Studies of Strategic Trade Policies* (Chicago: University of Chicago Press, 1993); Howard Pack and Kamal Saggi, "Is There a Case for Industrial Policy?" *The World Bank Research Observer* 21:2 (2006): 267.

41 Paul M. Sherer, "Thailand Trips in Reach for New Exports," *Wall Street Journal* (August 27, 1996): A8.

42 "Biting the Bullet," *The Economist* (September 23, 2017): 65–66.

43 Richard Brahm, "National Targeting Policies, High-Technology Industries, and Excessive Competition," *Strategic Management Journal* 16 (1995): 71–91.

44 Andrea E. Goldstein and Steven M. McGuire, "The Political Economy of Strategic Trade Policy and the Brazil-Canada Export Subsidies Saga," *The World Economy* 27:4 (2004): 541.

45 Theresa M. Greaney, "Strategic Trade and Competition Policies to Assist Distressed Industries," *The Canadian Journal of Economics* 32:3 (1999): 767.

46 Mertule Mariam, "The Young Continent," *The Economist* (December 12, 2015): 23–25.

47 "Demographic Change Will Have Big Economic Impacts," *The Economist* (September 26, 2016): 72.

48 United Nations, Department of Economic and Social Affairs, Population Division, *World Population Prospects 2019: Highlights* (New York: United Nations, 2019).

49 Greg Ip, "How Aging Japan Defied Demographics and Revived its Economy," *The Wall Street Journal* (January 11, 2019) (accessed January 29, 2020).

50 "The Magic of Migration," *The Economist* (November 16, 2019): special report 1–12.

51 Eduardo Porter and Karl Russell, "Migrants Are on the Rise Around the World, and Myths About Them Are Shaping Attitudes," *New York Times* (June 23, 2018): B1+.

52 "Migration: Foreign-Born Population," OECD, https://data.oecd.org/migration/foreign-born-population.htm (accessed January 26, 2020).

53 Sevil Sönmez, Yorghos Apostopoulos, Diane Tran, and Shantyana Rentrope, "Human Rights and Health Disparities for Migrant Workers in the UAE," *Health and Human Rights* 13:2 (2011).

54 "The Magic of Migration," *The Economist* (November 16, 2019): special report 1-12.

55 Sergio Peçanha and Timothy Wallace, "Around the Globe, a Desperate Flight from Turmoil," *New York Times* (June 21, 2015): 10.

56 "Statelessness: Nowhere to Call Home," *The Economist* (May 17, 2014): 58.

57 "The Magic of Migration," *The Economist* (November 16, 2019): special report 1-12.

58 Abhijit V. Banerjee and Esther Duflo, *Good Economics for Hard Times* (New York: PublicAffairs, 2019); see especially Chapter 2.

59 "The Magic of Migration," *The Economist* (November 16, 2019): special report 1-12.

60 Paul M. Vaaler, "Immigrant Remittances and the Venture Investment Environment of Developing Countries," *Journal of International Business Studies* 42:9 (December 2011): 1121–49.

61 James K. Jackson, "The Committee on Foreign Investment in the United States," Congressional Research Service Report, July 3, 2018; Katy Stech Ferek, "U.S. Panel Expanded Its Review Of Foreign Deals in '19," *Wall Street Journal* (July 31, 2020): A3.

62 Keith Head and John Ries, "Exporting and FDI as Alternative Strategies," *Oxford Review of Economic Policy* 20:3 (2004): 409–29.

63 Andrew E. Kramer, "Russian Farm, Chinese Farmer," *New York Times* (September 11, 2012): B1+.

64 See Frank D. Bean et al., "Circular, Invisible, and Ambiguous Migrants: Components of Differences in Estimates of the Number of Unauthorized Mexican Migrants in the United States," *Demography* 38:3 (2001): 411–22; United Nations Conference on Trade and Development, *World Investment*

Report 2000: Cross-Border Mergers and Acquisitions and Development (New York and Geneva: United Nations, 2000): 312.

65 Paul Windrum, Andreas Reinstaller, and Christopher Bull, "The Outsourcing Productivity Paradox: Total Outsourcing, Organisational Innovation, and Long Run Productivity Growth," *Journal of Evolutionary Economics* 19:2 (2009): 197–229.

66 June Kronholtz, "Immigrant Labor or Machines?" *Wall Street Journal* (December 19, 2006): A4.

67 "March of the Lettuce Bot," *The Economist* (December 1, 2012): monitor 5.

68 Theodore H. Moran, "Foreign Investment and Supply Chains in Emerging Markets: Recurring Problems and Demonstrated Solutions," Peterson Institute for International Economics, Working Paper WP 14–12 (December 2014): 1.

69 J. Duanmu and Y. Guney, "Heterogeneous Effect of Ethnic Networks on International Trade of Thailand: The Role of Family Ties and Ethnic Diversity," *International Business Review* 22:1 (2013): 126–39.

70 Paul Markillie, "Manufacturing the Future," *The Economist* (special issue, the world in 2013, no date): 128.

71 "3D Printing: Print Me a Pavilion," *The Economist* (December 5, 2015): 13–14.

72 We wish to thank Mauricio Calero, former manager of two Ecuadoran rose farms, for granting us interviews and supplying additional data. We would also like to thank Tyler Gill who, while an undergraduate student at the University of Miami, worked diligently in gathering information on the world's, and particularly Ecuador's, export market in roses. Other information came from Alka Kshirsagar, "This V-Day, Rouble Trouble for Roses," *Businessline* (February 13, 2015): n.p.; "Cut Flower Imports (FY 2014)," U.S. Customs and Border Protection, www.cbp.gov/newsroom/spotlights/2015-01-23-000000/cut-flowers (accessed March 1, 2016); Bob Sechler, "Fresh-Cut Flowers, Shipped by Boat?" *Wall Street Journal* (May 11–12, 2013): 3; "Holiday Statistics on Buying Flowers," www.aboutflowers.com/holiday-statistics.html (accessed March 1, 2016); Mick Conefry, "Roses with Altitude: Why Ecuador's Roses Stand Out," *FT.com* (April 10, 2015); "Our Rose Garden: The History of Roses," University of Illinois Extension, urbanext.illinois.edu/roses/history.cfm (accessed December 8, 2010); "The World Cut Flower Industry: Trends and Prospects," Sector Publications, www.ilo.org/public/english/dialogue/sector/papers/ctflower/139e1.htm; www.cia.gov/library/publications/the-world-factbook/geos/ec.html (accessed September 12, 2010); "Trade Map—International Trade Statistics: List of Importing Markets for a Product Exported by Ecuador," International Trade Center (ITC), www.trademap.org/tradestat/Country_SelProductCountry_TS.aspx (accessed February 4, 2011); "Hoja Verde: The Flower of Ecuador," TransFair Canada, transfair.ca/en/producers/profiles/hoja-verde (accessed February 3, 2011); Alena Maschke, "As Flower Imports Increase, Miami Remains Main Entry Point," *Naples News* (May 24, 2018), online edition (accessed February 9, 2019); Bryan Lufkin, "Why are Flowers so Expensive?" *BBC Worklife* (May 7, 2019), online edition (accessed January 15, 2020); Daniel Workman, "Flower Bouquet Exports by Country," www.worldstopexports.com (November 19, 2019) (accessed January 15, 2020).

Chapter 7

1 *Sources include the following:* USDA, National Agricultural Statistics Service, "Catfish Production," (February 2, 2018); Mississippi State University Extension Service, "Catfish Marketing," n.d., https://extension.msstate.edu/agriculture/catfish/catfish-marketing (accessed April 29, 2016); Terry Hanson and Dave Sites, "2013 U.S. Catfish Database," Fisheries and Allied Aquacultures Department Series No. 1 (April 2014); "Vietnam Catfish Exporters Forecast Gloomy Future As US Tightens Quality Control," *Thanhnien News* [Ho Chi Minh City] (December 15, 2015): n.p.; "Vietnam's Catfish Exports to the United States Still Safe This Year," *Vietnam NetBridge* (February 14, 2014): n.p.; Embassy of the Socialist Republic of Vietnam in the United States of America, "Vietnam Resumes Basa Catfish Exports to the US Market" (April 6, 2016), http://vietnamembassy-usa.org/relations/Vietnam-resumes-basa-catfish (accessed April 29, 2016); Melissa Martin, "New Tariff Could Protect Alabama's Catfish Industry," *Southeast Farm Press* (March 25, 2013): n.p.; Roy Roberson, "Golden Opportunity for US Agriculture in Vietnam," *Western Farm Press* (October 10, 2012): n.p.; Terry Hanson and Dave Sites, "U.S. Farm-Related Catfish Industry 2009 Review and 2010 Outlook," Unpublished report, Department of Fisheries and Allied Aquacultures, Auburn University (March 2011); "Catfish Farmers Face Shifting Tides of Imports, Costs," *Southeast Farm Press* (August 14, 2012): n.p.; Fred Kuchler, Barry Krissoff, and David Harvey, "Do Consumers Respond to Country-of-Origin Labelling?" *Journal of Consumer Policy* 33:4 (December 2010): 323–37; "Fishy Diplomacy with Hanoi," *Wall Street Journal* (September 21, 2010), online edition (accessed November 30, 2010); Bartholomew Sullivan, "Stakes High in Catfish Fight," *McClatchy – Tribune Business News* (October 31, 2010) (accessed November 30, 2010); "Fishy Tales; Charlemagne," *The Economist* 387: 8584 (June 14, 2008): 53; Paul Greenberg, "A Catfish by Any Other Name," *New York Times* (October 12, 2008): 72; Ben Evans, "Catfish Plan Risks Trade War," *Miami Herald* (July 2, 2009): 4C; Jeffrey H. Birnbaum, "House Floats Idea for Fish Inspections, But No One Is Biting," *Washington Post* (March 11, 2008): A17; Taras Grescoe, "Catfish with a Side of Scombroid," *New York Times* (July 15, 2007): WK13; Julie Wernau and Benjamin Parkin, "Catfish Gets Tangled in a Small-Fry Trade War," *Wall Street Journal* (September 21, 2018), online edition (accessed February 4, 2019); U.S. National Oceanic and Atmospheric Administration, *Fisheries of the United States, 2017* (accessed February 2, 2019).

2 Mary Amiti, Stephen J. Redding, and David E. Weinstein, "The Impact of the 2018 Tariffs on Prices and Welfare," *Journal of Economic Perspectives* 33:4 (Fall 2019): 187–210.

3 Nelson D. Schwartz and Quoctrung Bui, "Where Free Trade Hurts, Voters Seek Extremes," *New York Times* (April 26, 2016): A1+.

4 Christopher J. O'Leary, Randall W. Eberts, and Brian M. Pittelko, "Effects of NAFTA on US Employment and Policy Responses," *OECD Trade Policy Working Papers* 131 (February 2012).

5 Jim Tankersley, "Trump Tariff on Washers Created Jobs At High Price," *New York Times* (April 22, 2019): B1.

6 "Zero-Sum Grain," *The Economist* (December 15, 2018): 70–71.

7 Michael Hart, "Breaking Free: A Post-mercantilist Trade and Productivity Agenda for Canada," *C.D. Howe Institute Commentary* 357 (August 2012): 1–27.

8 This argument is most associated with the writings of Raul Prebisch, Hans Singer, and Gunnar Myrdal in the 1950s and 1960s. For a recent discussion, see P. Sai-wing Ho, "Arguing for Policy Space to Promote Development: Prebisch, Myrdahl, and Singer," *Journal of Economic Issues* 42:2 (June 2008): 509–16.

9 Dorothy Solinger and Yiyang Hu, "Welfare, Wealth and Poverty in Urban China: The Dibao and Its Differential Disbursement," *The China Quarterly* 211 (September 2012): 741–64.

10 Dani Rodrik, "Premature Deindustrialization," 21 (2016): 1–33 gives a detailed analysis of the changing structure of economies at different economic levels.

11 Benedict Ezema, "Effectiveness of Policy Responses to Terms of Trade Shocks in Selected African Countries," *International Journal of Business and Management* 7:8 (April 2012): 88–101.

12 Peter Navarro, "A Tariff Issue on Which Free and Fair Traders Can Agree," *Wall Street Journal* (May 29, 2019): A15.

13 Gerald K. Helleiner, "Markets, Politics, and Globalization: Can the Global Economy Be Civilized?" *Global Governance* (July–September 2001): 243; Marina Murphy, "EU Chemicals Need Flexibility: A Level Playing Field Should Be Established between the EU and U.S. Chemicals Industries," *Chemistry and Industry* (July 1, 2002): 9; Lisa Schmidt, "How U.S. Sees Trade Rows," *Calgary Herald* [Canada] (June 25, 2002): A2.

14 Annie Gowen, "U.S. Caviar with a Russian Accent," *Washington Post* (December 31, 2004): Metro, B1.

15 Greg Ip, "Globalization Is Down, but It's Not Out Yet," *Wall Street Journal* (April 29, 2020): A2;Gerard Baker, "Nations Push Back Against a Globalized World," *Wall Street Journal* (March 28–29, 2020): C6.

16 Emiko Terazono, "UN Warns Over Volatility in Food Prices," *Financial Times* (October 11, 2011): 20; Tennille Tracy, "Lawmaker Gets a Say on Gas Exports," *Wall Street Journal* (December 26, 2012): A4; Keith Johnson, "Geopolitical Benefit Raised in Debate on Exporting Gas," *Wall Street Journal* (May 6, 2013): A4; "Crude-Oil Exports: Binning the Ban," *The Economist* (March 28, 2015): 35–6; "Developing World Faces Food Crisis," *Wall Street Journal* (May 14, 2020): A9+.

17 John W. Miller, "U.S. Steel Makers Win Tariff Battle," *Wall Street Journal* (August 23–24, 2014): B2.

18 Jenna Smialek and Ana Swanson, "American Consumers, Not China, Are Paying for Trump's Tariffs," *New York Times* (January 6, 2020) (accessed January 12, 2020).

19 Jessica Brice and Christiana Sciaudone, "Luxe for Sale as Cartier, Prada Become Bargains in Brazil," *Bloomberg Business* (August 14, 2015): n.p.

20 "Who Pays?" *The Economist* (September 8, 2018): 25; Jenna Smialek and Ana Swanson, "American Consumers, Not China, Are Paying Trump's Tariffs," *New York Times* (January 6, 2020) (accessed February 3, 2020).

21 Sanchita B. Saxena, "American Tariffs, Bangladeshi Deaths," *New York Times* (December 12, 2012): A31.

22 Stephen Moore, "Tax Cut and Spend: The Profligate Ways of Congressional Republicans," *National Review* (October 1, 2001): 19.

23 Liam Pleven, "Pentagon in Race for Raw Materials," *Wall Street Journal* (May 3, 2010): A3+.

24 Lance Davis and Stanley Engerman, "Sanctions: Neither War nor Peace," *Journal of Economic Perspectives* 17:2 (Spring 2003): 187–97.

25 Susie Sell, "Promise and Pitfalls in Myanmar," *Asia's Newspaper for Media, Marketing and Advertising* (November 1, 2012): 42–3.

26 "The Amazon Rainforest: Cutting Down on Cutting Down," *The Economist* (June 7, 2014): 83–4.

27 "Too Smart by Half," *The Economist* (September 6, 2014): 29–30.

28 Anton Troianovski and Ellen Emmerentze, "Norway Fish Are Caught in Sanctions Clash," *Wall Street Journal* (August 8–9, 2014): A9.

29 Philip Shenon, "In Hanoi, U.S. Goods Sold but Not by U.S.," *New York Times* (October 3, 1993): A1.

30 Patrick Barta, "Black Gold," *Wall Street Journal* (August 16, 2006): A1+.

31 Thomas Erdbrink, "Iran Sanctions Take Unexpected Toll on Medical Imports," *New York Times* (November 3, 2012): A4+.

32 Jacob Weisberg, "Sanctions Help to Sustain Rogue States," *Financial Times* (August 3, 2006): 11.

33 Andrew M. Lemieux and Ronald V. Clarke, "The International Ban on Ivory Sales and Its Effects on Elephant Poaching in Africa," *The British Journal of Criminology* 49:4 (July 2009): 451–71; Bryan Christy, "Ivory Worship," *National Geographic* (October 2012): 28–61.

34 Bryan Christy and Brent Stirton, "Tracking Ivory," *National Geographic* (September 2015): 32–59.

35 Rostram J. Neuwirth, "The 'Culture and Trade Debate' Continues: The UNESCO Convention in Light of the WTO Reports in China—Publications and Audiovisual Products: Between Amnesia or Déjà Vu?" *Journal of World Trade* 44:6 (December 2010): 1333–56.

36 "Canadian Content," *Wikipedia*, https://en.wikipedia.org/wiki/Canadian_content (accessed May 1, 2016).

37 Gail L. Cramer, James M. Hansen, and Eric J. Wailes, "Impact of Rice Tariffication on Japan and the World Rice Market," *American Journal of Agricultural Economics* 81 (1999): 1149.

38 Kimiko de Freytas-Tamura, "East Africa Curbs Imports on the West's Hand-Me-Downs," *New York Times* (October 12, 2017): A4.

39 "Futile Fortress," *Financial Times* (August 26, 2003): 16.

40 Jonathan Weisman and Eric Lipton, "Air Skirmish in War Over Ex-Im Bank," *New York Times* (April 7, 2015): B1+.

41 "U.S.–EU Aircraft Subsidies Dispute Drags on, with No End in Sight in 2013," *Inside US Trade* 31:1 (January 4, 2013): n.p.; Jeffrey D. Kienstra, "Cleared for Landing: Airbus, Boeing, and the WTO Dispute over Subsidies to Large Civil Aircraft," *Northwestern Journal of International Law & Business* 33:3 (Summer 2012): 569–606.

42 John W. Miller, "WTO Warns Members Not to Undermine Trade," *Wall Street Journal* (March 27, 2009): A8; Joseph Stiglitz, "The Global Crisis, Social Protection and Jobs," *International Labour Review* 148:1/2 (June 2009): 1–13; "State Capitalism: Big Brother is Back," *The Economist* (November 3, 2012): 63–4.

43 "Milking Taxpayers," *The Economist* (February 14, 2015): 26, 28.

44 Colin O'Neill, "Will the Obama Administration Give Cotton Growers a New $10 Billion Subsidy," *AgMag Blog* (January 29, 2016), www.ewg.org/agmag/2016/01 (accessed May 1, 2016).

45 "No More Grand Bargains," *The Economist* (August 9, 2014): 10.

46 European Commission, *EU Agriculture Spending Focused on Results* (September 2015). For some data on the United States, see "At the Trough," *The Economist* (June 1, 2013): 32.

47 G. Chandrashekhar, "Should India Demand Farm Subsidy Cuts by Developed Nations?" *Businessline* (January 4, 2006): 1; Carmen G. Gonzalez, "The Global Food System, Human Rights, and the Environment," *GPSolo* 29:6 (November–December 2012): 72–3.

48 Chi-Chur Chao and Eden S. H. Yu, "Import Quotas, Tied Aid, Capital Accumulation, and Welfare," *Canadian Journal of Economics* 34 (2001): 661; Mark Rice, "Australia Must Join Other Countries in Untying Overseas Aid," *Australian Financial Review* (April 4, 2002): 59.

49 Yun Sun, "China's Aid to Africa: Monster or Messiah?" *Brookings East Asia Commentary* 75 (February 2014): n.p.

50 "An Opportunity to Support US Customs Valuations," *International Tax Review* (June 2012): n.p.

51 "Philippines/Thailand: Philippines Urges Thailand to Fully Comply with WTO Customs Valuation Ruling," *Asia News Monitor* [Bangkok] (May 19, 2012): n.p.

52 "National Import Specialist Addresses Outreach to the Public," *U.S. Customs Border Protection Today* (October–November 2006), retrieved July 13, 2007, from www.customs.ustreas.gov/xp?CustomsToday/2006/october_november/import_article; *Customs Bulletin and Decision* (June 27, 2007): 58.

53 Alexander Moens and Amos Vivancos Leon, "Mandatory Country of Origin Labeling: The Case for a Harmonized Canada–US Beef and Pork Regulatory Regime," *Fraser Forum* 4 (July–August 2012): 14–17.

54 "Target Corp., Staples Inc., and OfficeMax, Inc., Among Pencil Importers in the Subject of a False Claims Act Case Brought by The Cullen Law Firm, PLLC," *PR Newswire* [New York] (May 17, 2012): n.p.

55 Christopher Swann, "Shielding Sugar Industry 'Costs Thousands of Jobs,'" *Financial Times* (February 15, 2006): 6; Bryan Riley, "U.S. Trade Policy Gouges American Sugar Consumers," *Backgrounder #2914 on Trade* (June 5, 2014), www.heritage.org/research/reports/2014/06/us-trade-policy-gouging (accessed May 1, 2016); Ron Nixon, "American Candy Makers, Pinched by Inflated Sugar Prices, Look Abroad," *New York Times* (October 30, 2013): n.p.; Douglas A. Irwin, "The Return of the Protectionist Illusion," *Wall Street Journal* (July 2, 2012): A11.

56 Stephanie Strom, "United States and Mexico Reach Tomato Deal, Averting a Trade War," *New York Times* (February 3, 2013), www.nytimes.com/2013/02/04/business/united-states-and-mexico-reach-deal-on-tomato-imports.html (accessed April 21, 2014).

57 John R. Luckey, "Domestic Content Legislation: The Buy American Act and Complementary Little Buy American Provisions," *Congressional Research Service* 7:5700 (April 25, 2012).

58 Jeremy Grant and Ralph Minder, "Comment & Analysis: Agribusiness," *Financial Times* (February 1, 2006): 11.

59 Abhijit V. Banerjee and Esther Duflo, *Good Economics for Hard Times* (New York: PublicAffairs, 2019): 66.

60 Anita Chang, "Food Safety," *Miami Herald* (July 15, 2007): 18A.

61 Marie-Agnés Jouanjean, "Standards, Reputation, and Trade: Evidence from US Horticultural Import Refusals," *World Trade Review, suppl. Symposium Issue: Standards and Non-Tariff Barriers in Trade* 11:3 (July 2012): 438–61.

62 "Delays Reported in Customs-Clearance Procedures in China," *Jiji Press English News Service* [Tokyo] (September 20, 2012): n.p.

63 Dena Kouremetis, "Bartering for Survival," *Forbes/Tech* (October 22, 2012), www.forbes.com/sites/denakouremetis/2012/10/22/bartering-for-survival-have-i-got-a-deal-for-you/ (accessed May 1, 2016).

64 Mark J. Nackman, "A Critical Examination of Offsets in International Defense Procurements: Policy Options for the United States," *Public Contract Law Journal* 40:2 (Winter 2011): 511–29.

65 "Guns and Sugar," *The Economist* (May 25, 2013): 63–5.

66 Ralph G. Carter and Lorraine Eden, "Who Makes U.S. Trade Policy?" *International Trade Journal* 13:1 (1999): 53–100.

67 Eugene Salorio, "Trade Barriers and Corporate Strategies: Why Some Firms Oppose Import Protection for Their Own Industry," unpublished DBA dissertation, Harvard University, 1991.

68 *Sources include the following:* OECD (2015), *Health at a Glance 2015: OECD Indicators*, OECD Publishing, Paris, http://dx.doi.org/10.1787/health_glance-2015-en (accessed April 26, 2016); Jacquie McNish and Liz Hoffman, "Valeant's CEO Was Key Force on Pricing," *Wall Street Journal* (May 2, 2016): n.p.; Katie Thomas, "Under Fire Over Prices, Drug Makers Keep Raising Them," *New York Times* (April 27, 2016): B1+; Andrew Pollack, "Drug Goes From $13.50 a Tablet to $750, Overnight" (September 20, 2015), http://nyti.ms/1V3cJVc (accessed April 27, 2016); U.S. Food and Drug Administration, "Protecting and Promoting Your Health: Is It Legal for Me to Personally Import Drugs?" www.fda.gov/AboutFDA/Transparency/Basics/ucm194904.htm (accessed April

27, 2016); "Painful Pills," *The Economist* (September 26, 2015): 66, 68; Govind Persad, "The Medical Cost Pandemic: Why Limiting Access to Cost-Effective Treatments Hurts the Global Poor," *Chicago Journal of International Law* 15:2 (Winter 2015): 559–611; John Theriault, "Protecting the U.S. Medicine Supply: Integrating Approaches to Promote Safety," *Journal of Commercial Biotechnology* 19:4 (October 2013): 29–34; Todd Allen Wilson, "Grassley, McCain to HHS: Allow Case-by-Case Drug Imports From Canada," *InsideHealthPolicy.com* 7:47 (November 25, 2015): n.p.; Joshua M. Sharfstein and Aaron S. Kesselheim, "The Safety of Prescription Drugs," *Journal of the American Medical Association (JAMA)* 314:3 (July 21, 2015): 233–34; "HealthWarehuse.com Responds to Senator Klobucher & McCain on Reintroduction of Canadian Pharmacy Bill," *Business Wire* (January 27, 2015): n.p.; "The Council on Foreign Relations Holds a Discussion on Generic Drug Regulation and Politics of Pharmaceutical Pricing," *Political Transcript Wire* (February 19, 2016): n.p.; Liz Hamel, Mira Norton, Karen Pollitz, Larry Levitt, Gary Claxton, and Mollyann Brodie, "The Burden of Medical Debt: Results from the Kaiser Family Foundation/New York Times Medical Bills Survey" (January 5, 2016), http://kff.org/health-costs/report/the-burden-of-medical-debt-results-from-the-kaiser-family-foundationnew-york-times-medical-bills-survey/(accessed April 26, 2016); "Save Money on Your Meds," *Consumer Reports* 81:1 (January 2016): 13; "Pharmaceutical Companies and Drug Pricing," *Congressional Record—Senate* (October 5, 2015): S7118-S7119; Laurie McGinley, "Trump Administration to Explore Drug Imports to Counter Price Hikes," *Washington Post* (July 19, 2018), online edition (accessed February 8, 2019); "U.S. Unveils Plan to Import Lower-Priced Drugs from Canada," *The Guardian* (December 18, 2019), online edition (accessed February 3, 2020); Katie Thomas, "Trump Administration Takes First Step to Allow Drug Imports from Canada," *The New York Times* (December 18, 2019), online edition (accessed February 3, 2020); Stephanie Armour, "Executive Orders Renew Push to Cut Drug Costs," *Wall Street Journal* (July 25-26, 2020): A3.

Chapter 8

1 *Sources include the following:* http://www.annualreports.com/Company/toyota-motor-corp (accessed April 13, 2019); Stephen Power, "EU Auto Industry Faces Overhaul as Japanese Gain in Market Share," *Wall Street Journal* (October 14, 2004): A1; Mari Koseki, "Quota on Auto Exports to EC Curbed at 1.089 Million in '93," *Japan Times* (April 12–18, 1993): 14; Nick Maling, "Japan Poised for EU Lift of Export Ceiling," *Marketing Week* (May 6, 1999): 26; Todd Zaun and Beth Demain, "Leading the News: Ambitious Toyota, Buoyed by Europe, Sets Global Goals," *Wall Street Journal* (October 22, 2002): A3; Mark M. Nelson, Thomas F. O'Boyle, and E. S. Browning, "International—The Road to European Unity—1992: EC's Auto Plan Would Keep Japan at Bay—1992 Unification Effort Smacks of Protectionism," *Wall Street Journal* (October 27, 1988): A1; Toyota home page, "Toyota—Joining Europe," at www.toyota-europe.com/experience/the_company/toyota-ineurope.aspx (accessed May 10, 2007); Christoph Rauwald, "Leading the News: Toyota Sales in Europe Jump as Market Stalls," *Wall Street Journal* (March 16, 2007): 2.

2 Peter J. Buckley, Jeremy Clagg, Nicolas Forsans, and Kevin T. Reilly, "Increasing the Size of the 'Country': Regional Economic Integration and Foreign Direct Investment in a Globalised World Economy," *Management International Review* 41:3 (2001): 251–75.

3 Alan M. Rugman and Alain Verbeke, "A Perspective on Regional and Global Strategies of Multinational Enterprises," *Journal of International Business Studies* 35 (2004): 7.

4 Pankaj Ghemawat, "Distance Still Matters: The Hard Reality of Global Expansion," *Harvard Business Review* (September 2001): 3–11.

5 Bela Balassa, *The Theory of Economic Integration* (Homewood, IL: Richard D. Irwin, 1961): 40.

6 Op cit., Ghemawat.

7 For more information on the EU, check out its website at europa.eu (accessed April 1, 2019).

8 "About EFTA," www.efta.int (accessed April 1, 2019).

9 "EU Institutions and Other Bodies," europa.eu (accessed April 1, 2019).

10 "The European Parliament," europa.eu (accessed April 1, 2019).

11 "The European Court of Justice" in "Institutions and Bodies," europa.eu (accessed April 1, 2019).

12 Sam Schechner, Emily Glazer, and Valentina Pop, "EU Deepens Antitrust Probe of Facebook's Data Practices," *Wall Street Journal* (February 7, 2020): B1.

13 Sam Schechner, "Europe Gives Google a Major Privacy Fine," *Wall Street Journal* (January 22, 2019): B1.

14 Farhad Manjoo, "Challenge to Google: Innovation May Undercut the Case," *New York Times* (April 16, 2015): B1.

15 https://europa.eu/european-union/about-eu/countries_en#schengen (accessed on February 8, 2020).

16 Matthias Verbergt, "Belgium Tightens Border with France," *Wall Street Journal* (February 24, 2016): A12.

17 "Refugees in Greece: No Way Out," *The Economist* (February 27, 2016): 43.

18 "Forming an Orderly Queue," *The Economist* (February 6, 2016): 19.

19 Sudeep Reddy, Matthew Dalton, and Joann S. Lublin, "Broad Trade Deal on Table," *Wall Street Journal* (February 13, 2013); Annie Lowrey, "Sore Feelings on U.S. and Europe Begin Trade Talks," *New York Times* (July 9, 2013): B8.

20 Joshua Chaffin and James Politi, "Fractures Appear on Trade Pact," *Financial Times* (May 24, 2013): 2.

21 Jacob M. Schlesinger and Emre Peker, "U.S., EU Set Conflicting Goals for Looming Trade Talks," *Wall Street Journal* (January 14, 2019), www.wsj.com (accessed April 2, 2019).

22 https://ec.europa.eu/trade/policy/in-focus/ttip/index_en.htm (accessed on February 8, 2020).

23 Office of the United States Trade Representative, "United States-Mexico-Canada Trade Fact Sheet: Rebalancing Trade to Support Manufacturing," https://ustr.gov/trade-agreements/free-trade-agreements/united-states-mexico-canada-agreement/fact-sheets/rebalancing (accessed February 10, 2020).

24 Miriam Jordan, "Mexican Migration Reverses," *Wall Street Journal* (November 20, 2015): A3.

25 Mexican Automotive Industry Association and the U.S. Department of Commerce, Bureau of the Census, Foreign Trade Division. Mexico Country Commercial Guide, export.gov (accessed April 4, 2019).

26 Andres Oppenheimer, "While Pacific Alliance Thrives, Mercosur Withers," *The Miami Herald* (May 27, 2013).

27 Sebastian Sermiento-Saher, "The Pacific Alliance: The Americas' Bridge to Asia?" *Pacific Money: Economics and Business* (May 25, 2013), thediplomat.com/pacific-money/2013/05/25/the-pacific-alliance–the-americas-bridge-to-asia/ (accessed May 27, 2013).

28 https://www.statista.com/statistics/796245/gdp-of-the-asean-countries/ (accessed April 3, 2019).

29 "AFTA Doha," *The Economist* (September 6, 2008): 85.

30 Patrick Barta and Alex Frangos, "Southeast Asia Linking Up to Compete with China," *Wall Street Journal* (August 23, 2010): A2.

31 www.opec.org (accessed on April 9, 2019).

32 Barbara Weisel, "Trade Policy in the Asia Pacific after Trans- Pacific Partnership, *Insights* Vol. 19, No. 1 (Academy of International Business, 2019): 22–23.

33 http://worldpopulationreview.com/continents/sub-saharan-africa-population/ (accessed on April 9, 2019).

34 Joseph J. Bish, "Population Growth in Africa: Grasping the Scale of the Challenge," *The Guardian* (January 11, 2016), online edition (accessed March 12, 2016).

35 "Foreign Direct Investment in Africa," KPMG (June 1, 2012), www.kpmg.com/africa/en/issuesandinsights/articles-publications/pages/foreign-direct-investment-in-africa.aspx (accessed May 27, 2013).

36 Eleanor Albert, "China in Africa," *Council on Foreign Affairs* (last updated on July 12, 2017), https://www.cfr.org/backgrounder/china-africa (accessed April 11, 2019).

37 "Trade Within Africa: Tear Down the Walls," *The Economist* (February 27, 2016): 37.

38 Mariama Sow, "Foresight Africa 2016: Regional Integration in Sub-Saharan Africa" (The Brookings Institution, January 12, 2016), https://www.brookings.edu/blog/africa-in-focus/2016/01/12/foresight-africa-2016-regional-integration-in-sub-saharan-africa/ (accessed April 11, 2019).

39 Alan M. Field, "Showdown for CAFTA-DR," *Journal of Commerce* (April 11, 2005).

40 Gerard Butler, "The Great Brexit Breakdown," *The Wall Street Journal* (December 8–9, 2018): C1–2.

41 "The Real Danger of Brexit," *The Economist* (February 27, 2017): 8; "Next Stop: Brexit?", *The Economist* (March 12, 2016): 53; "The Brexit Delusion," *The Economist* (February 27, 2016): 16; Tim Montgomerie, "Brexit Strategy," *Wall Street Journal* (February 20–21): C1; Jenny Gross and Laurence Norman, "Britain Forges EU Deal, Sets Up Showdown at Home," *Wall Street Journal* (February 20–21): A1.

42 The United Nations, www.un.org/en/mainbodies/index.shtml (accessed March 12, 2016).

43 "About UNCTAD," unctad.org (accessed on February 11 2019).

44 *State of Commodity Dependence: 2019* (UNCTAD, October 5, 2019), especially pages 1–20.

45 "Annual Statistical Bulletin," OPEC, www.opec.org/opec_web/static_files_project/media/downloads/publications/ASB2012.pdf (accessed April 12, 2019).

46 *Sources include the following:* "Walmart Statement in Support of the U.S.-Mexico-Canada Agreement" (https://corporate.walmart.com/newsroom/2020/01/16/walmart-statement-in-support-of-the-u-s-mexico-canada-agreement); Interview with Francisco Suarez Mogollon, Director Institutional Relations, Walmart de Mexico y Centroamérica, June 3, 2011; Loretta Chao, "Chinese TV Giant Builds Up Base in Mexico," *Wall Street Journal* (March 3, 2016): B1; Dante Di Gregorio, Douglas E. Thomas, and Fernán González de Castilla, "Competition between Emerging Market and Multinational Firms: Walmart and Mexican Retailers," *International Journal of Management* 25:3 (September 2008): 532; Gabriela Lopez, "Mexico Probes Retail Competition as Walmex Dominates," *Reuters Company News* (May 29, 2002); "Walmart around the World," *The Economist* (December 6, 2001), www.economist.com/displayStory.cfm?Story_ID=895888; David Luhnow, "Crossover Success: How NAFTA Helped Walmart Reshape the Mexican Market," *Wall Street Journal* (August 31, 2001): A1; Alexander Hanrath, "Mexican Stores Wilt in the Face of US Group's Onslaught," *Financial Times* (August 14, 2002): 21; Richard C. Morais, "One Hot Tamale," *Forbes* (December 27, 2004): 134–47; Mike Troy, "Walmart International," *DSN Retailing Today* (December 13, 2004): 20–2; Ricardo Castillo Mireles, "Taking It to the Competition, Mexican Style," *Logistics Today* (December 2004): 10; "International Data Sheet," Walmart Stores, walmartstores.com (accessed June 15, 2011); *Walmart 2018 Annual Report*, www.walmart.com (accessed April 13, 2019); Matthew Boyle, "Walmart v. the World," *CNNMoney* (December 19, 2007); "CATALYST: Walmart's Distribution Juggernaut," *Businessline* (June 14, 2007): 1; Miguel Bustillo, "After Early Errors, Wal-Mart Thinks Locally to Act Globally," *Wall Street Journal* (August 14, 2009): A1; Miguel Bustillo, "Sam's Club Tests the Big-Box Bodega," *Wall Street Journal* (August 10, 2009): B1; https://corporate.walmart.com/our-story/our-business/international/walmart-canada; https://corporate.walmart.com/our-story/our-business/international/walmart-mexico.

Chapter 9

1 *Sources include the following:* Western Union, 2017 Annual Report; World Bank, *Migration and Remittances Factbook 2016* (Washington, DC: The International Bank for Reconstruction and Development/World Bank, December 2015); World Bank, Migration and Remittances: Recent Developments and Outlook (Washington, DC: The International Bank for Reconstruction and Development/World Bank, April 2018); Mark Scott, "Mobile Money Transfers Shake Up a Global Market," *New York Times* (June 8, 2015): B7; "The GCC in 2020: The Gulf and its People," Economist Intelligence Unit, 2009; "Remittances to Latin America and the Caribbean to Top $100 Billion a Year by 2010, IDB Fund Says," press release, Inter-American Development Bank (March 18, 2007); Marla Dickerson, "Cash Going to Mexico Likely to Start at a Bank," *Los Angeles Times* (February 14, 2007): 21; Miriam Jordan, "U.S. Banks Woo Migrants, Legal or Otherwise," *Wall Street Journal* (Eastern Edition) (October 11, 2006): B1; Ioan Grillo, "Wired Cash," *Business Mexico* 12:12/13:1 (2003): 44; Rosa Salter Rodriguez, "Money Transfers to Mexico Peak as Mother's Day Nears," *Fort Wayne* (IN) *Journal Gazette* (May 1, 2005): 1D; Karen Krebsbach, "Following the Money," *USBanker* (September 2002): 62; Nancy Cleeland, "Firms Are Wired into Profits," *Los Angeles Times* (November 7, 1997): 1; David Fairlamb, Geri Smith, and Frederik Blafour, "Can Western Union Keep On Delivering?" *Businessweek* (December 29, 2003): 57; Heather Timmons, "Western Union: Where the Money Is—In Small Bills," *Businessweek* (November 26, 2001): 40.

2 Sam Y. Cross, *All about the Foreign Exchange Market in the United States* (New York: Federal Reserve Bank of New York, 1998): 9.

3 Cross, *All about the Foreign Exchange Market*, 9.

4 Bank for International Settlements, "Triennial Central Bank Survey: Foreign Exchange Turnover in April 2019" (Basel: BIS, September 2019): 7.

5 Ibid.

6 John D'Antona Jr., "E-Trading in FX Outshines Voice," *Traders Magazine*, 27: 377 (July 2015), Proquest (accessed March 25, 2015).

7 Reuters financial glossary, glossary.reuters.com (accessed March 26, 2016).

8 Bank for International Settlements, "Triennial Central Bank Survey: Foreign Exchange Turnover in April 2019," 6.

9 Bank for International Settlements, "Triennial Central Bank Survey: Foreign Exchange Turnover in April 2019," 11.

10 Cross, *All about the Foreign Exchange Market*, 12.

11 www1.oanda.com/currency/live-exchange-rates (accessed February 12, 2020).

12 See "Foreign Exchange Poll 2009: Methodology," *Euromoney* (May 2009): 76.

13 "Euromoney FX Survey 2019 – Press Release," https://www.euromoney.com/Media/documents/euromoney/pdf/research/Euromoney-FX-Survey-2019-Press-Release.pdf (June 11, 2019; accessed February 12, 2020).

14 http://www.cmegroup.com/trading/fx/?utm_source=trading_flyout&utm_medium=fx&utm_campaign=flyout (accessed April 4, 2016).

15 https://www.theice.com/products/Futures-Options/FX (accessed February 12, 2020).

16 "The Collapse of Barings: A Fallen Star," *The Economist* (March 4, 1995): 19–21; Glen Whitney, "ING Puts Itself on the Map by Acquiring Barings," *Wall Street Journal* (March 8, 1995): B4; John S. Bowdidge and Kurt E. Chaloupecky, "Nicholas Leeson and Barings Bank Have Vividly Taught Some Internal Control Issues," *American Business Review* (January 1997): 71–7; "Trader in Barings Scandal Is Released from Prison," *Wall Street Journal* (July 6, 1999): A12; Ben Dolven, "Bearing Up," *Far Eastern Economic Review* (July 15, 1999): 47; "Nick Leeson and Barings Bank," *bbc.co.uk*, www.bbc.co.uk/crime/caseclosed/nickleeson.shtml (accessed May 19, 2005); Nick Leeson and Edward Whitley, *Rogue Trader* (London: Little, Brown, 1996): 272.

17 James B. Stewart, "Convictions Prove Elusive in 'London Whale' Trading Case," *New York Times* (July 17, 2015); Lucy McNulty and Gregory Zuckerman, "London Whale Breaks Silence," *Wall Street Journal* (February 2, 2016; accessed online March 28, 2016).

18 Steve Bills, "State St.'s Forex Deal a Lure for Hedge Funds," *American Banker* (January 23, 2007): 10.

19 Dave Michaels and Paul Vigna, "Digital Money vs. The Dollar," *Wall Street Journal*, September 23, 2019: R1.

20 Nathaniel Popper, "New Kid on the Blockchain," *New York Times* (March 28, 2016): B1; Robert McMillan, "IGBM Bets on Bitcoin Ledger," *Wall Street Journal* (February 16, 2016): B1; "Bitcoin's Schism: Stumbling Blocks," *The Economist* (December 12, 2015): 72; "List of Cryptocurrencies," *Wikipedia* (accessed March 18, 2019); coinmarketcap.com (accessed February 12, 2020).

21 *Sources include the following:* Keith Bradsher, "IMF Designates China's Renminbi Global Currency," *New York Times* (December 1, 2015): A1; Ian Talley, "China Joins World's Elite Currency Club," *Wall Street Journal* (December 1, 2015): A1; Justin Baer, "Group Promotes Trading of China Currency in U.S," *Wall Street Journal* (November 30, 2015): C3; Lingling Wei, Jason Douglas, and Chiara Albanese, "Yuan's Adventure Abroad Stumbles in London," *Wall Street Journal* (November 15, 2015): C1; Chiara Albanese, "China's Yuan Goes Global," *Wall Street Journal* (October 7, 2015): C12; Ira Iosebashvili and Biman Mukherji, "Markets Jolted by China Devaluation," *Wall Street Journal* (August 12, 2015): C1; Lingling Wei, "China Pushes Further to Widen Yuan Use," *Wall Street Journal* (June 16, 2015): C1; Lingling Wei, "New Signal on Easing Yuan's Peg to Dollar," *Wall Street Journal* (December 12–13, 2015): B1; Mia Lamar and Anjani Trivedi, "Wagers Against Yuan Face Risk from Central Bank," *Wall Street Journal* (January 14, 2016); Lingling Wei, "IMF Wants More Data From Beijing on Yuan," *Wall Street Journal* (March 23, 2016): C1; Tom Orlick, "Get Ready: Here Comes the Yuan," *Wall Street Journal* (June 2, 2011): C7; Peter Stein, "The Chinese Test Kitchen," *Wall Street Journal* (June 2, 2011): C8; Peter Stein and Shai Oster, "China Speeds Yuan Push," *Wall Street Journal* (April 20, 2011); Lingling Wei, "Beijing Considers New Hub for Yuan," *Wall Street Journal* (April 9–10, 2011): B1; "The Rise of the Redback," *The Economist* (January 22, 2011): 14; Shai Oster, Dinny McMahon, and Tom Lauricella, "Offshore Trading in Yuan Takes Off," *Wall Street Journal* (December 14, 2010): A1; Dinny McMahon, "Yuan Goes Electronic in Global Market Bid," *Wall Street Journal* (October 8, 2010): C1; Robert N. McCauley and Chang Shu, "Recent RMB policy and currency co-movements," Bank for International Settlements working paper number 727, June 2018; Mike Bird, "This Is How China Keeps a Firm Grip on the Yuan," *Wall Street Journal* (October 30, 2018; accessed March 6, 2019); William Mauldin,

Nick Timiraos, and Paul Kiernan,"U.S., China Escalate Trade War," *Wall Street Journal* (August 6, 2019): A1; Joshua Zumbrun and Kate Davidson,"U.S. Drops China's Label as Currency Manipulator," *Wall Street Journal* (January 14, 2020): A8; Sonali Das,"China's Evolving Exchange Rate Regime," *IMF Working Paper*, March 2019;"The 24-body Problem," *The Economist* (June 13, 2020): 60.

Chapter 10

1 *Sources include the following:* Angelina Rascouet,"Venezuela Needs Oil's Rally More Than Anyone as Economy Teeters," *Bloomberg.com* (April 8, 2016, accessed on that date); Andrew Rosati,"Venezuela Doesn't Have Enough Money to Pay for Its Money," *Bloomberg.com* (April 27, 2016; accessed April 28, 2016); Anatola Kumarev and Mayala Arman,"Venezuelans Seek Leader's Recall," *Wall Street Journal* (April 28, 2016): A10; CIA World Factbook (Washington, DC, CIA; accessed April 25, 2016); Brian A. Nelson,"Hugo Chavez: President of Venezuela," www.britanica.com (accessed April 28, 2016); Currency Converter, *oanda.com* (accessed April 27, 2016);"Spot the Difference," *The Economist* (April 2, 2016): 36; Kejal Vayas,"Venezuela Tries to Prop Up Crumbling Economy," *Wall Street Journal* (February 18, 2016): A9; Carolyn Cui and Sara Schaefer Munoz, "Venezuela Pulls Out All Stops for Debt," *Wall Street Journal* (February 25, 2016): C1; Juan Forero,"Venezuela Data Show World's Top Inflation," *Wall Street Journal* (February 19, 2016): A6;"Reasons to Celebrate," *The Economist* (December 12, 2015): 35; Kejal Vyas,"Venezuela Embraces the Dollar—Ambivalently," *Wall Street Journal* (May 30–31, 2015): A8; William Neuman,"Venezuela Announces Plan to Relax Currency Controls," *New York Times* (February 11, 2015): A10; Analtoly Kurmanaev and Maolis Castro,"Venezuela's Savage Suffering," *Wall Street Journal* (February 13–14, 2016): A1; Corina Pons,"Venezuela 2016 Inflation Hits 800 Percent, GDP Shrinks 19%: Document," *Reuters News*, January 20, 2017 (accessed March 31, 2019);"Venezuela 2017 Annual Inflation at 2,616 Percent: Opposition Lawmakers," *Reuters News* (January 8, 2018; accessed March 31, 2019); International Monetary Fund, *Annual Report on Exchange Arrangements and Exchange Restrictions 2017* (Washington, DC: IMF, 2017); Juan Forero, "Hyperinflation Shatters Venezuelan Manufacturing," *Wall Street Journal* (March 5, 2019; accessed March 31, 2019); Steve Hanke,"Venezuela's Hyperinflation Hits 80,000% per Year in 2018," *Forbes* (January 1, 2019; accessed March 31, 2019); Robert Rapier,"Charting the Decline of Venezuela's Oil Industry," *Forbes* (January 29, 2019; accessed March 31, 2019); Patrick Gillespie,"Half the Venezuelan Economy Has Disappeared," *CNN Money* (January 25 2018; accessed March 31, 2019); Kejal Vyas,"Caracas Reports Soaring Prices," *Wall Street Journal* (November 7, 2018; accessed March 31, 2019).

2 International Monetary Fund,"IMF Chronology," imf.org/external/np/exr/chron/chron.asp (accessed April 28, 2016).

3 IMF,"History," www.imf.org/external/about/history.htm (accessed April 28, 2016) and"The IMF at a Glance," https://www.imf.org/en/About/Factsheets/IMF-at-a-Glance (accessed March 25, 2019).

4 IMF,"Overview: What Do We Do?" imforg/external/about/overview.htm (accessed April 28, 2016).

5 "Quotas, Governors, & Voting Power," imf.org/data (accessed April 29, 2016).

6 Keith Bradsher,"I.M.F. Designates China's Renminbi Global Currency," *New York Times* (December 1, 2015): 1.

7 International Monetary Fund,"How the IMF Promotes Global Economic Stability," http://www.imf.org/external/np/exr/facts/globstab.htm (accessed April 29, 2016).

8 Julie Wernau and Matthieu Wirz,"World Bank Halts Aid to Mozambique," *Wall Street Journal* (April 28, 2016): C2.

9 International Monetary Fund, *Annual Report on Exchange Arrangements and Exchange Restrictions 2018* (Washington, DC: IMF, 2019): pp. 5–8.

10 Mary Anastasia O'Grady,"Argentina Needs the Dollar," *Wall Street Journal* (August 18, 2019; accessed March 9, 2020).

11 Ibid.

12 See the following for specific definitions of different degrees of flexibility in exchange rates: https://www.imf.org/external/np/mfd/er/2003/eng/1203.htm.

13 "The Euro: Who Can Join and When," http://ec.europa.eu/economy_finance/euro/adoption/who_can_join/index_en.htm (accessed April 30, 2016).

14 "The EU: Going Negative," *The Economist* (April 30, 2016): 9, 47.

15 Paul Masson and Catherine Patillo,"A Single Currency for Africa?" *Finance & Development* (December 2004): 9–15;"History of the CFA Franc," www.bceao.int/internet/bcweb.nsf/pages/umuse1 (accessed May 30, 2005); IMF,"The Fabric of Reform—An IMF Video," www.imf.org/external/pubs/ft/fabric/backgrnd.htm (accessed May 30, 2005).

16 Ann-Marie Gulde,"The CFA Franc Zone: Common Currency, Uncommon Challenges Overview" (Washington DC: IMF, 2008).

17 Elliot Smith,"West Africa's New 'Eco' Currency Sparks Division Over Timetable and Euro Peg," *CNBC online* (January 17, 2020; accessed February 26, 2020).

18 Isaac Imaka,"East Africans to Wait for 10 Years to Get Common Currency, Officials Say," *Daily Monitor* (May 27, 2013), www.monitor.co.ug/News/National/East-Africans-to-wait-for-10-years-to-get-common/-/688334/1864310/-/sg6wfrz/-/index.html (accessed June 18, 2013).

19 Elliott Smith,"West Africa's New 'Eco' Currency Sparks Division Over Timetable and Euro Peg," *CNBC online* (January 17, 2020; accessed February 26, 2020).

20 "Foreign Exchange" www.newyorkfed.org/markets/foreignex.html (accessed May 4, 2016).

21 "Currency Composition of Official Foreign Exchange Reserves (COFER)," International Monetary Fund, data.imf.org/cofer (accessed February 26, 2020).

22 Dietrich Domanski, Emanuel Kohlscheen, and Robin Moreno,"Foreign Exchange Market Intervention in EMEs: What Has Changed?" *BIS Quarterly Review*, Bank for International Settlements, September 2016: 65–79.

23 Neil MacLucas and Brian Blackstone,"Swiss Move Roils Global Markets," *Wall Street Journal* (January 16, 2015): A1.

24 Patrick McGroarty and Farai Mutsaka,"How to Turn 100 Trillion Dollars into Five and Feel Good About It," *Wall Street Journal* (May 11, 2011), online edition.

25 Steve Hanke,"Zimbabwe Introduces a New Currency and a Maxi-Devaluation," *Forbes* (February 22, 2019) online edition (accessed March 25, 2019); Victor Bhoroma,"Zimbabwe: Government Controls Fuelling the Black Market," *Zimbabwe Independent* (January 10, 2020), https://allafrica.com/stories/202001100386.html (accessed March 9, 2020); Gabriele Steinhauser and Bernard Mpofu,"Zimbabwe Shuts Exchange as Currency Deteriorates," *Wall Street Journal* (July 8, 2020): B12.

26 International Monetary Fund, *Annual Report on Exchange Arrangements and Exchange Restrictions 2018* (Washington, October 2019): 17.

27 Tim Callen,"Purchasing Power Parity: Weights Matter," *Finance & Development* (Washington, DC: IMF), as cited in http://www.imf.org/external/pubs/ft/fandd/basics/ppp.htm (accessed May 5, 2016).

28 Reid W. Click,"Contrarian Macparity," *Economics Letters* 53:2 (November 1996): 209–212.

29 "The Big Mac Index Shows Currencies Are Very Cheap Against the Dollar," *The Economist* (January 12, 2019) online edition (accessed March 25, 2019). For more information, see economist.com/bigmac.

30 "The Big Mac Index: Food for Thought," *The Economist* (May 27, 2004): 75; quoting Michael Pakko and Patricia Polland,"For Here or to Go? Purchasing Power Parity and the Big Mac" (St. Louis, MO: Federal Reserve Bank of St. Louis, January 1996).

31 Tommy Stubbington,"Torrent of Cash Exits the Eurozone," *Wall Street Journal* (March 23, 2015): A1.

32 Avantika Chilkoti and Caitlin Ostroff,"Coronavirus Pushes Some Emerging Markets to Brink of Default," *Wall Street Journal* (March 29, 2020; accessed March 29, 2020).

33 "Forecasting Currencies: Technical or Fundamental?" *Business International Money Report* (October 15, 1990): 401–02.

34 See Ian H. Giddy and Gunter Dufey,"The Random Behavior of Flexible Exchange Rates: Implications for Forecasting," *Journal of International Business Studies* 6:1 (1975): 1–32; Christopher J. Neely and Lucio Sarno,"How Well Do Monetary Fundamentals Forecast Exchange Rates?" *St. Louis Fed* (September/October 2002), 51–74, www.research.stlouisfed.org/publications/review/02/09/51-74Neely.pdf (accessed October 8, 2009).

35 Andrew C. Pollock and Mary E. Wilkie,"Briefing," *Euromoney* (June 1991): 123–24.

36 David A. Moss, *A Concise Guide to Macro Economics* (Boston: Harvard Business School Press, 2007): 131.

37 Sam Y. Cross, *All about the Foreign Exchange Market in the United States* (Federal Reserve Bank of New York, 1998): 114.

38 Sudeep Jain and Debiprasad Nayak,"Rupee Fall Hits India's Small Importers," *Wall Street Journal* [India] (June 18, 2013), online edition.

39 Theo Francis, "Dollar's Rise Puts Squeeze on American Companies," *Wall Street Journal* (January 21, 2015): A1.

40 International Monetary Fund, *World Economic Outlook* (October 2019); Appendix A.

41 "What America Can Learn from Sterling's Decline as a Reserve Currency," *The Economist* (October 3, 2015): 80.

42 Alex Frangos, "Chinese Foreign-Exchange Reserves Dive as Stresses Mount," *Wall Street Journal* (February 8, 2015): C6.

43 Samuel Shen and Andrew Galbraith, "China Constricts Capital Outflows with an Eye on Yuan Stability," *Reuters* (October 11, 2018; accessed March 31, 2019).

44 *Sources include the following:* Megumi Fujikawi, "Corporate Profits in Japan Bend to Yen," *Wall Street Journal* (February 18, 2016): B1; James Ramage and Anjani Trivedi, "Fumbling the Carry Trade," *Wall Street Journal* (March 12, 2015): C1; Yoko Kubota, "Weak Yen Fuels Toyota's Profit Even as Sales Dip," *Wall Street Journal* (August 5, 2015): B4; Takashi Nakamichi, "Japan Caught in Negative Rate Trap," *Wall Street Journal* (March 11, 2016): C3; Hiroko Tabuchi, "Weaker Yen Helps Sony Raise Its Profit Outlook," *Wall Street Journal* (April 26, 2013): B6; Mayumi Negishi and Daniel Inman, "Falling Yen Sets Stage for Windfall," *Wall Street Journal* (April 24, 2013): B6; Thomas Black, "Now, a Weak Link in the Global Supply Chain," *Businessweek* (March 21–27, 2011): 18; Hiroko Tabuchi, "Sony Warns of a Loss from Quake," *Wall Street Journal* (May 24, 2011) online edition; Jamie McGeever, "Dollar Gets Battered across the Board," *Wall Street Journal* (December 9, 2003): C17; Sebastian Moffett, "Japan's Yen Strategy Offers Economic Relief," *Wall Street Journal* (January 12, 2004): A2; Miyako Takebe, "Japan Plans to Keep Intervening in Markets to Hold Down the Yen," *Wall Street Journal* (March 17, 2004): B4E; Alan Beattie, "Japan and ECB Consider Joint Currency Move as Dollar Falls," *Financial Times* (December 2, 2004): 11; Sony 2008 Annual Report; Robert Flint, "Yen Gains on Dollar, Europe in Flight from Risk," *Wall Street Journal* (January 13, 2009): C2; Joanna Slater, Yuka Hayashi, and Peter Stein, "Move to Stem Yen's Rise Is Likely," *Wall Street Journal* (October 28, 2008): C1; Stanley Reed, "What's Driving Up the Dollar," *Businessweek* (December 8, 2008): 38; John Murphy and Hiroko Tabuchi, "Japan's Companies, Consumers, React to New Reality," *Wall Street Journal* (October 29, 2008): A13; John Murphy, "Toyota's Global Woes Start to Hit Home in Japan," *Wall Street Journal* (November 4, 2008): A10; Yumiko Ono and Andrew Monahan, "Japan Exports Fall 49% as U.S. Trade Plunges," *Wall Street Journal* (March 26, 2009): A7; John Murphy, Peter Stein, and Neil Shah, "Dollar Vexes Asian Central Banks," *Wall Street Journal* (May 26, 2009): C1; Sony Consolidated Financial Statements, for the fiscal year ended March 31, 2019 (available from www.sony.net).

Chapter 11

1 *Sources include the following:* "Taxing America Inc.: Pfiasco," *The Economist* (April 9, 2016): 63; Kevin Drabaugh, "Burger King to Save Millions in U.S. Taxes in Inversion: Study," *Reuters* (December 11, 2014; accessed May 9, 2016); Jon Hartley, "Burger King's Tax Inversion and Canada's Favorable Corporate Tax Rates," *Forbes* (August 25, 2014; accessed May 9, 2016); David Gelles, "Treasury Urges End to Foreign Tax Flights," *New York Times* (July 17, 2014): B1; Julie Hirschfeld Davis, "Obama Sidesteps Congress with Rules to Curb Corporate Flight," *New York Times* (September 23, 2014): B1; Liz Hoffman, "Inversion Rules Test Pending Deals," *Wall Street Journal* (April 6, 2016): B1; Jonathan D. Rockoff, "Pfizer, Allergan Move On," *Wall Street Journal* (April 7, 2016): B1; Richard Rubin and Liz Hoffman, "U.S. Sets Tougher Rules on Tax Deals," *Wall Street Journal* (April 5, 2016): 1; Michael J. de la Merced and Leslie Picker, "U.S. Crackdown on Inversions Is Tougher Than Expected," *New York Times* (April 6, 2016): B1; Michael J. de la Merced, David Gelles, and Leslie Picker, "Chief of Pfizer Defends Merger as Good for U.S.," *New York Times* (November 24, 2015): 1; Richard Rubin, "Treasury Plans New Anti-Inversion Plans," *Wall Street Journal* (November 19, 2015): B6; Richard Rubin, Jonathan D. Rockoff, and Dana Cimilluca, "Pfizer Girds for Fight on Tax-Saving Deal," *Wall Street Journal* (November 20, 2015): 1; Liz Hoffman and John D. McKinnon, "Takeovers See U.S. Losing Tax Revenue," *Wall Street Journal* (March 6, 2015): C1; Richard Rubin and Jonathan D. Rockoff, "New Tax Rules are Met With Protest," *Wall Street Journal* (April 7, 2016): 1; Julie Jargon and Mike Esterl, "Coffee Empire Adds Krispy Kreme," *Wall Street Journal* (May 10, 2016): B1.

2 Jonathan Berk, Peter De Marzo, and Jarrad Harford, *Fundamentals of Corporate Finance*, 2nd edition (Upper Saddle River, NJ: Pearson Prentice-Hall, 2012), 9–10.

3 "Theory versus the Real World," *Finance & Treasury* (April 26, 1993): 1.

4 Joseph P. F. Han, Sheridan Titman, and Garry Twite, "An International Comparison of Capital Structure and Debt Maturity Choices," *Journal of Finance and Quantitative Analysis* 47:1 (February 2013): 23–56.

5 Ibid., p. 33.

6 Abe de Jong, Rezaul Kabir, and Thuy Thu Nguyen, "Capital Structure around the World: The Roles of Firm and Country Specific Determinants," *Journal of Banking & Finance* 32 (2008): 1954–69.

7 Charles Forelle, "The Isle That Rattled the World – Tiny Iceland Created a Vast Bubble, Leaving Wreckage Everywhere When It Popped," *Wall Street Journal* (December 27, 2008): A1.

8 Basel Committee on Banking Supervision, Bank for International Settlements, bis.org, (accessed May 20, 2016).

9 Nu Skin Annual Report 2017.

10 Patrick McGuire, "A Shift in London's Eurodollar Market," *BIS Quarterly Review* (September 2004): 67.

11 Michael J. de La Merced, "Understanding LIBOR," *Wall Street Journal* (July 11, 2012): B3; David Enrich and Max Colchester, "Before Scandal, Clash Over Control of LIBOR," *Wall Street Journal* (September 11, 2012): A1.

12 "London Interbank Offered Rate (LIBOR) Definition," www.investopedia.com/terms.asp (accessed May 20, 2016) and ICE LIBOR, http://theice.com/iba/libor (accessed April 13, 2019) and Oliver Wyman, "Making the World's Most Important Number Less Important: LIBOR Transition," July 2018 Edition.

13 Oliver Wyman, "Making the World's Most Important Number Less Important: LIBOR Transition," July 2018 Edition.

14 Securities Industry and Financial Markets Association, "SIFMA 2020 Outlook: Trends in the Capital Markets."

15 Ibid.

16 Financial Market Series, *Bond Markets* (October 2012): 3 (accessed June 3, 2013).

17 Securities Industry and Financial Markets Association, "SIFMA 2019 Outlook: Trends in the Capital Markets."

18 Christopher Whittall, "In ECB Moves, Corporate Bonds Score Big," *Wall Street Journal* (March 11, 2016): C1.

19 Fiona Law, "Dim-Sum Bond Issuance Climbs," *Wall Street Journal*, online edition (accessed March 25, 2013).

20 Peter Stein, "'Dim Sum Bonds' on the Menu for Foreign Investors," *Wall Street Journal* (October 31, 2010), retrieved July 13, 2011, from http://wsj.com.

21 Anant Sundaram, "International Financial Markets," in *Handbook of Modern Finance*, ed. Dennis E. Logue (New York: Warren, Gorham, Lamont, 1994): F3–F4.

22 Jason Bush, "Gazprom Swiss Franc Bond Shows Reviving Demand for Russian Issues," *Reuters*, www.reuters.com/article/russia-gazprom-eurobond-idUSL5N16P2EH (accessed May 21, 2016).

23 "Sovereign Wealth Fund Rankings," The Sovereign Wealth Fund Institute, swfinstitute.com (accessed March 2, 2020).

24 Ibid.

25 Michael J. de la Merced, "Alibaba Raises Fund-Raising Target for I.P.O. to $21.8 Billion," *New York Times* (September 16, 2014): B4.

26 Saumya Vaishampayan and Min Zeng, "Stocks Near Elusive Record," *Wall Street Journal* (April 18, 2016): C1.

27 Saumya Vaishampayan, "Why Markets are in Chaos," *Wall Street Journal* (February 11, 2016): C1.

28 Corrie Driebusch and Riva Gold, "China Drags Down Markets," *Wall Street Journal* (January 8, 2016): 1.

29 Christopher Whittall and Riva Gold, "Investors Pull Out of Europe," *Wall Street Journal* (May 23, 2016): C1.

30 "Euroequity" *Investopedia* (accessed April 13, 2019).

31 Alexander Martin, "App IPO Priced at More Than $1 Billion," *Wall Street Journal* (July 11, 2016; accessed April 13, 2019).

32 3M Annual Report, 2018 and www.six-group.com/exchanges/shares/companies/issuer_list_en.html.

33 Procter & Gamble, "P&G Announces Delisting of its Shares from Euronext Paris," press release, www.pginvestor.com/Cache/1001249378.PDF?O=PDF&T=&Y=&D=&FID=1001249378&iid=4004124 (accessed April 19, 2019).

34 NYSE, "Current List of All Non-U.S. Issuers," February 28, 2019, www.nyse.com/publicdocs/nyse/data/CurListofallStocks.pdf (accessed April 8, 2019).

35 Elke Asen, "Corporate Tax Rates Around the World, 2019," The Tax Foundation (December 10, 2019; accessed March 2, 2020).

36 Deloitte, "International Tax and Business Guide: Germany" (2016), www.deloitte.com/taxguides.

37 David Cay Johnston, "Enron Avoided Income Taxes in 4 of 5 Years," *New York Times (Late Edition [East Coast])* (January 17, 2002): A1.

38 Urban Institute and Brookings Institution, Tax Policy Center, *Briefing Book*, p. 417.

39 OECD, *Transfer Pricing Guidelines for Multinational Enterprises and Tax Administrations 2017* (Paris: OECD Publishing, July 10, 2017; accessed April 17, 2019).

40 Ronald Fink, "Haven or Hell," *CFO Magazine* (March 2004), www.cfo.com/article.cfm/3012017 (accessed October 23, 2009); Helen Shaw, "Transfer Students," *CFO Magazine* (April 2007), www.cfo.com/article.cfm/8885626/c_8910395?f=insidecfo (accessed August 30, 2007).

41 IRS Publication 901, *U.S. Tax Treaties*, revised September 2016, www.irs.gov/pub/irs-pdf/p901.pdf.

42 Eric Pfanner, "European Countries Seek More Taxes from U.S. Multinational Companies," *New York Times* (November 19, 2012): B1.

43 Mark Scott, "Ireland Adjusts Its Corporate Tax Attraction," *New York Times* (November 16, 2016): B1.

44 IMF Monetary and Exchange Affairs Department, "IMF Background Paper: Offshore Financial Centers," www.imf.org/external/np/mae/oshore/2000/eng/back.htm#1, June 23, 2000.

45 Ibid.

46 "How the Heavyweights Shape Up," *Euromoney* (May 1990): 56.

47 "On or Off? It's a Matter of Degree," in "Places in the Sun: A Special Report on Offshore Finance," *The Economist* (February 24, 2007): 7.

48 OECD, *Harmful Tax Competition: An Emerging Global Issue* (Paris: OECD, 1998): 23.

49 OECD, *Harmful Tax Competition: An Emerging Global Issue* (Paris: OECD, 1998): 27.

50 OECD, *Overview or the OECD's Work on Countering International Tax Evasion* (Paris: OECD, August 11, 2009): 8; www.oecd.org/dataoecd/32/45/42356522.pdf (accessed October 23, 2009).

51 Eric Lipton, "Documents Show How Wealthy Hid Millions Abroad," *New York Times* (June 6, 2016): A1; Jesse Drucker, "U.S. Prosecutors Bring Their First Charges Over the Panama Papers," *New York Times* (December 4, 2018; accessed April 19, 2019).

52 Lucy Komisar, "Funny Money," *Metroactive News & Issues*, January 24, 2002, www.metroactive.com/papers/sonoma/01.24.02/offshorebanking-0204.html (accessed June 7, 2005).

53 Liz Rappaport, "Bank Settles Iran Money Case," *Wall Street Journal* (August 15, 2012): A1.

54 Nick Davis, "Tax Spotlight Worries Cayman Islands," *BBC News* (March 31, 2009), news.bbc.co.uk/go/pr/fr/-/2/hi/americas/7972695.stm (accessed October 23, 2009).

55 Eric Pfanner, "European Countries Seek More Taxes from U.S. Multinational Companies," *New York Times* (November 19, 2012): B1.

56 *Sources include the following:* Vindu Goel, Michael J. de la Merced, and Neil Gough, "Chinese Giant Alibaba Will Go Public, Listing in the U.S.," *New York Times* (May 6, 2014; accessed April 17, 2019); Michael J. de la Merced, "The Six Banks Leading Alibaba's Giant I.P.O.," *New York Times* (May 6, 2014; accessed April 17, 2019); Liyan Chen, Ryan Mac, and Brian Solomon, "Alibaba Claims Title for Largest Global IPO Ever with Extra Share Sales," *Forbes* (September 22, 2014; accessed April 8, 2019); Victor Luckerson, "Everything You Need to Know About Alibaba and Its Mega-IPO," *Time* (September 18, 2014; accessed April 8, 2019); "Alibaba IPO: The Biggest IPO in History," NYSE, www.nyse.com/network/article/Alibaba-Lists-on-the-NYSE (accessed April 8, 2019); Paul Hodgson, "Alibaba IPO: Shareholders Can Buy Shares, Not Influence," *Forbes* (September 18, 2014; accessed April 8, 2019); "Alibaba: A Dictatorship?" Chazen Global Insights, Columbia Business School (November 7, 2016; accessed April 8, 2019); Bruce Einhorn, "Masayoshi Son's $58 Billion Payday on Alibaba," *Bloomberg* (May 8, 2014; accessed April 17, 2019); Leena Rao, "The Most Expensive Sake that Alibaba's Jack Ma Ever Had," *Fortune* (September 25, 2015; accessed April 17, 2019); Rory Jones, "Aramco Adds to Record Listing," *Wall Street Journal* (January 13, 2020): B1; Stu Woo, "Alibaba Starts Strong in Hong Kong," *Wall Street Journal* (November 27, 2019): B4.

Chapter 12

1 *Sources include the following:* Vertica Bhardwaj, Megan Eickman, and Rodney C. Runyan. "A Case Study on the Internationalization Process of a 'Born-Global' Fashion Retailer," *The International Review of Retail, Distribution and Consumer Research* 21:3 (2011): 293–307; Paige L. Glovinsky and Jiyeon Kim, "Turning Customer Feedback into Commitment," *GSTF Business Review (GBR)* 4:2 (2015): 53; Min Jeong Seo, Minjeong Kim, and Kyu-Hye Lee, "Supply Chain Management Strategies for Small Fast Fashion Firms," *International Journal of Fashion Design, Technology and Education* 9:1 (2016): 51–61; Aline Buzzo and Maria José Abreu. "Fast Fashion, Fashion Brands & Sustainable Consumption." In *Fast Fashion, Fashion Brands and Sustainable Consumption* (Springer: Singapore, 2019): pp. 1–17; Mary Hanbury, "We Went Inside One of the Sprawling Factories Where Zara Makes Its Clothes. Here's How the World's Biggest Fashion Retailer Gets It Done," *Business Insider*, https://bit.ly/33BWpyo (accessed February 14, 2020); Vickie Elmer, "Issue: Fashion Industry Fashion Industry" (Sage Publishing Inc., 2019).

2 "Global Fashion Industry Statistics—International Apparel," *Fashion United*, www.fashionunited.com/global-fashion-industry-statistics-international-apparel.

3 John Fernie and David B. Grant. *Fashion Logistics: Insights into the Fashion Retail Supply Chain* (Kogan Page Publishers, 2019); Ian Urbina and Keith Bradsher, "Linking Factories to the Malls, Middleman Pushes Low Costs," *New York Times* 8 (2013). See also www.lifung.com/about-lf/our-reach/.

4 James C. Collins and Jerry I. Porras, *Built to Last: Successful Habits of Visionary Companies* (New York: Harper Business Essentials, 1994).

5 The Inditex Group, a Spanish apparel MNE, is the parent corporation of eight global retail chains, including Zara, Bershka, Massimo Dutti, Stradivarius, and Oysho. No matter the brand, the all-trendy, reasonably priced products are sold in attractive stores worldwide. Zara is the flagship, generating the bulk of total sales. Inditex runs operations from "The Cube," its gleaming, futuristic headquarters in Artexio, near La Coruña, a small, seaside town in northwest Spain about 300 miles from Madrid.

6 "Amancio Ortega," *Forbes*, www.forbes.com/profile/amancio-ortega/(accessed January 31, 2020).

7 The Inditex Group, a Spanish apparel MNE, is the parent corporation of eight global retail chains, including Zara, Bershka, Massimo Dutti, Stradivarius, and Oysho. Inditex is one of the world's largest fashion retailers with eight brands and over 6,700 stores. Zara is the crown jewel of Inditex, generating roughly two-thirds of total sales.

8 "Zara," Inditex.com, www.inditex.com/brands/zara (accessed February 1, 2020).

9 "Meet Amancio Ortega: The Third-Richest Man in the World," *Fortune*, https://bit.ly/2vGQ1tq (accessed April 2, 2016).

10 "Our Mission Statement," ZARA United States, https://go.zara/3diiR4b (accessed April 2, 2016).

11 Jane M. Folpe, "Zara Has a Made-to-Order Plan for Success," *Fortune, European Edition*, 142:5 (2000): 18.

12 "Zara Transforms Life in La Coruna—Business Insider." https://bit.ly/2vHw0TA (accessed February 1, 2020).

13 "Zara Clothing Company Supply Chain," *SCM Globe*, https://bit.ly/2WwqQVf (accessed February 15, 2020).

14 Derek Thompson, "Zara's Big Idea: What the World's Top Fashion Retailer Tells Us About Innovation," *The Atlantic*. https://bit.ly/3bkHeN3 (accessed November 13, 2012).

15 Pankaj Ghemawat, Jose Luis Nueno, and Melissa Dailey. *ZARA: Fast Fashion* (Boston, MA: Harvard Business School, 2003).

16 About three-quarters of the merchandise on display changes every three to four weeks, which corresponds to the average time between Zara customers' visits: 17 times a year, versus 3 to 4 visits per year for competitors.

17 Vivienne Walt, "Meet Amancio Ortega: The Third-Richest Man in the World," *Fortune* (January 14, 2013): 56–59.

18 "The Stars of Europe—Amancio Ortega, Chairman, Inditex," *Businessweek*, (June 11, 2001): 65.

19 "The Fashion Industry in Galicia: Understanding the 'Zara' Phenomenon," *European Planning Studies* 10 (2002).

20 Patrick Byrne, "Closing the Gap between Strategy and Results," *Logistics Management* (March 2004): 13.

21 "How We Classify Countries," *The World Bank*, from data.worldbank.org/about/country-classifications (accessed February 6, 2016).

22 Andrea Ovans, "What Is Strategy, Again?" *Harvard Business Review* (May 12, 2015).

23 Michael A. Hitt, R. Duane Ireland, and Robert E. Hoskisson. *Strategic Management Cases: Competitiveness and Globalization* (Cengage Learning, 2012).

24 Deborah Ancona, "Sensemaking: Framing and Acting in the Unknown," in *The Handbook for Teaching Leadership: Knowing, Doing, and Being*, eds. Scott Snook, Nitin Nohria, and Rakesh Khurana (Sage Publishing, 2012): 3–21.

25 Ad Krijnen, "The Toyota Way: 14 Management Principles from the World's Greatest Manufacturer," *Action Learning: Research and Practice*, 4:1 (2007): 109–111; Y. Monden, *Toyota Management System: Linking the Seven Key Functional Areas* (Routledge, 2019).

26 Karl E. Weick, Kathleen M. Sutcliffe, and David Obstfeld, "Organizing and the Process of Sensemaking," *Organization Science* 16:4 (2005): 409–21.

27 See B. Wernerfelt, "A Resource-Based View of the Firm," *Strategic Management Journal* (1984): 171–80.

28 "James C. Collins Quotes (Author of Good to Great)," GoodReads, www.goodreads.com/author/quotes/2826.James_C_Collins (accessed February 26, 2016); Peter Drucker, *The Effective Executive* (Routledge, 2018).

29 Jim Collins and Morten T. Hansen, *Great by Choice: Uncertainty, Chaos and Luck—Why Some Thrive Despite Them All* (Random House, 2011).

30 Birger Wernerfelt, "A Resource—Based View of the Firm," *Strategic Management Journal* 5, no. 2 (1984): 171–180.

31 Technically, a competency satisfies three conditions: It provides consumer benefits, it is difficult for competitors to imitate, and it is leveraged to different products and markets. The fact that rivals cannot easily match or replicate a firm's competencies serves as a powerful competitive advantage.

32 Creating value requires that an MNE develop a compelling value proposition (why a customer should buy its goods or use its services) that specifies its targeted markets (those customers for whom it creates goods or services).

33 Greg Linden, Jason Dedrick, and Kenneth L. Kraemer, "We Estimate China Only Makes $8.46 from an iPhone—and That's Why Trump's Trade War Is Futile," *The Conversation*, https://bit.ly/2xfsbVQ (accessed January 1, 2019). See also https://bit.ly/2Ub4Iyt and https://bit.ly/3dihLW7.

34 Henry Ford, Wikiquotes. Accessed February 20, 2020, from https://en.wikiquote.org/wiki/Henry_Ford.

35 Newley Purnell and Tripp Mickle, "'It's Been a Rout': Apple's iPhone Fall Flat in World's Largest Untapped Market," *Wall Street Journal*, https://on.wsj.com/3deABh3 (accessed December 18, 2018).

36 "Hungry Tiger, Dancing Elephant: How India Is Changing IBM's World," *The Economist* (April 4, 2007): 58–61.

37 "Profitable Growth: Target 2012 Annual Report," *Target Corporate* https://bit.ly/33Crjqp (accessed October 11, 2015).

38 See www.investopedia.com/terms/1/3_6_3_rule.asp; https://en.wikipedia.org/wiki/3-6-3_Rule.

39 Chet Miller and Laura B. Cardinal, "Strategic Planning and Firm Performance: A Synthesis of More than Two Decades of Research," *Academy of Management Journal* 37:6 (1994): 1649–65.

40 See Henry Mintzberg, *Rise and Fall of Strategic Planning* (Simon and Schuster, 1994); Robert M. Grant, "Strategic Planning in a Turbulent Environment: Evidence from the Oil Majors," *Strategic Management Journal* 24 (2003): 491–517; Phil Rosenzweig, *The Halo Effect: ... and the Eight Other Business Delusions That Deceive Managers* (Simon and Schuster, 2014).

41 The S&P 500 stock market index, maintained by S&P Dow Jones Indices, comprises 505 common stocks issued by 500 large-cap companies and traded on American stock exchanges, and covers about 75 percent of the American equity market by capitalization.

42 Ilan Mochari, "Why Half of the S&P 500 Companies Will Be Replaced in the Next Decade," *Inc.com* https://bit.ly/2WvNOMr (accessed March 23, 2016); Matthew De Silva, "The Art and Science of Stewarding the S&P 500," *Quartz*, https://bit.ly/2J4JUlS (accessed February 15, 2020).

43 "Schumpeter: Fail Often, Fail Well," *The Economist*, https://econ.st/2y2Eeq8 (accessed April 28, 2011).

44 Scott Barry Kaufman, "The Role of Luck in Life Success Is Far Greater Than We Realized," *Scientific American Blog Network*, https://bit.ly/33BRWw0 (accessed December 24, 2018). "If You're So Smart, What Virtue Rich? Turns Out It's Just Chance," *MIT Technology Review*, https://bit.ly/3deAq5n (accessed February 5, 2020).

45 Dan Kahneman and Daniel Lovallo, "Delusions of Success: How Optimism Undermines Executives' Decisions," *Harvard Business Review* (July 2003); Phil Rosenzweig, *The Halo Effect: ... and the Eight Other Business Delusions That Deceive Managers* (Simon and Schuster, 2014).

46 J. Manyika, S. Lund, J. Bughin, J. Woetzel, K. Stamenov, and D. Dhingra, *Digital Globalization: The New Era of Global Flows* (New York: McKinsey Global Institute, 2016).

47 Ibid., Lovallo and Kahneman, "Delusions of Success."

48 Ibid., Phil Rosenzweig, *The Halo Effect*; M. G. Haselton, D. Nettle, and D. R. Murray, The evolution of cognitive bias. In D. M. Buss (ed.), *The Handbook of Evolutionary Psychology*, 1–20 (New York: Wiley and Sons, 2015); D. Kahneman, D. Lovallo, and O. Sibony, "Before You Make That Big Decision," *Harvard Business Review*, *89*:6 (2011), 50–60.

49 "Apple Supply Chain Braces for Disruption From Coronavirus | Material Handling and Logistics," https://bit.ly/2wvbHJn (accessed March 23, 2020).

50 "Coronavirus and the Death of Xi's 'China Dream' | The Strategist" https://bit.ly/3991EqN; "Coronavirus Killed the 'China Dream' | The National Interest," https://bit.ly/2y2xcSg (all accessed March 23, 2020).

51 Ibid., J. Manyika, et al.

52 Nan Zhou and Mauro F. Guillén, "From Home Country to Home Base: A Dynamic Approach to the Liability of Foreignness," *Strategic Management Journal* 36:6 (2015): 907–17.

53 Janet C. Lowe, *Welch: An American Icon* (New York: Wiley and Sons, 2002).

54 W. Brian Arthur, "The Second Economy," *McKinsey Quarterly* (October 2011).

55 Heather Timmons, "Outsourcing to India Draws Western Lawyers," NYTimes.com, https://nyti.ms/2U85FqZ (accessed April 26, 2011).

56 John Markoff, "New Wave of Deft Robots Is Changing Global Industry," *New York Times* (August 18, 2012).

57 Eugene Demaitre, "China's Robotics Market: A Look Ahead to 2020," *The Robot Report*, https://www.therobotreport.com/chinese-robotics-market-look-ahead-2020/ (accessed, February 5, 2020); "Shirt Tales; Schumpeter," *The Economist* (January 5, 2019).

58 Hannah Jane Parkinson, "AI Can Write Just like Me. Brace for the Robot Apocalypse | Hannah Jane Parkinson," *The Guardian*, https://bit.ly/2QOOhpt (accessed February 15, 2019).

59 "The Future of Employment: How Susceptible Are Jobs to Computerisation?" Oxford Martin School, https://bit.ly/3bi4U4D (accessed October 13, 2015).

60 John Markoff, "New Wave of Deft Robots Is Changing Global Industry," NYTimes.com, https://nyti.ms/33GfLmb (accessed February 25, 2013).

61 "Coronavirus and 3D Printing - 3D Printing Media Network." https://bit.ly/2wvFLEK; "Meet The Italian Engineers 3D-Printing Respirator Parts for Free to Help Keep Coronavirus Patients Alive," *Forbes*, https://bit.ly/2UaLPeU (all accessed March 23, 2020).

62 "The Digitization of Manufacturing Will Transform the Way Goods Are Made—And Change the Politics of Jobs Too," *The Economist* (April 21, 2012): 56.

63 BofA Global Research, "*Tectonic Shifts in Global Supply Chains*," https://bit.ly/2QzT5P5 (accessed February 4, 2020).

64 "FDI in the United States, First Quarter 2018," https://bit.ly/3bdrGdJ (accessed February 18, 2019); "*FDI in the USA*," Bureau of Economic Analysis, https://www.selectusa.gov/FDI-in-the-US (accessed February 5, 2020).

65 *Encyclopaedia Britannica*, www.britannica.com/EBchecked/topic/1357503/cultural-globalization.

66 Walter Isaacson, *Steve Jobs* (Simon & Schuster, 2011).

67 Adrian Wooldridge, *Masters of Management: How the Business Gurus and Their Ideas Have Changed the World—for Better and for Worse* (HarperCollins, 2011).

68 Pankaj Ghemawat, "Distance Still Matters," *Harvard Business Review* 79:8 (2001): 137–47.

69 Lui Hebron and John F. Stack, *Globalization: Debunking the Myths* (Pearson Prentice Hall, 2008);

70 C. Prahalad and Y. Doz, *The Multinational Mission: Balancing Local Demands and Global Vision* (New York: Free Press, 1987).

71 "Google in Asia: Seeking Success," *The Economist*, https://econ.st/3aa4aOF, (accessed March 15, 2011).

72 "A Special Report on Entrepreneurship: Global Heroes," *The Economist*, www.economist.com/node/13216025 (accessed March 15, 2011).

73 Interestingly, a 150-pound bag of coffee beans might earn a farmer approximately $50. The "street value" of that same bag, once processed into approximately 10,000 cups of coffee and depending upon the outlet, is anywhere between $10,000 to $40,000.

74 Toby Gibbs, Suzanne Heywood, and Leigh Weiss, "Organizing for an Emerging World," *McKinsey Quarterly* (June 2012).

75 Theodore Levitt, "The Globalization of Markets," *Harvard Business Review* 61 (1983): 92–102.

76 C. Dörrenbächer and M. Geppert, *The Integration-Responsiveness Framework: A Review and Application of the Concept* (No. 1). Working paper (2016), https://bit.ly/2UvAxB0 (accessed February 22, 2020).

77 Jan Art Scholte, *Globalization: A Critical Introduction* (Palgrave Macmillan, 2005).

78 "Hungry Tiger, Dancing Elephant: How India Is Changing IBM's World," *The Economist* (April 4, 2007): 58–61.

79 Headquarters sent home-nation executives to run its satellite units. Expatriates typically commanded technical expertise but little cultural fluency and minimal foreign-language competency. Often, the only thing multinational about these executives was the location of their international assignment.

80 Harold Sirkin, James Hemerling, and Arindam Bhattacharya, *Globality: Competing with Everyone from Everywhere for Everything* (New York: Business Plus, 2008).

81 Ibid.

82 Yves Doz, Jose Santos, and Peter Williamson, *Global to Metanational: How Companies Win in the Knowledge Economy* (Cambridge, MA: Harvard Business School Press, 2001).

83 Keeley Wilson and Yves L. Doz, "10 Rules for Managing Global Innovation," *Harvard Business Review* (October 12, 2012).

84 "Globalization Feature: Why Being Multinational Is No Longer Enough," HBS Working Knowledge Archive, Harvard Business School, http://hbswk.hbs.edu/archive/2679.html (accessed March 7, 2016).

85 Andrew Kramer, "The Evolution of Russia, as Seen from McDonald's," NYTimes.com, https://nyti.ms/2xdxqW (accessed March 17, 2011).

86 Mark Scott, "Companies Born in Europe, but Based on the Planet," *New York Times* (June 12, 2012): B7.

87 Alison Coleman, "The Tel Aviv Tech Start-ups to Watch In 2018," *Forbes*, https://bit.ly/2xiGpVZ (accessed January 2, 2019); Greg Nichols, "Swiss Army Knife of Drones Gets $28.5m in Funding." ZDNet, https://zd.net/2J54Ade (accessed January 2, 2019).

88 O. Moen, R. Sorbeim, and T. Erikson, "Born Global Firms and Informal Investors: Examining Investor Characteristics," *Journal of Small Business Management* (October 2008): 536.

89 "Zoom Video Communications." *Wikipedia* (September 29, 2018), https://bit.ly/3dgmHuE (accessed December 24, 2018).

90 Pankaj Ghemawat, "Regional Strategies for Global Leadership," *Harvard Business Review* (December 2005).

91 Marc Singer, "Beyond the Unbundled Corporation," *McKinsey Quarterly* (Summer, 2001).

92 "2009 State of the Future," The Millennium Project, 22.

93 Ibid., Jim Collins, "Good to Great."

Chapter 13

1 *Sources include the following:* We'd like to acknowledge the invaluable assistance of Jonathan Fitzpatrick, former Executive V.P. and Chief Brand Operations Officer; Julio A. Ramirez, former Executive Vice President Global Operations; Arianne Cento, Senior Analyst, Global Communications; and Ana Miranda, Senior Manager Investor Relations, all with Burger King Corporation. Additional information came from Philip G. Gayle and Zijun Luo, "Choosing between Order-of-Entry Assumptions in Empirical Entry Models: Evidence from Competition between Burger King and McDonald's Restaurant Outlets," *The Journal of Industrial Economics* 63:1 (March 2015): 129–51; Julie Jargon, "Burger King: The Assetless Company," *Wall Street Journal* (August 2014): B1; Michael Stothard, "Burger King Swallows UP Quick Fast-Food Chain," *Financial Times* (September 29, 2015): 18; Avinder Batra, "Burger King Drops Tradition for Indian Taste Buds, Gets Vegetarian Delicacies on Its Menu," *The Economic Times* [New Delhi] (June 17, 2015): n.p.; "Seventh Time Lucky? Burger King," *The Economist* (August 30, 2014): 60; "Burger King Scouting for Locations in Major Siberian Cities," *Interfax: Russia & CIS Business and Financial Newswire* (January 22, 2013): n.p.; Elaine Walker, "Burger King Goes for New Look," *Miami Herald* (May 31, 2011): 1A–2A; Rebecca Ordish, "Testing the Franchising Waters in China," *The China Business Review* 33:6 (November–December 2006): 30–3; "Burger King Plans to Double Restaurant Count in Russia in 2011," *Interfax, Ukraine Business Daily* (Kiev) (November 17, 2010); "Negocio de Resturantes Aumenta 8% en Colombia," *Noticieras Financieras* (December 22, 2010); Business Monitor International, *Colombia Food & Drink Report Q1 2009* (London: Business Monitor International, 2009); Gemma Charles, "Burger King Adds First 'Value Meal' to Menu," *Marketing* (February 11, 2009): 3; "The Burger King® Brand Enters Colombia," *Business Wire* (December 13, 2007): n.p.; Danielle Wiener-Bronner, "How Burger King Fell Behind," *CNN Business* (November 13, 2018; accessed April 29, 2019); Chloe Sorvino, "Whopper of a Turnaround: At Burger King, the 3G Capital Model Actually Worked," *Forbes* (April 30, 2019; accessed May 5, 2019); Restaurant Brands International investor day presentation (May 15, 2019; accessed January 13, 2020).

2 Paul Glader, "GE Is Reassigning Veteran Rice to Job Focusing on Overseas Sales," *Wall Street Journal* (November 9, 2010): B2.

3 Thomas Hutzschenreuter and Martin Hommes, "What Determines the Speed of New Product Area International Rollout?" *Proceedings of the 54th Annual Meeting of the Academy of International Business* (June 30–July 3, 2012), emphasize the further need to consider location when companies add new products to their portfolios.

4 Shige Makino, Takehiko Isobe, and Christine M. Chan, "Does Country Matter?" *Strategic Management Journal* 25 (2004): 1027–43.

5 Tony W. Tong, Todd M. Alessandri, Jeffrey J. Reuer, and Asda Chintakananda, "How Much Does Country Matter? An Analysis of Firms' Growth Options," *Journal of International Business Studies* 39:3 (2008): 387–405.

6 Peter Enderwick, "The Imperative of Global Environmental Scanning," *AIB Insights* 11:1 (2011): 12–15.

7 Daniel R. Clark, Dan Li, and Dean A. Shepherd, "Country Familiarity in the Initial Stage of Foreign Market Selection," *Journal of International Business Studies*, 49:4 (2018): 442–472.

8 David Gonzalez, "Fried Chicken Takes Flight, Happily Nesting in U.S.," *New York Times* (September 20, 2002): A4; Joel Millman, "California City Fends Off Arrival of Mexican Supermarket," *Wall Street Journal* (August 7, 2002): B1+ illustrates how Gigante, a Mexican supermarket chain, has targeted U.S. cities with large Mexican populations.

9 Don E. Schultz, "China May Leapfrog the West in Marketing," *Marketing News* (August 19, 2002): 8–9.

10 Amol Sharma, "In India, Subsidies Upend Car Sales," *Wall Street Journal* (July 1, 2012): B1+.

11 Kejal Vyas, "Venezuelans Opt for Rum over Pricey Scotch," *Wall Street Journal* (August 13, 2014): B4.

12 "Africa's Middle Class Few and Far Between," *The Economist*, October 24, 2015, 43–44, refers to data from Pew Research Centre that just 6 percent of Africans qualify as middle class.

13 C. Denbour, "Competition for Business Location: A Survey," *Journal of Industry, Competition and Trade*, 8:2 (June 2008): 89–111.

14 Nicholas Casey, "In Mexico, Auto Plants Hit the Gas," *Wall Street Journal* (November 20, 2012): A1+; "The Rise of Mexico," *The Economist* (November 24, 2012): 14; Keith Bradsher, "Hello, Cambodia," *New York Times* (April 9, 2013): Business 1+.

15 Anil Khurana, "Strategies for Global R&D," *Research Technology Management* (March/April 2006): 48–59.

16 Michael Peel, "Bitter-Sweet Confections of Business in Nigeria," *Financial Times* (November 20, 2002): 10; "Dairy Farming in Nigeria: Uncowed," *The Economist* (June 6, 2015): 38.

17 G. Bruce Knecht, "Going the Wrong Way down a One-Way Street," *Wall Street Journal* (March 18, 2002): A1.

18 Alfredo J. Mauri and Arvind V. Phatak, "Global Integration as Inter-Area Product Flows: The Internationalization of Ownership and Location Factors Influencing Product Flows across MNC Units," *Management International Review* 41 (2001): 233–49.

19 Cynthia O'Murchu and Jan Cienski, "Multinationals Reap the Rewards," *Financial Times* (December 2, 2010): 9. For a description of the EU financial support, see European Commission, "Research Structures: EU Financial Support" (August 11, 2015), http://ec.europa.eu/research/infrastructure/index (accessed September 14, 2015).

20 Nicholas James Bailey, "MNE Bargaining Power Under Constrained Location Choices: Evidence from the Tourism Industry," *Proceedings of the 54th Annual Meeting of the Academy of International Business* (June 30–July 3, 2012).

21 Colin Kirkpatrick and Kenichi Shimamoto, "The Effect of Environmental Regulation on the Locational Choice of Japanese Direct Investment," *Applied Economics* 40:11 (June 2008): 1399; and George Z. Peng and Paul W. Beamish, "The Effect of National Corporate Responsibility Environment on Japanese Foreign Direct Investment," *Journal of Business Ethics* 80:4 (July 2008): 677–95.

22 Hoon Park, "Determinants of Corruption: A Cross-National Analysis," *Multinational Business Review* 11:2 (2003): 29–48.

23. Mario I. Kafouros, Peter J. Buckley, and Jeremy Clegg, "The Effects of Global Knowledge Reservoirs on the Productivity of Multinational Enterprises: The Role of International Depth and Breadth," *Research Policy* 41:5 (June 2012): 848–61.

24 John D. Daniels and James A. Schweikart, "Political Risk, Assessment and Management of," in *IEBM Handbook of International Business*, ed. Rosalie L. Tung (London: International Thomson Business Press, 1999): 502–14.

25 "Political Consultants: Risk Premiums," *The Economist* (May 21, 2016): 61.

26 Robert Wright, "Continuity Planning Is Strengthened," *Financial Times* (March 20, 2012): Risk Management/Supply Chain 1.

27 Jing-Lin Duanmu, "State-Owned MNCs and Host Country Expropriation Risk: The Role of Home State Soft Power and Economic Gunboat Diplomacy," *Journal of International Business Studies* 45:8 (2015): 1044–60.

28 Haig Simonian, "Venezuela to Pay Holcim $650M Compensation for Seized Assets," *Financial Times* (September 14, 2010): 17.

29 Lamine Chikhi, Dmitry Zhdannikov, and Ron Bousso, "Exxon's Talks to Tap Algeria Shale Gas Falter Due to Unrest – Sources," *Reuters* (March 20, 2019; accessed May 1, 2019).

30 This preference for liquidity is associated with options theory in the work of Robert C. Merton, Myron S. Scholes, and Fisher Black. For good, succinct coverage, see John Krainer, "The 1997 Nobel Prize in Economics," FRBSF Economic Letter No. 98–05 (February 13, 1998).

31 Sharon Terlep and Mike Ramsey, "Disaster in Japan: Supply Shortages Stall Auto Makers," *Wall Street Journal* (March 19, 2011): 9.

32 WHO, Public Health Mapping and GIS, Map Library, retrieved June 11, 2007, from gamapserver.who.int/mapLibrary/default.aspx. Also see World Health Organization, *World Health Statistics 2012* (Geneva: World Health Organization, 2012) for statistics on communicable and noncommunicable diseases by country.

33 KPMG Services Ltd. (2015) "Doing Business in Africa in Sickness and Health: A Focus on the Business and Economic of Ebola," http://www.kpmg.com/Africa/en/IssuesAndInsights/Articles-Publications/Documents/Business%20 1nd%20economics%20impact%20ofEbola.pdf (accessed August 3, 2016).

34 Julie Creswell and David Segal, "Companies Confront Zika Virus and Safety," *New York Times* (February 15, 2016): B1–B2.

35 Samantha Pearson, Ralph Oliver, and Robert Wright, "Business Take Stock as Zika Outbreak Spreads," *Financial Times*, February 16, 2016: 16.

36 Jeremy Page, Wenxin Fan, and Natasha Khan, "How It All Started: China's Early Coronavirus Missteps," *Wall Street Journal* (March 6, 2020; accessed March 29, 2020); Liza Lin, "How China Slowed Coronavirus: Lockdowns, Surveillance, Enforcers," *Wall Street Journal* (March 10, 2020; accessed March 29, 2020); Reshma Kapadia, "What the U.S. Can Learn from China's Response to the Coronavirus Pandemic," *Barron's* (March 20, 2020; accessed March 29, 2020).

37 Paul D. Ellis, "Does Psychic Distance Moderate the Market Size-Entry Sequence Relationship?" *Journal of International Business Studies* 39:3 (2008): 351–69; Katarina Blomkvist and Rian Drogendijk, "The Impact of Psychic Distance on Chinese Outward Foreign Direct Investment," *Management International Review* 53:5 (2013): 659–86; David W. Williams and Denis A. Grégoire, "Seeking Commonalities or Avoiding Differences? Re-conceptualizing Distance and Its Effects on Internationalization Decisions," *Journal of International Business Studies* 46:3 (2015): 253–84.

38 See Srilata Zaheer and Elaine Mosakowski, "The Dynamics of the Liability of Foreignness: A Global Study of Survival in Financial Services," *Strategic Management Journal* 18 (1997): 439–64; Stewart R. Miller and Arvind Parkhe, "Is There a Liability of Foreignness in Global Banking? An Empirical Test of Banks' X-Efficiency," *Strategic Management Journal* 23 (2002): 55–75.

39 Mikhail V. Gratchev, "Making the Most of Cultural Differences," *Harvard Business Review* (October 2001): 28–30.

40 John Cantwell, "Location and the Multinational Company," *Journal of International Business Studies* 40:1 (January 2009): 35–41; Nandini Lahiri, "Geographic Distribution of R&D Activity: How Does It Affect Innovation Quality?" *Academy of Management Journal* 53:5 (2010): 1194–209; and Lilach Nachum and Sangyoung Song, "The MNE as a Portfolio: Interdependencies in MNE Growth Trajectory," *Journal of International Business Studies* 42:3 (April 2011): 381–405.

41 Shige Makino and Eric W. K. Tsang, "Historical Ties and Foreign Direct Investment: An Exploratory Study," *Journal of International Business Studies* 42:4 (May 2011): 545–57.

42 Khanh T. L. Tran, "Blockbuster Finds Success in Japan," *Wall Street Journal* (August 19, 1998): A14; Cecile Rohwedder, "Blockbuster Hits Eject Button as Stores in Germany See Video-Rental Sales Sag," *Wall Street Journal* (January 16, 1998): B9A.

43 John A. Doukas and Ozgur B. Kan, "Does Global Diversification Destroy Firm Value?" *Journal of International Business Studies* 37 (2006): 352–71.

44 B. Kazaz, M. Dada, and H. Moskowitz, "Global Production Planning under Exchange-Rate Uncertainty," *Management Science* 51 (2005): 1101–09.

45 Mario I. Kafouros, Peter J. Buckley, and Jeremy Clegg, "The Effects of Global Knowledge Reservoirs on the Productivity of Multinational Enterprises: The Role of International Depth and Breadth," *Research Policy* 41:5 (June 2012): 848–61.

46 Edward B. Flowers, "Oligopolistic Reactions in European and Canadian Direct Investment in the United States," *Journal of International Business Studies* 7:2 (Fall–Winter 1976): 43–55; Frederick Knickerbocker, *Oligopolistic Reaction and Multinational Enterprise* (Cambridge, MA: Harvard University, Graduate School of Business, Division of Research, 1973); Keith Head, John C. Ries, and Thierry Mayer, "Revisiting Oligopolistic Reaction: Are Decisions on Foreign Direct Investment Strategic Complements?" *Journal of Economics & Management Strategy* 11:3 (2002): 453–72.

47 See J. Myles Shaver and Fredrick Flyer, "Agglomeration Economies, Firm Heterogeneity, and Foreign Direct Investment in the United States," *Strategic Management Journal* 21 (2000): 1175–93; Philippe Martin and Gianmarco I. P. Ottaviano, "Growth and Agglomeration," *International Economic Review* 42 (2001): 947–68; Edward E. Leamer and Michael Storper, "The Economic Geography of the Internet Age," *Journal of International Business Studies* 32 (2001): 641–65.

48 "Hard Faces: India's Diamond Polishers," *The Economist* (December 5, 2015): 40–41.

49 Heeyon Kim, "Should Birds of a Feather Flock Together? Agglomeration by Nationality as a Constraint in International Expansion," *AIB Insights* 15:3 (2015): 11–12; Exequiel Hernandez "Finding a Home Away from Home: Effects of Immigrants on Firms' Foreign Location Choice and Performance," *Administrative Science Quarterly* 59:1 (2014): 73–108.

50 Jedrzej George Frynas, Kamel Mellahi, and Geoffrey Allen Pigman, "First Mover Advantages in International Business and Firm-Specific Political Resources," *Strategic Management Journal* 27 (2006): 321–45; Makino, Isobe, and Chan, "Does Country Matter?"

51 Joel Millman, "PriceSmart to Restate Results Due to an Accounting Error," *Wall Street Journal* (November 11, 2003): B9.

52 "Economic Data: Funny Numbers," *The Economist* (October 24, 2015): 68.

53 "Maduro's Muzzle," *The Economist* (April 4, 2015): 32+.

54 Josh Zumbrun, "Sex, Drugs and a GDP Rethink," *Wall Street Journal* (June 9, 2014): 2; Liz Alderman, "Black Markets, Red-Light Districts and Measuring G.D.P.s in Europe," *New York Times* (July 10, 2014): Business 1+.

55 "China: Bottoms Up," *The Economist* (March 30, 2013): 43–4.

56 Andria Cheng, "Limited Brands Defends Its International Plan," *Market Watch* (October 19, 2011): n.p.

57 Azam Ahmed, "Suicide Bombers Attack a Red Cross Compound in Eastern Afghanistan," *New York Times* (May 30, 2014): A6.

58 Moisés Naím, "The Five Wars of Globalization," *Foreign Policy* (January–February 2003): 29–36.

59 Benjamin Bader and Nicola Berg, "An Empirical Investigation of Terrorism-Induced Stress on Expatriate Performance," *Proceedings of the 54th Annual Meeting of the Academy of International Business* (June 30–July 3, 2012).

60 "Doing Business in Dangerous Places," *The Economist* (August 14, 2004): 11.

61 Most of these variables are discussed in Igal Ayal and Jehiel Zif, "Marketing Expansion Strategies in Multinational Marketing," *Journal of Marketing* (Spring 1979): 84–94.

62 Makino, Isobe, and Chan, "Does Country Matter?"

63 Susan Freeman, Kate Hutchings, and Sylvie Chetty, "Born-Global and Culturally Proximate Markets," *Management International Review* 52 (2012): 425–60.

64 Nikki Tait, "Dana Set to Sell UK-Based Components Arm," *Financial Times* (November 29, 2000): 22.

65 Makino, Isobe, and Chan, "Does Country Matter?"; Bernard Simon, "Goodyear Sells Its Last Plantation," *Financial Times* (December 1, 2004): 18.

66 See Jean J. Boddewyn, "Foreign and Domestic Divestment and Investment Decisions: Like or Unlike?" *Journal of International Business Studies* 14:3 (Winter 1983): 28; Michelle Haynes, Steve Thompson, and Mike Wright, "The Determinants of Corporate Divestment in the U.K.," *Journal of Industrial Organization* 18 (2000): 1201–22; Jose Mata and Pedro Portugal, "Closure and Divestiture by Foreign Entrants: The Impact of Entry and Post-Entry Strategies," *Strategic Management Journal* 21 (2000): 549–62.

67 *Mexico Telecommunications Report* (Second Quarter 2015).

68 International Monetary Fund, *World Economic Outlook, September 2004* (Washington, DC: International Monetary Fund, 2004): 143–9.

69 Peter Hall, *Cities in Civilization: Culture, Technology, and Urban Order* (London: Weidenfeld & Nicholson, 1998).

70 "A Sense of Place," *The Economist* (October 27, 2012): Special Report on Technology and Geography, 6.

71 David Aviel, "The Causes and Consequences of Public Attitudes to Technology: A United States Analysis," *International Journal of Management* 18 (2001): 166.

72 *Sources include the following:* Amazon Annual Reports, 1998–2018; Mark Hall, "Amazon.com," *Encyclopaedia Britannica* online, November 1, 2018 (accessed May 8, 2019); Tim Carmody, "From Kindle to Fire: Why Amazon Needs to Go Global," www.wired.com (September 30, 2011; accessed May 9, 2019); "Strange Bedfellows: Waterstones and Amazon," *Economist* (May 26, 2012): 32; Jillian D'Onfro, "One of Amazon's Biggest Challenges for the New Year," *Business Insider* (January 22, 2015; accessed May 8, 2019); Leslie Hook, "Amazon's Prime Challenge Is International Growth," *Financial Times* (March 3, 2016; accessed May 8, 2019); Jan Dawson, "Amazon's International Growth Challenge" www.vox.com (May 11, 2015; accessed May 8, 2019); "Beyond Shopping; Amazon," *Economist* (October 28, 2017): 4; Alex Lee, "A Case Study on International Expansion: When Amazon went to China," www.medium.com (October 22, 2018; accessed May 8, 2019); "Home and Away; Going Global," *Economist* (October 28, 2017): 7; "Amazon's Efforts in Japan Remain Dogged," www.emarketer.com (July 5, 2017; accessed May 8, 2019); Jeannette Neumann and Laura Stevens, "Amazon's Out of Fashion in Europe," *Wall Street Journal* (May 1, 2018; accessed May 9, 2019); Morgan Stanley Research, "Amazon versus Alibaba: The Next Decade of Disruption" (May 2018; accessed May 8, 2019); Brad Haynes, "Amazon.com Plays Catch-UP in Brazil as Local Rivals Thrive," www.reuters.com (April 25, 2018; accessed May 8, 2019); Sangara Narayanan, "Amazon's International Expansion Takes a New Twist: The Online Retail and Technology Giant Has Fine-Tuned Its Expansion Strategy Outside the U.S." www.gurufocus.com (April 7, 2017; accessed May 8, 2019); Newley Purnell, "Bezos Invests Billions to Make Amazon a Top Player In India," *Wall Street Journal* (November 18, 2016; accessed May 11, 2019); Mohanbir Sawhney, "7 Ways Amazon Is Winning by Acting 'Globally' in India," *Forbes* (April 30, 2018; accessed May 8, 2019); "Why India Is Crucial to Amazon's Massive International Expansion Plans," *Forbes* (November 28, 2018; accessed May 8, 2019); "Briefing: Amazon: And on the Second Day...," *The Economist* (June 20, 2020):15-18.

Chapter 14

1 "Trade Data & Analysis | International Trade Administration," retrieved February 15, 2020, from https://www.trade.gov/trade-data-analysis. United States International Trade Association, Export Fact Sheet April 2015, www.trade.gov/press/press-releases/2015/export-factsheet-060315.pdf (accessed July 15, 2015).

2 Case developed based on profiles of company management, company activities, and country profiles reported at www.export.gov; United States International Trade Administration; United States Census Bureau, *Profile of U.S. Exporting Companies 2015–2016,* at www.census.gov/foreign-trade/aip/edbrel-0203.pdf; *Small & Medium-Sized Exporting Companies: Statistical Overview,* tse.export.gov/EDB/SelectReports.aspx?DATA=ExporterDB. SpinCent represents the reported experiences of active exporters as well as the observations expressed by their management. Please visit www.export.gov/articles/successstories/eg_success_story_021417.asp for an overview of the source documents.

3 By the way, these trade data combine imports and exports (i.e., a bit of double counting). Still, the upward trend powers on.

4 "World's Top Export Products." 2019. World's Top Exports. October 14, 2019 http://www.worldstopexports.com/worlds-top-export-products/ (accessed February 22, 2020).

5 "Economic Impact of International Students," www.iie.org/Research-and-Insights/Open-Doors/Data/Economic-Impact-of-International-Students (accessed December 21, 2018).

6 "World's Top Export Services in 2018." n.d. http://www.worldstopexports.com/worlds-top-export-services/ (accessed February 15, 2020).

7 Saeed Samiee and Peter Walters, "Segmenting Corporate Exporting Activities: Sporadic Versus Regular Exporters," *Journal of the Academy of Marketing Science* 19:2 (1991): 93–104.

8 Jakob Munch and Georg Schaur, "The Effect of Export Promotion on Firm-Level Performance," *American Economic Journal: Economic Policy* 10.1 (2018): 357–87; James H. Love and Stephen Roper, "SME Innovation, Exporting and Growth: A Review of Existing Evidence," *International Small Business Journal* 33:1 (2015): 28–48.

9 US Census Bureau, Foreign Trade Division, "US Census Bureau Foreign Trade," www.census.gov/foreign-trade/Press-Release/edb/2017/index.html? (accessed December 21, 2018). We see the same shares for the big importers in the United States.

10 A Profile of U.S. Importing and Exporting Companies, 2015–2016; Release Number: CB 18-54, USITC, www.census.gov/foreign-trade/Press-Release/edb/2016/text.pdf (accessed January 5, 2019); "Small and Medium-Sized Enterprises: Overview of Participation in U.S. Exports," January 2010; USITC, "Small and Medium-Sized Enterprises: U.S. and EU Export Activities, and Barriers and Opportunities Experienced by U.S. Firms," July 2010.

11 Richard Hoffman, "Small And Medium Enterprises in China," (July 4, 2018), https://ecovis-beijing.com/investment/smes-china/ (accessed December 20, 2018); "SMEs Keen on E-Commerce Exports - Business - Chinadaily.Com.Cn," www.chinadaily.com.cn/business/2016-12/24/content_27762503.htm (accessed December 21, 2018). "International Trade - Exports by Business Size - OECD Data," The OECD, http://data.oecd.org/trade/exports-by-business-size.htm (accessed December 21, 2018); Number of small to medium-sized enterprises in China from 2012 to 2020 (in millions), Statista, https://www.statista.com/statistics/783899/china-number-of-small-to-medium-size-enterprises/ (accessed February 29, 2020); Ministry of Commerce, "Small and Medium-Size Enterprises," People's Republic of China, http://english.mofcom.gov.cn/aarticle/zm/201205/20120508136044.html (accessed February 28, 2016).

12 B. Aw, M. Roberts, and D. Xu, "R&D Investment, Exporting, and Productivity Dynamics," www.econ.psu.edu/~mroberts/arxmarch2010.pdf (accessed December 18, 2012).

13 Özgur Uysal and Abdulakadir Said Mohamoud, "Determinants of Export Performance in East Africa Countries," *Chinese Business Review* 17.4 (2018): 168–178.

14 D. Crick, "UK SMEs' Motives for Internationalizing: Differences between Firms Employing Particular Overseas Market Servicing Strategies," *Journal of International Entrepreneurship* (2007): 11–23 (accessed May 15, 2011); H. T. Ngo, & P. A. Igwe (2019). Internationalization of Firms and Entrepreneur's Motivations: A Review and Research Agenda. *Societal Entrepreneurship and Competitiveness, Emerald Publishing Limited,* 29–46.

15 Coffee & More, LLC, www.export.gov/articles/successstories/eg_success_story_022775.asp (accessed May 15, 2011).

16 Certified Worldwide LLC, www.export.gov/articles/successstories/eg_success_story_020902.asp (accessed May 15, 2011).

17 USITC, "Small and Medium-Sized Enterprises: Overview of Participation in U.S. Exports," January 2010; USITC.

18 Elena Golovko and Giovanni Valentini, "Exploring the Complementarity between Innovation and Export for SME's Growth," *Journal of International Business Studies* 42 (2011): 362–80.

19 Domes International, www.export.gov/articles/successstories/eg_success_story_021027.asp (accessed May 15, 2011).

20 "Direct vs. Indirect Exporting," http://onlinefx.westernunion.com/business/learning-center/import-and-export/direct-vs-indirect-exporting/(accessed July 14, 2015).

21 "Global Development Horizons 2011—Multipolarity: The New Global Economy," *The World Bank,* http://siteresources.worldbank.org/INTGDH/Resources/GDH_CompleteReport2011.pdf (accessed May 30, 2011).

22 "Hey Big Spenders," *The World in 2012, The Economist,* www.economist.com/theworldin/2012 (accessed December 22, 2012).

23 "Asia's Future Is Now | McKinsey," https://www.mckinsey.com/featured-insights/asia-pacific/asias-future-is-now (accessed February 15, 2020).

24 Hans Gemunden, "Success Factors of Export Marketing: A Meta-Analytic Critique of the Empirical Studies," in *New Perspectives on International Marketing,* ed. S. Paliwoda (London: Routledge, 1991): 33–62; M.Y. Haddoud, P. Jones, and R. Newbery, "Export intention in developing countries: A configuration approach to managerial success factors," *Journal of Small Business Management* (October 2018), 1–29.

25 Jan Johanson and Jan-Erik Vahlne, "The Internationalization Process of the Firm: A Model of Knowledge Development and Increasing Foreign Market Commitments," *Journal of International Business Studies* (1977): 23–32; Daniel Sullivan and Alan Bauerschmidt, "Incremental Internationalization: A Test of Johanson and Vahlne's Thesis," *MIR: Management International Review* (1990): 19–30; Daniel Sullivan, "Measuring the Degree of Internationalization of a Firm," *Journal of International Business Studies* (1994): 325–42.

26 Guillermo García-Pérez, et al., "The Hidden Hyperbolic Geometry of International Trade: World Trade Atlas 1870–2013," *Scientific Reports* 6 (2016): 33441.

27 "Schumpeter: The Case against Globaloney," *The Economist* (April 23, 2011): 72.

28 Profile of Analytical Graphics, Inc., export.gov/articles/successstories/eg_main_033668.asp (accessed December 15, 2012).

29 Daniel Sullivan and Alan Bauerschmidt, "Incremental Internationalization: A Test of Johanson and Vahlne's Thesis," *Management International Review* (1990): 19–30.

30 McKinsey & Co. (1993), "Emerging Exporters: Australia's High Value-Added Manufacturing Exporters," Melbourne: Australian Manufacturing Council, catalogue.nla.gov.au/Record/2621131 (accessed May 17, 2011).

31 Examples cited in T. Koed Madsen and P. Servais, "The Internationalization of Born Globals: An Evolutionary Process?" *International Business Review* (1997): 561–83.

32 O. Moen, R. Sorbeim, and T. Erikson. "Born Global Firms and Informal Investors: Examining Investor Characteristics," *Journal of Small Business Management* (October 2008): 536.

33 "Zoom Video Communications." *Wikipedia* (September 29, 2018), https://en.wikipedia.org/w/index.php?title=Zoom_Video_Communications&oldid=861677545 (accessed December 24, 2018).

34 "Zady Takes Socially Conscious Fashion Global with Pitney Bowes' Borderfree," Pitney Bowes, http://news.pb.com/article_display.cfm?article_id=5632 (accessed July 31, 2015).

35 Evertek Computer Corp., www.export.gov/articles/successstories/eg_success_story_021490.asp (accessed May 15, 2011).

36 Ibid., Evertek.

37 Ibid., Evertek.

38 "A Profile of U.S. Importing and Exporting Companies, 2015–2016; Release Number: CB 18-54, USITC, www.census.gov/foreign-trade/Press-Release/edb/2016/text.pdf (accessed January 5, 2019).

39 Daniel Sullivan and Alan Bauerschmidt, "Incremental Internationalization: A Test of Johanson and Vahlne's Thesis," *Management International Review* (1990): 19–30.

40 J. Manyika, S. Lund, J. Bughin, J. R. Woetzel, K. Stamenov, and D. Dhingra, *Digital Globalization: The New Era of Global Flows (Vol. 4)* (San Francisco: McKinsey Global Institute, 2016); "Global Ecommerce Statistics and Trends to Launch Your Business Beyond Borders." n.d. Enterprise Ecommerce Blog - Enterprise Business Marketing, News, Tips & More, https://www.shopify.com/enterprise/global-ecommerce-statistics (accessed February 15, 2020); Bryan Bielefeldt, n.d. "Global Commerce | What Is International E-Commerce | Global Expansion," *Flow* (blog), https://www.flow.io/international-e-commerce/ (accessed February 15, 2020).

41 Scott Barry Kaufman, "The Role of Luck in Life Success Is Far Greater Than We Realized." Scientific American Blog Network, https://blogs.scientificamerican.com/beautiful-minds/the-role-of-luck-in-life-success-is-far-greater-than-we-realized/ (accessed December 24, 2018).

42 Mark Stein, "Export Opportunities Aren't Just for the Big Guys," *New York Times* (March 24, 2005): C1.

43 Vellus Products, www.export.gov/articles/successstories/eg_main_020763.asp (accessed May 15, 2011).

44 Mark Stein, "Export Opportunities Aren't Just for the Big Guys," *New York Times* (March 24, 2005): C1.

45 Profile of Analytical Graphics, Inc. at export.gov, export.gov/articles/successstories/eg_main_033668.asp (accessed Saturday, December 15, 2012).

46 A Profile of U.S. Importing and Exporting Companies, 2015–2016; Release Number: CB 18-54, USITC, www.census.gov/foreign-trade/Press-Release/edb/2016/text.pdf (accessed January 5, 2019); "Small and Medium-Sized Enterprises: Characteristics and Performance," United States International Trade Commission, Investigation No. 332-510, USITC Publication 4189, November 2010.

47 The World Counts. "Electronic Waste Facts," https://www.theworldcounts.com/challenges/planet-earth/waste/electronic-waste-facts(accessed February 16, 2020).

48 "Municipal Solid Waste Generation, Recycling and Disposal in the United States; Tables and Figures for 2012," U.S. EPA, February 2014, Tables 12–14, www.epa.gov/sites/production/files/2015-09/documents/2012_msw_fs.pdf.

49 "Africa Waste Trade," www1.american.edu/TED/oauwaste.htm (accessed May 4, 2011); Estimates for developed economies taken from Hazardous Waste Disposal, www.uos.harvard.edu/ehs/environmental/hw_faq_answers.shtml; Leslie Kaufman, "A Green Way to Dump Low-Tech Electronics," *New York Times* (June 30, 2009).

50 "Electronic Waste in Guiyu" *Wikipedia,* en.wikipedia.org/wiki/Electronic_waste_in_Guiyu (accessed December 22, 2012).

51 Elisabeth Rosenthal, "Recycled Battery Lead Puts Mexicans in Danger," NYTimes.com, www.nytimes.com/2011/12/09/science/earth/recycled-battery-lead-puts-mexicans-in-danger.html?pagewanted=all&_r=0 (accessed December 23, 2012).

52 Reported by Karl Schoenberger, "E-Waste Ignored in India," *Mercury News,* www.ban.org/ban_news/ewaste_ignored_031228.html (accessed May 4, 2011).

53 Brook Larmer, "E-Waste Offers an Economic Opportunity as Well as Toxicity," *The New York Times,* https://www.nytimes.com/2018/07/05/magazine/e-waste-offers-an-economic-opportunity-as-well-as-toxicity.html (accessed February 16, 2020); "GDP (Current US$) | Data," The World Bank, https://data.worldbank.org/indicator/NY.GDP.MKTP.CD?most_recent_value_desc=false (accessed February 16, 2020).

54 Matthew Khan, "Environmental and Urban Economics: October 2005," greeneconomics.blogspot.com/2005_10_01_archive.html (accessed February 25, 2013).

55 Rick LeBlanc, "Here Is a Look at E-Waste Recycling Facts and Figures," *The Balance Small Business,* www.thebalancesmb.com/e-waste-recycling-facts-and-figures-2878189 (accessed December 29, 2018); "After Dump, What Happens to Electronic Waste?" *NPR,* www.npr.org/2010/12/21/132204954/after-dump-what-happens-to-electronic-waste (accessed April 19, 2011).

56 "CTA Releases ECycling Leadership Initiative Annual Report," *Recycling Today,* www.recyclingtoday.com/article/cta-ecycling-leadership-initiative-2016-report/ (accessed December 29, 2018); "ERI to Team with CTA and Samsung for Free E-Waste Recycling Event Before CES 2020," December 27, 2019, https://www.businesswire.com/news/home/20191227005234/en/ERI-Team-CTA-Samsung-Free-E-Waste-Recycling.

57 "E-Waste Chokes Southeast Asia–Basel Action Network," www.ban.org/news/2018/11/5/e-waste-chokes-southeast-asia (accessed December 29, 2018); Michelle Castillo, "Electronic Waste: Where Does It Go and What Happens to It?" TIME.com, techland.time.com/2011/01/14/electronic-waste-where-does-it-go-and-what-happens-to-it/ (accessed February 25, 2013).

58 Elisabeth Rosenthal,"Recycled Battery Lead Puts Mexicans in Danger," *NYTimes.com*, www.nytimes.com/2011/12/09/science/earth/recycled-battery-lead-puts-mexicans-in-danger.html?pagewanted=all&_r=0 (accessed February 25, 2013).

59 Forti V. Baldé, V. Gray, R. Kuehr, and P. Stegmann,"The Global E-waste Monitor—2017, United Nations University (UNU), International Telecommunication Union (ITU) & International Solid Waste Association (ISWA), Bonn/Geneva/Vienna," http://collections.unu.edu/eserv/UNU:6341/Global-E-waste_Monitor_2017__electronic_single_pages_.pdf (accessed December 29, 2019); Helen Baulch,"Error: Dumping Does Not Compute," *Alternatives Journal* (Summer 2002): 2.

60 "The Digital Dump: Exporting Reuse and Abuse to Africa," *Basel Action Network*, www.ban.org/banreports/10-24-05/index.htm (accessed May 4, 2011).

61 Ibid., C. P. Baldé, V. Forti, V. Gray, R. Kuehr, and P. Stegmann.

62 Ibid., Brook Larmer.

63 Kaufman,"A Green Way to Dump Low-Tech Electronics";"The Politics of E-waste: A Cadmium Lining," *The Economist* (January 26, 2013): 56.

64 "Basel Convention Home Page," www.basel.int/ (accessed December 29, 2018);"Basel Action Network," Basel Action Network, www.ban.org/ (accessed December 29, 2018).

65 "World's Top Imports: Products and Countries," http://www.worldstopexports.com/worlds-top-imports-products-countries/ (accessed February 16, 2020).

66 Kenton, Will."Import." Investopedia, www.investopedia.com/terms/i/import.asp (accessed December 26, 2018).

67 A Profile of U.S. Importing and Exporting Companies, 2015–2016; Release Number: CB 18-54, USITC, www.census.gov/foreign-trade/Press-Release/edb/2016/text.pdf (accessed January 5, 2019); Andrew Bernard, Bradford Jensen, and Peter Schott,"Importers, Exporters, and Multinationals: A Portrait of Firms in the U.S. That Trade Goods," NBER Working Paper No. 11404, June 2005.

68 Andrew Bernard, Bradford Jensen, and Peter Schott,"Importers, Exporters, and Multinationals: A Portrait of Firms in the U.S. that Trade Goods," NBER Working Paper No. 11404, June 2005.

69 "Law of One Price," *Wikipedia*, retrieved December 25, 2018, from https://en.wikipedia.org/w/index.php?title=Law_of_one_price&oldid=875263329.

70 Pascal-Emmanuel Gobry,"Asian Scalpers Are Wiping out Apple's Supply of iPad 2s In New York," www.businessinsider.com/ipad-scalpers-new-york-2011-3 (accessed May 31, 2011).

71 Adapted from various sources, including"Small and Medium-Sized Enterprises: Characteristics and Performance," USITC Investigation No. 332–510, 2010; see also"Trade Barriers That U.S. Small and Medium-Sized Enterprises Perceive as Affecting Exports to the European Union," USITC Investigation No. 332–541.

72 John Kerr,"Exporters Need to Connect with Customers," *Logistics Management* (March 1, 2006): 41.

73 C. O'Gorman,"Strategy and the Small Firm," in *Enterprise and Small Business: Principles, Practice, and Policy*, eds. S. Carter and D. Jones-Evans (Harlow: Prentice Hall, FT Pearson, 2000).

74 "Food & Beverage Exporter Successes | Export.Gov," www.export.gov/article?id=Food-Beverage-Exporter-Successes (accessed December 28, 2018).

75 A Profile of U.S. Importing and Exporting Companies, 2015–2016; Release Number: CB 18-54, USITC, www.census.gov/foreign-trade/Press-Release/edb/2016/text.pdf (accessed January 5, 2019).

76 OECD, OECD-APEC paper on removing barriers to SME access to international markets (2006). See also Alan Bauerschmidt, Daniel Sullivan, and Kate Gillespie,"Common Factors Underlying Barriers to Export Studies in the U.S. Paper Industry," *Journal of International Business Studies*, 16:3 (1985): 111–23.

77 Irving A. Williamson, Shara L. Aranoff, Dean A. Pinkert, David S. Johanson, Meredith M. Broadbent, and F. Scott Kieff,"U.S. International Trade Commission," n.d., 168. Technically, a trade credit is an agreement where a customer can purchase goods on account (without paying cash), paying the supplier later. Usually when the goods are delivered, a trade credit is given for a specific number of days—30, 60, or 90."Open Account | Export.Gov," www.export.gov/article?id=Trade-Finance-Guide-Chapter-5-Open-Account (accessed December 27, 2018).

78 Eldrede T. Kahiya,"Five Decades of Research on Export Barriers: Review and Future Directions," *International Business Review* (2018), 27, 6: 1172–1188, https://doi.org/10.1016/j.ibusrev.2018.04.008

79 Ibid., Irving A. Williamson, et al.

80 Spectra Colors of NJ, retrieved May 15, 2011, from www.export.gov/articles/successstories/eg_success_story_023038.asp.

81 Kerr,"Exporters Need to Connect with Customers."

82 "Exporters Hit by Air Freight Restrictions," *Telegraph*, www.telegraph.co.uk/finance/yourbusiness/8860814/Exporters-hit-by-air-freight-restrictions.html (accessed December 21, 2012);"Known Consignor Scheme," Australian Government, Department of Homeland Affairs, https://www.homeaffairs.gov.au/about-us/our-portfolios/transport-security/air-cargo-and-aviation/air-cargo/known-consignor-scheme(accessed February 17, 2020).

83 U.S. Trade Representative,"2010 National Trade Estimate Report on Foreign Trade Barriers," 2010.

84 U.S. Department of Commerce, International Trade Administration,"Country Commercial Guide: Thailand," February 18, 2008, 64.

85 WTO,"Trade Policy Review: India," April 18, 2007, 147; WTO,"Trade Policy Review: India," April 18, 2007, 147;"India Supreme Court: Foreign Lawyers Cannot Practice Law in Country—JURIST—News—Legal News & Commentary," www.jurist.org/news/2018/03/india-supreme-court-foreign-lawyers-cannot-practice-law-in-country/ (accessed December 28, 2018).

86 "A 'Green Zone' for Firms in Ciudad Juárez: Business on the Bloody Border," *The Economist*, www.economist.com/node/21540262 (accessed December 22, 2012);"Canada and the United States: The Border Two-Step," *The Economist*, www.economist.com/node/21541421 (accessed December 22, 2012).

87 Specifically, see"Trading across Borders - Doing Business - World Bank Group," www.doingbusiness.org/en/data/exploretopics/trading-across-borders (accessed December 28, 2018).

88 "Trading Across Borders Topic Analysis - Doing Business - World Bank Group," https://www.doingbusiness.org/en/data/exploretopics/trading-across-borders/what-measured (accessed February 17, 2020).

89 "Trade.Gov - Trade Statistics." www.trade.gov/mas/ian/tradestatistics/index.asp (accessed December 28, 2018). In particular, see U.S. Trade Overview, 2016 for a summary profile of developments and general trends in international trade.

90 "Medical Exporter Success | Export.Gov," www.export.gov/article?id=Medical-Exporter-Success (accessed December 28, 2018).

91 Lee Li,"Joint Effects of Factors Affecting Exchanges Between Exporters and Their Foreign Intermediaries: An Exploratory Study," *Journal of Business & Industrial Marketing* (February–March 2003): 162–78.

92 See U.S. Department of Commerce, *Guide to Exporting, 1998*, p. 20; Philip MacDonald, *Practical Exporting and Importing*, 2nd edition (New York: Ronald Press, 1959): 30–40.

93 U.S. Department of Commerce, Guide to Exporting (Washington, DC: U.S. Government Printing Office, 1998): 63;"Global Freight Forwarding," *Transport Intelligence* (blog), www.ti-insight.com/product/global-freight-forwarding/ (accessed December 28, 2018);"Top 25 Freight Forwarders 2017: Digitization & E-Commerce Continue to Reshape the Marketplace," www.logisticsmgmt.com/article/top_25_freight_forwarders_2017_digitization_e_commerce_continue_to_reshape (accessed December 28, 2018).

94 *The Economist*."Why Have Containers Boosted Trade So Much?" https://www.economist.com/the-economist-explains/2013/05/21/why-have-containers-boosted-trade-so-much(accessed February 17, 2020).

95 Ibid., Certified Worldwide LLC.

96 Richard Armstrong,"The Top 40 3PLs 2010," *Logistics Quarterly Magazine* (2011)."Top 50 US and Global Third Party Logistics Providers (3PL) in 2017: Collaboration Is Now Paramount," https://www.logisticsmgmt.com/article/top_50_us_and_global_third_party_logistics_providers_3pl_in_2017_collaborat(accessed February 15, 2020.).

97 "Third-Party Logistics," Wikipedia, https://en.wikipedia.org/w/index.php?title=Third-party_logistics&oldid=872098645 (accessed December 5, 2018).

98 Costas Paris and Mike Sudal,"With Container Ships Getting Bigger, Maersk Focuses on Getting Faster," *Wall Street Journal* (December 20, 2018): sec. C Suite, www.wsj.com/articles/with-container-ships-getting-bigger-maersk-focuses-on-getting-faster-11545301800.

99 "Basic Question: To Export Yourself or to Hire Someone to Do It for You?" *Business America* (April 27, 1987): 14–17.

100 Quote from CEO Robert Allen, Coffee & More, LLC, www.export.gov/articles/successstories/eg_success_story_022775.asp (accessed May 15, 2011).

101 Profile of Analytical Graphics, Inc. at export.gov, export.gov/articles/successstories/eg_main_033668.asp (accessed December 15, 2012).

102 Julie Sloane, Justin Martin, and Alessandra Bianchi, "Small Companies That Play Big," *FSB Magazine* (November 1, 2006), quoting Ram Iyer.

103 Costas Paris and Mike Sudal, "With Container Ships Getting Bigger, Maersk Focuses on Getting Faster," *Wall Street Journal* (December 20, 2018): sec. C Suite, www.wsj.com/articles/with-container-ships-getting-bigger-maersk-focuses-on-getting-faster-11545301800.

104 Gary Hamel, *What Matters Now: How to Win in a World of Relentless Change, Ferocious Competition, and Unstoppable Innovation* (Wiley, 2012).

105 "Countertrade | World Problems & Global Issues | The Encyclopaedia of World Problems," http://encyclopedia.uia.org/en/problem/149679 (accessed December 29, 2018); Marco Sartor, Guido Orzes, Guido Nassimbeni, Fu Jia, and Richard Lamming, "International Purchasing Offices: Literature Review and Research Directions," *Journal of Purchasing and Supply Management* 20, no. 1 (2014): 1–17.

106 Various reports, www.Alibaba.com; "Amazon vs. Alibaba: How the E-Commerce Giants Stack Up in the Fight to Go Global," *CB Insights Research* (March 2, 2018), www.cbinsights.com/research/amazon-alibaba-international-expansion/.

107 Ming Zeng, "Alibaba and the Future of Business," *Harvard Business Review* (September 1, 2018), https://hbr.org/2018/09/alibaba-and-the-future-of-business.

108 "Fast as a Rabbit, Patient as a Turtle," Forbes.com, www.forbes.com/forbes/2000/0717/6602074a_print.html (accessed February 25, 2013).

109 "Alibaba and Amazon Look to Go Global," *The Economist* (October 28, 2017), www.economist.com/special-report/2017/10/28/alibaba-and-amazon-look-to-go-global.

Chapter 15

1 *Sources include the following:* J. Pla-Barber, F. León-Darder, and C. Villar, "The Internationalization of Soft-Services: Entry Modes and Main Determinants in the Spanish Hotel Industry," *Service Business* 5:2 (2011): 139–154; M. M. Massot, L. M. Vegas, and M. A. García, "Sol Meliá: Un Nuevo Paradigma en la Gestión Hotelera," in *Multinacionales Españolas II: Nuevas Experiencias de Internacionalización,* ed. J. J. Durán (Madrid: Pirámide, 1997): 73–110; www.meliahotelsinternational.com (accessed April 19, 2013); "Sol Meliá Absorbe la Cadena TRYP en una Operación Valorada en 72,500 Millones," *Cinco Días* (August 22, 2001) at www.cincodías.com (accessed January 5, 2013); "Sol Meliá Compra una Cadena en Alemania por 16.5 Millones," *Cinco Días* (November 9, 2007) at www.cincodias.com (accessed February 7, 2013); "La Cadena Sol Meliá Vende la Marca TRYP al Grupo Hotelero Americano Wyndham: La Operación, Cifrada en unos 32 Millones, No Implica la Transacción de Establecimientos," *Diario de Mallorca* (June 9, 2010) at www.diariodemallorca.es (accessed March 21, 2013); F. Contractor and S. Kundu, "Modal Choice in a World of Alliances: Analyzing Organizational Forms in International Hotel Sector," *Journal of International Business Studies* 29:2 (1998): 325–57; F. León-Darder, C. Villar, and J. Pla-Barber, "Entry Mode Choice in the Internationalization of the Hotel Industry: A Holistic Approach," *Service Industries Journal* 31:1 (2011): 107–22; "La Primera Aventura Británica de Escarrer—Meliá White House, un Hotel en Londres 'Made in Spain'," *Actualidad Económica* (September 23, 2002) at www.actualidad-economica.com (accessed February 7, 2013); "Sol Meliá Renueva su Portfolio en el Exterior con Siete Altas y Ocho Bajas," *Alimarket* (March 1, 2008) at www.alimarket.es (accessed January 19, 2013); "Sol MeliáControla Ya el 32% del Mercado Turístico Cubano," *El País* (May 16, 2005) at www.elpais.com (accessed March 21, 2013); "Sol Meliá Busca una Alianza para Crecer en EE.UU," *La Vanguardia* (September 18, 1999) at www.lavanguardia.es (accessed February 7, 2013); "Sol Meliá, Barceló y Blau Hotels Entrarán en China con la Gestión de Hoteles en Shanghai," *Cinco Días* (May 5, 1999) at www.cincodias.com (accessed January 5, 2013); "Sol Meliá, Barceló y Riu Descartan Nuevas Inversiones en Asia a Corto Plazo por la 'Complejidad' del Mercado," *Europa Press* (February 6, 2006) at www.europapress.es (accessed January 5, 2013); "Barceló Abandona la Gestión de su Primer Hotel en China," *Cinco Días* (January 5, 2001) at www.cincodias.com (accessed January 5, 2013); "Sol Meliá Entra en China de la Mano de un Grupo Local y otro de Cuba," *Cinco Días* (July 10, 2010) at www.cincodias.com (accessed January 5, 2013); "Meliá Apuesta por la Internacionalización en 2013 Para Reforzar su Liderazgo y Hacer Frente al Entorno," at www.meliahotelsinternational.com/es/sala-de-prensa/30012013/melia-apuesta-internacionalizacion-2013-reforzar-su-liderazgo-hacer-frente (accessed April 19, 2013); "Meliá Hotels International Anuncia en Kenia su Interés de Expansión en África Subsahariana," at www.meliahotelsinternational.com/es/sala-de-prensa/26092012/melia-hotels-international-anuncia-kenia-su-interes-expansion-africa; Joseph A. Mann, Jr. "Meliá Expanding in the Americas," *Miami Herald* (May 4, 2015): 13G.

2 Fidel León-Darder is Associate Professor and Cristina Villar is Assistant Professor, both in the Department of Management, Universitat de València (Spain).

3 "Looking to the Future," *Business Europe* 50:18 (October 1, 2010): 7; Birsen Altayli, "Turkish Auto Production and Exports to Hit Record – Association," *Reuters* (July 15, 2015), www.reuters.com/article/turkey-autos-idUSL5N0ZT0MD20150713#qEQKTil3mtCseYDl.97 (accessed December 4, 2015).

4 John Griffiths, "VW May Build Beetle in Europe to Meet Demand," *Financial Times* (November 11, 1998): 17.

5 Peter Marsh, "The World's Wash Day," *Financial Times* (April 29, 2002): 6.

6 "India–EU FTA to Include Tariff Reduction on Import of Vehicles," *Accord Fintech* [Mumbai] (May 20, 2011).

7 Jill Gabrielle Klein, "Us versus Them, or Us versus Everyone? Delineating Consumer Aversion to Foreign Goods," *Journal of International Business Studies* 33:2 (2002): 34563; and Jing Yang, "An Examination of Brand Equity Differences between Utilitarian and Hedonic Products," *International Journal of Marketing Studies* 7:4 (2015): 42–50.

8 John S. Hulland, "The Effects of Country-of-Brand and Brand Name on Product Evaluation and Consideration: A Cross-Country Comparison," *Journal of International Consumer Marketing* 11 (1999): 23–39; Ali Riza Apil and Erdener Kaynak, "Georgian Consumers' Evaluation of Products Sourced from European Union Member Countries," *International Journal of Commerce and Management* 20:2 (2010): 167–87.

9 "'Made in Australia' Label Confuses Shoppers: Choice Survey," *Asia Pulse* (May 18, 2011).

10 Peter J. Lane, Jane E. Salk, and Marjorie A. Lyles, "Absorptive Capacity, Learning, and Performance in International Joint Ventures," *Strategic Management Journal* 22 (2001): 1139–61.

11 *Internalization theory,* or holding a monopoly control over certain information or other proprietary assets, builds on earlier market-imperfections work by Ronald H. Coase, "The Nature of the Firm," *Economica* 4 (1937): 386–405. It has been noted by such writers as M. Casson, "The Theory of Foreign Direct Investment," Discussion Paper No. 50 (Reading, UK: University of Reading International Investment and Business Studies, November 1980); Alan M. Rugman, *Inside the Multinationals: The Economics of Internal Markets* (New York: Columbia University Press, 1981); David J. Teece, "Transactions Cost Economics and the Multinational Enterprise," Berkeley Business School International Business Working Paper Series No. IB-3 (1985); B. Kogut and U. Zander, "Knowledge of the Firm and the Evolutionary Theory of the Multinational Corporation," *Journal of International Business Studies* 24:4 (1993): 625–45; Peter W. Liesch and Gary A. Knight, "Information Internalization and Hurdle Rates in Small and Medium Enterprise Internationalization," *Journal of International Business Studies* 30:2 (1999): 383–96.

12 Eric M. Johnson, "Harnessing the Power of Partnerships," *Financial Times* (October 8, 2004): Mastering Innovation, Section 4.

13 Paul Marer and Vincent Mabert, "GE Acquires and Restructures Tungsram: The First Six Years (1990–1995)," *OECD, Trends and Policies in Privatization* III: 1 (Paris: OECD, 1996): 149–85; and their unpublished 1999 revision, "GE's Acquisition of Hungary's Tungsram."

14 Kalle Pajunen and Liang Fang, "Dialectical Tensions and Path Dependence in International Joint Venture Evolution and Termination," *Asia Pacific Journal of Management* 30:2 (2013): 577–600.

15 Kathy Chu, "L'Occitane Joins Alibaba's Tmall—French Skin-Care Brand Launches Store on Shopping Site in Move to Combat Unauthorized Sales," *Wall Street Journal* (December 10, 2014): n.a.; and Iolanda D'Amato and Thanos Papadimitriou, "Legitimate vs. Illegitimate: The Luxury Supply Chain and Its Doppelganger," *International Journal of Retail & Distribution Management* 41:11/12 (2013): 986–1007.

16 Stephen Magee, "Information and the MNC: An Appropriability Theory of Direct Foreign Investment," in Jagdish N. Bhagwati, ed., *The New International Economic Order* (Cambridge, MA: MIT Press, 1977): 317–40; C. W. Hill, L. P. Hwang, and W. C. Kim, "An Eclectic Theory of the Choice on International Entry Mode," *Strategic Management Journal* 11 (1990): 117–18; Ashish Arora and Andrea Fosfuri, "Wholly Owned Subsidiary versus Technology Licensing in the Worldwide Chemical Industry," *Journal of International Business Studies* 31:4 (2000): 555–72.

17 Jack Ewing, "The Royal Family Business," *New York Times* (December 4, 2013): B1+.

18 Fabio Gama "Managing Collaborative Ideation: The Role of Formal and Informal Appropriability Mechanisms," *International Entrepreneurship and Management Journal* 15:1 (March 2019): 97–118; Roger Strange and John Humphrey, "What Lies Between Market and Hierarchy? Insights from Internalization Theory and Global Value Chain Theory," *Journal of International Business Studies* 50:8 (October 2019): 1401–1413; and Graciela Corral de Zubielqui and Janice Jones, "The Influence of Trust and Collaboration with External Partners on Appropriability in Open Service Firms," *Journal of Technology Transfer* 44:2 (April 2019): 540–558.

19 Zaheer Kahn, Oded Shenkar, and Yong Kyu Lew, "Knowledge Transfer from International Joint Ventures to Local Suppliers in a Developing Economy," *Journal of International Business Studies* 46:6 (2015): 656–75; and Liliana Pérez-Nordtvedt, Debmalya Mukherjee, and Ben L. Kedia, "Cross-Border Learning, Technological Turbulence and Firm Performance," *Management International Review* 55:1 (2014): 32–51.

20 Anne-Wil Harzing, "Acquisitions versus Greenfield Investments: International Strategy and Management of Entry Modes," *Strategic Management Journal* 23:3 (2002): 211–27.

21 Jaideep Anand and Andrew Delios, "Absolute and Relative Resources as Determinants of International Acquisitions," *Strategic Management Journal* 23:2 (2002): 119–34.

22 Sergery Filippov, "Innovation and R&D in Emerging Russian Multinationals," *Economics, Management and Financial Markets,* 6:1 (March 2011): 182–206.

23 Geoff Dyer, Francesco Guerrera, and Alexandra Harney, "Chinese Companies Make Plans to Join the Multinational Club," *Financial Times* (June 23, 2005): 19.

24 "Beefed Up—The World's Largest Meat Company Is Brazilian, but Mostly Operates Abroad," *The Economist* (September 24, 2011): Special Report on the World Economy, 16.

25 Two such indications are from studies by Alan Gregory, which is cited in Kate Burgess, "Acquisitions in U.S. 'Disastrous' for British Companies," *Financial Times* (October 11, 2004): 18; and Ping Deng, "Absorptive Capacity and a Failed Cross-Border M&A," *Management Research Review* 33:7 (2010): 673–82.

26 John Child, David Faulkner, and Robert Pitethly, *The Management of International Acquisitions* (Oxford: Oxford University Press, 2001); Peter Martin, "A Clash of Corporate Cultures," *Financial Times* (June 2–3, 2001): Weekend section, xxiv.

27 "From Guard Shack to Global Giant," *The Economist* (January 12, 2013): 55–6.

28 Gabriel Baffour Awuah and Amal Mohamed, "Impact of Globalization: The Ability of Less Developed Countries' (LDCs') Firms to Cope with Opportunities and Challenges," *European Business Review* 23:1 (2011): 120–32; Rodney C. Shrader, "Collaboration and Performance in Foreign Markets: The Case of Young High-Technology Manufacturing Firms," *Academy of Management Journal* 44:1 (2001): 45–60.

29 Rahul Jacob, "Hong Kong Banks on New Disney Park for Boost," *Financial Times* (August 31, 2001): 6.

30 Paavo Ritala, "Coopetition Strategy—When Is It Successful? Empirical Evidence on Innovation and Market Performance," *British Journal of Management* 23:3 (September 2012): 307–24.

31 Phred Dvorak and Scott Kilman, "BHP Roils Potash Cartel," *Wall Street Journal* (August 25, 2010): 1.

32 John M. Connor, "Global Antitrust Prosecutions of Modern International Cartels," *Journal of Industry, Competition and Trade* 4:3 (2004): 239.

33 Luiz F. Mesquita and Sergio G. Lazzarini, "Horizontal and Vertical Relationships in Developing Economies: Implications for SMEs' Access to Global Markets," *Academy of Management Journal* 51:2 (2008): 359–80.

34 Destan Kandemir and G. Tomas Hult, "A Conceptualization of an Organizational Learning Culture in International Joint Ventures," *Industrial Marketing Management* 34:5 (2005): 440.

35 Robert F. Howe, "The Fall of the House of Mondavi," *Business 2.0* 6:3 (2005): 98.

36 Sebastian-Andrei Labes, "FDI Determinants in BRICs," *CES Working Papers* 13 (2015): 1–13.

37 Jia-Ruey Ou, "An Analytical Model for Innovating Localization Policy," *International Journal of Electronic Business Management* 8:2 (2010): 110–19.

38 Heather Berry, "Managing Valuable Knowledge in Weak IP Protection Countries," *Journal of International Business Studies* 48:7 (2017): 787–807.

39 "H&M Wins Back Name in Russia," *Managing Intellectual Property* (April 2007): 1; and Steven Seidenberg, "Trademark Squatting on the Rise in U.S." *Inside Counsel* (May 2010): n.p.

40 Julie Bennett, "Road to Foreign Franchises Is Paved with New Problems," *Wall Street Journal* (May 14, 2001): B10.

41 Pierre Dussauge, Bernard Garrette, and Will Mitchell, "Asymmetric Performance: The Market Share Impact of Scale and Link Alliances in the Global Auto Industry," *Strategic Management Journal* 25 (2004): 701–11; and Candace E. Ybarra and Thomas A. Turk, "Strategic Alliances with Competing Firms and Shareholder Value," *Journal of Management and Marketing Research* 6 (January 2011): 1–10.

42 Koen Dittrich and Geert Duysters, "Networking as a Means to Strategy Change: The Case of Open Innovation in Mobile Telephony," *Journal of Product Innovation Management* 24:6 (November 2007): 510–21.

43 Barry J. Dickinson, "Symbiotic Marketing: A Network Perspective," *Journal of Management and Marketing Research* 11 (September 2012): 1–27, offers many examples of horizontal alliances.

44 Viknesh Vijayenthiran, "Mercedes and Infiniti Form Mexican Joint Venture for Next-Generation Compact Car Production," *Motor Authority* (August 4, 2015), http://motorauthority.com/news/1028353 (accessed September 25, 2015).

45 Stefano Elia, Marcus M. Larsen, and Lucia Piscitello, "Entry Mode Deviation: A Behavioral Approach to Internalization Theory," *Journal of International Business Studies* 50:8 (October 2019): 1359–1371.

46 For an extensive discussion of these variables, see Farok J. Contractor and James Woodley, "How Do Alliance Partners Share the Value They Create? Determinants of the Value Split in International Technology Transfer Alliances," *Proceedings of the 54th Annual Meeting of the Academy of International Business* (Washington: 2012): n.p.

47 Melissa Maleske, "OFAC's Global Reach," *Inside Counsel* (August 2012): n.a.

48 Miguel Angel Asturias, *Strong Wind,* trans. Gregory Rabassa (New York: Delacorte Press, 1968): 112.

49 For an extensive treatise on the theory, see Robert A. Packenham, *The Dependency Movement: Scholarship and Politics in Development Studies* (Cambridge, MA: Harvard University Press, 1992). For some different national views of its validity, see Ndiva Kofele-Kale, "The Political Economy of Foreign Direct Investment: A Framework for Analyzing Investment Laws and Regulations in Developing Countries," *Law & Policy in International Business* 23:2/3 (1992): 619–71; and Stanley K. Sheinbaum, "Very Recent History Has Absolved Socialism," *New Perspectives Quarterly* 13:1 (1996).

50 Ravi Ramamurti, "The Obsolescing 'Bargaining Model'? MNC-Host Developing Country Relations Revisited," *Journal of International Business Studies* 32 (2001): 23; Yadong Luo, "Toward a Cooperative View of MNC-Host Government Relations: Building Blocks and Performance Implication," *Journal of International Business Studies* 32 (2001): 401.

51 Qing Liu, Ruosi Lu, and Chao Yang, "International Joint Ventures and Technology Diffusion: Evidence from China, *The World Economy* 43:1 (January 2020): 146+.

52 "Google and Samsung in Deal to Cooperate on Patents," *New York Times* (January 14, 2014): B4.

53 Fred Burton, Adam R. Cross, and Mark Rhodes, "Foreign Market Servicing Strategies of UK Franchisors: An Empirical Enquiry from a Transactions Cost Perspective," *Management International Review* 40:4 (2000): 373–400.

54 John K. Ryans, Jr., Sherry Lotz, and Robert Krampf, "Do Master Franchisors Drive Global Franchising?" *Marketing Management* 8:2 (1999): 33–8.

55 "Four Seasons Signs Management Contract with Three C Universal Developers," *Mint* [New Delhi] (April 21, 2011).

56 "Flagship Ventures Forms Strategic Innovation Partnerships with AstraZeneca, Nestlé Health Science and Bayer CropScience," *News Bites US – NASDAQ,* (May 6, 2015): n.p.

57 Daniel Michaels and Robert Wall, "Airbus-Boeing Speed Race Increasingly Takes Place on the Ground," *Wall Street Journal Online* (June 2015): 11, www.wsj.com/articles/airbus-boeing-speed-race-increasingly-takes-place-on-the-ground-1434042301 (accessed December 7, 2015).

58 "Essar Ports Announces Strategic Alliance with Port of Antwerp International," *PR Newswire* (May 31, 2012): n.p.

59 Luis Zalamea, "AeroRepublica, Copa Offer Details of New Alliance," *Aviation Daily* (March 11, 2005): 5.

60 Terrence Chea, "No Perfect Partnership," *Washington Post* (June 3, 2002): E1.

61 Anna Shaojie Cui, Roger J. Calantone, and David A. Griffith, "Strategic Change and Termination of Interfirm Partnerships," *Strategic Management Journal* 32:4 (April 2011): 402–23.

62 Mikhail Fridman, "BP Has Been Treating Russians as Subjects," *Financial Times* (July 7, 2008): 9.

63 David Ibison, "Culture Clashes Prove Biggest Hurdle to International Links," *Financial Times* (January 24, 2002): 17.

64 William H. Meyers, "Maxim's Name Is the Game," *New York Times Magazine* (May 3, 1987): 33–5; Christina Passariello, "Pierre Cardin Ready to Sell His Overstretched Label," *Wall Street Journal* (May 3, 2011): 1.

65 Ramit Plushnick-Masti, "German Firm Faulted for Taking Vitamin out of Baby Formula," *Miami Herald* (November 12, 2003): 19A.

66 Annette P. Tower, Kelly Hewett, and Anton P. Fenik, "The Role of Cultural Distance Across Quantiles of International Joint Venture Longevity," *Journal of International Marketing:* 27:4 (December 2019): 3–21.

67 Diana Elena Ranf, "Cultural Differences in Project Management," *Annales Universitatis Apulensis Series Oeconomica* 12:2 (2010): 657–62; and Marshall Geiger and Joyce van der Laan Smith, "The Effect of Institutional and Cultural Factors on the Perceptions of Earnings Management," *Journal of International Accounting Research* 9:2 (2010): 21–43.

68 James T. Areddy, "Danone Pulls Out of Disputed China Venture," *Wall Street Journal* (October 1, 2009): B1.

69 Gokhun Ertug, Ilya R. P. Cuypers, Niels G. Noorderhaven, and Ben B. Bensaou, "Trust Between International Joint Venture Partners: Effects of Home Countries," *Journal of International Business Studies* 44 (2013): 263–82.

70 Seung Ho Park and Gerardo R. Ungson, "The Effect of National Culture, Organizational Complementarity, and Economic Motivation on Joint Venture Dissolution," *Academy of Management Journal* 40:2 (April 1997): 279–307; Harry G. Barkema, Oded Shenkar, Freek Vermeulen, and John H. J. Bell, "Working Abroad, Working with Others: How Firms Learn to Operate International Joint Ventures," *Academy of Management Journal* 40:2 (April 1997): 426–42, found survival differences only for differences in uncertainty avoidance.

71 Riikka M. Sarala and Eero Vaara, "Cultural Differences, Convergence, and Crossvergence as Explanations of Knowledge Transfer in International Acquisitions," *Journal of International Business Studies* 41:8 (October–November 2010): 1365–90.

72 Tabuchi, loc. cit.

73 Akbar Zaheer, Exequiel Hernandez, and Sanjay Banerjee, "Prior Alliances with Targets and Acquisition Performance in Knowledge-Intensive Industries," *Organization Science* 21:5 (September–October 2010): 1072–91+.

74 Mike W. Peng and Oded Shenkar, "Joint Venture Dissolution as Corporate Divorce," *Academy of Management Executive* 16:2 (May 2002): 92–105.

75 Doug Cameron, "U.S. Airline Merger to Affect Alliances," *Wall Street Journal (Online)* (February 14, 2013): n.p.; Adrian Schofield, "JAL, British Airways Code-Share Another Step Toward Joint Venture," *Aviation Daily* 389:46 (September 5, 2012): n.p.; Anne Smith and Marie-Claude Reney, "The Mating Dance: A Case Study of Local Partnering Processes in Developing Countries," *European Management Journal* 15:2 (1997): 174–82.

76 Linda H.Y. Hsieh and Suzana B. Rodrigues, "Partner Trustworthiness and Ex Post Governance Choice in International Joint Ventures: The Role of Performance Satisfaction," *AIB 2012 Proceedings of 54th Annual Meeting* (Washington: June 30–July 3, 2012).

77 Africa Ariño and Jeffrey J. Reuer, "Designing and Renegotiating Strategic Alliance Contracts," *Academy of Management Executive* 18:3 (2004): 37–48.

78 Sanjiv Kumar and Anju Seth, "The Design of Coordination and Control Mechanisms for Managing Joint Venture–Parent Relationships," *Strategic Management Journal* 19:6 (June 1998): 579–99; T. K. Das and Bing-Sheng Teng, "Between Trust and Control: Developing Confidence in Partner Cooperation in Alliances," *Academy of Management Journal* 23:3 (July 1998): 491–512; Arvind Parkhe, "Building Trust in International Alliances," *Journal of World Business* 33:4 (1998): 417–37; Prashant Kale, Harbir Singh, and Howard Perlmutter, "Learning and Protection of Proprietary Assets in Strategic Alliances: Building Relational Capital," *Strategic Management Journal* 21:3 (March 2000): 217–37; and Dina Preston-Ortiz, "The Effects of Trust in Virtual Strategic-Alliance Performance Outcomes," unpublished doctoral dissertation (Phoenix: University of Phoenix, 2010).

79 Srilata Zaheer and Akbar Zaheer, "Trust across Borders," *Journal of International Business Studies* 37:1 (2006): 21.

80 Gary D. Burton, David Ahlstrom, Michael N. Young, and Yuri Rubanik, "In Emerging Markets, Know What Your Partners Expect," *Wall Street Journal* (December 15, 2008): R5.

81 Bharat Anand and Tarun Khanna, "Do Firms Learn to Create Value? The Case of Alliances," *Strategic Management Journal* 21:3 (March 2000): 295–315; Anthony Goerzen and Paul W. Beamish, "The Effect of Alliance Network Diversity on Multinational Enterprise Performance," *Strategic Management Journal* 26 (2005): 333–54; and Maurizio Zollo and Jeffrey J. Reuer, "Experience Spillovers Across Corporate Development Activities," *Organization Science* 21:6 (November–December 2010): 1195–1212.

82 Prashant Kale and Harbir Singh, "Managing Strategic Alliances: What Do . We Know Now and Where Do We Go from Here?" *Academy of Management Perspectives* 23:3 (August 2009): 45–62.

83 Rachelle C. Sampson, "Experience Effects and Collaborative Returns in R&D Alliances," *Strategic Management Journal* 26 (2005): 1009–31.

84. Christian Schwens, Florian B. Zapkau, Keith D. Brouthers, and Lina Hollender, "Limits to International Entry Mode Learning in SMEs," *Journal of International Business Studies* 49:7 (2018): 809–831.

85 John Kenneth Galbraith, *American Capitalism* (Boston: Houghton Mifflin, 1952): 91–2.

86 "Schumpeter: Managing Partners," *The Economist* (May 23, 2013): 57.

87 Eric H. Kessler, Paul E. Bierly, and Shanthi Gopalakrishnan, "Internal vs. External Learning in New Product Development: Effects of Speed, Costs and Competitive Advantage," *R & D Management* 30:3 (2000): 213–23.

88 Adrian Wooldridge, "Return of the Giants," *The Economist* (The World in 2013 edition): 25.

89 These are adapted from Arvind Parkhe, "Interfirm Diversity, Organizational Learning, and Longevity in Global Strategic Alliances," *Journal of International Business Studies* 22:4 (1991): 579–601.

90 *Sources include the following:* We wish to acknowledge the assistance of several American Airlines and oneworld executives, who, although wishing to remain anonymous, supplied useful information for and feedback on this case. Additional information came from "American Airlines to Operate Only Service between New York and Japan's Tokyo International Airport at Haneda after Historic Open Skies Agreement," *Entertainment Newsweekly* (March 4, 2011): 172; Andrea Ahles, "American Airlines, Japan Airlines Announce Joint Venture," *McClatchy–Tribune Business News* (January 12, 2011): n.p.; Julie Johnsson, "American Airlines Combining Pacific Flights with Japan Airlines," *McClatchy–Tribune Business News* (January 12, 2011): n.p.; "American to Move Its Asia–Pacific Regional Office to the Japan Airlines Building in Tokyo," *Journal of Transportation* (September 18, 2010): 26; "Japan Airlines and American Airlines Announce Joint Business Benefits for Trans-Pacific Consumers," *The Pak Banker* (January 11, 2011): n.p.; "Airline Profits to Tumble in 2011: IATA," *The Pak Banker* (June 8, 2011): n.p.; "Europe: Trans-Atlantic Alliances Are Set to Tighten," *Oxford Analytica Daily Brief Service* (January 3, 2008): 1; Alfred Kahn and Dorothy Robyn, "The Sky Must Be No Limit to Global Competition," *Financial Times* (February 15, 2006): 17; Bruce Bernard, "American Airlines Seeks OK for Trans-Atlantic Tie-up," *Journal of Commerce Online* (August 15, 2008); International Air Transport Association, *Annual Report* (2008); "Aer Lingus Set for Second oneworld," *Airline Business* 31:7 (2015): 43; Linda Ball, "Will Qater Pull Out of oneworld?" *Air Cargo World* 18: 6 (2015): 16.

Chapter 16

1 For the record, DuPont's trade name for PTFE is Teflon.

2 "Innovation Democracy: W. L. Gore's Original Management Model," *Management Innovation eXchange*, https://bit.ly/2I3qyNm (accessed March 16, 2016);

3 Deborah Ancona, Elaine Backman, Kate Isaacs,"Nimble Leadership," *Harvard Business Review* (July–August 2019), https://bit.ly/2uFqK2g.

4 The World's Best Multinational Workplaces ranking is the world's largest annual study of workplace excellence and identifies the top 25 best multinational companies in terms of workplace culture—"World's Best Multinational Workplaces." See Great Place to Work,"World's Best Workplaces 2017," United States, https://bit.ly/2Tzlupt (accessed January 8, 2019).

5 As noted on page 2 in W. L. Gore's Culture Press Kit: "These early influences helped pave the way for a company culture that by all accounts was ahead of its time. A place that believes in every individual and encourages experimentation, healthy risk taking, personal growth and development, and shared ownership for success. A place where we 'make money and have fun doing so' (to use Bill's own words). And a place where every Associate—not employee—has the power to make a difference, not just within the company but across industries and around the world. Gore was built on a dream, and our founders' vision continues to shape who we are today. See "Culture Press Kit," https://bit.ly/2T64aJu (accessed January 8, 2019).

6 Technically, the titles of president and secretary-treasurer were used only because they were required by the laws of incorporation.

7 Characteristics of a lattice structure include: Lines of communication are direct—person to person—with no intermediary; No fixed or assigned authority; Sponsors, not bosses; Natural leadership defined by followership; Objectives are set by those who must "make them happen"; Tasks and functions organized through commitments.

8 For those wondering how this happens, officially, the company explains "Associates (not employees) are hired for general work areas. With the guidance of their sponsors (not bosses) and a growing understanding of opportunities and team objectives, associates commit to projects that match their skills. All of this takes place in an environment that combines freedom with cooperation and autonomy with synergy. Everyone can earn the credibility to define and drive projects. Sponsors help associates chart a course in the organization that will offer personal fulfilment while maximizing their contribution to the enterprise. Leaders may be appointed but are defined by 'followership.' More often, leaders emerge naturally by demonstrating special knowledge, skill, or experience that advances a business objective."

9 "Culture Press Kit," https://bit.ly/2T64aJu (accessed January 8, 2020); "Gore Culture," W. L. Gore & Associates, https://bit.ly/384tMuG (accessed March 17, 2019).

10 Gary Hamel, "Innovation Democracy: W.L. Gore's Original Management Model," https://bit.ly/2TlELdH (accessed February 29, 2020).

11 "Culture Press Kit," https://bit.ly/2T64aJu (accessed February 14, 2020).

12 Quote extracted from "Gore Recognized as One of the World's Best Multinational Workplaces by Great Place to Work®," www.gore.com/en_xx/news/best-multinational-places-to-work-2014.html (accessed September 23, 2015).

13 Personal conversation, March 17, 2016, e-mail exchange.

14 For example, Gore has installed Project Management Office that conducts a leadership review of all projects every 6 months.

15 This unique kind of corporate structure has proven to be a significant contributor to Associate satisfaction and retention.

16 Quote extracted from "W. L. Gore & Associates: Developing Global Teams to Meet 21st-Century Challenges," http://webcache.googleusercontent.com/search?q=cache:ho6ojanol68J:cets.coop/moodle/pluginfile.php/179/mod_data/content/754/Gore_case26_C391-C405.pdf+&cd=1&hl=en&ct=clnk&gl=us (accessed September 23, 2015).

17 Courtney Young and Sumantra Ghoshal, *Organization theory and the multinational corporation* (Springer, 2016); Martin Dewhurst, Jonathan Harris, and Suzanne Heywood, "The Global Company's Challenge," *McKinsey Quarterly*, December 31, 2012, https://mck.co/2PC5WQt.

18 Aaron De Smet and Chris Gagnon, "8 Ways to Build a Future-Proof Organization | McKinsey & Company," June 4, 2018, https://mck.co/2veBaGu (accessed February 27, 2020).

19 Simon Clark and Margot Patrick, "HSBC to Cut 35,000 Jobs and $100 Billion of Assets," *Wall Street Journal*, https://on.wsj.com/3aiRgO1 (February 18 2020; accessed February 18, 2020).

20 "Walmart International Sales 1997–2019 and Number of Stores outside US in 201," https://corporate.walmart.com/our-story/our-business (accessed February 30, 2020).

21 Ian Urbina and Keith Bradsher, "Linking Factories to the Malls, Middleman Pushes Low Costs," *New York Times* 8 (2013).

22 "Hungry Tiger, Dancing Elephant: How India Is Changing IBM's World," *The Economist* (April 4, 2007): 58–61.

23 Alfred P. Sloan and John McDonald, eds., *My Years with General Motors* (New York: Doubleday, 1964).

24 Chris Bartlett, "MNCs: Get Off the Reorganization Merry-Go-Round," *Harvard Business Review* (March–April 1983): 88–101; Mike Geppert, Florian Becker-Ritterspach, and Ram Mudambi, "Politics and Power in Multinational Companies: Integrating the International Business and Organization Studies Perspectives," *Organization Studies* 37, no. 9 (2016): 1209–1225; Florian Becker-Ritterspach, Knut Lange, and Karin Lohr, "Reorganization in MNCs," *Challenges for European Management in a Global Context: Experiences from Britain and Germany* (2016): 68.

25 Craig W. Fontaine, "Organization Structure," *Human Resource Management Knowledge Base*, Northeastern University (August 2007).

26 Alfred Dupont Chandler, *Strategy and structure: Chapters in the history of the industrial enterprise*, Vol. 120 (MIT Press, 1990).

27 Lucia Darino, Bryan Hancock, and Kate Lazaroff-Puck, "Employee Motivation in the Age of Automation and Agility," December 9, 2019, https://bit.ly/2uHgnLm (accessed February 28, 2020).

28 Harold Sirkin, James Hemerling, and Arindam Bhattacharya, *Globality: Competing with Everyone from Everywhere for Everything* (New York: Business Plus, 2008).

29 Richard Daft, *Organization Theory and Design* (Cengage Learning, 2018); Andrea Whittle, Frank Mueller, Alan Gilchrist, and Peter Lenney, "Sensemaking, Sense-Censoring and Strategic Inaction: The Discursive Enactment of Power and Politics in a Multinational Corporation," *Organization Studies* 37, no. 9 (2016): 1323–1351.

30 "Nestlé Is Starting to Slim Down at Last," *Businessweek* (October 27, 2003): 56–8; "Daring, Defying, to Grow," *The Economist* (August 7, 2004): 55–7; Scott Keller and Mary Meaney, "Reorganizing to Capture Maximum Value Quickly | McKinsey" (accessed December 30, 2018).

31 Gunnar Hedlund, "Organization in-between: The Evolution of the Mother-Daughter Structure of Managing Foreign Subsidiaries in Swedish MNCs," *Journal of International Business Studies* 15:2 (1984): 109–123.

32 Ibid., Simon Clark and Margot Patrick.

33 Andria Cheng, "Nike Reorganizes into Six Geographic Regions: Faster-Growing China, Eastern Europe Regions to be Managed Separately," *MarketWatch* (March 20, 2009).

34 "Japanese Firms Push into Emerging Markets: The New Frontier for Corporate Japan," *The Economist* (April 19, 2011), www.economist.com/node/16743435.

35 See Toby Gibbs, Suzanne Heywood, and Leigh Weiss, "Organizing for an Emerging World," *McKinsey Quarterly* (June 2012).

36 Eric Rosenbaum, "IBM Artificial Intelligence Can Predict with 95% Accuracy Which Workers Are About to Quit Their Jobs," *CNBC* (April 3, 2019), https://cnb.cx/2TsKluL (accessed March 1, 2020).

37 John W. Hunt, "Is Matrix Management a Recipe for Chaos?" *Financial Times* (January 12, 1998): 10.

38 Scott Keller and Mary Meaney, "Reorganizing to Capture Maximum Value Quickly | McKinsey," https://mck.co/397X0tI (accessed December 30, 2018); Phil Rosenzweig, *The Halo Effect: How Managers Let Themselves Be Deceived* (New York, NY: Free Press, 2007).

39 Richard Hodgetts, "Dow Chemical CEO William Stavropoulos on Structure," *Academy of Management Executive* (May 30, 1999): 30.

40 Spin-Off Insights, "P&G: The Largest Organizational Change in 20 Years," *Seeking Alpha*, https://bit.ly/2VrImJN (November 19, 2018); "Procter & Gamble Unveils Simpler Management Structure," *Reuters* (November 8, 2018), https://reut.rs/2T41E6A.

41 "The New Organisation," *The Economist* (February 24, 2013): 63.

42 Christian Weinberg, "Why Lego Is Snapping Off 1,400 Jobs," *Just Sayin'* (blog), https://bit.ly/2Tkyv61 (September 6, 2017).

43 Aaron De Smet, Sarah Kleinman, and Kirsten Weerda, "Beyond Matrix Organization, the Helix Organization | McKinsey," https://mck.co/39eXe2b.

44 Hiroko Tabuchi and Brooks Barnes, "Sony Chief Is Still in Search of a Turnaround," *New York Times* (May 26, 2011): A1.

45 Statement from Jack Welch's Letter to Shareholders,"Boundaryless Company in a Decade of Change," reported in GE's 1990 *Annual Report.*

46 "Gore: Our Culture," www.gore.com/en_xx/aboutus/culture/ (accessed May 1, 2013); "W. L. Gore & Associates—Best Companies to Work For 2012," *Fortune,* money.cnn.com/magazines/fortune/best-companies/2012/snapshots/38.html (accessed May 1, 2013).

47 "The World According to Chambers," *The Economist* (August 27, 2009): 81–4.

48 "Tesla CEO Musk Says Company Is 'Flattening Management Structure' in Reorganization—WSJ," https://on.wsj.com/2T63l3f (accessed December 30, 2018).

49 Ibid., Spin-Off Insights, "P&G: The Largest Organizational Change in 20 Years."

50 General Stanley McChrystal, Tantum Collins, David Silverman, and Chris Fussell, *Team of Teams: New Rules of Engagement for a Complex World* (New York: Portfolio, 2015); ibid., De Smet and Gagnon.

51 W. Baker, "The Network Organization in Theory and Practice," in *Networks and Organizations,* eds. N. Nohria and R. Eccles (Cambridge, MA: Harvard Business School Press, 1992): 327–429.

52 "ING's Agile Transformation | McKinsey," https://mck.co/32ymJsN (accessed January 1, 2019).

53 Characteristics of a lattice structure include: Lines of communication are direct—person to person—with no intermediary; No fixed or assigned authority; Sponsors, not bosses; Natural leadership defined by followership; Objectives are set by those who must "make them happen"; Tasks and functions are organized through commitments.

54 Yves Doz and Keeley Wilson, *Managing Global Innovation: Frameworks for Integrating Capabilities around the World* (Harvard Business Press Books, 2012).

55 Gibbs, Toby, Suzanne Heywood, and Leigh Weiss, "Organizing for an Emerging World | McKinsey," https://mck.co/2PwEPGr (accessed January 4, 2019).

56 The *keiretsu* appeared in Japan during the "economic miracle" following World War II. Before Japan's surrender, Japanese industry was controlled by large family-controlled vertical monopolies called *zaibatsu.*

57 "Presidential Politics in South Korea: Bashing the Big Guys," *The Economist* (October 13, 2012): 49.

58 "The New, Improved Keiretsu," *Harvard Business Review,* https://hbr.org/2013/09/the-new-improved-keiretsu (accessed March 7, 2016).

59 "ING's Agile Transformation | McKinsey," https://mck.co/32wgkOO (accessed January 2, 2019).

60 Jenni L. Hebert, "The Identification of Leadership Competencies within a Global Virtual Organization" (PhD dissertation, The Chicago School of Professional Psychology, 2017).

61 Dmitry Ivanov, Boris Sokolov, and Joachim Kaeschel, "Structure Dynamics Control-Based Framework for Adaptive Reconfiguration of Collaborative Enterprise Networks," *International Journal of Manufacturing Technology and Management* 17 (2009): 23.

62 Áine Cain, "In a Leaked Video, Ikea US Head Apologizes for Restructuring That Store Employees Say Tanked Morale and Pit Them against Each Other," *Business Insider,* https://bit.ly/2uB20rQ (accessed December 30, 2018).

63 "Schumpeter: Corporate Burlesque," *The Economist* (November 3, 2012): 68.

64 Nicolai J. Foss, "Selective Intervention and Internal Hybrids: Interpreting and Learning from the Rise and Decline of the Oticon Spaghetti Organization," *Organization Science* 14 (May–June 2003): 331–50.

65 Patrick Kiger, "Hidden Hierarchies," *Workforce Management* (February 27, 2006): 24.

66 Frederick Winslow Taylor, *Scientific Management* (Routledge, 2004).

67 Karen Beaman, "An Interview with Christopher Bartlett," *Boundaryless HR: Human Capital Management in the Global Economy* (San Francisco: IHRIM Press, June 2002).

68 Darrell Rigby, "Bain & Company's 2005 Management Tools & Trends" (August 2, 2005), www.bain.com/management_tools.

69 Adam Lashinsky, "Chaos by Design," *Fortune* (October 2, 2006); Geoffrey Colvin, "Managing in Chaos," *Fortune* (October 2, 2006).

70 Lowell Bryan and Claudia Joyce, "The 21st-Century Organization," *The McKinsey Quarterly* 3 (2005).

71 Ibid., Martin Dewhurst, Jonathan Harris, and Suzanne Heywood.

72 Ibid., Aaron De Smet, Sarah Kleinman, and Kirsten Weerda; Tony Hsieh, "Holacracy and Self-Organization," *Zappos.com,* https://bit.ly/32Forsm (both accessed March 1, 2020).

73 Loren Cary, "The Rise of Hyperarchies," *Harvard Business Review* (March 2004).

74 Karl-Heinrich Grote and Erik K. Antonsson, eds., *Springer Handbook of Mechanical Engineering* (New York: Springer, 2009): 1344.

75 The Boston Consulting Group, "Reorganized Information Processing Vital to Improving U.S. Intelligence Capabilities," *BCG Media Releases* (May 6, 2007), www.bcg.com/news_media/news_media_releases.jsp?id=928.

76 Ibid., Lucia Darino, Bryan Hancock, and Kate Lazaroff-Puck.

77 In contrast, one could precisely design a structure that looks great on paper but struggles in the stress test of reality.

78 "The New Organisation," *The Economist* (February 24, 2013): 63; Yves Doz, "Managing Multinational Operations: From Organisational Structures to Mental Structures and from Operations to Innovations," *European Journal of International Management* 10, no. 1 (2016): 10–24.

79 More specifically, Grove reasoned: "Let chaos reign, then rein in chaos. Does that mean that you shouldn't plan? Not at all. You need to plan the way a fire department plans. It cannot anticipate fires, so it must shape a flexible organization that can respond to unpredictable events"; Michael E. Rock, "Case Example: Intel's Andy Grove," *CanadaOne* (October 31, 2007), www.canadaone.com/magazine/mr2060198.html.

80 "Innovations to Create New Streams of Profitable Growth," *Accenture Outlook,* www.accenture.com/in-en/outlook/Pages/outlook-journal-2010-less-is-new-more-innovation.aspx (accessed June 9, 2011).

81 "Starbucks Opens in India with Pomp and Tempered Ambition," *New York Times,* http://india.blogs.nytimes.com/2012/10/19/starbucks-opens-in-india-with-pomp-and-tempered-ambition/?_r=0 (accessed September 28, 2015).

82 Daniel Erasmus, "A Common Language for Strategy," *Financial Times* (April 5, 1999): 7–8.

83 Neil Perkins, "Agile Transformation at ING—A Case Study—Business Agility," https://bit.ly/2PF8PA0 (accessed March 2, 2020).

84 Michel Domsch and Elena Hristozova, eds., *Human Resource Management in Consulting* (New York: Springer, 2006).

85 Jakob Lauring and Ling Eleanor Zhang, "Knowledge Sharing Across National Cultural Boundaries and Multinational Corporations." In *The Palgrave Handbook of Knowledge Management,* pp. 381–407 (Palgrave Macmillan, Cham, 2018).

86 Innovations can arise anywhere within the firm's global network, not just at the center. The role of headquarters changes fundamentally.

87 Sumantra Ghoshal and Christopher Bartlett, "Changing the Role of Top Management: Beyond Structure to Process," *Harvard Business Review* 73 (January–February 1995): 93–4. "Corporate Spotlight Interview: 3M." https://bit.ly/2IcdsNR (accessed March 2, 2020).

88 F. Shipper, C. C. Manz, B. Nobles, and K. P. Manz, "Shared Entrepreneurship: Toward an Empowering, Ethical, Dynamic, and Freedom-Based Process of Collaborative Innovation," *Organization Management Journal,* 11:3 (2014): 133–46.

89 Acharya Ashwin, Ketan Chaudhry, J. Maxwell, and Matt Rosenstock, "Streamline Decision-Making for a Better Customer Journey | McKinsey & Company" (August 12, 2019), https://mck.co/2T4cs4s (accessed February 27, 2020).

90 Toby Gibbs, Suzanne Heywood, and Leigh Weiss, "Organizing for an Emerging World," *McKinsey Quarterly* (June 2012).

91 Pankaj Ghemawat, "Developing Global Leaders | McKinsey," https://mck.co/3ce8iyt (accessed January 4, 2019).

92 "The World According to Chambers," *The Economist* (August 27, 2009): 81–4.

93 Ibid., Dewhurst, Martin, Jonathan Harris, and Suzanne Heywood.

94 Sumantra Ghoshal, Gita Piramal, and Christopher A. Bartlett, *Managing Radical Change* (Penguin Books India, 2002): 318; Jack Welch and Suzy Welch, *Winning* (HarperCollins Publishers, 2005).

95 See H. Schwartz, "Matching Corporate Culture and Business Strategy," *Organizational Dynamics* 81:10 (1981): 30; J. B. Barney, "Organizational Culture: Can It Be a Source of Sustained Competitive Advantage?" *Academy of Management Review* 11:3 (1986).

96 Ibid., Martin Dewhurst, Jonathan Harris, and Suzanne Heywood.

97 Pankaj Ghemawat, "Developing Global Leaders | McKinsey," https://mck.co/32vzlB8 (accessed January 4, 2019).

98 Ibid., Dewhurst, Martin, Jonathan Harris, and Suzanne Heywood.

99 Pay is one thing, passion is another; see Stephen R. Covey and Rebecca R. Merrill, *The Speed of Trust: The One Thing That Changes Everything* (Simon and Schuster, 2006).

100 Chris Gagnon, Elizabeth John, and Rob Theunissen,"Organizational Health: A Fast Track to Performance Improvement | McKinsey," https://mck.co/2uFpXyk (accessed December 30, 2018).

101 Aaron De Smet and Chris Gagnon,"Company Organization in the Age of Urgency | McKinsey," https://mck.co/2VvyY82 (accessed December 30, 2018).

102 Richard Florida, *The Rise of the Creative Class* (New York: Basic Books, 2004); Charlotta Mellander and Richard Florida,"The Rise of the Global Creative Class," in *The Handbook of Global Science, Technology, and Innovation,* eds. Daniele Archibugi and Andrea Filipppetti (Wiley-Blackwell, 2015): 313–42.

103 Adam Bryant,"Google's 8-Point Plan to Help Managers Improve," NYTimes.com, www.nytimes.com/2011/03/13/business/13hire.html?hp (accessed March 12, 2011).

104 Cain, Áine,"In a Leaked Video, Ikea US Head Apologizes for Restructuring That Store Employees Say Tanked Morale and Pit Them against Each Other," *Business Insider,* https://bit.ly/39b0XOo (accessed December 30, 2018).

105 James Charles Collins, *Good to Great: Why Some Companies Make the Leap... and Others Don't* (New York: Random House, 2001).

106 Ibid.

107 Natalie Djodat and Dodo zu Knyphausen-Aufseß,"Revisiting Ghoshal and Bartlett's Theory of the Multinational Corporation as an Interorganizational Network," *Management International Review* 57, no. 3 (2017): 349–78.

108 Alison Maitland,"Bridging the Culture Gap," *Financial Times* (January 28, 2002): 8.

109 Ibid., Martin Dewhurst, Jonathan Harris, and Suzanne Heywood.

110 Tatiana Kostova,"Transnational Transfer of Strategic Organizational Practices: A Contextual Perspective," *Academy of Management Review* 24 (1999): 308–24.

111 "Staffing Globalisation: Travelling More Lightly," *The Economist* (June 23, 2006): 55.

112 Quote extracted from "Gore Recognized as One of the World's Best Multinational Workplaces by Great Place to Work®," www.gore.com/en_xx/news/best-multinational-places-to-work-2014.html (accessed September 23, 2015).

113 Martin Fackler,"The 'Toyota Way' Is Translated for a New Generation of Foreign Managers," *New York Times,* www.nytimes.com/2007/02/15/business/worldbusiness/15toyota.html (accessed August 5, 2010).

114 "The Toyota Way: Our Values and Way of Working," https://bit.ly/2wr0cSH (accessed March 2, 2020).

115 Ibid., Martin Fackler.

116 Rebecca Knight,"Corporate Universities: Move to a Collaborative Effort," *Financial Times* (March 19, 2007);"Book Review: Corporate Universities. Drivers of the Learning Organization—Kasper Spiro" (2016), http://kasperspiro.com/2015/05/11/book-review-corporate-universities-drivers-of-the-learning-organization/ (accessed January 7).

117 Aaron De Smet, Susan Lund, and William Schaninger,"Organizing for the Future | McKinsey," https://mck.co/2uBOF2B (accessed December 30, 2018).

118 Eric Rosenbaum,"IBM AI Can Predict with 95 Percent Accuracy Which Employees Will Quit," https://cnb.cx/37Zql8s (accessed April 3, 2019).

119 "Humanyze—Analytics for Better Performance," *Humanyze,* www.humanyze.com/ (accessed January 3, 2019);"Google's New Earbuds Can Translate 40 Languages," *BuzzFeed News,* https://bit.ly/2I3U4SY (accessed January 3, 2019).

120 Ibid, Eric Rosenbaum.

121 *Sources include the following:* www.jnj.com; J&J's 2007, 2008, 2009, 2010, 2011, 2012, 2013, 2014, 2015, 2016, 2017, 2018 Annual Reports;"8 Fun Facts About Our Credo—Johnson & Johnson's Mission Statement," *Content Lab—U.S.* (February 6, 2018), https://bit.ly/3855nF6;"Our Commitment to Innovation," *Content Lab—U.S.* (accessed January 3, 2019).

122 Thomas Sullivan,"A Tough Road: Cost to Develop One New Drug Is $2.6 Billion; Approval Rate for Drugs Entering Clinical Development Is Less Than 12%—Policy & Medicine" (June 21, 2019), https://bit.ly/3cjYhA0 (accessed February 29, 2020).

123 "A Big Company That Works," *Businessweek,* www.businessweek.com/stories/1992-05-03/a-big-company-that-works(accessed February 25, 2013).

124 Johnson & Johnson CEO William Weldon: Leadership in a Decentralized Company," Knowledge@Wharton, https://whr.tn/2uKEDfu (accessed March 2, 2020).

125 Management, Strategic, Global Focus, and North America,"Patients versus Profits at Johnson & Johnson: Has the Company Lost Its Way?" Knowledge@Wharton, https://whr.tn/39iMAYe (accessed March 2, 2020).

126 J&J's 2008 Annual Report,"Our Strategic Framework," Johnson & Johnson, www.jnj.com/caring/citizenship-sustainability/strategic-framework (accessed February 15, 2016).

127 Extracted from J&J 2007 Annual Report.

128 "8 Fun Facts About Our Credo—Johnson & Johnson's Mission Statement," *Content Lab—U.S.* (February 6, 2019), https://bit.ly/3855nF6.

129 From the CEO to the employees of the smallest unit, management believes that the people and their values are the firm's greatest assets. Senior executives note that rank-and-file workers have created product breakthroughs, process innovations, and customer insights. In and of itself, such praise is not terribly unusual. Many companies—perhaps even some that you have worked for—have likely expressed similar sentiments

Chapter 17

1 *Sources include the following:* Lisa Lockwood,"Tommy Hilfiger Is Official Sponsor of Hahnenkamm Ski Races, *Women's Wear Daily* (November 25, 2019):2; Jacob Gallagher,"How '90s Clothing Brands Are Using Retro Designs to Entice Millennials," *Wall Street Journal (online)* (October 29, 2018); Fred Gehring,"How I Did It ... Tommy Hilfiger's Chairman on Going Private to Spark a Turnaround," *Harvard Business Review* 93:7/8 (July/August 2015): 33–6; "PVH Corp Annual Shareholders Meeting—Final," *Fair Disclosure Wire* (June 18, 2015): 1–14;"Tommy Thriving Under PVH Ownership," *Women's Wear Daily* 203:82 (April 19, 2012): n/a; Joe Fernandez,"Fashion: Hilfiger to Use 'Delebs' for Silver Anniversary," *Marketing Week* (June 10, 2010): 4; Miles Socha and Joelle Diderich,"Hilfiger: American in Paris," *Women's Wear Daily,* 200:107 (November 18, 2010): n.p.;"Tommy Hilfiger," *Investment Weekly News* (April 23, 2011): 898; Michael Barbaro,"Macy's and Hilfiger Strike Exclusive Deal," *New York Times* (October 27, 2007): 1; Cathy Horyn,"Still Tommy after All These Years," *New York Times* (December 7, 2008): Sec. M3, 182; Teri Agins,"Costume Change," *Wall Street Journal* (February 2, 2007): A1+; Miles Socha,"Tommy Takes Paris," *DNR* (October 23, 2006): 26; Miles Socha,"Tommy's Latest Take," *WWD* (October 20, 2006): 1; Julie Naughton,"Hilfiger and Lauder Aim for Perfect 10," *WWD* (June 23, 2006): 4; Lisa Lockwood,"CEO Says Tommy to Now Trade Up," *WWD* (May 11, 2006): 3.

2 Stefan Schmid and Thomas Kotulla,"50 Years of Research on International Standardization and Adaptation—From a Systematic Literature Analysis to a Theoretical Framework," *IBIB Review* 20 (2011): 491–507.

3 "Tommy Hilfiger Thriving Under PVH Ownership," *WWD* (April 19, 2012): n.p.

4 Constantine S. Katsikeas, Saeed Damiee, and Marios Theodosiou,"Strategy Fit and Performance Consequences of International Marketing Standardization," *Strategic Management Journal* 27 (2006): 867–90.

5 Schmid and Kotulla,"50 Years of Research on International Standardization and Adaptation."

6 Karina R. Jensen,"Creating Global Innovation Opportunities through Cross-Cultural Collaboration," *The International Journal of Knowledge, Culture and Change Management* 10:10 (2011): 33–42.

7 Ruby P. Lee, Qimei Chen, Daekwan Kim, and Jean L. Johnson,"Knowledge Transfer between Multinational Corporations' Headquarters and Their Subsidiaries: Influences on and Implications for New Product Outcomes," *Journal of International Marketing* 16:2 (2008): 1–31.

8 Matt Moffett,"Learning to Adapt to a Tough Market, Chilean Firms Pry Open Door to Japan," *Wall Street Journal* (June 7, 1994): A10.

9 Margarita Stancati and Preetika Rana,"Hermès Goes Local with India Sari Launch," *Wall Street Journal* (October 12, 2011): n.p.

10 Peter Evans and Caitlan Reeg,"Personal-Care Firms Uncover New Markets," *Wall Street Journal* (May 20, 2014): B7.

11 Manoj K. Agarwal,"Developing Global Segments and Forecasting Market Shares: A Simultaneous Approach Using Survey Data," *Journal of International Marketing* 11:4 (2003): 56.

12 Rosalie L. Tung, "The Cross-Cultural Research Imperative: The Need to Balance Cross-National and Intra-National Diversity," *Journal of IBIB Studies* 39:1 (2008): 41–46; James Agarwal, Naresh Malhotra, and Ruth N. Bolton, "A Cross-National and Cross-Cultural Approach to Global Market Segmentation: An Application Using Consumers' Perceived Service Quality," *Journal of International Marketing* 18:3 (2010): 18–40.

13 Ed Hammond, "Red Bull: Where Marketing Goes into Overdrive," *Financial Times* (September 27, 2011): n.p.

14 "Ferrari Makes India Debut," *Wall Street Journal* (May 27, 2011): n.p.

15 Rebecca Rose, "Global Diversity Gets All Cosmetic," *Financial Times* (April 10–11, 2004): W11.

16 Constantine S. Katsikeas, Saeed Samiee, and Marios Theodosiou, "Strategy Fit and Performance Consequences of International Marketing Standardization," *Strategic Management Journal* 27 (2006): 867–90.

17 "Look What They've Done to My Brands," *The Economist* (November 17, 2012): 60.

18 Adam Janofsky, "Franchising: Why Burger King Is Selling a Squid-Ink Burger," *Wall Street Journal* (May 26, 2015): R4.

19 Laurie Burkitt, "Home Depot: Chinese Prefer 'Do-It-for-Me'" *Wall Street Journal* (September 15, 2012): B1.

20 Louise Lucas, "Multinationals Try to Make the Most of their Local Credentials," *Financial Times* (September 22, 2010): Peru section, 10.

21 Paul Sonne, Devon Maylie, and Drew Hinshaw, "With West Flat, Big Brewers Peddle Cheap Beer in Africa," *Wall Street Journal* (March 20, 2013): A1+.

22 Orit Gadiesh and Till Vestring, "The Consequences of China's Rising Global Heavyweights," *MIT Sloan Management Review* 49:3 (Spring 2008): 10–11.

23 Keith Bradsher, "India Gains on China among Multinationals," *International Herald Tribune* (June 12–13, 2004): 13.

24 Stefan Schmid and Thomas Kotulla, "To What Degree Should Firms Standardize or Adapt Their Product Mix Across Countries? New Empirical Results Based on the Strategic-Fit Approach," Paper presented at the Academy of AIB annual meeting, Washington, DC (2012).

25 Yonca Limon, Lynn R. Kahle, and Ulrich R. Orth, "Package Design as a Communications Vehicle in Cross-Cultural Values Shopping," *Journal of International Marketing* 17:1 (2009): 30–57.

26 "The World's Wash Day," *Financial Times*, 6.

27 "Nike Faces Marketing Challenge in China: Make Running Cool," *Advertising Age* (October 20, 2011): n.p.

28 Ian Austen and Stephanie Clifford, "North of the Border," *New York Times* (November 15, 2012): B1+.

29 Saeed Samiee, "International Marketing Strategy in Emerging-Market Exporting Firms," *Journal of International Marketing* 27:1 (March 2019): 20.

30 James A. Roberts and Chris Manolis, "Cooking Up a Recipe for Self-Control: The Three Ingredients of Self-Control and Its Impact on Impulse Buying," *Journal of Marketing Theory and Practice* 20:2 (Spring 2012): 173–88.

31 Jenny Wiggins and Chris Flood, "Coke to Shrink Size of Cans in Hong Kong," *Financial Times* (July 25, 2008): 18.

32 Edward W. Miles, "The Role of Face in the Decision Not to Negotiate," *International Journal of Conflict Management* 21:4 (2010): 400–14.

33 C. Gopinath, "Fixed Price and Bargaining," *Business Line* (July 15, 2002): 1.

34 Claude Cellich, "FAQ . . . about Business Negotiations on the Internet," *International Trade Forum* 1 (2001): 10–11.

35 Jan H. Schumann, Florian V. Wagenheim, Anne Stringfellow, Zhilin Yang, Vera Blazevic, Sandra Praxmarer, G. Shainesh, Marcin Komor, Randall M. Shannon, and Fernando R. Jiménez, "Cross-Cultural Differences in the Effect of Received Word-of-Mouth Referral in Relational Service Exchange," *Journal of International Marketing* 18:3 (2010): 62–80.

36 Loretta Chao, "PC Makers Cultivate Buyers in Rural China," *Wall Street Journal* (September 23, 2009): B1.

37 Jamie Anderson, Martin Kupp, and Ronan Moaligou, "Lessons from the Developing World," *Wall Street Journal* (August 17, 2009): R6.

38 Owen M. Bradfield, Caroline Parker, and Leonie Goodwin, "Sustaining Performance: Learning from Buyers' Experience," *Journal of Medical Marketing* 9:4 (October 2009): 343–53.

39 Ed Hammond, loc. cit.

40 Charles Goldsmith, "Dubbing in Product Plugs," *Wall Street Journal* (December 6, 2004): B1+.

41 Ouidade Sabri, Delphine Manceau, and Bernard Pras, "Taboo: An Underexplored Concept in Marketing: RAM," *Recherche et Applications en Marketing* 25:1 (2010): 59–85.

42 Amy Guthrie, "Mexico Hits Food Ads for Children," *Wall Street Journal* (August 22, 2016): B6.

43 Gemma Charles, "Don't Be a Code Breaker," *Marketing* (March 17, 2010): 17; Ernest Cyril De Run, "Attitudes Towards Offensive Advertising: Malaysian Muslims' Views," *Journal of Islamic Marketing* 1:1 (2010): 25–36.

44 Deborah Ball, "Women in Italy Like to Clean but Shun the Quick and Easy," *Wall Street Journal* (April 25, 2006): A1+.

45 Andrew Ward, "Home Improvements Abroad," *Financial Times* (April 6, 2006): 8.

46 Sarah Ellison, "Sex-Themed Ads Often Don't Travel Well," *Wall Street Journal* (March 31, 2000): B7.

47 Arvind Sahay, "Finding the Right International Mix," *Financial Times* (November 16, 1998): Mastering Marketing section, 2–3.

48 "Stalkers, Inc.," *The Economist* (September 13, 2014): 18.

49 *New Zealand Business* 18:11 (2004): 21–27.

50 Rita Marcella and Sylvie Davies, "The Use of Customer Language in International Marketing Communication in the Scottish Food and Drink Industry," *European Journal of Marketing* 38:11/12 (2004): 1382.

51 Moen Øystein, Iver Endresen, and Morten Gavlen, "Executive Insights: Use of the Internet in International Marketing: A Case Study of Small Computer Software Firms," *Journal of International Marketing* 11:4 (2003): 129–44.

52 "What Are Brands For?" *The Economist* (August 30, 2014): 57–8; Jo Roberts, "The 100 Most Valuable Global Brands," *Marketing Week* (May 24, 2012): 1+.

53 Tulin Erdem, Joffre Swait, and Ana Valenzuela, "Brands as Signals: A Cross-Country Validation Study," *Journal of Marketing* 70:1 (2006): 34; Desmond Lam, "Cultural Influence on Proneness to Brand Loyalty," *Journal of International Consumer Marketing* 19:3 (2006): 7.

54 Andreas B. Eisingerich and Gale Rubera, "Drivers of Brand Commitment: A Cross-National Investigation," *Journal of International Marketing* 18:2 (2010): 64–79.

55 Claudiu V. Dimofte, Johny K. Johansson, and Richard P. Bagozzi, "Global Brands in the United States: How Consumer Ethnicity Mediates the Global Brand Effect," *Journal of International Marketing* 18:1 (2010): 81–106.

56 Andrews Adugudaa Akolaa, "Cultural Diagnosis and By Passing: The Effect on Successful Internationalizaton," *Review of Business & Finance Case Studies* 3:1 (2012): 69–84.

57 Michael Wines, "Picking the Pitch-Perfect Brand Name in China," *New York Times* (November 12, 2011): A4.

58 Lee Simmons and Robert M. Schindler, "Cultural Superstitions and the Price Endings Used in Chinese Advertising," *Journal of International Marketing* 11:2 (2003): 101.

59 Miriam Jordan, "Sara Lee Wants to Percolate through All of Brazil," *Wall Street Journal* (May 8, 2002): A14+; "Sara Lee Buys Brazilian Out-of-Home Player Expresso Coffee: Sara Lee Reinforces its Leadership in Fast-Growing São Paulo and Rio de Janeiro Markets," *PR Newswire* [New York] (April 10, 2012): n.p.

60 Isabelle Schuiling and Jean-Noël Kapferer, "Executive Insights: Real Differences between Local and International Brands: Strategic Implications for International Marketers," *Journal of International Marketing* 12:4 (2004): 197.

61 Jan-Benedict, E. M. Steenkamp and Martijn G. de Jong, "A Global Investigation into the Constellation of Consumer Attitudes Toward Global and Local Products," *Journal of Marketing* 74 (November 2010): 18–40.

62 Saeed Samiee, Terrence A. Shimp, and Subash Sharma, "Brand Origin Recognition Accuracy: Its Antecedents and Consumers' Cognitive Limitations," *Journal of International Business Studies* 36 (2005): 379–97; George Balabanis and Adamantios Diamantopoulos, "Gains and Losses from the Misperception of Brand Origin: The Role of Brand Strength and Country-of Origin Image," *Journal of International Marketing* 19:2 (2011): 95–116; Helena F. Allman, Anton P. Fenik, Kelly Hewett, and Felicia N. Morgan, "Brand Image Evaluations: The Interactive Roles of Country of Manufacture, Brand Concept, and Vertical Line Extension Type," *Journal of International Marketing* 24:2 (June 2016): 1.

63 Daniel Laufer, Kate Gillespie, and David H. Silvera, "The Role of Country of Manufacture in Consumers' Attributions of Blame in an Ambiguous Product-Harm Crisis," *Journal of International Consumer Marketing* 21 (2009): 189–201.

64 Daniel Laufer, Kate Gillespie, and David H. Silvera, "The Role of Country of Manufacture in Consumers' Attributions of Blame in an Ambiguous Product-Harm Crisis," *Journal of International Consumer Marketing* 21 (2009): 189–201.

65 P. Sharma, "Country of Origin Effects in Developed and Emerging Markets: Exploring the Contrasting Roles of Materialism and Value Consciousness," *Journal of IBIB Studies*, 42:2 (2012): 285–306; Terence Motsi and Ji Eun Park, "Consumer Evaluation of Developing Country Products: The Moderating Role of Product Ethnicity," paper presented at the Academy of IBIB annual meeting, Washington, DC (2012); Zhongqi Jin, Richard Lynch, Samaa Attia, Bal Chansarkar, Tanses Gulsoy, and Paul Lapoule, "Antecedents of Home and Foreign Product Country Images in Developed and Developing Countries: A Comparative Study," paper presented at the Academy of IBIB annual meeting, Washington, DC (2012); Stephen Gould, Mike Chen-Ho Chao, Andreas Grein, and Rania Semaan, "The Biasing Effects of Country-of-Origin: A Cross-Cultural Application of Preference Reversals," paper presented at the Academy of IBIB annual meeting, Washington, DC (2012).

66 "Chin-Chin in China," *The Economist* (May 9, 2015): 44.

67 Seah Park, "LG's Kitchen Makeover," *Wall Street Journal* (September 22, 2004): A19.

68 Matthew Dalton, "Salty Issue in U.S.—European Trade Talks," *Wall Street Journal Online* (October 19, 2015).

69 Kevin McCallum, "Grape Debate," *Miami Herald* (March 27, 2009): 1C+.

70 "CEC Finalizing Report on SLAB Exports," *Business Wire* [New York] (November 30, 2012): n.p.; Don Hopey, "Rachel Carson's Book Turned the Environmental World on Its Ear 50 Years Ago," *McClatchy Tribune Business News* [Washington] (September 27, 2012): n.p.

71 Robert Kennedy, "Tobacco Firms Accused of Thwarting Controls," *McClatchy Tribune Business News* [Washington] (May 30, 2012): n.p.

72 Andrew Jacobs, "Big Tobacco Hooked Them Young, On," *New York Times* (March 15, 2019): B1+.

73 Andrew Jack, "Economic Reality Spurs Intervention: More Is Being Done to Tackle 'NTDs' as Research Reveals Their Impact on Countries' Growth," *Financial Times* (October 11, 2012): 2.

74 Rick Gladstone, "W.H.O. Deplores Delay in Ebola Vaccine," *New York Times* (November 4, 2014): A9.

75 Andrew Jack, "FDA to Stimulate Tropical Disease Research," *Financial Times* (May 1, 2008): 6.

76 Rebecca Perl, Nandita Murukutla, Jessica Occleston, Megen Bayly, and Mego Lien, "Responses to Antismoking Radio and Television Advertisements among Adult Smokers and Non-smokers Across Africa: Message-Testing Results from Senegal, Nigeria, and Kenya," *Tobacco Control* 24:6 (November 2015): 601.

77 Sebastien Sauve, "Pesticide Research Must Stay Transparent and Independent," *Bizcommunity.com [Capetown]:* (May 13, 2019) ABI/Inform from Proquest (accessed January 29, 2020).

78 Danny Hakim, "Banned Abroad," *New York Times* (February 24, 2015): Business 1+.

79 Daniel Greenfield, "DDT Might Have Stopped Zika, but Environmentalists Chose Mosquitos over People," *Frontpage Magazine* (January 28, 2016), www.frontpagemag.com/point/261639 (accessed June 10, 2016).

80 Michael Finkel, "Bedlam in the Blood: Malaria," *National Geographic* (July 2007): 63; and Richard Tren and Roger Bate, "Malaria and the DDT Story," *SSRN Working Paper Series* (April 2012).

81 Kevin Helliker, "Smokeless Tobacco to Get Push by Venture Overseas," *Wall Street Journal* (February 4, 2009): B1+.

82 "Smoke Signals," *The Economist* (April 23, 2016): 55–6.

83 "Coca-Cola Releases 2011–2012 Global Sustainability Report," *Professional Services Close-Up* (November 11, 2012).

84 Avery Johnson, "Drug Firms See Poorer Nations as Sales Cure," *Wall Street Journal* (July 7, 2009): A1+.

85 Andrew Jack, "Anti-Malaria Drug to Sell at Cost Price," *Financial Times* (March 2, 2007): 3; Jennifer Corbett Dooren, "Research to Target Neglected Diseases," *Wall Street Journal* (May 21, 2009): 16.

86 Susanna Khavul, Mark Peterson, Drake Mullens, and Abdul A. Rasheed, "Going Global with Innovations from Emerging Economies: Investment in Customer Support Capabilities Pays Off," *Journal of International Marketing* 18:4 (2010): 22–42.

87 Mobolaji Olaseni and Wale Alade, "Vision 20:2020 and the Challenges of Infrastructural Development in Nigeria," *Journal of Sustainable Development* 5:2 (February 2012): 63–76.

88 Tomasz Lenartowicz and Sridhar Balasubramanian, "Practices and Performance of Small Retail Stores in Developing Economies," *Journal of International Marketing* 17:1 (2009): 58–90.

89 Ibid.

90 J. A. Weber, "Comparing Growth Opportunities in the International Marketplace," *Management International Review* 1 (1979): 47–54; Van R. Wood, John R. Darling, and Mark Siders, "Consumer Desire to Buy and Use Products in International Markets: How to Capture It, How to Sustain It," *International Marketing Review* 16:3 (1999): 231–42.

91 "Mintel: India's Craving for Chocolate to Create Business Opportunities for Manufacturers," *Entertainment Close Up* (November 17, 2012): n.p.; Anu Kaimal, "What May Be the Reasons Why Per Capita Chocolate Consumption of India Is Comparatively Lower?" www.quora.com (accessed April 21, 2016).

92 Oliver Nieburg, "The New World of Chocolate: How Is Consumption in Emerging Markets Developing?" Confectionarynews.com (October 9, 2014) (accessed April 21, 2016).

93 Elizabeth Crawford, "5 Marketing Tactics Helping Premium Chocolate Sales Outpace Overall Category" (December 9, 2014), www.foodnavigator-usa-com/Markets/5 (accessed April 21, 2016).

94 Dermot Doherty, "Godiva's Sweet on China," *Miami Herald* (June 12, 2012): 6B.

95 Haig Simonian, "Nestlé Enriches Its Choc Value," *Financial Times* (March 24, 2006): 9.

96 "A Billion Shades of Grey," *The Economist* (April 26, 2014): 13.

97 Michiyo Nakamoto, "Japanese Fall out of Love with Luxury," *Financial Times* (June 3, 2009): 15.

98 Allen L. Hammond and C. K. Prahalad, "Selling to the Poor," *Foreign Policy* (May/June 2004): 30–7.

99 Stephanie Strom, "New Tack on Snacks," *New York Times* (June 13, 2012): B1+.

100 Kelvin Chan, "Foreign Vineyards Keen to Tap China Wine Market," *Miami Herald* (November 7, 2011): n.p.

101 For an excellent discussion of these traits and their interactions, see Mark Cleveland, Michel Laroche, and Nicolas Papadopoulos, "Cosmopolitanism, Consumer Ethnocentrism, and Materialism: An Eight-Country Study of Antecedents and Outcomes," *Journal of International Marketing* 17:1 (2009): 116–46.

102 Coauthor Professor Jon Jungbien Moon is at Korea University. *Sources include the following:* Muhammad Yunus, *Creating a World Without Poverty* (New York: Public Affairs, 2007); C. K. Prahalad, *The Fortune at the Bottom of the Pyramid* (Upper Saddle River, NJ: Wharton School Publishing, 2010); IMF World Economic Outlook Database, October 2018 (www.imf.org/en/Publications/WEO/Issues/2018/09/24/world-economic-outlook-october-2018) and World Bank Country Statistics (data.worldbank.org/country/bangladesh); Grameen Danone Foods Ltd. PowerPoint (Jan. 2012) available at www.danonecommunities.com; Grameen Intel TSI available at www.tsi.com.bd/about/who-we-are/(accessed March 17, 2019); Grameen Bank Annual Report, 2017; Danone Annual Report, 2017; Grameen UNIQLO, www.grameenuniqlo.com/who-we-are (accessed March 17, 2019); Grameen Veolia Water Ltd., www.muhammadyunus.org/index.php/social-business/grameen-veolia-water-ltd (accessed March 17, 2019); "GAIN and Grameen Danone: A Study About Nutrition," www.youtube.com/watch?v=EQJ0Qco7JhE (accessed on February 8, 2013); Sheridan Prasso, "Saving the World With a Cup of Yogurt," *Fortune* 155:2 (March 15, 2007): 44; John F. Jones, "Social Finance: Commerce and Community in Developing Countries," *International Journal of Social Economics* 37:6 (2010): 415–28; Nevin S. Scrimshaw, "History and Early Development of INCAP1, 2," *The Journal of Nutrition* 140:2 (February 2010): 394–96; Sarah Murray, "Yogurt Maker's Recipe for Funding Social Businesses," *Financial Times* (July 7, 2008): 16; Christina Passariello, "Danone Expands Its Pantry to Woo the World's Poor," *Wall Street Journal* (June 29, 2010): A1; Paul Bennet, "The Biggest Idea Might Be Learning to Think Small," *Financial Times* (December 31, 2009); Michael Fitzgerald, "As the World Turns," 133 *Fast Company* (March 2009): 33–4; Scheherazade Daneshkhu, "The Off-the-Wall Executive," *Financial Times* (November 22, 2010): 12; "Top CEOs Talk on Global Social Business in Germany," *The Global Express* [Dhaka] (November 12, 2010): n.p.; and Dean Nelson, "Pioneer Bank in Turmoil," *The Sunday Telegraph* [London] (February 13, 2011): 3.

Chapter 18

1 *Sources include the following:* Philip Elmer-DeWitt, "What's Really Going On at Apple's iPhone 5 Factory in Zhengzhou, China," *Fortune* (October 7, 2012), http://tech.fortune.cnn.com/2012/10/07/whats-really-going-on-at-apples-iphone-5-factory-in-zhengzhou-china/(accessed June 15, 2013); Kenneth

L. Kraemer, Greg Linden, and Jason Dedrick, "Capturing Value in Global Networks: Apple's iPad and iPhone," pcic.merage.uci.edu/papers/2011/Value_iPad_iPhone.pdf; Dedrick, Kraemer, and Linden, "The Distribution of Value in the Mobile Phone Supply Chain," pcic.merage.uci.edu/papers/2010/CellPhoneProfitability_Oct2010.pdf; G. Froud, S. Johal, A. Leaver, and K. Williams, "Apple Business Model: Financialization Across the Pacific," University of Manchester, Centre for Research in Socio-cultural Change (CRESC), Working Paper No. 111 (2012); B. Ganges and A. Van Assche, "Product Modularity and the Rise of Global Value Chains: Insights from the Electronics Industry," CIRANO Scientific Series, Montreal (2011): S64; Apple Inc., Form 10-K, September 29, 2012; Nick Wingfield, "Fixing Apple's Supply Lines," *New York Times* (April 2, 2012): B1; Catherine Rampell and Nick Wingfield, "In Shift of Jobs, Apple Will Make Some Macs in U.S.," *New York Times* (December 7, 2012): A1; "When the Jobs Inspector Calls," *The Economist* (March 31, 2012): 73; "Non-U.S. Share of Apple's Revenue from 1st Quarter 2006 to 2nd Quarter 2016," www.statista.com/statistics/263465/non-us-share-of-apples-revenue/(accessed June 6, 2016); "Apple Retail Stores," www.apple.com/retail/storelist/(accessed June 6, 2016).

2 "The Fourth Annual Global Survey of Supply Chain Progress," Computer Sciences Corporation (CSC) and *Supply Chain Management Review* (2006); Darrell Rigby, "Management Tools 2005," *Bain & Company* (2005): 58.

3 Council of Supply Chain Management Professionals, cscmp.org/about-us/supply-chain-management-definitions (accessed June 1, 2013).

4 Homin Chen and Tain-Jy Chen, "Network Linkages and Location Choice in Foreign Direct Investment," *Journal of International Business Studies* 29:3 (1998): 447.

5 Lauren Sherman, "It Takes a Village to Make a Barbie," *Forbes* (March 5, 2009), http://www.forbes.com/2009/03/05/barbie-design-manufacturing-business_numbers.html (accessed June 6, 2016).

6 Stanley E. Fawcett and Anthony S. Roath, "The Viability of Mexican Production Sharing: Assessing the Four Cs of Strategic Fit," *Urbana* 3:1 (1996): 29.

7 See S. C. Wheelwright, "Reflecting Corporate Strategy in Manufacturing Decisions," *Business Horizons* (1978): 21; S. C. Wheelwright, "Manufacturing Strategy: Defining the Missing Link," *Strategic Management Journal* 5 (1984): 77–91; Frank DuBois, Brian Toyne, and Michael D. Oliff, "International Manufacturing Strategies of U.S. Multinationals: A Conceptual Framework Based on a Four-Industry Study," *Journal of International Business Studies* 24:2 (1993): 313–14; Robert H. Hayes, Steven C. Wheelwright, and Kim B. Clark, *Dynamic Manufacturing* (New York: Free Press, 1988): 10–11.

8 Interview by author of Wall's Unilever personnel in Beijing, China (June 2006).

9 Christina Rogers, "Ford Aims to Raise Output from Mexico," *Wall Street Journal* (February 8, 2016): B3; Phoebe Wall Howard, "Ford Focus for 2019 gets Roomier, More Tech-Forward: Will No Longer Be Built in the U.S.," *Detroit Free Press*, www.usatoday.com/story/money/cars/2018/04/10/ford-focus-gets-new-look-more-room-and-tech/505491002/ (accessed April 16, 2019).

10 www.talapparel.com/en/tal-group (accessed April 16, 2019).

11 Kathy Chu, "China Loses Edge on Labor Costs," *Wall Street Journal* (December 3, 2015): B1.

12 Demetri Sevastopulo, "Shirt Tales from TAL, an Apparel Powerhouse," *Financial Times* (December 11, 2015), https://www.ft.com/content/f31b2d54-60de-11e3-916e-00144feabdc0 (accessed April 16, 2019).

13 Rogers, op. cit.

14 Rogers, op. cit.

15 Michael E. McGrath and Richard W. Hoole, "Manufacturing's New Economies of Scale," *Harvard Business Review* (May–June 1992): 94.

16 Christina Rogers and John D. Stoll, "Ford to Shift Work Abroad," *Wall Street Journal* (July 10, 2015): B1 and Kathy Chu, "Made in Vietnam Ready for Boost," *Wall Street Journal* (October 19, 2015): B1.

17 Evan Coman, "Which Manufacturers Are Bringing the Most Jobs Back to America," *USA Today* (June 6, 2018; accessed April 16, 2019).

18 Fawcett and Roath, "The Viability of Mexican Production Sharing," 29.

19 Amy Schoenfeld, "A Multinational Loaf," *New York Times* (June 20, 2007), www.nytimes.com/imagepages/2007/06/15/business/20070616_FOOD_GRAPHIC.html (accessed November 9, 2007).

20 Alexei Barrionuevo, "Globalization in Every Loaf," *New York Times* (June 16, 2007), www.nytimes.com/2007/06/16/business/worldbusiness/16food.html?partner=rssnyt&emc=rss (accessed November 9, 2007).

21 Masaaki Kotabe and Glen S. Omura, "Sourcing Strategies of European and Japanese Multinationals: A Comparison," *Journal of International Business Studies* (Spring 1989): 120–22.

22 Thomas L. Friedman, *The World Is Flat* (New York: Picador/Farrar, Straus and Giroux): 152.

23 Robert M. Monczka and Robert J. Trent, "Global Sourcing: A Development Approach," *International Journal of Purchasing and Materials Management* (Spring 1991): 3.

24 Doug Cameron, "Pentagon Hires Foreign Chips Supplier," *Wall Street Journal* (June 6, 2016): B3.

25 R. D'Aveni and D. Ravenscraft, "Economies of Integration versus Bureaucracy Costs: Does Vertical Integration Improve Performance?" *Academy of Management Journal* 37: 5 (1994): 1167–206; O. Williamson, "Vertical Integration and Related Variations on a Transaction-Cost Theme," in *New Developments in the Analysis of Market Structure*, eds. J. Stiglitz and G. Mathewson (Cambridge, MA: MIT Press, 1986): 149–95; O. Williamson, *The Economic Institutions of Capitalism* (New York: The Free Press, 1985): 85–130.

26 Russell Johnston and Paul R. Lawrence, "Beyond Vertical Integration—The Rise of the Value-Adding Partnership," *Harvard Business Review* (July–August 1988): 98.

27 Chester Dawson, "A 'China Price' for Toyota," *Businessweek* (February 21, 2005): 50–51.

28 Brian Tomey, "Understanding Japanese Keiretsu," *Investopedia* (March 9, 2018), www.investopedia.com/articles/economics/09/japanese-keiretsu.asp (accessed April 17, 2019).

29 List of Laptop Brands and Manufacturers (Wikipedia.com), en.wikipedia.org/wiki/List_of_laptop_brands_and_manufacturers (accessed April 18, 2019).

30 Rigby, "Management Tools 2005."

31 "Still Made in Japan," *Economist.com* (April 7, 2004), www.economist.com/printedition/displayStory. cfm?Story_ id=2571689 (accessed November 9, 2007).

32 "Still Made in Japan," *Economist.com*.

33 Paul Mozur, "Eye on Apple, Foxconn Bets Billions on Sharp," *New York Times* (March 31, 2016): B1.

34 Ralph Jennings, "Apple Contractor Foxconn Makes Gains with Its Own Brand of Phones in a Tough Market," *Forbes* (January 31, 2019), https://www.forbes.com/sites/ralphjennings/2019/01/31/apple-contractor-foxconn-makes-gains-with-its-own-brand-of-phones-in-a-tough-market/#f8a84472c48e (accessed February 18, 2019).

35 Adapted from Pete Engardio and Bruce Einhorn, "Outsourcing Innovation," *Businessweek* (March 21, 2005): 84–94.

36 IKEA Group FY18 Sustainability Report(accessed April 18, 2019) and https://preview.thenewsmarket.com/Previews/IKEA/DocumentAssets/525318.pdf (accessed April 18, 2019).

37 Apple Supplier Responsibility 2019 Progress Report, p. 50, www.apple.com/supplier-responsibility/pdf (accessed April 18, 2019).

38 Lynnley Browning, "Complex Law on Conflict Mineral," *New York Times* (September 8, 2015): B1.

39 Apple Supplier Responsibility, op. cit.

40 "Conflict Minerals Rule," *Government Accountability Office* (www.gao.gov/assets/680/672051.pdf), accessed April 18, 2019.

41 Monczka and Trent, "Global Sourcing: A Development Approach," 4–5.

42 Stanley E. Fawcett, "The Globalization of the Supply Environment," *The Supply Environment* 2 (Tempe, AZ: NAPM, 2000): 11.

43 Thomas L. Friedman, *The World Is Flat: a Brief History of the Twenty-First Century*, Release 3.0 (New York, NY: Picador, 2007): 77.

44 Richard Karpinski, "Wal-Mart Mandates Secure, Internet-Based EDI for Suppliers," *Internetweek.com* (September 12, 2002), www.internetweek.com/supplyChain/INW20020912S0011 (accessed October 1, 2002); R. Sridharan and Shamni Pande, "Surviving Wal-Mart," *Business Today* (July 29, 2007): 166.

45 Scott McCartney, "A New Way to Prevent Lost Luggage," *Wall Street Journal* (February 27, 2007): D1.

46 Vlad Krotov and Iris Junglas, "RFID as a Disruptive Innovation," *Journal of Theoretical and Applied Electronic Commerce Research* 3:2 (August 2008): 44.

47 Radio-Frequency Identification (RFID) Market 2018: Global Trends, Business Growth and Forecast Report basics: Segmentation, Application, Dynamics,

Development Status and Outlook 2023, *Market Watch* (March 27, 2018), www.marketwatch.com/press-release/radio-frequency-identification-rfid-market-2018-global-trends-business-growth-and-forecast-report-basics-segmentation-application-dynamics-development-status-and-outlook-2023-2018-07-27 (accessed April 18, 2019).

48 Karpinski, "Wal-Mart Mandates Secure, Internet-Based EDI for Suppliers."

49 Rob O'Bryne, "Blockchain Technology is Set to Transform the Supply Chain," *Logisticsbureau.com* (January 9, 2019), https://www.logisticsbureau.com/how-blockchain-can-transform-the-supply-chain/ (accessed February 18, 2020).

50 "Internet Growth Statistics," www. Internetworldstats.com/emarketing.htm (accessed April 18, 2019).

51 "Number of Active Daily Facebook Users Worldwide as of 4th Quarter 2019," Statista (https://www.statista.com/statistics/264810/number-of-monthly-active-facebook-users-worldwide/), accessed February 17, 2020.

52 Lee J. Krajewski, Manoj K. Malhotra, and Larry P. Ritzman, *Operations Management: Processes and Supply Chains,* 12th ed. (Boston, MA: Pearson Education, Inc., 2019): Chapter 3.

53 F. Robert Jacobs and Richard B. Chase, *Operations and Supply Management: The Core,* 4th Edition (New York: McGraw-Hill Irwin, 2017), Chapter 10.

54 Daniel Michaels and Robert Wall, "Boeing Aims to Restore Its Image," *Wall Street Journal* (April 17, 2019): B2.

55 "Takata Airbag Recall—Everything You Need to Know," *Consumer Reports,* updated on June 9, 2016, www.consumerreports.org/cro/news/2016/05/everything-you-need-to-know-about-the-takata-air-bag-recall/index.htm.

56 Hayes, Wheelwright, and Clark, *Dynamic Manufacturing,* 17.

57 Foster, *Managing Quality: Integrating the Supply Chain,* 6th edition (Upper Saddle River, NJ: Pearson, 2016).

58 Alastair Gale and Sean McLain, "Japan's Famed Manufacturing Model Is Facing a Crisis," *Wall Street Journal* (February 5, 2018), A1.

59 Foster, op. cit.

60 Krajewski, Malhortra, and Ritzman, op. cit.

61 Ibid, 101–103.

62 Alastair Gale and Sean McLain, "Japan's Famed Manufacturing Model Is Facing a Crisis," *Wall Street Journal* (February 5, 2018), A1.

63 Ibid.

64 Gabriel Kahn, Trish Saywell, and Quenna Sook Kim, "Backlog at West Coast Docks Keeps Christmas Toys at Sea," *Wall Street Journal* (October 21, 2002), www.wsj.com (accessed October 25, 2002).

65 Shawnee K. Vickery, "International Sourcing: Implications for Just-in-Time Manufacturing," *Production and Inventory Management Journal* (1989): 67.

66 "What Is Six Sigma?" www.isixsigma.com/new-to-six-sigma/getting-started/what-six-sigma/(accessed June 9, 2016).

67 Brian Hindo and Brian Grow, "Six Sigma: So Yesterday?" *Businessweek* (June 11, 2007): 11.

68 Robert McClusky, "The Rise, Fall and Revival of Six Sigma Quality," *Quality Focus* 4:2 (2000): 6.

69 International Organization for Standardization, "ISO Standards," www.iso.org (accessed April 19, 2019).

70 Yoko Kubota, "Coronavirus Exposes Businesses' Dependency on China," *Wall Street Journal* (February 19, 2020), A7; Tripp Mickle, "Apple Warns Coronavirus to Hit Sales," *Wall Street Journal* (February 18, 2020), A1.

71 This case was written by Manuel G. Serapio, Associate Professor and IB Program Director, Business School and Faculty Director of the University of Colorado Denver CIBER. The information on Nokero is from the author's personal interviews with Steve Katsaros, Founder and CEO of Nokero, and Tom Boyd, Director of Communications and Marketing, Nokero. Nokero's Steve Katsaros, Evan Husney, Tom Boyd, and Beth Polizzotto, University of Colorado Denver, provided research materials for the initial version of the case. Updates on the case were provided by Steve Katsaros, Hannah Ritchie, and Max Roser (2020). *Sources include the following:* "Access to Energy," *Published online at OurWorldInData.org.* Retrieved from 'https://ourworldindata.org/energy-access' [Online Resource] John Collins Rudolf, "A Solar Bulb May Light the Way," *New York Times* (June 25, 2010), http://green.blogs.nytimes.com/2010/06/25/a-solar-bulb-may-light-the-way/?_r=0 (accessed June 1, 2013); Jason Blevins, "The Power of Light," *The Denver Post* (July 10, 2010): 1; Tom Boyd, "A Year After Quake, Nokero and American Green Light Up Orphanage, Tent City in Haiti" (January 14, 2010), Nokero.com (accessed June 1, 2013); "Solar Powered Lightbulb Invented for World's Powerless" (January 8, 2013), http://nokero.com/ (accessed April 15, 2019).

Chapter 19

1 *Sources include the following:* "People on the Move," *Deseret News* (January 31, 1999): M02; Wells Fargo News Release, "Wells Fargo & Company and First Security Corporation Agree to Merge" (April 10, 2000), www.wellsfargo.com/press/firstsec20000410?year= 2000 (accessed November 20, 2007); follow-up interview with Ali Manbeian on April 25, 2019; GPS Capital Markets, www.gpsfx.com (accessed February 25, 2020).

2 "Chief Financial Officer—CFO," www.investopedia.com/terms/c/cfo.asp (accessed February 27, 2020).

3 Geert Hofstede, *Culture's Consequences: International Differences in Work-Related Values* (Beverly Hills: Sage, 1980): 327; Geert Hofstede and Michael H. Bond, "The Confucius Connection: From Cultural Roots to Economic Growth," *Organizational Dynamics* 16:4 (1988): 4; Geert Hofstede, Gert Jan Hofstede, and Michael Minkov, *Cultures and Organizations: Software of the Mind,* Third Edition (Maidenhead, England: McGraw-Hill, 2010): 561.

4 Sidney J. Gray, "Towards a Theory of Cultural Influence on the Development of Accounting Systems Internationally," *Abacus* (March 1988): 1.

5 European Union, "Third Countries/Convergence," ec.europa.eu/internal_market/accounting/third_countries/index_en.htm (accessed May 27, 2016).

6 "IFRS: About the Organisation," www.ifrs.org/The+organisation/IASCF+and+IASB.htm (accessed May 2, 2019).

7 IFRS Foundation "The Organisation, Trustees," www.ifrs.org/The+organisation/Trustees/Trustees.htm (accessed May 2, 2019).

8 IFRS Foundation, "About the IFRS Foundation and the IASB," www.ifrs.org/The-organisation/Pages/IFRS-Foundation-and-the-IASB.aspx (accessed May 2, 2019).

9 "Who Uses IFRS Standards" (IFRS Foundation, updated on April 25, 2018), www.ifrs.org/use-around-the-world/use-of-ifrs-standards-by-jurisdiction/#analysis (accessed February 27, 2020).

10 Financial Accounting Standards Board, "Memorandum of Understanding: The Norwalk Agreement," www.fasb.org/news/memorandum.pdf (accessed May 28, 2016).

11 FASB, "Convergence with the International Accounting Standards Board."

12 Securities and Exchange Commission, "About the SEC: What We Do," www.sec.gov/about/whatwedo.shtml (accessed May 2, 2019).

13 "Financial Reporting," (European Union), http://ec.europa.eu/info/business-economy/company-reporting-and-auditing/company-reporting/financial-reporting.en

14 "Finance and Economics: Speaking in Tongues," *The Economist* (May 19, 2007): 77–78.

15 "Uniform Rules for International Accounting Standards from 2005 Onwards," *European Parliament Daily Notebook,* Report on the Proposal for a European Parliament and Council Regulation on the Application of International Accounting Standards (COM 2001) 80-C5-0061/2001–2001/004 (COD), Doc.: A5-0070/2002, www.europarl.europa.eu/sides/getDoc.do?pubRef=-//EP//TEXT+PRESS+DN-20020312-1+0+DOC+XML+V0//EN&language=EN#SECTION5 (accessed October 21, 2009).

16 "Who Uses IFRS," op cit.

17 "Organization of the SEC," www.sec.gov/about/whatwedo.shtm#org (accessed May 30, 2016).

18 FASB, "Foreign Currency Translation," Statement of Financial Accounting Standards No. 52 (Stamford, CT: FASB, December 1981): 6–7.

19 www.ifrs.org/IFRSs/Pages/IFRS.aspx.

20 Coca-Cola, 2019 Form 10-K (Securities and Exchange Commission), p. 64.

21 David K. Eiteman, Arthur I. Stonehill, and Michael H. Moffett, *Multinational Business Finance,* 15th edition (Pearson: Upper Saddle Ridge, NJ:, 2019): Chapter 18.

22 "Working Capital," Investopedia.com/terms/w/workingcapital.asp (accessed May 3, 2019).

23 Mike Ramsey, "VW Chops Labor Costs in U.S.," *Wall Street Journal* (May 23, 2011): B1; Stephen Power, "BMW's Profit Softened in Quarter," *Wall Street Journal* (May 4, 2005): A12.

24 Tatyana Shumsky, "SEC Nods to Multinationals," *Wall Street Journal* (February 23, 2016): B5.

25 Ibid.

26 Michael Rapoport and Jean Eaglesham, "SEC Nears Settlement with China Auditors," *Wall Street Journal* (February 5, 2015): C3.

27 *Sources include the following:* Various annual reports of The Gap, H&M, and Inditex for 2015, accessed on May 26, 2016; Greg Petro, "The Future of Fashion Retailing," a three-part series, *Forbes*, www.forbes.com/sites/greg-petro/2012/10/23/the-future-of-fashion-retailing-part-1-uniqlo/, www.forbes.com/sites/gregpetro/2012/10/25/the-future-of-fashion-retailing-the-zara-approach-part-2-of-3/#I, www.forbes.com/sites/gregpetro/2012/11/05/the-future-of-fashion-retailing-the-hm-approach-part-3-of-3/ (accessed June 15, 2013); MarketLine Industry Profile, "Global Apparel Retail," February 2013.

Chapter 20

1 S. Green, F. Hassan, J. Immelt, M. Marks, and D. Meiland, "In Search of Global Leaders," *Harvard Business Review* 81:8 (2003): 44.

2 Brookfield GRS. "Career Impact of an Assignment—2016 Global Mobility Trends Survey" http://globalmobilitytrends.brookfieldgrs.com/ (accessed March 10, 2020).

3 "Migration: How Many People Are on the Move around the World?" *The Guardian*, September 10, 2018, sec. News.

4 Mark Schoeff Jr., "P&G Places a Premium on International Experience," *Workforce*, https://bit.ly/2wEJL5F (accessed February 25, 2013).

5 Ibid., Green, Hassan, Immelt, Marks, and Meiland.

6 Liz Wolgemuth, "What the Résumés of Top CEOs Have in Common | Careers | US News," https://bit.ly/2TNXHDj (accessed March 14, 2020).

7 Barbara Ettorre, "A Brave New World," *Management Review* 82:4 (April 1993): 10–16.

8 Martin Dewhurst, Matthew Pettigrew, and Ramesh Srinivasan. "How Multinationals Can Attract the Talent They Need | McKinsey," https://mck.co/39JbCAk (accessed January 4, 2019).

9 "Staffing Globalisation: Travelling More Lightly," *The Economist* (June 23, 2006): 67.

10 Adapted from Expat Insider 2019 Business Edition, "A Look at Global Talent Mobility Though Expat Eyes, Motivation for Relocation," InterNations Business Solutions, https://business.internations.org/expat-insider (accessed March 13, 2020).

11 "Globalisation: The Empire Strikes Back," *The Economist* (September 18, 2008): 51.

12 Melinda Ligos, "The Foreign Assignment: An Incubator, or Exile?" *New York Times* (October 22, 2000).

13 Mark Larson, "More Employees Go Abroad as International Operations Grow," *Workforce Management* (June 1, 2006): 12.

14 Joe Sharkey, "Global Economy Is Leading to More Dangerous Places," *New York Times* April 19, 2005): C3.

15 Stefan Schmid and Dennis Wurster. "International Work Experience: Is It Really Accelerating the Way to the Management Board of MNCs?" *International Business Review* 26, no. 5 (2017): 991–1008; Njål Andersen, "Mapping the Expatriate Literature: A Bibliometric Review of the Field from 1998 to 2017 and Identification of Current Research Fronts," *The International Journal of Human Resource Management* (2019): 1–38.

16 Sandra Jones, "Going Stateside: Once the Overseas Hitch Is Over, Homeward-Bound Expats Hit Turbulence," *Crain's Chicago Business* (July 24, 2000): 23.

17 "No Soft Landing for Returning Expats," Jemima Whyte, September 10, 2018, https://bit.ly/2Q3ck3g (accessed March 9, 2020).

18 Breakthrough to the Future of Global Talent Mobility—2016 Global Mobility Trends Survey, https://bit.ly/2Q0Het3 (accessed January 9, 2019). Joann S. Lublin, "Going Overseas for a Job? Coming Home Is the Hard Part," *Wall Street Journal* (September 5, 2017), https://on.wsj.com/2Wa9vBF.

19 Barry Newman, "Expat Archipelago," *Wall Street Journal* (December 12, 1995): A1.

20 Ibid., Breakthrough to the Future of Global Talent Mobility—2016 Global Mobility Trends Survey.

21 Ibid., Melinda Ligos.

22 Jeffrey Joerres, "Beyond Expats: Better Managers for Emerging Markets | McKinsey," https://mck.co/2IApsJi (accessed January 4, 2019).

23 "The World at Work," McKinsey Global Institute, www.mckinsey.com/insights/ (accessed December 27, 2012); David Jones, "The Importance of International Experience for CEOs," June 12, 2019, https://bit.ly/3cVDx1X (accessed March 14, 2020).

24 "The Rise and Rise of Overseas Experience for Today's CEO | DHR International," https://bit.ly/33tU6Od (accessed March 14, 2020).

25 Ibid., Mark Schoeff

26 Ibid., Green, Hassan, Immelt, Marks, and Meiland.

27 Ibid., Green, Hassan, Immelt, Marks, and Meiland.

28 Acharya Ashwin, Ketan Chaudhry, J. Maxwell, and Matt Rosenstock, "Streamline Decision-Making for a Better Customer Journey | McKinsey & Company," August 12, 2019, https://mck.co/2T4cs4s (accessed February 27, 2020).

29 Ibid., 2016 Global Mobility Trends Survey, See responses to query "International Assignment Failure: What Percentage of Your International Assignments fail?" "Reasons for Early Return from an Assignment: Select the Primary Reasons for Early Returns from International Assignments."

30 Ibid., Green, Hassan, Immelt, Marks, and Meiland.

31 See "World Investment Report 2018: Investment and New Industrial Policies," https://bit.ly/2VYHPzu (accessed January 6, 2019); "2018 BCG Local Dynamos: Emerging-Market Companies up Their Game." https://on.bcg.com/336tZfG (accessed January 9, 2019).

32 Ibid., 2016 Global Mobility Trends Survey/

33 Mercer Mobility, "Seven Dilemmas Facing the Future of Global Mobility," https://bit.ly/2Q4A2MD (accessed March 10, 2020).

34 For example, PricewaterhouseCoopers (PwC) found that more than 70 percent of millennials seek global opportunities. Hence, it offers its Early PwC International Challenge program (EPIC) to fast-track younger employees into international assignments. Candidates jump-start the process by completing an online assessment and consulting PwC's career pages. If selected, off one goes to a two-year assignment. Candidates, besides expediting career progression, improve executive skills and global orientation. PwC benefits by improving recruitment as well as fortifying its leadership pipeline.

35 Maike Andresen, Marshall Pattie, and Thomas Hippler. "What Does It Mean to Be a 'Self-Initiated' Expatriate in Different Contexts? A Conceptual Analysis and Suggestions for Future Research," *The International Journal of Human Resource Management* 31, 2020: 174–201. "Expat Explorer—Expat 2019 Global Report," HSBC, https://www.expatexplorer.hsbc.com/global-report/ (accessed March 10, 2020). Ibid., Mercer Mobility. "Mobile Millennials."

36 "Number of International Students in the United States Hits All-Time High," https://bit.ly/2IC0OTu (accessed March 10, 2020).

37 "Americans Look Overseas for Global MBA Courses and Diversity," *TOPMBA*, https://bit.ly/2xsbvuJ (accessed December 27, 2012).

38 Ibid., Expat Insider 2019 Business Edition, "A Look at Global Talent Mobility Through Expat Eyes;" see also "International Assignees by Gender: Estimate the Percentage of Your Current International Assignees by Gender;" "Where Are Women in the Expatriate Workforce," https://bit.ly/2TFFojT (accessed January 15, 2018).

39 "More Females Sent on International Assignment Than Ever Before, Survey Finds," https://bit.ly/3aMXK8h (accessed April 25, 2009).

40 Maria Bastida, "Yes, They Can Do It! Exploring Female Expatriates' Effectiveness," *European Research on Management and Business Economics* 24, no. 2 (2018): 114–120.

41 "Education in China," 2019. WENR, https://bit.ly/38GWamG (accessed March 10, 2020);

42 Martin Dewhurst, Jonathan Harris, and Suzanne Heywood. "The Global Company's Challenge | McKinsey," https://mck.co/2vJ0sNd (accessed January 4, 2019).

43 Ibid., 2016 Global Mobility Trends Survey, See response to query "Assignments to/from Headquarters Country: Estimate the Percentage of Your International Assignments to/from Headquarters Country."

44 Ibid., 2016 Global Mobility Trends Survey, See response to query "Pressure to Reduce Assignment Costs: In Response to Business and Economic Conditions That May Be Affecting Your Company, Has There Been an Effort to Reduce International Assignment Costs?"

45 Ibid., 2016 Global Mobility Trends Survey, See response to query "Single Status Assignments by Assignment Length: Estimate the Percentage of Single Status Assignments by Assignment Length (Short-Term vs. Long-Term Assignment)."

46 Eric Rosenbaum, "IBM Artificial Intelligence Can Predict with 95% Accuracy Which Workers Are about to Quit Their Jobs," *CNBC*, April 3, 2019, https://cnb.cx/2TsKluL (accessed March 1, 2020).

47 Maggie M. Cheng and Rick D. Hackett, "A Critical Review of Algorithms in HRM: Definition, Theory, and Practice," *Human Resource Management Review* (2019): 100698; Brookfield GRS. "Change in Requirement for Program Reporting, Global Mobility Trends Survey," http://globalmobilitytrends.brookfieldgrs.com/ (accessed March 10, 2020).

48 Adrian Wooldridge, "The Battle for the Best," *The Economist: The World in 2007.*

49 "Staffing Globalisation: Travelling More Lightly," *The Economist* (June 23, 2006).

50 "Why Toyota Has Flopped in China," *Business Insider*, http://globalmobilitytrends.brookfieldgrs.com/ (accessed January 6, 2013).

51 Ibid., Martin Dewhurst, Jonathan Harris, and Suzanne Heywood.

52 J. Kahn, "The World's Most Admired MNEs," *Fortune* (October 11, 1999): 267.

53 Ibid., J. Kahn.

54 William C. Weldon, "Chairman's Letter: To Our Shareholders," *Annual Report 2006.*

55 Ibid., "Why Toyota Has Flopped in China."

56 Ibid., Green, Hassan, Immelt, Marks, and Meiland.

57 "High-Tech Nomads: These Engineers Work as Temps on Wireless Projects All over the World," *Time* (November 26, 2001); B. Kedia and A. Mukherji, "Global Managers: Developing a Mindset for Global Competitiveness," *Journal of World Business* 34 (Fall 1999).

58 Ibid., Green, Hassan, Immelt, Marks, and Meiland.

59 Adam Hajo, Otilia Obodaru, Jackson G. Lu, William W. Maddux, and Adam D. Galinsky, "The Shortest Path to Oneself Leads around the World: Living Abroad Increases Self-Concept Clarity," *Organizational Behavior and Human Decision Processes* 145 (March 2018): 16–29. https://doi.org/10.1016/j.obhdp.2018.01.002.

60 Ibid., Candidate Readiness - Leadership Skills, 2016 Global Mobility Trends Survey, http://globalmobilitytrends.brookfieldgrs.com/ (accessed March 10, 2020).

61 Data results for query: "What Are the Criteria for Including a Candidate into the Candidate Pool?" "Mindful Mobility: Brookfield GRS' 2015 Global Mobility Trends Survey," https://bit.ly/2VYyXtr (accessed January 10, 2020).

62 "Mindful Mobility: Brookfield GRS' 2015 Global Mobility Trends Survey," https://bit.ly/332MDoS (accessed October 6, 2015), see query "International Assignment Objectives: Select the Primary Objectives for Sending Employees on Assignment."

63 "Breakthrough to the Future of Global Talent Mobility—2016 Global Mobility Trends Survey," Brookfield GRS. http://globalmobilitytrends.brookfieldgrs.com/ (accessed January 10, 2019).

64 "In Search of Global Leaders: View of Stephen Green, Group CEO, HSBC," *Harvard Business Review* (August 1, 2003).

65 "Business in China and the West: A Tale of Two Expats," *The Economist* (December 29, 2010).

66 Yari, Nooria, Erik Lankut, Ilan Alon, and Nicole Franziska Richter, "Cultural Intelligence, Global Mindset, and Cross-Cultural Competencies: A Systematic Review using Bibliometric Methods," *European Journal of International Management* (2020); Maike Andresen and Franziska Bergdolt, "A Systematic Literature Review on the Definitions of Global Mindset and Cultural Intelligence—Merging Two Different Research Streams," *The International Journal of Human Resource Management* 28, no. 1 (2017): 170–195.

67 Tsun-yan Hsieh, Johanne Lavoie, and Robert Samek, "Are You Taking Your Expatriate Talent Seriously?" *The McKinsey Quarterly* (Summer 1999).

68 Adapted from Expat Insider 2019 Business Edition, "A Look at Global Talent Mobility Though Expat Eyes, Biggest Concerns before Moving Abroad," InterNations Business Solutions, https://bit.ly/38QkimQ (accessed March 13, 2020); see also Karen Beaman, "2010–2011 Going Global Report," Jeitosa Group International, Adapted from Table 7, https://bit.ly/2TCK9KY.

69 "Before You Accept That Exciting Expat Assignment, Know This First," https://bit.ly/332Rvul (accessed March 9, 2020).

70 Jessica Twentyman, "An Expat Job Can Be a Move Too Far," FT.com, https://on.ft.com/2WjKN1A (accessed February 25, 2013).

71 S. Larson, "More Employees Go Abroad as International Operations Grow," Workforce.com, www.workforce.com/index.html (accessed April 27, 2009).

72 Kathy Gurchiek, "HR Best Practices Can Lead to a Better Expat Experience," SHRM, March 22, 2016, https://bit.ly/2IQKhA6 (accessed March 15, 2020).

73 Ibid., "Breakthrough to the Future of Global Talent Mobility—2016 Global Mobility Trends Survey."

74 "Mindful Mobility: Brookfield GRS' 2017 Global Mobility Trends Survey," *Brookfield GRS*, http://globalmobilitytrends.brookfieldgrs.com/ (accessed January 13, 2019).

75 "Reasons Why Expatriates Fail at Overseas Assignments," Atlas, https://bit.ly/2x0QEOz (accessed December 1, 2017).

76 "English Is Coming: The Adverse Side-Effects of the Growing Dominance of English," *The Economist* (February 14, 2009): 85.

77 Philip Oltermann, "Something in Common: Should English Be the Official Language of the EU? | Philip Oltermann," *The Guardian*, April 24, 2013, https://bit.ly/2PZw347 (accessed September 28, 2019).

78 M. Joseph, "India Faces a Linguistic Truth—English Spoken Here," *New York Times* (February 16, 2011); "Schumpeter: New Rules for Schools," *The Economist* (March 26, 2013).

79 "Lingua Franca," https://bit.ly/2VXYjYw (accessed February 25, 2016).

80 "MLA Data on Enrolments Show Foreign Language Study Is on the Decline," (March 19, 2018), https://bit.ly/3aE802 (accessed January 6, 2019).

81 European Commission, "Languages of Europe," *Education and Training*, https://bit.ly/2IMOi8Y (accessed July 18, 2007).

82 Doreen Carvajal, "In Many Business Schools, the Bottom Line is in English," *New York Times* (April 10, 2007), https://nyti.ms/3366gMT (accessed June 12, 2007).

83 "Machine Translation: Conquering Babel," *The Economist* (January 5, 2013): 63.

84 Jenna Wortham, "A Surge in Learning the Language of the Internet," NYTimes.com, https://nyti.ms/38Ni2Nu (accessed December 26, 2012).

85 "In Search of Global Leaders: View of Fred Hassan, Chairman and CEO, Schering-Plough," *Harvard Business Review* (August 1, 2003).

86 Lera Boroditsky, "How Language Shapes Thought," *The Long Now*, https://bit.ly/39TdPJl (accessed December 27, 2012); "For a Better Brain, Learn Another Language," *The Atlantic*, https://bit.ly/2TZ0rfS (accessed October 6, 2015).

87 "Enduring Voices Project," *National Geographic*, https://bit.ly/39Q6Fpp (accessed December 27, 2012).

88 "It's Time to Protect Chinese Language," *China Daily*, https://bit.ly/3aQGSNC (accessed December 27, 2012).

89 Ibid., Melinda Ligos.

90 Ibid., Mindful Mobility: Brookfield GRS' 2017 Global Mobility Trends Survey, See response to query "Approach to Long-Term Assignment Compensation: Approach Taken to Assignee Compensation Philosophy/Methodology for Long-Term Assignments (1 Year or Greater)."

91 "Business in China and the West: A Tale of Two Expats," *The Economist* (December 29, 2010).

92 Barney Jopson and Demetri Sevastopulo, "US Expats Given Hope of Lower Tax Bills," *Financial Times* (October 25, 2017), https://on.ft.com/2TATJh9 (accessed February 20, 2020); "Tax Nightmare for American Expats As IRS Treats Them Like Cheats - Bloomberg," November 26, 2019, https://bloom.bg/2VZM9hY (accessed March 9, 2020).

93 Ibid., Jemima Whyte.

94 Ibid., 2016 Global Mobility Trends Survey, See response to query "Career Impact of International Assignment: Upon Repatriation, What Is the Impact on the Assignee Career in Comparison to Peers without International Experience within your Company?"

95 "Repatriation Strategy Link to Career Management, 2016 Global Mobility Trends Survey," http://globalmobilitytrends.brookfieldgrs.com/ (accessed March 10, 2020).

96 "In Search of Global Leaders: View of Daniel Meiland, Executive Chairman, Egon Zehender International," *Harvard Business Review* (August 1, 2003).

97 M. Lazarova and P. Caligiuri, "Retaining Repatriates: The Role of Organizational Support Practices," *Journal of World Business* 36 (Winter 2001): 389–402.

98 Liz Bleacher, "Students Return from Study Abroad, Experience Reverse Culture Shock," *Delaware Review* (February 19, 2013).

99 Ibid., Kathy Gurchiek.

100 Source: "2016 Global Mobility Trends Survey," Brookfield GRS, https://bit.ly/38ABcWI (accessed March 11, 2020).

101 Expat Insider 2019 Business Edition, "A Look At Global Talent Mobility Though Expat Eyes," InterNations Business Solutions, https://business.internations.org/expat-insider (accessed March 13, 2020); Breakthrough to the Future of Global Talent Mobility—2016 Global Mobility Trends Survey, https://bit.ly/2Q0Het3, See responses to query "International Assignment Failure: What Percentage of Your International Assignments Fail?," "Reasons for Early Return from an Assignment: Select the Primary Reasons for Early Returns from International Assignments."

102 Vindu Goel, "IBM Now Has More Employees in India Than in the U.S," *The New York Times* (September 28, 2017), https://nyti.ms/39BTY13 (accessed January 24, 2019).

103 Ibid., Martin Dewhurst, Jonathan Harris, and Suzanne Heywood.

104 "Big US Firms Shift Hiring Abroad," *Wall Street Journal* (April 19, 2011).

105 "Financial Careers: Go East, Young Moneyman," *The Economist* (April 16, 2011).

106 "Up or Out: Next Moves for the Modern Expatriate," *The Economist Intelligence Unit*, https://bit.ly/2U3e3XL (accessed December 31, 2012).

107 Keith Bradsher, "A Younger India Is Flexing Its Industrial Brawn," *New York Times* (September 1, 2006): A1.

108 "Transparency International - India," https://www.transparency.org/country/IND (accessed January 6, 2019). "Transparency International—Country Profiles," www.transparency.org/country#IND (accessed January 15, 2016).

109 "More than 25 Million People Apply for Indian Railway Vacancies," *Reuters*, March 29, 2018, https://reut.rs/2IuW0V0 (accessed January 28, 2020).

Glossary

Absolute advantage: A free trade theory holding that different countries produce different things more efficiently than others.

Acceptable quality level (AQL): A concept of quality control whereby managers are willing to accept a certain level of production defects, which are dealt with through repair facilities and service centers.

Acquired advantage: An explanation of a country's competitive advantage based on either product or process technology.

Acquired group memberships: An individual affiliation not determined by birth, such as religion, political membership, and profession.

Active income: Income of a CFC that is derived from the active conduct of a trade or business, as specified by the U.S. Internal Revenue Code.

Ad valorem duty: A tax placed on the value of goods shipped internationally.

Advance import deposit: A form of foreign-exchange convertibility control where the government tightens control of import licenses and requires importers to make a deposit with the central bank.

American Depositary Receipt (ADR): A negotiable certificate issued by a U.S. bank in the United States to represent the underlying shares of a foreign corporation's stock held in trust at a custodian bank in the foreign country.

American terms: The practice of using the direct quote for exchange rates.

Andean Community (CAN): A South American form of economic integration involving Bolivia, Colombia, Ecuador, and Peru.

Appropriability theory: Explanation for denying rivals access to resources.

Arbitrage: The process of buying and selling foreign currency at a profit that results from price discrepancies between or among markets.

Arm's-length price: A price between two companies that do not have an ownership interest in each other.

Ascribed group memberships: Individual affiliations determined by birth, such as gender, family, age, ethnicity, and race.

Asia Pacific Economic Cooperation (APEC): A cooperation formed by 21 countries that border the Pacific Rim in Asia and the Americas to promote multilateral economic cooperation in trade and investment in the Pacific Rim.

Association of South East Asian Nations (ASEAN): A free trade area involving the Asian countries of Brunei, Cambodia, Indonesia, Laos, Malaysia, Myanmar, the Philippines, Singapore, Thailand, and Vietnam.

Balance sheet approach: Compensation plan that sets expatriate salaries to equalize purchasing power across countries.

Bank for International Settlements (BIS): A bank in Basel, Switzerland, that facilitates transactions among central banks; it is effectively the central banks' central bank.

Bargaining school theory: A premise that the terms of a foreign investor's operations depend on how much the investor and host country need each other.

Base currency: The currency whose value is implicitly 1 when a quote is made between two currencies; for example, if the Brazilian real is trading at 3.8 reals (reais) per dollar, the dollar is the base currency and the real is the terms currency.

Base of the Pyramid: The billions of people living on less than a few dollars per day yet who some see as the next market frontier of the global economy.

Bicultural: A description of someone who has internalized two different national cultures.

Bid (buy) rate: The amount a trader is willing to pay for foreign exchange.

Bilateral integration: A form of integration between two countries in which they agree to cooperate more closely, usually in the form of tariff reductions, but often in other areas as well.

Black market: The foreign-exchange market that lies outside the official market.

Born-global companies: Companies that start out with a global focus, usually because of their founders' international experience and knowledge of foreign markets through advances in communications.

Boundaries: In terms of political environments, an official or perceived point of separation that defines the boundary of a nation. In terms of organization structure, horizontal constraints that follow from having specific employees only do specific jobs in specific units as well as the vertical constraints that separate employees into specific levels of a precisely stipulated command-and-control hierarchy.

Boundarylessness: State whereby companies build organizations that eliminate the vertical, horizontal, and external boundaries that impede information flows and hinder developing relationships.

Brain drain: Outward migration of educated people, reducing productive resources in the country of origin.

Bretton Woods Agreement: An agreement among IMF countries to promote exchange-rate stability and to facilitate the international flow of currencies.

Bureaucratic control: System whereby an organization uses centralized authority to install rules and procedures to govern activities.

Capabilities: Distinct types of resources that improve the productivity of related resources owned by the firm.

Capitalism: An economic system characterized by private ownership, pricing, production, and distribution of goods.

Caribbean Community (CARICOM): A customs union in the Caribbean region.

Centralization: The degree to which high-level managers, usually above the country level, make strategic decisions and delegate them to lower levels for implementation.

Choice-of-law clause: A provision in a contract whereby the parties agree that a particular nation's laws will be used to interpret the agreement, even if they live in (or the agreement is signed in) a different nation.

Civil law: A body of rules that delineate private rights and remedies, and govern disputes between individuals in such areas as contracts, property, and family.

Clan control: System whereby an MNE relies on shared values among employees to idealize and enforce preferred behaviors.

Classical structures: Structural configurations that reflect scientific management perspectives, emphasizing precise roles, relationships, and responsibilities in the quest to maximize efficiency, standardization, and specialization.

CME Group: The world's leading and most diverse derivatives marketplace, dealing in future and options products for a wide variety of asset classes, including foreign exchange; formed in 2007 as a merger between the Chicago Mercantile Exchange and the Chicago Board of Trade.

Code of conduct: A set of principles guiding the actions of MNEs in their contacts with societies.

Collaborative arrangements: Companies' working together, such as in joint ventures, licensing agreements, management contracts, minority ownership, and long-term contractual arrangements.

Collectivism: Perspective that the needs of the group take precedence over the needs of the individual; encourages dependence on the organization.

Command economy: An economic system in which the political authorities make major decisions regarding the production and distribution of goods and services.

Commercial law: The area of law that governs the broad areas of business, commerce, and consumer transactions.

Common law: A legal system based on tradition, precedent, and custom and usage, in which the courts interpret the law based on those conventions.

Common market: A form of regional economic integration in which countries abolish internal tariffs, use a common external tariff, and abolish restrictions on factor mobility.

Communism: A political theory advocating class war and leading to a society in which all property is publicly owned and each person works and is paid according to their abilities and needs.

Commuter assignment: One where the expatriate travels between his home and host country at frequent intervals.

Comparable access argument: Also known as a fairness argument, it holds that industries are entitled to the same access to foreign markets as foreign industries have to theirs.

Comparative advantage: A free trade argument that global efficiency gains may result from trade if a country specializes in what it can produce most efficiently, even though other countries may have an absolute advantage.

Competencies: Special outlooks, skills, capabilities, or technologies that run through the firm's operations, weaving together disparate value activities into an integrated value chain.

Compound duty: A tariff based on both a valuation and the number of units traded.

Concentrated configuration: The design of a value chain whereby a particular activity is performed in one geographic location and serves the world from it.

Concentration strategy: A company first moves to only one or a few foreign countries, not going elsewhere until it develops a very strong involvement and competitive position.

Configuration: To set up, arrange, and disperse value activities to the ideal locations around the world so that the company can start and sustain operations.

Confirmed letter of credit: A letter of credit to which a bank in the exporter's country adds its guarantee of payment.

Consolidation: An accounting process in which financial statements of related entities, such as a parent and its subsidiaries, are combined to yield a unified set of financial statements; in the process, transactions among the related enterprises are eliminated so that the statements reflect transactions with outside parties.

Consortium: An organization owned by more than two firms.

Constitutional law: Law that is created and changed by the people.

Consumer ethnocentrism: Preference for local to global, such as seeking out local alternatives when buying products and services.

Contract manufacturer: A company that is responsible for manufacturing and delivering a product on behalf of another company with which it is contracted.

Control systems: Process by which managers compare performance to plans, identify differences, and, where found, assess the basis for the gap and implement corrective action; ensure that activities are completed in ways that support the company's strategy.

Controlled foreign corporation (CFC): A foreign corporation of which more than 50 percent of the voting stock is owned by U.S. shareholders (taxable entities that own at least 10 percent of the voting stock of the corporation).

Convergence: Efforts by the FASB and IASC to move toward a common global set of accounting standards.

Coopetition: Refers to situations in which competing firms collaborate on some portions of their operations.

Coordination by mutual adjustment: System whereby managers interact extensively with counterparts in setting common goals.

Coordination by plan: System that relies on general goals and detailed objectives to coordinate activities.

Coordination by standardization: System whereby rules and procedures apply to units worldwide, thereby enforcing consistency in the performance of activities in geographically dispersed units.

Coordination systems: Systems that synchronize the work responsibilities of the value chain so that the company uses its resources efficiently and makes decisions effectively.

Core values: Values so strong that they are not negotiable.

Corporate-level strategy: Decisions made to attain competitive advantage through the selection, integration, and management of a mix of businesses competing in several industries or product markets, often across multiple countries.

Cosmopolitanism: Openness to the world, thus high acceptance of foreign products.

Cost leadership strategy: Strategy whereby a firm sells its products at the average industry price to earn a profit higher than that of rivals or below the average industry prices to capture market share.

Countertrade: International trade by exchange of goods rather than by currency purchase.

Country-similarity theory: A trade theory that organizations place earlier and stronger emphasis on those countries most similar to their own.

Country of origin: Where products or services are created, which affects trade in that consumers may prefer to buy goods produced in one country rather than another usually because of quality perceptions or because of nationalism.

Court of Justice: Court made up of judges from each EU country that ensures laws are applied and interpreted the same way across member nations, confirms EU institutions are abiding by laws, and settles disputes between members.

Creeping expropriation: The progressive, incremental restriction of private property rights by a government through mechanisms involving legislation, regulation, and taxation.

Criminal law: Body of laws dealing with crimes against the public and members of the public.

Cross-licensing: An arrangement whereby companies exchange technology or other intangible property rather than compete with each other on every product in every market.

Cross rate: An exchange rate between two currencies used in the spot market and computed from the exchange rate of each currency in relation to a third currency, usually the U.S. dollar.

Cultural collision: A situation whereby contact among divergent cultures creates problems.

Cultural distance: A measurement based on cultural factors that indicates the relative similarity of countries culturally.

Cultural imperialism: The imposition of certain elements from an alien culture.

Culture: The shared values, attitudes, and beliefs of a group of individuals.

Culture shock: The frustration resulting from having to absorb a vast array of new cultural cues and expectations.

Currency swaps: The exchanges of principal and interest payments between two currencies.

Current-rate method: A method of translating foreign-currency financial statements that is used when the functional currency is that of the local operating environment.

Customary law: A legal system anchored in the wisdom of daily experience or great spiritual or philosophical traditions.

Customs broker: The profession that involves helping importers and exporters clear shipments through a nation's customs agencies.

Deal-focus (DF) culture: A culture in which people are primarily task oriented rather than relationship oriented.

Decentralization: The degree to which lower-level managers, usually at or below the country level, make and implement strategic decisions.

Democracy: A political system that relies on citizens' participation in the decision-making process.

Deontological approach: An approach that asserts that moral reasoning occurs independent of consequences.

***Dependencia* theory:** A theory holding that emerging economies have practically no power in their dealings with MNEs.

Developed economies: Economies marked by a comparatively higher standard of living, advanced technological infrastructure, and broader range of productive activities relative to developing economies.

Developing economies: Economies typically marked by low industrialization and low standard of living relative to other countries; also referred to as less developed or underdeveloped countries.

Diamond of national competitive advantage: A theory showing four features as important for countries' competitive superiority: demand conditions; factor conditions; related and supporting industries; and firm strategy, structure, and rivalry.

Differentiation strategy: A business strategy in which a company tries to gain a competitive advantage by providing a unique product or service, or providing a unique brand of customer service.

Digital divide: The gap between those who have ready access to computers and the Internet, and those who do not.

Direct exporting: Selling products to an independent party outside of the exporter's home country.

Direct investment: *See* foreign direct investment.

Direct quote: A quote expressed in terms of the number of units of the domestic currency given for one unit of a foreign currency.

Dispersed configuration: The design of a value chain whereby a particular activity is performed in many geographic locations and serves the world market from any to all of its units.

Distribution: The course—physical path or legal title—that goods take between production and consumption.

Diversification strategy: In the context of IB location, it describes a company's rapid movement into many foreign markets, gradually increasing its commitment within each one.

Divesting: This is also called harvesting. It is the process of reducing commitments in some countries because they have poorer performance prospects than do others.

Divisional structure: An organization that contains separate divisions based around individual product lines or based on the geographic areas of the markets served.

Draft (or commercial bill of exchange): An instrument of payment in international business that instructs the importer to forward payment to the exporter.

Dumping: Exporting below cost or below the home-country price.

Duty: A tax levied on a good shipped internationally (also known as a tariff).

Dynamic effects: The overall growth in the market and the impact on a company of expanding production and achieving greater economies of scale.

E-commerce: The use of the Internet to join together suppliers with companies and companies with customers.

Economic center of gravity: The average location of economic activity, measured 3-dimensionally, across geographies on Earth.

Economic exposure (operating exposure): The potential for change in expected cash flows that arises from the pricing of products, the sourcing and cost of inputs, and the location of investments.

Economic freedom: The absence of government coercion or constraint on the production, distribution, or consumption of goods and services beyond the extent necessary for citizens to protect and maintain liberty.

Economic Freedom Index: The systematic measurement of economic freedom in countries throughout the world; sponsored by the Heritage Foundation and the *Wall Street Journal*.

Economic integration: Political and economic agreements among nations in which preference is given to member countries, especially as they relate to the reduction of trade barriers.

Economic system: The system concerned with the allocation of scarce resources.

Economies of scale: The lowering of cost per unit as output increases because of allocation of fixed costs over more units produced.

Effective tariff: An argument that the manufactured portion of products from developing countries pay higher tariffs in developed countries than the stated tariff because the raw material component would have come in duty free.

Electronic data interchange (EDI): The electronic movement of money and information via computers and telecommunications equipment.

Embargo: A specific type of quota that prohibits all trade.

Emerging economies: Economies experiencing rapid growth, expanding industrialization, and improving standard of living.

Enterprise resource planning (ERP): Software that can link information flows from different parts of a business and from different geographic areas.

Equalization: Fundamental principle stating that an expatriate should neither overly prosper nor unduly suffer from working abroad.

Equity alliance: A collaborative arrangement in which at least one of the companies takes an ownership position (almost always minority) in the other(s).

Escalation of commitment: The more time and money companies invest in examining an alternative, the more likely they are to accept it, regardless of its merits.

Essential-industry argument: A rationale for protectionism contending that nations should apply trade restrictions to protect crucial domestic industries so that they are not dependent on foreign supplies during hostile political periods.

Ethnocentrism: A conviction that one's own practices are superior to those in other countries.

Ethnocentric framework: A staffing approach in which all key management positions, whether in the home country or abroad, are filled by home-country nationals.

Euro: The common currency of the European Union, although not all members have adopted the euro.

Eurobond: A bond sold in a country other than the one in whose currency it is denominated.

Eurocredit: A loan, line of credit, or other form of medium- or long-term credit on the Eurocurrency market that has a maturity of more than one year.

Eurocurrency: Any currency that is banked outside of its country of origin.

Eurocurrency market: An international wholesale market that deals in Eurocurrencies.

Eurodollar: U.S. dollar banked outside of the United States.

Euroequity market: The market for shares sold outside the boundaries of the issuing company's home country.

European Central Bank (ECB): Established July 1, 1998, the ECB is responsible for setting the monetary policy and for managing the exchange-rate system for all of Europe since January 1, 1999.

European Commission: The representatives of each member of the EU who run the different programs of the EU on a day-to-day basis.

European Council: Representatives of each member government of the EU responsible for passing laws and making and enacting major policies.

European Monetary System (EMS): A cooperative foreign-exchange agreement involving many members of the EU and designed to promote exchange-rate stability within the EU.

European Monetary Union (EMU): An agreement by participating European Union member countries that consists of three stages coordinating economic policy and culminating with the adoption of the euro.

European Parliament: Elected representatives of major parties in the EU who have legislative power, control over the budget, and supervision of executive decisions.

European terms: The practice of using the indirect quote for exchange rates.

European Union (EU): A form of regional economic integration among countries in Europe that involves a free trade area, a customs union, and the free mobility of factors of production that is working toward political and economic union. It is governed by the European Commission, the European Council, the European Parliament, and the Court of Justice.

Exchange rate: The price of one currency in terms of another currency.

Expatriate: Often reduced to "expat," refers to a person temporarily or permanently working in a country other than that of their country of origin.

Expatriate failure: Narrowly defined, it is the manager's premature return home due to poor performance. Broadly defined, it is the failure of the MNE's selection policies to identify individuals who succeed abroad.

Expatriate selection: The process of screening executives to find those with the greatest inclination and highest potential for a foreign assignment.

Export plan: Specification of the key issues that shape the success of exporting.

Export tariffs: Taxes collected on exports by the exporting country.

Exporting: The sale of goods or services produced by a company based in one country to customers that reside in a different country.

Export-led development: A country's promotion of industries with export potential so as to increase economic growth.

Extranet: The use of the Internet to link a company with outsiders.

Factor mobility theory: A theory focusing on why production factors move internationally, the effects of those movements on transforming factor endowments, and their impact on world trade.

Factor proportions theory: A theory maintaining that differences in countries' proportional endowments of labor, land, and capital explain differences in these endowments' costs and, thus, the export of products using abundant and cheaper inputs.

Favorable balance of trade: A country is exporting more than it imports.

FDI: An acronym for foreign direct investment.

Financial Accounting Standards Board (FASB): The private-sector organization that sets financial accounting standards in the United States.

First-mover advantage: Being first into a country enables a firm to more easily gain the best partners, best locations, and best suppliers.

Fisher Effect: The theory about the relationship between inflation and interest rates; for example, if the nominal interest rate in one country is lower than that in another, the first country's inflation should be lower so that the real interest rates will be equal.

Flexpatriates: Employees who conduct international assignments through frequent international business travel from their home markets rather than relocating to the host markets.

Foreign bonds: Bonds sold outside of the borrower's country but denominated in the currency of the country of issue.

Foreign Corrupt Practices Act (FCPA): A law that criminalizes certain types of payments by U.S. companies, such as bribes to foreign government officials.

Foreign direct investment (FDI): This is sometimes referred to simply as *direct investment*. It is an operation in which an investor holds a controlling interest in a foreign company.

Foreign exchange (FX): Checks and other instruments for making payments in another country's currency.

Foreign exchange control: A requirement that an individual or company must apply to government authorities for permission to buy foreign currency above some determined threshold amount.

Foreign-exchange market: The market where foreign exchange is traded; usually banks, nonbank financial institutions, and exchanges, such as the CME.

Forward discount: The amount by which the forward rate in a foreign currency is less than the spot rate, that is, the foreign currency is expected to weaken in the future.

Forward premium: The amount by which the forward rate in a foreign currency is greater than the spot rate, that is, the foreign currency is expected to strengthen in the future.

Forward rate: An exchange rate fixed in advance for an exchange of currencies beyond three days.

Franchising: A contract in which a company assists another on a continuous basis and allows use of its trademark.

Freight forwarders: Companies that facilitate the movement of goods from one country to another.

Functional currency: The currency of the primary economic environment in which an entity operates; useful in helping a firm determine how to translate its foreign currency financial statements into the current of the parent company.

Functional structure: An organization that is structured according to functional areas of business.

Fundamental forecasting: A forecasting tool that uses trends in economic variables to predict future exchange rates.

Future orientation: A willingness to delay gratification in order to reap more in the future.

Futures contract: An agreement between two parties to buy or sell a particular currency at a particular price on a particular future date, as specified in a standardized contract to all participants in that currency futures exchange.

FX swap: A simultaneous spot and forward transaction in foreign exchange.

GAAP (Generally Accepted Accounting Principles): The accounting standards accepted by the accounting profession in each country as required for the preparation of financial statements for external users.

Gap analysis: A tool used by a company to estimate potential sales for a given type of product and compare how emphasis on different marketing mix elements accounts for shortcomings in reaching the potential.

General Agreement on Tariffs and Trade (GATT): A global arrangement aimed at reducing barriers to trade, both tariff and nontariff; at the signing of the Uruguay round, the GATT was designated to become the World Trade Organization (WTO).

Geocentric staffing framework: Staffing perspective that seeks the best people for key jobs throughout the organization, regardless of nationality.

Geocentrism: A process of integrating home- and host-country practices as well as introducing some entirely new ones.

Global integration: The unification of distinct national economic systems into one global market.

Global mindset: Ability to absorb information, traditions, and norms from around the world and be able to conceptualize how to make an impact in all environments

Global strategy: A strategy that increases profitability by achieving cost reductions from experience curves and location economies.

Globality: The state of affairs where one competes with everyone, from everywhere, for everything.

Globalization: The widening and deepening of interdependent relationships among people from different nations. The term sometimes refers to the elimination of barriers to international movements of goods, services, capital, technology, and people that influence the integration of world economies.

Glorecalization: A portmanteau of **Glo**balization-**Re**gionalization-**Localization**; champions consistent global values and customized local tactics within a regional context.

Go-no-go decisions: Examining one opportunity at a time and pursuing it if it meets some threshold criteria.

Gray market: It is also called product diversion and refers to the selling and handling of goods through unofficial distributors.

Green economics: Transdisciplinary field that studies the interdependence and coevolution of human economies and natural ecosystems.

Gross domestic product (GDP): A monetary measure of the market value of all the final goods and services produced in a period of time, often annually.

Gross national income (GNI): The total domestic and foreign output claimed by residents of a country, consisting of gross domestic product, plus factor incomes earned by foreign residents, minus income earned in the domestic economy by nonresidents

Gross national product (GNP): The total of incomes earned by residents of a country, regardless of where the productive assets are located, in a given period.

Happynomics: Evaluating a country's performance and potential by directly considering peoples' life satisfaction.

Hard currencies: Currencies that are freely traded without many restrictions and for which there is usually strong external demand; often called freely convertible currencies.

Harvesting: This is also called divesting. It is the process of reducing commitments in some countries because they have poorer performance prospects than do others.

Hierarchy-of-needs theory: A motivation theory that people try to fulfill lower-level needs before moving on to higher-level ones.

High-context cultures: Where most people tend to understand and regard indirect information as pertinent.

Home-country national: Employees who are citizens of the country in which the company is headquartered.

Horizontal differentiation: Degree to which a company assigns specific tasks to specific people in specific activities, rather than having a few people cross-trained to carry out many responsibilities.

IB: An abbreviation for international business.

Idealism: A preference to establish overall principles before trying to resolve small issues.

Import or export license: A country's requirement that importers or exporters secure governmental permission before transacting trade. The license often controls access to foreign exchange at a government-specified exchange rate.

Import substitution: The restriction of imports to boost local production of products that would otherwise be imported.

Import tariffs: Taxes on traded goods imposed by the country in which international shipments enter.

Importing: The purchase of products by a company based in one country from sellers that reside in another.

Incoterms: A portmanteau of **In**ternational **Co**mmercial **Terms**; three-letter terms recognized and used worldwide in an attempt to prevent miscommunications in trade contracts.

Incremental internationalization: The view that as a company gains experience, resources, and confidence, it progressively exports to increasingly distant and dissimilar countries.

Indirect exporting: Exporting that is not handled directly by the manufacturer or producer but through an export agent, freight forwarder, or 3PL.

Indirect quote: An exchange rate given in terms of the number of units of the foreign currency for one unit of the domestic currency.

Individualism: A construct comparing people's preference to fulfill leisure time, build friendships, and improve skills independently and outside the organization as opposed to collectively and within the organization.

Industrial clusters: Groups of buyers and suppliers within the same industry located in the same geographic area in order to facilitate doing business.

Industrial policy: This is also known as a strategic trade policy. It is one in which a government identifies target industries to develop to be internationally competitive.

Industrialization argument: A trade protection argument that, although a country may develop an inefficient and non-globally competitive industrial sector, it will achieve economic growth by protecting the industrial sector so that the unemployed and underemployed people can work in industry.

Industry organization (IO): Field of economics that studies the strategic behavior of firms, the structure of markets, and their interactions.

Infant-industry argument: It holds that a government should shield an emerging industry from foreign competition by guaranteeing it a large share of the domestic market until it can compete on its own.

Inpatriate: An expatriate transferred from a foreign operation to the MNE's headquarters country.

Institutions: Systems of established and prevalent social rules that structure social interactions, such as language, money, law, systems of weights and measures, table manners, and organizations.

Integrated cost leadership-differentiation strategy: Simultaneously pursue providing unique but comparatively inexpensive goods or services by combining elements of the cost leadership and differentiation strategy.

Integration-Responsiveness (IR) Grid: Schema that helps managers measure the global and local pressures that influence the configuration and coordination of value chains.

Intellectual property (IP): Property in the form of patents, trademarks, service marks, trade names, trade secrets, and copyrights.

Intellectual property right (IPR): Ownership rights to intangible assets, such as patents, trademarks, copyrights, and know-how.

Interbank transactions: Foreign-exchange transactions that take place between commercial banks.

Interest arbitrage: Investing in debt instruments in different countries to take advantage of interest differentials. The investment is "covered" if the investor converts money into foreign exchange at the spot rate, invests it in the foreign market at a higher interest rate, and enters into a forward contract so that it can convert principal and interest back into the home currency and earn more than if that money had been invested in the home currency.

Internalization: Control through self-handling of foreign operations, primarily because such control is less expensive than to contract with an external organization.

International Accounting Standards Board (IASB): The international private-sector organization based in London that sets financial accounting standards for worldwide use.

International business: All commercial transactions that take place among countries.

International Financial Reporting Standards (IFRS): A set of accounting standards issued by the International Accounting Standards Board (IASB) and adopted by many countries, especially those in the European Union.

International Fisher Effect (IFE): The theory that the relationship between interest rates and exchange rates implies that the currency of the country with the lower interest rate will strengthen in the future.

International Human Resource Management (IHRM): The staffing function of the organization; includes the activities of human resources planning, recruitment, selection, performance appraisal, compensation, retention, and labor relations.

International Monetary Fund (IMF): A multigovernmental association organized in 1945 to promote exchange-rate stability and to facilitate the international flow of currencies.

International Organization of Securities Commissions (IOSCO): An international organization of securities regulators that supports the efforts of the IASB to establish comprehensive accounting standards.

International Organization for Standardization (ISO): An independent nongovernmental organization that helps develop international technical standards.

International reserves: Monetary assets held by central banks kept in three major forms: foreign-exchange reserves, IMF-related assets (including SDRs), and gold.

International strategy: The effort of managers to create value by transferring core competencies from the home market to foreign markets in which local competitors lack those competencies.

Jamaica Agreement: A 1976 agreement among countries that permitted greater flexibility of exchange rates, basically formalizing the break from fixed exchange rates.

Joint venture: An operation in which two or more companies share ownership. (There are also non-equity joint ventures.)

Lag strategy: An operational strategy that involves either delaying collection of foreign-currency receivables if the currency is expected to strengthen or delaying payment of foreign-currency payables if the currency is expected to weaken; the opposite of a lead strategy.

Laissez-faire: The concept of minimal government intervention in a society's economic activity.

Lead strategy: An operational strategy that involves either collecting foreign-currency receivables before they are due when the currency is expected to weaken or paying foreign-currency payables before they are due when the currency is expected to strengthen; the opposite of a lag strategy.

Legal system: The rules that regulate behavior, the processes that enforce the laws of a country, and the procedures used to resolve grievances.

Letter of credit (L/C): A precise document by which the importer's bank extends credit to the importer and agrees to pay the exporter.

Leverage: The amount of debt used to finance a firm's assets.

Liability of foreignness: Foreign companies' lower survival rate in comparison to local companies for many years after they begin operations.

Licensing agreements: Contracts whereby firms allow others to use some assets, such as trademarks, patents, copyrights, or expertise.

Local content: Refers to the percentage of a product that is produced in the host country.

Local responsiveness: The process of disaggregating a standardized whole into differentiated parts to improve responsiveness to local market circumstances.

Localization: Process whereby an expatriate retains a foreign assignment provided she accepts the status, and corresponding compensation, of a local hire.

Localization strategy: An approach that emphasizes responsiveness to the unique conditions prevailing in different national markets.

Location advantages: Cost advantages arising from performing a value activity in the optimal location.

Location economies: Cost advantages arising from performing a value activity in the optimal location.

Logistics management: That part of the supply chain process that plans, implements, and controls the efficient, effective flow and storage of goods, services, and related information from the point of origin to the point of consumption, to meet customers' requirements; sometimes called *materials management*.

London Interbank Offered Rate (Libor): The interest rate for large interbank loans of Eurocurrencies. It is the benchmark interest rate for many different types of loans, including home mortgages.

Low-context cultures: Where people generally regard as relevant only firsthand information that bears directly on the subject at hand.

Management contracts: Arrangements in which a company provides personnel to perform management functions for another organization.

Market capitalization: A common measure of the size of a stock market, which is computed by multiplying the total number of shares of stock listed on the exchange by the market price per share.

Market control: System whereby an MNE uses external market mechanisms to establish internal performance benchmarks and standards.

Market economy: An economic system in which resources are allocated and controlled by consumers who "vote" by buying goods; emphasizes minimal government involvement.

Masculinity–femininity index: A construct measuring attitudes toward achievement and the roles expected of genders.

Materialism: The importance of acquiring possessions as a means of self-satisfaction and happiness, as well as for the appearance of success.

Matrix structure: A structure in which foreign units report (by product, function, or area) to more than one group, each of which shares responsibility over the foreign unit.

Mercantilism: A trade theory holding that a country's wealth is measured by its holdings of "treasure," which usually means its gold.

Merchandise exports and imports: Tangible products—goods—that are respectively sent *out* of and brought *into* a country.

Mercosur: A major regional group in South America that includes Argentina, Brazil,

Paraguay, and Uruguay, and that is hampered by internal political issues.

Mission: Statement that defines the business, its objectives, and its approach to achieve them.

Mixed economy: An economic system characterized by some mixture of market and command economies; balances public and private ownership of factors of production.

Mixed legal system: A legal system that emerges when two or more legal systems function in a country.

Mixed structure: A structure that integrates various aspects of classical structures.

MNC: An acronym for multinational corporation or multinational company and a synonym for multinational enterprise.

MNE: An acronym for multinational enterprise.

Monochronic: A term to describe cultures in which most people normally prefer to work sequentially, such as finishing transactions with one customer before dealing with another.

Most-favored-nation (MFN) clause: A GATT (and now a WTO) requirement that a trade concession that is given to one country must be given to all other countries. Also known as "trade without discrimination."

Multicultural: Description of someone who has internalized more than two national cultures.

Multinational corporation or company (MNC): A synonym for a multinational enterprise (MNE).

Multinational enterprise (MNE): Usually signifies any company with foreign direct investments.

Multiple exchange-rate system: A means of foreign-exchange control whereby the government sets different exchange rates for different kinds of transactions.

Mutual recognition: The principle that a foreign registrant that wants to list and have its securities traded on a foreign stock exchange need only provide information prepared according to the GAAP of the registrant's country.

NASDAQ: The second-largest stock market in the United States that trades in equities, commodities, options, and futures. In the Nordic countries, it owns and operates the exchanges in Denmark, Finland, Iceland, Sweden, and has an exchange for commodities derivatives in Norway. It is known in the region as NASDAQ OMX.

Natural advantage: A reason for a competitive advantage in production that comes from countries' climatic conditions, access to certain natural resources, or availability of certain labor forces.

Nearshoring: Applies to bringing back or setting up production or services in a country close to the home country, often in a country that shares a common border.

Neoclassical structures: Apply different devices to resolve the shortcomings, such as conformity, rigidity, bureaucracy, and authoritarianism, often found in the classical formats of functional and divisional structures.

Neomercantilism: The running of a favorable balance of trade to achieve some social or political objective.

Net present value (NPV): The sum of the present values of the annual cash flows minus the initial investment.

Netting: The transfer of funds from subsidiaries in a net payable position to a central clearing account and from there to the accounts of the net receiver subsidiaries.

Network structure: Neoclassical structure whereby a small core organization outsources value activities to linked firms whose core competencies support greater innovation.

Non-tradable goods: Products and services that are seldom practical to export because of high transportation costs.

Normativism: A theory stating that universal standards of behavior (based on people's own values) exist that all cultures should follow, making nonintervention unethical.

North American Free Trade Agreement (NAFTA): A free trade agreement involving the United States, Canada, and Mexico that went into effect on January 1, 1994.

NYSE:ICE (Intercontinental Exchange): Also known as Intercontinental Exchange Inc., ICE owns and operates 23 regulated exchanges in the United States, Canada, and Europe, including the New York Stock Exchange and various derivatives exchanges. NYSE is the largest stock market in the world.

Offer (sell) rate: The amount for which a foreign-exchange trader is willing to sell a currency.

Offsets: *See* countertrade.

Offshore financial centers (OFCs): Cities or countries that provide large amounts of funds in currencies other than their own and are used as locations in which to raise and accumulate cash.

Offshore financing: The provision of financial services by banks and other agents to nonresidents.

Offshore manufacturing: Any investment that takes place in a country other than the home country.

Offshoring: The dependence on production in a foreign country, usually by shifting from a domestic source.

Oligopolistic reaction: In IB, it is a situation in which managers may purposely crowd a market to prevent competitors from gaining advantages there that they can use to improve their positions elsewhere.

Onshoring: Relocating operations from a foreign to a domestic location.

Operations: The conversion of inputs into outputs.

Operations management: Activities in the value chain that occur within the company.

Optimum-tariff theory: The imposition of an import tariff that leads a foreign producer to lower its export price.

Options: Foreign-exchange instruments that give the purchaser the right, but not the obligation, to buy or sell a certain amount of foreign currency at a set exchange rate within a specified amount of time.

Organization: The specification of the framework for work, development of the systems that coordinate and control what work is done, and the cultivation of a common workplace culture among employees.

Organization of the Petroleum Exporting Countries (OPEC): A producers' alliance among 13 petroleum-exporting countries that attempts to agree on oil production and pricing policies.

Organization structure: The formal arrangement of roles, responsibilities, and relationships within an organization.

Organizational culture: The shared meaning and beliefs that shape how employees interpret information, make decisions, and implement actions.

Outright forward transactions: Forward contracts that are not connected to spot transactions.

Outsourcing: Where one company contracts with another company to perform certain functions, including manufacturing and back-office operations. May be done in the company's home country or in another country (nearshoring or offshoring).

Pacific Alliance: A regional economic group in Latin America composed of Mexico, Colombia, Peru, and Chile. It is more favorable to trade and investment than other regional groups in South America.

Par value: In international finance, the benchmark value of a currency, originally quoted in terms of gold or the U.S. dollar and now quoted in terms of Special Drawing Rights.

Parent-country national: An expatriate sent from her or his home country to live and work in another.

Passive income: Income of a CFC that comes from sources other than those connected with the active conduct of a trade or business, such as holding company income; also called Subpart F income.

Payback period: The number of years required to recover the initial investment made.

Peripheral values: Those values that are less dominant and more pliable than core values.

Political freedom: The right to participate freely in the political process.

Political ideology: The body of complex ideas, theories, and aims that constitute a sociopolitical program.

Political risk: Potential changes in political conditions that may cause a company's operating positions to deteriorate.

Political spectrum: A conceptual structure that specifies and organizes various types of political ideologies.

Political system: The system designed to integrate a society into a viable, functioning unit.

Polycentric staffing framework: A staffing policy whereby a company relies on host country nationals to manage operations in their own country, while parent-country nationals staff corporate headquarters.

Polychronic: A term to describe cultures where most people are more comfortable when working simultaneously on a variety of tasks (multitasking).

Populism: Range of political approaches that appeal to "the people," often juxtaposing this group against the "elite."

Portfolio investment: A non-controlling financial interest in another entity.

Power distance: A measurement of employee preferences of interaction between superiors and subordinates.

Pragmatic: Describes cultures in which people focus more on details than on abstract principles.

Primary activities: The line activities that compose the value chain. Specifically, inbound logistics, operations, outbound logistics, marketing, and service.

Product diversion: It is also called the gray market and refers to the selling and handling of goods through unofficial distributors.

Product life cycle (PLC) theory of trade: The theory that states that the production location of certain manufactured products shifts as they go through their life cycle, particularly from developed to developing countries.

Protectionism: The collective, governmental actions to influence international trade.

Pull: A type of promotion that relies on mass media.

Purchasing power parity (PPP): A theory that explains exchange-rate changes as being based on differences in price levels in different countries. Also, the number of units of a country's currency to buy the same products or services in the domestic market that US$1 would buy in the United States.

Push: A type of promotion that uses direct selling techniques.

Quality: Meeting or exceeding the expectations of a customer.

Quota: A quantity limit of a product's import or export in a given time frame, typically per year.

Reconciliation: The process required in U.S. capital markets where a company from a foreign country reconciles its home country GAAP with U.S. GAAP.

Refugees: People living in a country other than their country of origin, who moved for political reasons—for example, because of persecution or war dangers—and usually become part of the labor pool where they live.

Regional integration: A form of integration in which a group of countries located in the same geographic proximity decide to cooperate.

Relationship-focus (RF) culture: A culture that puts dealings with friends ahead of business dealings.

Relativism: A theory stating that ethical truths depend on the groups holding them, making intervention by outsiders unethical. The belief that behavior has meaning and can be judged only in its specific cultural context.

Repatriate: A person who has returned to his or her place of birth or origin.

Repatriation: When expatriates return to their home country.

Reshoring: Firms' bringing operations back to their home countries from abroad and is sometimes called rightshoring.

Resource-based view: Each company has a unique combination of resources, capabilities, and competencies.

Resources: Inputs, owned or controlled by the MNE, that support its production process.

Reverse culture shock: The trauma of adjusting to one's own country after having become partial to aspects of life abroad that are not options back home.

Reverse-expats: Local managers who direct a company's emerging-market business and are rotated through some of the company's established operations outside of that market before returning home.

Royalties: Payments for the use of some assets, such as trademarks, patents, copyrights, or expertise.

Rule of law: The principle that every member of a society must follow the same laws.

Rule of man: Notion that the word and whim of the ruler, no matter how arbitrary, are law.

Safe haven: A country with low political risk, usually regarded as a good location for investment.

Scanning: A process in which managers examine many countries broadly—using information that is readily available, inexpensive, and fairly comparable—to narrow detailed analysis and travel to only the most promising ones.

Self-initiated expatriates: People who go to work in another country on their own initiative as compared to those sent by their companies.

Serendipity: Refers to the trigger of so-called accidental exporters who, responding to happenstance or odd circumstances, enter overseas markets by chance.

Service exports and imports: Non-merchandise international earnings and payments. They are also referred to as invisibles.

Shadow economy: Illicit economic activity, such as counterfeiting or unlicensed services, that exists alongside a country's official economy; also called the underground, informal, or parallel economy.

Sight draft: A commercial bill of exchange that requires payment to be made as soon as it is presented to the party obligated to pay.

Silent language: The exchange of messages through a host of nonspoken and nonwritten cues.

Six Sigma: A highly focused system of quality control that uses data and rigorous statistical analysis to identify "defects" in a process or product, reduce variability, and achieve as close to zero defects as possible.

Small and medium-sized enterprises (SMEs): Companies whose headcount or sale turnover falls below certain thresholds; in the United States, companies that employ fewer than 500 employees. Commonly expressed as "SME."

Smithsonian Agreement: A 1971 agreement among countries that resulted in the devaluation of the U.S. dollar, revaluation of other world currencies, a widening of exchange-rate flexibility, and a commitment on the part of all participating countries to reduce trade restrictions; superseded by the Jamaica Agreement of 1976.

Socialism: A system based on public ownership of the means of production and distribution of wealth.

Soft currencies: Currencies that are usually not fully convertible. Often these currencies are unstable and not very liquid.

Sourcing: The strategy that a company pursues in purchasing materials, components, and final products; sourcing can be from domestic and foreign locations and from inside and outside the company.

Sovereign wealth funds (SWFs): Pools of money from a country's reserve that are set aside for investment purposes;

usually related to natural resources such as oil.

Sovereignty: A country's freedom to "act locally" and without externally imposed restrictions.

Special drawing right (SDR): A unit of account issued to countries by the International Monetary Fund to expand their official reserves bases.

Specific duty: A tariff assessed on a per-unit basis.

Spillover effect: In the context of IB, a marketing program in one country that results in product awareness elsewhere, particularly in an adjacent country.

Spot rate: An exchange rate quoted for immediate delivery of foreign currency, usually within two business days.

Spot transactions: Foreign exchange transactions involving the exchange of currency the second day after the date on which the two foreign-exchange traders agree to the transaction.

Staffing framework: A systems view that articulates the internal structures and mechanisms of human resource management.

Stakeholders: The collection of groups, including stockholders, employees, customers, and society at large, that a company must satisfy to be successful.

State capitalism: An economic system whereby the state decides how, when, and where assets will be valued and resources allocated.

Static effects: The shifting of resources from inefficient to efficient companies as trade barriers fall.

Strategic alliance: Refers simply to companies' working together, such as in joint ventures and licensing agreements. However, the term sometimes refers to an agreement that is of critical importance to a partner or one that does not involve joint ownership.

Strategic planning: A comprehensive process that determines how the firm can best achieve its goals. An industry is composed of those companies engaged in a particular type of enterprise.

Strategic trade policy: Also known as an industrial policy. It is one in which a government identifies target industries to develop to be internationally competitive.

Strategy: An integrated and coordinated set of commitments of actions that reflects the company's present situation, identifies the direction it should go, and determines how it will get there.

Subpart F income: Income of a CFC that comes from sources other than those connected with the active conduct of a trade or business, such as holding company income; also called passive income.

Subsidies: Payments from the government to assist companies so they will be competitive.

Supply chain: The coordination of materials, information, and funds from the initial raw material supplier to the ultimate customer.

Supply chaining: Collaborating horizontally among suppliers, retailers, and customers to create value.

Support activities: The general infrastructure of the firm that anchors the day-to-day execution of the primary activities of the value chain.

Sustainability: The ability to meet the needs of the present without compromising the ability of future generations to meet their own needs, while taking into account what is best for the people and the environment.

Syndication: Cooperation by a lead bank and several other banks to make a large loan to a public or private organization.

Tariff: A tax levied on a good shipped internationally.

Technical forecasting: A forecasting tool that uses past trends in exchange rates themselves to spot future trends in rates.

Teleological approach: An approach based on the idea that decisions are made based on the consequences of the action.

Temporal method: A method of translating foreign-currency financial statements used when the functional currency is that of the parent company.

Terms currency: In a foreign exchange quote, the base currency is 1 and the terms currency gives you the number of units of that currency per one unit of the base currency. If a foreign exchange trader quotes USD/JPY, the dollar is the base currency and the yen is the terms currency. The quote will give you the number of Japanese yen per U.S. dollar. The quote is also shown as USDJPY=X.

Terms of trade: The quantity of imports that a given quantity of a country's exports can buy.

Theocratic law: A situation whereby a nation's legal system is based on whatever religious text the ruling religion abides by.

Theory of country size: Countries with larger land masses usually depend less on trade than smaller ones.

Third Wave of Democratization: Expression to capture the collective set of nations that moved from nondemocratic to democratic political systems during the 1970s through the 1990s.

Third-country national: An expatriate who is neither a citizen of the country in which they are working nor a citizen of the country where the company is headquartered.

3PL: Term that stands for third-party logistics; agents that develop state-of-the-art technology to help companies understand trade practices, identify opportunities, manage risks, and shepherd exports and imports from buyers to sellers.

Time draft: A commercial bill of exchange calling for payment to be made at some time after delivery.

TNC: An acronym for transnational company, a term used by the United Nations to refer to a multinational enterprise.

Total quality management (TQM): The process that a company uses to achieve quality, where the goal is elimination of all defects.

Totalitarianism: A political ideology characterized by the absence of widespread participation in decision making and suppression of political and civil freedoms.

TQM: *See* Total quality management.

Trade deficit: A country is importing more than it is exporting.

Trade surplus: A country is exporting more than it is importing.

Trans-Pacific Partnership: A potential regional economic trade group involving Australia, Brunei, Canada, Chile, Japan, Malaysia, Mexico, New Zealand, Peru, Singapore, and Vietnam.

Transaction exposure: Foreign-exchange risk arising because a company has outstanding accounts receivable or accounts payable that are denominated in a foreign currency.

Transfer price: A price on goods and services one member of a corporate family sells to another.

Transit tariffs: Taxes charged by countries through which international shipments move.

Translation: The restatement of financial statements from one currency to another.

Translation exposure: An exposure that occurs because exposed accounts—those translated at the balance-sheet or current exchange rate—either gain or lose value when the exchange rate changes.

Transnational company (TNC): A term used by the United Nations to refer to a multinational enterprise.

Transnational strategy: Configuring a value chain to exploit location economies as well as coordinate activities to leverage core competencies while simultaneously responding to local pressures.

Transpatriate: An expatriate "lifer" who tends to work in several countries over time and who has no true corporate "home."

Turnkey operations: Construction projects performed under contract and transferred to owners when they're operational.

Uncertainty avoidance: A country trait whereby most people feel uncomfortable with ambiguity.

Unfavorable balance of trade: A country is importing more than it is exporting.

United Nations Conference on Trade and Development (UNCTAD): A UN body that has been especially active in dealing with the relationships between developing and industrialized countries with respect to trade.

Unity-of-command principle: An unbroken chain of command and communication should flow from the CEO to the entry-level worker.

Utilitarianism: A consequences-based approach to moral reasoning that judges an action to be right if it does the most good to the most people.

Value: A measure of a firm's capability to sell what it makes for more than the costs incurred to make it; the ultimate purpose of strategy.

Value chain: The collective activities that occur as a product moves from raw materials through production to final distribution; the disaggregation of value creation.

VER: *See* voluntary export restraint.

Vertical differentiation: The specification of the degrees of centralization and decentralization of decision-making in an organization.

Vertical integration: The control of the different stages as a product moves from raw materials through production to final distribution.

Virtual structure: A form of company that acquires strategic capabilities by creating a temporary network of independent companies, suppliers, customers, and even rivals.

Vision: The idealization of what an MNE firm wants to be. It expresses, in broad terms, its ultimate goal.

Voluntary export restraint (VER): A quota variation whereby a country voluntarily reduces its companies' exports to another country.

World Trade Organization (WTO): The 125-member successor to GATT that is charged with reducing tariff and nontariff barriers to trade in goods, services, and investment among member nations.

Zero defects: The elimination of defects, which results in the reduction of manufacturing costs and an increase in consumer satisfaction.

Company and Trademark Index

Page references with "*f*" refer to figures; page references with "*m*" refer to maps; page references with "*t*" refer to tables; and page references with "n" refer to endnotes cited by number.

Name Index

Page references with "*f*" refer to figures; page references with "*m*" refer to maps; page references with "*t*" refer to tables; and page references with "n" refer to endnotes cited by number.

Subject Index

Page references with "*f*" refer to figures; page references with "*m*" refer to maps; page references with "*t*" refer to tables; and page references with "n" refer to endnotes cited by number.